1991/92	1992/93	1993/94	1994/95	1995/96	1996/97		Para No.
—	20%	20%	20%	20%	20%	Lower Rate	3
						Lower Rate limit	3
—	£2,000	£2,500	£3,000	£3,200	£3,900	(taxable income)	
25%	25%	25%	25%	25%	24%	Basic Rate	3, 5
						Basic Rate band	3, 5
£23,700	£21,700	£21,200	£20,700	£21,100	£21,600	(taxable income)	
						Basic Rate limit	3, 5
£23,700	£23,700	£23,700	£23,700	£24,300	£25,500	(taxable income)	
40%	40%	40%	40%	40%	40%	Higher Rate(s)	3, 5
						Wife's Earned Income Relief	22
—	—	—	—	—	—	Maximum	
						PERSONAL ALLOWANCES	
£3,295	£3,445	£3,445	£3,445	£3,525	£3,765	Single/Personal	14, 20
£1,720	£1,720	£1,720	£1,720	£1,720	£1,790	Married/Married couple's	15, 21
							14, 15, 23
£4,020	£4,200	£4,200	£4,200	£4,630	£4,910	Age—Single/Personal (65 or over)	
£4,180	£4,370	£4,370	£4,370	£4,800	£5,090	—Single/Personal (80/75 or over)	
£2,355	£2,465	£2,465	£2,665	£2,995	£3,115	—Married/Married couple's (65 or over)	
£2,395	£2,505	£2,505	£2,705	£3,035	£3,155	—Married/Married couple's (80/75 or over)	
£13,500	£14,200	£14,200	£14,200	£14,600	£15,200	—Income limit	
—	—	—	—	—	—	Housekeeper	24
£1,720	£1,720	£1,720	£1,720	£1,720	£1,790	Widow's bereavement	16
						Addition re child if claimant	17
£1,720	£1,720	£1,720	£1,720	£1,720	£1,790	single or claimant's wife ill	
						Dependent Relative Allowance	25
—	—	—	—	—	—	Certain women claimants	
—	—	—	—	—	—	Other claimants	
—	—	—	—	—	—	Income limit	
—	—	—	—	—	—	Services of Daughter (or Son)	26
£1,080	£1,080	£1,080	£1,200	£1,200	£1,250	Blind Persons	18
						CLASS 4 NIC	
6.3%	6.3%	6.3%	7.3%	7.3%	6%	—rate	
£5,900–	£6,120–	£6,340–	£6,490–	£6,640–	£6,860–	—band	
£20,280	£21,060	£21,840	£22,360	£22,880	£23,660		
						DISCRETIONARY TRUST INCOME	
10%	10%	—	—	—	—	additional rate	
—	—	35%	35%	35%	34%	flat rate	

Tolley's Income Tax 1996–97

81st Edition

by Glyn Saunders MA
and
David Smailes FCA
from an original text by
Eric L Harvey FCA

Tolley Publishing Company Limited

un A United News & Media publication

Published by
Tolley Publishing Company Ltd
Tolley House
2 Addiscombe Road
Croydon CR9 5AF England
0181-686 9141

Typeset by Interactive Sciences, Gloucester

Printed in Great Britain by The Bath Press, Somerset

About This Book

This is the 81st edition of Tolley's Income Tax. It includes the income tax provisions of the Finance Act 1996, relevant case law, statements by the Revenue and other official bodies, and further important information concerning income tax, up to the date of Royal Assent to that Act. A summary of the contents of the 1996 Act is included at Chapter 92.

Income and corporation tax law was consolidated in the Income and Corporation Taxes Act 1988, capital allowances legislation in the Capital Allowances Act 1990 and legislation relating to corporation tax on capital gains in the Taxation of Chargeable Gains Act 1992. A summary of the approach adopted to the citation of statutory references affected by the consolidations is included overleaf.

This book includes the income tax law and practice for at least six years (i.e. for 1990/91 onwards and sometimes earlier) and so provides comprehensive information for claims, late assessments etc. There is a twelve-year summary of rates and allowances inside the front cover. The inside back cover contains a table of tax rates for 1996/97 and a table of the main taxable social security benefits. An index and tables of leading cases and statutes provide quick reference to the subject and to the legislation.

Comments on this annual publication and suggestions for improvements are always welcomed.

TOLLEY PUBLISHING CO. LTD.

Consolidation of Tax Enactments

With effect generally for 1988/89 and subsequent years of assessment (and for companies' accounting periods ending after 5 April 1988), the *Taxes Acts* provisions relating to income tax and corporation tax are consolidated in the *Income and Corporation Taxes Act 1988* (*ICTA 1988*). The consolidation does not affect the application of the provisions concerned, but references to provisions which ceased to have effect before 6 April 1988 are omitted, as is the commencement date of the consolidated provisions (unless still relevant to application of the current provisions).

Tolley's Income Tax 1996/97, continues, as in previous years, to set out the position for the six years before 1996/97, i.e. for 1990/91 to 1995/96, but occasional references are still required to earlier years. In strictness, the legislation applicable to years before 1988/89 is that in force prior to the consolidation referred to above, and the Revenue (while acknowledging that 'on previous consolidation, inspectors, Commissioners and taxpayers alike got used to the new references in dealing with previous periods'), have indicated that claims etc. for those years should refer to the statute then applicable.

Accordingly, the approach which has been adopted to statutory references in this edition is as follows:

(i) References to current legislation invariably quote the *ICTA 1988* reference in the familiar form, i.e. '*Sec XXX*' to identify a section thereof and '*XX Sch*' to identify a Schedule thereto. Remaining references to the previous consolidation Act are in the form '*ICTA 1970, s XXX*' or '*ICTA 1970, XX Sch*'. Where there has been no change in the legislation in the last six years, no statutory reference other than that for *ICTA 1988* is quoted.

(ii) Where the legislation has changed during the last six years, the earlier provisions continue to be described in the text, and the appropriate earlier statutory reference is quoted. Legislation current during that six years but now repealed is similarly dealt with. Where any part of the current legislation was introduced during that six years, the commencement date is quoted, but the statutory reference for that date is generally omitted.

(iii) In any case where a claim or election for a year before 1988/89 may be involved, the appropriate earlier statutory reference is quoted. The earlier reference is also given in certain cases where the reference may have achieved a particular familiarity, e.g. in the case of *sections 154(2), 189* or *460 of ICTA 1970*.

(iv) Where a full pre-consolidation statutory reference is required, this may be obtained from Tolley's Income Tax 1987/88 or an appropriate earlier edition.

(v) The Table of Statutes in this edition includes all references to earlier legislation appearing in the text (as above). If a full Table of Derivations and Destinations in relation to *ICTA 1988* is required, this is published by HMSO, price £5, and is available (post free) from Tolley Publishing Co. Ltd.

A similar approach has been adopted on the consolidation of the enactments relating to capital allowances in the *Capital Allowances Act 1990*, which took effect generally for chargeable periods ending after 5 April 1990, and to those relating to corporation tax on capital gains in the *Taxation of Chargeable Gains Act 1992*, which took effect generally for chargeable periods beginning after 5 April 1992.

Contents

The following subjects are in the same alphabetical order in the book.
A detailed index and tables of cases and statutes are at the end of the book.

Contents

Contents

Abbreviations and References

References throughout the book to numbered sections and schedules are to the Income and Corporation Taxes Act 1988 unless otherwise indicated.

ABBREVIATIONS

ACT	=	Advance Corporation Tax.
CAA	=	Capital Allowances Act.
CA	=	Court of Appeal.
CCA	=	Court of Criminal Appeal.
CCAB	=	Consultative Committee of Accountancy Bodies.
CES	=	Court of Exchequer (Scotland).
Cf.	=	compare.
CGT	=	Capital Gains Tax.
CGTA 1979	=	Capital Gains Tax Act 1979.
CIR	=	Commissioners of Inland Revenue ('the Board').
Ch D	=	Chancery Division.
CJEC	=	Court of Justice of the European Communities.
CS	=	Scottish Court of Session.
DSS	=	Department of Social Security.
EC	=	European Communities.
EEC	=	European Economic Community.
EU	=	European Union.
Ex D	=	Exchequer Division (now absorbed into Chancery Division).
FA	=	Finance Act.
FII	=	Franked Investment Income.
HC	=	High Court.
HC(I)	=	High Court of Ireland.
HL	=	House of Lords.
ICAEW	=	Institute of Chartered Accountants in England and Wales.
ICTA	=	Income and Corporation Taxes Act.
IHT	=	Inheritance Tax.
IHTA 1984	=	Inheritance Tax Act 1984.
IR	=	Inland Revenue.
KB	=	King's Bench Division.
LIFFE	=	London International Financial Futures Exchange.
NI	=	Northern Ireland.
PC	=	Privy Council.
PDA	=	Probate, Divorce and Admiralty Division. (Now Family Division).
QB	=	Queen's Bench Division.
RI	=	Republic of Ireland (Eire).
s	=	Section.
SC(I)	=	Irish Supreme Court.
Sch	=	Schedule [*4 Sch 10* = 4th Schedule, paragraph 10].
Sec	=	Section.
SI	=	Statutory Instrument.
SP	=	Inland Revenue Statement of Practice.
Sp C	=	Special Commissioners.
SR&O	=	Statutory Rules and Orders.

SSAP	=	Statement of Standard Accounting Practice.
TCGA 1992	=	Taxation of Chargeable Gains Act 1992.
TMA	=	Taxes Management Act 1970.
VAT	=	Value Added Tax.
VATA 1994	=	Value Added Tax Act 1994.

REFERENCES

AER	=	All England Law Reports (Butterworth & Co. (Publishers) Ltd., 88 Kingsway, WC2B 6AB).
ATC	=	Annotated Tax Cases (Gee & Co. (Publishers) Ltd., South Quay Plaza, 183 Marsh Wall, London E14 9FS).
ITC	=	Irish Tax Cases (Government Publications, 1 and 3 G.P.O. Arcade, Dublin 1).
LTR	=	Law Times Reports.
SC	=	Special Commissioners.
SLR	=	Scottish Law Reporter.
SLT	=	Scots Law Times.
SSCD	=	Simon's Special Commissioners' Decisions (Butterworth & Co., as above).
STC	=	Simon's Tax Cases (Butterworth & Co., as above).
STI	=	Simon's Tax Intelligence (Butterworth & Co., as above).
TC	=	Official Tax Cases (H.M. Stationery Office, P.O. Box 276, SW8 5DT).
TLR	=	Times Law Reports ('The Times', New Printing House Square, 200 Gray's Inn Road, WC1X 8EZ).
TR	=	Taxation Reports (Gee & Co., as above).

The first number in the citation refers to the volume, and the second to the page, so that [1985] 1 AER 15 means that the report is to be found on page fifteen of the first volume of the All England Law Reports for 1985. Where no volume number is given, only one volume was produced in that year. Some series have continuous volume numbers.

Where legal decisions are very recent and in the lower courts, it must be remembered that they may be reversed on appeal. But references to the official Tax Cases ('TC') may generally be taken as final.

In English cases, Scottish and N. Irish decisions (unless there is a difference of law between the countries) are generally followed but are not binding, and Republic of Ireland decisions are considered (and vice-versa).

Acts of Parliament, Cmnd. Papers, 'Hansard' Parliamentary Reports and Statutory Instruments (SI) formerly Statutory Rules and Orders (SR & O)) are obtainable from H.M. Stationery Office (bookshop at 49, High Holborn, WC1V 6HB; orders to P.O. Box 276, London SW8 5DT). Telephone orders should be made to 0171-873 9090. **Hansard** references are to daily issues and do not always correspond to the columns in the bound editions. **N.B.** Statements in the House, while useful as indicating the intention of enactments, have no legal authority if the Courts subsequently interpret the wording of the Act differently, but see 4.7 APPEALS for circumstances in which evidence of parliamentary intent may be considered by the Courts.

BOOKS

Inland Revenue explanatory books and pamphlets may be obtained (free) from any local Inspector of Taxes. See list in Chapter 37.

Retention of Tolley's. Subscribers should preserve each year's edition of 'Tolley's' because the necessity of including considerable new material each year involves the omission of some older and less important matter.

Abbreviations and References

Tolley's Corporation Tax 1996/97 is the companion publication to Tolley's Income Tax and sets out the application of the taxing statutes to the income and capital gains of companies up to and including the 1996 Finance Act. £34.95.

Tolley's Capital Gains Tax 1996/97 is a detailed guide to the statutes and case law up to and including the 1996 Finance Act. In the same alphabetical format as Tolley's Income Tax and Tolley's Corporation Tax. £34.95.

Tolley's Inheritance Tax 1996/97 is a detailed guide to the statutes and case law up to and including the 1996 Finance Act. £29.95.

Tolley's Value Added Tax 1996/97 is a comprehensive guide to value added tax, covering legislation, Customs & Excise notices and leaflets and all other relevant information up to and including the 1996 Finance Act. £33.95.

Tolley's Tax Computations 1996/97 contains copious worked examples covering income tax, corporation tax, capital gains tax, inheritance tax and value added tax. £38.95.

Tolley's Tax Cases 1996 contains over 2,500 summaries of cases up to 1 January 1996 relevant to current legislation. £35.95.

Tolley's Practical Tax is an eight-page, fortnightly newsletter containing news, articles and items of practical use to all involved with UK tax. By subscription only.

1   Allowances and Tax Rates—Applicable to individuals

1.1   This chapter provides a general introduction to UK income tax. All rates and allowances for the fiscal year 1990/91 onwards are included in order to provide comprehensive information for claims etc. (and where a rate in force for 1990/91 commenced in an earlier year, that earlier year is shown). Changes are shown for and from the year in which they commenced with current rates etc. in **bold type**. A separate **twelve-year summary** of rates and allowances appears inside the front cover.

Headings in this chapter are:

1.2   The **Fiscal Year** (or 'year of assessment' or 'tax year') runs from **6 April to 5 April** (e.g. the fiscal year 1996/97 is from 6 April 1996 to 5 April 1997 inclusive). **Total Income** (see 1.6 below) less **Personal Allowances** (see 1.14 to 1.18 below) equals **Taxable Income**.

1.3   **RATES OF TAX—1996/97** [*Sec 1(2); FA 1996, s 72*]

	Rate	On Taxable Income	Cumulative tax
Lower Rate	20%	0–£3,900	£780
Basic Rate	24%	£3,900–£25,500	£5,964
Higher Rate	40%	Over £25,500	

Where income tax at the basic rate has been deducted from income, and that income is chargeable (in whole or part) at the lower rate, repayment of the excess tax deducted may be claimed. [*Sec 1(6A); FA 1992, s 9(8)*].

For 1993/94 and subsequent years, so much of total income as comprises income chargeable under Schedule F (i.e. UK company dividends etc. together with related tax credits), or income of the same nature received from non-UK resident companies, is generally chargeable at the lower rate to the extent that such income does not exceed the basic rate limit (treating it as the highest part of total income). For 1996/97 and subsequent years, this treatment is extended to savings income generally. [*Secs 1A, 207A; FA 1993, s 77; FA 1996, s 73, 41 Sch Pt V(1)*]. See 1.8(ii)(iii) below for detailed provisions.

See 80.5 SETTLEMENTS as regards rate applicable to certain trust income. See 1.13 below as to indexation of tax bands.

1.4   **EARLIER HISTORY**

For 1973/74 onwards, a unified income tax system replaced the previous dual structure of income tax and surtax on the incomes of individuals. A single graduated tax, comprising a

1.5 Allowances and Tax Rates—Applicable to individuals

basic rate and higher rates, became applicable to all income, whether earned or unearned, and an investment income surcharge commenced as an additional flat rate charge on investment incomes exceeding certain limits. [*FA 1971, ss 32–39 and 6, 7 Sch; FA 1972, ss 65 and 66*]. Earned income relief as such was abolished. [*FA 1971, s 32(2)*]. For 1978/79 and 1979/80 a lower rate applied to the first slice of taxable income. [*FA 1978, s 14; FA 1980, s 18(2)*]. The investment income surcharge was abolished for 1984/85 onwards. [*FA 1984, 7 Sch 1*].

For rates of tax for 1995/96 to 1990/91, see 1.5 below.

1.5 **RATES OF TAX—1995/96 TO 1990/91**

Lower, basic and higher rate for 1995/96 [*Sec 1(2); FA 1995, s 35; SI 1994 No 3012*]

	Rate	On Taxable Income	Cumulative tax
Lower Rate	20%	0–£3,200	£640
Basic Rate	25%	£3,200–£24,300	£5,915
Higher Rate	40%	Over £24,300	

Lower, basic and higher rate for 1994/95 [*Sec 1(2); FA 1994, s 75*]

	Rate	On Taxable Income	Cumulative tax
Lower Rate	20%	0–£3,000	£600
Basic Rate	25%	£3,000–£23,700	£5,775
Higher Rate	40%	Over £23,700	

Lower, basic and higher rate for 1993/94 [*Sec 1(2); FA 1993, s 51*]

	Rate	On Taxable Income	Cumulative tax
Lower Rate	20%	0–£2,500	£500
Basic Rate	25%	£2,500–£23,700	£5,800
Higher Rate	40%	Over £23,700	

Lower, basic and higher rate for 1992/93 [*Sec 1(2); FA 1992, ss 9, 10(1)(2)*]

	Rate	On Taxable Income	Cumulative tax
Lower Rate	20%	0–£2,000	£400
Basic Rate	25%	£2,000–£23,700	£5,825
Higher Rate	40%	Over £23,700	

Basic and higher rate for 1991/92 [*Sec 1(2); FA 1991, s 21(1)*]

	Rate	On Taxable Income	Cumulative tax
Basic Rate	25%	0–£23,700	£5,925
Higher Rate	40%	Over £23,700	

Basic and higher rate for 1990/91 [*Sec 1(2); FA 1990, s 17(1)*]

	Rate	On Taxable Income	Cumulative tax
Basic Rate	25%	0–£20,700	£5,175
Higher Rate	40%	Over £20,700	

1.6 **TOTAL INCOME**

of an individual is his statutory income from all sources, calculated in accordance with tax legislation. [*Sec 835*]. It consists of earned and investment (or unearned) income less certain charges etc. (see 1.7 to 1.9 below). See also 28 EXCESS LIABILITY.

Exemptions. See list under 29 EXEMPT INCOME.

1.7   EARNED INCOME

is income arising to an individual from

(i) any office or employment of profit, or property attached thereto. [*Sec 833(4)*]. (See *Recknell Ch D 1952, 33 TC 201*). Includes maternity pay (see 55.31 PAY AS YOU EARN).

(ii) the *personal* carrying on of a trade, profession or vocation (including certain POST-CESSATION RECEIPTS (60) chargeable under *Sec 103* or *Sec 104* [*Sec 107*]). [*Sec 833(4)*]. But does not include: a sleeping partnership; trustees carrying on business for minors, etc. (*Shiels' Trustees CS 1914, 6 TC 583*) (except, in practice, where a trustee carrying on such a business is himself a beneficiary—see also *Dale HL 1953, 34 TC 468*, and *White v Franklin CA 1965, 42 TC 283*); interest received by solicitor on bank deposits made out of clients' funds in his hands (*Brown v CIR HL 1964, 42 TC 42; Northend v White Ch D 1975, 50 TC 121*); Lloyd's underwriters, unless actively engaged in Lloyd's business and employed full time in the Room etc. (see 89 UNDERWRITERS).

(iii) deferred pay, pensions, etc., given in respect of past services (whether of the individual or individual's spouse or parent, or any deceased person, and regardless of whether or not the individual contributed to the pension, etc.), including Civil List pensions, voluntary pensions under *Sec 58(2)* or *Sec 133* (see 59.1 PENSIONS) and chargeable payments on retirement or removal from office (see 19.4 COMPENSATION FOR LOSS OF EMPLOYMENT). Also, annuities under RETIREMENT ANNUITIES AND PERSONAL PENSION SCHEMES (65) so far as attributable to contributions on which relief has been given. Also partnership retirement annuities as specified in *Sec 628* (see 53.5 PARTNERSHIPS). [*Sec 833(4)(5); FA 1988, 3 Sch 21*].

(iv) social security benefits (other than specified exemptions, see 82 SOCIAL SECURITY). [*Secs 150, 151, 617, 833(5)(c)*].

(v) annuities for giving up (after attaining age of 55) uncommercial agricultural land, see under 71.76 SCHEDULE D, CASES I AND II. [*Sec 833(5)(d)*].

(vi) inventor's income from patents [*Sec 529*] (see under 54 PATENTS).

(vii) distribution of assets of body corporate carrying on mutual business to certain recipients [*Sec 491(5)*], see Tolley's Corporation Tax under Mutual Companies.

(viii) sale of earnings for capital sum [*Sec 775(2)*], see 3.10 ANTI-AVOIDANCE.

(ix) know-how sale by non-trading vendor who devised it [*Sec 531(6)*], see 71.66 SCHEDULE D, CASES I AND II.

(x) furnished holiday lettings [*Sec 503*], see 74.4 SCHEDULE D, CASE VI.

1.8   INVESTMENT (OR UNEARNED) INCOME

is the income *other than earned income* included in the total income. It includes the following.

(i) **Annual Payments** either falling due before 15 March 1988, or made otherwise than by an individual, or made in pursuance of an 'existing obligation' (but see below 1995/96 onwards). This includes **annuities** (except that the capital portion of a purchased life annuity or annuity certain is exempt from tax, and certain retirement annuities are treated as earned income, see 1.7(iii) above), income from **deeds of covenant** (for 1994/95 and earlier years under existing obligations) and **maintenance payments** (alimony) under a Court Order or enforceable agreement. Such income is often received after deduction of income tax at the basic rate. (But most maintenance payments made after 5 April 1989 (see 47.15 MARRIED PERSONS) are made without deduction of tax as are certain annual payments made under tax avoidance schemes (see 3.19 ANTI-AVOIDANCE)). The gross amount of annual payments is assessable on the recipient but a credit is given for tax deducted (which means that if tax at the basic rate is deducted *and* the recipient is only liable to basic rate tax, there is no further liability).

An annual payment made by an individual, or by a Scottish partnership in which at least one partner is an individual, and falling due **after 14 March 1988**, other than where made in pursuance of an 'existing obligation', does not form part of the taxable income of the person to whom it is made or of any other person, but excluded are payments of interest, payments under charitable covenants, payments made for *bona fide* commercial reasons in connection with the payer's trade, profession or vocation and payments within 3.19 ANTI-AVOIDANCE. **For 1995/96 and subsequent years,** this rule also applies to payments treated as income of the payer under *Secs 660A, 660B* (see 80.13–80.17 SETTLEMENTS) *even if* made under an 'existing obligation', which means, for example, that a payment due and made after 5 April 1995 and a pre-15 March 1988 non-charitable deed of covenant will not count as the income of the recipient for tax purposes.

An '*existing obligation*' means a binding obligation under

(*a*)   a Court Order made, whether or not in the UK, before 15 March 1988, or applied for before 16 March 1988 and made before the end of June 1988, or

(*b*)   a deed executed, or written agreement made, before 15 March 1988 and received by an inspector of taxes before the end of June 1988, or

(*c*)   an oral agreement made before 15 March 1988, written particulars of which were received by an inspector before the end of June 1988, or

(*d*)   a Court Order or written agreement made after 14 March 1988 or (after 5 April 1993) a maintenance assessment under the Child Support Act 1991 (or NI equivalent) which replaces, varies or supplements an order or agreement within these provisions, but only if

(i)   the obligation is for a person to make periodical payments of maintenance (excluding instalments of a lump sum) to or for the benefit of his or her divorced or separated spouse, or to any person under 21 for his own benefit, maintenance or education, or to any person for the benefit etc. of a person under 21, and

(ii)   the previous order etc. was for the benefit etc. of the same person.

A payment to or for the benefit of a person who attained the age of 21 before the due date of the payment but after 5 April 1994 which is made in pursuance of an obligation within (*a*), (*b*) or (*c*) above is deemed *not* to have been made in pursuance of an existing obligation (and after 5 April 1995, payments within (*b*) and (*c*) above to those aged 18 and over are disregarded—see 47.15 MARRIED PERSONS). This treatment is extended to payments made after 5 April 1996, in pursuance of an obligation within (*a*) above, to or for the benefit of a child who attained the age of 21 before 6 April 1994.

Payments due after 5 April 1990 between a husband and wife at a time when they are living together are, notwithstanding (*a*)–(*d*) above, effectively regarded as being other than in pursuance of an existing obligation.

[*Sec 347A; FA 1988, s 36, 3 Sch 32; F(No 2)A 1992, s 62(2); FA 1994, s 79(2); FA 1995, 17 Sch 4(1); FA 1996, s 149; SI 1992 No 2642*].

For **1988/89,** a maximum deduction of £1,490 may be made, in arriving at total income, from maintenance payments received under an existing obligation from a divorced or separated spouse. For **1989/90** and subsequent years, maintenance payments received under existing obligations are taxable only to the extent of the aggregate amount of such payments received from the same person which formed part of the recipient's taxable income (before the above-mentioned deduction) for 1988/89; such payments will usually be receivable without deduction of tax at source (but see 47.15 MARRIED PERSONS for exceptions). In addition, where the payments are received from a divorced or separated spouse, the recipient may claim a maximum deduction equal to the difference between the married man's allowance (see 1.21 below) and the single person's allowance (see 1.20 below), or, for 1990/91 onwards, equal to the married couple's allowance (see 1.15 below). No deduction may be made, either for 1988/89 or for subsequent years, in respect of payments due at a time when the beneficiary has remarried. Payments received from a divorced or separated spouse include payments received by a third party for the benefit of the person concerned and payments received by that person for the maintenance of a child of the family, being a person under 21 who is a child of both parties to the marriage or has been treated by them both as a child of their family, but excluding a child who has been boarded out with them by a public authority or voluntary organisation. [*FA 1988, ss 37, 38, 40, 3 Sch 33; FA 1994, 26 Sch Pt V(1)*]. See also 47.15 MARRIED PERSONS.

(ii) **Dividends etc..** In addition to receiving the cash amount of a dividend or other qualifying distribution, a UK resident receives a 'tax credit' of a proportion of the dividend etc. received, found by the formula

$$\frac{I}{100 - I}$$

where I is the lower rate (for 1992/93 and earlier years, the basic rate) of income tax, expressed as a percentage, for the year of assessment. Thus for 1993/94 and subsequent years, with a lower rate of 20%, the tax credit is one-quarter of the dividend etc.. No tax credit is available in respect of 'foreign income dividends' within *ICTA 1988, Pt VI, Ch VA* (see Tolley's Corporation Tax under Foreign Income Dividends).

The income assessable on the UK resident is the sum of the dividend etc. and the attached tax credit, with the tax credit being available against the liability. For 1992/93 and earlier years (where the tax credit was equivalent to the basic rate liability), there was thus no further liability where the basic rate limit was not exceeded, and the tax credit was wholly or partly repayable where other income did not exhaust the lower rate band.

For **1993/94 onwards,** income from UK dividends etc. which would otherwise be chargeable at the basic rate is instead chargeable at the lower rate, so that the liability thereon is fully satisfied by the tax credit. The tax credit may be repaid if the allowances are not exhausted by other income, and if dividend etc. income exceeds the basic rate limit, it is taxed at the higher rate (with a tax credit at the lower rate). For this purpose, the dividend etc. income is (for 1996/97 onwards, together with other savings income, see (iii) below) treated as the top slice of total income (see (iii) below). These provisions apply equally to income consisting of foreign dividends etc. chargeable under Schedule D, Case V, which do not carry a tax credit, unless they are taxable on the remittance basis under *Sec 65(5)(b)* (see 73.5 SCHEDULE D, CASES IV AND V). [*Secs 1A, 14(3), 207A, 231(1), 833(3); FA 1993, ss 77, 78(1)(3); FA 1996, s 73, 41 Sch Pt V(1)*]. The definition of 'excess liability' throughout the *Taxes*

Acts is amended to take account of the lower rate charge on dividend and other savings income. See also 80.5 SETTLEMENTS as regards income of discretionary trusts.

Where a person (other than a UK resident company) is not entitled to a tax credit on a distribution, the amount received is not taxed at the lower rate (or, for 1992/93 and earlier years, at the basic rate), and any tax at a higher rate is reduced by tax at the lower rate (for 1992/93 and earlier years, the basic rate). The income is not available to cover tax on charges (see 1.9 below) and the notional tax deducted is not repayable. Where the non-entitlement to the tax credit in respect of a qualifying distribution arises from the recipient being non-UK resident or the dividend a 'foreign income dividend', the distribution is for these purposes grossed up at the lower rate of tax. [*Secs 233(1)(1A), 246C, 246D; F(No 2)A 1992, s 19(4); FA 1993, 6 Sch 2; FA 1994, 16 Sch 1; FA 1996, s 122(3)–(5), 6 Sch 5, 28, 27 Sch 2, 41 Sch Pt V(1)*]. See also 80.5 SETTLEMENTS as regards income of discretionary trusts.

Certain payments (and other items normally treated as distributions) made by a company for the redemption, repayment or purchase of its own shares are not treated as distributions [*Sec 219*] and consequently have no tax credit and are not treated as income (but see 71.81 SCHEDULE D CASES I AND II as regards dealers in securities). See Tolley's Corporation Tax regarding purchase by a company of its own shares.

A non-resident individual who claims personal allowances (see 51.11 NON-RESIDENTS AND OTHER OVERSEAS MATTERS) is entitled to a tax credit in respect of any qualifying distribution as if he were resident in the UK. [*Sec 232*].

Tax credits set off or repaid which ought not to have been set off or repaid may be assessed, the tax due on such an assessment being payable (subject to the normal appeal procedures) within 14 days after the issue of the notice of assessment. [*Sec 252*].

For foreign dividends paid through agents, see (70) SCHEDULE C.

(iii) **Savings income (including interest)**, which for 1996/97 and subsequent years is chargeable to income tax at the lower rate (provided in the case of an individual that it is not chargeable at the higher rate—see below). This applies to 'savings income' received by any person other than a discretionary trust (see 80.5 SETTLEMENTS) or unauthorised unit trust (see 90.2 UNIT TRUSTS). Where tax is deductible at source (see below) from savings income, then (regardless of the recipient's status) the deduction is at the lower rate. For these purposes, '*savings income*' comprises:

(*a*)   UK company dividends (see (ii) above);

(*b*)   any income chargeable under SCHEDULE D, CASE III (72), *except for* annuities and other annual payments that are not interest (see (i) above and 23.10 DEDUCTION OF TAX AT SOURCE) and rents etc. under *Secs 119* and *120* (re mines, quarries and electric wayleaves, see 23.14 DEDUCTION OF TAX AT SOURCE); *however*, purchased life annuities (see 23.11(*c*) DEDUCTION OF TAX AT SOURCE, and including those excluded under 23.11(*c*)(i)) are not excluded and the lower rate thus applies; and

(*c*)   foreign income chargeable under SCHEDULE D, CASES IV AND V (73) and equivalent either to income within (*b*) above but arising from securities or other possessions outside the UK or to dividends within (*a*) above, *except for* income so chargeable on the remittance basis (see 73.5 SCHEDULE D, CASES IV AND V) and payments made out of a foreign estate of a deceased person and chargeable under Case IV (see 22.3 DECEASED ESTATES).

Savings income is chargeable at the higher rate to the extent that it falls within an individual's higher rate band. If the income has suffered lower rate tax at source, excess liability is payable at the difference between the higher and lower rate. For the purpose of determining this extent, savings income is treated as the top slice of total income, but before taking into account income chargeable under *Sec 148* (payments on loss of office, see 19.5 COMPENSATION FOR LOSS OF EMPLOYMENT) or *Sec 547(1)(a)* (life assurance gains, see 45.13 LIFE ASSURANCE POLICIES). For 1993/94 to 1995/96 inclusive, this also applied, but only to dividend income (see (ii) above).

[*Secs 1A, 4(1A); FA 1996, s 73*].

Interest is receivable under deduction of tax at source where it is annual interest paid *by* a company (including a partnership of which a company is a member), *by* a local authority, or *to* a person whose usual place of abode is outside the UK. [*Sec 349(2)(3)*], including interest on company debentures and other securities. Bank and building society interest is excluded, but deduction of tax is imposed under separate provisions. See 8.3 BANKS and 9.5 BUILDING SOCIETIES for further details and for exceptions (and see 8.2 and 9.3, 9.4 for the position for 1990/91 and earlier years). Otherwise, interest is generally receivable gross. See 29.11 EXEMPT INCOME for interest on 'TESSAs' and other tax-exempt interest, and see also 33 GOVERN-MENT STOCKS.

(iv) **Property income** assessed under SCHEDULE A (68) and SCHEDULE D, CASE VI (74) other than from furnished holiday lettings (see 68.9).

Note. In the case of an individual carrying on a trade etc. investment income does not include (*a*) income from investment the proceeds of which, if sold, would be trading income or (*b*) interest on trade debts. [*FA 1971, s 32(4)*].

1.9 **CHARGES ON INCOME ETC.**

deductible, except where stated, in arriving at 'Total Income' as above comprise

(i) **Annual Payments** falling due before 15 March 1988 or within the exceptions referred to below. See 1.8(i) above for details of annual payments and 23 DEDUCTION OF TAX AT SOURCE (and 47.15 MARRIED PERSONS as regards maintenance payments) for the circumstances in which income tax at the basic or lower rate should be deducted. The payer, having deducted tax at source, will be assessed to that tax to the extent, if any, that it exceeds the tax he has borne on his income (see 2.5 ALLOWANCES AND TAX RATES—EXAMPLES). [*Sec 350(1)(1A); FA 1996, 6 Sch 8, 28*]. *If he fails to deduct tax*, he obtains no relief for the payment. [*Sec 276; FA 1994, 8 Sch 11*]. Certain payments under deeds of covenant and under maintenance agreements between parent and child are ineffective for the purposes of excess liability (i.e. excess of higher rates of income tax over basic rate) (see 80.28 SETTLEMENTS), and no deduction is made from 'Total Income' for excess liability purposes in those cases, nor for certain annual payments made under tax avoidance schemes (see 3.19 ANTI-AVOIDANCE).

An annual payment made by an individual, or by a Scottish partnership in which at least one partner is an individual, and falling due after 14 March 1988 is not a charge on the income of the person making it. Exceptions are

(*a*) payments under 'existing obligations' (see 1.8(i) above, and also 47.15 MARRIED PERSONS as regards 1994/95 and subsequent years),

(*b*) payments of interest,

(*c*) payments under charitable covenants,

(*d*) payments made for *bona fide* commercial reasons in connection with the payer's trade, profession or vocation, and

(*e*) payments within *Sec 125* (see 3.19 ANTI-AVOIDANCE).

1.10 Allowances and Tax Rates—Applicable to individuals

As regards (a) above, for 1995/96 and subsequent years a payment treated as income of the payer under *Secs 660A, 660B* (see 80.13–80.17 SETTLEMENTS) is not a charge on the income of the payer even if made under an 'existing obligation', which would apply for example to a payment due and made after 5 April 1995 under a pre-15 March 1988 non-charitable deed of covenant.

[Sec 347A(1)(2); FA 1988, s 36(1)(3); FA 1995, 17 Sch 4(1)].

See 47.15 MARRIED PERSONS for special rules regarding maintenance payments.

(ii) **Interest payable** by the taxpayer insofar as it is allowable for tax purposes and has not been allowed as a deduction in computing profits. Higher rate relief is denied in certain cases. For 1994/95 and subsequent years, most mortgage interest is relieved either by deduction at source under MIRAS or by way of a reduction in tax payable; such interest is *not* deductible in arriving at total income. See 43 INTEREST PAYABLE.

(iii) **Class 4 National Insurance contributions.** For 1995/96 and earlier years, a claim may be made to deduct 50% of such contributions an individual is liable to pay (as finally determined) in respect of the year of assessment. *[Sec 617(5); FA 1996, s 147].*

Charges as in (i) and, where applicable, (ii) above are deducted from investment income first, except that they may be deducted from earned income, if this is advantageous to the taxpayer, subject to any express provision to the contrary. *[Sec 835(4)].*

See also 28 EXCESS LIABILITY.

1.10 EXCESS LIABILITY

Certain income is subject to 'excess liability', which broadly means income tax in excess of the basic (or, where appropriate, lower) rate (i.e. the higher rate or rates plus, before 1984/85, the investment income surcharge). See under 28 EXCESS LIABILITY.

1.11 CLAIMS

Allowances unclaimed or not deducted from assessments (and relief for unused tax credits on dividends or tax suffered by deduction at source) may be claimed within five years after 31 January following the tax year for which the claim is made (for 1995/96 and earlier years, six years after the end of that tax year). *[TMA s 43; FA 1994, ss 196, 199(2)(a), 19 Sch 14].* See 17 CLAIMS. But relief is given only in respect of tax actually borne by the claimant, i.e., no relief on income the tax on which he is entitled to charge at the basic rate against, or deduct from any payment to, any other person. *[Secs 256(3)(c)(ii), 276; FA 1994, s 77(1), 8 Sch 11].* Allowances depend upon 'the facts as they exist at the time' and cannot afterwards be withdrawn (or fresh assessments made) by reason of facts 'which arose after the year of assessment' *(Dodworth v Dale KB 1936, 20 TC 285).*

See 7 BANKRUPTCY for claims by bankrupts.

1.12 NON-RESIDENTS

pay income tax at the full rates on chargeable income, with none of the following reliefs except those available to Commonwealth subjects etc. (see 51.11 NON-RESIDENTS AND OTHER OVERSEAS MATTERS) and under certain DOUBLE TAX RELIEF (25) agreements. See, however, 64.5 RESIDENCE, ORDINARY RESIDENCE AND DOMICILE as regards year permanent residence begins or ends.

1.13   INDEXATION OF PERSONAL RELIEFS AND TAX THRESHOLDS

Unless Parliament otherwise determines, the basic rate band, the higher rate bands (where applicable) and certain personal reliefs are increased by the same percentage as the percentage increase (if any) in the retail price index (or any substitute index) for the September preceding the year of assessment over that for the previous September (December in each case for 1993/94 and earlier years). The resultant figure in the case of tax bands and income limits is rounded up to the nearest £100 and in the case of the personal reliefs to the nearest £10. The personal reliefs affected are the personal allowance and married couple's allowance; the additional personal allowance in respect of children and the widow's bereavement allowance are both equal to the basic married couple's allowance.

The new figures are specified in a statutory instrument by HM Treasury before the year of assessment. [*Secs 1(4)(6), 257C, 259(2); FA 1988, s 33, 3 Sch 5; FA 1993, s 107*].

1.14   PERSONAL ALLOWANCE [*Sec 257; FA 1988, s 33; SI 1990 No 677; SI 1991 No 732; SI 1992 No 622; FA 1993, s 52; FA 1994, s 76; SI 1994 No 3012; FA 1995, s 36; SI 1995 No 3031; FA 1996, ss 74, 134, 20 Sch 13*]

The personal allowance is available to all claimants (subject to the rules relating to non-UK residents, see 51.11 NON-RESIDENTS AND OTHER OVERSEAS MATTERS).

For	1990/91	£3,005
For	1991/92	£3,295
From	1992/93	£3,445
For	1995/96	£3,525
For	**1996/97**	**£3,765**

Where the claimant is at any time in the year of assessment aged 65 (or aged 75) or over, or would have been but for his or her death in that year, a higher allowance is available. Where total income exceeds an income limit, that higher allowance is reduced by one half of the excess until the allowance is the same as the ordinary personal allowance. The income level at which the higher allowance ceases is shown in the right hand column below.

		Personal allowance		Income	Maximum income	
		65 to 74	75 or over	limit	65 to 74	75 or over
For	1990/91	£3,670	£3,820	£12,300	£13,630	£13,930
For	1991/92	£4,020	£4,180	£13,500	£14,950	£15,270
From	1992/93	£4,200	£4,370	£14,200	£15,710	£16,050
For	1995/96	£4,630	£4,800	£14,600	£16,810	£17,150
For	**1996/97**	**£4,910**	**£5,090**	**£15,200**	**£17,490**	**£17,850**

See 1.13 above as to indexation.

See 47.5 MARRIED PERSONS as regards certain transitional reliefs.

See 1.20 below for the single person's allowance which applied before 1990/91.

1.15   MARRIED COUPLE'S ALLOWANCE [*Secs 256, 257A; FA 1988, s 33; SI 1990 No 677; SI 1991 No 732; FA 1991, s 22; SI 1992 No 622; FA 1992, s 10(3); FA 1993, s 52; FA 1994, ss 77(1)(2)(6)–(10), 78, 8 Sch 1; SI 1995 No 3031; FA 1996, s 134, 20 Sch 14*]

The married couple's allowance is available (subject to the rules relating to non-UK residents, see 51.11 NON-RESIDENTS AND OTHER OVERSEAS MATTERS) to a claimant who is, at any time in the year of assessment, a married man whose wife is living with him (see 47.12

1.15 Allowances and Tax Rates—Applicable to individuals

MARRIED PERSONS). For polygamous marriages under Moslem law, see *Nabi v Heaton CA 1983, 57 TC 292*, in which, at the Revenue's request, the taxpayer's appeal from the Ch D decision against him was allowed by consent.

From 1990/91 £1,720
For **1996/97** £1,790

For 1994/95 and subsequent years, tax relief for the married couple's allowance is given at a reduced rate, 20% for 1994/95 and 15% thereafter. The allowance is no longer given as a deduction from total income, but is given instead by means of a reduction in the claimant's income tax liability. The reduction is the smaller of the specified percentage (i.e. 15% for 1996/97) of the allowance and what would otherwise be the claimant's total income tax liability. For this purpose, 'total income tax liability' is before deducting any double tax relief and excludes any basic rate tax deducted at source from charges on income or other payments (and is before giving credit for tax suffered at source on the claimant's income and tax credits on dividends). Other reductions in income tax liability are made before that for married couple's allowance.

Where the claimant or his wife is at any time in the year of assessment aged 65 (or aged 75) or over, or would have been but for his or her death in that year, a higher allowance is available (but with relief restricted, and calculated, as above). Where the claimant's total income exceeds an income limit, that higher allowance is reduced by one half of the excess (less any reduction made in the claimant's personal allowance age increase, see 1.14 above) until the allowance is the same as the ordinary married couple's allowance. The maximum income level at which the higher allowance ceases is shown in the right hand column below.

		Married couple's allowance		Income limit	Maximum income	
		65 to 74	75 or over		65 to 74	75 or over
For	1990/91	£2,145	£2,185	£12,300	£14,480	£14,860
For	1991/92	£2,355	£2,395	£13,500	£16,220	£16,620
From	1992/93	£2,465	£2,505	£14,200	£17,200	£17,620
For	1994/95	£2,665	£2,705	£14,200	£17,600	£18,020
For	1995/96	£2,995	£3,035	£14,600	£19,360	£19,780
For	**1996/97**	£3,115	£3,155	£15,200	£20,140	£20,580

The figures in the right hand column may vary where entitlement to the higher allowance is by virtue of the wife's age rather than the husband's, or where the wife is 75 or over.

No more than one allowance may be claimed for any year of assessment, and where marriage takes place during the year of assessment (and the husband had not previously in that year been entitled to the married couple's allowance), the allowance is reduced by one-twelfth for each fiscal month (i.e. ending on 5 May, 5 June, etc.) of the year ending before the date of the marriage.

A man marrying in a year of assessment and otherwise entitled to the additional personal allowance in respect of children (see 1.17 below) may elect that the marriage be disregarded for the purposes of both that allowance and the married couple's allowance. [*Sec 261; FA 1988, 3 Sch 6*].

Where death takes place during the year of assessment, the full allowance is available for that year. The allowance is not reduced if the husband remarries during the year in which his wife dies.

See 1.13 above as to indexation.

See 47.2, 47.5 MARRIED PERSONS as regards transfer of allowances and certain transitional reliefs.

See 1.21 below for the married man's allowance which applied before 1990/91.

1.16   **WIDOW'S BEREAVEMENT ALLOWANCE** [*Secs 256, 262; FA 1988, 3 Sch 7; F(No 2)A 1992, 5 Sch 7; FA 1994, s 77(1)(5)(8)(9), 8 Sch 9*]

Where a married man whose wife is living with him dies, his widow is entitled to an allowance for the year of his death, and for the following year provided she does not remarry before the beginning of that year, of an amount equal to the married couple's allowance (see 1.15 above) for the year, in addition to any other available reliefs. The allowance is still due if the couple stopped living together before the husband's death, provided that they separated in the year of death and are still married at the time of his death. (Revenue Independent Taxation Handbook, In 523, 524).

From   1990/91   £1,720
For   1996/97   £1,790

For 1993/94 and earlier years, the allowance is given as a deduction from total income. For 1994/95 and subsequent years, tax relief for the allowance is given at a reduced rate, 20% for 1994/95 and 15% thereafter, and is given by means of a reduction in the widow's income tax liability. The reduction is the smaller of the specified percentage (i.e. 15% for 1996/97) of the allowance and what would otherwise be the widow's total income tax liability. For this purpose, 'total income tax liability' is as defined in 1.15 above, except that it is before any reduction on account of married couple's allowance (see below).

Where a widow is entitled for the year of her husband's death both to the bereavement allowance and (as a result of an election (see 47.2 MARRIED PERSONS)) to the whole or part of the married couple's allowance, then, for 1993/94 and earlier years, the married couple's allowance is instead deducted from the late husband's total income of the year of death, to the extent that it does not exceed that income after all deductions other than those in respect of business expansion scheme investments (see 26 ENTERPRISE INVESTMENT SCHEME (AND BES)) and payments for which relief is obtained by deduction of basic rate tax in respect of retirement benefit or personal pension scheme contributions (66.5(*a*) RETIREMENT SCHEMES, 65.2 RETIREMENT ANNUITIES AND PERSONAL PENSION SCHEMES), relevant loan interest (23.13 DEDUCTION OF TAX AT SOURCE), MEDICAL INSURANCE (48) premiums, and vocational training costs (71.87 SCHEDULE D, CASES I AND II, 75.42 SCHEDULE E). Any such excess remains available to the widow. For 1994/95 and subsequent years, the married couple's allowance is given by way of reduction in the late husband's income tax liability of the year of death, to the extent that there is sufficient liability to cover it. The widow is entitled to a reduction by reference to any excess allowance.

1.17   **ADDITIONAL RELIEF IN RESPECT OF CHILDREN** [*Secs 256, 259–261A; FA 1988, ss 30, 35, 3 Sch 5, 6; F(No 2)A 1992, 5 Sch 5, 6; FA 1994, s 77(1)(3)(4)(8)(9), 8 Sch 6–8; FA 1996, s 134, 20 Sch 17, 18*]

A relief equal in amount to the married couple's allowance (see 1.15 above) (for 1989/90 and earlier years, to the difference between the married man's and single person's allowances, see 1.20, 1.21 below) is claimable by

(i)   any woman who is not throughout the year of assessment married and living with her husband,

(ii)   a man who is neither married and living with his wife for the whole or part of a year of assessment nor entitled to the transitional personal reliefs available to certain separated couples (see 47.5(*c*) MARRIED PERSONS), and

(iii)   a man who for the whole or part of a year of assessment is married, the wife being totally incapacitated (physically or mentally) throughout the year (for which see Revenue Independent Taxation Handbook, In 594),

who has a 'qualifying child' resident with him/her for the whole or part of the year.

From   1990/91   £1,720
For   **1996/97**   **£1,790**

Relief under (i) and (ii) above is not available for the year of separation, for which special provisions apply (see below), for 1993/94 and subsequent years.

For 1993/94 and earlier years, the additional relief is given as a deduction from total income. For 1994/95 and subsequent years, the relief is given at a reduced rate, 20% for 1994/95 and 15% for 1995/96 and subsequent years, and is given by means of a reduction in the claimant's income tax liability. The reduction is the smaller of the specified percentage (i.e. 15% for 1996/97) of the additional relief and what would otherwise be the claimant's total income tax liability. For this purpose, 'total income tax liability' is as defined in 1.15 above, except that it is before any reduction on account of married couple's allowance and/or widow's bereavement allowance.

A claimant is entitled to only one relief for a year of assessment no matter how many 'qualifying children' are resident with him/her during the year. A woman is not entitled to relief for a year of assessment during any part of which she is married and living with her husband unless the 'qualifying child' is resident with her during a part of the year when she is not married and living with her husband.

A man marrying in a year of assessment may claim that his marriage be disregarded for the purposes of both this relief and the married couple's allowance (see 1.15 above).

Where an unmarried couple live together as husband and wife at any time in the year of assessment, and they would both otherwise be entitled to claim the additional relief, then neither of them will be entitled to the relief in respect of any child other than the youngest of the children for whom either of them could otherwise claim relief, i.e. relief to the couple is restricted to one allowance.

A '*qualifying child*' must be born in, or under sixteen at the commencement of, the year of assessment or over sixteen and receiving full-time instruction at a university, college, school or other educational establishment or undergoing full-time training by an employer (for not less than two years) for a trade, profession or vocation (for 1995/96 and earlier years, the employer may be required to furnish particulars of such training). A child who enrols on a 2 year YTS training programme normally satisfies this latter condition. See generally Revenue Independent Taxation Handbook, In 653–655. The child must be resident with the claimant for the whole or part of the year, and must be a 'child of the claimant' or, if not, must be under eighteen and maintained for the whole or part of the year at the claimant's expense. 'Custody' of child is not required.

The Revenue consider that, to be 'resident with' the claimant, a child must have his or her home with the claimant. While it is possible for a child to have more than one home, it is not accepted that any short visit, e.g. for a holiday, makes the place so visited a home. (Revenue Tax Bulletin November 1992 p 44).

'*Child of the claimant*' includes a stepchild, an illegitimate child whose parents have married each other after his birth and a child adopted under the age of eighteen.

Age of child. A child is 'over sixteen' or 'over eighteen' at the beginning of a year of assessment if its sixteenth or eighteenth birthday falls either on the first day of that year (i.e. 6 April) or during the previous year.

Apportionment of the relief may be made between two or more persons as may be agreed between them or, failing agreement, in proportion to the length of the periods the child resided with them respectively during the year. Failing agreement, the apportionment is to be made by the appellate General Commissioners for the division in which one of the claimants resides (or Special Commissioners if none of the claimants resides in the United Kingdom). Each claimant is entitled to make oral or written representations.

The Board may direct that a claim to relief which requires apportionment be dealt with by the Commissioners. Where an individual is apportioned amounts in respect of two or more children, his total relief is limited to the lesser of the sum of those amounts and the full relief available for one child. An individual is not entitled to relief in respect of the same child as another person if he alone is entitled to relief in respect of another child.

Year of separation. For 1993/94 and subsequent years, the additional relief is available in the year of assessment of 'separation' to a spouse with whom a qualifying child resides during the year but after the separation, but not where it is already available to that spouse under (iii) above. The amount of the relief is reduced by any married couple's allowance available to the spouse (see 1.15 above, 47.2 MARRIED PERSONS), unless that allowance has been transferred to that spouse because the other spouse's income was insufficient fully to utilise the allowance (see 47.2 MARRIED PERSONS). Only one relief is available to a spouse, regardless of the number of qualifying children resident with the spouse. For 1994/95 and subsequent years, the relief is given at a reduced rate, and by means of an income tax reduction, as above.

Where another person is entitled to the additional relief in respect of the same child, whether under this or under the general provision, the total relief (which may not exceed the married couple's allowance) is apportioned between them (subject to the same procedural rules as apply in relation to the general provision above). '*Separation*' for these purposes means separation under a Court order or deed of separation or in circumstances that it is likely to be permanent.

1.18   **BLIND PERSONS** [*Sec 265; FA 1988, 3 Sch 8; FA 1990, s 18; FA 1994, s 82; FA 1996, ss 75, 134, 20 Sch 19*]

From	1990/91	£1,080
From	1994/95	£1,200
For	**1996/67**	**£1,250**

Allowance as above may be claimed if a person is, throughout the whole or part of the year, registered as blind under *National Assistance Act 1948, s 29* (or Scottish or NI equivalent).

For 1994/95 and subsequent years, by concession, a person becoming entitled to the blind person's allowance by being registered during the year will (subject to the normal time limit for claims) also be given the allowance for the previous year if, at the end of that year, the evidence on which the registration was based (e.g. the ophthalmologist's certificate) had already been obtained. (Revenue Pamphlet IR 1 (November 1995 Supplement), A86).

For transfer of allowances between spouses, see 47.2 MARRIED PERSONS.

1.19   For Life Assurance Relief, see 45.1 *et seq.* LIFE ASSURANCE POLICIES. For relief for medical insurance premiums, see 48 MEDICAL INSURANCE. For Mortgage Interest Relief, see 23.13 DEDUCTION OF TAX AT SOURCE and 43.6 *et seq.* INTEREST PAYABLE. For Retirement Annuity Relief and relief for Personal Pension Contributions, see 65 RETIREMENT ANNUITIES AND PERSONAL PENSION SCHEMES.

1.20   Allowances and Tax Rates—Applicable to individuals

1.20   **SINGLE PERSON'S ALLOWANCE** [*Sec 257(1)(b); ICTA 1970, s 8(1)(b) as amended; FA 1988, ss 25(1)(b), 33; SI 1989 No 467*]

(to an unmarried, separated or divorced person or widow(er))

For	1988/89	£2,605
For	1989/90	£2,785

Where election was made for separate taxation of wife's earned income (see 47.10 MARRIED PERSONS), the single allowance was given to both the husband and wife *instead* of the married allowance (see 1.21 below) being given to the husband and wife's earned income relief (see 1.22 below) being granted on wife's earnings.

The allowance is **abolished** for 1990/91 and later years. See now 1.14 above.

1.21   **MARRIED MAN'S ALLOWANCE** [*Sec 257(1)(a); ICTA 1970, s 8(1)(a) as amended; FA 1988, ss 25(1)(a), 33; SI 1989 No 467*]

(to a married man whose wife (not including common law wife, see *Rignell v Andrews Ch D 1990, 63 TC 312*) was living with him (see 47.12 MARRIED PERSONS) or was wholly maintained by him, see *Holmes v Mitchell Ch D 1990, 63 TC 718*). No married allowance if husband made maintenance etc. payments to his separated wife under Court Order or enforceable agreement which could be deducted from his income for tax purposes (see 47.15 MARRIED PERSONS).

For	1988/89	£4,095
For	1989/90	£4,375

Where marriage took place during the year of assessment (and the husband had not previously in that year been entitled to married allowance), the married allowance was reduced by one-twelfth of excess over single allowance for each fiscal month (i.e. ending 5 May, 5 June etc.) which ended before date of marriage. Thus, reduction per month was one-twelfth of £1,490 for 1988/89 and one-twelfth of £1,590 for 1989/90. [*Sec 257(8)*].

A man marrying in a year of assessment entitled to allowances under *Sec 259* (see 1.17 above) could, for that year, disclaim the higher married allowance and be treated as not married for the purpose of such allowances. [*Sec 261; ICTA 1970, s 15*].

Where a wife's income was, as was normally the case, treated as that of her husband (see 47.6 MARRIED PERSONS), any excess of the married allowance over the husband's income could, in effect, be set against the wife's income in addition to any wife's earned income relief (see 1.22 below).

The allowance is **abolished** for 1990/91 and later years. See now 1.15 above.

1.22   **WIFE'S EARNED INCOME RELIEF** [*Sec 257(6)(7); ICTA 1970, s 8(2) as amended; FA 1988, ss 25(1)(b), 33; SI 1989 No 467*]

Granted in respect of wife's own earned income, including social security retirement pension from her own contributions, unemployment benefit, and invalid care allowance paid to wife (but excluding any other social security benefits and any pension in respect of *husband's past services*). The relief was not available for the tax year in which the marriage occurred (unless on 6 April). Amount of relief as below, regardless of taxpayer's or wife's age.

For	1988/89	Amount of wife's earnings	maximum relief £2,605
For	1989/90	Amount of wife's earnings	maximum relief £2,785

14

Wife's earned income included a bona fide salary, paid to her as such, for genuine services rendered in her husband's business, and also her share of profit if actually in partnership with him. In *Thompson v Bruce KB 1927, 11 TC 607* held no allowance for alleged salary where not charged in accounts and no other evidence of payment. Also includes maternity pay [*Secs 150(b), 833(5)(c)*], see 55.31 PAY AS YOU EARN.

The relief is **abolished** for 1990/91 and later years. See now 1.14 above.

1.23   **AGE ALLOWANCE** [*Sec 257(2)–(6); ICTA 1970, s 8(1)(1A)(1B) as amended; FA 1988, ss 25(1)(c)–(g), 33; SI 1989 No 467; FA 1989, s 31*]

Where a person, or his wife, was aged 65 or more in a year of claim and had total income not exceeding the limit as below, an age allowance was given (instead of the ordinary single or married allowances in 1.20 and 1.21 above) as follows.

					Maximum	income
		Single	Married	Income limit	Single	Married
For	1988/89	£3,180	£5,035	£10,600	£11,463	£12,010
For	1989/90	£3,400	£5,385	£11,400	£12,630	£13,420

A higher rate of age allowance was given where a person, or his wife, was aged 75 or more (80 for 1988/89). The rates were as follows.

					Maximum	income
		Single	Married	Income limit	Single	Married
For	1988/89	£3,310	£5,205	£10,600	£11,658	£12,265
For	1989/90	£3,540	£5,565	£11,400	£12,910	£13,780

Where the total income exceeded the limit, the allowance was reduced by one-half of the excess (two-thirds for 1988/89 and earlier years) until the allowance was the same as the ordinary single or married allowance. The income level at which the allowance ceased to be effective is shown in the two right-hand columns above.

Note that any building society or bank interest received under deduction of composite rate tax was grossed up at basic rate and included in total income.

There was no age allowance where election was made for separate taxation of wife's earned income, and it did not apply to increase the amount of wife's earned income relief (see 1.22 above). Where marriage took place during the year of assessment (and the husband had not previously in that year been entitled to a married allowance), the married allowance (i.e. for 1989/90 £5,385 (or £5,565) less any reduction for income over £11,400) was reduced by one-twelfth of the excess over the single allowance (i.e. £3,400 (or £3,540) less any reduction or £2,785 if husband under 65) for each fiscal month (i.e. ending 5 May, 5 June etc.) which ended before the date of marriage. If taxpayer died in year of assessment in which he would have been 65 (or 75/80) or more, he was treated as having been of that age in that year.

The allowance is **abolished** for 1990/91 and later years. See now 1.14, 1.15 above.

2.1 Allowances and Tax Rates—Examples

2 Allowances and Tax Rates—Examples

The following examples illustrate the method of calculating tax payable for **1996/97**. References in brackets are to items above (under 1 ALLOWANCES AND TAX RATES).

2.1   A **Single Person** aged under 65 receives earned income of £15,000, net building society interest of £240 and national savings bank ordinary account interest (account opened in 1994/95) of £152. He pays interest of £2,000 on a £25,000 loan which was used to purchase his main residence and which is not within MIRAS.

		£	£
(1.7)	Earned income		15,000
(1.8(iii))	Building society interest received	240	
	Tax deducted	60	
		—	300
	National savings bank ordinary account interest (£152 less £70 exempt)		82
(1.6)	Total income		15,382
(1.14)	*Deduct* Personal allowance		3,765
	Taxable income		£11,617
(1.3)	Tax liability (non-savings income):		
	£3,900 at 20%		780.00
	£7,335 at 24%		1,760.40
(1.8(iii))	(savings income):		
	£382 at 20%		76.40
			£2,616.80
	Deduct Reduction for mortgage interest £2,000 at 15%		300.00
			£2,316.80
	Deduct BSI tax deducted		60.00
	Tax payable		£2,256.80

See 43.3 INTEREST PAYABLE for the rate of, and method of giving relief for, home loan interest.

2.2   **Repayment Claim.** A single person aged under 65 years receives earned income of £2,550 (no Schedule E tax having been deducted at source), plus dividends of £1,600 from UK companies (with related 1/4th tax credit of £400).

		£
(1.7)	Earned income	2,550
(1.8(ii))	Dividends, including tax credit (£1,600 + £400)	2,000
(1.6)	Total income	4,550
(1.14)	*Deduct* Personal allowance	3,765
	Taxable income	£785

(1.3)	Tax liability: £785 at 20%	157.00
	Deduct Tax credit on dividends as above	400.00
	Income tax repayable	£243.00

2.3 **Dividend taxation.** A Married man under 65 entitled to the full married couple's allowance has income from self-employment assessable in 1996/97 of £25,000. He also receives UK dividends in that year of £6,400 (with tax credit attached £1,600).

		£	£
(1.7)	Earned income	25,000	
(1.8.(ii))	Dividends (incl. tax credit)	8,000	
(1.6)	Total income	33,000	
(1.14, 1.15)	*Deduct* Personal allowance	3,765	
	Taxable income	29,235	
(1.3)	Tax liability on non-dividend income: £3,900 at 20%		780.00
	£17,335 at 24%		4,160.40
(1.8(ii))	Tax liability on dividends: (£25,500 − £21,235 =) £4,265 at 20%		853.00
	£3,735 at 40%		1,494.00
			7,287.40
(1.15)	*Deduct* Married couple's allowance £1,790 at 15%		268.50
			7,018.90
	Deduct Tax credit on dividends		1,600.00
	Income tax payable		£5,418.90

2.4 **Age increase in personal/married couple's allowance.** A married man aged 78 has a total income of £18,040 (which does not include any dividend or interest income).

		£	£
(1.6)	Total income	18,040	18,040
(1.14)	Income limit	15,200	
(1.15)			
	Excess	2,840	
(1.14)	Personal allowance (75 and over)	5,090	
	Less reduction for excess ($\frac{1}{2} \times 2,840$)	1,420	
		3,670	

2.5 Allowances and Tax Rates—Examples

Since this is below the basic personal allowance of £3,765, the reduction is limited to £1,325 and the full £3,765 is allowable 3,765

Taxable income £14,275

		£	£
(1.3)	Tax liability: £3,900 at 20%...................................		780.00
	£10,375 at 24%...................................		2,490.00
			3,270.00
(1.15)	*Deduct* Married couple's allowance £3,060 (see below) at 15%		459.00
	Tax payable		£2,811.00
(1.15)	Married couple's allowance (75 and over)		3,155
	Less reduction for excess...............................	1,420	
	less reduction in personal allowance	1,325	95
			£3,060

2.5 A **Widow**, aged 70, whose husband died in 1995/96 (and who has not remarried), receives a State pension of £3,175 in 1996/97 and has a national savings bank investment account (opened in January 1995) on which interest of £2,005 was credited in 1996/97. She makes a charitable donation of £76 per annum under deed of covenant.

		£	
(1.7)	Earned income...	3,175	
	National savings bank investment account interest.....................................	2,005	
		5,180	
(1.9)	*Deduct* Charges (gross): £76 × 100/76...............................	100	
(1.6)	Total income...	5,080	
(1.14)	*Deduct* Personal allowance (65 to 74).....................................	4,910	
	Taxable income	£170	
(1.3)	Tax liability: £170 at 20%		34.00
1.16	*Deduct* Widow's bereavement allowance £1,790 at 15% = £268.50 but restricted to...........................		34.00
			Nil
(1.9)	*Add* Basic rate tax retained on payment under covenant..		24.00
	Tax liability...		£24.00

2.6 **Transfer of married couple's allowance.** A married man aged 68 has a total income of £6,500 out of which he pays £1,000 allowable mortgage interest outside MIRAS. His wife, aged under 65, has a total income of £10,000. She elects to receive one-half of the basic married couple's allowance. Neither spouse has any interest or dividend income.

Husband £

(1.6)	Total income	6,500
(1.14)	Personal allowance	4,910
	Taxable income	£1,590

(1.3)	Tax liability: £1,590 at 20%	318.00
	Deduct Mortgage interest	
	£1,000 at 15%	150.00
		168.00
(1.15)	*Deduct* Married couple's allowance	
	(£3,115 − 1/2 × £1,790) = £2,220.	
	£2,220 at 15% = £333 but restricted to	168.00
	Tax payable	Nil

Wife

(1.6)	Total income	10,000
(1.14)	Personal allowance	3,765
	Taxable income	£6,235

(1.3)	Tax liability: £3,900 at 20%	780.00
	£2,335 at 24%	560.40
		1,340.40
(1.15)	*Deduct* Married couple's allowance (under election)	
	£895 at 15%	134.25
	Tax payable (subject to below)	£1,206.15

The unused balance of the husband's married couple's allowance is (£333 − £168) × 100/15 = £1,100. On a claim, this may be transferred to the wife, who will then be entitled to a further income tax reduction of £165 (£1,100 at 15%), reducing tax payable to £1,041.15.

2.7 **Husband with excess allowances: transitional relief.** (See 47.5 MARRIED PERSONS.) A man married on or before 6 April 1989 and under 65 has a total income of £1,000 in 1989/90 and 1990/91, £2,500 in 1991/92 and 1992/93, £3,250 in 1993/94 and £3,400 in 1994/95. His wife, also under 65, has earned income of £10,000 in each of those years. Each is entitled only to the normal personal reliefs. The surplus allowances available for transfer to the wife in 1990/91 were as follows.

2.7 Allowances and Tax Rates—Examples

		£	£
(1.15)	Married couple's allowance		1,720
	Less husband's total income for 1990/91	1,000	
(1.14)	*less* personal allowance	3,005	—
	Allowance transferable to wife		1,720
(1.20)	Husband's reliefs for 1989/90 (including		
(1.21)	wife's earned income relief)		7,160
	Less husband's 1990/91 total income	1,000	
(1.14)	wife's 1990/91 reliefs (including		
(1.15)	transferred married couple's allowance).........	4,725	5,725
	Transitional relief available to wife		1,435
	Total allowances available to wife are thus		
	personal allowance...		3,005
	married couple's allowance transferred...............		1,720
	transitional relief		1,435
			6,160

The surplus allowances available for 1991/92 were as follows.

		£	£
(1.15)	Married couple's allowance.......................................		1,720
	Less husband's total income for 1991/92	2,500	
(1.14)	*less* personal allowance	3,295	—
	Allowance transferable to wife		1,720
	Wife's transitional relief for 1990/91		1,435
(1.14)	*Less* wife's 1991/92 allowances (including		
(1.15)	transferred married couple's allowance		
	but excluding transitional allowance)	5,015	
(1.14)	*less* 1990/91 allowances (including		
(1.15)	transferred married couple's		
	allowance but excluding		
	transitional allowance)	4,725	290
			1,145
(1.14)	Husband's 1991/92 personal allowance.......................	3,295	
	Less 1991/92 total income.....................................	2,500	795
	Transitional relief available to wife		
	(lesser of £1,145 and £795)		795

	£	£
Total allowances available to wife are thus		
personal allowance...		3,295
married couple's allowance transferred..................		1,720
transitional relief...		795
		5,810

The surplus allowances available for 1992/93 were as follows.

(1.15)	Married couple's allowance.................................		1,720
	Less husband's total income for 1992/93	2,500	
(1.14)	*less* personal allowance...................................	3,445	—
	Allowance transferable to wife		1,720
	Wife's transitional relief for 1991/92		795
(1.14)	*Less* wife's 1992/93 allowances (including		
(1.15)	transferred married couple's allowance		
	but excluding transitional allowance).........................	5,165	
	less 1991/92 allowances (including transferred married couple's allowance but excluding transitional allowance)............................	5,015	150
			645
(1.14)	Husband's 1992/93 personal allowance........................	3,445	
	Less 1992/93 total income...	2,500	945
	Transitional relief available to wife (lesser of £645 and £945)...		645
	Total allowances available to wife are thus		
	personal allowance..		3,445
	married couple's allowance transferred..................		1,720
	transitional relief...		645
			5,810

The surplus allowances available for 1993/94 were as follows.

(1.15)	Married couple's allowance...		1,720
	Less husband's total income for 1993/94	3,250	
(1.14)	*less* personal allowance..	3,445	—
	Allowance transferable to wife		1,720
	Wife's transitional relief for 1992/93		645

2.7 Allowances and Tax Rates—Examples

		£	£
(1.14) (1.15)	*Less* wife's 1993/94 allowances (including transferred married couple's allowance but excluding transitional allowance)......................	5,165	
	less 1992/93 allowances (including transferred married couple's allowance but excluding transitional allowance)...........................	5,165	—
			645

		£	£
(1.14)	Husband's 1993/94 personal allowance.......................	3,445	
	Less 1993/94 total income.............................	3,250	195

Transitional relief available to wife
(lesser of £645 and £195).. 195

Total allowances available to wife are thus

	£
personal allowance..	3,445
married couple's allowance transferred...................	1,720
transitional relief..	195
	5,360

The surplus allowances available for 1994/95 were as follows.

		£	£
(1.14)	Wife's transitional relief for 1993/94.............		195
	Less wife's 1994/95 allowances given by deduction (excluding transitional allowance).................	3,445	
	less 1993/94 allowances (excluding transferred married couple's allowance and transitional allowance)........................	3,445	—
			195

		£	£
(1.14)	Husband's 1994/95 personal allowance........................	3,445	
	Less 1994/95 total income.............................	3,400	45

Transitional relief available to wife
(lesser of £195 and £45)................................ 45

Total allowances available to wife (by deduction from total income) are thus

	£
personal allowance..	3,445
transitional relief..	45
	3,490

In addition, she is entitled to the unused married couple's allowance of £1,720 at 20%, given by way of reduction in her income tax liability.

22

Note. For 1995/96 and subsequent years, no transitional relief is available as the increase in the wife's personal allowance for 1995/96 of (£3,525 – £3,445 =) £80 exceeds the £45 transitional relief available for 1994/95.

2.8 **Maintenance payments.** (See 47.15 MARRIED PERSONS.) Under a pre-15 March 1988 Court Order, a man makes maintenance payments (in full) to his ex-wife of £3,000 in 1993/94, 1994/95, 1995/96 and 1996/97. The payments due in 1988/89 (which were made under deduction of tax) were £2,500.

Ex-husband. The maintenance payments deductible for 1993/94 are limited to £2,500, the amount payable (before deduction of tax) in 1988/89.

In 1994/95, 1995/96 and 1996/97, relief continues to be given by reference to the above figure of £2,500. The first £1,720 is relieved at 20% in 1994/95 and at 15% in 1995/96, and is given by means of a reduction in tax liability. The balance of £780 is deductible in computing total income. For 1996/97, the first £1,790 is relieved at 15% by a reduction in tax liability, the balance of £710 being deductible in computing total income.

Ex-wife. Her income for all four years includes the maintenance payments, but limited to £2,500, the amount payable (before deduction of tax) in 1988/89. She is entitled to a deduction therefrom of £1,720 for the first three years, and of £1,790 for 1996/97.

Note. If the maintenance payments were under a post-14 March 1988 Order, the maximum deduction for the ex-husband for 1993/94 would be £1,720, and the maximum reduction in tax liability for 1994/95 and 1995/96 would be £1,720 at 20% or 15% respectively, and for 1996/97 £1,790 at 15% (with no amount deductible in computing total income). For all four years, the maintenance payments would be disregarded in calculating the ex-wife's income.

2.9 **Charges on income.** Z, a married man, has income and makes payments in the year to 5 April 1997 as follows.

	£	£
Earnings		37,400
Dividends plus tax credits		8,000
		45,400
Mortgage interest paid (under MIRAS)	net 1,700	
Deeds of covenant to charities	net 3,040	
		4,740
		£40,660

In October 1996, Z makes a settlement of £20,000 on his parents which produced income of £325 (received gross on a National Savings Bank investment account) in 1996/97. The capital is to revert to him on the death of the last surviving parent.

On 31 March 1997, Z makes a single gift to charity of £304.

Z's income tax liability for the year 1996/97 is

	£
Tax at lower and basic rates	
Income note (*a*)	45,725
Deduct Personal allowance	(3,765)
	£41,960

23

2.9   Allowances and Tax Rates—Examples

	£
Tax at 20% on £3,900 (lower rate band)	780.00
Tax at 24% on £30,060	7,214.40
Tax at 20% on dividends of £8,000	1,600.00
Deduct Tax retained at basic rate on	
covenants £4,400 at 24% note (*b*)	(1,056.00)
Tax retained at 15% on mortgage interest	(300.00)
Married couple's allowance £1,790 at 15%	(268.50)

	7,969.90

Tax at the higher rate	£
Basic rate tax band	21,600
Extension re charitable covenants note (*b*)	4,400
	26,000

	£
£3,900 at Nil (20% – 20%)	—
26,000 at Nil (24% – 24%)	—
4,060 at 16% (40% – 24%)	649.60
8,000 at 20% (40% – 20%)	1,600.00
£41,960	2,249.60

Total tax borne	£10,219.50

The position could be more simply laid out as follows.

	£
Income	45,725
Deduct Personal allowance	3,765
Taxable income	£41,960

Tax at 20% on £3,900	780.00
Tax at 24% on £26,000	6,240.00
Tax at 40% on £12,060	4,824.00
	£11,844.00
Deduct Married couple's allowance £1,790 at 15%	268.50
	£11,575.50

The figure of £11,575.50 will be reduced by tax paid under PAYE and by tax credits of £1,600 on dividends, with the balance payable by self-assessment. As Z has retained tax of £1,356 (£1,056 + £300) on payments, he has effectively suffered tax of £10,219.50 (£11,575.50 – £1,356) for the year.

Notes

(*a*)   Income arising from certain settlements of income only is treated as income of the settlor for both basic and higher rate taxes (see 80.16 SETTLEMENTS). Thus, £325 is added to Z's income.

24

(b)   The single donation to charity, being at least £250, is treated as if it were a covenanted payment equal to the grossed-up amount (£400) (see 15.8 CHARITIES). The gross equivalent of actual covenanted payments is £4,000 (£3,040 × 100/76).

(c)   Z's total income for tax purposes is £41,325 (£45,725 − £4,400 (charges on income, i.e. covenants and gift aid donation)).

3   Anti-Avoidance

Cross-references. See CAPITAL ALLOWANCES at 10.9, 10.22 and 10.38(iii) for sales between connected persons and 10.35 re certain leasing arrangements; 25 DOUBLE TAX RELIEF for amounts taxed abroad; 43.2(ii) INTEREST PAYABLE for certain interest; 45.5 LIFE ASSURANCE POLICIES for withdrawal of life assurance relief; 46.1 LOSSES for restrictions relating to the use of losses in a trade, profession or vocation; 46.10(*c*) LOSSES for restrictions on the use of losses arising from first-year allowances to leasing partnerships or under certain other arrangements; 52 OFFSHORE FUNDS; 53.14 PARTNERSHIPS in relation to certain company partnership arrangements; 68.27 and 68.28 SCHEDULE A for certain transactions in short leases; 74.6 *et seq.* SCHEDULE D, CASE VI for accrued income scheme; 80.13 to 80.29 SETTLEMENTS for provisions treating income of settlements as income of settlor.

For a detailed book on this subject, see Tolley's Anti-Avoidance Provisions.

3.1   **For the general approach of the Courts** to transactions entered into solely to avoid or reduce tax liability, leading cases are *Duke of Westminster v CIR HL 1935, 19 TC 490; W T Ramsay Ltd v CIR, Eilbeck v Rawling HL 1981, 54 TC 101; CIR v Burmah Oil Co Ltd HL 1981, 54 TC 200* and *Furniss v Dawson (and related appeals) HL 1984, 55 TC 324.* See also *Cairns v MacDiarmid CA 1982, 56 TC 556; Ingram v CIR Ch D, [1985] STC 835; Craven v White and related appeals HL 1988, 62 TC 1; Shepherd v Lyntress Ltd Ch D 1989, 62 TC 495; Moodie v CIR and Sinnett HL 1993, 65 TC 610; Hatton v CIR Ch D, [1992] STC 140; Ensign Tankers (Leasing) Ltd v Stokes HL 1992, 64 TC 617; Countess Fitzwilliam and Others v CIR and related appeals HL, [1993] STC 502;* and *Pigott v Staines Investment Co Ltd Ch D, [1995] STC 114.*

The classical interpretation of the constraints upon the Courts in deciding cases involving tax avoidance schemes is summed up in Lord Tomlin's statement in the *Duke of Westminster* case that '. . . every man is entitled if he can to order his affairs so that the tax attaching . . . is less than it otherwise would be.' The case concerned annual payments made under covenant by a taxpayer to his domestic employees, which were in substance, but not in form, remuneration. The judgment was thus concerned with the tax consequences of a single transaction, but in *Ramsay*, and subsequently in *Furniss v Dawson*, the Courts have set bounds to the ambit within which this principle can be applied in relation to modern sophisticated and increasingly artificial arrangements to avoid tax. *Ramsay* concerned a complex 'circular' avoidance scheme at the end of which the financial position of the parties was little changed, but it was claimed that a large CGT loss had been created. It was held that where a preconceived series of transactions is entered into to avoid tax, and with the clear intention to proceed through all stages to completion once set in motion, the *Duke of Westminster* principle does not compel a consideration of the individual transactions and of the fiscal consequences of such transactions taken in isolation.

The HL opinions in *Furniss v Dawson* are of outstanding importance, and establish, inter alia, that the *Ramsay* principle is not confined to 'circular' devices, and that if a series of transactions is 'preordained', a particular transaction within the series, accepted as genuine, may nevertheless be ignored if it was entered into solely for fiscal reasons and without any commercial purpose other than tax avoidance, even if the series of transactions as a whole has a legitimate commercial purpose.

However, in *Craven v White* the House of Lords indicated that for the *Ramsay* principle to apply all the transactions in a series have to be pre-ordained with such a degree of certainty that, at the time of the earlier transactions, there is no practical likelihood that the transactions would not take place. It is not sufficient that the ultimate transaction is simply of a kind that was envisaged at the time of the earlier transactions.

The inheritance tax case *Fitzwilliam v CIR* appears to further restrict the application of the *Ramsay* principle, in that the HL found for the taxpayer in a case in which all their

Lordships agreed that, once the scheme was embarked upon, there was no real possibility that the later transactions would not be proceeded with. There is, however, some suggestion that a decisive factor was that the first step in the transactions took place before the rest of the scheme had been formulated.

See ICAEW Guidance Note TR 588 'Furniss v Dawson' for guidance on the Revenue approach to the application of the principles outlined above.

Anti-avoidance legislation is intended to counteract transactions designed to avoid taxation, but *bona fide* transactions may sometimes be caught also. The provisions relating to individuals (some of which may also relate to companies) are detailed below and as further indicated in the cross-references above. For provisions relating only to companies, see Tolley's Corporation Tax, and see Tolley's Capital Gains Tax for CGT provisions.

3.2	Cancellation of tax advantages from certain transactions in securities. [*Secs 703–709*].
3.3	Sale of securities with arrangement to repurchase. [*Sec 729*].
3.4	Sale of right to annuities, dividends or interest. [*Sec 730*].
3.5	Treatment of price differential on sale and repurchase of securities. [*Secs 730A, 730B*].
3.6	Income received on securities held for one month or less. [*Secs 731–735*].
3.7	'Manufactured' dividends or interest after sale 'cum div'. [*Sec 737*].
3.8	Transfer of assets abroad. [*Secs 739–746*].
3.9	Trading transactions at other than market price. [*Sec 770*].
3.10	Capital sums received in lieu of earnings. [*Secs 775, 777, 778*].
3.11	Transactions in land. [*Secs 776–778*].
3.12	Land sold and leased back. [*Sec 779*].
3.13	Land sold and leased back. [*Sec 780*].
3.14	Leases of assets other than land. [*Secs 781, 783, 784*].
3.15	Leases of assets (other than land) previously owned for trade, etc., by taxpayer. [*Sec 782*].
3.16	Loan transactions. [*Sec 786*].
3.17	Persons exempt from tax (restrictions regarding pre-acquisition dividends, etc., received on 10% holdings). [*Secs 235, 236*].
3.18	Persons exempt from tax (restriction regarding certain bonus issues). [*Sec 237*].
3.19	Annual payments for non-taxable consideration. [*Sec 125*].
3.20	Dealings in commodity futures. [*Sec 399*].

3.2   CANCELLATION OF TAX ADVANTAGES FROM CERTAIN TRANSACTIONS IN SECURITIES [*Secs 703–709*]

Where, in consequence of transaction(s) in securities (including interests in companies not limited by shares, and such transaction(s) coupled with liquidation of a company), *combined with* any of the relevant circumstances mentioned below, a person is able to obtain a tax advantage, the Board of Inland Revenue may make adjustments counteracting that advantage (having first given notice of their intention to do so), unless the person concerned is able to show that the transactions were made (1) for bona fide commercial reasons or in the ordinary course of investment management, and (2) without tax advantages being their main object, or one of their main objects. [*Sec 703*]. For transactions before 6 April 1990, spouses are treated as nominees of each other. [*Sec 703(7)(8); FA 1988, 14 Sch Pt VIII*]. For 'transactions in securities' see *CIR v Joiner HL 1975, 50 TC 449* and for 'bona fide commercial reasons' see *CIR v Brebner HL 1967, 43 TC 705* and *Clark v CIR Ch D 1978, 52 TC 482*.

The relevant circumstances are those where a person:

3.2 Anti-Avoidance

A   in connection with (i) the distribution, transfer or realisation of a company's profits, income, reserves or other assets, or (ii) a sale or purchase of securities followed by the purchase or sale of the same or other securities, *receives an abnormal amount* (see definition below) *by way of dividend* (or other qualifying distribution, see *Sec 14(2)*) which is taken into account for purposes of (*a*) tax exemption or (*b*) setting-off losses against profits or income or (*c*) group relief (see *Sec 402*) or (*d*) calculating a company's advance corporation tax liability, or (*e*) the application of a surplus of franked investment income under *Sec 242* or *243*, or (*f*) payments within *Sec 348* or *349(1)*, or *(g)* setting against income of interest paid, or

B   in connection with A(i) and (ii) above, *becomes entitled to a deduction from profits because of a decrease in value of securities* held, formerly held, or sold which arises from payment of a dividend thereon or from any other dealing with a company's assets (or where another company obtains the benefit of such a deduction by way of group relief), or

C   in consequence of a transaction whereby (see *CIR v Garvin HL 1981, 55 TC 24* and *Bird v CIR HL 1988, 61 TC 238*, and contrast *Emery v CIR Ch D 1980, 54 TC 607*) another person has received or subsequently receives an abnormal amount (see definition below) by way of dividend, or has become, or subsequently becomes, entitled to a deduction, as in B above, *receives a consideration not taxable as income* (apart from the present provisions) representing the value of a company's trading stock, future receipts, or assets which are, or would otherwise have been, available for distribution (see *CIR v Brown CA 1971, 47 TC 217*) as dividend, and which, in the case of a company incorporated abroad, do not represent a return of capital to subscribers, or

D   in connection with the distribution of the profits, income, reserves or other assets of a company (including any body corporate) under the control of *five or fewer persons*, or whose shares are not listed and dealt in on the Stock Exchange (but excluding in either case any company under control of one or more companies to which D does not apply), *receives a consideration not taxable as income* as in C above, or

E   in connection with (i) the transfer of the assets of a company to which D above applies, to another such company, or (ii) a transaction in securities in which two or more such companies are concerned, receives, in the form of *share capital or securities* of such a company, any non-taxable consideration representing the value of distributable assets of such a company. (Adjustments under this heading may be made immediately if the consideration consists of securities or redeemable share capital, but in the case of non-redeemable share capital *not unless*, and until, *that capital is repaid* (including repayments in liquidation).)

As regards (D) above, there are provisions effective from 29 April 1996 for the additional exclusion of companies whose shares are dealt in on the Unlisted Securities Market, until the closure of that Market.

[*Sec 704; FA 1996, s 175*].

See Revenue Tax Bulletin November 1992 p 37 for the Revenue view on the application of these provisions in relation to payments of intra-group dividends outside any group income election.

For **other cases** under C and D above, see *CIR v Cleary HL 1967, 44 TC 399; Anysz v CIR Ch D 1977, 53 TC 601; Williams v CIR HL 1980, 54 TC 257; CIR v Wiggins Ch D 1978, 53 TC 639*. In determining 'under the control' in D, the relevant date is the date of the dividend (*CIR v Garvin* above).

An abnormal amount by way of dividend etc. is one which substantially exceeds either

(a)   a normal return on the consideration provided for the shares, with market value at time of acquisition used if less than consideration or if no consideration provided, and, in determining 'normal return', regard will be had to length of time the shares were held and other distributions received in respect of them, or

(b)   the proportion of the dividend arising during ownership (where the dividend is at a fixed rate and the recipient sells, disposes of, or acquires an option to sell, the securities within six months of purchase). [Sec 709(4)–(6)].

Tax advantage means any relief or repayment (or increases thereof) or avoidance or reduction of a charge or assessment to tax, whether effected by receipts accruing as non-taxable or by deductions from profits or gains. [Sec 709(1)].

For 'tax advantage' see CIR v Cleary HL 1967, 44 TC 399 (tax advantage obtained where taxpayers' company purchased shares from them) and contrast CIR v Kleinwort, Benson Ltd Ch D 1968, 45 TC 369 (no tax advantage where merchant bank purchased debentures with interest in arrear shortly before redemption) and Sheppard and another (Trustees of the Woodland Trust) v CIR (No 2) Ch D 1993, 65 TC 716 (no tax advantage where relief obtained by virtue of charitable exemption). As regards the latter case, however, the Revenue have indicated that they will continue to proceed under Sec 703 on the footing that tax-exempt bodies obtain a tax advantage whenever they receive abnormal dividends, since they consider that there would have been good grounds for challenging the decision had it not been for a defect in the assessment under appeal. (Revenue Tax Bulletin August 1993 p 90). For the quantum of the tax advantage, see Bird v CIR HL 1988, 61 TC 238.

Procedure:

(i)   The Board must notify person (or personal representatives if deceased [Sec 703(11)]) that they have reason to believe Sec 703 may apply to him in respect of transaction(s) specified in notification. [Sec 703(9)]. See Balen v CIR CA 1978, 52 TC 406. No assessment may be made later than six years after the chargeable period to which the tax advantage relates. [Sec 703(12)].

(ii)   Person notified may make, within 30 days, statutory declaration that in his opinion the section does not apply and state supporting facts and circumstances. [Sec 703(9)].

(iii)   The Board must then either take no further action or send declaration together with certificate that they see reason to take further action (and any counter-statement they wish to submit) to tribunal (appointed by Lord Chancellor) which will decide either (a) there is no prima facie case for proceeding further (against this the Crown cannot appeal) or (b) there is such a case. [Sec 703(10)]. The taxpayer is not entitled to see the Board's counter-statement nor to be heard by the tribunal (Wiseman v Borneman HL 1969, 45 TC 540). See also Howard v Borneman HL 1975, 50 TC 322 and Balen v CIR CA 1978, 52 TC 406.

(iv)   If tribunal decides there is a case, or if no statutory declaration is made by taxpayer, the Board will make adjustments to counteract the specified tax advantages and notify the taxpayer. [Sec 703(3)].

(v)   Taxpayer may, within 30 days, appeal to Special Commissioners against adjustments. After appeal has been heard and determined either side may appeal from that decision within 30 days for re-hearing by tribunal with usual rights of further appeal by case stated in the High Court. [Secs 705–705B; SI 1994 No 1813].

(vi)   The Board have power to require of any person information (within 28 days of written notice) relevant to transaction(s) which it appears to the Board may give rise to a liability on that person under these provisions. [Sec 708]. For the way in which the Board should exercise these powers, see R v CIR (ex p. Preston) HL 1985, 59 TC 1.

3.3 Anti-Avoidance

Advance corporation tax. There are provisions whereby income tax paid by a person under D or E above may be treated by a company as advance corporation tax. [*Sec 703(4)–(6); FA 1993, 6 Sch 12*].

Clearance. Taxpayer may take the initiative by submitting to the Board particulars of any transaction effected or contemplated; the Board may, within 30 days of receipt, call for further information (to be supplied within 30 days). Subject to this, they must notify their decision within 30 days of receipt of the particulars or further information, and if they are satisfied that no liability arises the matter is concluded as regards that transaction by itself, provided that all facts and material particulars have been fully and accurately disclosed. [*Sec 707*]. The Revenue is not obliged to give reasons for refusal of clearance but where the applicant has given full reasons for his transactions the main grounds for refusing clearance will be indicated. A refusal to give clearance indicates that counteraction would be taken if the transaction were completed. (Revenue Pamphlet IR 131, SP 3/80, 26 March 1980).

Applications for clearance should be directed to Inland Revenue, Section 703 Group, Special Investigations Section 2, 3rd Floor, SW Wing, Bush House, Strand, London WC2B 4QN. Where application is made in a single letter for clearance under *Sec 707* and under *Sec 215* (demergers) and/or *Sec 225* (company purchase of own shares), an additional copy or copies of the letter should be enclosed. Where application is also made for capital gains tax clearances, a copy of the letter should in addition be sent to Inland Revenue, Capital and Valuation Division (CGT), Sapphire House, 550 Streetsbrook Road, Solihull, West Midlands B91 1QU. (Revenue Press Release 9 August 1989).

3.3 **SALE OF SECURITIES WITH ARRANGEMENT TO REPURCHASE—INCOME ASSESSABLE ON SELLER** [*Sec 729*]

Where the owner of any securities sells them under an agreement (or option subsequently exercised) to buy them back (or 'similar securities' as defined) so that a dividend or interest thereon is paid to another person, that interest is treated for all tax purposes as his; if the transaction is carried out with a dealer, it is similarly ignored in the latter's accounts. This does not apply to Eurobonds (see 3.6(*a*) below) or to stock issued by a foreign government in a currency other than sterling, where both vendor and purchaser are dealers in securities, nor to income to which 3.16(ii) below applies. The Board have power to obtain information.

'Securities' are defined to exclude securities within the accrued income scheme (see 74.6 *et seq.* SCHEDULE D, CASE VI).

These provisions are **abolished** where the agreement is made on or after an appointed day (which will be the day appointed for the bringing into effect of *Sec 737A* (see 3.7 below) in relation to overseas securities). [*FA 1996, s 159(1)*].

3.4 **SALE OF RIGHT TO ANNUITIES, DIVIDENDS OR INTEREST—INCOME ASSESSABLE ON SELLER** [*Sec 730; FA 1996, 7 Sch 23*]

Where the owner of securities sells or transfers the right to the interest, dividends, annuities etc. therefrom *but not to the securities themselves*, such interest etc. (or the proceeds, when sold or realised in such a way that tax is deductible by virtue of *Sec 18(3B)* (see 72.2 SCHEDULE D, CASE III) (for 1995/96 and earlier years, and for accounting periods ending before 1 April 1996, under SCHEDULE C (70) or *Sec 123(3)*) is treated for tax purposes as income of that owner (or of the beneficiary entitled to the income) and no other person, for the fiscal year in which the right to receive the interest was sold. If the interest etc. on the securities is paid gross, an assessment under Schedule D, Case VI is made on the owner unless he shows that the proceeds of any sale etc. have been taxed as above. If tax would have been chargeable on the remittance basis on the interest etc. under Schedule D, Cases IV or

V, the Case VI assessment is correspondingly limited to the amounts remitted. The Board have power to obtain information.

This section applies chiefly to coupons sold through agents abroad not liable to deduct tax (Hansard 27 June 1938 col 1575), but it may have a wider application.

3.5   **TREATMENT OF PRICE DIFFERENTIAL ON SALE AND REPURCHASE OF SECURITIES** [*Secs 730A, 730B; FA 1995, s 80*]

Subject to the exception mentioned below, where a person (the 'original owner') has transferred securities to another person (the 'interim holder') under an agreement to sell them entered into on or after 1 May 1995, and the original owner or a CONNECTED PERSON (20) is required to buy them back under, or in consequence of the exercise of an option acquired under, the same or a 'related' agreement at a different price, the difference between the sale and repurchase price is treated for income and corporation tax purposes as a payment of interest which:

(*a*)   where the repurchase price is greater than the sale price, is made by the repurchaser on a deemed loan from the interim holder of an amount equal to the sale price; and

(*b*)   otherwise is made by the interim holder on a deemed loan from the repurchaser of an amount equal to the repurchase price.

In either case, the deemed interest is treated for income and corporation tax purposes as becoming due when the repurchase price becomes due and, accordingly, as paid when that price is paid. For income and corporation tax purposes (other than those of the current provisions and *Secs 737A, 737C* (see 3.7 below)), and for the purposes of *TCGA 1992* (unless *TCGA 1992, s 263A*, see below, applies), the repurchase price is treated as reduced by the amount of the deemed interest where (*a*) above applies or as increased by that amount where (*b*) above applies. For the purposes of *Sec 209(2)(d)(da)* (interest treated as a distribution, see Tolley's Corporation Tax under Distributions) any deemed interest payment under (*a*) above is deemed to be interest in respect of securities issued by the repurchaser and held by the interim holder.

The repurchase price, in a case where *Sec 737A* (see 3.7 below) applies (or would apply were it in force in relation to the securities in question) is that price which is or would be applicable by virtue of *Sec 737(3)(b), (9)* or *(11)(c)*. For corporation tax purposes, for accounting periods ending after 31 March 1996, deemed interest under these provisions is treated as payable under a loan relationship, in respect of which the debits and credits to be brought into account are trading or non-trading according to the extent to which the repurchase is in the course of activities forming an integral part of the company's trade. See Tolley's Corporation Tax under Gilts and Bonds. Previously, deemed interest was treated (if it would not otherwise be so) as yearly interest for the purpose of relief under *Sec 338* as a charge on income (see Tolley's Corporation Tax under Profit Computations). For other purposes, the Revenue generally accept that the deemed interest is short interest, except where it is clear that the transaction was entered into as a substitute for long term finance, and in particular where it is clear finance was arranged in this way specifically to avoid deduction of tax at source. (Revenue Tax Bulletin December 1995 p 266).

The exception referred to above disapplies these provisions (unless regulations under *Sec 737E*, see 3.7 below, otherwise provide) if the agreement(s) in question are non-arm's length agreements, or if all the benefits or risks arising from fluctuations in the market value of the securities accrue to, or fall on, the interim holder.

The Treasury has power to make regulations providing for an amount of deemed interest under these provisions to fall within the exemptions for pension business of insurance companies, for exempt approved pension schemes or superannuation funds or certain other

3.5 Anti-Avoidance

such schemes, or for funds held for personal pension schemes or retirement annuity contracts. See *SI 1995 No 3036* as regards payments after 1 January 1996.

[*Sec 730A; FA 1995, s 80(1)(5); FA 1996, 14 Sch 37*].

Where the above provisions apply (or would apply were the sale and repurchase price different), the acquisition and disposal by the interim holder, and (except where the repurchaser is or may be different from the original owner) the disposal and acquisition (as repurchaser) by the original owner, are disregarded for capital gains tax purposes. This does not, however, apply:

(A) where the repurchase price falls to be computed by reference to provisions of *Sec 737C* (see 3.7 below) which are not in force in relation to the securities when the repurchase price becomes due; or

(B) if the agreement(s) in question are non-arm's length agreements, or if all the benefits or risks arising from fluctuations in the market value of the securities accrue to, or fall on, the interim holder; or

(C) in relation to any disposal or acquisition of qualifying corporate bonds (see Tolley's Capital Gains Tax under Qualifying Corporate Bonds) where the securities disposed of by the original owner, or those acquired by him or another person as repurchaser, are not such bonds.

[*TCGA 1992, s 263A; FA 1995, s 80(4)(5)*].

Interpretation. For the above purposes, the following apply.

(i) Agreements are 'related' if entered into in pursuance of the same arrangement.

(ii) References to buying back securities include buying back similar securities, and 'repurchase' is construed accordingly. Securities are 'similar' if they give entitlement to the same rights against the same persons as to capital, interest and dividends, and to the same enforcement remedies.

(iii) 'Securities' has the same meaning as in *Sec 737A* (See 3.7 below).

[*Sec 730B; FA 1995, s 80(1)*].

The Treasury has broad powers to make regulations providing for the above provisions to apply with modifications (including exceptions and omissions) in relation to cases involving any arrangement for the sale and repurchase of securities where the obligation to repurchase is not performed, or the repurchase option not exercised, or where provision is made by or under any agreement:

(*a*) for different or additional securities to be treated as, or included with, securities which, for the purposes of the repurchase, are to represent securities transferred in pursuance of the original sale; or

(*b*) for any securities to be treated as not included with securities which, for repurchase purposes, are to represent securities transferred in pursuance of the original sale; or

(*c*) for the sale or repurchase price to be determined or varied wholly or partly by reference to fluctuations, in the period from the making of the agreement for the original sale, in the value of securities transferred in pursuance of that sale, or in the value of securities treated as representing those securities, or for any person to be required, where there are such fluctuations, to make any payment in the course of that period and before the repurchase price becomes due.

Regulations may also make such modifications in relation to cases where corresponding arrangements are made by an agreement, or by related agreements, in relation to securities which are to be redeemed in the period after their sale, those arrangements being such that the vendor (or a person connected with him), instead of being required to repurchase the securities or acquiring an option to do so, is granted rights in respect of the benefits that will accrue from their redemption. They may also provide for modifications in relation to cases involving any arrangement for the sale and repurchase of securities in relation to which there is an agreement which would not have been entered into by persons dealing at arm's length.

[*Sec 737E; FA 1995, s 83(1)*].

Although of wider general application, these provisions are introduced as part of a package of measures designed to facilitate an open market in the sale and repurchase of gilt-edged securities ('gilt repos'). See also 3.7 below, 33.3 GOVERNMENT STOCKS, 71.81 SCHEDULE D, CASES I AND II and Tolley's Corporation Tax under Income Tax in Relation to a Company.

3.6   **INCOME RECEIVED ON SECURITIES HELD FOR ONE MONTH OR LESS—or held for more than one month but not more than six months** *and either* **purchase or sale was not at current market price** *or* **agreement regarding sale was made at, or before, purchase** (see *Sec 731(3); FA 1996, 20 Sch 36*). [*Secs 731–735*].

Effects as regards various classes of recipient are as in (*a*) to (*d*) below.

In calculating period of one or six months, sale under prior option is regarded as a sale at option date [*Sec 731(4)*], and a sale of 'similar securities' is taken into account. [*Sec 731(5)(10)*]. Where the subsequent sale takes place after 24 July 1991, a purchase or sale effected as a direct result of the exercise of a 'qualifying option' (broadly, a traded or financial option within *CGTA 1979, s 137(9)*) is treated as being at current market price (and so excluded from these provisions) if the first buyer acquired, or became subject to, the option on arm's length terms. [*Sec 731(4A)–(4C); FA 1991, s 55*]. The '*appropriate amount*' is the pre-acquisition portion of the dividend, interest etc. calculated from last 'ex-div' day. [*Sec 735(3); FA 1996, 38 Sch 9*]. See *Sec 735(4)* (as amended) if no last 'ex-div' day. In the case of (*a*) below, the portion taken is of net interest after deduction of tax and the amounts of actual dividends. In the case of (*b*), (*c*) and (*d*) below, it is the gross amount of interest and the amounts of dividends plus related tax credits. In all cases, special rules apply in relation to foreign income dividends within *ICTA 1988, Pt VI, Ch VA*. [*Secs 731(9), 735(1)(2); FA 1994, 16 Sch 17*].

These provisions do not apply where the purchaser is required by the purchase agreement to make to the vendor, before his re-sale of the securities, a payment representative of the interest, or where the purchaser is treated by *Sec 737A(5)* (see 3.7 below) as being required to make a payment representative of a dividend on them, where the payment is required, or treated as required, to be made on or after 1 May 1995. [*Sec 731(2A); FA 1995, s 81*].

(*a*)   **Share dealers.** The net 'appropriate amount' of the interest etc. is treated for all tax purposes as a reduction of the purchase price, unless already caught by *Sec 729* (see 3.3 above). This treatment does not apply to overseas securities if *Sec 732(4)* complied with, nor where the securities are rights in a unit trust scheme (see 90.1 UNIT TRUSTS) and the subsequent sale is carried out in the ordinary course of business by the manager of the scheme, nor if the buyer is a dealer in Eurobonds. '*Eurobond*' means a security (i) which is neither preference stock nor preference share capital and (ii) which is issued in bearer form and (iii) which carries a right to interest at a fixed rate or at a rate bearing a fixed relationship to a standard published base rate and (iv) which carries no right to any other form of benefit whether in nature of interest, participation in profits or otherwise (but it may carry a right to convert into a security of another description or to subscribe for further securities, of any description) and (v) the interest on which is payable without deduction of income tax or similar foreign tax.

This provision does not apply to a dealer who is either

    (i)   a market maker in securities of the kind concerned, selling the securities in the ordinary course of business, or

    (ii)   in circumstances prescribed by Treasury regulations, either a recognised clearing house so prescribed or a member of a recognised investment exchange so prescribed, where the securities are sold after a date so prescribed in the ordinary course of business. *SI 1992 No 568* prescribes such circumstances in relation to The London Clearing House Ltd, and members of The London International Financial Futures Exchange (Administration and Management) trading in equity options on The London International Financial Futures and Options Exchange, from 22 March 1992.

[*Sec 732; FA 1990, s 53; FA 1991, s 56; FA 1996, 41 Sch Pt V(21)*].

Special exemptions apply in certain circumstances for dealers on the Tradepoint exchange. [*SI 1995 No 2050*].

See *Sec 731(7)(8)* regarding change in ownership, or commencement, of trade.

The Board may make regulations by statutory instrument, effective from a day to be appointed therein, imposing conditions for the exclusion of market makers to apply, and making appropriate provision in regard to recognised investment exchanges other than the Stock Exchange. [*Sec 738(1)*].

    (*b*)   **Person entitled to exemption from tax.** Exemption does not extend to the gross 'appropriate amount' of the interest etc. and any annual payment out of the interest etc. is treated as not paid out of taxed income. [*Sec 733*].

    (*c*)   **Traders other than share dealers** (whether company or not). The gross 'appropriate amount' of the interest etc. and tax thereon is ignored in calculating loss repayment claim under *Sec 380* or *381*. [*Sec 734(1)* and see 46.3 LOSSES].

    (*d*)   **Companies other than share dealers.** The gross 'appropriate amount' and tax thereon is ignored for tax purposes except that net equivalent is treated as capital distribution in calculation of chargeable gain. [*Sec 734(2)*].

'Securities' are defined to exclude those within the accrued income scheme (see 74.6 *et seq.* SCHEDULE D, CASE VI). [*Sec 731(9)*].

3.7   'MANUFACTURED' DIVIDENDS OR INTEREST

For payments made on or after different dates specified or to be specified by the Treasury by statutory instrument, the provisions of *Sec 736A, 23A Sch* (introduced by *FA 1991, s 58, 13 Sch*) have effect in relation to certain cases (see (*a*)–(*e*) below) where, under a contract or other arrangement for the transfer of shares or securities, a person is required to pay to the other party an amount representing a dividend or payment of interest thereon.

Where these provisions apply, the intention is that both payer and recipient of the amount in question should be in the same position, for tax purposes, as if the payment had in fact been a dividend or payment of interest. See *23A Sch 2–6* (as amended) for the detailed mechanism by which this is achieved in each case.

The circumstances in which these provisions apply are as follows.

    (*a*)   *Manufactured dividends on UK equities.* This applies where one of the parties to a transfer of UK equities is required to pay the other an amount (a '*manufactured dividend'*) representative of a dividend thereon. Special provisions apply in relation to foreign income dividends within *ICTA 1988, Pt VI, Ch VA*.

(*b*)   *Manufactured interest on UK securities.* This applies where one of the parties to a transfer of UK securities is required to pay the other an amount ('*manufactured interest'*) representative of a periodical payment of interest thereon. (See Tolley's Corporation Tax under Gilts and Bonds special cases for the corporation tax treatment of manufactured interest.)

(*c*)   *Manufactured overseas dividends.* This applies where one of the parties to a transfer of overseas securities (including quoted Eurobonds held in a recognised clearing system, see 23.3 DEDUCTION OF TAX AT SOURCE) is required to pay the other an amount (a '*manufactured overseas dividend'*) representative of an overseas dividend thereon.

(*d*)   *Dividends and interest passing through the market.* This applies where one of the parties to a transfer of securities, who is entitled to a dividend or periodical payment of interest either as registered holder of the securities or, directly or indirectly, from a person from whom he acquired them or to whom he transferred them, is required to pay the other an amount (a '*manufactured payment'*) representative of that dividend or interest.

(*e*)   *Unapproved manufactured payments.* This applies where a person makes a payment which is:

    (i)   a manufactured dividend, overseas dividend or interest payment (see (*a*)–(*c*) above) in connection with a stock lending arrangement which is excluded from the provisions of *Sec 129* (see 71.81 SCHEDULE D, CASES I AND II) by Treasury regulations under that *section* (see *SI 1993 No 2003*); or

    (ii)   any other manufactured dividend or interest payment, otherwise than in connection with a stock lending arrangement within *Sec 129* (see 71.81 SCHEDULE D, CASES I AND II), in respect of UK securities or equities, where the person making the payment is neither a market maker in relation to securities or equities of the kind in question nor, in circumstances prescribed in 'dividend manufacturing regulations' (see below), a recognised clearing house or a member of a recognised investment exchange (within *Financial Services Act 1986*) as so prescribed.

(*a*) above is brought into effect for payments made after 25 February 1992, (*b*) above for payments made after 29 June 1992, and (*c*) above for payments made after 21 April 1993.

As regards (*c*) above, the Board may arrange for manufactured overseas dividends to be paid without deduction of tax in certain cases where a double taxation agreement is in force with the territory in which the recipient of the dividend (not being UK resident) is resident. See *SI 1993 No 1957* as amended by *SI 1995 No 1551*.

There are provisions to counteract any artificial allocation of a payment between the manufactured dividend or interest and the associated stock lending fee.

The Treasury may make 'dividend manufacturing regulations' for the purposes of these provisions which may, *inter alia*, change the definition of an 'unapproved manufactured payment' in (*e*) above and extend the circumstances in which (*a*)–(*c*) above may apply. See *SI 1992 No 569, SI 1992 No 2074* (amended by *SI 1995 No 3221*), *SI 1993 No 2004* (amended by *SI 1995 No 1324*). [*Sec 736A, 23A Sch; FA 1991, s 58, 13 Sch 1; FA 1993, 6 Sch 19; FA 1994, ss 123(2)–(5)(7), 124; FA 1995, s 82; FA 1996, s 159(4)–(9), 14 Sch 52; SI 1992 No 173; SI 1992 No 1346; SI 1993 No 933*].

The Treasury has power to make regulations providing for any manufactured payment within *23A Sch* to be treated as falling within the exemptions for pension business of insurance companies, for exempt approved pension schemes or superannuation funds or certain other such schemes, or for funds held for personal pension schemes or retirement annuity contracts. [*Sec 737D; FA 1995, s 83(1)*]. See *SI 1995 No 3036* as regards payments after 1 January 1996.

Special regulations apply to transactions on the Tradepoint exchange. [*SI 1995 No 2052*].

Treatment of tax deducted. The existing *Sec 737* is amended in respect of payments made on or after a date or dates to be specified by Treasury statutory instrument, to have effect, subject to *23A Sch* (above), where one party to the transfer of shares or securities (not being a UK resident company) is required to pay to the other an amount representing a dividend (or other qualifying distribution) or a periodical payment of interest thereon. *Sec 350(1), 16 Sch* (see 23.3 DEDUCTION OF TAX AT SOURCE) apply as if such a payment were an annual payment made, after deduction of tax, other than out of profits or gains brought into charge to income tax. Where the payment is such that, in relation to a recipient chargeable to income tax, it would be chargeable under Schedule F (i.e. as a dividend), the deduction of tax is deemed to have been made at 22.5% for payments in 1993/94 and at the lower rate of income tax for subsequent payments. The charge under *Sec 350(1)* on the dividend manufacturer is then at the rate so applicable, rather than at the basic rate. After 5 April 1996, as a consequence of the introduction of a lower rate charge on 'savings income' (see 1.8(iii) ALLOWANCES AND TAX RATES), deduction at the lower rate is extended to all payments within these provisions.

The date specified in relation to manufactured dividends on UK equities (see (*a*) above) is 26 February 1992, that in respect of manufactured interest on UK securities (see (*b*) above) is 30 June 1992, and that in respect of manufactured overseas dividends (see (*c*) above) is 22 April 1993.

Excluded from the operation of *Sec 737* as above are:

(i) interest or a dividend (not being a qualifying distribution) payable gross;

(ii) a payment which, under stock exchange rules, is required to be equivalent to the gross interest or dividend (not being a qualifying distribution);

(iii) a 'manufactured overseas dividend' (see (*c*) above);

(iv) a payment made by a non-UK resident other than in the course of a trade carried on in the UK through a branch or agency or by a member of a recognised investment exchange prescribed in the regulations; and

(v) a manufactured dividend representing a foreign income dividend within *ICTA 1988, Pt VI, Ch VA*.

As regards (iv) above, if the payment is received by a UK resident (or a non-resident who receives it for the purposes of a trade carried on through a UK branch or agency), he is assessable and chargeable with the amount of income tax which the payer would have been required to account for and pay had he been UK resident. (For 1995/96 and earlier years, and for accounting periods ending before 1 April 1996, this applied only to UK resident recipients, and did not apply where the recipient showed that the payer was entitled to payment of the dividend, etc. either as registered holder of the shares or securities, or directly or indirectly from a person from whom he acquired, or to whom he transferred, the shares or securities, and who was entitled to the dividend, etc. as registered holder of the shares or securities.)

Also excluded, from 2 January 1996, is interest on gilt-edged securities (as defined under *TCGA 1992*), except that the Treasury has broad powers to make regulations bringing such interest within *Sec 737* with such modifications as may be specified.

No income or corporation tax relief is available, where *Sec 737* applies (other than to manufactured interest within *FA 1996, s 97*), for any amount required to be deducted from the payment on account of income tax.

'Dividend manufacturing regulations' (see above) may modify the above provisions in any case where a payment is made by a non-UK resident carrying on a trade in the UK through a branch or agency or by a member of a recognised investment exchange prescribed in the regulations. See *SIs 1992 Nos 569, 2074.*

[*Sec 737; FA 1991, s 58, 13 Sch 3; FA 1993, 6 Sch 16; FA 1994, 16 Sch 18; FA 1995, s 82; FA 1996, s 159(2)(9); 6 Sch 18, 14 Sch 38, 41 Sch Pt V(21); SI 1992 No 173; SI 1992 No 1346; SI 1993 No 933; SI 1995 No 2933*].

In relation to payments made before the date(s) from which *Sec 737* is amended as above, where one party to a contract for the sale of shares or securities is required to pay to the other an amount representing a dividend (or other qualifying distribution) or a periodical payment of interest thereon, *Sec 350(1), 16 Sch* (see 23.3 DEDUCTION OF TAX AT SOURCE) apply as if such a payment were an annual payment made, after deduction of tax, other than out of profits or gains brought into charge to income tax. This does not apply where:

(i) the payer is entitled to the interest, etc. either as the registered holder of the shares or securities or from a person from whom he purchased them;

(ii) the payment is of interest or of a dividend which is not a qualifying distribution and is payable gross (but this does not apply to certain building society interest);

(iii) the payment is, under stock exchange rules, required to be equivalent to the gross interest or dividend (not being a qualifying distribution);

(iv) payments are made by certain market makers dealing in the shares or securities concerned in the ordinary course of business; or

(v) the payment is made by a non-UK resident and the sale concerned was effected through a broker.

As regards (i) above, where the payer is UK resident and purchased the shares or securities (other than through a broker) from a non-UK resident, the condition is that the payer must either be entitled to the interest, etc. as the registered holder of the securities or show that he acquired the shares or securities, directly or indirectly, from a person who was so entitled.

As regards (v) above, however, unless the broker shows that the payer was entitled to the interest, etc. as the registered holder of the shares or securities, or that he acquired the shares or securities directly or indirectly from a person so entitled, *Sec 350(1)* applies as if the payment through the broker were an annual payment by the broker made, after deduction of tax, other than out of profits or gains brought into charge to income tax. [*Sec 737*].

The Revenue have appropriate information [*Sec 737(8)*] and regulatory [*Sec 738*] powers.

The charge under these provisions takes precedence over that under the accrued income scheme, see 74.33 SCHEDULE D, CASE VI.

Sale and repurchase of securities. *Sec 737, 23A Sch* (above) and the dividend manufacturing regulations thereunder apply where, on or after an appointed day (see below), a person (the 'transferor') agrees to sell any 'securities', and under the same agreement (or under another agreement under the same arrangement) he (or a person connected with him (within *Sec 839*)) is required to buy back the same or 'similar' securities, or acquires an option (which he subsequently exercises) to buy them back, and the following conditions are fulfilled:

3.7 Anti-Avoidance

(a) as a result of the transaction, a dividend on the securities is receivable by a person other than the transferor;

(b) the agreement(s) do not contain a requirement for an amount representative of the dividend to be paid to the transferor on or before the date the repurchase price becomes due; and

(c) it is reasonable to assume that the repurchase price took into account the fact that the dividend was receivable by a person other than the transferor.

They apply as if the person from whom the securities are repurchased (or from whom the transferor has the right to repurchase them) were required under the arrangements for transfer of the securities to pay the transferor an amount representative of the dividend mentioned in (a) above, and a payment were accordingly made by that person to the transferor on the date the repurchase price of the securities becomes due. For the corporation tax treatment of such deemed payments, see Tolley's Corporation Tax under Gilts and Bonds (special cases).

'*Securities*' means UK equities and securities and overseas securities (as under *23A Sch 1(1)*), and securities are '*similar*' if they carry the same entitlement as to capital and interest (or dividends) and the same enforcement remedies. References in *Sec 737A* to dividends are, in the case of UK securities, to periodical payments of interest, and in the case of overseas securities, to overseas dividends (as under *23A Sch 1(1)*).

The 'appointed day' is such day as the Treasury may by order appoint for this purpose, and different days may be appointed in relation to UK equities, UK securities and overseas dividends. In relation to UK equities and UK securities, it is 1 May 1995.

There are special provisions (in *Sec 737C*) for determining the amount of the deemed maufactured dividend or interest for these purposes, and for a corresponding adjustment to be made for tax purposes to the repurchase price of the securities.

[*Secs 737A, 737B, 737C; FA 1994, s 122; FA 1996, s 159(1)(3), 6 Sch 19, 28; SI 1995 No 1007*].

The Treasury has broad powers to make regulations providing for *Secs 737A to 737C* to apply with modifications (including exceptions and omissions) in relation to cases involving any arrangement for the sale and repurchase of securities where the obligation to repurchase is not performed, or the repurchase option not exercised, or where provision is made by or under any agreement:

(a) for different or additional securities to be treated as, or included with, securities which, for the purposes of the repurchase, are to represent securities transferred in pursuance of the original sale; or

(b) for any securities to be treated as not included with securities which, for repurchase purposes, are to represent securities transferred in pursuance of the original sale; or

(c) for the sale or repurchase price to be determined or varied wholly or partly by reference to fluctuations, in the period from the making of the agreement for the original sale, in the value of securities transferred in pursuance of that sale, or in the value of securities treated as representing those securities, or for any person to be required, where there are such fluctuations, to make any payment in the course of that period and before the repurchase price becomes due.

Regulations may also make modifications in relation to cases where corresponding arrangements are made by an agreement, or by related agreements, in relation to securities which are to be redeemed in the period after their sale, those arrangements being such that the vendor (or a person connected with him), instead of being required to repurchase the securities or acquiring an option to do so, is granted rights in respect of the benefits that will accrue from their redemption.

See *SI 1995 No 3220* as regards such modification in cases where securities are redeemed rather than being repurchased, and where other securities are substituted for those originally transferred.

[Sec 737E; FA 1995, s 83(1)].

See also 3.6 above and, as regards application of accrued income scheme to such securities, 74.24 SCHEDULE D, CASE VI.

3.8   **TRANSFER OF ASSETS ABROAD—**
income payable to person abroad assessable on UK resident in certain circumstances. *[Secs 739–746]*

Liability of transferor. Where, as a result of a transfer of assets, either alone or in conjunction with any associated operations (see below), income becomes payable to non-residents, or to persons not domiciled in the UK, then the following provisions apply.

(*a*)   If, by virtue of the transfer, either alone or in conjunction with associated operations (see *Vestey v CIR HL 1979, 54 TC 503* overruling *Congreve v CIR HL 1948, 30 TC 163;* and also *CIR v Pratt and Others Ch D 1982, 57 TC 1*), the transferor, being an individual ordinarily resident in the UK (at the time of the transfer, see *CIR v Willoughby Ch D, [1995] STC 143*), has power to enjoy, forthwith or in the future, any income of a non-resident or non-domiciled person which would be taxable if it were the income of the resident individual received in the UK, that income is deemed, for all tax purposes, to be the income of that individual.

(*b*)   If such a resident individual receives, or is entitled to, any capital sum by way of loan, etc. (see *Lee KB 1941, 24 TC 207*), or other non-income payment not for full consideration, which is in any way connected with the transfer, etc., the income which, by virtue of the transfer, etc., has become payable to the non-resident or non-domiciled person is deemed for all tax purposes to be income of the resident. A sum which a third person receives, or is entitled to receive, at the individual's direction or by assignment of the right to receive it, is treated as such a capital sum. There is no deemed income for a year of assessment in respect of a loan to the individual which has been wholly repaid before the beginning of that year.

These provisions do not apply if the Board are satisfied (subject to review by the Special Commissioners) that avoidance of tax was not a main purpose of the transfer or associated operations, or that they were *bona fide* commercial transactions not designed for the avoidance of tax. *[Secs 739, 741]*. For a case in which the Revenue's refusal of exemption under *Sec 741* was overturned on appeal, see *CIR v Willoughby Ch D, [1995] STC 143*.

For **1996/97 onwards**, where a non-UK resident or domiciled person realises a profit from the discount on a relevant discounted security (see 72.2 SCHEDULE D, CASE III), it is treated for these purposes as income of that person. *[FA 1996, 13 Sch 12]*.

For the above purposes an individual is deemed to have power to enjoy income of a non-resident or non-domiciled person if

(i)   the income is so dealt with by *any* person so as to benefit the individual at some point of time, whether as income or not, or

(ii)   the income increases the value to the individual of assets held by him or for his benefit, or

(iii)   the individual receives, or is entitled to receive, at any time any benefit provided out of the income, or out of money available by the effect of associated operations on that income or assets representing it, directly or indirectly, or

3.8 Anti-Avoidance

(iv) the individual may obtain beneficial enjoyment of the income in the event of the exercise of one or more powers, by whomsoever exercisable and whether with or without the consent of any other person, or

(v) the individual is able to control application of the income,

regard being had to the substantial effect of the transfer and associated operations and bringing into account all resultant benefits to the individual whether or not he has rights in law or equity to those benefits. [*Sec 742(2)(3)*].

Companies incorporated abroad, or regarded under double taxation arrangements as resident outside the UK, are, for this purpose, always to be treated as resident abroad, even if technically resident in UK. [*Sec 742(8); FA 1990, s 66*].

Reference to an individual includes the individual's wife or husband. Reference to income of a person non-resident or non-domiciled in the UK includes income of a company apportioned to him (plus advance corporation tax thereon) and is treated as payable to that person. [*Sec 742(9)(a)(d), (10)*].

For *premiums on leases etc.* in the case of persons resident in the Republic of Ireland but not in UK, see *Sec 746*.

Income falling under the above headings is, to the extent that it is not taxed by deduction or otherwise, assessable under Sch D, Case VI. A non-domiciled individual is only chargeable on any income *deemed* to be his if he would have been chargeable if it had in fact been his income. All deductions and reliefs to be given to the individual assessed as if he had actually received the income. If it is received subsequently, not again assessed. [*Sec 743; FA 1996, 6 Sch 20, 28*]. Appeals are to Special Commissioners. [*TMA s 31(3)(b)*].

The Board have power to demand from any person, under penalty, particulars of transactions where he acted for others (even if he considers no liability arises), and of what part he took in them. [*Sec 745; FA 1989, 12 Sch 17; FA 1995, 17 Sch 18; FA 1996, 37 Sch 2*]. These powers limited in the case of *solicitors* (but not accountants or others), and *bankers* are not obliged to furnish particulars of any *ordinary* banking transactions carried out in the *ordinary* course of a banking business. 'Bank' for this purpose is defined by *Sec 840A* (see 8.1 BANKS). See *Royal Bank of Canada Ch D 1971, 47 TC 565*, where held particulars required were not ordinary banking transactions and *Clinch v CIR QB 1973, 49 TC 52* for powers of Revenue.

See *Philippi v CIR CA 1971, 47 TC 75* for burden on taxpayer to prove that avoidance was not a purpose.

'*Associated operation*'. See *Sec 742(1)* and *Corbett's Exors CA 1943, 25 TC 305; Bambridge HL 1955, 36 TC 313* and *Fynn CD 1957, 37 TC 629*.

For general principles see the above cases and *Cottingham's Exors CA 1938, 22 TC 344; Beatty cases KB 1940, 23 TC 574; Lord Howard de Walden CA 1941, 25 TC 121; Aykroyd KB 1942, 24 TC 515; Latilla HL 1943, 25 TC 107; Sassoon CA 1943, 25 TC 154; Vestey's Exors HL 1949, 31 TC 1; Ramsden Ch D 1957, 37 TC 619; Chetwode v CIR HL 1977, 51 TC 647; Vestey (Nos 1 & 2) HL 1979, 54 TC 503; CIR v Schroder Ch D 1983, 57 TC 94; CIR v Brackett Ch D 1986, 60 TC 134, 639*.

Liability of non-transferor. Where, as a result of a transfer of assets, either alone or in conjunction with associated operations (see above), income becomes payable to a non-resident, or to a person not domiciled in the UK, *and* an individual ordinarily resident in the UK who is not liable as the transferor under *Sec 739* (see above) receives a benefit provided out of those assets, then the following provisions apply to benefits received and relevant income arising after 9 March 1981 irrespective of when the transfer or associated operations took place. They do not, however, apply if the Board are satisfied (subject to review by the Special Commissioners) that avoidance of tax was not a main purpose of the transfer or associated operations, or that they were *bona fide* commercial transactions not designed for the avoidance of tax (and see above). [*Secs 740(1), 741*].

For **1996/97 onwards**, where a non–UK resident or domiciled person realises a profit from the discount on a relevant discounted security (see 72.2 SCHEDULE D, CASE III), it is treated for these purposes as income of that person. [*FA 1996, 13 Sch 12*].

The value of the benefit, up to the amount of relevant income of years of assessment up to and including the year in which received, is treated as income of the resident individual for all tax purposes for that year and charged under Schedule D, Case VI. Any excess of benefit is carried forward against relevant income of subsequent years and taxed accordingly. [*Sec 740(2)(4)*].

'*Relevant income*' of a year of assessment is any income arising in that year to a non-resident or non-domiciled person and which by virtue of the transfer or associated operations mentioned above can directly or indirectly be used for providing a benefit for the resident individual or enabling a benefit to be provided for him. [*Sec 740(3)*].

An individual domiciled outside the UK is not taxable on a benefit not received in the UK in respect of any 'relevant income' on which, if he had received it, he would not, because of his domicile, have been taxable. *Sec 65(6)–(9)* (income applied outside UK treated in certain cases as received in UK, see 63.4 REMITTANCE BASIS) applies as if the benefit were income arising from possessions outside the UK. [*Sec 740(5)*].

The provisions of *Secs 742(8)–(10), 745* apply, see above.

Exclusion of double charge. No income can be charged more than once under the above provisions and where there is a choice as to persons to be assessed the Board may allocate income as appears just and reasonable. The Board's decision is appealable to the Special Commissioners. Income is treated as having been charged to tax

(A) in full, where charged under *Sec 739* as income;

(B) to the extent of the value of any benefit charged under (iii) above, and

(C) to the amount of relevant income taken into account in charging any benefit under *Sec 740*. [*Sec 744*].

Trustees and personal representatives. In relation to benefits received on or after 15 June 1989, relevant income for *Sec 740* purposes (see above) includes income arising to trustees or personal representatives before 6 April 1989, notwithstanding that one or more of the trustees or personal representatives was not resident outside the UK, unless they have been charged to tax in respect of that income. [*FA 1989, s 111(8)*].

Accrued income on certain securities. See 74.33 SCHEDULE D, CASE VI as regards deemed income arising on transfer of certain securities.

See also Tolley's Corporation Tax under Controlled Foreign Companies as regards *Secs 739, 740* relief in certain cases where a charge is made in respect of profits of such companies.

3.9 **TRADING TRANSACTIONS AT OTHER THAN MARKET PRICE—**
may be adjusted to market price if either a person holding the item as a fixed asset or any non-UK resident is involved. [*Sec 770*]

Where either the buyer or the seller (being a 'body of persons' or a partnership) is **controlled by the other party** to the contract, or both are such bodies controlled by the same person(s), any sale (including letting and hiring of property, grant or transfer of rights or licences, or giving of business facilities) at a price other than market price at the time of completion or, if earlier, of giving possession may (if the Board of Inland Revenue so direct) be adjusted by the Revenue as follows:

3.10 Anti-Avoidance

(i)   If the price is **below** market price, the latter is substituted in computing the *seller's* profits unless the buyer, being a UK resident trader, is entitled to deduct the price paid in computing his own profits.

(ii) If the price is **above** market price, the latter is substituted in computing the *buyer's* profits unless the seller, being a UK resident trader, would have to bring in, as a trade receipt, the price received. [*Sec 770*].

'*Control*', for this purpose, means power of a person (including nominees and certain connected persons, and their nominees), by shareholding or voting power (whether direct or through another company) or under articles of association, to secure that the company's affairs are conducted according to that person's wishes. It includes, for partnerships, the right to a share of more than one-half of the firm's assets or profits. For whether control at company meeting is necessary, see *Irving v Tesco Stores Holdings Ltd Ch D 1982, 58 TC 1*. As to trustee holdings, see *CIR v Lithgows CS 1960, 39 TC 270*. [*Secs 773(2)(3), 840*].

The Board may serve notices specifying the information required (with penalties for non-compliance) on a *company* if it or an associated company was party to a relevant transaction. If one party to a transaction which may be within *Sec 770* is a non-resident 51% subsidiary of a UK parent, notice may be served on the parent for access to the books, etc. of the subsidiary (subject to appeal to Special Commissioners). An inspector may in certain circumstances and with the Board's authority enter premises to examine books, etc.

Where a direction is given, all necessary adjustments are made, by assessment, repayment or otherwise, to give effect to it. [*Sec 770(3)*]. This applies equally to adjustment of open assessments (*Glaxo Group Ltd and Others v CIR CA, [1996] STC 191*). Appeals involving questions arising from directions are to that extent to be referred to and determined by the Special Commissioners. [*Sec 772(8)*].

Nothing in *Sec 770* is to affect the operation of any provisions of *CAA 1968*. [*Sec 773(1)*].

To assist foreign companies which operate or may be thinking of operating through a branch or subsidiary in the UK, the Revenue have available 'Transfer Pricing of Multinational Enterprises: Notes for Guidance' (Revenue Press Release 26 January 1981).

Arbitration Convention. The EEC Convention (*90/463/EEC*) on the elimination of double taxation in connection with the adjustment of profits of associated enterprises requires Member States to adopt certain procedures and to follow the opinion of an advisory commission in certain cases of dispute relating to transfer pricing adjustments. The Convention came into force on 1 January 1995. *Sec 815B* makes provision for domestic legislation and agreements to be over-ridden where necessary under the Convention, and *Sec 816(2A)* and *FA 1989, s 182A* provide the necessary information powers and confidentiality requirements in relation to disclosures of information to an advisory commission. [*F(No 2)A 1992, s 51*].

3.10   **CAPITAL SUMS RECEIVED IN LIEU OF EARNINGS** [*Secs 775, 777, 778*]

Where

(i)   transactions or arrangements are made (having as their *main* object, or one of their main objects, the avoidance or reduction of income tax) which enable some other person to enjoy profits, gains, income, copyrights, licences or rights, etc., deriving, directly or indirectly, from occupational activities, past or present, which an individual (whether resident in the UK or not [*Sec 775(9)*]) carries on wholly or partly in the UK, and

(ii)   in connection therewith, or in consequences thereof, that individual obtains, for himself or for some other person, *a capital amount* (i.e. any amount not otherwise includible in any computation of income for tax purposes [*Sec 777(13)*])

any such amount is (subject to certain exceptions, as below) to be treated as *earned income* of that individual, assessable under Schedule D, Case VI, arising when the capital sum is receivable (or, if it consists of property or a right, when it is sold or realised [*Sec 775(7)*]). [*Sec 775(1)–(3), (8)*].

Exemptions. Capital amounts from the disposal of

(*a*)   shares in a company, so far as their value is attributable to the value of the company's business as a going concern, or

(*b*)   assets (including goodwill) of a profession or vocation, or a share in a professional or vocational partnership, so far as their value is attributable to the value of the profession, etc., as a going concern.

But the above exemptions do not apply to any part of the capital amount which represents any part of the going-concern value of the business, profession, etc., as above, materially deriving from prospective income, etc., from the individual's activities in the occupation, whether as partner or employee, for which he has not received full consideration (disregarding all capital amounts). [*Sec 775(4)–(6)*].

Where the person charged to tax is not the one for whom the capital amount was obtained (see (ii) above) he may recover from the latter person any part of that tax which he pays (for which purpose the Revenue will supply, on request, a certificate of income in respect of which tax has been paid). [*Sec 777(8)*].

The various provisions applicable to *Sec 776*, which are listed in 3.11 below under 'General', also apply for purposes of this section.

3.11   **TRANSACTIONS IN LAND** [*Secs 776–778*]

The following provisions apply to all persons, whether UK residents or not, if all or any part of the land in question is in the UK. [*Sec 776(14)*].

Where

(*a*)   land (or any property deriving its value from land) is acquired with the sole or main object of realising a gain from disposing of it, or

(*b*)   land is held as trading stock, or

(*c*)   land is developed with the sole or main object of realising a gain from disposing of it when developed,

any capital gain from disposal of the land or any part of it (i.e. any amount not otherwise includible in any computation of income for tax purposes [*Sec 777(13)*]) which is realised (for himself or for any other person) by the person acquiring, holding or developing it (or by any connected person, as defined by *Sec 839* (see 20 CONNECTED PERSONS), or a person party to, or concerned in, any arrangement or scheme to realise the gain indirectly or by a series of transactions) is, subject as below, treated for all tax purposes as income of the person realising the gain (or the person who transmitted to him, directly or indirectly, the opportunity of making that gain [*Sec 776(8)*]) assessable, under Schedule D, Case VI, for the chargeable period in which the gain is realised. [*Sec 776(1)–(3)*]. See *Yuill v Wilson HL 1980, 52 TC 674* and its sequel *Yuill v Fletcher CA 1984, 58 TC 145; Winterton v Edwards Ch D 1979, 52 TC 655*; and *Sugarwhite v Budd CA 1988, 60 TC 679. Bona fide* transactions, not entered into with tax avoidance in view, may be caught by the legislation—see *Page v Lowther and Another CA 1983, 57 TC 199*.

3.11 Anti-Avoidance

'*Land*' includes buildings, and any estate or interest in land or buildings. [*Sec 776(13)(a)*].

'*Property deriving its value from land*' includes any shareholding in a company, partnership interest, or interest in settled property, deriving its value, directly or indirectly, from land, and any option, consent or embargo affecting the disposition of land. [*Sec 776(13)(b)*]. See, however, 'Exemptions' below.

Land is '*disposed of*' for the above purposes if, by any one or more transactions or by any arrangement or scheme (whether concerning the land or any property deriving its value therefrom), the property in, or control over, the land is effectively disposed of. [*Sec 776(4)*]. Any number of transactions may be treated as a single arrangement or scheme if they have, or there is evidence of, a common purpose. [*Sec 776(5)(b)*]. See also under 'General' below.

For the date of the capital gain where instalments involved, see *Yuill v Fletcher CA 1984, 58 TC 145.*

Exemptions.

(i)   An individual's gain made from the *sale, etc., of his residence* exempted from capital gains tax under *TCCA 1992, s 222* or which would be so exempt but for *TCGA 1992, s 224(3)* (acquired for purpose of making a gain). [*Sec 776(9)*].

(ii) A gain on the sale of *shares in a company holding land as trading stock* (or a company owning, directly or indirectly, 90% of the ordinary share capital of such a company) *provided that* the company disposes of the land by normal trade and makes all possible profit from it, and the share sale is not part of an arrangement or scheme to realise a land gain indirectly. [*Sec 776(10)* and see *Chilcott v CIR Ch D 1981, 55 TC 446*].

(iii) (If the liability arises solely under (c) above.) Any part of the gain fairly attributable to a period *before the intention was made* to develop the land. [*Sec 776(7)*].

Gains are to be computed 'as is just and reasonable in the circumstances', allowance being given only for expenses attributable to the land disposed of, and the following may be taken into account.

(A)   If a leasehold interest is disposed of out of a freehold, the Sch D, Case I treatment in such a case of a person dealing in land (see 71.76 SCHEDULE D, CASES I AND II).

(B)   Any adjustments under *Sec 99(2)(3)* for tax on lease premiums. [*Sec 776(6)*].

Where the computation of a gain in respect of the development of land (as under (*c*) above) is made on the footing that the land or property was appropriated as trading stock, that land, etc., is also to be treated for purposes of capital gains tax (under *TCGA 1992, s 161*) as having been transferred to stock. [*Sec 777(11)*].

Where, under *Sec 775* or *776*, tax is assessed on, and paid by, a person other than the one who actually realised the gain, the person paying the tax may recover it from the other party (for which purpose the Revenue will, on request, supply a certificate of income in respect of which tax has been paid). [*Sec 777(8)*].

Clearance. The person who made or would make the gain may (if he considers that (*a*) or (*c*) above may apply), submit to his Inspector of Taxes particulars of any completed or proposed transactions. If he does so the inspector must, within 30 days of receiving those particulars, notify the taxpayer whether or not he is satisfied that liability under this section does not arise. If the inspector is so satisfied no assessment can thereafter be made on that gain, provided that all material facts and considerations have been fully and accurately disclosed. [*Sec 776(11)*].

General. See *Sec 777(2)(3)* for provisions to prevent avoidance by the use of indirect means to transfer any property or right, or enhance or diminish its value, e.g., by sales at less, or more, than full consideration, assigning share capital or rights in a company or partnership or an interest in settled property, disposal on the winding-up of any company, partnership or trust, etc. For ascertaining whether, and to what extent, the value of any property or right is derived from any other property or right, value may be traced through any number of companies, partnerships and trusts, at each stage attributing property held by the company, partnership or trust to its shareholders, etc., 'in such manner as is appropriate to the circumstances'. [*Sec 777(5)*]. Where the person liable is non-resident, the Board may direct that any part of an amount taxable under these provisions on that person be paid under deduction of tax as if made other than out of taxable income. [*Sec 777(9)*].

For the above purposes the Revenue may require, under penalty, any person to supply them with any particulars thought necessary, including particulars of

(I)   transactions, etc., in which he acts, or acted, on behalf of others, and

(II)   transactions, etc., which in the opinion of the Revenue should be investigated, and

(III) what part, if any, he has taken, or is taking, in specified transactions, etc. (Under this heading a *solicitor* who has merely acted as professional adviser is not compelled to do more than state that he acted and give his client's name and address.) [*Sec 778*].

The transactions of which particulars are required need not be identified transactions (*Essex v CIR CA 1980, 53 TC 720*).

3.12   **LAND SOLD AND LEASED BACK—TAX DEDUCTIONS FOR RENT ARE LIMITED TO COMMERCIAL RENT** [*Sec 779; FA 1995, 6 Sch 27*]

Where, after 14 April 1964, land (or any interest or estate in land) is transferred from one person to another (by sale, lease, surrender or forfeiture of lease, etc.) and

(*a*)   under a lease of the land, or any part of it, granted then or subsequently by the transferee to the transferor, or

(*b*)   as a result of a transaction or transactions affecting the land or interest,

the transferor, or any person associated with him, becomes liable to pay any lease rent (including any premium treated as rent—see 68.28 SCHEDULE A), or rent charge on, or connected with, the land which would be allowable

(i)   as a deduction from trading profits, or

(ii)   in computing profits or losses under Case VI, or

(iii)   as a management expense under *Sec 75* or *Sec 76*, or

(iv)   against Schedule E emoluments, under *Sec 198(1)*, or

(v)   as a deduction in computing profits from woodlands, or

(vi)   in computing profits under Schedule A,

the allowance for tax purposes in respect of that rent or other payment (apart from any portion which properly relates to services, tenant's rates, or the use of assets other than land) is limited to the commercial rent of the land to which it relates for the period for which the payment is made. In the case of a lease, '*commercial rent*' means the open-market rent, at the time the actual lease was created, under a lease whose duration and repair terms are the same as under the actual lease but stipulating a rent payable at uniform intervals at a uniform rate, or progressively increasing proportionately to any increases provided by the actual lease. For other transactions, it is the open market rent which would be payable under a tenant's repairing lease (as defined by *Sec 779(12)*) for the period over which payments are to be made, or 200 years if they are for a longer period or are perpetual.

Any part of a payment which is disallowed under the above provisions may be carried forward as an addition to the next subsequent payment, and so on. All payments for the same period are amalgamated, including apportioned parts of periods which overlap. A payment for a period falling, wholly or partly, beyond one year from the date of payment is treated as being for the year commencing with the date on which it is paid. [*Sec 779(5)–(7)*].

'Associated persons'.

A.   Husband and wife, their relatives and spouses,

B.   the trustee of a settlement and the settlor or any person associated with him,

C.   a person and any body, or bodies of persons (including partnerships) which he, or any persons associated with him, or he and any persons associated with him, controls (as under *Sec 840*, see 20.8 CONNECTED PERSONS and note that, in the case of a partnership, control means the right to more than a half share in assets or income),

D.   any bodies of persons associated with the same person under C above,

E.   joint owners of the land, etc. the subject of disposal, including their associates,

F.   the transferor and any other transferor acting in concert, or reciprocally, with him, and their associates,

G.   any two or more companies participating in the reconstruction, or amalgamation, of a company or companies. [*Secs 779(11), 783(10); FA 1995, 17 Sch 19*].

3.13   **LAND SOLD AND LEASED BACK—PROPORTION OF CAPITAL SUM RECEIVED IS TO BE TAXED AS INCOME IN CERTAIN CIRCUMSTANCES** [*Sec 780; FA 1988, s 75*]

As regards arrangements as in *Sec 779* (see 3.12 above), made after 21 June 1971, where the lease when sold has no more than 50 years still to run and the period for which the premises are leased back is 15 years or less, the increased rent payable, so far as it does not exceed a commercial rent (see 3.12 above), is allowable as a deduction from profits, but of the consideration received by the lessee for giving up the original lease (or undertaking to pay an increased rent) a proportion equivalent to one-fifteenth of that consideration multiplied by the number of years by which the term of the lease-back falls short of 16 years will be treated as assessable income, not capital. Appropriate adjustment to be made where the lease-back is of part only of the property previously leased. For the above purposes the term of the new lease is deemed to end on any date whereafter the rent payable is reduced, or, if the lessor or lessee has power to determine the lease or the lessee has power to vary its terms, on the earliest date on which the lease can be so determined or varied.

3.14   **LEASES OF ASSETS OTHER THAN LAND—CAPITAL SUM RECEIVED BY PERSON WHO PAYS LEASE RENTALS IS TAXABLE—**
to the extent of tax allowances on such lease rentals. [*Secs 781, 783, 784*]

Where any payment under a lease, created after 14 April 1964, of any asset not falling under *Sec 779* (see 3.12 above) or *Sec 782* (see 3.15 below), is allowable

(i)   as a deduction from trading profits, or

(ii)   in computing profits or losses under Case VI, or in respect of woodlands, or

(iii)   as a management expense under *Secs 75, 76* or

(iv)   against Schedule E emoluments,

then if at any time the person making the payment has obtained, or obtains, a capital sum (i.e. any money, or money's worth, not chargeable as profits, etc., of a trade, profession, or from woodlands nor chargeable under Case VI) in respect of the lessee's interest in the lease (including by surrender to the lessor, assignment, subleasing, or receipt under insurance—and see *Sec 783*), or any person associated with the payer has obtained a capital sum for an interest in the asset, the recipient of that capital sum is assessed, under Sch D, Case VI, for the year in which the capital sum was obtained, on a figure equal to the amount of the payment under the lease which is allowable for tax purposes as above (or the effectively allowable part of it, where the whole or part of the period in which the payment would normally be allowed is not a basis period for assessment), subject to the overriding limitation that the amount(s) so charged shall not exceed the capital sum received (or, where the lease is a hire-purchase agreement, that sum less the recipient's capital expenditure on the asset—see *Sec 784*).

Apportionments are made in the case of recipients who are partners or persons with a joint interest in the asset. 'Associated persons' are as listed in A to E of 3.12 (relating to *Sec 779*) above. [*Sec 783(10)*]. Assessments to give effect to the above provisions may be made up to five years after 31 January following the tax year in which the allowable payment was made (for 1995/96 and earlier years, six years after the end of that tax year) or, for corporation tax purposes, six years after the end of the accounting period in which it was made. [*Sec 781(8); FA 1996, s 135, 21 Sch 21*].

3.15   **LEASES OF ASSETS (OTHER THAN LAND) PREVIOUSLY OWNED FOR TRADE ETC. BY TAXPAYER—**
Deductions for lease rentals are limited to commercial rent. [*Sec 782*]

Any payment under a lease, created after 14 April 1964, of any asset (other than land or an interest in land) which at any time prior to the lease was used for the purpose of the lessee's trade (or any other trade carried on by him) and was then owned by the person carrying on the trade in which it was used is limited, in computing profits or losses of the lessee's trade, to the commercial rent of the asset for the period covered by the payment, i.e. a rent representing a reasonable return, by uniform instalments at uniform intervals over the remainder of the asset's anticipated normal working life (as under *Sec 782(6)*), on its market value at the time the lease was created. *Sec 782(3)–(5)* contains similar provisions (disallowed payments carried forward etc.) to *Sec 780(4)–(6)*—see 3.12 above.

3.16   **LOAN TRANSACTIONS** [*Sec 786*]

Where, with reference to lending money or giving credit (or varying the terms of a loan or credit):

(i)   a transaction provides for the payment of an *annuity or other annual payment*—that payment is treated as if it were of annual interest. [*Sec 786(3)*];

(ii)   a transaction provides for the sale or transfer of any securities or other income-producing property and for the transferor's subsequent acquisition of, or of an option on, the same or any other property from the transferee—an amount equal to any income from the property transferred arising before repayment of the loan etc. is treated as income of the former owner, assessable under Schedule D, Case VI. This provision is **abolished** where the initial agreement for sale or transfer is made on or after an appointed day (which will be the day appointed for the bringing into effect

3.17 Anti-Avoidance

of *Sec 737A* (see 3.7 above) in relation to overseas securities). [*Sec 786(4); FA 1996, s 159(1)*];

(iii) any person *assigns, surrenders, waives or forgoes* income on property (without a sale or transfer of the property)—that person is assessable under Schedule D, Case VI, on a sum equal to the income assigned, surrendered, waived etc. [*Sec 786(5)*];

(iv) if credit is given for the purchase price of property and during the subsistence of the debt, the purchaser's rights to income from the property are suspended or restricted—he is treated for the purpose of (iii) above as if he had made a surrender of that income. [*Sec 786(6)*].

Transactions with CONNECTED PERSONS (20) are included.

3.17 **PERSONS EXEMPT FROM TAX—**
restriction regarding pre-acquisition dividends etc. received on 10% holdings. [*Secs 235, 236; FA 1993, s 78(6), 6 Sch 3*]

An exempt person will not be able to recover a tax credit in respect of any part of a distribution related to profits (as defined—see *Sec 236*) arising before acquisition of the shares if the shares held (together with any associated holding) are 10% or more of that class. The income will not then be exempt from tax and will become liable to tax, or, as the case may be, additional tax at the difference between the lower rate and the rate applicable to trusts (before 1993/94, at the additional rate) (see 80.5 SETTLEMENTS) in force when the distribution is made and will not be available for purposes of *Secs 348* and *349(1)*, nor may interest paid under *Sec 353* be set against it. These provisions do not apply to certain payments treated as qualifying distributions (see 3.18 below). See *CIR v Sheppard and another (Trustees of the Woodland Trust) (No 2) Ch D 1993, 65 TC 716* for attribution of profits to a distribution where waiver resulted in whole distribution being received although only 60% of shares held.

3.18 **PERSONS EXEMPT FROM TAX—**
restriction regarding certain bonus issues. [*Sec 237; FA 1993, 6 Sch 3; FA 1994, 9 Sch 2*]

Where 'bonus issues' are treated as a distribution by virtue of *Secs 209(3), 210,* or *211*, a recipient entitled to exemption from tax or the setting-off of losses against income shall have such bonus issue and related tax credit ignored in the repayment or loss calculation and be liable to tax as in 3.17 above on such bonus issue unless it represents a normal return, as defined. Such 'bonus issues' are not available for purposes of *Secs 348* and *349(1)*, nor may interest paid and otherwise deductible under *Sec 353* be set against them.

3.19 **ANNUAL PAYMENTS FOR NON-TAXABLE CONSIDERATION** [*Sec 125; FA 1989, s 109(2); FA 1995, 17 Sch 2, 29 Sch Pt VIII(8)*]

Any payment (whenever the liability to make it was incurred, but subject to exceptions as below) of an annuity or other annual payment charged with tax under SCHEDULE D, CASE III (72), not being interest, and made for a consideration which is *not wholly* included in the income for tax purposes of the person making the annual payment, shall be paid without deduction of tax and not allowed as a deduction from, or a charge on, his income for the purposes of income tax and corporation tax. Certain admission rights in return for annual payments to charities are disregarded for this purpose (see 15.6(*b*) CHARITIES).

Exceptions to the above provisions are any payments (i) which, for 1994/95 and earlier years, are income of the recipient within *Sec 674A(1)(a)(c)* or *Sec 683(1)(a)(c)* or *(6)* (to a former partner or his dependants under a partnership agreement or under a maintenance agreement or in consideration for the acquisition of a business) or, for 1995/96 onwards, which fall within 80.16(i) or (ii) SETTLEMENTS, or (ii) to an individual for surrendering, assigning or releasing an interest in settled property to a person having a subsequent interest or (iii) of any annuity granted in the ordinary course of a business of granting annuities or (iv) any annuity charged on an interest in settled property and granted before 30 March 1977 by an individual to a company whose business was wholly or mainly in acquiring such interests or which was carrying on life assurance business in the UK. For Scotland, reference to settled property refers to property held in trust. For position prior to these provisions see *CIR v Plummer HL 1979, 54 TC 1*, and *Moodie v CIR and Sinnett HL 1993, 65 TC 610*, in which the decision in *Plummer* on similar facts was reversed on *Ramsay* principles (see 3.1 above).

A payment to which these provisions apply is excluded from the *FA 1988* provisions as to the non-deductibility and exemption from tax of certain annual payments falling due after 14 March 1988 (see 1.8(i) and 1.9(i) ALLOWANCES AND TAX RATES).

3.20   **DEALING IN COMMODITY FUTURES—**
withdrawal of loss relief. [*Sec 399*]

Where there was a trade of dealing in commodity futures carried on in partnership in which one or more partners was a company and there were arrangements made or scheme effected (whether by the partnership agreement or otherwise) after 5 April 1976 so that the sole or main benefit expected from the partnership was tax relief under *Sec 380* (trading losses set-off against general income of an individual) or *Sec 393(2)* (trading losses set-off against total profits of a company) or *Sec 381* (losses in early years of a trade set-off against general income of an individual in earlier years), such relief will not be given. Where relief has been given, it will be withdrawn by an assessment under Schedule D, Case VI.

4 Appeals

(See also Revenue Pamphlet IR 37.)

Cross-references. See 6.8 BACK DUTY for investigatory powers of Revenue; 17.5 CLAIMS for appeals in respect of claims; 52.7 OFFSHORE FUNDS; 56.2 PAYMENT OF TAX for payment of tax pending appeal; 58.5, 58.6 and 58.7 PENALTIES for appeals relating to penalties and 64.8 RESIDENCE, ORDINARY RESIDENCE AND DOMICILE. See also 78 SELF-ASSESSMENT.

4.1   RIGHT OF APPEAL

The majority of appeals are against assessments, the right of appeal being conferred by *TMA s 31* but, with unimportant exceptions, the taxpayer may appeal against any formal decision by an inspector or the Board. In particular a decision on CLAIMS (17) may be appealed [*TMA s 42*] as may coding under PAY AS YOU EARN (55). [*1993 No 774, reg 11*]. Further, certain matters are dealt with as appeals, e.g. disputes as to the transfer price of trading stock on a discontinuance (see 71.82 SCHEDULE D, CASES I AND II).

Unless otherwise stated or required by the context, the following paragraphs apply to all appeals and matters treated as appeals, and not only to appeals against assessments.

An appeal once made cannot be withdrawn (*R v Special Commrs (ex p Elmhirst), CA 1935, 20 TC 381*) but see 4.4 below for the withdrawal of appeals by agreement and 4.7 below regarding appeals to the High Court.

As regards 1996/97 and subsequent years, see also 78.31 SELF-ASSESSMENT.

4.2   TIME LIMIT FOR APPEALS ETC.

An appeal *against an assessment* must be made within 30 days of the date of issue of the notice of assessment and state the grounds of appeal, but grounds not stated may be advanced at any hearing of the appeal if the Commissioners allow. [*TMA s 31(1), (5); F(No 2)A 1975, s 67(1)*]. An appeal against a decision on a claim must be made within 30 days of receipt of written notice of the decision except for certain overseas matters (see 64.8 RESIDENCE, ORDINARY RESIDENCE AND DOMICILE). There is no time limit for appeals against PAYE codings.

A **late appeal** may be accepted by the inspector if there is reasonable excuse for the delay and if he does not accept it he must refer the application to the Commissioners for their decision. [*TMA s 49*]. If they refuse, their decision is not subject to appeal by way of stated case (*R v Special Commrs (ex p Magill) QB (NI) 1979, 53 TC 135*), but is subject to judicial review (see *R v Hastings and Bexhill General Commrs and CIR (ex p Goodacre) QB, [1994] STC 799*, in which a refusal was quashed and the matter remitted to a different body of Commissioners).

As regards 1996/97 and subsequent years, see also 78.31 SELF-ASSESSMENT.

4.3   JURISDICTION OF COMMISSIONERS

As regards 1996/97 and subsequent years, see also 78.36 SELF-ASSESSMENT.

An appeal is made to the General or Special Commissioners. Notice of the appeal is given in writing to the appropriate inspector or officer of the Board. If not settled by agreement (4.4 below) it is heard by the Commissioners. Appeals relating to most personal allowances and certain other reliefs are heard only by the General Commissioners. [*TMA s 42, 2 Sch*]. Appeals against assessments made by the Board and assessments made under *Sec 350* (see 23.3 DEDUCTION OF TAX AT SOURCE), against any decision of the Board and relating to double taxation relief by agreement and a number of technical matters, mainly overseas matters or regarding financial bodies, are heard only by the Special Commissioners. [*TMA ss 31(3) as amended, 42, 2 Sch*]. Subject to this, the appeal is to the General Commissioners, unless the taxpayer elects for the Special Commissioners, either when the appeal is made or separately but within the time limit for making the appeal. Such an election is, however, disregarded if the appellant and the inspector so agree in writing before the appeal is determined, or if before the appeal is determined the inspector refers the election to the General Commissioners (after notifying the appellant) and they so direct. They must give such a direction unless satisfied that the appellant has arguments to present or evidence to adduce on the merits of the appeal. Such a direction may be revoked at any time before determination of the appeal if that condition is subsequently satisfied. The decision to give or revoke a direction is final. [*TMA ss 31(5A)–(5E), 46(1), 2 Sch 1A–1E; FA 1984, s 127, 22 Sch 3; SI 1984 No 1836*]. In deciding when to list an appeal for hearing, inspectors treat appeals to the Special Commissioners in exactly the same way as those to the General Commissioners. The taxpayer's agreement (or, failing that, the General Commissioners' direction) that an election for hearing by the Special Commissioners be disregarded will only be sought when a decision is needed to arrange the listing of the appeal for hearing, and then only where the inspector is satisfied that it is a delay appeal and not a contentious one. (Revenue Press Release 26 February 1990).

Appeals to the General Commissioners may, if the parties so apply and the Commissioners consent, be transferred to the Special Commissioners (and vice versa) despite the expiry of the time limit for election as above or the making of such an election. [*TMA s 44(3)*]. In addition, the General Commissioners may arrange that an appeal brought before them be transferred to the Special Commissioners, with the Special Commissioners' consent, if, after considering any representations made to them by the parties to the appeal, the General Commissioners consider that, because of the complexity of, or likely time required to hear, the appeal, it should be so transferred. [*TMA s 44(3A); FA 1984, s 127, 22 Sch 5; SI 1984 No 1836*].

Where an appeal against an assessment to tax on chargeable gains is on a question of the value of any land, or of a lease of land, then the question is determined on a reference to the Lands Tribunal. [*TMA s 47*].

Where the General Commissioners have jurisdiction, rules for prescribing the appropriate Division are in *TMA 3 Sch* as amended, although the parties may come to an agreement that the proceedings be brought before any body of General Commissioners specified in the agreement. [*TMA s 44(1)(2); FA 1988, s 133(2)*]. The Board may, however, direct that specified proceedings be brought before the General Commissioners for a specified division, provided that the inspector notifies the other party of the effect of that direction, unless

(i) the other party objects to the direction within 30 days of the service of the inspector's notice, or, in the case of an appeal, has elected for a hearing in the place where he ordinarily resides (see below), or

(ii) the proceedings are subject to the special rules applicable where more than one taxpayer may be a party to the proceedings.

Any such direction may be superseded by an agreement between the parties (as above). [*TMA s 44(1A)(1B); FA 1988 s 133(1)(3)*]. A list has been published of the division of General Commissioners with which the Board will, under these provisions, generally seek to link those tax offices dealing with substantial groups of companies and trusts. (Revenue Press Release 19 December 1988).

For appeals against *assessments* the broad effect of *TMA 3 Sch* is to designate the Division in which the appellant's trade etc. is carried on. If he has no trade etc., an employee may elect for the Division in which he ordinarily resides (or, in practice, any other Division he nominates), otherwise it is the Division in which he is employed (or, at the inspector's election, the Division in which the assessment was made). The election for Division of residence etc. must strictly be made by written notice not later than the notice of appeal, but the Revenue will in practice accede to a request by an employee subsequent to the appeal being made but before it is set down for hearing (and notwithstanding an election by the inspector as above) for the hearing to be in the Division in which he resides or in any other Division the employee nominates. See Revenue Tax Bulletin May 1993 p 70. If the taxpayer has no trade etc. or employment, the Division of residence applies, which also applies to appeals relating to personal allowances irrespective of the place of any trade etc. or employment. Corporation tax appeals are heard in the Division in which the company carries on its trade or where its head office is situated. These rules are, however, directory and not mandatory (*CIR v Adams CA 1971, 48 TC 67; Murphy v Elders Ch D 1973, 49 TC 135*) and a decision of the Commissioners cannot be invalidated for want of jurisdiction if there was no objection to jurisdiction before the decision. [*TMA s 44(4)*]. See also *R v Kingston & Elmbridge Commrs QB 1972, 48 TC 75; R v St Pancras Commrs QB 1973, 50 TC 365; Parikh v Birmingham North Commrs CA, [1976] STC 365.*

The Special Commissioners go on circuit to the chief provincial towns, but appeals to them may generally by arrangement be heard in London, which is usually more convenient if it is intended to engage counsel.

The Lord Chancellor has powers, by regulation, to provide for the transfer of appeals between the General and Special Commissioners or between General Commissioners for different divisions, and for varying the number of General or Special Commissioners required or permitted to hear appeals. Different provision may be made for different cases and different circumstances. [*TMA s 46A; F(No 2)A 1992, 16 Sch 3*]. See now *SI 1994 Nos 1811–1813* and 4.6 below.

In **Northern Ireland** all appeals were previously heard by the Special Commissioners except where the taxpayer elected (under *TMA s 59*) for private hearing by a single judge in County Court. However, from 3 April 1989, the system of General Commissioners described above was extended to NI, and the election for County Court hearing abolished. Outstanding appeals to the Special Commissioners were transferred to the General Commissioners unless the taxpayer elected to the contrary by notice in writing before 3 May 1989. [*FA 1988, ss 134, 135; SI 1989 No 473*].

4.4   **SETTLEMENT OF APPEALS BY AGREEMENT**

Where agreement, written or otherwise, has been reached at any time between the Revenue and the appellant or agent on his behalf on any appeal to General or Special Commissioners, against any assessment or decision under appeal, the assessment or decision as upheld, varied, discharged or cancelled by that agreement, is treated as if it had been determined on appeal, provided that (*a*) taxpayer may withdraw from the agreement by giving written notice within 30 days of making it, (*b*) verbal agreements reached are of no effect unless confirmed in writing by either side (the date of such confirmation then being the effective date of 'determination'). [*TMA s 54*]. The agreement must specify the figure for assessment or a precise formula for ascertaining it (*Delbourgo v Field CA 1978, 52 TC 225*). The inspector has no power unilaterally to 'vacate' an assessment (*Baylis v Gregory CA, [1987] STC 297*). An agreement as to partial set-off of a loss in a year of assessment does not bind the parties as to the amount of the loss carried forward and available in subsequent years (*Tod v South Essex Motors (Basildon) Ltd Ch D 1987, 60 TC 598*). For the extent to which further assessments are permissible if an appeal has been determined by agreement, see 5.3 ASSESSMENTS.

An agreement under *TMA s 54* does not prevent an assessment being revised to correct an error, where the effect of the error was that the common intention of the parties was not recorded by the agreement (*R v HMIT ex p Bass Holdings Ltd QB 1992, 65 TC 495*). An agreement based on a mutual mistake of fact was thereby vitiated, so that the taxpayer could proceed with his appeal (*Fox v Rothwell (Sp C 50), [1995] SSCD 336*).

A taxpayer cannot withdraw an appeal made to Commissioners (see 4.1 above) but if, having appealed, he, or his agent acting in that appeal, gives the inspector oral or written notice of his desire not to proceed, then, unless the inspector gives written notice of objection within 30 days thereof, the appeal is treated as if settled by agreement, as above, at the date of the taxpayer's notification. [*TMA s 54(4)*].

4.5   THE HANDLING OF TAXPAYERS' APPEALS

Appeal meetings must be notified to the appellant and the inspector (or other Revenue party) (see 4.6 below). In practice the inspector normally gives details of appeals ready for hearing to the clerk who, after consulting the inspector and, in important appeals, the taxpayer or his agent as appropriate, makes the necessary arrangements, notifies the inspector and issues notices of the hearing to the appellant. In some Divisions he may, by arrangement, also notify the appellant's agent.

Deferred delay appeals. In Revenue Press Release 25 January 1983, the Revenue announced a change of practice as regards the handling of appeals, in an effort to reduce the number of 'delay' hearings. The main elements are as follows.

(i)   The new approach applies to estimated assessments made under Schedules A or D or on taxed income after July 1982, where the tax charged is £10,000 or less. Schedule E, corporation tax and capital gains tax appeals are not affected.

(ii)   Provided that a reasonable payment on account has been agreed and that the business (or other source) is continuing, appeals are not normally listed for hearing until two years' accounts (or other information) are outstanding. Both years' appeals are then listed for hearing together after the June following the second year of assessment.

(iii) The fact that no pressure has been applied to obtain returns does not affect the Revenue's attitude to cases in which interest is chargeable under *TMA s 88* (see 42.5 INTEREST ON UNPAID TAX) or to the time limits for elections or claims.

In order to prepare for the introduction of SELF-ASSESSMENT (78), District Inspectors have been encouraged by the Board to agree a programme with local accountants to deal with deferred delay appeals, to ensure that taxpayers' affairs are brought up to date, although the above arrangements will continue where no such agreement is in operation. (ICAEW Technical Release TAX 1/95, 10 January 1995).

The procedural changes previously introduced in 1976 presumably still apply to other assessments. Under these, inspectors will, in general, bring to the Appeal Meetings during the first half of the calendar year only the following.

(a)   *Cases of gross delay* i.e. where there are unsettled appeals for more than one year and also where the reckonable date for interest purposes has passed (but some corporation tax assessments may be listed before the reckonable date where there is a long interval between the end of the accounting period and the due and payable date) and priority will be given where material amounts of interest on unpaid tax are likely to arise. At these hearings the inspector may be seeking the Commissioners' determination of the liability and will be unlikely to acquiesce in continued delay.

(b)   *Contentious cases*, which would also include, for example, some corporation tax cases where the real point of dispute lies in Schedule E and PAYE liabilities of the directors and where the accounts are necessary to resolve this, even though the corporation tax liability will be small.

(c) *Applications for postponement of tax pending appeal.* Inspectors will normally be selective and concentrate on worthwhile cases and will then usually contest any request for an adjournment pending production of accounts.

(d) *Appeals where the taxpayer is not professionally advised or represented.*

(CCAB Memorandum TR 181, 2 April 1976).

Under the earlier procedures, at least 15 months usually elapsed between the taxpayer's accounting date and the first listing for a Commissioners' hearing. At such hearings the onus was on the taxpayer or his agent to show cause for continued delay.

(CCAB Memorandum TR 181a, 4 November 1976).

4.6 APPEALS HEARD BY COMMISSIONERS

The Lord Chancellor has wide regulatory powers in relation to the practice and procedure to be followed in connection with appeals, including the power to make different provision for different cases and different circumstances. [*TMA ss 56B–56D; F(No 2)A 1992, 16 Sch 4; FA 1994, s 254*]. With effect from 1 September 1994, regulations are brought in governing the jurisdiction of the General Commissioners and the procedure for proceedings before them. [*SI 1994 No 1812*]. Similar regulations apply in relation to the Special Commissioners [*SI 1994 No 1811*], and *SI 1994 No 1813* makes consequential and complementary amendments to other enactments.

In relation to the General Commissioners, these regulations do not apply to any proceedings set down (or first set down) for hearing by notice given before 1 September 1994 if any party to those proceedings so elects (by notice to the Clerk to the Commissioners) prior to commencement of the hearing (or to the recommencement of adjourned proceedings which were commenced before 1 September 1994). They also do not apply to any proceedings under *TMA s 100C* (see 58.6 PENALTIES) in respect of which a summons was issued prior to 1 September 1994 to the defendant to appear before them at a time and place stated in the summons. Where these regulations *do* apply to proceedings set down (or first set down) for hearing by notice given before 1 September 1994, anything done in relation to those proceedings before that date which, if the proceedings had commenced on or after that date, could have been done pursuant to these regulations, is to have effect as if done pursuant to these regulations. [*SI 1994 No 1812, reg 1*].

In relation to the Special Commissioners, these regulations do not apply to any proceedings set down for hearing by notice given before 1 September 1994, or in respect of which a summons was issued before that date. [*SI 1994 No 1811, reg 1*].

Where these regulations do not apply, the jurisdictional and procedural rules were broadly similar, the most significant difference being the absence of the powers of the Special Commissioners to hear cases in public, to publish their decisions and to award costs in certain cases. For details of the earlier rules, see Tolley's Income Tax 1994/95 or earlier edition.

The remainder of this section deals with the rules applicable from 1 September 1994, and with the general and case law which is of continuing application.

(a) **General Commissioners.**

Constitution of Tribunal. Two or more, but not more than five, General Commissioners for a division may hear any proceedings. [*SI 1994 No 1812, reg 2*]. They will themselves decide which one of them will preside at the hearing. Where possible at least three will sit, and, with the consent of all the parties, proceedings may be continued by one or more of them. [*SI 1994 No 1812, reg 11*]. For the effect of personal business connection between a Commissioner and a party to proceedings, see *R v Holyhead Commrs (ex p Roberts) QB 1982, 56 TC 127*.

The Clerk to the Commissioners, who is frequently a local solicitor, normally attends the meeting to take minutes and to advise them as required, but a meeting without a Clerk would not be invalid (*Venn v Franks CA 1958, 38 TC 175*).

Preparation for hearing. *Listing and notice of hearing.* Except in relation to proceedings under *TMA s 100C* (see 58.6 PENALTIES), any party to the proceedings may serve notice on the Clerk to the Commissioners that he wishes a date for the hearing to be fixed, on receipt of which the Clerk must send notice to each party of the place, date and time of the hearing. Unless the parties otherwise agree, or the Commissioners otherwise direct, the date must not be earlier than 28 days after the date of the Clerk's notice. [*SI 1994 No 1812, reg 3*].

Witnesses. A General Commissioner, on the application of any party to the proceedings, may issue a witness summons (in Scotland, a witness citation) requiring any person in the UK either to attend the hearing of those proceedings to give evidence or to produce any relevant document in his possession, custody or power. The party applying for issue of the summons is responsible for its service (for which see *reg 4(3)*), and attendance may not be required within seven days of service unless the witness informs the Clerk that he accepts shorter notice. That party must also agree to meet the witness' reasonable travelling expenses. The witness may apply, by notice served on the Clerk, for the Commissioners to set aside the summons (in whole or part), on which application the party on whose application the summons was issued is entitled to be heard.

Except in Scotland, a witness so summoned to give evidence may only be cross-examined by the party on whose application the summons was issued if the Commissioners decide that the witness is a hostile witness and give leave.

A witness cannot be compelled to give evidence or produce documents which he could not be compelled to give or produce in an action in a court of law. An auditor or tax adviser (within *TMA s 20B(10)*) cannot be compelled to produce any document which he would not be obliged to deliver or make available by notice under *TMA s 20(3)* or *(8A)* (having regard to *TMA s 20B(9)–(13)*), and copies of, or of parts of, documents may similarly be produced in certain cases (see 6.8 BACK DUTY).

In the event of failure by a witness to attend in obedience to the summons, or refusal to be sworn or to affirm, or refusal to answer any lawful question or to produce a document he is required to produce by the summons, the Commissioners may summarily determine a penalty not exceeding £1,000, to be treated as tax charged by an assessment and due and payable.

[*SI 1994 No 1812, reg 4*].

Joint hearings. The Commissioners have powers to direct that two or more proceedings, in one or more divisions, with common issues be heard at the same time or consecutively within one division, either of their own motion or on an application by any of the parties to any of those proceedings. All the parties must be notified, and are entitled to be heard before such a direction is given. On the giving of a direction, the Clerk must send notice of its date and terms to all parties. [*SI 1994 No 1812, reg 6*]. The Commissioners have an inherent power to deal with two or more appeals simultaneously where the appellants' affairs are so intermingled as to be incapable of separation, and where they are satisfied that it would result in no injustice to either party (*Johnson v Walden; King v Walden CA, [1996] STC 382*).

Postponements and adjournments. The Commissioners may postpone or adjourn the hearing of any proceedings, the Clerk being responsible for notifying all parties of the place, date and time of the postponed or adjourned hearing (unless announced before an adjournment in the presence of all parties). Where a hearing is adjourned for the obtaining of further information or evidence, the Commissioners may direct the parties regarding the disclosure of such information or evidence prior to resumption. [*SI 1994 No 1812, reg 8*]. In *Packe v Johnson Ch D 1991, 63 TC 507*, a determination was quashed because of the Commissioners' refusal to consider all relevant information in deciding to refuse an adjournment at a second hearing.

Other matters in preparation for hearing. There are also regulations dealing with the agreement of documents [*reg 5*], the joinder of additional parties to the proceedings [*reg 7*] and the admission of expert evidence [*reg 9*].

Hearing and determination of proceedings. Hearings are in private, except that certain persons with official responsibilities may be present, and may remain present during, but not take part in, the Commissioners' deliberations. With the consent of the parties, the Commissioners may permit any other person to attend the hearing. [*SI 1994 No 1812, reg 13*].

Power to obtain information. The Commissioners may, at any time before final determination of the proceedings, serve on any party to the proceedings (other than the Revenue) notice requiring that party, within a specified time,

(i)   to deliver such particulars as may be required to determine any issue of the proceedings, and

(ii)   to make available for inspection by the Commissioners or by an officer of the Board such specified or described books, accounts, etc. in his possession or power as may, in their opinion, contain information relevant to the proceedings.

For unsuccessful challenges relating to the issue of notices under these and the similar powers previously contained in *TMA s 51*, see *Johnson v Blackpool General Commrs and CIR Ch D, [1996] STC 277*, *Eke v Knight CA 1977, 51 TC 121* and *Khan v Newport General Commrs and CIR Ch D, [1994] STC 972*.

The Commissioners may summarily determine a penalty (to be treated as tax charged in an assessment and due and payable) of up to £300 for failure to comply with such a notice, plus up to £60 per day for continuing failure after such a penalty is determined. Any officer of the Board (and the Commissioners in the case of (ii)) may, at all reasonable times, take copies of, or extracts from, any such particulars, books, etc.. [*SI 1994 No 1812, reg 10*].

Representation at hearing. A party to the proceedings may be represented by any person, except that the Commissioners may, if satisfied that there are good and sufficient reasons for doing so, refuse to permit a party to be represented by a particular person, not being a legally qualified person or a member of an incorporated society of accountants. In practice, most bodies of Commissioners permit the taxpayer to be represented by any person who they are satisfied is competent to present the appellant's case. The Revenue may be represented by a barrister, advocate, solicitor or any officer of the Board. [*SI 1994 No 1812, reg 12*]. The Revenue representative is normally an inspector. The secretary or 'other proper officer' represents a company (the liquidator if in liquidation). [*TMA s 108*].

Failure to attend hearing. Where a party fails to attend or be represented at a hearing of which he has been duly notified, the Commissioners may postpone or adjourn a hearing or (unless satisfied that there is good and sufficient reason for such failure, and after considering any written or other representations) hear and determine the proceedings. [*SI 1994 No 1812, reg 14*]. Determinations in the absence of the taxpayer or his agent have been upheld where notice of the meeting was received by the appellant (*R v Tavistock Commrs (ex p Adams) QB 1969, 46 TC 154; R v Special*

Commr (ex p Moschi) CA, [1981] STC 465 and see *Fletcher & Fletcher v Harvey CA 1990, 63 TC 539*), but Commissioners were held to have acted unreasonably in refusing to re-open proceedings when taxpayer's agent was temporarily absent when the appeal was called (*McKerron Ltd CS 1979, 52 TC 28*). Where the taxpayer was absent through illness, a determination was quashed because the Commissioners, in refusing an adjournment, had failed to consider whether injustice would thereby arise to the taxpayer (*R v Sevenoaks Commrs (ex p Thorne) QB 1989, 62 TC 341* and see *Rose v Humbles CA 1971, 48 TC 103*). See also *R v O'Brien (ex p Lissner) QB, 1984 STI 710* where the determination was quashed then the appellant had been informed by the inspector that the hearing was to be adjourned.

Procedure and evidence at hearing. The Commissioners have wide discretion as to the manner in which the proceedings are conducted, and should seek to avoid inappropriate formality. They may require any witness to give evidence on oath or affirmation, and may admit evidence which would be inadmissible in a court of law. Evidence may be given orally or, if they so direct, by affidavit or statement recorded in a document (and they may, on their own motion or on the application of any party, at any stage require the personal attendance as a witness of the maker of such a statement or affidavit or the person who recorded the statement). They may take account of the nature and source of any evidence, and the manner in which it is given, in assessing its truth and weight. The parties may be heard in any order, but are entitled to give evidence, to call witnesses, to question witnesses (including other parties who give evidence), and to address the Commissioners both on the evidence and on the subject matter of the proceedings. [*SI 1994 No 1812, reg 15*]. A party to the proceedings cannot insist on being examined on oath (*R v Special Commrs (in re Fletcher) CA 1894, 3 TC 289*). False evidence under oath would be perjury under criminal law (*R v Hood Barrs CA. [1943] 1 AER 665*). A taxpayer was held to be bound by an affidavit he had made in other proceedings. (*Wicker v Fraser Ch D 1982, 55 TC 641*). A remission to Commissioners to hear evidence directed at the credit of a witness was refused in *Potts v CIR Ch D 1982, 56 TC 25*. Rules of the Supreme Court under which evidence can be obtained from a witness abroad cannot be used in proceedings before the Commissioners (*In re Leiserach CA 1963, 42 TC 1*). As to hearsay evidence under *Civil Evidence Act 1968*, see *Forth Investments Ltd Ch D 1976, 50 TC 617* and *Khan v Edwards Ch D 1977, 53 TC 597*.

The inspector is entitled to ask the Commissioners to exercise their powers to increase an assessment, and to adduce evidence in support of his application (*Glaxo Group Ltd and others v CIR CA, [1996] STC 191*).

The Commissioners are under no obligation to adjourn an appeal for the production of further evidence (*Hamilton v CIR CS 1930, 16 TC 28; Noble v Wilkinson Ch D 1958, 38 TC 135*), and were held not to have erred in law in determining assessments in the absence abroad of the taxpayer (*Hawkins v Fuller Ch D 1982, 56 TC 49*).

The taxpayer has no general right to conduct his appeal in writing without attending the hearing (*Banin v Mackinlay CA 1984, 58 TC 398*), although written pleadings may, at the Commissioners' discretion, be taken into account (*Caldicott v Varty Ch D 1976, 51 TC 403*).

In reaching their decision, the Commissioners may not take into account matters appropriate for application for judicial review (*Aspin v Estill CA 1987, 60 TC 549*). They do not generally have the power to review on appeal the exercise of a discretion conferred on the Revenue by statute (see *Slater v Richardson & Bottoms Ltd Ch D 1979, 53 TC 155; Kelsall v Investment Chartwork Ltd Ch D 1993, 65 TC 750*) (although in certain cases such power of review is itself statutory; see e.g. *SI 1993 No 743, reg 10(4)*, which in effect reversed the decision in *Richardson & Bottoms Ltd* above).

4.6 Appeals

For the extent to which Commissioners may use their local knowledge, see *Forest Side Properties (Chingford) Ltd v Pearce CA 1961, 39 TC 665*.

Onus of proof. The onus is on the appellant to displace an assessment (but see 6.2 BACK DUTY for onus on Crown to prove fraud or wilful default to support extended time limit assessments). See *Brady v Group Lotus Car Companies plc CA 1987, 60 TC 359* where onus of proof remained with taxpayer where amount of normal time limit assessment indicated contention of fraud. The general principle emerges in appeals against estimated assessments in 'delay cases' (see 4.5 above) which are the bulk of appeals heard by the General Commissioners. For examples of cases in which the Commissioners have confirmed estimated assessments in the absence of evidence that they were excessive, see *T Haythornthwaite & Sons Ltd v Kelly CA 1927, 11 TC 657; Stoneleigh Products Ltd v Dodd CA 1'948, 30 TC 1; Rosette Franks (King St) Ltd v Dick Ch D 1955, 36 TC 100; Pierson v Belcher Ch D 1959, 38 TC 387*. In a number of cases, the Courts have supported the Commissioners' action in rejecting unsatisfactory accounts (e.g. *Cain v Schofield Ch D 1953, 34 TC 362; Moll v CIR CS 1955, 36 TC 384; Cutmore v Leach Ch D 1981, 55 TC 602; Coy v Kime Ch D 1986, 59 TC 447*) or calling for certified accounts (e.g. *Stephenson v Waller KB 1927, 13 TC 318; Hunt & Co v Joly KB 1928, 14 TC 165; Wall v Cooper CA 1929, 14 TC 552*). In *Anderson v CIR CS 1933, 18 TC 320*, the case was remitted where there was no evidence to support the figure arrived at by the Commissioners (which was between the accounts figure and the estimated figure assessed), but contrast *Bookey v Edwards Ch D 1981, 55 TC 486*. The Commissioners are entitled to look at each year separately, accepting the appellant's figures for some years but not all (*Donnelly v Platten CA (NI) 1980, [1981] STC 504*). Similarly, the onus is on the taxpayer to substantiate his claims to relief (see *Eke v Knight CA 1977, 51 TC 121; Talib v Waterson Ch D, [1980] STC 563*).

For the standard of proof required in evidence, see *Les Croupiers Casino Club v Pattinson CA 1987, 60 TC 196*.

The Commissioners' decision. The Revenue representative must not be present while the Commissioners are deliberating their decision unless the other party or parties (or their representative(s)) are also present (*R v Brixton Commrs KB 1912, 6 TC 195*). The Commissioners' determination was quashed where the Clerk had discussed the case with Revenue representatives between hearing and announcement of determination (*R v Wokingham Commrs (ex p Heron) QB, 1984 STI 710*).

If it appears to the Commissioners that the appellant has been over- or under-charged by any assessment under appeal, they must reduce or increase that assessment accordingly, but otherwise the assessment stands good. A determination of income assessable determines the appeal; if the Commissioners alter the assessment, they are not obliged to determine the revised tax payable. [*TMA s 50(6)–(8); SI 1994 No 1813*]. Only the assessment by which the taxpayer was overcharged may be reduced under *TMA s 50(6)*. Any decision is by a majority of the Commissioners hearing the proceedings, with the presiding Commissioner having a casting vote where necessary. The final determination may be announced orally at the end of the hearing or may be reserved. In either case, the Clerk to the Commissioners must send to each party a notice (including details of the procedure for appeals from the General Commissioners) setting out the determination, and unless the determination was given at the hearing, the date of such notice is the date of the determination. [*SI 1994 No 1812, reg 16*]. Where the Clerk announced the decision wrongly, it was held that the correct decision stood good (*R v Morleston & Litchurch Commrs KB 1951, 32 TC 335*) (and see below under *Miscellaneous: Irregularities*).

Where Commissioners determined appeals in principle and held a further hearing to adjust assessments, their action in refusing to admit further evidence for the taxpayer at the later hearing was upheld (*R v St Marylebone Commrs (ex p Hay) CA 1983, 57 TC 59*). They are entitled, however, to alter their decision in principle at a later hearing (*Larner v Warrington Ch D 1985, 58 TC 557*). See also *Gibson v Stroud Commrs Ch D 1989, 61 TC 645.*

A decision of the Commissioners is not legally binding on them or any other Commissioners in any other proceedings, even on appeal by the same taxpayer against a similar assessment for another year (*CIR v Sneath CA 1932, 17 TC 149* and cf. *Edwards v 'Old Bushmills' Distillery HL 1926, 10 TC 285; Abdul Caffoor Trustees PC 1961, 40 ATC 93*).

Review of the Commissioners' final determination. A decision of the Commissioners is generally final and conclusive [*TMA s 46(2)*], but the Commissioners may review and set aside or vary their final determination on the application of any party or of their own motion where they are satisfied that either

(1)   it was wrongly made as a result of administrative error, or

(2)   a party entitled to be heard failed to appear or be represented for good and sufficient reason, or

(3)   relevant information had been supplied to the Clerk or to the appropriate inspector or other Revenue officer prior to the hearing but was not received by the Commissioners until after the hearing.

A written application for such a review must be made to the Commissioners not later than 14 days after the date of the notice of the determination (or by such later time as the Commissioners may allow), stating the grounds in full. Where the Commissioners propose of their own motion to review a determination, they must serve notice on the parties not later than 14 days after the date of the notice of the determination.

The parties are entitled to be heard on any such review or proposed review. If practicable, the review is to be determined by the Commissioners who decided the case, and if they set aside the determination, they may substitute a different determination or order a rehearing before the same or different Commissioners. A decision to vary or substitute a final determination is to be notified in the same way as the original determination (see above).

[*SI 1994 No 1812, reg 17*].

See 4.8 below as regards application for judicial review where the Commissioners have acted unfairly or improperly.

Special procedure. *Proceedings relating to tax on chargeable gains.* Where material, the market value of an asset or the apportionment of an amount or value is, if so required by any party, to be recorded in the final determination. They may be proved in any proceedings relating to tax on chargeable gains by a certificate signed by the Clerk to the Commissioners (in certain cases the clerk or registrar of another tribunal), or by the inspector where the appeal was settled by agreement, stating the material particulars. [*SI 1994 No 1812, reg 18*].

Reference to other tribunals. Certain questions relating to the value of land or of an interest in land may be referred to the appropriate Lands Tribunal, and similarly in relation to unquoted shares to the Special Commissioners (see *TMA s 47*). The instant proceedings may be determined without awaiting the outcome of such referral. [*SI 1994 No 1812, reg 19*].

Miscellaneous. *Irregularities.* Any irregularity resulting from failure to comply with regulations or with any Commissioners' direction given before a final determination is reached, shall not, of itself, render the proceedings void, and before reaching that determination the Commissioners may, and if they consider that any person has been prejudiced by the irregularity must, give such direction as they think just to cure or waive any irregularity which comes to their attention. Clerical errors in any document recording a direction or decision of the Commissioners may be corrected by any of the Commissioners concerned (or by the Clerk if all the Commissioners have died or ceased to be Commissioners) by certificate under his hand. [*SI 1994 No 1812, reg 24*].

Notices must be in writing unless the Commissioners authorise them to be given orally. [*SI 1994 No 1812, reg 25*].

Service of any notice or document (other than a witness summons, see above) may be by post, by (legible) facsimile transmission etc. or by delivery at the proper address. [*SI 1994 No 1812, reg 26(1)*]. The persons and addresses to whom and which a document may be sent or delivered are set out in *reg 26(2)(3)*, and the provisions for substituted or waived service in certain cases in *reg 27*.

Penalties. Any appeal against summary penalties determined under regulations as above lies to the High Court (in Scotland, the Court of Session). [*TMA s 53; SI 1994 No 1813*].

Guidance notes for General Commissioners issued by the Lord Chancellor's department, on the law relevant to their duties and on how the many aspects of those duties may be carried out in practice, are available to ICAEW members from Accountancy Books, PO Box 620, Central Milton Keynes, MK9 2JX (price £5).

(*b*)   **Special Commissioners**

The provisions applicable to the General Commissioners (see (*a*) above) apply equally to the Special Commissioners, with the following variations.

Constitution of Tribunal. Any one, two or three of the Special Commissioners may hear any proceedings. If two or three Commissioners are sitting, the Presiding Special Commissioner, or, if he is not sitting, the Commissioner nominated by him, shall preside at the hearing. With the consent of all parties, proceedings may be continued by any one or two of the Commissioners unless the Presiding Special Commissioner otherwise directs. [*SI 1994 No 1811, regs 2, 13*].

Preparation for hearing. *Listing and notice of hearing.* Before notifying the parties of the place, date and time of a hearing, the Clerk to the Commissioners must satisfy himself that the Special Commissioners have jurisdiction over the proceedings and that he has sufficient particulars for determination. The Presiding Special Commissioner may direct that such notifications are not to be sent. [*SI 1994 No 1811, reg 3*].

General power to give directions. The Commissioner(s) have wide direction-giving powers, on the application of any of the parties to proceedings or of their own motion. Applications by the parties (otherwise than during the hearing) must be in writing to the Clerk, and if not made with the consent of all the parties, must be served by the Clerk on any affected party, who may object. [*SI 1994 No 1811, reg 4*].

Witnesses. The maximum penalty which the Commissioner(s) may summarily determine for failure to attend or refusal to be sworn or affirm, to answer any lawful question or to produce documents as required is £10,000. [*SI 1994 No 1811, regs 5, 24(2)*].

Preliminary hearing. Where it appears to a Special Commissioner that any proceedings would be facilitated by holding a preliminary hearing, he may, on the application of a party or of his own motion, give directions for such a hearing to be held. The Clerk to the Special Commissioners must give to all the parties 14 days notice (or such shorter time as the parties agree or the Commissioner sees fit to impose) of the time and place of the hearing. On a preliminary hearing, the Commissioner has wide direction-giving powers, and may, if the parties so agree, determine the proceedings without any futher hearing. [*SI 1994 No 1811, reg 9*]. See below as regards powers of Commissioner to obtain information on preliminary hearing of any proceedings.

Hearing and determination of proceedings. *Hearings in public or private.* Hearings before the Special Commissioner(s) are in public, unless any party applies by notice to the Clerk for the hearing (or any part) to be in private. A Revenue application for a private hearing requires in addition a direction by a Special Commissioner. The rules for attendance at a private hearing follow those before the General Commissioners (as above). [*SI 1994 No 1811, reg 15*].

Power to obtain information. The powers of General Commissioners to obtain information apply to both a preliminary hearing before a Special Commissioner and to the hearing of the proceedings, except that the specific penalty provisions for failure to comply with a notice do not apply (although the general penalty for failure to comply with Commissioner's direction, see below, *does* apply). [*SI 1994 No 1811, regs 10, 24(1)*].

The Commissioners' decision. The recording of the Commissioner(s)' decision must contain a statement of the facts found and the reasons for the determination. After reserving the final determination, the Commissioner(s) may give a written decision in principle on one or more of the issues arising, and adjourn the making of the final determination until after that decision has been issued and any further questions arising from it have been agreed by the parties or decided by the Commissioner(s) after hearing the parties. A decision in principle must contain a statement of the facts and the reasons for the decision, and these need not be repeated in the document recording the final determination. [*SI 1994 No 1811, reg 18*].

Review of the Commissioners' decision in principle may proceed in the same way as a review of a final determination. [*SI 1994 No 1811, reg 19*].

Publication of decisions in principle or final determinations. The Presiding Special Commissioner may arrange for the publication of such reports of decisions in principle and final determinations as he considers appropriate. If the proceedings (or any part) were held in private, he must ensure that the report is in a form which, so far as possible, prevents the identification of any person whose affairs are dealt with. [*SI 1994 No 1811, reg 20*]. An application for non-publication of a decision on the grounds of inadequate anonymity, or for publication of a short summary only, was refused by the Presiding Special Commissioner in *Y Co Ltd v CIR (Sp C 69), [1996] SSCD 147.* The policy on anonymisation was quoted as: 'In cases where anonymisation is required, the Presiding Special Commissioner will seek to achieve this in co-operation with the parties. If a decision or determination cannot be anonymised to the complete satisfaction of the party requiring it, the Presiding Special Commissioner's policy is to report it in as anonymised a form as he, in consultation with the Special Commissioner[s] deciding the case, considers to be appropriate. To this there is one exception, which is that no report will be published where the decision cannot be effectively anonymised and to report it would defeat the ends of justice, e.g. where particulars of a secret process would otherwise have to be disclosed or in cases where minors were involved. The Presiding Special Commissioner will consider cases falling outside this exception on their merits.' A substantial number of cases (amounting to well over 50 in the first year from early 1995) is now reported, and these are referred to in the text of this publication where relevant. The Special Commissioners expect to have their attention drawn in appropriate cases to any of their previous published decisions which is relevant, unless superseded by a higher court decision. The Revenue consider that, whilst not creating any binding legal precedent, these decisions may be relevant in other cases, particularly if not appealed against, but that it would be inappropriate to enter into any discussion of a case which is, or may be, the subject of appeal to the High Court. (Revenue Tax Bulletin October 1995 pp 258, 259).

Orders for costs. The Commissioner(s) may make an order awaiting costs (in Scotland expenses) of, or incidental to, the hearing of any proceedings against any party who has, in their opinion, acted wholly unreasonably in connection with the hearing, but not without giving that party the opportunity of making representations against the award. The award may be of all or part of the costs of the other party or parties, such costs to be taxed in the county court (in Scotland the sheriff court) if not agreed. In Northern Ireland, the Commissioners may determine the costs. [*SI 1994 No 1811, reg 21*].

Penalty for failure to comply with Commissioner(s)' direction. The Commissioner(s) may summarily determine a penalty of up to £10,000 for any such failure, to be treated as if it were tax charged in an assessment and due and payable. [*SI 1994 No 1811, reg 24(1)(3)*].

An **explanatory booklet** 'Appeals and Other Proceedings before the Special Commissioners' (October 1994) dealing with procedural and other points is available free of charge from the Clerk to the Special Commissioners, 15/29 Bedford Avenue, London WC1B 3AS (tel. 0171–631 4242).

4.7   APPEALS TO THE HIGH COURT

Prior to the determination of an appeal by the Commissioners, the Court may be prepared to consider an application seeking a determination as to whether the Revenue may make use of certain 'tax-altering' provisions in relation to the assessments under appeal (*Balen v CIR Ch D 1976, 52 TC 406; Beecham Group plc v CIR Ch D 1992, 65 TC 219*). In general, 'there is an absolute exclusion of the High Court's jurisdiction only when the proceedings seek relief which is more or less co-extensive with adjudicating on an existing open assessment . . . the more closely the High Court proceedings approximate to that in their substantial effect, the more ready the High Court will be, as a matter of discretion, to decline jurisdiction.' (*Glaxo Group Ltd and others v CIR Ch D, [1995] STC 1075*).

Case stated procedure — General Commissioners. Within 30 days of the date of final determination of an appeal (or of the variation or substitution of such a determination, see above), any party dissatisfied with the determination as being erroneous in point of law (for which see e.g. *Billows v Robinson CA, [1991] STC 127*) may serve notice on the Clerk requiring the Commissioners to state and sign a case for the opinion of the High Court (in Scotland the Court of Session, in Northern Ireland the Court of Appeal (NI)), setting forth the facts and final determination of the Commissioners. See *Grainger v Singer KB 1927, 11 TC 704* as regards receipt of the case. The 30 day time limit for requesting a case does not apply to the payment of the fee (*Anson v Hill CA 1968, 47 ATC 143*). The Commissioners may serve notice on the person who required the stated case requiring him, within 28 days, to identify the question of law on which he requires the case to be stated. They may refuse to state a case until such notice is complied with, or if they are not satisfied that a question of law is involved, or if the requisite fee (see below) has not been paid. A requirement for a case to be stated becomes invalid if the determination to which it relates is set aside or varied. [*SI 1994 No 1812, regs 20, 23*].

A fee of £25 is payable to the Clerk by the person requiring the case before he is entitled to have it stated. [*TMA s 56(3); SI 1994 No 1813*]. A single case may have effect as regards each of a number of appeals heard together (*Getty Oil Co v Steele and related appeals Ch D 1990, 63 TC 376*).

If the taxpayer dies, his personal representatives stand in his shoes (*Smith v Williams KB 1921, 8 TC 321*).

Although the case stated procedure envisages the determination of the proceedings before the Commissioners, where an appeal has been decided in principle but there may be considerable delay in reaching figures for the formal determination, the Court will accept a case stated in principle (see e.g. *Rank Xerox Ltd v Lane HL 1979, 53 TC 185*).

The case stated procedure is not open to a successful party to an appeal (*Sharpey-Schafer v Venn Ch D 1955, 34 ATC 141*), but where another party requires a case, the successful party may invite the Commissioners to include in the case an additional question relating to another ground on which the Commissioners had found against it (*Gordon v CIR CS 1991, 64 TC 173*). In the case of a partnership, the procedure is available to any one of the partners, with or without the consent of the others (*Re Sutherland & Partners appeal CA, [1994] STC 387*).

Consideration of draft case. Within 56 days of receipt of a notice requiring a stated case (or of the Commissioners being satisfied as to the question of law involved), the Clerk must send a draft of the case to all the parties. Written representations thereon may be made to the Clerk by any party within 56 days after the draft case is sent out, with copies to all the other parties, and within a further 28 days further representations may similarly be made in response. Any party to whom copies of representations are not sent may apply to the Clerk for a copy. The validity of a case after it has been stated and signed (see below), and of any subsequent proceedings, is not affected by a failure to meet these time limits or by a failure to send copies of representations to all parties. [*SI 1994 No 1812, reg 21*].

An application for the taxpayer's name to be withheld was refused (*In re H Ch D 1964, 42 TC 14*) as was an application for the deletion of a passage possibly damaging the taxpayer (*Treharne v Guinness Exports Ltd Ch D 1967, 44 TC 161*). An application for judicial review on the ground that the case did not cover all matters in dispute was refused in *R v Special Commrs (ex p Napier) CA 1988, 61 TC 206*. In *Danquah v CIR Ch D 1990, 63 TC 526*, an application for the statement of a further case was refused where the case did not set out all the questions raised by the taxpayer in the originating motion by which he had sought an order directing the Commissioners to state a case. The proper course was for the taxpayer to apply for remission of the case for amendment under *TMA s 56(7)*. See also *Consolidated Goldfields plc v CIR Ch D 1990, 63 TC 333* (dealt with further below) in which a request to remit a case to the Commissioners for further findings of fact was refused.

Preparation and submission of final case. As soon as may be after the final date for representations (see above), the Commissioners, after taking into account any representations, must state and sign the case. In the event of the death of a Commissioner, or of his ceasing to be a Commissioner, the case is to be signed by the remaining Commissioner(s) or, if there are none, by the Clerk. The case is then sent by the Clerk to the person who required it to be stated, and the other parties notified accordingly.

In England, Wales and Scotland, the party requiring the case must transmit it to the High Court (in Scotland, the Court of Session) within 30 days of receiving it, and at or before the time he does so must notify each of the other parties that the case has been stated on his application and send them a copy of the case. The fact that the same case may have been transmitted timeously by another party, where there are cross-appeals, does not relieve the appellant of the requirement to transmit the case timeously if his appeal is to be heard (*Petch v Gurney CA, [1994] STC 689*). The 30 day time limit (under the similar earlier provisions of *TMA s 56(4)*) is mandatory (*Valleybright Ltd (in liquidation) v Richardson*

4.7 Appeals

Ch D 1984, 58 TC 290; Petch v Gurney CA, [1994] STC 689), and may run from the date the case is received by the taxpayer's authorised agent (*Brassington v Guthrie Ch D 1991, 64 TC 435*). The notification (and copy) to the other parties is required only to give 'adequate notice' of the appeal and not to be 'too long delayed' (*Hughes v Viner Ch D 1985, 58 TC 437*). In Northern Ireland, slightly different rules apply (and see *CIR v McGuckian CA (NI), [1994] STC 888*).

[*SI 1994 No 1812, regs 22, 23*].

The High Court (or Court of Session or Court of Appeal (NI)) hears and determines any question(s) of law arising on the case, and may reverse, affirm or amend the determination of the Commissioners, or may remit the matter to the Commissioners with the opinion of the Court thereon, or may make such other order as seems to it fit. In certain circumstances, this may include the power to uphold an assessment as if it had been made under a section other than that under which it was in fact made (*CIR v McGuckian CA (NI), [1994] STC 888*). The Court may also cause the case to be sent back for amendment (see further below). An appeal from the decision of the High Court lies (in England and Wales) to the Court of Appeal and thence (with leave) to the House of Lords. In certain cases, 'leap-frog' appeals direct from the High Court to the House of Lords may be permitted under *Administration of Justice Act 1969, s 12* (see e.g. *Fitzleet Estates Ltd v Cherry HL 1977, 51 TC 708*). In the case of an appeal against a decision on an appeal against an assessment, tax must be paid in accordance with the Commissioners' decision. Following the decision on appeal, any tax overpaid is refunded with such interest as the Court may allow, and any amount undercharged is due and payable 30 days after the inspector issues a notice of the amount due. [*TMA s 56(6)–(9)*].

Once set down for hearing, a case cannot be declared a nullity (*Way v Underdown CA 1974, 49 TC 215*) or struck out under *Order 18, rule 19 of the Rules of the Supreme Court* (*Petch v Gurney CA, [1994] STC 689*), but the appellant may withdraw (*Hood Barrs v CIR (No 3) CA 1960, 39 TC 209*, but see *Bradshaw v Blunden (No 2) Ch D 1960, 39 TC 73*). Where the appellant was the inspector and the taxpayer did not wish to proceed, the Court refused to make an order on terms agreed between the parties (*Slaney v Kean Ch D 1969, 45 TC 415*).

The Court may, however, return a case for amendment. [*TMA s 56(7)*]. In *Consolidated Goldfields plc v CIR Ch D 1990, 63 TC 333*, the taxpayer company's request that the High Court remit a case to the Commissioners for further findings of fact was refused. Although the remedy was properly sought, it would only be granted if it could be shown that the desired findings were (*a*) material to some tenable argument, (*b*) reasonably open on the evidence adduced, and (*c*) not inconsistent with the findings already made. See also *Carvill v CIR Ch D, [1996] STC 126*. However, in *Fitzpatrick v CIR C/S 1990, [1991] STC 34*, a case was remitted where the facts found proved or admitted, and the contentions of the parties, were not clearly set out, despite the taxpayer's request for various amendments and insertions to the case, and in *Whittles v Uniholdings Ltd Ch D, [1993] STC 671*, remission was appropriate in view of the widely differing interpretations which the parties sought to place on the Commissioners' decision (and the case was remitted a second time (see *[1993] STC 767*) to resolve misunderstandings as to the nature of a concession made by the Crown at the original hearing and apparent inconsistencies in the Commissioners' findings of fact). See also *Bradley v London Electric plc Ch D, [1996] STC 231*. If a case is remitted, the taxpayer has the right to attend any further hearing by the Commissioners (*Lack v Doggett CA 1970, 46 TC 497*) but the Commissioners may not, in the absence of special circumstances, admit further evidence (*Archer-Shee v Baker CA 1928, 15 TC 1; Watson v Samson Bros Ch D 1959, 38 TC 346; Bradshaw v Blunden (No 2) Ch D 1960, 39 TC 73*), but see *Brady v Group Lotus Car Companies plc CA 1987, 60 TC 359* where the Court directed the Commissioners to admit further evidence where new facts had come to light suggesting the taxpayers had deliberately misled the Commissioners. Errors of fact in the case may be amended by agreement of the parties prior to hearing of the case (*Moore v Austin Ch D 1985, 59 TC 110*). See *Jeffries v Stevens Ch D 1982, 56 TC 134* as regards delay between statement of case and motion for remission.

A new question of law may be raised in the Courts on giving due notice to the other parties (*Muir v CIR CA 1966, 43 TC 367*) but the Courts will not admit evidence not in the stated case (*Watson v Samson Bros Ch D 1959, 38 TC 346; Cannon Industries Ltd v Edwards Ch D 1965, 42 TC 625; Frowd v Whalley Ch D 1965, 42 TC 599*, and see *R v Great Yarmouth Commrs (ex p Amis) QB 1960, 39 TC 143*).

Following the decision in *Pepper v Hart HL 1992, 65 TC 421* (see 75.13 SCHEDULE E), the Courts are prepared to consider the parliamentary history of legislation, or the official reports of debates in Hansard, where all of the following conditions are met.

(*a*)   Legislation is ambiguous or obscure, or leads to an absurdity.

(*b*)   The material relied upon consists of one or more statements by a Minister or other promoter of the Bill together if necessary with such other parliamentary material as is necessary to understand such statements and their effect.

(*c*)   The statements relied upon are clear.

For the requirements preliminary to reference to extracts from Hansard in any hearings, see Supreme Court Practice Direction issued 20 December 1994 (*1995 STI 98*).

Many Court decisions turn on whether the Commissioners' decision was one of fact supported by the evidence, and hence final. The Court will not disturb a finding of fact if there was reasonable evidence for it, notwithstanding that the evidence might support a different conclusion of fact. The leading case is *Edwards v Bairstow & Harrison HL 1955, 36 TC 207*, in which the issue was whether there had been an adventure in the nature of trade. The Commissioners' decision was reversed on the ground that the *only* reasonable conclusion from the evidence was that there had been such an adventure. For a recent discussion of the application of this principle, see *Milnes v J Beam Group Ltd Ch D 1975, 50 TC 675*.

A Court decision is a binding precedent for itself or an inferior Court except that the House of Lords, while treating its former decisions as normally binding, may depart from a previous decision should it appear right to do so. For this see *Fitzleet Estates Ltd v Cherry HL 1977, 51 TC 708*. Scottish decisions are not binding on the High Court but are normally followed. Decisions of the Privy Council and of the Irish Courts turning on comparable legislation are treated with respect. A Court decision does not affect other assessments already final and conclusive (see 5.5 ASSESSMENTS) but may be followed, if relevant, in the determination of any open appeals against assessments and in assessments made subsequently irrespective of the years of assessment or taxpayers concerned (*Re Waring decd Ch D, [1948] 1 AER 257; Gwyther v Boslymon Quarries Ltd KB 1950, 29 ATC 1; Bolands Ltd v CIR SC(I) 1925, 4 ATC 526*). Further, a Court decision does not estop the Crown from proceeding on a different basis for other years (*Hood Barrs v CIR (No 3) CA 1960, 39 TC 209*). A general change of practice consequent on a Court decision may affect error or mistake relief (see 17.6 CLAIMS) or retrospective Schedule E assessments under *Sec 206* (see 75.1(3) SCHEDULE E).

For joinder of CIR in non-tax disputes, see *In re Vandervell's Trusts HL 1970, 46 TC 341*.

Special Commissioners. In the case of an appeal to the Special Commissioners, if the appellant or the Revenue is dissatisfied in point of law with a decision (whether in principle or on final determination) or with a decision varying or substituting such a decision, appeal may be made to the High Court. Under *Order 55* of the Supreme Court Practice, the appeal must be lodged in the High Court within 28 days from the date on which notice of the decision is given. Further appeal may be made to the Court of Appeal and thence (with leave) to the House of Lords. A 'leap-frog' appeal to the Court of Appeal may be made if all the parties agree, the Commissioners certify that a point of law is involved relating wholly or mainly to the construction of an enactment which was fully argued and considered before them, and the leave of the Court of Appeal has been obtained. In Scotland appeals are to the Court of Session, in Northern Ireland to the Court of Appeal (NI), and thence in either case to the House of Lords. When a decision against which an appeal has been made is set aside or varied (see above), the appeal is treated as withdrawn.

In the case of an appeal against a decision on an appeal against an assessment, tax must be paid in accordance with the Commissioners' decision. Following the decision on appeal, any tax overpaid is refunded with such interest as the Court may allow, and any amount undercharged is due and payable 30 days after the inspector issues a notice of the amount due. [*TMA ss 56A, 58; SI 1994 No 1813*].

For the general statutory provisions and case law applicable equally to Special Commissioners, see above in relation to General Commissioners.

4.8   **JUDICIAL REVIEW (PREROGATIVE ORDERS)**

A taxpayer who is dissatisfied with the exercise of administrative powers may in certain circumstances (e.g. where the Revenue has exceeded or abused its powers or acted contrary to the rules of natural justice, or where the Appeal Commissioners have acted unfairly or improperly) seek a remedy in one of the prerogative orders of mandamus, prohibition or certiorari. This is now done by way of application for judicial review under *Supreme Court Act 1981, s 31* and *Order 53 of the Rules of the Supreme Court.*

The issue on an application for leave to apply for judicial review is whether there is an arguable case (*R v CIR (ex p Howmet Corporation and another) QB, [1994] STC 413*). The procedure is generally used where no other, adequate, remedy, such as a right of appeal, is available. See *R v Special Commrs (ex p Stipplechoice Ltd) (No 1) CA 1985, 59 TC 396, R v HMIT (ex p Kissane and Another) QB, [1986] STC 152, R v Sevenoaks Commrs (ex p Thorne) QB 1989, 62 TC 341* and *R v Hastings and Bexhill General Commrs and CIR (ex p Goodacre) QB, [1994] STC 799.*

There is a very long line of cases in which the courts have consistently refused applications where a matter should have been pursued through the ordinary channels as described above. See, for example, *R v Special Commrs (ex p Morey) CA 1972, 49 TC 71; R v Special Commrs (ex p Emery) QB 1980, 53 TC 555; R v Walton General Commrs (ex p Wilson) CA; [1983] STC 464; R v Special Commrs (ex p Esslemont) CA, 1984 STI 312; R v Brentford Commrs (ex p Chan) QB 1985, 57 TC 651; R v CIR (ex p Caglar) QB, [1995] STC 741.* See also, however, *R v HMIT and Others (ex p Lansing Bagnall Ltd) CA 1986, 61 TC 112* for a successful application where the inspector issued a notice under a discretionary power on the footing that there was a mandatory obligation to do so, and *R v Ward, R v Special Commr (ex p Stipplechoice Ltd) (No 3) QB 1988, 61 TC 391*, where insufficient notice given of revision of an accounting period under *Sec 12(8)* prior to appeal hearing.

In *R v CIR (ex p J Rothschild Holdings) CA 1987, 61 TC 178*, the Revenue were required to produce internal documents of a general character relating to their practice in applying a statutory provision, but in *R v CIR (ex p Taylor) CA 1988, 62 TC 562* discovery of internal Revenue correspondence was refused as there was no material indication that it had any bearing on the question of whether the decision taken by the inspector could be challenged. In *R v CIR (ex p Unilever plc) CA, 1996 STI 320*, an application for judicial review for a Revenue decision to refuse a late loss relief claim was successful. The Revenue's refusal was 'so unreasonable as to be, in public law terms, irrational' in view of an administrative procedure established with the company over many years of raising assessments on estimates of net taxable profits, adjusted when the final accounts became available without regard to the loss claim time limit. A confirmation by the local inspector that capital allowances were available in relation to an enterprise zone property trust scheme was not binding where the promoters were aware that clearance applications were required to be made to a specialist department, and failed to disclose that the scheme involved 'artificial provisions' (*R v CIR (ex p Matrix Securities Ltd) HL, [1994] STC 272*). As regards informal advice by the Revenue generally, they were not bound by anything less than a clear, unambiguous and unqualified representation (*R v CIR (ex p MFK Underwriting Agencies Ltd) QB 1989, 62 TC 607*). See generally 35.6 INLAND REVENUE: ADMINISTRATION See also *R v CIR (ex p Camacq Corporation) CA 1989, 62 TC 651*, where a Revenue decision to revoke its authorisation to pay a dividend gross was upheld, and *R v CIR (ex p S G Warburg & Co Ltd) QB, [1994] STC 518*, where a decision not to apply a published practice was upheld.

See 6.8 BACK DUTY as regards challenges to the validity of notices under *TMA s 20*.

The first step is to obtain leave to apply for judicial review from the High Court. Application for leave is made ex parte to a single judge who will usually determine the application without a hearing. The Court will not grant leave unless the applicant has a sufficient interest in the matter to which the application relates. See *CIR v National Federation of Self-employed and Small Businesses Ltd HL 1981, 55 TC 133* for what is meant by 'sufficient interest' and for discussion of availability of judicial review generally, and cf. *R v A-G (ex p ICI plc) CA 1986, 60 TC 1*.

Time limit. Applications must be made **within three months** of the date when the grounds for application arose. The Court has discretion to extend this time limit where there is good reason, but is generally very reluctant to do so. See e.g. *R v HMIT (ex p Brumfield and Others) QB 1988, 61 TC 589*. Grant of leave to apply for review does not amount to a ruling that application was made in good time (*R v Tavistock Commrs (ex p Worth) QB 1985, 59 TC 116*).

4.9   **COSTS**

Costs may be awarded by the Courts in the usual way. In suitable cases, e.g. 'test cases', the Revenue may undertake to pay the taxpayer's costs. There is no general provision for the award of costs of appearing before Commissioners, but see 4.6 above as regards award of costs of Special Commissioners' hearings against parties acting 'wholly unreasonably'. Costs awarded by the Courts may include expenses connected with the drafting of the Stated Case (*Manchester Corporation v Sugden CA 1903, 4 TC 595*). Costs of a discontinued application for judicial review were refused where the Revenue was not informed of the application (*R v CIR ex p Opman International UK QB 1985, 59 TC 352*). Law costs of appeals not allowable for tax purposes (*Allen v Farquharson KB 1932, 17 TC 59; Rushden Heel* and *Smith's Potato* cases *HL 1948, 30 TC 298 & 267*, and see *Spofforth KB 1945, 26 TC 310*).

5 Assessments

Cross-references. See 71.3 SCHEDULE D, CASES I AND II for bases of assessments on business profits. As regards particular assessments see also 6 BACK DUTY; 28.1 EXCESS LIABILITY; 53 PARTNERSHIPS; 75 SCHEDULE E and 55 PAY AS YOU EARN for assessments on employment income; 80 SETTLEMENTS for assessment on trust income. See also 78 SELF-ASSESSMENT.

5.1   ASSESSMENTS

Assessments to tax are made by inspectors, or their delegates [*TMA s 113(1A)(1B)*] and notices of assessment are served, which must also state the date issued and the time limit for making APPEALS (4). [*TMA s 29(1)(2)(5); F(No 2)A 1975, s 44(5)*]. Assessments may, where income is charged for a year of assessment on the amount arising in that year, be raised during the year, subject to later adjustment. [*TMA s 29(1)(c); FA 1988, s 119*]. The assessment must include a statement of the tax actually payable (*Hallamshire Industrial Finance Trust Ltd v CIR Ch D 1978, 53 TC 631*). A taxpayer may request the inspector to provide a copy of any assessment to an agent. (Revenue Press Release 18 December 1973). An assessment becomes binding if not appealed against within 30 days of the date of issue. [*TMA s 31; F(No 2)A 1975, s 67(1)*]. The inspector's power of assessment is not limited to persons or sources of income within the area of his tax office (*R v Tavistock Commrs (ex p Adams) CA 1971, 48 TC 56*). See 4.3 APPEALS for jurisdiction of Commissioners on appeal.

In the absence of a satisfactory return the inspector may make an assessment to the best of his judgment. [*TMA s 29(1)(b)*]. As to this, see *Van Boeckel v C & E Commrs QB 1980, [1981] STC 290*, relating to the comparable VAT provision of *FA 1972, s 31(1)*, *Blackpool Marton Rotary Club v Martin CA 1989, 62 TC 686* and *Phillimore v Heaton Ch D 1989, 61 TC 584*.

An assessment defective in form or containing errors may be validated by *TMA s 114(1)* if the person and income assessed are apparent, e.g. where the person assessed was later found to have received the income as trustee (*Martin v CIR CS 1938, 22 TC 330*). See also *Fleming v London Produce Co Ltd Ch D 1968, 44 TC 582*, *Hart v Briscoe Ch D 1977, 52 TC 53* and *Vickerman v Mason's Personal Representatives Ch D 1984, 58 TC 39*. But where the assessment was under Schedule D, Case VII it was held that *TMA s 114(1)* could not be used to treat the assessment as under Case I (*Bath & West Counties Property Trust Ltd v Thomas Ch D 1977, 52 TC 20*, although for special reasons, including the Crown option between Cases, the Court used its powers under *TMA s 56(6)* to alter the assessment, for which see also *CIR v McGuckian CA(NI), [1994] STC 888*) or to validate an assessment where wrong year of assessment had been entered through a copying error (*Baylis v Gregory CA, [1987] STC 297*).

Income under Schedules A or D is assessable on the person receiving or entitled to it. [*Secs 21(1), 59(1)*]. Trustees, guardians, etc. are assessable in respect of income of incapacitated persons including minors (see 16.3 CHILDREN) and there are provisions for charging non-residents through agents, etc. (see 51.4 NON-RESIDENTS AND OTHER OVERSEAS MATTERS) but these provisions do not preclude the non-resident himself being assessed if he can be reached (*CIR v Huni KB 1923, 8 TC 466; Whitney v CIR HL 1925, 10 TC 88*).

An assessment once made cannot be 'vacated' (*Baylis v Gregory*, above).

5.2   CHOICE BY REVENUE

In making assessments, the Revenue has an option, where more than one Case of Sch D is applicable, to elect to tax under the Case which is most advantageous to it (*Liverpool London and Globe Insurance Co v Bennett HL 1913, 6 TC 327*). This case related to unremitted foreign interest, which could not then be assessed under Case IV, but the Revenue successfully contended that it formed part of the taxpayer's *'trading profits'* assessable under Case I (and cf. *Butler v Mortgage Co of Egypt CA 1928, 13 TC 803*).

But there is no such power of selection between the Schedules. 'A subject matter of taxation properly assessed ... under one Schedule, cannot be brought into assessment under another Schedule' (Lord Dunedin and Lord Tomlin in *Salisbury House Estate v Fry HL 1930, 15 TC 266*). And see *Sywell Aerodrome Ltd v Croft KB 1941, 24 TC 126; Mitchell & Edon v Ross HL 1961, 40 TC 11*.

5.3 **FURTHER ASSESSMENTS ON 'DISCOVERY'**

If an inspector or the CIR 'discover' that income has not been assessed or has been under-assessed or that excessive relief has been given, a further assessment can be made. [*TMA s 29(3)(4)*]. The existence of an assessment under appeal capable of being increased and determined in the correct amount does not preclude the making of a further assessment and the consequent determination of both the original assessment and the further assessment (*Duchy Maternity Ltd v Hodgson Ch D 1985, 59 TC 85*). Discovery has been given a very wide meaning by the Courts. There is a discovery by the inspector if he comes to the honest conclusion that there has been under-assessment (*R v Kensington Commrs (ex p Aramayo) HL 1915, 6 TC 279, 613; R v St Giles, etc. Commrs (ex p Hooper) KB 1915, 7 TC 59*). It has been established in a number of cases that *a change of opinion* or rectification of an error by the Revenue, including an arithmetical error in calculating the tax, without the ascertainment of any new facts amounts to discovery and this is so notwithstanding that the former opinion had been notified to the taxpayer (*Brodie's Trustees v CIR KB 1933, 17 TC 432; Williams v Grundy Trustees KB 1933, 18 TC 271; British Sugar Mfrs Ltd v Harris CA 1937, 21 TC 528; CIR v Mackinlay's Trustees CS 1938, 22 TC 305; Steel Barrel Co Ltd v Osborne (No 2) CA 1948, 30 TC 73; Commercial Structures Ltd v Briggs CA 1948, 30 TC 477; Jones v Mason Investments Ch D 1966, 43 TC 570; Vickerman v Mason's Personal Representatives Ch D 1984, 58 TC 39*). (See 56.6 PAYMENT OF TAX for remission of tax in cases of official error.) A further assessment may be made on incomplete information supplied on behalf of the taxpayer (*McLuskey's Executrix v CIR CS 1955, 36 TC 163*) and successive further assessments are permissible (*Cansick v Hochstrasser Ch D 1961, 40 TC 151*). See also *Beatty v CIR Ch D 1953, 35 TC 30; Multipar Syndicate Ltd v Devitt KB 1945, 26 TC 359*. A Court decision does not estop the Crown from proceeding on a different basis for other years (*Hood Barrs v CIR (No 3) CA 1960, 39 TC 209*).

If in the determination of an appeal *including a determination by agreement* (see 4.4 APPEALS) a matter has been adjudicated or agreed, the Revenue cannot re-open the matter by making a further assessment (*Cenlon Finance Co Ltd v Ellwood HL 1962, 40 TC 176*). However, the matter must have been dealt with specifically (*Kidston v Aspinall Ch D 1963, 41 TC 371; Young v Duthie Ch D 1969, 45 TC 624; Skinner v Berry Head Lands Ltd Ch D 1970, 46 TC 377; Parkin v Cattell CA 1971, 48 TC 462*) or clearly have been raised by implication, so that an inspector of average experience must have appreciated it was being made (*Scorer v Olin Energy Systems Ltd HL 1985, 58 TC 592*). A further assessment is not precluded where an appeal was settled by an agreement based on trading profits which were incorrectly stated (*Gray v Matheson Ch D 1993, 65 TC 577*).

The Revenue have issued a Statement of Practice setting out their view of the application in practice of the case law outlined above. The following are listed as specific circumstances in which there are clearly no grounds for *not* making discovery assessments:

(a) profits or income have not earlier been charged to tax because of any form of fraudulent or negligent conduct;

(b) the inspector has been misled or misinformed in any way about the particular matter at issue;

5.4 Assessments

(c)   there is an arithmetical error in a computation which had not been spotted at the time agreement was reached, and which can be corrected by the making of an in date discovery assessment;

(d)   an error is made in accounts and computations which it cannot reasonably be alleged was correct or intended, e.g. the double deduction from taxable profits of a particular item (say group relief).

The Statement of Practice also makes it clear that, by concession, the principles determining the making of a further assessment following settlement of an appeal by agreement will also be applied where agreement is reached prior to the issue of an assessment. Also by concession, whether or not there has been an appeal, a discovery assessment will not be made where, although the matter in question may not have been the subject of a specific agreement within the case law principles outlined above, the inspector's decision was based on full and accurate disclosure and was a tenable view, so that the taxpayer could reasonably have believed the inspector's decision to be correct. (Revenue Pamphlet IR 131, SP 8/91, 26 July 1991).

See 17.7 CLAIMS as regards the making of claims, etc. relevant to further assessments.

See 78.15 SELF-ASSESSMENT as regards 'discovery' assessments for 1996/97 and subsequent years.

5.4   DOUBLE ASSESSMENT

'The taxing acts . . . nowhere authorise the Crown to take Income Tax twice over in respect of same source for same period of time' (Lord Sumner in *English Sewing Cotton Co HL 1923, 8 TC* at *513*). An *alternative* income tax assessment may, however, be raised in respect of transactions already the subject of a final CGT assessment (*Bye v Coren CA 1986, 60 TC 116*), and where more than one of a number of alternative assessments become final and conclusive, the Crown may institute collection proceedings in respect of any one (but not more than one) of them (*CIR v Wilkinson CA 1992, 65 TC 28*). For alternative assessments generally, see *Lord Advocate v McKenna CS, [1989] STC 485*.

Where there has been double assessment for the same cause and for the same chargeable period a claim may be made to the Board (with right of appeal to the Commissioners having jurisdiction to hear appeals against the assessment, or the later of the assessments, to which the appeal relates) for the overcharge to be vacated. [*TMA s 32*]. See 17.6 CLAIMS for Error or Mistake relief.

5.5   FINALITY OF ASSESSMENTS

An assessment cannot be altered after the notice has been served except in accordance with the express provisions of the *Taxes Acts*. [*TMA s 29(6)*]. As regards the figure for the income assessed, the principal provisions are as those for APPEALS (4.4). Other examples are certain of the bases of assessment provisions, e.g. *Sec 62(10)*, enabling an assessment to be reduced in the opening years of a business. Where over-assessment results from an *error or mistake* in a return, see 17.6 CLAIMS. An assessment as determined on appeal or not appealed against is final and conclusive.

5.6   SOCIAL SECURITY CONTRIBUTIONS

Class 4 contributions (which are levied on profits etc.) are shown separately on notices of assessment under Schedule D. See 82.7 SOCIAL SECURITY.

5.7   **TIME LIMITS**

An assessment or additional assessment cannot be made later than six years from the end of the tax year to which it relates (or accounting period in the case of a company) [*TMA s 34*] except in cases of fraudulent or negligent conduct (for 1982/83 and earlier years, cases of fraud, wilful default or neglect) [*TMA ss 36–41; FA 1989, s 149*, see 6.4 BACK DUTY] or where there is specific statutory provision for later assessment (including Sch E assessments on delayed remuneration, see *TMA s 35* and 75.1 SCHEDULE E). But assessments on personal representatives in respect of deceased's income before death must be made within three years after end of tax year in which death occurred. [*TMA s 40(1)*]. See also 6.5 BACK DUTY regarding deceased persons.

For 1996/97 and later years, the general time limit is five years after 31 January following the tax year and the time limit where the taxpayer is deceased is three years after 31 January following the tax year of death (see 78.30 SELF-ASSESSMENT).

An assessment is made on the date on which the inspector authorised to make it signs a certificate in the appropriate assessments volume that he made certain assessments including the assessment in question (*Honig v Sarsfield CA 1986, 59 TC 337*).

5.8   **TOLERANCE LIMIT OF ASSESSMENT**

Where pensioners and single women under 65 have no income apart from the standard Social Security pension, and such pension exceeds the single person's allowance, no direct assessment will be made on the excess if the tax payable is £75 or less. This tolerance is to minimise work which is cost ineffective. But if an assessment has to be made in any event (for instance because the taxpayer has asked for it to check his tax position) any underpayment is collected in the normal way even if it is less than the assessing tolerance (Revenue Pamphlet IR 131, A12). See 56.7 PAYMENT OF TAX for tolerances on repayment of tax.

5.9   **BASES OF ASSESSMENT**

The summary on the following page is subject to the detailed explanations in the other sections of this book under the headings shown in the first column, and particularly, as regards Schedule D, to adjustments in cases of **change of accounting period** (adjustment of preceding year's assessment), **new business** (adjustment of first, second and third years' assessments), **new source of income** (adjustment of first, second and (sometimes) third years' assessments), **discontinuance of business** (adjustment of last three years' assessments), **cessation of certain sources of income or death** (adjustment of last two years' assessments), **losses in trading or farming, change of ownership of business** (adjustment of last three and next three years' assessments). The Finance Act 1994 introduces a **current year basis of assessment for Schedule D** with effect as noted in the summary below.

The adjustments regarding new and discontinued sources of income apply to **each item** of **untaxed income**, such as changes in War Loan holdings, purchase or sale of foreign stocks and shares etc., etc. Thus in many cases of income of this kind, adjustments will be required every year, and it will be necessary to prepare the annual return forms and check assessments carefully. This is of no application where the current year basis of assessment (see above) is in force.

Where overseas items are concerned, the REMITTANCE BASIS (63) applies in certain circumstances. In some other circumstances percentage deductions may be made in arriving at assessable income, see 64.2 RESIDENCE, ORDINARY RESIDENCE AND DOMICILE.

Assessments on companies are on an actual basis. See Tolley's Corporation Tax. For full details of capital gains tax, see Tolley's Capital Gains Tax.

5.9   Assessments

Assessed under	Source	Basis on which Assessed
Schedule A	Rents receivable from lands, houses, buildings etc.	Rents or receipts arising in the tax year.
B	The *occupation* of Woodlands managed on a commercial basis for profit, where no election made for assessment under Sch D. Abolished after 5 April 1988.	One-third gross annual value.
C	Government and public authority Stocks etc.	Actual interest etc. paid.
Sch D, Case I	Trades etc.	Usually on profits based on annual account ending in preceding tax year.*
„ „ II	Professions and vocations.	Usually on profits based on annual account ending in preceding tax year.*
„ „ III	War Loan and other Government Stocks, Deposit Interest, Treasury Bills, Discounts etc. not taxed at source.	Usually on amount arising in preceding tax year.**
„ „ IV	Overseas securities	Usually on amount arising in preceding tax year.**
„ „ V	Overseas possessions.	
„ „ VI	Sundry profits not included above, such as letting furnished houses, guaranteeing a loan, underwriting etc. (where not a *trade* etc. assessable under Case I).	Usually on actual profits for tax year.
Schedule E	Offices and Employments, Pensions etc. other than foreign pensions.	Total income from the particular employment etc., for current tax year.
Schedule F	From 6 April 1973. Dividends and certain other distributions, plus tax credits, from companies resident in the UK.	Actual dividends etc. payable in tax year.
Capital Gains Tax	Chargeable gains.	Actual gains for tax year.

*   For 1994/95 and subsequent years (subject to opening years rules) as regards trades, professions and vocations commenced after 5 April 1994 and for 1996/97 for those commenced on or before that date (subject to transitional provisions), usually on profits based on annual account ending in current tax year.

**   For 1994/95 and subsequent years as regards income from a source first arising after 5 April 1994 and otherwise for 1996/97 and subsequent years (subject to transitional provisions), usually on amount arising in current tax year.

6   Back Duty

Cross-reference. See 71.28 SCHEDULE D, CASES I AND II for in-depth examination of business accounts. See also 78 SELF-ASSESSMENT.

6.1   BACK DUTY CLAIMS

Such claims are made by the Inland Revenue where they consider tax has been lost by a taxpayer's fraudulent or negligent conduct (or by his fraud or wilful default or by his neglect). In such cases, the normal time limits for assessment are extended (see 6.4 below), interest is chargeable on the understated tax (see 6.6 below) and PENALTIES (58) are incurred which the Board may mitigate.

The Revenue have published a Code of Practice (No 2, published February 1993 and available from local tax offices) setting out their standards for the way in which investigations are conducted and the rights and responsibilities of taxpayers. Codes of Practice 8 and 9, dealing with Special Compliance Office Investigations in cases other than suspected serious fraud and cases of such fraud respectively, were published in January 1995 and are available from the Special Compliance Office, Angel Court, 199 Borough High Street, London SE1 1HZ.

For the validity of tax amnesties see *CIR v National Federation of Self-employed and Small Businesses Ltd HL 1981, 55 TC 133.*

6.2   FRAUD OR WILFUL DEFAULT

See 6.4 below as regards the replacement of 'fraud, wilful default or neglect' assessments by 'fraudulent or negligent conduct' assessments. The later expression is not defined, and the following cases may be of continued assistance in this respect.

Unexplained capital increases or admitted omissions may be held evidence of fraud or wilful default (*Amis v Colls Ch D 1960, 39 TC 148; Woodrow v Whalley Ch D 1964, 42 TC 249; Hudson v Humbles Ch D 1965, 42 TC 380; Hillenbrand CS 1966, 42 TC 617; Young v Duthie Ch D 1969, 45 TC 624; James v Pope Ch D 1972, 48 TC 142*; and cf. *Brimelow v Price Ch D 1965, 49 TC 41*). Taxpayer's deliberate exclusion of wife's income when making return held wilful default (*Brown v CIR Ch D 1965, 42 TC 583*) but not where husband unaware of wife's omissions (*Wellington v Reynolds Ch D 1962, 40 TC 209*). Wilful default may be by agent (*Clixby v Pountney Ch D 1967, 44 TC 515; Pleasants v Atkinson Ch D 1987, 60 TC 228*). Where Commissioners found fraud on the basis of the inspector's evidence at a hearing which the taxpayer or his agent did not attend, the case was remitted to be heard by different Commissioners (*Ottley v Morris Ch D 1978, 52 TC 375*).

The onus of proving fraud or wilful default is on the Crown but the onus is on the taxpayer to prove the assessments are excessive (*Johnson v Scott CA 1978, 52 TC 383; Jonas v Bamford Ch D 1973, 51 TC 1; Nicholson v Morris CA 1977, 51 TC 95* and cf. *Barney v Pybus Ch D 1957, 37 TC 106* and *R v Spec Commrs (ex p Martin) CA 1971, 48 TC 1*). Acceptance of an inadequate estimated assessment may amount to wilful default (*Nuttall v Barrett Ch D 1992, 64 TC 548*). Once the unreliability of one year's accounts has been demonstrated, the Commissioners are entitled to make their own estimate for other years (*Brittain v Gibbs Ch D 1986, 59 TC 374*). For the standard of proof required, see *Les Croupiers Casino Club v Pattinson CA 1987, 60 TC 196*. For finding required of Commissioners, see *Rea v Highnam Ch D 1990, 63 TC 287*.

6.3 Back Duty

6.3 NEGLECT

See 6.4 below as regards the replacement of 'fraud, wilful default or neglect' assessments by 'fraudulent or negligent conduct' assessments.

Neglect means negligence or a failure to give any notice, make any return or to produce or furnish any document or other information required by or under the *Taxes Acts*. [*TMA s 118 as enacted*]. See the note at 67.1 RETURNS as regards reasonable excuse for failure to make returns.

6.4 EXTENDED TIME LIMITS

Note. See also 78.30 SELF-ASSESSMENT as regards assessments for 1996/97 and subsequent years.

Except where specifically provided, the normal time limit for assessments is 6 years after the tax year concerned. [*TMA s 34*]. In certain cases, however, extended limits apply to assessments for the purpose of making good a loss of tax.

Assessments made after 26 July 1989 relating to 1983/84 and subsequent years (or to accounting periods ending after 31 March 1983). Where the loss of tax arises due to the *fraudulent or negligent conduct* of a person (or of a person acting on his behalf), an assessment may be made at any time not later than 20 years after the end of the chargeable period to which it relates. Individual partners of an individual responsible for fraudulent or negligent conduct may similarly be assessed for such years in respect of partnership profits. If the person assessed so requires, the assessment may give effect to reliefs or allowances to which he would have been entitled had he made the necessary claims within the relevant time limits (excluding certain elections for the transfer inter-spouse of the married couple's allowance). [*TMA s 36; FA 1989, s 149; F(No 2)A 1992, 5 Sch 9(2)*]. In the case of personal representatives of offenders, such assessments in respect of deceased's income before death must be made within three years after the tax year in which he died. [*TMA s 40(2)*]. See 5.7 ASSESSMENTS as regards the date an assessment is made.

Assessments made before 27 July 1989 or relating to 1982/83 and earlier years (or to accounting periods ending before 1 April 1983). Where an assessment for any year (a 'normal year') has been made within six years thereafter for the purpose of making good tax lost by a taxpayer's *fraud, wilful default or neglect*, assessments for any of the six years prior to that 'normal year', for recovering tax lost by his neglect, may, by leave of a General or Special Commissioner, be made at any time up to the end of the tax year following that in which tax under the assessment for the normal year is finally determined. [*TMA ss 118(4), 37(3), 41(1)*]. In the case of personal representatives of offenders, such assessments in respect of deceased's income before death must be made within three years after the tax year of death. [*TMA s 40(2)*]. Granting of leave by a Commissioner does not involve a hearing, and taxpayer is not entitled to appear or be heard (*Day v Williams CA 1969, 46 TC 59; Pearlberg v Varty HL 1972, 48 TC 14* and *Nicholson v Morris CA 1977, 51 TC 95*). For jurisdiction of Commissioners see *CIR v Adams CA 1971, 48 TC 67; Murphy v Elders Ch D 1973, 49 TC 135* and cf. *F Lack Ltd v Doggett CA 1970, 46 TC 524*. See also *R v Spec Commrs (ex p Morey) CA 1972, 49 TC 71* (use of prerogative orders disapproved) but contrast *R v Spec Commrs (ex p Stipplechoice Ltd) (No 1) CA 1985, 59 TC 396* where judicial review was granted in the absence of any other adequate remedy (and see *R v Spec Commrs (ex p Stipplechoice Ltd) (No 2) QB 1986, 59 TC 396* for the decision against the taxpayer on that review). The decision in *O'Mullan v Walmsley QB (NI) 1965, 42 TC 573* that such assessments are invalid unless the assessment for the 'normal year' was expressly stated to be for making good tax lost by fraud, default or neglect was not followed in *Thurgood v Slarke Ch D 1971, 47 TC 130*. 'What matters is not the purpose of the assessor but of the assessment.' See also *R v Spec Commrs (ex p Rogers) CA 1972, 48 TC*

46; Knight v CIR CA 1974, 49 TC 179 and *R v Holborn Commrs (ex p Rind) QB 1974, 49 TC 656.*

If the person to be assessed so requires, the assessment may give effect to reliefs or allowances to which he would have been entitled had the necessary claims been made within the relevant time limits. [*TMA s 37(8)*].

Once an assessment (under *TMA ss 37(3), 41(1)*, or, being one of a number of assessments not more than six years apart, under *TMA s 36*, above) has been made more than six years after the end of a tax year (an 'earlier year') an assessment for any year up to six years before that earlier year may be made for recovering tax lost by taxpayer's neglect, but only by leave of the General or Special Commissioners on their being satisfied (on a Revenue application, at which taxpayer may appear and be heard) that reasonable grounds exist for believing that tax for that year has been so lost.

Applications to Commissioners for this purpose may be made up to the end of the tax year following final determination of liability under the assessment for the 'earlier year'. This provision applies separately to income tax and capital gains tax. [*TMA s 37*].

Adaptation of these provisions to partnerships is provided by *TMA s 38*.

Married couples. Where total income of 1990/91 or any subsequent year is increased as a result of fraudulent or negligent conduct assessments, this does not affect the validity of any blind person's allowance or certain other allowances transferred from husband to wife which are determined by reference to total income or given as a reduction in total income tax liability. The husband's allowances are correspondingly reduced. [*TMA s 37A; FA 1988, 3 Sch 30; FA 1989, s 149(4); F(No 2)A 1992, 5 Sch 9(3); FA 1994, 8 Sch 13*].

6.5   **Deceased persons.** Assessments on deceased's income or capital gains arising or accruing before death must be made within three years after the tax year in which he dies. [*TMA s 40(1)*]. Assessments for any of the six years of assessment preceding that of death, for the purpose of making good tax lost by deceased's fraudulent or negligent conduct, may also be made within the same time limit, but not later. [*TMA s 40(2); FA 1989, s 149(4)*]. See 78.30 SELF-ASSESSMENT as regards 1996/97 and later years. If the deceased was in *partnership* valid assessments on the partnership may be made outside that limit, but will be enforceable only against the surviving partners (*Harrison v Willis CA 1965, 43 TC 61*). See 5.7 ASSESSMENTS as regards the date an assessment is made.

6.6   **INTEREST ON UNDERPAID TAX**

Note. The provisions described below do not apply where the new self-assessment interest provisions of *Sec 86* have effect (see 78.22 SELF-ASSESSMENT). [*FA 1996, 18 Sch 4, 17(3)(4)*].

Where an assessment is made for making good tax lost through

(*a*)   a 'failure' to give a notice, make a return, or provide a document or other information, or

(*b*)   an error in any information or return, etc. supplied

after 26 July 1989, the tax attributable to that failure or error is chargeable with interest, if an inspector or the Board so determines. '*Failure*' includes failure to do something at a particular time or within a particular period; and the exclusion in *TMA s 118(2)* (see 67.1 RETURNS) does not apply. [*TMA s 88(1)(7); FA 1989, ss 159, 160(1)*].

A determination under these provisions can be made at any time within six years of the end of the chargeable period for which the tax is charged, or within three years of the final determination of the amount of that tax. Notice of the determination must specify

6.6 Back Duty

    (i)   the date of issue,

    (ii)   the amount of tax carrying interest, and the assessment by which it was charged,

    (iii)   the date when, for *TMA s 88* purposes, it ought to have been paid, and

    (iv)   the time within which an appeal against the determination may be made.

The general APPEALS (4) provisions apply, except for *TMA s 50(6)–(8)* (see 4.6(*c*)(*e*) APPEALS). On appeal, the Commissioners can set aside or confirm the determination, or alter it in respect of the amount of tax or the date. For collection purposes, an interest certificate may be supplied by the inspector, or other officer of the Board, and the collector. [*TMA ss 70(3), 88A; FA 1989, s 160(2)(3)*].

Where an assessment is made for making good tax lost by fraud, wilful default or neglect (see 6.2, 6.4 above) which occurred **before 27 July 1989**, the tax attributable to that fraud, etc. is chargeable with interest. [*TMA s 88(1)*]. The amount of interest is certified by the General or Special Commissioners under *TMA s 70(3)*, following an application by the Revenue at which the taxpayer is entitled to appear and be heard (*Nicholson v Morris CA 1977, 51 TC 95*). There is no appeal by way of case stated (*R v Holborn Commissioners (ex p Rind) QB 1974, 49 TC 656*). For the limited extent to which regard should be had to events after the making of an assessment in determining whether *TMA s 88* applies, see *Billingham v Myers CA, 1996 STI 595*.

Tax carrying interest under TMA s 88 does not also carry interest under *TMA s 86* (see 42.1 INTEREST ON UNPAID TAX). It is payable gross (and not deductible for tax purposes) from the date when the tax ought to have been paid (but without the alternative of 30 days after the date of issue of the notice of assessment, see 56.1 PAYMENT OF TAX) to the date of actual payment. The Board have power to mitigate interest payable and to stay or compound any recovery proceedings. [*TMA ss 88–90; FA 1989, s 161*]. See also 58 PENALTIES and 67.2 RETURNS, and note that the provisions of *TMA s 88* are applied to underpaid Class 4 national insurance contributions by *Social Security Contributions and Benefits Act 1992, 2 Sch 6* (see also *Social Security (Consequential Provisions) Act 1992, 4 Sch 1, 8, 9*).

Rates of interest are generally as for INTEREST ON UNPAID TAX (42), i.e. as follows.

3% p.a. for periods up to 18 April 1967
4% p.a. from 19 April 1967 to 30 June 1974
9% p.a. from 1 July 1974 to 31 December 1979
12% p.a. from 1 January 1980 to 30 November 1982
8% p.a. from 1 December 1982 to 30 April 1985
11% p.a. from 1 May 1985 to 5 August 1986
8.5% p.a. from 6 August 1986 to 5 November 1986
9.5% p.a. from 6 November 1986 to 5 April 1987
9% p.a. from 6 April 1987 to 5 June 1987
8.25% p.a. from 6 June 1987 to 5 September 1987
9% p.a. from 6 September 1987 to 5 December 1987
8.25% p.a. from 6 December 1987 to 5 May 1988
7.75% p.a. from 6 May 1988 to 5 August 1988
9.75% p.a. from 6 August 1988 to 5 October 1988
10.75% p.a. from 6 October 1988 to 5 January 1989
11.5% p.a. from 6 January 1989 to 5 July 1989
12.25% p.a. from 6 July 1989 to 5 November 1989
13% p.a. from 6 November 1989 to 5 November 1990
12.25% p.a. from 6 November 1990 to 5 March 1991
11.5% p.a. from 6 March 1991 to 5 May 1991
10.75% p.a. from 6 May 1991 to 5 July 1991
10% p.a. from 6 July 1991 to 5 October 1991

9.25% p.a. from 6 October 1991 to 5 November 1992
7.75% p.a. from 6 November 1992 to 5 December 1992
7% p.a. from 6 December 1992 to 5 March 1993
6.25% p.a. from 6 March 1993 to 5 January 1994
5.50% p.a. from 6 January 1994 to 5 October 1994
6.25% p.a. from 6 October 1994 to 5 March 1995
7% p.a. from 6 March 1995 to 5 February 1996
6.25% p.a. from 6 February 1996 onwards.

Interest factor tables for use as ready reckoners in calculating interest on overdue tax are published by the Revenue and updated as rates change. (Revenue Press Release 25 January 1996).

6.7   UNDERSTATED PROFITS ETC.

The measure of understated profits, etc., is calculated from the available data, but if this is unsatisfactory, on the increase of capital from year to year, with adjustments for cost of living, etc. See for this, cases mentioned at 6.2 and 6.4 above and *Deacon v Roper Ch D 1952, 33 TC 66; Horowitz v Farrand Ch D 1952, 33 TC 221; Moschi v Kelly CA 1952, 33 TC 442; Kilburn v Bedford Ch D 1955, 36 TC 262; Roberts v McGregor Ch D 1959, 38 TC 610; Chuwen v Sabine Ch D 1959, 39 TC 1; Erddig Motors Ltd v McGregor Ch D 1961, 40 TC 95; Hellier v O'Hare Ch D 1964, 42 TC 155; Hurley v Young Ch D 1966, 45 ATC 316; Hope v Damerel Ch D 1969, 48 ATC 461; Driver v CIR CS 1977, 52 TC 153; Kovak v Morris CA 1985, 58 TC 493* and cf. *Rose v Humbles CA 1971, 48 TC 103.* For a case in which similar principles were applied in determining directors' true remuneration, see *Billows v Robinson Ch D 1989, 64 TC 17.*

Inspectors will not automatically insist on annual capital statements (see above) where understated profits can be measured satisfactorily in other ways, such as by use of expected rates of gross trading profits. (Revenue Press Release 1 August 1977).

A certificate of full disclosure may be required by the Revenue from a taxpayer during a back duty enquiry stating that complete disclosure has been made of, *inter alia*, all: banking, savings and loan accounts, deposit receipts, Building Society and Co-operative Society accounts; investments including Savings Certificates and Premium Bonds and loans (whether interest bearing or not); other assets, including cash and life assurance policies, which taxpayer and his wife now possess, or have possessed, or in which they have or have had any interest or power to operate or control during a stated period; gifts in any form, by taxpayer or wife to children or to other persons during stated period; sources of income and all income derived therefrom and of all facts bearing on liability to income tax, capital gains tax and other duties for the stated period. Great care must be exercised before signing such a certificate since subsequent discovery of an omission could lead to heavy penalties.

Independent taxation. Inspectors will respect the right of confidentiality between husband and wife under independent taxation in all cases, including investigation cases. However, the underlying interdependence remains and inspectors, in investigating one spouse, may need information from or concerning the other. Although inspectors will make every effort to avoid unwarranted disclosure and the gratuitous passing of information, it remains open to them to take such action as is necessary to enable them to perform their duties. In effect, married persons are in the same position with regard to confidentiality as are single persons.

Husbands remain liable for tax, etc. on the wife's income or gains for years prior to the introduction of independent taxation. The inspector will, however, normally agree to the wife settling any such liability personally. (ICAEW Memorandum TR 778, 8 January 1990).

6.8 **INVESTIGATORY POWERS**

With effect from 27 July 1989, *FA 1989, ss 142–148* amend *TMA ss 20–20D* to extend the Revenue's powers to obtain the production of accounts, books and other information. The revised powers are described below.

For these purposes, '*document*' means anything in which information of any description is recorded, but does not include personal records or journalistic material (within *Police and Criminal Evidence Act 1984, ss 12, 13*) (and those exclusions apply also to particulars contained in such records or material). The documents concerned are those in the possession or power of the person receiving the notice. Photographic, etc. facsimiles may be supplied provided the originals are produced if called for, and documents relating to any pending tax appeal need not be delivered. There are special provisions relating to computer records (see *FA 1988, s 127*). Documents in a person's 'possession or power' are those actually in existence at the time the notice is given, and not any which would have to be brought into existence in order to satisfy the notice.

(*a*) Where an **inspector** is of the reasonable opinion that documents contain, or may contain, information relevant to any tax liability of a person he may (with the Board's authority and the consent of a General or Special Commissioner (who is excluded from subsequent appeal proceedings)) by notice in writing require that person to deliver such documents to him (but only after that person has been given reasonable opportunity to produce them). For challenges to the validity of notices, see *R v CIR (ex p T C Coombs & Co) HL 1991, 64 TC 124; R v CIR (ex p Taylor) CA 1988, 62 TC 562; (No 2) CA 1990, 62 TC 578*; also *Kempton v Special Commrs and CIR Ch D, [1992] STC 823*, where the validity of the notice was confirmed although the only evidence on which the inspector relied related to omissions from the returns of a fellow director of the taxpayer concerned.

(*b*) An **inspector** may similarly by notice in writing require a person to furnish him with such particulars as he may reasonably require as being relevant to any tax liability of that person (again after reasonable opportunity has been given for their production).

(*c*) An **inspector** may similarly by notice in writing require any other person (including the Director of Savings) to deliver to him (or, if the person so elects, make available for inspection by a named officer of the Board) documents relevant to any tax liability of a taxpayer. A copy of the notice must be sent to the taxpayer concerned unless, in a case involving suspected fraud, a General or Special Commissioner directs otherwise. Production of documents originating more than six years before the notice cannot be required (unless the Commissioner who gave consent to the notice specifically allows it on being satisfied there is reasonable ground for believing loss of tax through fraud).

A notice cannot require the production by a statutory auditor of his audit papers, nor by a tax adviser of communications with a client (or with any other tax adviser of his client) relating to advice about the client's tax affairs. This exemption does not, however, apply to explanatory documents concerning any other documents prepared with the client for, or for delivery to, the Revenue, unless the Revenue already has access to the information contained therein in some other document. Similarly, where a notice does not identify the taxpayer to which it relates (see below), the exemption does not apply to any document giving the name or address of any taxpayer to whom the notice relates (or of a person acting on their behalf) unless the Revenue already has access to the information contained therein. Where the exemption is so disapplied, either the document must be delivered or made available to the Revenue or a copy of the relevant parts must be supplied (which parts must be available if required for inspection). The Revenue's application of these provisions in practice is set out in a Statement of Practice (Revenue Pamphlet IR 131, SP 5/90, 11 April 1990). In particular, it is made clear that accountants' working papers will be called for only where voluntary access has not been obtained and it is considered absolutely necessary in order to determine whether a client's accounts or returns are complete and correct. Requests for access may on occasion extend to the whole or a particular part of the working papers, rather than just to information explaining specific entries, and the Revenue will usually be prepared to visit the accountants' or clients' premises to examine the papers and to take copies or extracts. These restrictions on the use of its powers by the Revenue do not apply in the circumstances described under (*d*) below.

'*Taxpayer*' includes an individual who has died (but any notice must be given within six years of the death) and a company which has ceased to exist.

A notice may, subject to conditions, be given which does not specify the taxpayer to whom it relates, with the specific consent of a Special Commissioner, and subject to appeal (within 30 days) by the person on whom it is served on the ground that it would be onerous for him to comply with it.

(*d*)   An inspector may similarly by notice in writing (with the Board's authority and the consent of a Circuit judge in England and Wales, a sheriff in Scotland or a County Court judge in NI) require a tax accountant (i.e. a person who assists another in the preparation of returns, etc. for tax purposes) who has been convicted of a tax offence or incurred a penalty under *TMA s 99* (see 58.3 PENALTIES) (in relation to which no appeal is pending) to deliver documents relevant to any tax liability of any of his clients. The notice must be issued within twelve months of the final determination of the conviction or penalty award.

(*e*)   The **Board** may require, by notice in writing, a person to deliver or furnish, to a named officer of theirs, documents or information as specified in (*a*) and (*b*) above. Notices will not, however, be given under this power unless there are reasonable grounds for believing that that person may have failed, or may fail, to comply with any provision of the *Taxes Acts*, and that any such failure is likely to have led, or to lead, to serious prejudice to the proper assessment or collection of tax.

Where notice under (*a*), (*b*) or (*c*) above is given after 3 May 1994, the taxpayer concerned must be provided with a written summary of the inspector's reasons for applying for consent to the giving of the notice (unless, in the case of (*c*), a Commissioner has directed that the taxpayer need not be sent a copy of the notice itself). Such a summary may exclude information which might identify an informant, or which the Commissioner is satisfied might prejudice the assessment or collection of tax, although a summary written so as not to compromise these requirements should nevertheless be provided. However, in a case within (*c*) above, the courts refused to quash such a notice where no written summary had been provided to the taxpayers whose liabilities were under investigation (*R v CIR (ex p Continental Shipping Ltd and Atsiganos SA) QB, 1996 STI 602*).

For guidance on the question of whether documents and records are the property of the client or of the accountant, see ICAEW Memorandum TR 781, 23 February 1990.

The notice must specify or describe the documents or particulars required, the time limit for production (generally not less than 30 days) and, except as above, the name of the taxpayer or client, as appropriate; and the person to whom they are delivered may take copies. There are severe penalties for the falsification, concealment, disposal or destruction of a document which is the subject of a notice or formal request (see (*a*) above), unless strict conditions and time limits are observed. [*TMA ss 20–20BB, 20D; FA 1989, ss 142–145, 148, 168(2); FA 1990, s 93; FA 1994, s 255; Civil Evidence Act 1995, 1 Sch 6*]. For failure to comply with a notice, see 58.4 PENALTIES.

6.9 Back Duty

Notices given on or after 26 July 1990 (other than those under (*d*) above and those which relate to an unnamed taxpayer) may relate to tax liabilities in EEC member States other than the UK. [*FA 1990, s 125(1)(2)(6)*].

6.9 **Search and Seizure.** Where there is reasonable suspicion of serious tax fraud the Board may apply to a Circuit judge, etc. (as in 6.8(*d*) above) for a warrant to enter premises within 14 days to search and to seize any things which may be relevant as evidence. There are detailed procedural rules governing searches and the removal of documents, etc. [*TMA ss 20C, 20CC, 20D; FA 1989, ss 146, 147*]. The warrant need not specify the suspected fraud or the documents, etc., searched for (*Rossminster Ltd HL 1979, 52 TC 160*).

6.10 **Barristers, advocates or solicitors.** A notice under 6.8(*a*), (*b*), (*c*) or (*d*) above to a barrister, advocate or solicitor can be issued only by the Board and he cannot (without his client's consent) be required to deliver under 6.8(*c*) and (*d*) documents protected by professional privilege nor are such documents subject to the powers of search and seizure. [*TMA ss 20B(3)(8), 20C(4); FA 1989, s 146(4)*]. See *R v CIR (ex p Goldberg) QB 1988, 61 TC 403* as regards nature of documents subject to privilege, but note that the decision in that case was doubted in *Dubai Bank Ltd v Galadari CA, [1989] 3 WLR 1044*, a non-tax case.

6.11 **OFFERS BY TAXPAYER**

Where back duty arises, the taxpayer may offer a sum in full settlement of liability for tax, interest and penalties. The practice of the Board of Inland Revenue in cases of tax fraud is as follows.

(i) The Board may accept a money settlement instead of instituting criminal proceedings in respect of fraud alleged to have been committed by a taxpayer.

(ii) They can give no undertaking that they will accept a money settlement and refrain from instituting criminal proceedings even if the case is one in which the taxpayer has made full confession and has given full facilities for investigation of the facts. They reserve to themselves full discretion in all cases as to the course they pursue.

(iii) But in considering whether to accept a money settlement or to institute criminal proceedings, it is their practice to be influenced by the fact that the taxpayer has made a full confession and has given full facilities for investigation into his affairs and for examination of such books, papers, documents or information as the Board may consider necessary.

(Revenue Press Release 18 October 1990).

See *CIR v Nuttall CA 1989, 63 TC 148* for confirmation of power to enter into such agreements. Amounts due under such an agreement which are unpaid may be pursued by an action for a debt, but the Crown does not rank as a preferential creditor in respect of the sums due (*Nuttall* above; *CIR v Woollen CA 1992, 65 TC 229*).

See generally Revenue Pamphlet IR 73 as regards negotiation of settlements.

Relief for retirement annuity premiums and personal pension contributions. Where an offer as above is made and accepted by the Board in settlement of liabilities which include tax on relevant earnings assessable for a year which ended more than six years earlier, unused retirement annuity and personal pension relief (see 65.9 RETIREMENT ANNUITIES AND PERSONAL PENSION PLANS) which would have arisen if an assessment had been made on such earnings may be set against premiums or contributions paid within six months of acceptance of the offer on election by the taxpayer, within the same six months, for such relief to be given. Relief is, however, only available to the extent that the premiums or contributions exceed the maximum applying for the year of assessment in which they are paid, although the normal time limits apply in relation to the payment of premiums up to that maximum (see 65.8 RETIREMENT ANNUITIES AND PERSONAL PENSION PLANS). This practice also applies where assessments have been made and appealed against but the appeals have not been formally determined, if the tax for the years concerned is included in the settlement. (Revenue Pamphlet IR 131, SP 9/91, 31 July 1991, replacing SP 9/80, which dealt only with retirement annuities).

---

7 Bankruptcy

7.1 **Income received by trustee during bankruptcy is not income of bankrupt for purposes of claiming personal allowances, etc.** (*Fleming CS 1928, 14 TC 78*). Trustee is assessable on such income including profits of bankrupt's business continued by him notwithstanding requirement to hand over to creditors (*Armitage v Moore QB 1900, 4 TC 199*). And see *Hibbert v Fysh CA 1962, 40 TC 305* (bankrupt assessable on remuneration retainable by him). The trustee continues generally to act following the death (undischarged) of the bankrupt as if he or she were still alive.

See 56.5 PAYMENT OF TAX for Crown Priority and 58.9 PENALTIES for penalties awarded against a bankrupt. See also Tolley's Capital Gains Tax under Settlements.

8 Banks

8.1 For the tax treatment of banks themselves, and for certain exemptions, see Tolley's Corporation Tax (under Banks).

Interest payable in UK to a UK bank, and interest paid by a UK bank, are both payable gross (see 23.3(ii) DEDUCTION OF TAX AT SOURCE) except as detailed in 8.2 and 8.3 below, but payments by individuals to banks of certain home mortgage interest are made after deduction of tax, see 23.13 DEDUCTION OF TAX AT SOURCE. For savings bank interest etc., see 29.11 EXEMPT INCOME.

In general, the term 'bank' is defined by reference to the carrying on of a *bona fide* banking business, but for certain purposes it is specially defined as:

(*a*)   the Bank of England;

(*b*)   an institution authorised under the *Banking Act 1987*;

(*c*)   a European authorised institution (within the *Banking Co-ordination (Second Council Directive) Regulations 1992*) in relation to the establishment of a branch of which the requirements of *2 Sch 1* of those regulations have been complied with; or

(*d*)   an international organisation of which the UK is a member and which is designated as a bank for the particular purpose by Treasury order.

See 3.8 ANTI-AVOIDANCE, 15.5 CHARITIES, 23.3(ii) DEDUCTION OF TAX AT SOURCE, 67.4 RETURNS. [*Sec 840A; FA 1996, 37 Sch 1(1)*].

Returns. Banks must make returns of interest paid to depositors, see 67.4 RETURNS.

8.2   **COMPOSITE RATE SCHEME—1990/91 AND EARLIER YEARS** [*Secs 479–483*]

For 1990/91 and earlier years, where a recognised bank or other deposit-taker (including the Bank of England, the Post Office (but not the National Savings Bank), a company successor to a trustee savings bank, a Scottish savings bank or any other person (or class of person) specified by Treasury statutory instrument in relation to any or all 'relevant deposits') makes a payment of, or credits, interest on a 'relevant deposit', it must deduct therefrom, and account to the Revenue for, tax thereon at the 'composite rate' determined as for building society payments (see 9.3 BUILDING SOCIETIES). [*Secs 479(1), 481(2), 482(1)*]. The Treasury have prescribed for this purpose the British Railways Board (*SI 1984 No 1801*) and local authorities (excluding parish or community councils) (*SI 1985 No 1696*).

A '**relevant deposit**' (subject to the exclusions below) is a deposit in respect of which either (*a*) the person beneficially entitled to any interest is an individual (or the persons so entitled are all individuals), or, in Scotland, is a partnership all the partners of which are individuals, or (*b*) the person entitled to it receives it as the personal representative of a deceased individual (but note particularly the ordinary residence requirement at (xi) below).

Excluded are:

(i)   deposits in respect of which a CERTIFICATE OF DEPOSIT (13) has been issued for £50,000 or more (or foreign equivalent at the time the deposit is made) not repayable within seven days;

(ii)   non-transferable fixed deposits of £50,000 or more (or foreign equivalent at the time the deposit is made) to be repaid in full at the end of a specified period of not less than seven days;

(iii)   debentures (as defined in *Companies Act 1985, s 744*);

(iv) loans made *by* a deposit-taker in the ordinary course of his business;

(v) debts on securities listed on a recognised stock exchange;

(vi) deposits in a 'general client account deposit', i.e. a client account, other than an account for specific clients, if the depositor is required by law to make payments representing interest to any of the clients whose money it contains;

(vii) Lloyd's UNDERWRITERS (89) premiums trust funds;

(viii) deposits by Stock Exchange money brokers (recognised by the Bank of England) in the course of business as such a broker;

(ix) deposits held at non-UK branches of UK resident deposit-takers;

(x) deposits with non-UK resident deposit-takers held other than in UK branches; and

(xi) deposits in respect of which any person beneficially entitled to any interest thereon, or entitled to receive the interest in his capacity as a personal representative, or to whom it is payable, has declared in writing to the deposit-taker that the individual mentioned above (or all those individuals) is not (or are not) ordinarily resident in the UK, or was not so ordinarily resident at the time of his death. The declaration must be in such form, and contain such information, as is required by the Board, and must include an undertaking to notify the deposit-taker should any individual concerned become ordinarily resident in the UK, and the Revenue have powers to review all declarations received by a deposit-taker. A certificate by the deposit-taker is required in cases where a declaration of non-ordinary residence does not include the depositor's permanent address. A declaration in similar terms given to a building society (see 9.4(*a*) BUILDING SOCIETIES) which converts to company status (see 9.8 BUILDING SOCIETIES) will be treated for this purpose as having been made to the successor company. (Revenue Pamphlet IR 1, A69).

The deposit-taker must treat all deposits as relevant deposits unless satisfied to the contrary, but if so satisfied may treat a deposit as not being a relevant deposit until he comes into possession of information reasonably indicative that the deposit is, or may be, a relevant deposit.

The Treasury and the Board are given wide powers to amend the legislation by statutory instrument, in particular in relation to the declaration required at (xi) above. [*Secs 481(3)–(6), 482(2)–(7), (11), (12)*].

Tax position of recipient. Where an interest payment falls to be made under deduction of composite rate tax as above, the recipient is treated as having received income for the year of payment equal in amount to that received grossed up at the basic rate of income tax, and no liability to basic rate tax arises thereon (although higher rate liability will arise where appropriate). The notional basic rate tax paid cannot be repaid, but the payment received (*not* grossed up) is treated as brought into charge to income tax in applying *Secs 348, 349* (see 23.2 DEDUCTION OF TAX AT SOURCE). [*Sec 479(2)–(4)*].

Tax position of deposit-taker. The collection procedure of *16 Sch* applies, *mutatis mutandis*, to payments of interest on relevant deposits (as above). In outline, returns are required at quarterly intervals, and tax is due without assessment within 14 days of the date of making the return. For company deposit-takers, income tax suffered by deduction in a return period may be set against liability of the period under these provisions. [*Sec 479(5)–(7)*].

Transitional provisions on commencement of scheme.

(*a*) A CERTIFICATE OF DEPOSIT (13) issued before 13 March 1984 on which interest is payable after 5 April 1985 is not a relevant deposit (see above). [*Sec 482(8)*].

(*b*) A non-transferable fixed deposit made before 6 July 1984, to be repaid in full on a specified date after 5 April 1985 or (where interest is payable only on repayment of the deposit) on demand or on notice, is not a relevant deposit (see above). [*Sec 482(9)*].

(*c*) Up to and including 5 April 1988, a declaration made before 6 July 1984 under *TMA s 17* (see 67.4 RETURNS) containing an undertaking as required under (xi) above satisfies that requirement. [*FA 1984, 8 Sch 6(4)*].

(*d*) Where an existing deposit comes within the composite rate scheme (as above), the SCHEDULE D, CASE III (72) rules apply as if the source ceased on its coming within the scheme. If, however, it came within the scheme on 6 April 1985, the 1983/84 assessment (if any) on that source may not be adjusted from the preceding to the current year basis (see 72.4(*c*) SCHEDULE D, CASE III). [*Sec 480(1)(2)(4)*].

(*e*) Where a deposit which is a source of income ceases to be within the composite rate scheme (as above), the SCHEDULE D, CASE III (72) rules apply as if the source commenced on its ceasing to be within the scheme. [*Sec 480(3)(4)*].

8.3 **DEDUCTION OF TAX FROM INTEREST—1991/92 AND SUBSEQUENT YEARS** [*Secs 480A–482; FA 1990, 5 Sch 7–12; SI 1990 No 2232; FA 1991, ss 75, 82; SIs 1992 Nos 12–15; F(No 2)A 1992, 8 Sch 4; SI 1992 No 3234; FA 1993, ss 59, 183(2); SI 1994 No 295; FA 1995, s 86; SI 1995 No 1370*]

Any 'deposit-taker' paying or crediting interest on a 'relevant deposit' must deduct therefrom a sum representing income tax thereon (at the lower rate (before 1996/97, the basic rate) for the year of assessment in which the payment is made), unless the conditions for gross payment contained in *The Income Tax (Deposit-takers) (Interest Payments) Regulations 1990* (*SI 1990 No 2232*) (see below) are met. Income tax chargeable under SCHEDULE D, CASE III (72) on such interest is computed on the full amount of the interest arising in the year. *Sec 349* (see 23.3 DEDUCTION OF TAX AT SOURCE) does not apply to such payments.

The deposit-taker must treat all deposits as relevant deposits unless satisfied to the contrary, but if so satisfied may treat a deposit as not being a relevant deposit until he comes into possession of information reasonably indicative that the deposit is, or may be, a relevant deposit.

For these purposes, '*deposit-taker*' means the same as under 8.2 above, except that all local authorities are included, trustee savings bank company successors and Scottish savings banks are excluded insofar as they do not come within one of the other categories and, from 1 January 1993, a 'European deposit-taker' within *regulation 82(3)* of *SI 1992 No 3218* is included. '*Relevant deposit*' similarly has the same meaning as under 8.2 above, except that:

(A) for payments made after 6 April 1996, it may include a deposit, interest on which arises to the trustees of a discretionary or accumulation trust (as under *Sec 686*, see 80.5 SETTLEMENTS). This does not apply to deposits made before 6 April 1995 unless the deposit-taker has, between that date and the making of the interest payment, been notified by the Board or by the trustees that the interest is income of such a trust (and the Board has wide information powers in relation to such notices). The form of notification by the trustees is laid down by *SI 1995 No 1370*, under which payments may continue to be made gross for up to 30 days after receipt of notice (whether by the trustees or by the Revenue) where deduction within that period has not become reasonably practicable. Notification may be cancelled by the Revenue where appropriate. There are transitional provisions treating the source as ceasing where a payment on a deposit made before 6 April 1996 is brought within the scheme before 6 April 1998. The exclusion under 8.2(xi) above applies where a trustee has declared that the trustees are non-UK resident and have no reasonable grounds for believing that any beneficiary (as widely defined) is a UK ordinarily resident individual or a UK resident company (with the usual undertakings being required in relation to notification of changes affecting such a declaration); and

(B)   in the cases of the exclusions at 8.2(i) and (ii) the deposit must be repayable within five years and no minimum repayment period is imposed, and certain deposits in respect of which a certificate of deposit could be, but has not been, issued, but which otherwise meet the conditions under 8.2(i), are also excluded.

In the case of depositors who make the appropriate declaration for their deposit to be excluded from being a relevant deposit (see 8.2(xi) above) to a deposit-taker other than a bank, the normal deduction rules under *Sec 349(2)* are disapplied by *Sec 349(3)(h)* (introduced by *FA 1993, s 59*) as they are disapplied in the case of banks by *Sec 349(3)(a)* (and see Revenue Press Release 21 January 1993).

The collection procedure of *16 Sch* applies, *mutatis mutandis*, to such payments whether or not the deposit-taker is UK-resident.

The Inland Revenue Financial Intermediaries and Claims Office may be contacted for technical advice in relation to the basic rate tax scheme on 0151–472 6156.

Gross payment may be made where the person beneficially entitled to the interest is UK ordinarily resident (see 64.6 RESIDENCE, ORDINARY RESIDENCE AND DOMICILE) and has supplied the appropriate certificate to the deposit-taker to the effect that he is unlikely to be liable to income tax for the year of assessment in which the payment is made or credited (taking into account for this purpose all interest arising in the year of assessment concerned which would, in the absence of such a certificate, be received under deduction of lower or basic rate tax). The certificate must be in prescribed form and must contain the name, permanent address, date of birth and (where applicable) national insurance number of the person beneficially entitled to the interest, and the name (and if necessary branch) of the deposit-taker and account number. It must also contain an undertaking to notify the deposit-taker if the person beneficially entitled to the payment becomes liable to income tax for the year in which the payment is made or credited. Revenue Explanatory Leaflet IR 110 outlines the conditions for certification (which are described in detail below) and contains the appropriate Form R85(1990) on which application may be made (and of which further copies may be obtained from banks, building societies, post offices and tax offices). Leaflet IR 111 explains the procedure for reclaiming tax deducted where no Form R85(1990) is in effect, and contains the appropriate claim Form R95(1991).

Such a certificate may only be given by:

(i)   a depositor aged 16 or over at the beginning of the year of assessment in which the payment is made or credited, or who attains age 16 during that year, who is beneficially entitled to the payment; or

(ii)   the parent or guardian of a person beneficially entitled to the payment who is under 16 at the beginning of that year; or

(iii) a person authorised by power of attorney to administer the financial affairs of the person beneficially entitled to the payment; or

(iv)   (from 30 January 1992) the parent, guardian, spouse, son or daughter of a mentally handicapped person, or any person appointed by a court to manage the affairs of a mentally handicapped person; or

(v)   (from 4 March 1994) a person appointed by the Secretary of State to receive benefits on behalf of a person who is for the time being unable to act.

8.3 Banks

A certificate may not be given where the payment is treated as income of a parent of the person beneficially entitled to the payment, or where the Board has issued a notice in relation to the account concerned requiring deduction of tax (see below).

The certificate must be supplied before the end of the year of assessment in which the payment is made or credited, or, in the case of a certificate given by a person who will attain 16 years of age during a year of assessment, before the end of that year.

A person who, after 24 July 1991, gives such a certificate fraudulently or negligently, or fails to comply with any undertaking contained in the certificate, is liable under *TMA s 99A* (introduced by *FA 1991, s 82*) to a penalty up to £3,000.

Tax deducted from payments in a year prior to receipt of a certificate relating to that year may be refunded, and a like amount recovered by the deposit-taker from the Board, provided that a certificate of deduction of tax (see 23.7 DEDUCTION OF TAX AT SOURCE) has not been furnished to the depositor prior to receipt of the gross payment certificate.

In Revenue Press Release 13 August 1992, the Revenue position as regards incorrect certification for gross payment was explained. In asking those who had registered to reconsider their position (and, if appropriate, to ask for their registration with the bank or building society to be cancelled), the Revenue made clear that where, as a result of their audited sample, cases of incorrect registration were identified, gross payment would cease and tax (and possibly interest and penalties) would be imposed in respect of any interest already received. No interest and penalties would be applied in cases of simple misunderstanding of the position, and a penalty would be considered only where false or fraudulent declarations had knowingly been made on the registration form (or there had been a deliberate failure to cancel the registration).

A certificate ceases to be valid:

(a)   where the deposit-taker is notified (as above) that the person beneficially entitled to the payment is liable to income tax for the year in which the payment is made;

(b)   where it was given by a parent or guardian, at the end of the year of assessment in which the person beneficially entitled to the payment attains 16 years of age;

(c)   where it was given by a person who attained 16 years of age during the year of assessment in which a payment was made or credited, but who was not the holder of the account to which the certificate relates, and that person fails to become the holder before the first payment is made or credited after the end of that year of assessment;

(d)   where the deposit-taker is notified that the person by or on whose behalf the certificate was given has died; and

(e)   where the Board, having reason to believe that a person beneficially entitled to a payment of interest has become liable to income tax, give notice requiring the deposit-taker to deduct tax from payments of interest made, more than 30 days after the issue of the notice (or from earlier payments, if practicable), to or for the benefit of that person on a specified account held by or on behalf of that person.

A notice under (e) above must be copied to the person to whom it refers, and a further certificate in respect of the account referred to in the notice may not be given by or on behalf of that person (unless the notice is subsequently cancelled, see below).

A notice under (e) above may be cancelled (and the deposit-taker and person referred to in the notice so informed) if the Board are satisfied that the person referred to in the notice was not at the date of the notice, and has not since become, liable to income tax, or is no longer so liable.

Deposit-takers may make written application for deduction of tax to apply, notwithstanding the above provisions, in relation to accounts which before 6 April 1991 had ceased to be available to persons desiring to open a new account.

Certificates of non-liability given by a building society which converts to company status are, by concession, treated as having been given to the successor company. (Revenue Pamphlet IR 1, A69).

Joint accounts. The position as regards certification by each of joint holders of an account is considered separately. Payments are apportioned equally to each joint holder, and tax deducted in respect of that part of a payment to which certification does not apply. The deposit-taker may, however, deduct tax from the whole of payments in respect of joint accounts where certification does not apply to all the joint holders, after giving notice to the Board of its intention to do so (which notice the deposit-taker may subsequently cancel).

Information. The Board may by notice require any deposit-taker (within not less than 14 days) to furnish them with such information (including books, records etc.) as they require, in particular

(I)   for verification of payments made without deduction of tax and of the validity of certification for gross payment, and

(II) for verification of the amount of tax deducted from payments of interest (but this does not include copies of books, records etc. from which the depositor can be ascertained).

Copies of the deposit-taker's books, records etc. must be made available when required by the Board. Certificates for gross payment must be retained for at least two years after they expire.

Subject to *FA 1989, s 182(5)* (see 36.3 INLAND REVENUE: CONFIDENTIALITY OF INFORMATION), information obtained under these provisions may not be used other than for the purposes of the provisions or for the ascertainment of the tax liability of the deposit-taker or of the person beneficially entitled to interest paid without deduction of tax to whom the information relates.

The Board may also make regulations providing for the exclusion from its information powers of accounts held by non-UK ordinary residents or non-UK resident trustees.

For Revenue audit powers and further information powers, see *SIs 1992 Nos 12, 15.*

The Revenue have published a Code of Practice (No 4, published July 1993) setting out their standards for the carrying out of inspections of tax deduction schemes operated by financial intermediaries.

9 Building Societies

9.1 For years up to and including 1985/86, a Building Society normally entered into special arrangements with the Revenue resulting in the consequences set out in 9.3 and 9.4 below. [*ICTA 1970, ss 343, 344*].

For the years 1986/87 to 1990/91 inclusive, this system was replaced by regulations made by statutory instrument by the Board, although the revised system operated on broadly similar lines to the previous arrangements. [*Sec 476*]. The regulations are contained in *The Income Tax (Building Societies) Regulations 1986, SI 1986 No 482* and *(Amendment) Regulations 1987, SI 1987 No 844* and *1988, SI 1988 No 1011*.

For 1991/92 and subsequent years, a new system is introduced under which building societies deduct lower or basic rate tax from interest payments unless a certificate is supplied to the effect that the recipient is unlikely to be liable to income tax for the year. [*Sec 477A; FA 1990, s 30, 5 Sch*]. Regulations provide for the detailed implementation of the new scheme (see *The Income Tax (Building Societies) (Dividends and Interest) Regulations 1990, SI 1990 No 2231*).

For these purposes, a building society is one within the meaning of the *Building Societies Act 1986*. [*Sec 832(1)*].

9.2 **Returns.** Building societies are required to make returns of dividends and interest paid to investors. [*TMA s 17; SI 1986 No 482; FA 1990, s 92; SI 1990 No 2231; F(No 2)A 1992, s 29*]. See 67.4 RETURNS.

9.3 **INTEREST AND DIVIDENDS PAID TO INVESTORS—1990/91 AND EARLIER YEARS**

Interest and dividends are paid to investors without any deduction for income tax. [*Sec 476(5)(a)*]. Apart from certain payments which are made gross (see 9.4 below), the building society is required to account for and pay to the Revenue an amount representing income tax partly at a reduced rate known as the composite rate (22% for 1990/91), and partly at the basic rate, in respect of grossed-up payments of dividends, interest and certain annual payments. 'Interest and dividends paid to investors' for this purpose are such payments in respect of shares in, or deposits with or loans to, the society, including qualifying distributions in respect thereof. [*Sec 476(1); SI 1986 No 482; SI 1989 No 2339*].

Tax position of recipient—if an individual ordinarily resident in the UK.

(i) The recipient is not liable to income tax at the basic rate thereon. [*Sec 476(5)(c)*].

(ii) The recipient is liable (if his total income is high enough) to the excess of the higher rate(s) of income tax over the basic rate on the amount received grossed up at the basic rate (e.g. amount received £75, basic rate 1990/91 25%, grossed-up amount is £100), which is treated as income of the year of payment. [*Sec 476(6)*].

(iii) The recipient is not entitled to any tax repayment in respect of such interest or dividends. [*Sec 476(5)(b)*]. But see below as to exempt pension funds and see also 22.3 DECEASED ESTATES.

(iv) The amounts received (not grossed) are, in applying *Secs 348, 349(1)* (see 23.2 DEDUCTION OF TAX AT SOURCE), treated as taxed income received. [*Sec 476(5)(d)*].

(v) The amounts received (not grossed) must be shown on tax returns.

Tax position of recipient—if a company or unincorporated body such as a club etc.

Liability to corporation tax arises on the amount received grossed up at the basic rate of income tax, but a credit is given against this liability for the amount of such grossing up. The credit may be repaid where appropriate. [*Sec 476(3)*].

Tax position of recipient—if an exempt pension fund (but see 9.4 below).

The special provisions under *Sec 476(5)(b)* do not apply to pension funds exempt from tax under *Secs 592(2), 613(4), 614(1)–(3), 620(6)* or *643(2)*. The amount received is treated as paid or credited after deduction of tax which may then be reclaimed. [*Sec 476(7)*].

9.4   **Interest and dividends payable gross.** For 1986/87 to 1990/91 inclusive, interest and dividends are payable gross (i.e. the building society does not have to account for composite or basic rate tax in respect of them) where, at the time of payment, they fall into one of the following categories.

(*a*)   A payment to an individual not ordinarily resident in the UK who is beneficially entitled to the payment, or jointly so entitled with other such individuals.

(*b*)   A payment to trustees of a trust in the income of which no person has an interest apart from individuals not ordinarily resident in the UK.

(*c*)   A payment to personal representatives in respect of an investment (or another investment representing an investment) forming part of the estate of a deceased person who was not ordinarily resident in the UK at the time of his death.

(*d*)   A payment to a charity exempt under *Sec 505(1)(c)*.

(*e*)   A payment to an exempt friendly society under *Sec 460*.

(*f*)   A payment to a pension fund all of whose income is exempt under *Sec 592(2)*.

(*g*)   A payment of interest on a bank loan.

(*h*)   A payment under a CERTIFICATE OF DEPOSIT (13) issued after 5 April 1983 under which the society is obliged within five years of issue to pay £50,000 or more (exclusive of interest); or on a non-transferable sterling deposit of £50,000 or more for a fixed period of less than five years. Such certificates of deposit and other non-transferable deposits may be denominated in a foreign currency, the equivalent £50,000 limit being determined at the time of the deposit. [*SI 1987 No 844; SI 1989 No 36*].

(*i*)   A payment under a SAYE scheme within *Sec 326(3)*.

(*j*)   A payment to a non-resident in respect of certain 'quoted Eurobonds' (see 23.3(ii) DEDUCTION OF TAX AT SOURCE).

(*k*)   A payment on a deposit by a subsidiary of a building society with its parent society (where an election for gross payment is in force). [*SI 1987 No 844*].

(*l*)   A payment for the purposes of an approved personal pension scheme (see 65.5 RETIREMENT ANNUITIES AND PERSONAL PENSION SCHEMES). [*SI 1988 No 1011*].

(*m*)   A payment made on a loan by one building society to another. [*SI 1989 No 36*].

(*n*)   A payment in respect of a general client deposit account (see 8.2(vi) BANKS). [*SI 1989 No 36*].

Scottish partnerships consisting only of individuals not ordinarily resident in the UK are within the requirements at (*a*) and (*b*) above. A payment within (*a*)–(*f*) or (*l*) above may not be made gross unless the society has a written declaration in a prescribed form from the

9.5 Building Societies

investor certifying that the relevant conditions are met. Where payments are made gross, liability arises on the recipient under SCHEDULE D, CASE III (72). The commencement and cessation provisions of *Sec 66(3)* and *Sec 67* apply where any building society investment (other than a 'quoted Eurobond') respectively ceases to be or becomes a '*relevant investment*', i.e. one where dividends or interest payable in respect of it are sums in respect of which the society is required to account for and pay an amount representing income tax at the composite or basic rate. A building society investment in existence on 6 April 1986 which was not a relevant investment on that date is treated as a new source of income acquired on that date, and the commencement provisions apply accordingly. [*Secs 476(1)(11), 477; FA 1986, s 47(7); SI 1986 No 482*].

9.5 **INTEREST AND DIVIDENDS PAID TO INVESTORS—1991/92 AND SUBSEQUENT YEARS** [*Sec 477A; FA 1990, 5 Sch 4, 10; SI 1990 No 2231; FA 1991, ss 52, 75, 82, 11 Sch; SIs 1992 Nos 10, 11, 2915; SI 1995 No 1184; SI 1996 No 223*]

Except in the case of certain marketable securities (see below), building societies are required under regulations (*SI 1990 No 2231*) made under *Sec 477A* to deduct a sum representing income tax (at the lower rate (before 1996/97, the basic rate) for the year of assessment in which the payment is made) thereon from all payments or credits of dividends or interest in respect of shares in, deposits with or loans to the society, unless gross payment is authorised under the conditions described below. The deduction requirements of *Sec 349* (see 23.3 DEDUCTION OF TAX AT SOURCE) do not apply to such payments. Whether or not gross payment applies, such interest etc. is chargeable under SCHEDULE D, CASE III (72) on the current year basis.

The Inland Revenue Financial Intermediaries and Claims Office may be contacted for technical advice in relation to the tax deduction scheme on 0151–472 6156.

Gross payment applies in the same cases as are described at 9.4 above, except that:

(*a*) in the case of non-transferable time deposits within 9.4(*h*) made after 5 April 1991, the terms must prevent partial withdrawals of or additions to the deposit;

(*b*) gross payment also applies where the person beneficially entitled to the interest is UK ordinarily resident (see 64.6 RESIDENCE, ORDINARY RESIDENCE AND DOMICILE) and has supplied the appropriate certificate to the society to the effect that he is unlikely to be liable to income tax for the year of assessment in which the payment is made or credited (taking into account for this purpose all interest arising in the year of assessment concerned which would, in the absence of such a certificate, be received under deduction of lower or basic rate tax);

(*c*) (with effect from 30 January 1992) 9.4(*j*) is deleted and gross payment is applied also to payments to local authorities and to Lloyd's underwriters' premium trust funds;

(*d*) (with effect from 14 December 1992) gross payment is applied to all payments to companies (defined to include all bodies corporate and unincorporated associations other than partnerships and local authority associations), health service bodies (within *Sec 519A*) and trustees of unit trust schemes (within *Financial Services Act 1986, s 75(8)*). Also with effect from that date, gross payment is extended to payments in respect of a '*qualifying deposit right*' (as defined below);

(*e*) (with effect from 14 December 1992) the investor certification requirements are extended to most companies and to unit trust scheme trustees;

(*f*) (with effect from 4 March 1994) 9.4(*f*) is amended to refer to a payment to a retirement benefits scheme approved under *Sec 592(1)* (see 66.1 RETIREMENT SCHEMES) or whose application for approval is under consideration;

(*g*)   (with effect from 4 March 1994) gross payment is applied to a payment in respect of an investment held at a non-UK branch;

(*h*)   (with effect from 3 May 1995) gross payment is applied to deemed interest payments under *Sec 730A(2)* (price differential on sale and repurchase of securities, see 3.5 ANTI-AVOIDANCE); and

(*i*)   (with effect from 6 April 1996) gross payment is applied to payments to trustees of a discretionary or accumulation trust (within *Sec 686*, see 80.5 SETTLEMENTS) where the trustees are non-UK resident and all beneficiaries (as widely defined) are either non-UK ordinarily resident individuals (or Scottish partnerships comprising such individuals) or non-UK resident companies.

The conditions for certification, and related information powers etc., are similar to those described at 8.3 BANKS.

Marketable securities. Dividends or interest paid after 24 July 1991 in respect of shares or securities (other than 'qualifying certificates of deposit' or a 'qualifying deposit right') listed, or capable of being listed, on a recognised stock exchange when the dividend, etc. became payable are not within the regulations under *Sec 477A* referred to above, but are subject to deduction of tax under *Sec 349* unless the securities are 'quoted Eurobonds' within *Sec 124* (see 23.3 DEDUCTION OF TAX AT SOURCE). 'Permanent interest bearing shares' (see Tolley's Corporation Tax under Building Societies) issued by a society are within these provisions.

A '*qualifying certificate of deposit*' is a CERTIFICATE OF DEPOSIT (13) for £50,000 or more (exclusive of interest) (or foreign equivalent at the time of the deposit) repayable within five years. A '*qualifying deposit right*' is a right to receive an amount in pursuance of a deposit of money under an arrangement made after 16 July 1992 under which no certificate of deposit has been issued, although the person entitled to the right could call for the issue of such a certificate, which otherwise meets the same conditions as a qualifying certificate of deposit. [*Secs 349(3A)(3B)(4), 477A(1A); FA 1991, 11 Sch 1, 2; F(No 2)A 1992, 8 Sch 2, 3*].

Code of Practice. The Revenue have published a Code of Practice (No 4, published July 1993) setting out their standards for the carrying out of inspections of tax deduction schemes operated by financial intermediaries.

9.6   INTEREST PAYABLE TO BUILDING SOCIETIES

Payments to a building society in respect of advances normally comprise capital repayment plus interest. The interest portion will generally be 'relevant loan interest' which will be paid under deduction of tax by most borrowers (see 23.13 DEDUCTION OF TAX AT SOURCE). Otherwise, no tax is deductible from such payments but the payer is given tax relief (subject to certain restrictions, see 43.5 *et seq.* INTEREST PAYABLE) on the interest portion each year (either by adjustments in PAYE coding or by discharge or repayment).

Where building society interest is paid in connection with a trade, profession or vocation and the payer's income is not sufficient for relief to be given in full, any unrelieved balance may be carried forward against subsequent profits as under *Sec 385*, or used in a terminal loss claim under *Sec 388*. [*Sec 390*]. See under 46 LOSSES.

9.7   TAX LIABILITY OF A BUILDING SOCIETY ITSELF

See Tolley's Corporation Tax (under Building Societies).

9.8 Building Societies

9.8   TRANSFER OF BUILDING SOCIETY BUSINESS TO COMPANY

The acquisition by members of shares on such a transfer is granted certain reliefs from capital gains tax and from treatment as a distribution. [*FA 1988, s 145, 12 Sch; TCGA 1992, ss 216, 217*]. See Tolley's Corporation Tax under Building Societies.

Declarations made as to the ordinary residence of depositors (see 9.4(*a*) above) and certificates of non-liability given to societies (see 9.5(*b*) above) are treated as having been made or given to the successor company. (Revenue Pamphlet IR 1, A69).

10   Capital Allowances

10.1   Capital allowances (balancing charges) are a deduction from (addition to) the profits etc. of trades, professions, employments, vocations, offices and occupation of woodlands assessed under Schedule D, in arriving at the taxable amount. The amount of depreciation charged in the accounts of a business is not so allowed. For *income tax* purposes, for 1996/97 and earlier years as regards trades etc. commenced before 6 April 1994, most capital allowances are *deducted from the assessment* and not treated as expenses in the accounts. [*CAA 1990, s 140 as originally enacted*]. For income tax purposes, for 1994/95 and subsequent years as regards trades etc. commenced after 5 April 1994 and for 1997/98 and subsequent years as regards trades etc. commenced on or before that date, and for corporation tax purposes, capital allowances (or balancing charges) are treated as trading expenses (or receipts) of the period of account (see 10.2(xi) below), or for corporation tax the accounting period, to which they relate. [*CAA 1990, ss 140, 144; FA 1994, s 211*]. See also 10.2(vi) and (vii) below. See Tolley's Corporation Tax for matters with special relevance to companies.

Capital allowances are granted in respect of certain types of expenditure detailed in 10.3 to 10.52 below.

Headings in this chapter are as follows.

10.2   **MATTERS OF GENERAL APPLICATION**

(i)   **Composite sales** may be apportioned by Commissioners despite separate prices attributed in sale agreement. [*CAA 1990, ss 150, 151*]. See *Fitton v Gilders & Heaton Ch D 1955, 36 TC 233*, and *Wood v Provan CA 1968, 44 TC 701*.

(ii) **Subsidies.** All expenditure met, or to be met, directly or indirectly by the Crown or by any government or public or local authority (except through Regional Development Grants or NI equivalent (for which see *SI 1995 No 611* and predecessor orders)) is treated as not having been incurred by any person, so that no capital allowance is due in respect of it.

A contribution by any other person is generally ignored, unless the contributor could himself obtain a capital allowance in respect of it under *CAA 1990, s 154* (see below), or obtain a deduction against trading profits, in which case the recipient's expenditure is reduced by the amount of the contribution in determining his capital allowances. [*Secs 91(9), 532(1); CAA 1990, s 153*]. Where a contribution is towards expenditure on dredging (10.7 below), however, the person incurring the expenditure will receive full allowances only if the contributions are made for the purposes of that person's trade. [*CAA 1990, s 134(8)*]. Certain contributions by pools promoters towards football ground improvements are disregarded despite being an allowable deduction in the pools promoter's trade (see 71.84 SCHEDULE D, CASES I AND II). [*FA 1990, s 126*]. Scientific research capital allowances (10.52 below) are not available where expenditure is met by a contribution by any other person. [*CAA 1990, s 153(1)(4)*].

Contributors towards capital expenditure on an asset may receive allowances where the contribution is for the purposes of the contributor's (or his tenant's) trade, profession or vocation, and where the expenditure would, apart from the contribution, have attracted capital allowances, as if the asset were at all material times used for trade purposes (so that balancing adjustments do not apply to such contributions). The allowances are such as would have been made if the contribution had been expended on the provision for the contributor's trade of a similar asset. On a transfer of the trade, or part thereof, the allowances (or part) are passed to the transferee.

Certain contributions towards expenditure by a sewerage authority on the provision of an asset to be used in the treatment of trade effluents also attract allowances.

No allowances are available to the contributor, however, where the person incurring the expenditure and the contributor are CONNECTED PERSONS (20).

These provisions do not apply to mineral depletion allowances (10.49(*a*) below), cemeteries and crematoria (10.5 below), scientific research allowances (10.52 below) or dredging (10.7 below), although contributions towards dredging are treated as expenditure by the contributor on that dredging. [*CAA 1990, ss 134(8), 154, 155; Sec 532*].

(iii) **Time expenditure incurred.** Capital expenditure (other than that constituted by an 'additional VAT liability'—see (v) below) is generally treated, for capital allowance purposes, as incurred on the date on which the obligation to pay becomes unconditional, whether or not payment is in whole or part required to be made by some later date, *except that* it is treated as incurred on a later date in the following circumstances.

(*a*) Where any part of the expenditure is required to be paid on or by a date more than four months after the date determined as above, it is treated as incurred on that later date.

(*b*) Where an obligation to pay becomes unconditional earlier than in accordance with normal commercial usage, with the sole or main benefit expected being that, under these provisions, the expenditure would be treated as incurred in an earlier chargeable or basis period, it is instead treated as incurred on the date on or before which it is required to be paid.

(c)   Where any other provision requires expenditure to be treated as incurred on a later date than that laid down by these provisions (including (a) and (b) above), the expenditure is treated as incurred on that later date.

[*CAA 1990, s 159(2)(3)(5)–(8); FA 1991, 14 Sch 14; FA 1994, 26 Sch Pt V(24)*].

Where, as a result of an event such as the issuing of a certificate, an obligation to pay becomes unconditional before one month has elapsed after the start of a chargeable or basis period, but the asset concerned has become the property of, or is otherwise attributed under the contract to, the person having the obligation at or before the end of the immediately preceding chargeable or basis period, the obligation is treated as becoming unconditional immediately before the end of that earlier period. [*CAA 1990, s 159(4); FA 1994, 26 Sch Pt V(24)*].

(iv)   **Exclusion of double allowances.** Where an allowance is made to a person under one of the codes of allowances listed below, he cannot obtain an allowance under another of those codes, in respect of either the same expenditure or expenditure in respect of an asset to which the first-mentioned allowance relates, nor can such expenditure qualify for machinery and plant allowances (see 10.28 below). Similarly, neither an amount of capital expenditure qualifying for machinery and plant allowances nor an asset to which it relates can qualify for any of the allowances listed. The allowances in question are

(a)   industrial buildings allowances (10.10–10.23 below);

(b)   allowances for expenditure on dredging (10.7 below);

(c)   agricultural buildings allowances (10.3 below);

(d)   scientific research allowances (10.52 below);

(e)   allowances for mines and oil wells (10.39–10.46 below);

(f)   allowances for dwelling-houses let on assured tenancies (10.9 below).

[*CAA 1990, s 147; FA 1993, 13 Sch 13*].

These provisions do not prevent the purchaser of an asset from claiming allowances on a different basis from the vendor, where alternative bases of claim are permissible. (Revenue Capital Allowances Manual, CA 1060).

(v)   **VAT capital goods scheme.** Under the VAT capital goods scheme, the input tax originally claimed on the acquisition of certain capital assets is subject to amendment within a specified period of adjustment in accordance with any increase or decrease in the extent to which the asset is used in making taxable, as opposed to exempt, supplies for VAT purposes. The items covered by the scheme are limited to land and buildings (or parts of buildings) worth £250,000 or more and computers (and items of computer equipment) worth £50,000 or more. See Tolley's Value Added Tax under Capital Goods for a full description of the scheme.

Special capital allowances provisions apply where a VAT adjustment is made under the capital goods scheme. [*FA 1991, s 59; 14 Sch*]. These affect allowances for industrial buildings, machinery and plant and scientific research, and the provisions specific to each are described in the appropriate sections of this chapter. General definitions and provisions are described below.

'*Additional VAT liability*' and '*additional VAT rebate*' in relation to any capital expenditure mean, respectively, an amount which a person becomes liable to pay or an amount which he becomes entitled to deduct by way of adjustment under any 'VAT capital items legislation' (as defined) in respect of input tax on an asset on the

10.2 Capital Allowances

construction or provision of which the expenditure was wholly or partly incurred. Generally (but see below), such a liability or rebate is to be regarded as incurred or made on the last day of the 'relevant VAT interval'. The '*relevant VAT interval*' is that one of the periods of which, under the VAT capital items legislation, the applicable VAT period of adjustment consists, in which occurred the increase or decrease in use giving rise to the additional VAT liability or rebate.

For the purpose *only* of determining the chargeable period for which a capital allowance or balancing charge may be made in respect of it (or for which it is to be brought into account in connection with the making of such allowances or charges), an additional VAT liability or rebate is to be regarded as incurred or made at a time (referred to below as the relevant time) determined as follows:

(*a*)   where a VAT return (in which the liability or rebate is accounted for) is made to Customs and Excise, the relevant time is a time within the chargeable period or its basis period which includes the last day of the period covered by that return;

(*b*)   if, before the making of a return as in (*a*) above, Customs and Excise assess the liability or rebate as due or repayable, the relevant time is the day on which the assessment is made;

(*c*)   if the trade (or profession, vocation, employment etc. — see 10.24 below) is permanently discontinued (or treated as such for tax purposes) before the liability or rebate has been accounted for in a VAT return and before the making of an assessment as in (*b*) above, the relevant time is the last day of the chargeable period related to the discontinuance.

Where an allowance or charge falls to be determined by eference to a proportion only of the expenditure incurred or a proportion only of what that allowance or charge would otherwise have been, any allowance or charge in respect of an additional VAT liability or rebate in respect of that expenditure is similarly apportioned.

[*CAA 1990, s 159A; FA 1991, 14 Sch 14; FA 1994, 26 Sch Pt V(24)*].

(vi)   **Periods of account/chargeable periods.** For 1994/95 and subsequent years as regards trades, etc. commenced after 5 April 1994 and for 1997/98 and subsequent years as regards trades, etc. commenced on or before that date, capital allowances given in taxing the trade, etc. are, for income tax purposes, given by reference to 'periods of account' (see 10.1 above). Previously, they were calculated by reference to the basis period for the year of assessment for which they were made. A '*period of account*' means a period for which accounts are made up, except that where such a period exceeds 18 months, it is deemed to be split into two or more periods of account, beginning on, or on an anniversary of, the date on which the actual period begins. Where, exceptionally, there is an interval between two periods of account, it is deemed to form part of the first such period, and where two periods of account overlap, the common period is deemed to form part of the first period only. For non-traders, a period of account is a year of assessment. [*CAA 1990, ss 140, 160; FA 1994, ss 211, 212(1)*]. Consequentially, references in the capital allowances provisions to the basis period for a chargeable period are repealed, and such references in this chapter should be construed accordingly. [*FA 1994, ss 211(2), 213(1), 214(5), 26 Sch Pt V (24)*].

Any reference in the capital allowances provisions to a chargeable period is, for income tax purposes, a reference to a period of account, except that for 1996/97 and earlier years as regards trades, etc. commenced before 6 April 1994, it is a reference to a year of assessment. For corporation tax purposes, a chargeable period is an accounting period. [*CAA 1990, s 161(2); FA 1994, ss 211(2), 212(2)*].

(vii) **Transitional rule on changeover to new system.** 10.1 above mentions the change to the system for dealing with capital allowances for income tax purposes, i.e. a change from treating an allowance as a deduction from the Schedule D, Case I or II assessment to treating it as a trading expense. For trades, etc. commenced before 6 April 1994 and continuing beyond 5 April 1997, any capital allowances claimed for 1996/97 and earlier years but unrelieved (due to an insufficiency of profits) are treated as trading expenses for the first period of account (see (vi) above) ending after 5 April 1997. [*FA 1994, 20 Sch 9*].

10.3   **AGRICULTURAL BUILDINGS AND WORKS**

After 31 March 1986, a new code of capital allowances applies to qualifying expenditure on agricultural buildings and works, replacing the provisions in *CAA 1968, ss 68, 69*, subject to transitional provisions (see below). [*CAA 1990, ss 122–133*].

Qualifying buildings, etc. Writing-down and (in certain cases) initial allowances (see below) are given in respect of capital expenditure incurred on the construction, reconstruction, alteration or improvement of farmhouses (but see below), farm or forestry buildings, cottages, fences or other works (such as drainage and sewerage works, water and electricity installations or land reclamation) for the purposes of husbandry or forestry. [*CAA 1990, ss 123, 124(1), 124A, 131; FA 1993, 12 Sch 2, 3*]. See below as regards ending of forestry allowances. *'Husbandry'* includes any method of intensive rearing of livestock or fish on a commercial basis for the production of food for human consumption [*CAA 1990, s 133(1)*] and, normally, the use of land for the growing of bulbs (Tolley's Practical Tax 1986 p 23). Cottages occupied by retired farm workers and buildings constructed to provide welfare facilities for employees may qualify for allowances, as may farm shops to the extent that they sell produce of the farm. (Revenue Capital Allowances Manual, CA 4533, 4534).

Qualifying expenditure. Allowances are available where a person has a 'major interest' in any agricultural or forestry land (but see below) and incurs capital expenditure as set out above for the purposes of husbandry or forestry on that land, excluding any proportion of such costs relating to the land itself. The asset does not have to be on the land in question, e.g. a farmworker's cottage in a nearby village might qualify. (Revenue Capital Allowances Manual, CA 4504). *'Agricultural land'* is land, buildings etc. in the UK occupied wholly or mainly for the purposes of husbandry (as above), and *'forestry land'* is woodlands in the UK (and buildings occupied with, and for the purposes of, those woodlands) which are the subject of an election for taxation under Schedule D (see 69 SCHEDULE B—WOODLANDS—the election ceased to be available after 14 March 1988, subject to transitional provisions). A *'major interest'* in land means the fee simple estate in the land or an agreement to acquire that interest (or Scottish equivalent) or a lease. A creditor who has conveyed or assigned an interest in land by way of security will still be treated as entitled to the interest provided that he has a related right of redemption. [*CAA 1990, ss 123, 125, 131, 133(1)(4)(6)(7)*]. On **farmhouses** a maximum of only one-third of expenditure may be taken into account for allowances and, in general, expenditure on other assets only partly used for agricultural, etc. purposes is only eligible in such proportion as is just. Partial use may include occupation by a part-time farm worker. (Revenue Capital Allowances Manual, CA 4532). [*CAA 1990, ss 124(1)(2), 124A(4); FA 1993, 12 Sch 2, 3*]. For the meaning of 'farmhouse', see *Lindsay v CIR CS 1953, 34 TC 289; CIR v Whiteford & Sons CS 1962, 40 TC 379; Korner v CIR HL 1969, 45 TC 287* and Revenue Capital Allowances Manual, CA 4530 (including the circumstances in which it may be accepted that a farm has two farmhouses). For what constitutes capital expenditure on the construction of a farmhouse or other agricultural building, see Revenue Capital Allowances Manual, CA 4515, 4516.

Buildings, etc. bought unused. Similar provisions apply as in the case of industrial buildings (see 10.12 below). [*CAA 1990, ss 127, 127A; FA 1993, 12 Sch 5, 6*].

10.3 Capital Allowances

Market gardening, whether of plants and flowers or for the production of food, is treated in the same way as farming for allowance purposes, and a house which is the centre of such operations is treated as a farmhouse (see above). (Revenue Capital Allowances Manual, CA 4509).

Forestry land. Allowances (under the current or old code (see below)) in respect of forestry land or use cease for chargeable periods beginning after 19 June 1989. Allowances for 1989/90 or for company accounting periods straddling that date are apportioned on a time basis to the part ending on that date and to the other part, those apportioned to the other part not being made.

Where an election for Schedule D treatment of forestry income (see 69.2 SCHEDULE B—WOODLANDS) is in force for a chargeable period beginning before 6 April 1993, allowances continue to be available notwithstanding the above. Where the period concerned is a company accounting period ending after 5 April 1993, allowances given otherwise than in taxing a trade are time-apportioned, those falling in the part of the period after that date not being made. Allowances given in taxing a trade are similarly denied by virtue of the transitional provisions referred to at 69.3 SCHEDULE B—WOODLANDS. Initial allowances under *CAA 1990, s 124A* (see below) are not available in respect of expenditure incurred for the purposes of forestry. [*CAA 1990, s 131; FA 1993, 12 Sch 9*].

Initial allowances. An initial allowance is available in respect of qualifying expenditure incurred under a contract entered into in the twelve-month period **1 November 1992 to 31 October 1993 inclusive** or for the purpose of securing compliance with obligations incurred under a contract entered into during that period, but not for expenditure incurred under a contract entered into for the purpose of securing compliance with obligations under a contract entered into before 1 November 1992. The qualifying building must come to be used for the purposes of husbandry before 1 January 1995, and, if this condition is not satisfied or if the building first comes to be used for purposes other than husbandry, any initial allowance given will be withdrawn. The initial allowance is **20%** of the expenditure incurred, and is given for the chargeable period related to the incurring of the expenditure. For income tax purposes and, as regards company accounting periods ended after 30 September 1993, for corporation tax purposes, either a smaller initial allowance may be claimed or the initial allowance not claimed at all; for earlier accounting periods, a company may disclaim the initial allowance in whole or in part by giving written notice to the inspector within two years after the end of the accounting period concerned. [*CAA 1990, s 124A(1)–(3) (5)–(7); FA 1993, 12 Sch 3*].

Writing-down allowances are made at **4% p.a.** during a period of 25 years beginning on the first day of the chargeable period (see 10.2(vi) above) relating to the incurring of the expenditure, so as to give aggregate allowances (including any initial allowance) up to the amount of that expenditure. Any expenditure remaining unallowed at the end of the writing-down period by virtue of these provisions and, where appropriate, by virtue of the granting of proportionate allowances for the chargeable period during which the writing-down period ends, is additionally allowed for that chargeable period. If the buildings, etc. in fact come to be first used other than for the purposes of husbandry or forestry, no writing-down allowance can be made in respect of the related expenditure and any allowance previously given is withdrawn. A writing-down allowance is given for the same chargeable period as an initial allowance under *CAA 1990, s 124A* (see above) in respect of the same expenditure, but only if the building etc. comes to be used for the purposes of husbandry before the end of that chargeable period. [*CAA 1990, ss 123, 124(2), 124B, 126(6); FA 1993, 12 Sch 3, 4(3)*]. If the conditions are met when the expenditure is incurred and the first use is for the purposes of husbandry, allowances continue throughout the writing-down period without regard to any change of use of the building in later years. (Revenue Capital Allowances Manual, CA 4566).

Transfer of relevant interest. Where a person entitled to allowances in respect of capital expenditure as above ceases to own the 'relevant interest' in the land (or part) concerned giving rise to that entitlement, and another person acquires that interest, the right to the writing-down allowances (or part) is transferred to the new owner of the interest (proportionate allowances being given where the transfer falls during a chargeable or basis period of either the former or the new owner). The right to an initial allowance is not transferred to the new owner (subject to the provisions referred to above for buildings etc. bought unused). [*CAA 1990, s 126(1)–(3); FA 1993, 12 Sch 4(1)(2); FA 1994, 26 Sch Pt V(24)*].

The *'relevant interest'* is the major interest in the land to which the person who incurred the expenditure was entitled when he incurred it (the interest in reversion to all others where two or more major interests in the land were held). A major interest remains the relevant interest where a lease, etc. is created to which the interest is subject, and, where a lease which is a relevant interest is surrendered or reverts, the interest into which it merges becomes the relevant interest (unless a new lease takes effect on the extinguishment). [*CAA 1990, ss 125(2)–(4), 126(4)*]. If a new lease is granted to the former lessee, the new lease is treated as a continuation of the old lease. If it is granted to a person other than the former lessee, the relevant interest is treated as acquired by the new lessee if he makes a payment to the former lessee for the assets representing the expenditure in question. In any other case, the landlord under the former lease is treated as acquiring the relevant interest. [*CAA 1990, s 126(5)*].

Balancing events. A *'balancing event'* occurs when the relevant interest in land is acquired by another person (see above) or when the building, etc. on construction of which the expenditure was incurred is demolished, destroyed, or otherwise ceases to exist as such, *provided that* a written election to that effect is made. The election must be made (i) for income tax for 1996/97 onwards (subject to (ii) below), within twelve months after 31 January following the tax year in which ends the chargeable period related to the occurrence of the balancing event, (ii) for income tax for 1996/97 only as regards trades etc. commenced before 6 April 1994 and as respects events in the basis period for that year, on or before 31 January 1999, and (iii) for income tax for earlier years and for corporation tax, within two years after the end of such chargeable period. The election must be made jointly in the case of acquisition of the relevant interest, but otherwise by the former owner only. An election may not be made by a person outside the charge to UK tax, nor if the sole or main benefit of an acquisition was the obtaining of an allowance (but ignoring *CAA 1990, s 157*, see below). [*CAA 1990, s 129; FA 1993, 12 Sch 8; FA 1994, 26 Sch Pt V(24); FA 1996, s 135, 21 Sch 33*].

Where a balancing event occurs in a chargeable or basis period for which an allowance would otherwise have been available, no such allowance is made, but a balancing adjustment arises for that period on or to the person entitled to the relevant interest immediately before the balancing event. If the residue of expenditure immediately before the balancing event (i.e. after deducting any allowances previously given) exceeds any sale, compensation, etc. receipts, a balancing allowance equal to that excess is made. If any sale, compensation, etc. receipts exceed that residue, a balancing charge is made equal to the excess (but limited to the allowances previously given to the person on whom the charge arises). Allowances made to a husband before 6 April 1990 in respect of his wife's relevant interest are treated as having been made to the wife for these purposes on a balancing event on or after that date. [*CAA 1990, s 128; FA 1993, 12 Sch 7; FA 1994, 26 Sch Pt V(24)*].

Where a balancing event occurs on the transfer of the relevant interest, the writing-down allowances available to the new owner consist of the residue of expenditure (see above) immediately before the balancing event, plus any balancing charge or less any balancing allowance consequent on that event, spread over the period from the balancing event to the end of the original 25 year writing-down period. [*CAA 1990, s 129(3); FA 1994, 26 Sch Pt V(24)*].

Making of allowances and charges. An initial, writing-down or balancing adjustment for a chargeable period is given or made in taxing a trade. If no trade is carried on in that chargeable period, then, for 1995/96 and subsequent years for income tax purposes, allowances and charges are treated as expenses and receipts of a Schedule A business (see 68.4 SCHEDULE A) or, where the taxpayer is not, in fact, carrying on such a business, of a deemed Schedule A business. For 1994/95 and earlier years for income tax purposes, and continuing for corporation tax purposes, allowances are given by discharge or repayment of tax, primarily against agricultural or (where applicable, see above) forestry income and income which is the subject of a balancing charge. A balancing charge is made under Schedule D, Case VI for income tax or treated as agricultural etc. income of a company. [*CAA 1990, s 132; FA 1995, 6 Sch 35*]. Allowances are given in taxing a trade in accordance with *Sec 140* in the same way as for industrial buildings allowances to traders (see 10.17 below). See also 10.2(vi) and (vii) above.

Double allowances. See 10.2(iv) above.

There are **connected person** and **anti-avoidance provisions** in respect of certain balancing events, similar to those applicable to industrial buildings allowances (see 10.22(i) below). [*CAA 1990, ss 130, 133(8)(9), 157, 158(5)*].

Transitional provisions. The former provisions of *CAA 1968, ss 68, 69* continue to apply to expenditure incurred before 1 April 1987 under a contract entered into before 14 March 1984 by the person incurring the expenditure. [*CAA 1990, ss 122, 133(3)*].

'Old scheme' for expenditure incurred before 1 April 1986. Writing-down allowances are (and initial allowances, in certain cases, were) given by way of discharge or repayment of tax (and not in taxing a trade), primarily against assessments on agricultural or forestry income. Any balance of allowances due for a year of assessment may be carried forward without time limit against future such income, or may (on a claim within two years of the end of the year of assessment) be set against other income of the year of assessment or of the following year. [*CAA 1968, ss 68(1)(2)(3), 71*]. See above as regards ending of forestry allowances.

An *initial allowance of 20%* of expenditure incurred (after 11 April 1978) could be claimed for the year of assessment following the year to 31 March (or such other date as was agreed with the inspector) in which the expenditure was incurred. An individual was able to claim a specified reduced amount. [*CAA 1968, s 68(1)(3A)(6); FA 1978, s 39*].

For expenditure for which an initial allowance was available as above (and for pre-12 April 1978 expenditure), a *writing-down allowance of 10%* may be claimed annually for the year of assessment for which the initial allowance was available and subsequent years, until the initial and writing-down allowances exhaust the expenditure. If the conditions are met when the expenditure is incurred, allowances continue throughout the writing-down period without regard to any change of use of the building in later years, and even if it is destroyed. (Revenue Capital Allowances Manual, CA 4656). In the case of sales, transfers of property, change of tenants, etc., the transferee takes over the writing-down allowances for the remainder of the writing-down period, the allowance for the year of sale, etc. being apportioned. [*CAA 1968, s 68(1)(4)(5); CA 1990, s 122*]. See also *Sargaison v Roberts Ch D 1969, 45 TC 612*.

10.4   *Example*

Farmer Jones prepares accounts annually to 31 December and has incurred the following expenditure

		£
12.1.90	Extension to farmhouse	12,000
3.6.91	Construction of cattle court	15,000
26.4.93	Erection of barn	10,000
15.10.96	Replacement barn for that acquired on 26.4.93 which was destroyed by fire in September 1996. The insurance proceeds totalled £6,600	20,000

The agricultural buildings allowances are as follows.

Date of expenditure	Cost	Residue brought forward	Allowances Initial 20%	WDA 4%	Residue carried forward
	£	£	£	£	£
1991/92 (basis period — year to 31.12.90)					
12.1.90	4,000			160	3,840
				—	—
1992/93 (basis period — year to 31.12.91)					
12.1.90	4,000	3,840		160	3,680
3.6.91	15,000			600	14,400
	£19,000	£3,840		£760	£18,080
1993/94 (basis period — year to 31.12.92)					
12.1.90	4,000	3,680		160	3,520
3.6.91	15,000	14,400		600	13,800
	£19,000	£18,080		£760	£17,320
1994/95 (basis period — year to 31.12.93)					
12.1.90	4,000	3,520		160	3,360
3.6.91	15,000	13,800		600	13,200
26.4.93	10,000		2,000	400*	7,600
	£29,000	£17,320	£2,000	£1,160	£24,160
1995/96 (basis period — year to 31.12.94)					
12.1.90	4,000	3,360		160	3,200
3.6.91	15,000	13,200		600	12,600
26.4.93	10,000	7,600		400	7,200
	£29,000	£24,160		£1,160	£23,000

(i) No election for a balancing adjustment

Date of expenditure	Cost	Residue brought forward	Initial 20%	WDA 4%	Residue carried forward
1996/97 (basis period — two years to 31.12.96)					
12.1.90	4,000	3,200		160	3,040
3.6.91	15,000	12,600		600	12,000
26.4.93	10,000	7,200		400	6,800
15.10.96	20,000			800	19,200
	£49,000	£23,000		£1,960	£41,040

(ii) Election for a balancing adjustment

Date of expenditure	Cost	Residue brought forward	Allowances		Residue carried forward
			Initial 20%	WDA 4%	
	£	£	£	£	£
1996/97 (basis period — two years to 31.12.96)					
12.1.90	4,000	3,200		160	3,040
3.6.91	15,000	12,600		600	12,000
15.10.96	20,000			800	19,200
	£39,000	£15,800		£1,560	£34,240

Balancing allowance

	£
Proceeds	6,600
Written-down value	7,200
Balancing allowance	£600

* In order to qualify for a writing-down allowance in addition to an initial allowance in 1994/95, the original barn must be brought into use before 6 April 1995.

10.5 CEMETERIES AND CREMATORIA [*Sec 91*]

Cemeteries. In computing profits etc. of a trade consisting of or including the carrying on of a cemetery, a deduction as a trading expense of any period is allowed for

(i) *cost of land* (including cost of levelling, draining or making suitable) *sold for interments*, or in relation to which *interment rights are sold*, in that period, and

(ii) a *proportion* (based on ratio of number of grave spaces sold in the period to that number plus those still available) of the *residual capital expenditure* at the end of the period. *Capital expenditure* for this purpose is expenditure on any building or structure (excluding dwelling houses) and underlying or surplus land, likely to have little or no value when the cemetery is full. (Certain expenditure before the 1954/55 basis period is excluded.) The *residue* is the balance of such expenditure after deducting amounts previously allowed under this section and any sale or insurance etc. receipts in respect of assets (the subject of such expenditure) sold or destroyed.

Changes of ownership of the trade (whether otherwise treated as a discontinuance or not) are ignored—allowances continue as they would to the original trader. [*Sec 91(5)*].

For the treatment of lump sums for grave maintenance, etc., see Revenue Inspector's Manual, IM 2061–2063.

Crematoria attract similar allowances, substituting memorial garden plots for cemetery land, grave-spaces or interments. [*Sec 91(7)*]. See also *Bourne v Norwich Crematorium Ch D 1967, 44 TC 164.*

For the treatment of expenditure and receipts in connection with the provision of niches and memorials, see Revenue Inspector's Manual, IM 2071, 2072.

10.6   *Example*

GE, who operates a funeral service, owns a cemetery for which accounts to 31 December are prepared. The accounts to 31.12.96 reveal the following

(i)	Cost of land representing 110 grave spaces sold in period	£3,400
(ii)	Number of grave spaces remaining	275
(iii)	Residual capital expenditure on buildings and other land unsuitable for interments	£18,250

	The allowances available are	£
(*a*)	Item (i)	3,400
(*b*)	$\dfrac{110}{110+275} \times £18,250$	5,214
		£8,614

Note

(*a*)   £8,614 will be allowed as a deduction in computing GE's Schedule D, Case I profits for the accounting period ending on 31 December 1996.

10.7   **DREDGING** [*CAA 1990, ss 134, 135*]

Writing-down, balancing and, in certain cases, initial allowances (see below) may be claimed for capital expenditure on **dredging** incurred for the purposes of a *qualifying trade* (provided that neither industrial buildings allowances (see 10.10 below) nor machinery and plant allowances (see 10.24 below) are available in respect of the same expenditure).

'*Dredging*' must be done in the interests of navigation, and either

(i)   the qualifying trade must consist of the maintenance or improvement of navigation of a harbour, estuary or waterway, or

(ii)   the dredging must be for the benefit of vessels coming to, leaving or using docks or other premises used in the qualifying trade.

It includes removal, by any means, of any part of, or projections from, any sea or inland water bed (whether then above water or not), and the widening of any inland waterway.

A '*qualifying trade*' is one either within (i) above or within the industrial buildings allowance definitions at 10.11(*a*)–(*c*) below. Expenditure only partly for a qualifying trade is apportioned as may be just, and for this purpose, where part only of a trade qualifies, the qualifying and non-qualifying parts are treated as separate trades.

Initial allowances are given for the year of assessment in whose basis period (see 71.3 SCHEDULE D, CASES I AND II) the expenditure is incurred at the following rates.

From   6 April 1956—10%
From 15 April 1958—15% (5% where certain investment allowances were payable between 8 April 1959 and 16 January 1966).

[*CAA 1968, s 67(1)(a)(8), 1 Sch*].

10.8 Capital Allowances

Initial allowances are **abolished** for expenditure incurred **after 31 March 1986,** unless incurred before 1 April 1987 under a contract entered into before 14 March 1984 by the person incurring the expenditure. [*FA 1985, s 61*].

Expenditure incurred for a trade before it is carried on, or in connection with a dock etc. before it is occupied for a qualifying trade, attracts allowances as if the trade was carried on, or the dock etc. occupied, when the expenditure was incurred. The initial allowance is then given for the first year of assessment in whose basis period both the trade is carried on and the dock etc. occupied. [*CAA 1968, s 67(7); CAA 1990, s 134(7)*].

Writing-down allowances are given to the person for the time being carrying on the trade, at a rate fixed by the date expenditure was incurred, until initial and writing-down allowances exhaust the expenditure. The rates are

Before 6 November 1962—2% p.a.
From 6 November 1962—4% p.a.

The writing-down allowances are first given in the period for which initial allowances are (or would have been) given. In any year of assessment for only part of which a person is chargeable to income tax in respect of the trade, the annual writing-down allowance is apportioned on a time basis, but this is of no application where allowances fall to be treated as trading expenses (see 10.1 above). [*CAA 1990, ss 134(1), 135(2), 146; FA 1994, ss 211(2), 213(9), 26 Sch Pt V(24)*].

A **balancing allowance** is given for the year of assessment of *permanent discontinuance* of the trade, equal to expenditure incurred less initial and writing-down allowances given, to the person last carrying on the trade. The allowance includes expenditure incurred before 6 April 1956, but in relation to such expenditure, all possible allowances (other than initial allowances) are deemed to have been given in respect of 1955/56 and earlier years as if the provisions introduced by *FA 1956* had always been in force. [*CAA 1990, s 134(2)(3)*].

Permanent discontinuance includes sale of the business (unless it is a sale between CONNECTED PERSONS (20), or without change of control, or one the sole or main benefit of which appears to be a capital allowance advantage, see *CAA 1990, s 157*), but not deemed discontinuance under *Sec 113* (change in person(s) carrying on trade) or certain corporation tax provisions. [*CAA 1990, s 134(4)*].

Excess allowances. Where the allowances for a year of assessment exceed the assessment for the year, the balance may be carried forward without time limit while the trade continues. Alternatively, allowances may create or enhance a trade loss. See 46 LOSSES generally. [*CAA 1990, s 140 as originally enacted*]. This is of no application where allowances fall to be treated as trading expenses (see 10.1 above).

10.8   *Example*

D is the proprietor of an estuary maintenance business preparing accounts to 30 June. Expenditure qualifying for dredging allowances is incurred as follows.

	£
Year ended 30.6.93	4,000
Year ended 30.6.94	5,000

On 2 January 1997, D sells the business to an unconnected third party. The Revenue do not revise the 1994/95 and 1995/96 assessments under *ICTA 1988, s 63*.

The allowances available are

Date of expenditure	Cost	Residue brought forward	Allowances WDA 4%	Residue carried forward
	£	£	£	£
1994/95 (basis period — year ended 30.6.93)				
1993	4,000	—	160	3,840
1995/96 (basis period — 1.7.93 – 5.4.96)				
1993	4,000	3,840	160	3,680
1994	5,000	—	200	4,800
			£360	
1996/97 (basis period — 6.4.96 – 2.1.97, nine months)				
1993	4,000	3,680	($\frac{9}{12}$) 120	3,560
1994	5,000	4,800	($\frac{9}{12}$) 150	4,650
			270	£8,210
Balancing allowance			8,210	
Total allowances (1996/97)			£8,480	

10.9 **DWELLING-HOUSES LET ON ASSURED TENANCIES** [*CAA 1990, ss 84–97*]

Legislation was introduced by *FA 1982* to give capital allowances on expenditure incurred by an *'approved body'* (i.e. a body specified by the Secretary of State under *Housing Act 1980, s 56(4)*), on the construction of buildings consisting of, or including, dwelling-houses let on assured and certain other tenancies, after 9 March 1982 and before 1 April 1987 (subsequently extended until **31 March 1992**). [*CAA 1990, ss 84(1), 96(3)*]. The provisions were substantially modified following repeal of the relevant sections of the *Housing Act 1980* by the *Housing Act 1988*.

A *qualifying dwelling-house* is a dwelling-house let on a tenancy being an assured tenancy within *Housing Act 1980, s 56* (or, not being an assured shorthold tenancy, within *Housing Act 1988*) and continues to qualify at any time when

(i)   it is subject to a regulated tenancy or a housing association tenancy (as defined in the *Rent Act 1977*), and

(ii) the landlord under the tenancy either is or has been an approved body.

[*CAA 1990, ss 86(1)(2)(4), 97(1)*].

A dwelling-house does not qualify

(a)   unless the landlord is a company (applicable to expenditure contracted and incurred after 4 May 1983, or where a person other than a company becomes entitled to the 'relevant interest' after that date) and either is entitled to the relevant interest in the dwelling-house or is the person who incurred the capital expenditure on the construction of the building containing it; or

10.9 Capital Allowances

(b) if the landlord is a housing association approved under *Sec 488* (co-operative housing association) or is a self-build society under the *Housing Associations Act 1985*; or

(c) if the landlord and tenant, or a company of which the tenant is a director, are CONNECTED PERSONS (20); or

(d) if the landlord is a close company and the tenant is a participator, or associate of a participator, in that company; or

(e) if the tenancy is part of a reciprocal arrangement between the landlords or owners of different dwelling-houses designed to counter the restrictions in (c) or (d) above. [*CAA 1990, s 86*].

Capital expenditure appropriate to a dwelling-house is limited to £60,000 if it is in Greater London and £40,000 elsewhere, and is:

(A) where the building consists of a single qualifying dwelling-house, the whole of the expenditure on its construction;

(B) where the dwelling-house forms part of a building, (i) the proportion of capital expenditure attributable to that dwelling-house, and (ii) such proportion of the capital expenditure on any common parts of the building as is just and reasonable, but not exceeding one-tenth of the amount in (i). [*CAA 1990, s 96(1)(2)*].

The acquisition of, or of rights in or over, any land is not included in expenditure incurred on the cost of construction of a building for these purposes. [*CAA 1990, s 97(2)*].

Any capital expenditure incurred on repairs is treated as if incurred on the construction for the first time of that part of the building. [*CAA 1990, s 93(1)*].

Buildings bought unused. The provisions in *CAA 1990, s 91* are similar to those in *CAA 1990, s 10*, for which see 10.12, 10.13 below.

Subsidies. See 10.2(ii) above.

After the coming into force of the *Housing Act 1988, Pt I*, any assured tenancy (other than an assured shorthold tenancy) for the purposes of that *Act* is treated as an assured tenancy within the *Housing Act 1980, s 56*, but only in relation to capital expenditure incurred on the building either

(I) before 15 March 1988 (or under a contract entered into before that date) by a company which was on that date an approved body (see above) or by the vendor to such a company of the relevant interest in the building sold before use, or

(II) by a company as in (I) which, before 15 March 1988, bought or contracted to buy the relevant interest in the building. [*CAA 1990, s 84(2)(3)*].

Initial allowances were, and **writing-down allowances** are, given in a similar manner, at similar rates and under similar conditions as for industrial buildings, for which see 10.13, 10.14 below. [*FA 1982, 12 Sch 1; FA 1984, s 58, 12 Sch 3; CAA 1990, ss 85, 87(7)(8); FA 1994, s 213(7), 26 Sch Pt V(24)*]. Initial allowances available only by reason of *Housing Act 1980, s 56B* (as enacted by *Housing and Planning Act 1986*), and to which effect could not otherwise be given, could, on a claim before 1 April 1988, be given effect. [*F(No 2)A 1987, s 72(2)*].

References to 'temporary disuse' [*CAA 1990, s 89(2)*], 'residue of expenditure' [*CAA 1990, s 90*], and 'relevant interest' should be taken as they apply for industrial buildings allowances, but it should be noted that the creation of a subsidiary interest (e.g. leasehold out of freehold) does not transfer the relevant interest. [*CAA 1990, s 95*].

Balancing allowances and charges are made in a similar manner and under similar conditions as for industrial buildings in *CAA 1990, s 4* (see 10.15 below). [*CAA 1990, ss 87, 88; FA 1994, 26 Sch Pt V(24)*].

Where *cessation of qualifying use occurs* otherwise than by sale or transfer of the relevant interest, that interest is treated as having been sold at the time of cessation at the open market price. [*CAA 1990, s 89(1)*].

Making of allowances and charges. Allowances and charges are made in a similar way as they apply to lessors and licensors of industrial buildings, for which see 10.17 below. [*CAA 1990, ss 92, 140–145; FA 1995, 6 Sch 34*].

Holding over by lessee etc. Where the relevant interest in relation to the capital expenditure incurred on the construction of a building is an interest under a lease, the following provisions apply. The lease will be treated as continuing where (i) with the consent of the lessor, a lessee remains in possession of any building after his lease ends and without a new lease being granted, (ii) where a lease ends and a new lease is granted to the same lessee under an option available in the first lease, and (iii) where a lease ends and another lease is granted to a different lessee who pays a sum to the first lessee (i.e. the transaction is treated as an assignment). However, where a lease ends and the lessor pays any sum to the lessee in respect of the building, the transaction is treated as if the lease had come to an end by reason of its surrender in consideration of the payment. [*CAA 1990, s 94*].

Double allowances. See 10.2(iv) above.

Connected persons and other anti-avoidance provisions. The provisions of *CAA 1990, ss 157, 158* apply to certain sales as they apply to sales of industrial buildings (see 10.22 below) but an election is only available if both the seller and the buyer are, at the time of the sale (or, for sales after 14 January 1989, were at any earlier time), approved bodies. Due to a drafting error, the original provisions allowed such an election only if that condition was *not* fulfilled, and an election made before 1 April 1983 on that basis remains valid. [*F(No 2)A 1983, s 6(2)*]. Any transfer of relevant interest which is not a sale will be treated as a sale other than at market price under these provisions but there is no balancing allowance or charge if the dwelling-house is treated as having been sold for a sum equal to the residue of expenditure before the sale. [*CAA 1990, ss 87(5), 88(4)*].

10.10   **INDUSTRIAL BUILDINGS**

Allowances are given in respect of certain capital expenditure (see 10.12 below) on industrial buildings or structures (see 10.11 below), and are available to traders and to lessors and licensors of industrial buildings for use by traders. The main elements of the scheme of allowances are dealt with as follows

10.11	Qualifying buildings	10.17	Making of allowances and
10.12	Qualifying expenditure		charges
10.13	Initial allowances	10.18	Hotels
10.14	Writing-down allowances	10.19	Enterprise zones
10.15	Balancing allowances and	10.21	Small workshops
	charges	10.22	General matters

10.11   **Qualifying buildings.** An 'industrial building or structure' is a building etc., or part of a building etc., in use either

(*a*)   for the purposes of a trade, or part of a trade (which must be a self-contained part, see Revenue Capital Allowances Manual, CA 1310, 1311), consisting of

    (i)   the manufacture or processing of goods or materials, or

    (ii)   after 9 March 1982, the maintaining or repairing of goods or materials (but not goods etc. employed by the person carrying out the repair or maintenance in any trade or undertaking unless that trade etc. itself qualifies the building as an industrial building etc.), or

(iii)   the storage of (*a*) raw materials for manufacture, (*b*) goods to be processed, (*c*) goods manufactured or processed but not yet delivered to any purchaser, or (*d*) goods on arrival in the UK from a place outside (for chargeable periods ended before 6 April 1990, goods on arrival by sea or air into the UK), or

(iv)   the working of mines, oil wells, etc. or foreign plantations, or

(v)   agricultural operations on land not occupied by the trader, or

(vi)   catching fish or shellfish; or

(*b*)   for the purposes of

(i)   a trade, or part of a trade, carried on in a mill, factory or other similar premises, or

(ii)   a transport, dock, inland navigation, water, sewerage, electricity, hydraulic power, bridge or tunnel undertaking, or

(iii)   in relation to any chargeable or basis period ending after 5 April 1991, a toll road undertaking or, for expenditure incurred after 5 April 1995, a 'highway undertaking' (see below); or

(*c*)   for the welfare of workers employed in a trade or undertaking within (*a*) or (*b*) above; or

(*d*)   as a sports pavilion for the welfare of workers employed in any trade; or

(*e*)   as a qualifying hotel (see 10.18 below).

A building the whole of which is in use partly for qualifying and partly for non-qualifying purposes may qualify for allowances in full provided that the qualifying use is at least 10% of the total use. (Revenue Capital Allowances Manual, CA 1328). See also *Saxone Lilley & Skinner (Holdings) Ltd* below.

Excluded from the definition of 'industrial buildings or structure' are buildings etc. in use as, or as part of, dwelling-houses, retail shops, showrooms, offices or hotels (but see 10.18 below as regards expenditure on hotels after 11 April 1978), or on buildings etc. for purposes ancillary thereto, except that (1) where only part of a building, representing 25% (10% for expenditure incurred before 16 March 1983 or deemed so incurred under *CAA 1990, s 10(1)(2)*, see 10.12 below) or less of the total cost, falls within these exclusions, the whole building continues to qualify, and (2) buildings etc. constructed for occupation by, or welfare of, employees in mines, oil wells, etc. or foreign plantations, and likely to have little or no value on the ending of the working of the mine etc. or of the foreign concession, also qualify. Note that when alterations, extensions etc. or changes in use result in the 25% limit in (1) being exceeded, no amendment is made to allowances for basis periods before that of the change, and allowances continue to be available in respect of that part of the building etc. not excluded. Similarly, where the 25% condition commences to be met, allowances are available for the whole of the building etc. only for the basis period of the change and subsequent basis periods. See Revenue Capital Allowances Manual at CA 1344 for what is an 'office' for these purposes, and at CA 1350–1354 for purposes 'ancillary' to those of a retail shop. In *Girobank plc v Clarke Ch D, 1996 STI 451*, a bank document and data processing centre was held to be an office.

Buildings etc. *outside the UK* can only qualify if the trade for which they are in use is assessable under Sch D, Case I or Case V. A building etc. used by more than one licensee of the same person only qualifies if each of the licensees uses the building, or his part of it, for the purposes of a trade as above under licences granted after 9 March 1982. [*CAA 1990, ss 14, 18; FA 1991, s 60(4)(10); FA 1993, s 113(6); FA 1995, ss 99(5), 101*].

A '*highway undertaking*' (see (*b*)(iii) above) means so much of any undertaking relating to the design, building, financing and operation of roads as is carried on for the purposes of, or in connection with, the exploitation of 'highway concessions'. A '*highway concession*', in relation to a road, means any right, in respect of public use of the road, to receive sums from the Government, or, in the case of a toll road, the right to charge tolls. [*CAA 1990, s 21(5AA); FA 1995, s 99(7)*].

(*c*) above is regarded by the Revenue as including canteens, day nurseries, garages, hard tennis courts, hostels and indoor sports halls. It does not, however, include buildings excluded as above from being industrial buildings or structures (e.g. a grocery shop with extended hours for the convenience of workers, or holiday accommodation). Also as regards (*c*) above, the workers for whose welfare a building is provided must be workers engaged directly in the productive, manufacturing or processing side of the business, rather than office staff or management, although the whole of a building provided for staff generally may qualify provided use by production workers is not negligible. Similarly use by outsiders as well as workers does not exclude the building from relief. (Revenue Capital Allowances Manual, CA 1304–1307).

For cases in which industrial buildings allowances were **refused** see *Dale v Johnson Bros KB(NI) 1951, 32 TC 487* (warehouse—contrast the non-tax case *Crusabridge Investments Ltd v Casings International Ltd Ch D 1979, 54 TC 246*); *CIR v National Coal Board HL 1957, 37 TC 264* (colliery houses capable of alternative use); *Bourne v Norwich Crematorium Ch D 1967, 44 TC 164* (furnace chamber, etc.); *Abbott Laboratories Ltd v Carmody Ch D 1968, 44 TC 569* (separate administrative block); *Buckingham v Securitas Properties Ltd Ch D 1979, 53 TC 292* (building used for wage packeting); *Vibroplant Ltd v Holland CA 1981, 54 TC 658* (depots of plant hire contractor, but now see (*a*)(ii) above); *Copol Clothing Co Ltd v Hindmarch CA 1983, 57 TC 575* (inland storage of goods imported in containers); *Carr v Sayer Ch D 1992, 65 TC 15* (quarantine kennels, claimed under (*a*)(iii)(*d*) above); and *Girobank plc v Clarke Ch D, 1996 STI 451* (bank document and data processing centre held to be an office, although within (*a*)(i) above).

For cases where allowances were **granted**, see *CIR v Lambhill Ironworks Ltd CS 1950, 31 TC 393* (drawing office); *Kilmarnock Equitable Co-operative Society Ltd v CIR CS 1966, 42 TC 675* (coal packing not ancillary to retail shop); and *Saxone Lilley & Skinner (Holdings) Ltd v CIR HL 1967, 44 TC 122* (warehouse for shoes both bought and manufactured).

Temporary disuse. A building etc. which falls temporarily out of use after a period in which it qualified as an 'industrial building or structure' is treated as continuing to so qualify during disuse. [*CAA 1990, s 15*]. All disuse other than that preceding demolition or dereliction is in practice regarded as temporary.

10.12   **Qualifying expenditure** is the cost of construction of the building etc. including the cost of preparing, cutting, tunnelling or levelling land, but excluding expenditure on the land itself or on rights therein. [*CAA 1990, ss 1(1), 21(1)*]. The fees of professionals involved in the design and construction of the building (e.g. architects, quantity surveyors and engineers) are also included. (Revenue Capital Allowances Manual, CA 1035). Expenditure on repairs which is, exceptionally, disallowable in computing profits is treated as the cost of constructing that part of the building [*CAA 1990, s 12*], and the cost of preparing etc. land as a site for the installation of machinery or plant is, if no relief would otherwise be available under industrial buildings or machinery and plant allowances, treated as attracting allowances as if the machinery or plant were a building. [*CAA 1990, s 13*]. Where, for the purpose of erecting a new building on the same site, costs are incurred in demolishing an existing building, and the costs cannot be taken into account in calculating a balancing adjustment (see 10.15 below) on the demolished building (e.g. because more than 25 (or 50) years has elapsed since the building was first used), the demolition costs may be treated as expenditure on construction of the new building. (Revenue Capital Allowances Manual, CA 1034, 1244).

With effect in relation to any chargeable period or its basis period ending after 26 July 1989, roads on an industrial trading estate will be treated as industrial buildings or structures. [*CAA 1990, s 18(8)*]. Previously, a similar rule operated by extra-statutory concession (see Revenue Pamphlet IR 1, B3). See 10.25 below for certain expenditure on existing buildings treated as being on machinery or plant.

The following are considered by the Revenue to be excluded from being qualifying expenditure: expenditure on obtaining planning permission (although if a builder's costs are inclusive of such expenditure, no apportionment will be made); capitalised interest; public enquiry costs; land drainage and reclamation and landscaping; and legal expenses. (Revenue Capital Allowances Manual, CA 1036, 1039, 1042).

Abortive expenditure. Expenditure (including professional fees) incurred on the construction of a building which never becomes an industrial building, etc. (e.g. because it is never completed) cannot be qualifying expenditure. (Revenue Capital Allowances Manual, CA 1035, 1051).

Buildings bought unused. If the 'relevant interest' (see 10.14 below) in a building etc. is sold before it is used, the purchaser (the last purchaser if more than one before the building is used) is treated as having incurred on its construction, at the time the purchase becomes payable, the lesser of the actual cost of construction and the net purchase price of the interest (excluding any part attributable to the land, see Revenue Capital Allowances Manual, CA 1119). Where the original expenditure was incurred by a builder as part of his trade of constructing such buildings with a view to sale, the purchaser's deemed construction cost is the net purchase price paid by him or, if there have been previous sales unused, the lesser of the net purchase price paid by him and the net price paid to the builder on the first sale. (Note that this latter provision does not apply for agricultural buildings allowances purposes, for which the provisions are otherwise similar.) [*CAA 1990, s 10(1)–(3)*]. Except where the purchase price is specially defined by virtue of an election under *CAA 1990, s 11* (see 10.14 below), the net purchase price of the interest includes acquisition costs, i.e. legal fees, surveyors' fees and stamp duty. (Revenue Capital Allowances Manual, CA 1118).

The initial allowance under *CAA 1990, s 2A* (see 10.13 below) can be claimed by the purchaser (or last purchaser) of an unused building regardless of the date of sale providing some or all the actual construction expenditure falls within those provisions, i.e. it is incurred in, broadly, the year ending 31 October 1993. It can also be claimed where the actual construction expenditure was incurred by a builder (as above) *at any time* before 1 November 1993, the sale occurs between 1 November 1992 and 31 October 1993 inclusive and the vendor has been entitled to the relevant interest since before 1 November 1992. Such construction expenditure is deemed for these purposes to fall within *section 2A*. In both circumstances, it remains a condition that the building comes to be used before 1 January 1995 (see 10.13 below). Where only part of the actual construction expenditure is within *section 2A*, the purchaser's deemed construction cost is computed as above and then divided into a *section 2A* element qualifying for the initial allowance and a residual element qualifying only for writing-down allowances. The *section 2A* element is the proportion of the deemed expenditure that corresponds to the proportion of actual construction expenditure that is within *section 2A*. [*CAA 1990, ss 10(3A), 10C(1)–(10); FA 1993, s 113(3)(4)*].

Appropriation from trading stock. A building appropriated by a builder from trading stock to capital account (with a corresponding market value credit to profit and loss) and let as an industrial building, etc. is eligible for writing-down allowances based on the construction cost (rather than on the transfer value). Initial allowances are not available in these circumstances. (Revenue Capital Allowances Manual, CA 1212).

Arrangements affecting the value of purchased interest. Where certain 'arrangements' have been entered into relating to, or with respect to, any interest in or right over a building, etc., special rules apply for determining any amount which is to be taken to be:

(*a*)   for the purposes of *CAA 1990, ss 10–10C* (buildings bought unused or, after use, from original builder or, in certain cases, within two years after first use (see above and 10.19 below)), the sum paid on the sale of the relevant interest, and

(*b*)   for the purposes of *CAA 1990, ss 1–8* (allowances and charges generally, see above and 10.13–10.19 below), the amount of any sale, etc. moneys payable, where a person is deemed under any of *CAA 1990, ss 10–10C* to have incurred expenditure on the construction of the building, etc. of an amount equal to the price paid on a sale of the relevant interest.

The '*arrangements*' in question are those

(i)   entered into at or before the 'specified time',

(ii)   having the effect at that time of enhancing the value of the relevant interest in the building, etc., and

(iii)   containing any provision having an artificial effect on pricing,

and as regards (iii) above, arrangements are treated as containing such a provision to the extent that they go beyond what, at the time they were entered into, it was reasonable to regard as required by the prevailing market conditions in similar arm's length transactions.

The '*specified time*' is the time of the fixing of the sale price:

(A)   in relation to the determination of an amount within (*a*) above, for the sale in question; and

(B)   in relation to the determination of an amount within (*b*) above, for the sale by reference to which the amount of the deemed expenditure fell to be determined under any of *CAA 1990, ss 10–10C*.

Where these provisions apply, the amount falling to be determined is reduced to the extent that, on a just apportionment, the sale price or the amount of the sale, etc. moneys is more than it would have been if the arrangements had not contained the provision in (iii) above.

These provisions apply to determinations after 28 November 1994, unless the 'specified time' (see above) would be the time of the fixing of a sale price which either became payable before 29 November 1994 or, being an amount becoming payable before 6 April 1995, was fixed by a contract entered into before 29 November 1994. [*FA 1995, s 100*].

10.13   **Initial allowances.** In general, initial allowances were **abolished** for expenditure incurred after 31 March 1986, or after 31 March 1987 in the case of expenditure incurred after 13

10.13 Capital Allowances (Industrial Buildings)

March 1984 under a contract entered into before 14 March 1984 by the person incurring the expenditure. [*FA 1984, 12 Sch 1*]. However, they continue to be available

(*a*)   at a rate of 100% for certain expenditure in enterprise zones (see 10.19 below), and

(*b*)   at a rate of 20% for certain expenditure incurred in, broadly, the year ending 31 October 1993 (see further below),

and to any additional VAT liability (see 10.2(v) above) in respect of such expenditure.

[*CAA 1990, ss 1(1), 2A; FA 1991, 14 Sch 2*]. The general rules governing availability of initial allowances are described below.

Initial allowances were reintroduced by *FA 1993* and are available in respect of qualifying expenditure (see 10.12 above) incurred under a contract entered into in the twelve-month period 1 **November 1992 to 31 October 1993 inclusive** or for the purpose of securing compliance with obligations incurred under a contract entered into during that period, but not for expenditure incurred under a contract entered into for the purpose of securing compliance with obligations under a contract entered into before 1 November 1992. See also below for the rules generally governing availability of initial allowances, which apply equally to these provisions. The qualifying building must come to be used before 1 January 1995, and, if this condition is not satisfied, any initial allowance given will be withdrawn. The initial allowance is **20%** of the expenditure incurred. These provisions do not apply where initial allowances would otherwise be available, i.e. under (*a*) or (*b*) above. They do apply to qualifying hotels (see 10.18 below), and also in respect of any 'additional VAT liability' (see 10.2(v) above) incurred in respect of expenditure falling within these provisions. [*CAA 1990, s 2A; FA 1993, s 113(1)*].

Initial allowances are available to a person incurring qualifying expenditure (see 10.12 above) on a building etc. which is to be in use as an 'industrial building or structure' (see 10.11 above) for a trade carried on by that person or by his lessee or, for licences granted after 9 March 1982, by his licensee. [*CAA 1968, s 1(1) (1A); FA 1982, s 74; CAA 1990, s 1(1)(4)*]. See also 10.12 above as regards buildings bought unused. An initial allowance is given for the chargeable period related to the incurring of the expenditure. [*CAA 1990, s 1(1)*]. Expenditure for the purposes of a trade incurred by a person about to carry it on is treated as if incurred on the day the trade is actually commenced, but this applies only for the purpose of determining the chargeable period for which the allowance may be made (and not, for example, to determine the availability or otherwise of an initial allowance under *CAA 1990, s 2A*–see above). [*CAA 1968, s 1(6); CAA 1990, s 1(10)*]. See also 10.12 above as regards buildings bought unused and 10.2(iii) above generally as to the time at which expenditure is treated as being incurred.

The *rate* of allowance depends on the date on which the expenditure was actually incurred [*FA 1980, s 75(5); FA 1981, s 73(3); FA 1984, 12 Sch 1; CAA 1990, ss 6(5), 19(6)*], except that in the case of expenditure deemed under *CAA 1968, s 5(1)* to have been incurred on the construction of a building bought unused (see 10.12 above) (and disregarding the 20% allowance introduced by *FA 1993* (see above)),

(i)   the reduced rates of allowance for expenditure incurred after 13 March 1984 apply as if the expenditure was incurred at the latest time any expenditure was in fact incurred on its construction [*FA 1984, 12 Sch 1*], and

(ii)   otherwise, where such expenditure is deemed to have been incurred after 10 March 1981, the deemed date governs the rate of allowance [*FA 1981, s 73(3)*].

The **rates** of initial allowance (other than that introduced by *FA 1993*–see above) are

After 5 April 1944	—10%
After 5 April 1952	—Nil
After 14 April 1953	—10%
After 6 April 1954	—Nil
After 17 February 1956	—10%
After 14 April 1958	—15%
After 7 April 1959	— 5%
After 16 January 1966	—15%
After 5 April 1970	—30% (40% if building in development or intermediate area or N. Ireland)
After 21 March 1972	—40%
After 12 November 1974	—50% (20% on hotels and 100% in enterprise zones and on certain small workshops, from later dates, see 10.18, 10.19 and 10.21 below)
After 10 March 1981	—75% (—as above—)
After 13 March 1984	—50% (—as above, omitting reference to workshops from 27 March 1985—)
After 31 March 1985	—25% (—as above—)

Initial allowances may be claimed in whole or part by individuals and partnerships and, for accounting periods ended after 30 September 1993, by companies. For earlier accounting periods, companies may disclaim all or part of such allowances by notice in writing within two years of the end of the accounting period. [*FA 1981, s 73(2); CAA 1990, s 1(5); FA 1990, 17 Sch 2*].

Initial allowances are withdrawn if, when the building etc. comes to be used, it is not an 'industrial building or structure'. [*CAA 1968, s 1(5); CAA 1990, s 1(6)*].

10.14   **Writing-down allowances** are available where a qualifying building (see 10.11 above) is in use as such (or in temporary disuse following such use, see 10.11 above) at the end of a chargeable period (formerly basis period—see 10.2(vi) above). They are available to the person entitled to an interest which is the 'relevant interest' in the building at the end of that period. For this purpose, an entitlement to a highway concession (see 10.11 above) in respect of a road constitutes an interest in the road. A writing-down allowance can be given for the same chargeable period as an initial allowance (see 10.13 above) in respect of the same expenditure. There is no provision for partial claims (see Revenue Capital Allowances Manual, CA 1211), although this does not apply to corporation tax claims.

For expenditure incurred between 6 April 1946 and 5 November 1962 inclusive, the rate of allowance is 2% p.a.

For expenditure incurred **after 5 November 1962**, the rate of allowance is 4% p.a. (but see 10.19, 10.21 below as regards 25% annual allowances in certain cases).

The allowances are calculated on the qualifying expenditure (see 10.12 above) incurred, and continue until the 'residue of expenditure' is nil. The annual writing-down allowance is available in full where the expenditure is incurred during the basis period, but is proportionately reduced or increased where the chargeable period is less or more than twelve months. [*CAA 1990, s 3(1)(2)(4)(5); FA 1991, s 60(3); FA 1994, s 213(2), 26 Sch Pt V(24); FA 1995, s 99(2)*]. For lessors of industrial buildings, however, the basis period is the year of assessment itself, so that the full allowance is available regardless of the date of commencement of letting in the year. [*CAA 1990, s 160(5); FA 1994, s 212(1)*].

Where an 'additional VAT liability' (see 10.2(v) above) is incurred in respect of any qualifying expenditure, the amount of the liability qualifies for writing-down allowances as if it were additional capital expenditure incurred on the construction in question; the 'residue of expenditure' is increased by that amount at the time the liability is incurred. For chargeable or basis periods ending after the time the liability is incurred, writing-down allowances are given of the proportion of the residue of expenditure immediately after that time which the length of the chargeable period bears to the length of the period from the date of the incurring of the liability to the 25th anniversary of the first use of the building for any purpose. Similar provisions apply where an 'additional VAT rebate' (see 10.2(v) above) is made, the residue being reduced by the amount thereof (but see 10.15 below where the rebate exceeds the residue). [*CAA 1990, ss 3(2A)–(2C), 8(12A); FA 1991, 14 Sch 3, 5(2); FA 1994, 26 Sch Pt V(24)*].

If the 'relevant interest' in a building is sold, and the sale is an event which may give rise to a balancing adjustment under *CAA 1990, s 4(1)* (see 10.15 below), subsequent writing-down allowances are given to the purchaser and are calculated on the 'residue of expenditure' immediately after the sale, spread over the period from the date of sale to the 25th anniversary of the first use of the building for any purpose (50th anniversary for expenditure incurred before 6 November 1962). [*CAA 1990, s 3(3); FA 1994, 26 Sch Pt V(24)*].

For a sale *before 18 December 1980* (or pursuant to a contract made before that date) at a time when the building etc. was not in use as an 'industrial building or structure', so that no balancing adjustment arose (see 10.15 below), writing-down allowances to the purchaser (for subsequent basis periods at the end of which the building etc. has reverted to use as an 'industrial building or structure') continue at the rate after the most recent sale while in use as an 'industrial building or structure' or, if there has been no such sale, the full 4% (or 2%) rate. [*CAA 1968, s 2; FA 1981, s 74*].

'*Residue of expenditure*' is original capital expenditure

minus all industrial buildings and scientific research allowances (see 10.52 below) granted, including balancing allowances, and

minus 'notional writing-down allowances' for periods, following first use of the building for any purpose and including, where appropriate, periods before 1946/47, at the end of which the building etc. was not in use as an 'industrial building or structure', and

plus any balancing charges made, and

plus or *minus* any 'additional VAT liability' or 'additional VAT rebate' (see 10.2(v) above) incurred or made in respect of that expenditure.

Where the Crown is entitled to the relevant interest for a period immediately before a sale etc., allowances and charges which could have been made if the building had been in use by a non-corporate trader entitled to that interest for that period are taken into account for this purpose. This treatment applies also to prior entitlement by any person not within the charge to UK tax.

Where a balancing charge arises on the excess of allowances given over adjusted net cost following a sale after non-qualifying use (see 10.15 below), the residue after the sale is restricted to the net sale proceeds. [*CAA 1990, ss 3(2A)(b), 8; FA 1991, 14 Sch 3(1), 5; FA 1994, s 213(3), 26 Sch Pt V(24)*].

'*Notional allowances*' are calculated on the original qualifying expenditure or, if the building etc. has subsequently been sold in circumstances such that a balancing adjustment might have arisen under *CAA 1990, s 4(1)* (see 10.15 below), at the appropriate rate following that sale. [*CAA 1990, s 8(7)*].

'*Relevant interest*' is, in relation to any expenditure incurred on the construction of the building or structure, the interest (freehold or leasehold) in that building etc. to which the person who incurred the expenditure was entitled when he incurred it. Where a person incurs expenditure on a road in respect of which he is entitled to a highway concession (see 10.11 above) and does not otherwise have an interest in the road, the highway concession is the relevant interest in relation to that expenditure. The creation of a subsidiary interest (e.g. leasehold out of freehold) does not transfer the relevant interest. [*CAA 1990, s 20; FA 1991, s 60(5); FA 1995, s 99(6)* and *Woods v R M Mallen (Eng) Ltd Ch D 1969, 45 TC 619*].

But where a long lease is granted out of a 'relevant interest' the lessor and the lessee may jointly elect for allowances to apply to the leasehold interest. The grant of the lease is then regarded as a sale to the lessee, the capital sum as the purchase price, and the lessee's interest as replacing all the lessor's relevant interest. The election is not available if lessor and lessee are 'connected persons' (unless the lessor has statutory functions) or if the sole or main benefit which may be expected to accrue to the lessor is a balancing allowance (see 10.15 below). The election must be in writing to the inspector within two years after the date on which the lease takes effect. [*CAA 1990, s 11*].

Buildings bought after use. Where a person carrying on a trade, consisting wholly or partly of the construction of buildings or structures with a view to their sale, incurs expenditure on such a construction and after the building has been used, he sells the relevant interest in the course of the trade, the purchaser is entitled to allowances as if the original expenditure had been capital expenditure and all appropriate writing-down allowances and balancing allowances or charges (see 10.15 below) had been made to or on the vendor. Normally, the effect will be that the purchaser obtains allowances on the lesser of the net purchase price and the cost of construction. This provision applies in any case where the purchase price becomes payable after 26 July 1989. [*CAA 1990, s 10(4)(5)*]. Previously, a similar rule operated by extra-statutory concession. (Revenue Pamphlet IR 1, B20).

10.15   **Balancing allowances and charges.** A balancing allowance or charge may arise when a building etc. is sold, destroyed or permanently put out of use, or when the 'relevant interest' (see 10.14 above) is lost on termination of a lease or foreign concession, or when a highway concession (see 10.11 above) is brought to or comes to an end (see also below), *provided that* that event occurs within 25 years (50 years for expenditure incurred before 6 November 1962) of the building's first being used. On a sale etc. **after 17 December 1980** (unless pursuant to a contract made on or before that date) of a building etc. which has been an industrial building or structure (or used for scientific research, see 10.52 below) throughout the 'relevant period', the balancing adjustment is calculated as follows. If the 'residue of expenditure' (see 10.14 above) immediately before the sale etc. exceeds the proceeds of any sale, insurance, salvage or compensation, the difference is allowed as a balancing allowance; if it is less, the difference is the subject of a balancing charge. [*CAA 1990, s 4(1)–(4); FA 1995, s 99(3)*]. Where the building etc. has at any time in the 'relevant period' been neither an 'industrial building or structure' nor in use for scientific research, a balancing charge will be made to recover all allowances given where the proceeds of sale, insurance, salvage or compensation equal or exceed the 'capital expenditure'. Where these proceeds are nil or less than the 'capital expenditure', a balancing allowance will be given (or a balancing charge made) on the excess of the 'adjusted net cost' of the building etc. over the allowances given (or vice versa). For this purpose, the allowances given include all industrial buildings, scientific research, and mills, factories or exceptional depreciation allowances, and any balancing charge raised may not exceed the total of such allowances, less any balancing charges previously made. Allowances made to a husband before 6 April 1990 in respect of his wife's relevant interest are treated as having been made to the wife for this purpose on a balancing event on or after that date.

'*Relevant period*' means the period beginning at the time when the building was first used for any purpose and ending with the event giving rise to the balancing adjustment, unless there have been previous sales, when the relevant period begins on the day following the last sale.

'*Capital expenditure*' means the expenditure incurred on the construction of the building (less any balancing charge made in respect of an 'additional VAT rebate'—see below) or, in the case of a 'second-hand' building, the residue of expenditure (see 10.14 above) at the beginning of the relevant period, together (in either case) with the net cost of demolition (as under *CAA 1990, s 8(12)*, see below) if appropriate.

'*Adjusted net cost*' means the amount by which capital expenditure exceeds the proceeds, reduced in the proportion that the period of qualifying use bears to the relevant period. [*CAA 1990, s 4(5)–(12); FA 1991, 14 Sch 4(4)(5); FA 1994, 26 Sch Pt V(24)*].

Successive sales etc. during non-use as industrial building. Where there are two or more sales etc. in a period during which a building etc. is not an 'industrial building or structure', a balancing adjustment arises only on the first such sale etc. [*CAA 1990, s 4(2); FA 1991, 14 Sch 4(2)*].

Additional VAT rebate. Where an 'additional VAT rebate' (see 10.2(v) above) is made in respect of qualifying expenditure, and this exceeds the residue of expenditure (see 10.14 above), a balancing charge, equal to the excess, will be made. [*CAA 1990, s 4(1)(e)(2A); FA 1991, 14 Sch 4(1)(3)*].

In the case of a *highway concession* (see above), no balancing adjustment arises (and writing-down allowances continue) where, on the coming to an end of the concession, the period for which it was granted is extended, i.e. the person entitled to it is granted a renewal of the concession in respect of the whole or part of a road, or he or a CONNECTED PERSON (20) is granted a new concession in respect of the same road (or part of it or a road of which it is part). Where the extension relates to part only of a road, a 'just and reasonable' apportionment is made to determine the expenditure in respect of which a balancing adjustment arises. [*CAA 1990, s 4(2AA)(2AB); FA 1995, s 99(4)*].

On a sale etc. **before 18 December 1980** (or pursuant to a contract made before that date), a balancing adjustment arose only when the building etc. was in use as an 'industrial building or structure' at the time of the sale etc. Any balancing adjustment which did arise was calculated as follows. If the 'residue of expenditure' (see 10.14 above) immediately before the sale etc. exceeded the proceeds of any sale, insurance, salvage or compensation, the difference was allowed as a balancing allowance; if it was less, the difference was the subject of a balancing charge, subject to two restrictions:

(*a*)   the charge may not exceed the total of industrial buildings, scientific research, and mills, factories or exceptional depreciation allowances given; and

(*b*)   where during any part of the 'relevant period' (see below) the building etc. has not attracted writing-down or scientific research allowances, the charge is reduced to the proportion which the parts of the 'relevant period' which were included in basis periods for which such allowances were given bears to the whole of the 'relevant period'. For this purpose the '*relevant period*' is the period from first use of the building to date of the sale etc. or, if that date is not the last day of a basis period, the most recent day before the sale etc. which was the last day of a basis period.

A restriction similar to that in (*b*) above could be placed on balancing allowances on election by the vendor. [*CAA 1968, s 3 as originally enacted*].

Demolition. The net cost (after crediting sales of materials and scrap) of demolition borne by the person concerned is added to 'residue of expenditure' for balancing allowance and balancing charge calculations. [*CAA 1990, s 8(12)*]. Where this is not possible (e.g. because more than 25 (or 50) years has elapsed since the building was first used), and if the holder of the relevant interest demolishes the building for the purpose of erecting a new building on the same site, the demolition costs may be treated as expenditure by the holder on construction of the new building. (Revenue Capital Allowances Manual, CA 1034, 1244).

See also 10.22(i) below as regards certain transactions between connected persons and other anti-avoidance provisions.

10.16   *Examples*

Initial and writing-down allowances and balancing adjustments
Prior to commencing business on 1 June 1993, P incurred the following expenditure.

	£
10.1.93 Plot of land	5,000
20.2.93 Clearing and levelling site	2,000
20.4.93 Construction of factory	50,000
	£57,000

The factory was brought into use for a qualifying purpose on commencement of trade, remained in such use until 1 May 1996, when it was sold to Y for £55,000, being £48,000 for the factory and £7,000 for the land. P drew up accounts annually to 31 May, and did not elect for the second and third years of assessment to be taxed on an actual basis. Y draws up accounts to 30 April, having commenced trading on 1 May 1996, and uses the factory for a qualifying purpose.

The allowances available to P are as follows.

Year of assessment			Residue of expenditure
			£
1993/94	Qualifying expenditure		52,000
	Initial allowance	20% of £52,000	(10,400)
	Writing-down allowance	4% of £52,000	(2,080)
			39,520
1994/95,	Writing-down allowance		
1995/96	for 2 years	4% of £52,000 × 2	(4,160)
			35,360
1996/97	Writing-down allowance		—
	Sale proceeds		(48,000)
	Balancing charge		£12,640

The allowances available to Y are as follows.

Date of first use	1.6.93
Date of purchase by Y	1.5.96
Number of years remaining	22 years 1 month
Residue of expenditure	£48,000

Y is therefore entitled to writing-down allowances of £2,174 p.a. until total allowances reach £48,000. His first writing-down allowance will be given for the period of account 1.5.96 to 30.4.97.

10.16 Capital Allowances (Industrial Buildings)

Notes

(*a*)   Writing-down allowances are first due in 1993/94, being P's first chargeable period, but are *not* restricted to the length of the basis period (which runs from 1 June 1993 to 5 April 1994) (see 10.14 above).

(*b*)   No allowances are due on the cost of the land (see 10.12 above).

(*c*)   P's basis period for 1996/97 is the two years to 31 May 1996 (see 71.20 SCHEDULE D, CASES I AND II) so the balancing event on 1 May 1996 falls into 1996/97.

Non-qualifying purposes and balancing adjustments
A, B and C entered into partnership in 1974 and prepare accounts annually to 31 March. The partnership incurred £40,000 of capital expenditure in 1980 on the construction of a building which was brought into use as an industrial building on 1 April 1981. After three years of use for a qualifying industrial purpose, it was used for three years, from 1 April 1984 to 31 March 1987, for non-qualifying purposes after which the original qualifying activity was resumed until the building was destroyed by fire.

The fire occurred on 1 October 1995 with an insurance recovery of (i) £50,000 (ii) £35,000. The partnership's 1996/97 industrial buildings allowance position will be as follows.

1996/97 Balancing charge

(i)   *Proceeds exceed cost*

Actual allowances given	note (*a*)	£37,600
Balancing charge		£37,600

		£
(ii) *Proceeds less than cost*		
Net cost (£40,000 − £35,000)		5,000
Reduction $\dfrac{3y}{14y\ 6m}$	note (*b*)	(1,034)
Adjusted net cost		3,966
Allowances given	note (*a*)	37,600
Excess		£33,634
Balancing charge		£33,634

Notes

(*a*)   Allowances given in previous years are

	£
Initial allowance £40,000 × 50%	20,000
Writing-down allowances £40,000 × 4% × 11	17,600
	£37,600

Writing-down allowances would not have been given for the three years 1985/86 to 1987/88 as the building was not an industrial building at the end of the basis period for each of those years (see 10.14 above).

118

(*b*)   In example (ii), the net cost is reduced by the proportion which the period of non-qualifying use bears to the total period from first use to date of balancing event (see 10.15 above).

10.17   **Making of allowances and charges.** Allowances to traders are given as a deduction in taxing the trade (but see below), and must be claimed in the annual return [*CAA 1990, s 140(3); FA 1994, s 211*] or, more commonly in practice, in computations accompanying accounts in support of a return. A highway undertaking (see 10.11 above) is treated as a trade. [*CAA 1990, ss 21(5A), 140(6), 140(11) as originally enacted; FA 1991, s 60(6)(8); FA 1994, s 211; FA 1995, s 99(8)*]. See 17.6 CLAIMS as regards error or mistake relief claims following omission. For 1996/97 and earlier years as regards trades commenced before 6 April 1994, allowances are calculated by reference to events in the basis period for the year of assessment of claim (see 71.3 SCHEDULE D, CASES I AND II), except that

(*a*)   where basis periods overlap, expenditure in the common period is treated as incurred only in the earlier period,

(*b*)   expenditure in an interval between two basis periods is treated as incurred in the later period unless it is the period of permanent discontinuance of the trade, in which case it is treated as incurred in the earlier period.

[*CAA 1990, s 160 as originally enacted*].

If the deduction exceeds the assessment for the year, the balance may be carried forward to following years, until exhausted, while the trade continues. [*CAA 1990, s 140(4) as originally enacted*]. Alternatively, allowances may create or enhance a trade loss, see 46 LOSSES generally and 46.10(*e*) LOSSES for restrictions on use of allowances.

Balancing allowances to, and charges on, traders are made in the same way, the latter normally by separate assessment.

For 1994/95 and subsequent years as regards trades commenced after 5 April 1994 and for 1997/98 and subsequent years as regards trades commenced on or before that date, allowances and charges to traders are treated as trading expenses and receipts [*CAA 1990, s 140; FA 1994, s 211*] and are calculated by reference to events in periods of account (see 10.2(vi) above). See 10.2(vii) above as regards transitional relief for unused allowances carried forward under *CAA 1990, s 140(4) as originally enacted* (see above).

Where a balancing adjustment arises on the sale etc. of a building after the cessation of trade, then, for 1995/96 and subsequent years for income tax purposes, allowances and charges are treated as expenses and receipts of a Schedule A business (see 68.4 SCHEDULE A) or, where the lessor is not, in fact, carrying on such a business, of a deemed Schedule A business. For 1994/95 and earlier years for income tax purposes, and continuing for corporation tax purposes, any allowance is given by discharge or repayment of tax (see below), and any charge is raised as below for lessors. [*CAA 1990, s 15(2)(2A); FA 1995, 6 Sch 30*].

Where a balancing charge falls to be made on any person following a period of temporary disuse of a building, and the most recent use was as an industrial building, etc. for the purposes of a trade carried on by that person which has since ceased, the charge is treated as a post-cessation receipt for the purposes of *Sec 105* (allowable deductions from post-cessation receipts, see 60.1 POST-CESSATION ETC. RECEIPTS AND EXPENDITURE) (without prejudice to the deduction of any amounts allowable against the balancing charge under other provisions). This applies where the balancing charge falls to be made on or after 29 April 1996, but similar reliefs were previously available by extra-statutory concession (see Revenue Pamphlet IR 1, B19). [*CAA 1990, s 15A; FA 1996, 39 Sch 1(2)(4)*].

Lessors (and licensors) of industrial buildings etc. may claim allowances for a year of assessment under the normal claims procedure (see 17 CLAIMS). For 1995/96 and subsequent years for income tax purposes, allowances and balancing charges are treated as expenses and receipts of a Schedule A business (see 68.4 SCHEDULE A) or, where the lessor is not, in fact, carrying on such a business, of a deemed Schedule A business. For 1994/95 and earlier years for income tax purposes, and continuing for corporation tax purposes, allowances are given by discharge or repayment of tax, primarily against income from (or balancing charges on) leased industrial buildings etc. Any balance of allowances may be carried forward and set against such income and charges without time limit, or, for income tax, may alternatively be claimed against other income of the same or the following year of assessment. Such a claim had to be made within two years of the end of the year of assessment for which relief is claimed. An election may, in practice, be withdrawn within the time limit for making it, provided that the corresponding liability has not been settled and agreed. Late elections may be accepted where an in-date indication of an intention to elect has in effect been accepted by the inspector. (Revenue Capital Allowances Manual, CA 156, 157). Balancing charges are raised under Sch D, Case VI for income tax and treated as Schedule A income for corporation tax. [*CAA 1990, ss 9(1A)–(6), 141; FA 1994, 26 Sch Pt V(24); FA 1995, 6 Sch 29*]. (For corporation tax relief against profits generally, see Tolley's Corporation Tax under Capital Allowances.)

Tenancies. Where, after 26 March 1980, capital expenditure is incurred on a qualifying building (see 10.11 above) and its first use is by a tenant-occupier for the purposes of a trade, the initial allowance is given for the period in which the expenditure is incurred, even if the tenancy commences on a later date. Expenditure before 27 March 1980 qualified for the allowances when the tenancy began or is treated as incurred on that date if the tenancy had not then begun. [*CAA 1968, s 1(4); FA 1980, s 76; CAA 1990, ss 1(1), 161(2)*].

Double allowances. See 10.2(iv) above.

For allowances to companies generally, see Tolley's Corporation Tax.

10.18   **Hotels.** Expenditure incurred after 11 April 1978 and before 1 April 1986, or before 1 April 1987 under a contract entered into before 14 March 1984 by the person incurring the expenditure, on construction or extension of a qualifying hotel attracts an initial allowance of 20% and **writing-down allowances** of 4% p.a.. The 20% initial allowance under *CAA 1990, s 2A* for expenditure incurred in, broadly, the year ending 31 October 1993 (see 10.13 above) applies equally to qualifying hotels. Subsequent expenditure attracts the writing-down allowance only. For this purpose, expenditure incurred before a trade commenced was not treated under *CAA 1968, s 1(6)* as incurred after the date it was in fact incurred, and expenditure on a building bought unused was treated as having been incurred at the latest time any expenditure was in fact incurred on its construction. Certain expenditure on fire safety and thermal insulation may be treated as on machinery and plant, see 10.25 below.

A '*qualifying hotel*' must: (i) have accommodation in building(s) of a permanent nature; (ii) be open for at least four months during April–October; (iii) have at least ten letting bedrooms, i.e. private bedrooms for letting to the public generally and not normally in same occupation for more than a month; (iv) offer sleeping accommodation consisting wholly or mainly of letting bedrooms and (v) its services must normally include providing breakfast and evening meals, making beds and cleaning rooms. The provision of breakfast and dinner must be offered as a normal event in the carrying on of the hotel business and must not be exceptional or available only on request. (Revenue Pamphlet IR 131, SP 9/87, 22 September 1987). Buildings provided for the welfare of employees are regarded as part of a qualifying hotel but not accommodation for an individual (including a partner) or his household carrying on the hotel, unless under 25% of the total cost (10% for expenditure incurred or deemed incurred before 16 March 1983).

Qualification under the above conditions is by reference to the twelve months ending with the last day of the taxpayer's chargeable or basis period or, if the hotel's trade commences (or fully qualifies) during such period, the twelve months from the commencing or qualifying date. Qualification ceases when the trade ceases. An hotel in temporary disuse (see 10.11 above) ceases to qualify two years after the end of the basis period in which it fell out of use. An hotel outside the UK may qualify provided that the profits, etc. are assessable under Sch D, Case I.

Balancing adjustments arise on the first sale etc. falling within *CAA 1990, s 4* (see 10.15 above) (whether or not the hotel is at the time a 'qualifying hotel') or, if the hotel ceases to qualify and there is no such sale etc. within two years of the end of the chargeable period (formerly basis period—see 10.2(vi) above) in which it ceases to qualify, at the end of that two years, when the hotel is treated as having been sold at open market value. [*FA 1978, s 38, 6 Sch; FA 1985, s 66; CAA 1990, ss 7, 19; FA 1990, 13 Sch 1; FA 1994, 26 Sch Pt V(24)*].

10.19   **Enterprise zones.** An 'enterprise zone' is an area designated as such by the Secretary of State (or Department of the Environment for Northern Ireland). [*CAA 1990, s 21(4)*]. Areas designated are as follows.

Zones whose ten-year life expires after 31 March 1995

Ashfield, see East Midlands (No 7)
Barnsley, see Dearne Valley
Bassetlaw, see East Midlands (No 4)
Dearne Valley (Nos 1 to 6) (from 3 November 1995, *SI 1995 No 2624*)
Derbyshire (NE), see East Midlands (Nos 1 to 3)
Doncaster, see Dearne Valley
Easington, see East Durham
East Durham (Nos 1 to 6) (from 29 November 1995, *SI 1995 No 2812*)
East Midlands (Nos 1 to 3) (from 3 November 1995, *SI 1995 No 2625*)
East Midlands (No 4) (from 16 November 1995, *SI 1995 No 2738*)
East Midlands (No 7) (from 21 November 1995, *SI 1995 No 2758*)
Holmewood, see East Midlands (Nos 1 to 3)
Inverclyde (from 3 March 1989, *SI 1989 No 145*)
Kent (NW) (zones 6 and 7 only) (from 10 October 1986, *SI 1986 No 1557*)
Lanarkshire (Hamilton) (from 1 February 1993, *SI 1993 No 23*)
Lanarkshire (Monklands) (from 1 February 1993, *SI 1993 No 25*)
Lanarkshire (Motherwell) (from 1 February 1993, *SI 1993 No 24*)
Rotherham, see Dearne Valley
Sunderland (Castletown and Doxford Park) (from 27 April 1990, *SI 1990 No 794*)
Sunderland (Hylton Riverside and Southwick) (from 27 April 1990, *SI 1990 No 795*)
Tyne Riverside (North Tyneside) (from 19 February 1996, *SI 1996 No 106*)

Zones whose ten-year life expired before 1 April 1995

Allerdale, see Workington (Allerdale)
Arbroath, see Tayside (Arbroath)
Belfast (from 21 October 1981, *SR 1981 No 309*)
Clydebank (from 3 August 1981, *SI 1981 No 975*)
Corby (from 22 June 1981, *SI 1981 No 764*)
Delyn (from 21 July 1983, *SI 1983 No 896*)
Dudley (Round Oak) (from 3 October 1984, *SI 1984 No 1403*)
Dudley (not Round Oak) (from 10 July 1981, *SI 1981 No 852*)
Dundee, see Tayside (Dundee)
Flixborough, see Glanford (Flixborough)

10.19 Capital Allowances (Industrial Buildings)

Gateshead (from 25 August 1981, *SI 1981 No 1070*)
Glanford (Flixborough) (from 13 April 1984, *SI 1984 No 347*)
Glasgow (from 18 August 1981, *SI 1981 No 1069*)
Hartlepool (from 23 October 1981, *SI 1981 No 1378*)
Invergordon (from 7 October 1983, *SI 1983 No 1359*)
Isle of Dogs (from 26 April 1982, *SI 1982 No 462*)
Kent (NW) (from 31 October 1983, *SI 1983 No 1452* (zones 1 to 5 only))
Lancashire (NE) (from 7 December 1983, *SI 1983 No 1639*)
Liverpool (Speke) (from 25 August 1981, *SI 1981 No 1072*)
London, see Isle of Dogs
Londonderry (from 13 September 1983, *SR 1983 No 226*)
Lower Swansea Valley (from 11 June 1981, *SI 1981 No 757*)
Lower Swansea Valley (No 2) (from 6 March 1985, *SI 1985 No 137*)
Middlesbrough (Britannia) (from 8 November 1983, *SI 1983 No 1473*)
Milford Haven Waterway (North Shore) (from 24 April 1984, *SI 1984 No 443*)
Milford Haven Waterway (South Shore) (from 24 April 1984, *SI 1984 No 444*)
Newcastle (from 25 August 1981, *SI 1981 No 1071*)
Rotherham (from 16 August 1983, *SI 1983 No 1007*)
Salford Docks (from 12 August 1981, *SI 1981 No 1024*)
Scunthorpe (Normanby Ridge and Queensway) (from 23 September 1983, *SI 1983 No 1304*)
Speke, see Liverpool (Speke)
Swansea, see Lower Swansea Valley and Lower Swansea Valley (No 2)
Tayside (Arbroath) (from 9 January 1984, *SI 1983 No 1816*)
Tayside (Dundee) (from 9 January 1984, *SI 1983 No 1817*)
Telford (from 13 January 1984, *SI 1983 No 1852*)
Trafford Park (from 12 August 1981, *SI 1981 No 1025*)
Wakefield (Dale Lane and Kingsley) (from 23 September 1983, *SI 1983 No 1305*)
Wakefield (Langthwaite Grange) (from 31 July 1981, *SI 1981 No 950*)
Wellingborough (from 26 July 1983, *SI 1983 No 907*)
Workington (Allerdale) (from 4 October 1983, *SI 1983 No 1331*)

Advantageous provisions apply to expenditure on the construction of an industrial building or structure, a qualifying hotel or a commercial building or structure, which is incurred (or contract entered into) within ten years of the inclusion of the site in an enterprise zone. Expenditure incurred more than 20 years after a site was first included in an enterprise zone does not attract enterprise zone allowances, regardless of when the contract for the expenditure was entered into. [*CAA 1990, ss 1(1)(2), 17A; FA 1990, 13 Sch 1; F(No 2)A 1992, 13 Sch 10*].

'*Qualifying hotel*' has the same meaning as in *CAA 1990, s 19*, see 10.18 above. (Note that any hotel not qualifying under this heading will qualify as a commercial building.)

'*Commercial building or structure*' means a building or structure, other than an industrial building or a qualifying hotel, which is used for the purposes of a trade, profession or vocation or as an office for any purpose, but does not include any building in use as, or as part of, a dwelling house. [*CAA 1990, s 21(5)*].

The allowances given are as follows.

An initial allowance of 100% is given but an individual or partnership or, for accounting periods ended after 30 September 1993, a company need not claim the full amount; for earlier accounting periods, a company may disclaim all or part of the initial allowance by notice in writing to the inspector within two years after the relevant accounting period. If any part of the initial allowance is not claimed then **writing-down allowances at 25%** p.a. of cost on the straight line basis will apply to the unclaimed balance. [*CAA 1990, ss 1, 6; FA 1990, 17 Sch 2*].

For the above purposes, the following special rules apply.

(i) *Date expenditure incurred.* *CAA 1990, s 1(10)* (pre-trading expenditure treated as incurred on first day of trading, see 10.13 above) does not apply in determining whether expenditure attracts enterprise zone allowances (i.e. whether it is incurred at a time when the building etc. is in an enterprise zone).

As regards buildings bought unused, where the purchase price becomes payable after 15 December 1991, the normal rules under *CAA 1990, s 10* apply (see 10.12 above), except that:

(*a*) where some or all of the actual construction expenditure is incurred (or incurred under a contract entered into) within ten years of the inclusion of the site in an enterprise zone, a corresponding proportion of the purchaser's deemed expenditure is treated as giving rise to entitlement to enterprise zone allowances, notwithstanding that it may be deemed to have been incurred outside that ten-year period;

(*b*) where (*a*) does not apply, the purchaser's deemed expenditure is treated as not giving rise to entitlement to enterprise zone allowances, notwithstanding that it may be deemed to have been incurred during the ten-year period.

Where some of the actual construction expenditure falls within (*a*) above and some or all of the balance would qualify for a 20% initial allowance by virtue of the provisions in 10.12 above, the above provisions and those in 10.12 above interact. The purchaser can thus obtain a 100% enterprise zone initial allowance on part of his deemed expenditure and the 20% initial allowance on another part or, where appropriate, on the balance.

Where the purchase price of a building bought unused became payable before 16 December 1991, *CAA 1990, s 10(1)* does not apply, and the Revenue accept this as allowing the purchaser to treat his expenditure as having been incurred (or incurred under a contract entered into) on the date(s) the actual construction expenditure was incurred (or contract entered into). (Revenue Press Release 16 December 1991). [*CAA 1990, ss 10A, 10C(11); F(No 2)A 1992, 13 Sch 2–7, 14; FA 1993, s 113(4)*].

(ii) *Buildings purchased within two years of first use.* Where some or all of the construction expenditure on a building first used after 15 December 1991 is incurred (or incurred under a contract entered into) within ten years of the inclusion of the site in an enterprise zone, and the 'relevant interest' (see 10.14 above) is sold during the two years (but see below) following the first use of the building (whether or not there have been any sales while the building was unused), then on that sale (or the first such sale) the normal balancing allowance or charge rules apply to the vendor (see 10.15 above), but the purchaser is deemed to have incurred expenditure on purchase of a building bought unused (see 10.12 and (i) above). A proportion of the deemed expenditure corresponding to the proportion of the actual construction expenditure which was incurred within ten years of the inclusion of the site in the enterprise zone is treated as giving rise to entitlement to enterprise zone allowances, notwithstanding that it may be deemed to have been incurred outside the ten-year period. The balance of the deemed expenditure does not attract enterprise zone allowances. If the purchase is directly from a person who constructed the building in the course of a trade of constructing such buildings for sale, the part of the purchaser's deemed expenditure which does *not* attract enterprise zone allowances is calculated by reference to the actual expenditure of the vendor if that is less than the price actually paid by the purchaser. [*CAA 1990, s 10B; F(No 2)A 1992, 13 Sch 8, 9, 15*]. The two year period is extended to 31 August 1994 where it would otherwise end within the period beginning 13 January 1994 and ending 31 August 1994, and the relevant interest is sold within that period and outside the two year period. [*FA 1994, s 121*].

(iii) *Machinery and plant* which is to be an integral part of a building will not be subject to the restriction of first-year allowances to lessors under *CAA 1990, s 22(4)* (see 10.35(*a*) below) (and see now below).

(iv) *Balancing charge on realisation of capital value.* Where capital expenditure on construction of a building etc. in an enterprise zone has been incurred (or is deemed to have been incurred) under a contract entered into after 12 January 1994 (or which becomes unconditional after 25 February 1994), and 'capital value' is received in respect of the building etc., a balancing charge (but not a balancing allowance) may arise. This applies generally where the payment is made (or an agreement to make it made) seven years or less after the date of the agreement relating to the expenditure (or the date on which that agreement became unconditional). Where, however, there are certain guaranteed exit arrangements, it applies throughout the normal balancing adjustment period (i.e. 25 years from first use, see 10.15 above).

'*Capital value*' is realised when a sum is paid which is attributable to an interest in land to which the relevant interest in the building etc. in question is or will be subject, e.g. where a lease is granted out of the relevant interest, unless *CAA 1990, s 11* (see 10.14 above) applies to the grant of that interest. There are detailed provisions as to the form and amount of the capital value, and as to its attribution to the grant of the interest. See Revenue Capital Allowances Manual, CA 1440 *et seq.*.

[*CAA 1990, s 4(1)(dd)(9A), 4A; FA 1994, s 120*].

An 'additional VAT liability' (see 10.2(v) above) incurred in respect of qualifying expenditure, within ten years of the inclusion of the site in the enterprise zone, is itself qualifying expenditure for the chargeable period related to the incurring of the liability. [*CAA 1990, s 1(1A); FA 1991, 14 Sch 1*]. Where a 100% initial allowance was not claimed on the expenditure to which the additional VAT liability relates, a 100% allowance may nevertheless generally be claimed for the additional VAT liability. If less than the full 100% allowance is claimed for the additional VAT liability, writing-down allowances for the whole of the expenditure on the building, etc. in question will be recomputed as under 10.14 above, resulting in a substantial reduction in the rate of annual allowance. See Revenue Capital Allowances Manual, CA 1216.

For balancing adjustments after non-qualifying use, see 10.15 above. For transfers between connected persons, etc., see 10.22(i) below.

For the special treatment for tax purposes of investors in enterprise zone property trusts, see *SI 1988 No 267* and *SI 1992 No 571*.

Machinery or plant. Expenditure on machinery or plant, or on thermal insulation treated as machinery or plant under *CAA 1990, s 67*, which is to be an integral part of an industrial or commercial building in an enterprise zone may be treated as part of the expenditure on construction of the building, and so attract the 100% initial allowance (see 10.2(iv) above). A claim for expenditure on machinery or plant, etc. to be so treated does not prevent a subsequent purchaser of the building from claiming machinery and plant allowances on that expenditure and industrial buildings allowances on the fabric of the building. (Revenue Capital Allowances Manual, CA 1060).

10.20 *Examples*

(i)

In 1994, J, a builder, incurs expenditure of £400,000 on the construction of a building in a designated enterprise zone. The whole of the expenditure was incurred (or contracted for) within ten years of the site's first being included in the zone. In January 1995, he sells the building unused to K for £600,000 (excluding land). In February 1995, K lets the building to a trader who immediately brings it into use as a supermarket. K claims a reduced initial allowance of £50,000. In March 1997, he sells the building to L for £750,000 (excluding land).

K's allowances are as follows.

			Residue of expenditure
		£	£
1994/95	Qualifying expenditure		600,000
	Initial allowance (maximum 100%)	50,000	
	Writing-down allowance 25% of £600,000	150,000	
	Total IBA due	200,000	(200,000)
1995/96	Writing-down allowance	150,000	(150,000)
			250,000
1996/97	Writing-down allowance	—	—
	Sale proceeds		(750,000)
			£500,000
	Balancing charge (restricted to allowances given)		£350,000

Notes

(a)   K's qualifying expenditure would normally be the lesser of cost of construction and the net price paid by him for the building. However, on purchase from a builder, whose profit on sale is taxable as a trading profit, his qualifying expenditure is equal to the net price paid for the relevant interest (excluding the land). See 10.12, 10.19(i) above.

(b)   K's allowances as a non-trader will be given by way of discharge or repayment of tax primarily against letting income from buildings qualifying for IBAs. For 1995/96 onwards, allowances and balancing charges are treated as expenses and receipts of a Schedule A business. See 10.17 above. K could have claimed a 100% initial allowance in 1994/95 if he had so wished.

(c)   Providing the building continues to be used for a qualifying purpose, L can claim writing-down allowances over the remainder of the 25-year writing-down period. His qualifying expenditure is restricted to £600,000, i.e. the residue of expenditure (£250,000) plus the balancing charge on K. See 10.14 above.

(d)   In this example, the first sale after the building was first used took place just over two years after the date of first use. If the sale had taken place within two years after first use, the balancing charge on K would have been computed in the same manner, but L could have claimed an initial allowance and 25% writing-down allowances as if he had bought the building unused. His qualifying expenditure would again have been restricted to £600,000, being the lesser of the price paid by him for the relevant interest in the building and that paid on the original purchase by K from the builder. See 10.19(ii) above.

10.20   Capital Allowances (Industrial Buildings)

(ii)
The facts are as in (i) above, except that, of the £400,000 construction expenditure actually incurred, only £360,000 is incurred (or contracted for) within ten years of the site's first being included in an enterprise zone, and the first sale occurred after the expiry of that ten-year period.

K's qualifying expenditure of £600,000 (arrived at as in (i) above) is divided into an enterprise zone element and a non-enterprise zone element.

The enterprise zone element is

$$£600,000 \times \frac{360,000}{400,000} = \underline{£540,000}$$

The non-enterprise zone element is   £600,000 − £540,000 = £60,000

The non-enterprise zone element does not qualify for enterprise zone allowances. See 10.19(i) above. (It could have qualified for normal IBAs if the building had been an industrial building.)

K's allowances are as follows.

		£	Residue of expenditure £
1994/95	Qualifying expenditure (enterprise zone element)		540,000
	Initial allowance (maximum 100%)	50,000	
	Writing-down allowance (25% of £540,000)	135,000	
		185,000	(185,000)
1995/96	Writing-down allowance	135,000	(135,000)
			220,000
1996/97	Writing-down allowance	—	—
	Sale proceeds £750,000 × $\frac{540,000}{600,000}$		(675,000)
			£455,000
	Balancing charge (restricted to allowances given)		£320,000

L's qualifying expenditure is £540,000, i.e. the residue of £220,000 plus the balancing charge of £320,000 on K.

Note

(a)   The apportionment of sale proceeds in 1996/97 is considered to be a 'just apportionment' as required by *CAA 1990, s 21(3)*.

10.21   **Small and very small workshops.** Expenditure incurred after 26 March 1980 and before 27 March 1985 on the construction of an industrial building (or permanently separated part of a larger building, intended and suitable for separate occupation, but common facilities are excepted) of, before 27 March 1983, 2,500 square feet or less, and, after 26 March 1983 and before 27 March 1985, 1,250 square feet or less of gross internal floor space (including ancillary works) qualified for an initial allowance of 100% with similar rights to reduce or disclaim this and receive writing-down allowances of 25% as described in 10.19 above. Similarly the provisions stated at (i), (iii) in 10.19 above applied also to small workshops. [*FA 1980, s 75, 13 Sch Pt I; FA 1982, s 73*]. (Revenue Pamphlet IR 131, SP 6/80, 9 July 1980). For balancing adjustments after non-qualifying use, see 10.15 above. For transfers between connected persons, etc., see 10.22(i) below.

See Revenue Pamphlet IR 131, SP 4/80, 26 March 1980 for the application of these provisions where individual units in a larger development did not exceed 2,500 square feet.

The limit of 1,250 square feet could be exceeded in certain cases where existing buildings were converted into separate units. [*FA 1983, s 31*].

10.22   **General matters**

(i)   *Connected persons and other anti-avoidance provisions.* Special provisions apply to sales of industrial buildings etc. where

(*a*)   the sale results in no change of control, or

(*b*)   the sole or main benefit apparently arising is the obtaining of an industrial buildings allowance.

For transfers after 10 March 1981 (unless contracted for on or before that date), (*a*) is extended to cover also sales between CONNECTED PERSONS (20), and transfers other than by way of sale, and (*b*) includes cases where the anticipated benefit is a reduction in a charge or the *increase* of an allowance. Normally, where these provisions apply, market value is substituted for purchase price (if different). However, for transactions within (*a*) but not (*b*), the parties may elect for the substitution of the residue of expenditure (see 10.14 above) if this is lower than market value, and for any subsequent balancing charge on the buyer to be calculated by reference to allowances given to both buyer and seller. Such an election is *not* available if the circumstances are such that an allowance or charge which otherwise would or might fall, in consequence of the sale, to be made to or on *any* of the parties to the sale cannot fall to be made. For sales after 28 July 1988, the election must be made within two years after the sale. The election also covers qualifying hotels and commercial buildings etc. in enterprise zones. For sales of industrial buildings etc. before 16 March 1993 (or under a pre-16 March 1993 contract or a contract entered into for the purpose of securing compliance with obligations under a pre-16 March 1993 contract) the circumstances in which an election was not available were that either party was non-UK resident and that an allowance or charge could not be made to or on *that* party in consequence of the sale. [*CAA 1990, ss 21(6)(7), 157, 158; FA 1993, s 117(2)(4)(5); FA 1994, s 119(1)*].

Balancing allowances (see 10.15 above) are restricted on sales after 13 June 1972 where the relevant interest (see 10.14 above) in an industrial building etc. is sold subject to a subordinate interest (e.g. in a sale and lease-back) and either

(1)   the seller, the purchaser of the interest, and the grantee of the subordinate interest (or any two of them) are CONNECTED PERSONS (20), or

(2)   the sole or main benefit appears to be the obtaining of an industrial buildings allowance.

In such cases the net sale proceeds are increased, in determining any balancing allowance, by

(A) where less than a commercial rent is payable under the subordinate interest, the difference between actual sale proceeds and open market value had a commercial rent been payable, and

(B) the amount of any premium receivable for the grant of the subordinate interest and not chargeable under *Sec 34* (see 68.27 SCHEDULE A),

but not by more than is required to eliminate any balancing allowance. The residue of expenditure (see 10.14 above) following the sale is, however, calculated as if the balancing allowance had been made without the application of these provisions. [*CAA 1990, s 5*].

(ii) *Double allowances.* See 10.2(iv) above.

(iii) *Partnerships* are entitled to industrial buildings allowances in respect of qualifying expenditure (see 10.12 above) on industrial buildings or structures (see 10.11 above).

On a change of partnership, if the trade is treated as continuing, unexhausted allowances are carried forward, and subsequent balancing adjustments (see 10.15 above) made as if the new partnership had carried on the trade before the change. Allowances continue to be calculated as though there had been no change, being apportioned between the old and the new partnerships for the year of assessment of the change. If however the trade is treated as ceasing, only continuing partners may carry forward their share of unexhausted allowances, as a loss to set against their future profit shares. [*CAA 1990, s 152(3)*]. See also (iv) below as regards allowances on successions to trades.

(iv) *Successions.* Where a trade changes hands (other than in certain partnership changes (see (iii) above)) unexhausted allowances may not be carried forward to the new owner. Unless the change is not treated as a permanent cessation (see 53.6 PARTNERSHIPS), any asset transferred, without being sold, to the new owner for continuing use in the trade is treated as sold at open market value on the date of change, although no initial allowance is available to the new owner. [*CAA 1990, s 152(1)(2)*].

10.23 **'KNOW-HOW'** [*Sec 530*]

Expenditure on acquiring 'know-how' for use in a trade (expenditure before commencement of the trade being treated as incurred on commencement) attracts **writing-down** and **balancing allowances** (as below), insofar as it is not otherwise deductible for income or corporation tax purposes. [*Sec 530(1)(7)*]. For expenditure incurred after 31 March 1986, a balancing charge may arise (see below). For receipts arising from sales of know-how, see generally 71.66 SCHEDULE D, CASES I AND II.

'*Know-how*' means any industrial information and techniques of assistance in (*a*) manufacturing or processing goods or materials, (*b*) working, or searching, etc. for, mineral deposits, or (*c*) agricultural, forestry or fishing operations. [*Sec 533(7)*].

Expenditure incurred before 1 April 1986

A *writing-down allowance* of one-sixth per annum of the expenditure incurred is available during the six years beginning with the chargeable period in whose basis period the expenditure was incurred. A *balancing allowance* is given of the expenditure unallowed on the trade ceasing during that six years. [*Sec 530(6)(8)*].

Expenditure incurred after 31 March 1986

For any chargeable period for which a trader has 'qualifying expenditure' exceeding any 'disposal value' to be brought into account, a *writing-down allowance* is made of 25% of the excess (proportionately reduced or increased where the period is less or more than one year, or if the trade has been carried on for part only of a chargeable period) except that a *balancing allowance* of the whole of the excess is made if the chargeable period is that of permanent discontinuance of the trade. If qualifying expenditure is less than the disposal value to be brought into account, a *balancing charge* is made on the trader in the amount of the difference.

'*Qualifying expenditure*' of a chargeable period is the aggregate of any capital expenditure on know-how incurred before the end of the chargeable period or its basis period which has not, in whole or part, previously formed part of qualifying expenditure, and any unallowed balance of expenditure brought forward from the previous chargeable period.

The *disposal value* to be brought into account for any chargeable period is the net proceeds of any sale in that period or its basis period (including any consideration for a restrictive covenant connected with the disposal) of know-how on which the trader incurred expenditure for use in a trade carried on by him.

[*Secs 530(2)–(5), 531(8); FA 1994, s 214(6), 26 Sch Pt V(24)*].

Excess allowances may be used as under Dredging (10.7 above).

10.24　**MACHINERY AND PLANT**

Allowances are available in respect of certain capital expenditure on machinery and plant etc. (see 10.25 below) to the person incurring the expenditure, where the machinery or plant etc. is provided

(i)　for the purposes of a trade carried on by him, or

(ii)　for letting (insofar as not included in (i) above) other than for use in a dwelling-house or flat.

[*CAA 1990, ss 22(1), 24(1), 61(1)*].

For this purpose, provision for the purposes of a profession or vocation, or the occupation of woodlands assessable under Schedule D, or necessarily for use in the performance of the duties of an office or employment, or for use in estate management or the management of investment companies etc., satisfies the requirement for provision for the purposes of a trade. [*CAA 1990, s 27*]. See 75.43 SCHEDULE E for special provisions relating to private cars used partly for the purposes of an office or employment. Plant provided by a vicar so as to give visual sermons was held not to comply with the requirement that it be provided necessarily for use in the performance of his duties (*White v Higginbottom Ch D 1982, 57 TC 283*). Expenditure on assets used for providing business entertainment (other than for certain overseas customers) is, however, excluded. [*Sec 577(1)(c)*].

Allowances in respect of leased assets are available to the lessor and not the lessee, irrespective of the accounting treatment adopted. (Revenue Press Release 27 October 1986). For a case in which leasing arrangements did not amount to a trade, see *Gold Fields Mining and Industrial Ltd v GKN (United Kingdom) plc Ch D, [1996] STC 173*.

Unless otherwise specified, the provisions described below apply to expenditure incurred after 26 October 1970. See 10.37 below as regards expenditure incurred on or before that date and certain other expenditure subject to the earlier provisions.

The main elements of the scheme of allowances are dealt with as follows.

10.25 Capital Allowances (Machinery and Plant)

10.25 **Eligible expenditure.** The capital expenditure eligible for allowances includes that on alteration of existing buildings incidental to the installation of machinery or plant for trade purposes [*CAA 1990, s 66*], on demolition of machinery etc. which it replaces [*CAA 1990, s 62*], and, in practice, on its removal from one site to another.

'*Capital expenditure*' excludes any sums allowed as deductions in computing the claimant's profits and any sums payable under deduction of tax. [*CAA 1990, s 159(1)*].

Whether the machinery or plant is new or secondhand is generally irrelevant (but see 10.38(iii) below as regards certain sales between connected persons etc.).

Meaning of machinery or plant: leading cases. Machinery and plant are not statutorily defined. *Machinery* is accordingly given its ordinary meaning, but *plant* has been considered in many cases. It includes apparatus kept for permanent employment in the trade, but a line is drawn between that which performs a function in the business operations (which may be plant) and that which provides the place or setting in which these operations are performed (which is not). See *Cole Bros Ltd v Phillips HL 1982, 55 TC 188* (electric wiring and fittings in department store held not to be plant) and *St. John's School v Ward CA 1974, 49 TC 524* (prefabricated school buildings held not to be plant) and contrast *CIR v Barclay, Curle & Co Ltd HL 1969, 45 TC 221* (dry docks, including cost of excavation, held to be plant) and *CIR v Scottish & Newcastle Breweries Ltd HL 1982, 55 TC 252* (lighting and decor of licensed premises held to be plant). If an item used for carrying on a business does not form part of the premises and is not stock-in-trade, then it is plant (*Wimpy International Ltd v Warland CA 1988, 61 TC 51*).

Permanent employment demands some degree of durability, see *Hinton v Maden & Ireland Ltd HL 1959, 38 TC 391* (shoe manufacturer's knives and lasts, average life three years, held to be plant). In practice, a life of two years or more is generally sufficient.

Held to rank as plant. Movable office partitions (*Jarrold v John Good & Sons Ltd CA 1962, 40 TC 681*); mezzanine platforms installed in a warehouse (but not ancillary lighting) (*Hunt v Henry Quick Ltd Ch D 1992, 65 TC 108*); swimming pools for use on caravan site (*Cooke v Beach Station Caravans Ltd Ch D 1974, 49 TC 514*); grain silos (*Schofield v R & H Hall Ltd CA(NI) 1974, 49 TC 538*); barrister's books (*Munby v Furlong CA 1977, 50 TC 491*); Building Society window screens (*Leeds Permanent Building Society v Proctor Ch D 1982, 56 TC 293*); light fittings (*Wimpy International Ltd v Warland CA 1988, 61 TC 51*).

In relation to certain 'qualifying films' (broadly, British or European films, see 71.57 SCHEDULE D, CASES I AND II), a *film production* business producing and retaining a master print of a film with an anticipated life of two years or more may elect to treat the cost as capital expenditure on plant. See *Ensign Tankers (Leasing) Ltd v Stokes HL 1992, 64 TC 617* for relief to investor in film production partnership. Otherwise, see now 71.57 SCHEDULE D, CASES I AND II for relief of production costs treated as revenue expenditure and for special relief for preliminary expenditure.

Held not to be plant. Stallions (*Earl of Derby v Aylmer KB 1915, 6 TC 665*); wallpaper pattern books (*Rose & Co Ltd v Campbell Ch D 1967, 44 TC 500*); canopy over petrol-filling station (*Dixon v Fitch's Garage Ltd Ch D 1975, 50 TC 509*); ship used as floating restaurant

(*Benson v Yard Arm Club Ltd CA 1979, 53 TC 67*); false ceilings (*Hampton v Fortes Autogrill Ltd Ch D 1979, 53 TC 691*); a football stand (*Brown v Burnley Football Co Ltd Ch D 1980, 53 TC 357*); an inflatable tennis court cover (*Thomas v Reynolds Ch D 1987, 59 TC 502*); shop fronts, wall and floor coverings, suspended floors, ceilings and stairs, etc. (*Wimpy International Ltd v Warland, Associated Restaurants Ltd v Warland CA 1988, 61 TC 51*); permanent quarantine kennels (allowances having been granted for movable kennels) (*Carr v Sayer Ch D 1992, 65 TC 15*); lighting ancillary to mezzanine platform installation qualifying as plant (*Hunt v Henry Quick Ltd Ch D 1992, 65 TC 108*); a planteria (a form of glasshouse, see also below) (*Gray v Seymours Garden Centre (Horticulture) CA, [1995] STC 706*); access site and wash hall containing car wash equipment (*Attwood v Anduff Car Wash Ltd Ch D, [1996] STC 110*).

In *McVeigh v Arthur Sanderson & Sons Ltd Ch D 1968, 45 TC 273*, held that cost of blocks etc. of a wallpaper manufacturer (admitted to be plant) should include something for the designs but the designs, following *Daphne v Shaw KB 1926, 11 TC 256*, were not plant. (*Daphne v Shaw* has since been overruled by *Munby v Furlong* above.)

Interest etc. on money borrowed to finance purchases of plant and charged to capital, held not eligible for capital allowances (*Ben-Odeco Ltd v Powlson HL 1978, 52 TC 459* and cf *Van Arkadie v Sterling Coated Materials Ltd Ch D 1982, 56 TC 479*). It is understood that the Revenue consider this exclusion to apply also to architects' fees and preliminary expenses on plant included in building works. (Tolley's Practical Tax 1983 p 28.)

Cable television. The cost of provision and installation of ducting in connection with construction of cable television networks is regarded as expenditure on machinery or plant. (Revenue Press Release 15 March 1984).

Glasshouses are likely to be accepted as plant only where, during construction, sophisticated environmental control systems are permanently installed, incorporating e.g. a computer system controlling heating, temperature and humidity control, automatic ventilation systems and automatic thermal or shade screens. (Revenue Tax Bulletin November 1992 p 46). See for example *Gray v Seymours Garden Centre (Horticulture) CA, [1995] STC 706*, where a 'planteria' was held to be premises.

Certain expenditure on buildings is treated for capital allowance purposes as being on machinery and plant (unless a deduction could be obtained otherwise).

(i)   *Fire safety expenditure* incurred in a trade in taking steps specified in a notice under *Fire Precautions Act 1971, s 5(4)* (or which might have been so specified but were in fact specified in a letter or other document from the fire authority on application for a fire certificate under that *Act*) and similarly for expenditure incurred in order to avoid restriction of use of premises by an order under *section 10* of that *Act*. [*CAA 1990, s 69*]. Applies by Order to hotels and boarding houses (*SI 1972 No 238*) and to premises of factories, offices, shops and railways with minimum of 10 employees (*SI 1976 No 2009*). *Lessors of such premises* may claim allowances on contributions towards tenants' qualifying expenditure (under *CAA 1990, s 154*) or own similar direct expenditure. All these provisions also apply by concession to NI. (Revenue Pamphlet IR 1, B16.)

(ii)   *Thermal insulation of existing industrial building.* If the expenditure is by a person letting the building (otherwise than in course of trade), then,

(a)   for 1995/96 and subsequent years for income tax purposes, the allowances are given as expenses of a Schedule A business (see 68.4 SCHEDULE A), the letting being deemed to be in connection with such a business whether or not such a business is, in fact, carried on; and

(b)   for 1994/95 and earlier years for income tax purposes, and continuing for corporation tax purposes, the allowances are primarily against income (I) from any industrial building taxed under Schedule A, or (II) arising from a balancing charge on an industrial building. [*Sec 32(1B)(1C); CAA 1990, s 67; FA 1994, 26 Sch Pt V(24); FA 1995, 6 Sch 8(3), 32*].

(iii) *Sports ground expenditure* incurred by a trade to comply with a safety certificate issued or to be issued under the *Safety of Sports Grounds Act 1975* or certified by local authority as falling within requirements if such certificates had been applied for. Also, expenditure incurred after 31 December 1988 by a trade in respect of a 'regulated stand' (as defined by the *Fire Safety and Safety of Places of Sport Act 1987*) to comply with a safety certificate (as defined by that *Act*) issued for the stand or to take steps specified by the local authority as being necessary under the terms, or proposed terms, of such a safety certificate issued, or to be issued, by it. [*CAA 1990, s 70*]. See also 10.2(ii) above as regards certain contributions to expenditure.

(iv) *Quarantine premises.* Expenditure incurred before 16 March 1988 (or before 1 April 1989 under a contract entered into before 16 March 1988) by a trader to alter or replace authorised quarantine premises (as defined under the *Diseases of Animals Act 1950*) to comply with legal requirements. [*FA 1980, s 71; FA 1985, 14 Sch 15; FA 1988, s 94*].

On any disposal the disposal value (see 10.30 below) of (i)–(iv) above is taken as nil.

(v) *Hotels and restaurants.* The Revenue regard as eligible for capital allowances expenditure on *apparatus* to provide electric light or power, hot water, central heating, ventilation or air conditioning, alarm and sprinkler systems. Also on cost of hot water pipes, baths, wash basins etc. Also expenditure on alterations to *existing* buildings which is incidental to the installation of plant and machinery. (CCAB Statement, 9 August 1977.) See now *Cole Bros Ltd v Phillips HL 1982, 55 TC 188* and *CIR v Scottish & Newcastle Breweries Ltd HL 1982, 55 TC 252*.

See below for provisions restricting allowances for certain expenditure on buildings and structures.

Expenditure on security assets. Expenditure incurred after 5 April 1989, by an individual, or partnership of individuals, carrying on a trade, profession or vocation, in connection with the provision for or use by the individual, or any of them, of a security asset (being an asset which improves personal security), is treated as if it were capital expenditure on machinery or plant qualifying for writing-down allowances (see 10.28 below). On any disposal the disposal value (see 10.30 below) is taken as nil. These provisions do not apply where the expenditure is otherwise eligible, either by means of writing-down allowances or as a Schedule D, Case I or II deduction, for tax relief. They apply only where certain conditions, very similar to those described in 71.80 SCHEDULE D, CASES I AND II, are satisfied, both as regards the provision or use of the asset and the type of asset that may qualify. An appropriate proportion of the expenditure may qualify in cases where the asset is intended to be used only partly to improve personal physical security. [*CAA 1990, ss 71, 72*]. See also 75.35 SCHEDULE E.

Computer software. Where capital expenditure is incurred after 9 March 1992 on the acquisition of computer software for trade purposes, the software, if it would not otherwise be machinery or plant, is treated as such for capital allowance purposes. Similarly where capital expenditure is incurred after that date in acquiring for trade purposes a right to use or otherwise deal with computer software, both the right and the software are treated as machinery or plant provided for trade purposes and (so long as entitlement to the right continues) as belonging to the person incurring the expenditure.

Where, after 9 March 1992, a right is granted to another person to use or deal with the whole or part of software or rights which are treated as machinery or plant, and the consideration for the grant consists of (or would if it were in money consist of) a capital sum, a disposal value (see 10.28 below) has to be brought into account (unless the software or rights have previously begun to be used wholly or partly for non-trade purposes, or the trade for which they were used has been permanently discontinued). The amount of the disposal value to be brought into account is the net consideration in money received for the grant, plus any insurance moneys or other capital compensation received in respect of the software by reason of any event affecting that consideration, except that open market value is substituted where

(a)   the consideration for the grant was not, or not wholly, in money, or

(b)   no consideration, or money consideration less than open market value, was given for the grant.

(b) does not, however, apply where there is a Schedule E charge in respect of the grant of the right, or where the person to whom the right is granted can obtain machinery or plant or scientific research allowances for his expenditure.

Where a disposal value falls to be calculated in relation to software or rights over which a right has previously been granted as above, that disposal value is increased by the disposal value taken into account in relation to that grant in determining whether it is to be limited by reference to the capital expenditure incurred (see 10.28 below). [*CAA 1990, ss 24(6A), 26(1)(ea)(eb)(ec)(2AA), 67A; F(No 2)A 1992, s 68; FA 1994, 26 Sch Pt V(24)*].

See also 71.71 SCHEDULE D, CASES I AND II.

Enterprise zones. Expenditure on machinery or plant which is to be an integral part of an industrial or commercial building in an enterprise zone may qualify for 100% industrial buildings allowance. See 10.19 above.

Notification of expenditure. A new time limit is introduced by *FA 1994* which applies to expenditure incurred on machinery or plant. A claim for first-year allowances or writing down allowances in respect of such expenditure cannot be made unless notice of the expenditure is given to the Revenue, in such form as may be required by the Board (see below). The time limit within which notice must be given is (i) for income tax for 1996/97 onwards (subject to (ii) below), twelve months after 31 January following the tax year in which ends the chargeable period concerned, (ii) for income tax for 1996/97 only as regards trades etc. commenced before 6 April 1994, the period up to and including 31 January 1999, and (iii) for income tax for earlier years and for corporation tax (where, in both cases, the chargeable period ended on or after 30 November 1993), within two years after the end of the chargeable period concerned. For chargeable periods ending before 30 November 1993, the notice condition is met if (i) the expenditure was included in a tax computation given to the inspector before that date, or (ii) notice of the expenditure is given to the inspector, in such form as may be required by the Board (see below), not later than *three* years after the end of the relevant chargeable period (or, if that period ends after 30 November 1990, before 3 May 1994 if later).

The period within which the notice or computation is required may be extended in any particular case at the Board's discretion, but this will not be done routinely. The criteria for acceptance of a late notification are as follows.

(1)   There must be good reason, arising out of circumstances beyond the taxpayer's and agent's control, why notification could not be given timeously.

(2)   In the case of a large construction project extending over several years and involving expenditure on a variety of assets, including machinery and plant, it may be impossible to complete final allocation of the expenditure between different classes of asset timeously. In such cases, refinement of the allocation will be accepted after the time limit has passed provided that reasonable estimates have been made within the time limit and there is no undue delay in finalising the details.

(3)   The application for extension, and notification of the expenditure involved, must be made within a reasonable period (normally no more than three months) after the expiry of the circumstances giving rise to late notification.

(4)   The following will *not* constitute acceptable reasons for late notification.

(*a*)   Oversight or negligence on the part of the taxpayer or agent.

(*b*)   Delay for any reason except where (1) above applies.

(*c*)   The taxpayer's absence or illness, unless it arose at a critical time preventing timeous notification, there was good reason for notification not being given before the absence or illness, (in the case of absence) there was a good reason why the taxpayer was unavailable, and there was no one else who could have given timeous notification on the taxpayer's behalf.

(Revenue Pamphlet IR 131 (October 1995 Supplement), SP 6/94, 4 August 1994).

Where the time limit has not been met for a particular chargeable period, the expenditure concerned may still form part of the qualifying expenditure for a subsequent period where the time limit for that period has not expired and the machinery or plant still belongs to the claimant at some time in that period or (where relevant) its basis period. A failure to meet the deadline cannot be rectified by an error or mistake claim under *TMA s 33*.

Form of notification. No form of notification is specified. Generally, it will be sufficient if the expenditure is included in a tax computation. It will, however, be advisable to give enough information to identify the asset concerned, as well as the amount of the expenditure, without listing each and every item where large numbers of similar assets are purchased. Where revenue expenditure in a profit computation is subsequently recategorised as machinery or plant expenditure, the original computation will be regarded as notice of the expenditure for these purposes. Inclusion of the expenditure in a document prepared primarily for non-tax purposes (e.g. annual accounts or valuation reports) will not be sufficient. Where, exceptionally, tax computations are not available in time to meet the deadline, the inspector may be notified separately in writing before it expires, such notification to include as a minimum the aggregate amount of the expenditure on which a claim may be made. (Revenue Pamphlet IR 131 (October 1995 Supplement), SP 6/94, 4 August 1994; Revenue Press Release 17 December 1993).

Before 30 November 1993, notification will be regarded as having been made where there is reasonable evidence to suggest that the inspector had been informed in writing of the incurring of the expenditure. As a minimum, the notice must have stated the aggregate amount of the expenditure concerned. It would have been acceptable to have included the expenditure in a tax computation, but just including it in the accounts would not have been sufficient by itself. (Revenue Press Release 17 December 1993).

[*FA 1994, s 118, 26 Sch Pt V(24); FA 1996, s 135, 21 Sch 48*].

10.26   **Restrictions on eligible expenditure.** For expenditure incurred after 29 November 1993 (subject to transitional provisions, see below), *CAA 1990, AA1 Sch* is introduced by *FA 1994, s 117* to exclude certain expenditure from the definition of machinery and plant for capital allowance purposes. Assets which have been held to be plant under specific court decisions will continue to qualify for machinery and plant allowances, and assets not covered by the *FA 1994* provisions remain subject to prevailing case law on plant. (Revenue Press Release 17 December 1993).

Transitional provisions. Expenditure is not affected by the *FA 1994* provisions where it is incurred before 6 April 1996 in pursuance of a contract entered into either before 30 November 1993 or for the purposes of securing compliance with obligations under a contract entered into before that date. [*FA 1994, s 117(2)*].

Expenditure on buildings which does not qualify for allowances. Expenditure on the construction or acquisition of a building will not qualify for machinery and plant allowances where it is incurred after 29 November 1993 (subject to the above transitional provisions). For these purposes the expression 'building' includes:

(a)   any assets forming an integral part of the building;

(b)   any assets which do not form an integral part of the building because they are movable or for some other reason, but are nevertheless of a kind which are normally incorporated into buildings; and

(c)   any of the following:

   (i)   walls, floors, ceilings, doors, gates, shutters, windows and stairs;

   (ii)   mains services, and systems, of water, electricity and gas;

   (iii)   waste disposal systems;

   (iv)   sewerage and drainage systems;

   (v)   shafts or other structures in which lifts, hoists, escalators and moving walkways are installed; and

   (vi)   fire safety systems.

'Electrical systems' include lighting systems.

[*CAA 1990, AA1 Sch 1(1)(2)(4), 5(1); FA 1994, s 117(1)*].

Expenditure on buildings not excluded from qualifying for allowances. Expenditure incurred on the construction or acquisition of any assets listed in (1) to (20) below, of which (1) to (16) are included in the expression 'building', is not excluded from qualifying for machinery and plant allowances.

(1)   Electrical, cold water, gas and sewerage systems provided mainly to meet the particular requirements of the trade, or provided mainly to serve particular machinery or plant used for the purposes of the trade.

(2)   Space or water heating systems; powered systems of ventilation, air cooling or air purification; and any ceiling or floor comprised in such systems.

(3)   Manufacturing or processing equipment; storage equipment, including cold rooms; display equipment; and counters, checkouts and similar equipment.

(4)   Cookers, washing machines, dishwashers, refrigerators and similar equipment; washbasins, sinks, baths, showers, sanitary ware and similar equipment; and furniture and furnishings.

(5)   Lifts, hoists, escalators and moving walkways.

(6)   Sound insulation provided mainly to meet the particular requirements of the trade.

(7)   Computer, telecommunication and surveillance systems (including their wiring or other links).

(8)   Refrigeration or cooling equipment.

(9)   Sprinkler equipment and other equipment for extinguishing or containing fire; fire alarm systems.

(10)   Burglar alarm systems.

(11)   Strong rooms in bank or building society premises; safes.

(12)   Partition walls, where moveable and intended to be moved in the course of the trade.

(13) Decorative assets provided for the enjoyment of the public in the hotel, restaurant or similar trades.

(14) Advertising hoardings; and signs, displays and similar assets.

(15) Swimming pools (including diving boards, slides and structures on which such boards or slides are mounted).

(16) Any machinery (including devices for providing motive power) not within any other item in (1) to (15) above.

(17) Any cold store.

(18) Any building provided for testing aircraft engines run within the building.

(19) Any caravan provided mainly for holiday lettings.

(20) Any moveable building intended to be moved in the course of the trade.

An asset does not fall within (1) to (16) above if its principal purpose is to insulate or enclose the interior of the building or to provide an interior wall, a floor or a ceiling which (in each case) is intended to remain permanently in place.

'Electrical systems' include lighting systems.

[*CAA 1990, AA1 Sch 1(3)(4), 5(1); FA 1994, s 117(2)*].

Expenditure on structures not qualifying for allowances. 'Structure' means a fixed structure of any kind, other than a building. [*CAA 1990, AA1 Sch 5(1)(a); FA 1994, s 117(1)*]. A structure is 'any substantial man-made asset' (see Revenue Press Release 17 December 1993).

Expenditure on the construction or acquisition of a structure or other assets listed in (A) to (G) below, or on any works involving the alteration of land, will not qualify for machinery and plant allowances where it is incurred after 29 November 1993 (subject to the above transitional provisions).

(A) Any tunnel, bridge, viaduct, aqueduct, embankment or cutting.

(B) Any way or hard standing, such as a pavement, road, railway or tramway, a park for vehicles or containers, or an airstrip or runway.

(C) Any inland navigation, including a canal or basin or a navigable river.

(D) Any dam, reservoir or barrage (including any sluices, gates, generators and other equipment associated with it).

(E) Any dock (and see below).

(F) Any dike, sea wall, weir or drainage ditch.

(G) Any structure not in (A) to (F) above, with the exception of an industrial structure (other than a building) that is or is to be an industrial building or structure within the meaning of *CAA 1990, s 18* (see 10.11 above), which is slightly amended for this purpose.

As regards (E) above, 'dock' includes any harbour, wharf, pier, marina or jetty, and any other structure in or at which vessels may be kept or merchandise or passengers may be shipped or unshipped.

[*CAA 1990, AA1 Sch 2(1)(2)(4), 5(1); FA 1994, s 117(1)*].

Expenditure on structures not excluded from qualifying for allowances. Expenditure incurred on assets listed in (I) to (XII) below or on the construction or acquisition of any asset of a description within any of the items in (1) to (16) above is not excluded from qualifying for machinery and plant allowances.

(I) Dry docks.

(II) Any jetty or similar structure provided mainly to carry machinery or plant.

(III) Pipelines, or underground ducts or tunnels with a primary purpose of carrying electricity cables.

(IV) Towers provided to support floodlights.

(V) Any reservoir incorporated into a water treatment works or any service reservoir of treated water for supply within any housing estate or other particular locality.

(VI) Silos provided for temporary storage or on the construction or acquisition of storage tanks.

(VII) Slurry pits or silage clamps.

(VIII) Fish tanks or fish ponds.

(IX) Rails, sleepers and ballast for a railway or tramway.

(X) Structures and other assets for providing the setting for any ride at an amusement park or exhibition.

(XI) Fixed zoo cages.

(XII) Expenditure on the alteration of land for the purpose only of installing machinery or plant.

[*CAA 1990, AA1 Sch 2(3)(4); FA 1994, s 117(1)*].

Interests in land. Expenditure on the construction or acquisition of machinery or plant does not include expenditure on the acquisition of any interest in land incurred after 29 November 1993 (subject to the above transitional provisions), but this restriction does not apply to any asset which is so installed or otherwise fixed in or to any description of land as to become, in law, part of that land. The definition of 'land' in the *Interpretation Act 1978, 1 Sch* is accordingly amended for these purposes to omit the words 'buildings and other structures', but otherwise 'interest in land' for these purposes has the same meaning as that for fixtures under leases in *CAA 1990, s 51* (see 10.34 below). [*CAA 1990, AA1 Sch 3, 5; FA 1994, s 117(1)*].

General exemptions. Expenditure falling within *CAA 1990, ss 67, 67A, 68, 69, 70, 71* (relating to thermal insulation, computer software, films, tapes and discs, fire safety, safety of sports grounds and security assets, see 10.25 above) is not affected by the above provisions. [*CAA 1990, AA1 Sch 4; FA 1994, s 117(1)*].

Glasshouses. Nothing in the above provisions affects the question of whether expenditure on the construction or acquisition of any glasshouse for growing plants is expenditure on the provision of machinery or plant, where the glasshouse is designed so that the required environment (that is air, heat, light, irrigation and temperature) is controlled automatically by devices incorporated into its structure. [*CAA 1990, AA1 Sch 5(2); FA 1994, s 117(1)*].

10.27   **First-year allowances** were available (and see further below as regards their temporary reinstatement) for the basis period (see 10.32 below) in which expenditure on machinery and plant (see 10.25 above) was incurred, provided that the machinery etc. belonged to the claimant at some time during that period (but see 10.38(vii) below as regards certain expenditure by a lessee), and that that period was not also the period of permanent discontinuance of the trade. [*CAA 1990 s 22(1); FA 1971, s 41(1)*]. 'Belongs' has its ordinary meaning and normally entails a right of disposition over the thing possessed. See also *Bolton v International Drilling Co Ltd Ch D 1982, 56 TC 449, Ensign Tankers (Leasing)*

10.27 Capital Allowances (Machinery and Plant)

Ltd v Stokes HL 1992, 64 TC 617 and *Melluish v BMI (No 3) Ltd HL, [1995] STC 964*. However, following the decision in *Stokes v Costain Property Investments Ltd CA 1984, 57 TC 688*, specific provisions were introduced to determine entitlement to allowances for machinery or plant which are fixtures (see 10.34 below). For a case in which allowances in respect of leased machinery were refused because the leasing arrangements did not amount to a trade, see *Gold Fields Mining and Industrial Ltd v GKN (United Kingdom) plc Ch D, [1996] STC 173*.

Expenditure incurred for the purposes of, and prior to the commencement of, a trade is treated as incurred on the first day of trading, except that this does not apply to impose the reduced rates of first-year allowance applicable after 13 March 1984, or for the purposes of the provisions described at 10.34 below as regards entitlement to allowances. [*CAA 1990, s 83(2); FA 1971, s 50(4); FA 1984, 12 Sch 2(4); FA 1985, s 59(7)*]. Instalment payments under contract are 'incurred' as they fall due. See 10.2(iii) generally as regards the date on which expenditure is treated as having been incurred.

The **rates** of allowance are

After 26 October 1970	—60%	*After* 13 March 1984	—75%
After 19 July 1971	—80%	*After* 31 March 1985	—50%
After 21 March 1972	—100%		

First-year allowances were generally **abolished** for expenditure **after 31 March 1986**, although they continue at the 100% rate for expenditure incurred before 1 April 1987 under a contract entered into before 14 March 1984 either by the person incurring the expenditure or by another person (the 'lessee') who had arranged to lease the machinery or plant from the person incurring the expenditure (the 'lessor'), where the lessor had either taken over the lessee's obligations under the contract or entered into a new contract discharging those obligations (payments under such a new contract being treated as under the original contract for these purposes). [*FA 1971, s 42; FA 1972, s 67; FA 1984, s 58, 12 Sch 2*]. They continue to be available at the 100% rate, however, for any 'additional VAT liability' (see 10.2(v) above) incurred in respect of such expenditure at a time when the machinery or plant is provided for the purposes of the trade (the allowance being given for the chargeable period related to the incurring of the liability). [*CAA 1990, ss 22, 23; FA 1991, 14 Sch 6; FA 1994, 26 Sch Pt V(24)*]. See also 10.35 below as regards rented television sets.

First-year allowances are reinstated at a rate of **40%** in respect of expenditure incurred **after 31 October 1992 and before 1 November 1993** (and any 'additional VAT liability' (see 10.2(v) above) incurred, at whatever time, in respect of such expenditure), subject to the general conditions of *CAA 1990, s 22(1)* (see above) being satisfied. *CAA 1990, s 83(2)* (pre-trading expenditure–see above) is disregarded in determining for this purpose the date on which expenditure is incurred. [*CAA 1990, s 22(1)(3B); FA 1993, s 115(1)(2)*].

First-year allowances are **not** given on the following:

(i) **Cars** and road vehicles, unless they are

    (*a*) of a type constructed primarily for carrying goods, or

    (*b*) of a type unsuitable for use, and not commonly used, as private vehicles, or

    (*c*) provided wholly or mainly for a trade of hire to, or carriage of, members of the public (i.e. not where hiring etc. is limited to a certain class of customers, such as business connections or group companies).

As regards (*b*) above, see Schedule E benefits case of *Gurney v Richards Ch D, [1989] STC 682* (fire brigade car equipped with flashing light held within excluded class), decided on similarly worded legislation (see 75.15 SCHEDULE E). See also *Bourne v*

Auto School of Motoring Ch D 1964, 42 TC 217 (driving school cars) and *Roberts v Granada TV Rental Ltd Ch D 1970, 46 TC 295* (mini-vans, etc.).

(*c*) above applies only if the vehicle was either not normally on hire etc. to the same person (or a person connected with him, see 20 CONNECTED PERSONS) for a period of thirty or more consecutive days or for ninety or more days in any twelve month period; or was provided to a person who himself satisfied those conditions in using it wholly or mainly for a trade of hire etc. to members of the public (e.g. a taxi driver). These restrictions do not, however, apply to vehicles supplied for the use of persons receiving a social security mobility allowance, disability living allowance or war pensioners' mobility supplement and certain other like payments. [*CAA 1990, ss 22(4)(b), 36; FA 1971, s 43; F(No 2)A 1979, s 14; FA 1984, s 61; SI 1984 No 2060; SI 1991 No 2874*].

(ii)   Assets involved in certain partnership changes and other successions (see 10.38(viii), (xi) below). [*CAA 1990, ss 77, 78; FA 1971, 8 Sch 13, 15(3)*].

(iii) Assets acquired in sales between connected persons (as under *Sec 839*, see 20 CONNECTED PERSONS), or in sale and lease-back transactions, or in transactions the sole or main benefit of which would be the obtaining of capital allowances. [*CAA 1990, s 75; FA 1971, 8 Sch 3, 4; FA 1972, s 68*]. See also 10.38(iii) below.

(iv)   Assets attracting investment grants which, although withdrawn after 26 October 1970, continued to apply to certain prior contracts. Ships, however, were granted first-year allowances on expenditure less investment grant. [*FA 1971, 8 Sch 1*].

(v)   (With respect to chargeable periods whose basis periods ended before 1 April 1985), assets disposed of without having been brought into use for trade purposes (any allowances previously given being withdrawn). [*FA 1971, s 41(2); FA 1985, s 55(2)*]. Such assets are to be regarded as never having qualified for allowances (*Burman v Westminster Press Ltd Ch D 1987, 60 TC 418*).

(vi)   Certain assets used for leasing (see 10.35 below).

Partial use for non-trade purposes results in first-year allowances being scaled down as is just and reasonable. [*CAA 1990, s 79; FA 1971, 8 Sch 5; FA 1985, 14 Sch 2*]. See 10.28(C) below as regards writing-down allowances in such cases.

Claims. An individual or partnership may claim all or any part of the allowances available for a year of assessment. In practice, such claims may be revised, even after the related assessment has become final, if they are made early in the year and circumstances change before the end of the year (e.g. as a result of a personal relief becoming available) (see Revenue Pamphlet IR 131 (October 1995 Supplement), A26). For accounting periods ending after 30 September 1993, companies may similarly claim all or part of the first-year allowances available; for earlier accounting periods, first-year allowances are given without claim to companies, who may (within two years of the end of the chargeable period) elect for all, or any part, of the allowances for the chargeable period to be disclaimed. Although such a disclaimer strictly relates to the total of the allowances for the period, where the period begins on or before and ends after 13 March 1984 the Revenue will concessionally allow a disclaimer relating only to first-year allowances in respect of expenditure incurred after that date (see Tolley's Practical Tax 1985, p 31). [*CAA 1990, s 22(7); FA 1971, s 41(3); FA 1990, 17 Sch 3*].

This provision does not, however, apply to **ships**, for which the trader may by notice in writing require the postponement of the whole allowance to a later period or periods or, in the case of a company for an accounting period ended before 1 October 1993, disclaim it, or may require the allowance to be reduced, in which case he may also require that reduced allowance to be postponed. The time limit within which notice must be given is (i) for income tax for 1996/97 onwards (subject to (ii) below), twelve months after 31 January following the tax year in which ends the chargeable period for which the allowance is due, (ii) for income tax for 1996/97 only as regards trades etc. commenced before 6 April 1994, twelve months after 31 January following the chargeable period, and (iii) for income tax for earlier years and for corporation tax, two years after the end of the chargeable period. With respect to expenditure incurred before 1 April 1985, these provisions applied only to expenditure on new ships. Also, in respect of expenditure incurred before 14 March 1984, a claim in respect of a new ship could only require the postponement of all or part of the allowance, and postponed allowances could not be claimed in a later period if 10.35(g) below applied. Where a previous owner of a ship was denied first-year allowances through disposing of the ship without its having been brought into use for trade purposes, his ownership was ignored in determining whether the ship was 'new'. [*CAA 1990, s 30; FA 1971, 8 Sch 8; FA 1980, 12 Sch 1(2); FA 1984, s 59; FA 1985, s 58(1); FA 1989, 13 Sch 15; FA 1990, 17 Sch 7; FA 1993, 13 Sch 3; FA 1996, s 135, 21 Sch 27*]. See 10.28(B) below as regards writing-down allowances for ships.

10.28   **Writing-down allowances** are available for any chargeable period (see 10.2(vi) above) other than that of permanent discontinuance to any person who has incurred expenditure on machinery etc. (see 10.25 above) which belongs or has belonged to him (but see 10.38(vii) below as regards certain expenditure by a lessee) (and which, in relation to chargeable periods whose basis periods end before 1 April 1985, is or has been in use for trade or leasing purposes). [*CAA 1990, s 24(1); FA 1971, s 44(1); FA 1985, s 55(2)*]. See 10.27 above and 10.34 below for meaning of 'belongs'. See 10.38(iii) below as regards restrictions under connected persons and other anti-avoidance provisions.

The allowance is **25% p.a.** (proportionately reduced or increased where the chargeable period is less or more than one year, or if the trade has been carried on for part only of a chargeable period) of the excess of 'qualifying expenditure' over 'disposal value' for that period. [*CAA 1990, s 24(2); FA 1994, s 213(4)*].

Qualifying expenditure of a chargeable period whose basis period ends after 31 March 1985 is the sum of:

(i)   the residue of qualifying expenditure brought forward from the preceding chargeable period;

(ii)   the balance, after deducting any first-year allowance (see 10.27 above) given, of any expenditure which has not formed part of the qualifying expenditure for any previous chargeable period, and which does not qualify for a first-year allowance (ignoring any failure to claim or any disclaimer) for the chargeable period in question;

(iii)   the balance, after deducting the first-year allowance, of any expenditure in respect of which a first-year allowance is made where a 'disposal value' (see below) falls to be brought in, in respect of the machinery or plant on which the expenditure was incurred, in the chargeable period in question; and

(iv)   net cost during the basis period for the chargeable period under review of demolition of machinery and plant not replaced by the trader.

[*CAA 1990, ss 25(1)(5)(6), 62; FA 1990, 17 Sch 6; FA 1994, 26 Sch Pt V(24)*].

Where an 'additional VAT liability' (see 10.2(v) above) is incurred in respect of expenditure qualifying for writing-down allowances, at a time when the machinery or plant in question is provided for the purposes of the trade, it is itself expenditure (on the machinery or plant in question) qualifying for writing-down allowances. [*CAA 1990, s 24(1A); FA 1991, 14 Sch 7(1)*].

For a chargeable period whose basis period ended before 1 April 1985, expenditure on machinery or plant is only brought into qualifying expenditure if the machinery or plant was or had been in use for trade purposes in or before the basis period for the chargeable period in question. Also, (iii) above does not apply, but there is instead an addition to qualifying expenditure of the cost less 'disposal value' of any machinery or plant sold in the basis period for the chargeable period under review without having been brought into use for trade purposes.

[*FA 1971, s 44(4), 8 Sch 4, 14; FA 1985, 14 Sch 3(2), 5*].

As regards (ii) above, expenditure incurred by a trader after 13 March 1984 which qualifies for a first-year allowance in a chargeable period is *not* excluded from being qualifying expenditure of that period where either

(1)   the trader, not having claimed the first-year allowance, so elects (for chargeable periods ended before 1 October 1993, this applied only to traders other than companies), or

(2)   the trader (being a company) disclaimed the first-year allowance for an accounting period ended before 1 October 1993, or

(3)   part of the first-year allowance was disclaimed or a reduced allowance required to be given (see 10.27 above),

in which case the fraction of the total expenditure corresponding to the proportion of the available first-year allowances not taken may be included in qualifying expenditure. The time limit for the election in (1) above is (i) for income tax for 1996/97 onwards (subject to (ii) below), twelve months after 31 January following the tax year in which the chargeable period ends, (ii) for income tax for 1996/97 only as regards trades etc. commenced before 6 April 1994, twelve months after 31 January following the chargeable period, and (iii) for income tax for earlier years and for corporation tax, two years after the end of the chargeable period. [*CAA 1990, s 25(2)(3)(4)(9); FA 1990, 17 Sch 6; FA 1996, s 135, 21 Sch 26*].

Disposal value for a chargeable period whose basis period ends after 31 March 1985 is that calculated for any machinery or plant provided for trade purposes which belongs to the trader at some time in the basis period, and in respect of which, in that basis period, one of the following events occurs, being the first such event to occur.

(i)   The machinery or plant ceases to belong to the trader.

(ii)   He loses possession of it, and it is reasonable to assume the loss is permanent.

(iii)   It ceases to exist as such.

(iv)   It begins to be used wholly or partly other than for trade purposes (but see (B) below).

(v)   The trade is, or is treated as, permanently discontinued.

For a chargeable period whose basis period ended before 1 April 1985, disposal value is brought in for any machinery or plant which, after being in use for trade purposes, ceased to belong to the trader, or ceased permanently to be used for trade purposes, in the basis period.

The amount to be brought into account depends upon the nature of the event.

10.28 Capital Allowances (Machinery and Plant)

(*a*) On a sale, it is the net sale proceeds plus any insurance or capital compensation received by reason of any event which affected the sale price (but see (*b*) below).

(*b*) On a sale at less than market value, market value is substituted for the actual sale price, unless the buyer can claim machinery and plant or scientific research allowances for his expenditure, or is charged to tax under Schedule E in respect of the sale.

(*c*) On demolition or destruction, it is the net amount received for the remains plus any insurance or capital compensation receipts.

(*d*) On permanent loss, it is any insurance or capital compensation receipts.

(*e*) On permanent discontinuance of the trade preceding an event in (*a*)–(*d*) above, it is the value under (*a*)–(*d*) as appropriate.

(*f*) On any other event, it is open market value (except that no disposal value is brought in when machinery etc. was given away resulting in a charge on the recipient under Schedule E).

Where an 'additional VAT rebate' (see 10.2(v) above) is made in respect of expenditure qualifying for allowances, a disposal value equal to the amount of that rebate must be brought into account for the chargeable period related to the making of the rebate.

The disposal value may not, however, exceed the cost (reduced by any 'additional VAT rebates' (see above), and if the event is itself the making of an additional VAT rebate, by any other disposal value previously brought into account) (but see 10.38(iii) below as regards certain transactions between connected persons). [*CAA 1990, ss 24(6)–(8), 26; FA 1971, s 44(5)(6); FA 1985, 14 Sch 3(3); FA 1991, 14 Sch 7(2), 8; FA 1994, 26 Sch Pt V(24)*].

The exemptions under (*b*) and (*f*) above where there is a charge to tax under Schedule E apply where there would be such a charge but for the exemptions under *Sec 188* (see 19.6 COMPENSATION FOR LOSS OF EMPLOYMENT (AND DAMAGES)). (Tolley's Practical Tax 1984 p 114).

Claims. For accounting periods ended before 1 October 1993, writing-down allowances are given without claim to companies (but see *Elliss v BP Northern Ireland Refinery Ltd CA 1986, 59 TC 474*, where it was held that a company may renounce such allowances). For accounting periods ending after 13 March 1984, it is specifically provided that a company may (by notice in writing within two years after the end of the period) either disclaim an allowance or claim a reduced allowance. Individuals or partnerships, in claiming allowances, may claim all, none or any part of the allowances available. The same applies to companies for accounting periods ending after 30 September 1993. [*CAA 1990, s 24(3)(4); FA 1990, 17 Sch 5*]. In practice, individual or partnership claims may be revised after the related assessment has become final if they are made early in the year of assessment and circumstances change before the end of the year (e.g. as a result of a personal relief becoming available) (see Revenue Pamphlet IR 131 (October 1995 Supplement), A26).

Items not included in 'pool' of qualifying expenditure are

(A) *Motor cars costing over £12,000* acquired for purposes of a trade (other than vehicles constructed primarily for carrying goods, unsuitable as private vehicles, or provided for a trade of public hire or conveyance, see 10.27(i) above). The car is treated as being acquired for the purposes of a *separate and distinct trade* commencing immediately after the beginning of the basis period related to the incurring of the expenditure and ending when the car begins to be used for purposes other than those of the actual trade. Writing-down allowances are calculated on this basis but are

142

limited to a *maximum of £3,000 a year* (proportionately reduced or increased for chargeable periods of less or more than a year). The allowances, or charges, are made to, or on, the actual trade.

For expenditure incurred or treated as incurred before 11 March 1992 or under a contract entered into before that date, the figures are £8,000 and £2,000 respectively.

Where a car of which the *retail price when new* exceeded £12,000 is *hired* for business purposes, the hire charge is treated for tax purposes as reduced in the proportion which £12,000 plus one-half of the excess bears to that original price. For hire expenditure under a contract entered into before 11 March 1992, the figure is £8,000 in each case. The restriction does not apply if the car is within the exceptions listed at (a)–(c) under 10.27(i) above. The restriction also does not apply to any separate maintenance charge explicitly specified in the contract (see Tolley's Practical Tax 1986 p 63). Any subsequent rental rebate (or other release within *Sec 94*, see 71.44 SCHEDULE D, CASES I AND II) is reduced for tax purposes in the same proportion as the hire charge restriction. (This applies where the rebate etc. is made on or after 29 April 1996, but similar relief was previously available by extra-statutory concession (see Revenue Pamphlet IR 1, B28).) [*CAA 1990, ss 34–36; F(No 2)A 1992, s 71; FA 1994, s 213(5)(6); FA 1996, 39 Sch 1(3)(4)*]. As regards hire purchase agreements under which there is an option to purchase for a sum not more than one per cent of the retail price when new, the finance charge element, which strictly falls within the definition of a hire charge, is excluded from this restriction. [*CAA 1990, s 35(3)(4); FA 1991, s 61*].

Motor cars costing £12,000 (£8,000) or less must be included in the separate 'pool' mentioned in 10.35(a) below. [*CAA 1990, s 41(1)(c)*].

(B)   *Ships*. Where a trader incurs expenditure on a ship for trade purposes (not for a deemed trade of letting, see (E) below), the ship is treated for writing-down allowances as if provided for a notional separate 'single ship trade'. Allowances and charges which would be made in the single ship trade are made for the same period in the actual trade. For expenditure incurred after 26 July 1989, these provisions do not apply where the ship is provided for leasing or otherwise for letting on charter, unless it appears that the ship will be used in the 'requisite period' only for a 'qualifying purpose' (as defined in 10.35(d) below), and do not apply where the overseas leasing provisions in 10.35 below apply.

The single ship trade is treated as being permanently discontinued at the time when the ship begins to be used wholly or partly for non-trade purposes. If, before that time, it starts to be used in the 'requisite period' other than for a 'qualifying purpose' (as defined in 10.35(c)(d) below), the trade is treated as ceasing when it starts to be so used. Where, as a result, a disposal value falls to be brought in, no balancing adjustment is made in the single ship trade, but a corresponding adjustment is made in the actual trade by an addition to qualifying expenditure or the bringing in of a disposal value. If the ship ceases to belong to the trader without having been brought into use for the trade, the single ship trade is again treated as being permanently discontinued, but in addition writing-down allowances previously given or postponed are withdrawn and the corresponding amount added to the qualifying expenditure of the actual trade.

A trader may elect for any of the following.

(i)   Postponement, in whole or part, of allowances to a later period.

(ii)   That the separate trade provisions shall not apply, the balance of qualifying expenditure being added to the actual trade.

(iii)   That any part of the expenditure be transferred to the pool of the actual trade.

The time limit within which notice of any of the above must be given is (i) for income tax for 1996/97 onwards (subject to (ii) below), twelve months after 31 January following the tax year in which ends the chargeable period concerned, (ii) for income tax for 1996/97 only as regards trades etc. commenced before 6 April 1994, twelve months after 31 January following the chargeable period, and (iii) for income tax for earlier years and for corporation tax, two years after the end of the chargeable period. Where, as a result of (ii) above, there is deemed to be a permanent discontinuance of the single ship trade, no balancing adjustment is made in respect of that trade, but an addition to or subtraction from the qualifying expenditure of the actual trade is made.

[*CAA 1990, ss 31–33; FA 1990, 17 Sch 8; FA 1994, 26 Sch Pt V(24); FA 1996, s 135, 21 Sch 28, 29*].

See also 10.30 below as regards balancing charges on disposals of ships.

(C)   *Partial use for other purposes.* Where machinery or plant is acquired for trade purposes but will also be used for other purposes, a first-year allowance, where available, can be given but is scaled down as is just and reasonable. Writing-down allowances, etc., similarly scaled down, will be calculated primarily as if the machinery were acquired for a separate 'notional' trade starting at the commencement of the basis period in which it is acquired for the purposes of the actual trade and being permanently discontinued when the machinery starts to be used wholly for purposes other than those of the actual trade. If an asset in use wholly for trade purposes begins to be used partly for other purposes, it is treated as permanently ceasing to be used for the purposes of the (actual) trade at the beginning of the period of the change in use, so that its open market value (see (f) above) is deducted from qualifying expenditure and is treated as the acquisition cost in the 'notional' trade. [*CAA 1990, s 79; FA 1990, 17 Sch 14; FA 1994, 26 Sch Pt V(24)*]. See also *Kempster v McKenzie Ch D 1952, 33 TC 193* and *G H Chambers (Northiam Farms) Ltd v Watmough Ch D 1956, 36 TC 711* as regards adjustment for any element of personal choice.

(D)   Where *contributions are received* as reimbursement of day-to-day depreciation. [*CAA 1990, s 80*]. See 10.38(xii) below.

(E)   *Machinery etc., on lease.* A person incurring expenditure on machinery, etc., which he lets otherwise than in the course of a trade, and not for use in a dwelling-house, is treated as if he had incurred that expenditure in a *separate trade* beginning at the commencement of the first letting and not ending until letting permanently ceases. [*CAA 1990, s 61; FA 1994, 26 Sch Pt V(24)*]. See 10.35 below as regards restrictions in making allowances and 10.38(vii) below as regards machinery, etc. a lessee is required to provide under his lease.

(F)   *Short-life assets.* Allowances for expenditure incurred by a trader after 31 March 1986 on such an asset are calculated as if the asset was acquired for a separate notional trade, which is permanently discontinued when the asset starts to be used wholly or partly for purposes other than those of the actual trade. The allowances are given, and charges made, for the corresponding chargeable period in the actual trade. If, following a permanent discontinuance of the notional trade on which a balancing allowance arose (see 10.30 below), an 'additional VAT liability' (see 10.2(v) above) is incurred in respect of the asset, a further balancing allowance of that amount is given for the chargeable period related to the incurring of the liability.

The Revenue accept that it may not be practicable for individual computations to be maintained for every short-life asset, especially where they are held in very large numbers. Statement of Practice SP 1/86 sets out examples of acceptable bases of computation where the inspector is satisfied that the actual life in the business of a distinct class of assets with broadly similar average lives, before being sold or scrapped, is likely to be less than five years.

The trader may elect in writing for any machinery or plant (except as below) to be a *short-life asset*. The election is irrevocable and the time limit within which it must be made is (i) for income tax for 1996/97 onwards (subject to (ii) below), twelve months after 31 January following the tax year in which ends the chargeable period in which the expenditure (or earliest expenditure) is incurred, (ii) for income tax for 1996/97 only as regards trades etc. commenced before 6 April 1994, as regards expenditure incurred in the basis period for that year, the period up to and including 31 January 1999, and (iii) for income tax for earlier years and for corporation tax, two years after the end of the chargeable period or (for income tax only) its basis period.

In general, inspectors will require sufficient information in support of an election to minimise the possibility of any difference of view at a later date (e.g. on a disposal) about what was and was not covered by the election, and to ensure that assets are not in any of the excluded categories (see below). Where separate identification of short-life assets acquired in a chargeable period is either impossible or impracticable, e.g. similar small or relatively inexpensive assets held in very large numbers, perhaps in different locations, then the information required in support of the election may be provided by reference to batches of acquisitions. (Revenue Pamphlet IR 131, SP 1/86, 15 January 1986).

The following can *not* be short-life assets.

   (i) A ship.
   (ii) A motor-car within 10.27(i) or 10.28(A) above.
   (iii) An asset leased other than in the course of a trade.
   (iv) An asset used partly for non-trade purposes.
   (v) An asset the subject of a 'wear and tear' subsidy.
   (vi) An asset received by way of gift or whose previous use by the trader did not attract capital allowances (see 10.38(v)(ix) below).
   (vii) Machinery or plant provided for leasing unless likely to be used in the 'requisite period' only for a 'qualifying purpose' (as defined in 10.35(c)(d) below), excluding in any case vehicles within 10.35(AA) below.
   (viii) A leased asset within *CAA 1990, s 43* (see 10.35(f) below).
   (ix) A rented television set within the transitional provisions in 10.35 below.
   (x) An asset leased outside the UK within 10.35 below.

As regards (vii) above, if, before the notional trade is otherwise treated as permanently discontinued, the asset starts to be used in the 'requisite period' other than for a 'qualifying purpose', the notional trade is treated as ceasing when it starts to be so used. No balancing adjustment is made in the actual trade, but the qualifying expenditure in the notional trade at the start of the period is added to qualifying expenditure for the actual trade (or, if it is 'old expenditure' (see 10.35 below), added to the special pool in 10.35(*a*) below).

If a disposal value does not fall to be brought into account (other than by virtue of the grant of certain computer software rights (see 10.25 above) or an 'additional VAT rebate' (see above)) on the notional trade within four years of the end of the chargeable period related to the incurring of the expenditure (or earliest expenditure), then in the first chargeable period ending thereafter (or in its basis period) the notional trade is treated as being permanently discontinued. No balancing adjustment is made, but the trader's qualifying expenditure for that period in his actual trade is increased by the balance of qualifying expenditure in the notional trade.

Also if, before the notional trade is treated as permanently discontinued, the asset is disposed of to a connected person within *Sec 839* (see 20 CONNECTED PERSONS), the asset is treated as continuing to be subject to an election made under these provisions at the time the original election was made. If the trader and the connected person so elect (not more than two years after the end of the chargeable period in which, or in the basis period for which, the disposal occurred), the disposal is treated as at a price equal to the notional trade qualifying expenditure of the period of the disposal, and *CAA 1990, s 75* (see 10.38(iii) below) does not apply. If no election is made, the normal connected person rules apply (see 10.38(iii) below), but the bar on substituting market value for a lesser sale price where the buyer is entitled to capital allowances (see (*b*) above) is lifted. [*CAA 1990, ss 37, 38; FA 1991, 14 Sch 9; F(No 2)A 1992, s 68(7); FA 1993, 13 Sch 4; FA 1994, 26 Sch Pt V(24); FA 1996, s 135, 21 Sch 30*].

10.29   *Example*

Short-life assets
A, who prepares trading accounts to 30 June each year, buys and sells machines as follows.

	Cost	Date of acquisition	Disposal proceeds	Date of disposal
Machine X	£20,000	30.4.94	£10,000	1.10.96
Machine Y	£25,000	1.9.93	£4,000	1.12.99

A elects under *CAA 1990, s 37* for both machines to be treated as short-life assets. His pool of qualifying expenditure brought forward at the beginning of 1995/96 is £80,000.

A's capital allowances are as follows.

	Pool £	Machine X £	Machine Y £	Allowances £
1995/96 (basis period 1.7.93–30.6.94)				
WDV b/f	80,000			
Additions		20,000	25,000	
FYA 40%			(10,000)	10,000
WDA 25%	(20,000)	(5,000)	—	25,000
	———	———	———	———
	c/f 60,000	c.f 15,000	c/f 15,000	£35,000
	———	———	———	———

	Pool £	Machine X £	Machine Y £	Allowances £
	b/f 60,000	b/f 15,000	b/f 15,000	
1996/97 (basis period 1.7.94–30.6.96)				
WDA	(15,000)	(3,750)	(3,750)	£22,500
	45,000	11,250	11,250	
Period of account 1.7.96–30.6.97				
Disposal		(10,000)		
Balancing allowance		£1,250		1,250
WDA	(11,250)		(2,813)	14,063
				£15,313
	33,750		8,437	
Period of account 1.7.97–30.6.98				
WDA	(8,437)		(2,109)	£10,546
	25,313		6,328	
Period of account 1.7.98–30.6.99				
WDA	(6,328)		(1,582)	£7,910
	18,985		4,746	
Period of account 1.7.99–30.6.2000				
Transfer to pool	4,746		(4,746)	
	23,731		—	
Disposal	(4,000)			
	19,731			
WDA	(4,933)			£4,933
WDV c/f	£14,798			

Notes

(a)   The basis period for 1996/97 is extended, this being the transitional year for the changeover to the current year basis of assessment (see 71.20 SCHEDULE D, CASES I AND II).

(b)   The chargeable period related to the incurring of the expenditure on both machines in this example is the tax year 1995/96. The fourth anniversary of the end of that chargeable period is 5 April 2000. The balance of expenditure on Machine Y is thus transferred to the pool in the period of account ended 30 June 2000, this being the first chargeable period ending after 5 April 2000.

10.30   **Balancing allowances and charges.** A balancing charge will be made in any chargeable period (including that of permanent discontinuance of the trade (or notional trade)) in which disposal value exceeds qualifying expenditure (see 10.28 above), and will be equal to the excess. [*CAA 1990, s 24(2)(5)*].

A balancing allowance will arise, only in the period of permanent discontinuance of the trade (or notional trade), of the whole of any excess for the period of qualifying expenditure over disposal value (see 10.28 above). [*CAA 1990, s 24(2)(b)*].

Where machinery etc. has been *partly used for non-trade purposes*, and is thus treated as in use for a separate notional trade (see 10.28(C) above), any balancing adjustment is reviewed on a just and reasonable basis in the light of allowances given and non-trade use. [*CAA 1990, s 79(5); FA 1994, 26 Sch Pt V(24)*].

Deferment of balancing charges on ships. With effect for chargeable periods or basis periods ending after 20 April 1994, balancing charges on ships may be deferred and set against subsequent expenditure on ships for a maximum of six years from the date of disposal. A claim for deferment of the whole or part of a balancing charge may be made by a trader where an event within 10.28(i)–(iii) above (events giving rise to disposal value) occurs after 20 April 1994 with respect to a 'qualifying ship' (the old ship). A *'qualifying ship'* is, broadly, a ship of a sea-going kind of 100 gross registered tons or more, excluding ships of a kind used or chartered primarily for sport or recreation (but passenger ships and cruise liners are not so excluded) and oil/gas rigs etc.. The provisions also apply to ships of less than 100 tons in cases where the old ship is totally lost or is damaged beyond worthwhile repair. A ship brought into use in the trade on or after 20 July 1994 must within three months of first use (unless disposed of during those three months) be registered in the UK, the Channel Islands, Isle of Man, a colony (as to which see Revenue Tax Bulletin April 1995 p 208), a European Union State or a European Economic Area State and must continue to be so until at least three years from first use or, if earlier, until disposed of to an unconnected person. The old ship must not be one that falls to be excluded from the main pool of qualifying expenditure under the provisions for leased assets (see 10.28(E) above and 10.35(*a*) below), assets used only partly for the trade (see 10.28(C) above) or assets attracting a subsidy towards wear and tear (see 10.38(xii) below).

The balancing charge on the old ship is in effect calculated as if allowances had been granted, and the charge arises, in a separate single ship trade, with appropriate assumptions where that is not the case (see *CAA 1990, s 33B; FA 1995, s 94*).

Deferment is achieved by increasing qualifying expenditure by the amount deferred, thus reducing the excess of disposal value over qualifying expenditure. The *maximum deferment* is the *lowest* of (i) the amount treated as brought into account in respect of the old ship under *Sec 33B* (see above), (ii) the amount to be expended on new shipping (see below), so far as not already set against an earlier balancing charge, in the six years starting with the date of disposal of the old ship, (iii) the total balancing charge for the chargeable period in question (excluding charges on certain assets held outside the main pool of qualifying expenditure, and (iv) the amount needed to reduce the trading profit to nil (disregarding losses brought forward), no deferment being possible if no such profit has been made. Where current year basis does not yet apply, capital allowances (other than any brought forward) and balancing charges are treated as trading expenses and receipts of the basis period in determining the profit or loss for the purpose of (iv) above. If the amount actually expended within (ii) above turns out to be less than the amount deferred, the amount of the deficiency is reinstated as a balancing charge for the chargeable period to which the claim relates.

Where an amount is expended on new shipping within the six-year period allowed and is identified by the trader or, in default, determined by the inspector as to be attributed to any part of an amount deferred, an amount equal to the amount so matched is brought into account as a disposal value of the single ship trade (see 10.28(B) above) for the chargeable period in which (or in the basis period for which) the expenditure is incurred, thus reducing the amount on which writing-down allowances may be claimed. No amount of expenditure can be attributed to a deferment if there is earlier expenditure on new shipping within the said six-year period which has not been atrributed to that or earlier deferments. An attribution may be varied by the trader by notice to the inspector within a specified time (see *CAA 1990, s 33F(3)* and *FA 1995, s 98(6)(b)*).

For the purposes of these provisions, an amount is expended on new shipping if it is capital expenditure, incurred by the claimant wholly and exclusively for the purposes of the trade, on a ship (the new ship) which will be a qualifying ship (see above) for at least three years from first use or, if earlier, until disposed of to an unconnected person. Expenditure is treated as incurred by the claimant if it is incurred by a successor to his trade following a partnership change (see 53.6 PARTNERSHIPS) or company reconstruction (see Tolley's Corporation Tax) in consequence of which the trade was not treated as discontinued. Expenditure incurred on a ship which has belonged to either the trader or a connected person within the previous six years or which is incurred mainly for tax avoidance reasons does not qualify. The new ship must be one to which the 'single ship trade' provisions at 10.28(B) above apply. If an election is made to disapply those provisions or transfer expenditure to the main pool (see 10.28(B)(ii)(iii) above), the expenditure in question is deemed never to have been expenditure on new shipping (but must nevertheless be taken into account in matching expenditure with deferments, so that either election prevents further matching of amounts already deferred). Expenditure does not qualify if the overseas leasing provisions at 10.35 below come to apply to the new ship.

For income tax purposes, where current year basis applies, the claim for deferment must be made within twelve months after 31 January following the year of assessment in which the chargeable period of deferment ends. Where current year basis does not yet apply, the claim must be made within two years after the end of that chargeable period. For corporation tax purposes, the provisions relating to capital allowances claims apply also to claims for deferment. Where a claim for deferment is found to be erroneous as a result of subsequent circumstances, the trader must, within three months of the end of the chargeable period in which those circumstances first arise, notify the inspector accordingly (failure to do so incurring a penalty under *TMA s 98*). A claim cannot be made until on or after a date to be appointed by the Treasury; the period for making a claim will be extended, where it would otherwise end earlier, until twelve months after the appointed day.

Where the disposal giving rise to the balancing charge occurs **on or after 29 April 1996**, there is provision for the balancing charge to be set against expenditure on new shipping by another member of the same *group of companies* as the shipowner (within *ICTA 1988, Pt X, Ch IV*, see Tolley's Corporation Tax under Groups of Companies). Such expenditure is, however, excluded where the ship ceases to belong to the fellow group member without being brought into use for trade purposes, or where, within three years of being so brought into use, a disposal value falls to be brought in in respect of the ship (although these exclusions do not apply in the case of total loss of, or commercially irreparable damage to, the ship). Expenditure is similarly excluded where the group relationship between the two companies ceases after the expenditure is incurred and within three years after the commencement of trade use (again disregarding events after the total loss etc. of the ship). Claims, assessments and adjustments relating to this extended relief may not be made before a day appointed for the purpose by the Treasury, but may then relate to times before that day, and all such claims, etc. made within twelve months of that day are valid nowithstanding any other time limits.

[*CAA 1990, ss 33A–33F; FA 1995, ss 94–98; FA 1996, 35 Sch*].

10.31   *Example*

Writing-down allowances, motor cars, partial non-business use, acquisitions from connected persons and balancing adjustments

A is in business as a builder and demolition contractor. He normally makes up his accounts to 5 April, but makes up accounts for the two years to 5 April 1997 as the basis for the 1996/97 assessment (see 71.20 SCHEDULE D, CASES I AND II). The accounts reveal the following additions and disposals.

	£
Additions	
Plant	
Dumper Truck	5,000
Excavator	32,000
Bulldozer	20,000
	£57,000
Fittings	
Office furniture	£2,000
Motor Vehicles	
Land Rover	6,000
Van	5,000
Car 1 (used by A)	12,200
Car 2 (no private use)	2,000
	£25,200

Disposals	Cost £	Proceeds £
Excavator	32,000	30,000
Digger loader	15,000	4,000
Car (Audi)	5,200	4,200
Fittings	3,500	500
	£55,700	£38,700

The dumper truck was bought second-hand from Q, brother of A, but had not been used in a trade. The truck had originally cost Q £6,000, but its market value at sale was only £2,000.

The excavator was sold without having been brought into use.

The bulldozer and car 2 were both purchased from P, father of A and had originally cost P £25,000 and £3,500 respectively. Both assets had been used for trading purposes. In both cases the price paid by A was less than the market value.

The Audi sold and the new car 1 are both used for private motoring by A. Private use has always been 30%.

The capital allowances for 1996/97 are

		Pool	Car pool	Motor Vehicles		Total allowances
		25%	25%	Audi	Car 1	
		£	£	£	£	£
WDV b/f (say)		7,500		3,900		
Additions						
Plant (excavator)	note (*a*)	2,000				
Plant (dumper truck)	note (*b*)	2,000				
Plant (bulldozer)	note (*c*)	20,000				
Fittings		2,000				
Vehicles (Land Rover, van)		11,000				
Vehicles (cars)	note (*d*)		2,000		12,200	
Disposals						
Plant (digger)		(4,000)				
Fittings		(500)				
Audi				(4,200)		
		40,000	2,000	(300)	12,200	
Allowances						
WDA	note (*e*)	(10,000)	(500)		(3,000)	13,500
30% private use restriction (car 1)						(900)
WDV c/f		£30,000	£1,500		£9,200	
Total allowances						£12,600
Balancing charge (Audi) £300 less 30% private use						£(210)

Notes

(*a*)   Writing-down allowances are available even though an asset is disposed of without being brought into use, always provided that the expenditure was incurred for the purposes of the trade (see 10.28 above) and the appropriate notification is made under *FA 1994, s 118* (see 10.25 above). Where disposal takes place in the same period as acquisition, the addition to the pool is effectively the excess of cost over disposal value.

(*b*)   Qualifying expenditure on the dumper truck is restricted to the lowest of
   (i)   open market value;
   (ii)   capital expenditure incurred by the vendor (or, if lower, by a person connected with him);
   (iii)   capital expenditure incurred by the purchaser.

See 10.38(iii) below.

(c)   Qualifying expenditure on the bulldozer is the lesser of A's actual expenditure and the disposal value brought into account in the vendor's computations (see 10.38(iii) below). (The vendor's disposal value would have been open market value but for the fact that the purchaser is himself entitled to claim capital allowances on the acquisition (see 10.28 above).) A's qualifying expenditure is thus equal to his actual expenditure. The same applies to the purchase of Car 2.

(d)   Car 1, by virtue of its costing over £12,000, is not pooled (see 10.28(A) above). Car 2 is separately pooled by virtue of *CAA 1990, s 41(1)(c)(2)* (see 10.35(a) below). See note (c) above as regards the amount of qualifying expenditure to be brought into account in respect of Car 2. The Audi was not pooled as it was used partly for non-trade purposes (see 10.28(C) above).

(e)   The writing-down allowance on Car 1 is restricted to £3,000 before adjustment for private use (see 10.28(A) above).

10.32   **Making of allowances and charges.** Allowances due to **traders** (other than companies) are given as a deduction in taxing the trade (but see below), and not as a deduction in arriving at the profits of the trade. [*CAA 1990, ss 73, 140(1)(2) as originally enacted*]. Allowances must be claimed in the annual return [*CAA 1990, s 140(3); FA 1994, s 211*] or, more commonly in practice, in computations accompanying accounts in support of a return. (This applies equally to companies for accounting periods ending after 30 September 1993. [*CAA 1990, s 145A, A1 Sch; FA 1990, s 102, 16 Sch*]. See Tolley's Corporation Tax.) See 17.6 CLAIMS as regards error or mistake relief claims following omission. For 1996/97 and earlier years as regards trades commenced before 6 April 1994, allowances are calculated by reference to events in the basis period for the year of assessment of claim (see 71.3 SCHEDULE D, CASES I AND II), except that

(a)   where basis periods overlap, expenditure in the common period is treated as incurred only in the earlier period, and

(b)   expenditure in an interval between two basis periods is treated as incurred in the later period unless it is the period of permanent discontinuance of the trade, in which case it is treated as incurred in the earlier. [*CAA 1990, s 160 as originally enacted*].

Any excess of allowances over profits for a year of assessment may be carried forward without time limit against future profits of the trade. [*CAA 1990, s 140(4) as originally enacted*]. Alternatively, allowances may create or augment a trade loss, see 46 LOSSES generally and 46.10(c)(d)(e) for restrictions on use of allowances.

For 1994/95 and subsequent years as regards trades commenced after 5 April 1994 and for 1997/98 and subsequent years as regards trades commenced on or before that date, allowances to **traders** are treated as trading expenses [*CAA 1990, s 140; FA 1994, s 211*] and are calculated by reference to events in periods of account (see 10.2(vi) above). See 10.2(vii) above as regards transitional relief for unused allowances carried forward under *CAA 1990, s 140(4) as originally enacted* (see above).

Allowances due to individual or partnership **non-trading lessors** are given on a claim for a year of assessment by way of discharge or repayment of tax, primarily against income from letting machinery or plant. Any excess of allowances over such income for a year of assessment may be carried forward without time limit against future such income. Allowances on expenditure incurred before 27 March 1980 (or under a contract entered into before that date where the machinery etc. is brought into use before 28 March 1982) may, on election within twelve months after 31 January following the tax year for which relief is given (for 1995/96 and earlier years, two years after the end of that tax year), be set against the lessor's other income of the year of assessment or of the following year, provided that the machinery etc. is at some time in the year of assessment used for the purposes of a trade carried on by the lessee. An election may, in practice, be withdrawn within the time limit for making it, provided that the corresponding liability has not been settled and agreed. Late elections may be accepted where an in-date indication of an intention to elect has in effect been accepted by the inspector. (Revenue Capital Allowances Manual, CA 156, 157). [*CAA 1990, ss 73(2)(4), 141; FA 1971, s 48; FA 1980, s 70(3); FA 1995, 6 Sch 33; FA 1996, s 135, 21 Sch 34*].

Balancing charges are assessed on traders and (under Schedule D, Case VI) on non-trading lessors, again by reference to events in the appropriate basis period (or year of assessment). For 1994/95 and subsequent years as regards trades commenced after 5 April 1994 and for 1997/98 and subsequent years as regards trades commenced on or before that date, charges on traders are treated as trading receipts and are calculated by reference to events in periods of account (see 10.2(vi) above). A charge arising on the disposal etc. of machinery or plant purchased (or treated as purchased) before 27 October 1970 (see 10.37 below) may be postponed by deducting from it the cost of machinery etc. bought in replacement, other than machinery etc. either used partly for non-trade purposes, or the subject of wear and tear subsidies (see 10.38(xii) below), or motor cars costing over £12,000. [*CAA 1990, ss 24(5), 73, 140; CAA 1968, s 40; FA 1971, 8 Sch 17; FA 1994, s 211, 26 Sch Pt V(24); FA 1995, 6 Sch 33*].

Schedule A business. With effect for 1995/96 and subsequent years (subject to transitional provisions), the above provisions concerning allowances to and charges on non-trading lessors do not apply for income tax purposes where the letting of machinery or plant is connected with the carrying on of a Schedule A business (see 68.3, 68.4 SCHEDULE A). In such a case, allowances/charges are made in taxing the business and treated as expenses/receipts of the business. [*Sec 32(1B); FA 1995, 6 Sch 8(3)*].

10.33   *Examples*

Basis periods under preceding year basis
S commenced business on 1 May 1991 preparing accounts annually to 30 April. The following expenditure was incurred.

	Plant £	Motor Car £
Period 1.5.91 – 5.4.92	10,000	4,000 (no private use)
Period 6.4.92 – 30.4.92	2,000	
Period 1.5.92 – 31.10.92	3,500	
Period 1.11.92 – 30.4.93	4,000	
Period 1.5.93 – 31.10.93	1,500	
Period 1.11.93 – 30.4.94	4,500	

An item of plant was sold for £500 (original cost £1,000) on 27.4.92.

Profits will be assessed as follows
1991/92   Period 1.5.91 – 5.4.92 (actual)
1992/93   Year ended 30.4.92 (first 12 months)
1993/94   Year ended 30.4.92 (preceding year)
1994/95   Year ended 30.4.93 (preceding year)
1995/96   Year ended 30.4.94 (preceding year)

The capital allowances are

	Qualifying for FYAs £	Pool £	Pool for cars £	Total £
1991/92 (basis period 1.5.91 – 5.4.92)				
Plant		10,000		
Motor car			4,000	
		10,000	4,000	
Allowances				
WDA 25% × $\frac{11}{12}$		(2,292)	(917)	£3,209
WDV at 5.4.92		7,708	3,083	
1992/93 (basis period 6.4.92 – 30.4.92)				
Plant		2,000		
Disposals		(500)		
		9,208	3,083	
Allowances				
WDA 25%		(2,302)	(771)	£3,073
WDV at 5.4.93		6,906	2,312	
1993/94 (no basis period)				
Allowances				
WDA 25%		(1,727)	(578)	£2,305
WDV at 5.4.94		5,179	1,734	
1994/95 (basis period 1.5.92 – 30.4.93)				
Plant	4,000	3,500		
	4,000	8,679	1,734	
Allowances				
FYA 40%	(1,600)			1,600
WDA 25%		(2,170)	(434)	2,604
	2,400	6,509	1,300	
Transfer to pool	(2,400)	2,400		
WDV at 5.4.95		c/f 8,909	c/f 1,300	
Total allowances 1994/95				£4,204

	Qualifying for FYAs	Pool	Pool for cars	Total
	£	£	£	£
		b/f 8,909	b/f 1,300	
1995/96 (basis period 1.5.93 – 30.4.94)				
Plant	1,500	4,500		
	1,500	13,409	1,300	
Allowances				
FYA 40%	(600)			600
WDA 25%		(3,352)	(325)	3,677
	900	10,057	975	
Transfer to pool	(900)	900		
WDV at 5.4.96		£10,957	£975	
Total allowances 1995/96				£4,277

Notes

(a)   The period 1.5.91–5.4.92 falls into the profits basis periods for 1991/92, 1992/93 and 1993/94. It will therefore form the capital allowances basis period for the first year, 1991/92.

(b)   The period 6.4.92–30.4.92 falls into the profits basis periods for both 1992/93 and 1993/94. Again, for capital allowances, the overlap will fall into the earlier year, 1992/93.

(c)   In 1991/92, $\frac{11}{12}$ths of a full year's writing-down allowance will be given because the business was in operation for only eleven months of that period (see 10.28 above). If a first-year allowance had been available, it would not have fallen to be restricted in this way.

Changeover from preceding year to current year basis of assessment.
Transitional year. Interval between basis periods
S continues to trade beyond the turn of the century. He has the following expenditure on machinery and plant in the three years to 30 April 1997.

	Plant £	Motor Car £
Year ended 30 April 1995	3,043	
Year ended 30 April 1996	2,300	4,800
Year ended 30 April 1997	6,400	

The new car was a replacement for the old, which was traded in at a value of £775. There continued to be no private use of either car. An item of plant was sold for £300 in the year to 30 April 1995.

10.33 Capital Allowances (Machinery and Plant)

The capital allowances for the years 1996/97 and 1997/98 are as follows.

	Pool £	Pool for cars £	Total allowances £
1996/97 (basis period 1.5.94 – 30.4.96)			
WDV at 6.4.96	10,957	975	
Additions	5,343		
Disposals	(300)	(775)	
Balancing allowance		£200	200
	16,000		
Addition		4,800	
Allowances			
WDA 25%	(4,000)	(1,200)	5,200
WDV c/f	12,000	3,600	
Total allowances 1996/97			£5,400
Period of account 1.5.96 – 30.4.97			
Additions	6,400		
	18,400	3,600	
Allowances			
WDA 25%	(4,600)	(900)	£5,500
WDV c/f	£13,800	£2,700	

Notes

(a) The capital allowances basis period for 1996/97 is the period on the profits of which income tax falls to be computed (*CAA 1990, s 160(2) as originally enacted*), which in this case is the two years to 30 April 1996 under the transitional rules (see 71.20 SCHEDULE D, CASES I AND II).

(b) The capital allowances of £5,400 for 1996/97 are deductible from the averaged profit for that year (see 71.20 SCHEDULE D, CASES I AND II) in arriving at the taxable profit. The capital allowances are not themselves subject to averaging.

(c) For 1997/98 and subsequent years (for businesses commenced before 6 April 1994), capital allowances are given by reference to periods of account (see 10.2(vi) above and the examples below). The allowances of £5,500 for the year to 30 April 1997 are deductible as a trading expense in arriving at the taxable profit for that year. The profit thus arrived at is taxable in 1997/98 on a current year basis, with overlap relief accruing for that part of the profit (*before* capital allowances) which arose before 6 April 1997 (see 71.22 SCHEDULE D, CASES I AND II).

Periods of account

James commences business on 1 October 1994 preparing accounts initially to 30 September. He changes his accounting date in 1996, preparing accounts for the 15 months to 31 December 1996. The following capital expenditure is incurred.

	Plant £	Motor Car £
Year ended 30 September 1995	12,000	4,000 (no private use)
Period ended 31 December 1996	7,500	
Year ended 31 December 1997	4,000	

An item of plant is sold for £500 (original cost £1,000) on 25 September 1996.

Profits *before* capital allowances but otherwise as adjusted for tax purposes are as follows.

	£
Year ended 30 September 1995	18,000
Period ended 31 December 1996	25,000
Year ended 31 December 1997	24,000

The capital allowances are

	Pool £	Pool for cars £	Total allowances £
Year ended 30.9.95			
Qualifying expenditure	12,000	4,000	
WDA 25%	(3,000)	(1,000)	£4,000
WDV at 30.9.95	9,000	3,000	
15 months ended 31.12.96			
Additions	7,500		
Disposals	(500)		
	16,000		
WDA 25% × 15/12	(5,000)	(938)	£5,938
WDV at 31.12.96	11,000	2,062	
Year ended 31.12.97			
Additions	4,000		
	15,000		
WDA 25%	(3,750)	(516)	£4,266
WDV at 31.12.97	£11,250	£1,546	

10.33 Capital Allowances (Machinery and Plant)

Taxable profits for the accounting periods concerned are

	Before CAs £	CAs £	After CAs £
Year ended 30 September 1995	18,000	4,000	14,000
Period ended 31 December 1996	25,000	5,938	19,062
Year ended 31 December 1997	24,000	4,266	19,734

Taxable profits for the first four years of assessment of the business are

	£	£
1994/95 (1.10.94–5.4.95) (£14,000 × 6/12)		7,000
1995/96 (y/e 30.9.95)		14,000
1996/97 (1.10.95–31.12.96)	19,062	
Deduct Overlap relief £7,000 × 3/6	3,500	
		15,562
1997/98 (y/e 31.12.97)		19,734

Notes

(a)   For businesses commencing after 5 April 1994 (and with effect for 1997/98 and subsequent years as regards businesses commenced before 6 April 1994), capital allowances are calculated by reference to periods of account and are treated as trading expenses (see 10.1, 10.2(vi) above).

(b)   Where a period of account exceeds 12 months, writing-down allowances are proportionately increased (see 10.28 above).

Period of account exceeding 18 months
Bianca commenced business on 1 October 1994 preparing accounts initially to 30 June. She changes her accounting date in 1996/97, preparing accounts for the 21 months to 31 March 1997. The following capital expenditure is incurred.

	Plant £	Motor Car £
Period ended 30 June 1995	24,000	16,000 (no private use)
Period ended 31 March 1997	10,000	
Year ended 31 March 1998	2,150	

Of the £10,000 of expenditure incurred in the 21-month accounting period to 31 March 1997, £3,000 was incurred in the 12 months to 30 June 1996 and £7,000 in the nine months to 31 March 1997.

An item of plant is sold for £675 (original cost £1,000) on 3 November 1996.

Profits *before* capital allowances but otherwise as adjusted for tax purposes are as follows.

	£
Period ended 30 June 1995	30,000
Period ended 31 March 1997	75,000
Year ended 31 March 1998	50,000

The capital allowances are

	Pool £	Car £	Total allowances £
9 months ended 30.6.95			
Qualifying expenditure	24,000	16,000	
Allowances			
WDA 25% × 9/12	(4,500)		4,500
WDA £3,000 × 9/12		(2,250)	2,250
WDV at 30.6.95	19,500	13,750	
Total allowances			£6,750
12 months ended 30.6.96			
Additions	3,000		
	22,500		
Allowances			
WDA 25%	(5,625)		5,625
WDA £3,000		(3,000)	3,000
WDV at 30.6.96	16,875	10,750	
Total allowances			£8,625
9 months ended 31.3.97			
Additions	7,000		
Disposals	(675)		
	23,200		
WDA 25% × 9/12	(4,350)	(2,016)	£6,366
WDV at 31.3.97	18,850	8,734	
Year ended 31.3.98			
Additions	2,150		
	21,000		
WDA 25%	(5,250)	(2,184)	£7,434
WDV at 31.3.98	£15,750	£6,550	

Taxable profits for the accounting periods concerned are

	Before CAs £	CAs £	After CAs £
Period ended 30 June 1995	30,000	6,750	23,250
Period ended 31 March 1997	75,000	(8,625 + 6,366)	60,009
Year ended 31 March 1998	50,000	7,434	42,566

Taxable profits for the first four years of assessment of the business are

	£	£
1994/95 (1.10.94 – 5.4.95) (£23,250 × 6/9)		15,500
1995/96 (1.10.94 – 30.9.95):		
1.10.94 – 30.6.95	23,250	
1.7.95 – 30.9.95 (£60,009 × 3/21)	8,573	
		31,823
1996/97 (1.10.95 – 31.3.97) (£60,009 × 18/21)	51,436	
Deduct Overlap relief	15,500	
		35,936
1997/98 (y/e 31.3.98)		42,566

Notes

(a) Where a period of account for capital allowances purposes would otherwise exceed 18 months, it is broken down into shorter periods, the first beginning on the first day of the actual period and each subsequent period beginning on an anniversary of the first day of the actual period. No period can therefore exceed 12 months. See 10.2(vi) above.

(b) The capital allowances computed for the notional periods of account referred to in (a) above are deductible in aggregate in arriving at the adjusted profit for the actual accounting period.

(c) An accounting period exceeding 18 months cannot normally result in an immediate change of basis period. However, the conditions of *Sec 62A* do not have to be satisfied if the change of accounting period occurs in the second or third year of assessment of a new business, as in this example. See 71.15 SCHEDULE D, CASES I AND II.

10.34   **Entitlement to allowances for fixtures.** For expenditure incurred after 11 July 1984 (but excluding expenditure under a contract entered into on or before that date, or pursuant to an obligation in a lease, or agreement for a lease, entered into on or before that date), there are special provisions to determine entitlement to allowances on fixtures which, by law, become part of the building or land on which they are installed or otherwise fixed. A dispute may arise as to whether fixtures have, in law, become part of a building or land. Where two or more persons' tax liabilities are affected by the outcome of such a dispute, the question is determined *for tax purposes* by the Special Commissioners, before whom all those persons are entitled to appear and be heard or to make written representations. [*CAA 1990, s 51(1)(7)(8)*].

These provisions determine to whom fixtures belong for allowance purposes in each of the various circumstances described at (a)–(g) below, and deny allowances to any other person in respect of those fixtures (except to a person contributing towards the capital expenditure, see 10.2(ii) above). Where fixtures are accordingly treated as ceasing to belong to a person at any time without being permanently severed from the land, and the interest as a result of which they were previously treated as belonging to him continues in existence (or would do so but for being merged in another interest), the fixtures are treated as being sold at that time for capital allowance purposes. The *deemed sale price* of the fixtures is

(1) on a sale of the qualifying interest at open market value or higher, or where the purchaser's expenditure can be taken into account for capital allowance purposes, that part of the sale price which falls (or would, if there were an entitlement, fall) to be treated for capital allowance purposes as on the provision of the fixtures;

(2)   on the grant of a lease out of the qualifying interest, so much of the consideration for the lease as falls to be treated for capital allowance purposes as expenditure by the lessee on the provision of the fixtures;

(3)   if neither (1) nor (2) applies, the amount which, if that interest were sold in the open market at that time, would be treated for capital allowance purposes as expenditure by the purchaser on provision of the fixtures (ignoring the event giving rise to the deemed sale).

[*CAA 1990, ss 51(1)(8), 59(1)–(6)*].

There are also special rules for determining the disposal value to be brought in where the qualifying interest expires, where the trade ceases, and where the fixtures start to be used for non-trade purposes. [*CAA 1990, s 59(7)–(9)*].

The expenditure by the new owner of the fixtures which attracts capital allowances is restricted to any disposal value brought in on the former owner. [*CAA 1990, s 59(10)(11)*].

For these purposes an '*interest in land*' is

(i)   the fee simple estate in the land;

(ii)   in Scotland, the estate or interest of the proprietor of the *dominium utile* (in the case of property other than feudal property, the owner);

(iii)   any leasehold estate in, or in Scotland lease of, the land;

(iv)   an easement or servitude;

(v)   a licence to occupy land;

and any agreement to acquire an interest as at (i)–(iv) above. Where an interest is conveyed or assigned by way of security subject to a right of redemption, the interest is treated as continuing to belong to the person having the redemption right. [*CAA 1990, s 51(3)(4)*].

(*a*)   *Expenditure incurred by holder of interest in land.* Where a person having an interest in land incurs capital expenditure on fixtures which become part of that land, either for trade or for leasing purposes, then, subject to (*b*)–(*f*) below, the fixtures are treated as belonging to that person. If there are two or more such persons, with different interests, the only interest to be taken into account for this purpose is

(i)   an easement or servitude, or any agreement to acquire same;

(ii)   if (i) does not apply to any of those interests, a licence to occupy the land;

(iii)   if neither (i) nor (ii) applies to any of those interests, that interest which is not directly or indirectly in reversion on any other of those interests in the land (in Scotland, that of whichever of those persons has, or last had, the right of use of the land).

[*CAA 1990, s 52*].

(*b*)   *Expenditure incurred by equipment lessor.* Where an equipment lessor incurs capital expenditure on fixtures for leasing, and an agreement is entered into for lease of the fixtures, otherwise than as part of the land to which they are attached, to another person for the purposes of a trade carried on by him or for leasing, an election may be available to the lessor and lessee. Provided that, if the expenditure had been incurred by the lessee, the fixtures would under (*a*) above have been treated as belonging to him (for which see *Melluish v BMI (No 3) Ltd HL, [1995] STC 964*), they may jointly elect in writing for the fixtures to be treated as belonging to the lessor and not to the lessee. The time limit for the election is (i) for income tax for

1996/97 onwards (subject to (ii) below), within twelve months after 31 January following the tax year in which ends the lessor's chargeable period in which the expenditure is incurred, (ii) for income tax for 1996/97 only as regards trades etc. commenced before 6 April 1994, on or before 31 January 1999, and (iii) for income tax for earlier years and for corporation tax, within two years after the end of the lessor's chargeable period in which, or in the basis period for which, the expenditure was incurred. No election is available if lessor and lessee are CONNECTED PERSONS (20).

The Revenue used to take the view that the election was available even if the lessee had not yet commenced the trade in question at the time the lease was entered into. They now take the view that an election is not valid in these circumstances, but will continue to apply their previous practice where the parties committed themselves to a transaction in reliance thereon. (Revenue Tax Bulletin October 1994 p 166).

See also (g) below.

Such an agreement as is described above, or a lease entered into pursuant to such an agreement, is referred to below as an *'equipment lease'*. [*CAA 1990, s 53; FA 1996, s 135, 21 Sch 31*].

(c)   *Expenditure included in consideration for acquisition of existing interest in land.* Where a person acquires a pre-existing interest in land to which fixtures are attached, for a consideration in part treated for capital allowance purposes as being expenditure on provision of the fixtures, and either no person had previously been entitled to allowances on the fixtures, or any person previously so entitled is or has been required to bring in a disposal value (other than by virtue of an 'additional VAT rebate'—see 10.2(v) above) in respect of them, then the fixtures are treated as belonging to the person acquiring the interest. This applies equally where the fixtures in question were previously let under an 'equipment lease' (see (*b*) above) and, in connection with the acquisition, the purchaser pays a capital sum to discharge the lessee's obligations under that lease. [*CAA 1990, s 54; FA 1991, 14 Sch 10*].

(d)   *Expenditure incurred by incoming lessee: election to transfer right to allowances.* Where a person with an interest in land to which fixtures are attached grants a lease (or enters into an agreement for a lease) and, apart from (*f*) below, he would (or if chargeable to tax would) be entitled, for the chargeable period relating to the grant of the lease (or the agreement), to capital allowances in respect of the fixtures, and the consideration given by the lessee falls in part to be treated for capital allowance purposes as expenditure on the provision of the fixtures, an election may be available to the lessor and lessee. They may jointly elect (in writing within two years of the date on which the lease or agreement takes effect) that, from the grant of the lease (or the agreement), the fixtures are treated as belonging to the lessee and not to the lessor. No election is, however, available if lessor and lessee are CONNECTED PERSONS (20), or if it appears that the sole or main benefit to the lessor from the grant of the lease (or the agreement) and the election would be enhanced capital allowances or a reduced balancing charge. [*CAA 1990, ss 52, 55, 57(5)*].

(e)   *Expenditure incurred by incoming lessee: lessor not entitled to allowances.* Where (*d*) above does not apply because the lessor is not entitled to capital allowances in respect of the fixtures, and at the time of grant of the lease (or the agreement) no person has previously become so entitled, and before that time the fixtures have not been used for trade purposes by the lessor or by a person connected with him (see 20 CONNECTED PERSONS), then the fixtures are treated as belonging to the lessee. [*CAA 1990, ss 52, 56*].

(*f*) *Cases where fixture is to be treated as ceasing to belong to a particular person.* Where a person to whom fixtures are treated as belonging under (*a*), (*c*), (*d*) or (*e*) above ceases for any reason to have the interest giving rise to that treatment, the fixtures are at that time treated as ceasing to belong to him for capital allowance purposes. An agreement to acquire an interest and the interest subsequently acquired under the agreement are treated for this purpose as the same interest. Similarly, an interest into which the interest in question is merged, or an interest consisting of a new lease or licence following termination of a previous lease or licence which was the interest in question, is treated as the same interest as the interest in question. If the interest in question is a lease, and the lessee remains in possession with the lessor's consent following its termination without a new lease, the interest is treated as continuing as long as the possession continues.

Where, under these provisions, fixtures are treated as ceasing to belong to a person on termination of a lease or licence, they are treated as commencing to belong to the lessor or licensor immediately before the termination.

Where fixtures treated under these provisions as belonging to a person are severed from the land to which they are attached, they are treated as ceasing to belong to that person, unless they in fact belong to him. [*CAA 1990, s 57*].

(*g*) *Special provisions as to equipment lessors.* Where an election is made under (*b*) above, and either

(i) the lessor assigns his rights under the equipment lease; or

(ii) the lessee's financial obligations under the lease are discharged,

then the fixtures are treated as ceasing to belong to the lessor by reason of a sale by him.

If (i) above applies, then, from the time of the assignment, the fixtures are treated as belonging to the assignee for capital allowance purposes, and the consideration for the assignment treated as consideration for the fixtures. If the assignee makes any further assignment, he is treated under this provision as if he were the original lessor.

If (ii) above applies and a capital sum is paid in consideration of the discharge, that sum is treated as consideration for the fixtures, and the fixtures are treated from the time of the payment as belonging to the lessee (or to any other person in whom his obligations under the lease have become vested). [*CAA 1990, s 58*].

10.35 **Leasing of machinery and plant.** Legislation regarding capital allowances on machinery and plant provided for leasing was first introduced in 1980 and was mainly concerned with restricting the availability of first-year allowances. Further legislation introduced in 1982 restricted, and in some cases prohibited, writing-down allowances on machinery and plant leased to non-UK resident lessees in certain circumstances. Following the phasing out of first-year allowances, much of the original legislation was no longer appropriate and the leasing provisions were widely amended by the *Finance Act 1986* but so as to broadly retain those relating to overseas leasing. For the purposes of applying the 1986 changes expenditure incurred after 31 March 1986 (with the exceptions below) was designated 'new expenditure'. The current provisions are contained in *CAA 1990, ss 39–50*.

For the purposes of these provisions, a 'lease' includes a sub-lease, with 'lessor' and 'lessee' being construed accordingly, and 'leasing' is regarded as including the letting of any asset on hire or of a ship on charter (and see *Barclays Mercantile Industrial Finance Ltd v Melluish Ch D 1990, 63 TC 95* at (*d*) below). [*CAA 1990, s 50(1)(2)*].

10.35 Capital Allowances (Machinery and Plant)

'*New expenditure*' means expenditure incurred after 31 March 1986 on machinery and plant other than certain cars costing £12,000 or less (see (*a*) below), provided that it is not 'old expenditure'. '*Old expenditure*' means the following.

(A) Certain expenditure incurred before 1 April 1987 for which a first-year allowance (other than the temporary 40% allowance under *CAA 1990, s 22(3B)*) would (apart from the leasing restrictions) be available (see 10.27 above).

(B) Certain expenditure incurred before 1 June 1986 on 'television sets' (to which separate provisions applied—see below).

(C) Certain expenditure on acquisition of an asset by a person connected with (see 20 CONNECTED PERSONS), or succeeding to a trade carried on by, the person who originally incurred expenditure on its acquisition before 1 April 1986.

[*CAA 1990, s 50(3); FA 1993, 13 Sch 11(1)*].

Assets leased outside the UK. The provisions described below apply to both 'new' and 'old expenditure' on the provision of machinery or plant which at any time in the 'requisite period' is leased to a person who

(1) is not resident in the UK, and

(2) does not use the machinery etc. exclusively for earning profits chargeable to UK tax, being either profits from a trade carried on in the UK or from exploration or exploitation activities carried on in the UK or its territorial sea.

For the purpose of (2) above, profits chargeable to UK tax do not include profits in respect of which the trader etc. is entitled to tax relief under a double taxation agreement. This does not apply in the case of leases entered into before 16 March 1993 for which, in addition, the use of the machinery etc. does not have to be *exclusively* for the purposes stated. The provisions do not apply where the leasing is either 'short-term leasing' (see (*e*) below) or, as regards 'new expenditure' only, the leasing of a ship, aircraft or transport container used for a 'qualifying purpose' by virtue of *CAA 1990, s 39(6)–(9)* (see (*d*) below). [*CAA 1990, ss 42(1)(8), 50(3A); FA 1993, s 116(2)–(4)*]. The provisions apply to expenditure incurred on or after 10 March 1982. There was an exclusion for expenditure consisting of payments made under a contract entered into before that date or, under certain conditions relating to arrangements in existence at that date, before 1 April 1984, provided in either case that the machinery was brought into use before 1 April 1985. [*FA 1982, s 70(10)(12)*].

The provisions referred to above are as follows.

(*a*) *Restriction of writing-down allowances and separate pooling.* Writing-down allowances on machinery or plant within these provisions are restricted to **10% p.a.** (instead of the normal 25% p.a.). [*CAA 1990, s 42(2)*]. For this purpose, the machinery etc. is treated as being provided for a separate notional trade, i.e. it is separately pooled. The notional trade is regarded as permanently discontinued when all items in the separate pool begin to be used wholly or partly for purposes other than those of the actual trade (or are disposed of, lost or cease to exist). A lessor need not claim the full amount of writing-down allowances. When machinery and plant in the separate pool is disposed of to a CONNECTED PERSON (20) (otherwise than on an occasion when the trade is treated as continuing) the 'disposal value' is its open market value or, if lower, its original cost, and the person acquiring it may claim allowances on the same value. [*CAA 1990, s 41(1)–(3)(5); FA 1990, 17 Sch 9*].

The above separate pooling provisions do not apply to cars costing over £12,000, assets used partially for non-trade purposes and assets for which contributions are received towards wear and tear, all of which remain outside the main pool of qualifying expenditure in any case (see 10.28(A)(C) above, 10.38(xii) below). The restriction on writing-down allowances *does* so apply. *Cars costing £12,000 or less*

(£8,000 for expenditure incurred or treated as incurred before 11 March 1992), and which are not leased so as to be otherwise within these provisions, must also be included in a separate pool under *Sec 41* but *not* the same pool as that used for leased assets. [*CAA 1990, ss 41(1)(c)(4)(6), 42(2)*]. The car pool will also include any 'old expenditure' on machinery and plant provided for leasing which is precluded by *CAA 1990, s 22(4)(c)* from qualifying for a first-year allowance (or would have been if a first-year allowance had not already been precluded by *CAA 1990, s 75* (sales between connected persons etc.)). [*CAA 1990, s 41(1)(b)*].

(b)   *Prohibition of allowances.* No writing-down or balancing allowances are available in respect of expenditure to which the overseas leasing provisions apply if the machinery etc. is used other than for a 'qualifying purpose' (see (*d*) below) and

  (i)   there is more than one year between consecutive payments due under the lease, or

  (ii)   any payments other than periodical payments are due under the lease or under any collateral agreement, or

  (iii) any payment expressed monthly under the lease or any collateral agreement is not the same as any other such payment, but disregarding variations due to changes in rates of tax, capital allowances, interest which is linked with rates applicable to inter-bank loans or changes in premiums for insurances of any kind by a person not connected with the lessor or lessee, or

  (iv)   either the lease is for a period exceeding thirteen years or there is any provision for its extension or renewal or for the grant of a new lease so that the leasing period could exceed thirteen years, or

  (v)   at any time, the lessor or CONNECTED PERSON (20) could be entitled to receive from the lessee or any other person a payment (not insurance moneys) of an amount determined before expiry of the lease and referable to the value of the machinery etc. at or after that expiry (whether or not the payment relates to a disposal of the machinery etc.).

[*CAA 1990, s 42(3)*].

Where allowances (including any first-year allowance) have been made (and not fully withdrawn under the excess relief provisions in (*g*) below) but by reason of any event in the 'requisite period' (see (*c*) below) are found to be prohibited as above (assuming, where relevant, first-year allowances to be so prohibited), the net allowances are clawed back by means of a balancing charge. For this purpose only, the allowances made on an item of 'new expenditure' are determined as if that were the only item, i.e. as if it had not been pooled with any other item of machinery etc. Where an item was acquired from a CONNECTED PERSON (20), or as a part of a series of transactions with connected persons, allowances made to those persons are also taken into account in computing the balancing charge, with any actual consideration on a connected persons transaction being ignored and with the amount of such allowances being adjusted as is 'just and reasonable in the circumstances' where balancing allowances/charges have already been made in respect of the item in question. This does not apply in the case of transactions between connected persons on which the trade was treated as continuing under *Secs 113(2)* or *114(1)* (partnership changes treated as a continuation) or *Sec 343(2)* (company reconstruction without change of ownership) or *CAA 1990, s 77(1)* (succession to trade before 30 July 1988 between connected persons). [*CAA 1990, s 42(3)–(9); FA 1993, 13 Sch 6*].

(c)   '*Requisite period*'. The '*requisite period*', for 'new expenditure' and for 'old expenditure' falling within the overseas leasing provisions and not used for a 'qualifying purpose' (see (*d*) below), is the period of ten years after the asset is first brought into use by the person who incurred the expenditure, but ends earlier if the asset ceases to belong to that person (but ignoring a disposal to a CONNECTED PERSON (20) or on a partnership change which is treated as a continuation under *Sec 113(2)* or disregarded under *Sec 114(1)*). For other 'old expenditure', the '*requisite period*' is one of four years, with the same rule as above for earlier disposals. For leases entered into before 16 March 1993, what would otherwise have been a ten-year maximum requisite period was reduced to a maximum of four years if the machinery etc. was used for a 'qualifying purpose' (see (*d*) below); for later leases, this applies only in defining the '*requisite period*' for the purposes of the provisions for writing-down allowances on ships (see 10.28(B) above) and the short-life asset provisions (see 10.28(F) above). [*CAA 1990, s 40(4)(5); FA 1993, s 116(1)*].

(*d*) '*Qualifying purpose*'. Machinery or plant on which a person (the buyer) has incurred expenditure is used for a '*qualifying purpose*' at any time if, at that time:

(i) it is used by a lessee for the purposes of a trade (other than leasing), the buyer's expenditure was 'new expenditure' and had the lessee bought the machinery etc. himself at that time, and incurred 'new expenditure' in doing so, it would have fallen to be wholly or partly included in his qualifying expenditure for writing-down allowances; or

(ii) it is used by a lessee for the purposes of a trade (other than leasing), the buyer's expenditure was 'old expenditure' and had the lessee bought the machinery etc. himself at that time, and incurred capital expenditure in doing so, he would have been entitled to a first-year allowance (disregarding the withdrawal of such allowances after 31 March 1986 (see 10.27 above) and ignoring double allowances provisions (see 10.38(iv) below)); or

(iii) the buyer uses it for 'short-term leasing' (see (*e*) below); or

(iv) the lessee uses it for 'short-term leasing' and is either UK resident or so uses it in the course of a trade carried on in the UK; or

(v) the buyer uses it for the purposes of a trade other than leasing.

For the purposes of (iii) and (v) above, where during the 'requisite period' (see (*c*) above) an asset is disposed of to a connected person, or on a partnership change treated as a continuation under *Sec 113(2)* or disregarded under *Sec 114(1)*, the new owner is treated as the 'buyer'. [*CAA 1990, s 39(1)–(5)(10); FA 1993, 13 Sch 5(1)*].

As regards (i) and (ii) above, the use by the lessee must be *wholly* for the purposes of a trade otherwise than for leasing, but the word 'leasing' is to be construed in accordance with the narrow test applicable to leases of land, so that distribution agreements entered into by film lessee companies were not leases for these purposes but arrangements entered into in the ordinary course of the lessees' businesses (*Barclays Mercantile Industrial Finance Ltd v Melluish Ch D 1990, 63 TC 95*).

Without prejudice to (i)–(v) above, a ship is also used for a '*qualifying purpose*' at any time when it is let on charter in the course of a trade of operating ships if the lessor is resident, or carries on his trade, in the UK and is responsible as principal (or appoints another person to be responsible in his stead) for navigating and managing the ship and for defraying substantially all its expenses except those directly incidental to a particular voyage or charter period. The same applies with necessary modifications in relation to aircraft. However, neither ship nor aircraft chartering qualifies if the main object, or one of them, of the chartering (or of a series of transactions of which the chartering was one) was the obtaining by any person of a first-year allowance or, for 'new expenditure' only, an unrestricted writing-down allowance. A transport container is also used for a '*qualifying purpose*' at any time when it is leased in the course of a trade carried on in the UK or by a UK resident if either the trade is one of operating ships or aircraft and the container is at other times used by the trader in connection with such operation, or the container is leased under a succession of leases to different persons who, or most of whom, are not connected with each other. [*CAA 1990, s 39(6)–(9); FA 1993, 13 Sch 5(2)*].

(*e*)   '*Short-term leasing*' means leasing an item of machinery or plant in such a manner

    (i)   that (A) the number of consecutive days for which it is leased to the same person will normally be less than 30 and (B) the total number of days to the same person in any period of 12 months will normally be less than 90, or

    (ii)   that (A) the number of consecutive days for which it is leased to the same person will not normally exceed 365 and (B) the aggregate of the periods for which it is leased to lessees not falling within (*d*)(i)(ii) above will not exceed 2 years in the 'requisite period' (see (*c*) above) or, where the requisite period exceeds 4 years, in any period of 4 consecutive years falling within the 'requisite period'.

For the above purposes, persons who are connected with each other (see CONNECTED PERSONS (20)) will be treated as the same person and where machinery or plant is leased from a pool of items of similar description and not separately identifiable, all the items in the pool may be treated as used for short-term leasing if substantially the whole of the items in the pool are so used. [*CAA 1990, s 40(1)–(3)*].

(*f*)   *Joint lessees.* Where machinery or plant on which 'new expenditure' has been incurred

    (i)   is leased (otherwise than by 'permitted leasing'—see below) to two or more persons jointly, and

    (ii)   at least one of the joint lessees is a person within (1) and (2) above,

the normal 25% writing-down allowance, and where applicable the temporary 40% first-year allowance, is due only to the extent that it appears that the profits of the trade or trades (other than leasing) in which the item is used during the 'requisite period' (see (*c*) above), or the period of the lease if shorter, will be chargeable to income tax or corporation tax. The part of the expenditure so qualifying for normal allowances is treated as if it were expenditure on a separate item of machinery etc. with the remaining part treated as expenditure within the overseas leasing provisions, with such apportionments as are necesary. [*CAA 1990, s 43; FA 1993, 13 Sch 7*]. Excess relief is recoverable under (*g*) below if at any time in the requisite period while the item is so leased, no lessee uses it for the purposes of such a trade or if, at the end of the requisite period, it appears that the actual extent of such trade use was less than anticipated. In the latter case the amount of excess relief recoverable is in proportion to the reduction in use and any disposal value subsequently brought into account is apportioned to the extent of such trade use as determined at the end of the requisite period. [*CAA 1990, s 44; FA 1993, 13 Sch 8*]. Broadly similar provisions apply in relation to both first-year and writing-down allowances on 'old expenditure'. [*CAA 1990, s 45*].

'*Permitted leasing*' means 'short-term leasing' (see (*e*) above) or the leasing of a ship, aircraft or transport container which is used for a 'qualifying purpose' by virtue of *CAA 1990, s 39(6)–(9) (see (d) above).* [*CAA 1990, s 50(3)*].

10.35 Capital Allowances (Machinery and Plant)

(g) *Recovery of excess relief.* Where 'new expenditure' has qualified for the normal 25% writing-down allowance (or the temporary 40% first-year allowance) and the machinery or plant is at any time in the 'requisite period' (see (c) above) used for the purpose of leasing to a non-resident within (1) and (2) above, otherwise than by 'permitted leasing' (see (f) above), any 'excess relief' is recovered. This is achieved by means of a balancing charge of an amount equal to the excess relief, to be made on the person to whom the item then belongs, for the chargeable period in which, or in the basis period for which, the change of use occurs. The item is removed from the general pool of qualifying expenditure by means of a disposal value equal to the item's written-down value for capital allowances purposes. The sum of the excess relief and the disposal value is then regarded as qualifying expenditure for the next chargeable period in the separate notional trade for assets leased overseas (see (a) above). The '*excess relief*' is the excess, if any, of the allowances made, up to and including the chargeable period in question, over the maximum writing-down allowances that could have been made if the expenditure had been within (a) or (b) above from the outset. The allowances made are determined for this purpose as if the item in question were the only item, i.e. as if it had not been pooled with any other item of machinery etc.

Where the person on whom the balancing charge falls to be made acquired the item in question from a CONNECTED PERSON (20), or as part of a series of transactions with connected persons, normal writing-down allowances and any first-year allowance made to those persons are taken into account in computing the excess relief, with any actual consideration on a connected persons transaction being ignored and with the amount of excess relief being adjusted as is 'just and reasonable in the circumstances' where balancing allowances/charges have already been made in respect of the item in question. This does not apply in the case of transactions between connected persons on which the trade was treated as continuing under *Secs 113(2)* or *114(1)* (partnership changes treated as a continuation) or *Sec 343(2)* (company reconstruction without change of ownership) or *CAA 1990, s 77* (succession to trade between connected persons). Where relief has been obtained by means of a balancing allowance instead of claiming (or by disclaimer of) a normal writing-down allowance or first-year allowance, excess relief is recovered under these provisions suitably modified.

In the case of ships, any allowance deferred (see 10.27, 10.28(B) above) may not be made for any chargeable period in or after which the change of use occurs, but is instead treated as qualifying expenditure for the next chargeable period in the separate notional trade.

[*CAA 1990, s 46; FA 1990, 17 Sch 10; FA 1993, 13 Sch 9; FA 1994, 26 Sch Pt V(24)*].

Broadly similar recovery rules apply to both first-year and writing-down allowances on 'old expenditure'. As regards first-year allowances, these rules apply when any non-qualifying use of the leased assets occurs during the requisite period. [*CAA 1990, s 47; FA 1990, 17 Sch 11; FA 1994, 26 Sch Pt V(24)*].

(h) *Information* (e.g. names of lessees) must be provided to the Revenue under *CAA 1990, s 48* where 'new expenditure' on machinery or plant has qualified for a normal 25% writing-down allowance and/or the temporary 40% first-year allowance and the item is leased (other than by 'permitted leasing'—see (f) above), at any time in the 'requisite period' (see (c) above), to a non-resident within (1) and (2) above, or to joint lessees at least one of whom is such a person. The time limit for providing the information is three months after the end of the chargeable period or basis period in which the item is first so leased, extended to 30 days after the informant came to know that the item was being so leased (if he could not reasonably have been expected to know earlier). [*CAA 1990, ss 48(2)–(7), 50(3); FA 1993, 13 Sch 10; FA 1994, 26 Sch Pt V(24)*]. Broadly similar information provisions apply under *CAA 1990, s 49* in respect of 'old expenditure'.

Where 'new expenditure' has not yet qualified for a normal writing-down allowance and the item is used for permitted leasing to a non-resident within (1) and (2) above, a claim for a writing-down allowance thereon must be accompanied by a certificate describing the permitted leasing. This also applies to the temporary 40% first-year allowance. [*CAA 1990, ss 48(1)(7), 50(3); FA 1990, 17 Sch 12; FA 1993, 13 Sch 10*].

Restriction of first-year allowances. 'New expenditure' is not automatically precluded from qualifying for the temporary 40% first-year allowance under *CAA 1990, s 22(3B)* for expenditure incurred after 31 October 1992 and before 1 November 1993 (see 10.27 above), but *is* so precluded if:

(I)   it appears that the expenditure would fall within the provisions for assets leased outside the UK (see above); or

(II)   the expenditure is incurred after 13 April 1993 and each of the following conditions is satisfied:

(*a*)   a first-year allowance would have been precluded under the provisions below if the expenditure had been 'old expenditure'; and

(*b*)   the person to whom the machinery etc. is to be, or is, leased, or a person connected with him, used the machinery etc. for any purpose at any time before its provision for leasing.

[*CAA 1990, s 22(6A); FA 1993, s 115(3)*].

As regards 'old expenditure', machinery or plant provided for leasing does not qualify for a first-year allowance unless it appears that it will be used *only* for a 'qualifying purpose' (see (*d*) above) during the 'requisite period' (see (*c*) above). This exclusion does not apply to the provision of

(AA) vehicles wholly or mainly for use by persons in receipt of certain social security mobility allowances/supplements and disability living allowances, or

(BB) machinery or plant which is to be an integral part of a building qualifying for enterprise zone allowances (see 10.19 above), or

(CC) machinery or plant fixed to a building or land of which the person incurring the expenditure is the lessor, where a transfer of his interest in the building etc. would operate to transfer his interest in the machinery etc.

[*CAA 1990, s 22(4)(c)(5)(6)(11)*].

For 'old expenditure' only, *information* must be provided to the Revenue under *CAA 1990, s 23*.

See (*f*) above for the position where machinery or plant is leased under certain circumstances to joint lessees. See (*g*) above for recovery of excess relief, including first-year allowances.

10.36   Capital Allowances (Machinery and Plant)

Temporary provisions for 'foreign to foreign' leasing. The first-year allowance was restricted to 25%, and separate pooling applied, for expenditure incurred after 23 October 1979 and before 1 June 1980 if the machinery or plant was at any time in the requisite period being leased under a finance lease (as defined) to a non-UK resident who did not use it for the purposes of a trade carried on in the UK or for exploration or exploitation activities in a designated area of the continental shelf. [*FA 1980, s 72(4), 12 Sch Pt I*].

Transitional provisions for television or viewdata etc. sets. First-year allowances were not precluded for expenditure on a television set or viewdata receiver (as defined) or teletext receiver (as defined) where the expenditure was incurred *and* delivery made to the person incurring it during a transitional period starting on 1 June 1980 and ending on 31 May 1984 for a television set and 31 May 1986 for a teletext or viewdata receiver. For expenditure incurred after 9 March 1982, the provisions were extended to cover teletext and viewdata adaptors. If sets were used other than for a 'qualifying purpose' (see (*d*) above) (for example, if they were used for leasing to a private individual) within the 'requisite period' (see (*c*) above), first-year allowances, normally 100%, were reduced to 75% and 50% respectively for sets delivered (to the person incurring the expenditure) in the penultimate year and final year of the transitional period, and separate pooling applied. The general reductions in first-year allowances for expenditure incurred after 13 March 1984 (see 10.27 above) did not apply to such expenditure. [*FA 1980, s 72(5), 12 Sch Pt II; FA 1982, s 77; FA 1983, s 33*].

10.36   *Examples*

Separate pooling
L has a leasing business preparing accounts annually to 31 May. In the year to 31 May 1994, his expenditure included the following.

		£
(i)	Machine 1, leased to M Ltd, a UK resident company for the purposes of its trade	20,000
(ii)	Machine 2, leased to N, a UK resident individual, for private use	8,000
(iii)	Machine 3, leased to P, a non-UK resident, for his overseas trade	16,000
(iv)	Fixtures and fittings for use in L's business	2,000
(v)	Motor car used by L entirely for business	6,000

All the above expenditure was incurred before 1 November 1993. At 6 April 1995, there is a written-down value of £40,000 brought forward in L's machinery and plant pool.

The leasing in (iii) above is neither 'short-term leasing' (see 10.35(*e*) above) nor the leasing of a ship, aircraft or transport container to be used for a 'qualifying purpose' (see 10.35(*d*) above).

L's capital allowances for 1995/96, assuming no capital expenditure for the year to 31 May 1994 other than as listed above, are as follows.

	Expenditure qualifying for FYAs £	Main Pool £	Car Pool £	Pool for overseas leasing £	Total allowances £
WDV b/f		40,000			
Additions					
(i) (ii) (iv)	30,000				
(iii) (v)			6,000	16,000	
FYA 40%	(12,000)				12,000
WDA 25%		(10,000)	(1,500)		11,500
WDA 10%				(1,600)	1,600
Transfer to pool	(18,000)	18,000			
WDV c/f		£48,000	£4,500	£14,400	
Total allowances					£25,100

Notes

(a)   Machines 1 and 2 go into the general pool for machinery and plant, as do the fixtures and fittings. Machine 3 goes into a separate pool by virtue of its falling within *CAA 1990, s 42* (assets leased outside the UK). The car also goes into a separate pool. See 10.35(*a*) above.

(b)   The writing-down allowance for Machine 3 is restricted to 10%. A first-year allowance is not available for Machine 3.

Recovery of excess relief

M, who has a 30 September accounting date, incurred expenditure of £16,000 in March 1992 on a machine leased to Q Ltd, a company trading in the UK. In May 1995, Q Ltd terminated the lease and M then leased the machine, with effect from June 1995, to P Ltd, a company resident in Panama, for the purposes of its trade there. The leasing was not 'permitted leasing'.

A balancing charge arises in 1996/97 (basis period two years to 30.9.96, see 71.20 SCHEDULE D, CASES I AND II) as follows.

Actual allowances

	£	Total allowances £
Expenditure (year ended 30.9.92)	16,000	
WDA 25% for 1993/94	4,000	4,000
	12,000	
WDA 25% for 1994/95	3,000	3,000
	9,000	
WDA 25% for 1995/96	2,250	2,250
	6,750	
WDA 25% for 1996/97	1,688	1,688
Residue of expenditure	£5,062	
Total allowances claimed		£10,938

10.37   Capital Allowances (Machinery and Plant)

Notional allowances

	£	Total allowances £
Expenditure (year ended 30.9.92)	16,000	
WDA 10% for 1993/94 note (*a*)	1,600	1,600
	14,400	
WDA 10% for 1994/95	1,440	1,440
	12,960	
WDA 10% for 1995/96	1,296	1,296
	11,664	
WDA 10% for 1996/97	1,166	1,166
	£10,498	
Notional allowances		£5,502

Balancing charge, equal to the excess of actual allowances over notional allowances, for 1996/97 note (*b*)		£5,436

M will then be deemed to have incurred qualifying expenditure of £10,498 (equal to the residue of expenditure plus the balancing charge) for the year ending 30.9.97, i.e. the chargeable period following that in the basis period for which the change of use arose, and will then be entitled to writing-down allowances of 10% for that and subsequent chargeable periods. The expenditure will constitute, or form part of, a separate pool.

Notes

(*a*)   Notional writing-down allowances are restricted to 10% notwithstanding the fact that the machine was used for a qualifying purpose up to May 1995. It is leased to a person within 10.35(1) and (2) above at some time in the requisite period.

(*b*)   In practice, the machine would originally have been included in the general pool for machinery and plant. For the purpose of calculating the balancing charge, it is assumed to have been the only item of machinery and plant qualifying for writing-down allowances. In 1996/97, a disposal value equal to the residue of expenditure (£5,062) must be deducted from the pool.

10.37   **'Old scheme' before 27 October 1970.** A different system of reliefs and charges (the 'old scheme') applies to expenditure before 27 October 1970 and to certain later expenditure (see below). A summary is given below, see Tolley's Income Tax 1981/82 or earlier editions for more detailed coverage. Most machinery etc. subject to old scheme was, however, brought into the 'pool' of qualifying expenditure under the current scheme (see 10.28 above) following the *FA 1976* provisions (see below).

(*a*)   *Expenditure after 26 October 1970 to which old scheme applies* is that on machinery etc.

   (i)   purchased from a connected person (within *Sec 839*, see 20 CONNECTED PERSONS) who incurred his expenditure before 27 October 1970; or

    (ii)   purchased from a person who incurred his expenditure before 27 October 1970, where the sole or main benefit from the transaction(s) appears to be the obtaining of relief under the current scheme; or

    (iii)   first brought into use by the purchaser after 26 October 1970, where the later expenditure consists of hire purchase instalments; or

    (iv)   purchased in a sale and lease-back transaction from a person who incurred his expenditure before 27 October 1970; or

    (v)   which belonged (or was treated as belonging) to the purchaser at any time before 27 October 1970.

(iv) and (v) apply only to expenditure incurred after 13 June 1972.

[*FA 1971, s 40(2)(3); FA 1972, s 68(1)*].

(*b*)   *FA 1976 'pooling' provisions.* Commencing with the first basis period (first accounting period for a company) ending after 5 April 1976, any balance of unallowed expenditure incurred up to 26 October 1970 is to be added to the 'pool' of unallowed expenditure incurred after that date (see 10.28 above) except for

    (i)   ships.

    (ii)   cars where writing-down allowances are restricted (see (*c*)(iii) below).

    (iii)   items with partial use for other purpose (see 10.28(C) above).

    (iv)   items leased (see (*c*)(iv) below).

    (v)   items on which subsidies are received for wear and tear (see 10.38(xii) below).

    (vi)   items on which the alternative method of calculating writing-down allowances has been used (see (*c*)(ii) below).

    (vii)   items on hire purchase contracts which are uncompleted at beginning of the first basis (or accounting) period mentioned above.

    (viii)   items where an election is made (within two years from end of first period affected) for these provisions not to apply. The election is irrevocable.

The writing-down allowance (for (ii) to (vii) above) will be at 25% and ships (at (i) above) will continue to receive free depreciation. [*FA 1976, s 39, 15 Sch*].

(*c*)   *System of allowances.*

    (i)   An *initial allowance* of (from 15 April 1958) 30% (10% where an investment allowance was also available) was made. [*CAA 1968, s 18, 1 Sch 1*].

    (ii)   *Writing-down allowances* were granted for a basis period at the end of which machinery etc. was in use for the trade etc. Various rates applied, and a 'normal' (written-down value) method, an 'alternative' (straight-line) method and a 'special' (mines, oil wells etc.) method were available. New ships could be depreciated freely. [*CAA 1968, ss 19–31, 4 Sch*].

    (iii)   *Cars* did not attract initial allowances (except with restrictions similar to those in 10.27(i) above). The maximum writing-down allowance was £500. [*CAA 1968, ss 18(3), 32, 2 Sch*].

    (iv)   *Lessees of plant* were entitled to writing-down allowances only on a 'just and reasonable' proportion of capital expenditure incurred, provided that they were responsible for its maintenance and bore the cost of wear and tear. [*CAA 1968, s 43*]. Special provisions applied to lessees of ships. [*CAA 1968, s 43(2)*]. *Lessors of plant* could claim a capital allowance of the wear and tear borne by them in any basis period. [*CAA 1968, s 42*].

(v)   *Hire purchase.* Initial allowances were given on the capital portion of each instalment, writing-down allowances on the capital portion of the full price for any basis period at the end of which the machinery etc. was in use for trade etc. purposes. [*CAA 1968, ss 18(7), 19(1), 20(1)*].

(*d*)   *Balancing allowance or charge* arises when machinery etc. (not transferred to 'pool' under *FA 1976* provisions, see (*b*) above) ceases to belong to the trader, or permanently ceases to be used for the trade, or when the trade is permanently discontinued. [*CAA 1968, s 33(1)*].

The amount of the allowance or charge is the difference between (A) the sum of all sale, insurance, salvage or compensation proceeds, and (B) the 'expenditure still unallowed', i.e. the original cost less all initial, annual, scientific research and exceptional depreciation allowances already made on the plant (including previous balancing allowances). [*CAA 1968, ss 33, 41, 86*]. But where demolition of plant etc. gives rise, or might give rise, to a balancing allowance or charge, the net cost of demolition (after crediting sales of materials or scrap) is added to the 'expenditure unallowed' as above. [*CAA 1968, s 36*]. A balancing charge cannot exceed the total of allowances previously given [*CAA 1968, s 33(5)*] and may be postponed by deducting from it cost of plant bought in replacement, but allowances in respect of that plant are then calculated on the reduced amount. [*CAA 1968, s 40; FA 1971, 8 Sch 17*].

Machinery etc. is to be treated as if sold at open-market price if

(i)   it is given away, or sold at less than market price, or

(ii)   it ceases to be used for a trade by being transferred to other use, or is retained by the transferor on a transfer of a trade not treated as a discontinuance, or

(iii)   on permanent discontinuance of the trade it is retained or given away, or sold at less than market price. [*CAA 1968, s 34*].

But these provisions do not apply if the gift or sale at less than market price is already caught by *CAA 1968, s 78* (sales between controlled bodies) or by *ICTA 1970, s 196, FA 1976, Pt III* or *ICTA 1988, Pt V, Ch II* ('benefits in kind', see 75.11 *et seq.* SCHEDULE E), or is, in certain circumstances, between partners. [*CAA 1968, ss 34, 44, 79(2)*]. Also, former and subsequent owners may jointly elect to continue calculations on written-down value, but in that case any subsequent balancing adjustments will be calculated by reference to original cost. [*CAA 1968, s 35*].

10.38   Machinery and plant—General matters.

(i)   *Abortive expenditure.* When a person is entitled to the benefit of a contract under which he incurs capital expenditure on the provision of machinery or plant for trade purposes, and he shall or may become the owner of the machinery or plant on performance of the contract, the machinery or plant is treated as belonging to him. [*CAA 1990, s 60(1)(a)*]. Capital allowances are accordingly available for the expenditure as it is incurred, and if the person ceases to be entitled to the benefit of the contract without becoming the owner of the machinery or plant, the provisions described at (vi) below crystallise a deemed disposal of the machinery or plant. [*CAA 1990, s 60(2)*].

(ii)   *Car leasing* (see 10.27(i) above). Where a car is sold to the lessee or his nominee or connected person at less than the open market value at the end of the leasing contract, or some other variation of the traditional kind of contract, the Revenue will consider what adjustment may be necessary to the tax liabilities of the taxpayers affected. The adjustments may be to treat the car as stock-in-trade of the lessor rather than an asset qualifying for capital allowances, or substituting the open market value for the sale proceeds, or disallowing the lessee's rental payments as not being wholly and exclusively for the trade, or taxing any benefit obtained by the person connected with the lessee who acquires the car (Revenue Press Release 26 July 1978). See special legislation re leasing in 10.35 above and re motor cars costing over £12,000 in 10.28(A) above.

(iii) *Connected persons and other anti-avoidance measures.* See 10.27(iii) above as regards first-year allowance restrictions, and 10.37(*a*) above as regards certain expenditure to which current scheme does not apply. See 20 CONNECTED PERSONS for a definition of that term.

    (*a*)   For disposals of machinery etc. acquired as a result of transaction(s) between connected persons, the disposal value (see 10.28 above) may not exceed the greatest cost incurred on it by any of the participants in the transaction(s) (after deducting any 'additional VAT rebates', see 10.2(v) above, made to the participant). [*CAA 1990, s 26(3)(4); FA 1991, 14 Sch 8(3)*].

    (*b*)   Where machinery etc. is purchased from a connected person, or in a sale and lease-back transaction, or in transaction(s) from which the sole or main benefit appears to be the obtaining of an allowance under the current provisions, no first-year allowances are given, and writing-down allowances and balancing adjustments ignore any excess of the expenditure (including any 'additional VAT liability' incurred in respect thereof—see 10.2(v) above) incurred over the disposal value to be brought into account on the seller. Where no disposal value is so brought into account (e.g. where the seller is non-UK resident), allowances are given on the smallest of

    (1)   open market value on acquisition,

    (2)   the purchaser's expenditure, and

    (3)   the capital expenditure, if any, incurred by the seller or any person connected with him,

with modifications to allow for 'additional VAT liabilities' and 'rebates'—see 10.2(v) above.

These restrictions do not apply to the supply of unused machinery etc. in the ordinary course of trade. Also, where the machinery etc. has not before the sale been used in a trade carried on by the seller or any person connected with him, first-year allowances *are* given, on the smallest of (1), (2) and (3) above.

These provisions apply to contracts for future delivery and hire purchase contract assignments as they apply to direct sales. [*CAA 1990, ss 75, 76; FA 1991, 14 Sch 11*].

The 'sole or main benefit' restriction referred to above does not apply to straightforward finance leasing transactions (*Barclays Mercantile Industrial Finance Ltd v Melluish Ch D 1990, 63 TC 95*).

See (xi) below as regards successions to trades between connected persons.

(iv) *Double allowances.* See 10.2(iv) above.

(v) A *gift of machinery etc.*, brought into use after 26 July 1989 for the purposes of the donee's trade, entitles the donee to writing-down allowances, as if he had purchased it from the donor, from the basis period in which he first so uses it. Allowances will, subject to (iii) above, be calculated on open market value at the time when brought into use. [*CAA 1990, s 81(1)–(3)*]. Previously, it was necessary for the gift to have resulted in open market value being brought into account on the donor as disposal value, although in practice, allowances were generally also available where the plant was not used for trade purposes by the donor. [*CAA 1990, s 81(4)*]. Where the gift is brought into use between 1 November 1992 and 31 October 1993 inclusive, the donee's deemed expenditure qualifies for the 40% first-year allowance introduced by *FA 1993* (see 10.27 above). [*CAA 1990, s 81(1A); FA 1993, 13 Sch 12(1)*].

(vi) *Hire purchase.* If machinery etc. acquired under hire purchase agreement is brought into trade use on acquisition, the full capital cost (i.e. excluding the hire or interest element) attracts capital allowances immediately. Any such capital payments made *before* the machinery etc. is brought into use attract allowances as they fall due. If the contract is not completed, and the trader does not in fact become the owner, the machinery etc. is treated as ceasing to belong to him when he loses the benefit of the contract. He must then bring in as its disposal value (see 10.28 above) any consideration, compensation etc. he may receive, plus, if the machinery etc. has been brought into trade use, the capital element of all instalments not paid, subject to an overall limit of the full cost of the machinery etc. under the contract. [*CAA 1990, s 60*]. See 10.28(A) above as regards hire purchase agreements relating to certain motor cars.

(vii) A *lessee required to provide machinery etc.* under the terms of his lease, and using it for trade purposes, is treated as if he owned it, but after termination of the lease, any disposal value (see 10.28 above) on disposal etc. is brought into account on the *lessor*, not the lessee. This does not, however, apply where the machinery, etc. becomes, by law, part of the building in which it is installed or attached (see 10.34 above) under a lease entered into after 11 July 1984 unless pursuant to an agreement made on or before that date. [*CAA 1990, s 61(4)*].

(viii) *Partnerships* are entitled to allowances on assets used for the partnership trade, and either owned by the partnership or owned by a partner and not let to the partnership.

On a *change of partnership*, if the trade is treated as continuing, unexhausted allowances are carried forward and subsequent balancing adjustments (see 10.30 above) made as if the new partnership had carried on the trade before the change. Allowances continue to be calculated as though there had been no change, being apportioned between the old and the new partnership for the year of assessment of the change. If however the trade is treated as ceasing, only continuing partners may carry forward their share of unexhausted allowances, as a loss to set against their future profit shares (but see 10.1 above as regards changes for 1994/95 onwards for trades etc. commenced after 5 April 1994 and for 1997/98 onwards as regards trades etc. commenced on or before that date). [*CAA 1990, ss 65, 78(3)(4)*].

See also (xi) below as regards allowances on successions to trades.

(ix) *Previous use outside trade.* Where a trader brings into use for the trade machinery etc. which he previously owned for purposes not entitling him to machinery and plant allowances in respect of the trade, allowances (excluding first-year allowances) are calculated as if the trader had, on bringing it into use for the trade, incurred expenditure on its acquisition of its open market value on a sale at that time. This treatment does not apply to machinery etc. previously used only for the purposes specified in 10.49(*b*) and (*c*) below which applied before 1 April 1986 in relation to mines, oil wells, etc. In such a case, the full cost is treated as expenditure incurred when the machinery is brought into trade use. Where the machinery etc. is brought into use between 1 November 1992 and 31 October 1993 inclusive, the trader's deemed expenditure qualifies for the 40% first-year allowance introduced by *FA 1993* (see 10.27 above). First-year allowances are not, however, available where machinery etc. is transferred from one trade to another carried on by the same person and is brought into use in the second trade after 13 April 1993. [*FA 1971, 8 Sch 7; FA 1985, 14 Sch 8; CAA 1990, s 81; FA 1993, 13 Sch 12*].

(x)   *Renewals basis* is generally available as an alternative to capital allowances as above. A deduction is allowed in computing profits of the cost of a replacement item less the proceeds of sale (or scrap value) of the item replaced. Where, however, the replacement item is an improvement on that replaced, the deduction is restricted to the cost of replacing like with like. See *Caledonian Railway Co v Banks CES 1880, 1 TC 487; Eastmans Ltd v Shaw HL 1928, 14 TC 218; Hyam v CIR CS 1929, 14 TC 479.*

Cost of renewals of trade implements, utensils etc. allowed as a deduction under *Sec 74(d)*, but cf. *Hinton v Maden & Ireland Ltd HL 1959, 38 TC 391* and also see *Peter Merchant Ltd v Stedeford CA 1948, 30 TC 496* (provision for future renewals not allowable). Replacement of parts is allowed under general principles so far as identity of machinery etc. is retained. For further details of 'renewals basis' and change from renewals basis to normal capital allowances, see Revenue Pamphlet IR 1, B1.

(xi) *Successions.* Where a trade changes hands (other than in certain partnership changes (see (viii) above)) unexhausted allowances may not be carried forward to the new owner. Unless the change is not treated as a permanent cessation (see 53.6 PARTNERSHIPS), any asset transferred, without being sold, to the new owner for continuing use in the trade is treated as sold at open market value on the date of change, although no first-year allowance (where otherwise applicable) is available to the new owner.

If a beneficiary succeeds to a trade under a deceased proprietor's will or intestacy, he may elect for written-down value to be substituted (if less) for the open market value. [*CAA 1990, s 78; FA 1990, 13 Sch 3*].

Where the old and new owners are 'connected' with each other, each is within the charge to UK tax on profits of the trade, and the successor is not a dual resident investing company (see *Sec 404*), they may elect, within two years of the date of change, for any machinery or plant continuing to be used in the trade to be treated as transferred at a price giving rise to no balancing allowance or charge, and for allowances to be given to the successor disregarding the change of ownership. For this purpose, persons are *'connected'* if

(a)   they are CONNECTED PERSONS (20) within *Sec 839*, or

(b)   one of them is a partnership in which the other has the right to a share of assets or income, or both are partnerships in both of which some other person has the right to such a share, or

(c)   one of them is a body corporate over which the other has control (within *Sec 840*), or both are bodies corporate, or one a body corporate and one a partnership, over both of which some other person has control.

An election in relation to a succession occurring after 26 July 1989 will preclude the application of *CAA 1990, s 78* (see above) and the similar provisions in *CAA 1990, s 41* (see 10.35(e) above).

In relation to successions occurring before 29 July 1988, such an election (with similar effect) can only be made where the old and new owners are CONNECTED PERSONS (20) within *Sec 839*, but the requirement that both are within the charge to

UK tax is omitted, and the restriction on dual resident investing companies did not apply before 1 April 1987. No time limit is specified for such an election. [*CAA 1990, s 77*].

(xii) *Wear and tear allowances.* Where any sums, not otherwise taxable on the recipient, are payable to him, directly or indirectly, by any other person in respect of, or to take account of, the wear and tear of plant or machinery used in the recipient's trade, no capital allowances are available for that plant or machinery. Where the sums only partially offset that wear and tear, a first-year allowance, where available, can be given, but scaled down as is just and reasonable. Writing-down allowances are calculated as if the machinery were used solely for a separate 'notional' trade and only a just proportion allowed against the actual trade. Balancing adjustments are similarly debarred or restricted. [*CAA 1990, s 80; FA 1990, 17 Sch 15*]. See 10.2(ii) above as regards certain other subsidies.

10.39 **MINES, OIL WELLS**

The original capital allowances for mines, oil wells, etc. contained in *CAA 1968, ss 51–66, 5, 6 Schs* (the '*old code*', see 10.49 below) are repealed **after 31 March 1986** and a new code introduced for expenditure incurred in a 'trade of mineral extraction' after that date, subject to transitional provisions (see 10.47 below) which may apply to certain expenditure incurred before 1 April 1987. [*CAA 1990, Pt IV*]. For these purposes, any accounting or basis period beginning on or before 31 March 1986 and ending after that date is split into two such periods, the first ending on that date and the second commencing on 1 April 1986. [*FA 1986, s 55(3)(4)*].

A '*trade of mineral extraction*' is a trade consisting of or including the working of a source of '*mineral deposits*', i.e. such deposits of a wasting nature including any natural deposits or geothermal energy capable of being lifted or extracted from the earth. [*CAA 1990, s 121(1)(2)*].

The main elements of the new code are dealt with as follows.

10.40 Qualifying expenditure
10.41 Limitations on qualifying expenditure
10.42 Writing-down allowances
10.43 Disposal receipts
10.44 Balancing allowances and charges
10.45 Making of allowances and charges
10.46 Machinery and plant allowances
10.47 Transitional provisions
10.49 'Old scheme' before 1 April 1986

10.40 **Qualifying expenditure.** The new code applies to '*qualifying expenditure*', i.e. expenditure on

(*a*) '*mineral exploration and access*' (i.e. searching for or discovering and testing the mineral deposits of any source, or winning access to any such deposits),

(*b*) acquisition of a '*mineral asset*' (i.e. any mineral deposits or land comprising mineral deposits, or any interest in or right over such deposits or land),

(*c*) construction of any works, in connection with the working of a source of mineral deposits, which are likely to become of little or no value when the source ceases to be worked, and

(*d*) construction of works which are likely to become valueless when a foreign concession under which a source of mineral deposits is worked comes to an end.

Included in (a) above is abortive expenditure on seeking planning permission for the undertaking of mineral exploration and access or the working of mineral deposits. Expenditure on the acquisition of, or of rights in or over, mineral deposits or the site of a source of such deposits falls into (b) rather than (a) above. [CAA 1990, ss 105(1)(7), 121(1)].

Qualifying expenditure also includes certain contributions, for the purposes of a trade of mineral extraction carried on outside the UK, to the cost of accommodation outside the UK for employees engaged in working a source, and related public and welfare services and facilities, provided that the buildings etc. are likely to be of little or no value when the source ceases to be worked, that the expenditure does not result in the acquisition of an asset, and that relief is not due under any other provision of the Tax Acts. Net expenditure incurred on the 'restoration' of a mining site within three years of the cessation of the trade is also qualifying expenditure, treated as incurred on the last day of trading, unless relieved elsewhere. [CAA 1990, ss 108, 109].

The following are, however, not qualifying expenditure.

(i)   Expenditure on, or treated as being on, machinery or plant (except certain pre-trading expenditure, see below).

(ii)   Expenditure on acquisition of, or of rights in or over, the site of works as in (c) or (d) above.

(iii)   Expenditure on works constructed wholly or mainly for processing the raw products, unless the process is designed to prepare the raw products for use as such.

(iv)   Expenditure on buildings and structures for occupation by or welfare of workers.

(v)   Expenditure on construction of any part of a building or structure for use as an office where such expenditure exceeds one-tenth of the capital expenditure on the whole building.

[CAA 1990, s 105(4)(5)].

Time expenditure incurred. The normal rules (see 10.2(iii) above) apply, and, additionally, pre-trading expenditure is generally treated as incurred on the first day of trading, although expenditure within (a) above may not thereby become qualifying expenditure. Certain net expenditure on machinery or plant sold, demolished, destroyed or abandoned before commencement of a trade of mineral extraction is treated as qualifying expenditure incurred on the first day of the mineral extraction trade. Certain other expenditure on mineral exploration and access incurred before commencement of a trade of mineral extraction is treated as incurred on the first day of that trade (i.e. where another trade was previously carried on). [CAA 1990, ss 105(2), 106, 107, 120(1)(2)].

10.41   **Limitations on qualifying expenditure.** Where expenditure includes the acquisition of an interest in land, an amount equal to the 'undeveloped market value' of the land is excluded. 'Undeveloped market value' is the open market value of the land at the time of acquisition ignoring the mineral deposits and assuming that development of the land (other than that already begun or for which planning permission has already been granted by a general development order) is, and will remain, unlawful. Where the undeveloped market value includes the value of buildings which are subsequently demolished or otherwise permanently cease to be used, their value, excluding the land, less the amount of any capital allowances received in respect of them, is treated as qualifying expenditure incurred at the time of cessation of use. The special provisions regarding the time of acquisition of land (see 10.40 above) do not apply for these purposes. [CAA 1990, s 110].

Where a deduction has been allowed under Sec 87 in respect of a premium under a lease (see 68.28 SCHEDULE A), the qualifying expenditure allowable in respect of acquisition of the interest in land to which the premium relates is correspondingly reduced. [*CAA 1990, s 111*].

Qualifying expenditure is also restricted where the asset is acquired from another person, and either that person or an earlier previous owner incurred expenditure on it in connection with a trade of mineral extraction. Broadly, the amount qualifying is limited to the amount of expenditure incurred by the most recent previous owner who used it in connection with a trade of mineral extraction, net of any allowances made to or on that person. Where the asset is a mineral asset in the UK, no restriction applies

(*a*)   if the asset was acquired under a contract for sale made before 16 July 1985 from a person who incurred expenditure on it in connection with a trade of mineral extraction, or

(*b*)   if no previous owner after 31 March 1986 has incurred expenditure on it in connection with a trade of mineral extraction.

Where an asset representing expenditure on mineral exploration or access is acquired from a person who incurred that expenditure without carrying on a trade of mineral extraction, qualifying expenditure is restricted to the expenditure incurred by the seller.

A similar restriction applies where assets are transferred between companies under common control, unless an election is made under *CAA 1990, s 158* for the transfer to be treated as made at tax written-down value.

If the expenditure includes the cost of an oil licence, the qualifying expenditure is limited to the amount of the original licence fee paid.

In any case where the expenditure is incurred both in mineral exploration and access and in the acquisition of a mineral asset, the qualifying amount in respect of the former is limited to the amount incurred by the previous trader in that respect. [*CAA 1990, ss 113–118*].

10.42   **Writing-down allowances.** After 31 March 1986 the following allowances are given in respect of qualifying expenditure incurred in connection with a trade of mineral extraction in a chargeable or basis period, or treated as so incurred, net of any disposal receipts (see 10.43 below).

Acquisition of a mineral asset (see 10.40(*b*) above) and
certain pre-trading expenditure   **10% p.a.**
Other qualifying expenditure   **25% p.a.**

Allowances for subsequent chargeable periods are calculated by applying the same percentages to the balance of expenditure after adjustment for disposal receipts and allowances and charges given or made for earlier periods. [*CAA 1990, s 98; FA 1994, s 213(8)*].

10.43   **Disposal receipts.** When an asset, in respect of the acquisition of which a person has incurred qualifying expenditure, permanently ceases to be used in a trade of mineral extraction carried on by him (by disposal or otherwise), the disposal value calculated as under *CAA 1990, s 26* (see 10.28 above) must be brought into account. A mineral asset is treated as ceasing to be so used at any time when it begins to be used in a way which constitutes development which is neither development for the purposes of a trade of mineral extraction carried on by him nor '*existing permitted development*', i.e. development lawfully carried out prior to the acquisition or for which planning permission is granted by a general development order (or foreign equivalent). Where the qualifying expenditure has been restricted in accordance with the rules regarding acquisition of an interest in land (see 10.41 above) the disposal value is correspondingly restricted. Any capital receipt is similarly brought into account to the extent that it is attributable to qualifying expenditure. [*CAA 1990, ss 99, 112; FA 1994, 26 Sch Pt V(24)*].

10.44   **Balancing allowances and charges.** A balancing charge arises in any chargeable period in which, or in whose basis period, the sum of disposal receipts (see 10.43 above) for that and earlier periods and the net allowances made for earlier periods in respect of any qualifying expenditure exceeds the expenditure. The charge is on the lesser of that excess and the net allowances made for earlier periods.

A balancing allowance arises for any chargeable period in which any of the following circumstances apply.

(*a*)   On permanent discontinuance of the trade.

(*b*)   On permanent cessation of the working of certain mineral deposits. If two or more mineral assets derive from a single asset, the adjustment will not arise until the deposits comprised in all the assets concerned cease to be worked.

(*c*)   Where neither (*a*) nor (*b*) applies, but a disposal receipt falls to be brought into account as in 10.43 above.

(*d*)   In respect of certain pre-trading expenditure where the machinery or plant is sold, etc., or the mineral exploration and access has ceased, before commencement of the trade of mineral extraction.

(*e*)   Where a person incurs expenditure on mineral exploration and access in respect of search, exploration or inquiry and does not then or subsequently commence a related trade of mineral extraction.

(*f*)   Where qualifying expenditure has been incurred consisting of a contribution to the cost of temporary overseas employee accommodation and related public and welfare services and facilities, and the buildings or works permanently cease to be used in connection with a trade of mineral extraction.

(*g*)   Where assets are lost, cease to exist as such, or begin to be used for another purpose outside the trade of mineral extraction.

The amount of the balancing allowance is the excess of the qualifying expenditure over the sum of disposal receipts of that and earlier periods and the net allowances made for earlier periods.

The excess of any demolition costs over monies received for the remains of an asset representing qualifying expenditure is added to that expenditure for the purposes of balancing adjustments and is not then treated as expenditure incurred on any replacement asset. [*CAA 1990, ss 100–103; FA 1994, 26 Sch Pt V(24)*].

10.45   **Making of allowances and charges.** All allowances and charges under these provisions are made in taxing the trade of mineral extraction. [*CAA 1990, s 104*]. The miscellaneous and general provisions of *CAA 1990* generally apply to allowances under the new code, which are in most cases treated in the same way as other capital allowances for the purposes of other provisions in the *Tax Acts*.

10.46   **Machinery and plant allowances.** Machinery and plant is normally excluded from relief under the current provisions, but certain pre-trading expenditure may qualify (see 10.40

above). [*CAA 1990, ss 105(4), 106*]. The normal machinery and plant rules (see 10.24 *et seq.* above) apply to machinery and plant provided for the purposes of mineral exploration and access, subject to the necessary minor modifications. Where such expenditure is incurred prior to the date of commencement of the trade of mineral extraction, it is treated as sold immediately before that date and as re-acquired on that date. The capital expenditure on re-acquisition is deemed to be the actual expenditure previously incurred. [*CAA 1990, s 63*].

10.47 **Transitional provisions.** An irrevocable election could be made for initial allowances under the old code to continue to apply to expenditure incurred, by a person carrying on a trade of mineral extraction, in the year ending 31 March 1987 under a contract entered into by that person before 16 July 1985 in respect of which, but for the new code of allowances, an initial allowance would have been available under *CAA 1968, s 56*. The old code of allowances then continue to apply until 31 March 1987.

The election had to be made in writing within two years after the end of the chargeable or basis period in which the expenditure (or the first part of the expenditure after 31 March 1986) was incurred. Where an election was made, the new code applies after 31 March 1987 instead of 31 March 1986. [*FA 1986, 14 Sch 2*].

Where expenditure had not been fully relieved under the provisions of *CAA 1968, ss 57, 60* and *61*, the balance is treated for allowance purposes under the new code as incurred on the '*relevant day*' (i.e. the day from which the new code applies to the expenditure in question). Where such expenditure had been fully relieved but the asset or assets so acquired continue in use after the relevant day, the expenditure is treated as having been incurred on the relevant day, with allowances equal to the expenditure having been made under the new code, for the purposes of subsequent balancing adjustments. [*FA 1986, 14 Sch 4; CAA 1990, s 119(3)*].

Expenditure on mineral exploration and access, or on acquisition of mineral assets, or on construction of certain works, which did not qualify for allowances under the old code because either the trade, or output from the source, had not commenced, or for some other reason, is treated as incurred on 1 April 1986 and relieved as appropriate under the new code.

Special rules apply where the old code expenditure on a mineral asset included the acquisition of an interest in land, allowing the value of that interest to remain within the relievable expenditure where some relief had already been given under the old code, but bringing that value into account when calculating subsequent balancing adjustments. [*FA 1986, 14 Sch 5–7; CAA 1990, s 119(2)(3)*].

In making balancing adjustments where old code expenditure has been brought under the new code, allowances given under the old code will be taken into account together with those given under the new code. [*CAA 1990, s 119(4)(5)*].

10.48 *Example*

X has for some years operated a mining business with two mineral sources, G and S. Accounts are prepared to 30 September. On 31 December 1996 the mineral deposits and mineworks at G are sold at market value to Z for £80,000 and £175,000 respectively. A new source, P, is purchased on 30 April 1997 for £170,000 (including land with an undeveloped market value of £70,000) and the following expenditure incurred before the end of the accounting period ended 30 September 1997.

		£
Machinery and plant		40,000
Construction of administration office		25,000
Construction of mining works which are likely		
to have little value when mining ceases		50,000
Staff hostel		35,000
Winning access to the deposits		150,000
		£300,000

During the year to 30 September 1997, X incurred expenditure of £20,000 in seeking planning permission to mine a further plot of land, Source Q. Permission was refused.

Residue of expenditure brought forward		£
(based on accounts to 30 September 1996)		
Mineral exploration and access	– Source G	170,000
	– Source S	200,000
Mineral assets	– Source G	95,250
	– Source S	72,000

The mineral extraction allowances due for the year ending 30.9.97 are

Source G	£	£
Mineral exploration and access		
WDV b/f	170,000	
Proceeds	175,000	
Balancing charge	£5,000	(5,000)
Mineral assets		
WDV b/f	95,250	
Proceeds	80,000	
Balancing allowance	£15,250	15,250
Source S		
Mineral exploration and access		
WDV b/f	200,000	
WDA 25%	(50,000)	50,000
WDV c/f	£150,000	
Mineral assets		
WDV b/f	72,000	
WDA 10%	(7,200)	7,200
WDV c/f	£64,800	
Source P		
Mineral exploration and access		
Expenditure	150,000	
WDA 25%	(37,500)	37,500
WDA c/f	£112,500	c/f 104,950

10.49   Capital Allowances (Mines, Oil Wells)

	£	£
		b/f 104,950
Mineral assets		
Expenditure	100,000	
WDV 10%	(10,000)	10,000
WDV c/f	£90,000	
Mining works		
Expenditure	50,000	
WDA 25%	(12,500)	12,500
WDV c/f	£37,500	
Source Q		
Mineral exploration and access		
Expenditure	20,000	
WDA 25%	(5,000)	5,000
WDV c/f	£15,000	
Total allowances (net of charges)		£132,450

Notes

(*a*)   Allowances are not due on either the office or staff hostel although the hostel may qualify for industrial buildings allowances (see 10.11 above). Machinery and plant qualify for machinery and plant allowances (see 10.24 above) rather than for mineral extraction allowances (see 10.46 above).

(*b*)   Abortive expenditure on seeking planning permission is qualifying expenditure as if it were expenditure on mineral exploration and access (see 10.40 above).

(*c*)   The undeveloped market value of land is excluded from qualifying expenditure and from disposal receipts (see 10.41, 10.43 above).

10.49   **'Old scheme' before 1 April 1986.** For capital allowances on plant and machinery used in mines, etc., see above and *CAA 1968, s 23*, for special method applicable to expenditure up to 26 October 1970. Allowances were also given for capital expenditure on the following.

(*a*)   [1963/64 onwards]. Acquiring UK mineral deposits, land comprising them or rights over such land [*CAA 1968, s 60*].

Writing-down allowances were given as follows—

First 10 years of working source...........1/2 'royalty value' of output in the chargeable period or its basis period.

Next 10 years (i.e. up to 20)................1/4th 'royalty value' of output in the chargeable period or its basis period.

Thereafter...1/10th 'royalty value' of output in the chargeable period or its basis period.

'*Royalty value*' means amount of reasonable royalties on output in chargeable or basis period that would be payable if the source had been acquired under lease, expiring after that output produced, less any royalties actually payable. [*CAA 1968, s 60(11)*].

Total writing-down allowances including those deemed to have been made before 1963/64, plus capital receipts not to exceed amount of capital outlay. Where a source ceased to be worked, a balancing charge, or allowance, limited to the part appropriate to years after 1962/63, was made on the difference between the cost of acquiring the source (less its residual market value, etc.) and the total of allowances.

(b) Searching for, discovering, testing or winning access to deposits [*CAA 1968, s 51(2)(a)*] including plant, etc., so used (but not if initial or annual allowances had at any time previously been made in respect of that plant). [*CAA 1968, s 52*].

Capital allowances for such plant were given only on the diminution in its value attributable to its use in searching for, discovering, etc., the deposits. [*CAA 1968, 5 Sch 1, 2*]. See *CAA 1968, s 59* for restriction if purchase was not from mining concern etc. Outlay by mining etc. concerns on searching for, discovering, etc., deposits which were abandoned without the source being worked was allowed as a revenue expense as were unsuccessful planning applications for permission to explore and successful applications where the exploration itself was unsuccessful. [*CAA 1968, s 62;* Revenue Pamphlet IR 131, SP 4/78, 6 November 1978].

(c) Construction of works likely to be of little or no value when the source was no longer worked, or when a foreign concession under which the source was worked came to an end. [*CAA 1968, ss 51(2)(b), 56*].

(d) Cost of acquiring mineral deposits abroad (or rights over them) [*CAA 1968, s 53*], or of acquiring land abroad in connection with working a mine, etc., under a foreign concession, if likely to be valueless, at the end of the concession, to the person then working it. [*CAA 1968, s 54*]. But not including plant, industrial buildings etc. Where land etc. purchased from UK resident, allowances restricted to his cost. [*CAA 1968, 5 Sch 3–5*].

(e) (Overseas mines, etc., only.) Capital sums contributed, after 5 April 1952, towards the cost of the buildings, services and works ancillary thereto occupied by or giving welfare facilities for employees or their dependants, if those buildings, etc., were likely to be of little or no value when working of the source ceased. But no allowance for expenditure resulting in the *acquisition of a capital asset* by the person making it or if other allowances due. Allowance of one-tenth of the expenditure was given in each of 10 years, commencing with the year in the basis period for which the contribution was made (for corporation tax, beginning with the chargeable period in which the expenditure was incurred). [*CAA 1968, s 61*].

There were provisions for continuation to successor for balance of the relevant years. [*CAA 1968, s 61(3)(4)*].

Allowable expenditure under the above headings did not include the following.

(i) Cost of the site or the deposits (except as under (a) or (d) above).

(ii) Machinery or plant (other than under (b) or (e) above).

(iii) Processing works, other than for preparing the raw material.

(iv) Buildings for workers' occupation or welfare, except for (e) above.

(v) Buildings (or parts thereof, if exceeding 1/10th) used as offices. [*CAA 1968, s 51(3)(4)*].

10.50 Capital Allowances

(A) **Initial Allowances.** (*Applicable only to expenditure under (c) above.*)

Rate of allowance. 40% on expenditure incurred after 14 April 1953. (The 40% rate was reduced to 20% where expenditure (before 17 January 1966) also qualified for investment allowance.) [*CAA 1968, s 56, 1 Sch 1(2)(c)*].

The rate was increased to 100% (or such lesser amount as the taxpayer specified) on expenditure incurred after 26 October 1970 on the construction of works in a *development area* or in N. Ireland. [*FA 1971, s 52*].

(B) **Writing-down allowances** (other than under (*a*) and (*e*) above). Calculated each year as a fraction of '*residue of expenditure*' (cost less previous allowances, other than investment allowances and less capital receipts not resulting in balancing allowance or charge) corresponding to the ratio that *output in chargeable period or 'basis period'* bore to the sum of that output plus '*potential future output*'. Minimum allowance one-twentieth, but in respect of expenditure incurred after 3 April 1963, and before 17 January 1966, on constructing works in, or providing plant, etc., for use in, a former '*development district*' the taxpayer could himself specify the fraction to be applied. Except in this latter case, adjustments including revision of allowances for final six years, claimable when source ceased to be worked or concession came to an end. [*CAA 1968, s 57*].

(C) **Balancing allowances or charges** (with modifications in the case of sources worked before 6 April 1952) were made if assets included above were sold to a buyer who continued to work the whole or part of the source. [*CAA 1968, s 58*]. 'Residue of expenditure', included net cost (after crediting sales of materials and scrap) of demolition falling on the person concerned. [*CAA 1968, s 55*]. Such buyer received writing-down allowances on lesser of purchase price or 'residue of expenditure' immediately after sale. [*CAA 1968, s 58(7)*]. For expenditure incurred prior to commencement of trading, and for treatment of assets, as above, acquired from a person who had not worked the source, see *CAA 1968, s 59*.

Except for (*a*) above, there were provisions for the substitution of open market value for sale consideration on certain '**sole or main benefit**' transactions, **sales without change of control** and **sales between connected persons** subject in the latter cases to an election for residue of expenditure to be substituted instead. [*CAA 1968, s 78, 7 Sch 1, 4*].

Allowances were **given in taxing the trade**, in the same way as machinery and plant allowances are given to traders (see 10.32 above).

10.50 PATENT RIGHTS

Writing-down allowances are available, and **balancing adjustments** made, in respect of capital expenditure on

(*a*) purchase of patent rights (i.e. the right to do or authorise the doing of anything which would, apart from that right, be a patent infringement), or

(*b*) obtaining a right to acquire future patent rights,

provided that either the allowance falls to be made in taxing the purchaser's trade or any income receivable in respect of the rights would be liable to tax. Expenditure incurred by a person for the purposes of a trade he is about to carry on is treated as incurred on the first day of trading, provided that the rights are still held at that time. [*Secs 520–523, 528; FA 1994, 26 Sch Pt V(24)*].

Expenditure incurred after 31 March 1986

For any chargeable period (see 10.2(vi) above) for which a person has 'qualifying expenditure' exceeding any 'disposal value' to be brought in, a writing-down allowance of 25% of the excess (proportionately reduced or increased if the period is less or more than one year or the allowance falls to be made in taxing a trade carried on for only part of a chargeable period) is made, except that a *balancing allowance* of the whole of the excess is made where:

(a)   the chargeable period is that of permanent discontinuance of the trade in taxing which the allowance falls to be made; or

(b)   (a) above does not apply but during the period the last of the patent rights, expenditure on which has been taken into account in determining qualifying expenditure and which have not been wholly disposed of, comes to an end without any such rights being revived.

For any chargeable period for which a person's qualifying expenditure is less than the disposal value to be brought in, a *balancing charge* is made on him on the amount of the difference. [*Sec 520(1), (4)–(6); FA 1994, s 214(4)*].

'Qualifying expenditure' for a chargeable period is the aggregate of any capital expenditure on patent rights incurred before the end of the chargeable period or its basis period which has not, in whole or part, previously formed part of qualifying expenditure, and any unallowed balance brought forward from the previous chargeable period. [*Sec 521(1); FA 1994, 26 Sch Pt V(24)*].

A *disposal value* falls to be brought in for a chargeable period in which, or in the basis period for which, a person sells the whole or part of any patent rights on the purchase of which he has incurred capital expenditure. The value to be brought in is the net sale proceeds, except that:

(1)   the sale proceeds to be brought in shall not exceed the capital expenditure incurred on purchase of the rights; and

(2)   where the rights were acquired as a result of a transaction between CONNECTED PERSONS (20) (or a series of such transactions), (1) above shall have effect as if it referred to the highest capital expenditure incurred on the purchase of those rights by any of those connected persons. [*Sec 521(2)–(4); FA 1994, 26 Sch Pt V(24)*].

Connected persons and anti-avoidance. Where a person incurs capital expenditure after 26 July 1989 on the purchase of rights either from a connected person (see 20 CONNECTED PERSONS), or so that it appears that the sole or main benefit from the sale and any other transactions would have been the obtaining of an allowance under these provisions, the amount of that expenditure taken into account in determining any writing-down allowance or balancing allowance or charge to or on the purchaser may not exceed an amount determined as follows:

(I)   where a disposal value (see above) falls to be brought into account, an amount equal to that value;

(II)   where no disposal value falls to be brought into account, but the seller receives a capital sum chargeable under Schedule D, Case VI (see 54.5 PATENTS), an amount equal to that sum;

(III)   in any other case, an amount equal to the smallest of

(i)   open market value of the rights;

(ii)   the amount of capital expenditure, if any, incurred by the seller on acquiring the rights;

(iii)   the amount of capital expenditure, if any, incurred by any person connected with the seller on acquiring the rights.

[*Sec 521(5)–(7); FA 1989, 13 Sch 27*]. Previously, the restriction was by reference to the disposal value only. See also (2) above.

10.50 Capital Allowances

Expenditure incurred before 1 April 1986

This expenditure is allowable in full, by equal annual instalments (or pro rata for shorter periods), over the shortest of

(i)   seventeen years,

(ii)   the period of the rights purchased, and

(iii)   if the rights purchased begin a year or more after the date from which the patent became effective, and are not for a specified period, seventeen years less the number of complete years from the patent becoming effective to the rights being purchased (minimum writing-down period one year),

beginning with the year of assessment in whose basis period the expenditure is incurred. [*Sec 522(3)–(5)*].

Balancing adjustments arise where, before the end of the writing-down period (see above), any of the following events occur.

(A)   The rights come to an end without subsequently being revived.

(B)   The rights (or remaining rights) are sold, the net proceeds of sale being

    (i)   less than the unallowed expenditure, or

    (ii)   greater than the unallowed expenditure.

(C)   Part of the rights is sold, the net proceeds of sale being greater than the unallowed expenditure.

Where (A) or (B)(i) apply, a *balancing allowance* is given on the unallowed expenditure (less net sale proceeds, if any) provided that writing-down allowances have been given in respect of the rights (or would have been given but for the sale etc.).

Where (B)(ii) or (C) apply, a *balancing charge* is made on the excess of net sale proceeds over unallowed expenditure (but limited to allowances granted in respect of the rights).

Where part of the rights is sold but (C) does not apply, writing-down allowances for the year of assessment in whose basis period the sale takes place and subsequent years are recalculated after deducting net sale proceeds from the unallowed expenditure before the period of the sale.

Balancing allowances and charges are given or made for the year of assessment in whose basis period the related event occurs, and no writing-down allowance is made for that year. [*Sec 523*].

Connected persons and anti-avoidance. There are provisions for the substitution of open market value for sale consideration on certain 'sole or main benefit' transactions, sales without change of control and sales between connected persons, subject in the latter cases to an election for unallowed expenditure to be substituted instead. [*CAA 1990, ss 157, 158; Sec 532*]. However, where the inventor is the seller, no such election is available unless he sells to own controlled company at less than market value, in which case allowances and charges (and, if the purchaser agrees, capital gains tax) may be based on actual price paid (Revenue Pamphlet IR 1, B17).

Making of allowances and charges. *Traders,* using patent rights for purposes of a trade chargeable under Schedule D, Case I, may claim allowances and suffer charges in taxing the trade. Excess allowances may be used as under Dredging (10.7 above); this is of no application where allowances fall to be treated as trading expenses (see 10.1 above).

Non-traders may only set allowances against income from patents, excess allowances being carried forward without time limit. Balancing charges are assessed under Schedule D, Case VI. [*Sec 528; FA 1994, 26 Sch Pt V(24)*].

Trading partnerships and successions are treated in the same way as for industrial buildings allowances (see 10.22(iii)(iv)).

See 54 PATENTS for treatment of patent royalties and capital sums received, and 71.72 SCHEDULE D, CASES I AND II for trading income and expenses re patents.

10.51   *Example*

P, who prepares accounts to 31 December, acquires three new patent rights for trading purposes.

	Date	Term	Cost
Patent 1	20.2.87	20 years	£6,800
Patent 2	19.4.94	15 years	£4,500
Patent 3	5.10.95	5 years	£8,000

On 1.10.89 P sold his rights under patent 1 for £5,000 and on 1.12.96 he sold part of the rights under patent 2 for £2,000.

The allowances for each patent are

Patent 1
	£
Expenditure	6,800
1988/89 (basis period — y/e 31.12.87)	
WDA $\frac{1}{17} \times$ £6,800	(400)
	6,400
1989/90	
WDA $\frac{1}{17} \times$ £6,800	(400)
	6,000
1990/91 (basis period — y/e 31.12.89)	
Disposal proceeds	(5,000)
Balancing allowance	£1,000

Patents 2 and 3	Pool	WDA
1995/96 (basis period — y/e 31.12.94)	£	£
Expenditure (patent 2)	4,500	
WDA 25%	(1,125)	£1,125
	3,375	
1996/97 (basis period — 2 years to 31.12.96 — see 71.20		
SCHEDULE D, CASES I AND II)		
Expenditure (patent 3)	8,000	
Disposal proceeds (patent 2)	(2,000)	
	9,375	
WDA 25%	(2,344)	£2,344
WDV c/f	£7,031	

10.52   **SCIENTIFIC RESEARCH** [*CAA 1990, ss 136–139*].

Capital expenditure incurred by a trader on 'scientific research' related to the trade, and undertaken directly or on his behalf (i.e. by an agent or other person in a similar contractual relationship, see *Gaspet Ltd v Elliss CA 1987, 60 TC 91*), attracts a **100% allowance.** A just apportionment may be made of expenditure which partly qualifies. The allowance is also available where the expenditure is incurred before commencement of the trade. An 'additional VAT liability' (see 10.2(v) above) incurred, in respect of qualifying expenditure, before the asset ceases to belong to the trader is itself qualifying expenditure.

For 1996/97 and earlier years as regards trades commenced before 6 April 1994, the allowance may be deducted in taxing the trade for the year of assessment in whose basis period the expenditure is incurred, except that

(i)   where basis periods overlap, expenditure in the common period is treated as incurred only in the earlier period,

(ii)   expenditure in an interval between two basis periods is treated as incurred in the later period, unless it is the period of permanent discontinuance of the trade, in which case it is treated as incurred in the earlier period, and

(iii) expenditure incurred before commencement of the trade gives rise to an allowance for the year of assessment in which the trade is commenced.

For 1994/95 and subsequent years as regards trades commenced after 5 April 1994 and for 1997/98 and subsequent years as regards trades commenced on or before that date, the allowance is deducted as a trading expense of the chargeable period (see 10.2(vi) above) in which the expenditure is incurred (or, in the case of pre-trading expenditure, the chargeable period beginning with commencement of trade).

No allowances are available in respect of expenditure on the acquisition of, or of rights in or over, *land* except insofar as, on a just apportionment, the expenditure is referable to such acquisition of a building or other structure already constructed on the land, or of machinery or plant which forms part of such a building, etc..

Expenditure on provision of a *dwelling* does not qualify for allowances, except that where not more than one quarter of the expenditure (disregarding any 'additional VAT liability' or 'rebate'—see 10.2(v) above) on a building consisting partly of a dwelling and partly of a building used for scientific research is justly apportionable to the dwelling, the whole of the expenditure may be the subject of allowance.

[*CAA 1990, ss 137, 140(1)(2)(5); FA 1985, s 63(7); FA 1991, 14 Sch 12; FA 1994, ss 211, 213(10)*].

'*Scientific research*' is defined as activities in the fields of natural or applied science for the extension of knowledge. [*CAA 1990, s 139(1)*]. Any question of whether, and to what extent, any activities constitute scientific research, or any asset is used for scientific research, is ultimately referred to the Secretary of State for a final decision. [*CAA 1990, s 139(3)*]. For the Revenue approach to such questions, see Revenue Capital Allowances Manual, CA 5000–5011.

A **balancing adjustment** arises when an asset representing allowable scientific research expenditure ceases to belong to the trader. The 'disposal value' of the asset, up to a maximum of the amount of the expenditure (less any 'additional VAT rebate' falling to be treated as a trading receipt—see below), is normally treated as a trading receipt accruing at the time of the event giving rise to the adjustment or, if earlier, immediately before permanent discontinuance of the trade. A deduction may similarly be given for net demolition costs in respect of assets destroyed. Where, however, the event giving rise to the adjustment takes place before the chargeable period for which an allowance in respect of the expenditure is due (disregarding any allowance due in respect of an 'additional VAT liability'—see above), an allowance is instead made of the excess (if any) of the expenditure over the disposal value and is allowed in taxing the trade for the chargeable period of that event. The amount of the *'disposal value'* depends on the nature of the event giving rise to the adjustment:

(1)   if the asset is sold at open market value or higher, it is the sale proceeds;

(2)   if the asset is destroyed, it is the sum of any compensation received and any receipts for the remains of the asset *less* any demolition costs;

(3)   in any other event, it is the open market value.

In the event of a sale, the asset ceases to belong to a person at the earlier of the time of completion and the time when possession is given.

An 'additional VAT rebate' (see 10.2(v) above) made in respect of allowable scientific research expenditure before the asset in question ceases to belong to the trader is treated as a trading receipt accruing for the chargeable period related to the making of the rebate or, if earlier, immediately before permanent discontinuance of the trade.

[*CAA 1990, ss 138(1)–(5)(8), 139(4); FA 1991, 14 Sch 13*].

Double allowances, etc. See 10.2(iv) above. No balancing charge is made on a sale giving rise to an industrial building or machinery and plant balancing charge (see 10.15, 10.30 above), and balancing allowances are similarly restricted for chargeable or basis periods ending before 27 July 1989. [*CAA 1990, s 138(6)(7); FA 1994, 26 Sch Pt V(24)*].

Excess allowances may be used as under dredging (see 10.7 above).

Connected persons and other anti-avoidance provisions apply to substitute open market value for sale consideration on certain 'sole or main benefit' transactions, sales without change of control and sales between connected persons. For most sales, the election referred to at 10.22(i) above is available, with the result that an asset representing expenditure for which the 100% allowance has been made will be treated as transferred for nil consideration. [*CAA 1990, ss 157, 158; FA 1993, s 117(3)–(5); FA 1994, s 119(1)*].

For expenditure of a revenue nature, see 71.79 SCHEDULE D, CASES I AND II.

10.53   *Example*

C is in business manufacturing and selling cosmetics, and he prepares accounts annually to 30 June. For the purposes of this trade, he built a new laboratory adjacent to his existing premises, incurring the following expenditure.

		£
April 1992	Laboratory building	50,000
June 1992	Technical equipment	3,000
March 1993	Technical equipment	4,000
June 1993	Plant	2,500
August 1995	Extension to existing premises comprising 50% further laboratory area and 50% sales offices.	30,000

In July 1993 a small fire destroyed an item of equipment originally costing £2,000 in June 1992; insurance recoveries totalled £3,000. In March 1994, the plant costing £2,500 was sold for £1,800.

The allowances due are

10.53 Capital Allowances

	£
1993/94 (basis year ended 30.6.92)	
Laboratory building	50,000
Technical equipment	3,000
Plant note (*a*)	700
	£53,700

1994/95 (basis year ended 30.6.93)	
Technical equipment	£4,000

1995/96 (basis year ended 30.6.94)
No allowance due, but balancing adjustment of £2,000 arises (note (*b*)).

1996/97 (transitional year)	
Extension	£15,000

Notes

(*a*)   As the plant was sold prior to 1994/95, the year in which an allowance would have been obtained, no allowance is due for that year. Instead, an allowance (£700) based on the excess of the cost (£2,500) over proceeds (£1,800) is made for the chargeable period, i.e. the tax year, in which the sale took place.

(*b*)   The destruction of the equipment in the year to 30 June 1994 results in a balancing adjustment limited to the allowance originally given. The deemed trading receipt is assessable in 1995/96.

11   Capital Gains Tax

For full details of CGT provisions, see Tolley's Capital Gains Tax. For date due see 56.1(*e*) PAYMENT OF TAX. See also 78.19 SELF-ASSESSMENT.

11.1   CAPITAL GAINS TAX (CGT)

The legislation applying to individuals and companies was consolidated by the *Taxation of Chargeable Gains Act 1992* (*TCGA 1992*) and references to that Act are given throughout this book where appropriate. For full details see Tolley's Capital Gains Tax.

11.2   EXCLUSION OF AMOUNTS OTHERWISE TAXED

Gains for CGT purposes are calculated exclusive of receipts chargeable to income tax or corporation tax (except items giving rise to balancing charges for CAPITAL ALLOWANCES (10) purposes). However, the capitalised value of a rentcharge, ground annual, feu duty or other series of income receipts can be taken into account for CGT purposes. [*TCGA 1992, s 37*].

11.3   RATE OF CGT

For 1988/89 and subsequent years of assessment, the rate of CGT is, except as follows, equal to the basic rate of income tax or, for an individual liable to higher rate tax on any part of his income, the higher rate (see 1.3 ALLOWANCES AND TAX RATES). Where there is no higher rate liability, but the amount chargeable to CGT exceeds the unused part of the basic rate band (see 1.3 ALLOWANCES AND TAX RATES), the CGT rate on the excess is equal to the higher rate of income tax. Similarly, where part or all of the lower rate band is unused, a corresponding part of the chargeable gains is taxed at the lower rate.

For 1988/89 and 1989/90 only, the rate of CGT on a married woman's chargeable gains is that which would apply if they were her husband's (and as the top slice if the husband has chargeable gains of his own). Thereafter, husband and wife are treated separately for CGT purposes.

The rate of CGT applicable to gains accruing to trustees of accumulation and discretionary settlements is the sum of the basic and additional rates of income tax (see 80.5 SETTLEMENTS).

In determining for these purposes whether income is liable at the higher rate of income tax, and the unused part of the basic rate band, account is taken of various provisions of the *Income Tax Acts* requiring additions to or deductions from total income. [*TCGA 1992, ss 4–6; F(No 2)A 1992, s 23; FA 1994, 26 Sch Pt V; FA 1995, 29 Sch Pt VIII(8)*].

For 1993/94 and subsequent years, special computational provisions apply for a year of assessment for which all or part of an individual's lower rate band is utilised by dividend income (or, for 1996/97 onwards, 'savings income'—see 1.8(iii) ALLOWANCES AND TAX RATES) and he has chargeable gains. The effect is to allocate to the gains that part of the lower rate band which is so utilised, with the individual's basic rate limit for income tax then being reduced by the amount so allocated. [*TCGA 1992, s 4(3A)(3B); FA 1993, 6 Sch 22; FA 1996, 6 Sch 27, 28*].

11.4   SET-OFF OF INCOME TAX RELIEFS AGAINST CAPITAL GAINS

See 46.5 LOSSES for set-off of trading losses against capital gains for 1991/92 and subsequent years of assessment. See 60.4 POST-CESSATION ETC. RECEIPTS AND EXPENDITURE for relief for certain post-cessation expenditure incurred after 28 November 1994, and 75.23 for relief for certain post-employment expenditure for 1995/96 and subsequent years of assessment.

12 Cash Basis

12.1   Business profits should be computed on an earnings basis (see 71 SCHEDULE D, CASES I AND II) but in practice the cash basis (where profits measured by excess of cash receipts over cash outlay, ignoring debtors and creditors, accruals, unbilled or uncompleted work) or some other recognisable basis short of a full earnings basis, is accepted for individuals or partnerships carrying on professions or vocations (*not trades*) if desired and provided the profits computed on the new basis will not, taking one year with another, differ materially from the profits computed on the earnings basis. The Revenue do, however, insist on the earnings basis for the first three accounting years of a new profession including one treated as new on a partnership change (see 53.6 PARTNERSHIPS) and, on the change to a cash etc. basis, require a written undertaking that bills for services rendered for work done will be issued at regular and frequent intervals. See *Walker v O'Connor (Sp C 74), 1996 STI 709* for a case in which the cash basis was held not to be permissible in opening years.

The change must be a complete one. For example, receipts after the change for work done before the change must be brought into account on the cash basis notwithstanding that they have already been brought into the earnings basis (*Morrison CS 1932, 17 TC 325*) and similarly expenses accrued due but unpaid which were debited in the accounts on the earnings basis may again be charged in the subsequent accounts on the cash basis when they are paid. Receipts after a cessation or change of basis which would otherwise escape assessment are assessable as post-cessation receipts etc. (see 60 POST-CESSATION ETC. RECEIPTS AND EXPENDITURE). *Note.* There is no relief for this 'double charge' on any later charge to post-cessation receipts.

A change from the cash basis to the earnings basis will be accepted but not a subsequent claim to revert to a cash basis (Revenue Pamphlet IR 131, A27). The above does not apply to barristers, see below.

See *Rankine v CIR CS 1952, 32 TC 520*, for limitation of Revenue's rights of revision on change-over of basis and *Wetton, Page & Co v Attwooll Ch D 1962, 40 TC 619*, for Revenue's rights to insist on earnings basis notwithstanding use of cash basis in other years. See also *McCash & Hunter v CIR CS 1955, 36 TC 170* (outgoing partner's share of receipts when cash basis applies).

Barristers are normally assessed on a cash basis but may elect to change to the earnings basis (or adopt that basis from commencement of practice). The earnings basis need not include work in progress. A change to the earnings basis or cessation of practice will attract a charge on POST-CESSATION ETC. RECEIPTS AND EXPENDITURE (60) (Revenue Pamphlet IR 131, A3).

13   Certificates of Deposit

13.1   A certificate of deposit is any document relating to money, in any currency, which has been deposited with the issuer or some other person, being a document which recognises an obligation to pay a stated amount to bearer or to order, with or without interest, and being a document by the delivery of which, with or without endorsement, the right to receive that stated amount, with or without interest, is transferable. [Sec 56(5)]. It does not include bearer bonds. (CCAB Memorandum June 1973).

13.2   Profits or gains (other than in respect of interest) on certificates of deposit acquired after 6 March 1973 will be taxable under Schedule D, Case VI (if not taxable as a trading receipt). A loss on a certificate of deposit can be offset against interest assessable in respect of it. These provisions do not apply to exempt pension funds and charities. [Secs 56(1)(a)(2)(3), 398].

13.3   Where, in a transaction in which no certificate of deposit or security (as defined by TCGA 1992, s 132) is issued, but an amount becomes payable with interest (by a bank, similar institution or person regularly engaging in similar transactions), then if the right to receive the amount or interest is disposed of or exercised, any profit (or loss) will be treated as in 13.2 above. [Sec 56(1)(b)]. Where a right to receive an amount (with or without interest) in pursuance of a deposit of money comes into existence without a certificate of deposit, but the person entitled to the right could call for the issue of such a certificate, a profit (or loss) on disposal of the right before the issue of such a certificate is similarly treated as in 13.2 above. [Sec 56A; F(No 2)A 1992, 8 Sch 1].

13.4   13.1–13.3 above do not apply for corporation tax purposes for accounting periods ending after 31 March 1996 (subject to transitional provisions). [Sec 56(4A)(4B); FA 1996, 14 Sch 6]. See now Tolley's Corporation Tax under Gilts and Bonds.

14   Certificates of Tax Deposit

14.1   A taxpayer (including partnerships, companies and personal representatives) may make deposits, evidenced by Certificates of Tax Deposit, with Collectors of Taxes for the subsequent payment of tax generally (other than PAYE and tax deducted from payments to construction sub-contractors and, from 1 October 1993, corporation tax—see further below). If a deposit is tendered in respect of any liability, that liability will be treated as paid on the later of the certificate date and the normal due date for that liability (see 57 PAYMENT OF TAX). The minimum initial deposit is £2,000 with minimum additions of £500. Deposits of £100,000 or over must be made by direct remittance to the Bank of England.

Series 7 Certificates, introduced from 1 October 1993, are not available for purchase for use against corporation tax liablities. Certificates purchased before that date (i.e. Series 6 Certificates) continue to be available against the full range of liabilities under the Series 6 prospectus until 30 September 1999. (Revenue Press Release 27 August 1993).

Interest, which is payable gross but taxable, will accrue for a maximum of six years from the date of deposit to the date of payment of tax or, if earlier, the 'deemed due date' for payment of the liability against which the deposit (plus accrued interest) is set. For income tax, the 'deemed due date' is 1 January in the year of assessment for which the tax is payable if it is payable in one sum, or 1 January in that year and 1 July in the following year where it is payable in two instalments, or 1 December in that following year where it is charged at a rate other than the basic rate on income from which tax has been deducted (other than under PAYE), or is treated as having been paid or deducted, or on income chargeable under 76 SCHEDULE F. A deposit may be withdrawn for cash at any time but will then receive a reduced rate of interest. Where a certificate is used in settlement of a tax liability, interest at the higher rate up to the normal due date may be less than interest at the encashment rate up to the reckonable date. In such circumstances the taxpayer may instruct the Collector to calculate interest on the latter basis. (ICAEW Technical Release TAX 13/93, 30 June 1993). The rates of interest, published by the Treasury, and calculated by reference to the rate on comparable investment with the Government, vary with the size and period of the deposit, and the rate payable on a deposit is adjusted to the current rate on each anniversary of the deposit.

Deposits are not transferable except to personal representatives of a deceased person or by a company for tax payable by other members of a group of companies. It is understood that certificates held in the name of a partnership may, with written authorisation from all the partners, be used in settlement of partners' individual liabilities. (Tolley's Practical Tax 1993 p 183).

Compensation for withdrawal of deposit for cash following introduction of independent taxation. Where, on or after 6 April 1990, a deposit made before that date has been withdrawn for cash, and within a month either side of the date of the withdrawal a 'qualifying tax liability' was discharged wholly or partly by a payment made other than by use of a certificate, a claim may be made to the Board for compensation. A '*qualifying tax liability*' is so much of a liability for 1990/91 or a later year, being a year of assessment at some time during which the person liable for the tax was married to the depositor, as could, had it been a liability of the depositor, have been settled by the application of the deposit which was withdrawn for cash (as above). The amount of the compensation is in effect the difference between the interest added to the cash withdrawal and the interest which would have been added if the certificate had at the time of the withdrawal been used to pay tax. Where the amount of the withdrawal (including interest) exceeds the amount of the qualifying tax liability, the compensation is correspondingly reduced. In addition, interest will be added for the period from the withdrawal for cash until payment of the compensation at the rate(s) of INTEREST ON UNPAID TAX (42). The compensation (but not the additional interest) is chargeable to tax under Case III of Schedule D. All qualifying tax liabilities payment of which could give rise to compensation as above in relation to the same cash withdrawal are aggregated for these purposes, and liabilities are disregarded to the extent that they have been taken into account in relation to a compensation claim relating to a different cash withdrawal. [*FA 1995, s 157*]. From the date of the announcement of the compensation arrangements, holders of certificates purchased before 6 April 1990 may use them to meet either their own or their spouse's tax liabilities and receive the higher rate of interest. (Hansard Written Answers 13 May 1994 Vol 243 Col 256).

Rates of interest are given at 14.2, 14.3 and 14.4 below. Information on current rates may be obtained from the Reuters Monitor Service, Page Index TREG and TREH, from any Collector of Taxes, or from Inland Revenue Finance Division (CTD) on Worthing (01903) 700222 ext 2064/5.

14.2   The rates of interest on date of deposit or anniversary on Series 6 and Series 7 Certificates for deposits of under £100,000 (and, before 16 November 1992, for other deposits withdrawn for cash) are (from 1 January 1990 to 31 March 1996)

	Used to pay tax	Withdrawals for cash
1 January 1990–7 October 1990	$11\frac{1}{2}$%	5%
8 October 1990–13 February 1991	$10\frac{1}{2}$%	5%
14 February 1991–27 February 1991	10%	5%
28 February 1991–24 March 1991	$9\frac{1}{2}$%	5%
25 March 1991–14 April 1991	9%	5%
15 April 1991–27 May 1991	$8\frac{1}{2}$%	5%
28 May 1991–14 July 1991	8%	5%
15 July 1991–4 September 1991	$7\frac{1}{2}$%	5%
5 September 1991–22 September 1992	7%	5%
23 September 1992–19 October 1992	$5\frac{1}{2}$%	5%
20 October 1992–15 November 1992	$4\frac{3}{4}$%	4%
16 November 1992–26 January 1993	$3\frac{1}{2}$%	$1\frac{3}{4}$%
27 January 1993–23 November 1993	$2\frac{3}{4}$%	$1\frac{1}{4}$%
24 November 1993–8 February 1994	$1\frac{3}{4}$%	1%
9 February 1994–12 September 1994	$1\frac{1}{2}$%	$\frac{3}{4}$%
13 September 1994–7 December 1994	2%	1%
8 December 1994–2 February 1995	$2\frac{1}{2}$%	$1\frac{1}{4}$%
3 February 1995–13 December 1995	3%	$1\frac{1}{2}$%
14 December 1995–18 January 1996	$2\frac{1}{2}$%	$1\frac{1}{4}$%
19 January 1996–10 March 1996	$2\frac{3}{4}$%	$1\frac{1}{2}$%
11 March 1996 onwards	$2\frac{1}{2}$%	$1\frac{1}{4}$%

14.3   The rates of interest on date of deposit or anniversary on Series 6 or Series 7 Certificates for deposits of £100,000 or more used to meet a scheduled liability are (from 1 January 1990 to 31 March 1996)

14.4 Certificates of Tax Deposit

	Under 1	1 but under 3	3 but under 6	6 but under 9	9 but under 12
		Period of deposit in months			
1 January 1990–7 October 1990	$11\frac{1}{2}$%	13%	13%	13%	13%
8 October 1990–13 February 1991	$10\frac{1}{2}$%	12%	12%	12%	$11\frac{1}{2}$%
14 February 1991–27 February 1991	10%	12%	11%	$10\frac{1}{2}$%	$10\frac{1}{2}$%
28 February 1991–24 March 1991	$9\frac{1}{2}$%	$11\frac{1}{2}$%	11%	$10\frac{1}{2}$%	10%
25 March 1991–14 April 1991	9%	11%	$10\frac{1}{2}$%	10%	10%
15 April 1991–27 May 1991	$8\frac{1}{2}$%	11%	$10\frac{1}{2}$%	10%	$9\frac{1}{2}$%
28 May 1991–14 July 1991	18%	$10\frac{1}{2}$%	10%	$9\frac{1}{2}$%	$9\frac{1}{2}$%
15 July 1991–4 September 1991	$7\frac{1}{2}$%	10%	$9\frac{1}{2}$%	9%	9%
5 September 1991–5 May 1992	7%	$9\frac{1}{2}$%	9%	9%	9%
6 May 1992–22 September 1992	$6\frac{1}{2}$%	9%	9%	$8\frac{1}{2}$%	$8\frac{1}{2}$%
23 September 1992–19 October 1992	$5\frac{1}{2}$%	8%	$7\frac{1}{2}$%	$7\frac{1}{4}$%	7%
20 October 1992–15 November 1992	$4\frac{3}{4}$%	7%	$6\frac{1}{2}$%	$6\frac{1}{4}$%	6%
16 November 1992–26 January 1993	$3\frac{1}{2}$%	6%	$5\frac{1}{2}$%	5%	5%
27 January 1993–23 November 1993	$2\frac{3}{4}$%	$5\frac{1}{4}$%	5%	$4\frac{3}{4}$%	$4\frac{1}{2}$%
24 November 1993–8 February 1994	$1\frac{3}{4}$%	$4\frac{1}{4}$%	4%	$3\frac{3}{4}$%	$3\frac{3}{4}$%
9 February 1994–12 September 1994	$1\frac{1}{2}$%	4%	$3\frac{3}{4}$%	$3\frac{3}{4}$%	$3\frac{1}{2}$%
13 September 1994–7 December 1994	2%	$4\frac{3}{4}$%	$4\frac{3}{4}$%	5%	$5\frac{1}{2}$%
8 December 1994–2 February 1995	$2\frac{1}{2}$%	$5\frac{1}{4}$%	$5\frac{1}{2}$%	$5\frac{3}{4}$%	6%
3 February 1995–13 December 1995	3%	$5\frac{3}{4}$%	$5\frac{3}{4}$%	6%	$6\frac{1}{4}$%
14 December 1995–18 January 1996	$2\frac{1}{2}$%	$5\frac{1}{2}$%	5%	5%	$4\frac{3}{4}$%
19 January 1996–10 March 1996	$2\frac{3}{4}$%	$5\frac{1}{4}$%	$4\frac{3}{4}$%	$4\frac{3}{4}$%	$4\frac{1}{2}$%
11 March 1996 onwards	$2\frac{1}{2}$%	5%	$4\frac{3}{4}$%	$4\frac{3}{4}$%	$4\frac{1}{2}$%

14.4 The rates of interest on date of deposit or anniversary on Series 6 or Series 7 Certificates for deposits of £100,000 or more withdrawn for cash are (from 16 November 1992 to 31 March 1996)

	Under 1	1 but under 3	3 but under 6	6 but under 9	9 but under 12
		Period of deposit in months			
16 November 1992–26 January 1993	$1\frac{3}{4}$%	3%	$2\frac{3}{4}$%	$2\frac{1}{2}$%	$2\frac{1}{4}$%
27 January 1993–23 November 1993	$1\frac{1}{4}$%	$2\frac{1}{2}$%	$2\frac{1}{2}$%	$2\frac{1}{4}$%	$2\frac{1}{4}$%
24 November 1993–8 February 1994	1%	$2\frac{1}{2}$%	2%	2%	$1\frac{3}{4}$%
9 February 1994–12 September 1994	$\frac{3}{4}$%	2%	2%	$1\frac{3}{4}$%	$1\frac{3}{4}$%
13 September 1994–7 December 1994	1%	$2\frac{1}{2}$%	$2\frac{1}{2}$%	$2\frac{1}{2}$%	$2\frac{3}{4}$%
8 December 1994–2 February 1995	$1\frac{1}{4}$%	$2\frac{3}{4}$%	$2\frac{3}{4}$%	3%	3%
3 February 1995–13 December 1995	$1\frac{1}{2}$%	3%	3%	3%	$3\frac{1}{4}$%
3 February 1995–13 December 1995	$1\frac{1}{2}$%	3%	3%	3%	$3\frac{1}{4}$%
14 December 1995–18 January 1996	$1\frac{1}{4}$%	$2\frac{3}{4}$%	$2\frac{1}{2}$%	$2\frac{1}{2}$%	$2\frac{1}{2}$%
19 January 1996–10 March 1996	$1\frac{1}{2}$%	$2\frac{3}{4}$%	$2\frac{1}{2}$%	$2\frac{1}{2}$%	$2\frac{1}{4}$%
11 March 1996 onwards	$1\frac{1}{4}$%	$2\frac{1}{2}$%	$2\frac{1}{2}$%	$2\frac{1}{2}$%	$2\frac{1}{4}$%

15 Charities

(See also Revenue Pamphlets IR 64 and IR 65, 'Giving to Charity: How businesses/individuals can get tax relief', IR 75, 'Tax Reliefs for Charities' and IR 113, 'Gift Aid—A Guide for Donors and Charities'.)

Cross-references. See 13.2 CERTIFICATES OF DEPOSIT for exemption of gains; 30 EXEMPT ORGANISATIONS for other exempt organisations; 71.53 SCHEDULE D, CASES I AND II for employees seconded to charities.

15.1 CHARITY, CHARITABLE PURPOSES—GENERAL PRINCIPLES

'Charity' means any body of persons or trust established for charitable purposes only. [*Sec 506(1)*]. The meaning of charity is also governed by general law. Under the *Recreational Charities Act 1958, s 1* the provision, in the interest of social welfare, of facilities for recreation or other leisure time occupation, is deemed to be charitable (subject to the principle that, unless the trust is for the relief of poverty (*Dingle v Turner HL 1972, 1 AER 878*), a trust or institution to be charitable must be for the public benefit). Charities may be registered under the *Charities Act 1960*. The CIR as an interested party may appeal to the High Court against a decision of the Charity Commissioners and *Charities Act 1960, s 9* (as amended by *FA 1986, s 33*) provides for the exchange of information between the Charity Commissioners and the CIR.

Subject to the above, what is a charity rests largely on judicial interpretation. A leading case is *Special Commrs v Pemsel HL 1891, 3 TC 53* in which Lord Macnaghten laid down that 'charity' should be given its technical meaning under English law and comprises 'four principal divisions; trusts for the relief of poverty, trusts for the advancement of education, trusts for the advancement of religion and trusts beneficial to the community and not falling under any of the preceding heads. The trusts last referred to are not the less charitable . . . because incidentally they affect the rich as well as the poor'. In the same case it was held that in relation to tax the English definition should be applied to Scottish cases (and cf. *Jackson's Trustees v Lord Advocate CS 1926, 10 TC 460* and *CIR v Glasgow Police Athletic Assn HL 1953, 34 TC 76*). The concept of 'charity' may change with changes in social values (cf. *CIR v Trustees of Football Association Youth Trust HL 1980, 54 TC 413*).

The charity reliefs are not available to overseas charities (*Gull KB 1937, 21 TC 374; Dreyfus Foundation Inc v CIR HL 1955, 36 TC 126*).

Where land given for educational and certain other charitable purposes ceases after 16 August 1987 to be used for such purposes and, under the *Reverter of Sites Act 1987*, is held by the trustees on a trust for sale for the benefit of the revertee, then unless the revertee is known to be a charity, there is a deemed disposal and reacquisition for capital gains purposes, which may give rise to a chargeable gain. Any income arising from the property will be liable to income tax, and a chargeable gain may also arise on a subsequent sale of the land. By concession, where the revertee is subsequently identified as a charity or disclaims all entitlement to the property (or where certain orders are made by the Charity Commissioners or the Secretary of State), provided that charitable status is re-established within six years of the date on which the land ceased to be held on the original charitable trust, any capital gains tax paid as above in the interim period will be discharged or repaid (with repayment supplement where appropriate) as will any income tax (provided that the income charged was used for charitable purposes). Partial relief will be given where the above conditions are only satisfied in respect of part of the property concerned. A request by the trustees for postponement of the tax payable will be accepted by the Revenue where the revertee has not been identified and this concession may apply. (Revenue Pamphlet IR 1 (November 1995 Supplement), D47).

15.2 Charities

The *Charitable Trusts (Validation) Act 1954* provides for validating as charitable a pre-1953 trust if its property was in fact applied for charitable purposes only, notwithstanding that the trust also authorised its application for non-charitable purposes (cf. *Vernon & Sons Ltd Employees Fund v CIR Ch D 1956, 36 TC 484; Buxton v Public Trustees Ch D 1962, 41 TC 235*).

A donation by one charity to another has been applied for charitable purposes even though merely added to the funds of the other charity (*Helen Slater Charitable Trust Ltd CA 1981, 55 TC 230*).

The application of income to the making of loans at interest to the subsidiaries from whom the income was derived was held to be for charitable purposes in *Nightingale Ltd v Price (Sp C 66), [1996] SSCD 116.*

As regards the time at which charitable purposes arise, see *Guild and Others (as Trustees of the William Muir (Bond 9) Ltd Employees' Share Scheme) v CIR CS 1993, 66 TC 1* (trustees of share scheme required to repay loans out of proceeds of distribution and to apply balance to charitable purposes; held not to apply proceeds of distribution for charitable purposes).

For general restrictions on reliefs, see 15.5 below.

The Revenue have issued a booklet 'Guidelines on the Tax Treatment of Disaster Funds' (obtainable free of charge from Inland Revenue, FICO (Trusts and Charities), St John's House, Merton Road, Bootle, Merseyside L69 9BB (tel. 0151–472 6000 ext. 7016) or FICO (Scotland), Trinity Park House, South Trinity Road, Edinburgh EH5 3SD (tel. 0131–551 8127)) to help people organising disaster appeal funds to decide what form their fund should take and to deal with any tax implications. See generally Revenue publication 'Fund-Raising for Charity' (10.5(*c*) below), which also in particular replaces paras 27 and 28 of this booklet.

A leaflet 'Setting up a Charity in Scotland' is also available free of charge from Inland Revenue FICO (Scotland), who may be contacted for enquiries on whether a body is charitable.

A 'Charity Fund-raising Pack' is available free of charge from FICO (Charity Technical), St John's House, Merton Road, Bootle, Merseyside L69 9BB (tel. 0151–472 6036/6037/6055/6056) or FICO (Scotland) (as above). It contains three booklets: 'Trading by Charities' (an Inland Revenue booklet, see 15.4 (*c*) below); 'VAT—Charities' (Customs and Excise); and 'Charities and Fund-raising: A Summary' (Charity Commissioners). The Charity Commissioners for England and Wales have also published more comprehensive advice for charity trustees in 'Charities and Fund-raising' (CC20), available from any of their offices, including St Alban's House, 57–60 Haymarket, London SW1Y 4QX. Detailed guidance on the use of professional fund-raisers and commercial participation is available in the Home Office publication 'Charitable Fund-raising: Professional and Commercial Involvement' (ISBN 0 11 341133 2, £5.50 from HMSO, tel. 0171–873 9090).

The Revenue have published a Code of Practice (No 5, published July 1993) setting out their standards for the carrying out of inspections of charities' records.

15.2 CHARITY, CHARITABLE PURPOSES—EXAMPLES

Relevant cases are summarised below under appropriate headings.

(*a*) **Almshouse.** Inmates need not be destitute (*Mary Clark Home Trustees v Anderson KB 1904, 5 TC 48*).

(*b*) **Arts.** A musical festival association and the Royal Choral Society have been held to be charitable (*Glasgow Musical Festival Assn CS 1926, 11 TC 154; Royal Choral Socy*

200

v CIR CA 1943, 25 TC 263) but not companies formed to produce plays in association with the Arts Council (*Tennent Plays Ltd v CIR CA 1948, 30 TC 107*) or with the aim of furthering the theatre and dramatic taste (*Associated Artists Ltd v CIR Ch D 1956, 36 TC 499*).

(c)   **Benevolent funds, etc.** for the relief of widows and orphans of members held charitable (*Society for the Relief of Widows and Orphans of Medical Men KB 1926, 11 TC 1; Baptist Union, etc. Ltd v CIR KB (NI) 1945, 26 TC 335*) but not a death benefit fund (*Royal Naval etc. Officers' Assn Ch D 1955, 36 TC 187*) nor a fund set up to promote the formation of mutual provident associations (*Nuffield Foundation v CIR; Nuffield Provident Guarantee Fund v CIR KB 1946, 28 TC 479*).

(d)   **Education.** A trust for the advancement of education does not require an element of poverty to be charitable (*R v Special Commrs (ex p University College of N. Wales) CA 1909, 5 TC 408*). The technical college of a trade association was held to be charitable (*Scottish Woollen Technical College v CIR CS 1926, 11 TC 139*) as was the Students' Union of a medical college (*London Hospital Medical College Ch D 1976, 51 TC 365*) and a trust to promote sports in schools, etc. (*CIR v Trustees of Football Association Youth Trust HL 1980, 54 TC 413*). See also *Educational Grants Assn Ltd CA 1967, 44 TC 93; Abdul Caffoor Trustees v Ceylon Income Tax Commr PC 1961, 40 ATC 93*. For 'public school' see (h) below.

(e)   **Hospital.** A Friendly Society's convalescent home was exempted (*Royal Antediluvian Order of Buffaloes v Owens KB 1927, 13 TC 176*).

(f)   **Political and similar objects** (including the reform of the law) are not charitable purposes. Objects held not to be charitable include the reform of the law on vivisection (*National Anti-Vivisection Socy HL 1947, 28 TC 311*) and temperance (*Temperance Council etc. of England KB 1926, 10 TC 748*), simplified spelling (*Hunter 'C' Trustees v CIR KB 1929, 14 TC 427*), fostering Anglo–Swedish relations (*Anglo-Swedish Socy v CIR KB 1931, 16 TC 34*), Jewish resettlement (*Keren Kayemeth Le Jisroel Ltd v CIR HL 1932, 17 TC 27*) and a memorial fund for Bonar Law (*Bonar Law Memorial Trust v CIR KB 1933, 17 TC 508*).

(g)   **Professional associations etc.** Professional associations are generally not admitted to be established for charitable purposes; they benefit their members, any wider public advantage being incidental (*R v Special Commrs (ex p Headmasters' Conference) KB 1925, 10 TC 73; General Medical Council v CIR CA 1928, 13 TC 819; Geologists' Assn v CIR CA 1928, 14 TC 271; Midland Counties Institution of Engineers v CIR KB 1928, 14 TC 285; General Nursing Council for Scotland v CIR CS 1929, 14 TC 645; Master Mariners (Honourable Company of) v CIR KB 1932, 17 TC 298*). But contrast *Institution of Civil Engineers v CIR CA 1931, 16 TC 158*, where the Institution was held to be charitable, any benefit to members being incidental. Members' clubs and social clubs are not charitable (*Scottish Flying Club v CIR CS 1935, 20 TC 1; Sir H J Williams's Trustees v CIR HL 1947, 27 TC 409*). An agricultural society for the general promotion of agriculture was held charitable (*CIR v Yorkshire Agricultural Socy CA 1927, 13 TC 58*) but not a statutory Pig Marketing Board (*Pig Marketing Board (Northern Ireland) v CIR KB (NI) 1945, 26 TC 319*) nor a society to promote foxhound breeding (*Peterborough Royal Foxhound Show Socy v CIR KB 1936, 20 TC 249*) (but it was given relief under a predecessor to *Sec 510* on its annual show—see 30.1 EXEMPT ORGANISATIONS).

(h)   **Public school.** A school may be for the public benefit and qualify for the relief notwithstanding that it derives substantial receipts from fees (*Blake v Mayor etc. of London CA 1887, 2 TC 209; Ereaut v Girls' Public Day School Trust Ltd HL 1930, 15 TC 529*, and contrast *Birkenhead School Ltd v Dring KB 1926, 11 TC 273*). A Quaker school exclusively for children of members of the Society of Friends was

15.3 Charities

refused relief (*Ackworth School v Betts KB 1915, 6 TC 642*) but a Roman Catholic school which admitted non-catholic pupils qualified for relief (*Cardinal Vaughan Memorial School Trustees v Ryall KB 1920, 7 TC 611*).

(*i*) **Religion.** Charitable relief was refused for trusts to advance the 'religious, moral, social and recreative life' of Presbyterians in Londonderry (*Londonderry Presbyterian Church House Trustees v CIR CA(NI) 1946, 27 TC 431*), for the promotion and aiding of 'Roman Catholicism' in a particular district (*Ellis v CIR CA 1949, 31 TC 178*) and for the 'religious, educational and other parochial requirements' of the Roman Catholic inhabitants of a parish (*Cookstown Roman Catholic Church Trustees v CIR QB (NI) 1953, 34 TC 350*). In each case, the objects included non-charitable elements which prevented the whole being charitable. Relief was also refused to the Oxford Group (*Oxford Group v CIR CA 1949, 31 TC 221*).

(*j*) **Miscellaneous.** A nursing home (*Peebleshire Nursing Assn CS 1926, 11 TC 335*) and a holiday home (*Roberts Marine Mansions Trustees CA 1927, 11 TC 425*) providing services for members etc. at reduced fees held to be charitable, as was a non-profit-making company for publishing law reports (*Incorpd. Council of Law Reporting v A-G CA 1971, 47 TC 321*). Relief refused to a trust to maintain an historic building because it also had a non-charitable object (*Trades House of Glasgow v CIR CS 1969, 46 TC 178*) and to a Society established mainly with philanthropic objects which, in the event, were not achieved (*Hugh's Settlement Ltd v CIR KB 1938, 22 TC 281*). The inclusion of an object 'to promote the development of industry, commerce and enterprise' did not prevent the objects as a whole of a Training and Enterprise Council from being charitable (*Oldham TEC v CIR (Sp C 44), [1995] SSCD 273*).

15.3 SPECIFIC EXEMPTIONS AND RELIEFS FROM TAX

Subject to the restrictions at 15.5 below, the specific exemptions are as below.

Claims can be made, generally within the time limit at 17.4 CLAIMS, to Inland Revenue, FICO (Trusts and Charities), St John's House, Merton Road, Bootle, Merseyside L69 9BB or, in Scotland, FICO (Scotland), Trinity Park House, South Trinity Road, Edinburgh EH5 3SD. [*Sec 505(1)*].

(i) **Schedules A and D.** Profits or gains in respect of rents or other receipts from an estate, interest or right in or over any land (whether in the UK or elsewhere) vested in any person for charitable purposes are exempt to the extent they are applied to charitable purposes only. [*Sec 505(1)(a); FA 1996, s 146(2)(5)*]. For 1995/96 and earlier years (and company accounting periods ended on or before 31 March 1996), the exemption did not strictly apply to rents etc. from land outside the UK, but such rents were exempt by concession. (Revenue Pamphlet IR 1, B9). Also, the legislation specifically referred to 'lands . . . belonging to a hospital, public school or almshouse, or vested in trustees for charitable purposes'. The special relief to hospitals etc. could often be covered by the relief to trusts for charitable purposes (cf. *Scottish Woollen Technical College v CIR CS 1926, 11 TC 139*) and was in any case of reduced importance since the abolition by *FA 1963* of the Schedule A charge on owner-occupied property.

(ii) **Schedule B (before 6 April 1988).** Lands occupied by a charity are exempt. [*Sec 505(1)(b); FA 1988, 14 Sch Pt V*].

(iii) Income of a charity, or applicable for charitable purposes under an Act of Parliament, charter, decree, deed of trust or will, is exempt so far as applied to charitable purposes and consisting of **Schedule C** income, **Schedule D, Case III** income (or equivalent overseas income within **Schedule D, Case IV or V**), **Schedule D, Case V** income consisting of distributions which would be within Schedule F if the paying company were UK resident or distributions within **Schedule F**. For 1995/96 and earlier years (and company accounting periods ended on or before 31 March 1996), the Schedule D exemption strictly applied only to yearly interest and annual payments but was extended by concession as noted at 15.4(*a*) below. Schedule C income of trustees which is applicable towards repairs of any cathedral, college, church, chapel etc., is also exempt so far as applied to those purposes only. For 1996/97 and subsequent years, the charge (and corresponding exemptions) under Schedule C are transferred to Schedule D. [*Sec 505(1)(c)(d); FA 1996, s 146(3)(5), 7 Sch 19*]. Also see Notes at 15.4 below.

Schedule F transitional relief. The tax credit attached to qualifying distributions was reduced from one-third of the distribution in 1992/93 to one-quarter in 1993/94 (and is to continue to be calculated by reference to the lower rate of income tax for subsequent years). [*FA 1993, s 78(1)(3)*]. As a transitional relief for charities (and for other bodies similarly treated under *Sec 507* (see 30.3, 30.9, 30.14 EXEMPT ORGANISATIONS) or *Sec 508* (see 77.1 SCIENTIFIC RESEARCH ASSOCIATIONS)), a compensatory payment may be claimed by the charity etc. in respect of qualifying distributions made by UK companies between 6 April 1993 and 5 April 1997 inclusive, and in respect of which the charity etc. is entitled to payment of the attached tax credit. The payment is in addition to payment of the tax credit itself, and is treated for the purposes of *Sec 252* (see Tolley's Corporation Tax under Advance Corporation Tax) as if it were a payment of tax credit.

The claim must be made within two years after the end of the chargeable period in which the distribution is made. Where (and to the extent that) the claim is accepted, the charity etc. will be entitled to be paid by the Board, out of money provided by Parliament, a proportion of the amount or value of the distribution as follows:

(*a*)   one-fifteenth for a distribution made in 1993/94;

(*b*)   one-twentieth for a distribution made in 1994/95;

(*c*)   one-thirtieth for a distribution made in 1995/96;

(*d*)   one-sixtieth for a distribution made in 1996/97.

Any entitlement to a payment under these provisions is subject to a power of the Board to determine, whether before or after the payment is made, and having regard to *Secs 236, 237* and *703* (see 3.17, 3.18 and 3.2 *et seq.* ANTI-AVOIDANCE respectively), that the charity etc. is to be treated as not entitled to the payment or to a part of it. An appeal may be made against any such decision by written notice to the Board within 30 days of receipt of written notification of the decision, the appeal being to the Special Commissioners.

[*FA 1993, s 80*].

Claims for payments under these transitional arrangements should be made on a special claim form R68(TR), to be completed in addition to the usual form (R68) claiming payment of tax credits on dividends.

(iv)   **Schedule D.** Profits of trades carried on (in the UK or elsewhere) by, and applied solely for purposes of, charities are exempted *if either* (*a*) the trade is exercised in the course of carrying out a primary purpose of the charity, *or* (*b*) the work is mainly carried on by its beneficiaries. [*Sec 505(1)(e); FA 1996, s 146(4)(5)*]. For 1995/96 and earlier years (and company accounting periods ended on or before 31 March 1996), the extension of the exemption to overseas trades applied only by concession. (Revenue Pamphlet IR 1, B9). Also see Notes at 15.4 below.

15.4 Charities

Lotteries. For 1995/96 and subsequent years, lottery profits applied solely to the charity's purposes are exempt, provided that the lottery is promoted and conducted in accordance with *Lotteries and Amusements Act 1976, s 3* or *s 5* (or NI equivalent). [*Sec 505(1)(f); FA 1995, s 138*]. Similar relief for earlier periods is given on a concessional basis. (Revenue Press Release 11 July 1994).

Underwriting commissions are taxable, whether chargeable under Schedule D, Case I (as trading income) or Case VI. Where, however, a charity has been granted exemption from tax on commissions chargeable under Case VI for 1995/96 or earlier years, such treatment will not be disturbed. From 6 April 1996, all such exemption will cease. See Revenue Tax Bulletin December 1995 p 265.

(v) **Capital Gains.** Charities are exempt from capital gains tax on gains applicable, and applied, for charitable purposes. [*TCGA 1992, s 256(1)*]. But this exemption does not apply to gains arising where property which ceases to be subject to charitable trusts is then deemed to have been sold, and immediately re-acquired, at market value. Any CGT on such gains may be assessed within three years after the year of assessment in which the cessation occurs. [*TCGA 1992, s 256(2)*]. See also 44.5, 44.6 INTEREST RECEIVABLE for exemption from charge in respect of deep discount securities and 52.8 OFFSHORE FUNDS as regards certain offshore gains.

(vi) Charities are exempt from tax on offshore income gains—see 52.8 OFFSHORE FUNDS.

(vii) **Charitable unit trust schemes** are excluded from the normal income tax treatment of unauthorised unit trusts, and are thus able to pass on their income to participating charities without deducting tax. [*SI 1988 No 267; SI 1994 No 1479*].

15.4 Notes

(a) The Schedule D exemptions at 15.3(iii) and (iv) above as they applied before 1996/97 (and for company accounting periods ended on or before 31 March 1996) were concessionally extended to bank interest whether yearly or not, to gross building society interest and dividends, to profits on discounting transactions within Case III of Schedule D, and to other overseas income not strictly exempt. (Revenue Pamphlet IR 1, B9). Now superseded by *FA 1996, s 146.*

Where under a will a business was bequeathed to trustees to carry it on and pay the net profits to a charity, the amounts so paid were held to be annual payments (*R v Special Commrs (ex p Shaftesbury Homes) CA 1922, 8 TC 367*). In *Lawrence v CIR KB 1940, 23 TC 333* copyright royalties held to be annual payments. For annual payments generally, see 23.10 DEDUCTION OF TAX AT SOURCE.

(b) For restrictions on the Schedule F relief at 15.3(iii) above, see 3.17 and 3.18 ANTI-AVOIDANCE.

(c) The Schedule D exemption is not a general one and hence does not extend to e.g. trades not within 15.3(iv) above or Case VI income (cf. *Grove v Young Men's Christian Association KB 1903, 4 TC 613* and *Rotunda Hospital, Dublin v Coman HL 1920, 7 TC 517*).

Profits from bazaars, jumble sales, gymkhanas, carnivals, etc., arranged by *voluntary organisations or charities* for raising funds for charity are not taxed if the public are aware of the charitable purpose and the organisation or charity is not regularly carrying on these trading activities and is not in competition with other traders and the profits are transferred to charities or otherwise applied for charitable purposes. (Revenue Pamphlet IR 1, C4). For regular trading within Case I see *British Legion,*

Peterhead Branch v CIR CS 1953, 35 TC 509. (In practice the Revenue may in such cases allow a reasonable deduction for services, etc. provided free.) For annual shows of agricultural societies see 30.1 EXEMPT ORGANISATIONS.

See 15.3(iv) above as regards lotteries.

A 'Charity Fund-raising Pack' is available (see 15.1 above for details), which in particular includes a Revenue publication 'Trading by Charities' (available separately) giving advice on the tax treatment of particular types of trade commonly carried on by charities. This incorporates the guidance given in the earlier Revenue booklet 'Fund-raising for Charities' (still available free of charge from FICO (Trusts and Charities) (see 15.1 above)) as to the type of fund-raising activities covered by extra-statutory concession C4 and the conditions the activities must satisfy, detailing the kind of profits covered by the concession and the consequences if an event is not covered by it, and offering a helpline which charities may phone for further advice.

(d)   For trades held to be within 15.3(iv) above, see *Glasgow Musical Festival Assn CS 1926, 11 TC 154; Royal Choral Society v CIR CA 1943, 25 TC 263* and *Dean Leigh Temperance Canteen Trustees v CIR Ch D 1958, 38 TC 315.*

(e)   The Board have powers to require the production of books, documents etc. relevant to any claim made after 16 July 1992 for exemption under *Sec 505(1)* (see 15.3 above), *Sec 507* (see 30.3, 30.9, 30.14 EXEMPT ORGANISATIONS) or *Sec 508* (see 77.1 SCIENTIFIC RESEARCH ASSOCIATIONS) leading to the repayment of income tax or the payment of tax credit. [*F(No 2)A 1992, s 28*].

15.5   **Non-qualifying expenditure.** A restriction of the exemptions in 15.3 above applies in any chargeable period in which a charity

(a)   has 'relevant income and gains' of £10,000 or more (but see below) which exceed the amount of its 'qualifying expenditure', and

(b)   incurs, or is treated as incurring, 'non-qualifying expenditure'.

Where (a) and (b) above apply, exemption under *Sec 505(1)* and *TCGA 1992, s 256* is not available for so much of the excess at (a) as does not exceed the 'non-qualifying expenditure' incurred in that period. Where the exemption is not so available, the charity may, by notice in writing, specify which items of its 'relevant income and gains' are wholly or partly to be attributed to the amount concerned (covenanted payments to the charity, see 15.6 below, being treated as a single item). If, within 30 days of a request to do so, the charity does not give such notice, the Board determines the attribution. [*Sec 505(3)(6); FA 1995, 17 Sch 7*].

The £10,000 *de minimis* limit in (a) above is proportionately reduced where a chargeable period is less than twelve months, and does not apply where two or more charities acting in concert are engaged in transactions aimed at tax avoidance and where the Board, by notice in writing, so direct. An appeal, as against a decision on a claim, may be made against such a notice. [*Sec 505(4)(7)(8)*].

'*Relevant income and gains*' means the aggregate of

(i)   income which, apart from *Sec 505(1)*, would not be exempt from tax, together with any income which is taxable notwithstanding *Sec 505(1)*, and

(ii)   gains which, apart from *TCGA 1992, s 256*, would be chargeable gains, together with any gains which are chargeable gains notwithstanding *section 256*. [*Sec 505(5)*].

'*Non-qualifying expenditure*' is expenditure other than 'qualifying expenditure'. If the charity invests any funds in an investment which is not a 'qualifying investment', or makes

15.5 Charities

a loan (not as an investment) which is not a 'qualifying loan', the amount invested or lent is treated as non-qualifying expenditure. Where the investment or loan is realised or repaid in whole or in part in the chargeable period in which it was made, any further investment or lending of the sum realised or repaid in that period is, to the extent that it does not exceed the sum originally invested or lent, ignored in arriving at non-qualifying expenditure of the period.

Where the aggregate of the qualifying and non-qualifying expenditure incurred in a chargeable period (the '*primary period*') exceeds the relevant income and gains of that period, so much of the excess as does not exceed the non-qualifying expenditure constitutes '*unapplied non-qualifying expenditure*'. Except to the extent (if any) that it represents the expenditure of 'non-taxable sums' received in the primary period, the unapplied non-qualifying expenditure may be treated as non-qualifying expenditure of a chargeable period ending not more than six years before the end of the primary period. '*Non-taxable sums*' are donations, legacies and other sums of a similar nature which, apart from *Sec 505(1)* and *TCGA 1992, s 256*, are not within the charge to tax.

Where an amount of unapplied non-qualifying expenditure (the '*excess expenditure*') falls to be treated as non-qualifying expenditure of earlier periods, it is attributed only to those periods in which, apart from the attribution in question but taking account of any previous attribution, the relevant income and gains exceed the aggregate of the qualifying and non-qualifying expenditure in that period; and such attribution is not to be greater than the excess. Attributions are made to later periods in priority to earlier periods. Any excess expenditure which cannot be attributed to an earlier period is ignored altogether for attribution purposes. Adjustments by way of further assessments, etc. are made in consequence of an attribution to an earlier period. [*Sec 506(1), (4)–(6), 20 Sch Pt III*].

'*Qualifying expenditure*' is expenditure incurred for charitable purposes only. A payment made (or to be made) to a body situated outside the UK is not qualifying expenditure unless the charity concerned has taken all reasonable steps to ensure that the payment will be applied for charitable purposes. Expenditure incurred in a particular period may be treated as incurred in another period if it is properly chargeable against income of that other period and is referable to commitments (contractual or otherwise) entered into before or during that other period. [*Sec 506(1)–(3)*].

'*Qualifying investments*' are the following.

(A) Investments within *Trustee Investments Act 1961, Sch 1, Pts I, II (para 13 (mortgages, etc.) excepted) and III.*

(B) Investments in a common investment fund established under *Charities Act 1960, s 22* (or NI equivalent) or similar funds under other enactments.

(C) Investments in a common deposit fund established under *Charities Act 1960, s 22A* or similar funds under other enactments (from 1 September 1992).

(D) Any interest in land other than a mortgage, etc.

(E) Shares or securities of a company listed on a recognised stock exchange (within *Sec 841*) or dealt in on the Unlisted Securities Market.

(F) Units in unit trusts within *Financial Services Act 1986.*

(G) Deposits with a recognised bank or licensed institution (but see below) in respect of which interest is payable at a commercial rate, but excluding a deposit made as part of an arrangement whereby the bank, etc. makes a loan to a third party.

(H) CERTIFICATES OF DEPOSIT (13) within *Sec 56(5).*

(I) Loans or other investments as to which the Board are satisfied, on a claim, that the loans or other investments are made for the benefit of the charity and not for the avoidance of tax (whether by the charity or by a third party). Loans secured by mortgage, etc. over land are eligible.

Deposits within (G) above (and money placed within (3) below) on or after 29 April 1996 must be with a bank within *Sec 840A* (see 8.1 BANKS) rather than with a recognised bank or licensed institution.

'Qualifying loans'. A loan which is not made by way of investment is a qualifying loan if it is one of the following.

(1) A loan made to another charity for charitable purposes only.

(2) A loan to a beneficiary of the charity which is made in the course of carrying out the purposes of the charity.

(3) Money placed on a current account with a recognised bank or licensed institution (as in (G) above) otherwise than under arrangements as in (G) above.

(4) A loan, not within (1) to (3) above, as to which the Board are satisfied, on a claim, that the loan is made for the benefit of the charity and not for the avoidance of tax (whether by the charity or by a third party).

[*20 Sch Pts I, II; Charities Act 1992, 6 Sch 17; SI 1992 No 1900; FA 1996, 37 Sch 2, 5, 10, 38 Sch 6*].

Payments between charities. Any payment received by one charity from another, other than in return for full consideration, which would otherwise not be chargeable to tax (and which is not of a description within any of the relieving provisions of *Sec 505(1)*, see 15.3 above), is chargeable to tax under Schedule D, Case III, but is eligible for relief under *Sec 505(1)(c)* (see 15.3(iii) above) as if it were an annual payment. [*Sec 505(2)*].

15.6 **COVENANTS**

A *'covenanted payment to charity'* is a payment under a covenant in favour of a body of persons or trust established for charitable purposes only (including any of the bodies mentioned in *Sec 507*—see 30.3, 30.9, 30.14 EXEMPT ORGANISATIONS) and under which the annual payments become payable for a period which can exceed three years. The covenant must not be for a consideration in money or money's worth and can only be terminable within the three-year period with the consent of the charity. [*Sec 347A(7)(8); FA 1995, 17 Sch 4(2)*].

(*a*) **'Tax-free' subscriptions to charities.** If made by deed of covenant legally binding taxpayer to pay for a period capable of exceeding three years such a sum as, after deduction of tax at the basic rate, will leave a stated amount, the charity benefits by treating that *gross* sum as its income and claiming refund of the difference as tax deducted from it. An expiring deed must be renewed immediately if arrangement is desired to continue; relief to charity refused on payments made between expiry of old deed and coming into operation of new. See 80.23 SETTLEMENTS as regards continuation of relief for payments under certain revocable covenants where the power of revocation could have, but has not, been exercised (and see Revenue Press Release 24 March 1993 for guidance on the use of revocable covenants). See 80.21 and 80.28 SETTLEMENTS regarding additional tax relief for higher rate taxpayers and effectiveness of deed of covenant generally. The provisions covered at 80.21, 80.23 and 80.28 have no application for 1995/96 and later years. See 15.8 below as regards certain donations treated as made under covenant. See *Racal Group Services Ltd v Ashmore CA, [1995] STC 1151* for an unsuccessful attempt retrospectively to amend a deed to achieve the intended effect for tax purposes.

(*b*) Covenanted payments must be **pure income** in the hands of the charity and not a payment by the covenantor for goods, services or benefits to him (see 23.10

15.7 Charities

DEDUCTION OF TAX AT SOURCE and *Campbell & Anor v CIR HL 1968, 45 TC 427; National Book League CA 1957, 37 TC 455; Taw & Torridge Festival Socy Ltd v CIR Ch D 1959, 38 TC 603*). In relation to charities (and certain bodies treated as charities) for the preservation of property or the conservation of wildlife, certain admission rights in return for payments to the charity are ignored for this purpose. [*FA 1989, s 59*]. Generally, in the case of ordinary small subscriptions, benefits available to subscribers up to 25% of the subscription are ignored. (Revenue Press Release 20 March 1990).

(c) The long-standing practice of the Revenue, to accept **retrospective validation** of payments made earlier in the tax year in which the deed was made, ceases for covenants made after 30 July 1990. This follows the decision in *Morley-Clarke v Jones CA 1985, 59 TC 567*, see 47.15 MARRIED PERSONS. (Revenue Pamphlet IR 131, SP 4/90, 20 March 1990).

(d) The insertion of **escape clauses** in a deed which enable the covenantor of his own volition to terminate the covenant without the consent of the charity concerned (e.g. where payments cease on the covenantor voluntarily ceasing to work for his current employer) may invalidate the covenant for tax purposes. Covenants which have been accepted by the Revenue as valid, and on which repayments of tax have been made, but which are invalid as a result of escape clauses, will continue to be treated as effective until they expire, but covenantors contemplating inserting such clauses in deeds should take legal advice before doing so. (Revenue Pamphlet IR 131, SP 4/90, 20 March 1990).

(e) For **claims** relating to deeds of covenant by individuals, a charity may, from 1 July 1992, provide a composite certificate covering all payments, accompanied by completed forms R185 (Covenant) for all first-year payments. For covenants by companies, forms R185(AP) are required for all payments, as are the deeds of covenant for first claims. Previously, in the case of covenants by individuals, forms R185(AP) were required for all years where the amount was more than £400 net (£175 before 6 April 1990), although required only with the first claim for smaller covenants, and the deeds were also required with first claims. Proper records must be kept in support of claims, and should be retained for up to six years after the expiry of covenants. (Revenue Press Releases 20 March 1990, 7 May 1992). See generally the Charity Tax Pack obtainable from Inland Revenue, FICO (Trusts and Charities), St John's House, Merton Road, Bootle, Merseyside L69 9BB.

(f) To minimise any delay in making **repayments** of tax to charities, the Revenue may, in appropriate circumstances, be prepared provisionally to repay tax apparently suffered by deduction before the full verification procedure has been completed. (Revenue Pamphlet IR 131, SP 3/87, 26 March 1987).

(g) A **claim for repayment** of tax deducted from covenanted donations was refused where the claim was made more than six years after the end of the years of assessment within which the payments were due, although the payments had in fact been made within the six years preceding the date of claim (*CIR v Crawley Ch D 1986, 59 TC 728*).

15.7 **PAYROLL DEDUCTION SCHEME** [*Sec 202; FA 1990, s 24; FA 1993, s 68; FA 1996, s 109*]

An employee may make charitable donations of up to £1,200 in any year of assessment (£600 in 1990/91, 1991/92 and 1992/93, £900 in 1993/94, 1994/95 and 1995/96) by deduction from wages or salaries subject to PAYE (55). Tax relief will be allowed as if the amounts so deducted were allowable expenses, provided that

(a) the scheme is of a kind approved by the Board,

(*b*)   the employer is authorised by the employee to deduct from pay donations requested to be paid to a charity or charities,

(*c*)   the deductions constitute gifts by the employee and are not under deeds of covenant, and

(*d*)   the employer pays the donations to an approved agent, who pays them to a charity (or charities), or the employer pays them directly to a charity (or charities) approved by the Board as an agent for the purpose of paying sums to other charities.

Administrative regulations may be made by statutory instrument regarding such matters as

(i)   the grant or withdrawal of approval by the Board of schemes and agents, and appeals to the Special Commissioners against the Board's decision,

(ii)   the requirements of terms of schemes and qualifications of agents,

(iii) the production of documents and records by a participating employer or agent within a specified time, and

(iv)   production of other information to the Revenue.

The first such regulations are contained in *The Charitable Deductions (Approved Schemes) Regulations 1986 (SI 1986 No 2211)*.

Penalties apply for failure to comply with (iii) and (iv) above under *TMA s 98*.

A Prospectus 'Charities—Payroll Giving Schemes' was published by the Revenue in June 1986 giving details of the tax relief proposals.

Lists of approved agency charities have been issued by the Revenue, and will be added to from time to time. (Revenue Press Releases 11 March 1987, 11 May 1987, 16 July 1987, 5 October 1987).

Administrative costs. Voluntary contributions made by an employer to assist a charitable agency with its costs in managing a payroll giving scheme on the employer's behalf are deductible in computing the profits of a trade, profession or vocation, or as management expenses of an investment company. [*Sec 86A; FA 1993, s 69*]. This applies to expenditure incurred by the employer after 15 March 1993, but a similar deduction was previously allowed by concession. (Revenue Pamphlet IR 1, B32).

15.8   **QUALIFYING DONATIONS** [*FA 1990, ss 25, 94; FA 1991, s 71(5)(6); F(No 2)A 1992, s 26(2)(4); FA 1993, s 67(2)(4)*]

Where an individual makes a 'qualifying donation' to a charity after 30 September 1990, it is treated as if it were a covenanted payment made at the same time as the gift, i.e. as if it were a payment of the corresponding grossed-up amount paid under deduction of basic rate tax. Higher rate relief is available where appropriate in respect of the grossed-up amount. Where the covenanted payment, had it been made, would not, or not wholly, have been payable out of income taxed at the basic (or higher) rate, the basic rate tax deemed to have been deducted (or the difference between that tax and tax at the lower rate), or a corresponding proportion thereof, is assessable on the donor.

Secs 348 et seq. (annual payments) (see 23.1 *et seq.* DEDUCTION OF TAX AT SOURCE) do not apply to such deemed payments. The charity may, however, claim repayment of the tax deemed to have been deducted in the normal way (see 15.6(*a*) above).

A gift is a '*qualifying donation*' if:

(*a*)   it takes the form of a payment of a sum of money and is not subject to a condition as to repayment;

(*b*)   it is not in fact a covenanted payment to charity;

(*c*)   it is not made under the payroll deduction scheme (see 15.7 above);

(*d*)   either

      (i)   neither the donor nor a person connected with him (see 20 CONNECTED PERSONS) receives a benefit in consequence of the gift, or

      (ii)   the aggregate value of all such benefits so received in consequence of the gift does not exceed one-fortieth of the amount of the gift, and the total value of such benefits so received in respect of that gift and any other gifts made by the donor to the charity earlier in the year of assessment does not exceed £250;

(*e*)   it is not conditional on, or associated with, or part of an arrangement involving, the acquisition of property by the charity from the donor or a person connected with him, otherwise than by way of gift;

(*f*)   it is not less than £250 (£400 in relation to gifts made after 6 May 1992 and before 16 March 1993, £600 in relation to gifts made before 7 May 1992) or, in relation to gifts made before 19 March 1991, more than £5,000,000 (together with any other qualifying donations made by the same donor earlier in the year of assessment);

(*g*)   the donor is UK resident at the time of the gift; and

(*h*)   the donor gives to the charity a certificate in prescribed form (i.e. Form R190(SD)) in relation to the gift, to the effect that the gift satisfies (*a*) to (*g*) above, and that the tax deemed to have been deducted has been or will be accounted for, either directly or by payment out of taxed income.

The release of a loan not for consideration and not under seal cannot amount to a gift of money (see *Battle Baptist Church v CIR and Woodham (Sp C 23), [1995] SSCD 176*).

The Board have powers to inspect the records of the charity in relation to repayment claims in respect of qualifying donations (the specific powers in *FA 1990, s 94* being replaced after 16 July 1992 by the general powers under *F(No 2)A 1992, s 28*, see 15.4(*e*) above).

For a similar relief available to company donors, see Tolley's Corporation Tax under Charities. See generally Revenue Pamphlet IR 113.

16   Children

16.1   Child allowances were phased out from 1977/78 onwards by the introduction of the non-taxable child benefit. The remaining allowance is the additional personal allowance in respect of children, see 1.17 ALLOWANCES AND TAX RATES.

16.2   All the income of a child is assessable on him (subject to below) and he has full entitlement to personal allowances and reliefs. In most cases only the personal allowance (see 1.14 ALLOWANCES AND TAX RATES) will be claimable.

16.3   Returns and claims may be made by a child in respect of income within his control but otherwise these are the responsibility of his parent, guardian, tutor or any trustee [*TMA ss 72, 118*] who is also liable for payment of any tax in default of payment by the child, with right of recovery. [*TMA s 73*]. Where assessment should primarily be made on the guardian, tutor or trustee, an assessment in the name of the child is not precluded (*R v Newmarket Commrs (ex p Huxley) CA 1916, 7 TC 49*).

16.4   If a parent makes a settlement in favour of his child, then the income arising thereon is treated (subject to certain exceptions) as that of the parent and not of the child for tax purposes. The definition of 'settlement' for this purpose is wide enough to cover gifts e.g. of money, or shares. See 80.17, 80.20 SETTLEMENTS. See also the other provisions in 80.13 to 80.29 SETTLEMENTS whereby income of a settlement can be treated as that of the settlor for tax purposes.

16.5   Any reference to a child in the *Tax Acts*, is to be construed as including reference to an adopted child. [*Sec 832(5)*].

16.6   **Contingency claims in respect of income up to 5 April 1969** in relation to certain settlements, see 80.12 SETTLEMENTS.

17   Claims

Cross-references. See ALLOWANCES AND TAX RATES at 1.11 onwards for claims to personal allowances and reliefs; 25 DOUBLE TAX RELIEF for claims under DTR agreements etc.; 43 INTEREST PAYABLE for relief for interest paid; 51.11 NON-RESIDENTS AND OTHER OVERSEAS MATTERS for reliefs claimable by non-residents; 53.6 PARTNERSHIPS where change of partners or proprietors; 64.7 RESIDENCE, ORDINARY RESIDENCE AND DOMICILE for residence, etc. claims; 80 SETTLEMENTS for claims by beneficiaries and contingent trust claims. See also 78 SELF-ASSESSMENT.

17.1   Claims may be made to the local Inspector of Taxes (or to the Board of Inland Revenue in certain specified cases) whenever the *Taxes Acts* provide for relief to be given or other thing to be done. Any error or mistake in a claim may be rectified by a supplementary claim. [*TMA s 42(1)(2)(8)*].

Claims are personal matters and (except in the case of trustees for persons under disability etc.) can be made only by the person entitled to the relief (cf. *Fulford v Hyslop Ch D 1929*,

17.2 Claims

8 ATC 588). For claims to personal allowances etc. by persons receiving tax-free annuities, see 23.17 DEDUCTION OF TAX AT SOURCE. See 67.2 RETURNS for signing of claims by attorney.

Where an official form is provided for use in making a claim or election, it is permissible to fill out a photocopy of the blank form, provided that, where double sided copying is not available, all the pages (including any notes) are present and attached in the correct order. Although such copying is in strictness a breach of HMSO copyright, this will only be pursued if forms are copied on a large scale for commercial gain. (Revenue Pamphlet IR 131, SP 5/87, 15 June 1987). See also 67.2 RETURNS.

17.2 TAX REPAYMENT CLAIMS

For an example of claims for repayment of tax, see 2.2 ALLOWANCES AND TAX RATES—EXAMPLES. Forms for making repayment claims can be obtained from the local Inspector of Taxes (whose address in case of difficulty can be obtained from the Secretary, Inland Revenue, Somerset House, London WC2R 1LB) or by completing Form R95(D) (which is included in Revenue Pamphlet IR 112). A non-resident should apply to the Inland Revenue, Financial Intermediaries and Claims Office, Foreign Division, 1st Floor, St John's House, Merton Road, Bootle, Merseyside L69 9BB.

It is now the practice to dispense in some cases with claim forms, provided the annual return form (see 67.2 RETURNS) is correctly filled up and sufficient tax deduction vouchers (e.g. dividend counterfoils) at the appropriate rate (lower or basic) are sent to the inspector to cover the amount reclaimable for that year.

Where an individual's income is comprised of UK dividends (which have related tax credits) and other income taxed by deduction, there is no need to wait until the end of the tax year. The claim can be sent in as soon as sufficient income has been received to cover both the allowances claimed and any 'charges' on the income (see 1.9 ALLOWANCES AND TAX RATES). Alternatively, interim claims may be made for part allowances. However, repayments are only made during the tax year where the total involved exceeds £50. Claims for lesser amounts will not be processed until either the amount exceeds £50 or, if earlier, the end of the tax year. (Revenue Press Release 29 March 1989).

Late claims. Where an over-payment of tax has arisen because of official error, and there is no doubt or dispute as to the facts, claims to repayment of tax are accepted outside the statutory time limits. (Revenue Pamphlet IR 1, B41).

17.3 ADDITIONAL ALLOWANCES

The inspector should be notified promptly of additional allowances so that relief can be given in the current PAYE coding or other assessments.

17.4 TIME LIMITS FOR CLAIMS

See 86 TIME LIMITS—5 APRIL 1997 and 87 TIME LIMITS—MISCELLANEOUS for details. **Unless otherwise prescribed, a claim for 1995/96 or an earlier year must be made within six years** of the end of the tax year ('year of assessment') to which it relates (or the end of the accounting period, in the case of a company). [*TMA s 43(1)*]. Such claims for the tax year 1990/91 must accordingly be made by 5 April 1997. See, however, 86.1(*e*)(i) TIME LIMITS—5 APRIL 1997 as regards claims following late assessment. See also 15.6(*g*) CHARITIES as regards claims in relation to late payments under covenant. See also 17.7 below.

For 1996/97 and later years (under self-assessment), this general time limit is reduced, for income tax and capital gains tax purposes, to five years after 31 January following the year of assessment to which the claim relates. The six-year limit remains unchanged for corporation tax purposes. [*TMA s 43(1); FA 1994, ss 196, 199(2)(a), 19 Sch 14*].

17.5   APPEALS IN RESPECT OF CLAIMS

An unfavourable decision by the inspector, or Board, on a claim, may be appealed against in writing within 30 days of receipt of written notice of the decision or within three months on matters affecting non-residents relating to (*a*) personal reliefs or (*b*) residence, ordinary residence or domicile or (*c*) exemption of pension funds for overseas employees. Appeals from decision of the inspector are to the General Commissioners or (at taxpayer's option) to the Special Commissioners, and those from decision of the Board to the Special Commissioners. [*TMA s 42, 2 Sch*]. See under 4 APPEALS for this and for appeals to the High Court. See also 78.34, 78.36 SELF-ASSESSMENT as regards 1996/97 and subsequent years.

17.6   ERROR OR MISTAKE RELIEF [*TMA s 33*]

Relief may be claimed in writing, within six years after the end of the year of assessment in which the assessment was made, against any over-assessment due to an error or mistake (including an omission) in any return or statement. The relief is given because the return etc. was wrong and hence does not apply where the assessment is not on the basis of the return. No relief is allowed if the return or statement was made in accordance with the basis or practice generally prevailing at the time, or if the relevant circumstances of the case render relief inequitable.

The relief, which is given by repayment, is determined by the Board with appeal from them to the Special Commissioners and from them, but only on a point of law arising in connection with the computation of the income or gains, to the High Court. (See *Rose Smith & Co Ltd v CIR KB 1933, 17 TC 586; Carrimore Six Wheelers Ltd CA 1944, 26 TC 301* and *CA 1947, 28 TC 422; Arranmore Investment Co Ltd v CIR CA(NI) 1973, 48 TC 623*.)

For relief for double assessment, see 5.4 ASSESSMENTS. For re-opening of accounts in respect of 'late' receipts and payments, see 71.28 SCHEDULE D, CASES I AND II. For alteration of past claims on farming and market gardening profits, see 71.56 SCHEDULE D, CASES I AND II.

17.7   FURTHER ASSESSMENTS

In the case of a discovery leading to a further assessment under *TMA s 29(3)* (see 5.3 ASSESSMENTS) or *Sec 412(3)* (group relief recovery, see Tolley's Corporation Tax under Groups of Companies) which is made after 26 July 1989, and is not for making good a loss of tax attributable to fraudulent or negligent conduct (see 6.4 BACK DUTY),

(*a*)   any 'relevant' claim, election, application or notice which could have been made or given within the normal time limits may be made or given within one year of the end of the chargeable period in which the assessment is made, and

(*b*)   any 'relevant' claim, etc. previously made or given, except an irrevocable one, can, with the consent of the person(s) by whom it was made or given (or their personal representatives), be revoked or varied in the manner in which it was made or given.

Certain elections for the transfer inter-spouse of the married couple's allowance are excluded from this treatment.

A claim, etc. is '*relevant*' to an assessment for a chargeable period if

(i)   it relates to, or to an event occurring in, the chargeable period, and

(ii)   it, or its revocation or variation, reduces, or could reduce,

(A)   the increased tax liability resulting from the assessment, or

(B)   any other liability of the person for that chargeable period or a later one ending not more than one year after the end of the period in which the assessment is made.

The normal APPEALS (4) provisions apply, with any necessary modifications.

If the making, etc. of a claim, etc. (as above) would alter another person's tax liability, the consent of that person (or his personal representatives) is needed. If such alteration is an increase, the other person cannot make, etc. a claim, etc. under the foregoing provisions.

If the reduction, whether resulting from one or more than one claim, etc., would exceed the additional tax assessed, relief is not available for the excess. If the reduction, so limited, involves more than one period, or more than one person, the inspector will specify by notice in writing how it is to be apportioned; but within 30 days of the notice (or last notice if more than one person is involved) being given, the person, or persons jointly, can specify the apportionment by notice in writing to the inspector. [*TMA ss 43A, 43B; FA 1989, s 150; F(No 2)A 1992, 5 Sch 9(4); FA 1993, 14 Sch 2*].

---

18   Clubs and Societies

18.1   A club or society is liable to corporation tax on its taxable income and capital gains which includes interest received and profits from trading activities with non-members (see under 50 MUTUAL TRADING). See *CIR v Worthing Rugby Football Club Trustees CA 1987, 60 TC 482* and *Blackpool Marton Rotary Club v Martin Ch D 1988, 62 TC 686* and, for non-proprietary members' golf clubs, Revenue Tax Bulletin August 1994 p 156. For a case in which the Special Commissioner declined to make a distinction between profits arising from ordinary members and those arising from associate members, see *Westbourne Supporters of Glentoran Club v Brennan (Sp C 22), [1995] SSCD 137*. Generally, see Revenue explanatory pamphlet IR 46 'Clubs, Societies and Associations'.

18.2   **Holiday clubs and thrift funds** formed annually are not legally entitled to relief, but where income is received which has not been subjected to composite rate tax, tax assessed on income paid or applied to members is restricted to the tax charge which would have arisen had the members received the income directly. (See Revenue Pamphlet IR 1, C3.)

18.3   **Loan and Money Societies.** Society must account for income tax at average rate (calculated by reference to the average rate which would be applicable if investors were charged directly) on dividends etc. grossed up at that average rate, after taking into account contributions from members to meet management expenses. The grossed-up amount is deductible in computing corporation tax liability of society. (Revenue Pamphlet IR 1, C2.)

18.4   **Lotteries etc.** See 71.30 SCHEDULE D, CASES I AND II.

18.5   **Sporting clubs—VAT repayments.** See Revenue Tax Bulletin April 1995 p 209.

19   Compensation for Loss of Employment (and Damages)

Cross-references. See 59.4 PENSIONS for war service payments etc.; 71.47 SCHEDULE D, CASES I AND II ('Compensation, Damages etc.—Receipts') and 71.46 ('Compensation, Damages etc.—Payments') for treatment in relation to trading profits and 71.53 for allowability of payments to employees; 75.32 SCHEDULE E for Redundancy Payments, 75.34 for Restrictive Covenants, 75.41 for certain payments to MPs etc. and 75.45 for wages in lieu of notice.

19.1   The following paragraphs apply to lump sums paid on termination of an office or employment and, at 19.7 below, to the reduction of an award for damages by reference to the tax liability.

19.2   **SUMS RECEIVABLE ON TERMINATION OF OFFICE OR EMPLOYMENT— SUMMARY**

In determining the correct treatment for tax purposes of a sum receivable by a director or employee on termination of his office or employment, it is first necessary to see whether it is taxable under the general rules of SCHEDULE E (75). See 19.3 below for an outline of the principles to be applied. If it is within the general rules, it is taxable in full under PAYE (55) at the time of the payment.

If it is not within the general rules of Schedule E, such a sum will generally be taxable under that Schedule by the special legislation in *Sec 148*. See 19.4, 19.5 below for the application of *Sec 148*, and 19.6 below for exemptions.

19.3   **COMPENSATION FOR LOSS ETC. OF OFFICE OR EMPLOYMENT— GENERAL TAX LAW**

The following principles apply in determining whether a sum received in compensation for loss, etc. of office or employment is taxable under the general rules of SCHEDULE E (75). See 19.4 *et seq.* below as regards such payments not within these rules.

Any payment made to a director or employee by way of reward for services, past, present or future, is within the general charge. It was considered by the Revenue that this could include any termination payment received under the terms of a contract of service, or where there was an expectation of receiving such a payment firm enough to allow the payment to be viewed as part of the reward for services (see e.g. Revenue Pamphlet IR 131, SP 1/81, 10 March 1981). In *Mairs v Haughey HL, [1993] STC 569*, however, it was held that a non-statutory redundancy payment would not be within the general Schedule E charge, being compensation for the employee's not being able to receive emoluments from the employment rather than emoluments from the employment itself. (The case concerned a payment for the waiver of a contingent right to such a payment, which was to be accorded the same tax treatment.) Following the decision in *Mairs v Haughey*, SP 1/81 was replaced by Revenue Statement of Practice SP 1/94. This acknowledges that lump sum payments under a non-statutory redundancy scheme are liable to income tax only under *Sec 148*, provided that they are genuinely made solely on account of redundancy as defined in *Employment Protection (Consolidation) Act 1978, s 81*, whether the scheme is a standing scheme forming part of the conditions of service or an *ad hoc* scheme devised to meet a particular situation. SP 1/94 indicates, however, that the Revenue is concerned to distinguish payments which are in reality terminal bonuses or other reward for services, which are fully taxable under the general Schedule E rules, and that in view of the often complex arrangements for redundancy, and the need to consider each scheme on its own facts, employers may submit proposed schemes (together with any explanantory letter to be sent to employees) to the inspector for advance clearance. (Revenue Pamphlet IR 131 (October 1995 Supplement), SP 1/94, 17 February 1994).

19.4 Compensation for Loss of Employment (and Damages)

The following decided cases reflect the different approaches the courts have adopted in relation to such compensation. Proper compensation for loss of office is usually exempt (see *Clayton v Lavender Ch D 1965, 42 TC 607*) except where payable under service agreement (see *Dale v De Soissons CA 1950, 32 TC 118*) or under rights conferred by company's articles (*Henry v Foster CA 1932, 16 TC 605*). But an agreed sum payable for waiving such rights was held not assessable (*Hunter v Dewhurst HL 1932, 16 TC 605*), as also a payment in lieu of agreed pension (*Wales v Tilley HL 1943, 25 TC 136*). Payment in settlement of claim re breach of service contract also exempt (*Du Cros v Ryall KB 1935, 19 TC 444*), but cf. *Carter v Wadman CA 1946, 28 TC 41*. Voluntary payments on retirement held to be personal testimonials and not assessable (*Cowan v Seymour CA 1919, 7 TC 372; Mulvey v Coffey HC(I) 2 ITC 239*). A transfer fee paid by his old club to a professional footballer held to be assessable under general Sch E rules and not as a termination payment (*Shilton v Wilmshurst HL 1991, 64 TC 78*).

Wages in lieu of notice are not generally assessable, but see 75.45 SCHEDULE E for further consideration of such payments. Compare *Duff v Barlow KB 1941, 23 TC 633; Carter v Wadman CA 1946, 28 TC 41; Henley v Murray CA 1950, 31 TC 351; Clayton v Lavender Ch D 1965, 42 TC 607*; in which sums paid on cessation of office in lieu of future income held not to be assessable. *Hofman v Wadman KB 1946, 27 TC 192* in which the decision was against the taxpayer was not followed in *Clayton v Lavender*. But the following items paid during continuance of office were held liable: agreed sum paid to director to remain in office (*Prendergast v Cameron HL 1940, 23 TC 122*); for surrender of rights to fees or commission (*Leeland v Boarland KB 1945, 27 TC 71; Wilson v Daniels KB 1943, 25 TC 473; Bolam v Muller KB 1947, 28 TC 471* and *McGregor v Randall Ch D 1984, 58 TC 110*); and for accepting lower fees (*Wales v Tilley HL 1943, 25 TC 136*). See also *Williams v Simmonds Ch D 1981, 55 TC 17*. Payments under *Employment Protection (Consolidation) Act 1978*, or NI equivalent, are exempt from tax [*Sec 579*] but must be included for the purposes of *Sec 148* (in practice, similar treatment is given to non-statutory redundancy payments under certain conditions), see 19.5 below. A proposed supplementary redundancy payment which, following a change in circumstances, was made to all employees whether or not made redundant, was held to be assessable under the general Schedule E rules where made to employees not made redundant (*Allan v CIR; Cullen v CIR CS, [1994] STC 943*).

Sum paid as compensation for loss of benefit under an abandoned refuse salvage scheme held assessable (*Holland v Geoghegan Ch D 1972, 48 TC 482*).

See 3.10 ANTI-AVOIDANCE regarding capital sums received in lieu of earnings. [*Sec 775*].

19.4 COMPENSATION FOR LOSS OF OFFICE AND OTHER TERMINAL PAYMENTS—SPECIAL LEGISLATION

The general legal position in 19.3 above is modified by special legislation as explained in 19.5, 19.6 below. A payment taxable under any other provisions is not within this special legislation, but *a compensation payment which does not fall within the special legislation nevertheless remains subject to the general law.*

For the interaction of these provisions and *Gourley* principles (see 19.7 below) see *Stewart v Glentaggart Ltd CS 1963, 42 ATC 318; Bold v Brough QB, [1963] 3 AER 849* and *Parsons v BNM Laboratories Ltd CA, [1963] 2 AER 658.*

19.5 TERMINAL PAYMENTS WITHIN SEC 148 CHARGE

Subject to the specific exceptions and reliefs below, Schedule E applies to any payment or valuable consideration (not otherwise taxable) made or given, whether under legal obligation or not, by any person to the holder or past holder of any office or employment, or to his executors, his spouse, relatives or dependants, directly or indirectly in connection with his ceasing to hold the office or employment, or with any change in its functions or emoluments, or by way of commutation of periodical payments otherwise arising therefrom. Treated as earned income received as at the date of cessation or change as above or, in cases of commutation, at date effected. Executors are liable. Payer required to notify Revenue in writing within 30 days of end of year of assessment in which payment is made. [*Sec 148(1)–(5), (7)*].

The value of the provision of a car for a limited period following termination was held to be within *Sec 148*, by reference to the period for which it was actually made available (rather than the longer period for which the original termination agreement provided) (*George v Ward (Sp C 30), [1995] SSCD 230*).

Sec 148 is an independent Schedule E charging provision, not confined to the rules of the Cases under *Sec 19(1)* (see 75.1 SCHEDULE E) (*Nichols v Gibson Ch D, [1994] STC 1029*).

A statutory redundancy payment is included for the purpose of *Sec 148*. [*Sec 580(3)*]. For the position as regards a payment under a non-statutory redundancy scheme, see 19.3 above.

Where, as part of an arrangement relating to the termination of an employment, both parties agree that the employer will make a special contribution into an approved retirement benefit scheme on behalf of the employee the Revenue will not charge under *Sec 148* provided the benefits are within the limits provided by the scheme. A similar exemption will apply to the purchase of an annuity for the employee so long as the transaction is approved under *ICTA 1988, Pt XIV*. See 66.4 RETIREMENT SCHEMES. (Revenue Pamphlet IR 131, SP 2/81, 10 March 1981).

For the above purposes, two or more payments to the same person re the same office, or different offices under same or associated employers (as defined in *Sec 188(7)*) or successors, are treated as one, the provisions applying to each such payment after deducting the exempt amount (see 19.6(i) below) rateably or, if falling in different fiscal years, from the earliest first. [*Sec 188(5)*].

For MPs see *Sec 190*, and for European MPs, 75.41 SCHEDULE E.

Expenses incurred by taxpayer in obtaining an award for unfair dismissal or securing fresh employment held not deductible (*Warnett v Jones Ch D 1979, 53 TC 283*).

See 75.23 for exemption from *Sec 148* for payment made to reimburse the employee for cost of indemnity insurance or certain liabilities relating to the employment.

As to whether *compensation to auditor* and others falls within *Sec 148*, see 75.24 SCHEDULE E.

19.6 EXCEPTIONS AND RELIEFS FROM SEC 148 CHARGE

    (i) The first £30,000 of the payment. [*Sec 188(4)*].

    (ii) Payments made under an obligation incurred before 6 April 1960. [*Sec 148(6)*].

    (iii) Payment where cessation arises from death, injury or disability of the holder of the office. [*Sec 188(1)(a)*]. 'Disability' covers not only a condition resulting from a sudden affliction but also continuing incapacity to perform the duties of an office or employment arising out of the culmination of a process of deterioration of physical or mental health caused by chronic illness. (Revenue Pamphlet IR 131, SP 10/81, 3 November 1981). See e.g. *Horner v Hasted Ch D, [1995] STC 766* (relief refused).

    (iv) Sums chargeable under *Sec 313* (restrictive covenants, see 75.34 SCHEDULE E). [*Sec 188(1)(b)*].

(v) Benefits provided before 1 December 1993, or on or after that date under retirement benefit schemes entered into before that date and not varied on or after that date, for the provision of which the holder has been charged under *ICTA 1970, s 220* or *Sec 595*. [*Sec 188(1)(c); FA 1994, s 108(7)(8)*]. (See also now 66.9 RETIREMENT SCHEMES.).)

(vi) Benefits under schemes described in *ICTA 1970, s 221(1)(2)* or *Sec 596(1)* (see 66 RETIREMENT SCHEMES) [*Sec 188(1)(d)*], but payments for loss of office, or loss or diminution of earnings, are exempted only if the loss etc. is due to ill-health or the payment is properly a benefit earned by past service. [*Sec 188(2)*].

(vii) Terminal grants, gratuities (including commutation of annual sums), etc. to *HM Forces*. [*Sec 188(1)(e)*].

(viii) Benefit from Commonwealth overseas government superannuation schemes, or compensation for loss of career etc., due to constitutional changes there, paid to a former public servant of that territory (for certain definitions see *Overseas Development and Cooperation Act 1980*). [*Sec 188(1)(f)*].

(ix) Payments where certain foreign service is included. [*Sec 188(3)*].

(x) A special contribution by an employer into an approved retirement benefit scheme or an approved personal pension scheme (or purchase of an approved annuity from a Life Office) to provide benefits for the employee as part of an arrangement relating to the termination of an employment. (Revenue Pamphlet IR 131, SP 2/81, 10 March 1981).

(xi) Legal costs. Where an employee takes action to recover compensation for loss of office etc., any legal costs recovered from the employer are strictly chargeable under *Sec 148*, without any deduction for the costs incurred. By concession, tax will not be charged on such recovered costs where either:

(*a*) the dispute is settled without recourse to the courts, and the costs are paid direct to the employee's solicitor under the settlement agreement, in full or partial discharge of the solicitor's bill of costs incurred by the employee only in connection with the termination of the employment; or

(*b*) the dispute goes to court, and the costs are paid in accordance with a court order (including where they are paid direct to the employee).

Other professional costs, such as accountancy fees, are not covered by this concession, but it does cover legal costs incurred by the employee's solicitor in consulting other professionals for the specific claim or in paying the expenses of expert professional witnesses. (Revenue Pamphlet IR 1, A81; Revenue Tax Bulletin October 1994 p 170).

A payment in pursuance of an obligation incurred before 10 March 1981 may, by election by written notice within, for 1996/97 and later years, five years after 31 January following the tax year of payment (for earlier years, six years after the end of the tax year of payment) be granted certain reliefs from *Sec 148* under the provisions generally applicable before that date. [*11 Sch Pt II; FA 1996, s 135, 21 Sch 24*].

19.7 DAMAGES—REDUCTION FOR TAX

Tax liability is taken into account in fixing *damages* for injury, see *British Transport Commission v Gourley HL 1955, 34 ATC 305*. For application of *Gourley* principle see *West Suffolk CC v W Rought Ltd HL 1956, 35 ATC 315* and contrast *Stoke-on-Trent City Council v Wood Mitchell & Co Ltd CA 1978, [1979] STC 197* (compulsory purchase of land); *Lyndale Fashion Mfrs v Rich CA 1972, [1973] STC 32* (tax on damages calculated as if top slice of income after expenses deducted); *In re Houghton Main Colliery Ch D 1956, 23 ATC 320* (lump sum payable re pensions); *Stewart v Glentaggart CS 1963, 42 ATC 318; Parsons v BNM Labs CA 1963, 42 ATC 200* (damages for wrongful dismissal); *McGhie & Sons v BTC QB 1962, 41 ATC 144* (prohibition from mining under railway—cf. 71.47(*c*) SCHEDULE D, CASES I AND II); and *John v James Ch D, [1986] STC 352* (no deduction for tax paid by defendant on sums wrongfully retained or for tax plaintiff would have been liable for on these sums or on compound interest award). But cf. *Spencer v Macmillan's Trustees CS 1958, 37 ATC 388* (breach of contract). A PAYE refund was deducted in *Hartley v Sandholme QB, [1974] STC 434*. In a case involving taxable damages paid to a large group of Lloyd's Names, it was held that the fact that certain of the Names would receive a tax benefit, due to the differential tax rates applicable to the damages and the corresponding loss reliefs, did not require a departure from the general principle that no account is to be taken of taxation where both damages and lost profits are taxable (*Deeny and others v Gooda Walker Ltd QB, [1995] STC 439*).

As regards whether interest on awarded damages should take account of the extent to which the damages are taxable, see *Deeny and others v Gooda Walker Ltd (in liquidation) and others (No 4) QB, [1995] STC 696*.

20   Connected Persons

[*Sec 839 as amended*]

20.1   For many tax purposes, certain persons are treated as being so closely involved with each other that they must either be viewed as the same person or that transactions between them must be treated differently from transactions 'at arm's length'. These 'connected persons' are defined for tax purposes as below.

20.2   **An individual** is connected with his spouse or with relatives (including their spouses) of his or his spouse. It appears that a widow or widower is no longer a spouse (*Vestey's Exors and Vestey v CIR HL 1949, 31 TC 1*). Spouses divorced by decree nisi remain connected persons until the decree is made absolute (*Aspden v Hildesley Ch D 1981, 55 TC 609*). See definition of relative in 20.8 below.

20.3   **A trustee of a settlement**, in his capacity as such, is connected with

(*a*)   the settlor (if an individual) (see 20.8 below), and

(*b*)   any person connected with the settlor (if within (*a*)), and

(*c*)   a body corporate connected with the settlement (see 20.8 below).

20.4   **A partner** is connected with the person with whom he is in partnership and with the spouse or relative of that person except in connection with acquisitions and disposals of partnership assets made pursuant to bona fide commercial arrangements.

20.5   **A company is connected with another company if**

(*a*)   the same person controls both, or

20.6 Connected Persons

(b)   one is controlled by a person who has control of the other in conjunction with persons connected with him, or

(c)   a person controls one company and persons connected with him control the other, or

(d)   the same group of persons controls both, or

(e)   the companies are controlled by separate groups which can be regarded as the same by interchanging connected persons.

20.6   **A company is connected with another person who** (either alone or with persons connected with him) **has control of it.** It is understood that the Revenue will accept that a partnership and a company under common control are connected in relation to the treatment for capital allowances of assets transferred on a succession (Tolley's Practical Tax 1981 p 142).

20.7   **Persons acting together to secure or exercise control of a company** are treated in relation to that company as connected with each other and with any other person acting on the direction of any of them to secure or exercise such control. For the meaning of 'acting together to secure or exercise control', see *Steele v European Vinyls Corp (Holdings) BV Ch D, [1995] STC 31.* Control may be 'exercised' passively. See *Floor v Davis HL 1979, 52 TC 609.*

20.8   '*Company*' includes any body corporate, unincorporated association or unit trust scheme (within *Secs 469, 470*). It does not include a partnership.

'*Control*' is as defined by *Sec 416* (see Tolley's Corporation Tax, under Close Companies) but see below as regards *Sec 840* definition.

'*Relative*' means brother, sister, ancestor or lineal descendant.

'*Settlement*' includes any disposition, trust, covenant, agreement, arrangement or, for 1995/96 onwards, transfer of assets. [*Sec 681(4) (repealed); Sec 660G(1); FA 1995, 17 Sch 1*]. See also 80.15 SETTLEMENTS.

'*Settlor*' is any person by whom the settlement was made or who has directly or indirectly (or by a reciprocal arrangement) provided, or undertaken to provide, funds for the settlement. [*Sec 681(4) (repealed); Sec 660G(1)(2); FA 1995, 17 Sch 1*].

'*A body corporate connected with the settlement*' is a close company (or one which would be close if resident in the UK) the participators in which include the trustees of the settlement, or a company of which such a close company etc. has control. 'Control' is as defined in *Sec 840*, i.e. the power of a person by shareholding or voting power (whether directly or through another company), or under Articles of Association or other regulating document, to secure that the company's affairs are conducted according to his wishes. [*Sec 681(5) (repealed); Secs 682A(2), 839(3A); FA 1995, 17 Sch 11, 20*].

21 Construction Industry Tax Deduction Scheme

See also Revenue Pamphlets IR 14/15, IR 40, IR 71, IR 109, IR 116, IR 117 and IR 148.

21.1 REQUIREMENT TO DEDUCT TAX FROM PAYMENTS

Where a *contractor* carrying on a business which includes construction work makes any payment (other than under a contract of employment) to, or to the nominee of, a *sub-contractor* (i.e. one under a duty to carry out, or to furnish his own, or others', labour in the carrying out of, construction operations) under a contract relating to construction operations in the UK or on offshore installations, *the payer must deduct*, and pay over to the Revenue, 24% (25% before 1 July 1996) of so much of the payment (excluding VAT) as does not represent the cost of materials, unless the recipient has a sub-contractor's tax certificate (often referred to as an 'exemption certificate') from the Revenue. The amount which may be paid without the 24% (25%) deduction is limited where the recipient holds a form 714S certificate (see 21.2 below). If the recipient is a nominee then he, the person who nominated him and the person for whose labour the payment is made must all have sub-contractor's tax certificates if a deduction is to be avoided. [*Secs 559(1)–(4), 560(1), 561(1), 567(1)(b); FA 1988, s 28; FA 1996, s 72(3)*]. See 21.5 below for changes to be made to the certification scheme, probably in August 1998, and for the mandatory registration card to be simultaneously introduced for sub-contractors not holding an exemption certificate.

It is understood that the 'cost of materials' which may be excluded in determining the amount subject to deduction may include a reasonable commercial charge for plant supplied by the sub-contractor for the period of the contract. (Tolley's Practical Tax 1986 p 158.)

A **contractor** is any person carrying on a business which includes construction operations; any local authority; any development corporation or new town commission; the Housing Corporation; any housing association or trust; the Scottish Special Housing Association; and the Northern Ireland Housing Executive. It includes a person who is himself a sub-contractor in relation to construction operations, e.g. a gang-leader.

A contractor is also any person carrying on a business at any time if his average annual expenditure on construction operations in the three years up to the end of his last period of account exceeded £250,000 or, where the business was not being carried on at the beginning of that three-year period, if his total expenditure on such operations up to the end of that last period of account exceeded £750,000. A person who is a contractor under these provisions will continue within that definition until he satisfies the Board that his expenditure on construction operations has been below £250,000 in each of three successive years beginning in or after that period of account. For the purposes of these expenditure limits, where a trade is transferred from one company to another and *Sec 343* (no change of ownership) applies, the transferor's expenditure will be treated as the transferee's, with apportionment by the Board (subject to appeal) when only part of the trade is transferred. [*Secs 559(1), 560(2)–(5)*].

Small contracts. Concessionally, where local managers of the above contractor organisations (not being building contractors in the construction industry) commission small contracts with a total value (excluding the cost of materials) of up to £250, the tax deduction scheme will not operate, provided that the organisation applies to its local inspector for the necessary arrangements to be made. (Revenue Pamphlet IR 1, B23).

Construction operations are widely defined to cover installing heating, lighting, drainage, etc. systems, internal cleaning of buildings in the course of their construction, alteration or repair, and internal or external painting, as well as constructing, altering, repairing or

21.2 Construction Industry Tax Deduction Scheme

demolishing buildings, walls, roadworks, etc., but to *exclude* drilling for oil or gas, mining operations, the professional work of architects, surveyors, etc., the installation, etc. of sculptures, murals, and other artistic works, signwriting, advertisements, seating, blinds, shutters, security and public address systems and the manufacture of components for heating, lighting, drainage, etc. systems. The Treasury may add to these categories by order made by statutory instrument. [*Sec 567*]. Carpet fitting is outside the scope of the scheme. (Revenue Pamphlet IR 131, SP 12/81, 20 November 1981). For detailed guidance on the scope of 'construction operations', see Appendix B to Revenue Pamphlet IR 14/15.

21.2 **APPLICATION FOR SUB-CONTRACTOR'S TAX CERTIFICATE**
(For renewal applications, see 21.3 below.)

For a sub-contractor's tax certificate to be issued, the Revenue must be satisfied that the sub-contractor is carrying on a construction business (which may include the furnishing of labour for construction operations) in the UK with proper premises, equipment, stock and other facilities. Where a business has not yet, or only just, started, the inspector can approve an application subject to some evidence of the actual commencement of the business, and review the position after three months (see Tolley's Practical Tax 1980 p 157). There must be a bank account through which the business is substantially conducted and proper records must be kept.

A **company applicant** must also have a satisfactory record of compliance with all its taxation, National Insurance and Companies Act obligations in the three years prior to its application. In particular, a check is normally made that all tax due has been paid; that any returns, etc. required of the company as a contractor under the scheme have been made; that accounts required by the inspector have been submitted; that the record of National Insurance contributions is up to date; that the company is registered with, and has made the required annual returns to, the Registrar of Companies; and that there have been no unreasonable delays in complying with these requirements. 'Minor and technical' failings not giving rise to doubts about future compliance may be ignored at the Board's discretion.

The Board may also, in certain cases where there is a limited history of construction operations or where there has been a change of control, issue a direction under *Sec 561(6)* that the directors (and, if the company is close, the beneficial shareholders) must satisfy the conditions imposed on individual applicants (for a full certificate, not the conditions for a special form 714S certificate, see below). Such a direction is normally made only where, after reviewing the directors' (and, if appropriate, shareholders') files, the inspector proposes to refuse a certificate to the company under *Sec 561*. The procedure is for a letter to be sent to the company, requesting that the directors (and shareholders) sign and return forms of authority allowing the inspector to disclose details of their personal tax and National Insurance affairs to the company. Until all such authorities requested are returned, no further action is taken by the inspector in relation to the company's application. When they have all been received, a formal notice of refusal is issued (unless the inspector's doubts about the directors (or shareholders) have in the intervening period been assuaged). Where the introduction of a new shareholder into a close private company results in a change of control, the company must notify the inspector of the new shareholder within 30 days.

There is in addition a requirement that there be 'reason to expect' that the company will comply with future tax, National Insurance and Companies Act obligations. Except in the case of certain renewal applications (see 21.3 below), this requirement is usually only used by the Revenue in conjunction with one or more of the other conditions in refusing a certificate.

Some practical advice on applications by overseas-controlled companies is contained in Revenue Tax Bulletin August 1992 p 30.

An **individual applicant** (including a partner) has to meet an additional requirement, that he must have been employed or trading in the UK for the preceding three years or for a continuous period of three years in the preceding six years. The active seeking of work while unemployed does not satisfy this requirement (see *Phelps v Moore Ch D 1980, 53 TC 433* and *Jones v Lonnen Ch D 1981, 54 TC 714*). Where there is an intervening period between such employment (or trading) and the application, the applicant must show that he has not worked in the UK (or specify the period that he has so worked) and produce evidence of any period abroad. In considering the three-year requirement, the Board may ignore periods of unemployment totalling not more than six months.

For individuals (including partners), the requirement for a satisfactory tax and National Insurance record applies to the necessary three-year period of employment or trading and to the intervening period (if any) between that three-year period and the date of application, and includes the satisfaction of any foreign tax liabilities in those periods. Any company of which the individual had control (as defined by *Sec 840*, see 20.8 CONNECTED PERSONS) during those periods must also satisfy those conditions in respect of any accounting period ending within those periods. There must be 'reason to expect' that the applicant will comply with future tax and National Insurance obligations, and 'minor and technical' failings may again be ignored at the Board's discretion.

Special certificate. For individual applicants (excluding partners), application may be made for a special certificate, form 714S, if either of the following applies.

(i)   The three-year employment condition can only be met by treating as period(s) of employment period(s) of full-time education or training at a school or other establishment. The full-time education, etc. must have ceased at the date of application.

(ii)   The applicant supplies to the Revenue a guarantee in a form and amount prescribed by Regulations.

(It is understood that the Revenue do not consider any payment for the guarantee at (ii) above to be deductible in computing trading profits, see Tolley's Practical Tax 1982 p 119.)

The Regulations relating to the issue of form 714S certificates provide for a maximum weekly payment without the 24% (25%) deduction of £150 (any excess to be paid under the 24% (25%) deduction); for special vouchers to be supplied by the sub-contractor to the contractor; and for the guarantee, on which the Revenue may call in a variety of circumstances, to be in an amount of £2,500 for each year of validity of the certificate. [*Secs 561–565; SI 1993 No 743, Regs 26, 29, 32, 42, 2 Sch*].

21.3   SUB-CONTRACTOR'S TAX CERTIFICATE RENEWAL APPLICATIONS

Sub-contractors' tax certificates are normally valid for three years, although shorter or slightly longer periods may be authorised to bring groups of companies to a common expiry date. Form 714S certificates (see above) may be issued for shorter periods. However, pending the introduction of changes to the scheme from a date not earlier than 1 August 1998 (see 21.5 below), certificates issued or renewed up to early 1998 will show an expiry date of 31 July 1998. (Revenue Press Release 1 March 1995).

The requirements for the issue of a renewal certificate are the same as on a first application, except as below.

For **company applicants**, a direction that the directors (and, if appropriate, shareholders) must satisfy the conditions imposed on individual applicants can only be made where, for any reason, the company has not carried on a business including construction operations throughout the three years prior to its renewal application. In practice, where a director or shareholder appears to the Revenue unsatisfactory but such a direction cannot be made, the Revenue may invoke the 'reason to expect' requirement (see 21.2 above).

For **individual applicants**, the requirement for a three-year period of employment or trading in the UK does not apply on applications for renewal of a full certificate. Where a special certificate form 714S was previously held, application must be made as for a new certificate. [*Secs 561(6), 562(3)*].

21.4   **MISCELLANEOUS**

Administration. Detailed administrative arrangements for the operation of the scheme were consolidated in *The Income Tax (Sub-contractors in the Construction Industry) Regulations 1993 (SI 1993 No 743)* which took effect on 6 April 1993. References in the remainder of this chapter to regulations are, except where otherwise stated, to those consolidated regulations as subsequently amended. The arrangements for accounting for deductions and for interest on unpaid or overpaid tax broadly follow those for PAYE (see 55.8 PAY AS YOU EARN), and there are detailed provisions governing the form and use of sub-contractor's tax certificates. See also below under 'Failure to deduct and under-deduction'. Further regulations may be made by statutory instrument. [*Sec 566*]. See Revenue Pamphlets IR 71 and IR 109 as regards inspection of contractors' records and negotiation of settlements. The Revenue have published a Code of Practice (No 3, published February 1993 and available from local tax offices) setting out their standards for the way in which inspections of contractors' records are conducted and the rights and responsibilities of taxpayers.

Appeals. There is a right of appeal (to the Commissioners, within 30 days) against the refusal or cancellation of a sub-contractor's tax certificate, and the Commissioners have the jurisdiction to review the exercise of any discretionary powers by the Board. [*Sec 561(9)*]. See also below under 'Failure to deduct and under-deduction' and 'Assessment'.

Cancellation. A certificate may at any time be cancelled by the Board, and its surrender demanded, if it was issued on false information, or has been misused by the holder, or if the holder no longer meets the requirements for the issue of a certificate or if, in the case of a company, there has been a change of control (within *Sec 840*) and the information required concerning that change has not been furnished. [*Sec 561(8)*].

Penalties for fraudulent attempts to obtain or misuse a certificate may be up to £5,000, and proceedings may be commenced up to three years after the date of an offence. [*Sec 561(10)–(12)*]. Penalties under *TMA s 98A* apply in cases of failure to make required end-of-year returns. These are, however, being phased in over a number of years, see 58.4 PENALTIES. See also 58.7 PENALTIES as regards negotiated settlements.

If **exemption is not obtained**, the recipient will be treated for tax purposes as having received the full amount, the tax deducted being treated as a payment by that person in respect of the income or corporation tax liability on the profits of the trade in the year of assessment or accounting period in which the deduction was made. In the case of an individual, any excess is treated as a payment on account of his Class 4 contributions under the *Social Security Acts*. [*Sec 559(4)(5); Reg 20*]. See also *Woodcock v Bonham Ch D 1980, 53 TC 326*. To the extent that any liability for a year of assessment is met by tax deducted in that year, no interest charge will arise under *TMA s 86* or *s 88* in e.g. a case of failure to notify liability.

Failure to deduct and under-deduction. If the contractor fails to deduct the tax, he is nevertheless liable for the tax which should have been deducted (see *Ladkarn Ltd v McIntosh Ch D 1982, 56 TC 616*). However, where the Collector is satisfied that the contractor took reasonable care, and that the failure was due to an error made in good faith or to a genuine belief that the payment was not subject to deduction, the Collector may waive the liability. An appeal may be made (within 30 days) against a decision not so to waive liability. Liability in respect of such failure may also be waived at the contractor's request where the inspector is satisfied that the sub-contractor to whom the payment was made either was not chargeable to tax thereon or has made the appropriate return and paid the tax and any Class 4 contributions. [*Reg 10*].

See Revenue Pamphlets IR 71 and IR 109 as regards inspection of contractors' records and negotiation of settlements.

Assessment. If the inspector considers it necessary to do so in all the circumstances, he may raise an assessment on the contractor in any amount which, to the best of his judgment, the contractor is liable to pay under the scheme regulations. The assessment is treated in the same way as an income tax assessment for assessment, appeal and recovery purposes. Tax is due and payable 14 days after the date of the assessment. [*Reg 14*]. Tax unpaid on such assessments made after 19 April 1988 and in respect of any year prior to 1992/93 carries interest at the prescribed rate (see 42.1 INTEREST ON UNPAID TAX) from 14 days after the end of the year of assessment to which the assessment relates (or from 19 April 1988 if later). [*Reg 15*]. In respect of tax for 1992/93 and subsequent years, similar provisions as regards interest on unpaid and overpaid tax apply as in 55.8 PAY AS YOU EARN. [*Regs 16–18*].

21.5   **Future changes.** With effect for payments made **on or after a day to be appointed** for the purpose (which must be **after 31 July 1998**), a number of changes are made to the scheme, with the intention of restricting eligibility for exemption from tax deduction by the application of a minimum turnover requirement for sub-contractors. At the same time, the rate of tax deducted is to be adjusted so as to be closer to the effective rate of tax and Class 4 national insurance contributions for most sub-contractors. The introduction of paperless systems is also to be encouraged. In outline, the changes are as follows.

(*a*)   The 24% deduction is to be replaced by a deduction of a percentage determined by the Treasury by order, which may not exceed the basic rate.

(*b*)   A minimum anticipated annual turnover (to be prescribed by regulation, and in the case of firms or companies broadly geared to the number of individuals who are partners or directors) is to be a precondition for the issue of an exemption certificate. In the case of companies, certain subsidiaries are exempted from this requirement.

(*c*)   The limited certificates for school leavers and where a bank guarantee is in force are to be withdrawn.

(*d*)   A general exemption from deduction is provided where conditions to be prescribed are met in relation to a payment under any contract and to the person making the payment.

(*e*)   All public offices and departments of the Crown, and such statutory bodies as are designated in regulations, are to be treated as contractors for the purposes of the deduction scheme.

(*f*)   The average annual expenditure on construction operations which renders the person incurring the expenditure a contractor for the purposes of the deduction scheme is to be increased from £250,000 to £1,000,000.

(*g*)   The conditions for an exemption certificate for an individual partner in a firm are generally to be aligned with those for sole traders, insofar as they relate to the circumstances of the individual. The individual conditions relating to the length of

21.5 Construction Industry Tax Deduction Scheme

time the business has been carried on are to be removed, and a number of minor changes made relating to the requirement for a satisfactory record of compliance in the case of both individuals and firms.

(*h*)   The fine (maximum £5,000) on summary conviction for certain fraudulent attempts to obtain or misuse an exemption certificate is replaced by a penalty up to £3,000.

[*FA 1995, s 139, 27 Sch*].

For the draft regulations enacting the above changes, see Revenue Press Release 1 March 1995.

Registration cards. FA 1996, s 178 gives the Board powers to make regulations for the introduction of a mandatory registration card system for sub-contractors not holding an exemption certificate, and provides for penalties for failures under the regulations. It is proposed to introduce the new system at the same time as the changes to the certification scheme described above come into effect. In outline, the proposed system is as follows.

(i)   The registration card will carry the sub-contractor's name and photograph, the tax reference and (probably) the national insurance number.

(ii)   Contractors will be required to check cards before making payments under deduction.

(iii)   In the case of a sub-contractor who had not previously applied for a card, a short period will be allowed for him to obtain one.

(iv)   The cards will be available on request to anyone working, or intending to work, in the construction industry.

(v)   A penalty of up to £3,000 will apply for failure by a contractor to take the necessary steps to require the production of registration cards and to check their validity, or to make accurate returns in relation to registration card payments (unless there were reasonable grounds for accepting the validity of a card and all reasonable steps were taken to ensure the correctness of the return).

See Revenue Press Release 28 November 1995 (REV 38) and *Sec 566(2A)–(2F)* introduced by *FA 1996, s 178*.

22   Deceased Estates

Cross-references. See 28.6 EXCESS LIABILITY, 42.6 INTEREST ON UNPAID TAX and 43.6 and 43.23 INTEREST PAYABLE.

22.1   Personal representatives of a deceased person (being either executors appointed under the will or administrators if there was no will) are assessable for all tax due from the deceased to the date of his death. [*Secs 60(8), 62(9), 63(3) as originally enacted; Sec 60(4); TMA s 74; FA 1994, s 200*]. Personal allowances may be claimed in full for the year of death.

Income may be assessed and charged on and in the name of any one or more of the personal representatives to whom it arises and any subsequent personal representatives of the deceased. [*FA 1989, s 151*].

See 71.9 SCHEDULE D, CASES I AND II for discontinuance of a business on death and 71.36 for trading (or not) by the executors. See 6.4 and 6.5 BACK DUTY for time limits for assessments. See Tolley's Capital Gains Tax for capital gains tax position on death.

22.2   Personal representatives are also liable to income tax at the basic rate on income which they receive subsequent to the death. Dividends falling due after death are treated as the income of the estate, and not of the deceased, for all tax purposes, including exemption claims, although they accrued before the death (*Reid's Trustees v CIR CS 1929, 14 TC 512; CIR v Henderson's Exors CS 1931, 16 TC 282*), and the same principle applies in respect of interest payments, including bank and building society interest, falling due after the date of death. An exception is interest falling within the accrued income scheme (see 74.15 SCHEDULE D, CASE VI). The accrued annuity to the date of death of an annuitant is income of his estate and not his income (*Bryan v Cassin KB 1942, 24 TC 468*) and similarly as to the accrued income of which he was life-tenant (*Wood v Owen KB 1940, 23 TC 541; Stewart's Exors v CIR Ch D 1952, 33 TC 184*).

22.3   **Income from deceased estates during administration.** [*Secs 695–702*]. Residuary income of an estate comprises aggregate income therefrom *less* interest and annual payments charged thereon, sums payable out of residue under law of intestacy, admissible expenses of administration and any income from assets vesting during or on completion of administration. [*Sec 697(1), 701(6)*]. An annual payment falling due after 14 March 1988 and made by personal representatives in satisfaction of a liability of the deceased is treated as if made by an individual for the purpose of applying the provisions of *FA 1988, s 36* excluding such payments from being a charge on income (see 1.9(i) ALLOWANCES AND TAX RATES). [*Sec 347A(3); FA 1988, s 36(1)*].

Limited interests (e.g. life tenants). Sums paid to a beneficiary *during administration* are treated as his income for the tax year of payment. Any amount which remains payable in respect of the limited interest *on completion of administration* after 5 April 1995 is deemed to have been paid to the beneficiary as income for the tax year in which the administration period ends or, if that interest has ceased earlier (because of the beneficiary's death), as income for the tax year in which the interest ceased. Where the administration period ended before 6 April 1995, the beneficiary's income for each tax year covered by the administration period was revised, by additional assessment or repayment of tax, to the proportion allocated to that year on a time basis of the income deemed to have *accrued* from day to day throughout the administration period. [*Secs 695(2)(3), 700; FA 1995, 18 Sch 2*]. **Absolute interests.** Sums paid to a beneficiary *during administration* and after 5 April 1995 are treated as his income for the tax year of payment except to the extent that aggregate payments of income for that and earlier years (including any made before 6 April 1995) exceed the beneficiary's aggregate entitlement to the residuary income of the estate for that and earlier years. If *on completion of administration* after 5 April 1995 the aggregate income entitlement exceeds the aggregate payments of income, the excess is deemed to have been paid to the beneficiary immediately before the end of the administration period. Payments to a beneficiary before 6 April 1995 were treated as his income for the tax year to which they related (not necessarily the year of payment). On completion of administration before 6 April 1995, the beneficiary's income for each tax year covered by the administration was revised to his actual ascertained share of the estate residuary income *arising* in that year. [*Secs 696(3)–(3B)(5), 700; FA 1995, 18 Sch 3*].

In each case payments out of a UK estate are 'grossed-up' at the basic or lower rate, as appropriate (see 1.8(ii)(iii) ALLOWANCES AND RATES), and treated as received under deduction of such tax. For this purpose, payments are assumed to be made out of the beneficiary's share of income bearing tax at the basic rate before they are made out of his share of income bearing tax at the lower rate. Payments out of a foreign estate are directly assessed, without grossing, under Schedule D, Case IV (although, for 1995/96 onwards, certain sums treated as having suffered tax at source, e.g. life assurance gains, 'foreign income dividends' and UK stock dividends, *are* grossed up). [*Secs 246D(1)–(3A), 695(4), 696(3)–(6), 699A, 701(3A); FA 1993, 6 Sch 11; FA 1994, 16 Sch 1; FA 1995, s 76(1)(4); FA 1996, 6 Sch 5*]. Income bearing tax at the lower rate is treated in the hands of the recipient as chargeable as 'savings income' (before 1996/97, dividend income) (see 1.8(ii)(iii) ALLOWANCES AND RATES), except that income paid indirectly through a trustee and taxable under *Sec 698(3)* on the ultimate recipient is instead so treated in the hands of the trustee (unless it is within *Sec 686*, see 80.5 SETTLEMENTS). [*Sec 698A; FA 1993, 6 Sch 11(2); FA 1996, 6 Sch 17*].

Charities and individuals with an absolute interest in the residue of an estate may claim repayment of the tax included in the grossed-up payments even though the estate income includes building society interest or other income which has not borne the full basic rate of tax. (Revenue Pamphlet IR 131, SP 7/80, 16 July 1980). In computing estate residuary income for 1995/96 onwards in the case of an absolute interest, any excess of allowable deductions over income for any year is carried forward and treated as an allowable deduction of the following year. [*Sec 697(1A); FA 1995, 18 Sch 4(1)(3)*]. Previously, by concession, such an excess was allowed in computing the net residuary income of the preceding or succeeding years for higher rate tax. (Revenue Pamphlet IR 1, A13). If the total benefits received by a beneficiary with an absolute interest on completion of administration after 5 April 1995 are less than the amount taken to be his residuary income, the deficiency is applied in reducing the said amount, firstly for the tax year in which the administration ends, then for the previous year and so on. Previously, such a deficiency was applied in reducing proportionately the income for each tax year covered by the administration period. [*Sec 697(2); FA 1995, 18 Sch 4(2)(3)*].

Assessments may be made or adjusted and relief may be claimed by virtue of these provisions within, for 1996/97 and later years, three years after 31 January following the year of assessment in which administration was completed (for earlier years, three years following the end of that year of assessment). [*Sec 700(3); FA 1996, s 135, 21 Sch 20*].

By concession, a residuary legatee, or legatee with a limited interest, who is not resident or not ordinarily resident in the UK may claim to have his tax liability on income from the estate adjusted to what it would be if such income had arisen to him directly from the respective sources of residuary income. A claim must be made not later than three years after the end of the year of assessment in which the administration of the estate is completed, or within six years of the end of the year of assessment in which the estate income arose, whichever is the later. (Revenue Pamphlet IR 1, A14). However, where the legatee is resident in a country with which the UK has a double taxation agreement, and the 'Other Income' Article in that agreement gives sole taxing rights in respect of such income to that country, the above concession does not apply, and the tax paid by the personal representatives will be repaid to the legatee, subject to the conditions in the Article being met. (Revenue Pamphlet IR 131, SP 3/86, 2 April 1986).

The treatment of rights held by personal representatives in relation to other deceased estates, and of successive interests in the residue of an estate, are dealt with in *Sec 698(1)–(2); FA 1995, 18 Sch 5*. Discretionary payments out of the income of the residue of an estate, whether made directly by the personal representatives or through a trustee etc., are income of the recipient when paid. [*Sec 698(3)*]. This applies whether the payments are out of income as it arises, or out of income arising to the personal representatives in earlier years and retained pending exercise of the discretion. See Revenue Pamphlet IR 131 (October 1995 Supplement), SP 4/93, 16 March 1993, under which claims and supplementary claims on this basis are invited for 1986/87 onwards.

For Revenue information powers, see *Sec 700(4)*. A personal representative has a duty to supply a beneficiary on request with a statement of income and tax borne for a year of assessment. [*Sec 700(5)(6); FA 1995, 18 Sch 6*].

For relief from overlapping of inheritance tax and excess liability on accrued income, see 28.6 EXCESS LIABILITY.

22.4   *Examples*

Limited interest

Mrs D died on 5 January 1994 leaving her whole estate with a life interest to her husband and then the capital to her children on his death. The administration of the estate was completed on 7 February 1996. Mr D received payments on account of income of £1,200 on 30 September 1994, £2,500 on 31 December 1995, £1,050 on 7 February 1996 and £300 on 31 May 1996.

The actual income and deductible expenses of the estate were as follows.

	1993/94 (from 6.1.94)	1994/95	1995/96 (to 7.2.96)
	£	£	£
Dividends received (net)	750	2,400	2,000
Other income (gross)	400	600	200
Basic rate tax thereon	(100)	(150)	(50)
Expenses	(150)	(450)	(400)
Net income available for distribution	£900	£2,400	£1,750

D's income from the estate for tax purposes is calculated as follows.

	1993/94	1994/95 Basic rate income	1994/95 Lower rate income	1995/96 Basic rate income	1995/96 Lower rate income
	£	£	£	£	£
Gross income	Nil	1,000	562	200	4,625
Basic rate tax		(250)	112	(50)	
Lower rate tax					(925)
Net income	Nil	£750*	£450*	£150**	£3,700**

22.4 Deceased Estates

*   The payments to the beneficiary in each year must be allocated between (i) income bearing tax at the basic rate and (ii) income bearing tax at the lower rate, (i) taking priority over (ii). Total basic rate income for 1993/94 and 1994/95 is £750 (£400 + £600 − £100 − £150), so £750 of the £1,200 payment in 1994/95 is deemed to have been made out of basic rate income.

**   Total basic rate income for the three tax years is £900 (£400 + £600 + £200 − £100 − £150 − £50) of which £750 was paid out in 1994/95 leaving £150 of the 1995/96 payments to be allocated to basic rate income. The balance of the 1995/96 payments (£2,500 + £1,050 + £300 − £150 = £3,700) is deemed to have been made out of lower rate income.

Note

(a)   The £300 paid in May 1996 is deemed to have been paid in 1995/96, being the tax year in which the administration period ends.

Absolute interest

C died on 5 July 1994 leaving his estate of £400,000 divisible equally between his three children. The income arising and administration expenses paid in the administration period which ends on 25 January 1997 are as follows.

	Period to 5.4.95		Year to 5.4.96		Period to 25.1.97
	£	£	£	£	£	£
Dividends received (net)		15,000		8,850		3,000
Administration expenses chargeable to income		(1,500)		(750)		(300)
		13,500		8,100		2,700
Other income (gross)	10,000		3,200		1,000	
Basic rate tax thereon payable by executors	(2,500)		(800)		(250)	
		7,500		2,400		750
Net income distributed		£21,000		£10,500		£3,450
Each child's share		£7,000		£3,500		£1,150

Dates and amounts of payments to *each* child are as follows.

	Payment £	Allocated to tax years (see 22.3 above)
30.4.95	5,000	1995/96
16.10.95	3,000	1995/96
21.6.96	2,000	1996/97
22.1.97	1,000	1996/97
30.7.97	650	1996/97

The children's income for tax purposes is as follows.

	1994/95	1995/96	1996/97
Each child's share			
of basic rate income	Nil	3,300.00*	250.00
Basic rate tax	Nil	1,100.00	83.33
Gross basic rate income	Nil	£4,400.00	£333.33

* £(7,500 + 2,400) × 1/3 =£3,300

	1994/95	1995/96	1996/97
Each child's share			
of lower rate income	Nil	4,700.00	3,400.00
Lower rate tax	Nil	1,175.00	850.00
Gross lower rate income	Nil	£5,875.00	£4,250.00

Notes

(a)   Each beneficiary would receive tax certificates (Forms R185E) showing the gross amount of his entitlement and the tax paid by the executors for each of the three tax years. Where the estate has income bearing tax at the lower rate (i.e. savings income—before 1996/97, dividend income), the tax certificate should show such income separately from income which has borne tax at the basic rate.

(b)   In the hands of a beneficiary, estate income which has borne tax at the lower rate is treated as income within *Sec 1A* (before 1996/97, *Sec 207A*). Therefore, the beneficiary will have a further liability only to the extent that the income exceeds the basic rate limit but will be able to reclaim tax at only 20% to the extent that the income is covered by personal reliefs.

(c)   Payments to a beneficiary of an estate are deemed to be made out of his share of income bearing tax at the basic rate in priority to his share of income bearing tax at the lower rate. Therefore, administration expenses chargeable to income are effectively relieved primarily against lower rate income.

22.5   **Residence of personal representatives.** See 64.5 RESIDENCE, ORDINARY RESIDENCE AND DOMICILE for special provisions where personal representatives are partly UK resident and partly non-UK resident.

22.6   Otherwise the tax position in respect of deceased estates is similar to that of settlements (or trusts as they are often called) and reference should be made to the following items under 80 SETTLEMENTS which contain details of tax cases relating to both deceased estates and settlements.

80.3 Assessments on trust income.   80.9 Annuities etc. out of capital.
80.7 Personal position of trustee.   80.10 Foreign trust income.
80.8 Income of beneficiaries.   80.11 Claims by trustees and beneficiaries.

23 Deduction of Tax at Source

Cross-references. See 3.19 ANTI-AVOIDANCE re annual payments for non-taxable consideration; 8 BANKS and 9 BUILDING SOCIETIES for interest; 15.6 CHARITIES regarding deeds of covenant; 21 CONSTRUCTION INDUSTRY TAX DEDUCTION SCHEME; 25.6 DOUBLE TAX RELIEF for reduced rate of deduction on payments abroad, 25.5(*a*) for alimony payable by non-resident; 32 FUNDING BONDS; 33.3 GOVERNMENT STOCKS for certain payments gross; 43 INTEREST PAYABLE; 44 INTEREST RECEIVABLE; 48 MEDICAL INSURANCE; 49 MINERAL ROYALTIES; 51.8 NON-RESIDENTS AND OTHER OVERSEAS MATTERS for non-resident entertainers and sportsmen; 55 PAY AS YOU EARN; 65.2 RETIREMENT ANNUITIES AND PERSONAL PENSION SCHEMES for personal pension scheme contributions; 66.5 RETIREMENT SCHEMES for additional voluntary contributions and for refunds of pension and superannuation contributions; 71.87 SCHEDULE D, CASES I AND II and 75.42 SCHEDULE E as regards vocational training costs; 75.34 SCHEDULE E for payments for restrictive covenants; 80.5 SETTLEMENTS for distributions from discretionary and accumulation trusts; 89 UNDERWRITERS for transfers to special reserves.

23.1   Income tax (at the basic or lower rate, whichever is applicable) *may* legally be deducted by the payer from certain annuities and other annual payments and certain royalties, which are paid out of taxed income, within the terms of *Sec 348* (see 23.2 below) and *must* be deducted from the payments listed in 23.3 below. Tax may also be deducted from certain mortgage loan interest, see 23.13 below. See Revenue Tax Bulletin February 1996 pp 277–280 for a list showing the rate at which tax should be deducted from various types of payment made after 5 April 1996 and for commentary on the various deduction arrangements.

The **payer** thus obtains tax relief other than at the higher rate in respect of such payments. He may also be able to deduct the payments as charges on income in arriving at his EXCESS LIABILITY (28). For **companies** the payments may rank as charges on income for corporation tax, see Tolley's Corporation Tax under Profit Computations.

The **recipient** has, because of the deduction of tax, suffered income tax at the basic or lower rate (whichever is applicable) on the income. If he is not liable, or not wholly liable, on such income at that rate, he can recover from the Revenue any excess tax suffered so far as not adjusted in direct assessments on him. On the other hand, if his total income is high enough, further liability will arise on him at the higher rate of income tax. See 1.8(iii) ALLOWANCES AND TAX RATES for the circumstances in which the recipient is liable at the lower rate (as opposed to the basic rate) on savings income for 1996/97 and later years.

A payment made under deduction of tax is income (equal to the grossed-up equivalent) of the year of assessment by reference to the basic or lower rate of tax for which tax is deducted from the payment, without regard to the period of accrual (and see *CIR v Crawley 1986, 59 TC 728*). [*Sec 835(6); FA 1996, 6 Sch 24, 28*].

For the deduction of tax from VAT-inclusive amounts, see Revenue Inspector's Manual, IM 3900.

Headings in this chapter are as follows.

23.2   **CIRCUMSTANCES WHERE PAYER <u>MAY</u> DEDUCT TAX** [*Sec 348*]

The permissible tax deduction, as 23.1 above, applies to

(*a*)   any annuity or other annual payment charged with tax under SCHEDULE D, CASE III (72), not being interest (but see 1.8(i) ALLOWANCES AND TAX RATES for certain annual payments excluded from the charge to tax, 23.9 below re alimony, maintenance, separation allowances, etc., 23.13 below for certain relevant loan interest, and also see 3.19 ANTI-AVOIDANCE re annual payments made for non-taxable consideration and 80.5 SETTLEMENTS re payments out of discretionary trusts),

(*b*)   (i)   any royalty or other sum paid in respect of the user of a patent, and

(ii)   electric line wayleaves [*Sec 120*] and (before 1 May 1995) mining rents and royalties [*Sec 119; FA 1995, s 145*] (see 23.14 below),

provided that the payment is wholly out of profits or gains brought into charge to income tax. (N.B. As the profits of UK companies are not charged to income tax, *Sec 348* does not apply to them and payments by them will be within *Sec 349*—see 23.3 below.)

The payer is entitled to deduct tax and it will be detrimental to himself if he fails to do so. See 23.8 below regarding omission to deduct tax.

The tax deductible is at the basic rate for the year in which the payment became due, irrespective of the date of actual payment. Where the payment would constitute 'savings income' (see 1.8(iii) ALLOWANCES AND TAX RATES) of the recipient (whatever his status), deduction is at the lower rate instead for 1996/97 and subsequent years (although the only type of payment within *Sec 348* to which this should apply is a purchased life annuity). [*Sec 4; FA 1996, s 73(2)–(4), 6 Sch 2, 28*]. (Cf. *Re Sebright Ch D 1944, 23 TC 190.*) It is accordingly income of the recipient of the year when due—an important point if the recipient wishes to claim repayment of the tax deducted (*Crawley v CIR Ch D 1986, 59 TC 728*).

23.3   **CIRCUMSTANCES WHERE PAYER <u>MUST</u> DEDUCT TAX** [*Secs 349, 350*]

Income tax *must* be deducted from the following.

(i)   Payments specified in 23.2(*a*) and (*b*) above which are not payable, or not wholly payable, out of profits or gains brought into charge to income tax. [*Sec 349(1)*]. See 74.2 SCHEDULE D, CASE VI as regards certain payments to theatrical 'angels'.

The payer must deduct tax from such payments, and must inform the Revenue, who will make an assessment to collect that tax. Appeals against that assessment are to the Special Commissioners. [*TMA s 31(3)*]. Payments by UK companies are within *Sec 349(1)* but the tax is accounted for under *16 Sch*, see Tolley's Corporation Tax.

23.3 Deduction of Tax at Source

The obligation to deduct is upon 'the person by or through whom' the payment is made and see *Rye & Eyre v CIR HL 1935, 19 TC 164; Aeolian Co Ltd v CIR KB 1936, 20 TC 547* and *Howells v CIR KB 1939, 22 TC 501*. But liability under *Sec 350* does not arise until the annual payment is actually 'paid'.

Tax is deductible at the basic rate in force at the time of payment. Where the payment would constitute 'savings income' (see 1.8(iii) ALLOWANCES AND TAX RATES) of the recipient (whatever his status), deduction is at the lower rate instead for 1996/97 and subsequent years (but the same comment applies as in 23.2 above as regards application). [*Sec 4; FA 1996, s 73(2)–(4), 6 Sch 2, 28*].

Where a payment from which tax should have been deducted is made in full, there is no right to recover the under-deduction by deduction from later payments (*Tenbry Investments Ltd v Peugeot Talbot Motor Co Ltd Ch D, [1992] STC 791*).

If a payment is made in a later year than the year when due and it could have been wholly or partly made out of taxed income in that due year, an allowance will be made in any assessment to collect the tax for the tax which could have been deducted if the payment had been made when due. (Revenue Pamphlet IR 1, A16).

The profits or gains to be taken into account are those assessed (or received less tax) for the year of assessment in which the payment was made. Hence, except where the concession A16 applies, accumulated income of previous years cannot be taken into account (*Luipaard's Vlei Estate v CIR CA 1930, 15 TC 573*) and, for a trader, the Case I assessment for the year after deducting any losses forward and capital allowances is taken into account irrespective of the actual profits of the year (*A-G v Metropolitan Water Board CA 1927, 13 TC 294; Trinidad Petroleum Development Co Ltd v CIR CA 1936, 21 TC 1*). For the individual, *Sec 349(1)* will normally be applicable only if his annual payments, etc. exceed his aggregate income of the year (cf. *CIR v Plummer HL 1979, 54 TC 1*). However, trustees may be liable under *Sec 350* where annual payments etc. are made out of capital of the trust fund irrespective of the trust income, see 80.9 SETTLEMENTS.

Loss Relief. Where payments are made under deduction of tax but the payer has no income assessable to income tax the tax deducted will be collected by assessment under *Sec 350*. But if this position arises by reason of a loss sustained in a trade, etc. in the year, or brought forward, a sole trader or partnership may treat amounts so assessed as if they were trading losses under *Sec 385* and carry them forward for computing profits of the same business for the following years, except where they fall into the list given under 46.18(*a*) LOSSES. [*Sec 387*].

(ii) Yearly interest of money chargeable to tax under SCHEDULE D, CASE III (72) but only if paid

    (*a*) by a company or local authority (otherwise than in a fiduciary or representative capacity), or

    (*b*) by or for a partnership of which a company is a member, or

    (*c*) to a person whose usual place of abode is outside the UK. [*Sec 349(2); FA 1996, 14 Sch 18*].

As regards (*c*) above, tax need not be deducted from payments of interest to the UK branch of a non-resident company trading in the UK through that branch, where the branch profits are liable to corporation tax under *Sec 11* and not exempted under a double tax treaty. (Revenue Tax Bulletin August 1993 p 87).

For advances made on or after 29 April 1996, interest payable on an advance from a bank (within *Sec 840A*, see 8.1 BANKS) within the charge to corporation tax in respect of it, and interest paid by such a bank in the ordinary course of its business, is excluded. Previously, the exclusion applied to interest payable in the UK on an advance from a bank carrying on a *bona fide* banking business in the UK (see *Hafton Properties Ltd v McHugh Ch D 1986, 59 TC 420*) or paid by such a bank in the ordinary course of such a business (for which see Revenue Pamphlet IR 131, SP 12/91, 9 October 1991). There are transitional provisions preserving relief as regards interest payable or paid on or after 29 April 1996 on an advance made before that day. *[Sec 349(3)(a)(b)(3AA)(3AB); FA 1996, 37 Sch Pt II]*. See, however, 23.13 below as regards 'relevant loan interest' and 8.2, 8.3 BANKS as regards special deduction schemes. See 8.3 BANKS also for exclusion from *Sec 349(2)* of certain interest payments by bodies other than banks where those payments are not within the special deduction scheme. *[Sec 349(3)(h); FA 1993, s 59]*.

As regards payments by building societies, only interest and dividends paid after 24 July 1991 on certain 'marketable securities' is within *Sec 349*. *[Sec 349(2)(3A); FA 1991, 11 Sch 1]*. See BUILDING SOCIETIES (9) generally and at 9.5 in particular. Interest paid to a society is payable gross unless it is 'relevant loan interest', see 23.13 below. *[Sec 369(1); FA 1994, s 81(3)]*.

Interest paid on '*quoted Eurobonds*' (i.e. listed securities carrying a right to interest and issued by a company in bearer form) is also excluded where either:

(I) the payment is made by or through a person who is not in the UK; or

(II) where (I) above does not apply, either

(i) the bond is held in a 'recognised clearing system' (as designated by the Board), or

(ii) the beneficial owner of the bond is non-UK resident and is beneficially entitled to the interest.

The Board has regulatory powers to disapply (II) above unless certain declarations confirming eligibility are received by the payer or the Board has issued the appropriate notice. Before 29 April 1996, different requirements applied in relation to (II) above. *[Secs 124, 841A; FA 1996, 7 Sch 26, 29 Sch 4, 38 Sch 6, 41 Sch Pt V(19)]*. See also Revenue Pamphlet IR 131, SP 8/84, 18 October 1984, as regards the application of these provisions; Revenue Press Release 1 August 1984 as regards designation as a 'recognised clearing system'; and *FA 1989, s 116* (repealed by *FA 1996, 41 Sch Pt V(3)*) as regards certain payments of interest to Netherlands Antilles subsidiaries which were treated as being within *Sec 124*.

Tax is deductible at the lower rate (for 1995/96 and earlier years, the basic rate) in force for the tax year in which payment is made. *[Sec 4; FA 1996, s 73(2)–(4), 6 Sch 2, 28]*.

For the procedure under which companies pay income tax so deducted to the Revenue, see *16 Sch* and Tolley's Corporation Tax.

(iii) The following, as under (i) above, except that they cannot qualify for the loss relief described.

(a) Rents paid to non-residents chargeable under Schedule A or Schedule D, Case VI. *[Secs 42A, 43; FA 1995, s 40(3); SI 1995 No 2902]*. Special provisions apply from 6 April 1996. See 68.24 SCHEDULE A.

(b) Sale of British patent rights by a non-resident. *[Sec 524]*. See 54 PATENTS.

(c) Copyright royalties, public lending right payments and design royalties payable to a non-resident. *[Secs 536, 537, 537B; FA 1995, s 115(10)]*. See 23.15 below and 51.10 NON-RESIDENTS AND OTHER OVERSEAS MATTERS.

(iv) (For 1995/96 and earlier years) income charged under SCHEDULE C (70). *[Sec 44, 3 Sch; FA 1996, 7 Sch 7, 27]*.

23.4 Deduction of Tax at Source

(v)   UK public revenue and foreign dividends etc. paid in UK through an agent (see 23.12 below).

23.4 DEDUCTION OF TAX UNDER FOREIGN AGREEMENTS, OR BY NON-RESIDENTS

UK tax legislation cannot alter rights not within the jurisdiction of UK courts. See *Keiner v Keiner QB 1952, 34 TC 346* (tax not deductible from alimony under American agreement paid by UK resident ex-husband to non-resident ex-wife); *Bingham v CIR Ch D 1955, 36 TC 254* (maintenance payments under foreign Court Order not deductible in arriving at total income as tax not deductible); *Westminster Bank v National Bank of Greece HL 1970, 46 TC 472* (interest on foreign bonds paid in London by guarantor held within Case IV and tax not deductible). But where under a UK contract a non-resident paid interest to another non-resident and the payer died, held his executors (resident in UK) must deduct tax from interest they paid (*CIR v Broome's Exors KB 1935, 19 TC 667*). And where 'free of tax' alimony was payable under UK agreements, etc., payments by the ex-husband no longer resident in the UK were held to have been paid subject to deduction of tax, the onus being on the Crown to collect the tax if the payments were within *Sec 349* (*Stokes v Bennett Ch D 1953, 34 TC 337*). See also *CIR v Ferguson HL 1969, 46 TC 1*.

23.5 RATE OF TAX DEDUCTIBLE

For *Sec 348* purposes, the basic (or lower) rate when payment becomes **due** applies, see 23.2 above.

For *Sec 349* purposes, the basic (or lower) rate when payment is **made** applies, see 23.3(i) and (ii) above.

In other words, the tax deductible is at the basic (or lower) rate in force for the year in which the payment is due if paid out of taxed profits or gains or, in any other case, the rate for the year in which the payment is made.

For 1995/96 and earlier years, tax is deductible at the basic rate. This continues for 1996/97 and later years except where the payment would constitute 'savings income' (including interest) (see 1.8(iii) ALLOWANCES AND TAX RATES) of the recipient (whatever his status), in which case tax is deductible at the lower rate. [*Sec 4; FA 1996, s 73(2)–(4), 6 Sch 2, 28*].

23.6 ALTERATIONS IN TAX RATE

Where deductions are made by reference to a tax rate greater or less than the rate subsequently fixed for the tax year:

(*a*)   **under-deductions** in respect of any half-yearly or quarterly payments of interest, dividends or other annual payments, other than company dividends and other distributions, are charged under Schedule D, Case III (for 1995/96 and earlier years, under Schedule D, Case VI). [*Sec 821(1); FA 1996, 6 Sch 22, 28*];

(*b*)   **under-deductions** in respect of copyright royalties or public lending right payments paid to non-residents, patent royalties and mining rents etc. under *Secs 119* and *120*, rent, interest, annuities and other annual payments may be deducted from future payments or, if none, recovered from the payee. [*Sec 821(2)(3)*]. See *Nesta v Wyatt KB 1940, 19 ATC 541*;

(*c*)   **over-deductions** of tax under *Sec 349* or from interest on government securities can generally be recovered from the Revenue provided that the tax has been accounted for and no adjustment made between the parties. See *Provisional Collection of Taxes Act 1968, s 2*; and

(d)   **over-deductions** of tax by a 'body corporate' on interest (not being a distribution) on its securities may be adjusted in the next payment but any repayments must be made no later than a year from the passing of the Act imposing the tax, and enure to the benefit of the person entitled at date of adjustment or repayment. [*Sec 822; FA 1996, 6 Sch 23, 28*].

23.7   CERTIFICATE OF TAX DEDUCTED

A certificate of tax deducted under *Secs 339, 348, 349, 480A* or *687* (re payments under discretionary trusts), or under regulations made under *Sec 477A* (*SI 1990 No 2231*, see 9.5 BUILDING SOCIETIES) must be given by payer upon written request by recipient. [*Sec 352; FA 1990, 5 Sch 11*].

23.8   OMISSION TO DEDUCT TAX

(a)   The provisions for the deduction of tax do not preclude assessment of the recipient if tax is not deducted (*Glamorgan County Quarter Sessions v Wilson KB 1910, 5 TC 537; Renfrew Town Council v CIR CS 1934, 19 TC 13; Grosvenor Place Estates Ltd v Roberts CA 1960, 39 TC 433*). These cases were decided when the legislation (cf. *subsection (1)(a)* (as originally enacted) of *ICTA 1970, s 52* (the predecessor to *Sec 348*)) precluded assessment on the recipient if the payment was out of taxed income. This provision was abolished for 1973/74 onwards by *FA 1971, 14 Sch Pt II*. However where in a case within *Sec 348* (23.2 above) tax is not deducted, the Crown nevertheless effectively collects from the payer the tax he failed to deduct [*Secs 3, 256(3)(c)(ii), 276(1)(1A); FA 1994, s 77(1), 8 Sch 11*] and does not need to have recourse to the recipient.

(b)   Tax not deducted at the time of payment cannot generally be recovered afterwards. For this see *Shrewsbury v Shrewsbury CA 1907, 23 TLR 224; Re Hatch Ch D 1919, 1 Ch 351; Ord v Ord KB 1923, 39 TLR 437; Taylor v Taylor CA 1937, 16 ATC 218; Brine v Brine KB 1943, 22 ATC 177; Hemsworth v Hemsworth KB 1946, 25 ATC 466; Tenbry Investments Ltd v Peugeot Talbot Motor Co Ltd Ch D, [1992] STC 791*. But where trustees omitted to deduct tax from annuities through an honest error of fact, not an error of law, they were authorised to recoup the tax from future payments (*Re Musgrave, Machell v Parry Ch D, [1916] 2 Ch 417*). See also *Turvey v Dentons (1923) Ltd QB 1952, 31 ATC 470*. Only net amount of alimony available to satisfy contra account (*Butler v Butler CA 1961, 40 ATC 19*). See also *Fletcher v Young CS 1936, 15 ATC 531; Hollis v Wingfield CA 1940, 19 ATC 98*.

(c)   The Courts may rectify documents shown not to embody the intentions of the parties. For cases where rectification sought in relation to deduction of tax see *Burroughes v Abbott Ch D 1921, 38 TLR 167; Jervis v Howle & Talke Colliery Co Ltd Ch D 1936, 15 ATC 529; Fredensen v Rothschild Ch D 1941, 20 ATC 1; Van der Linde v Van der Linde Ch D 1947, 26 ATC 348; Whiteside v Whiteside CA 1949, 28 ATC 479*.

(d)   Where a person having the right to do so does not deduct tax under *Sec 348* from annual payments such as maintenance payments to another person under a Court Order or other legally binding agreement, concessionary relief is available equal to the amount of any repayment which would have been due to the recipient had the right to deduct tax been properly exercised. (Revenue Pamphlet IR 1, A52). The concession is of limited application after 5 April 1989. See also 47.15 MARRIED PERSONS.

(e)   A penalty of £50 is incurred by refusal to allow the deduction of tax, and any 'agreement' not to deduct is void to that extent. [*TMA s 106*]. See 23.17 below for 'free of tax' payments.

23.9   Deduction of Tax at Source

23.9   ALIMONY, MAINTENANCE, SEPARATION ALLOWANCES, ETC.

falling due before 6 April 1989, and chargeable to tax under SCHEDULE D, CASE III (72), were subject to deduction of tax under *Secs 348, 349(1)* in the normal way, whether they arose under a Court Order or under an agreement (including a parol agreement—see *Peter's Exors v CIR CA 1941, 24 TC 45*). If paid (i) under an overseas agreement or Court Order or (ii) by a non-resident, see 23.4 above. For 'free of tax' payments see 23.16 and 23.17(*d*) below.

Payments falling due in the year 1989/90 and subsequently must normally be made *without deduction of tax. [FA 1988, s 38(7)]*. Exceptions were payments made before 6 April 1996 to, or for the maintenance of, a child aged 21 or over where made under a Court Order or payments made before 6 April 1995 to or for a child aged 18 or over where made under an agreement, *where such payments were made under an 'existing obligation'* (see 1.8(i) ALLOWANCES AND TAX RATES). Such payments were subject to deduction of tax under *Secs 348, 349(1)*.

23.10   ANNUAL PAYMENTS, ETC.

The broad rule is that annual payments are recurrent payments which, in the hands of the recipient, are 'pure income profit' and not e.g. elements in the computation of the profits of the recipient. Leading cases are *Earl Howe v CIR CA 1919, 7 TC 289* (insurance premiums under covenant not annual payments) and *CIR v Epping Forest Conservators HL 1953, 34 TC 293* (yearly contributions to meet the deficiencies of a charity held to be annual payments). Payments for the use of chattels not annual payments (*In re Hanbury, decd CA 1939, 38 TC 588*). See also *CIR v Whitworth Park Coal Co Ltd HL 1959, 38 TC 531*. Payments to a County Council under deed of covenant in consideration of the Council's paying special school fees of the covenantor's handicapped child held not annual payments (*Essex County Council v Ellam CA 1989, 61 TC 615*). The profits of a business bequeathed to a charity were held to be annual payments (*R v Special Commrs (ex p Shaftesbury Homes) CA 1922, 8 TC 367*). For covenanted subscriptions see *CIR v National Book League CA 1957, 37 TC 455* and *Taw & Torridge Festival Society Ltd v CIR Ch D 1959, 38 TC 603* (but see also 15.6(*b*) CHARITIES). Covenanted payments to a charity as part of arrangements under which it acquired the business of the payer not annual payments (*Campbell v CIR HL 1968, 45 TC 427*). Payments by a film company of a share of certain receipts as part of arrangements for cancellation of a contract were annual payments (*Asher v London Film Productions Ltd CA 1943, 22 ATC 432*) as were payments under a guarantee of the dividends of a company (*Aeolian Co Ltd v CIR KB 1936, 20 TC 547; Moss Empires Ltd v CIR HL 1937, 21 TC 264*). But not payments by the principal subscribers to a newsfilm service to make good its operating deficit (*British Commonwealth International Newsfilm Agency Ltd v Mahany HL 1962, 40 TC 550*).

Instalments of the purchase price of a mine held not annual payments (Foley v Fletcher 1858, 7 WR 141) nor instalment repayments of a debt (*Dott v Brown CA 1936, 15 ATC 147*). Where the Secretary of State for India acquired a railway in consideration of annuities for 48 years, tax held to be deductible only from the interest element actuarially ascertained (*Scoble v Secretary of State for India HL 1903, 4 TC 478, 618* and cf. the two *East India Rly.* cases at *21 TLR 606* and *40 TLR 241*). Similarly where shares were sold for payments over 125 years, the actuarially ascertained interest element in the payments was held to be income in the hands of the recipient for surtax (*Vestey v CIR Ch D 1961, 40 TC 112*). See also *Goole Corporation v Aire, etc. Trustees KB 1942, 21 ATC 156* (tax held deductible from interest element in yearly payments to local authority to meet street repairs). In *CIR v Church Commissioners HL 1976, 50 TC 516* rent charges paid as the consideration for property were held wholly income and not (as contended for Crown) partly income and partly capital. The HL judgments are an important review of the possibility of dissecting periodical payments in return for valuable consideration between income and capital and

Vestey v CIR above, although not overruled, was called 'the high water of dissection cases' (Lord Wilberforce) and some of the reasoning in it was not approved. See also *Chadwick v Pearl Life Insce KB 1905, 21 TLR 456.* For reimbursement of expenditure calculated by reference to an interest factor, see *Re Euro Hotel (Belgravia) Ltd Ch D 1975, 51 TC 293* and *Chevron Petroleum (UK) Ltd v BP Petroleum Development Ltd Ch D 1981, 57 TC 137.*

Payments in satisfaction of the transfer of a business, etc., and based on profits held not to be annual payments in *CIR v Ramsay CA 1935, 20 TC 79* and *CIR v Ledgard KB 1937, 21 TC 129* but contrast *CIR v Hogarth CS 1940, 23 TC 491.* Payments of a percentage of receipts over 40 years for the use of a secret process held to be annual payments (*Delage v Nugget Polish Co Ltd KB 1905, 21 TLR 454*) as were quarterly payments for the use of a firm's name etc. (*Mackintosh v CIR KB 1928, 14 TC 15*). See also *CIR v 36/49 Holdings Ltd CA 1943, 25 TC 173.* Where a business was bequeathed for life and the trustees were directed to carry a percentage of the profits to reserve, the amounts set aside were held to be annual payments (*Stocker v CIR KB 1919, 7 TC 304*).

In *Watkins v CIR KB 1939, 22 TC 696,* payments by a husband for the maintenance of his wife (of unsound mind) were held not to be annual payments. See 23.9 above for alimony payments. Payments to trustees as 'remuneration' are annual payments (*Baxendale v Murphy KB 1924, 9 TC 76; Hearn v Morgan KB 1945, 26 TC 478*) but not Sch E remuneration (*Jaworski v Institution of Polish Engineers CA 1950, 29 ATC 385*).

For amounts taxable under *Sec 775* or *Sec 776* (see 3.10 and 3.11 ANTI-AVOIDANCE), if the person entitled is resident abroad the Revenue may direct that they be treated as annual payments subject to deduction of tax under *Sec 349(1)*. [*Sec 777(9)*].

See also 3.19 ANTI-AVOIDANCE where certain annual payments are made for non-taxable consideration.

23.11   **ANNUITIES**

(*a*)   **General.** In the absence of provisions to the contrary annuities are (i) within SCHEDULE D, CASE III (72) unless payable under foreign contracts etc. (when they are foreign possessions within SCHEDULE D, CASE IV (73), (ii) subject to deduction of tax under *Secs 348, 349(1)* and (iii) this is so notwithstanding that the annuity may have been granted for valuable and sufficient consideration. Hence, (iv) an annuity cannot be dissected between the capital, if any, in consideration of the annuity and an 'interest element'. For a full discussion of this, see the HL opinions in *CIR v Church Commissioners HL 1976, 50 TC 516.* See also 23.10 above. For tax-free annuities see 23.17 below.

Statutory exceptions to this general rule are below.

(*b*)   **Annuities for non-taxable consideration.** See 3.19 ANTI-AVOIDANCE.

(*c*)   **Purchased life annuities.** The capital element in such annuities, whenever purchased, is **not treated as income** (except where, for other tax purposes, a lump sum payment has to be taken into account in computing profits or losses). Applies to any *life annuity* (i.e., one payable for a period ending with, or ascertainable only by reference to, the end of a life—notwithstanding that it may also end at a fixed term, or on the happening of a contingency, during the life or may extend beyond the end of the life) *purchased for money or money's worth* from a person whose business is to grant life annuities—but **not including any annuity**

(i)   treated, for other tax purposes, as being partly payment or repayment of a capital sum, or

(ii)   bought with sums ranking for relief under provisions for retirement annuities (see 65 RETIREMENT ANNUITIES AND PERSONAL PENSION SCHEMES) or as life assurance premiums, etc. under *Secs 266, 273* (see 45.1 *et seq.* LIFE ASSURANCE POLICIES), or

(iii)   purchased under direction in a will, or in substitution for an annuity charged on income of settled property, or

(iv)   purchased under any sponsored superannuation scheme (see *Sec 624* and 66 RETIREMENT SCHEMES), or retirement annuity scheme (see 65 RETIREMENT ANNUITIES AND PERSONAL PENSION SCHEMES), or in recognition of services, past or present, in any employment, or

(v)   payable under approved personal pension arrangements (see 65 RETIREMENT ANNUITIES AND PERSONAL PENSION SCHEMES). [*Secs 656(1), 657*].

Subject as below, the *capital element* is constant throughout and is, normally, that part of an annuity payment which bears to the full amount the same proportion as the purchase price of the annuity bears to the actuarial value of the total annuity payments, based on mortality tables but excluding any element of discounting, and calculated as at the date the first payment begins to accrue. For prescribed mortality tables see *SI 1956 No 1230* as amended by *SI 1991 No 2808*, and *Rose v Trigg Ch D 1963, 41 TC 365*.

Where the term but not the amount of the annuity does not depend solely on the duration of a life or lives, the calculation of the capital element is varied as may be just, and where the purchase price covers more than a pure annuity, that price is similarly apportioned.

But where the *amount* of any annuity payment depends on a contingency other than the duration of a life or lives the exempt capital element will not be calculated as above but will be arrived at by spreading the purchase price of the annuity rateably over its expected term (as at the date the first annuity payment begins to accrue) and allocating to each annuity payment a part corresponding to the length of the period for which the annuity payment is made. [*Sec 656; FA 1991, s 76*]. If the capital element exceeds the annuity payment, the excess may be carried forward for allowance in determining the capital element in the next payment or payments. (See Revenue Pamphlet IR 1, A46).

Sellers of annuities are notified of annuities affected by *Sec 656(1)–(4)* and of the capital element in them: until then they continue to deduct tax and account for it, where appropriate, as before. Any tax over- or under-deducted from payments made before the notification is repaid to or charged on the payee, subject to time limits. [*Sec 656(5)(6)*, and *IT (Purchased Life Annuities) Regulations 1956 (SI 1956 No 1230)*, and *Amendment Regulations 1960 (SI 1960 No 2308)* and *1990 (SI 1990 No 626)*].

For 1996/97 and subsequent years, the income element of a purchased life annuity is chargeable to income tax at the lower rate (to the extent that it does not fall within an individual's higher rate band) and tax is deductible at source at the lower rate (see 1.8(iii) ALLOWANCES AND TAX RATES).

As to tax on sale, surrender, etc., of rights under a life annuity contract see 45.15 LIFE ASSURANCE POLICIES and *Secs 542, 543*.

Other life, or terminable, annuities are taxed under *Sec 348*.

(*d*)   **Annuities out of approved superannuation funds.** See 66.5(*d*) RETIREMENT SCHEMES.

(*e*)   **'Capital and income'** policies are those where in the event of death within a selected period, a lump sum and an annuity for the rest of the period is paid. The annuity may (conditionally) be treated as instalments of capital, not subject to tax deduction. Some companies arrange for return of part of *capital* over a number of years, followed by an ordinary annuity subject to tax deduction. But if assigned or settled for benefit of a third party see 80.9 SETTLEMENTS.

(*f*) For **children's education policies** see *Perrin v Dickson CA 1929, 14 TC 608* in which the yearly payments were held to be a return of the premiums with interest, only the interest being taxable. The decision was questioned in *Sothern-Smith v Clancy CA 1940, 24 TC 1*. Purchased life annuities are now regulated, see (*c*) above.

23.12 **DIVIDENDS AND INTEREST**

Banks, etc. See 8 BANKS.

British companies etc. See 1.8 (iii) ALLOWANCES AND TAX RATES.

Building societies. See 9 BUILDING SOCIETIES.

Government Stock. See 33 GOVERNMENT STOCKS, 70 SCHEDULE C.

Local authority and statutory corporation stock. Tax is deductible under *Sec 349(2)* (see 23.3(ii) above) but not if borrowing is in foreign currency (or, for securities issued before 6 April 1982, in the currency of a territory outside the scheduled territories) and Treasury so direct. Interest is then exempt from income tax (but not corporation tax) if the beneficial owner is not resident in UK. [*Secs 349(2), 581*].

Foreign dividends (including foreign Government or public revenue dividends) are generally subject to deduction of tax under the paying and collecting agents arrangements under *Secs 118A–118K* introduced by *FA 1996, s 156, 29 Sch* and associated regulations. There are reliefs *inter alia* for payments to non-UK residents, or to non-UK resident trustees of certain discretionary or accumulation trusts for non-UK resident beneficiaries, for certain payments held in 'recognised clearing systems' (see 23.3(ii) above), for dividends payable by non-UK resident companies to UK companies holding 10% or more of the voting power in the paying company, and for various payments constituting exempt income in the hands of the recipient. For 1995/96 and earlier years (and for company accounting periods ending before 1 April 1996), similar provisions applied by the inclusion of such payments within SCHEDULE C (70).

23.13 **MORTGAGE INTEREST ('MIRAS')**

Mortgage interest on home loans may be paid after deduction of tax if the interest is 'relevant loan interest' paid by a 'qualifying borrower' to a 'qualifying lender'. This scheme is commonly known as MIRAS: Mortgage Interest Relief At Source.

For interest payments falling due before 6 April 1994, tax is deducted at the basic rate (for the year in which the payment becomes due). This continues to be the case for 1994/95 and subsequent years where the loan is within (*a*)(ii) below (loans to purchase life annuities). Otherwise, the deduction is at 20% for interest due in 1994/95 and 15% for interest due in 1995/96 and subsequent years. No further tax relief is available, but nor is tax relief clawed back if the borrower has insufficient liability to cover it. In general, the reduced rates of relief apply to interest payments made (and due) after 5 April 1994, but where advance payments were made after 29 November 1993 and before 6 April 1994 of interest due after 5 April 1994, the rate of deduction is determined by reference to the date the payment becomes due, rather than the payment date.

Payments of 'relevant loan interest' made after 5 April 1994 (whenever falling due), and advance payments as above, are not deductible in computing total income. As regards earlier payments, where personal reliefs (except relief for life assurance premiums and relief for deferred annuities) exceeded total income, the excess was deducted from an amount of notional income charged at basic rate, so that qualifying borrowers who were not liable to tax on their income nevertheless received tax relief (by retention of tax deducted) on that excess (although see the definition of 'qualifying borrowers' below as regards certain tax exemptions). Borrowers liable to income tax only at the lower rate, or whose interest payments exceeded their income chargeable at the basic rate, similarly received full basic rate relief. Interest payments after 5 April 1991 do not attract relief from income tax at the higher rate(s) (but see below as regards certain bridging loans). Such relief for payments on or before that date was given in PAYE codings and tax assessments by deducting from total income the gross interest paid and charging a similar amount of notional income to basic rate tax.

It is understood that relief under MIRAS may be claimed retrospectively where interest under a mortgage meeting all the qualifying conditions for inclusion in the scheme was paid outside MIRAS, and relief for the interest thereby lost (e.g. where there was no taxable income). (Tolley's Practical Tax 1993 p 120).

Qualifying lenders are able to recover from the Government the tax deducted from interest payments received. Where the lender was not entitled to such a payment, and the payment, or the claim on which it was made, was made on or after 27 July 1993, the Board may assess and recover such overpayments and obtain interest and penalties where appropriate.

Relevant loan interest is not deductible from profits etc. under Schedule D, Case I or II or VI. [*Secs 74(o), 369; FA 1991, s 27(2); F(No 2)A 1992, s 19(3)(5); FA 1993, s 58, 6 Sch 1; FA 1994, s 81(3)–(7), 9 Sch 1; FA 1996, 18 Sch 6, 17(1)–(4)(8)*]. Form Miras 5, a certificate of interest paid, is available on demand from the lender, although building societies normally notify the tax office direct.

For a general explanation of the scheme, see Revenue Pamphlet IR 63 'Mortgage interest relief at source'.

'**Relevant loan interest**' is interest which is paid and payable in the UK to a 'qualifying lender', where

(*a*) it is interest on

　(i) loans for purchase of land, caravan or houseboat *in the UK* which, when the interest is paid, is used 'wholly or to a substantial extent' (see below) as the only or main residence of the borrower under *Secs 354(1), 355* (as altered for this purpose), see 43.6 INTEREST PAYABLE, or where the borrower resides in job-related accommodation within *Sec 356*, see 43.16 INTEREST PAYABLE; or

　(ii) loans to a borrower aged 65 or over to purchase life annuities secured on land *in the UK* under *Sec 365*, see 43.24 INTEREST PAYABLE; or

　(iii) an option mortgage in respect of which an option notice was in force on 31 March 1983 and to which the conditions in (*a*)(i) above apply (with minor modifications), and

(*b*) apart from the current provisions, the whole of the interest in (*a*)(i) or (*a*)(ii) above (ignoring the tax relief limit—see 43.10 INTEREST PAYABLE) would be eligible for relief under *Sec 353* (see 43.3 INTEREST PAYABLE) or would be deductible from profits etc. under Schedule D, Case I or II or VI.

The election referred to in 43.3 INTEREST PAYABLE (where interest is dually eligible for relief) also has effect for determining whether interest falls within (*a*)(i) above.

[*Sec 370; FA 1988, s 42(3)(c); FA 1994, 9 Sch 10; FA 1995, 29 Sch Pt VIII(2)*].

The Revenue normally regard the condition in (*a*)(i) above as satisfied if at least two-thirds of the property is used as the borrower's main residence. (Revenue Tax Bulletin August 1995 p 230). See *R v Inspector of Taxes (ex p. Kelly) CA 1991, 64 TC 343* for disallowance of interest on mixed purpose loans.

Interest on home improvement loans and on loans for the purchase of property to be used, wholly or substantially, as the only or main residence of the borrower's dependent relative or separated or former spouse is relevant loan interest if it would be eligible for tax relief (see 43.6 *et seq.* INTEREST PAYABLE), that is, broadly speaking, if the loan was made, or deemed to be made, before 6 April 1988, and if within (*b*) above.

If non-qualifying expenditure is added to otherwise qualifying loans, the loans must be taken out of MIRAS. In practice, however, lenders may treat as qualifying expenditure sums advanced:

(1) by miscellaneous debits to the borrower's account by virtue of the mortgage deed or rules, e.g. buildings insurance premiums, legal costs in the event of arrears, or realisation expenses;

(2) to pay premiums due on indemnity insurance, mortgage protection and guarantee policies, or loan protection policies (including limited costs of incidental sickness and redundancy cover); or

(3) to pay costs of mortgage deed preparation, stamp duty, valuation and survey fees, and legal costs.

(MIRAS 30 (1995) para 10.22).

Certain administration fees charged to loan account are similarly disregarded, up to £300 in the first year and £150 p.a. thereafter. (MIRAS 30 (1995) para 10.23).

Where unauthorised arrears of interest are capitalised, the loan should strictly be excluded from the MIRAS scheme as being of a mixed quality. In practice, such action will only be taken where, when the loan is recalculated, the capitalised interest exceeds the greater of 12 months' arrears and £1,000, and no satisfactory arrangements have been made to reduce the arrears. Even then, in certain cases of hardship, no action will be taken. (MIRAS 30 (1995) paras 10.4, 10.5). See also 43.10 INTEREST PAYABLE as regards extension of the tax relief limit by up to £1,000 where interest is capitalised.

In relation to interest paid before 16 March 1993, if a *bridging loan* was raised for the purchase of another dwelling with a view to the previous dwelling being disposed of, then interest payable in respect of the previous dwelling within twelve months of raising the bridging loan continued to be eligible for relief under these provisions. The Board could extend the twelve months. See 43.6 INTEREST PAYABLE as regards the continuation of higher rate relief after 5 April 1991 for interest in respect of the previous dwelling where the bridging loan was (or was treated as having been) made on or before that date. [*Sec 371; FA 1991, s 27(4)(5); FA 1993, s 57(4)(b)*]. See now 43.7 INTEREST PAYABLE

Interest on a *home improvement loan* (i.e. a loan applied wholly in improving or developing land or buildings or in paying off another similar loan), if otherwise eligible (see 43.6 *et seq.* INTEREST PAYABLE), is *not* relevant loan interest unless

(i) it is paid to a building society or a local authority or the NI Housing Executive, or

(ii) the qualifying lender has given notice to the Board that he is prepared to have such loans, made after such date as specified in the notice, brought within the tax deduction scheme, or

(iii) it is interest to which (*a*)(iii) above applies. [*Sec 372*].

Loans over the tax relief limit. (See 43.10 INTEREST PAYABLE.) Interest on such loans is not relevant loan interest unless all the loans to be taken into account are by the same qualifying lender, and only interest on loans up to the limit is then relevant loan interest. For loans made before 6 April 1987, there is an additional requirement that the lender has given notice to the Board that he is prepared to have such loans brought within the tax deduction

23.13 Deduction of Tax at Source

scheme. [*Sec 373(1)–(5); FA 1988, s 42(3)(d)*]. See also 43.10 INTEREST PAYABLE as regards extension of the limit by up to £1,000 where interest is capitalised.

Joint borrowers. Interest on a loan which is to joint borrowers who are not husband and wife (i.e. living together and not separated) is not relevant loan interest unless each of the borrowers is a qualifying borrower and in relation to each of them, considered separately, the whole of that interest is relevant loan interest. [*Sec 373(6)(7)*].

'Penalty' interest charged on the early redemption of a loan within MIRAS is not relevant loan interest (although this does not apply to interest charged for the whole of the month in which redemption occurs). Similarly a penalty charged for changing the terms of a loan, including a penalty for changing from a fixed to a variable rate, is not relevant loan interest. However, a replacement loan need not be regarded as mixed purpose merely because, in part, it replaces such a charge. (MIRAS 30 (1995), para 10.46).

Option to deduct interest under Schedule A. Where for 1995/96 and subsequent years a qualifying borrower carries on or proposes to carry on a Schedule A business (see 68.4 SCHEDULE A) and gives notice to the Board that relevant interest on a loan is to be deducted in computing profits, interest paid on that loan after the date specified in the notice is to be paid outside MIRAS. The notice is irrevocable and must be given within 22 months after the end of the tax year in which the specified date falls. The Board must notify the lender, and there are provisions whereby any tax deducted by the borrower after the specified date can be reclaimed by the Revenue and reimbursed to the lender. The loan remains outside MIRAS until the Board gives notice to both borrower and lender that it is to be brought back within the scheme, which they will do only when the Schedule A business is permanently discontinued or the proposal to carry it on is finally abandoned. [*Sec 375A; FA 1995, 6 Sch 18*].

Property used for both residential and business purposes. See 43.2 INTEREST PAYABLE for Revenue Extra-statutory Concession applicable where part of a borrower's main residence is used for business (including a Schedule A business) purposes. The concession applies equally to a loan within MIRAS. (Revenue Pamphlet IR 1 (November 1995 Supplement), A89). This is, however, subject to the property being used 'wholly or to a substantial extent' as the borrower's residence (see (*a*)(i) above). Where this condition is satisfied, *all* the interest qualifies for relief through MIRAS (subject to the £30,000 maximum). Where the part of the loan attributed to residential use under Concession A89 is less than £30,000, all or part of the interest attributed to the business use will have been relieved through MIRAS. The business deduction is reduced accordingly (see Revenue Tax Bulletin August 1995 pp 230–232 for worked examples).

A **'qualifying borrower'** is an individual who pays 'relevant loan interest'. In relation to interest paid at a time when an individual (or spouse, if not permanently separated) holds an office or employment the emoluments from which would otherwise be chargeable to tax under Case I, II or III of Schedule E, the individual is **not** a qualifying borrower if he or she has some special exemption or immunity (e.g. diplomatic) from such charge. [*Sec 376(1)–(3)*]. The exclusion of EEC employees from the scheme by virtue of their Schedule E exemption does not conflict with Community law (*Tither v CIR CJEC, [1990] STC 416*). Where a borrower dies, the loan should be removed from MIRAS immediately the lender is advised of the death by the personal representatives, except in the case of the death of a joint married borrower where the surviving borrower continues to use the property as the only or main residence. (MIRAS Central Unit Guidance Letter 31 May 1989).

A **'qualifying lender'** is any of the following: a building society; a local authority; the Bank of England; the Post Office; an insurance company authorised to carry on long-term business (e.g. life assurance) in the UK; a company successor to a trustee savings bank; a registered or incorporated friendly society or branch; a development corporation; the Commission for the New Towns; the Housing Corporation; Housing for Wales; the

Northern Ireland Housing Executive; the Scottish Special Housing Association; the Development Board for Rural Wales; the Church of England Pensions Board; and an existing lender under the mortgage option scheme.

With effect from 3 May 1994, the Board may also register as a qualifying lender any of the following bodies: a recognised bank or licensed deposit-taking institution; an insurance company authorised to carry on general insurance business in the UK; a 90% subsidiary of any such bank, institution or company; and any other body whose activities and objects it considers qualify the body for inclusion. The registration may apply generally or only in relation to a particular description of loan, and applies from a specified date, and the terms of registration may be varied by the Board. Registration may be cancelled where it appears to the Board that an application for registration by the lender concerned would be refused. At least 30 days notice is required to be given of variation or cancellation. There is a right of appeal (within 30 days) to the Special Commissioners against a refusal, variation or cancellation of registration. Applications for registration should be made to Inland Revenue, FICO (Savings and Investments), 3rd Floor, St John's House, Merton Road, Bootle, Merseyside L69 9BB, stating the grounds on which the applicant qualifies and giving their full legal title or registered name.

An updated Register of Qualifying Lenders was published on 14 November 1995 and is available for inspection at Tax Enquiry Centres, or may be purchased (price £1 post free) from Inland Revenue, Reference Library, New Wing, Somerset House, Strand, London WC2R 1LB or by personal callers at the Public Enquiry Room, West Wing, Somerset House.

Before the introduction of registration for such qualifying lenders, the Treasury had prescriptive powers, under which numerous orders were made. Bodies which were so prescribed immediately before 3 May 1994 were automatically entered in the initial Register published on 4 July 1994, and were deemed to have been registered in the intervening period.

[*Secs 376(4)–(6), 376A; Housing Act 1988, 17 Sch 115; F(No 2)A 1992, 9 Sch 3; FA 1994, s 142*].

Administration of the tax deduction scheme. The scheme does not apply to any relevant loan interest unless

(*a*)   the borrower, or each joint borrower, has given notice to the lender in the prescribed form certifying (i) that he is a qualifying borrower and (ii) that the interest is relevant loan interest and (iii) such other matters as may be prescribed; or

(*b*)   the Board have notified the lender and the borrower that the interest may be paid under deduction of tax; or

(*c*)   the interest is on a loan which was, on 31 March 1983, an option mortgage loan; or

(*d*)   the loan was made before the commencement date (see above), and is of a description specified by regulations made by the Board.

Where any of the above requirements are met, tax may be deducted from the interest: on and after the date of the notice in (*a*); on and after the date specified in the Board's notification in (*b*), and where that date is retrospective the Board may repay the amount which was under-deducted from interim interest paid (subject to recovery powers for amounts wrongly repaid); on and after the commencement date (see above) for (*c*) and (*d*). [*Secs 374, 375(8)(8A); FA 1995, s 112(4)*].

Where the relevant loan interest is payable to a building society or other specified qualifying lender under a loan agreement requiring combined payments (i.e. a number of regular payments which are part repayment of capital and part payment of interest) on a loan made before 1 April 1983, the qualifying lender may give notice to the qualifying borrower that each net payment (i.e. each payment from the interest element of which tax has to be deducted) will be of the same amount (unless there is a change in the deductible rate of income tax or in the rate of interest charged by the borrower) and that payments will be determined so as to secure that the period of the loan remains unchanged. The borrower may, however, give counter-notice that each net payment must be of the same amount (again subject to deductible tax rate or interest rate changes) and that the amount of each combined payment must not exceed what would have been the amount of the first combined payment, less tax, after the giving of notice by the lender, apart from these provisions. If such notice is given the borrower may, whenever he chooses, make additional capital repayments so as to secure repayment of the loan within a period not shorter than that originally agreed. Subsequent variations may be made by agreement. [*Sec 377; FA 1994, s 81(8)*]. A qualifying lender may be specified for these purposes by the Treasury by order made by statutory instrument. The orders made before commencement of the deduction scheme are *The Income Tax (Interest Relief) (Specified Qualifying Lenders) (No 1) Order 1982 (SI 1982 No 1630); Order 1983 (SI 1983 No 93). [Sec 378]*.

Where, on or after 1 May 1995, tax is deducted from interest which has never been relevant loan interest or which is paid otherwise than by a qualifying borrower, the interest is treated as such providing either condition (*a*) or condition (*b*) above is fulfilled. The tax deducted is, however, recoverable from the borrower by assessment. Interest is chargeable under *TMA s 88* (see 6.6 BACK DUTY), where relevant (see 78.22 SELF-ASSESSMENT), by reference to a due date of 1 December following the tax year in which the deduction was made. Where the borrower fraudulently or negligently makes a false statement or representation, he will be liable to a penalty not exceeding the amount of tax consequently deducted. [*Sec 374A; FA 1995, s 112(1)(5); FA 1996, 18 Sch 7, 17(5)(6)*].

If at any time interest ceases to be relevant loan interest or a person ceases to be a qualifying borrower, the borrower must notify the lender, and where tax has been deducted from a payment made between that time and the notification the payment is treated as relevant loan interest, but any excess relief or deduction above proper entitlement is recoverable from the borrower by assessment, with potential interest and, for deductions made on or after 1 May 1995, penalties.

If a qualifying lender has reason to believe that interest is no longer relevant loan interest or a borrower is no longer a qualifying borrower, he must inform the Board. Failure to do so incurs penalties.

Form Miras 3, available from the lender, enables the borrower to claim tax relief where a qualifying loan is excluded from MIRAS.

Where it appears to the Board that any qualifying condition under the scheme is not, or may not be, fulfilled, they must give notice to the lender and the borrower and the tax deduction scheme will not apply to the relevant loan interest due between dates specified in the notice and any subsequent notice. [*Sec 375(1)–(7); FA 1994, 9 Sch 11; FA 1995, s 112(2)(3)(5); FA 1996, 18 Sch 8, 17(1)*].

Where interest is treated as relevant loan interest only by virtue of *Sec 375(2)*, it may nevertheless be deductible against total income or for Schedule D, Case I or II purposes if it would be so deductible under general principles. [*Secs 74(o), 369(3); FA 1994, s 81(4), 9 Sch 1*].

The Inland Revenue may disclose information about option mortgages to the Secretary of State or the Department of the Environment for Northern Ireland or to an authorised officer of either of them. [*Sec 375(9)(10)*].

The Treasury may make regulations to apply the above provisions to housing associations and self-build societies which borrow from qualifying lenders and the Board may make regulations regarding the administration of the scheme, its application to personal representatives and trustees, the inspection of records, appeals and generally. [*Sec 378*]. The first such regulations made by the Board deal mainly with the bringing of loans into the scheme; with 'limited loans' (broadly those over the interest relief limit—see 43.10 INTEREST PAYABLE); with variations of amounts due under existing loans brought within the scheme; with the reimbursement of lenders for tax deducted by borrowers; and with information and penalty powers and appeal procedures. [*The Income Tax (Interest Relief) Regulations 1982 (SI 1982 No 1236) as amended*]. The *(No 2) Regulations 1983 (SI 1983 No 311)* supplement the principal regulations, and the *(No 3) Regulations 1985 (SI 1985 No 1252)* amend the procedures for bringing limited loans into the scheme. The (*Housing Associations) Regulations 1988 (SI 1988 No 1347)* and (*Amendment) Regulations 1995 (SI 1995 No 1212)* deal with housing associations and self-build societies, replacing the earlier (*Housing Associations) Regulations 1983 (SI 1983 No 368)* as amended.

Interest paid by a housing association or self-build society is not relevant loan interest if

(A)   it is interest on a home improvement loan made on or after 6 April 1988 (and not deemed to have been made before that date), or

(B)   by virtue of *FA 1988, s 44* (loans for residence of dependent relative, etc.) it would not be relevant loan interest if paid by a member of the association or society.

(See 43.6 *et seq.* INTEREST PAYABLE.) [*FA 1988, ss 43(3), 44(6)*].

An explanatory lenders booklet (MIRAS 30) is available to existing MIRAS lenders and those thinking about coming into the scheme.

The Revenue have published a Code of Practice (No 4, published July 1993) setting out their standards for the carrying out of inspections of tax relief at source schemes operated by financial intermediaries.

The Inland Revenue Financial Intermediaries and Claims Office may be contacted in relation to MIRAS on 0151–472 6160 to 6167 as regards repayments or 0151–472 6155 for technical advice.

23.14   **RENTS ETC. UNDER SECTIONS 119 AND 120**

Under *Sec 119*, where rent (as defined) was payable before 1 May 1995 for any 'easement' (as defined) 'used, occupied or enjoyed' in connection with any of the 'concerns' specified in *Sec 55(2)*, tax is deductible as for patent royalties, see 23.15(*b*) below. See *New Sharlston Collieries CA 1936, 21 TC 69; Hope CS 1937, 21 TC 116* and *Fitzwilliam's Collieries Co v Phillips HL 1943, 25 TC 430*. Payments made on or after that date are made gross. [*FA 1995, s 145*]. If the rent is paid in produce of the concern the recipient is charged, on its value, under Schedule D, Case III. [*Sec 119(2)*].

Sec 119(2) held to cover value of coals received free (*Baillie CS 1936, 20 TC 187*) and payments under short-term agreements for the extraction of, respectively (*a*) all sand and gravel, and (*b*) all coal, on certain lands (*Stratford v Mole & Lea KB 1941, 24 TC 20* and *Old Silkstone Collieries Ltd v Marsh KB 1941, 24 TC 20*. Cf. *Craigenlow Quarries Ltd CS 1951, 32 TC 326*). But not payments for extracting fluorspar from old lead mining dumps (*Rogers v Longsdon Ch D 1966, 43 TC 231*) or shingle from foreshore (*Duke of Fife's Trustees v Geo. Wimpey CS 1943, 22 ATC 275*) because there was no 'concern'. For cases involving sales of slag etc. but not rents etc. within *Sec 119*, see 71.70 SCHEDULE D, CASES I AND II.

The provisions of *Sec 122* (see 49 MINERAL ROYALTIES) altering the taxation treatment of recipients of mineral royalties and rents do not displace the payer's obligation to deduct income tax at the basic rate when paying those royalties, etc. [*Sec 122(1)*].

Deduction at source as above continues to apply to rents for easements in connection with electric telegraph or telephone wires or cables (including poles, pylons, related apparatus and transformers) except, by payer's election, to sums of £2.50 p.a. or under (which are then assessable on recipient under Schedule D, Case III) but if any such rent is paid under deduction of tax by a person carrying on a radio relay service the payment is nevertheless deductible in calculating profits for Schedule D, Case I but for purposes of *Secs 348* and *349* is deemed not to be payable out of taxed profits. [*Sec 120*].

Other property rentals, including ground rents, are payable in full and assessable on recipient, see 68 SCHEDULE A.

23.15   **ROYALTIES**

(*a*)   **Copyright royalties, public lending right payments** and **design royalties** paid to non-residents are taxed by deduction under *Sec 349(1)*. [*Secs 536, 537, 537B; FA 1995, s 115(10)*]. Payer is assessable, even if he has not deducted the tax (*Rye & Eyre v CIR HL 1935, 19 TC 164*). See 51.10 NON-RESIDENTS AND OTHER OVERSEAS MATTERS.

(*b*)   **Patent royalties** are payable under deduction of tax. [*Secs 348(2), 349(1)(b)*]. Instalments of fixed amount for five-year use of patent held capital (*Desoutter Bros Ltd KB 1936, 15 ATC 49*). A lump sum payment on signing a ten-year agreement held capital but ten fixed yearly payments royalties (*CIR v British Salmson Aero Engines Ltd CA 1938, 22 TC 29*). Awards by a Royal Commission for use of inventions and patents in 1914–1918 war held patent royalties (*Constantinesco v Rex HL 1927, 11 TC 730; Mills v Jones HL 1929, 14 TC 769*). See also *Jones v CIR KB 1919, 7 TC 310; Wild v Ionides KB 1925, 9 TC 392; International Combustion Ltd v CIR KB 1932, 16 TC 532* and cf. *Rank Xerox Ltd v Lane HL 1979, 53 TC 185*.

For the treatment of capital sums for the acquisition or from the sale of patents, see 54 PATENTS.

(*c*)   **Mining royalties,** see 23.14 above.

23.16   **TAX-FREE ARRANGEMENTS**

An agreement which provides for an annual payment without deduction of tax is void [*TMA s 106(2)*] but a provision to pay interest at a stated rate after deduction of tax is treated as requiring payment at the gross rate. [*Sec 818(2)*]. An agreement to make payments 'free of tax' is not avoided by *TMA s 106(2) (CIR v Ferguson HL 1969, 46 TC 1*). See 23.17 below for tax-free annuities.

23.17   **TAX-FREE ANNUITIES ETC.**

(*a*)   **General.** A direction under a will or settlement for an annuity to be paid 'free of tax' (or similar wording) is a direction to pay an annuity of such an amount which after deduction of the tax will produce the specified figure (cf. *CIR v Ferguson HL 1969, 46 TC 1*). This is a matter, however, in which it is important the wording used should express clearly and unambiguously what is intended. The large number of court cases referred to below have arisen mostly because of the imprecision of the relevant wording.

The wording was held *not* to confer freedom from tax in *Abadam v Abadam 1864, 10 LT 53* ('payable without any deduction whatsoever'); *Shrewsbury v Shrewsbury Ch D 1906, 22 TLR 598* ('clear of all deductions'); *In re Loveless Ch D 1918, 34 TLR 356* ('clear'); *In re Well's Will Trusts Ch D 1940, 19 ATC 158* ('clear of all deductions'); *In re Best's Marriage Settlement Ch D 1941, 20 ATC 235* ('such a sum as shall after deductions'); *CIR v Watson CS 1942, 25 TC 25* (annuity payable out of 'whole free residue' of income); *In re Hooper Ch D 1944, 1 AER 227* ('free of all duty . . . and

. . . free of all deductions whatsoever'); *In re Wright Ch D 1952, 31 ATC 433* ('net'). The wording was held to confer freedom from tax in *In re Buckle 1894, 1 Ch 286* ('free of legacy duty and every other deduction' under a codicil to a will in which originally 'clear of all deductions whatsoever, except income tax'); *In re Shrewsbury Estate Acts CA 1923, 40 TLR 16* ('clear of all deductions whatsoever for taxes or otherwise'). *In re Hooper* above was not followed in *In re Cowlishaw Ch D 1939, 18 ATC 377* where the wording was similar, but in a later case (*In re Best's Marriage Settlement* above) *Cowlishaw* was described as special to its context.

(*b*)   **Surtax/excess liability.** All the decisions below relate to super-tax or surtax but it would seem that, suitably adapted, they are equally applicable to excess liability (see 28.1 EXCESS LIABILITY). Here it is relevant that an annuity is investment income.

An annuity of a sum such 'as after deduction of the income tax' would give the prescribed amount was held not to be free of super-tax (*In re Bates Ch D 1924, 4 ATC 518*). However an annuity 'free of income tax' was held to be free of surtax on the ground that surtax was an additional income tax and there was no indication in the will to restrict the wording to 'income tax as known for many years'. The previous decision was distinguished as there the wording referred to 'deduction' and surtax was not deductible at source (*In re Reckitt CA 1932, 11 ATC 429*; followed in *Prentice's Trustees CS 1934, 13 ATC 612*). A direction to pay an annuity free of super-tax was held to cover surtax (*In re Hulton Ch D 1930, 9 ATC 570*).

The surtax is normally taken as the part of the annuitant's total surtax proportionate to the ratio of the annuity grossed at the standard rate to the annuitant's total income (*In re Bowring 1918, 34 TLR 575*; followed in *In re Doxat 1920, 125 LT 60* and other cases). In *Baird's Trustees CS 1933, 12 ATC 407* the surtax was calculated on the basis that the annuity was the annuitant's only income, but this decision was distinguished in *Richmond's Trustees 1935 CS, 14 ATC 489* and *In re Bowring* was followed. See also *In re Horlick's Settlement CA 1938, 17 ATC 549*.

The surtax/excess liability borne on behalf of the annuitant by the trust fund is itself, grossed-up, income in his hands (*Meeking v CIR KB 1920, 7 TC 603; Lord Michelham's Trustees v CIR CA 1930, 15 TC 737*. See also *Shrewsbury & Talbot v CIR KB 1936, 20 TC 538* and compare *CIR v Duncanson KB 1949, 31 TC 257*). The practice is to treat the liability so borne for year 1 as an addition for grossing-up purposes to the annuity for year 2.

(*c*)   **Tax repayments of annuitants.** In a tax-free annuity the question arises whether the benefit conferred on the annuitant should be limited to the tax actually suffered by him after taking into account his allowances etc.

Where the annuity under a will was 'free of income tax' it was held that the annuitant must hand to the trustees a part of the tax repaid to her on account of her reliefs, in proportion to the ratio of the net annuity to her net income after tax (*In re Pettit, Le Fevre v Pettit Ch D 1922, 38 TLR 787*). But where the annuity was expressed to be of such an amount as after deduction of the tax at the current rate would give the prescribed sum it was held, distinguishing *In re Pettit*, that the annuitant was entitled to retain any tax repaid to him (*In re Jones Ch D 1933, 12 ATC 595*). For cases in which these two decisions were considered and applied as appropriate to the precise wording of the provision of the annuity, see *Richmond's Trustees CS 1935, 14 ATC 489; In re Maclennan CA 1939, 18 ATC 121; In re Eves Ch D 1939, 18 ATC 401; Rowan's Trustees CS 1939, 18 ATC 378; In re Jubb Ch D 1941, 20 ATC 297; In re Tatham Ch D 1944, 23 ATC 283; In re Williams Ch D 1945, 24 ATC 199; In re Bates's Will Trusts Ch D 1945, 24 ATC 300; In re Arno CA 1946, 25 ATC 412. Tatham* and *Arno* give useful reviews of the subject as does *CIR v Cook HL 1945, 26 TC 489* (in which it was held that the Revenue must repay the tax on the grossed-up amount of a tax-free annuity notwithstanding that the annuitant would not be liable to tax if the annuity was not grossed-up and that the whole of the repayment would be handed over to the trustees). The annuitant must, if required by the trustees, exercise his right to repayment (*In re Kingcombe Ch D 1936, 15 ATC 37*). If the annuitant is a married woman *In re Pettit* applies to tax repayable to the husband but, if necessary, she must apply for separate assessment (*In re Batley CA 1952, 31 ATC 410*). It applies to loss relief (*In re Lyons CA 1951, 30 ATC 377*). For the effect of an *In re Pettit* refund on the annuitant's total income for surtax see *CIR v Duncanson KB 1949, 31 TC 257*.

(*d*)   **Tax-free alimony etc. payments.** The *In re Pettit* rule (see (*c*) above) does not apply to tax-free Court Orders and in *CIR v Ferguson HL 1969, 46 TC 1*, Lord Diplock explicitly refrained from deciding whether it applied to a separation agreement. Whether a free of tax Court Order would confer freedom from surtax/ excess liability does not seem to have arisen. Subject to the foregoing (*a*), (*b*) and (*c*) above apply, where appropriate, to tax-free alimony payments, etc.

For tax-free alimony payments by non-residents, see *Ferguson* above and *Stokes v Bennett Ch D 1953, 34 TC 337*.

(*e*)   For **overseas taxes** under tax-free annuities, see *Re Frazer Ch D 1941, 20 ATC 73* and compare *Havelock v Grant KB 1946, 27 TC 363*.

23.18   VOLUNTARY ALLOWANCES

Not assessable on recipient (unless a misnomer for payments for services). But *voluntary pensions* by employers are assessable on recipient under Schedule E and tax is deductible by employers (see 55 PAY AS YOU EARN and 59.4 PENSIONS). See 23.9 above regarding alimony and separation allowances.

24 Diplomatic, etc. Immunity—Individuals and Organisations

24.1   *Diplomatic Agents* (i.e. heads of mission or members of diplomatic staff) of foreign states
(recognised by HM Government, see *Caglar v Billingham (Sp C 70), [1996] SSCD 150*)
are exempt from tax except on income or capital gains arising from *private* investments or
immovable property in the UK under *Diplomatic Privileges Act 1964*. Similar exemption is
given to *Agents-General* and their staffs [*Sec 320; TCGA 1992, s 11*] (and see Revenue
Pamphlet IR 1, A39 as regards certain Hong Kong officials). *Consuls* and *official agents* of
foreign States in UK (not British subjects or citizens of Eire and not trading) are exempt
on income from their official employment [*Sec 321*] and are also, subject to Order in
Council, exempt under SCHEDULE D, CASES IV AND V (72) (and, for 1995/96 and earlier years,
treated as non-resident under *Secs 48* and *123(4)* as regards foreign dividends), provided
they are permanent employees or were not ordinarily resident in UK immediately prior to
that employment. [*Sec 322; FA 1990, 14 Sch 4; FA 1996, 7 Sch 15*]. See also *Consular
Relations Act 1968*.

International organisations (e.g. the United Nations (*SI 1974 No 1261*)), their representatives, officers, members of committees, persons or missions etc. may be specified by Order
in Council as exempt from certain taxes under *International Organisations Act 1968*. Also
other bodies under the *European Communities Act 1972* (e.g. the North Atlantic Salmon
Conservation Organisation (*SI 1985 No 1773*)) and certain financial bodies under the
Bretton Woods Agreements Act 1945 (e.g. the International Monetary Fund (*SI 1946 No 36*)).
Also exemption from income tax is given to the remuneration of the Commissioners of the
European Communities and their staffs under *Art. 13 of Chap. V of the Protocol on the
Privileges and Immunities of the European Communities*. See *Hurd v Jones CJEC, [1986] STC
127* as regards exemption of certain payments out of Community funds, although see now
SI 1990 No 237. See also *Tither v CIR CJEC, [1990] STC 416*, where exclusion of EEC
official from MIRAS scheme upheld. The Treasury may also designate any of the
international organisations of which the UK is a member for the purpose of exemption
from various requirements for the deduction of tax from payments made in the UK (see e.g.
SI 1991 No 1694 designating The European Bank for Reconstruction and Development
and *SI 1992 No 2655*). [*Sec 582A; FA 1991, s 118; FA 1996, 7 Sch 22, 29 Sch 6*].

See 64 RESIDENCE, ORDINARY RESIDENCE AND DOMICILE for definition of resident etc.

25 Double Tax Relief

[Secs 788–816]

(See also Revenue Pamphlet IR 6.)

Cross-reference. See generally 51 NON-RESIDENTS AND OTHER OVERSEAS MATTERS.

25.1 Where the same income is liable to be taxed in both the UK and another country, relief may be available

    (a) under the specific terms of a double tax agreement between the UK and that other country—see 25.2 below [*Sec 788*];

    (b) under special arrangements with Eire—see 25.3 below; or

    (c) under the unilateral double tax relief provisions contained in UK tax legislation—see 25.4 below. [*Sec 790*].

25.2 **DOUBLE TAX AGREEMENTS** [*Secs 788, 789*]

A list is given below of the bilateral agreements made by the UK which are currently operative. Representations on points interested parties would like to see addressed in negotiating particular treaties, or on other matters relating to the treaty negotiation programme or the treaty network, should be addressed to David Harris, Inland Revenue, International Division, Room 314, Strand Bridge House, 138–142 Strand, London WC2R 1HH.

Under these agreements certain classes of income derived from those countries by UK residents are given complete exemption from income taxes in the country from which they arise and reciprocal exemption from UK income tax or corporation tax is given to similar income derived from the UK by residents of those countries. Exemption may also be granted in respect of capital gains taxes, as provided for by *TCGA 1992, s 277*, and in respect of corporation tax on capital gains.

Other classes of income or gain derived from those countries are not exempted, or only partially exempted, by the agreements and in these cases relief from UK income tax, etc., is generally given in the agreement (but to UK residents only [*Sec 794*]) in the form of a credit, calculated by reference to the foreign tax suffered, which is set against and reduces the UK tax chargeable on the doubly-taxed income or gain. [*Sec 793*]. See example in 25.8 below.

Double tax agreements normally contain a provision enabling a taxpayer who considers that the action of a tax authority has resulted, or will result, in taxation not in accordance with the agreement to present his case to the competent authority in his state of residence. The UK competent authority is the Inland Revenue, and the address to which all relevant facts and contentions should be sent is International Division, Strand Bridge House, 138–142 Strand, London WC2R 1HH.

In *R v CIR (ex p. Commerzbank AG) QB, [1991] STC 271*, INTEREST ON OVERPAID TAX (41) was held not to fall within the scope of double tax agreements, although on a reference to the European Court of Justice (see *[1993] STC 605*), the Court upheld the view that, in the case of companies resident in EC Member States, such discrimination against non-UK resident companies was prevented by the relevant Articles of the Treaty of Rome. See also 41.1 INTEREST ON OVERPAID TAX as regards treatment of EC resident individuals following this decision, and Revenue Double Taxation Relief Manual, DT 1950 *et seq.* for Revenue approach to non-discrimination claims generally.

Agreements under *Sec 788* making provision in relation to interest may also have a provision dealing with cases where, owing to a special relationship, the amount of interest paid exceeds the amount which would have been paid in the absence of that relationship, and requiring the interest provision to be applied only to that lower amount. In relation to interest paid after 14 May 1992, any such special relationship provision has to be construed:

(*a*)   as requiring account to be taken of all factors, including whether, in the absence of the relationship, the loan would have been made at all, or would have been in a different amount, or a different rate of interest and other terms would have been agreed. This does not apply, however, where the special relationship provision expressly requires regard to be had to the debt on which the interest is paid in determining the excess interest, and accordingly expressly limits the factors to be taken into account, and in the case of a loan by one company to another, the fact that it is not part of the lending company's business to make loans generally is disregarded; and

(*b*)   as requiring the taxpayer either to show that no special relationship exists or to show the amount of interest which would have been paid in the absence of that relationship.

[*Sec 808A; F(No 2)A 1992, s 52*].

Under many double tax agreements, **employees working in the UK,** who are resident in the overseas country but not resident in the UK, and who are not physically present in the UK for more than 183 days in the year of assessment, are exempt from UK tax on earnings paid by or on behalf of a non-UK resident employer. For this purpose, fractions of days are counted. (CCAB Memorandum TR 508, 9 June 1983). This exemption does not usually apply to public entertainers (and see now 51.4(*b*) NON-RESIDENTS AND OTHER OVERSEAS MATTERS), nor, under certain agreements, does it extend to employees working on the UK continental shelf (see Revenue Press Release 3 March 1989). For employees commencing a work assignment in the UK after 1 July 1995, and in all cases for 1996/97 onwards, claims will be refused where the cost of an employee's remuneration is borne by a UK resident company acting as the 'economic employer'. This would apply where, for example, the employee is seconded to the UK company, which obtains the benefit and bears the risks in relation to work undertaken by the employee, and to which the non-resident employer recharges the remuneration costs. It would also apply where the non-resident employer carries on a business of hiring out staff to other companies. (Revenue Tax Bulletin June 1995 p 220).

The specific provisions of the particular agreement concerned must be examined carefully. For relevant Court decisions, see Tolley's Tax Cases.

Where double tax relief applies no deduction for foreign tax is allowed in assessing the foreign income or gain [*Secs 795(2), 811(2)*] but if a taxpayer elects not to take credit allowable by an agreement, any foreign tax paid on that income in the place where it arises is *deductible* from the income for purposes of UK assessment, *except* that it is not so deductible where the UK assessment is on the basis of *remittances* to the UK. [*Secs 805, 811*]. Where tax on overseas income is not relieved, or is only partly relieved, under an agreement, unilateral relief (see 25.4 below) will normally apply. Where income of a UK close company is apportioned to a non-resident he will normally be exempt from UK income tax in respect of the apportioned income if his UK dividend income is relieved from UK higher rate tax under a double tax agreement. (Revenue Pamphlet IR 1, B22).

The following provisions supersede those of *Sec 790* (Unilateral Relief) to the extent, and as from the operative dates, specified in the various reciprocal agreements currently operative with the countries and territories that follow—(*SI* numbers in round brackets).

25.2 Double Tax Relief

Antigua (1947/2865; 1968/1096), **Australia** (1968/305; 1980/707), **Austria** (1970/1947; 1979/117; 1994/768), **Azerbaijan** (1995/762) from 6 April 1996 (UK) and 1 January 1996 (Azerbaijan),

Bangladesh (1980/708), **Barbados** (1970/952; 1973/2096), **Belarus** (1995/2706) (and see note below), **Belgium** (1987/2053) from 6 April 1990 (UK) and 1 January 1990 (Belgium), **Belize** (1947/2866; 1968/573; 1973/2097), **Bolivia** (1995/2707) from 6 April 1996 (UK) and 1 January 1996 (Bolivia), **Bosnia-Hercegovina** (see note below), **Botswana** (1978/183), **British Honduras** (see Belize), **Brunei** (1950/1977; 1968/306; 1973/2098), **Bulgaria** (1987/2054), **Burma** (see Myanmar),

Canada (1980/709; 1980/780; 1980/1528; 1985/1996; 1987/2071), **China** (1981/1119; 1984/1826), **Croatia** (see note below), **Cyprus** (1975/425; 1980/1529), **Czech Republic** (see note below),

Denmark (1980/1960; 1991/2877),

Eire (see 25.3 below), **Egypt** (1980/1091), **Estonia** (1994/3207) from 6 April 1995 (UK) and 1 January 1995 (Estonia),

Falkland Islands (1984/363; 1992/3206), **Faroe Islands** (1961/579; 1971/717; 1975/2190), **Fiji** (1976/1342), **Finland** (1970/153; 1980/710; 1985/1997; 1991/2878), **France** (1968/1869; 1973/1328; 1987/466; 1987/2055),

Gambia (1980/1963), **Germany** (1967/25; 1971/874), **Ghana** (1993/1800, and see note below) from 6 April 1995 (UK) and 1 January 1995 (Ghana), **Greece** (1954/142), **Grenada** (1949/361; 1968/1867), **Guernsey** (1952/1215; 1994/3209), **Guyana** (1992/3207) from 6 April 1993 (UK) and 1 January 1992 (Guyana),

Hungary (1978/1056),

Iceland (1991/2879) from 6 April 1992 (UK) and 1 January 1992 (Iceland), **India** (1981/1120; 1993/1801), **Indonesia** (1994/769) from 6 April 1995 (UK) and 1 January 1995 (Indonesia), **Isle of Man** (1955/1205; 1991/2880; 1994/3208), **Israel** (1963/616; 1971/391), **Italy** (1990/2590) from 6 April 1991 (UK) and 1 January 1991 (Italy), **Ivory Coast** (1987/169),

Jamaica (1973/1329), **Japan** (1970/1948; 1980/1530), **Jersey** (1952/1216; 1994/3210),

Kazakhstan (1994/3211) from 6 April 1993 (UK) and 1 January 1993 (Kazakhstan), **Kenya** (1977/1299), **Kiribati and Tuvalu** (1950/750; 1968/309; 1974/1271), **Korea (South)** (1978/786),

Lesotho (1949/2197; 1968/1868), **Luxembourg** (1968/1100; 1980/567; 1984/364),

Macedonia (see note below), **Malawi** (1956/619; 1964/1401; 1968/1101; 1979/302), **Malaysia** (1973/1330; 1987/2056), **Malta** (1995/763) from 6 April 1996 (UK) and 1 January 1996 (Malta), **Mauritius** (1981/1121; 1987/467), **Mexico** (1994/3212) from 6 April 1994, **Montserrat** (1947/2869; 1968/576), **Morocco** (1991/2881), **Myanmar** (1952/751),

Namibia (1962/2788; 1967/1490), **Netherlands** (1967/1063; 1980/1961; 1983/1902; 1990/2152), **New Zealand** (1984/365), **Nigeria** (1987/2057), **Norway** (1985/1998),

Pakistan (1987/2058), **Papua New Guinea** (1991/2882) from 6 April 1992 (UK) and 1 January 1992 (Papua New Guinea), **Philippines** (1978/184), **Poland** (1978/282), **Portugal** (1969/599),

Romania (1977/57), **Russia** (see note below),

St. Christopher (St. Kitts) and Nevis (1947/2872), **Sierra Leone** (1947/2873; 1968/1104), **Singapore** (1967/483; 1978/787), **Slovak Republic** (see note below), **Slovenia** (see note below), **Solomon Islands** (1950/748; 1968/574; 1974/1270), **South Africa** (1969/864), **South West Africa** (see Namibia), **Spain** (1976/1919; 1995/765), **Sri Lanka** (1980/713), **Sudan** (1977/1719), **Swaziland** (1969/380), **Sweden** (1961/619; 1984/366), **Switzerland** (1978/1408; 1982/714; 1994/3215),

Thailand (1981/1546), **Trinidad and Tobago** (1983/1903), **Tunisia** (1984/133), **Turkey** (1988/932),

Uganda (1993/1802) from 6 April 1994 (UK) and 1 January 1994 (Uganda), **Ukraine** (1993/1803) from 6 April 1994 (UK) and 1 January 1994 (Ukraine) (and see note below), **U.S.A.** (1946/1331; 1955/499; 1961/985; 1980/568; 1980/779, 1994/1418), **U.S.S.R.** (see note below), **Uzbekistan** (1994/770) from 6 April 1995 (UK) and 1 January 1995 (Uzbekistan) (and see note below),
Vietnam (1994/3216) from 6 April 1995 (UK) and various dates (Vietnam),
Yugoslavia (see note below),
Zambia (1972/1721; 1981/1816), **Zimbabwe** (1982/1842).

Shipping & Air Transport only—Algeria (Air Transport only) (1984/362), Argentina (1949/1435), Belarus (see note below), Brazil (1968/572), Cameroon (Air Transport only) (1982/1841), China (Air Transport only) (1981/1119), Ethiopia (Air Transport only) (1977/1297), Iran (Air Transport only) (1960/2419), Jordan (1979/300), Kuwait (Air Transport only) (1984/1825), Lebanon (1964/278), Russia (see note below), Saudi Arabia (Air Transport only) (1994/767) from 3 October 1994, Venezuela (1979/301; 1988/933), U.S.S.R. (see note below), Ukraine (see note below), Uzbekistan (see note below), Zaire (1977/1298).

(*Notes. Czechoslovakia.* The Convention published as *SI 1991 No 2876*, which took effect from 6 April 1992 (UK) and 1 January 1992 (Czechoslovakia), is treated as remaining in force between the UK and, respectively, the Czech Republic and the Slovak Republic. (Revenue Pamphlet IR 131, SP 5/93, 19 March 1993).

Ghana. The Convention published as *SI 1978 No 785* was subsequently found never to have been ratified in Ghana and consequently never to have had effect. The Arrangement published as *SR&O 1947 No 2868* with the Gold Coast accordingly continued in effect, and was reapplied from 6 April 1991 until such time as the new Convention (*SI 1993 No 1800*) came into effect. For the period from 6 April 1977 to 5 April 1991, whichever is more favourable to the taxpayer may be applied, out-of-date claims under the 1947 Arrangement being accepted for this purpose. (Revenue Press Release 31 January 1991).

U.S.S.R. The Convention published as *SI 1986 No 224* (which also continued in force the air transport agreement published as *SI 1974 No 1269*) is to be regarded as in force between the UK and Ukraine, Uzbekistan, the Russian Federation and Belarus until the coming into force of, respectively, *SI 1993 No 1803*, *SI 1994 No 770*, *SI 1994 No 3213* and *SI 1995 No 2706*. As regards the other former Soviet Republics, the UK will continue to apply the provisions of that Convention on the basis that it is still in force until such time as new arrangements take effect with particular countries. (Revenue Tax Bulletin May 1994 pp 132, 133).

Yugoslavia. The Convention published as *SI 1981 No 1815* is treated as remaining in force between the UK and, respectively, Croatia, Slovenia and Macedonia. The position as regards Bosnia-Hercegovina and the remaining Yugoslav republics remains to be established. (Revenue Pamphlet IR 131, SP 6/93, 19 March 1993).)

25.3   **EIRE** [*Sec 68; FA 1994, s 207(5); SI 1976 Nos 2151 and 2152; SI 1995 No 764*]

A Convention and Protocol 1976 replaced previous provisions between UK and Eire (the Republic of Ireland (RI)). Shipping and air transport profits, certain trading profits not arising through a permanent establishment, interest, royalties, pensions (other than Government pensions and salaries which are normally taxed by the paying Government only) are taxed in the country of residence. Salaries, wages and other similar remuneration (including directors) is taxed in the country where earned unless the employer is non-resident and the employee is present for not more than 183 days in the fiscal year and is not paid by a permanent establishment.

Where income is taxable in both countries, relief is given in the country of residence for the tax payable in the country of origin.

25.4 Double Tax Relief

The recipient of a dividend from a company resident in the other country is entitled to the related tax credit (except where the recipient is a company which controls, alone or with associates, 10% or more of the voting power of the paying company). Income tax up to 15% of aggregate of dividend and tax credit may be charged in country of source (but not on charity or superannuation scheme exempt in other country).

Capital gains on immovable property (and assets of a permanent establishment or fixed base) are taxed in country where situate, and gains on other property in the taxpayer's country of residence with credit given in the other country if also taxed there.

A further Convention relates to inheritance tax (previously capital transfer tax) (UK) and capital acquisitions tax (RI). Relief attaches to the property subject to the charge and is given by each country allowing a credit against its own tax if the property is situated in the other country.

25.4 **UNILATERAL RELIEF BY UK** [*Secs 790, 794*]

Taxes, other than those for which credit is available under the bilateral double tax agreements in 25.2 above, payable under the law of any territory outside the UK (and see 25.3 above for Eire) and computed by reference to income or gain *arising in that territory* are allowed (to the extent defined below) as a credit against UK income tax or corporation tax paid on that income or gain by UK residents. Relief is only available against UK tax chargeable under the same Schedule and Case as that under which the foreign income on which the foreign tax was borne is chargeable (*George Wimpey International Ltd v Rolfe Ch D 1989, 62 TC 597*). Where appropriate an apportionment must be made to determine what part of income may be regarded as 'arising in' the overseas territory, and in making that apportionment it is the principles of UK tax law which are to be applied (see *Yates v GCA International Ltd and cross-appeal Ch D, 1991, 64 TC 37* and Revenue Pamphlet IR 131, SP 7/91, 26 July 1991). The machinery and limits (with modifications as below) are substantially the same as those under which the bilateral agreements operate and the credit given is, basically, such as would be allowable were a double taxation agreement in force with the territory concerned. [*Secs 790(1)–(4), 794*]. See example in 25.8 below.

The modifications are:

(*a*) The foreign taxes must be charged on income or profits and correspond to income tax or corporation tax in the UK, but may include similar taxes payable under the law of a province, state or part of a country, or a municipality or other local body. [*Sec 790(12)*]. See *Yates v GCA International Ltd and cross-appeal Ch D, [1991] STC 157* where a tax imposed on gross receipts less a fixed 10% deduction was held to correspond to UK income tax or corporation tax. Following that decision, the Revenue amended their practice with effect from 13 February 1991. (Revenue Pamphlet IR 131, SP 7/91, 26 July 1991). Previously, all foreign taxes computed by reference to a proportion of the gross fee or contractual income, such that the tax could not reasonably be regarded as corresponding to a tax on net profits, were automatically excluded from relief. For claims made on or after 13 February 1991, and earlier claims unsettled at that date, foreign taxes will be examined to determine whether, in their own legislative context, they serve the same function as UK income and corporation taxes in relation to business profits, and are thus eligible for unilateral relief. Revenue Pamphlet IR 146 lists those overseas taxes which the Board consider admissible or inadmissible for relief as at 31 December 1994 (although see Revenue Tax Bulletin August 1995 p 244 as regards South African secondary tax on companies). Current information may be obtained on 0171–438 6643.

(*b*) The restriction to tax on '*income or gain arising in the territory*' does not apply in the case of the Channel Islands or the Isle of Man, and credit is given for CI or IOM tax if the claimant is resident for the particular year of assessment or accounting period either in the UK or the Channel Islands, or IOM as the case may be. [*Secs 790(5)(a), 794(2)(a)*].

(*c*)   Income from personal or professional services performed in a territory is deemed to arise in that territory, and credit for overseas tax on income from employments, etc. (where duties wholly or mainly performed in the overseas territory) is given against income tax under Schedule E on that income if the claimant is resident for the year of assessment either in UK or in the overseas territory. [*Secs 790(4), 794(2)(b)*].

(*d*)   Where an overseas company carries on a banking business through a UK branch or agency and suffers foreign tax on interest on a foreign loan made through that branch etc., double tax relief is available as if the UK branch were a UK bank. Tax payable in a country where the overseas company is taxable by reason of its domicile, residence or place of management is excluded. [*Sec 794(2)(c)*].

Foreign tax levied by reference to the value of assets employed to produce income chargeable to UK tax may, in practice, be allowed as a business expense under normal Schedule D, Case I rules. (Revenue International Tax Handbook, ITH 602).

25.5   **SPECIFIC MATTERS**

(*a*)   **Alimony.** Where alimony payments etc. under UK Court Order or agreement (technically a UK source) are made by an overseas resident, concessional relief by way of credit is allowed where (i) the payments are made out of the overseas income of the payer and subject to tax there, (ii) UK income tax if deducted from the payments is duly accounted for, and (iii) the payee is resident in the UK and effectively bears the overseas tax. (Revenue Pamphlet IR 1, A12).

(*b*)   (i)   **Amounts assessable in UK on the remittance basis.** Where double tax credit for foreign tax is allowable in respect of it, any income which is assessable on the basis of *remittance* is treated, for UK assessment purposes, as increased by the *foreign tax* on that income (but ignoring any notional tax under (*h*) below). [*Sec 795(1)(3)*].

(ii)   **Amounts assessable in UK on the arising basis.** Where income or gain is assessable to income tax or corporation tax on the basis of the full amount arising (not on remittance as in (i) above), and double tax credit is allowable in respect of foreign tax suffered on it, *no deduction* may be made for foreign tax on that, or any other, income or gain.

If the income is a dividend, credit is given for foreign taxes deducted from the dividend plus (either if provided for under the specific terms of a double tax agreement *or* if covered by unilateral relief under *Sec 790(6)*, which only applies to UK recipient companies with 10% holdings, etc., in the overseas company) 'underlying tax', being overseas taxes paid on the profits of the paying company (but ignoring any notional tax under (*h*) below). If credit for underlying tax is available, then the dividend is grossed-up by such tax for UK assessment purposes. [*Sec 795(2)*]. See further details in Tolley's Corporation Tax.

(iii)   **If the taxpayer does not take any credit** by way of either bilateral or unilateral relief, or if no UK double tax credit is otherwise allowable in respect of foreign income, any foreign tax paid on that income in the place where it arises is deductible from the income for purposes of UK assessment, *except* where the UK assessment is on the basis of *remittances* to the UK. [*Secs 805, 811*].

25.5 Double Tax Relief

(c) **Business Profits.** Where a UK resident pays tax in an overseas country on *business profits* arising there, that tax is allowed as a business expense if no double tax credit is allowable against UK tax on those profits, or the right to credit is forgone.

(d) **Capital Gains.** Relief for foreign taxes on *capital gains* is given against, and is limited to, the amount of UK capital gains tax on those gains. [*TCGA 1992, s 277*]. Capital gains accruing to companies are subject to corporation tax, and relief is available accordingly.

(e) **Claims** for credit under double tax arrangements must be made within, for 1996/97 and later years, five years after 31 January following the tax year in which the income or gain falls to be charged to tax (for earlier years, six years after the end of that tax year) or, for corporation tax purposes, six years after the end of the accounting period concerned. [*Sec 806(1); FA 1996, s 135, 21 Sch 23*]. Claims in respect of overlap profits (see (j) below) must be made within, for 1996/97 and later years, five years after 31 January following the latest tax year for which relief is due (for earlier years and also as regards claims in respect of opening years (see (j) below), six years after the latest such tax year). [*Sec 804(7); FA 1996, s 135, 21 Sch 22*].

Claims for credit must be sent to the inspector responsible for the relevant assessment but other claims for relief are made to the Board. [*Sec 788(6)*]. For appeals, see 64.8 RESIDENCE, ORDINARY RESIDENCE AND DOMICILE. Pending final agreement a provisional allowance can usually be obtained on application to the inspector.

(f) **Exchange rate.** Foreign tax is normally converted into sterling at the rate of exchange obtaining on the date it became payable. (Revenue Double Taxation Relief Manual, DT 845). Where part of foreign tax repaid and sterling was devalued in the period between payment and repayment, held relief due on net tax in foreign currency at the old rate (*Greig v Ashton Ch D 1956, 36 TC 581*).

(g) **Limit on Relief.** Where income is chargeable to *UK income tax*, credit for foreign tax suffered on that income is set against the income tax chargeable in respect of the doubly-taxed income. [*Secs 790(4), 793*]. But the relief is limited to the *difference* between the income tax (before double tax relief, but after any other income tax reduction) which would be borne by the claimant

    (i)   if he were charged on his *total income* (computed as in (b) above), and

    (ii)   if he were charged on that income *excluding* the income in respect of which the credit is to be allowed. [*Sec 796; FA 1994, 8 Sch 12*].

In no case may total double tax credits exceed the total income tax payable by the claimant for the year of assessment (less any income tax he is entitled to charge against any other person). [*Sec 796(3)*].

(h) **Notional Tax.** Under *Sec 788(5)* it may be provided that any tax which would have been payable in a foreign country but for a relief under the law of that territory given with a view to promoting industrial, commercial, scientific, educational or other development therein is nevertheless treated for purposes of credit against UK tax as if it had been paid. For example, credit is given for tax given up by Singapore under Singapore *Economic Expansion Incentives (Relief from Income Tax) Act 1967* (Revenue Press Release 9 May 1969) and by Malaysia under *Secs 21, 22, 26* of *Malaysian Investment Incentives Act 1968* (Revenue Press Release 5 March 1970). Similar relief may also be given where expressly provided in an agreement. [*Sec 788(5)(b)*]. For restrictions on relief available to banks in respect of such notional tax, see Tolley's Corporation Tax under Double Tax Relief.

(j) **Opening and Closing Years** [*Sec 804 as originally enacted*]. The following provisions apply for 1995/96 and earlier years as regards trades, professions and vocations commenced, and other sources of income first arising, before 6 April 1994 (see also (*n*) below). Credit for foreign tax paid in respect of income arising in the first three years of assessment on a new source of income (including, for Cases I & II of Schedule D, any period overlapping the end of those three years if the profits of that period affect the assessment for a later year) is allowed against UK income tax chargeable for any year in respect of that income, notwithstanding that credit for that foreign tax has already been allowed in an earlier year.

There are overriding provisions limiting the credit allowable for any year by reference to the total of credit due for all the relevant years above, and for cases where the number of UK periods of assessment exceeds the number of foreign periods. Also provision for recovery, by Case VI assessment, of excessive credit arising from operation of the ceased source rules so far as any income fails thereunder to enter into any basis period for assessment.

Overlap profits [*Sec 804; FA 1994, s 217; FA 1996, s 135, 21 Sch 22*]. For 1994/95 and subsequent years as regards trades, etc. commenced after 5 April 1994 and for 1996/97 and subsequent years as regards those commenced on or before that date, provisions similar to those above apply by reference to 'overlap profits' (see 71.19 SCHEDULE D, CASES I AND II) arising in taxing a trade, etc. Recovery of excess credit applies where, and to the extent that, relief is given for overlap profits either on cessation of the trade or on a change of accounting date resulting in a basis period of longer than twelve months. Recovery is achieved by reducing the credit otherwise available for the year of relief and, if there is still an excess, by assessment under Case VI.

See also (*n*) below.

(*k*)   **Partnerships.** It was held in the case of *Padmore v CIR CA 1989, 62 TC 352* that, where profits of a non-UK resident partnership were exempt under the relevant double tax treaty, the profit share of a UK resident partner was thereby also exempt. This decision was, however, reversed by subsequent legislation with retrospective effect, see 53.15 PARTNERSHIPS.

(*l*)   **Royalties and 'know-how' payments.** Notwithstanding that credit for overseas tax is ordinarily given only against income which arises (or is deemed to arise) in the overseas territory concerned, the Revenue treatment as regards this class of income is as follows.

Income payments made by an overseas resident to a UK trader for the use, in that overseas territory, of any *copyright, patent, design, secret process or formula, trade mark, etc.*, may be treated, for credit purposes (whether under double tax agreements or by way of unilateral relief) as income arising outside the UK—*except* so far as they represent consideration for services (other than merely incidental) rendered in the UK by the recipient to the payer (Revenue Pamphlet IR 1, B8).

For the treatment of sales of 'know-how' etc., see 71.66 SCHEDULE D, CASES I AND II.

(*m*)   **Transfer pricing.** Under EEC Convention *90/463/EEC*, Member States are required to adopt certain procedures, and to follow the opinion of an advisory commission, in transfer pricing disputes. *Sec 815B* makes provision for domestic legislation and double tax agreements to be overridden where necessary under the Convention (which came into force on 1 January 1995). [*F(No 2)A 1992, s 51*]. See 3.9 ANTI-AVOIDANCE.

(*n*)   **Transitional provisions on changeover from preceding year to current year basis of assessment.** Special provisions apply as regards trades, professions and vocations commenced before 6 April 1994 and sources of income within Schedule D,

25.6 Double Tax Relief

Cases IV and V first arising before that date, where the trade, etc. or other source continues (uninterrupted) beyond 6 April 1997.

(1) Where the assessment for 1996/97 is itself computed under the transitional rules in 71.20 SCHEDULE D, CASES I AND II or 73.9 SCHEDULE D, CASES IV AND V (such that a percentage of the profits/income of an extended basis period is charged to tax), any credit for foreign tax is similarly computed.

(2) Where credit has been given for foreign tax in respect of the opening years of assessment under *Sec 804 as originally enacted* (see (*j*) above) and the trade or other source later ceases, recovery of any excess credit is made by assessment under Case VI. The excess credit is calculated as if no income had escaped tax under the transitional rules mentioned in (1) above and as if (1) above had itself not applied.

(3) Where the trade, etc. ceases in 1997/98 or 1998/99 and either of the directions in 71.24 SCHEDULE D, CASES I AND II is given, or the source of Case IV or V income ceases before 6 April 1998, (1) and (2) above do not apply and *Sec 804* has effect as originally enacted (see (*j*) above).

(4) In applying the transitional rules mentioned in (1) above, any double tax relief to be given by deduction under *Sec 811* because no credit is allowable (see (*b*)(iii) above) is given *before* applying the appropriate percentage.

[*FA 1994, 20 Sch 10–14; FA 1995, s 122(4)(5)*].

25.6   **PAYMENTS ABROAD BY UK RESIDENTS**

Under *SI 1970 No 488* (as amended) a UK resident paying to a resident of a country with which the UK has a double tax agreement income which under that agreement is wholly or partially relieved (other than a dividend or other distribution by a company) may be required, by notice from the Board of Inland Revenue, to make such payments without deducting UK income tax, or under deduction of tax at, or not exceeding, a specified rate. Applications for such relief from deduction should be sent to Inland Revenue, FICO (International), Fitzroy House, PO Box 46, Nottingham NG2 1BD. Where a notice is given, the payer, if otherwise chargeable with, or liable to account for, tax on such payments (under *Sec 349*, etc., see 23.3 DEDUCTION OF TAX AT SOURCE) is exempted from that liability if the notice requires him to pay the income gross, and in other cases need account for tax only at the rate specified. The payer may, nevertheless, treat the gross amount of the payment as a loss for relief purposes, while if the payment is made by a company it is treated for purposes of *Sec 338(4)* as if tax has been deducted from it and accounted for under *Sec 349*. Where the payer would have been entitled (under *Sec 348*) to retain the tax deducted (as having made the payment out of income subjected to income tax) he is given, against the income tax otherwise payable by him for that year, an allowance equal to the additional tax which, but for the notice, he would have been entitled to deduct from the payment.

For Revenue practice in relation to claims for payment of interest to non-residents without deduction of tax, and in particular where payments are made in full in advance of the issue (or refusal) of a gross payment notice, see Revenue Tax Bulletin August 1994 p 153.

Under *SI 1973 No 317*, the Revenue may make arrangements with a UK resident company whereby it may pay to a non-resident shareholder that part of the tax credit relating to a dividend to which he is entitled under the terms of a double tax agreement. See Tolley's Corporation Tax (under Double Tax Relief).

25.7   **COMPANIES**

Companies enjoy the benefit of the foregoing double tax reliefs and they can in certain circumstances claim relief for underlying taxes in respect of overseas dividends receivable by them (being the overseas taxes borne by the paying company on its profits). See 25.5(*b*)(ii) above and Tolley's Corporation Tax (under Double Tax Relief).

25.8   **EXAMPLE OF RELIEF BY CREDIT**

A single man has, for 1996/97, UK earnings of £15,000 and foreign income from property of £2,000 on which foreign tax of £400 has been paid. He is entitled to the personal allowance of £3,765.

(*a*)   *Tax on total income*

Earnings	15,000	
Income from property	2,000	(foreign tax £400)
	17,000	
Personal allowance	3,765	
Taxable income	£13,235	
Tax on £13,235 @ 20/24%	£3,020.40	

(*b*)   *Tax on total income less foreign income*

Earnings	15,000
Personal allowance	3,765
Taxable income	£11,235
Tax on £11,235 @ 20/24%	£2,540.40

The difference in tax between (*a*) and (*b*) is £480. The foreign tax is less than this and full credit of £400 is available against the UK tax payable. If the foreign tax was £600, the credit would be limited to £480 and the balance of £120 would be unrelieved.

26 Enterprise Investment Scheme (and BES)

(See also Revenue Pamphlets IR137 and (as regards the BES) IR51 and IR85.)

26.1   The Enterprise Investment Scheme ('EIS') was introduced by *FA 1994, s 137, 15 Sch* in respect of shares issued on or after 1 January 1994. It 'revives' the earlier legislation governing the Business Expansion Scheme ('BES'), which was withdrawn by *F(No 2)A 1992* for shares issued after 31 December 1993, but with substantial amendment. The EIS is described at 26.2 *et seq.* below. The BES is dealt with at 26.17 *et seq.* below.

Revenue practices and concessions which apply to the BES are, where relevant, carried forward to the EIS.

The EIS is dealt with in this chapter under the following headings.

26.2   **CONDITIONS FOR RELIEF**

A 'qualifying individual' is eligible for relief under the EIS if

(*a*)   'eligible shares' in a 'qualifying company' for which he has subscribed are issued to him,

(*b*)   those shares are issued to raise money for the purpose of a 'qualifying business activity', and

(*c*)   the money so raised (or all but an insignificant amount of it) is employed wholly for that purpose by the end of the twelve months following the issue or, if the only 'qualifying business activity' falls within 26.6(*a*) below, and if later, by the end of the twelve months starting when the company (or subsidiary) began to carry on the 'qualifying trade'.

[*Sec 289(1)(3); FA 1994, 15 Sch 2*].

Relief is denied unless the shares are subscribed and issued for *bona fide* commercial purposes and not as part of a scheme or arrangement a main purpose of which is the avoidance of tax. [*Sec 289(6); FA 1994, 15 Sch 2*].

Relief is available where eligible shares are held on a bare trust for two or more beneficiaries as if each beneficiary had subscribed as an individual for all of those shares, and as if the amount subscribed by each was the total subscribed divided by the number of beneficiaries. [*Sec 311(2); FA 1994, 15 Sch 26(a)*].

Relief is also available where shares are subscribed for by a nominee for the individual claiming relief, including the managers of an investment fund approved by the Board for this purpose (an '*approved fund*'). With regard to an approved fund closed for the acceptance of further investments, the provisions of *Secs 289A, 289B* (dealing with the form and attribution of relief, see 26.8 below) apply as if the eligible shares were issued at the time at which the fund was closed, provided that the amount subscribed on behalf of the individual for eligible shares issued within six months after the closure of the fund is not less than 90% of the individual's investment in the fund. [*Sec 311(1)(2A)(2B); FA 1988, s 53; FA 1994, 15 Sch 26(b)*]. The Revenue have published guidelines setting out the principal criteria used in deciding whether to approve an investment fund for this purpose, and covering the procedures to be followed in applying for approval. They are available free of charge from Brian Lodde, Inland Revenue, Company Tax Division, Room M22, West Wing, Somerset House, London WC2R 1LB.

For the date on which shares are issued, see *National Westminster Bank plc v CIR; Barclays Bank plc v CIR HL, [1994] STC 580.*

26.3   A '*qualifying individual*' is an individual who subscribes for the 'eligible shares' on his own behalf and who (except as below) is not at any time in the 'relevant period' 'connected with' the issuing company. He is '*connected with*' the issuing company if he or an '*associate*' (within *Sec 417(3)(4)* but excluding a brother or sister) is either:

(*a*)   an employee, partner, or director of, or an employee or director of a partner of, the issuing company or any 'subsidiary'; or

(*b*)   an individual who directly or indirectly possesses or is entitled to acquire (whether he is so entitled at a future date or will at a future date be so entitled)

(i)   more than 30% of the voting power, the issued ordinary share capital, or the loan capital and issued share capital of the issuing company or any 'subsidiary' (loan capital including any debt incurred by the company for money borrowed, for capital assets acquired, for any right to income created in its favour, or for insufficient consideration, but excluding a debt incurred for overdrawing a bank account in the ordinary course of the bank's business), or

(ii)   such rights as would entitle him to more than 30% of the assets of the issuing company or any 'subsidiary' available for distribution to the company's equity holders (as under *18 Sch 1, 3*—see Tolley's Corporation Tax under Groups of Companies); or

(*c*)   an individual who has control (as defined by *Sec 840*, see 20.8 CONNECTED PERSONS) of the issuing company or any 'subsidiary'; or

(*d*)   an individual who subscribes for shares in the issuing company as part of an arrangement providing for another person to subscribe for shares in another company with which, were that other company an issuing company, the individual (or any other individual party to the arrangements) would be connected as above,

and rights or powers of associates are taken into account as regards (*b*)–(*d*) above.

As regards (*b*) (i) above, an investor who acquires one of two subscriber shares in a company from company formation agents will, by concession, not be regarded as being connected with the company solely because, until further shares are issued, he holds 50% of the company's issued share capital, provided that the company enters into no other transactions in the meanwhile. (Revenue Pamphlet IR 1 (November 1995 Supplement), A76).

A '*subsidiary*' for these purposes is a company more than 50% of whose ordinary share capital is at any time in the 'relevant period' owned by the issuing company, regardless of when that condition came to be fulfilled, and whether or not it is fulfilled while the individual falls within (*a*)–(*d*) above in respect of it.

As regards (*a*) above, directorships are taken into account only where the individual or an associate (or a partnership of which either of them is a member) receives or is entitled to receive, during the 'relevant period', a payment (whether directly or indirectly or to his order or for his benefit) from the issuing company or a 'related person' other than by way of

(i)   payment or reimbursement of allowable expenditure under Schedule E,

(ii)   interest at no more than a commercial rate on money lent,

(iii)   dividends, etc. representing no more than a normal return on investment,

(iv)   payment for supply of goods at no more than market value,

(v)   rent at no more than a reasonable and commercial rent for property occupied, or

(vi)   any reasonable and necessary remuneration for services rendered (other than secretarial or managerial services, or those rendered by the payer) which is chargeable under Schedule D, Case I or II,

and a '*related person*' is any company of which the individual or an associate is a director and which is a subsidiary of the issuing company, or a partner of the issuing company or a subsidiary, 'subsidiary' for this purpose requiring ownership of more than 50% of ordinary share capital at some time in the 'relevant period'.

For these purposes, in the case of a person who is both a director and an employee of a company, references to him in his capacity as a director include him in his capacity as an employee, but otherwise he is not treated as an employee.

The '*relevant period*' for these purposes is that beginning with the incorporation of the company (or, if later, two years before the date of issue of the shares) and ending five years after the date of issue of the shares.

An individual who is connected with the issuing company may nevertheless qualify for relief if he is so connected only by reason of his (or his associate's) being a director of (or of a partner of) the issuing company or any subsidiary receiving, or entitled to receive, remuneration (including any benefit or facility) as such, provided that:

(A)   the remuneration (leaving out any within (vi) above) is reasonable remuneration for services rendered to the company as a director;

(B)   he subscribed for eligible shares in the company at a time when he had never been either connected with the issuing company or an employee of any person who previously carried on the trade, business, profession or vocation carried on by the issuing company,

and where those conditions are satisfied in relation to an issue of eligible shares, subsequent issues are treated as fulfilling (B) where they would not otherwise do so, provided that they are made within five years of the date of the last issue which did fulfil (B).

Parallel trades. For shares issued **before 29 November 1994**, relief may be denied if, on the date of issue of the shares (or, if later, the date on which the company commences trading) the individual is both one of a group of persons who either control the company (within *Sec 416*) or together own more than a half share (determined as under *Sec 344(1)(a)(b)(2)(3)*) in the trade carried on by the company, and also, individually or as one of a group, so controls another company or has such an interest in another trade, business, profession or vocation. Where the trade (or a substantial part of it) carried on by the issuing company is concerned with the same or similar types of property or provides the same or similar services or facilities, and serves substantially the same outlets or markets, as the other trade etc. or the trade etc. carried on by the other company, the individual will not qualify for relief in respect of any shares in the issuing company. Rights and powers of associates are taken into account, as are trades etc. carried on by companies more than 50% of whose ordinary share capital is, at the relevant date (as above), owned by the company concerned.

[*Secs 291, 291A, 291B, 292, 312(1)(1A)(a); FA 1994, 15 Sch 5, 6; FA 1995, s 66(2)*].

26.4   '*Eligible shares*' are new ordinary shares which, for five years after issue, carry no present or future preferential right to dividends or to assets on a winding-up or to be redeemed. [*Sec 289(7); FA 1994, 15 Sch 2*].

26.5   A '*qualifying company*' may be resident in the UK or elsewhere. It must, throughout the 'relevant period' (see 26.6 below), be 'unquoted' and either

(*a*)   it must exist wholly for the purpose of carrying on one or more 'qualifying trades' (see 26.7 below) (disregarding purposes incapable of having any significant effect on the extent of the company's activities), or

(*b*)   its business must consist of holding shares or securities of, or making loans to, 'qualifying subsidiaries' (see 26.14 below), with or without the carrying on of one or more qualifying trades.

In relation to similar provisions under the BES, a company falling within (*a*) for part of the relevant period and within (*b*) for the remainder was regarded as meeting the condition throughout the period. (ICAEW Technical Memorandum TR831, 19 April 1991).

A company is '*unquoted*' if none of its shares, etc. are listed on a recognised stock exchange or on a foreign exchange designated for the purpose, or dealt in on the Unlisted Securities Market or outside the UK by such means as may be designated for the purpose. Securities on the Alternative Investment Market ('AIM') are treated as unquoted for these purposes. (Revenue Press Release 20 February 1995). If it is unquoted at the time of the share issue, it does not cease to be unquoted in relation to those shares because any shares etc. of the company subsequently become so listed, or start to be dealt in by any means designated by an order made after the date of the share issue.

Although a winding-up or dissolution in the relevant period generally prevents a company meeting the above conditions, they are deemed met if the winding-up or dissolution is for *bona fide* commercial reasons and not part of a scheme a main purpose of which is tax avoidance, provided that any net assets are distributed to members (or dealt with as *bona vacantia*) before the end of the relevant period or (if later) the end of three years from the commencement of winding-up.

The company must not at any time in the relevant period either

(i)   have share capital which includes any issued shares not fully paid up (or which would not be fully paid up if any undertaking to pay cash to the company at a future date were disregarded), or

(ii)   control another company (other than a 'qualifying subsidiary', see 26.14 below) or be controlled by another company ('control' being as defined by *Sec 416*, and being considered with or without connected persons within *Sec 839*), or

(iii)   be a 51% subsidiary of another company, or have a 51% subsidiary (other than a 'qualifying subsidiary', see 26.14 below) (by reference to the holding of more than 50% of ordinary share capital), or

(iv)   be capable of falling within (ii) or (iii) by virtue of any arrangements.

[*Secs 293, 312(1)–(1E); FA 1994, 15 Sch 7*].

Land and buildings. Subject to an exemption for small issues (see below), there is an additional exclusion if, at any time during the relevant period **and before 29 November 1994**, the value of the company's 'interests in land' (or, where lower, the value of those interests immediately after the issue of the shares, adjusted as below) exceeds half the value of all its assets (or such other fraction as the Treasury may substitute by statutory instrument). The value of those interests is for this purpose the aggregate of the market values of each such interest less debts secured thereon (including by floating charges), unsecured debts not falling due within twelve months and any amount paid up in respect of shares carrying a present or future preferential right to the company's assets on a winding-up. The value of the company's assets as a whole is similarly the aggregate market value less the company's debts and liabilities (including any amount paid up in respect of shares carrying a present or future preferential right to the company's assets on a winding-up, but excluding any other share capital, share premium account or reserves). Any question, on appeal, of the value of an interest in land is determined by the appropriate Lands Tribunal.

An 'interest in land' is valued on the assumption that there is no source of mineral deposits in the land exploitable other than by opencast mining or quarrying, and ignoring any oil exploration borehole.

Where the company is a member of a partnership, the value of any 'interest in land' held by the partnership is apportioned as on a dissolution of the partnership.

A qualifying company and its subsidiaries are treated as one company for these purposes, but ignoring any debts and liabilities between such companies.

'*Interest in land*' is widely defined to include rights related to land, and rights to obtain an interest etc. from another which depend on that other's ability to grant the interest etc., but excludes the interest of a creditor secured by any mortgage or charge over land. Valuation of such an interest excludes any plant or machinery which is, in law, part of the land etc..

The adjustments referred to above to the value of the company's interests in land held immediately after the issue of the shares are:

(A)   the addition of the cost(s) (i.e. consideration given, ignoring any discount for postponement of right to receive it) of any subsequent acquisitions of interests in land, and of any enhancement expenditure relating to interests in land; and

(B)   the deduction of any consideration for the disposal of, or grant of any interest out of, any interest in land, or derived from the ownership of interests in land (but excluding rent).

The value of an interest falls to be adjusted where the interest is under a lease at rent exceeding a full market rent. Contingent liabilities are disregarded unless and until the Board is satisfied that they have become enforceable and have been (or are being) enforced, whereon the necessary adjustments are made.

These restrictions do not apply where the total raised by the issue in question and any other issue in the previous twelve months does not exceed £50,000 and where that limit is exceeded, they apply only to the excess. The figure of £50,000 is reduced where, at any time in the relevant period, the company (or a subsidiary) carries on a trade in partnership, or in a joint venture, with another company.

Any restriction of relief under these provisions is apportioned amongst the qualifying individuals subscribing for otherwise eligible shares in proportion to their subscriptions, subject to determination on appeal by the General (or, in certain cases, the Special) Commissioners.

These restrictions ceased to apply with effect from 29 November 1994.

[*TMA s 47B; Secs 293(8A)(8B), 294–296, 312(1A); FA 1988, s 52; FA 1994, 15 Sch 8, 9; FA 1995, s 66(3)*].

Advance provisional approval. A company may submit its proposals for using the EIS to the inspector who normally deals with its tax affairs. If satisfied as to the purposes for which the money raised will be used, the company's status as a qualifying company and the eligibility of the shares to be issued under the proposals, the inspector may grant advance provisional approval, of which investors may be informed, although in the end the question of whether the company qualifies for the scheme is one of fact which cannot be determined in advance. (Revenue Pamphlet IR 137, page 30).

26.6   Any of the following is a '*qualifying business activity*' in relation to the issuing company, provided that, at any time in the 'relevant period' when it is carried on, it is carried on 'wholly or mainly in the UK'.

    (*a*)   The issuing company or any subsidiary (within *Sec 308*, see 26.14 below) carrying on a 'qualifying trade' which it is carrying on on the date of issue of the shares, or preparing to carry on such a trade which, on the date of issue of the shares, it intends to carry on 'wholly or mainly in the UK' and which it begins to carry on within two years after that date.

    (*b*)   The issuing company or any subsidiary carrying on either research and development or oil exploration which it is carrying on on the date of issue of the shares, or which it begins to carry on immediately afterwards, and from which it is intended will be derived a 'qualifying trade' which the company or a subsidiary will carry on 'wholly or mainly in the UK'.

As regards (*b*) above, in relation to oil exploration, there are further conditions relating to exploration and appraisal or development licences. 'Research and development' includes any activity intended to result in a computer program or a patentable invention under the *Patents Act 1977* (see Revenue Pamphlet IR 137, page 27).

The '*relevant period*' for these purposes is the period beginning with the date of issue of the shares and ending either three years after that date or, where (*a*) above applies and the company (or subsidiary) was not carrying on the 'qualifying trade' on that date, three years after the date on which it begins to carry on the trade.

[*Secs 289(2)(4)(5)(8), 312(1A)(b); FA 1994, 15 Sch 2*].

In considering whether a trade is carried on '*wholly or mainly in the UK*', the totality of the trade activities is taken into account. Regard will be had, for example, to the locations at which assets are held, and at which any purchasing, processing, manufacturing and selling is done, and to the places at which the employees customarily carry out their duties. No one of these factors is itself likely to be decisive in any particular case. Accordingly a company may carry on some such activities outside the UK and yet satisfy the requirement, provided that the major part of them, that is over one-half of the aggregate of these activities, takes place within the UK. Thus relief is not excluded solely because some or all of a company's products or services are exported, or because its raw materials are imported, or because its raw materials or products are stored abroad, or because its marketing facilities are supplied from abroad. Similar principles apply in considering the trade(s) carried on by a company and its qualifying subsidiaries.

In the particular case of a ship chartering trade, the test is satisfied if all charters are entered into in the UK and the provision of crews and management of the ships while under charter take place mainly in the UK. If these conditions are not met, the test may still be satisfied depending on all the relevant facts and circumstances.

(Revenue Pamphlet IR 131 (October 1995 Supplement), SP 2/94, 9 May 1994, revised by Revenue Press Release 14 September 1995).

26.7   To be a '*qualifying trade*' a trade may not, at any time in the 'relevant period' (as defined in 26.6 above), consist to a substantial extent of, or of a combination of:

(*a*)   dealing in land, commodities or futures, or in shares, securities or other financial instruments; or

(*b*)   dealing in goods otherwise than in an ordinary trade of wholesale or retail distribution (see below); or

(*c*)   banking, insurance or any other financial activities; or

(*d*)   oil extraction activities (but without prejudice to relief in respect of oil exploration (see 26.6(*b*) above) for which the activities would otherwise qualify); or

(*e*)   leasing or letting or receiving royalties or licence fees; or

(*f*)   providing legal or accountancy services; or

(*g*)   providing services or facilities for any trade, profession or vocation concerned in (*a*) to (*f*) and carried on by another person (other than a parent company), where one person has a 'controlling interest' in both trades.

Adventures and concerns in the nature of trade, and trades not carried on commercially and with a view to the realisation of profits, are also generally excluded.

The Revenue regard as 'substantial' for the above purposes a part of a trade which consists of 20% or more of total activities, judged by any reasonable measure (normally turnover or capital employed). (Revenue Inspectors' Manual, IM 6997). Similarly, as regards (*a*) above, it is understood that it was not intended to exclude from relief what is mainly a building trade, despite the technical position that what the builder sells is the land with the buildings on it. (Tolley's Practical Tax 1984 p 206).

As regards (*b*) above, a trade of wholesale or retail distribution is a trade consisting of the offer of goods for sale either to persons for resale (or processing and resale) (which resale must be to members of the general public) by them ('*wholesale*') or to the general public ('*retail*'), and a trade is not an ordinary wholesale or retail trade if it consists to a substantial extent of dealing in goods collected or held as an investment (or of that and any other activity within (*a*)–(*g*) above), and a substantial proportion of such goods is held for a significantly longer period than might reasonably be expected for a vendor trying to dispose of them at market value. Whether such trades are 'ordinary' is to be judged having regard to the following features, those under (A) supporting the categorisation as 'ordinary', those under (B) being indicative to the contrary.

(A)   (i)   The breaking of bulk.

(ii)   The purchase and sale of goods in different markets.

(iii) The employment of staff and incurring of trade expenses other than the cost of goods or of remuneration of persons connected (within *Sec 839*) with company carrying on such a trade.

(B)   (i)   The purchase or sale of goods from or to persons connected (within *Sec 839*) with the trader.

(ii)   The matching of purchases with sales.

(iii) The holding of goods for longer than might normally be expected.

(iv)   The carrying on of the trade at a place not commonly used for wholesale or retail trading.

(v)   The absence of physical possession of the goods by the trader.

As regards (e) above, a company engaged throughout the relevant period in the production of original master films, tapes or discs is not excluded from the scheme by reason only of its receipt by way of trade of royalties or licence fees, provided that all royalties and licence fees received by it in the relevant period are in respect of films etc. produced by it in that relevant period or in respect of by-products arising therefrom. The company may also be engaged in the distribution of films produced by it in the relevant period. Similarly royalties and licence fees attributable to research and development which a company carrying on a trade has engaged in throughout the relevant period do not prevent the trade being a qualifying trade.

Also as regards (e) above, a trade will not be excluded by reason only of its consisting of letting ships, other than oil rigs or pleasure craft (as defined), on charter, provided that

(i)   the company beneficially owns all the ships it so lets,

(ii)   every ship beneficially owned by the company is UK-registered,

(iii)   throughout the relevant period, the company is solely responsible for arranging the marketing of the services of its ships, and

(iv)   in relation to every letting on charter, certain conditions as to length and terms of charter, and the arm's length character of the transaction, are fulfilled,

and if any of (i)–(iv) above is not fulfilled in relation to certain lettings, only those lettings are taken into account in determining whether a substantial part of the trade consists of activities within (a)–(g) above.

In relation to (e) above, the Revenue has given its views on the scope of the exclusions in its Tax Bulletin. The leasing and letting exclusion covers all cases where (subject to reasonable conditions imposed by the trader) the customer is free to use the property as his own. Where this is not so—e.g. the hire of chauffeur-driven cars, or storage of articles by the trader in warehouses or safes—the exclusion does not apply. Royalties and licence fees are received where property rights are exploited by the company granting permission to another to make use of the property. In the case of royalties, the exclusion applies regardless of whether the company itself brought that property into existence (although see above as regards film and research and development royalties and licence fees). In the case of licence fees, the grant of the right to use the property is often incidental to the supply of services, and the exclusion does not apply in such cases. Similarly where, although there is no direct provision of services, continuous work is required to keep the property in a fit state for use, the question to be considered is whether such work is or is not greater than the work involved in obtaining the fees. The Revenue thus consider that receipts from an actively supervised gymnasium, with trainers in attendance to advise on personal fitness programmes and the use of equipment, are not licence fees, whereas receipts from letting out tennis courts to the general public by the hour are licence fees. The description of what is in effect a season ticket for the use of property as a membership fee (e.g. in the case of some sports clubs) does not affect the status of the payments. (Revenue Tax Bulletin August 1995 pp 240, 241).

As regards (g) above, a person has a 'controlling interest' in a trade carried on by a company if he controls (within Sec 416) the company; or if the company is close and he or an 'associate' is a director of the company and the owner of, or able to control, more than 30% of its ordinary share capital; or if at least half of its ordinary share capital is directly or indirectly owned by him. In any other case it is obtained by his being entitled to at least half of the assets used for, or income arising from, the trade. In either case, the rights and powers of a person's 'associates' are attributed to him. 'Associate' is as under Sec 417(3)(4), but excluding brothers and sisters.

26.8   Enterprise Investment Scheme (and BES)

The Treasury may, by statutory instrument, amend any of the above conditions.

[*Secs 297, 298; FA 1994, 15 Sch 10, 11*].

26.8   **FORM OF RELIEF**

Relief is (except as below) given for the year of assessment in which the shares were issued, by a reduction in what would otherwise be the individual's income tax liability by the lesser of

(*a*)   tax at the lower rate (currently 20%) for the year on the amount (or aggregate amounts) subscribed for eligible shares in respect of which he is eligible for relief, and

(*b*)   an amount sufficient to reduce that liability to nil.

In determining what would otherwise be the individual's income tax liability for the year for these purposes, no account is taken of:

(i)   any income tax reduction in respect of personal reliefs (see 1.15, 1.16, 1.17 ALLOWANCES AND TAX RATES) or qualifying maintenance payments (see 47.15 MARRIED PERSONS);

(ii)   any income tax reduction in respect of interest relief (see 43.5 INTEREST PAYABLE);

(iii)   any income tax reduction in respect of medical insurance (see 48.1 MEDICAL INSURANCE);

(iv)   any reduction of liability to tax by way of DOUBLE TAX RELIEF (25); or

(v)   any basic rate tax on income the tax on which the individual is entitled to charge against any other person or to deduct, retain or satisfy out of any payment.

Where shares in respect of which the individual is eligible for relief are issued before 6 October in a year of assessment, he may claim relief as if up to one half of the shares had been issued in the preceding year of assessment, subject to an overall limit of £15,000 on the amount of subscriptions which may be so treated. See 78.33 SELF-ASSESSMENT for general provisions regarding claims for payments made in one year of assessment to be carried back to an earlier year.

[*Sec 289A(1)–(5); FA 1994, 15 Sch 2*].

Relief for loss on disposal. Sec 574 (see 46.19 LOSSES), which grants income tax relief for certain losses on shares in unquoted trading companies, applies on the disposal by an individual of shares to which relief is attributable (see below) as it applies to shares in 'qualifying trading companies' under that *section. Secs 575(1)(3), 576(2)(3)* are similarly applied for this purpose. [*Sec 305A; FA 1994, 15 Sch 20*].

Attribution of relief to shares. Subject to any reduction or withdrawal of relief (see 26.12 *et seq.* below), where an individual's income tax liability is reduced for a year of assessment as above by reason of an issue or issues of shares made (or treated as made) in that year, the income tax reduction is attributed to that issue or those issues (being apportioned in the latter case according to the amount subscribed for each issue). Issues of shares by a company to an individual on the same day are treated as a single issue for this purpose. A proportionate amount of the reduction attributed to an issue is attributed to each share in the issue (and adjusted correspondingly for any subsequent bonus issue).

An issue to an individual part of which is treated as having been made in the preceding year (as above) is for all purposes (other than the minimum subscription limit, see 26.10 below) treated as two separate issues, one made on a day in the previous year.

Where relief attributable to an issue of shares falls to be withdrawn or reduced, the relief attributable to each of the shares in question is reduced to nil (if relief is withdrawn) or proportionately reduced (where relief is reduced).

[*Sec 289B; FA 1994, 15 Sch 2*].

On a *reorganisation of share capital* falling within *TCGA 1992, s 126(2)(a)* (i.e. where shares or debentures are allotted in proportion to an existing holding), the relief attributable to shares is reduced where both the amount subscribed for the shares and their market value immediately before the reorganisation exceed their market value immediately after the reorganisation. The reduction is in the same proportion as the lower of those two excesses bears to the amount subscribed for the shares. A similar reduction applies where, at any time in the 'relevant period' (see 26.3 above), rights on such a reorganisation are disposed of, and the reduction would have applied had the rights not been disposed of but the allotment made by virtue of the rights. No reduction applies, however, where the reorganisation occurred, or the rights were disposed of, after 28 November 1994. [*Sec 305; FA 1994, 15 Sch 19, FA 1995, s 66(4)*].

For the purposes of INTEREST ON OVERPAID TAX (41), any repayment of tax is treated as being in respect of tax payable in the year of assessment in which the shares are issued or, if later, the year in which the issuing company (or subsidiary) completed its first four months' trading (or, where relevant, ceased trading). [*Sec 289A(9); FA 1994, 15 Sch 2*]. For 1996/97 and subsequent years, see 78.33 SELF-ASSESSMENT.

26.9   *Examples*

Mr Jones is a married man with a salary of £30,000 per annum and no other income. In 1995/96 he subscribes for ordinary shares in two unquoted companies issuing shares under the enterprise investment scheme (EIS).

A Ltd was formed by some people in Mr Jones' neighbourhood to publish a local newspaper. 200,000 ordinary £1 shares were issued at par in August 1995 and the company started trading in September 1995. Mr Jones subscribed for 16,000 of the shares. Mr Jones becomes a director of A Ltd in September 1995, receiving director's fees of £5,000 per annum (£2,500 in 1995/96), a level of remuneration which is considered reasonable for services rendered by him to the company in his capacity as a director.

B Ltd, which is controlled by an old friend of Mr Jones, has acquired the rights to manufacture in the UK a new type of industrial cleaning solvent and requires additional finance. Mr Jones subscribed for 8,000 ordinary £1 shares at a premium of £1.50 per share in October 1995. The issue increases the company's issued share capital to 25,000 ordinary £1 shares.

Mr Jones will obtain tax relief in 1995/96 as follows.

Amount eligible for relief

		£
A Ltd	notes (*a*) and (*b*)	16,000
B Ltd	note (*c*)	Nil
Total (being less than the maximum of £100,000)		£16,000

26.9   Enterprise Investment Scheme (and BES)

Relief given   note (*d*)

	£
Salary	30,000
Director's remuneration (A Ltd)	2,500
Total income	32,500
Deduct Personal allowance	3,525
Taxable income	£28,975

Tax payable:

3,200 @ 20%	640.00
21,100 @ 25%	5,275.00
4,675 @ 40%	1,870.00
	7,785.00
Deduct EIS relief £16,000 @ 20%	3,200.00
	4,585.00
Deduct Married couple's allowance £1,720 @ 15%	258.00
Net tax liability	£4,327.00

Notes

(*a*)   Mr Jones is entitled to relief on the full amount of his investment in A Ltd regardless of the amount of relief claimed by other investors.

(*b*)   The fact that Mr Jones becomes a paid director of A Ltd *after* an issue to him of eligible shares does not prevent his qualifying for relief in respect of those shares providing his remuneration as a director is reasonable and he is not otherwise connected with the company (see 26.3 above).

(*c*)   Mr Jones is not entitled to relief against his income for his investment of £20,000 in B Ltd. As a result of the share issue he owns more than 30% of the issued ordinary share capital (8,000 out of 25,000 shares) and is therefore regarded as connected with the company and denied relief. See 26.3 above.

In 1996/97 Mr Jones subscribes for shares in three more unquoted companies trading in the UK and issuing shares under the EIS.

C Ltd is a local company engaged in the manufacture of car components. It issues a further 200,000 ordinary £1 shares at £1.80 per share in June 1996 and Mr Jones subscribes for 5,000 shares costing £9,000, increasing his stake in the company to 2%. He had originally held 9,000 shares, acquired by purchase at arm's length in May 1994 for £10,800.

D Ltd has been trading as a hotel and restaurant company for several years and requires an injection of capital to finance a new restaurant. Mr Jones and three other unconnected individuals each subscribe for 12,500 ordinary £1 shares at par in November 1996. The balance of 80,000 shares are held by Mr Jones' sister and niece.

E Ltd is an electronics company controlled by two cousins of Mr Jones. The company is seeking £1 million extra capital to enable it to expand and take advantage of new computer technology and raises it via the EIS. Mr Jones subscribes for 85,000 ordinary £1 shares at par in December 1996.

If he makes the optimum claims Mr Jones will obtain tax relief as follows

1995/96

C Ltd   note (*a*)   £4,500 @ 20% =   £900

1996/97

Amount eligible for relief

	£
C Ltd (£9,000 – £4,500 carried back)	4,500
D Ltd	12,500
E Ltd	85,000
Total	£102,000

But amount eligible for relief restricted to subscriptions of   £100,000

Relief given

	£
Salary	30,000
Director's remuneration	5,000
Total income	35,000
Deduct Personal allowance	3,765
Taxable income	£31,235

Tax payable:

3,900 @ 20%	780.00
21,600 @ 24%	5,184.00
5,735 @ 40%	2,294.00
	8,258.00

Deduct EIS relief:
£100,000 @ 20% = £20,000, but
restricted to   8,258.00

Net tax liability   Nil

Attribution of relief to shares   note (*b*)

	£
C Ltd shares $\dfrac{4,500}{102,000} \times £8,258$	364
D Ltd shares $\dfrac{12,500}{102,000} \times £8,258$	1,012
E Ltd shares $\dfrac{85,000}{102,000} \times £8,258$	6,882
	£8,258

26.10 Enterprise Investment Scheme (and BES)

Notes

(a) Since the C Ltd shares were issued before 6 October 1996, Mr Jones may elect to carry back up to half the amount subscribed, subject to an overriding maximum of £15,000, to the preceding tax year. The relief will be given in addition to that previously claimed for 1995/96 (see the example above). If Mr Jones had previously claimed relief on say £98,000 in 1995/96 the amount carried back would be restricted to £2,000 as relief in any one year may not be given on subscriptions of more than £100,000. See 26.8 above and 26.10 below.

(b) Relief is restricted in this example by (i) the £100,000 maximum (see (a) above) and (ii) an insufficiency in Mr Jones' tax liability. The relief attributable to each issue of shares (which will be relevant in the event of a disposal of the shares or withdrawal of relief—see 26.12 below) is found by apportioning the income tax reduction by reference to the amounts subscribed for each issue. (For this purpose, half of the C Ltd shares are regarded as having been separately issued in the previous year.) The relief so attributed to each issue is then apportioned equally between all the shares comprised in that issue. See 26.8 above.

(c) The unused married couple's allowance may be transferred to Mr Jones' wife under *ICTA 1988, s 257BB* (see 47.2 MARRIED PERSONS).

26.10 **LIMITS ON RELIEF**

(See 26.15 below as regards relief for married persons.)

Except in the case of investments through 'approved funds' (see 26.2 above), relief is restricted to investments of £500 or more in any one company in any year of assessment.

For 1994/95 and subsequent years, there is in all cases an upper limit of £100,000 on the amount in respect of which an individual may obtain relief in a year of assessment (regardless of whether the shares were issued in that year or in the following year). For 1993/94, the limit under the BES of £40,000 applies to the aggregate of relief under both schemes. [*Sec 290, 311(3); FA 1988, s 53; FA 1994, 15 Sch 3*].

There is also a restriction on the total amount of eligible shares which may be issued by a company within a specified period (see below) and attract relief. Where the money raised in such a period exceeds £1,000,000 the excess does not qualify for relief. The period specified is the longer of

(a) six months ending with the date of issue of the shares, and

(b) the period from the preceding 6 April to the date of issue.

Amounts raised which do not attract relief because the subscriber was not a qualifying individual (see 26.3 above), or had exceeded his personal limit or invested under the permitted minimum (see above), or because of an earlier application of these provisions, are not taken into account for the purposes of this restriction.

The limit is increased to £5,000,000 where the only qualifying trade(s) carried on by the issuing company (or by its subsidiaries) consist wholly or substantially wholly of operating or letting on charter ships other than oil rigs or pleasure craft, subject to similar conditions as apply to lettings of such ships in respect of there being a qualifying trade (see 26.7 above).

The £1,000,000 and £5,000,000 limits may be varied by Treasury order.

For the purposes of the above limits, amounts raised under the BES scheme are also taken into account.

Where, at any time in the 'relevant period' (see 26.6 above), the company issuing the shares (or a subsidiary) carries on any trade or part in partnership, or as a joint venture, with a company or companies (with or without other persons), the limit of £1,000,000 or £5,000,000 (as above) is divided by the total number of companies (but counting the issuing company and its subsidiaries as a single company) which are members of the partnership or parties to the joint venture.

Where these provisions restrict the amount of relief available to two or more individuals, the total relief available is apportioned amongst them according to the respective amounts subscribed for shares giving rise to the restriction and which would otherwise be eligible for relief.

[*Sec 290A; FA 1988, s 51(1); FA 1994, 15 Sch 4*].

26.11   CLAIMS FOR RELIEF

A claim for relief in respect of eligible shares issued by a qualifying company in a year of assessment cannot be allowed until the trade (or research and development or oil exploration) has been carried on for four months, but may otherwise be given at any time when it appears that the relief conditions may be satisfied. Where, for *bona fide* commercial reasons and not as part of a scheme or arrangement a main purpose of which was tax avoidance, a company carries on a trade for less than four months by reason of its being wound up or dissolved, a claim may be allowed after the trade so ceases. [*Sec 289A(6)–(8); FA 1994, 15 Sch 2*].

A claim for relief must be made not earlier than the end of the four-month period referred to above, and, for 1995/96 and earlier years, not later than twelve months after an inspector authorises the issue of a certificate (Form EIS 3) by the company. For 1996/97 and later years, the claim must be made not later than the fifth anniversary of 31 January following the year of assessment for which relief is claimed. The claimant must have received the said certificate before making the claim, and for shares issued before 6 April 1996 the certificate had to accompany the claim. The certificate must state that the conditions for relief, in respect of the company and the trade etc., are satisfied in relation to the eligible shares in question. A certificate may not be issued without the inspector's authority, nor where a notice under *Sec 310(2)* (see 26.16 below) has been given to the inspector. For appeal purposes, the inspector's refusal to authorise a certificate is treated as the refusal of a claim by the company.

Before issuing such a certificate, the company must supply to the inspector a statement (Form EIS 1) that those conditions were fulfilled from the beginning of the 'relevant period' (see 26.6 above), and that statement must contain such information as the Board may reasonably require, and a declaration that it is correct to the best of the company's knowledge and belief. The statement must be furnished to the inspector within two years after the end of the year of assessment in which the shares in question were issued (or, if the four-month period referred to above ends in the following year, within two years after the end of that four-month period).

If a certificate or statement is made fraudulently or negligently, or a certificate was issued despite being prohibited (as above), the company is liable to a fine of up to £3,000.

Special provisions (see *Sec 311(4)–(6)*) apply in relation to the issue of certificates where shares are held through an approved fund (see 26.2 above).

No application for postponement of tax pending appeal can be made on the ground that relief is due under these provisions unless a claim has been duly submitted.

For the purposes of INTEREST ON UNPAID TAX (41), tax charged by an assessment is regarded as due and payable notwithstanding that relief is subsequently given on a claim under these provisions, but is regarded as paid on the date on which a claim is made resulting in relief being granted, unless it was either in fact paid earlier or not due and payable until later. Interest is not refunded in respect of any subsequent discharge or repayment of tax giving effect to relief under these provisions.

[Secs 306, 311(4)–(6); FA 1994, 15 Sch 21; FA 1996, ss 134, 135, 20 Sch 22, 23, 21 Sch 7].

26.12 RESTRICTION OR WITHDRAWAL OF RELIEF

The following provisions apply to restrict or withdraw relief in certain circumstances. References to a reduction of relief include its reduction to nil, and references to the withdrawal of relief in respect of any shares are to the withdrawal of the relief attributable to those shares (see 26.8 above). Where no relief has yet been given, a reduction applies to reduce the amount which apart from the provision in question would be the relief, and a withdrawal means ceasing to be eligible for relief in respect of the shares in question. *[Sec 312(4); FA 1994, 15 Sch 27].*

Where an event giving rise to complete withdrawal of relief occurs at the same time as a disposal at a loss, the disposal is regarded as occurring first, so that relief may be only partially withdrawn (as below). (Revenue Inspectors' Manual, IM 7024).

Disposal of shares. Where eligible shares are disposed of (or an option granted the exercise of which would bind the grantor to sell them) before the end of the 'relevant period' (see 26.3 above):

(a)   if the disposal is at arm's length, relief attributable to those shares (see 26.8 above) is withdrawn or, if that relief exceeds an amount equal to lower rate tax (for the year in which the relief was given) on the disposal consideration, reduced by that amount;

(b)   otherwise, the relief is withdrawn.

Where the relief attributable to the shares was less than the lower rate of tax for the year of issue on the amount subscribed for the issue, the amount referred to in (a) above is correspondingly reduced.

Relief is also withdrawn where, during the relevant period, an option is granted to the individual, the exercise of which would bind the grantor to purchase the shares.

For these purposes, disposals are identified with shares of the same class issued earlier before shares issued later. Where shares are exchanged (without consideration) so that *TCGA 1992, s 127* applies to treat the new shares as the same asset as the old, this applies equally for the above purposes.

[Sec 299; FA 1994, 15 Sch 12].

See, however, 26.15 below as regards transactions between married persons.

Loan linked investments. Relief is denied where

(a)   a loan is made to the individual subscribing for shares or to an 'associate' (see 26.3 above) by any person at any time in the 'relevant period' (see 26.3 above), and

(b)   the loan would not have been made, or would not have been made on the same terms, if he had not subscribed, or had not been proposing to subscribe, for the shares.

The granting of credit to, or the assignment of a debt due from, the individual or associate is counted as a loan for these purposes.

[Sec 299A; FA 1993, s 111(1); FA 1994, 15 Sch 13].

For this restriction to apply, the test is whether the lender makes the loan on terms which are connected with the fact that the borrower (or an associate) is subscribing for eligible shares. The prime concern is why the lender made the loan rather than why the borrower applied for it. Relief would not be disallowed, for example, in the case of a bank loan if the bank would have made a loan on the same terms to a similar borrower for a different purpose. But if, for example, a loan is made specifically on a security consisting of or including the eligible shares (other than as part of a broad range of assets to which the lender has recourse), relief would be denied. Relevant features of the loan terms would be the qualifying conditions to be satisfied by the borrower, any incentives or benefits offered to the borrower, the time allowed for repayment, the amount of repayments and interest charged, the timing of interest payments, and the nature of the security. (Revenue Pamphlet IR 131 (October 1995 Supplement), SP 3/94, 9 May 1994, revised by Revenue Press Release 14 September 1995).

Value received from company. Where an individual subscribes for eligible shares in a company, and during the 'relevant period' (see 26.3 above) (and whether before or after the issue), 'receives value' from the company, any relief attributable to those shares (see 26.8 above) and not previously reduced in respect of the 'value received' is withdrawn or, if that relief exceeds an amount equal to lower rate tax (for the year in which the relief was given) on the 'value received', reduced by that amount. That amount is correspondingly reduced where the relief attributable to the shares was less than the lower rate of tax for the year of issue on the amount subscribed for the issue.

The above applies equally to 'value received' from a company which is a 51% subsidiary of the issuing company (i.e. a company more than 50% of whose ordinary share capital it owns) at any time in the relevant period (whether before or after the value is received).

An individual *'receives value'* from a company if it:

(*a*)   repays, redeems or repurchases any part of his holding of its share capital or securities, or makes any payment to him for giving up rights on its cancellation or extinguishment; or

(*b*)   repays any debt to him other than one incurred by the company on or after the date on which he subscribed for the shares which are the subject of relief and otherwise than in consideration of the extinguishment of a debt incurred before that date; or

(*c*)   pays him for the cancellation of any debt owed to him other than an *'ordinary trade debt'* (i.e. one incurred for normal trade supply of goods or services on normal trade credit terms (not in any event exceeding six months)) or one in respect of a payment falling within 26.3(i) or (vi) above; or

(*d*)   releases or waives any liability of his to the company (which it is deemed to have done if discharge of the liability is twelve months or more overdue) or discharges or undertakes to discharge any liability of his to a third person; or

(*e*)   makes a loan or advance to him (defined as including the deferring by him of any debt either to the company (other than an 'ordinary trade debt' (as above)) or to a third person but assigned to the company) which has not been repaid in full before the issue of the shares; or

(*f*)   provides a benefit or facility for him; or

(*g*)   transfers an asset to him for no consideration or for consideration less than market value, or acquires an asset from him for consideration exceeding market value; or

(*h*)   makes any other payment to him except one either falling within 26.3(i)–(vi) above or in discharge of an 'ordinary trade debt' (as above); or

(*i*)   is wound up or dissolved in circumstances such that the company does not thereby cease to be a 'qualifying company' (see 26.5 above), and he thereby receives any payment or asset in respect of ordinary shares held by him.

However, an individual does *not* receive value from a company by reason only of the payment to him (or to an associate) of reasonable remuneration (including any benefit or facility) for services as a company director, and for this purpose, if the individual is also an employee of the company, references to him in his capacity as a director include him in his capacity as an employee.

The amount of value received by the individual is that paid to or receivable by him from the company; or the amount of his liability extinguished or discharged; or the difference between the market value of the asset and the consideration (if any) given for it; or the net cost to the company of providing the benefit. In the case of value received within (*a*), (*b*) or (*c*) above, the market value of the shares, securities or debt in question is substituted if greater than the amount receivable.

Additionally, the individual '*receives value*' from the company if any person connected with the company (within 26.3 above) purchases any shares or securities of the company from him, or pays him for giving up any right in relation to such shares or securities. The value received is the amount receivable or, if greater, the market value of the shares, etc..

All payments or transfers, direct or indirect, to, or to the order of, or for the benefit of, an individual or 'associate' (see 26.3 above) are brought within these provisions, as are payments, etc. made by any person connected with the company (within *Sec 839*).

[*Secs 300, 301, 312(1); FA 1994, 15 Sch 14, 15*].

Value received other than by claimant. Relief is also restricted or withdrawn where an individual has obtained relief attributable (see 26.8 above) to eligible shares in a company, and during the 'relevant period' (see 26.3 above) the company (or any company more than 50% of whose ordinary share capital it owns) repays, redeems or repurchases any of its share capital belonging to a member other than (i) the individual or (ii) another individual whose relief is thereby withdrawn or reduced (as above), or makes any payment to any such member for giving up rights on the cancellation or extinguishment of any of its share capital. The relief is withdrawn or, if it exceeds an amount equal to lower rate tax (for the year in which the relief was given) on the sum receivable by the member (or, if greater, the nominal value of the share capital concerned), reduced by that amount. That amount is correspondingly reduced where the relief attributable to the shares was less than the lower rate of tax for the year of issue on the amount subscribed for the issue.

This restriction of relief does not apply to the redemption, within twelve months of issue, of any share capital of nominal value equal to the authorised minimum issued to comply with *Companies Act 1985, s 117* (or NI equivalent) where the company subsequently issues eligible shares.

Where in the relevant period, a member of the issuing company receives, or is or may become entitled to receive, any 'value' from the company or a 51% subsidiary (as above), then in applying the 30% test under 26.3(*b*)(i) at any subsequent time, the following amounts are treated as reduced:

(*a*) the amount of the company's ordinary share capital;

(*b*) the amount of that capital which, under 26.3(*b*), the individual directly or indirectly possesses or is entitled to acquire; and

(*c*) the amount at (*a*) not included in (*b*).

The reduction in (*b*) and (*c*) above is in each case the same proportion of the total amount as the value received by the member(s) entitled to the shares comprising the amount bears to the sum subscribed for those shares. The reduced amount at (*a*) is the sum of those at (*b*) and (*c*).

A member receives or is entitled to receive '*value*' where any payments, etc. are made to him which, if made to an individual, would fall within (*d*)–(*h*) above, excluding those within (*h*) made for full consideration. The amount of value received is as described above in relation to such payments, etc..

The capital *'relevant'* to a provision is those shares whose proportion of the total issued ordinary share capital is in each case compared with the appropriate percentage of that capital.

[*Sec 303; FA 1994, 15 Sch 17*].

Replacement capital. Relief attributable (see 26.8 above) to any shares in a company held by an individual is withdrawn if, at any time in the 'relevant period' (see 26.3 above), the company (or any subsidiary, as specially defined for this purpose) begins to carry on as its trade, business, profession or vocation (or part) a trade, etc. (or part) previously carried on at any time in that period otherwise than by the company or a subsidiary, or acquires the whole or the greater part of the assets used for a trade, etc. previously so carried on, and the individual is a person who, or one of the group of persons who together, either

(a)   owned more than a half share (ownership and, if appropriate, respective shares being determined as under *Sec 344(1)(a)(b)(2)(3)* (see Tolley's Corporation Tax under Losses) at any such time in the trade etc. previously carried on, and also own or owned at any such time such a share in the trade etc. carried on by the company, or

(b)   control (within *Sec 416*), or any such time have controlled, the company, and also, at any such time, controlled another company which previously carried on the trade, etc..

For these purposes, interests, etc. of 'associates' (see 26.3 above) are taken into account. There are special rules relating to shares held by certain directors of, or of a partner of, the issuing company or any subsidiary.

Relief is also withdrawn if the company, at any time in the relevant period, comes to acquire all the issued share capital of another company, and where the individual is a person who, or one of a group of persons who together, control or have, at any such time, controlled the company and who also, at any such time, controlled the other company.

[*Sec 302; FA 1994, 15 Sch 16*].

Assessments for withdrawing or reducing relief are made under Schedule D, Case VI for the year of assessment for which the relief was given. Relief may not be withdrawn on the grounds that the company is not a qualifying company (see 26.5 above), or that the requirements as to the purpose of the issue or the application of the proceeds are not fulfilled (see 26.2(*b*)(*c*) above), unless either the company has given notice under *Sec 310* (see 26.16 below) or the inspector has given notice to the company of his opinion that relief was not due (against which notice the company may appeal as though it were refusal of a claim by the company). Such notice by the inspector may not be given, nor any assessment withdrawing relief be made, more than six years after the end of the year of assessment in which the period mentioned in 26.2(*c*) above ends or, if later, the event giving rise to withdrawal occurs, but this restriction is without prejudice to the extension of time limits in cases of fraudulent or negligent conduct (see 6.4 BACK DUTY). No assessment may be made by reason of any event occurring after the death of the person to whom the shares were issued.

Where a person has made an arm's length disposal of all the ordinary shares issued to him by a company in respect of which relief has been given, no assessment may be made in respect of those shares by reason of any subsequent event unless he is at the time of that event 'connected with' the company (as under 26.3 above).

The reckonable date for the purposes of INTEREST ON UNPAID TAX (42) (or, where the self-assessment interest provisions have effect, the relevant date—see 78.22 SELF-ASSESSMENT)

26.13 Enterprise Investment Scheme (and BES)

is the date on which the event took place which gave rise to the withdrawal of relief, *except that*:

(a) where relief is withdrawn under the general anti-avoidance provision of *Sec 289(6)* (see 26.2 above), it is the date on which relief was granted or, if relief was given under PAYE, 5 April in the year of assessment in which relief was given;

(b) where relief is withdrawn due to failure to meet the condition at 26.2(c) above, it is the date on which relief was granted; and

(c) where relief is withdrawn as a result of the grant of an option the exercise of which would bind the grantor to purchase the shares (see above), it is the date of grant of the option.

[*Sec 307; FA 1989, s 149(4); FA 1993, s 111(3); FA 1994, 15 Sch 22; FA 1996, 18 Sch 5, 17(3)*].

26.13 *Examples*

In June 1997, Mr Jones, the investor in 26.9 above, sells 12,000 ordinary £1 shares in C Ltd (see 26.9 above), in an arm's length transaction, for £30,000.

The position is as follows.

Income tax

	£
1995/96	
Relief attributable to 2,500 shares treated as issued in 1995/96:	
2,500 shares at £1.80 per share = £4,500 @ 20%	900

Consideration received $\left(\dfrac{2,500}{12,000} \times £30,000 \right) = £6,250$ @ 20% $\qquad$ 1,250

	£
Excess of consideration over relief	£350
Relief withdrawn—Schedule D, Case VI assessment	£900

	£
1996/97	
Relief attributable to 500 shares	
500/2,500 × £364	73

Consideration received

$\left(\dfrac{500}{12,000} \times £30,000 \right) = £1,250 \times 73/(900 \text{ @ } 20\%) = £507$ @ 20% $\qquad$ 101

	£
Excess of consideration over relief	£28
Relief withdrawn—Schedule D, Case VI assessment	£73

Capital gains tax

1997/98	£	£
Disposal proceeds (12,000 shares)		30,000
Cost: 9,000 shares acquired May 1994	10,800	
3,000 shares acquired June 1996	5,400	16,200
Unindexed gain		13,800
Indexation allowance:		
£10,800 × (say) 0.15 (May 1994 to June 1997)	1,620	
£5,400 × (say) 0.05 (June 1996 to June 1997)	270	
		1,890
Chargeable gain		£11,910

Notes

(a)   For both income tax and capital gains tax purposes, a disposal is matched with acquisitions on a first in/first out basis (see 26.12 above and Tolley's Capital Gains Tax). Thus, the 12,000 shares sold in June 1997 are matched with 9,000 shares purchased in May 1994 and with 3,000 of the 5,000 EIS shares subscribed for in June 1996. For income tax purposes, 2,500 of the 5,000 EIS shares are treated as having been issued in 1995/96 (by virtue of Mr Jones' carry-back claim—see 26.9 above). Therefore, those shares are treated as disposed of in priority to those on which relief was given in 1996/97.

(b)   EIS relief is withdrawn if shares are disposed of before the end of the requisite five-year period. In this example, relief attributable to the shares sold is fully withdrawn as consideration received, reduced as illustrated, exceeds the relief attributable. See the example below for where the reverse applies. The consideration is reduced where the relief attributable (A) is less than tax at the lower rate on the amount subscribed (B), and is so reduced by applying the fraction A/B. See 26.12 above.

(c)   Relief is withdrawn by means of a Schedule D, Case VI assessment for the year(s) in which relief was given (see 26.12 above).

(d)   The capital gain on the disposal is fully chargeable as the shares are not held for the requisite five-year period (see Tolley's Capital Gains Tax).

In December 1997 Mr Jones disposes of his 12,500 ordinary £1 shares in D Ltd (see 26.9 above), in an arm's length transaction, for £10,000.

The position is as follows.

Income tax

1996/97	£
Relief attributable to shares sold	1,012
Consideration received £10,000 × $\dfrac{1,012}{£12,500 \times 20\%}$ = £4,048 @ 20%	810
Excess of relief over consideration	£202
Relief withdrawn—Schedule D, Case VI assessment	£810

Capital gains tax

1997/98

	£	£
Disposal proceeds (December 1997)		10,000
Cost (November 1996)	12,500	
Less Relief attributable to shares:		
£1,012 − £810	202	
		12,298
Allowable loss		£2,298

Notes

(*a*) The EIS relief withdrawn is limited to the consideration received, reduced as illustrated, at the lower rate of tax for the year for which relief was given. If the disposal had been made otherwise than by way of a bargain made at arm's length, the full relief would have been withdrawn. See 26.12 above.

(*b*) An allowable loss may arise for capital gains tax purposes on a disposal of EIS shares, whether or not the disposal occurs within the requisite five-year period. In computing such a loss, the allowable cost is reduced by EIS relief attributable to the shares (and not withdrawn). See Tolley's Capital Gains Tax.

(*c*) A loss, as computed for capital gains tax purposes, may be relieved against income on a claim under *Sec 574* (losses on unquoted shares—see 46.19 LOSSES).

26.14 **SUBSIDIARY COMPANIES**

The existence of certain subsidiaries in the 'relevant period' (see 26.6 above) does not prevent the parent being a qualifying company (see 26.5 above). The conditions imposed on any such subsidiary are:

(*a*) that it must either exist wholly, or substantially wholly, for the purpose of carrying on one or more qualifying trades (see 26.7 above), or be a 'property managing' or 'dormant' subsidiary; and

(*b*) (i) the qualifying company, or another of its subsidiaries, must possess at least 90% of both the issued share capital and the voting power, and be beneficially entitled to at least 90% of the assets available for distribution to equity holders on a winding-up etc. (see *18 Sch 1, 3*) and of the profits available for distribution to equity holders,

  (ii) no other person may have control (within *Sec 840*, see 20.8 CONNECTED PERSONS) of the subsidiary, and

  (iii) no arrangements may exist whereby (i) or (ii) could cease to be satisfied.

The condition at (*b*) above must continue to be satisfied until the end of the relevant period, except that the winding-up or dissolution, during that period, of the subsidiary or of the qualifying company does not prevent those conditions being satisfied, provided that the winding-up etc. meets the conditions applied in relation to qualifying companies (see 26.5 above). The conditions are also not regarded as ceasing to be satisfied by reason only of the disposal of the interest in the subsidiary within the relevant period if it can be shown to be for *bona fide* commercial reasons and not part of a tax avoidance scheme.

A '*property managing*' subsidiary is one which exists wholly (or substantially wholly) for the purpose of holding and managing property used by the qualifying company, or a subsidiary, for the purposes of a qualifying trade or trades carried on by the qualifying company or a subsidiary, or for the purposes of research and development from which such a qualifying trade is intended to be derived.

A *'dormant'* subsidiary is one with no corporation tax profits, and no part of whose business consists in the making of investments.

[*Sec 308; FA 1994, 15 Sch 23, 24*].

26.15   MARRIED PERSONS

The provisions for withdrawal of relief on the disposal of shares in respect of which relief has been given (see 26.12 above) do not apply to transfers between spouses living together. On any subsequent disposal or other event, the spouse to whom the shares were so transferred is treated as if he or she were the person who subscribed for the shares, and as if his or her liability to income tax had been reduced in respect of those shares by the same amount, and for the same year of assessment, as applied on the subscription by the transferor spouse. Any assessment for reducing or withdrawing relief is made on the transferee spouse. [*Sec 304; FA 1994, 15 Sch 18*].

26.16   MISCELLANEOUS

Capital gains tax. In determining the gain or loss on a disposal of eligible shares to which any relief is attributable (see 26.8 above):

(a)   if a loss would otherwise arise, the consideration the individual is treated as having given for the shares is treated as reduced by the amount of the relief;

(b)   if the disposal is after the end of the 'relevant period' (see 26.3 above) and a gain would otherwise arise, the gain is not a chargeable gain (although this does not prevent a loss arising in these circumstances from being an allowable loss). Where the reduction in liability in respect of the issue of the shares was less than the amount corresponding to lower rate income tax on the amount subscribed for the shares (other than because there is insufficient income tax liability to make full use of the relief), there is a corresponding reduction in the amount of the gain which is not chargeable.

Where a gain (or part of a gain) on a disposal is not a chargeable gain under (b) above, but the income tax relief on the shares disposed of is reduced on account of value received from the company by the claimant or by other persons (see 26.12 above) before the disposal but after 28 November 1994, then a corresponding proportion of the gain is brought back into charge.

The identification rules of *Sec 299* (see 26.12 above) apply for the above purposes.

See further *TCGA 1992, ss 150, 150A, 150B, 164M, 164MA* as amended and introduced by *FA 1994, 15 Sch 28–34* and *FA 1995, 13 Sch 1–3*. See also Tolley's Capital Gains Tax under Shares and Securities.

Deferred charge on re-investment. TCGA 1992, s 150C, 5B Sch (introduced by *FA 1995, 13 Sch 4*) applies where:

(a)   a chargeable gain accrues to an individual after 28 November 1994 on the disposal of any asset (or under the current provisions (see below) or on the occurrence of certain events in relation to venture capital trust investments, see *TCGA 1992, 5C Sch 4, 5* introduced as *FA 1995, 16 Sch 4, 5*);

(b)   the individual makes a 'qualifying investment'; and

(c)   the individual is UK resident or ordinarily resident both when the chargeable gain accrues to him and when he makes the 'qualifying investment', and is not, at the latter time, regarded as resident outside the UK for the purposes of certain double taxation arrangements.

A '*qualifying investment*' is a subscription for shares to which EIS relief is attributable within twelve months before or three years after the time of the accrual of the chargeable gain in question (either time limit being extendible by the Board), and, if before, provided that the shares are still held at that time.

Broadly, the provisions allow a claim for the chargeable gain to be rolled over into the EIS shares, and for the gain to become chargeable on certain events in relation to those shares (including, in particular, on their disposal). For the detailed provisions, see *TCGA 1992, 5B Sch 2–6*, introduced by *FA 1995, 13 Sch 4(3)*, and see Tolley's Capital Gains Tax under Re-investment in Shares Relief.

Information. Certain events leading to withdrawal must be notified to the inspector, generally within 60 days, by either the individual who received the relief, the issuing company, or any person connected with the issuing company having knowledge of the matter. The inspector may require such a notice and other relevant information where he has reason to believe it should have been made. The penalty provisions of *TMA s 98* apply for failure to comply.

The inspector also has broad powers to require information in other cases where relief may be withdrawn, restricted or not due. The requirements of secrecy do not prevent his disclosing to a company that relief has been given or claimed on certain of its shares. [*Sec 310; FA 1993, s 111(2); FA 1994, 15 Sch 25*].

26.17   **BUSINESS EXPANSION SCHEME**

As indicated at 26.1 above, the predecessor to the Enterprise Investment Scheme, the Business Expansion Scheme ('BES') ceased to apply to shares issued after 31 December 1993, although the BES legislation has been 'revived' to apply to the EIS. In view of the numerous amendments, the provisions applicable to the BES are described fully at 26.18 *et seq.* below. Statutory references are to the provisions before amendment by *FA 1994, 15 Sch*.

The BES is dealt with in this chapter under the following headings.

26.18   **Conditions for relief.** A 'qualifying individual' who subscribes for 'eligible shares' in a 'qualifying company' issued after 5 April 1983 and before 1 January 1994 may claim income tax relief on his investment, provided that the purpose of the issue is to raise money for a 'qualifying trade' carried on by the company (or by certain subsidiaries of the company, see 26.27 below) or which it intends to carry on and in fact commences within two years of the issue. For shares issued after 5 April 1985 and before 1 January 1994, the money may alternatively (or in addition) be raised for 'research and development', to be carried on by the company (or, for shares issued after 18 March 1986 and before 1 January 1994, by a subsidiary of the company), from which the 'qualifying trade' is intended to be derived, and which is being carried on at or immediately after the time of issue of the shares. [*Secs 289(1)(a)–(c), (8)(a)(ii), 308; F(No 2)A 1992, s 38*].

For the date on which shares are issued, see *National Westminster Bank plc v CIR; Barclays Bank plc v CIR HL, [1994] STC 580.*

See 26.26, 26.29 below for denial of relief in certain cases.

'*Research and development*' means any activity intended to result in a patentable invention or computer program. [*Sec 312(1)*].

For shares issued after 25 July 1986 and before 1 January 1994, the relief is extended to the raising of money for oil exploration from which a 'qualifying trade' is intended to be derived and which is being carried on by the company (or by a subsidiary) at or immediately after the time of issue of the shares. The exploration must be carried out solely within the area to which an exploration licence granted to the company (or to a subsidiary) applies, and that licence must be held throughout the three years from the date of issue of the shares. Neither the company nor any subsidiary may, at the time of issue of the shares, hold an appraisal or development licence relating to the same area, but where such a licence is granted in the three years following the issue of the shares, that licence and the exploration licence are treated as a single exploration licence for the purposes of these provisions. Also, for these purposes only, a trade consisting to any substantial extent of oil extraction activities may be a 'qualifying trade' notwithstanding the exclusion of such trades from the general provisions (see 26.22(*d*) below). [*Secs 289(1)(d), (2), (3), 297(9); F(No 2)A 1992, s 38*].

For shares issued after 28 July 1988 and before 1 January 1994, the relief is further extended to the raising of money by a company which, or a subsidiary of which, carries on, or intends to carry on, '*qualifying activities*', i.e. activities consisting of or connected with the provision and maintenance of certain dwelling-houses let, or to be let, by the company on 'qualifying tenancies', provided that those activities are conducted, throughout the '*relevant period*' (i.e. the period of four years from date of issue of the shares), on a commercial basis with a view to profit. All dwelling-houses are included except:

(*a*)   those with a 'market value' exceeding £85,000 (£125,000 in Greater London) (both figures variable by Treasury Order);

(*b*)   those unfit for human habitation or sub-standard (within *Housing Act 1985, ss 604, 508* or Scottish or NI equivalent);

(*c*)   those already let, i.e.

    (i)   where, before the '*relevant date*' (i.e. the date on which the company or a subsidiary first acquired an interest in the house or the related land), the company or any of its subsidiaries had made arrangements for letting the whole or part of the house in question, or

    (ii)   where at that date the whole or part of the house in question was let, or

    (iii)   where after that date the whole or any part of the house in question has been let other than on a 'qualifying tenancy';

(*d*)   those already qualifying for relief, i.e. a dwelling-house within these provisions in which an interest has been owned by another company (or subsidiary) at any time since that company issued shares qualifying for relief under these provisions; or

(*e*)   those qualifying for writing-down allowances under *CAA 1990, s 85* (see 10.9 CAPITAL ALLOWANCES).

For shares issued after 9 March 1992, (*c*) above is modified so as not to exclude certain prior lettings (or prior arrangements for lettings) to persons who had previously been 'owner-occupiers' (as defined) of the dwelling-houses concerned.

Companies or subsidiaries which are registered housing associations are excluded from the above provisions.

'*Market value*' for the purpose of (*a*) above is the expected open market sale price of the dwelling-house at the time of issue of the shares (or, if later, at the date when the company or a subsidiary first acquired an interest in the property), but on the assumptions that it was then in the same state as at the date of the valuation and that the sale was with vacant possession and was on specified terms as to title (see *FA 1988, 4 Sch 13(4)*). For valuations before 20 March 1990, an additional assumption had to be made that the locality in which the property is situated was then in the same state as at the date of the valuation as regards occupation and use of other premises in the locality, transport services and other local facilities and amenities.

A '*qualifying tenancy*' is a tenancy which is, for the purposes of the *Housing Act 1988* (or Scottish or NI equivalent), an assured tenancy other than an assured shorthold tenancy (in Scotland, an assured tenancy other than a short assured tenancy, in NI, a tenancy complying with prescribed requirements and conditions), except that neither a tenancy granted for a premium within *TCGA 1992, 8 Sch*, nor a tenancy of a dwelling-house in relation to which an option to purchase has been granted to the tenant or an 'associate' (see 26.19(iii) below) of his, can be a qualifying tenancy. [*FA 1988, s 50, 4 Sch; FA 1990, s 73; F(No 2)A 1992, s 40*].

Relief is allowed only when the company (or subsidiary) has carried on the trade, research and development, exploration or activities for four months. If, before the trade has been carried on for four months, the company (or subsidiary) is dissolved or wound up for bona fide commercial reasons, and not as part of a scheme the main purpose (or one such purpose) of which was tax avoidance, relief will nevertheless be available (except in the case of a company carrying on 'qualifying activities', see above). [*Sec 289(8)(13); FA 1988, 4 Sch 2*].

Relief is available where eligible shares issued after 18 March 1986 are held on a bare trust for two or more beneficiaries as if each beneficiary had subscribed as an individual for all of those shares, and as if the amount subscribed by each was the total subscribed divided by the number of beneficiaries. [*Sec 311(2)*].

Relief is also available where shares are subscribed for by a nominee for the individual claiming relief, including the managers of an investment fund approved by the Board for this purpose (an '*approved fund*'). With regard to an approved fund closing after 15 March 1988 (i.e. when no further investments in it are to be accepted after that date) relief is given to an individual (see 26.23, 26.24 below), and certain provisions relating to married couples (see 26.28 below) applied, as if the eligible shares were issued at the time at which the fund was closed, provided that the amount subscribed on behalf of the individual for eligible shares issued within six months of closure of the fund is not less than 90% of the individual's investment in that fund. [*Sec 311(1)(2A)(2B)(3); FA 1988, s 53*]. Detailed guidance on the criteria and related matters for approval of such funds are available from Inland Revenue, Company Tax Division (Business Expansion Scheme), Room 109, New Wing, Somerset House, London WC2R 1LB.

26.19 A '*qualifying individual*' must be resident and ordinarily resident in the UK at the time of the issue, must subscribe for the shares on his own behalf, and must not, at any time in the 'relevant period', be 'connected with' the issuing company (or a subsidiary of that company). He is so '*connected with*' any company

(i) of which he is an employee, partner or director, or of a partner of which he is an employee or director, except that as a director he is only 'connected with' a company from which he (or a partnership of which he is a member) receives or is entitled to receive, during the five years following the issue, a payment other than by way of

(*a*) payment or reimbursement of allowable expenditure under Schedule E,

(*b*) interest at a commercial rate on money lent,

    (*c*)   dividends, etc. representing a normal return on investment,

    (*d*)   payment for supply of goods at no more than market value, or

    (*e*)   any reasonable and necessary remuneration for services rendered (other than secretarial or managerial services, or those rendered by the company itself) which is chargeable under Schedule D, Case I or II;

(ii)   (in relation to 'qualifying activities', see 26.18 above) if he occupies, or is a tenant of, a dwelling-house in which the company has an interest superior to any he holds;

(iii)   of which an associate (as defined by *Sec 417(3)(4)* but excluding a brother or sister) meets any of the conditions at (i) or (ii) above;

(iv)   if he directly or indirectly possesses or is entitled to acquire

    (*a*)   more than 30% of its voting power, its issued ordinary share capital, or its loan capital and issued share capital together (loan capital including any debt incurred by the company for money borrowed, for capital assets acquired, for any right to income created in its favour, or for insufficient consideration, but excluding a debt incurred by overdrawing a bank account in the ordinary course of the bank's business), or

    (*b*)   rights entitling him to more than 30% of its assets available for distribution to the company's equity holders (as defined at *18 Sch 1, 3*—see Tolley's Corporation Tax under Groups of Companies); or

(v)   of which he has control (as defined by *Sec 840*, see 20.8 CONNECTED PERSONS);

and in applying (iv) and (v), rights and powers of his associates (restricted as in (iii) above) are attributed to him.

An investor who acquires one of two subscriber shares in a company from company formation agents will, by concession, not be regarded as being connected with the company by virtue of (iv)(*a*) above solely because, until further shares are issued, he holds 50% of the company's issued share capital, provided that the company enters into no other transactions in the meanwhile. (Revenue Pamphlet IR 1 (November 1995 Supplement), A76).

For shares issued after 5 April 1986, an individual treated under *Sec 132(4)(a)* as performing the duties of his employment in the UK (see 75.2(i) SCHEDULE E) is treated for this purpose as resident and ordinarily resident in the UK.

A '*subsidiary company*' is included within (i) to (v) above if it is a subsidiary during the relevant period, whether or not it becomes a subsidiary before, during or after the year of assessment in respect of which the individual claims relief and whether or not it is a subsidiary during the time that the circumstances in (i) to (v) above exist.

'*Relevant period*' in this context means the period from the date of incorporation of the company (or, if later, two years before the shares were issued) to five years after the issue of the shares.

Relief is denied where reciprocal arrangements are made aimed at circumventing this provision.

Parallel trades. Relief may be denied in respect of shares in a company issued after 18 March 1986 where, on the date of issue of the shares (or, if later, the date on which the company commences trading), the individual subscribing for the shares is both one of a group of persons who either control the company (within *Sec 416*) or together own more than a half share (determined as under *Sec 344(1)(a)(b), (2), (3)*) in the trade, business, profession or vocation carried on by the company and also, individually or as one of a group, has such an interest in another company. Where a substantial part of the trade, etc. carried on by the issuing company or by a subsidiary is concerned with the same or similar types of property or provides the same or similar services or facilities, and serves substantially the same outlets or markets, as the other company's trade, etc., no relief is available in respect of the shares subscribed for. Rights and powers of associates (see 26.19(iii) above) are taken into account.

This restriction does not apply in respect of a company carrying on 'qualifying activities' (see 26.18 above).

See 26.20 below for similar restrictions applying for shares issued before 19 March 1986.

[*Secs 289(12), 291, 309(5); FA 1988, 4 Sch 4, 5*].

26.20   A '*qualifying company*' must be incorporated in the UK. It must throughout the 'relevant period' be unquoted, be resident only in the UK, and must either

(*a*)   exist (or exist mainly) either to carry on one or more 'qualifying trades' 'wholly or mainly in the UK' or to carry on 'qualifying activities' (see 26.18 above), or

(*b*)   consist of holding shares or securities of, or making loans to, 'qualifying subsidiaries' (see 26.27 below), with or without either the carrying on of one or more 'qualifying trades' 'wholly or mainly in the UK' or the carrying on of 'qualifying activities'.

A company falling within (*a*) for part of the 'relevant period' and within (*b*) for the remainder is regarded as meeting this condition throughout the 'relevant period'. (ICAEW Technical Memorandum TR 831, 19 April 1991).

For shares issued after 18 March 1986, the qualifying trade(s) carried on by the company and its qualifying subsidiaries must, as a whole, be carried out 'wholly or mainly in the UK'. Although a winding-up or dissolution in the 'relevant period' generally prevents a company meeting these conditions, they are deemed met if the winding-up or dissolution is for *bona fide* commercial reasons and not part of a scheme the main purpose (or one such purpose) of which is tax avoidance, *provided that* any net assets are distributed to its members (or dealt with as *bona vacantia*) before the end of the 'relevant period' or (if later) the end of three years from the commencement of winding-up.

'*Relevant period*' in this context means the period from the date of issue of the shares to three years after that date or, if later, three years after the 'qualifying trade' was commenced following issue of the shares. The alternative later date does not apply to shares issued wholly or partly for research and development (see 26.18 above). The period is four years from the date of issue in relation to a company carrying on 'qualifying activities' (see 26.18 above).

In considering whether a trade is carried on '*wholly or mainly in the UK*', the totality of the trade activities is taken into account. Although no one factor is likely to be decisive, such things as the locations at which capital assets are held, and where purchasing, processing, manufacturing and selling is done, and the places where employees customarily carry out their duties will, for example, be relevant. A company may carry on some such activities outside the UK and yet satisfy the requirement that the major part, that is to say more than one-half, of the trade activities as a whole takes place in the UK. Thus relief is not excluded solely because some or all of a company's products or services are exported, or because its raw materials are imported, and the warehousing of raw materials, the storage of products pending sale or the availability of marketing facilities outside the UK would similarly not be sufficient by themselves to deny relief. Similar principles apply in considering the trade(s) carried on by a company and its qualifying subsidiaries.

In the particular case of a ship chartering trade, the test is satisfied if all charters are entered into in the UK and the provision of crews and management of the ships while under charter take place mainly in the UK. If these conditions are not met, the test may still be satisfied depending on all the relevant facts and circumstances. (Revenue Pamphlet IR 131, SP 4/87, 23 April 1987). The 'crew provision and management' test replaces an earlier 'port of call' test, but where relief was given under that earlier test, it will not be withdrawn if the revised test is not satisfied. (Revenue Pamphlet IR 131, SP 7/86, 12 September 1986; Revenue Press Release 23 April 1987).

A company is 'unquoted' if none of its shares, stocks or debentures is listed on the Stock Exchange or dealt in on the Unlisted Securities Market.

The company must also not at any time in the relevant period either

(i) have share capital which includes any issued shares not fully paid-up; or

(ii) control another company (other than a 'qualifying' subsidiary, see 26.27 below), or be controlled by another company (control being as defined by *Sec 416*, and being considered with or without connected persons under *Sec 839* (see 20 CONNECTED PERSONS)); or

(iii) be a 51% subsidiary of another company or itself have a 51% subsidiary (other than a 'qualifying' subsidiary, see 26.27 below); or

(iv) be capable of falling within (ii) or (iii) by virtue of any arrangements.

Parallel trades. For shares issued before 19 March 1986, there was an additional exclusion if an individual who, after 5 April 1983, had acquired a 'controlling interest' in the company's trade, or the trade of any subsidiary of the company, also had or had had such an interest in another trade concerned with similar goods or services, or serving a similar market, at any time in the period from two years before to three years after the later of the date of issue of the shares and the date the company or subsidiary commenced the trade. This restriction did not apply where the *same* trade was previously carried on by the person with the 'controlling interest' as was subsequently carried on by the 'qualifying company'. (Tolley's Practical Tax 1985 p 31).

In the case of a trade carried on by a company, a person has a '*controlling interest*' if he controls (within the definition of *Sec 416*) the company; or if the company is close and he is a director of the company and the owner of, or able to control, more than 30% of its ordinary share capital; or if at least half of its ordinary share capital is directly or indirectly owned by him or by an 'associate' of his. In any other case it is obtained by his being entitled to at least half of the assets used for, or income arising from, the trade. In either case, the rights and powers of any person's 'associates' are attributed to the person. '*Associate*' is as defined at 26.19(iii) above.

Simplified provisions apply in relation to shares issued after 18 March 1986 by disqualification from relief of certain individuals (see 26.19 above).

Land and buildings. For shares issued after 18 March 1986 other than by a company carrying on 'qualifying activities' (see 26.18 above), subject to an exemption for small issues, there is an additional exclusion if, at any time during the relevant period **and before 29 November 1994**, the value of the company's 'interests in land' (or, where lower, the value of those interests immediately after the issue of the shares, adjusted as below) exceeds half the value of all its assets (or such other fraction as the Treasury may substitute by statutory instrument). The value of those interests is for this purpose the aggregate of the market values of each such interest less debts secured thereon (including floating charges), unsecured debts not falling due within twelve months and any amount paid up in respect of shares carrying a present or future preferential right to the company's assets on its winding-up. The value of the company's assets as a whole is similarly the aggregate market value less the company's debts and liabilities (including any amount paid up in respect of shares carrying a present or future preferential right to the company's assets on its winding-up, but excluding any other share capital, share premium account or reserves). Any question, on appeal, of the value of an interest in land is determined by the appropriate Lands Tribunal.

An 'interest in land' is valued on the assumption that there is no source of mineral deposits in the land exploitable other than by opencast mining or quarrying. Where the company is a member of a partnership, the value of any 'interest in land' held by the partnership is apportioned as on a dissolution of the partnership. A qualifying company and its subsidiaries are treated as one company for these purposes, but ignoring any debts and liabilities as between such companies.

'*Interest in land*' is widely defined to include rights related to land, and rights to obtain an interest, etc. from another which depend on that other's ability to grant the interest, etc., but excludes the interest of a creditor secured by any mortgage or charge over land. Valuation (after 28 July 1988) of such an interest excludes any plant or machinery which is, in law, part of the land, etc.

The adjustments (referred to above) to the value of the company's interests in land held immediately after the issue of the shares are:

(1)   the addition of the cost(s) (i.e. consideration given, ignoring any discount for postponement of right to receive it) of any subsequent acquisitions of interests in land, and of any enhancement expenditure relating to interests in land; and

(2)   the deduction of any consideration for the disposal of, or grant of any interest out of, any interest in land, or derived from the ownership of interests in land (but excluding rent).

The value of an interest falls to be adjusted where the interest is under a lease at rent exceeding a full market rent. Contingent liabilities are disregarded unless and until the Board is satisfied that they have become enforceable and have been (or are being) enforced, whereon the necessary adjustments are made.

These restrictions do not apply where the total raised by the issue in question and any other issue in the previous twelve months (but not before 19 March 1986) does not exceed £50,000, and where it does exceed £50,000 they apply only to the excess. The figure of £50,000 is reduced where, at any time in the relevant period, the company (or a subsidiary) carries on a trade in partnership, or in a joint venture, with another company.

Any restriction of relief under these provisions is apportioned amongst the qualifying individuals subscribing for otherwise eligible shares in proportion to their subscriptions, subject to determination on appeal by the General (or, in certain cases, the Special) Commissioners.

These restrictions ceased to apply with effect from 29 November 1994.

[*Secs 289(12), 293–296, 298(1)(2), 312(1)(2); TMA s 47B; FA 1988, s 52, 4 Sch 2(4), 6, 7; FA 1995, s 68(2)*].

26.21   '*Eligible shares*' means new ordinary shares which, for five years after issue, carry no present or future preferential rights to dividends or assets (on a winding-up) or to be redeemed. [*Sec 289(4)*].

26.22   A '*qualifying trade*' may not at any time in the 'relevant period' (as defined in 26.20 above) consist to any 'substantial' extent of, or (for shares issued after 18 March 1986) of a combination of

(*a*)   dealing in commodities, shares, securities, land or futures; or

(*b*)   dealing in goods otherwise than in an ordinary trade of wholesale or retail distribution (see below); or

(c)   banking, insurance or any other financial activities; or

(d)   in relation to shares issued after 25 July 1986, oil extraction activities (but without prejudice to relief in respect of oil exploration (see 26.18 above) for which the activities would otherwise qualify); or

(e)   leasing or letting or receiving royalties or licence fees; or

(f)   providing legal or accountancy services; or

(g)   providing services and facilities for any trade, profession or vocation concerned in (a) to (f) and carried on by another person (other than a parent company), where one person has a 'controlling interest' (see 26.20 above) in both trades; or

(h)   in relation to shares issued after 13 March 1984 and before 19 March 1986, farming; or

(j)   in relation to shares issued after 19 March 1985 and before 19 March 1986, 'property development', i.e. development of land by a company which has, or has had, an interest in it (as defined, including certain rights to acquire land but excluding ordinary interests of creditors), with the sole or main object of realising a gain on its disposal.

Adventures and concerns in the nature of trade, and trades not carried on commercially and with an expectation of profits, are also generally excluded.

It is understood that the Revenue regard as 'substantial' a part of a trade which consists of 20% or more of total turnover. (Tolley's Practical Tax 1987 p 162).

As regards (a) above, it is not intended to exclude from relief what is mainly a building trade, despite the technical position that what the builder sells is the land with the buildings on it. (Tolley's Practical Tax 1984 p 206). (See, however, (j) above, itself replaced after 18 March 1986 by the 'land and buildings' provisions described at 26.20 above.)

As regards (b) above, a trade of wholesale or retail distribution is a trade consisting of the offer of goods for sale either to persons for resale (or processing and resale) (which resale must, for shares issued after 18 March 1986, be to members of the general public) by them ('wholesale') or to the general public ('retail') and, for shares issued after 18 March 1986, a trade is not an ordinary wholesale or retail trade if it consists to a substantial extent of dealing in goods collected or held as an investment (or of that and any other activity within (a)–(j) above), and a substantial proportion of such goods is held for a significantly longer period than might reasonably be expected to dispose of them at market value. Whether such trades are 'ordinary' is to be judged having regard to the following features, those under (A) supporting the categorisation as 'ordinary', those under (B) being indicative to the contrary.

(A)   (i)   The breaking of bulk.

(ii)   The purchase and sale of goods in different markets.

(iii)   The employment of staff and incurring of trade expenses other than the cost of goods or of remuneration of persons connected (see 20 CONNECTED PERSONS) with a company carrying on such a trade.

(B)   (i)   The purchase or sale of goods from persons connected (as in (A)(iii) above) with the trader.

(ii)   The matching of purchases with sales.

(iii)   The holding of goods for longer than might normally be expected.

(iv)   The carrying on of the trade at a place not commonly used for wholesale or retail trading.

(v)   The absence of physical possession of the goods by the trader.

As regards (e) above, with effect from 26 July 1984 a company engaged in the production of original master films, tapes or discs is not excluded from the scheme by reason only of its receipts by way of trade of royalties or licence fees in respect of films, etc. produced by it or in respect of by-products arising therefrom. In relation to shares issued after 16 March 1987, the company may also be engaged in the distribution of films produced by it in the relevant period, but the royalties or licence fees must relate to films, etc. produced by it in that period.

Similarly, after 19 March 1985 royalties and licence fees attributable to research and development (see 26.18 above) which a company carrying on a trade has engaged in throughout the relevant period do not prevent the trade being a qualifying trade.

Also as regards (e) above, for shares issued after 18 March 1986, a trade will not be excluded by reason only of its consisting of letting ships, other than oil rigs or pleasure craft (as defined), on charter, provided that

(i)   the company beneficially owns all ships it so lets,

(ii)   every ship beneficially owned by the company is UK registered,

(iii)   throughout the relevant period (as defined in 26.20 above) the company is solely responsible for arranging the marketing of the services of its ships, and

(iv)   in relation to every letting on charter, certain conditions as to length and terms of charter, and the arm's length character of the transaction, are fulfilled.

If any of the conditions at (i)–(iv) above is not fulfilled in relation to certain lettings, only those lettings are taken into account in determining whether a substantial part of the trade consists of activities within (a)–(j) above.

The Treasury may, by statutory instrument, amend any of the above conditions.

[Secs 289(12), 297, 298].

26.23   **Method of giving relief.** Relief is given on the amount subscribed (subject to certain limits, see 26.24 below) as a deduction, in the year of assessment of the share issue (but see below), from total income after any other deductions including personal allowances. It does not affect the computation of total income for the purposes of age allowance or dependent relative income limits, life assurance premium limit, and top-slicing relief on life policy etc. gains (or, where previously available, on lease premiums, termination payments and stock relief clawbacks). [Sec 289(5)(14)].

In relation to shares issued after 5 April 1987, relief in respect of shares issued before 6 October in a year of assessment may be claimed partly for the year of assessment of the share issue and partly for the preceding year. The deduction for the preceding year may not exceed one half of the total relief in respect of the shares, and the total of relief carried back to the preceding year may not exceed £5,000 in any year of assessment. [Sec 289(6)(7)]. See 26.18 above as regards time of issue of certain shares subscribed for through approved funds.

For repayment supplement purposes (see 41 INTEREST ON OVERPAID TAX) any repayment of tax is treated as being in respect of tax payable in the year of assessment in which the shares are issued or, if later, the year in which the issuing company completed its first four months' trading (see 26.18 above). [Sec 289(15)].

For treatment of married persons, see 26.28 below.

26.24   **Limits on relief.** (See 26.28 below as regards relief for married persons.)

Except in the case of investments through 'approved funds' (see 26.18 above), relief is restricted to investments of £500 or more in any one company in a year of assessment. In all cases, there is an upper limit of £40,000 on the relief which may be given to an individual for a year of assessment. [*Secs 290, 311(3)*]. For 1993/94, the £40,000 limit applies to the aggregate of relief under both the BES and the EIS (see 26.1 *et seq.* above). [*FA 1994, 15 Sch 3(3)*].

For shares issued after 15 March 1988, there is also a restriction on the total amount of eligible shares which may be issued by a company within a specified period (see below) and attract relief. Where the money raised in such a period exceeds £750,000 (£500,000 before 1 May 1990), the excess does not qualify for relief. The period specified is the longer of

(*a*)   six months ending with the date of issue of the shares, and

(*b*)   the period from the preceding 6 April to the date of issue.

As regards (*a*) above, shares issued before 16 March 1988 are taken into account for these purposes. There are, however, transitional provisions where shares are issued after 15 March 1988 but before 6 April 1988 in pursuance of a prospectus published or written offer made before 15 March 1988, increasing the permitted maximum to £1,000,000 in relation to the shares so issued.

Amounts raised which do not attract relief because the subscriber was not a qualifying individual (see 26.19 above), or had exceeded his personal limit or invested under the permitted minimum (see above), or because of an earlier application of these provisions, are not taken into account for the purposes of this restriction.

The limit is increased to £5,000,000 where the only qualifying trade(s) carried on by the issuing company (or by its subsidiaries) consist wholly or substantially wholly of operating or letting over charter ships other than oil rigs or pleasure craft, subject to similar conditions as apply to lettings of such ships in respect of their being a qualifying trade (see 26.22 above). The limit is also increased to £5,000,000 in the case of a company carrying on 'qualifying activities' (see 26.18 above), i.e. broadly the letting of assured tenancy housing.

The £750,000 (£500,000) and £5,000,000 permitted maxima may be varied by Treasury order.

Where, at any time within the 'relevant period' (see 26.20 above), the company issuing the shares (or a subsidiary) carries on any trade or qualifying activities (or part thereof) in partnership, or as a joint venture, with a company (with or without other persons), the appropriate permitted maximum (as above) is divided by the total number of companies (but counting the issuing company and its subsidiaries as one company) which are members of the partnership or parties to the joint venture.

Where these provisions restrict the amount of relief available to two or more individuals, the total relief available is apportioned between them according to the respective amounts subscribed for shares giving rise to the restriction. [*Sec 290A; FA 1988, s 51, 4 Sch 3; SI 1990 No 862*].

26.25   **Claims for relief.** A claim for relief in respect of any shares issued by a company in a year of assessment must be made not earlier than the date on which relief becomes allowable (see 26.18 above), and must be made within two years of the end of that year of assessment (or, if later, within two years of the end of the initial period of trading giving rise to eligibility for relief, see 26.18 above). It must be accompanied by a certificate (Revenue Form BES 3) issued by the company stating that the conditions for relief, in respect of the company and the trade or activities, are satisfied in relation to these shares. Before issuing such a certificate, the company must supply to the inspector a statement that those conditions were fulfilled from the beginning of the relevant period (as defined in 26.19 or 26.20 above as appropriate), and such statement must contain such information as the Board may reasonably require and be in such form as the Board may direct (i.e. Revenue Form BES 1 (New)), and must contain a declaration that it is correct to the best of the company's knowledge and belief. It is the Revenue's view (see Revenue Tax Bulletin August 1992 p 31) that Form BES 1 (New) can be submitted immediately after issuing the shares, even though the money raised has not yet been used, provided that the qualifying trade or activities have actually been carried on for the requisite four month period. A certificate may not be issued without the inspector's authority, nor where a notice under *Sec 310(2)* (see 26.29 below) has been given to the inspector. For appeal purposes, the inspector's refusal to authorise a certificate is treated as the refusal of a claim by the company. If such a certificate or statement is made fraudulently or negligently, or should not have been made (see above), the company is liable to a fine of up to £3,000 (before 27 July 1989, £250 or £500 in the case of fraud). The provisions are suitably modified where relief is claimed on shares held by an 'approved fund' (see 26.18 above).

No application for postponement of tax pending appeal on the ground that relief under the current provisions is due can be made unless a claim has been duly submitted.

For the purpose of calculating interest on overdue tax (see 42 INTEREST ON UNPAID TAX), tax charged by an assessment is regarded as due and payable notwithstanding that relief is subsequently given on a claim under these provisions, but is regarded as paid on the date on which a claim is made which results in relief being granted, unless it was either in fact paid earlier or not due and payable until later. Interest is not refunded in consequence of any subsequent discharge or repayment of tax giving effect to relief under these provisions. [*Sec 306; FA 1988, 4 Sch 10; FA 1989, s 170(3)(6)*].

26.26 **Restriction or withdrawal of relief.** Relief allowed in the 'relevant period' (as defined at 26.19 or 26.20 above as appropriate) may be withdrawn if on any subsequent event it appears that the claimant was not entitled to relief. [*Sec 289(10)*].

Where an event giving rise to complete withdrawal of relief occurs at the same time as a disposal at a loss, the disposal is regarded as occurring first, so that relief may be only partially withdrawn (as below). (Revenue Inspector's Manual, IM 6600).

Loan linked investments. For claims made after 15 March 1993, relief is denied in respect of shares issued after 15 March 1993 where

(a) a loan is made to the individual subscribing for the shares or to an 'associate' (within *Sec 417(3)(4)* but excluding a brother or sister) by any person at any time in the relevant period (as defined in 26.19 above), and

(b) the loan would not have been made, or would not have been made on the same terms, if he had not subscribed, or had not been proposing to subscribe, for the shares.

The granting of credit to, or the assignment of a debt due from, the individual or an associate of his is counted as a loan for these purposes.

[*Sec 299A; FA 1993, s 111*].

For the date on which shares are issued, see *National Westminster Bank plc v CIR; Barclays Bank plc v CIR HL, [1994] STC 580.*

For this restriction to apply, the test is whether the lender makes the loan on terms which are connected with the fact that the borrower (or an associate) is subscribing for eligible shares. The prime concern is why the lender made the loan rather than why the borrower applied for it. Relief would not be disallowed, for example, in the case of a bank loan if the bank would have made a loan on the same terms to a similar borrower for a different purpose. But if, for example, a loan is made specifically on a security consisting of or including the eligible shares (other than as part of a broad range of assets to which the lender has recourse), relief would be denied. Relevant features of the loan terms would be the qualifying conditions to be satisfied by the borrower, any incentives or benefits offered to the borrower, the time allowed for repayment, the amount of repayments and interest charged, the timing of interest payments, and the nature of the security. (Revenue Pamphlet IR 131 (October 1995 Supplement), SP 3/94, 9 May 1994, revised by Revenue Press Release 14 September 1995).

Disposal of shares. Where an individual disposes of shares, on the purchase of which relief was obtained, before the end of the 'relevant period' (as defined in 26.19 above), then

(*a*)   if the disposal is not at arm's length, all relief is withdrawn;

(*b*)   otherwise, relief is withdrawn to the extent of the amount or value of consideration received.

Relief is also withdrawn in respect of options granted after 18 March 1986, the exercise of which would bind the grantor to purchase any shares (a 'put' option), where the option is granted during the relevant period (as above) to the individual who subscribed for the shares.

Sales out of, and options over, a holding of ordinary shares of any class in a company on only part of which relief has been obtained are treated as relating to shares on which relief has been obtained rather than others, and to those on which relief has been obtained under the original provisions rather than those on which relief has been obtained under the current provisions. Subject to this, where a holding includes shares attracting relief but issued at different times, shares issued earlier are deemed disposed of before those issued later. Shares are treated as being of the same class only if they would be so treated if dealt with on the Stock Exchange.

For these purposes, in relation to options granted after 18 March 1986, the grant of an option the exercise of which would bind the grantor to sell the shares (a 'call' option) is treated as a disposal of the shares. The grant of such an option to the proprietor of the company will not result in withdrawal of relief provided that full market value will be received on exercise of the option. (Revenue Press Release 18 March 1986).

Where, on a capital reorganisation, new shares or debentures are allotted (without payment) in proportion to a holding of shares which have attracted relief, and are treated for capital gains tax as being the same asset, the disposal of the new shares or debentures is treated as a disposal of shares which have attracted relief. [*Sec 299*].

See, however, 26.28 below as regards transactions between married persons.

Value received from company. Subject to the above, entitlement to relief in respect of shares issued by a company is reduced by the amount of any 'value received' from the company (including any company which, during the 'relevant period', is a subsidiary of that company, whether it becomes a subsidiary before or after the individual receives any value from it) during the 'relevant period' (as defined in 26.19 above). Value received is disregarded for these purposes to the extent that it has already resulted in a reduction of relief.

An individual '*receives value*' from a company if it:

(i)   repays, redeems or repurchases any part of his holding of its share capital or securities, or makes any payment to him for the cancellation of rights; or

(ii)   repays any debt to him other than one incurred by the company on or after the date on which he subscribed for the shares which are the subject of relief and otherwise than in consideration of the extinguishment of a debt incurred before that date; or

(iii) pays him for the cancellation of any debt owed to him other than an '*ordinary trade debt*'—i.e. one incurred for normal trade supply of goods or services on normal trade credit terms (not in any event exceeding six months)—or one in respect of a payment falling within 26.19(i)(*a*) or (*e*) above; or

(iv) releases or waives any liability of his to the company (which it is deemed to have done if discharge of the liability is twelve months or more overdue) or discharges or undertakes to discharge any liability of his to a third person; or

(v) makes a loan or advance to him (defined as including the incurring by him of any debt either to the company (other than an 'ordinary trade debt'—see (iii) above) or to a third person but assigned to the company) which, in relation to shares issued after 18 March 1986, has not been repaid in full before the issue of the shares; or

(vi) provides a benefit or facility for him; or

(vii) transfers an asset to him for no consideration or for consideration less than market value, or acquires an asset from him for consideration exceeding market value; or

(viii) makes any other payment to him except one either falling within 26.19(i)(*a*)–(*e*) above or in discharge of an 'ordinary trade debt' (see (iii) above); or

(ix) is wound up or dissolved in circumstances such that the company does not thereby cease to be a 'qualifying company' (see 26.20 above), and he thereby receives any payment or asset in respect of ordinary shares held by him.

The amount of value received by the individual is that paid to or receivable by him from the company; or the amount of his liability extinguished or discharged; or the difference between the market value of the asset and the consideration (if any) given for it; or the net cost to the company of providing the benefit. In the case of value received within (i), (ii) or (iii) above, the market value of the shares, securities or debt in question is substituted if greater than the amount receivable.

Additionally, the individual 'receives value' from the company if any person 'connected with' the company (see 26.19 above) purchases any shares or securities of the company from him, or pays him for giving up any right in relation to such shares or securities. The value received is the amount receivable, or, if greater, the market value of the shares, etc.

All payments or transfers, direct or indirect, to, or to the order of, or for the benefit of, an individual or an 'associate' (as defined at 26.19(iii) above) of his are brought within these provisions, as are payments, etc. made by any person connected with the company.

Any reduction in relief is apportioned between eligible shares as appears just and reasonable to the inspector or, on appeal, the Commissioners. For shares issued before 19 March 1986, however, relief is, where appropriate, withdrawn or withheld in respect of shares issued earlier before shares issued later. [*Secs 300, 301, 309(8)*].

Value received other than by claimant. Relief is also reduced where, in the 'relevant period' (as defined in 26.19 above), the issuing company (including a subsidiary at any time during the relevant period) repays, redeems or repurchases any of its share capital belonging to any member other than (i) the individual, or (ii) another individual whose relief is thereby withdrawn or reduced (see above). The reduction is the amount receivable by the member or, if greater, the nominal value of the share capital in question (with relief being restricted in proportion to the relief otherwise available where two or more individuals are involved). Under the current provisions, this restriction of relief does not apply in relation to the redemption on a date fixed before 15 March 1983 of any share capital, nor in relation to the redemption, within twelve months of issue, of any shares issued after 5 April 1983 to comply with *Companies Act 1985, s 117* or NI equivalent (public company not to do business unless certain requirements as to share capital complied with). The rules for identification of shares to which a reduction of relief applies are as described above in relation to value received from the company.

Where, in the 'relevant period', a member of the issuing company receives, or is entitled to receive, any 'value' from the company, then in applying the percentage limits referred to at 26.19(iv) above, the following amounts are treated as reduced—

(i)   the amount of the company's issued ordinary share capital;

(ii)   the amount of that capital 'relevant' to the provisions in question; and

(iii)   the amount at (i) not included in (ii).

The reduction in (ii) and (iii) is in each case the same proportion of the total amount as the 'value' received by the member(s) entitled to the shares comprising the amount bears to the sum subscribed for those shares. The reduced amount at (i) is the sum of those at (ii) and (iii).

The capital '*relevant*' to a provision is those shares whose proportion of the total issued ordinary share capital is in each case compared with the appropriate percentage of that capital.

A member receives '*value*' from the company where any payments, etc. are made to him which, if made to an individual, would fall within (iv) to (viii) inclusive above, excluding those within (viii) made for full consideration. The amount of value received is as defined above. [*Secs 303, 309(4)(8)*].

Replacement capital. An individual is not entitled to relief in respect of shares issued by a company where, at any time in the relevant period (as defined in 26.19 above), the company (or a subsidiary) either begins to carry on a business (or part) previously carried on at any such time otherwise than by the company or a subsidiary, or acquires the whole or greater part of the assets used for a business so carried on, and the individual is a person who, or one of the group of persons who together, either

(i)   owned more than a half share (ownership and, if appropriate, respective shares being determined as under *Sec 344(1)(a)(b), (2), (3)* (see Tolley's Corporation Tax under Losses)) at any such time in the business previously carried on, and also own or owned at any such time such a share in the business carried on by the company, or

(ii)   control, or at any such time have controlled, the company, and also, at any such time, controlled another company which previously carried on the trade.

For these purposes, the interests, rights and powers of a person's associates (as defined by *Sec 417(3)(4)* but excluding a brother or sister) are attributed to that person.

An individual is similarly not entitled to relief in respect of shares in a company which, at any time in the relevant period, comes to acquire all the issued share capital of another company, and where the individual is the person who, or one of the persons who together, control or have, at any such time, controlled the company and who also, at any such time, controlled the other company. [*Sec 302; FA 1988, 4 Sch 9*].

Assessments for withdrawing relief are made under Schedule D, Case VI for the year of assessment for which relief was given, and will rank as earned income if the relief withdrawn was out of earned income (CCAB Memorandum TR 511, 31 August 1983). Where relief in respect of an issue has been claimed for each of two years of assessment (see 26.23 above), relief is withdrawn in respect of the earlier year in priority to the later year. If the event giving rise to the withdrawal occurred after the date of claim, assessments may be made at any time within six years after the end of the year of assessment in which the event occurs, without prejudice to the extension of the time limits in cases of fraudulent or negligent conduct (see 6.4 BACK DUTY). No assessment may be made by reason of any event occurring after the death of the person to whom the shares were issued.

Where a person has made an arm's length disposal of all the ordinary shares issued to him by a company in respect of which relief has been given, no assessment may be made in respect of those shares by reason of any subsequent event unless he is at the time of that event 'connected with' the company (as defined in 26.19 above).

The reckonable date for the purpose of INTEREST ON UNPAID TAX (42) (or, where the self-assessment interest provisions apply, the relevant date—see 78.22 SELF-ASSESSMENT) is the date on which the event took place which gave rise to the withdrawal of relief, *except that* where relief is withdrawn under the anti-avoidance provisions (see 26.29 below), it is the date on which relief was granted unless the relief was given under PAYE, in which case it is 5 April in the year of assessment in which relief was so given. [*Sec 307; FA 1989, s 149(4); FA 1993, s 111(3); FA 1996, 18 Sch 5, 17(3)*].

26.27 **Subsidiary companies.** The existence of certain subsidiaries does not prevent the parent being a 'qualifying company' (see 26.20 above), and a 'qualifying trade' (see 26.22 above) or 'qualifying activities' (see 26.18 above) being carried on by the subsidiary may enable shares issued by the parent to attract relief under the current provisions. The necessary modifications to those provisions apply where such a subsidiary company exists. [*Secs 308, 309; FA 1988, 4 Sch 11, 12*].

In relation to shares issued after 18 March 1986, the conditions imposed on any such subsidiary are that it (or each of them) must exist wholly (or substantially so) for the purpose of carrying on one or more qualifying trades, or be a 'property managing' or 'dormant' subsidiary, and that, until the end of the relevant period (as defined in 26.20 above):

(*a*)   the qualifying company, or another of its subsidiaries,

    (i)   possesses at least 90% of both the issued share capital and voting power,

    (ii)   is beneficially entitled to at least 90% of the assets available for distribution to equity holders on a winding-up, etc. (as to which see *18 Sch 1, 3*),

    (iii)   is beneficially entitled to at least 90% of the profits of the subsidiary available for distribution to equity holders (as above);

(*b*)   no other person has control (as defined by *Sec 840*, see 20.8 CONNECTED PERSONS) of the subsidiary; and

(*c*)   no arrangements exist whereby (*a*) or (*b*) above could cease to be satisfied.

In the case of a company or subsidiary carrying on 'qualifying activities' (i.e. the provision and maintenance of private rented housing, see 26.18 above), the conditions are that the subsidiary (or each of them) must either

(A)   be a 'dormant' subsidiary or exist wholly (or substantially so) for the purpose of carrying on substantially only 'qualifying activities', or

(B)   exist wholly (or substantially so) for the purposes of holding and/or managing a single block of flats more than half of which are let by the qualifying company or any of its subsidiaries in the course of 'qualifying activities',

and, until the end of the relevant period (as defined in 26.20 above), (*a*)–(*c*) above must be satisfied (in the case of subsidiaries within (B) above, substituting 51% for 90% in each case).

A '*property managing*' subsidiary is one which exists wholly (or substantially so) for the purpose of holding and managing property used by the qualifying company, or a subsidiary, for the purposes of a qualifying trade or trades carried on by the qualifying company or a subsidiary, or for the purposes of research and development from which such a qualifying trade is intended to be derived.

A *'dormant'* subsidiary is one with no corporation tax profits, and no part of whose business consists in the making of investments.

The winding-up or dissolution, in the relevant period, of the subsidiary or of the qualifying company does not prevent the above conditions being satisfied, provided that the winding-up, etc. meets the conditions applied in relation to qualifying companies (see 26.20 above). Those conditions are also not regarded as ceasing to be satisfied by reason only of the disposal of the interest in the subsidiary within the relevant period if it can be shown to be for *bona fide* commercial reasons and not part of a tax avoidance scheme. [*Sec 308; FA 1988, 4 Sch 11; F(No 2)A 1992, s 39*].

For shares issued before 19 March 1986, the conditions imposed until the end of the relevant period on any subsidiary are that

(i)   the 'qualifying company' possesses all the issued share capital and voting power,

(ii)   no other person has control (as defined by *Sec 840*, see 20.8 CONNECTED PERSONS), and

(iii) no arrangements exist whereby (i) and (ii) could cease to be satisfied,

and that it was incorporated in the UK and itself satisfies all the conditions for being a 'qualifying company' as regards residence and purpose and is an unquoted company and not wholly or partly a holding company (see 26.20 above). The winding-up or dissolution, in the relevant period, of the subsidiary or of the qualifying company does not prevent the above conditions being met, provided that the winding-up etc. meets the conditions applied in relation to qualifying companies (see 26.20 above). [*Sec 308(6)*].

26.28   **Married persons.** For **1990/91** and subsequent years of assessment, full reliefs are given separately to husbands and wives, whether or not they are living together. Relief is not withdrawn (see 26.26 above) on inter-spouse transfers while they are living together. On any later disposal to a third person of shares previously the subject of an inter-spouse transfer *inter vivos*, however, the normal provisions for withdrawal apply, the assessment being made on the transferor in relation to the later disposal.

Where relief was given for 1989/90 or earlier in respect of shares issued to a married man or woman who was living with his/her spouse at the time of issue, and it falls to be withdrawn by virtue of a disposal of the shares by the spouse who subscribed for them, the assessment withdrawing relief is made on the spouse making the disposal by reference to the reduction of tax flowing from the relief, regardless of the allocation of the relief for the year for which it was given.

Relief may be carried back (see 26.23 above) from 1990/91 to 1989/90 on election by either husband or wife, provided that they were married and living together both when the shares were subscribed for and throughout 1989/90. The relief is then set against the husband's total income for 1989/90, the overall and carry-back relief limits applying jointly to husband and wife for that year (see below). [*Sec 304(5)(6); FA 1988, 3 Sch 12*].

See 26.18 above as regards the deemed time of issue of shares subscribed for through approved funds.

For **1989/90** and earlier years of assessment, relief in respect of any amount subscribed by a married woman for shares issued to her at a time when she was living with her husband, and at which any income of hers was included as his income, is given against his total income, subject to any separate assessment application or wife's earnings election. The limits on relief are applied to them jointly, except that in the year of assessment of divorce or of ceasing to live together, or on the husband's death, the remainder of the year after such an event is treated as a separate year of assessment in respect of shares subscribed for by the wife after the event.

If either a separate assessment application or a wife's earnings election was in force for a year of assessment for which relief is claimed in respect of shares subscribed for by the wife, the relief applicable to her subscriptions is allocated to her under the relevant provision. If relief is claimed for the same year in respect of shares subscribed for by the husband, and the joint limit on relief is exceeded, the available relief is divided in proportion to the otherwise eligible subscriptions.

The provisions for one spouse's reliefs to be set against the other's income in the year of marriage (see 47.11(c) MARRIED PERSONS) are extended to relief under these provisions, limited, in the case of the wife's reliefs, to those in respect of shares subscribed for during any part of a year of assessment in which they were living together.

Relief is not withdrawn (see 26.26 above) on transfers between spouses when they were living together, but the normal provisions for withdrawal apply on any later disposal before 1990/91 to a third person of shares previously transferred between spouses. If, following a transfer of shares between spouses, and without those shares having been transferred to a third person, the husband and wife were divorced or ceased to live together, any assessment later required to withdraw relief in respect of those shares will be made on the transferee.

Where a husband and wife were divorced or ceased to live together, and relief falls to be withdrawn before 1990/91 on a disposal, by the original subscriber, of shares subscribed for and issued while they were married and living together, the assessment will be made on the disponor by reference to the reduction of tax flowing from the amount of relief, regardless of any allocation of that reduction under the separate assessment provisions and of any allocation of reliefs in the year of marriage (see above). [*Secs 280, 304 as originally enacted*].

26.29   **Miscellaneous.** *Anti-avoidance.* Relief otherwise due to an individual is denied where shares are issued other than for *bona fide* commercial reasons or as part of a scheme the main purpose (or one such purpose) of which was tax avoidance. [*Sec 289(11)*].

Capital gains tax considerations. In relation to shares issued after 18 March 1986, in respect of which relief has been given and not withdrawn, any gain or loss on a disposal of the shares as a result of which relief is not withdrawn is not a chargeable gain or allowable loss for capital gains tax purposes. This applies on a subsequent disposal to a third party where eligible shares have previously been transferred on a no gain/no loss basis between spouses, but where either *TCGA 1992, s 135* or *s 136* would otherwise apply on a share exchange, etc., it will only apply if relief is withdrawn (except, after 28 November 1994, where the new holding is, broadly, in a company which has issued BES or EIS shares).

In relation to shares issued before 19 March 1986, on a disposal, other than between spouses, of shares in respect of which relief has been given and not withdrawn, the allowable expenditure for capital gains tax purposes is determined without regard to that relief, except that where the expenditure exceeds the consideration (i.e. a loss), the expenditure is reduced by the lesser of (*a*) the amount of that relief and (*b*) the excess. Where *TCGA 1992, s 135* or *s 136* would otherwise apply in relation to an exchange of such shares after 5 April 1988 and before 1 January 1990, an election may be made (before 6 April 1991) for the *section* not to apply (unless the relief is withdrawn). This results from a consolidation error in *ICTA 1988* which was subsequently corrected with retrospective effect apart from the availability of this election.

Identification of securities for these purposes is as under 26.26 above.

Where only part of a holding of ordinary shares has attracted relief, and there has been a reorganisation of share capital within *TCGA 1992, s 126*, the new holding of shares is treated as two new holdings, one identified with shares attracting relief, the other with the remainder of the shares originally held. In relation to reorganisations after 18 March 1986, a new holding is treated as if it consists of the shares in respect of which relief has been given, both for the purposes of capital gains tax relief and for the rules regarding disposal of shares (see 26.26 above). On certain reorganisations involving allotment of shares for payment, however, *TCGA 1992, ss 127–130* do not apply, and the reorganisation is treated as a disposal in the usual way, and relief may be reduced (with a corresponding adjustment to the capital gains tax base cost). [*Sec 305; FA 1990, 14 Sch 17, 19; TCGA 1992, ss 39(3), 150; FA 1995, ss 68(3), 69; FA 1996, s 134, 20 Sch 54*]. For detailed coverage, see Tolley's Capital Gains Tax under Shares and Securities.

Information. Certain events leading to withdrawal of relief must be notified to the inspector, generally within 60 days, by either the individual who received the relief, the issuing company, or any person connected with that company having knowledge of the matter. The inspector may require such a notice and other relevant information where he has reason to believe it should have been made. The penalty provisions of *TMA s 98* apply for failure to comply.

The inspector also has broad powers to require information in other cases where relief may be withdrawn, restricted, or not due. The requirements of secrecy do not prevent his obtaining such information as he requires. [*Sec 310; FA 1993, s 111(2)*].

27   European Community Legislation

27.1   Statements of the European Council and European Commission are graded under the *EEC Treaty* as follows.

(*a*)   **Regulations** are binding in their entirety and have general effect in all Member States. They are directly applicable in the legal systems of Member States and do not have to be implemented by national legislation.

(*b*)   **Directives** are binding as to result and their general effect is specific to named Member States. The form and methods of compliance are left to individual Member States, which are normally given a specific period in which to implement the necessary legislation.

(*c*)   **Decisions** are binding in their entirety and are specific to a Member State, commercial enterprise or private individual. They take effect on notification to the addressee.

(*d*)   **Recommendations and opinions** are not binding and are directed to specific subjects on which the Council's or Commission's advice has been sought.

27.2   European Community law is effective in the UK by virtue of *European Communities Act 1972, s 2*, and the European Court of Justice has held that 'wherever the provisions of a Directive appear . . . to be unconditional and sufficiently precise, those provisions may . . . be relied upon as against any national provision which is incompatible with the Directive insofar as the provisions define rights which individuals are able to assert against the State' (*Becker v Finanzamt Munster-Innenstadt [1982] 1 CMLR 499*). Judgments in the European Court of Justice also have supremacy over domestic decisions, even if the proceedings commenced in another Member State.

27.3   In contrast to the extensive application of EC legislation in the VAT sphere, direct taxes are currently subject to only the following three measures.

(*a*)   *Council Regulation 2137/85* (25 July 1985) concerning European Economic Interest Groupings.

(*b*)   *Directive 90/434/EEC* (23 July 1990) concerning mergers, divisions, transfers of assets and exchanges of shares concerning companies of different Member States.

(*c*)   *Directive 90/435/EEC* (23 July 1990) concerning distributions of profits to parent companies.

As regards (*a*), see the related UK legislation at 53.19 PARTNERSHIPS. As regards (*b*), the UK legislation is dealt with in Tolley's Corporation Tax under Capital Gains, and a minor consequential amendment at 81.11 SHARE INCENTIVES AND OPTIONS. As regards (*c*), a minor amendment is dealt with at 23.12 DEDUCTION OF TAX AT SOURCE. The Revenue Consultative Document on EC Direct Tax Measures published in December 1991 sets out the manner in which (*b*) and (*c*) are considered to be implemented by these legislative changes.

In addition to the above, *Convention 90/436/EEC* (23 July 1990), concerning arbitration in double taxation disputes arising from transfer pricing adjustments, came into force on 1 January 1995. See 3.9 ANTI-AVOIDANCE, 25.5(*m*) DOUBLE TAX RELIEF and 36.2(*o*), 36.3 INLAND REVENUE: CONFIDENTIALITY OF INFORMATION.

27.4   Three further *Directives* have been proposed, concerning interest and royalty payments between parent and subsidiary companies, relief for losses of branches or subsidiaries in other Member States, and carry-over of losses of undertakings. The first has now been withdrawn, and there is currently little prospect of progress on adoption of the other two.

28   Excess Liability

Cross-references. See 1.3 ALLOWANCES AND TAX RATES for current unified tax rates (basic and higher) and 1.4 for a description of the changeover to unified income tax in 1973/74.

28.1   'Excess Liability' means income tax in excess of the basic rate. It thus comprises the higher rate or rates plus, before 1984/85, the investment income surcharge. See 1.3 ALLOWANCES AND TAX RATES. For 1992/93 and subsequent years, the definition is adjusted to take account of the lower rate band, and similarly for 1993/94 and subsequent years, it is adjusted to take account of the application of the lower rate of tax to dividend income (and, for 1996/97 onwards, savings income) insofar as such income does not exceed the basic rate limit (see 1.8(ii)(iii) ALLOWANCES AND TAX RATES). Although it is only so defined for certain specific purposes of the *Taxes Acts*, it is used for convenience in this chapter to refer to all such liabilities.

Returns, assessments and appeals. There is no provision for a return of total income for the purposes of excess liability. The ordinary annual return (see 67.2 RETURNS) will enable the total income and the relevant deductions—see 28.2(*a*) below—to be ascertained. The normal provisions for ASSESSMENTS (5) and APPEALS (4) apply to excess liability as they do to basic rate liability. Where the income is received untaxed, any appropriate excess liability is included with the basic and lower rate liability in the assessment on the income or, as regards Schedule E income, dealt with under PAY AS YOU EARN (55). The excess rate liability on other income is separately assessed. [*Sec 5(4); FA 1994, 26 Sch Pt V(23); FA 1996, 6 Sch 3, 28*]. For due dates of payment and related matters, see 56.1 PAYMENT OF TAX. See also 78.17 to 78.20 SELF-ASSESSMENT.

Relationship to surtax. Excess liability replaced surtax which, similarly, was charged by reference to the total income of individuals. Court decisions on appeals against assessments to surtax (or its predecessor, super-tax) apply to excess liability where the relevant legislation is now applicable to it, and the majority of cases referred to below (and in other parts of this work to which reference is made) do in fact involve surtax etc. appeals.

28.2   **INCOME CHARGEABLE TO EXCESS LIABILITY—GENERAL**

(*a*)   Excess liability is charged by reference to the total income of an individual and any investment income included in it. [*Sec 1(2)*]. Total income is the aggregate income from all sources. [*Sec 835(1)*]. 'Charges on income' (28.4 below), personal allowances given by deduction [*Sec 256; FA 1994, s 77(1)*], any interest payments eligible for relief by deduction and any other such reliefs, e.g. allowable LOSSES (46), are deducted to give the amount on which the excess liability is calculated.

The personal allowances are deducted after any other deductions and will not reduce the investment income surcharge payable for years of assessment before 1984/85 unless they exceed in aggregate the earned income plus the investment income covered by the nil rate. Subject to this and to any express provisions to the contrary (e.g. those providing for the order in which losses are to be allowed), the deductions are treated as reducing income of different descriptions in the order which results in the greatest tax reduction. [*Sec 835(3)–(5); FA 1971, s 34(4)*]. Hence for years before 1984/85 if there is any investment income surcharge liability, charges on income or interest will normally be deducted against investment income first.

For what is investment income see 1.8 ALLOWANCES AND TAX RATES.

(*b*)   There are various provisions under which amounts not within the normal charging rules of the Schedules and Cases are nevertheless to be treated as income of a person, or income of one person is to be deemed income of another. This legislation includes the following.

(i) Much of the ANTI-AVOIDANCE (3) legislation.

(ii) *ICTA 1988, Pt XI, Ch III* under which the undistributed income of close companies could be apportioned to shareholders, etc. For this see Tolley's Corporation Tax. See Revenue Pamphlet IR 131, A36 for restriction of excess liability where income apportioned after winding-up of company. *Chapter III was repealed by FA 1989.*

(iii) The settlements legislation in *Secs 660–689*. See 80.13 *et seq.* SETTLEMENTS.

For other provisions relating specifically to excess liability, see 28.3 below.

(*c*) **Assessments** which have become *final and conclusive* for income tax are also final and conclusive in estimating total income. [*Sec 835(7)*].

(*d*) **Dividends, interest, annual payments, etc. receivable.** Income received under deduction of tax is income of the year by reference to which the rate of tax is determined, irrespective of the period over which it accrued, and similarly for dividends within Schedule F. [*Sec 835(6)(a); FA 1996, 6 Sch 24, 28*]. Where securities are sold through the Stock Exchange, the interest or dividend for the period spanning the date of sale is income of the vendor or purchaser according to whether they were sold ex- or cum-dividend etc. irrespective of the period of accrual (cf. *Wigmore v Summerson KB 1925, 9 TC 577* and *CIR v Oakley KB 1925, 9 TC 582*). But see 28.3(*c*) below as regards certain sales cum-dividend etc. and 74.6 *et seq.* SCHEDULE D, CASE VI as regards the accrued income scheme. Where the transfer of shares bequeathed under a will was delayed, dividends paid before the transfers were held to be income of the legatee (*CIR v Hawley KB 1927, 13 TC 327*). But where the controlling shareholder of a company set up a scheme under which the employees were contingently entitled to shares he owned, the dividends were held to be his pending the contingency (*CIR v Parsons CA 1928, 13 TC 700*). See also *Spence v CIR CS 1941, 24 TC 311* where dividends on shares sold and later recovered because of fraudulent misrepresentation by the purchaser were held to be income of the vendor.

Income due is not assessable before it is received (*Lambe v CIR KB 1933, 18 TC 212*, mortgage interest due but not received from company in hands of receiver not assessable) and this is so even though the non-receipt is because right to the income has not been exercised (*Dewar v CIR CA 1935, 19 TC 561; Woodhouse v CIR KB 1936, 20 TC 673*). But where a shareholder refused to accept dividends tendered to her, surtax assessments including the dividends were upheld (*Dreyfus v CIR Ch D 1963, 41 TC 441*). See also *St Lucia Usines v Colonial Treasurer PC 1924, 4 ATC 112*.

Interest receivable on National Savings Certificates and on Tax Reserve Certificates is exempt. Special treatment applies to certain interest from Building Societies (see 28.3(*a*) below), to certain bank deposit interest (see 8.2 BANKS), and to interest from National Savings Banks (see 29.11(iv) EXEMPT INCOME).

(*e*) **Partnership income.** A partner's share of the partnership profits (arrived at as in 53.5 PARTNERSHIPS), is part of his total income, any higher rate liability on the share being included in the partnership assessment (where relevant—see 53.3 PARTNER-SHIPS). Where the ownership of partnership profits was subject to a future contingency and they were meanwhile carried to suspense, it was held that the profits could not meanwhile be assessed to super-tax (*Franklin v CIR KB 1930, 15 TC 464*). Similarly, amounts payable under a partnership agreement to the widow of a deceased partner, but not paid, were held not to be income of the widow (*Lebus's Exors CA 1946, 27 TC 136*). In *Dreyfus v CIR CA 1929, 14 TC 560*, it was held that the taxpayer's share of the profit of a French 'société en nom collectif' was not part of his total income.

(*f*) **Settlements.** Where the legislation at (*b*)(iii) above does not apply, the income of a beneficiary under a settlement or trust (including a will trust) falls to be determined under general principles. For this see SETTLEMENTS at 80.8 and also at 80.10 for foreign trust income, 80.5 for discretionary and accumulation trusts, 80.9 for annuities and other annual payments and 23.17 DEDUCTION OF TAX AT SOURCE for 'free of tax' annuities. For income from deceased estates during administration see 22.3 DECEASED ESTATES.

(*g*) **Other matters.** A balancing charge is part of total income (*CIR v Lloyds Bank (Scott's Exors) Ch D 1963, 41 TC 294*). For income assigned for certain purpose see *CIR v Paterson CA 1924, 9 TC 163* and *Perkins' Exors v CIR KB 1928, 13 TC 851* (in which the income was held to be income of the assignor) and compare *Wolverton v CIR HL 1931, 16 TC 467*. For case where the ownership of income was in dispute, see *Shenley v CIR KB 1945, 27 TC 85*.

In *Vestey v CIR Ch D 1961, 40 TC 112* the taxpayer sold shares of an estimated value of £2m for £5.5m payable in equal instalments over 125 years. He was held to be assessable to surtax on the interest element in the instalments, calculated on actuarial lines. (Some of the reasoning in this decision was not approved by the HL in *CIR v Church Commissioners HL 1976, 50 TC 516*.)

28.3   INCOME CHARGEABLE TO EXCESS LIABILITY—PARTICULAR PROVISIONS

(*a*) The following are treated as income not liable to basic rate income tax but (after grossing-up at the basic rate) are subject to excess liability.

(i) Interest paid or credited before 6 April 1991 from BUILDING SOCIETIES (9). [*Sec 476(5)(c)*].

(ii) Close company loans to a participator or associate of a participator, which are released or written off in 1992/93 or earlier. [*Sec 421*].

(iii) Restrictive covenant payments in respect of pre-9 June 1988 undertakings, in connection with an office or employment. [*Sec 313*]. See 75.34 SCHEDULE E.

(iv) Bank deposit interest paid or credited before 6 April 1991 and subject to composite rate tax (see 8.2 BANKS). [*Sec 479(2)(b)*].

As regards (ii), for 1993/94 and subsequent years, such loans are grossed up at the lower rate of income tax and taxed as if they were dividends (see 1.8(ii) ALLOWANCES AND RATES) (but with no entitlement to repayment of the notional tax credit). [*Sec 421; FA 1993, s 77(4); FA 1996, s 122(6), 6 Sch 9, 28*].

(*b*) **Gains on 'non-qualifying' insurance policies, etc.** are subject to excess liability, with top-slicing relief. See 45.13 LIFE ASSURANCE POLICIES.

28.4   CHARGES ON INCOME

(*a*) **General.** The term 'charges on income' is derived from *TMA s 8(8)* (as originally enacted). The deduction, subject to (*b*) below, is for annuities or other annual payments (other than interest), patent royalties and certain mining, etc. rents and royalties payable under DEDUCTION OF TAX AT SOURCE (23) out of the income. [*Sec 3*].

28.5 Excess Liability

In *Bingham v CIR Ch D 1955, 36 TC 254* a deduction was refused for alimony payable under a foreign Court Order as the payer was not empowered to deduct tax at source (cf. *Keiner v Keiner QB 1952, 34 TC 346*). Tax is deductible only if the payment is 'pure income profit' in the hands of the recipient and not e.g. an element entering into the computation of his business receipts. Hence a deduction was refused for insurance premiums payable under covenant on policies lodged as part of a mortgage security (*Earl Howe v CIR CA 1919, 7 TC 289*).

Where an interest in a business is transferred in consideration for periodical payments based on subsequent profits, whether the payments are 'annual payments' rests on the facts. See *Ramsay CA 1935, 20 TC 79* and *Ledgard KB 1937, 21 TC 129* in which a deduction was refused and contrast *Hogarth CS 1940, 23 TC 491*. Whether a payment is an 'annual payment' may arise in a number of contexts other than in arriving at total income. See 23.10 DEDUCTION OF TAX AT SOURCE for other cases.

(b) **Statutory modifications** of the general rule include the following.

    (i) The settlements legislation, in particular, for 1994/95 and earlier years, *Secs 660–662*, under which income under certain dispositions is treated as income of the settlor, *Secs 663–671*, dealing similarly with settlements on children and certain revocable settlements, and *Secs 683, 684*, which broadly prohibit the deduction for excess liability of annual payments by a settlor other than for certain specified purposes. See 80.21–80.23, 80.28 SETTLEMENTS. These provisions are replaced for 1995/96 and later years by those at 80.13–80.17 SETTLEMENTS under which certain income of a settlement may fall to be treated for all tax purposes as that of the settlor.

    See 15.6 CHARITIES, 80.21, 80.28 SETTLEMENTS for the definition of, and special treatment accorded to, covenanted payments to charity.

    (ii) Annual payments made for a non-taxable consideration and not involving a settlement within the legislation (*CIR v Plummer HL 1979, 54 TC 1*) are payable in full and are not deductible for excess liability purposes. [*Sec 125*]. See 3.19 ANTI-AVOIDANCE.

    (iii) Payments due after 14 March 1988 under non-charitable covenants, unless, for 1994/95 and earlier years, made under an 'existing obligation' (see 1.8(i) ALLOWANCES AND TAX RATES, and see also 47.15 MARRIED PERSONS) are not, in any case, charges on income. [*Sec 347A; FA 1988, s 36; FA 1995, 17 Sch 4(1)*]. See 15.6 CHARITIES, 80.21, 80.28 SETTLEMENTS as regards charitable covenants.

(c) **Timing and method of deduction.** Charges are deducted for the year which determines the rate of tax deductible, see 23.5 DEDUCTION OF TAX AT SOURCE. [*Sec 835(6)(b)*]. For the order of allowance against different types of income see 28.2(a) above.

28.5 INTEREST PAYABLE

Interest payable does not rank as a 'charge on income' within 28.4 above for income tax purposes, but may be allowable either as a deduction in computing business profits or as a deduction in arriving at total income or as a reduction in income tax liability. For this see 43 INTEREST PAYABLE. For the corporation tax position, see Tolley's Corporation Tax under Profit Computations.

28.6   **OVERLAP BETWEEN EXCESS LIABILITY AND INHERITANCE TAX ON A DEATH**

Where, on a death, income accrued at the death is treated both as capital of the estate for inheritance tax purposes and as residuary income of the estate in the hands of a beneficiary having an absolute interest in the residue, in arriving at the excess liability of the beneficiary the residuary income is reduced by the grossed-up amount of the inheritance tax attributable to the excess of the accrued income over any liabilities taken into account in both valuing the estate and arriving at the residuary income. [*Sec 699; FA 1993, 6 Sch 6; FA 1996, 6 Sch 13, 28*].

28.7   **OVERSEAS MATTERS**

There are no special provisions regarding the excess liability treatment of non-residents or overseas income and accordingly the normal rules apply unless modified by double tax agreements. Subject to any such relevant agreement a non-resident will be within the charge to excess liability as regards his UK income (see *Brooke v CIR CA 1917, 7 TC 261*) and is assessable in his own name if he can be served with a notice of assessment (cf. *CIR v Huni KB 1923, 8 TC 466; Whitney v CIR HL 1925, 10 TC 88*). If a non-resident is relieved from UK tax at the higher rate(s) on dividends received from UK companies under a double tax agreement, he is also normally exempted from UK income tax on any close company income apportioned to him. (Revenue Pamphlet IR 1, B22). Note that apportionment was abolished for company accounting periods beginning after 31 March 1989.

For the treatment of personal allowances, see 51.11 NON-RESIDENTS AND OTHER OVERSEAS MATTERS.

29 Exempt Income

Cross-references. See 1 ALLOWANCES AND TAX RATES for the various personal allowances against income and 1.8(i) for certain annual payments not treated as taxable income; 1.8 CLAIMS for repayment of tax suffered; 23.11(*c*) DEDUCTION OF TAX AT SOURCE for exemption of capital portion of purchased life annuities; 30 EXEMPT ORGANISATIONS; 64.2 RESIDENCE, ORDINARY RESIDENCE AND DOMICILE for certain percentage deductions; 59.4 PENSIONS; 74.4 SCHEDULE D, CASE VI for relief for furnished room lettings; 80.29 SETTLEMENTS—re maintenance funds for historic buildings; 89 UNDERWRITERS for transfers to special reserve funds.

The following income is exempt from income tax and any tax suffered may be reclaimed.

29.1   **Adoption allowances** paid under the *Adoption Allowance Regulations 1991* (or Scottish equivalent) which would otherwise be regarded as annual payments within SCHEDULE D, CASE III (72) are not taxable. (Revenue Pamphlet IR 1, A40).

29.2   **Compensation for loss of employment etc. up to £30,000.** See 19.4 COMPENSATION FOR LOSS OF EMPLOYMENT for details of exemptions and reliefs for these and other terminal payments at the end of an employment.

29.3   **Compensation for mis-sold personal pensions etc. (and interest thereon).** Exemption from both income tax and capital gains tax is conferred on the receipt at any time of a capital sum (which may include a sum otherwise chargeable to income tax) by way of compensation for loss, or likely loss, caused by certain 'bad investment advice' concerning personal pensions etc. '*Bad investment advice*' is investment advice (as defined by *Financial Services Act 1986, 1 Sch 15*) in respect of which an action has been or may be brought against the adviser for negligence, breach of contract or fiduciary obligation or by reason of a contravention actionable under *Financial Services Act 1986, s 62.* The exemption applies where a person (whether or not the person suffering loss), acting on such advice at least some of which was given after 28 April 1988 and before 1 July 1994 (at which date new regulatory safeguards came into force), either

(*a*)   joined a personal pension scheme or took out a retirement annuity contract (see 65 RETIREMENT ANNUITIES AND PERSONAL PENSION SCHEMES) whilst eligible, or reasonably likely to become eligible, to join an occupational pension scheme (i.e. an approved retirement benefits scheme, relevant statutory scheme or pre-6 April 1980 approved superannuation scheme—see 66.1, 66.13 RETIREMENT SCHEMES FOR EMPLOYEES); or

(*b*)   left, or ceased to pay into, an occupational pension scheme and instead joined a personal pension scheme or took out a retirement annuity contract; or

(*c*)   transferred to a personal pension scheme his accrued rights under an occupational pension scheme; or

(*d*)   left an occupational pension scheme and instead entered into arrangements for securing relevant benefits (see 66.1 RETIREMENT SCHEMES FOR EMPLOYEES) by means of an annuity contract with an insurance company.

Interest on the whole or part of a capital sum within the above exemption is itself exempt from income tax to the extent that it covers a period ending on or before the earliest date on which the amount of the capital sum is first determined, whether by agreement or by a court, tribunal, commissioner, arbitrator or appointee.

[*FA 1996, s 148*].

29.4   **Damages and compensation for personal injury.** Income tax relief is available where an agreement is made settling a claim or action for damages for personal injury (as widely defined) under which the damages are to consist wholly or partly of periodical payments, or where a court order incorporates such terms. This applies equally in relation to interim court order payments and voluntary payments on account. Periodical payments received **on or after 29 April 1996** (irrespective of when the agreement or order was made or took effect) are not regarded as income for income tax purposes, and are paid without deduction of tax under *Sec 348(1)(b)* or *Sec 349(1)* (see 23.2, 23.3 DEDUCTION OF TAX AT SOURCE). This applies as regards the person ('A') entitled to the damages under the agreement or order, and also

(*a*)   any person receiving the payments on behalf of A; and

(*b*)   any trustee receiving the payments on trust for A's benefit under a trust under which A is (during his lifetime) the sole beneficiary,

and sums paid on to (or for the benefit of) A by a person within (*b*) above are not regarded as A's income for income tax purposes.

Any or all of the periodical payments may (if the agreement etc., or a subsequent agreement, so provides) be under one or more annuities purchased or provided for (or for the benefit of) A by the person otherwise liable for the payments.

The above provisions apply equally to annuity payments under a compensation award under the Criminal Injuries Compensation Scheme. The Treasury may also apply them (with any necessary modifications) to any other scheme or arrangement making similar provision. [*Secs 329AA, 329AB; FA 1996, s 150, 26 Sch*].

For payments received **before 29 April 1996 and after 1 May 1995,** broadly similar provisions apply. Where a person received a sum as, or on behalf of, the annuitant under an annuity purchased for him pursuant to a 'qualifying agreement' (whenever made), that sum is not regarded as income for income tax purposes, and is paid without deduction of tax under *Sec 349(1)* (see 23.3 DEDUCTION OF TAX AT SOURCE). Similar relief applies to annuities pursuant to qualifying awards under the Criminal Injuries Compensation Scheme.

An agreement is a '*qualifying agreement*' if it is made settling a claim or action for personal injury (including any disease and any physical or mental impairment), and if the damages under the agreement are to consist wholly or partly of periodical payments, to be received by the person entitled to them as the annuitant under one or more annuities purchased for him by either the person against whom the claim or action was brought or his insurer. Claims or actions under the *Fatal Accidents Act 1976* or NI equivalent are included. Payments under the annuity or annuities must correspond in amount and timing to the periodical payments under the agreement. The periodical payments may be for the life of the claimant, for a specified period or of a specified number or minimum number, or include payments of more than one of those descriptions. The amounts of the periodical payments (which need not be at a uniform rate or intervals) may be specified in the agreement, with or without provision for increases, or may be adjustable in a specified manner to preserve their real value, or may be partly so specified and partly so adjustable.

Where an agreement would be a qualifying agreement but for the fact that the substitution of the annuity payments for the periodical payments is under a later agreement and from a future date, the later agreement is a '*qualifying agreement*'. Similarly, where the person liable to make the periodical payments (or his insurer) purchases an annuity or annuities, which is or are assigned to the claimant under a later agreement, that later agreement is the '*qualifying agreement*'. The requirements described above as to payments under the annuity or annuities and the periodical payments apply to such qualifying agreements with the necessary modifications.

[*Secs 329A, 329B, 329C; FA 1995, s 142; Criminal Injuries Compensation Act 1995, s 8*].

29.5 **Foreign service allowance** to a person in the service of the Crown representing compensation for the extra cost of living abroad. [*Sec 319*].

29.6 **Gallantry awards.** Annuities and additional pensions paid by virtue of holding the award to holders of the Victoria Cross or the George Cross are exempt, as are additional pensions paid to holders of the Military Cross, the Distinguished Flying Cross, the Distinguished Conduct Medal, the Conspicuous Gallantry Medal, the Distinguished Service Medal, the Military Medal or the Distinguished Flying Medal and annuities paid to holders of the Albert Medal or the Edward Medal. [*Sec 317*].

29.7 **German and Austrian annuities and pensions for victims of Nazi persecution** under German or Austrian law are not treated as income for any income tax purpose. [*Sec 330*].

29.8 **Housing grants.** Except where the expense recouped is deductible from profits, amounts received, under any relevant Act, towards expenses incurred, by the recipient or another, in providing, maintaining or improving residential accommodation are not assessable. [*Sec 578*].

29.9 Income from **international organisations** may be exempt under specific provisions, see 24 DIPLOMATIC IMMUNITY.

29.10 Annual payments under certain **insurance policies.** Where an individual's insurance policy provides income benefits which may be payable for more than one year, those benefits constitute annual payments within SCHEDULE D, CASE III (72). In practice, tax has not been collected where insurance benefits are provided in times of sickness, disability or unemployment to meet existing specified obligations such as loan repayments. (Revenue Press Release REV 6, 28 November 1995). Also, by concession, sickness benefits which compensate for lost earnings are generally exempt for the first twelve months. (Revenue Pamphlet IR 1, A83). Before 6 April 1994, a somewhat wider concession applied. (Revenue Pamphlet IR 1, A26). See 71.63 SCHEDULE D, CASES I AND II, 75.37 SCHEDULE E for details of both concessions.

Annual payments falling to be made after 5 April 1996 under certain policies are exempt from income tax under new statutory provisions (and see also below as regards earlier payments). The exemption, described below, will most commonly apply to mortgage payment protection insurance, permanent health insurance, creditor insurance (to meet existing commitments, possibly including domestic utility bills, in event of accident, sickness, disability or unemployment) and certain kinds of long-term care insurance (but only where the policy is taken out before the need for care becomes apparent). (Revenue Press Release REV 6, 28 November 1995).

The exemption is generally restricted to payments that would otherwise be taxed under Schedule D, Case III or, in the case of equivalent non-UK policies, Schedule D, Case V. Payments to be taken into account in computing business profits are thus excluded. However, where an employer takes out a group policy to meet the cost of employees' sick pay and the policy would otherwise qualify under these provisions, the proportion of any payment attributable (on just and reasonable apportionment) to employees' contributions to premiums is exempt from Schedule E. The exemption does not apply if any premiums under the policy (disregarding in the case of the Schedule E exemption an employer's share of premiums) have to any extent qualified for tax relief, either as a deduction from total income or in computing income from any source (e.g. business profits).

For an annual payment to qualify for the exemption:

(a)   it must be made under a policy (or part of a policy) providing insurance against a 'qualifying risk';

(b)   the provisions of the policy which insure against that risk must be 'self-contained';

(c)   the policy must make no provision for payments relating to that risk other than for a period throughout which the 'relevant conditions of payment' are satisfied; and

(d)   the provisions of the policy relating to that risk must always have been such that the insurer runs a genuine risk of loss (i.e. proceeds payable must be capable of exceeding premiums received plus an investment return on those premiums).

A '*qualifying risk*' is either a risk of physical or mental illness, disability, infirmity or defect (including a risk of an existing condition deteriorating) or a risk of loss of employment (including loss of self-employment). The persons at risk may include the insured, his spouse and, for policies connected with the meeting of liabilities under an identified transaction, a person jointly liable with the insured or his spouse.

The '*relevant conditions of payment*' are satisfied for as long as the illness etc. or unemployment continues (including in the case of illness etc. any related period of convalescence or rehabilitation) or for as long as the income of the insured etc. (apart from benefits under the policy) is less, in circumstances so insured against, than it otherwise would be. If any such period ends as a result of the death of the insured etc., it is extended to any period immediately following (so that benefits paid to the deceased's spouse or estate are brought within the exemption).

The requirement for the relevant provisions of the policy to be '*self-contained*' is an anti-avoidance measure. The provisions of a policy covering different kinds of benefits are self-contained unless the terms of the policy (possibly including the fixing of the amount of premiums), or the way in which they are given effect, in relation to the qualifying risk would have been significantly different if the policy insured only against the qualifying risk (except where the only difference is that certain benefits are applied for reducing other benefits under the policy). A broadly similar rule applies where there are multiple policies. In each case, regard must be had to all the persons for whose benefit insurance is provided against the qualifying risk.

There are provisions enabling benefits relating to illness etc. to qualify for the exemption if paid under an individual policy derived from and superseding an employer's group policy where an employee has left the employment as a consequence of the occurrence insured against.

The exemption also applies to annual payments falling due before 6 April 1996, whether or not made before that date, provided that the only or main purpose of the policy was to secure that the insured would be able to meet liabilities arising from identified transactions (actual or proposed, and including credit arrangements and services to residential premises) none of which could be entered into after any of the circumstances insured against arose, and that the policy provided for the right to annual payments to cease when all liabilities in question were discharged.

[*Secs 580A, 580B; FA 1996, s 143*].

29.11 Exempt Income

29.11   **Interest—**

(i)   on damages for personal injuries or death [*Sec 329*] including similar interest awarded by a foreign court if also exempt from tax in that country (Revenue Pamphlet IR 1, A30).

(ii)   on certain UK government stocks held by non-residents (see 33.2 GOVERNMENT STOCKS) and certain borrowings in foreign currency by local authorities and certain STATUTORY BODIES (83) (see 23.12 DEDUCTION OF TAX AT SOURCE).

(iii)   on **tax-exempt special savings accounts ('TESSAs').** Bonuses are also exempt. An account is a 'TESSA' if the following conditions (and any others specified by regulation by the Board) are satisfied when the account is opened.

(*a*)   It must be opened by an individual aged 18 or more.

(*b*)   It must be with a building society or an institution authorised under *Banking Act 1987*; it must not be a joint account and must not be held on behalf of another person; it must be identified as a TESSA, and the account-holder must not simultaneously hold another TESSA; and it must not be 'connected with' any other account. An account is '*connected with*' another if either was opened with reference to the other, or with a view to enabling or facilitating the opening of the other on particular terms, and the terms on which either was opened would have been significantly less favourable to the holder if the other had not been opened. In relation to TESSAs opened after 1 January 1996, accounts may be held with certain European authorised institutions entitled to accept deposits in the UK (which must, however, appoint UK tax representatives or make similar arrangements for discharging their duties under the scheme). By concession, accounts opened on or before that date may be transferred to such institutions after that date. (Revenue Press Release 21 December 1995).

(*c*)   There must not be a notice in force given by the Board to the society or institution prohibiting it from operating new TESSAs.

(*d*)   It must be transferable from one society or institution to another which is entitled to, and does, operate TESSAs, on terms agreed between the account-holder and any society or institution concerned.

As regards the requirement at (*b*) above that the account must not be held on behalf of another person, in Scotland, by concession, a *curator bonis* may open a TESSA on behalf of an incapacitated person aged 18 or more, whose name must, however, be shown on the application form. Any details given in returns etc. by the bank or building society holding the account must be those of the incapacitated person and not those of the *curator bonis*. (Revenue Pamphlet IR 1, A79).

A society or institution intending to operate or to cease to operate TESSAs must comply with notification requirements. The Board have powers (subject to appeal) to prohibit a society or institution from operating TESSAs. An application by an individual for a TESSA must contain information specified by regulation, and a statement that false statements in connection with the application may result in penalties or prosecution. On a transfer within (*d*) above, the transferor must supply the transferee with details of the account as specified by regulation.

An account continues to be a TESSA for five years from its being opened (or until the earlier death of the account-holder), or until any of the conditions set out above ceases to be satisfied or any of the following events occurs.

(I) The deposit of more than £3,000 in the first twelve months the account is open, of more than £1,800 in any succeeding twelve-month period, or of more than £9,000 in total.

(II) A withdrawal reducing the balance on the account below the aggregate of earlier deposits and lower or basic rate income tax (whichever is applicable) on any interest or bonus previously paid on the account. The rate applicable is the lower rate, except as regards interest etc. paid or credited before 6 April 1996 where it is the basic rate (being in each case the rate in force for the tax year in which the interest etc. was paid or credited).

(III) The assignment of any rights of the account-holder in respect of the account or the use of such rights as security for a loan.

When an account ceases to be a TESSA (other than on the expiry of the five-year period from its opening or the death of the account-holder), the *Income Tax Acts* have effect as if, immediately after it so ceased, the account were credited with an amount of interest equal to the interest and bonuses payable during the period it was a TESSA.

The Board have the necessary regulatory powers to require information, both aggregate and individual, and the maintenance and inspection of records, and to impose certain requirements as to UK tax representation on European authorised institutions. Penalties apply in relation to notices under those powers.

Follow-up TESSAs. Where a TESSA reaches the end of its five year life (without having ceased to be tax-exempt) and the total amount deposited was over £3,000, the holder may, within the following six months, open another 'follow-up' TESSA in which the maximum deposit in the first twelve months is the total amount deposited in the earlier TESSA (excluding any accumulated interest in that account). An account is not connected with another account (see (*b*) above) merely because it is a follow-up account.

[*Secs 326A–326D; FA 1990, s 28; TCGA 1992, s 271(4); FA 1995, ss 62, 63; FA 1996, 6 Sch 7; SI 1990 No 2361; SI 1995 Nos 1929, 3236, 3239; SI 1996 No 844*].

The Inland Revenue Financial Intermediaries and Claims Office may be contacted for technical advice in relation to TESSAs on 0151–472 6157.

See generally Revenue Pamphlet IR 114.

(iv) to the extent of the first £70 for each individual of **National Savings Bank** interest on deposits other than investment deposits. [*Sec 325*].

(v) on **Government Savings Certificates**. See 33.6 GOVERNMENT STOCKS.

(vi) on **Save As You Earn** (SAYE) certified contractual savings schemes (bonuses under such schemes also being exempt), provided (for schemes certified after 30 November 1994 and for contracts entered into after that date under earlier schemes) that they are linked to share option schemes (see 81.8 SHARE INCENTIVE AND OPTIONS). SAYE schemes may be offered by a wide range of providers, including (for schemes established after 1 May 1995) certain European authorised institutions. Treasury authorisation is required for the operation of such schemes. [*Sec 326, 15A Sch; FA 1990, s 29, 14 Sch 5; FA 1995, s 65, 12 Sch; SI 1995 No 1778*].

(vii) on overpaid inheritance tax. [*IHTA 1984, ss 233(3), 235(2)*].

(viii) on certain repayments, see 41 INTEREST ON OVERPAID TAX.

(ix) being loan interest paid by its members to a credit union. [*Sec 487; FA 1996, 14 Sch 31*].

29.12 Exempt Income

Interest and dividends paid or credited before 6 April 1991 by BUILDING SOCIETIES (9) and certain other income (see 28.3(*a*) EXCESS LIABILITY) is exempt from basic rate income tax only.

29.12 **Job release allowances** paid under scheme described in the *Job Release Act 1977* which provides for payment of allowances for periods beginning not earlier than one year before pensionable age. [*Sec 191*]. Note that allowances paid for periods beginning more than one year before pensionable age are taxable under SCHEDULE E (75). [*Sec 150(a)*]. The scheme was wound up in January 1988, although allowances in payment may continue until pensionable age.

29.13 **Long service awards** to employees, within limitations set out in 75.26 SCHEDULE E.

29.14 **Luncheon vouchers** if the conditions shown in 75.30 SCHEDULE E are complied with.

29.15 **Members of Parliament.** The following payments made pursuant to a Commons resolution are disregarded as income for tax purposes:

(i) accommodation allowances paid for additional overnight expenses incurred in performing parliamentary duties (and see 75.29 SCHEDULE E); and

(ii) reimbursed costs (paid after 31 December 1991) relating to travel between the UK and certain European Community institutions. (See generally 75.43 SCHEDULE E.)

[*Sec 200; FA 1993, s 124*].

Additionally, for 1996/97 and subsequent years, ministers and certain other office-holders in the UK government are exempt from tax under SCHEDULE E (75) in respect of the provision of transport or subsistence to them or their families or households by or on behalf of the Crown, or the re-imbursement of expenditure on such provision. 'Transport' for this purpose includes any car (with or without a driver) and any other benefit in connection with such a car (including fuel). 'Subsistence' includes food, drink and temporary accommodation. The exemption does *not* extend to the provision of mobile telephones (see 75.16 SCHEDULE E). [*Sec 200AA; FA 1996, s 108*].

29.16 **Miners'** free coal or cash in lieu thereof is exempt by concession. (Revenue Pamphlet IR 1, A6).

29.17 **Non-residents** are exempt from tax on income and capital gains from: certain GOVERNMENT STOCKS (33); securities of the Inter-American Development Bank [*Sec 583*]; securities of the OECD Support Fund [*OECD Support Fund Act 1975, s 4*] and certain other international organisations designated by statutory instrument [*Sec 324*], including the Asian Development Bank (*SI 1984 No 1215*), the African Development Bank (*SI 1984 No 1634*), the European Bank for Reconstruction and Development (*SI 1991 No 1202*) and any of the European Communities or the European Investment Bank (*SI 1985 No 1172*); and from certain pensions, see 59.4 PENSIONS. See also 25.2 DOUBLE TAX RELIEF.

29.18 Certain **overseas income** is exempt from UK tax under specific DOUBLE TAX RELIEF (25) agreements. If not so exempt, double tax relief may nevertheless be claimable. In some circumstances, overseas income is only assessable on the REMITTANCE BASIS (63). See also 51 NON-RESIDENTS AND OTHER OVERSEAS MATTERS.

29.19 Certain **pensions** are exempt, see 59.4 PENSIONS.

29.20   **Personal equity plans.** A 'qualifying individual' may subscribe a specified maximum to a personal equity plan to which no-one else may subscribe. Revised regulations came into force on 6 April 1989 (the *1989 Regulations*) (subsequently amended) modifying the original provisions (the *1986 Regulations*).

A '*qualifying individual*' must be 18 years of age or over, and either resident and ordinarily resident in the UK or a non-resident Crown employee serving overseas whose duties are treated as performed in the UK (see 75.2(i) SCHEDULE E). Subscriptions may be made to only one general plan and one 'single company plan' (see below) in any tax year. From 6 April 1996, a *curator bonis* appointed in Scotland for a qualifying individual suffering from incapacity may subscribe to a plan in his capacity as such, regardless of any subscription he may make in another capacity.

Under the *1989 Regulations*, a maximum of £6,000 may be invested through a 'plan manager' in a personal equity plan in any tax year. For so long as the various conditions continue to be met, dividends and interest on securities are tax-free (and the plan manager may reclaim the related tax credits). There is no capital gains tax liability (nor is there relief for losses) on the sale of an investment under the plan.

Up to £3,000 per tax year may be invested in a 'single company plan' (often known as a 'corporate PEP') in addition to any investment in a general plan as described above. A '*single company plan*' allows investment only in shares of one designated company, and an additional condition imposed is that substantially the whole of the cash subscribed to the plan, or from realisation of plan shares, must be reinvested in plan shares within 42 days, or transferred (with interest) to the investor within 14 days thereafter.

Regulations impose certain requirements as to UK tax representation on European authorised institutions and certain other European plan managers.

Conditions applicable to both 'general' and 'single company' plans. All transactions involving plan investments must be carried out at open market prices, and investments may not be purchased from the plan investor or spouse. Subscription to a plan must be by payment of cash to the plan manager for investment by him, except that

(a)   qualifying shares allotted under public offers, and

(b)   (in relation to single company plans, see below) certain shares acquired under employee share schemes,

may be transferred into plans. As regards (a) above, the shares must be transferred to the plan within 42 days of allotment, and their cost included within the overall investment limit. This applies also to shares in a building society issued on conversion to plc status. The fact that a new issue may take the form of separate offers on slightly different terms (e.g. to employees or customers of the issuing company) does not prevent the shares being eligible for transfer into a plan. (Revenue Press Releases 6 October 1989, 17 October 1990).

Cash held in a plan must be within the overall limit, must be held in sterling and must be invested in a designated account with a deposit-taker or building society (see 8 BANKS, 9 BUILDING SOCIETIES). Interest is paid gross and will be exempt from tax altogether, so long as it is eventually invested in plan shares, securities or unit trusts. (Revenue Press Release 17 October 1990). If interest etc. exceeding £180 in a year is paid by the plan manager to or for the plan investor in respect of cash held within a plan, the plan manager must account for a sum representing lower rate (before 1996/97 basic rate) tax on all such interest payments in the year; the interest payments are for all purposes treated as interest taxable under SCHEDULE D, CASE III (72) in the year in which they arise, the lower or basic rate liability on which is satisfied as above.

General plans. The investments which may be purchased, made or held under a general plan after 5 July 1995 are:

(i) ordinary shares in UK-incorporated companies (other than investment trusts) listed on a recognised stock exchange in an EU Member State or dealt in on the Unlisted Securities Market (but not the Alternative Investment Market, see Revenue Press Release 20 February 1995);

(ii) '*qualifying EC shares*' (i.e. shares issued by a company incorporated in a Member State other than the UK and listed on a recognised stock exchange in a Member State), provided that they form part of the authorised share capital of the company, carry no fixed, guaranteed or secured redemption rights or preferential rights to dividends or to company property in a liquidation, and are neither shares carrying no right to a profit share other than fixed dividends nor shares carrying no right to fixed dividends but carrying a right of conversion into shares which do carry such a right. The company must not be an open-ended investment company within *Financial Services Act 1986, s 75(8)*, and must not derive the principal part of its income from shareholdings each of which represents 10% or less of the voting power in the company concerned;

(iii) shares other than ordinary shares, issued by a company incorporated in a Member State and quoted on a recognised stock exchange in a Member State, not being shares in an investment trust or an authorised credit institution (as defined, and including the European equivalent);

(iv) securities (i.e. any loan stock or similar security, whether secured or unsecured) issued by a company incorporated in the UK, not being securities of an investment trust or an authorised credit institution (as defined), provided that:

   (*a*) at the date of issue and throughout the period of the loan they either carry a right to interest at a fixed percentage rate (or a series of consecutive such rates) or carry no right to interest;

   (*b*) they are denominated in sterling;

   (*c*) judged at the date when first held under the plan, the terms of issue do not require the loan to be repaid or the security to be re-purchased or redeemed, or allow the holder to so require except in circumstances unlikely to occur, within five years;

   (*d*) the securities are not deep gain securities within *FA 1989, 11 Sch* and do not fall to be treated as such by virtue of *FA 1989, 11 Sch 21(2), 22(2), 22A(2)* or *22B(3)* (see 44.7 INTEREST RECEIVABLE); and

   (*e*) at least one of the following conditions is satisfied:

      (I) the ordinary shares in the issuing company are quoted on a recognised stock exchange in a Member State;

      (II) the securities are so quoted; or

      (III) the issuing company is a 75% subsidiary (within *Sec 838*) of a company whose ordinary shares are so quoted;

(v) units in an authorised unit trust (as specially defined and excluding certain pension schemes with restricted investment powers ('feeder funds') and schemes which may invest wholly in warrants ('warrant funds')), provided that at least 50% in value of the investments held by the trust are either

   (I) ordinary shares in UK-incorporated companies (other than investment trusts),

   (II) qualifying EC shares and shares within (iii) above (or shares which would be such shares if quoted on a recognised stock exchange in a Member State),

(III) securities which would be within (iv) above if the condition in (iv)(*c*) required the judgement to be made when they were first acquired by the unit trust, and disregarding the condition in (iv)(*e*), and

(IV) shares in (and securities meeting the conditions in (iv)(*a*)–(*d*) above of) an investment trust 50% of the value of the investments of which are within (I) or (II) above, or would be within (III) above if the date in question were that on which the securities were first acquired by the investment trust;

(vi) units in a fund of funds (i.e. a unit trust scheme investing in authorised unit trusts) where at least 50% of the investments held by those trusts are within (v)(I)–(III) above;

(vii) shares in (and securities meeting the conditions in (iv)(*a*)–(*d*) above of) an investment trust (including a 'split-level' trust, see Revenue Press Release 3 May 1989) 50% of the value of the investments of which are either within (v)(I)–(IV) above or units in unit trusts at least 50% of the investments held by which are within (v)(I)–(III) above;

(viii) subject to an overall limit of one-quarter of the maximum subscription (less any amounts payable for qualifying investment trust shares allotted under public offers, see (*a*) above, and transferred to the plan), investments not within (v)–(vii) above which meet the following conditions:

(A) in the case of units in authorised unit trusts, 50% of the investments held by the trust are either ordinary shares in UK-incorporated companies (other than investment trusts) or 'other quoted shares' (i.e. shares listed on a recognised stock exchange which satisfy the conditions applicable to qualifying EC shares under (ii) above), or shares in investment trusts at least 50% of whose investments are such ordinary or other quoted shares;

(B) in the case of funds of funds, at least 50% of the investments held by the constituent unit trusts are ordinary shares in UK-incorporated companies (other than investment trusts) or other quoted shares (as in (A) above); and

(C) in the case of investment trusts, at least 50% of the investments held by the trust are either ordinary shares in UK-incorporated companies (other than investment trusts) or other quoted shares (as in (A) above), or units in authorised unit trusts 50% of the value of whose investments are such ordinary or other quoted shares; or

(ix) cash.

An occasional inadvertent fall below the 50% levels referred to in (v)–(viii) above will generally be disregarded, see Revenue Press Release 3 May 1989.

Cash received by the plan manager from dividends, disposals etc. may be reinvested in any qualifying investments within (i)–(vii) above, and in unit trusts, funds of funds and investment trusts *not* within (v)–(vii) above provided that the market value of such investments does not immediately thereafter exceed one-quarter of the market value of all plan investments.

Certain investments held on 5 April 1990 which failed to meet the test for qualification ('non-qualifying investments') may continue to be held under a plan, provided that

(*a*) the total of such investments made during 1989/90 and held at that date did not exceed £2,400, and

(*b*) apart from the reinvestment of proceeds of sale of non-qualifying investments, the amount invested in non-qualifying investments in 1990/91 did not exceed £900, and

(c)   after 5 April 1991, the total amount invested in authorised unit trusts, funds of funds and investment trusts does not exceed one-quarter of the subscription limit.

Single company plans. The investments which may be purchased, made or held under a single company plan are:

(i)   where the company designated for the purposes of the plan is a UK company (other than an investment trust or venture capital trust) quoted on a recognised stock exchange or dealt in on the Unlisted Securities Market, ordinary shares in the company, and ordinary shares or 'qualifying EC shares' 'representing' those shares;

(ii)   provided that the designated company is not an open-ended investment company within *Financial Services Act 1986, s 75(8)*, and does not derive the principal part of its income from shareholdings each of which represents 15% or less by value of its investments, 'qualifying EC shares' issued by the company, and 'qualifying EC shares' or ordinary shares within (i) above 'representing' those shares;

(iii)   investments in units comprising ordinary shares or 'qualifying EC shares' in the designated company (restricted as in (i) or (ii) above respectively) which are 'paired' with ordinary shares or 'qualifying EC shares' in another company meeting the condition in (i) or (ii) above respectively; or

(iv)   cash.

In addition, the plan investor may subscribe to a plan by transferring to the plan manager shares in the designated company which were appropriated to the plan investor under an approved profit-sharing scheme or acquired by exercise of options under a SAYE share option scheme (see 81.6, 81.8 SHARE INCENTIVES AND OPTIONS). Shares acquired under SAYE schemes must be transferred in within 90 days of exercise of the option, those appropriated under profit-sharing schemes within 90 days of the earlier of the date the plan investor directed the trustees of the scheme to transfer the shares to him and the 'release date' in relation to the shares (see 81.6 SHARE INCENTIVES AND OPTIONS). The sum of the market value of shares so transferred to a plan and of the cost of any new issue shares so transferred (see general conditions above) must, together with any cash subscribed, be within the overall subscription limit for the single company plan.

'*Qualifying EC shares*' are shares issued by a company incorporated in a Member State other than the UK and officially listed on a recognised stock exchange in a Member State. Shares '*represent*' other shares when there is a company reorganisation under which, for capital gains tax purposes, they are (or would but for being plan investments be) equated with the other shares. Shares in two companies are '*paired*' where it is provided in their governing instruments that no share in either company may be acquired otherwise than as part of a unit comprising one share in each company, such units being offered for sale at the same time and at the same price or, where sales are in more than one country, at a broadly equivalent price.

Cash received by the plan manager from dividends, disposals etc. may be reinvested in other shares within (i)–(iii) above. Where the cash arises in respect of shares transferred in from a profit-sharing or SAYE share option scheme (see above), it may be re-invested in similar shares even where they are not otherwise qualifying investments.

Pre–1990 plans. Plans under the *1986 Regulations* operated by reference to calendar years rather than tax years. There was an overall limit of £3,000 (£2,400 before 22 April 1988) per year of which the greater of £540 (£420 before 22 April 1988) and one-quarter of the plan subscription could be invested in investment trusts and authorised unit trusts.

[*Secs 333, 333A; TCGA 1992, s 151; FA 1991, s 70; FA 1993, s 85; FA 1995, s 64; SI 1986 No 1948; SI 1989 No 469; SI 1990 No 678; SI 1991 Nos 733, 2774; SI 1992 No 623; SI 1993 No 756; SI 1995 Nos 1539, 3287; SI 1996 No 846*].

General. A list of registered plan managers may be obtained by sending a self-addressed A4 size envelope to (or calling at) Inland Revenue, Public Enquiry Room, West Wing, Somerset House, London WC2R 1LB. The list is updated quarterly. An information pack on personal equity plans aimed at plan managers is available from the Inland Revenue Library, Mid-Basement, Somerset House, price £3.50.

The Inland Revenue Financial Intermediaries and Claims Office may be contacted in relation to personal equity plans on 0151–472 6110 as regards repayments or 0151–472 6157 for technical advice.

See generally Revenue Pamphlet IR 89.

29.21   **Profit-related pay** under a registered scheme is wholly or partly exempt within certain limits. See 75.31 SCHEDULE E.

29.22   **Redundancy payments** under *Employment Protection (Consolidation) Act 1978* (or NI equivalent). [*Sec 579*]. See also 75.32 SCHEDULE E.

29.23   **Repayment supplement** in respect of income tax or capital gains tax repayments (see 41 INTEREST ON OVERPAID TAX) or VAT repayments (under *VATA 1994, s 79*, see Tolley's Value Added Tax under Payment of Tax) is disregarded for income tax purposes. [*Secs 824(8), 827(2)*].

29.24   Certain lump sums under RETIREMENT ANNUITIES AND PERSONAL PENSION SCHEMES (65) and RETIREMENT SCHEMES (66).

29.25   **Sandwich courses.** Where an employee is released by employer to take a full-time educational course at a university, technical college or similar institution open to the public at large, payments for periods of attendance may be treated as exempt from income tax. Conditions are (i) that the course lasts at least one academic year, with an average of at least 20 weeks per year of full-time attendance, and (ii) that the rate of payment does not exceed the greater of (*a*) £7,000 p.a. (£5,500 before 6 April 1992, £5,000 before 6 April 1989) and (*b*) the rate of payment an individual in similar personal circumstances would have received as a grant from one of the public awarding bodies on a scale fixed by the Secretary of State for Education and Science (e.g. a Research Council Studentship). For this purpose, university fees etc. paid or reimbursed by employer are ignored. Where the rate of payment exceeds the limit, the full payments are taxable, but where a rate of payment is increased during a course, only subsequent payments are taxable, and periods where payments are thus taxable nonetheless count towards the requisite periods of attendance. (Revenue Pamphlet IR 131, SP 4/86, 8 August 1986; Revenue Press Releases 12 April 1989, 18 November 1992). See 75.42 SCHEDULE E as regards certain training courses.

29.26   **Scholarship** income and bursaries. [*Sec 331*]. In *Clayton v Gothorp Ch D 1971, 47 TC 168*, discharge of loan made by employer for training course held not scholarship income but was emoluments. See 29.25 above and 75.20 SCHEDULE E for where scholarship awarded by employer of parent etc. Covenanted 'parental contributions' under *Education Act 1962* not an educational endowment (*Gibbs v Randall Ch D 1980, 53 TC 513*).

29.27   Certain **Social Security** benefits (see 82 SOCIAL SECURITY) and corresponding foreign benefits. (Revenue Pamphlet IR 1 (November 1995 Supplement), A24). Disabled Person's Vehicle Maintenance Grants under *National Health Service Act 1977, 2 Sch 2* or corresponding Scottish or NI Act. [*Sec 327*]. Also Sickness and Disablement Benefits from Approved and Friendly Societies to the extent specified in Revenue Pamphlet IR 1, A26.

29.28 Exempt Income

29.28   For 1995/96 and earlier years, discounts on **Treasury securities** issued after 6 March 1973 are exempt from tax under Schedule D, Case III [*Sec 126; FA 1996, 41 Sch Pt V(3)*] without this exemption resulting in a charge under Schedule D, Case VI. They are still chargeable to tax if they constitute trading profits. This exemption does not apply to Treasury Bills, to 'deep discount securities' issued by public bodies or 'deep gain securities' (see 44.5, 44.7 INTEREST RECEIVABLE), or to certain gilt-edged securities which are treated as deep discount or deep gain securities. [*FA 1989, s 95; FA 1996, 41 Sch Pt V(3)*]. See now 72.2 SCHEDULE D, CASE III (and Tolley's Corporation Tax under Gilts and Bonds as regards accounting periods ending after 31 March 1996).

29.29   **Wages in lieu of notice** in most instances. See 75.45 SCHEDULE E.

29.30   **War Gratuities, Bounties or Gratuities** to men and women voluntarily re-enlisting; training bounties to reservists; mess and ration allowances, training expenses, allowances and efficiency bounties to members of reserve and auxiliary forces [*Sec 316*] but Civil Defence Corps bounties are not exempt because these are paid by local authorities and therefore not 'out of the public revenue' (*Lush v Coles Ch D 1967, 44 TC 169*).

29.31   **War widows etc.** Pensions payable in respect of death due to (*a*) service in the armed forces, including before 3 September 1939 or (*b*) wartime service in the merchant navy or (*c*) war injuries, and similar pensions payable by foreign governments, are exempt from tax. The exemption also applies to the amount of any other pension which replaces an exempt pension withheld or abated. [*Sec 318*].

29.32   **Wound and disability pensions** to HM Forces. [*Sec 315*]. See 59.4(ii) PENSIONS.

30   Exempt Organisations

Exemption is given to the organisations etc. below to the extent indicated.

30.1   **Agricultural societies** established to promote 'the interests of agriculture, horticulture, livestock breeding or forestry' are exempt from tax on profits or gains 'from any exhibition or show held for the purposes of the society . . . if applied solely to the purposes of the society'. [*Sec 510*]. See *Peterborough Royal Foxhound Show Society v CIR KB 1936, 20 TC 249; Glasgow Ornithological Assn CS 1938, 21 TC 445*. An agricultural society may also qualify for charitable relief, see 15.2(*g*) CHARITIES.

30.2   **Non-resident central banks** as specified by Order in Council are exempt from tax on certain classes of income [*Sec 516*] and the issue departments of the Reserve Bank of India and the State Bank of Pakistan are exempt from all taxes. [*Sec 517; TCGA 1992, s 271(8)*].

30.3   **The British Museum** and **Natural History Museum** may claim exemption as if they were charities. [*Sec 507; TCGA 1992, s 271(6)(a); FA 1989, s 60; Museums and Galleries Act 1992, 8 Sch 1(8)(9)*].

30.4   **Charities** are generally exempt but see full details under 15 CHARITIES.

30.5   CLUBS AND SOCIETIES (18). There is restriction of liability in a few special circumstances.

30.6   **The Crown** is not generally within the taxing Acts; see *Sec 49(2)* and *Sec 829(2)*. See *Sec 829* as amended by *FA 1993, s 122* as to assessment, deduction and payment of tax by Crown public offices and departments.

30.7   Under DIPLOMATIC IMMUNITY ETC. (24), there are certain exemptions.

30.8   FRIENDLY SOCIETIES (31) have certain exemptions.

30.9   **Historic Buildings and Monuments Commission for England** may claim exemption as if it were a charity. [*Sec 507; TCGA 1992, s 271(7)*].

30.10   **Housing Associations** and approved self-build societies have certain exemptions. [*Secs 488, 489*]. See Tolley's Corporation Tax.

30.11   **International Maritime Satellite Organisation.** An overseas signatory is exempt in respect of any receipt from the Organisation. [*Sec 515; TCGA 1992, s 271(5)*].

30.12   **Local authorities,** local authority associations and health service boards, as defined by *Secs 842A, 519(3), 519A* respectively as amended, are exempt. [*Secs 519, 519A as amended; TCGA 1992, s 271(3)*].

30.13   MUTUAL TRADING (50). There are some special tax provisions.

30.14   **National Heritage Memorial Fund** may claim exemption as if it were a charity. [*Sec 507; TCGA 1992, s 271(7)*].

30.15 Exempt Organisations

30.15   SCIENTIFIC RESEARCH ASSOCIATIONS (77) are generally exempt.

30.16   Some STATUTORY BODIES (83) receive a measure of exemption.

30.17   Approved **Superannuation Funds, personal pension schemes** etc. are exempt from tax on investment income and on chargeable gains arising on investments the income of which is exempt from tax. See 65 RETIREMENT ANNUITIES AND PERSONAL PENSION SCHEMES and 66 RETIREMENT SCHEMES. Income from, or from transactions relating to, futures and options contracts is within the exemption. See further 71.32 SCHEDULE D, CASES I AND II.

30.18   TRADE UNIONS (88), including employers' associations and Police Federations, which are registered are exempt on provident benefit income under certain conditions.

30.19   Authorised UNIT TRUSTS (90), investment trusts and VENTURE CAPITAL TRUSTS (91) are exempt from corporation tax on their chargeable gains. [*TCGA 1992, s 100(1); FA 1995, s 72(2)*].

30.20   **Visiting forces** and associated civilians from designated countries. [*Sec 323; FA 1990, 14 Sch 4*].

31   Friendly Societies

31.1   Friendly societies are within the charge to corporation tax on income and capital gains. There are, however, exemptions from tax for:

(i)   unregistered societies with incomes not exceeding £160 p.a.; and

(ii)   registered or incorporated societies, in respect of 'tax exempt life or endowment business'.

[Secs 459, 460(1)(2); F(No 2)A 1992, 9 Sch 4, 5].

Incorporated societies, following enactment of the *Friendly Societies Act 1992*, attract the same exemptions etc. as registered societies, and there are provisions to ensure that no tax charges arise on the incorporation of a registered society under that *Act*. [FA 1992, 9 Sch; Secs 461A–461C, 465A; TCGA 1992, ss 217A–217C].

'*Tax exempt life or endowment business*' is broadly life or endowment business consisting of the granting of annuities of annual amounts not exceeding £156, or of the assurance of gross sums under contracts under which the total premiums payable in any twelve-month period do not exceed a maximum figure as follows:

for contracts made after 30 April 1995	£270
for contracts made after 24 July 1991 and before 1 May 1995	£200
for contracts made after 31 August 1990 and before 25 July 1991	£150
for contracts made after 31 August 1987 and before 1 September 1990	£100

For contracts made after 13 March 1984 and before 1 September 1987, the limit on the assurance of gross sums was by reference to the amount of the gross sum assured, and was set at £750. For contracts made before 14 March 1984, the limit was £500, and that on the granting of annuities £104. Where the premium under a contract made after 31 August 1987 and before 1 May 1995 is increased by a variation after 24 July 1991 and before 1 August 1992 or after 30 April 1995 and before 1 April 1996, the contract is to be treated for these purposes as having been made at the time of the variation. In determining these limits, no account is taken of any bonus or addition declared upon an assurance or accruing thereon by reference to an increase in the value of any investments, or of any bonus or addition declared upon an annuity. In relation to premium limits, so much of any premium as relates to exceptional risks of death is disregarded, as is 10% of premiums payable more frequently than annually. [Sec 460(2)(c)(d), (3)–(6); FA 1990, s 49(1)(2); FA 1991, 9 Sch 1; F(No 2)A 1992, 9 Sch 5; FA 1995, 10 Sch 1]. For detailed requirements for exemption, see Tolley's Corporation Tax under Friendly Societies.

31.2   **Individual limit.** The total amount of business which a person may have outstanding with registered or incorporated friendly societies is limited:

(i)   to an annuity or annuities totalling not more than £156 p.a. (£416 p.a. where all the contracts were made before 14 March 1984); and

(ii)   to a gross sum assured under a contract or contracts under which the total premiums payable in any twelve-month period do not exceed any of the following limits:

for all contracts	£270
for contracts made after 24 July 1991 and before 1 May 1995	£200
for contracts made after 31 August 1990 and before 25 July 1991	£150
for contracts made before 1 September 1990	£100

unless all the contracts were made before 1 September 1987. For these purposes, a premium under an annuity contract made before 1 June 1984 by a 'new society' (see

31.3 below) is brought into account as if the contract were for the assurance of a gross sum. For contracts made before 1 September 1987, a limit was imposed by reference to the gross sum(s) assured, the limit being £750 (£2,000 if all the contracts were made before 14 March 1984). Where the premium under a contract made after 31 August 1987 and before 1 May 1995 is increased by a variation after 24 July 1991 and before 1 August 1992 or after 30 April 1995 and before 1 April 1996, the contract is to be treated for these purposes as having been made at the time of the variation. No account is, however, taken of (a) so much of any premium as relates to exceptional death risk, (b) 10% of premiums payable more frequently than annually, and (c) £10 of the premiums payable in a twelve month period under any contract made before 1 September 1987 by a society which is not a 'new society' (see 31.3 below).

The restrictions on both gross sum and annuity contracts are applied without taking into account any bonus or addition declared upon an assurance or accruing thereon by reference to an increase in the value of any investments. An annuity contract made before 1 June 1984 by a 'new society' is for these purposes treated as providing both the annual sum assured and a gross sum equal to 75% of the premiums which would be payable if the annuity ran its full term or the person died at age 75. [*Sec 464; FA 1990, s 49(3)(4); FA 1991, 9 Sch 3; F(No 2)A 1992, 9 Sch 11; FA 1995, 10 Sch 2*]. If, after 18 March 1985, a person obtains a policy which causes his contracts to exceed the above limits, the policy will not be a 'qualifying policy' (see 31.3 below), but without affecting earlier policies. [*15 Sch 6*].

31.3   **Qualifying policies** attract income tax relief on the premiums paid (for insurances made before 14 March 1984), and the proceeds are generally free of any income tax charge (see 45.1, 45.13 LIFE ASSURANCE POLICIES). Except as below, all policies issued by friendly societies before 19 March 1985 in the course of tax exempt life or endowment business (see 31.1 above) are qualifying policies. [*ICTA 1970, 1 Sch 3 as originally enacted*]. A policy issued *or varied* after 18 March 1985 is a qualifying policy only if it satisfies the conditions in *15 Sch 3, 4 as amended*. Broadly, these are the same as the conditions imposed under *Sec 462* on policies which a friendly society may issue in the course of its tax exempt life or endowment business (see Tolley's Corporation Tax under Friendly Societies), but in addition the minimum sum assured must be at least 75% of the total premiums payable, and contracts made before 25 July 1991 with a 'new society' must be with a person over the age of 18. [*15 Sch 3(1); FA 1991, 9 Sch 4*]. For the detailed application of the 75% test, see *15 Sch 3(5)–(11)*.

Certain policies issued under contracts made before 20 March 1991, and expressed at the outset not to be made in the course of tax-exempt life or endowment business, were subsequently determined to have been within the statutory definition of that business. A similar situation arose in relation to certain contracts for qualifying policies assumed, at the outset of the contract, not to be made in the course of tax-exempt life or endowment business (without being expressed either to be or not to be so). Where the society so elects (before 1 August 1992), profits attributable to such contracts are treated as not being within the exemption. [*Sec 462A; FA 1991, 9 Sch 2*]. However, such an election does not affect the tax position of the member holding the policy. By concession, the member will be taxed on the basis of the original assumption he will have been given that no charge to tax would arise on the surrender or maturity of the policy. (Revenue Press Release 12 June 1991). See Tolley's Corporation Tax under Friendly Societies for details of the society's election.

A '*new society*' is a society which either was registered after 3 May 1966 or was registered in the three months before that date but did not carry on any life or endowment business during that period (or a successor incorporated society). [*Sec 466(2); F(No 2)A 1992, 9 Sch 14(5)*].

If any rights under a health insurance policy (within *Friendly Societies Act 1974, 1 Sch 1*) issued by a new society (see above) are wholly or partly surrendered after 18 March 1985, the policy ceases to be a qualifying policy. [*15 Sch 4(3)(b)*].

31.4 **Non-qualifying policies.** A gain on a chargeable event in respect of a policy which is not a qualifying policy (see 31.3 above), or in respect of certain life annuity contracts, may give rise to a charge to income tax (see 45.13 LIFE ASSURANCE POLICIES). If such a gain arises on a policy issued in the course of a society's tax exempt life or endowment business (see 31.1 above), it is chargeable to basic and higher rates of income tax, with no deemed payment of basic rate liability, and with 'top-slicing relief' (see 45.13 LIFE ASSURANCE POLICIES) applying only to the higher rate tax. [*Secs 540, 542, 550; FA 1987, s 30(8)*].

31.5 **Qualifying distributions.** If a society registered after 31 May 1973, with certain exceptions, or one registered before that date if the registrar so directs, makes a payment to a member (in excess of his contributions and not in the course of life or endowment business), this is a qualifying distribution for income and corporation tax purposes (see Tolley's Corporation Tax under Distributions). [*Sec 461(2)(3)*].

31.6 **Status of certain life insurance policies.** Following a High Court decision in a non-tax case, certain types of contract entered into by life insurance companies and friendly societies, under which the return on death is no greater, or not significantly greater, than on a surrender at the same time, may not in law be life insurance policies. The previously accepted tax status of such policies is to be confirmed, by legislation if necessary. (Revenue Press Release 20 November 1994).

31.7 See 3.17 ANTI-AVOIDANCE for restriction of tax recovery regarding pre-acquisition dividends, etc. on 10% holdings, and 3.18 regarding certain bonus issues.

32   Funding Bonds

32.1   Funding Bonds etc. issued in respect of interest by any Government, public authority or institution, or company are treated as income equal to bonds' value when issued; but their eventual redemption is not treated as a payment of the interest. 'Bonds' includes 'stocks, shares, securities or certificates of indebtedness'. Persons by or through whom the bonds are issued and who, if the amount treated as income had been an actual payment of interest, would have been required to deduct tax therefrom, must retain a proportionate amount of these bonds equal to tax at the lower rate (for 1995/96 and earlier years, the basic rate) on their value, and are accountable to the Revenue accordingly, with the right to tender the bonds in payment. Where retention is impracticable they may be relieved of liability on their furnishing a list of recipients, who are then assessed direct under Schedule D, Case VI. [*Sec 582; FA 1996, s 134, 6 Sch 14, 20 Sch 32*].

33   Government Stocks

Cross-references. See 3 ANTI-AVOIDANCE for dividend-stripping and bond-washing transactions; 14 CERTIFICATES OF TAX DEPOSIT; 23 DEDUCTION OF TAX AT SOURCE; 70 SCHEDULE C for the position of paying and collecting agents.

33.1   GENERAL TAX PROVISIONS

The provisions of *FA 1996, ss 80–105, 8–15 Schs* introduced a new taxation regime for corporation tax purposes for gilt-edged and other securities. Broadly, for accounting periods ending after 31 March 1996, all interest and profits or losses in respect of securities is brought in on revenue account, either on an accruals or on a mark-to-market basis. This regime **does not apply for income tax.** However, for 1996/97 and subsequent years for income tax purposes, a new simplified regime (see 72.2 SCHEDULE D, CASE III) is introduced for dealing with discounts on securities, replacing the existing deep discount, deep gain and qualifying convertible securities provisions (see 44.5, 44.7, 44.8 INTEREST RECEIVABLE) and taking precedence over the accrued income scheme (see 74.6 *et seq.* SCHEDULE D, CASE VI). There continues to be a capital gains tax exemption for gilt-edged and most other securities.

For 1996/97 and subsequent years (and for company accounting periods ending after 31 March 1996), Government and foreign securities are chargeable under Schedule D, Case III, IV or V as appropriate, and are subject to the paying and collecting agents arrangements under *Secs 118A–118K* (introduced by *FA 1996, s 156, 29 Sch*) and associated regulations. Previously (but generally to similar effect) they were chargeable under SCHEDULE C (70).

33.2   INTEREST—TAX EXEMPTION FOR NON-RESIDENTS

The Treasury has powers to issue securities ('FOTRA securities') on terms that the profits or gains arising from the securities are exempt from tax provided that they are beneficially owned by persons not ordinarily resident in the UK (see RESIDENCE, ORDINARY RESIDENCE AND DOMICILE (64)). The following stocks are currently exempt.

9 % Conversion 2000	$7\frac{3}{4}$% Treasury 2012/15
9 % Conversion 2011	8 % Treasury 2003
$9\frac{1}{2}$% Conversion 2001*	8 % Treasury 2002/06
$9\frac{3}{4}$% Conversion 2003*	8 % Treasury 2013
$13\frac{1}{4}$% Exchequer 1996	$8\frac{1}{2}$% Treasury 2000*
7 % Treasury Convertible 1997	$8\frac{1}{2}$% Treasury 2007
$2\frac{1}{2}$% Treasury Index-linked 2024	$8\frac{3}{4}$% Treasury 1997
$4\frac{1}{8}$% Treasury Index-linked 2030	$8\frac{3}{4}$% Treasury 2017
$4\frac{3}{8}$% Treasury Index-linked 2004	9 % Treasury 1994
$4\frac{5}{8}$% Treasury Index-linked 1998	9 % Treasury 2008
$5\frac{1}{2}$% Treasury 2008/12	9 % Treasury 2012
6 % Treasury 1999	$9\frac{1}{2}$% Treasury 1999
$6\frac{1}{4}$% Treasury 2010	$12\frac{3}{4}$% Treasury 1995
$6\frac{3}{4}$% Treasury 1995/98	$13\frac{1}{4}$% Treasury 1997
$6\frac{3}{4}$% Treasury 2004	$15\frac{1}{4}$% Treasury 1996
7 % Treasury 2001	$15\frac{1}{2}$% Treasury 1998
$7\frac{1}{4}$% Treasury 1998	$3\frac{1}{2}$% War Loan
$7\frac{3}{4}$% Treasury 2006	Floating rate Treasury 1999

Further and current information relating to exempt stocks may be obtained from Gilt-Edged and Money Markets Division, Bank of England, Threadneedle Street, London EC2R 8AH (tel. 0171–601 4540). A restricted market operates in those stocks marked with an asterisk because of the small amounts still in issue.

Provided that any conditions imposed are complied with, nothing in the *Tax Acts* over-rides such exemption, although this does not confer any exemption from charge where income is treated under anti-avoidance provisions as income of a UK resident, etc. (see 80.16, 80.17 SETTLEMENTS, 3.8 ANTI-AVOIDANCE). See *FA 1996, s 154, 28 Sch*. For 1995/96 and earlier years (and for company accounting periods ending before 1 April 1996), *Sec 47* (which is repealed by *FA 1996, 28 Sch 1*) applied to broadly similar effect.

If interest forms part of the profits of a UK trade, exemption does not generally apply (depending on the Treasury conditions of issue) (see *Owen v Sassoon Ch D 1950, 32 TC 101*).

See 51.9 NON-RESIDENTS AND OTHER OVERSEAS MATTERS for the special position of *non-resident banks, insurance companies and dealers in securities* carrying on business in the UK.

For the exemption of non-residents from income tax on interest on local authority securities expressed in a foreign currency, see 23.12 DEDUCTION OF TAX AT SOURCE.

33.3   INTEREST—DEDUCTION OF TAX

Interest on UK government stocks is payable under deduction of income tax, except as indicated below. The procedure whereby paying agents deduct and account for tax, previously under 70 SCHEDULE C is, from 1996/97 onwards, dealt with under *Secs 118A–118K* (introduced by *FA 1996, s 156, 29 Sch*) and regulations thereunder.

The Treasury may direct that interest on certain securities should be paid gross [*Sec 50(1); 51AA; FA 1996, s 155*] but the recipient may nevertheless apply to the Bank of England for income tax to be deducted. [*Sec 50(2)*].

Interest on the following Government stocks (although not exempt) is paid without deduction of tax.

33.4   Government Stocks

(i) $3\frac{1}{2}$% War Loan.

(ii)   Registered stocks and bonds on the National Savings Stock Register.

(iii)   Stocks held through any Savings Bank.

The Treasury also has powers to make regulations for gross payment of interest on government stocks held by corporate bodies and in certain other circumstances under specified arrangements, and for periodic accounting for tax on such interest. (These powers relate to the 'gilt repos' market introduced on 2 January 1996.) See *SI 1995 Nos 2934, 3223, 3224, 3225, SI 1996 No 21* (all as amended). [*Secs 51A, 51B; FA 1995, ss 77, 78; FA 1996, 6 Sch 4; SI 1995 No 2932*]. See Tolley's Corporation Tax under Income Tax in Relation to a Company.

CHARITIES (15) are generally exempt and will receive payments gross after evidence to the paying agent of charitable status. [*Sec 118D(5); FA 1996, 29 Sch 1*].

33.4   DISCOUNT ON TREASURY SECURITIES

For 1995/96 and earlier years (and for company accounting periods ending before 1 April 1996), discount on Treasury securities issued after 6 March 1973 is exempt from tax under Schedule D, Case III without this giving rise to a charge under Schedule D, Case VI [*Sec 126; FA 1996, 41 Sch Pt V(3)*] but is still chargeable to tax if it constitutes trading profits. This exemption does not apply to Treasury Bills, to 'deep discount securities' issued by public bodies or 'deep gain securities' (see 44.5, 44.7 INTEREST RECEIVABLE), or to certain gilt-edged securities which are treated as deep discount or deep gain securities. [*FA 1989, s 95; FA 1996, 41 Sch Pt V(3)*]. See now 72.2 SCHEDULE D, CASE III and Tolley's Corporation Tax under Gilts and Bonds.

33.5   PREMIUM SAVINGS BONDS

Prizes are free of both income tax and capital gains tax.

33.6   SAVINGS CERTIFICATES

All income arising from savings certificates (as defined) (and including index-linked) and tax reserve certificates is exempt from tax except from

(i)   savings certificates purchased by or on behalf of a person in excess of the amount authorised under the regulations of the particular issue, or

(ii)   Ulster savings certificates, unless the holder is resident and ordinarily resident in NI when the certificates are repaid or he was so resident and ordinarily resident when he purchased them. [*Sec 46*]. By concession, where repayment is made after the death of the holder, who was resident and ordinarily resident in NI when he purchased them, the exemption is allowed. (Revenue Pamphlet IR 1, A34).

34   Herd Basis

See generally Revenue Pamphlet IR 9 'The tax treatment of Livestock—The Herd Basis'.

34.1   Animals and other living creatures kept for the purposes of farming or similar trades (e.g. animal or fish breeding) are generally treated as trading stock (see 71.82 SCHEDULE D, CASES I AND II) unless an election is made under *Sec 97* and *5 Sch* for the 'herd basis' to apply. [*Sec 97, 5 Sch 1, 9(1)(2)*]. Animals etc. are exempt from capital gains tax as wasting assets within *TCGA 1992, s 45*.

34.2   **Availability of election for herd basis.** An election for the herd basis may apply to animals etc., whether kept singly or as part of a production herd or flock etc., which are kept wholly or mainly for the sale of products of living animals or of their young. [*5 Sch 1(2), 8(1)(5), 9(2)(4)*]. It may in practice apply to a share in a single production animal used for the purposes of a herd and to a share in animals forming part of a herd. (Revenue Pamphlet IR 1, B37). An election must apply to all herds consisting of animals of the same species (irrespective of breed), kept for production of products of the same kind, which are kept by the farmer making the election, including herds which he ceased to keep before, or first keeps after, the making of the election. [*5 Sch 2(1), 8(6)*].

34.3   An election for the herd basis **may not apply** to animals kept wholly or mainly for farm work or for public exhibition or racing or other competitive purposes. [*5 Sch 7, 9(5)*]. Immature animals are not treated as part of a herd for these purposes unless the land on which the herd is kept is such that the replacement of animals which die or cease to form part of the herd can only be by animals bred and reared on that land (e.g. acclimatised hill sheep), and then only to the extent that they are necessarily bred and maintained in the herd for the purposes of replacement. Female animals become mature when they produce their first young (and laying birds when they first lay). [*5 Sch 8(2)–(4), 9(3)*].

34.4   The **election must be made** in writing, specifying the class of herd to which it applies. As respects 1996/97 and subsequent years, the election must be made not later than:

    (*a*)   for individual farmers, twelve months after 31 January following the qualifying year of assessment, i.e. the first tax year (excluding that in which the trade commences) in the basis period for which a production herd of the class specified was first kept by the individual; and

    (*b*)   for partnerships, twelve months after 31 January following the year of assessment in which ends the qualifying period of account, i.e. the first period of account during the whole or part of which a production herd of the class specified was first kept by the partnership.

For corporation tax purposes, as respects accounting periods ending on or after the appointed day for the introduction of self-assessment for companies (see Tolley's Corporation Tax under Assessments and Appeals), the time limit is two years after the end of the qualifying accounting period, i.e. the first accounting period during the whole or part of which a production herd of the class specified was first kept by the company.

[*5 Sch 2(2)(3)(6); FA 1994, ss 196 199(2), 19 Sch 43(1)(3)*].

See, however, 34.8 below as regards compulsory slaughter.

The election is irrevocable and has effect for, respectively, the qualifying year of assessment, period of account or accounting period (see above) and subsequently. For individuals, the election also has effect for the tax year in which the trade commenced if that year

34.5 Herd Basis

immediately precedes the qualifying year of assessment. [*5 Sch 2(4)–(6); FA 1994, 19 Sch 43(2)(3)*].

Previously, the election had to be made within two years after the end of either

(i) the first period of account for which an account was made up for farming, or

(ii) the first year of assessment or company accounting period for which farming profits were chargeable under Schedule D, Case I (or loss relief given under *Sec 380, Sec 393(2)* or *Sec 393A(1)*) and in which (or, where applicable, in the basis period for which) a production herd of the class specified in the election was kept,

and had effect from the first year of assessment or company accounting period affected by it. [*5 Sch 2(2)–(4), 8(7)*].

Where there is a change in the persons carrying on a trade, then whether or not there is a continuation election (see 53.6 PARTNERSHIPS), a further election is required if the herd basis is to continue to apply. (Revenue Tax Bulletin May 1992 p 20).

See 34.5 below as regards renewal of right of election where there is a five-year gap in keeping a herd of a particular class.

34.5 **Consequences of election.** Where a herd basis election is in force, the animals in the herd are in effect treated as capital assets. The initial cost of the herd and of additions to the herd is not deductible as a trading expense, and its value is not brought into account. A profit or loss on the sale within a twelve-month period (without replacement, see 34.6 below) of the whole or a substantial (i.e. normally 20% or more) part of the herd is similarly not brought into account. Where, however, within five years of such a sale, another herd of the same class is (or begins to be) acquired (or replacement animals are or begin to be acquired), the normal replacement provisions (see 34.6 below) apply, the proceeds of the sale being treated as received at the time of the corresponding acquisition(s). However, the sale, for reasons beyond the farmer's control, of animals subsequently replaced by animals of inferior quality may not give rise to a greater trading receipt than the amount allowed as a deduction in respect of the replacement animals. [*5 Sch 3(1)(2)(8)(9)*].

Where a farmer ceases to keep any herd of a particular class for a period of at least five years, he is thereafter treated as if he had never previously kept a herd of that class. [*5 Sch 4*].

The addition to a herd of an animal previously treated as trading stock, otherwise than by way of replacement (see 34.6 below), gives rise to a trading receipt equal to the cost of acquiring or breeding it and rearing it to maturity. [*5 Sch 3(3)*]. In practice, if the animal is included in stock at market value (being lower than cost), that figure will similarly be substituted as the trading receipt on appropriation to the herd.

The sale without replacement (see 34.6 below) of an animal from a herd gives rise to a trading profit or loss, calculated by reference to the cost of acquiring or breeding it (or its market value if acquired other than for valuable consideration) and of rearing it to maturity. [*5 Sch 3(10)*].

34.6 **Replacement animals.** The replacement of an animal dying or ceasing to be a member of a herd gives rise to a trading receipt of any proceeds of sale of the animal replaced, and a trading deduction of the cost of the replacement animal (so far as not otherwise allowable under Schedule D, Case I) but limited to the cost of an animal of similar quality to that replaced. Where the animal replaced was compulsorily slaughtered, and the replacement animal is of inferior quality, the trading receipt is restricted to the amount of the corresponding deduction. [*5 Sch 3(4)–(6)*]. See 34.5 above as regards animals not replaced. Whether a particular animal brought into the herd replaces an animal disposed of for these purposes is a question of fact, requiring a direct connection between the disposal and the later addition rather than a simple restoration of numbers. As a practical matter, inspectors will accept that replacement treatment is appropriate where animals are brought into the herd within twelve months of the corresponding disposal. Where the interval is more than twelve months, there is unlikely to be sufficient evidence to support the necessary connection where the new animal is bought in. Where animals are home bred, however, a longer interval may be reasonable where e.g. there is insufficient young stock to replace unexpected disposals. (Revenue Tax Bulletin October 1994 p 169).

Where the whole herd is replaced, this is treated as the replacement of a number of animals, being the smaller of the number in the old herd and in the new. [5 Sch 3(7)]. Where the new herd is the larger, the net increase will be treated as additions to the herd. Where the new herd is the smaller, but not substantially so (i.e. the provisions described in 34.5 above in relation to a substantial reduction do not apply), the net reduction in the number of animals is treated as giving rise to a corresponding sale without replacement (see 34.5 above). [5 Sch 3(11)].

34.7   **Insurance, compensation, etc.** Any reference to sale proceeds in the foregoing provisions includes a reference, in the case of the death or destruction of an animal, to insurance or compensation moneys received and to proceeds of carcase sales. [5 Sch 3(12)].

34.8   **Compulsory slaughter.** Where compensation is received for the whole, or a substantial part (i.e. normally 20% or more), of a herd compulsorily slaughtered by order under animal diseases laws, the farmer may, notwithstanding the time limits in 34.4 above, elect for the herd basis to apply. As respects 1996/97 and subsequent years, the election must be made not later than:

(a)   for individual farmers, twelve months after 31 January following the qualifying year of assessment, i.e. the first year of assessment in the basis period for which the compensation falls (or would otherwise fall) to be taken into account as a trading receipt; and

(b)   for partnerships, twelve months after 31 January following the year of assessment in which ends the qualifying period of account, i.e. the first period of account in which the compensation falls (or would otherwise fall) to be taken into account as a trading receipt.

For corporation tax purposes, as respects accounting periods ending on or after the appointed day for the introduction of self-assessment for companies (see Tolley's Corporation Tax under Assessments and Appeals), the time limit is two years after the end of the qualifying accounting period, i.e. the first accounting period in which the compensation falls (or would otherwise fall) to be taken into account as a trading receipt. The election has effect for, respectively, the qualifying year of assessment, period of account or accounting period and subsequently.

Previously, the election was for the herd basis to apply for the year of assessment for which the compensation receivable was (or would otherwise have been) assessable and all subsequent years. Notice of election had to be given within two years of the end of that year, except that where that year was the second year of assessment of a new business, notice of election could (for income tax only) be given not later than the giving of any notice under Sec 62(2) for the current year basis of assessment to apply (see 71.4 SCHEDULE D, CASES I AND II). Where the compensation was relevant to a loss relief claim under Sec 380 for an earlier year, the election applied also for such an earlier year.

[5 Sch 6; FA 1994, ss 196, 199(2), 19 Sch 43(4)].

34.9 Herd Basis

34.9 **Anti-avoidance.** There are provisions for the prevention of avoidance of tax in the case of a transfer between connected persons or where the sole or main benefit relates to its effect on a herd basis election. [*5 Sch 5*].

34.10 **Information, etc.** Where an election has effect, returns may be required as to the animals, and products thereof, kept by any person affected by the election. Repayments etc. may be made as required to give effect to the election. [*5 Sch 10, 11*].

34.11 *Example*

A farmer acquires a dairy herd and elects for the herd basis to apply. The movements in the herd and the tax treatment are as follows.

Year 1	No	Value
		£
Mature		
Bought @ £150	70	10,500
Bought in calf @ £180		
(Market value of calf £35)	5	900
Immature		
Bought @ £75	15	1,125

Year 1	Value
Herd Account	£
70 Friesians	10,500
5 Friesians in calf (5 × £(180 − 35))	725
75 Closing balance	£11,225

Trading Account	£
5 Calves (5 × £35)	175
15 Immature Friesians	1,125
Debit to profit and loss account	£1,300

Year 2	No	Value
		£
Mature		
Bought @ £185	15	2,775
Sold @ £200 note (*a*)	10	2,000
Died	3	—
Immature		
Born	52	—
Matured @ 60% of market value of £200 note (*a*)	12	1,440

Herd Account   £

75	Opening balance		11,225
	Increase in herd		
15	Purchases	2,775	
12	Transferred from trading stock	1,440	
27		4,215	
(13)	Replacement cost £4,215 × 13/27	2,029	
14	Non-replacement animals cost		2,186
89	Closing balance		£13,411

Trading Account   £

Sale of 10 mature cows replaced   (2,000)
Transfer to herd — 14 animals   (2,186)
Cost of 13 mature cows purchased to replace those
  sold/deceased ($\frac{13}{15}$ × £2,775)   2,405

Net credit to profit and loss account   note (*b*)   £(1,781)

Year 3

	No	Value
		£
Mature		
Jerseys bought @ £250	70	17,500
Friesians slaughtered @ £175	52	9,100
Immature		
Friesians born	20	—
Matured		
Friesians @ 60% of market value of £190 note (*a*)	15	1,710

			Value
Herd Account			£
89	Opening balance		13,411
	Increase in herd		
18	Jerseys		4,500
52	Improvement Jerseys @	£250	
	less Market value of Friesians (say)	185	
52@		65	3,380
	Transfer from trading stock		
15	Friesians		1,710
122	Closing balance		£23,001

34.11 Herd Basis

Trading Account	£
Compensation	(9,100)
Transfer to herd	(1,710)
Purchase of replacements note (*c*) (52 × £185)	9,620
Net credit to profit and loss account	£ (1,190)

Year 4

The farmer ceases dairy farming and sells his whole herd.

	No	Value
		£
Mature		
Jersey sold @ £320	70	22,400
Friesians sold @ £200	52	10,400
Immature		
Friesians sold @ £100	65	6,500

Herd Account		£
Opening balance		23,001
52	Friesians	
70	Jerseys	
(122)	Sales	(32,800)
–	Profit on sale note (*d*)	£(9,799)

Trading Account	£
Sale of 65 immature Friesians	(6,500)
Credit to profit and loss account	£(6,500)

Notes

(*a*) The use of 60% of market value was originally by agreement between the National Farmers' Union and the Revenue (see now Revenue Business Economic Note 19: Farming—Stock Valuation for Income Tax purposes, at paragraph 7.2). Alternatively, the actual cost of breeding or purchase and rearing could be used.

(*b*) As the cost of rearing the 12 cows to maturity will already have been debited to the profit and loss account, no additional entry is required to reflect that cost. Due to the fact that the animals were in opening stock at valuation and will not be in closing stock, the trading account will in effect be debited with that valuation.

(*c*) The cost of the replacements is restricted to the cost of replacing like with like.

(*d*) Provided these animals are not replaced by a herd of the same class within five years the proceeds will be tax-free (see 34.5 above).

35 Inland Revenue: Administration

35.1   The levying and collection of income tax, surtax and capital gains tax is administered by the **Commissioners of Inland Revenue** (normally referred to as the Board), Somerset House, London WC2R 1LB. [*TMA s 1(1)*].

Under them are local **inspectors of taxes,** permanent civil servants with an expert knowledge of tax law, who are responsible for making most assessments, and dealing with claims and allowances, and *to whom all enquiries should be addressed.*

35.2   **Collectors of Taxes** are also permanent civil servants and their duties for the most part relate only to the collection of tax. [*TMA ss 60–70*].

35.3   **Commissioners.** Except as otherwise provided, assessments are made by inspectors [*TMA s 29*] but appeals against such assessments are heard by

(*a*)   the General Commissioners (local persons appointed on a voluntary basis by the Lord Chancellor or, in Scotland, by the Secretary of State) [*TMA s 2; FA 1975, s 57; FA 1988, s 134(1)*], or

(*b*)   the Special Commissioners (full-time civil servants, being barristers, advocates or solicitors etc. of at least ten years' standing, appointed for this purpose) [*TMA s 4; FA 1984, s 127, 22 Sch 1; Courts and Legal Services Act 1990, 10 Sch 30*].

The Lord Chancellor has powers, by regulation, to change the names by which the General and Special Commissioners are to be referred to. [*F(No 2)A 1992, s 75*].

See 4.3, 4.6 APPEALS as regards jurisdiction of Commissioners and the conduct of appeals before them.

35.4   **'Care and management' powers.** For the validity of amnesties by the Board, see *CIR v National Federation of Self-Employed and Small Businesses Ltd HL 1981, 55 TC 133.* INLAND REVENUE EXTRA-STATUTORY CONCESSIONS (38) have been the subject of frequent judicial criticism (see Lord Edward Davies' opinion in *Vestey v CIR (No 1) HL 1979, 54 TC 503* for a review of this) but their validity has never been directly challenged in the Courts. In *R v HMIT (ex p Fulford-Dobson) QB 1987, 60 TC 168*, a claim that the Revenue had acted unfairly in refusing a concession where tax avoidance was involved was rejected, but the taxpayer's right to seek judicial review of a Revenue decision to refuse the benefit of a concession was confirmed in *R v HMIT (ex p Brumfield and Others) QB 1988, 61 TC 589.* A decision by the Revenue to revoke its authorisation to pay a dividend gross was upheld in *R v CIR (ex p Camacq Corporation) CA 1989, 62 TC 651.* For a general discussion of the Board's care and management powers and an example of a ruling by the Court that the Board had exercised a discretionary power reasonably, see *R v CIR (ex p Preston) HL 1985, 59 TC 1.* Where a discretionary power is given to the Revenue, it is an error in law to proceed on the footing that the power is mandatory (*R v HMIT and Others (ex p Lansing Bagnall Ltd) CA 1986, 61 TC 112*). See also *R v CIR (ex p J Rothschild Holdings) CA 1987, 61 TC 178,* where the Revenue were required to produce internal documents of a general character relating to their practice in applying a statutory provision.

The Revenue policy of selective prosecution for criminal offences in connection with tax evasion does not render a decision in a particular case unlawful or *ultra vires,* provided that the case is considered on its merits fairly and dispassionately to see whether the criteria for prosecution were satisfied, and that the decision to prosecute is then taken in good faith for the purpose of collecting taxes and not for some ulterior, extraneous or improper purpose (*R v CIR (ex p Mead and Cook) QB 1992, 65 TC 1*).

35.5 Inland Revenue: Administration

35.5 **Equitable liability.** For the circumstances in which the Revenue may accept a reduced sum in respect of certain assessed liabilities, see 56.9 PAYMENT OF TAX.

35.6 **Inland Revenue rulings.** For the extent to which taxpayers may rely on guidance given by the Revenue, see the letter from the Deputy Chairman to the various professional bodies following the decision in *Matrix-Securities Ltd v CIR HL, [1994] STC 272*. A code of practice in this area is to be published, and a consultative document on proposals for a system of post-transaction rulings was issued on 12 May 1994. A further consultative document exploring the options for an advance rulings system is to be issued in due course. (Revenue Tax Bulletin August 1994 p 137). Meanwhile, a pilot exercise to test the proposed scheme has been in operation (and will continue until 31 August 1995) in certain tax offices in Bristol and Swindon. (Revenue Press Release 17 November 1994).

35.7 **Taxpayer's Charter.** The Board of Inland Revenue and HM Customs and Excise have jointly produced a Taxpayer's Charter setting out the principles they try to meet in their dealings with taxpayers, the standards they believe the taxpayer has a right to expect, and what people can do if they wish to appeal or complain. Copies are available from local tax or collection offices and from local VAT offices.

A series of codes of practice, setting out the standards of service people can expect in relation to specific aspects of the Revenue's work, is published to support the Taxpayer's Charter. Each code states the standards which the Revenue sets itself and the rights of taxpayers in particular situations. The first three, covering the conduct of tax investigations (see 6.1 BACK DUTY), the conduct of inspections of employers' PAYE records (see 55.1 PAYE), and mistakes by the Revenue (see 35.8 below), were published in February 1993, and are available from local tax offices. Codes 4 and 5, relating to financial intermediaries and charities (see 15.1 CHARITIES) respectively, were published in July 1993, copies being sent to the institutions concerned. Codes 6 and 7, on collection of tax generally and collection from employers and construction industry contractors, were published in November 1994 and are available from local tax offices. Codes 8 and 9, on Special Compliance Office Investigations in cases other than suspected serious fraud and cases of such fraud respectively, were published in January 1995 and are available from the Special Compliance Office, Angel Court, 199 Borough High Street, London SE1 1HZ. Code 10, on the provision by the Revenue of information and advice, was published in June 1995 and is available from local tax offices.

35.8 **Revenue error.** Code of Practice 1 (see 35.7 above), 'Mistakes by the Inland Revenue' (revised April 1996), gives general advice on the circumstances in which compensation may be claimed from the Revenue as a consequence of Revenue error. (The code also refers to waivers of tax under Extra-statutory Concession A19, see 56.6 PAYMENT OF TAX.) These fall into three categories.

(*a*) *Delays in replying to letters or other enquiries*, where, without good reason, there is a delay totalling six months or more (over and above the 28 days within which replies should normally be given).

(*b*) *Serious error*, e.g. the adoption of a wholly unreasonable view of the law, or the pursuit of enquiries into obviously trivial matters, or a simply or trivial mistake which the Revenue should have known could lead to far more serious consequences.

(*c*) *Persistent error*, even though not serious, e.g. where a mistake is continued after it has been pointed out, or the same type of mistake keeps being made, or there are a lot of unconnected mistakes within a year or in connection with a period of assessment.

In cases within (*a*), interest on overdue tax will be waived, and repayment supplement paid, for the period of the delay, and reasonable costs resulting from the delay reimbursed. Where (*b*) or (*c*) applies, the Revenue will reimburse reasonable loss or expense incurred directly because of the error, including professional and personal expenses and lost earnings, and incidental expenses such as postal and telephone charges. In exceptional circumstances, consolatory payments may also be made.

Repayment claims resulting from mistakes by the Revenue or any other Government department will be accepted up to 20 years after the year affected by the mistake.

35.9   **Revenue Adjudicator.** A taxpayer who is not satisfied with the Revenue response to a complaint has the option of putting the case to an independent Adjudicator for the Inland Revenue. The adjudicator's office opened on 1 May 1993, and will consider complaints about the Revenue's handling of a taxpayer's affairs, e.g. excessive delays, errors, discourtesy or the exercise of Revenue discretion, where the events complained of occurred after 5 April 1993. Matters subject to existing rights of appeal are excluded.

From 1 April 1995, the adjudicator will also investigate complaints about Customs and Excise.

The address is Adjudicator's Office for the Inland Revenue and Customs and Excise, 3rd Floor, Haymarket House, 28 Haymarket, London SW1Y 4SP (tel. 0171-930 2292). A leaflet 'How to complain about the Inland Revenue' is obtainable from that office in a number of different languages.

Complaints normally go to the adjudicator only after they have been considered by the Controller of the relevant Revenue office, and where the taxpayer is still not satisfied with the response received. The alternatives of pursuing the complaint to the Revenue's Head Office, to an MP, or (through an MP) to the Ombudsman continue to be available. The adjudicator reviews all the facts, considers whether the complaint is justified, and, if so, makes recommendations as to what should be done. The Revenue will normally accept the recommendations 'unless there are very exceptional circumstances'.

The adjudicator publishes an annual report to the Board.

(Revenue Press Release 17 February 1993).

35.10   **Open Government.** Under the Government's 'Code of Practice on Access to Government Information', the Revenue (in common with other Government departments) is to make information about its policies and decisions more widely available. Revenue Pamphlet IR 141 ('Open Government') sets out the information to be made available, and how it may be obtained, and the basis on which a fee may be charged in certain circumstances to offset the cost of providing the information. Copies of the Code of Practice may be obtained by writing to Open Government, Room 417b, Office of Public Service and Science, 70 Whitehall, London SW1A 2AS (tel. 0345 223242). The Revenue has also published its own Code of Practice on the provision of information and advice (see 35.7 above).

As part of the Revenue's response to this process, all internal Revenue guidance manuals are to be made available for purchase (subject to the withholding of certain material under the exemptions in the code of practice). These are in the main to be published by Tolley Publishing Co Ltd, to whom application may be made for the relevant details of pricing and purchase arrangements.

36 Inland Revenue: Confidentiality of Information

36.1 The Revenue consider that the confidentiality of information maintained by their Department 'is essential to their traditional approach to their task and is deeply embedded in their practice'. (*Royal Commission on Standards of Conduct in Public Life 1976, para 111*). All officers of the Inland Revenue, together with General and Special Commissioners, are required to make declarations that information received in the course of duty will not be disclosed except for the purposes of such duty or for the purposes of the prosecution of revenue offences or as may be required by law. [*TMA s 6, 1 Sch*]. As to production in Court proceedings of documents in the possession of the Revenue, see *Brown's Trustees v Hay CS 1897, 3 TC 598; In re Joseph Hargreaves Ltd CA 1900, 4 TC 173; Shaw v Kay CS 1904, 5 TC 74; Soul v Irving CA 1963, 41 TC 517; H v H HC 1980, 52 TC 454*. For the overriding of confidentiality by the public interest in the administration of justice, see *Lonrho plc v Fayed and Others (No 4) CA 1993, [1994] STC 153*.

36.2 The Inland Revenue are authorised to disclose information to the following.

(*a*) **Charity Commissioners for England and Wales.** There are wide powers under which information may be exchanged between the Charity Commissioners and the Commissioners of Inland Revenue, in particular enabling the Revenue to disclose details of institutions which they consider to have been carrying on non-charitable activities or applying funds for non-charitable purposes. [*Charities Act 1992, ss 9, 52*].

(*b*) **Business Statistics Office of the Department of Industry** or to the **Department of Employment.** The Revenue are authorised to disclose, for the purposes of statistical surveys, the names and addresses of employers and employees and the number of persons employed by individual concerns. [*FA 1969, s 58; F(No 2)A 1987, s 69; SI 1990 No 1840*].

(*c*) **Tax authorities of other countries.** The Revenue are authorised to disclose information where it is necessary to do so for the operation of double taxation agreements [*Sec 816; TCGA 1992, s 277(4); IHTA 1984, s 158(5)*] and agreements may provide for such exchange, particularly in relation to prevention of fiscal evasion. [*Sec 788(2)*]. Disclosure may also be made to the tax authorities of other member States of the EC which observe similar confidentiality and use only for tax purposes. [*FA 1978, s 77; FA 1990, s 125(5)(6)*]. See also the 'working arrangement' between USA and UK in Revenue Press Release 2 March 1978.

(*d*) **Customs and Excise.** The Revenue and the Customs and Excise are authorised to disclose information to each other for the purpose of their respective duties. [*FA 1972, s 127*].

(*e*) **Occupational Pensions Board.** The Revenue are authorised to disclose information about pension schemes. [*Social Security Act 1973, s 89(2)*].

(*f*) **Social Security Departments.** The Revenue may, under the authority of the Commissioners of Inland Revenue, disclose information obtained in connection with the assessment or collection of income tax to any officer entitled to receive it in connection with the operation of any of the benefit Acts. Where the taxpayer is chargeable under Case I or II of Schedule D in respect of a trade etc., the only information which may be disclosed relating to that trade etc. is that concerning its commencement or cessation or the identity of the trader(s). [*Social Security Act 1986, s 59; Social Security and Housing Benefit Act 1987, s 25; Social Security Administration Act 1992, s 122*]. The Revenue will also supply to such officers the names and addresses of absent parents and, where appropriate, their employers, in cases where they are liable under the *Social Security Acts* to maintain lone parent families receiving income support. (Revenue Press Release 9 May 1990).

(g) **Assistance to police investigation into suspected murder or treason.** [*Royal Commission on Standards of Conduct in Public Life 1976, para 93*].

(h) **Non-UK resident entertainers and sportsmen.** In connection with the deduction of tax from certain payments to such persons, the Board may disclose relevant matters to any person who appears to the Board to have an interest. [*Sec 558(4)*].

(i) **Land Registry.** Particulars of land and charges. [*Land Registration Act 1925, s 129*].

(j) **Department of Environment.** Information regarding option mortgages and qualification of housing associations for certain grants. [*FA 1982, s 26, 7 Sch 12; Housing Associations Act 1985, s 62*].

(k) **Parliamentary Commissioner for Administration.** Information required for the purposes of his investigations. [*Parliamentary Commissioner Act 1967, s 8*].

(l) **National Audit Office.** Information required for the purposes of the Office's examinations. [*National Audit Act 1983, s 8*].

(m) **Data Protection.** Any information necessary for the discharge of the Registrar's or Tribunal's functions. [*Data Protection Act 1984, s 17*].

(n) **Secretary of State for Scotland and Scottish Housing Association.** Information regarding status of housing associations and refusals of charitable exemption. [*Tenants' Rights etc. (Scotland) Act 1980, s 1*].

(o) An **advisory commission** set up under the EEC Convention (*90/463/EEC*) on the elimination of double taxation in connection with the adjustment of profits of associated enterprises (see 3.9 ANTI-AVOIDANCE). [*Sec 816(2A); F(No 2)A 1992, s 51(2)*].

36.3   It is a criminal offence for a person to disclose information held by him in the exercise of tax functions about any matter relevant to tax in the case of an identifiable person. This does not apply if (or if he believes) he has lawful authority or the information has lawfully been made available to the public, or if the person to whom the matter relates has consented. [*FA 1989, s 182; FA 1995, 29 Sch Pt VIII(16)*]. Similar provisions apply to members of an advisory commission set up under the EEC Convention on transfer pricing arbitration (see 3.9 ANTI-AVOIDANCE). [*FA 1989, s 182A; F(No 2)A 1992, s 51(3)*].

37 Inland Revenue Explanatory Pamphlets Etc.

The Board publish explanatory pamphlets (with supplements from time to time) on Inland Revenue taxes. These are listed below, with the date of the latest edition in brackets, and are obtainable free of charge from any office of HM Inspector of Taxes, unless otherwise stated. As regards Inland Revenue internal guidance manuals, see 35.10 INLAND REVENUE: ADMINISTRATION.

IR 1   Extra-Statutory Concessions as at 31 August 1995 (June 1994 with November 1995 Supplement).

IR 6   Double Taxation Relief for Companies (March 1994).

IR 9   The Tax Treatment of Livestock: The Herd Basis (April 1984 with Insert).

IR 12   Occupational Pension Schemes—Notes on Approval (January 1995). (Obtainable from The Controller, Pension Schemes Office (Supplies Section), Inland Revenue, Yorke House, PO Box 62, Castle Meadow Road, Nottingham NG2 1BG). Price £10.00.

IR 14/15   Construction Industry Tax Deduction Scheme (September 1992).

IR 16   Share Acquisitions by Directors and Employees—Explanatory Notes (March 1994).

IR 17   Share Acquisitions by Directors and Employees (March 1994).

IR 20   Residents and Non-residents—Liability to Tax in the United Kingdom (November 1993).

IR 24   Class 4 National Insurance Contributions (November 1993).

IR 26   Income Tax Assessments on Business Profits—Changes of Accounting Date (April 1982).

IR 28   Starting in Business (October 1993).

IR 33   Income Tax and School Leavers (August 1992).

IR 34   Income Tax—PAYE (August 1994).

IR 37   Income Tax and Capital Gains Tax: Appeals (March 1995).

IR 40   Construction Industry: Conditions for Getting a Sub-contractor's Tax Certificate (July 1992).

IR 41   Income Tax and the Unemployed (October 1991).

IR 42   Lay-offs and Short-time Work (June 1992).

IR 43   Income Tax and Strikes (July 1992).

IR 45   Income Tax, Capital Gains Tax and Inheritance Tax: What Happens when Someone Dies (May 1995).

IR 46   Income Tax and Corporation Tax: Clubs, Societies and Associations (August 1991).

IR 53   PAYE for Employers: Thinking of Taking Someone On? (April 1995).

IR 56   Employed or Self-employed? (May 1995).

IR 57   Thinking of Working for Yourself? (May 1992).

IR 58   Going to Work Abroad? (April 1992).

IR 60   Income Tax and Students (March 1995).

IR 64   Giving to Charity: How Businesses can get Tax Relief (November 1993).

IR 65   Giving to Charity: How Individuals can get Tax Relief (November 1993).

IR 68	Accrued Income Scheme (December 1990).
IR 69	Expenses: Form P11D—How to Save Yourself Work (March 1994).
IR 71	PAYE Inspections: Employers' and Contractors' Records (May 1993).
IR 72	Inland Revenue Investigations: The Examination of Business Accounts (May 1995).
IR 73	Inland Revenue Investigations: How Settlements are Negotiated (January 1994).
IR 75	Tax Reliefs for Charities (June 1987).
IR 76	Personal Pension Schemes: Guidance Notes (1991). (Obtainable (free) as IR 12 above).
IR 78	Personal Pensions (December 1991).
IR 80	Income Tax and Married Couples (June 1994).
IR 83	Independent Taxation: A Guide for Tax Practitioners (January 1990). (Obtainable from Public Enquiry Room, West Wing, Somerset House, Strand, London WC2R 1LB (tel. 0171-438 6420/6425)).
IR 87	Rooms to Let: Income from Letting Property (November 1994).
IR 89	Personal Equity Plans (December 1995).
IR 90	A Guide to Tax Allowances and Reliefs (August 1994).
IR 91	A Guide for Widows and Widowers (June 1992).
IR 92	Income Tax: A Guide for One-parent Families (September 1993).
IR 93	Separation, Divorce and Maintenance Payments (June 1994).
IR 95	Income Tax: Shares for Employees—Profit-sharing Schemes (March 1994).
IR 96	Income Tax: Profit-sharing Schemes—Explanatory Notes (March 1994). (Obtainable as IR 83 above).
IR 97	Income Tax: Shares for Employees—SAYE Share Options (March 1994).
IR 98	Income Tax: SAYE Share Option Schemes—Explanatory Notes (March 1994). (Obtainable as IR 83 above).
IR 99	Income Tax: Shares for Employees—Executive Share Options (March 1994).
IR 100	Income Tax: Executive Share Option Schemes—Explanatory Notes (March 1994). (Obtainable as IR 83 above).
IR 103	Tax Relief for Private Medical Insurance (January 1995).
IR 104	Simple Tax Accounts (April 1993).
IR 105	How Your Profits are Taxed (July 1994).
IR 106	Capital Allowances for Vehicles and Machinery (April 1990).
IR 109	PAYE Inspections and Negotiations: Employers' and Contractors' Records—How Settlements are Negotiated (May 1993).
IR 110	A Guide for People with Savings (April 1995).
IR 113	Gift Aid: A Guide for Donors and Charities (July 1994). (Obtainable from Inland Revenue, FICO (Trusts and Charities), St John's House, Merton Road, Bootle, Merseyside L69 9BB).
IR 114	TESSA: Tax-free Interest for Taxpayers (December 1995).
IR 115	Tax and Childcare (October 1992).

37 Inland Revenue Explanatory Pamphlets Etc.

IR 116	Guide for Subcontractors with Tax Certificates (September 1992).
IR 117	A Subcontractor's Guide to the Deduction Scheme (September 1992).
IR 119	Tax Relief for Vocational Training (April 1995).
IR 120	You and the Inland Revenue (March 1995). (Special versions of this leaflet are available relating to the Special Compliance Office, the Financial Intermediaries and Claims Office and the Pension Schemes Office. The first is available from the office at Angel Court, 199 Borough High Street, London SE1 1HZ, the second from Fitz Roy House, PO Box 46, Castle Meadow Road, Nottingham NG2 1BD, the third from Yorke House, PO Box 62, Castle Meadow Road, Nottingham NG2 1BG. The leaflet is available in a range of languages and in Braille, large print and audio tape formats.)
IR 121	Income Tax and Pensioners (February 1992).
IR 122	Volunteer Drivers (June 1995).
IR 123	Mortgage Interest Relief—Buying your Home (May 1994).
IR 125	Using Your Own Car for Work (April 1996).
IR 126	Corporation Tax Pay and File—A General Guide (June 1993).
IR 127	Are You Paying too much Tax on Your Savings? (April 1995).
IR 128	Corporation Tax Pay and File: Company Leaflet (July 1993).
IR 129	Occupational Pension Schemes—An Introduction (June 1995).
IR 131	Statements of Practice as at 30 June 1995 (July 1994 with October 1995 Supplement).
IR 132	Taxation of Company Cars from 6 April 1994: Employers' Guide (October 1993).
IR 133	Income Tax and Company Cars from 6 April 1994—A Guide for Employees (November 1993).
IR 134	Income Tax and Relocation Packages (June 1994).
IR 136	Income Tax and Company Vans—A Guide for Employees and Employers (March 1994).
IR 137	The Enterprise Investment Scheme (October 1994).
IR 138	Living or Retiring Abroad? (October 1995).
IR 139	Income from Abroad? (October 1995).
IR 140	Non-resident Landlords, their Agents and Tenants (December 1995).
IR 141	Open Government (May 1995).
IR 142	Self Assessment—An Introduction (September 1994).
IR 144	Income Tax and Incapacity Benefit (February 1995).
IR 146	Double Taxation Relief—Admissible and Inadmissible Taxes (March 1995).
IR 148	Construction Industry: Are your Workers Employed or Self-employed? (October 1995).
IR 150	Taxation of Rents—A Guide to Property Income (March 1996).
CGT 4	Capital Gains Tax—Owner-occupied houses (November 1989).
CGT 6	Capital Gains Tax—Retirement Relief on Disposal of a Business (May 1992).
CGT 11	Capital Gains Tax and Small Businesses (February 1990).

CGT 13	Capital Gains Tax—Indexation Allowance for Quoted Shares (January 1991).
CGT 14	Capital Gains Tax—An Introduction (May 1992).
CGT 15	Capital Gains Tax—A Guide for Married Couples (November 1990).
CGT 16	Capital Gains Tax—Indexation Allowance: Disposals after 5 April 1988 (August 1989).
IHT 1	Inheritance Tax (January 1991). (Obtainable from Capital Taxes Office, Ferrers House, PO Box 38, Castle Meadow Road, Nottingham NG2 1BB and other Capital Taxes Offices in Nottingham, Edinburgh and Belfast).
IHT 2	Inheritance Tax on Lifetime Gifts (May 1993).
IHT 3	An Introduction to Inheritance Tax (September 1992).
IHT 8	Alterations to an Inheritance following a Death (February 1993).
CB(1)	Setting up a Charity in Scotland (March 1993). (Obtainable from Inland Revenue, FICO (Scotland), Trinity Park House, South Trinity Road, Edinburgh EH5 3SD).
480	Income Tax—Notes on Expenses Payments and Benefits for Directors and Certain Employees (1994).
P7	Employer's Guide to PAYE (1995).
SAT 1	The New Current Year Basis of Assessment, explaining how the new system will replace the existing rules of assessment for the self-employed. Also available on disk. (Obtainable from Inland Revenue Reference Library, New Wing, Somerset House, Strand, London WC2R 1LB.) (1995) Price £7.50.
SAT 2	Self-Assessment—The Legal Framework, explaining how the rules on the assessment and collection of income and capital gains taxes will change. Also available on disk. (Obtainable from Inland Revenue Reference Library, New Wing, Somerset House, Strand, London WC2R 1LB.) (1995) Price £5.00.
SAT 3	Self-Assessment—What it will mean for Employers (1995). Free.
SA/BK1	Self-Assessment—A General Guide (June 1995).
SA/BK2	Self-Assessment—A Guide for the Self-Employed (June 1995).
SA/BK3	Self-Assessment—A Guide to Keeping Records for the Self-Employed (June 1995).
SA/BK4	Self-Assessment—A General Guide to Keeping Records (February 1996).
—	Thinking of Employing a Domestic Worker or Nanny? (1994).
—	List of bodies approved by the Inland Revenue under *Sec 201* (subscriptions to professional bodies). (Obtainable from Inland Revenue Reference Library, New Wing, Somerset House, Strand, London WC2R 1LB). Price £5.00.
—	Register of Qualifying Lenders under the MIRAS scheme. (Obtainable from Inland Revenue Library, Room 3A, New Wing, Somerset House, London WC2R 1LB). Price £1.00.
—	Explanatory notes on the provisions of *ICTA 1988, Pt XVII, Ch IV* (Controlled Foreign Companies). (Obtainable from Inland Revenue Reference Library, New Wing, Somerset House, Strand, London WC2R 1LB). Price £10.00.
—	Charities—Payroll Giving Schemes, explaining how the proposals for tax relief are expected to work. (Obtainable from Public Enquiry Room, West Wing, Somerset House, Strand, London WC2R 1LF (tel. 0171-438 6420/6425)). Free.
—	Guidelines on the Tax Treatment of Disaster Funds, giving guidelines on the organisation of disaster appeal funds. (Obtainable from Inland Revenue, FICO (Trusts

and Charities), St John's House, Merton Road, Bootle, Merseyside L69 9BB (tel. 0151-472 6000) or FICO (Scotland), Trinity Park House, South Trinity Road, Edinburgh EH5 3SD (tel. 0131-551 8127)). Free.

— Trading by Charities, explaining how the trading activities of charities are treated for tax purposes (see 15.1, 15.4(c) CHARITIES). (Obtainable from Inland Revenue, FICO (Charity Technical), St John's House, Merton Road, Bootle, Merseyside L69 9BB (tel. no. 0151-472 6036/6037/6055/6056) or FICO (Scotland), Trinity Park House, South Trinity Road, Edinburgh EH5 3SD (tel. 0131-551 8127).) Free.

— Fund-raising for Charity, giving guidance on the operation of Extra-statutory Concession C4 (see 15.4(c) CHARITIES). (Obtainable from Inland Revenue, FICO (Trusts and Charities), St John's House, Merton Road, Bootle, Merseyside L69 9BB (tel. no. 0151-472 6000) or FICO (Scotland), Trinity Park House, South Trinity Road, Edinburgh EH5 3SD (tel. 0131-551 8127.) Free.

— Personal equity plan information pack, containing a Treasury guide for plan managers and technical specification. (Obtainable from Inland Revenue Reference Library, New Wing, Somerset House, Strand, London WC2R 1LB). Price £3.50.

— Profit-related pay schemes: guidance notes for employers and model rules. (Obtainable from Profit-Related Pay Office, Inland Revenue, St Mungo's Road, Cumbernauld, Glasgow G67 1YZ). Free.

— The tax treatment of top-up pension schemes. (Obtainable from Inland Revenue Library, Mid-Basement, Somerset House, London WC2R 1LB). Price £1.50.

— Business economic notes. See 71.28 SCHEDULE D, CASES I AND II.

— Codes of Practice. See 35.7 INLAND REVENUE: ADMINISTRATION.

— How to complain about the Inland Revenue. (Obtainable from the Revenue Adjudicator's Office, see 35.9 INLAND REVENUE: ADMINISTRATION). Free.

'Appeals and Other Proceedings before the Special Commissioners' (October 1994) dealing with procedural and other points is available free of charge from the Clerk to the Special Commissioners, 15/29 Bedford Avenue, London WC1B 3AS (tel. 0171–631 4242).

The Board also issue Press Releases ('Revenue Press Releases') and Statements of Practice (SP). Summaries of, and references to, these are included in this Part under the appropriate subject and in the following two chapters.

38   Inland Revenue Extra-Statutory Concessions

The following is a summary of the current concessions published in the Revenue Pamphlet IR 1 (1994 with November 1995 Supplement) or subsequently announced, insofar as they relate to subjects dealt with in this book. It should be borne in mind that in a particular case there may be special circumstances which will require to be taken into account in considering the application of a concession. A concession will not be given in any case where an attempt is made to use it for tax avoidance (and see *R v HMIT (ex p Fulford-Dobson) QB 1987, 60 TC 168*). See also 35.4 INLAND REVENUE: ADMINISTRATION.

A.   **APPLICABLE TO INDIVIDUALS**

A1   **Flat rate allowances for cost of tools and special clothing** may be claimed. See 75.25 SCHEDULE E.

A2   **Meal vouchers.** Certain vouchers are exempt from income tax. See 75.30 SCHEDULE E.

A4   **Directors' travelling expenses.** Certain expenses paid by employers are not assessable. See 75.13(ix), 75.43 SCHEDULE E.

A5   **Expenses allowances and benefits in kind.**

(*a*)   Removal expenses paid by employer in certain circumstances are not assessable. See 75.13(x) SCHEDULE E.

(*b*)   Bridging loans provided by employer in certain circumstances are not assessable. See 75.13(x), 75.17 SCHEDULE E.

Withdrawn after 5 April 1993, subject to transitional arrangements.

A6   **Miners: free coal and allowances in lieu** are exempt from income tax.

A7   **Business (or other source of income) passing to spouse on death of trader.** Discontinuance provisions are not enforced. (Withdrawn following the introduction of a current year basis of assessment.) See 71.9 SCHEDULE D, CASES I AND II, 72.4 SCHEDULE D, CASE III.

A8   **Loss relief for capital allowances unused on the cessation of a business.** Capital allowances brought forward are used to reduce the profits of the final year. See 46.7 LOSSES.

A9   **Doctors' and dentists' superannuation contributions** under NHS are allowable as deductions under Schedule D but alternatives apply where premiums for retirement annuities are also paid. See 66.11 RETIREMENT SCHEMES.

A10   **Overseas pension schemes.** Income tax is not charged on certain lump sums on termination of employment overseas. See 59.4(vi) PENSIONS.

A11   **Residence in the UK: year of commencement or cessation of residence.** Liability to tax is computed by reference to the period of residence in that year. (Revised by Revenue Press Release 29 January 1996.) See 64.5 RESIDENCE, ORDINARY RESIDENCE AND DOMICILE.

A12   **Double taxation relief: alimony etc. under UK court order or agreement: payer resident abroad.** Relief by way of credit is allowed in certain circumstances. See 25.5(*a*) DOUBLE TAX RELIEF.

A13   **Administration of estates: deficiencies of income allowed against income of another year.** (Obsolete for 1995/96 onwards). See 22.3 DECEASED ESTATES.

A14   Deceased person's estate: residuary income received during the administration period. A legatee resident abroad may have his tax liability on estate income adjusted as if the income had arisen to him directly. See 22.3 DECEASED ESTATES.

A16   Annual payments (other than interest) paid out of income not brought into charge to income tax. If payment is made in a year later than when due, and it could have been made out of taxed income in that due year, an allowance will be made (when collecting under *Sec 350*) for the tax which the payer would have been entitled to deduct (under *Sec 348*) and retain if the payment had been made at the due date. See 23.3(i) DEDUCTION OF TAX AT SOURCE.

A17   Death of taxpayer before due date for payment of tax. Interest on tax overdue may not begin to run until after probate or letters of administration are obtained. See 42.6 INTEREST ON UNPAID TAX.

A19   Arrears of tax arising through official error. Relief is given. (Revised by Revenue Press Releases 26 April 1994, 11 March 1996.) See 56.6 PAYMENT OF TAX for current details.

A20   Cessation of trade, profession or vocation. Where a person reduces his business activities to qualify for a National Insurance retirement pension, cessation and commencement provisions may be applied to his business. (Of limited application following abolition of earnings rule from 1 October 1989.) See 71.9 SCHEDULE D, CASES I AND II.

A21   Schedule A: deferred repairs: property passing from husband to wife (or vice versa) on death. Expenditure on maintenance or repairs attributable to ownership of the deceased spouse is allowable to the surviving spouse. (Withdrawn with effect from 6 April 1995.) See 68.15 SCHEDULE A.

A22   Long service awards are exempt from tax within limitations. See 75.26 SCHEDULE E.

A24   Foreign social security benefits. Payments by foreign governments to UK residents which correspond to UK benefits exempt under *Sec 617(1)(2)* will also be exempt from tax. See 29.27 EXEMPT INCOME, 82.4 SOCIAL SECURITY.

A25   Crown Servants engaged overseas may be exempted from UK tax. See 75.2(i) SCHEDULE E.

A26   Sick benefits. The practice as regards assessment is explained. Superseded by new concession from 6 April 1994. See 29.10 EXEMPT INCOME, 75.37 SCHEDULE E.

A27   Mortgage interest relief: temporary absences from mortgaged property. Absences of up to one year, or longer if occasioned by employment, are ignored in determining if a property is an only or main residence. See 43.6, 43.15 INTEREST PAYABLE.

A29   Farming and market gardening: relief for fluctuating profits. For this purpose, 'farming' includes the intensive rearing of livestock or fish on a commercial basis for the production of food for human consumption. See 71.56 SCHEDULE D, CASES I AND II.

A30   Interest on damages for personal injuries (foreign court awards) will be exempt from income tax if also exempt in the country in which award made. See 29.11(i) EXEMPT INCOME.

A31   Life assurance premium relief by deduction: pre-marriage policies: premium relief after divorce continues where one party pays on life of the other. See 45.4 (*j*) LIFE ASSURANCE POLICIES.

Inland Revenue Extra-Statutory Concessions   38

A32　Tax relief for life assurance premiums: position of certain pension schemes which are unapproved after 5 April 1980. Relief is continued. See 45.10(ii) LIFE ASSURANCE POLICIES.

A33　Lump sum retirement benefits: changes after 5 April 1980. Previous tax exemption is continued under certain conditions. See 66.12 RETIREMENT SCHEMES.

A34　Ulster savings certificates: certificates encashed after death of registered holder. Accumulated interest is exempt from income tax if the deceased was resident and domiciled in NI at time of purchase. See 33.6 GOVERNMENT STOCKS.

A35　Mortgage interest relief: year of marriage. Relief continues where one spouse vacates own mortgaged house to live in mortgaged house of other spouse. Superseded by *FA 1993, s 57*. See 43.12 INTEREST PAYABLE.

A36　Close companies in liquidation: distributions in respect of share capital. Where income after commencement of winding-up is apportioned for purposes of liability to higher rate tax (including investment income surcharge), the resulting liability of a participator will be restricted to the excess, if any, over the capital gains tax paid by him which is attributable to that income when received as a distribution in respect of share capital. Similarly, where such apportionment is made to the beneficiary of a trust or residuary legatee of an estate, account will be taken of any relevant capital gains tax paid by the trustees or the administrators. In either case, an adjustment may be made where the company met the income tax liability on the apportioned income. See 28.2 (*b*)(ii) EXCESS LIABILITY and Tolley's Corporation Tax.

A37　Tax treatment of directors' fees received by partnerships and other companies. Under certain conditions, such fees may be included in the Schedule D assessment of the partnership, see 75.24 SCHEDULE E, or in the corporation tax assessment of the other company, see 75.1(1) SCHEDULE E.

A38　Retirement annuity relief: death and disability benefits. An individual in a scheme providing a pension only on death or disability will not be treated as being in pensionable employment. See 65.12 RETIREMENT ANNUITIES AND PERSONAL PENSION SCHEMES.

A39　Exemption for Hong Kong officials. Relief under *Sec 320* (see 24.1 DIPLOMATIC IMMUNITY) is extended to salaries of certain Hong Kong officials working in the UK.

A40　Adoption allowances, under approved schemes, are not taxable. See 29.1 EXEMPT INCOME.

A41　Qualifying life assurance policies: statutory conditions may be relaxed in certain circumstances. See 45.12 (*h*) LIFE ASSURANCE POLICIES.

A42　Chargeable events: loans to policyholders may not be treated as partial surrenders in certain circumstances. See 45.15 (*f*) LIFE ASSURANCE POLICIES.

A43　Interest relief: investment in partnerships and close companies may continue to attract relief where the partnership is incorporated or the close company's shares reorganised. See 43.19–43.22 INTEREST PAYABLE.

A44　Education allowances under Overseas Service Aid Scheme, payable to officers in the public service of certain overseas territories, which the UK government has undertaken to exempt from income tax, are so exempted. See 75.2(i) SCHEDULE E.

A45　Life assurance policies: variation of term assured policies. A term assurance policy for a term of ten years or less will not be disqualified under *15 Sch 17(2)(b), 18* because of a reduction in the rate of premium to less than half as a result of a similar reduction in the sum assured or an extension of the term (resulting in a total term still not exceeding ten years). See 45.12(*d*) LIFE ASSURANCE POLICIES.

A46 **Variable purchased life annuities: carry forward of excess of capital element.** Any excess of the capital element over the annuity payment may be carried forward for allowance in determining the capital element in future payments. See 23.11(*c*) DEDUCTION OF TAX AT SOURCE.

A47 **House purchase loans made by life offices to staffs of insurance associations** may be treated in the same way as loans by a life office to a full-time employee. See 45.15(*f*) LIFE ASSURANCE POLICIES.

A49 **Widow's pension paid to widow of Singapore nationality, resident in the UK, whose husband was a UK national employed as a Public Officer by the Government of Singapore** is included in the exemption provided by *Sec 616(1)*. See 59.2 PENSIONS.

A51 **Repayment supplement: life assurance premium relief.** The repayment supplement provisions (see 41.1 INTEREST ON OVERPAID TAX) apply also to repayments of excessive clawback under *Secs 268, 269* (see 45.5 LIFE ASSURANCE POLICIES) and to relief by repayment under *14 Sch 6(1)* where relief is not obtained by deduction (see 45.1 LIFE ASSURANCE POLICIES).

A52 **Maintenance payments: concessionary relief.** Where a person fails to deduct tax under *Sec 348* from annual payments made under a Court Order or other legally binding agreement, relief may concessionally be granted equal to the amount of repayment which would have been due to the recipient had the right to deduct tax been properly exercised. See 23.8 DEDUCTION OF TAX AT SOURCE, 47.15 MARRIED PERSONS.

A55 **Arrears of foreign pensions,** or increases thereof, granted retrospectively may, where they are chargeable on the arising basis under Schedule D, Case V and it is advantageous to the taxpayer, be taxed as if the arrears arose in the years to which they relate, rather than being assessed in one sum as they arise. See 59.2 PENSIONS.

A56 **Benefits in kind: tax treatment of accommodation provided by employers.** The rules are modified in relation to Scotland. See 75.29 SCHEDULE E.

A57 **Suggestion schemes.** Awards to employees under such schemes are not charged to tax provided that certain conditions are satisfied. See 75.26 SCHEDULE E.

A58 **Travelling and subsistence allowance when public transport disrupted.** Such allowances, or the provision of facilities by the employer, are not charged to tax. See 75.13(v), 75.43 SCHEDULE E.

A59 **Home to work travel of severely disabled employees.** Provision of transport facilities or financial assistance is not charged to tax. See 75.13(vi), 75.15, 75.43 SCHEDULE E.

A60 **Agricultural workers' board and lodging** will, subject to conditions, not be charged to tax even where a higher wage in lieu could be taken. See 75.7 SCHEDULE E.

A61 **Clergymen's heating and lighting etc. expenses.** Certain sums paid or reimbursed are not charged to tax. See 75.9 SCHEDULE E.

A62 **Pensions to employees disabled at work.** The excess over the normal ill health retirement pension is not charged to tax. See 59.4(iii) PENSIONS.

A63 **External training courses—expenses borne by employer.** Certain such expenses do not give rise to a charge to tax on the employee. See 75.42 SCHEDULE E.

A64 **External training courses—expenses borne by an employee** may be allowed as a deduction. See 75.42 SCHEDULE E.

A65 **Workers on offshore oil and gas rigs or platforms—free transfers from or to mainland.** No charge to tax arises in respect of such transfers or certain mainland accommodation and subsistence. See 75.13(viii), 75.43 SCHEDULE E.

A66 **Employees' late night journeys from work to home.** Where the cost of occasional journeys is borne by the employer, the employee will not, subject to various conditions, be charged to tax on the benefit he receives. See 75.13(vii), 75.43 SCHEDULE E.

A67 **Payments to employees moved to higher cost housing areas** may be exempted from tax, subject to certain conditions. Withdrawn after 5 April 1993, subject to transitional arrangements. See 75.29 SCHEDULE E.

A68 **Payments out of a discretionary trust which are emoluments taxable under Schedule E.** Trustees may reclaim tax on certain payments to beneficiaries. See 80.5 SETTLEMENTS.

A69 **Composite rate tax: non-resident depositors.** Certain declarations made to a society are treated as having been made to a successor company. See 8.2, 8.3 BANKS, 9.8 BUILDING SOCIETIES.

A70 **Small gifts to employees by third parties and staff Christmas parties** may be exempted from income tax. (Revised by Revenue Press Release 1 November 1995.) See 75.13(xvi), 75.26 SCHEDULE E.

A71 **Company cars for family members.** In relation to the car scale charge: (*a*) a double charge is prevented where cars are supplied to members of the same family by the same employer; and (*b*) the charge is apportioned where use is shared. See 75.15 SCHEDULE E.

A72 **Pension schemes and accident insurance policies.** The exemption from the benefits charge for provision of death or retirement benefits is extended to all family and household beneficiaries. See 75.13(iii) SCHEDULE E.

A73 **Lloyd's underwriters: repayment of tax withheld where there is an overall loss.** Tax deducted by the managing agent may be repaid to the Name. See 89.5 UNDERWRITERS.

A74 **Meals provided for employees** may escape charge to tax as a benefit. See 75.13(iv) SCHEDULE E.

A75 **Theatrical entertainers: transition to Schedule E.** New rules apply from 6 April 1990, but with concessional transitional treatment of certain established entertainers. See 75.24 SCHEDULE E.

A76 **Business expansion scheme and enterprise investment scheme subscriber shares.** Relief will not be denied to subscribers for such shares because they may, for a short period, hold in excess of 30% of the issued share capital. See 26.3, 26.19 ENTERPRISE INVESTMENT SCHEME (AND BES).

A77 **Motor mileage allowances paid to volunteer drivers.** Only part of the mileage profit will be taxed for periods before 1995/96. See 74.2 SCHEDULE D, CASE VI.

A78 **Residence in the UK: accompanying spouse.** A concessional treatment is introduced for the determination of the residence and ordinary residence status of spouses accompanying individuals in full-time employment abroad. See 64.5, 64.6 RESIDENCE, ORDINARY RESIDENCE AND DOMICILE.

A79   **Tax exempt special savings accounts (TESSAs).** A *curator bonis* in Scotland may open a TESSA on behalf of an incapacitated person. See 29.11 EXEMPT INCOME.

A80   **Blanket partnership continuation elections.** Elections covering all future partnership changes (until withdrawn) may be accepted in the case of certain large partnerships. See 53.6 PARTNERSHIPS.

A81   **Termination payments and legal costs.** Certain legal costs recovered from the employer will not be charged under *Sec 148*. See 19.6(x) COMPENSATION FOR LOSS OF EMPLOYMENT (AND DAMAGES).

A82   **Repayment supplement to individuals resident in EC Member States** will be paid in certain cases following the decision in the *Commerzbank AG* case. See 41.4 INTEREST ON OVERPAID TAX.

A83   **Benefits under permanent health insurance policies.** Benefits under self-funded policies may be exempt for the first twelve months. (Supersedes Concession A26 above.) See 71.63 SCHEDULE D, CASES I AND II, 75.37 SCHEDULE E. See now the statutory provisions at 29.10 EXEMPT INCOME.

A84   **Allowances paid to Detached National Experts** on secondment to the European Commission are exempt from income tax. See 75.2(i) SCHEDULE E.

A85   **Transfers of assets by employees and directors to employers and others.** Certain employer's transaction costs will not be charged as a benefit. See 75.13(xxi) SCHEDULE E.

A86   **Blind person's tax allowance.** The allowance will be granted for the year before registration where the evidence on which registration was based was available at the end of that year. See 1.18 ALLOWANCES AND TAX RATES.

A87   **Loss relief on accounts basis.** The long-standing practice of allowing loss relief under *Sec 380* on the accounts basis rather than the strict fiscal year basis is confirmed. See 46.11 LOSSES.

A88   **Cessation adjustment where loss relief has been allowed on accounts basis.** Relief will be given for certain losses otherwise falling not to attract relief. See 46.11 LOSSES.

A89   **Mortgage interest relief—property used for residential and business purposes.** Interest relief may be obtained both under *Sec 353* and as a deduction in computing profits and losses. See 23.13 DEDUCTION OF TAX AT SOURCE, 43.2 INTEREST PAYABLE.

A90   **Jobmatch pilot scheme.** Payments and training vouchers provided under the scheme are exempt from income tax. See 82.4 SOCIAL SECURITY.

The following concessions await publication in IR 1.

A91   **Living accommodation provided by reason of employment.** A charge will not be raised under *Sec 146* where the *Sec 145* charge was based on the full market rent, and the combined charge under those *sections* will be restricted where the accommodation is provided to more than one director or employee. (Revenue Press Release 28 November 1995). See 75.29 SCHEDULE E.

A92   **TESSAs—European authorised institutions.** Accounts opened before 2 January 1996 may be transferred to such institutions on or after that date. (Revenue Press Release 21 December 1995). See 29.11(iii) EXEMPT INCOME.

A93   Payments from offshore trusts to minor unmarried child of settlor: claim by settlor for credit of tax paid by trustees against his liability to tax on income distributed to or for the benefit of the child will be allowed. (Revenue Press Release 25 January 1996). See 80.5 SETTLEMENTS.

B.   CONCESSIONS APPLICABLE TO INDIVIDUALS AND COMPANIES

B1   Machinery and plant: changes from 'renewals' to 'capital allowances' basis. Capital allowances may be claimed provided all items of the same class are changed to new basis. See 10.38(ix) CAPITAL ALLOWANCES.

B3   Industrial buildings allowance: private roads on industrial trading estates may attract relief. Now superseded by *CAA 1990, s 18(8)*. See 10.12 CAPITAL ALLOWANCES.

B4   Maintenance and repairs of property obviated by alterations etc.: Schedule A assessments. The estimated cost of the repairs etc. may be allowed. See 68.15 SCHEDULE A.

B5   Maintenance expenses of owner-occupied farms not carried on on a commercial basis may be claimed under *Sec 33*. See 71.56 SCHEDULE D, CASES I AND II.

B7   Benevolent gifts by traders are allowable in certain circumstances. See 71.83 SCHEDULE D, CASES I AND II.

B8   Double tax relief: income consisting of royalties and 'know-how' payments arising to a UK resident from abroad. See 25.5(*l*) DOUBLE TAX RELIEF.

B9   Bank interest, etc. received by charities is exempt. Now superseded by *FA 1996, s 149*. See 15.3(i)(iii)(iv), 15.4(*a*) CHARITIES.

B10   Income of contemplative religious communities or of their members, having a common fund and not being charities, is partly regarded as income of each monk or nun up to £2,730 each for 1993/94 (£2,669 for 1992/93; £2,619 for 1991/92; £2,518 for 1990/91; £2,327 for 1989/90; £2,142 for 1988/89; £1,986 for 1987/88). For 1995/96 and subsequent years, the allowable figure is set at the basic personal allowance for the year (see 1.14 ALLOWANCES AND TAX RATES). Where the aggregate of 'allowable figures' exceeds income of the community, the excess may be set against chargeable gains of that or (in the case of an excess arising in a year up to and including 1994/95) a subsequent year.

B11   Compensation for compulsory slaughter of farm animals may be treated as profits spread over the following three years. See 71.56 SCHEDULE D, CASES I AND II.

B13   Untaxed interest paid to non-residents. No action is taken to recover the tax unless an agent is chargeable or a set-off is available against a tax claim. See 51.3 NON-RESIDENTS AND OTHER OVERSEAS MATTERS.

B15   Borrowing and lending of securities with repayment in other securities of the same description is not a disposal for either Schedule D, Case I or capital gains where it is standard practice designed to preserve a market in securities etc. Now superseded by *Sec 129*. See 71.81 SCHEDULE D, CASES I AND II.

B16   Fire safety: capital expenditure incurred on certain trade premises (a) in Northern Ireland, and (b) by lessors. (*a*) Provisions relating to fire safety expenditure in UK are extended to NI, and (*b*) relief is allowed where lessor incurs the expenditure himself, if similar expenditure by the tenant would have qualified for relief. See 10.25(i) CAPITAL ALLOWANCES.

38   Inland Revenue Extra-Statutory Concessions

B17   **Capital allowances: sale of invented patent to an associate.** Where an inventor sells a patent to his own controlled company at less than open market value, the actual sale price is taken for assessment and capital allowances, and (subject to the purchaser's agreement) for capital gains tax. See 10.50 CAPITAL ALLOWANCES.

B18   **Payments out of discretionary trusts.** Beneficiaries may claim certain reliefs as if they had received the income out of which the payment was made directly. See 80.5 SETTLEMENTS.

B19   **Capital allowances for buildings: balancing charge after cessation of trade.** The assessment under Schedule D, Case VI may be off-set by trading losses and unused capital allowances. Now superseded by *CAA 1990, s 15A*. See 10.17 CAPITAL ALLOWANCES.

B20   **Capital allowances for buildings: sales by property developers of buildings which have been let.** Writing-down allowances are made to the purchaser even though the developer's expenditure on construction has been on revenue account. Now superseded by *CAA 1990, s 10(4)(5)*. See 10.14 CAPITAL ALLOWANCES.

B22   **Close companies: non-resident participators: apportionment.** A non-resident is normally exempted from UK income tax on any close company income apportioned to him if his dividend income from UK companies is relieved from UK tax at the higher rates under a double tax agreement. See 25.2 DOUBLE TAX RELIEF, 28.7 EXCESS LIABILITY.

B23   **Construction industry tax deduction scheme: exclusion of certain small payments.** Local managers may commission small contracts without operating the scheme. See 21.1 CONSTRUCTION INDUSTRY TAX DEDUCTION SCHEME.

B25   **Schedule D, Case V losses.** Relief is extended in certain cases. See 73.3 SCHEDULE D, CASES IV AND V.

B27   **Approved employee share schemes: jointly owned companies.** A scheme operated by a jointly owned company may nevertheless be granted approval. See 81.2 SHARE INCENTIVES AND OPTIONS.

B28   **Leased cars costing over £12,000: rebate of hire charges** will be treated as non-taxable in the same proportion as the hire charges were themselves disallowed under *CAA 1990, s 35(2)*. Now superseded by *CAA 1990, s 35(2A)*. See 10.28(A) CAPITAL ALLOWANCES.

B29   **Treatment of income from caravan sites where there is both trading and associated letting income.** In such circumstances the receipts from caravan pitch site income and from letting caravans may be treated as receipts of the trading activities. See 68.4 SCHEDULE A, 74.4 SCHEDULE D, CASE VI.

B30   **Income from property in Scotland: property managed as one estate.** The tax treatment will continue to be by reference to 1978 gross rateable values where appropriate. See 68.7(e) SCHEDULE A—PROPERTY INCOME.

B31   **Capital allowances: plant or machinery which is a fixture in a business building situated within an enterprise zone** may attract 100% initial allowances. Now superseded by *FA 1989, 13 Sch 28*. See 10.19 CAPITAL ALLOWANCES.

B32   **Payroll giving schemes: administrative costs.** Certain payments by employers to meet the costs of approved agencies will be deductible as trade expenses. Now superseded by *FA 1993, s 69*. See 15.7 CHARITIES.

B35   **Borrowing and lending of securities: gilt lending to redemption.** Certain transactions are treated as being within *Sec 129*. See 71.81 SCHEDULE D, CASES I AND II.

B36   Borrowing and lending of securities: replacement loans. Certain transactions are treated as being within *Sec 129*. See 71.81 SCHEDULE D, CASES I AND II.

B37   The herd basis: shares in animals. The herd basis may be applied to a share in an animal in the same way as if the share were a whole animal. See 34.2 HERD BASIS.

B38   Tax concessions on overseas debts. Relief may be available where they form part of profits assessable under Schedule D, Case I or Case II. See 71.90 SCHEDULE D, CASES I AND II.

B39   Contributions to overseas pension schemes. Employer contributions otherwise denied relief are allowed in certain circumstances. Now superseded by *FA 1989, s 76(6A)–(6C)*. See 66.10 RETIREMENT SCHEMES.

B40   UK investment managers acting for non-resident clients. The exemptions of *TMA, ss 78(2), 82* are extended in certain cases. See 51.4(*b*) NON-RESIDENTS AND OTHER OVERSEAS MATTERS.

B41   Claims to repayment of tax. Where an over-payment of tax has arisen because of official error, and there is no doubt or dispute as to the facts, claims to repayment of tax are accepted outside the statutory time limit (generally six years from the end of the tax year concerned). See 17.2 CLAIMS.

B42   'Free gifts' and insurance contracts. Certain incentive gifts offered in connection with the issue of insurance policies are disregarded. See 45.6 LIFE ASSURANCE POLICIES.

B43   Alterations to old pension funds. Certain minor rule amendments may be made without loss of exemption. See 66.13 RETIREMENT SCHEMES.

B44   Profit-related pay: extraordinary items. Existing treatment of certain items in the statutory profit and loss account is preserved following the replacement of SSAP6 by FRS3. See generally 75.31(K) SCHEDULE E.

B45   Automatic penalties for late company and employers' and contractors' end-of-year returns. A temporary short period of grace is allowed for submission of annual returns following the introduction of automatic penalties. See 58.4 PENALTIES.

The following concessions await publication in IR 1.

B46   Automatic penalties for late company and employers' and contractors' end-of-year returns. A short period of grace is allowed for submission of annual returns. (Revenue Press Release 14 September 1995). See 58.4 PENALTIES.

B47   Furnished lettings of dwelling houses—wear and tear of furniture. As an alternative to the renewals basis, an allowance of 10% of rent may be claimed. (Replaces Statement of Practice A 19.) (Revenue Press Release 28 September 1995). See 68.8 SCHEDULE A, 74.4 SCHEDULE D, CASE VI.

C.   CONCESSIONS APPLICABLE TO COMPANIES ETC.

C1   Credit for underlying tax: dividends from trade investments in overseas companies. (*a*) A few UK double tax agreements provide relief for underlying tax on income from ordinary portfolio investments and where these are in force, credit is also given for underlying taxes along a chain of shareholdings (see 25.5(*b*) DOUBLE TAX RELIEF). (*b*) Insurance companies in receipt of dividends from overseas companies, in which there is at least 10% control of voting power or the dividend is referable to insurance business of the UK company, are given credit for underlying taxes along a chain of shareholdings. See Tolley's Corporation Tax.

C2   **Loan and money societies.** There is restricted liability to tax on dividends and interest to members. See 18.3 CLUBS AND SOCIETIES.

C3   **Holiday clubs and thrift funds.** There is restricted liability to tax on profits or interest to members. See 18.2 CLUBS AND SOCIETIES.

C4   **Trading activities for charitable purposes.** Profits are not taxed under certain conditions. See 15.4(*c*) CHARITIES.

C19   **Stock lending by pension funds.** Certain payments in lieu of dividends or interest are exempted from tax. See 66.5(*b*) RETIREMENT SCHEMES.

D.   **CONCESSIONS RELATING TO CAPITAL GAINS**

D27   **Earn-outs.** The capital gains concession concerning the application of *TCGA 1992, s 135* to takeovers including an earn-out element is extended to trading profits of financial concerns. See 71.81 SCHEDULE D, CASES I AND II.

D46   **Relief against income for capital losses on the disposal of unquoted shares in a trading company.** Relief will be allowed in certain cases where a company without assets is dissolved and either no distribution is made during winding-up, or no final distribution is made. See 46.19 LOSSES.

D47   **Temporary loss of charitable status due to reverter of school and other sites.** Liabilities which may arise in the period before charitable status is re-established will be discharged or repaid. See 15.1 CHARITIES.

39   Inland Revenue Press Releases

The following is a summary in date order of Press Releases referred to in this Part (other than those containing Statements of Practice, as to which see 40 INLAND REVENUE STATEMENTS OF PRACTICE). Certain pre-18 July 1978 Press Releases were reissued as Statements of Practice on 18 June 1979 (see 40 INLAND REVENUE STATEMENTS OF PRACTICE).

Copies of any individual Press Release may be obtained from Inland Revenue, Public Enquiry Room, Somerset House, Strand, London WC2R 1LB (tel. 0171-438 6420/6425/7772). A charge (currently £75) is made for Press Releases (including Extra-Statutory Concessions and Statements of Practice) mailed weekly throughout a calendar year. To receive Press Releases, application can be made to Tolley Publishing Co Ltd, Tolley House, 2 Addiscombe Road, Croydon, Surrey CR9 5AF (tel. 0181-686 9141). A separate application is needed to subscribe to the Revenue's Tax Bulletin for an annual charge of £20, which should be made to Inland Revenue, Finance Division, Barrington Road, Worthing, West Sussex BN12 4XH.

9.5.69	**Double tax agreement with Singapore: matching of incentive reliefs.** Credit is given against UK tax for tax given up by Singapore to pioneer industries. See 25.5(*h*) DOUBLE TAX RELIEF.
5.3.70	**Double tax agreement with Malaysia: matching of incentive reliefs.** Credit is given against UK tax for tax given up by Malaysia to pioneer industries. See 25.5(*h*) DOUBLE TAX RELIEF.
18.12.73	**Copies of notices of assessment.** A taxpayer may request the inspector to provide a copy of any assessment to an agent. See 5.1 ASSESSMENTS.
15.10.76	**Examination of business accounts.** Notes of the approach adopted by the Revenue. See 71.28 SCHEDULE D, CASES I AND II.
1.8.77	**Investigation of incorrect business accounts and tax returns.** The Revenue's practice in such investigations is explained. See 6.7 BACK DUTY, 58.7 PENALTIES and 71.28 SCHEDULE D, CASES I AND II.
2.3.78	**Double taxation: exchange of information with the U.S.A.** Notes on the 'working arrangement' with the U.S. Internal Revenue Service. See 36.2(*c*) INLAND REVENUE: CONFIDENTIALITY OF INFORMATION.
26.7.78	**Car leasing schemes.** Where a car is sold to the lessee etc. at less than the open market value at the end of the contract, the Revenue will consider what adjustments may be necessary to the tax liabilities affected. See 10.38(ii) CAPITAL ALLOWANCES.
26.7.79	**Administrative simplification to help pensioners.** The Revenue are notified by the Department of Health and Social Security of the amounts of retirement and widows pensions. See 82.3 SOCIAL SECURITY.
16.6.80	**Life assurance premium relief: 15 Sch 14: disqualification of certain life policies.** Guidance is given as to the application of this legislation. See 45.11 LIFE ASSURANCE POLICIES.
26.1.81	**Transfer pricing of multinational enterprises: notes for guidance.** See 3.9 ANTI-AVOIDANCE.
4.2.81	**Life assurance premiums paid to the UK branch of an overseas life office.** Relief is available. See 45.4(*c*) LIFE ASSURANCE POLICIES.
13.2.81	**Travelling and subsistence allowances paid to site-based staff employees in the construction and allied industries.** Revenue practice is explained and extended. See 75.43 SCHEDULE E.

39   Inland Revenue Press Releases

25.6.81   **Sick pay.** The taxation of sick pay under *Sec 149* will not apply to sums received under sick pay policies to the extent that premiums are paid by employees for their own benefit. See 75.37 SCHEDULE E.

25.6.82   **Deep discounted and indexed stock.** The Revenue's views on the taxation of rolled-up interest are stated. See 44.9 INTEREST RECEIVABLE.

25.1.83   **Deferred listing of delay appeals.** See 4.5 APPEALS.

30.3.83   **'Freelance' workers in the film and allied industries.** Revised treatment of such workers operates from 6 April 1983. See 75.24 SCHEDULE E.

13.3.84   **Net of tax pay.** Special forms and tax tables are available to employers. See 75.40 SCHEDULE E.

15.3.84   **Cable television: capital allowances** are available on ducting. See 10.25 CAPITAL ALLOWANCES.

17.5.84   **Furnished holiday lettings and caravans.** The application of *Sec 503* to caravan lettings is clarified. See 68.4, 68.9 SCHEDULE A, 74.4 SCHEDULE D, CASE VI.

31.7.84   **Offshore funds: applications for certification as a distributing fund.** The procedure is explained. See 52.7 OFFSHORE FUNDS.

1.8.84   **Sec 124: interest on quoted Eurobonds.** The requirements for designation as a 'recognised clearing system' are outlined. See 23.3 DEDUCTION OF TAX AT SOURCE.

2.11.84   **Incentive awards and prizes for employees: taxed award schemes.** See 75.40 SCHEDULE E.

11.6.85   **Approved employee share option schemes: share restrictions.** The Revenue practice is revised. See 81.6, 81.8 SHARE INCENTIVES AND OPTIONS.

23.7.85   **Extra-statutory concession: benefits in kind: the tax treatment of accommodation provided for employees.** Annual value is in practice taken as gross rateable value. See 68.7(*e*) SCHEDULE A.

18.3.86   **Business Expansion Scheme.** The grant of certain options will not result in withdrawal of relief. See 26.26 ENTERPRISE INVESTMENT SCHEME (AND BES).

15.4.86   **Voluntary lifeboatmen: tax treatment of call-out fees.** See 55.43 PAYE.

27.10.86   **Capital allowances: changes in accounting practice for plant and machinery under lease or subject to hire purchase.** The tax treatment is unaffected. See 10.24 CAPITAL ALLOWANCES.

11.3.87   **Payroll giving scheme for charities: approval of agency charities.** A list of approved agency charities is published, and will be added to from time to time. See 15.7 CHARITIES.

11.5.87   **Payroll giving schemes for charities: approval of agency charities.** Additions are made to the list published on 11 March 1987. See 15.7 CHARITIES.

16.7.87   **Payroll giving schemes for charities: approval of agency charities.** Additions are made to the lists previously published. See 15.7 CHARITIES.

5.10.87   **Payroll giving scheme for charities: approval of agency charities.** Additions are made to the lists previously published. See 15.7 CHARITIES.

28.10.87   **Payments to employees moved to higher cost housing areas.** Statement of Practice SP 1/85 is republished as an extra-statutory concession. See 75.29 SCHEDULE E.

22.12.87   **Inland Revenue further guidance on profit-related pay.** See 75.31 SCHEDULE E.

22.1.88   **Life assurance: variation of qualifying policies.** After 24 February 1988, the Revenue will not certify, as qualifying policies, any new life assurance policies which allow for variations such that, under contract law, a new policy would be created. See 45.12 LIFE ASSURANCE POLICIES.

1.2.88   **Annual return form for profit-related pay.** The form of return to be used is published. See 75.31 SCHEDULE E.

4.2.88   **Occupational pensions: publication of Inland Revenue model rules and guidance notes for simplified occupational pension schemes.** See 66.4 RETIREMENT SCHEMES.

15.3.88   **Alimony, maintenance, etc.: retrospective Court Orders.** Revenue Statement of Practice SP 6/81 will not apply to Court Orders made or varied after 30 June 1988. See 47.15 MARRIED PERSONS.

15.3.88   **Reduction of basic rate of income tax.** The consequences are outlined, including the adjustments to be made where tax is deducted from certain payments. See 23.6 DEDUCTION OF TAX AT SOURCE.

30.3.88   **Payments to employees moved to a higher cost housing area.** The limit referred to in extra-statutory concession A67 is reduced. See 75.29 SCHEDULE E.

14.4.88   **Unapproved employee share schemes.** A charge will not normally arise under *FA 1988, s 78* in respect of 'equity ratchets'. See 81.4(*a*) SHARE INCENTIVES AND OPTIONS.

2.9.88   **New tax unit for agricultural gangmasters.** See 71.56(*c*) SCHEDULE D, CASES I AND II.

8.11.88   **Payments to employees moved to a higher cost housing area.** The limit referred to in extra-statutory concession A67 is increased. See 75.29 SCHEDULE E.

19.12.88   **Tax appeals and other proceedings: place of hearing by General Commissioners.** See 4.3 APPEALS.

3.2.89   **Profit-related pay simplified.** A number of modifications are introduced either prior to enactment or by concession. See 75.31 SCHEDULE E.

22.2.89   **Payments to employees moved to a higher cost housing area.** The limit referred to in extra-statutory concession A67 is increased. See 75.29 SCHEDULE E.

3.3.89   **Double taxation: taxation of certain non-residents working on the UK continental shelf.** See 25.2 DOUBLE TAX RELIEF.

14.3.89   **Measures based on recommendations of the Keith Committee.** Transitional provisions apply to penalties for late submission of PAYE, etc. returns. See 58.4 PENALTIES.

29.3.89   **Cutting the cost of handling claims for repayment of income tax.** From 6 April 1989, repayments under £50 will not be made during the tax year to which the claim relates. See 17.2 CLAIMS, 56.7 PAYMENT OF TAX.

12.4.89   **Scholarship and apprenticeship schemes for employees.** The exempt limit under Revenue Statement of Practice SP 4/86 is increased to £5,500 p.a.. See 29.25 EXEMPT INCOME.

3.5.89   **Personal equity plans: relaxations to 75% test.** See 29.20 EXEMPT INCOME.

19.7.89   **Tax relief for medicial insurance.** The permissible benefits are outlined. See 48.6 MEDICAL INSURANCE.

28.7.89   **FA 1989: the new simpler system of assessment for earnings.** Notes on the operation of PAYE. See 55.1 PAY AS YOU EARN, 75.1 SCHEDULE E.

39   Inland Revenue Press Releases

28.7.89	**Stock lending: Treasury regulations replace existing concession** from 18 August 1989. See 71.81 SCHEDULE D, CASES I AND II.
1.8.89	**Setting Revenue rates of interest** for repayment supplement, overdue tax, and official rate purposes. The rates are in future to be set automatically by reference to a formula based on certain bank base lending rates. See 41.1 INTEREST ON OVERPAID TAX, 42.1 INTEREST ON UNPAID TAX.
9.8.89	**Transfer of Head Office work from London to Solihull.** The addresses for various clearance applications are set out. See 3.2 ANTI-AVOIDANCE.
6.10.89	**Personal equity plans: new issue shares** on slightly different terms from those offered to the general public will not thereby be excluded from transfer into a plan. See 29.20 EXEMPT INCOME.
7.11.89	**Simpler accounts for small businesses.** From April 1990, businesses with a turnover under £10,000, and landlords with gross rental income under £10,000, may submit simplified three-line accounts. See 68.6 SCHEDULE A, 71.28 SCHEDULE D, CASES I AND II.
10.11.89	**Abolition of domestic rates and introduction of community charge.** The tax consequences are outlined. See 68.15 SCHEDULE A, 71.53, 71.77 SCHEDULE D, CASES I AND II, 75.7, 75.9, 75.10, 75.29 SCHEDULE E.
27.11.89	**Payments to employees moved to a higher cost housing area.** The limit referred to in extra-statutory concession A67 is increased. See 75.29 SCHEDULE E.
18.1.90	**Incentives for employees: improvements to the taxed award scheme.** Schemes may cover higher rate as well as basic rate liabilities. See 75.40 SCHEDULE E.
26.2.90	**Elections for an appeal to be heard by the Special Commissioners.** The circumstances in which an inspector will seek to have such an appeal heard by the General Commissioners are explained. See 4.3 APPEALS.
20.3.90	**New tax reliefs to encourage charitable giving.** Certain benefits available to subscribers to charitable organisations are ignored for the purposes of relief for covenanted payments, and the requirements for deeds of covenant outlined. See 15.6(*b*)(*e*) CHARITIES, 80.21 SETTLEMENTS.
9.4.90	**Payments to employees moved to a higher cost housing area.** The limit referred to in extra-statutory concession A67 is increased. See 75.29 SCHEDULE E.
19.4.90	**Benefits in kind: valuation of living accommodation provided for employees in England and Wales.** The consequences of the ending of the domestic rates system are outlined. See 75.29 SCHEDULE E.
9.5.90	**Tracing of absent parents: Inland Revenue assistance to DSS.** The Revenue will supply to the DSS information relating to such parents where they are liable to maintain lone-parent families on income support. See 36.2(*f*) INLAND REVENUE: CONFIDENTIALITY OF INFORMATION.
21.6.90	**Taxation of motor mileage allowances.** Amendments are made to the Fixed Car Profit Scheme. See 75.43 SCHEDULE E.
17.10.90	**Changes to personal equity plans.** Pending the issue of revised regulations, certain changes to the rules for qualifying investments are applied by concession. The treatment of interest following abolition of composite rate tax is outlined. See 29.20 EXEMPT INCOME.
18.10.90	**Co-operation in investigations—'Hansard leaflet'.** The Board's practice in relation to acceptance of money settlements is explained. See 6.11 BACK DUTY.

20.11.90   **Payments to employees moved to a higher cost housing area.** The limit referred to in extra-statutory concession A67 is decreased. See 75.29 SCHEDULE E.

22.11.90   **Benefits in kind—employer-provided living accommodation.** Revenue practice is revised where employees are provided with more than one property. See 75.29 SCHEDULE E.

12.12.90   **PAYE—'K' codes.** A new code, prefix 'K', is to be introduced from 6 April 1993 in cases where non-PAYE emoluments exceed allowances. See 55.4 PAY AS YOU EARN.

31.1.91   **Double taxation: Ghana.** The 1977 Convention was never formally ratified in Ghana, and has therefore never had effect in place of the 1947 Arrangement. See 25.2 DOUBLE TAX RELIEF.

19.3.91   **Business gifts to educational establishments—new relief.** The earlier 'technical education' relief is replaced. See 71.53 SCHEDULE D, CASES I AND II.

19.3.91   **Quarterly payments for small employers** of PAYE and NIC are to be introduced from 6 April 1991. See 55.8 PAY AS YOU EARN.

26.3.91   **Taxation of motor mileage allowances.** Details of the operation of the Fixed Profit Car Scheme for 1991/92 are given. See 75.43 SCHEDULE E.

5.4.91   **Benefits in kind: loans provided by employers.** A new basis of determining the official rate of interest is introduced from 6 April 1991. See 75.16 SCHEDULE E.

11.4.91   **Finance lease rental payments.** A new statement of practice (SP 3/91) is issued, and some aspects of finance leases clarified. See 71.67 SCHEDULE D, CASES I AND II.

30.5.91   **Payments to employees moved to a higher cost housing area.** The limit referred to in extra-statutory concession A67 is decreased. See 75.29 SCHEDULE E.

12.6.91   **Finance Bill: friendly societies—tax-exempt policies.** An extra-statutory concession applies in relation to certain wrongly classified policies. See 31.3 FRIENDLY SOCIETIES.

24.10.91   **PAYE 'K' codes.** Some amendments are made to arrangements for the proposed new code following consultation. See 55.4 PAY AS YOU EARN.

30.10.91   **Payments to employees moved to a higher cost housing area.** The limit referred to in extra-statutory concession A67 is decreased. See 75.29 SCHEDULE E.

1.11.91   **Simpler accounts for small businesses: increase in the numbers who can benefit.** The limit for the submission of three-line accounts is increased to £15,000 from 6 April 1992. See 68.6, 68.19 SCHEDULE A, 71.28 SCHEDULE D, CASES I AND II

16.12.91   **Enterprise zone capital allowances.** By concession, certain amounts payable before 16 December 1991 for the purchase of unused buildings are treated as incurred on the date the construction expenditure was incurred. See 10.19 CAPITAL ALLOWANCES.

10.2.92   **Claims to repayment of tax.** Late claims arising as a result of official error are admitted by extra-statutory concession. See 17.2 CLAIMS 56.6 PAYMENT OF TAX.

10.3.92   **Taxation of motor mileage allowances.** Details of the operation of the Fixed Profit Car Scheme for 1992/93 are given. See 75.43 SCHEDULE E.

7.5.92   **Charitable giving.** The requirements for repayment claims relating to deeds of covenant are revised. See 15.6(e) CHARITIES.

8.6.92   **Tax relief on earnings of people working abroad.** Revenue practice in relation to years prior to 1992/93, following the changes made by *F(No 2)A 1992, s 54*, is explained. See 75.3(A) SCHEDULE E.

13.8.92   **Tax on savings—getting it right.** The Revenue's attitude to cases of incorrect registration for gross payment of interest is explained. See 8.3 BANKS.

39   Inland Revenue Press Releases

12.11.92	**Enhanced capital allowances for machinery, plant and buildings.** First-year and initial allowances are reintroduced generally for a limited period. See 10.3, 10.13, 10.18, 10.27 CAPITAL ALLOWANCES.
18.11.92	**Scholarship and apprenticeship schemes at universities and technical colleges.** Revenue Statement of Practice SP 4/86 is amended and reprinted with an increased exemption limit. See 29.25 EXEMPT INCOME.
21.12.92	**Enhanced capital allowances for machinery, plant and buildings.** The temporary reinstatement of initial allowances for agricultural and industrial buildings (see Revenue Press Release 12 November 1992 above) is also to apply to buildings purchased unused from traders in buildings. See 10.3, 10.13 CAPITAL ALLOWANCES.
21.1.93	**Deposit interest: amendment to tax deduction at source rules.** Deduction will not be required from interest paid by deposit-takers other than banks to certain non-ordinarily resident individuals. See 8.3 BANKS.
21.1.93	**Taxation of in-house benefits in kind.** The Revenue explain how they intend to deal with such benefits following the decision in *Pepper v Hart*. See 75.13 SCHEDULE E.
29.1.93	**Payments to employees moved to a higher cost housing area.** The limit referred to in extra-statutory concession A67 is decreased. See 75.29 SCHEDULE E.
17.2.93	**Remission of tax in cases where information has not been used within a reasonable time.** The income limits for remission are increased. See 56.6 PAYMENT OF TAX.
16.3.93	**Reform of tax relief for relocation packages.** The transitional arrangements relating to the phasing out of the previous extra-statutory concessions, and aspects of the new statutory relief, are explained. See 75.13(x), 75.29(A)(ii), 75.33 SCHEDULE E.
16.3.93	**Council tax: income tax and corporation tax implications.** See 68.15 SCHEDULE A, 71.53, 71.77 SCHEDULE D, CASES I AND II, 75.7, 75.10(*a*), 75.29 SCHEDULE E.
16.3.93	**Temporary residents in the UK—available accommodation.** The circumstances in which such accommodation is taken into account in determining residence status are explained. See 64.5 RESIDENCE, ORDINARY RESIDENCE AND DOMICILE.
23.3.93	**Taxation of motor mileage allowances.** Details of the operation of the Fixed Profit Car Scheme for 1993/94 are given. See 75.43 SCHEDULE E.
24.3.93	**Charitable giving: covenants.** Guidance is given concerning revocable covenants. See 15.6(*a*) CHARITIES.
1.4.93	**Payments to the Inland Revenue by electronic funds transfer** are treated as received one working day before value is received by the Revenue. See 56.1 PAYMENT OF TAX.
14.4.93	**New statutory exemption for relocation packages.** Aspects of the operation of the provisions introduced by *FA 1993*, and of the phasing out of the previous extra-statutory concessions, are explained. See 75.13(x), 75.29(A)(ii), 75.33 SCHEDULE E.
19.5.93	**Interest and penalties on employers' and contractors' deductions.** Deadlines of 19 June 1993 and 19 May 1994 are set for submission without penalty of 1992/93 and 1993/94 returns respectively. See 58.4 PENALTIES.
23.7.93	**Tax repayments to EC resident companies.** Claims to repayment supplement may be made following the *Commerzbank AG* decision. See 41.1 INTEREST ON OVERPAID TAX.
27.8.93	**Certificates of tax deposit.** A new Series 7 Certificate, which is not available against corporation tax liabilities, is introduced from 1 October 1993. See 14.1 CERTIFICATES OF TAX DEPOSIT.

27.9.93	**Company cars—list prices.** The Revenue requirements for determining the list price of existing cars are explained. See 75.15(i) SCHEDULE E.
23.11.93	**Reform of tax relief for relocation packages: transitional arrangements.** Amendments are made to extra-statutory concessions A5 and A67 and to the arrangements for settlement of open cases. See 75.13(x), 75.29(A), 75.33 SCHEDULE E.
17.12.93	**Capital allowances for machinery and plant.** The *FA 1994* provisions restricting the availability of allowances, and requiring notification of expenditure, are explained. See 10.25, 10.26 CAPITAL ALLOWANCES.
17.12.93	**Lloyd's: basis of assessment for individual names: transitional administrative arrangements.** See 89.2 UNDERWRITERS.
2.2.94	**Tax treatment of interest paid by Government departments.** Following the decision in *Esso Petroleum Co Ltd v MOD*, no steps will be taken to seek out, nor make further payments to, the recipients of payments of interest other than on securities before the date of the decision. See 70.1 SCHEDULE C.
31.3.94	**Self-assessment—transition to current year basis: anti-avoidance provisions** to counter movements between accounts after 31 March 1994 are to be introduced. See 72.4 SCHEDULE D, CASE III.
26.4.94	**Arrears of tax arising through official error.** Extra-statutory Concession A19 is revised. See 56.6 PAYMENT OF TAX.
11.7.94	**Charities: tax treatment of lotteries.** Provisions exempting certain lottery income for 1995/96 onwards were introduced in the 1995 Finance Bill. Exemption for earlier years continues to be granted on a concessional basis. See 15.3(iv) CHARITIES.
21.7.94	**Company cars—cash alternatives.** The legislation introduced in the 1995 Finance Bill is aimed at preventing avoidance of national insurance contributions by the offer of cash alternatives to company car provision. See 75.15 SCHEDULE E.
8.9.94	**Individuals coming to the UK to take up employment—administrative measures.** Procedures following arrival in the UK are explained. See 64.5 RESIDENCE, ORDINARY RESIDENCE AND DOMICILE.
17.11.94	**Inland Revenue rulings—pilot exercise.** See 35.6 INLAND REVENUE: ADMINISTRATION.
29.11.94	**Self-assessment.** Deduction of tax from payments to non-resident landlords will not be required where the tax is included in payments on account made under self-assessment arrangements. See 68.24 SCHEDULE A.
29.11.94	**Taxation of income from property and self-assessment.** The renewals basis or wear and tear allowances will continue to be available for furnished lettings under the new Schedule A regime introduced by *FA 1995*. See 68.8 SCHEDULE A.
29.11.94	**Self-assessment: transition to current year basis—anti-avoidance provisions.** Guidance on the Revenue interpretation of certain expressions used in the legislation is contained in the commentary published with the draft legislation. See 71.20 SCHEDULE D, CASES I AND II.
29.11.94	**Investment managers.** Extra-statutory concession B40 may continue to apply until 5 April 2005 in certain cases which fall outside the *FA 1995* provisions limiting the chargeable income of non-residents. See 51.1 NON-RESIDENTS AND OTHER OVERSEAS MATTERS.
30.11.94	**Life insurance policy investments.** The tax status of certain policies is to be confirmed, by legislation if necessary. See 31.6 FRIENDLY SOCIETIES, 45.12(*j*) LIFE ASSURANCE POLICIES.

39   Inland Revenue Press Releases

4.1.95   **Trusts and settlements—simplification of income tax 'benefit to settlor' rules.** See 80.13 *et seq.* SETTLEMENTS.

10.2.95   **Schedule A transitional proposals.** Guidance notes on the introduction of the *FA 1995* provisions. See 68.22 SCHEDULE A.

17.2.95   **Finance Bill 1995, Clause 114, 23 Schedule: investment managers.** See 51.6 NON-RESIDENTS AND OTHER OVERSEAS MATTERS.

20.2.95   **The Stock Exchange alternative investment market (AIM)—tax reliefs for investment in companies joining AIM.** Shares in such companies are treated as unquoted for tax purposes. See 26.5 ENTERPRISE INVESTMENT SCHEME, 29.20(i) EXEMPT INCOME, 46.19 LOSSES, 91.3 VENTURE CAPITAL TRUSTS.

1.3.95   **Taxation of subcontractors in the construction industry—exemption certificate.** Pending changes to the conditions for issue, certificates will be valid up to 31 July 1998 only. See 21.3 CONSTRUCTION INDUSTRY TAX DEDUCTION SCHEME.

1.3.95   **Taxation of subcontractors in the construction industry—draft regulations** are published for the changes to be made to the scheme not earlier than 1 August 1998. See 21.5 CONSTRUCTION INDUSTRY TAX DEDUCTION SCHEME.

31.3.95   **Personal equity plans.** Draft regulations permitting investment in certain corporate bonds are published. See 29.20 EXEMPT INCOME.

16.5.95   **Personal incidental expenses—guidance for employers** on the practical application of the *FA 1995* provisions. See 75.43 SCHEDULE E.

14.7.95   **Profit-related pay—interest and penalties** may apply for late and incorrect returns for 1994/95 and subsequent years. See 75.31 SCHEDULE E.

17.7.95   **Withdrawal of tax relief for approved executive share option schemes.** It was announced that all income tax reliefs under such schemes were to be withdrawn from 17 July 1995, but see now Revenue Press Release 27 July 1995 (below). See 81.9 SHARE INCENTIVES AND OPTIONS.

27.7.95   **Approved executive share option schemes.** Income tax reliefs under such schemes are withdrawn for options granted on or after 17 July (subject to transitional provisions) (replacing Revenue Press Release 17 July 1995 (above)). See 81.9 SHARE INCENTIVES AND OPTIONS.

14.9.95   **Automatic penalties for late company and employers' and contractors' end-of-year returns.** By concession, a short period of grace is allowed for submission of annual returns. See 58.4 PENALTIES.

14.9.95   **Venture capital trusts.** (i) Inadvertent breaches of the 70% 'qualifying holdings' limit will not generally result in withdrawal of approval. See 91.2 VENTURE CAPITAL TRUSTS. (ii) Certain Statements of Practice are extended to cover venture capital trust reliefs. See 26.6, 26.12, 26.26 ENTERPRISE INVESTMENT SCHEME (AND) BES, 91.3(*b*), 91.5 VENTURE CAPITAL TRUSTS.

28.9.95   **Furnished lettings: wear and tear allowance—concession.** Statement of Practice A19 is revised and re-issued. See 68.8 SCHEDULE A, 74.4 SCHEDULE D, CASE VI.

19.10.95   **Insurance comissions rebated to ordinary policyholders will not be taxed.** Statement of Practice SP 5/95 is to be revised. See 71.63 SCHEDULE D, CASES I AND II.

1.11.95   **Extension of tax exemption for Christmas parties and small gifts.** Extra-statutory concession A70 is revised. See 75.13(xvi), 75.26 SCHEDULE E.

28.11.95   **Tax exemption for sickness or unemployment insurance payments (REV 6).** Certain benefits meeting specified existing obligations are in practice tax free. See 29.10 EXEMPT INCOME, 71.63 SCHEDULE D, CASES I AND II, 75.37 SCHEDULE E.

28.11.95   **Improvements to all-employee share schemes (REV 7).** Three-year SAYE scheme contracts are to be introduced, and the minimum monthly contribution reduced to £5. See 81.8 SHARE INCENTIVES AND OPTIONS.

28.11.95   **Tax treatment of compensation for mis-sold personal pensions (REV 23).** Compensation awards may be applied to top up the personal pension or retirement annuity contract. See 65.15 RETIREMENT ANNUITIES AND PERSONAL PENSION SCHEMES.

28.11.95   **Taxation of car and mileage allowances (REV 32).** FPCS rates may be used in calculating taxable profits and allowable deductions in respect of business use of an employee's private car. See 75.43 SCHEDULE E.

28.11.95   **Living accommodation provided by reason of employment (REV 35).** By concession, a charge will not be raised under *Sec 146* where the *Sec 145* charge was based on the full market rent, and the combined charge under those *sections* will be restricted where the accommodation is provided to more than one director or employee. See 75.29 SCHEDULE E.

28.11.95   **Subcontractors in the construction industry—registration cards (REV 38).** Details of the proposed scheme are announced. See 21.5 CONSTRUCTION INDUSTRY TAX DEDUCTION SCHEME.

21.12.95   **TESSAs—European authorised institutions.** By concession, accounts opened before 2 January 1996 may be transferred to such institutions on or after that date. See 29.11(iii) EXEMPT INCOME.

25.1.96   **Interest factor tables** for repayment supplement and overdue tax are published by the Revenue. See 6.6 BACK DUTY, 41.1 INTEREST ON OVERPAID TAX, 42.1 INTEREST ON UNPAID TAX.

25.1.96   **Payments from offshore trusts to minor unmarried child of settlor: claim by settlor for credit of tax paid by trustees** against his liability to tax on income distributed to or for the benefit of the child will be allowed by concession. See 80.5 SETTLEMENTS.

29.1.96   **Personal residence tax rules—concession relating to temporary visitors.** Extra-statutory Concession A11 is revised. See 64.5 RESIDENCE, ORDINARY RESIDENCE AND DOMICILE.

11.3.96   **Giving up tax where there are Revenue delays in using information.** Extra-statutory Concession A19 is revised, the income scale being abolished. See 56.6 PAYMENT OF TAX.

21.3.96   **Carry-back of personal pension contributions made in 1996/97.** Contributions carried back to 1995/96 will be taken into account in determining the interim payment required for 1996/97. See 78.17 SELF-ASSESSMENT.

1.4.96   **Interest and repayment interest—effective date of payment of tax and NICs.** See 56.1 PAYMENT OF TAX.

4.4.96   **Self-assessment—early settlement of a deceased taxpayer's tax affairs or those of a trust or estate following cessation.** Returns will, on request, be issued before the end of the tax year, and early written confirmation given if there is to be no enquiry into the return. See 78.5, 78.11 SELF-ASSESSMENT.

29.4.96   **Bovine spongiform encephalopathy (BSE) and farm stock taking valuations.** The Revenue approach is clarified, and special arrangements instituted in the short term. See 71.56 SCHEDULE D, CASES I AND II.

40 Inland Revenue Statements of Practice

The following is a summary of those Statements of Practice published in Revenue Pamphlet IR 131 (or October 1995 Supplement), or subsequently announced, which are referred to in this book.

Statements are divided into those originally published before 18 July 1978 (which are given a reference letter (according to the subject matter) and consecutive number, e.g. A34) and later Statements (which are numbered consecutively in each year, e.g. SP 6/94).

Certain Statements marked in IR 131 as obsolete continue to be referred to in the text (having been relevant within the last six years), and the original source is quoted in such cases, as it is where the Statement awaits inclusion in IR 131.

Copies of individual SP-denominated Statements are available free of charge from Public Enquiry Room, West Wing, Somerset House, Strand, London WC2R 1LB (large SAE to accompany postal applications).

As regards Inland Revenue internal guidance manuals, see 35.10 INLAND REVENUE: ADMINISTRATION.

A1	**Deeds of covenant.** This states Revenue's requirements when examining deeds for validity and repayment claims. (Hansard 19 November 1947 Col 193; 30 July 1959 Col 148; 6 April 1977 Cols 1375–6). See 80.21 SETTLEMENTS.
A3	**Barristers: the cash basis.** Although normally assessed on a cash basis, barristers may elect to change to the earnings basis. See 12.1 CASH BASIS.
A4	**Partnerships: change in membership.** Where a continuation election is made it may be revoked within the original time limit for making the election. See 53.6 PARTNERSHIPS.
A6	**Schedule E: VAT.** For PAYE purposes, VAT is excluded from payments for services supplied by a person holding an office in the course of carrying on a trade, profession or vocation. See 55.42 PAY AS YOU EARN.
A7	**Benefits in kind and VAT.** Expenses and other benefits chargeable on an employee include VAT, if any. See 55.9 PAY AS YOU EARN, 75.13 SCHEDULE E.
A8	**Stock dividends.** The interpretation of *Sec 251(2)* is clarified. (Amended in October 1995 Supplement.) See 84.1 STOCK DIVIDENDS.
A9	**Schedule E assessments: repayment supplement.** Attribution of repayments etc. between years. See 41.1 INTEREST ON OVERPAID TAX.
A10	**Airline pilots.** Revenue practice re duties deemed to be performed in the UK. See 75.2 SCHEDULE E.
A12	**Assessing tolerance.** Where the only income is the standard Social Security pension which exceeds the single person's allowance, no direct assessment is made if the tax payable is £75 or less. See 5.8 ASSESSMENTS and 75.1(2) SCHEDULE E.
A13	**Completion of return forms by attorneys.** In cases of illness, infirmity or old age of the taxpayer, the Revenue will accept the signature of an attorney who has full knowledge of the taxpayer's affairs. See 67.2 RETURNS.
A16	**Living expenses abroad: Schedule D, Cases I and II.** A UK resident living abroad for the purposes of his trade etc. will have his personal living expenses allowed. See 71.88 SCHEDULE D, CASES I AND II.
A19	**Furnished lettings: wear and tear allowance.** Revenue practice when giving wear and tear allowances is stated. (Re-classified as concession, see 38.B47 INLAND REVENUE EXTRA-STATUTORY CONCESSIONS.) See 68.8 SCHEDULE A, 74.4 SCHEDULE D, CASE VI.

A25 **Separate taxation of wife's earnings, Sec 287; extension of time limits.** The Revenue will extend the time limit in cases of serious personal difficulties etc. See 47.10 MARRIED PERSONS.

A26 **Capital allowances on machinery and plant: amendment of claim by an individual trader.** An individual (or partnership) may be allowed to revise his claim in certain circumstances. (Amended in October 1995 Supplement.) See 10.27(vi), 10.28 CAPITAL ALLOWANCES.

A27 **Accounts on a cash basis.** See 12.1 CASH BASIS.

A30 **Settlements: benefit to settlor's future spouse.** An explanation is given of the concept 'possible future spouse'. See 80.25 SETTLEMENTS.

A32 **Goods taken by traders for personal consumption.** The Revenue's practice in applying *Sharkey v Wernher* is stated. See 71.82 SCHEDULE D, CASES I AND II.

A33 **Relief for interest payments: loans applied in acquiring an interest in a partnership.** Salaried partners in a professional firm may claim relief in certain circumstances. See 43.22 INTEREST PAYABLE.

A34 **Relief for interest payments: loans for purchase or improvement of land.**

    (*a*)   Husband and wife living together are given relief for interest paid by either even if the property is owned wholly or partly by the other.

    (*b*)   A person who inherits property subject to a mortgage is entitled to tax relief for mortgage interest if, and only if, the person from whom he inherited the property was so entitled.

See 43.12 INTEREST PAYABLE.

B1 **Treatment of VAT.** Guidance on the general principles applied in dealing with VAT in tax computations. (Amended in October 1995 Supplement.) See 71.91 SCHEDULE D, CASES I AND II.

B6 **Goods sold subject to reservation of title.** Such goods should normally be treated as purchases in the buyer's accounts and sales in the supplier's accounts provided that both parties agree. See 71.82 SCHEDULE D, CASES I AND II.

C1 **Lotteries and football pools.** Where part of the cost of a ticket is to be donated to a club, etc., that part is, in certain circumstances, not treated as a trading receipt. See 71.30 SCHEDULE D, CASES I AND II.

SP 3/78 **Close companies: income tax relief for interest on loans applied in acquiring an interest in a close company.** Relief continues after company ceases to be close. See 43.19 INTEREST PAYABLE.

SP 4/78 **Mining companies: expenditure on planning permission applications.** The cost of unsuccessful applications etc. will be allowed. See 10.49(*b*) CAPITAL ALLOWANCES.

SP 3/79 **Payment of life assurance premiums on which commission is payable to the policyholder.** (Superseded by SP 5/95 below.) See 71.63 SCHEDULE D, CASES I AND II.

SP 4/79 **Life assurance premium relief—children's policies.** This is relaxed by SP 11/79 below. See 45.4(*g*) LIFE ASSURANCE POLICIES.

SP 7/79 **Benefits in kind: cheap loans—advances for expenses** to an employee will not be a taxable benefit provided certain conditions are met. See 75.17 SCHEDULE E.

SP 8/79 **Compensation for acquisition of property under compulsory powers.** Reimbursement of revenue costs are trading receipts. See 71.47(*d*) SCHEDULE D, CASES I AND II.

SP 11/79   **Life assurance premium relief—children's policies.** Relief will be given in certain circumstances on premiums on policies taken out by children under twelve. See 45.4(*g*) LIFE ASSURANCE POLICIES.

SP 1/80   **Legal entitlement and administrative practices** relating to tax overpaid. (Superseded by SP 6/95 below.) See 56.7 PAYMENT OF TAX.

SP 3/80   **Sec 707: Cancellation of tax advantages from certain transactions in securities: procedure for clearance in advance.** The procedure is explained. See 3.2 ANTI-AVOIDANCE.

SP 4/80   **Industrial buildings allowance: industrial workshops constructed for separate letting to small businesses.** A global basis will be used for giving allowances. See 10.21 CAPITAL ALLOWANCES.

SP 6/80   **Small workshops allowance.** Clarifies eligibility for the allowance. (Revenue Press Release 9 July 1980). See 10.21 CAPITAL ALLOWANCES.

SP 7/80   **Deceased persons' estates: income received during the administration period: claims to repayment of tax** by residuary legatees are extended. (Revenue Press Release 16 July 1980). See 22.3 DECEASED ESTATES.

SP 9/80   **Investigation settlements: retirement annuity relief.** Entitlement to relief where an investigation is settled by voluntary offer. (Revenue Press Release 19 September 1980). See 6.11 BACK DUTY. Now replaced by SP 9/91, see below.

SP 10/80   **Mortgage interest relief: year of marriage.** Relief may be granted on more than one property. (Revenue Press Release 24 September 1980). See 43.12 INTEREST PAYABLE.

SP 11/80   **Liability on gains arising on life and capital redemption policies and life annuities.** Non-residents will not be charged in certain circumstances. See 45.13 LIFE ASSURANCE POLICIES.

SP 15/80   **Maintenance payments: payment of school fees.** Relief may be given to a parent paying fees direct to a school as part of a Court Order. See 47.15 MARRIED PERSONS.

SP 16/80   **Lorry drivers: relief for expenditure on meals** where there is a full-time travelling appointment. Also refers to subsistence etc. allowances when working temporarily away from home. See 75.43 SCHEDULE E.

SP 1/81   **Non-statutory redundancy payments** will be liable only under *Sec 148* in certain circumstances. Superseded by SP 1/94 below. See 19.3 COMPENSATION FOR LOSS OF EMPLOYMENT.

SP 2/81   **Contributions to retirement benefit schemes on termination of employment.** Such payments by the employer on behalf of an employee will not be chargeable under *Sec 148*. See 19.5, 19.6(x) COMPENSATION FOR LOSS OF EMPLOYMENT.

SP 5/81   **Expenditure on farm drainage.** The net cost of restoring drainage is allowable as revenue expenditure. See 71.56(*b*) SCHEDULE D, CASES I AND II.

SP 6/81   **Maintenance payments under Court Orders: retrospective dating.** Payments before the date of the Order can be taken into account for tax purposes under certain circumstances. (Revenue Press Release 8 September 1981). The practice ceases for Orders made or varied after 30 June 1988 (Revenue Press Release 15 March 1988). See 47.15 MARRIED PERSONS.

SP 10/81   **Payments on account of disability resulting in cessation of employment.** The interpretation of 'disability' in *Sec 188(1)(a)* is extended. See 19.6(iii) COMPENSATION FOR LOSS OF EMPLOYMENT.

SP 11/81   **Additional redundancy payments.** Allowance under *Sec 90* will also apply to a partial discontinuance of a trade. See 71.53 SCHEDULE D, CASES I AND II.

SP 12/81   **Construction industry tax deduction scheme: carpet fitting.** Carpet fitting is considered to be outside the scope of the scheme. See 21.1 CONSTRUCTION INDUSTRY TAX DEDUCTION SCHEME.

SP 1/82   **Interaction of income tax and inheritance tax on assets put into settlement.** Income of a settlement will not be treated as income of the settlor solely because the trustees have power to pay, or do pay, inheritance tax on assets put into the settlement by the settlor. See 80.15(*e*) SETTLEMENTS.

SP 5/83   **Use of Schedules in making personal tax returns.** The Revenue requirements are detailed. See 67.2 RETURNS.

SP 1/84   **Trade unions: provident benefits: legal and administrative expenses.** See 88.1 TRADE UNIONS.

SP 2/84   **Payments to redundant steel workers** will be taxed under Schedule E. (Revenue Press Release 24 February 1984). See 75.32 SCHEDULE E.

SP 5/84   **Employees resident but not ordinarily resident in the UK: liability under Schedule E, Cases II and III.** Revenue practice on apportionment of emoluments between UK and non-UK duties of an employment is explained. See 75.2 SCHEDULE E.

SP 6/84   **Non-resident lessors: FA 1973, s 38.** The conditions under which profits of such lessors of mobile drilling rigs, etc. are exempt from tax are outlined. See 51.13 NON-RESIDENTS AND OTHER OVERSEAS MATTERS.

SP 8/84   **Sec 124: interest on quoted Eurobonds.** The application of the provisions is explained. See 23.3 DEDUCTION OF TAX AT SOURCE, 51.3 NON-RESIDENTS AND OTHER OVERSEAS MATTERS.

SP 1/85   **Tax treatment of certain payments to employees moved to higher housing cost areas.** Such payments may be exempted from tax. (Revenue Press Release 18 January 1985). Reissued 28 October 1987 as an extra-statutory concession. See 75.29 SCHEDULE E.

SP 4/85   **Income tax: relief for interest on loans used to buy land occupied for partnership business purposes.** Relief may be available where interest is paid by the partnership, and a similar practice may apply to controlling directors' loans to purchase land occupied by the company. See 43.3 INTEREST PAYABLE.

SP 6/85   **Income tax: incentive awards: calculation of the amount assessable.** The basis on which expenses are included is outlined. See 75.44(*a*) SCHEDULE E.

SP 1/86   **Capital allowances: machinery and plant: short-life assets.** Guidance is given on some practical aspects of the arrangements in *CAA 1990, ss 37, 38.* See 10.28(F) CAPITAL ALLOWANCES.

SP 2/86   **Offshore funds.** Various aspects of the legislation are clarified. See 52.3, 52.4, 52.5 OFFSHORE FUNDS.

SP 3/86   **Income tax: payments to a non-resident from UK discretionary trusts or UK estates during the administration period: double taxation relief.** A change of practice replaces extra-statutory concessions A14 and B18 in certain cases. See 22.3 DECEASED ESTATES, 80.5 SETTLEMENTS.

SP 4/86   **Scholarship and apprenticeship schemes for employees.** Certain payments to employees attending full-time educational courses are exempt from income tax. See 29.25 EXEMPT INCOME.

SP 7/86   **Business Expansion Scheme: overseas activities.** The requirement that trade(s) be carried on 'wholly or mainly in the UK' is clarified. (Revenue Press Release 12

September 1986). See 26.20 ENTERPRISE INVESTMENT SCHEME (AND BES). Now super-seded by SP4/87, see below.

SP 9/86   **Income tax: partnership mergers and demergers.** The application of the succession rules is explained. (Amended in October 1995 Supplement.) See 53.8 PARTNERSHIPS.

SP 1/87   **Exchange rate fluctuations.** The Revenue practice following the *Marine Midland* decision is explained. See 71.55 SCHEDULE D, CASES I AND II.

SP 3/87   **Repayment of tax to charities on covenanted and other income.** See 15.6(*f*) CHARITIES.

SP 4/87   **Business Expansion Scheme: ship chartering and overseas activities.** SP 7/86 (see above) is revised. See 26.20 ENTERPRISE INVESTMENT SCHEME (AND BES).

SP 5/87   **Tax returns: the use of substitute forms.** The conditions for acceptance of facsimile and photocopied returns and other forms are set out. See 17.1 CLAIMS, 67.2 RETURNS.

SP 9/87   **Capital allowances: hotels: FA 1978, s 38.** The Revenue interpretation of the provision of breakfast and evening meals by a qualifying hotel is set out. See 10.18 CAPITAL ALLOWANCES.

SP 2/88   **Civil tax penalties and criminal prosecution cases.** The Revenue practice as regards pursuit of such penalties is set out. See 58.10 PENALTIES.

SP 5/88   **Taxation of car telephones provided by employers.** The position as regards charge as a benefit in kind is explained. (Revenue Press Release 22 July 1988). See 75.15 SCHEDULE E.

SP 6/89   **Delay in rendering tax returns: interest on overdue tax: TMA s 88.** SP 3/88 above is revised to remove the 'reasonable excuse' waiver. See 67.2 RETURNS.

SP 8/89 (Revised)   **Independent taxation: mortgage interest relief time limit for married couples' allocation of interest elections.** The normal application of Revenue discretion to extend the time limits is explained. See 43.12 INTEREST PAYABLE.

SP 3/90   **Stocks and long-term contracts.** The Revenue practice as regards bases of valuation and changes therein is explained. See 71.82 SCHEDULE D, CASES I AND II.

SP 4/90   **Charitable covenants.** Revised practices in relation to retrospective validation and escape clauses are explained. See 15.6(*c*)(*d*) CHARITIES.

SP 5/90   **Accountants' working papers.** The Revenue's approach to the use of its information powers in relation to accountants' working papers is explained. See 6.8 BACK DUTY.

SP 2/91   **Residence in the UK: visits extended because of exceptional circumstances.** Extra days spent in the UK may be ignored for certain purposes. See 64.5 RESIDENCE, ORDINARY RESIDENCE AND DOMICILE.

SP 3/91   **Finance lease rental payments.** The practice in relation to deduction of rental payments is explained. See 71.67 SCHEDULE D, CASES I AND II.

SP 4/91   **Tax returns.** The principles followed by the Revenue in designing tax returns and determining the information required in them are explained. See 67.1 RETURNS.

SP 7/91   **Double taxation: business profits: unilateral relief.** The practice as regards admission of foreign taxes for unilateral relief is revised. See 25.4 DOUBLE TAX RELIEF.

SP 8/91   **Discovery assessments.** The Revenue practice as regards the making of further assessments following 'discovery' is explained. See 5.3 ASSESSMENTS.

SP 9/91   **Investigation settlements: retirement annuities and personal pension relief.** Special premium relief is given where an investigation is settled by voluntary offer. See 6.11 BACK DUTY.

SP 12/91   **Income tax: 'in the ordinary course' of banking business.** The Revenue interpretation of this expression is explained. See 23.3 DEDUCTION OF TAX AT SOURCE.

SP 13/91   **Ex gratia awards made on termination of an office or employment by retirement or death.** A revised practice, and extended system of approval, applies after 31 October 1991. (Amended in October 1995 Supplement.) See 66.12 RETIREMENT SCHEMES.

SP 14/91   **Tax treatment of transactions in financial futures and options.** The circumstances in which such transactions will be considered to constitute trading are outlined. See 71.32 SCHEDULE D. CASES I AND II.

SP 15/91   **Treatment of investment managers and their overseas clients.** The Revenue view of the application of *TMA s 78* is explained. See 51.4(*b*) NON-RESIDENTS AND OTHER OVERSEAS MATTERS.

SP 16/91   **Accountancy expenses arising out of accounts investigations.** Revenue practice on the allowance of such expenses is explained. See 71.68 SCHEDULE D, CASES I AND II.

SP 17/91   **Residence in the UK: when ordinary residence is regarded as commencing where the period to be spent here is less than three years.** See 64.6 RESIDENCE, ORDINARY RESIDENCE AND DOMICILE.

SP 18/91   **Foreign earnings deduction.** A change is made to the interpretation of the rules governing the deduction. See 75.3 SCHEDULE E.

SP 1/92   **Directors' and employees' emoluments: extension of time limits for relief on transition to receipts basis of assessment.** Revenue practice is explained. See 75.1 SCHEDULE E.

SP 6/92   **Accident insurance policies: chargeable events and gains on policies of life insurance.** Certain accident insurance policies will no longer be considered policies of life insurance for these purposes. See 45.13 LIFE ASSURANCE POLICIES.

SP 7/92   **Profit-related pay—use of pool determination formulae** will not normally meet the scheme registration requirements after 2 August 1992. See 75.31 SCHEDULE E.

SP 9/92   **Partnerships: circumstances in which late elections will be accepted.** (Amended in October 1995 Supplement.) See 53.6 PARTNERSHIPS.

SP 1/93   **Tax treatment of expenditure on films and certain similar assets.** Guidance on procedural points relating to relief for film production and preliminary expenditure. (Incorporates updated guidance from SP 2/83 and SP 2/85.) See 71.57 SCHEDULE D, CASES I AND II.

SP 4/93   **Deceased persons' estates: discretionary interests in residue.** Payments out of income of the residue are treated as income of the recipient for the year of payment, whether out of income as it arises or out of income arising in earlier years. (Amended in October 1995 Supplement.) See 22.3 DECEASED ESTATES.

SP 5/93   **UK/Czechoslovakia double taxation Convention.** The Convention is regarded as applying to the Czech and Slovak Republics. See 25.2 DOUBLE TAX RELIEF.

SP 6/93   **UK/Yugoslavia double taxation Convention.** The Convention is regarded as applying to Croatia and Slovenia, the position of Bosnia-Hercegovina and the remaining Yugoslav republics being uncertain. See 25.2 DOUBLE TAX RELIEF.

SP 15/93   **Business tax computations rounded to nearest £1,000** will be accepted from certain large businesses. See 71.28 SCHEDULE D, CASES I AND II.

40   Inland Revenue Statements of Practice

SP 1/94   **Non-statutory redundancy payments.** Revenue practice following the decision in *Mairs v Haughey* is explained. Supersedes SP 1/81 above. See 19.3 COMPENSATION FOR LOSS OF EMPLOYMENT.

SP 2/94   **Enterprise investment scheme and venture capital trust scheme—location of activity.** The requirement that trade(s) be carried on 'wholly or mainly in the UK' is clarified. (Revised by Revenue Press Release 14 September 1995). See 26.6 ENTERPRISE INVESTMENT SCHEME (AND BES), 91.3(*b*) VENTURE CAPITAL TRUSTS.

SP 3/94   **Business expansion scheme, enterprise investment scheme, capital gains tax reinvestment relief and venture capital trust scheme—loans to investors.** The requirements for denial of relief on loan-linked investments are explained. (Revised by Revenue Press Release 14 September 1995). See 26.12, 26.26 ENTERPRISE INVESTMENT SCHEME (AND BES), 91.5 VENTURE CAPITAL TRUSTS.

SP 4/94   **Enhanced stock dividends received by trustees of interest in possession trusts.** The Revenue view on the tax treatment of such dividends is explained. See 84.6 STOCK DIVIDENDS.

SP 6/94   **Capital allowances—notification of expenditure on machinery and plant made outside the normal time limit.** The general criteria are explained. See 10.25 CAPITAL ALLOWANCES.

SP 5/95   **Taxation of receipts of insurance and personal pension scheme commissions.** The Revenue view of the taxation consequences of a number of different arrangements is set out. (Supersedes SP 3/79 above.) See 71.63 SCHEDULE D, CASES I AND II.

SP 6/95   **Legal entitlement and administrative practice** in relation to repayments of tax is revised (superseding SP 1/80 above). See 56.7 PAYMENT OF TAX.

SP 7/95   **Venture capital trusts—value of gross assets.** The Revenue's general approach to the valuation of gross assets in determining whether a holding is a 'qualifying holding' is explained. (Revenue Press Release 14 November 1995). See 91.3(*e*) VENTURE CAPITAL TRUSTS.

SP 8/95   **Venture capital trusts—default terms in loan agreements.** Certain event of default clauses will not disqualify a loan from being a security for the purposes of approval. (Revenue Press Release 14 November 1995). See 91.2 VENTURE CAPITAL TRUSTS.

SP 1/96   **Obligation to notify chargeability to income tax for tax years 1995/96 onwards.** Employees are relieved in certain circumstances of the obligation to notify chargeability in respect of benefits, etc.. (Revenue Press Release 1 February 1996). See 78.4 SELF-ASSESSMENT.

SP 2/96   **Pooled cars: incidental private use.** The Revenue interpretation of the requirement that private use of pooled vehicles be 'merely incidental' to business use is explained. (Revenue Press Release 29 March 1996). See 75.15(v) SCHEDULE E.

SP 3/96   **ICTA 1988, s 313—termination payments made in settlement of employment claims.** The circumstances in which a charge will not arise are clarified. (Revenue Press Release 4 April 1996). See 75.34 SCHEDULE E.

41   Interest on Overpaid Tax

[*Sec 824; FA 1988, 13 Sch 7; FA 1989, ss 110(5), 114(4), 158(2), 178, 179; SI 1978 No 1117; SI 1979 No 1687; SI 1982 No 1587; SI 1985 No 563; SI 1986 Nos 1181, 1832; SI 1987 Nos 513, 898, 1492, 1988; SI 1988 Nos 756, 1278, 1621, 2185; SI 1989 Nos 1000, 1297; SI 1993 No 753*]

41.1   The provisions described below apply where the tax repayable relates to 1995/96 and earlier years (and to 1996/97 in the case of tax repayable to a partnership commenced, or deemed to commence, before 6 April 1994). As regards later years, see 78.23 SELF-ASSESSMENT.

A repayment (or set-off) to an individual by the Revenue of income tax (including tax credits and tax deducted under PAYE), surtax, capital gains tax or the special charge under *FA 1968, Pt IV*, repaid more than twelve months after the year of assessment to which it relates, carries tax-free interest ('a repayment supplement'), which will not be a person's income for any tax purpose, provided that the individual was resident in the UK for that year of assessment. In relation to repayments made before 6 April 1993, repayment supplement applies only where the repayment amounts to £25 or more for a year of assessment. From 19 April 1993, repayment supplement applies also to Class 4 national insurance contributions (see 82.7 SOCIAL SECURITY).

The **rates of interest** are, from 18 August 1989, adjusted automatically by reference to changes in the average of base lending rates of certain clearing banks, and are announced in Revenue Press Releases. (Revenue Press Release 1 August 1989). Before that date, they were prescribed by statutory instrument. The rates so determined are as follows.

> 6% p.a. before 6 April 1974
> 9% p.a. from 6 April 1974 to 5 January 1980
> 12% p.a. from 6 January 1980 to 5 December 1982
> 8% p.a. from 6 December 1982 to 5 May 1985
> 11% p.a. from 6 May 1985 to 5 August 1986
> 8.5% p.a. from 6 August 1986 to 5 November 1986
> 9.5% p.a. from 6 November 1986 to 5 April 1987
> 9% p.a. from 6 April 1987 to 5 June 1987
> 8.25% p.a. from 6 June 1987 to 5 September 1987
> 9% p.a. from 6 September 1987 to 5 December 1987
> 8.25% p.a. from 6 December 1987 to 5 May 1988
> 7.75% p.a. from 6 May 1988 to 5 August 1988
> 9.75% p.a. from 6 August 1988 to 5 October 1988
> 10.75% p.a. from 6 October 1988 to 5 January 1989
> 11.5% p.a. from 6 January 1989 to 5 July 1989
> 12.25% p.a. from 6 July 1989 to 5 November 1989
> 13% p.a. from 6 November 1989 to 5 November 1990
> 12.25% p.a. from 6 November 1990 to 5 March 1991
> 11.5% p.a. from 6 March 1991 to 5 May 1991
> 10.75% p.a. from 6 May 1991 to 5 July 1991
> 10% p.a. from 6 July 1991 to 5 October 1991
> 9.25% p.a. from 6 October 1991 to 5 November 1992
> 7.75% p.a. from 6 November 1992 to 5 December 1992
> 7% p.a. from 6 December 1992 to 5 March 1993
> 6.25% p.a. from 6 March 1993 to 5 January 1994
> 5.50% p.a. from 6 January 1994 to 5 October 1994
> 6.25% p.a. from 6 October 1994 to 5 March 1995
> 7% p.a. from 6 March 1995 to 5 February 1996.
> **6.25% p.a. from 6 February 1996 onwards.**

41.2 Interest on Overpaid Tax

Interest factor tables for use as ready reckoners in calculating repayment supplement are published by the Revenue and updated as rates change. (Revenue Press Release 25 January 1996).

The interest will run to the end of the tax month (i.e. sixth day of one calendar month to fifth day of following month) in which the repayment order is issued and will commence as follows.

Tax originally paid	*Interest commences*
More than 12 months after year of assessment	From end of year of assessment in which tax was paid
In any other case	From end of 12 months following year of assessment

Where a repayment relates to tax paid in two or more years of assessment, it shall be treated, as far as possible, as representing later rather than earlier years.

Repayments relating to claims under *ITA 1952, s 228* (income accumulated under trusts, see 80.12 SETTLEMENTS) are treated as repayment of tax paid for the year of assessment in which the contingency happened.

Repayment supplement is not paid in respect of out of date claims, since the amount repaid is regarded as an *ex gratia* payment made without acceptance of any legal liability. (Revenue Claims Manual, RM 5104).

Schedule E tax deducted under PAYE will be attributed to the year of assessment in which deducted, and repayments will be attributed to particular years according to regulations made by the Board, but without affecting interest on amounts which might become less than £25 for any year (where relevant). See Revenue Pamphlet IR 131, A9 and *SI 1975 No 1283*. A repayment supplement is paid when the total repayment of £25 or more is divided between husband and wife who individually receive less than £25 (*SI 1978 No 1117 para 5*) where this limit remains relevant.

The above provisions also apply to partnerships, trusts and deceased estates, but not to repayments of post-war credits or amounts paid by order of a court having power to allow interest (for which see 56.2 PAYMENT OF TAX). They are extended to repayments of excessive clawback of life assurance premium relief, and to relief by repayment for such premiums where relief is not obtained by deduction (see 45.5, 45.1 LIFE ASSURANCE POLICIES). (Revenue Pamphlet IR 1, A51).

In *R v CIR (ex p. Commerzbank AG) QB, [1991] STC 271*, repayment supplement was held not to fall within the scope of double tax agreements, although on a reference to the European Court of Justice (see *[1993] STC 605*), the Court upheld the view that, in the case of companies resident in EC Member States, such discrimination against non-UK resident companies was prevented by the relevant Articles of the Treaty of Rome. For repayment supplement payable to non-UK EC resident companies following this decision, see Revenue Press Release 23 July 1993. By concession, repayment supplement will also be added to tax repayments to non-UK EC resident individuals on the same basis as applies to UK resident individuals. The concession will also apply to repayments of income tax to individuals since 12 July 1987, and equally to partnerships, trustees and personal representatives. Claims should be sent to Inland Revenue, FICO (International), Room 2004, Lynwood Road, Thames Ditton, Surrey KT7 0DP or St John's House, Merton Road, Bootle, Merseyside L69 9BB (to the latter address in the case of claims relating to repayments made by other offices). (Revenue Pamphlet IR 1, A82).

See also 55.8 PAY AS YOU EARN.

41.2   **Unauthorised demands for tax.** There is a general right to interest under *Supreme Court Act 1981, s 35A* in a case where a taxpayer submits to such an unauthorised demand, provided that the payment is not made voluntarily to close a transaction (*Woolwich Equitable Building Society v CIR HL 1992, 65 TC 265*). (*Note.* The substantive decision against the Revenue which gave rise to the repayment was subsequently upheld in the HL. See *R v CIR (ex p. Woolwich Equitable Building Society) HL 1990, 63 TC 589.*)

41.3   **Revenue error.** The Revenue have published a Code of Practice (No 1, published February 1993 and available from local tax offices) setting out the circumstances in which they will consider paying a repayment supplement on money owed to the taxpayer for any period during which there has been undue delay on the part of the Revenue. See 35.8 INLAND REVENUE: ADMINISTRATION.

41.4   **Over-repayments.** Where a repayment supplement has been overpaid it may be recovered by an assessment under Schedule D, Case VI. See 56.8 PAYMENT OF TAX.

42 Interest on Unpaid Tax

Cross-references. See also 55.8 PAY AS YOU EARN and 78.22 SELF-ASSESSMENT.

42.1   The provisions of *TMA s 86* described below, and in 42.2, apply where the tax payable relates to 1995/96 and earlier years (and to 1996/97 in the case of tax payable by a partnership commenced, or deemed to commence, before 6 April 1994). However, they do not apply where an assessment for 1995/96 or earlier is made on or after 6 April 1998. Where these provisions cease to apply, they are replaced by those at 78.22 SELF-ASSESSMENT.

For notices of assessment for Schedules A, C, D and E and to excess liability on taxed investment income, if tax is not paid on the date it becomes due and payable (see 56.1 PAYMENT OF TAX), interest is chargeable from that date (even if it is a non-business day) on *each assessment*. In relation to notices of assessment issued (or Schedule E tax demands made) before 19 April 1993, the Board may remit interest of £30 or less arising on any assessment. [*TMA s 86(1)(2)(5)(6) as amended; FA 1989, s 158(1)(a); SI 1993 No 753*]. *Note.* Interest arising on 'any assessment' includes the *aggregate* of interest on *each* instalment of tax payable on an assessment under Schedule D, Case I or II (Tolley's Practical Tax 1982 p 9).

From 19 April 1993, interest under *TMA s 86* applies also to Class 4 national insurance contributions (see 82.7 SOCIAL SECURITY). Previously, only *TMA s 88* interest applied (see 6.6 BACK DUTY).

Rates of interest are, from 18 August 1989, adjusted automatically by reference to changes in the average of base lending rates of certain clearing banks, and are announced in Revenue Press Releases. (Revenue Press Release 1 August 1989). Before that date, they were prescribed by statutory instrument. The rates so determined are as follows.

   6% p.a. from 19 April 1969 to 30 June 1974
   9% p.a. from 1 July 1974 to 31 December 1979
   12% p.a. from 1 January 1980 to 30 November 1982
   8% p.a. from 1 December 1982 to 30 April 1985
   11% p.a. from 1 May 1985 to 5 August 1986
   8.5% p.a. from 6 August 1986 to 5 November 1986
   9.5% p.a. from 6 November 1986 to 5 April 1987
   9% p.a. from 6 April 1987 to 5 June 1987
   8.25% p.a. from 6 June 1987 to 5 September 1987
   9% p.a. from 6 September 1987 to 5 December 1987
   8.25% p.a. from 6 December 1987 to 5 May 1988
   7.75% p.a. from 6 May 1988 to 5 August 1988
   9.75% p.a. from 6 August 1988 to 5 October 1988
   10.75% p.a. from 6 October 1988 to 5 January 1989
   11.5% p.a. from 6 January 1989 to 5 July 1989
   12.25% p.a. from 6 July 1989 to 5 November 1989
   13% p.a. from 6 November 1989 to 5 November 1990
   12.25% p.a. from 6 November 1990 to 5 March 1991
   11.5% p.a. from 6 March 1991 to 5 May 1991
   10.75% p.a. from 6 May 1991 to 5 July 1991
   10% p.a. from 6 July 1991 to 5 October 1991
   9.25% p.a. from 6 October 1991 to 5 November 1992
   7.75% p.a. from 6 November 1992 to 5 December 1992
   7% p.a. from 6 December 1992 to 5 March 1993
   6.25% p.a. from 6 March 1993 to 5 January 1994

5.50% p.a. from 6 January 1994 to 5 October 1994
6.25% p.a. from 6 October 1994 to 5 March 1995
    7% p.a. from 6 March 1995 to 5 February 1996.
6.25% p.a. from 6 February 1996 onwards.

[*TMA s 89; FA 1989, ss 178, 179; SI 1974 No 966; SI 1979 No 1687; SI 1982 No 1587; SI 1985 No 563; SI 1986 Nos 1181, 1832; SI 1987 Nos 513, 898, 1492, 1988; SI 1988 Nos 756, 1278, 1621, 2185; SI 1989 Nos 1000, 1297*].

Interest factor tables for use as ready reckoners in calculating interest on overdue tax are published by the Revenue and updated as rates change. (Revenue Press Release 25 January 1996).

See under 56.1 PAYMENT OF TAX for the date on which tax is treated as having been paid, and under 56.3 PAYMENT OF TAX for collection.

Interest is payable gross and recoverable (as if it were tax charged and due and payable under the assessment to which it relates) as a Crown debt; it is not deductible from profits or income [*TMA ss 69, 90*] and is refundable to the extent that tax concerned is subsequently discharged (and any repayment may be treated as a discharge for this purpose). [*TMA s 91; FA 1996, 18 Sch 4(2), 17(3)(4)*].

42.2   **Assessments against which appeal is made.** On application by the taxpayer, the inspector may agree (or the Commissioners may determine) that part of the tax charged by an assessment may be postponed (see 56.2 PAYMENT OF TAX). Any tax which is *not postponed* then becomes due and payable as if it were tax charged by an assessment notice of which was issued on the date of the determination or agreement and against which there had been no appeal. On the determination of the substantive appeal, any *postponed tax* or *extra tax* becomes due and payable as if it were tax charged by an assessment notice of which was issued on the date on which the inspector issues to the appellant a notice of the total amount payable in accordance with the determination, and against which there had been no appeal. [*TMA 1970, s 55(3)(6)(9); FA 1989, s 156(2)*].

Interest on postponed and non-postponed tax and, for notices of assessment issued after 30 July 1982, on an increased liability following settlement of the appeal, then runs from a 'reckonable date' which is the date on which the tax becomes due and payable (see 56.2 PAYMENT OF TAX) *unless* that date is later than the date given by the following Table, in which case the reckonable date is the later of the date given by the Table and the date on which the tax under the assessment would have been due and payable had there been no appeal against it (any additional tax being treated as if it had been charged by the original assessment) (see 56.1 PAYMENT OF TAX). The Table referred to above is as follows.

Description of tax	*Latest date*
Income tax under Schedules A or D	1 July following the end of the year of assessment.
Higher rate tax and investment income surcharge on income taxed at source (other than under PAYE)	for tax in respect of 1980/81 and later years, 1 June following the December after the end of the year for which assessed (for tax in respect of years before 1980/81, 1 January following the end of the year for which assessed).
Capital gains tax	for tax in respect of 1980/81 and later years, 1 June following the December after the end of the year for which assessed (for tax in respect of years before 1980/81, 1 January following the end of the year for which assessed).

42.2 Interest on Unpaid Tax

See under 70 SCHEDULE C for related provisions. [*TMA s 86; FA 1989, s 156(1)*]. For Schedule E assessments, the reckonable date is strictly 14 days after the first application by the Collector for payment, but it is understood that, in the event of an appeal, the due date is recalculated to 14 days after the issue of a fresh demand note.

Example

Mr X has a business assessable under Schedule D, Case I. On 25 November 1995 he receives an estimated assessment for 1995/96 showing a tax liability of £21,000. He appeals on 20 December and also applies for postponement of tax of £5,000 which is agreed by the inspector on 14 January 1996. He pays the first instalment of tax £8,000 (one-half) on 1 March 1996 and the second instalment on 1 July 1996. The appeal is determined by the Commissioners on 31 July 1996 and on 5 August 1996 the inspector issues notice of the total tax payable of £23,000 (an increase of £2,000). Mr X pays the amount outstanding £7,000 on 30 September 1996.

The dates of consequence are as follows

(i) Due dates of payment had there been no appeal:	One-half on 1 January 1996 One-half on 1 July 1996
(ii) Revised due dates of payment of non-disputed sum (£16,000) and dates from which interest will run:	One-half (£8,000) on 13 February 1996 (30 days after agreement) One-half (£8,000) on 1 July 1996
(iii) Due date of determined balance—£7,000:	4 September 1996 (30 days after notice of tax payable)
(iv) Date from which interest will run on determined balance:	1 July 1996 (the 'reckonable date')

Note. The due date of the first non-disputed payment of £8,000 is also postponed (from 1 January to 13 February 1996). Although the tax in dispute is not payable until 4 September 1996, interest will run (on both the tax postponed and the increase) from the previous 1 July until paid. The total interest payable is thus

$$8{,}000 \times \frac{17}{366} \times 6.25\% = \qquad 23.22$$

$$7{,}000 \times \frac{91}{365} \times 6.25\% = \qquad \underline{109.08}$$

$$\underline{\underline{£132.30}}$$

Interest on tax becoming due after determination of an appeal by the Courts. Any outstanding tax charged in accordance with the Commissioners' decision must be paid before an appeal can be heard by the High Court, and if on the determination of the appeal further tax is found to be chargeable, it becomes due and payable thirty days from the date on which the inspector issues to the taxpayer a notice of the total amount payable. [*TMA s 56(9) as amended*]. Interest under *TMA s 86*, however, runs from the later of the Table date (see above) and the date on which the tax would have become due and payable if charged by the original assessment (without an appeal being made). [*TMA s 86 (3A); FA 1989, s 156(1)*]. If a taxpayer in NI exercised his right to appeal to the county court instead of to the Commissioners, the same rule applies if a case is stated for the opinion of the Court of Appeal in NI. [*TMA s 59(6) as amended*]. See now 4.3 APPEALS as regards NI appeals.

Revenue error. The Revenue have published a Code of Practice (No 1, published February 1993 and available from local tax offices) setting out the circumstances in which they will consider waiving a charge to interest on unpaid tax where there has been undue delay on the part of the Revenue. See 35.8 INLAND REVENUE: ADMINISTRATION.

42.3   COMPANIES

The provisions in 42.1 above apply to corporation tax for accounting periods ending before 1 October 1993. Special provisions apply to advance corporation tax and to income tax deducted from payments made by a company. See Tolley's Corporation Tax.

42.4   EXCHANGE RESTRICTIONS

Where foreign income cannot be remitted to UK due to government action in the country of origin, and tax thereon is held over by agreement with the Board, interest ceases to run from the date when the Board were first in possession of relevant facts—*no interest* if that date within three months after tax due. Interest recommences from the date of any subsequent demand, but this *latter* interest remitted if payment made within three months of demand. [*TMA s 92*]. See 51.14 NON-RESIDENTS AND OTHER OVERSEAS MATTERS.

42.5   TAX LOST THROUGH FAULT OF TAXPAYER

Where an assessment is made for making good tax lost through taxpayer failure or error (previously, by fraud, wilful default or neglect of the taxpayer), the tax is chargeable with interest under *TMA s 88* and not under *TMA s 86*, at 42.1 above, from the date when the tax ought originally to have been paid. See 6.6 BACK DUTY. This no longer applies where the new self-assessment interest provisions of *Sec 86* have effect (see 78.22 SELF-ASSESSMENT).

42.6   EXECUTORS

Executors unable to pay tax before obtaining probate may have concessional treatment so that interest on tax falling due after the date of death runs from 30 days after the date on which probate or letters of administration are obtained. (Revenue Pamphlet IR 1, A17).

42.7   VALUE ADDED TAX, INSURANCE PREMIUM TAX AND LANDFILL TAX

Interest on overdue or under-declared VAT, insurance premium tax or landfill tax is not allowed as a deduction for income or corporation tax purposes. [*Sec 827(1)(1B)(1C); FA 1994, 7 Sch 31; FA 1996, 5 Sch 40*].

43 Interest Payable

Cross-references. See 3.16 ANTI-AVOIDANCE; 8 BANKS; 9 BUILDING SOCIETIES; 23 DEDUCTION OF TAX AT SOURCE; 28.5 EXCESS LIABILITY for interest on loans to pay insurance premiums; 32 FUNDING BONDS for interest paid by issue of bonds; 42 INTEREST ON UNPAID TAX; 70 SCHEDULE C regarding paying and collecting agents for government stocks etc.

Note. See Tolley's Corporation Tax under Gilts and Bonds for the special provisions applicable for accounting periods ending after 31 March 1996 to all profits and losses in respect of company 'loan relationships'.

The headings in this chapter are as follows.

43.1 DEDUCTION OF TAX FROM INTEREST PAYMENTS

In general, tax is deductible from annual interest paid by companies but not by individuals (except on certain home mortgage loans, etc.), but see details under 23.3(ii) and 23.13 DEDUCTION OF TAX AT SOURCE. See also 8.2, 8.3 BANKS and 9.3, 9.5 BUILDING SOCIETIES.

43.2 BUSINESS INTEREST PAYABLE

Interest incurred wholly and exclusively for business purposes is an allowable deduction from profits assessable under Schedule D, Case I or II (including interest on money borrowed for use as capital in the business, see *Sec 74(f)*). [*Secs 74(m), 817(1)(b)*]. Interest incurred wholly and exclusively for the purposes of a Schedule A business (for 1995/96 onwards, subject to transitional provisions) is similarly an allowable deduction from the profits of that business (see 68.3, 68.5 SCHEDULE A). [*Sec 21(3); FA 1995, s 39*].

Exceptions are as follows.

(i) **Interest payable to non-residents** is deductible only so far as it is payable at a reasonable commercial rate [*Sec 74(n)*] and either

(a)   is paid under deduction of tax in accordance with *Sec 349*, see 23.3(ii) DEDUCTION OF TAX AT SOURCE (in which case the gross amount of the interest is deductible from profits, see *Sec 82(5)*), or

(b)   is contractually payable abroad (and is in fact so paid) by a UK resident sole trader or partnership either on a liability incurred for purposes of the foreign activities of the trade, etc., or in a currency other than sterling (for securities issued before 6 April 1982, in the currency of a territory outside the scheduled territories). But deduction of interest in these circumstances is not permitted if the recipient is a partner in the trade, or both payer and recipient are under common control.

This restriction does not apply in the case of a Schedule A business. [*Sec 82; FA 1995, 6 Sch 13*].

(ii) **Anti-avoidance.** Where interest is paid, no relief will be allowed, if, at any time, a scheme has been effected or arrangements made such that the sole or main benefit expected to accrue was a reduction in tax liability by means of the relief. [*Sec 787*]. See also *Cairns v MacDiarmid CA 1982, 56 TC 556*.

(iii) **'Relevant loan interest'**, see 23.13 DEDUCTION OF TAX AT SOURCE.

The restrictions in 43.3 *et seq.* below do not apply to interest deductible in computing business profits, but if interest so deductible is also allowable within those restrictions, relief may instead be claimable under *Sec 353*. See 43.3 below as to this. Where interest wholly and exclusively for business purposes is dealt with under *Sec 353* but not wholly relieved because of insufficiency of income, the unrelieved interest can be treated as a trading loss. [*Sec 390*]. See 46.18(*b*) LOSSES.

Where part of a borrower's main residence is used exclusively for business purposes, then by concession, for 1995/96 onwards (but reflecting pre-existing practice), a loan to buy the property may be treated as proportionally divided into two separate loans, mortgage interest relief (see 43.3 below) and relief for interest as a business (including a Schedule A business) deduction being available respectively. Where the exclusive business use occurs only sometimes (but for a significant amount of time), the concession still applies but with duration of use also taken into account in apportioning the loan. (Revenue Pamphlet IR 1 (November 1995 Supplement), A89. See 23.13 DEDUCTION OF TAX AT SOURCE for the MIRAS (mortgage interest relief by deduction at source) position, and see Revenue Tax Bulletin August 1995 pp 229–232 for worked examples.

Schedule D, Case VI. Where profits are assessable under Schedule D, Case VI, it is understood that in practice interest incurred wholly and exclusively for the purposes of earning those profits (e.g. on money borrowed to purchase properties let furnished) is an allowable deduction.

43.3   **RELIEF FOR INTEREST PAID—GENERAL**

Subject to the provisions in this and the following paragraphs, relief for interest may be given *for income tax purposes* for the year of assessment in which paid. For interest paid by companies within the charge to corporation tax, see Tolley's Corporation Tax. For the exclusion of double relief where the interest ranks as business interest, see 43.25 below.

For payments made **after 5 April 1994** (whenever falling due), *subject to the restrictions in* 43.5 *et seq.* below, relief is given on interest paid; the restrictions in (*a*) – (*d*) below no longer

43.3 Interest Payable

apply, except for the comments in (*a*) below on hire purchase charges. [*Sec 353(1); FA 1994, s 81(1)*].

For payments made **before 6 April 1994**, *subject to the further restrictions in* 43.5 *et seq.* below, relief is given on the following.

(*a*) **Annual interest** chargeable to tax under SCHEDULE D, CASE III (72) on the recipient. [*Sec 353(1)(a) as originally enacted*]. This will include annual interest paid to local authorities or charities and exempt in their hands, since such interest is chargeable under Case III although not assessed on the recipients under Case III.

'**Short interest**', i.e. interest other than annual interest, is not deductible except as in (*b*) to (*d*) below. For what is short interest, see *Hay CS 1924, 8 TC 636; Frere HL 1964, 42 TC 125; Corinthian Securities Ltd v Cato CA 1969, 46 TC 93; Minsham Properties Ltd v Price Ch D 1990, 63 TC 570.*

Hire purchase charges (the excess of the hire purchase payments over the cash price) are not interest and therefore not within this relief. (Some hire purchase agreements may specify that the whole balance of the rental after the initial payment is payable within seven days but will leave the hirer the option of paying that balance over a defined period on interest terms. At the date the option is exercised a loan is created and the interest on that loan is true interest under *Sec 353* and will qualify for relief if other relevant conditions are satisfied e.g. on a residential caravan.)

(*b*) **Bank interest** (payable in UK or RI on an advance from a bank carrying on *bona fide* banking business in UK or RI). [*Sec 353(1)(b) as originally enacted*]. Includes interest paid to the Channel Islands branch of a UK bank (*Maude v CIR KB 1940, 23 TC 63*) but not interest paid by a guarantor (*Holder HL 1932, 16 TC 540*) nor interest debited by bank for a year in which borrower made no payments into the account (*Paton v CIR HL 1938, 21 TC 626*). See also *Torrens v CIR KB(NI) 1933, 18 TC 262*.

(*c*) Interest payable in UK or RI on an advance from a person *bona fide* carrying on business as a **member of The Stock Exchange.** [*Sec 353(1)(b) as originally enacted*].

(*d*) Interest payable in UK or RI on an advance from a person *bona fide* carrying on the business of a **discount house** in the UK or RI. [*Sec 353(1)(b) as originally enacted*].

Relief is also given on the following (whenever paid).

(*i*) **Interest on loan for property bought by partner for partnership use.** Where a partner takes out a loan (other than an overdraft) to purchase land (including buildings, etc.) which he permits the partnership to use for business purposes, and the partnership pays the interest on the loan and charges it in its accounts, the payment is regarded as a rent for the use of the land. It is thus an allowable expense in computing partnership profits.

The rental income in the partner's hands will then be regarded as covered by the interest for which he is liable, assuming the interest would qualify for relief under 43.15 below if paid by him. No deduction is allowed in computing partnership profits where no rent or interest is paid by the partnership. (Revenue Pamphlet IR 131, SP 4/85, 5 February 1985).

Refusal of application of the benefit of this practice was approved (in judicial review proceedings) where a bank loan to a partnership was made in conjunction with an interest-free loan by the partnership to an individual partner to enable him to purchase land for partnership use (*R v HMIT (ex p Brumfield and Others) QB 1988, 61 TC 589*).

See 43.15 below where rent is paid by the partnership to the partner.

(ii) **Interest on loan for property bought by controlling director for company use.** The Statement of Practice referred to at (i) above also deals with occupation by a company for business purposes of land, etc. owned by a controlling director. Where the company pays the interest on a loan (other than an overdraft) taken out by the director to purchase the land, the payments may be treated as emoluments of the director, and hence as an allowable expense to the company. Since the director receives no rent, he obtains no relief for the interest paid on the loan against such emoluments. Where the company pays neither rent nor interest, no deduction is allowable from company profits.

See 43.15 below where rent is paid by the company to the controlling director.

No relief is given to the extent that the interest exceeds a reasonable commercial rate. [*Sec 353(3)(b)*].

Where interest is business interest (see 43.2 above), see 43.25 below for the exclusion of double relief, 43.2 above where property used for both residential and business purposes and 46.18 LOSSES for the treatment of unrelieved interest as a trading loss.

No relief is given if the interest is within the anti-avoidance provisions of *Sec 787*, see 43.2 (ii) above.

Note. Where tax is deductible from interest which is 'relevant loan interest' (see 23.13 DEDUCTION OF TAX AT SOURCE) the provisions under *Sec 353* above do not apply. [*Sec 353(2)*].

Rate of relief and method of giving relief. For interest payments made **before 6 April 1994**, relief was given by way of a deduction in computing total income. [*Sec 353(1) as originally enacted*]. Therefore, relief was generally at the borrower's marginal tax rate, but see 43.5 below for the abolition of higher rate relief for payments after 5 April 1991 on certain categories of loan.

For payments made **after 5 April 1994** (whenever falling due), interest on certain types of loan continues to be relieved by deduction and thus to attract relief at marginal rates. The categories of loan in question are those for the purpose of

(A) purchasing property let at a commercial rent (not generally applicable after 1994/95—see 43.15 below), the deduction being available only against letting income,

(B) purchasing machinery or plant (see 43.18 below),

(C) purchasing an interest in, or, where appropriate, making a loan or advance to, a close company, co-operative, an employee-controlled company or a partnership (see 43.19 to 43.22 below), or

(D) paying inheritance tax (see 43.23 below).

However, interest on the categories of loan listed below is relieved by way of reduction in income tax liability and no longer reduces total income. **Interest within (I) and (II) below attracts relief at 20% for 1994/95 and 15% for 1995/96 and subsequent years (the**

43.4 Interest Payable

rate being determined by reference to the year of actual payment, regardless of when payment was due). **Interest within (III) below continues to attract relief at the basic rate of tax in force for the year of payment** (e.g. 24% for 1996/97). The loans in question are those for the purchase of

   (I)   the borrower's only or main residence (see 43.6 to 43.12, and also 43.17, below),

   (II)   a residence intended to become the borrower's only or main residence, where the borrower lives in job-related accommodation (see 43.16 below), or

   (III)   a life annuity, where the loan is secured on land (see 43.24 below).

The reduction in liability is the smaller of the applicable percentage (as above) of the amount of interest eligible for relief and what would otherwise be the borrower's total income tax liability. For this purpose, 'total income tax liability' is as defined in 1.15 ALLOWANCES AND TAX RATES, except that it is before any reductions on account of personal reliefs and maintenance payments (where such items are also relieved by way of reduction in income tax liability— see 1.15 to 1.17 ALLOWANCES AND TAX RATES and 47.15 MARRIED PERSONS).

Where, for any tax year, an amount of interest is eligible for relief partly as a deduction and partly as a reduction in liability (for example, because the loan is a mixed loan or there is a change in the use of a property), it is apportioned by reference to the proportions of the amount borrowed (not the amount still outstanding) applied for different purposes and, where relevant, the different uses to which property is put from time to time.

Where particular interest payments would be eligible for relief both under (A) above and under (I) or (II) above, they will be treated as eligible under (A) above (so that relief is given by deduction) unless the borrower elects to the contrary. Such an election must take effect from the commencement of dual eligibility or from the beginning of a later tax year, remains in force until withdrawn with effect from the beginning of a tax year, and applies to all such interest payments made while it has effect. An election or withdrawal must be made by written notice, specifying the effective date, before the end of the tax year following that in which the effective date falls. See Revenue Tax Bulletin December 1994 p 173 for general commentary on the election. The provisions dealing with such dual eligibility are not relevant, and are repealed, following the repeal of the provisions at 43.15 below (interest on loans to purchase let property). For 1995/96 onwards, a borrower who is eligible for mortgage interest relief in respect of a let property may choose each year whether to claim such relief (restricted to 15% on a maximum of £30,000) or to deduct the interest in computing the profits of the Schedule A business. As regards inclusion of the loan within MIRAS (mortgage interest relief by deduction at source), see 23.13 DEDUCTION OF TAX AT SOURCE.

[*Sec 353(1A) – (1H); FA 1994, s 81(2); FA 1995, s 42(2), 29 Sch Pt VIII(2)*].

43.4   *Example*

Scott is a married man with the following details for 1996/97: Schedule D, Case II £15,585, bank deposit interest (net) £640, dividend income (net) £960, investment made under enterprise investment scheme (EIS) £500, interest paid gross on a £40,000 endowment mortgage taken out some years ago for purchase of main residence £3,600, payment under charitable deed of covenant (net) £45. Scott's wife has no income.

Scott's tax liability for 1996/97 is computed as follows.

	£
Schedule D, Case II	15,585
Bank deposit interest (gross)	800
Dividends plus tax credits	1,200
	17,585
Deduct Charges (covenanted donation) (gross)	60
Total income	17,525
Deduct Personal allowance	3,765
Taxable income	£13,760

Tax payable;	
3,900 @ 20%	780.00
7,860 @ 24%	1,886.40
2,000 @ 20%	400.00
13,760	3,066.40
Deduct EIS relief £500 @ 20%	100.00
	2,966.40

Deduct Mortgage interest relief:

$$£3,600 \times \frac{30,000}{40,000} = 2,700 \text{ @ } 15\% \qquad 405.00$$

	2,561.40
Deduct Married couple's allowance:	
£1,790 @ 15%	268.50
	2,292.90
Add Basic rate tax retained on covenanted donation	15.00
Total tax liability	2,307.90
Deduct Tax suffered at source on bank deposit interest	(160.00)
Tax credits on dividends	(240.00)
Net tax liability	£1,907.90

43.5   RELIEF FOR INTEREST PAID—RESTRICTED CATEGORIES OF LOAN —GENERAL PROVISIONS

Tax relief for interest paid on private borrowings will only be granted if the loan falls within any of the categories below (and even then will not be given on overdrafts, credit card or similar arrangements). [*Sec 353(1)(3)(a)*].

Relief is not granted unless the loan proceeds are so applied within a reasonable time (which, in the case of eligible home improvement loans, the Revenue appear to consider means the work being done within six months before or after the loan is provided). Nor if the loan proceeds are used for some other purpose first. The giving of credit can be treated as a loan. Proportionate relief is granted where part only of a debt fulfils the required conditions. [*Sec 367(2)–(4)*].

Relief is granted on loans replacing either prior eligible loans under 43.6, 43.15, 43.16 and 43.19–43.24 below or loans which would have been eligible but for their inclusion in the MIRAS deduction scheme (see 23.13 DEDUCTION OF TAX AT SOURCE). [*Sec 354(1)(c)*]. See

43.6 Interest Payable

Lawson v Brooks Ch D 1991, 64 TC 462 for denial of relief for loan replacing overdraft relating to expenditure otherwise eligible for relief.

For loans to persons other than building societies or local authorities, claims to relief must be supported by a statement by the lender of the date and amount of the debt, the name and address of the debtor and the interest paid in the year of assessment. [*Sec 366*]. See generally Revenue Tax Bulletin April 1995 p 210.

Higher rate relief. Interest payments after 5 April 1991 on a loan for the purchase of

(*a*)   the borrower's only or main residence (see 43.6 *et seq*. below), or

(*b*)   a residence intended to become the borrower's only or main residence, where the borrower lives in job-related accommodation (see 43.16 below), or

(*c*)   a life annuity, where the loan is secured on land (see 43.24 below),

do not attract relief from income tax at the higher rate(s). See 23.13 DEDUCTION OF TAX AT SOURCE for the application of this restriction in relation to loans within the MIRAS scheme. See 43.6 below for relief for certain bridging loans. [*Sec 353(4)(5); FA 1991, s 27(1); F(No 2)A 1992, s 19(3); FA 1993, 6 Sch 1; FA 1994, 9 Sch 3*].

See 43.3 above for further reductions, applying for 1994/95 and later years, in the rate of tax relief for interest within (*a*) and (*b*) above.

43.6   **LOANS FOR PURCHASING PROPERTY AS ONLY OR MAIN RESIDENCE**

Relief is given for interest paid on a loan for the purchase of land by a person owning an estate or interest in the property, where the property is at the time the interest is paid used as the **only or main residence of the borrower**. Where that condition is not satisfied, relief is granted if the interest is paid less than twelve months after the loan and the property is so used within that twelve months. The Inland Revenue have power to extend such periods if it appears reasonable for them to do so. [*Secs 354(1)(a), 355(1)(a)(2)(3)*]. For what is the main residence, see *Frost v Feltham Ch D 1980, 55 TC 10.*

See 43.5 above for denial of higher rate relief for interest payments after 5 April 1991 (but see below as regards certain bridging loans). See 43.3 above for the restriction of tax relief to 20% for 1994/95 and 15% thereafter, and for the method of giving such relief.

Concessionally, temporary absences of up to one year are left out of account in determining whether a property is used as the owner's only or main residence for purposes of allowing mortgage interest relief. Up to four years are allowed if a person's employment requires him to move from a property occupied before his departure as his only or main residence for a period not expected to exceed four years and there is reasonable expectation of his return to the property. Where an individual has moved his home abroad by reason of his employment as a Crown servant (within *Sec 132(4)(a)*, see 75.2(i) SCHEDULE E), the concession applies without the four year time limit. The concession will also apply if a person acquires an interest in property, (e.g. by exchange of contracts) but is prevented from occupying it as his home by his move, or if a property is purchased and occupied for at least three months during a period of leave from an overseas tour of duty. The four year period will re-apply if the property is reoccupied for at least three months. If the property is let during the owner's absence, the benefit of the concession may be claimed, where appropriate, if this is more favourable than claiming a deduction in computing the Schedule A business profits (or, before 6 April 1995, relief against the lettings income) (see 43.15 below). (Revenue Pamphlet IR 1 (November 1995 Supplement), A27).

Interest on an overdraft on the security of the deed of a residence is not allowable (*Walcot-Bather v Golding Ch D 1979, 52 TC 649*).

Additional interest charges. 'Penalty' interest charged on the early redemption of a loan within MIRAS does not qualify for relief (although this does not apply to interest charged for the whole of the month in which redemption occurs). Similarly a penalty charged for changing the terms of a loan, including a penalty for changing from a fixed to a variable rate, does not qualify for relief. However, a replacement loan need not be regarded as mixed purpose merely because, in part, it replaces such a charge. (MIRAS 30 (1995), para 10.46).

Administration fees. An allowance in respect of such fees reasonably incurred in arranging or servicing a qualifying loan will be regarded as qualifying expenditure up to £300 in respect of the first year of a loan, and up to £150 p.a. thereafter. (MIRAS 30 (1995) para 10.23).

Deceased persons. Interest paid by personal representatives of a deceased person, or by trustees of a settlement made by his will, is eligible for relief if the deceased used the property as his only or main residence at his death (or he resided in job-related living accommodation and the property was used by him as a residence or where he intended to use it in due course as his only or main residence) and, at the time the interest is paid, the property is used as the only or main residence of the widow or widower or, for interest paid before 6 April 1988, a dependent relative (or the widow or widower resides in job-related living accommodation and the property is used by such a relative or is intended to be used as the only or main residence). Interest paid after 5 April 1988 at a time when the property is used as the only or main residence of a dependent relative qualifies for relief only if the deceased died before 6 April 1988 *and* the property was so used by the dependent relative before that date. [*Sec 358; FA 1988, s 44(4)*]. Interest paid by a person who has inherited property subject to a mortgage is allowable only if it was allowable when paid by the person from whom he inherited. See Revenue Pamphlet IR 131, A34.

House exchanges. Where houses are exchanged, so long as any loan on the old property is redeemed and a new loan on the new property taken out, the new loan (including any further loan to meet the difference in value) qualifies for relief in the normal way. (MIRAS 30 (1995) para 10.25).

43.7   **Temporary relief following cessation of residence.** Relief under 43.6 above generally requires that, at the time the interest is paid, the land etc. is used as the only or main residence of the payer. Where the land etc. ceases at any time to be used as the only or main residence, and the borrower's intention at that time is to take steps within the following twelve months with a view to its disposal, that condition will be treated as satisfied until the end of those twelve months or, if earlier, until the borrower abandons his intention to dispose of the land etc. The Board may direct that the period of twelve months be extended in any particular case if it appears reasonable to do so.

Relief for interest on another loan used by the borrower for the purchase of a new property is eligible for relief to the extent it would be if no interest were payable on the loan on the former residence (in particular in relation to the qualifying limit, see 43.10 below).

These provisions apply to interest paid **on or after 16 March 1993.** Where the condition ceased to be satisfied before that date, the power of the Board to extend the twelve month relief period is exercisable irrespective of when the period began. Where an extension had previously been granted under the earlier relief described below, the Board's power of extension under the new provisions is deemed to have been exercised so that the new relief applies at least until the end of the extended period under the earlier provisions. The suspension of the abolition of higher rate relief (see below) similarly continues to apply where it would have applied under an extension of the relief period under the earlier provisions, or where an extension under the new provisions applies to a loan which fell

43.8 Interest Payable

within the earlier provisions, but ceases to apply as regards interest paid after 5 April 1994.

[*Sec 355(1A)(1B); FA 1993, s 57; FA 1994, 9 Sch 12*].

For interest paid **before 16 March 1993**, a more limited relief was available where a loan was made for the purchase of another residence, to be used as the only or main residence, with a view to the previous residence being disposed of. Under this, relief continued to be available on an existing loan (and was granted separately up to the qualifying maximum, see 43.10 below, on the new loan) for twelve months after the making of the new loan, regardless of whether the previous property continued to be used as the only or main residence. Again the twelve month period could be extended at the Board's discretion. The higher rate relief restriction which generally applies to interest payments after 5 April 1991 (see 43.5 above) did not apply to interest on the existing loan where the new loan was made before 6 April 1991 (or was applied in pursuance of a binding contract entered into before that date and was made in pursuance of an offer made before that date). [*Secs 354(5)(6), 356D(9); FA 1988, s 42(1); FA 1991, s 27(3)(5); FA 1993, s 57(4)(5)*]. Relief was only available provided that the new residence was occupied as the only or main residence within the twelve month (or extended) period (*Hughes v Viner Ch D 1985, 58 TC 437*).

See also 75.17 SCHEDULE E for bridging loans from employers and reimbursement of interest paid.

43.8 **Home improvement loans.** Interest paid on 'home improvement loans' is also eligible for relief, subject to the general requirements described above and below, if either paid before 6 April 1988 or paid after 5 April 1988 on a loan made before 6 April 1988. A loan made after 5 April 1988 is deemed to have been made before 6 April 1988 if it is proved by written evidence that it is made in pursuance of an offer made by the lender before that date, such offer being either in writing or evidenced by a note or memorandum made by the lender before that date. A '*home improvement loan*' means a loan to defray money applied in improving or developing land or buildings on land, otherwise than by the erection of a new building (which is not part of an existing residence) on land which immediately before the improvement or development began had no building on it. The definition is extended to include a loan replacing, directly or indirectly, such a loan (so that a replacement loan taken after 5 April 1988 does not attract relief). [*Secs 354(1)(b), 355(1)(a), (2A)–(2C); FA 1988, s 43(1)*]. Where interest on such a loan continues to qualify for relief for 1994/95 and later years, it does so at the reduced rate applicable for loans used to purchase the borrower's only or main residence, relief being given by way of reduction in tax liability (see 43.3 above).

43.9 **Dependent relatives, former or separated spouses.** Interest paid either before 6 April 1988 or after 5 April 1988 on loans made before 6 April 1988 (subject to the further condition below) is also eligible for relief where the property is, at the time the interest is paid (or within a twelve month, or longer, period as described above), used as the only or main residence of

   (i)   a dependent relative (incapacitated by old age or infirmity from maintaining himself, or the widowed, separated or divorced mother) of the borrower or his spouse, the residence being provided rent-free and without other consideration, or

   (ii)   a separated (under Court Order, deed of separation or in circumstances likely to be permanent) or former spouse.

The further condition for interest paid after 5 April 1988 on a pre-6 April 1988 loan is that interest paid on the loan at a 'relevant time' was eligible for relief *only* because the property concerned was used as the only or main residence of *the same* dependent relative or former or separated spouse. '*Relevant time*' means either the last time when interest was paid on the loan before 6 April 1988 or, if no such interest was paid before that date, any time within twelve months (or such longer period as the Board may allow in the circumstances of a particular case) after the date on which the loan was made, except that the latter time does not apply if, at any time after the loan was made and before the property comes to be used as the only or main residence of the dependent relative, etc., the property is used for any other purpose. A loan made after 5 April 1988 is deemed to have been made before 6 April 1988 in certain circumstances, these being identical to those described above for home improvement loans. [*Sec 355(1)(a); FA 1988, s 44(1)–(3)(5)*]. Where interest on such a loan continues to qualify for relief for 1994/95 and later years, it does so at the reduced rate applicable for loans used to purchase the borrower's only or main residence, relief being given by way of reduction in tax liability (see 43.3 above).

43.10 **Limit on amount of loan eligible for relief.** For payments made after 31 July 1988 of '*qualifying interest*' (i.e. interest eligible for relief under 43.6–43.9 above or 43.16 below), the 'qualifying maximum' amount of loan on which interest may attract relief (currently £30,000) applies per residence (the '*residence basis*') rather than (as previously) per person. [*Secs 356C(1), 356D(1), 367(5); FA 1988, s 41; FA 1989, s 46; FA 1990, s 71; FA 1991, s 26; FA 1992, s 10(4); FA 1993, s 55; FA 1994, s 80, 9 Sch 7; FA 1996, s 76*]. The residence basis does not apply to a payment of qualifying interest if

(*a*) the payment is under a loan made before 1 August 1988,

(*b*) qualifying interest was payable in relation to the residence for 1 August 1988 by someone other than the person making the payment or his spouse,

(*c*) qualifying interest is payable in respect of the residence throughout the period from 1 August 1988 to the date of payment by the person making the payment or by his spouse, and

(*d*) someone other than the person making the payment or his spouse owns an estate, interest or property in the residence throughout the period in (*c*) above, and, at any time during that period, at least one such person is a person by whom qualifying interest is payable in respect of the residence at some time within the period.

A loan made after 31 July 1988 is treated as if made before 1 August 1988 if it is proved by written evidence both that it was made in pursuance of an offer made before that date and either made in writing or evidenced by a note or memorandum made by the lender before that date, and that it was used to defray money applied in pursuance of a binding contract entered into before that date. In relation to such loans, for the purpose of (*b*)–(*d*) above, the date on which interest first becomes payable (or the latest of such days where more than one loan is involved) is substituted for 1 August 1988. Where these exceptions to the residence basis apply to payments of qualifying interest under one loan, they also apply to such payments made under other loans if made by the same person or by his spouse in respect of the same residence in the same 'period'. The qualifying maximum in respect of a loan excepted as above is restricted to the lesser of £30,000 and the amount on which interest was payable immediately before 1 August 1988 or, if later, the first day for which interest is payable. Payments of interest which is qualifying interest due only to the residence in question being the only or main residence of a dependent relative or former or separated spouse of the person making the payment (but see 43.9 above for the restricted circumstances in which such interest is eligible for relief) are also excepted from the residence basis. Where payments of qualifying interest would otherwise be excepted from the residence basis, the persons liable to pay such interest may jointly elect that the residence basis should apply to all qualifying interest paid by any person in relation to the residence, such election being irrevocable. For 1996/97 and later years, the election must be made within twelve months after 31 January following the year of assessment in which falls the first 'period' for which it is made. Previously, an election first had effect for the period *in which* it was made.

References above to a spouse do not include, except where stated, a separated spouse.

[*Secs 356C, 357(1A)–(1C); FA 1988, s 42(1)(2); FA 1996, s 135, 21 Sch 9*].

Where the residence basis does apply to a payment of qualifying interest, and all the interest payable for any 'period' in relation to a 'residence' is payable by one person, relief is available in full to the extent that the amount on which it is payable does not exceed the qualifying maximum. Where the interest payable for any 'period' in relation to a 'residence' is payable by more than one person, relief is available to each payer only to the extent that the amount on which the interest is payable by him does not exceed the 'sharer's limit' for the 'period' in his case. Prior loans on which interest is similarly eligible for relief operate to reduce the relief available in any event, and joint loans are for these purposes divided equally between the parties to the loan in determining the amount on which each pays interest. [*Secs 356A(1)(2), 356D(6)–(8)*].

'*Residence*' for these purposes means a building or part thereof occupied or intended to be occupied as a separate residence, or a caravan or house-boat. A building or part of a building designed for permanent use as a single residence is treated as a single residence even if it is temporarily divided into two or more parts which are, or are to be, occupied as separate residences.

A '*period*', in relation to any person, begins with any of the following:

(i)   a day which is the first day for which qualifying interest is payable by any person in respect of the residence in question (notwithstanding that such interest may previously have been payable in respect of the residence);

(ii)   a day immediately following a day on which any other person ceased to be liable for qualifying interest (notwithstanding that such interest continues to be payable in respect of the residence);

(iii)   the beginning of a year of assessment,

and ends with the day immediately preceding the next day within (i)–(iii) above or, if sooner, with the last day for which the person concerned is liable to pay qualifying interest.

[*Sec 356D(2)(3); FA 1988, s 42(1)*].

The '*sharer's limit*' for any period is the amount arrived at by dividing the qualifying maximum for the year of assessment in which the period falls by the number of persons liable to pay qualifying interest for the period in respect of the residence. (Interest treated as falling within 43.15 below by virtue of the dual eligibility provisions in 43.3 above was treated as qualifying interest for the purpose of determining the number of persons so liable.) If, however, any person's limit then exceeds the amount on which he actually pays interest and another person's limit falls short of the amount on which he pays interest, the limits are adjusted accordingly, any excess being eliminated and any shortfall thereby reduced. Where two or more persons have shortfalls, the total excess is apportioned between them on a pro rata basis. [*Secs 356A(2)–(8), 356D(4); FA 1988, s 42(1); FA 1994, 9 Sch 6; FA 1995, 29 Sch Pt VIII(2)*]. See 43.12 below for special provisions relating to married couples.

In determining whether the amount on which interest is payable exceeds the qualifying maximum or any sharer's limit, no account is taken of any interest which has been added to the capital and which does not exceed £1,000. [*Secs 356D(10), 357(6); FA 1988, s 42(1)*].

For interest paid before 1 August 1988, the limitation of relief by reference to the qualifying maximum applied as it does on or after that date under the residence basis where all the qualifying interest payable in relation to a residence is payable by one person, i.e. generally the £30,000 limit was available in full to all individual payers, subject to special provisions in relation to married couples, see 43.12 below. Joint loans (other than to married couples) were for these purposes apportioned in the proportion that each borrower paid the interest. For later interest payments excluded from the residence basis under the transitional arrangements described above, similar rules apply, subject to the special restrictions described above. [*Sec 357; FA 1988, s 42; FA 1994, 9 Sch 7*].

43.11   *Examples*

On 1 April 1996, Mr Romeo and Miss Juliet took out a joint mortgage for £65,000 for the purchase of a London flat to be used as their main residence. Gross interest paid in 1996/97 amounts to £5,850.

Interest relief for 1996/97

Mr Romeo
Amount on which interest is payable	£32,500
Sharer's limit—£30,000 (qualifying maximum) ÷ 2 =	£15,000
Interest paid	£2,925

Relief restricted to $£2,925 \times \dfrac{15,000}{32,500} =$ £1,350

Miss Juliet
Identical calculation—relief restricted to   £1,350

Adjustment of sharer's limits
Three friends, A, B and C, decide to pool their resources and buy a house to be shared as their main residence. Each contributes his own savings and obtains a mortgage to fund the balance of his one-third share of the purchase price. The mortgages are all taken out in May 1996 and the amounts thereof, and interest paid thereon for 1996/97, are as follows.

	Mortgage	Interest payable (gross)
	£	£
A	7,000	560
B	14,000	1,120
C	16,000	1,280

Each has a sharer's limit of £10,000 (£30,000 ÷ 3). As A's limit exceeds the amount on which he pays interest, the excess is divided between B and C each of whose limits falls short of the amount on which he pays interest. B and C have shortfalls of £4,000 and £6,000 respectively, a total shortfall of £10,000, so A's excess of £3,000 is divided between them as follows.

43.12 Interest Payable

B— $\frac{4}{10}$ × £3,000 = £1,200 (revised sharer's limit £11,200)
C— $\frac{6}{10}$ × £3,000 = £1,800 (revised sharer's limit £11,800)

A's sharer's limit is reduced to £7,000.

Interest relief for 1996/97 is then calculated as follows.

A— $\dfrac{7,000}{7,000}$ × £560 =   £560

B— $\dfrac{11,200}{14,000}$ × £1,120 =   £896

C— $\dfrac{11,800}{16,000}$ × £1,280 =   £944

43.12 **Married couples.** Special provisions apply in relation to married couples who are not separated under Court Order or deed of separation or in circumstances such that the separation is likely to be permanent.

Application of qualifying maximum. **For 1990/91** and subsequent years of assessment, a husband and wife who are not separated may jointly elect that, for the year in question (or for a period within that year), qualifying interest payable by either or both of them be allocated between them in whatever proportions they choose, and that either of their sharer's limits (see 43.10 above) be increased by any amount specified (with a corresponding reduction in the other's limit). The election must be made in prescribed form (i.e. form 15 (1990)) within twelve months after 31 January following the first year of assessment for which it is to apply, and, once made, continues to have effect for subsequent years until withdrawn. A notice of withdrawal may be given by either husband or wife in prescribed form (i.e. form 15–1 (1990)) within twelve months after 31 January following the first year of assessment for which it is to apply, and has effect for subsequent years (without prejudice to the right to make a fresh election). For 1995/96 and earlier years, election or withdrawal had to be made within twelve months of the end of the year of assessment concerned. All such time limits may be extended by the Revenue, having regard to the circumstances in any particular case. This discretion will normally be exercised where the lateness was due to sickness, absence abroad or serious personal difficulties, or to the unavailability (through no fault of the taxpayers or their advisors) of information essential to the decision to make or withdraw the election (Revenue Pamphlet IR 131, SP 8/89, 1 February 1990).

Where a married couple who are not separated have two residences, so that the husband pays interest on one, being his main or intended main residence, and the wife similarly pays interest on the other, the residence that was purchased first is to be regarded as the couple's only or main residence, the other residence being treated as the only or main residence of neither of them.

[*Secs 356B, 367(1); FA 1988, s 42(1), 3 Sch 14; FA 1995, s 42(2); FA 1996, s 135, 21 Sch 8*].

See generally Revenue Pamphlet IR 86.

For 1989/90 and earlier years:

(*a*)   where the residence basis (see 43.10 above) did not apply, loans to the borrower's spouse were treated as those of the borrower (unless they were separated, as above). [*Sec 357(3)*]. Relief was given for interest paid by either spouse, regardless of the actual ownership of the property (see Revenue Pamphlet IR 131, A34);

(b)   where the residence basis did apply, any qualifying interest payable by a married woman not separated from her husband was normally regarded as payable by her husband. Where the husband was so regarded as paying, or actually did pay, interest, and someone other than the married couple also paid qualifying interest in respect of the same residence, qualifying interest was treated as payable by the wife, whether or not it actually was, thus increasing the number of people amongst whom the qualifying maximum was to be divided in arriving at each person's sharer's limit. The limit applicable to the wife was then added to the husband's limit. However, where husband and wife had opted for separate assessment under *Sec 283* or for separate taxation under *Sec 287* (see 47.9, 47.10 MARRIED PERSONS), the husband and wife could instead jointly make an election similar to, and subject to the same conditions as, that available for 1990/91 onwards (see above). In any event, the rule for 1990/91 onwards where a married couple have two residences (see above) applies. [*Sec 356B; FA 1988, s 42(1)*].

Year of marriage. If one spouse goes to live in the other spouse's home which is being purchased under a mortgage and sells his or her own property, the interest for the period the property is vacant will be allowed, concessionally, in addition to the interest on the loan for the new matrimonial home, provided that the property is sold within twelve months from the date it is vacated (Revenue Pamphlet IR 1, A35).

Where two people, each buying a main residence before marriage with the aid of a loan, buy a joint residence and sell their existing properties, the bridging loan provisions (see 43.6 above) will be regarded as applying to all three properties, whether or not the relevant property continues to be used as the owner's only or main residence (Revenue Pamphlet IR 131, SP 10/80, 24 September 1980).

See also 43.7 above as regards more general relief from 16 March 1993.

43.13   **Substitution of security.** Interest relief as under 43.6 above is extended in certain cases where a person purchases an estate or interest in land etc. (the '*new estate*') after 15 March 1993, and a 'security substitution arrangement' takes effect after that date in connection with the purchase.

A '*security substitution arrangement*' is an arrangement under which:

(a)   the new estate becomes security for an existing loan or loans, and another estate etc. ceases to be security for the loan(s);

(b)   the other estate etc. was not absorbed into, or given up to obtain, the new estate;

(c)   immediately before the arrangement took effect, interest on the loan(s) was eligible for relief under 43.6 above or 43.16 below (job-related accommodation); and

(d)   had the loan(s) been applied in purchasing the new estate, interest would have been so eligible for relief.

Where there is more than one loan and one or more of them would not satisfy (c) above, these provisions are applied only in relation to such of the loans as do fall within (c) above.

Where the above conditions are met, then as regards interest paid on the loan after the time the new estate became security for the loan, the loan is treated for the purposes of 43.6 above as if:

(i)   it had been made at that time; and

(ii)   the amount then outstanding (insofar as it did not exceed the 'relevant amount') had been used at that time to purchase the new estate,

and similarly where two or more loans are the subject of such arrangements.

43.14 Interest Payable

The *'relevant amount'* is generally an amount equal to the purchase price of the new estate. The definition varies, however, where there is a loan (referred to below for convenience as an 'additional loan') eligible for relief under 43.6 above or 43.16 below, and actually used to any extent to purchase the new estate at or before the time the security substitution took place, or treated under an earlier security substitution arrangement as if before that time it had been so used. In those circumstances, the *'relevant amount'* is the difference between the purchase price of the new estate and the amount of the additional loan(s).

These provisions do not apply where the amount of any additional loan(s) (as above) equals the purchase price of the new estate. Where an additional loan is or was only partly used (or treated as used) in purchasing the new estate, it is only taken into account for the above purposes to the extent that it is or was or was treated as so used.

The exclusion from relief under 43.6 above of interest within the MIRAS scheme (see 23.13 DEDUCTION OF TAX AT SOURCE) does not affect the determination of eligibility for the purposes of these provisions.

[*Secs 357A, 357C(1)–(3); FA 1993, s 56; FA 1994, 9 Sch 7; FA 1995, s 42(2)*].

Treatment of loans following security substitution. Where, after the above provision has applied to treat a loan as having been used to defray the purchase cost of a new estate, a new loan is actually used to any extent for that purpose and would otherwise be eligible for relief under 43.6 above or 43.16 below, such relief is restricted. As regards interest paid on the new loan after the time it is so used (the *'material time'*), any part so used is eligible for relief only to the extent that it does not exceed the 'applicable amount', and relief for a number of such loans is similarly restricted in the aggregate. The *'applicable amount'* is the difference between the purchase price of the new estate and any earlier eligible loans or part loans in respect of the purchase (including those eligible by virtue of an earlier application of these provisions). [*Sec 357B; FA 1993, s 56; FA 1994, 9 Sch 7; FA 1995, s 42(2)*].

Joint purchases. Where the purchase is a joint purchase, and any of the money applied in the purchase is not attributable to all the joint purchasers, these provisions apply to the share of the new estate, and the attributable part of the purchase cost, of each of the purchasers to whom it is attributable. [*Sec 357C(4)–(6); FA 1993, s 56*].

43.14 *Example*

James has outstanding the following loans (all with the same lender).

	£
House purchase (main residence)	80,000
Home improvement loan 1 (made before 6 April 1988)	20,000
Home improvement loan 2 (made in 1991)	3,000

In October 1996, James arranges to sell his home for £90,000 and to buy a new home for £95,000. The lender agrees to substitute the new property as security for the three existing loans and to make a further advance of £5,000 to cover the difference between the proceeds of the old property and the cost of the new. The new arrangements all take effect from 6 October 1996.

Interest rates charged by the lender throughout 1996/97 were 8% on both the original house purchase loan and the new advance and 10% on both home improvement loans.

The interest qualifying for tax relief for 1996/97 is calculated as follows.

6.4.96–5.10.96 (six months)

	£
£80,000 × 8% × $\frac{6}{12}$	3,200
£20,000 × 10% × $\frac{6}{12}$	1,000
Total interest on qualifying loans	£4,200

$$\text{Allowable interest} = £4,200 \times \frac{30,000}{100,000} = \qquad £1,260$$

6.10.96–5.4.97 (six months)

The existing loans, restricted as below but disregarding home improvement loan 2 which is a non-qualifying loan, are regarded as having been made on 6.10.95 for the purchase of the new property.

The existing loans qualifying for relief are restricted to the lesser of

(i)   the amount of the qualifying loans outstanding (i.e. £100,000), and

(ii)   the purchase price of the new property (£95,000) *less* the loan actually used in purchasing the new property (£5,000) (i.e. £90,000).

The total loans outstanding (disregarding home improvement loan 2) are £105,000. Of this amount, £90,000 qualifies as above and the new advance of £5,000 qualifies under normal principles. Therefore, £95,000 of the total loans is a qualifying loan and the balance of £10,000 is not.

Allowable interest is calculated as follows.

					£
85,000 × 8% × $\frac{6}{12}$	=	3,400 × 95/105	=		3,076
20,000 × 10% × $\frac{6}{12}$	=	1,000 × 95/105	=		905
£105,000	total interest	£4,400	qualifying interest		£3,981

$$\text{Allowable interest} = £3,981 \times \frac{30,000}{95,000} = \qquad £1,257$$

Total allowable interest 1996/97 £(1,260 + 1,257)   £2,517

43.15   LOANS FOR PURCHASING PROPERTY LET AT A COMMERCIAL RENT

Relief is given for interest paid **before 6 April 1995** (see below) on a loan for the purchase of land by a person owning an estate or interest in the property where the property is, in any period of 52 weeks comprising the time at which the interest is payable and falling wholly or partly within the year of assessment, **let at a commercial rent** for more than 26 weeks and, when not so let, either available for letting at such a rent *or* used as in 43.6 above *or* prevented from being so available or used by construction or repair work. [*Sec 355(1)(b); FA 1995, s 42(1)*]. Interest is also eligible under this paragraph on loans applied in improving or developing land. Interest falling within *Sec 355(1)(b)* is allowable only against income from letting that or any other land, but unallowed interest may be carried forward against such income (while the land in respect of which the interest is paid continues to be eligible) of the following and subsequent years of assessment (but see below). [*Sec 355(4); FA 1994, 9 Sch 4; FA 1995, 29 Sch Pt VIII(2)*].

If an individual lets his property at a commercial rent whilst he is away, the benefit of the concession re temporary absences in 43.6 above may be claimed, where appropriate, if this is more favourable than a claim for relief against letting income. (Revenue Pamphlet IR 1 (November 1995 Supplement), A27). If the loan is within the MIRAS scheme, this should not prevent relief being obtained against the letting income, where appropriate, provided that an adjustment is made for the MIRAS relief. (Taxation Vol 125, No 3269 p 707, 20 September 1990). See 43.3 above for the election available for 1994/95 onwards where interest is eligible both under these provisions and under those in 43.6 above.

Interest may generally be relieved under these provisions against rent paid by a partnership to a partner, or by a company to a controlling director, in respect of land owned by the partner or director occupied for business purposes by the partnership or company. See 43.3(i)(ii) above where the interest is in these circumstances paid by the partnership or company direct.

Repeal of above provisions. The provisions of *Sec 355(1)(b)* and *355(4)* are repealed with effect in relation to interest paid on or after 6 April 1995. With effect for 1995/96 and subsequent years, interest incurred wholly and exclusively for the purposes of a Schedule A business (see 68.4 SCHEDULE A) is an allowable deduction as an expense in arriving at the profits of that business. Extra-statutory Concession A27 (referred to above) continues to apply if the benefit of the concession is more favourable than a deduction in arriving at the Schedule A business profits. A borrower who is eligible for mortgage interest relief in respect of a let property may choose each year whether to claim such relief (restricted to 15% on a maximum of £30,000) or to deduct the interest in computing the Schedule A business profits. As regards inclusion of the loan within MIRAS (mortgage interest relief by deduction at source), see 23.13 DEDUCTION OF TAX AT SOURCE.

For 1995/96 only,

(*a*) if under transitional provisions a source of property income ceasing in that year falls to be taxed otherwise than in accordance with the new Schedule A rules (see 68.3 SCHEDULE A and, in the case of property outside the UK, 73.4 SCHEDULE D, CASES IV AND V), and

(*b*) the source includes any land etc. satisfying the condition of *Sec 355(1)(b)* (see above).

interest paid before the time of cessation continues to be deductible under the above provisions. Unrelieved interest brought forward from 1994/95 and earlier years may also be relieved in 1995/96 against income from a source within (*a*) above. [*FA 1995, s 42(3)–(5)*]. Otherwise, such unrelieved interest is relievable in 1995/96 and subsequent years as a Schedule A loss (see 68.13(C) SCHEDULE A). See also 68.22 SCHEDULE A for Revenue policy where some interest would otherwise be unrelieved on the transition from relief on a payments basis to relief on an accruals basis.

43.16 **LOANS FOR PURCHASING PROPERTY WHERE BORROWER IN JOB-RELATED LIVING ACCOMMODATION**

Relief is given for interest paid on a loan for the purchase of land by a person owning an estate or interest in the property who is in **job-related living accommodation** at the time the interest is paid, provided that:

(i) the property is used by him as a residence, or is so used within twelve months of the loan if the interest is paid within that time; or

(ii) the property is intended to be used in due course as his only or main residence.

Relief can relate to only one property in the case of any one borrower.

See 43.5 above as regards denial of higher rate relief for interest payments after 5 April 1991. See 43.3 above for the restriction of tax relief to 20% for 1994/95 and 15% thereafter, and for the method of giving such relief.

As regards 'home improvement loans', rules identical to those described in 43.6 above apply, as they do to restrict the amount of loans eligible for relief by reference to a qualifying maximum.

'*Job-related living accommodation*' is living accommodation which is provided to a person or spouse either:

(A)   by reason of employment where (*a*) it is necessary for the proper performance of his duties for the employee to reside in the accommodation, or (*b*) the employment is such that it is customary for employees to be provided with accommodation for the better performance of their duties, or (*c*) there is a special threat to the employee's security, and he resides in the accommodation as part of special security arrangements in force; or

(B)   under an arm's length contract requiring him or his spouse to carry on a trade, profession or vocation on premises or other land provided (under a tenancy or otherwise) by another person and to live on the premises or on other premises provided by that other person.

Neither (A)(*a*) nor (A)(*b*) above applies to accommodation provided to a director by a company, or associated company, unless he has no material interest (5% with or without associates) in the company of which he is a director *and either* he is a full-time working director *or* the company is non-profit making (i.e. it does not carry on a trade, nor is its main function the holding of investments or other property) *or* the company is a charity. (B) above does not apply if the accommodation is provided, wholly or in part, by a company in which the borrower or spouse has a material interest (as above), or by any person(s) with whom the borrower or spouse is in partnership. [*Sec 356; FA 1988, s 43(2); FA 1994, 9 Sch 5; FA 1995, s 42(2)*].

It is understood that certain accommodation occupied by Ministry of Defence employees who extend their overseas tour beyond four years may be regarded as job-related for these purposes (Tolley's Practical Tax 1986 p 167).

43.17   **LOANS FOR PURCHASING PROPERTY—GENERAL MATTERS**

In relation to the reliefs described at 43.6–43.16 above, land includes buildings, caravans (as below) and house-boats in UK or Eire (but not elsewhere, see *Ockendon v Mackley Ch D 1982, 56 TC 1*). [*Sec 354(1)*]. Loans replacing a prior eligible loan are themselves eligible. [*Sec 354(1)(c)*]. See, however, 43.8 above as regards replacement home improvement loans. '*Improving or developing*' includes capital expenditure on making-up, sewering, lighting etc., adjoining or service roads. Also making good dilapidations in existence at the time of the purchase, but not other maintenance or repairs (but see below). [*Sec 354(2); FA 1995, 29 Sch Pt VIII(1)*]. Before 1991/92, a *caravan* only qualified if it was a large caravan (i.e. over 22 ft long or $7\frac{1}{2}$ ft wide) or if it, together with the land on which it stood, was a rateable hereditament on which rates were paid by the owner (or spouse) as occupier. [*Secs 354(3), 367(1); FA 1991, s 28*]. If the interest in land is a rentcharge etc. or an interest as chargee or mortgagee, the interest payable is not eligible (this has no effect for, broadly, 1995/96 and subsequent years). [*Sec 354(4); FA 1995, 29 Sch Pt VIII(2)*]. A tenant occupier who is in the process of purchasing property with money advanced by the landlord on loan is treated as the owner of that property in relation to any interest paid on the loan before the property actually passes to him. [*Sec 354(7)*]. There are provisions preventing avoidance by sales between husband and wife, or connected persons etc. [*Sec 355(5)*].

The further provisions in *Sec 367(2)–(4)* (see 43.5 above) apply to all loans within 43.6–43.23.

The Revenue have indicated that the following are considered to be '*improvements*' for these purposes.

Home extensions/Loft conversions	Installing kitchen or bedroom units fixed
Insulation of roofs/walls	to and part of the building
Connection to main drainage	Installation of bathrooms, showers,
Landscaping gardens	etc.
Major reconstruction, e.g.	Recovering/Reconstructing a roof
conversion to flats	Construction of swimming pools,
Rebuilding a facade	saunas, etc.
Inserting or renewing damp-proof	Underpinning
course	Renewing electrical installations
Extensive repointing,	Dry rot, wet rot or timber treatment
pebble-dashing, texture-coating or	Extensive replacement of guttering
stone-cladding	Installation of fire or burglar alarms
Erecting garages, garden sheds,	Fire precaution works
greenhouses or fences	Laying driveways, patios or paths
Double glazing/Replacement of	Permanent installation of water
windows and doors	softening equipment
Central or solar heating installations	Replacement of one form of central
(excluding portable and night	heating with another (e.g. moving
storage radiators not fixed to a	from oil to gas)
permanent spar outlet)	

(Taxation Vol 114, No 2988 p 483, 30 March 1985).

Caravans acquired under a hire purchase agreement may concessionally attract relief subject to certain conditions. The local inspector should be consulted as to the current position.

Loan replacing *bank overdraft*. Where an eligible property is acquired by means of an overdraft which is within twelve months replaced by a loan, the Board will concessionally allow relief for the loan interest if it can be demonstrated that the overdraft was used solely for the property acquisition (Revenue Pamphlet IR 11, para 33). (*Note.* Although IR 11 is no longer available, it is understood that this concession still applies, see Tolley's Practical Tax 1990 p 15.) See *Lawson v Brooks Ch D 1991, 64 TC 462* for denial of relief for loan replacing overdraft where the overdraft was not a 'temporary accommodation'.

43.18   LOANS FOR PURCHASING MACHINERY OR PLANT

Relief is given for interest paid on a loan for the purchase of machinery or plant

(*a*)   for use in the trade, etc., of a partnership of which the individual is a member and which is entitled to capital allowances on that machinery under *CAA 1990, s 65*, or

(*b*)   for the purposes of an *office or employment* he holds, and in respect of which he is entitled to capital allowances under *CAA 1990, Pt II* (or would be so entitled but for some contribution made by his employer) (but see 75.43 SCHEDULE E for special provisions relating to use of private car for such purposes).

Relief is not so granted on interest payable more than three years after the end of the year of assessment in which the debt was incurred, and is applied to a proportionate part of the interest where use is in part other than in (*a*) or (*b*) above. [*Sec 359*].

43.19   LOANS FOR PURCHASING INTEREST IN CLOSE COMPANY

Relief is given for interest paid on a loan for the purchase of ordinary shares in, or making a loan to, a close company, provided that the borrower is an individual either (i) with, together with certain associates, a 'material interest' (broadly more than 5% of ordinary share capital at the date of payment of the interest) in the close company or (ii) when the interest is paid, the individual holds any ordinary shares of the close company and (between purchase or loan and relevant interest payment) he has worked for the greater part of his time in the actual management or conduct of the business of that close company or an associated company. As regards this last condition, the facts of each particular case have to be considered, but individuals will normally be regarded as meeting the requirement if they are directors or have significant managerial or technical responsibilities. They must, however, be involved in the overall running and policy-making of the company as a whole—responsibility for just a particular area is not sufficient. (Revenue Tax Bulletin November 1993 p 102). See also Revenue Inspector's Manual IM 3804. If the company exists wholly or mainly to hold investments or property, the individual must not reside in property of the company unless he has worked for the greater part of his time in the actual management or conduct of that company or an associated company. [*Secs 360, 360A(1), 363(4); FA 1989, s 48*]. The associates whose interests are taken into account in applying the 'material interest' test for loans made after 5 April 1987 do not include the trustees of profit sharing schemes under *FA 1978* (see 81.6, 81.7 SHARE INCENTIVES AND OPTIONS), and for loans made after 26 July 1989 do not generally include the trustees of an employee benefit trust (as defined), as a beneficiary of which the borrower has an interest in shares or obligations of the company, unless the 5% ordinary share capital test would be satisfied without their inclusion (for which purpose certain payments received from the trust are treated as giving rise to beneficial ownership of ordinary share capital). Certain other variations in the general definition of 'associate' in *Sec 360A(2)* apply to loans made before 14 November 1986. [*Secs 360(4), 360A(2)–(7), 9 Sch 39; FA 1989, s 48*].

Relief is denied in respect of shares issued after 13 March 1989 if a claim is made to relief under the enterprise investment scheme or the business expansion scheme (see 26 ENTERPRISE INVESTMENT SCHEME (AND BES)) in respect of those shares by the person acquiring them or spouse. [*FA 1989, s 47*].

For interest paid before 27 July 1989, the close company (see Tolley's Corporation Tax) must be either (*a*) a trading company, (*b*) a member of a trading group, or (*c*) a company with 75% of its income comprising estate or trading income, interest, dividends or other distributions from a 51% subsidiary (see definition in *Sec 838*) within (*a*), (*b*) or (*c*). [*Secs 360(1)(a), (2)(a), 424(4)*]. Although this condition is to be met at the time the shares are acquired (or the loan made) as well as when the interest is paid, it would appear that the Revenue may allow relief in respect of a vehicle close company formed to acquire a trading company (Tolley's Practical Tax 1984 p 114). For interest paid on or after 27 July 1989, the condition is replaced by a requirement that, both at the time the shares are acquired (or the loan made) and throughout the accounting period in which the interest is paid, the close company comply with *Sec 13A(2)* (as introduced by *FA 1989, s 105*) and thus satisfies the conditions for not being a close investment-holding company (see Tolley's Corporation Tax under Close Companies). [*FA 1989, 12 Sch 12*]. The Revenue's practice in the case of investment in a start-up trading company is to allow relief so long as trading commences within a reasonable time after the investment is made, provided that the company remains close when trading starts. (ICAEW Technical Release TAX 15/92, 23 October 1992).

Where shares were subscribed for in a 'shell' company to enable it to acquire a business, but the business had not been acquired at the time of the subscription, it could fairly be said that the company existed for the purpose of carrying on that business, so that interest on a loan for the purchase of the shares qualified for relief under these provisions (*Lord v Tustain Ch D 1993, 65 TC 761*).

If relief is claimed on a loan to a close company, the money must be used within a reasonable time for the purposes of its business (or that of an associated close company as defined above). [*Secs 360(1)(b), 367(2)*]. Capital recoveries by the individual (by sale or repayment of ordinary shares, repayment by the company of its loan, or the assignment of the debt due from it etc.) are treated as a reduction of the loan with corresponding reduction of the

43.20 Interest Payable

interest allowable. [*Sec 363(1)–(3)*]. The interest will continue to be allowed if the company ceases to be close after the application of the loan monies (Revenue Pamphlet IR 131, SP 3/78, 19 October 1978). Conversely, it is understood that relief will be given where a loan is used to purchase shares in an 'open' company which by that acquisition becomes a close company (Tolley's Practical Tax 1981 p 99).

Interest paid by the guarantor of a bank loan to a close company is not within the relief (*Hendy v Hadley Ch D 1980, 53 TC 353*).

Interest on a loan applied to the purchase of a close company's convertible loan stock can qualify for relief under these provisions. Relief will, however, cease from the date on which the loan stock is converted to ordinary share capital, since this constitutes a capital recovery (see above). (Revenue Tax Bulletin February 1992 p 13).

Relief on a loan qualifying as above will not be discontinued where shares in the close company are exchanged for, or replaced by, shares in another close company, or by shares in a co-operative (see 43.20 below), or by shares in an employee-controlled company (see 43.21 below), provided that relief would have been available if the loan had been a new loan taken out to invest in the new entity. The usual restriction applies where any capital recovered from the close company is not used to repay the loan. (Revenue Pamphlet IR 1 (November 1995 Supplement), A43).

43.20 LOANS FOR PURCHASING INTEREST IN CO-OPERATIVE

Relief is given for interest paid on a loan for the purchase of a share or shares in, or making a loan to, a co-operative. Such relief only applies to interest on a loan made after 10 March 1981 and the individual must (between purchase or loan and the relevant interest payment) have worked for the greater part of his time as an employee of the co-operative, or of a subsidiary of that body, which continues to be a co-operative when the interest is paid. A loan to a co-operative must be used wholly and exclusively for the purposes of the business of that body or of a subsidiary. Capital recoveries by the individual (by sale or replacement of the shares, repayment by the co-operative of its loan, or the assignment of the debt due from it etc.) are treated as a reduction of the loan with corresponding reduction of the interest allowable.

'*Co-operative*' (and '*subsidiary*') means a common ownership enterprise or a co-operative enterprise as defined in the *Industrial Common Ownership Act 1976, s 2*. [*Secs 361(1)(2), 363*].

Relief on a loan qualifying as above will not be discontinued where shares in the co-operative are exchanged for, or replaced by, shares in another co-operative, or by shares in a close company (see 43.19 above), or by shares in an employee-controlled company (see 43.21 below), provided that relief would have been available if the loan had been a new loan taken out to invest in the new entity. The usual restriction applies where any capital recovered from the co-operative is not used to repay the loan. (Revenue Pamphlet IR 1 (November 1995 Supplement), A43).

43.21 LOANS FOR PURCHASING INTEREST IN EMPLOYEE-CONTROLLED COMPANY

Relief is given for interest paid on a loan for the purchase of any part of the ordinary share capital of an employee-controlled company by an individual, provided that:

(a) the company is, from the date of purchase of the shares to that of payment of the interest, resident only in the UK, unlisted on the Stock Exchange, and either a trading company (i.e. its business consists wholly or mainly of the carrying on of trade(s)) or the holding company of a trading group (i.e. the business of its 75% subsidiaries, taken together, consists wholly or mainly of carrying on trade(s));

(b) the shares are acquired before, or not later than twelve months after, the company becomes an 'employee-controlled company';

(c) the company is an 'employee-controlled company' throughout a period of at least nine months in the year of assessment in which the interest is paid, unless it is the year in which it first becomes an employee-controlled company;

(d) the individual (or spouse, but see further below) is a full-time employee of the company (i.e. works for the greater part of his time as an employee or director of the company or of a 51% subsidiary) from the date of application of the loan proceeds to the date of payment of the interest (or, if the interest is paid after cessation of the employment, the later of the date of cessation and twelve months before the interest payment date i.e. interest is eligible for relief for twelve months after full-time employment ceases);

(e) the individual has, from the date of application of the loan proceeds to the interest payment date, not recovered any capital from the company other than amounts treated as reducing the loan (see below).

Capital recoveries by the individual (by sale or replacement of the shares, repayment of the loan, etc.) are treated as reducing the loan and, correspondingly, the interest allowable.

A company is an *employee-controlled company* if more than 50% of both the issued share capital and the voting power is beneficially owned by full-time employees (see (d) above) (or spouses, but see below) of the company, but ignoring the excess over 10% of any holding of a person (and spouse, but see below) which exceeds 10% of either issued share capital or voting power. Where an individual and spouse are *both* full-time employees, this 10% test is applied to each separately ignoring the other's holding.

As regards (d) above and the definition of employee-controlled company, for interest paid after 5 April 1990 (unless the loan was used before that date as required for relief under these provisions) neither the employment of a spouse nor the shares held by a spouse are taken into account in determining whether the conditions for relief for interest paid on such loans are met. Replacement loans made after that date attract interest relief only if the loan replaced was applied after that date or would have attracted relief if it had been applied after that date. [*Secs 361(3)–(8), 363; FA 1988, 3 Sch 15*].

Relief on a loan qualifying as above will not be discontinued where shares in the employee-controlled company are exchanged for, or replaced by, shares in another such company, or by shares in a close company (see 43.19 above), or by shares in a co-operative (see 43.20 above), provided that relief would have been available if the loan had been a new loan taken out to invest in the new entity. The usual restriction applies where any capital recovered from the company is not used to repay the loan. (Revenue Pamphlet IR 1 (November 1995 Supplement), A43.)

43.22   **LOANS FOR PURCHASING INTEREST IN PARTNERSHIP**

Relief is given for interest on a loan for the purchase of a share of, or making an advance to, a partnership to an individual who (throughout the period between application of the proceeds of the loan and payment of relevant interest) has been a member of the partnership otherwise than as a limited partner. If relief is claimed on a loan to the partnership, the money must be used for the purposes of its trade, profession or vocation. [*Sec 362*]. Salaried partners in a professional firm who are allowed independence of action in handling the affairs of clients and so to act that they will be indistinguishable from general partners in their relations with clients, can claim relief. (See Revenue Pamphlet IR 131, A33.)

Capital recoveries by the individual (from sale of his partnership interest, repayment of capital or loan etc.) are treated as a reduction of the loan with corresponding reduction of the interest allowable. [*Sec 363*].

43.23   Interest Payable

Relief on a loan qualifying as above will not be discontinued where the partnership is incorporated into a close company (see 43.19 above), a co-operative (see 43.20 above) or an employee-controlled company (see 43.21 above), or there is a partnership reconstruction involving a merger or demerger, provided that relief would have been available if the loan had been a new loan taken out to invest in the new entity. The usual restriction applies where any capital recovered from the partnership is not used to repay the loan. (Revenue Pamphlet IR 1 (November 1995 Supplement), A43).

Anti-avoidance measures on changeover to current year basis of assessment. Where

(*a*)   the transitional rules at 71.20 SCHEDULE D, CASES I AND II apply to determine the basis period for 1996/97 for a partnership business commenced before 6 April 1994 (other than where, exceptionally, the 1996/97 assessment is on an actual basis), and

(*b*)   a claim for interest relief is made by a partner under the above provisions in respect of a loan made after 31 March 1994 to defray money contributed or advanced to a partnership (but *not* to purchase an interest in the partnership),

there is a restriction on the amount of interest eligible for relief on any of the loan proceeds contributed or advanced to the partnership otherwise than wholly or mainly for *bona fide* commercial reasons (which does not include the obtaining of a tax advantage) or wholly or mainly for a purpose other than the reduction of the partnership's borrowings for a period falling wholly or partly within the transitional period (see 71.20 SCHEDULE D, CASES I AND II). Relief for interest paid in respect of the transitional period on that part of the loan proceeds is restricted to the appropriate percentage (as defined in 71.20 SCHEDULE D, CASES I AND II) of that interest. This does not apply if the aggregate amount of that interest is less than an amount to be prescribed by regulations shortly before 5 April 1997. These provisions apply to interest on a replacement loan as they would have applied in respect of the original loan. The discovery provisions of *TMA ss 29, 30B* apply with the same modifications and related time limits as in 71.20 SCHEDULE D, CASES I AND II. [*FA 1995, s 123, 22 Sch 2, 11, 21(2)*].

Further anti-avoidance provisions apply where a claim for interest relief under the above provisions is made by a partner for 1997/98 in respect of a loan made after 31 March 1994 and there is a transitional overlap profit (see 71.22 SCHEDULE D, CASES I AND II) on the changeover to the current year basis. Subject to a *de minimis* limit (as above), that partner's transitional overlap profit (as reduced where applicable by the anti-avoidance provisions at 71.22) is reduced by the amount of interest paid in respect of the transitional overlap period (see 71.22 SCHEDULE D, CASES I AND II) on any part of the loan proceeds which was contributed or advanced by him to the partnership otherwise than wholly or mainly for *bona fide* commercial reasons or wholly or mainly for a purpose other than the reduction of partnership borrowings for a period falling wholly or partly within the transitional overlap period. Similar notice provisions and time limits apply as in 71.22 as to the amendment of a self-assessment to give effect to the foregoing. [*FA 1995, 22 Sch 5, 12*].

43.23   **LOANS TO PAY INHERITANCE TAX**

Relief is given for interest on a loan to personal representatives to pay inheritance tax or estate duty before a grant of representation or confirmation (payable on delivery of the affidavit etc.), or interest thereon, on personalty of which the deceased was competent to dispose at his death (and which passes to the personal representatives as such, or would if it were situate in UK). The interest must be paid in respect of the period of one year from the making of the loan. Unrelieved interest in a year of assessment can be carried to previous year(s) of assessment and then, if still unrelieved, to succeeding years of assessment. [*Sec 364*].

43.24   **LOANS FOR PURCHASING LIFE ANNUITY**

Relief is given for interest on a loan for the purchase of a life annuity by a borrower aged 65 or over under a scheme in which 90% or more of the proceeds of the loan are applied to the purchase by the borrower of an annuity ending with his death (or the last death of two or more annuitants aged 65 or over which include the borrower). The loan must be secured on land in the UK or Eire in which the borrower or one of the annuitants owns an estate or interest. Interest is not eligible unless payable by the borrower or one of the annuitants.

See 43.5 above as regards denial of higher rate relief for interest payments after 5 April 1991. See 43.3 above for the method of giving relief for 1994/95 and subsequent years.

As regards loans made from 27 March 1974 onwards (*a*) the borrower or each of the annuitants must use the land as his only or main residence when the interest is paid and (*b*) relief is granted on loans up to £30,000 only, with apportionment where payable by two or more annuitants. In relation to interest paid **after 15 March 1993**, where the condition at (*a*) ceases at any time to be satisfied, and it is intended to take steps, within the twelve months following cessation of use as the only or main residence, with a view to disposal of the land, the condition will be treated as satisfied until the end of those twelve months or, if earlier, until the intention to dispose of the land is abandoned. The twelve month period may be extended at the Board's discretion in any particular case (irrespective of whether the period began before 16 March 1993).

[*Secs 357(1), 365; F(No 2)A 1983, s 3; FA 1984, s 22; FA 1985, s 37; FA 1986, s 20; FA 1987, s 25; FA 1988, s 41; FA 1989, s 46; FA 1990, s 71; FA 1991, s 26; FA 1992, s 10(4); FA 1993, ss 55, 57(3)(5); FA 1994, s 80; FA 1996, s 76*].

43.25   **EXCLUSION OF DOUBLE RELIEF**

Provisions for exclusion of double relief or relief by different methods are in *Sec 368*. The general rule is that any interest relieved under *Sec 353* is not deductible for any other purpose. If a payment of interest on a debt has been allowed under 43.2 above in computing the profits of a period, no relief can be given under *Sec 353* on that payment and on any interest on the same debt in any years of assessment for which the period is the basis period (see 71.4 SCHEDULE D, CASES I AND II onwards). Conversely, if a payment of interest has been relieved under *Sec 353*, that payment cannot be deducted in computing profits for any year of assessment and any payment of interest on the same debt cannot be deducted in computing the profits for assessment for the year in which *Sec 353* relief was given. For these purposes, all business overdrafts are treated as one debt. [*Sec 368; FA 1994, 9 Sch 9; FA 1995, 6 Sch 17*]. Also, if any interest is eligible for deduction of tax at source as 'relevant loan interest' (see 23.13 DEDUCTION OF TAX AT SOURCE), then relief under *Sec 353* will not apply. [*Sec 353(2)*]. See 43.2 above for concession where property used for both residential and business purposes.

44 Interest Receivable

Note. See Tolley's Corporation Tax under Gilts and Bonds for the special provisions applicable for accounting periods ending after 31 March 1996 to all profits and losses in respect of company 'loan relationships'.

44.1 Interest is receivable gross unless tax is deductible under *Sec 349* (see 23.3(ii) DEDUCTION OF TAX AT SOURCE) or under paying and collecting agent arrangements (see SCHEDULE C (70)) or unless received from a building society (see 9.3, 9.5 BUILDING SOCIETIES) or from a bank (see 8.2, 8.3 BANKS) without a gross payment certificate being in force.

44.2 The recipient of interest is assessable thereon under SCHEDULE D, CASE III (72), or under SCHEDULE D, CASES IV AND V (73) if the interest is from abroad, which see at 72.4 and 73.9 respectively as regards basis of assessment, and in particular for adjustments for opening and closing years. See 71.65 SCHEDULE D, CASES I AND II for the assessment of interest received in the course of a business.

Interest received under deduction of tax (see 44.1 above) is income of the year of assessment in which the payment falls due, without regard to the period of accrual.

44.3 A list of certain types of interest which are exempt from tax is shown in 29.11 EXEMPT INCOME.

44.4 See 3 ANTI-AVOIDANCE for transactions regarding the transfer of interest etc., and see 74.6 *et seq.* SCHEDULE D, CASE VI as regards the accrued income scheme.

44.5 **DEEP DISCOUNT SECURITIES**

For **1995/96 and earlier** years, and for accounting periods ending **before 1 April 1996**, the discount element on 'deep discount securities' is brought into charge to income tax or corporation tax (rather than to capital gains tax or corporation tax on chargeable gains) on 'disposal' or redemption. [*Sec 57, 4 Sch*]. The provisions are replaced, **for 1996/97 onwards**, by the income tax provisions of *FA 1996, 13 Sch* (see 72.2 SCHEDULE D, CASE III), and, for accounting periods ending **after 31 March 1996**, by the corporation tax provisions of *FA 1996, Pt IV, Ch II* (see Tolley's Corporation Tax under Gilts and Bonds).

A '*deep discount security*' is a redeemable security issued by a company after 13 March 1984 at a discount exceeding either 15% of the amount payable on redemption overall or $\frac{1}{2}$% per annum to the earliest possible redemption date. Shares, index-linked securities and securities within *Sec 209(2)(c)* (see Tolley's Corporation Tax under Distributions) are excluded. Also excluded are securities issued after 31 July 1990 by a company which are convertible into share capital in a company (whether or not the issuing company), securities issued after that date where the terms of issue provide more than one date for redemption at the option of the holder, and securities which were qualifying convertible securities (see 44.8 below) at the time of issue. The amount payable on redemption excludes any amount payable by way of interest.

In relation to a security issued in a currency other than sterling, the level of discount is tested in the currency of issue. (Revenue Tax Bulletin November 1993 p 100). For securities issued with a period to maturity of less than a year, the $\frac{1}{2}$% p.a. test is applied pro rata to the length of the period. (Revenue Tax Bulletin November 1993 p 101).

A redeemable security issued by a '*public body*' (i.e. a government or public or local authority, not being a company, in the UK or elsewhere) at a deep discount (as above) is also a '*deep discount security*' unless it is

(*a*) an index-linked security, or

(*b*) a 'gilt-edged security' (as defined for capital gains tax purposes) issued before 14 March 1989 (or under the same prospectus as a gilt-edged security issued before that date) or issued, other than on the original issue, under a prospectus under which no securities were issued before that date, where all the securities on the original issue are gilt-edged securities and not deep discount securities, or

(*c*) not a gilt-edged security, and was issued under the same prospectus as any other security issued previously which is not a deep discount security.

As regards (*b*) and (*c*) above, certain securities which would, apart from those provisions, be deep discount securities are generally treated as such where at some time the aggregate nominal value of securities issued under the same prospectus which would (apart from (*b*) or (*c*) above) be deep discount securities exceeds that of those which would not, and the deemed treatment applies to events occurring after that time as if the securities in question had been issued and acquired as such.

Where securities issued by a company before 14 March 1984 are exchanged, on or after that date, for new securities which would otherwise be deep discount securities, the new securities are *not* deep discount securities if

(1) the original securities would not have been deep discount securities if issued after 13 March 1984;

(2) the earliest redemption date of the new securities is not later than that for the original securities; and

(3) the amount payable on redemption of the new securities does not exceed that on the original securities.

[*4 Sch 1, 19–21; FA 1989, 10 Sch 2, 7; FA 1990, s 59, 10 Sch 26*].

A '*disposal*' of a deep discount security is as defined for capital gains tax purposes (see Tolley's Capital Gains Tax under Disposals), but also includes the occasion of a conversion or exchange of securities within *TCGA 1992, s 132* or *s 135(3)*, and a deemed disposal immediately before the death of the holder. However, unless the security converted or exchanged is a 'chargeable security' within the coupon-stripping provisions (see 44.6 below), conversion or exchange, for no consideration other than the new securities, into securities which are also deep discount securities, and for which the earliest redemption date is no later than that for the original securities, is not a disposal for these purposes. In this case the 'accrued income' is carried forward to the new holding of securities. The conversion or exchange of a 'chargeable security' is always a disposal for these purposes. [*4 Sch 7*].

The **charge** to income or corporation tax is on the 'accrued income' attributable to the period from acquisition to disposal, and is under Schedule D, Case III or Case IV. The REMITTANCE BASIS (63) applies to a Case IV charge on a non-UK domiciled person or on a non-UK ordinarily resident British or Irish subject, by reference to sums remitted in the year of assessment of charge. Otherwise, the charge is on the amount arising from disposals in the year of assessment. See, however, 44.6 below as regards the charge on certain securities issued to exploit this delayed charge.

The '*accrued income*' is the aggregate of 'income elements' of each 'income period' (or part) in the period of ownership.

44.5 Interest Receivable

'*Income element*' for an 'income period' is the amount obtained by the formula

$$\frac{A \times B}{100} - C$$

where A is the issue price plus 'income elements' of all previous 'income periods'.

B is the 'yield to maturity', i.e. the annual percentage appreciation rate (compounded at the end of each 'income period') required for the issue price to grow to the redemption value at the earliest possible redemption date, after allowing for any interest payments.

C is the interest (if any) attributable to the 'income period'.

'*Income period*' is the period to which any interest is attributable, or, if no interest is payable, the year to anniversary of issue of the security, or shorter period from such an anniversary or the date of issue to the earliest redemption date. Where a period of ownership includes part of an 'income period', the income element is apportioned on a straight line basis.

The company issuing the security (and a public body issuing such a security after 31 July 1989) is required to state on the bond certificate the amount of the income element for each income period in the security's life. Redemption proceeds are payable gross, without deduction of tax under *Secs 348–350* or *Sec 123*.

[*4 Sch 1, 4, 13; FA 1989, 10 Sch 6*].

On **early redemption** (or **winding-up** of an issuing company), the accrued income attributable to the period of ownership ending on the redemption (or on a payment being made in respect of the security in the winding-up) is the amount paid on the redemption (or winding-up) *less* either (i) the issue price, or (ii) if the security was not acquired by the holder on its issue, the sum of the issue price and the accrued income from its issue to the holder's acquisition of it. [*4 Sch 11, 11A; FA 1989, 10 Sch 4, 5*]. See, however, 44.6 below as regards certain securities issued by companies subject to charge on accrued income at the end of each income period during the period of ownership.

For **capital gains tax** purposes (or for the purposes of corporation tax on chargeable gains):

(i) consideration for the disposal is reduced by the amount of the accrued income during the period of ownership (and any excess of that accrued income over actual consideration is treated as enhancement expenditure immediately before the disposal);

(ii) on a conversion or exchange of securities (see above) any sum payable to the beneficial owner in addition to the new holding is treated in the same way as the consideration at (i) above;

(iii) on a 'no gain-no loss' disposal, the deemed consideration is increased by the accrued income arising during the disponer's period of ownership; and

(iv) capital gains tax identification rules are applied.

[*TCGA 1992, s 118*]

Exemptions. No charge arises under these provisions where

(A) the amount otherwise chargeable is applicable and applied for charitable purposes, or

(B) either

(i) immediately before the disposal the security was held for the purposes of an exempt approved retirement benefits scheme (see 66.4 RETIREMENT SCHEMES), or

(ii)   the disposal was a stock lending transfer within *Sec 129(3)* (see 71.81 SCHEDULE D, CASES I AND II).

[4 Sch 14, 15, 16; FA 1989, 10 Sch 7].

Miscellaneous points

(a)   *Time of disposal.* Where a transaction in deep discount securities is under a contract, it takes place at the time the contract is made, or, if the contract is conditional, at the time at which the condition is satisfied. *[4 Sch 8].*

(b)   *Letters of allotment.* A security comprised in any letter of allotment or similar instrument is treated as issued unless the right to the security is provisional and has still to be accepted. *[4 Sch 1(3)].*

(c)   *Issuing company deduction.* For the deduction of the discount in the issuing company's computation, see Tolley's Corporation Tax under Profit Computations. Broadly, the company is allowed a deduction in each accounting period of the income elements in income periods ending in the accounting period. *[4 Sch 5].*

(d)   *Identification of securities* disposed of follows the capital gains tax rules in *TCGA 1992, s 108* (see Tolley's Capital Gains Tax under Indexation). *[4 Sch 12].*

(e)   *Trustees* on whom a charge arises under these provisions on a disposal are chargeable at the rate applicable to trusts (see 80.5 SETTLEMENTS) for the year of the disposal, except to the extent that they are trustees of a non-authorised unit trust (see 90.1 UNIT AND INVESTMENT TRUSTS) of which the amount charged is treated as income. *[4 Sch 17; FA 1989, 10 Sch 7; FA 1993, 6 Sch 18].*

(f)   UNDERWRITERS (89). For the underwriting year 1993 and earlier years, an underwriter is treated as absolutely entitled as against the trustees to securities forming part of his premiums trust fund (within *Sec 457; FA 1993, s 184(1)*). Securities held in premiums trust funds are to be regarded as disposed of by the trustees at market value on 31 December and as reacquired by them at market value on 1 January (commencing with 31 December 1989 and 1 January 1990) provided that they actually form part of the fund at the end of 31 December or the beginning of 1 January, as appropriate. For this purpose, stock lending transactions (see 71.81 SCHEDULE D, CASES I AND II) may be required to be disregarded, so that securities transferred are treated as still forming part of the fund. Where taxable income arises under these provisions in respect of securities forming part of a premiums trust fund, it is taxable in accordance with the rules in *Sec 450(1)* (see 89.4 UNDERWRITERS) rather than for the year of assessment in which the disposal occurs. The deemed disposal and reacquisition apply equally for capital gains tax purposes. For the underwriting year 1994 and subsequent years, the deep discount security provisions have no application to premiums trust funds. For 1992/93 and subsequent years, they also have no application to new-style special reserve funds under *FA 1993* (see 89.8(b) UNDERWRITERS). They continue to apply with respect to ancillary trust funds (see 89.3 UNDERWRITERS). For the purposes of the application of the provisions to ancillary trust funds and old-style special reserve funds, the underwriter is treated as absolutely entitled as against the trustees to securities forming part of the fund. There is no deemed disposal on death in respect of securities forming part of any of the above-mentioned funds. *[4 Sch 18; TCGA 1992, s 118(5)(6); FA 1989, s 96(2), 10 Sch 7; FA 1993, ss 176(3)(b), 183(5)(6), 23 Sch Pt III(12)].*

(g)   *New issues.* Where

(i)   securities of a particular kind are issued (being the original issue of securities of that kind),

(ii)   new securities of the same kind are issued subsequently, and after 18 March 1991,

(iii)   a sum (the 'extra return') is payable by the issuer in respect of each new security, to reflect the fact that interest is accruing on the old securities and calculated accordingly, and

(iv)   the issue price of each new security includes an element (separately identified or not) representing payment for the extra return,

then, for the purposes of the deep discount security provisions, the issue price of each new security is deemed to exclude the extra return referred to at (iii) above. [*4 Sch 11B; FA 1991, 12 Sch 3, 5*].

(*h*)   *Interest etc. on debts between associated companies or to associates of banks.* Certain debts owed by non-UK resident companies (or certain third parties) to UK resident 'associated' companies (within *Sec 416*), or by any company to a UK resident company associated with a company carrying on a UK banking business, are classed as 'qualifying debts'. Where the debt on a deep discount security is a qualifying debt, it is treated as transferred for the purposes of the above provisions on becoming or ceasing to be a qualifying debt, at the end of each accounting period, and on the provisions in question coming into force. [*FA 1993, ss 61, 62, 64, 66; FA 1995, ss 88, 89*]. See Tolley's Corporation Tax under Profit Computations for the detailed provisions.

These provisions are **abolished** for **1996/97 onwards** and (subject to transitional provisions) for accounting periods ending **after 31 March 1996**. [*FA 1996, 14 Sch 50, 15 Sch 19, 41 Sch Pt V(3)*]. See now 72.2 SCHEDULE D, CASE III and see Tolley's Corporation Tax under Gilts and Bonds.

44.6   **'Coupon-stripping'.** For 1995/96 and earlier years and for accounting periods ending before 1 April 1996, a special basis of charge applies to deep discount securities (see 44.5 above) issued by a company after 18 March 1985 which are *'chargeable securities'*, i.e. where they were issued in any of the following circumstances.

(*a*)   (i)   Immediately before the issue, the issuing company held (i.e. had a beneficial interest in) 'relevant securities' representing at least 75% of the market value of all its assets; or

       (ii)   the terms of issue were determined by reference to (without necessarily reflecting) the terms of issue of 'relevant securities' which the issuing company was holding or intended to acquire.

(*b*)   (i)   The criteria in (*a*) would apply if 'relevant securities' included 'UK corporate bonds'; and

       (ii)   the criteria in (*a*) would have applied if such bonds had been deep discount securities when acquired.

(*c*)   Neither (*a*) nor (*b*) above applies, and at any time during the first income period of securities of the particular kind (i.e. which are, or would be, dealt in on a stock exchange as being of the same kind), the company's assets include 'relevant securities' representing at least 75% of the market value of all its assets.

(*d*)   The security was issued on a conversion or exchange falling within *TCGA 1992, ss 132, 135(3), 136(1)* (see Tolley's Capital Gains Tax under Shares and Securities) and the original securities were within (*a*) or (*b*) above or this provision, or were within (*c*) above where the condition therein had been fulfilled in their case by the time of the conversion or exchange.

The company must state on the bond certificate of any security within (*a*), (*b*) or (*d*) above that tax is chargeable under these provisions.

'*Relevant securities*' means securities within the accrued income provisions of *Sec 710 et seq.* (see 74.6 *et seq.* SCHEDULE D, CASE VI) but excluding '*UK corporate bonds*', i.e. sterling securities issued by a UK resident company (and not convertible into or redeemable in any other currency) the debt on which represents (and has always represented) a normal commercial loan (as defined in *18 Sch 1(5)*—see Tolley's Corporation Tax under Groups of Companies).

Where a person acquires a chargeable security, there is a **charge** under Schedule D, Case III or Case IV (as appropriate) *on the current year basis* at the end of each 'income period' (see 44.5 above) falling wholly or partly within the period of ownership. The charge is on an amount equal to the 'income element' (see 44.5 above) for the income period (or the part thereof falling within the period of ownership).

On a **disposal** or deemed disposal (see 44.5 above) of the chargeable security, the total amount charged under these provisions is deducted from the income otherwise chargeable under 44.5 above (without, however, affecting the Capital Gains Tax position). Similarly, the total amount charged under these provisions is deducted from the accrued income in arriving at the charge on early redemption or on winding-up.

CHARITIES (15) are exempt from any charge under these provisions on any amount applicable and applied for charitable purposes.

[*4 Sch 2, 3, 4(1), 11(2), 14; TCGA 1992, s 118*].

See 44.5 above as regards abolition and replacement of these provisions.

44.7   **DEEP GAIN SECURITIES**

For **1995/96 and earlier** years, and for accounting periods ending **before 1 April 1996**, where there is a 'transfer' of a 'deep gain security' for an amount exceeding the acquisition cost, an amount equal to the difference (net of any acquisition or transfer costs) is treated as income of the transferor, chargeable to tax under Schedule D, Case III or IV, arising in the year of assessment of the transfer and assessable on the current year basis. '*Transfer*' is defined but specifically excludes the conversion of a security into share capital in a company. The amount obtained for the transfer includes any amount to which the transferor is entitled, whether or not he actually obtains that amount. A similar charge arises where a 'deep gain security' is redeemed. [*FA 1989, 11 Sch 4, 5, 6; FA 1990, 10 Sch 27(2)*]. The provisions are replaced, **for 1996/97 onwards**, by the income tax provisions of *FA 1996, 13 Sch* (see 72.2 SCHEDULE D, CASE III), and, for accounting periods ending **after 31 March 1996**, by the corporation tax provisions of *FA 1996, Pt IV, Ch II* (see Tolley's Corporation Tax under Gilts and Bonds).

Trustees on whom a charge arises under these provisions are chargeable at the rate applicable to trusts (see 80.5 SETTLEMENTS) for the year of the disposal, except to the extent that they are trustees of a non-authorised unit trust (see 90.1 UNIT AND INVESTMENT TRUSTS) of which the amount charged is treated as income. [*FA 1989, 11 Sch 11; FA 1993, 6 Sch 20*].

On the death of the person entitled to a 'deep gain security', there is a deemed market value transfer to his personal representatives immediately before his death, and the personal representatives are similarly treated as transferring a security at market value on a transfer of the security to a legatee (as widely defined). Transfers between CONNECTED PERSONS (20), whenever made, are similarly treated as at market value, as are any transfers other than for money's worth or other than at arm's length. Foreign currency transactions and costs are translated into sterling on the day of the transfer (or redemption) or acquisition by reference to the London closing rate of exchange for that day. [*FA 1989, 11 Sch 7, 8, 9, 12*].

A '*deep gain security*' is a redeemable security which meets the following conditions.

(*a*) At the time of issue (and assuming redemption) the amount payable on redemption (or on any one of a number of possible occasions of redemption) might constitute a 'deep gain'. For this purpose, 'redemption' does not include:

    (i) any redemption which may be made before maturity only at the option of the issuer;

    (ii) for securities issued before 13 November 1991, any redemption which may be made before maturity otherwise than by exercise by the holder of the security of an option exercisable only on the effluxion of time or the happening of an event which (judged at the time of the security's issue) is certain or likely to occur;

    (iii) for securities issued after 12 November 1991, any redemption which may be made before maturity otherwise than at the option of the holder of the security, and as regards which (judged at the time of the security's issue) the event occasioning redemption

        (A) is such that, if it occurred and there was no provision for redemption, the interests of the holder of the security at the time of the occurrence might be adversely affected,

        (B) is neither certain nor likely to occur, and

        (C) is not one of a number of events occasioning or allowing redemption before maturity at least one of which is certain or likely to occur,

    and provided that the obtaining of a tax advantage by any person is not the main benefit or one of the main benefits expected to accrue from the provision for redemption.

    (A) above is fulfilled if it is fulfilled by reference to any one potential holder, whether or not it is fulfilled by reference to other potential holders. In determining whether (B) or (C) is fulfilled in a case where the security is one which, under the terms of issue, can be converted into or exchanged for a security of a different kind, neither condition is treated as fulfilled unless it is fulfilled having regard only to circumstances in which (judged at the time of issue of the security) the right to convert or exchange cannot be, or is unlikely to be, exercised;

    (iv) for securities issued after 12 November 1991, any redemption which may be made before maturity at the option of the holder of the security and as regards which (judged at the time of the security's issue) the conditions in (iii) above are fulfilled in relation to the event allowing the option to be exercised.

Where, however, a security which would be a deep gain security but for (iii) or (iv) above is redeemed before maturity, it is treated, as regards the redemption, as if it were, and had been acquired as, a deep gain security, where either:

    (1) it was, immediately before redemption, held by a person connected with the issuer (within *Sec 839*, see 20 CONNECTED PERSONS); or

    (2) it was transferred in the period of one year before the redemption by a person so connected with the issuer.

(*b*) The security is neither a deep discount security (see 44.5 above); nor a company share; nor a 'qualifying indexed security'; nor a 'convertible security'; nor is it a gilt-edged security (as defined for capital gains tax purposes) which either

(i)   was issued before 14 March 1989, or under the same prospectus as any gilt-edged security issued before that date, or

(ii)   was issued, other than on the original issue, under a prospectus under which no securities were issued before 14 March 1989, where all the securities on the original issue are gilt-edged securities and not deep gain securities;

nor is it a security, other than a gilt-edged security, which was issued under the same prospectus as any other security issued earlier which is not a deep gain security.

As regards (ii) above and the paragraph which follows it, certain securities which would, apart from those provisions, be deep gain securities are generally treated as such where at some time the aggregate nominal value of securities issued under the same prospectus which would (apart from (ii) above and the paragraph following it) be deep gain securities exceeds that of those which would not, and the deemed treatment applies to events occurring after that time as if the securities in question had been acquired as such.

An amount payable on redemption constitutes a '*deep gain*' if the issue price is less than that amount (excluding any amount payable by way of interest) by more than 15% of that amount (excluding interest) or one-half per cent per annum of that amount (excluding interest) for each complete year between issue and redemption. [*FA 1989, 11 Sch 1, 19A, 20, 21, 21A; FA 1990, s 57; F(No 2)A 1992, 7 Sch 2, 4, 5*].

A '*qualifying indexed security*' is a security which, under the terms of issue (including those on which it may be offered by an agent or underwriter), satisfies the following conditions.

(i)   The amount payable on redemption (excluding interest) must be precisely determined by the retail prices index (or foreign currency local equivalent), although the adjustment may lag behind the period in question by up to eight months. Securities quoted on a recognised stock exchange at the time of issue or, for securities issued after 8 June 1989, within one month thereafter (or on 8 June 1989 if issued on or before that date) may alternatively satisfy this condition where the amount payable on redemption is linked to a quoted share prices index. In relation to securities issued before 9 June 1989, this condition is not prevented from being satisfied by a guaranteed minimum amount being payable on redemption provided that either

(a)   the minimum amount does not constitute a deep gain (as above), or

(b)   the minimum amount arises only in 'qualifying circumstances'.

Also, this condition is not prevented from being satisfied by a guaranteed minimum amount equal to a specified percentage (being no greater than 10) of the issue price being payable on redemption or, for securities issued after 8 June 1989, where the amount to be paid on redemption in any of the circumstances in (b) above is to be not more than the issue price.

(ii)   There must be no provision for redemption in, or conversion into, a different currency.

(iii)   Indexed interest (the indexation of which must meet conditions similar to those in (i) above) must be payable at least annually at not less than a reasonable commercial rate.

(iv)   The issue must have a stated life of not less than five years from the date of issue, and within that five year period the holder must not be able to require the purchase or repurchase of the security, or its conversion or redemption (in the latter case other than in 'qualifying circumstances').

44.7 Interest Receivable

The Revenue consider that, as regards (i) above, the share prices index used must relate to the exchange on which the security is quoted, and that as regards (iii) above, the index in question must be applied directly to the interest payable, i.e. without any formula restriction and not e.g. in inverse proportion to index movements. (Revenue Tax Bulletin February 1995 p 196).

The following are *'qualifying circumstances'*.

(I)   There is a fundamental change, detrimental to the interests of the holder of the security, in the rules of index in question.

(II) The index ceases to be published without comparable replacement.

(III) For securities issued before 13 November 1991, any circumstances except those in which the holder of the security exercises an option exercisable only on the effluxion of time or the happening of an event which (judged at the time of issue) is certain or likely to occur.

(IV) For securities issued after 12 November 1991, any circumstances for redemption which may be made before maturity otherwise than at the option of the holder of the security and as regards which the conditions set out at (*a*)(iii) above are fulfilled.

(V)   For securities issued after 12 November 1991, any circumstances for redemption which may be made before maturity at the option of the holder of the security and as regards which the conditions set out at (*a*)(iv) above are fulfilled.

Where the issuer and the holder agree (after 13 March 1989) to vary the terms under which it is held, and, had the terms as so varied applied on issue, the security would be a deep gain security, it is treated as having been acquired as such from the date of the agreement.

The Treasury has power by regulations to modify any of the above conditions. [*FA 1989, 11 Sch 2, 22, 23; FA 1990, s 58; F(No 2)A 1992, 7 Sch 3*].

A *'convertible security'* is a security issued by a company before 9 June 1989 under the terms of which it can be converted into or exchanged for share capital (by whatever name called) in that or any other company, and in relation to which the following condition is satisfied at some time in the period of one month following the day of issue. The condition is that either

(A)   the security was quoted on a recognised stock exchange, or

(B)   share capital in the company into whose shares the security may be converted or exchanged (but not necessarily those shares themselves) was so quoted, or

(C)   both (A) and (B) are satisfied (though not necessarily at the same time). [*FA 1989, 11 Sch 3*].

Convertible securities: special rules. A security which at the time of issue is a 'qualifying convertible security' (see 44.8 below) but would otherwise be a deep gain security is treated as not being a deep gain security. If, however, it ceases to be a qualifying convertible security, then, as regards any subsequent event in relation to it, including a transfer or acquisition, it is treated as if it were a deep gain security and had been acquired as such (whenever it was acquired). Where a security which would otherwise have been a deep discount security (see 44.5 above) ceases to be a qualifying convertible security, it is similarly treated, as regards subsequent events, as if it were, and had been acquired as, a deep gain security. [*FA 1989, 11 Sch 22A, 22B; FA 1990, 10 Sch 27*].

Exemptions apply as for deep discount securities (see 44.5 above). [*FA 1989, 11 Sch 14, 15, 16*].

Miscellaneous points

(1) *Accrued income scheme.* A transfer within these provisions is excluded from charge under the accrued income scheme (see 74.6 *et seq.* SCHEDULE D, CASE VI). [*FA 1989, 11 Sch 17*].

(2) *Deduction of tax* under *Secs 123, 348–350* (see 23 DEDUCTION OF TAX AT SOURCE) does not apply to the proceeds of redemption of a deep gain security. [*FA 1989, 11 Sch 18*].

(3) *Foreign domiciliaries* (and Commonwealth and Irish citizens not ordinarily resident in the UK) chargeable under Schedule D, Case IV are assessed on the remittance basis. [*FA 1989, 11 Sch 13*].

(4) *Identification of securities* follows the capital gains tax rules of *TCGA 1992, s 108*. [*FA 1989, 11 Sch 19*].

(5) *Underwriters.* Special provisions apply to disposals of securities forming part of the trust funds of Lloyd's UNDERWRITERS (89). These are broadly similar to those relating to deep discount securities (see 44.5 above). [*FA 1989, 11 Sch 10; FA 1993, ss 176(3)(c), 183(5)(6); 23 Sch Pt III(12)*].

(6) *New issues.* In the circumstances set out in 44.5(*g*) above, the issue price, for the purposes of the deep gain security provisions, is adjusted as there mentioned. [*FA 1989, 11 Sch 3A; FA 1991, 12 Sch 4, 5*].

(7) *Securities without a particular redemption date.* In the case of such securities, all the provisions of *FA 1989, 11 Sch* which refer to 'redemption before maturity', 'redeemed before maturity' or 'redemption which may be made before maturity' are to be read as if the words 'before maturity' were omitted. [*FA 1989, 11 Sch 22C; F(No 2)A 1992, 7 Sch 6*].

(8) *Interest etc. on debts between associated companies or to associates of banks.* Certain debts owed by non-UK resident companies (or certain third parties) to UK resident 'associated' companies (within *Sec 416*), or by any company to a UK resident company associated with a company carrying on a UK banking business, are classed as 'qualifying debts'. Where the debt on a deep gain security is a qualifying debt, it is treated as transferred at market value for the purposes of the above provisions on becoming or ceasing to be a qualifying debt, at the end of each accounting period, and on the provisions in question coming into force. [*FA 1993, ss 61, 62, 65; FA 1995, ss 88, 89*]. See Tolley's Corporation Tax under Profit Computations for the detailed provisions.

These provisions are **abolished** (subject to transitional provisions) for **1996/97 onwards** and for accounting periods ending **after 31 March 1996**. [*FA 1996, 14 Sch 57, 15 Sch 20, 41 Sch Pt V(3)*]. See now 72.2 SCHEDULE D, CASE III and see also Tolley's Corporation Tax under Gilts and Bonds. The **transitional provisions** for income tax purposes apply where a person (the 'relevant person') held a qualifying indexed security on 5 April 1996 (31 March 1996 in the case of certain authorised unit trust holdings) and did not dispose of it on that date, and does not otherwise fall to be treated for capital gains tax purposes as having disposed of it on that date, and a 'relevant event' occurs. A *'relevant event'* occurs on the first occasion after that date when the relevant person (or a spouse to whom the security has been transferred within *TCGA 1992, s 58*) is treated for capital gains tax purposes as disposing of the security (or of any asset falling to be treated as the same as the security) other than on an inter-spouse transfer. In those circumstances, the chargeable gain or allowable loss which would have accrued to the relevant person on a disposal at market value on 5 April 1996 (or 31 March 1996) is brought into account as accruing to the person making the disposal constituting the relevant event, in the year of assessment in which that event occurs. If a qualifying indexed security held both on and immediately after 5 April 1996 (or 31 March 1996) is a 'relevant discounted security' within *FA 1996, 13 Sch* (see 72.2

SCHEDULE D, CASE III), its acquisition on or before that date is treated for the purposes of that *Schedule* as having been at its market value on that date. [*FA 1996, 15 Sch 27–29*].

44.8 QUALIFYING CONVERTIBLE SECURITIES

For **1995/96 and earlier** years, and for accounting periods ending **before 1 April 1996**, securities issued after 8 June 1989 which are convertible into the ordinary share capital of the issuing company, give the investor an option to put the security back to the issuer and meet certain qualifying conditions ('*qualifying convertible securities*') are excluded from the rules for deep gain securities (see **44.7** above). A person disposing of such a security by putting it back to the issuer or transferring it before the expiry of a put option is, however, chargeable to income tax or corporation tax on the income components accruing while he has held it. [*FA 1990, s 56, 10 Sch*]. The provisions are replaced, **for 1996/97 onwards**, by the income tax provisions of *FA 1996, 13 Sch* (see **72.2** SCHEDULE D, CASE III), and, for accounting periods ending **after 31 March 1996**, by the corporation tax provisions of *FA 1996, Pt IV, Ch II* (see Tolley's Corporation Tax under Gilts and Bonds).

A security issued by a company after 8 June 1989 is a '*qualifying convertible security*' at the time of its issue if it meets each of the following conditions.

(*a*)   It is not a share, is redeemable and its issue does not fall, wholly or partly, to be treated, by virtue of *Sec 209(2)(c)*, as, or as part of, a company distribution (see Tolley's Corporation Tax under Distributions).

(*b*)   It is quoted on a recognised stock exchange or is so quoted within one month after the issue date.

(*c*)   Under the terms of the issue

  (i)   the security can be converted into ordinary share capital (as defined by *FA 1990, 10 Sch 11(5)*) in the issuing company,

  (ii)   it carries either no right to interest or a right to interest at a fixed (not variable) rate determined at the time of issue, and

  (iii)   any amount payable, either on redemption (at any time) or by way of interest, is payable in the currency in which the issue price is denominated.

(*d*)   At the time of issue, the security is subject to one (and one only) 'qualifying provision for redemption'.

(*e*)   The yield to redemption (as defined by *FA 1990, 10 Sch 9*) for the 'relevant redemption period' represents no more than a reasonable commercial return. The '*relevant redemption period*' is the 'redemption period' which ends with the day on which the occasion for redemption under the 'qualifying provision for redemption' falls.

(*f*)   The security is either a deep discount security (see **44.5** above) or a deep gain security (see **44.7** above), but only because of the 'qualifying provision for redemption'. *4 Sch 21* and *FA 1989, 11 Sch 22B(1)*, which prevent a qualifying convertible security from being a deep discount or deep gain security, are to be disregarded for this purpose.

(*g*)   The obtaining of a tax advantage within *Sec 709(1)* (see **3.2** ANTI-AVOIDANCE) by any person is not the main benefit, or one of the main benefits, that might be expected to accrue from issuing the security.

(*h*)   Where the security carries a right to interest, the first (or only) interest payment day must fall either one year or six months after the day of issue, and subsequent interest payment days (if any) must continue to fall at yearly or six-monthly intervals respectively.

Having satisfied the above conditions at the time of issue, a security continues to be a qualifying convertible security unless at any time

(i)   it becomes subject to a new qualifying provision for redemption and the conditions in *FA 1990, 10 Sch 4(3)* are not satisfied, or

(ii) any of the prohibited events listed below occurs in relation to the security,

in which case the security ceases to be a qualifying convertible security at the time in question. Any of the following is a prohibited event.

(A)   The security ceases to be quoted on a recognised stock exchange.

(B)   It becomes subject to a provision under which either of the conditions at (*c*)(ii) or (iii) above will no longer be satisfied.

(C)   It becomes subject to a provision which would be a 'qualifying provision for redemption' but for the fact that the conditions at (II) and (III) below are not fully satisfied.

(D)   There is a time when more than 10% of the securities issued, under the prospectus under which the security concerned was issued, are held by companies which are at that time linked companies within the meaning of *FA 1988, 11 Sch 4* (see Tolley's Corporation Tax under Capital Gains).

[*FA 1990, 10 Sch 2–5, 9, 11*].

A '*qualifying provision for redemption*', in relation to a security, is a provision which

(I)   provides for redemption before maturity only at the option of the person holding the security for the time being,

(II) provides for such redemption on one occasion only, which must occur on the last day of an 'income period', and

(III) is such that the amount payable on the exercise of the option is fixed (not variable), is determined at the time the security becomes subject to the provision and constitutes a 'deep gain'.

[*FA 1990, 10 Sch 1*].

The amount payable on redemption on exercise of the option under a provision for redemption constitutes a '*deep gain*' if the issue price is less than that amount (excluding any amount payable by way of interest) by more than 15% of that amount (excluding interest) or one-half per cent per annum of that amount (excluding interest) for each complete year between day of issue and the occasion for redemption under the provision concerned. Where, however, the security became subject to one or more qualifying provisions for redemption before becoming subject to the provision concerned, the above applies with the substitution of 'base amount' for 'issue price' and of 'base day' for 'day of issue'. The '*base amount*' is the amount payable on redemption on exercise of the option provided for by the previous qualifying provision for redemption or, if there was more than one, the one to which the security last became subject. The '*base day*' is the day on which the occasion for redemption falls under that previous, or last, qualifying provision for redemption. [*FA 1990, 10 Sch 6, 11(2)*].

An '*income period*' is the inclusive period from day of issue to the first (or only) interest payment day or any period from one interest payment day to the next. Where the security carries no right to interest, an income period is any period of one year ending with an anniversary of the day of issue. [*FA 1990, 10 Sch 7*].

A '*redemption period*' is the inclusive period from the day of issue to the day on which falls the first (or only) occasion for redemption under a qualifying provision for redemption, or any period beginning with a day after that on which one such occasion falls and ending with the day on which the next such occasion falls. [*FA 1990, 10 Sch 8*].

A **chargeable event** occurs where there is either a 'transfer' or a redemption (in exercise of the option under a qualifying provision for redemption) of a security which at that time is a qualifying convertible security and, in the case of a transfer, is subject to at least one qualifying provision for redemption under which the occasion for redemption has not arrived. ('*Transfer*' is defined but specifically excludes a transfer made on the conversion of a security into ordinary share capital of a company.) The 'chargeable amount' is treated as income of the person making the transfer or exercising the option, chargeable to tax under Schedule D, Case III or IV, arising in the year of assessment in which the chargeable event occurs and assessable on a current year basis. [*FA 1990, 10 Sch 10, 12*].

The '*chargeable amount*' is the lesser of the amount obtained on transfer or redemption (excluding interest), by the person making the transfer or entitled to the security immediately before redemption, and the 'total income element'. Except in cases where transfers are deemed to be at market value, i.e. on death, transfers between connected persons etc. or deemed transfers by trustees of Lloyd's premium trust funds, any amount which a person is entitled to obtain, but does not obtain, on transfer or redemption is treated for this purpose as having been obtained. [*FA 1990, 10 Sch 13*].

The '*total income element*' is the sum of the 'income elements' for each income period (if any) the whole of which, and the 'partial income elements' for each income period (if any) part of which, consists of or falls within the ownership period, i.e. the period from date of acquisition to date of chargeable event. The '*income element*' for an income period is the amount obtained by the formula

$$\frac{A \times B}{100} - C$$

where A is the issue price plus income elements of all previous income periods.
B is the figure included in the percentage representing the yield to redemption for the redemption period which consists of the income period or in which the income period falls.
C is the amount of interest (if any) payable for the income period.

The '*partial income element*' for an income period is the income element for that period apportioned in accordance with the number of days in that income period which consist of or fall within the ownership period. [*FA 1990, 10 Sch 14, 15*].

Exemptions apply as for deep discount securities (see 44.5 above). [*FA 1990, 10 Sch 21–23*].

Miscellaneous points

(1) Provisions broadly similar to those for deep gain securities (see 44.7 above) apply as regards *death*, transfers to *legatees*, transfers between CONNECTED PERSONS (20) etc. and transfers by *trustees*. [*FA 1990, 10 Sch 16, 17, 19; FA 1993, 6 Sch 21*].

(2) Special provisions apply to securities forming part of the trust funds of Lloyd's UNDERWRITERS (89). These are broadly similar to those relating to deep discount securities (see 44.5 above). [*FA 1990, 10 Sch 18; FA 1993, ss 176(3)(d), 183(5)(6), 23 Sch Pt III(12)*].

(3) Provisions identical to those described at (3) and (4) in 44.7 above, as regards *foreign domiciliaries etc.* and *identification of securities*, apply in respect of qualifying convertible securities. [*FA 1990, 10 Sch 20, 24*].

(4)   *Issuing company deduction*. Where a qualifying convertible security is redeemed in circumstances such that a chargeable event occurs, the excess of the amount paid on redemption (excluding interest) over the issue price may be deducted in the issuing company's computation for the account period of redemption. See also Tolley's Corporation Tax under Profit Computations. [*FA 1990, 10 Sch 25*].

These provisions are **abolished** for **1996/97 onwards** and (subject to transitional provisions) for accounting periods ending **after 31 March 1996**. [*FA 1996, 14 Sch 58, 15 Sch 21, 41 Sch Pt V(3)*]. See now 72.2 SCHEDULE D, CASE III and see Tolley's Corporation Tax under Gilts and Bonds.

44.9   **Deep discounted and indexed stock.** In as far as it is not within the specific legislation at 44.5 *et seq.* above, the Revenue consider that the discount on deep discounted stock (i.e. stock issued at a price well below par value and with a low interest rate) represents the reward for the use of the money over the period of the loan and as such will be treated, when it is paid on redemption, as chargeable to tax as rolled-up interest in the lender's hands and allowable against the borrower's profits for corporation tax purposes (whether or not there have been intermediate transactions during the life of the stock).

Corporate stock issued on an indexed basis and bearing a reasonable commercial rate of interest will generally be treated as follows:

(*a*)   if the indexation constitutes a capital uplift of the principal on redemption to take account of no more than the fall in real value because of inflation, the lender (other than a bank or financial concern) will be liable only to capital gains tax on the uplift and the borrowing company will have no deduction against its profits.

(*b*)   if the indexation applies to the interest element and additional sums of interest are rolled-up to be paid with the capital on redemption, the indexed and the rolled-up interest, when paid, will be given the same treatment as non-indexed interest.

(Revenue Press Release 25 June 1982).

Following the repeal of the provisions described at 44.5–44.8 above, and their replacement, for 1996/97 onwards, by the income tax provisions of *FA 1996, 13 Sch* (see 72.2 SCHEDULE D, CASE III), and, for accounting periods ending after 31 March 1996, by the corporation tax provisions of *FA 1996, Pt IV, Ch II* (see Tolley's Corporation Tax under Gilts and Bonds), these considerations no longer apply.

45 Life Assurance Policies

The headings in this chapter are as follows.

45.1   LIFE ASSURANCE PREMIUM RELIEF

Relief for premiums paid on qualifying life assurance policies (see 45.3 below) ceases to be available for insurances made after 13 March 1984, other than certain deferred annuity contracts (see 45.3(i) below), certain part payments to friendly societies (see 45.3(ii) below) and certain industrial assurance policies (see 45.12(*b*) below). See 65.4 RETIREMENT ANNUITIES AND PERSONAL PENSION SCHEMES as regards certain types of life assurance contract for persons not in pensionable employment which continue to attract full relief against income. Relief ceases for a contract made before 14 March 1984 if the policy is terminated or varied (including the exercise of an option to change the terms of the policy) so as to increase the benefits secured or extend the term of the insurance (disregarding increased benefits in consideration of the cessation of house to house collection of premiums). [*Sec 266(3)(c), 14 Sch 8(3)–(8); FA 1996, s 167(5)(6)*].

Tax relief where applicable is generally given to UK residents (except children under 12), whether they have taxable income or not, by deduction from admissible premiums (see 45.3 below) up to certain limits (see 45.2 below). The deduction is 12½% (but see 45.3(ii) below where relief is by reduction of total income). The deductions will normally be calculated by the life offices etc. (who will recover from the Board) without a specific claim being required. The Board may make regulations to implement this scheme of 'premium relief by deduction'. [*Sec 266(4)(5), 14 Sch 7; FA 1988, s 29; FA 1996, 18 Sch 11(3)(4), 17(1)–(4)(8)*]. Under the scheme relief will normally be allowed without the intervention of a tax office and PAYE taxpayers do not require a coding allowance for premiums.

The Inland Revenue Financial Intermediaries and Claims Office may be contacted in relation to life assurance premium relief on 0151–472 6169 as regards repayments or 0151–472 6152 for technical advice.

45.2   Limits on amounts of admissible premiums

Relief is not given on premiums to the extent that they exceed

(*a*)   **£1,500 or one-sixth of total income**, whichever is the greater. [*Sec 274(1)*]. See also 45.4(*j*) below for married persons and 1.6 ALLOWANCES AND TAX RATES for definition of total income.

(*b*)   £100 for policies not securing a capital sum at death. [*Sec 274(2)*].

The restrictions in (*a*) and (*b*) are not to take into account any additional 'war insurance premiums'. [*Sec 274(4); FA 1996, s 134, 20 Sch 20*]. Where the limits seem likely to be exceeded by the deductions, the Board may require some premiums to be paid in full. Any over- or under-deductions in a year will be adjusted by assessment or claim to repayment. [*14 Sch 4–6; FA 1996, 18 Sch 11(2), 17(5)(7)*].

45.3   Subject to the cessation of relief for policies made after 13 March 1984 (see 45.1 above), **admissible premiums** are as follows.

    (i)   **Life assurance premiums** (and payments under **contracts for deferred annuities** (but see 45.4(*b*) below and note limit at 45.2(*b*) above)) paid by an individual in respect of policies (or deferred annuities) on either the individual's own life or that of his spouse. The insurance or contract must be made by the individual. Policies effected after 19 March 1968 must be 'qualifying policies', see 45.6 below. [*Sec 266(1)–(3)*]. See RETIREMENT ANNUITIES AND PERSONAL PENSION SCHEMES (65) for the special provisions relating to such annuities.

    (ii)   Proportion of members' contributions to trade unions allocated to superannuation benefits in addition to any portion allocated to funeral benefits or life assurance.

         Relief is given by deducting one-half of the portion from total income. A similar deduction applies to a part payment to a registered or incorporated friendly society in respect of an eligible insurance or contract (excluding certain sickness, etc. insurances or contracts made after 31 August 1996). The deduction applies also to payments to an organisation of persons in police service provided the allocated portion is £20 or more per annum. [*Sec 266(6)(7)(13); F(No 2)A 1992, 9 Sch 2; FA 1996, s 171(3)(4)*].

    (iii)   Statutory deductions from salary for deferred pension to widow or widower or provision for children after claimant's death, including similar compulsory deductions under any contract of employment—the relief for such deductions being given at the full basic rate. [*Sec 273; FA 1988, 3 Sch 10*].

Employers' contributions under retirement schemes not approved by the Revenue may be relieved in some circumstances as if they were life assurance premiums paid by the employee, see 66.2 RETIREMENT SCHEMES.

45.4   **Notes**

    (*a*)   Policies as under 45.3(i) above are only eligible for relief if they secure capital sum at *death* whether or not in conjunction with any other benefit e.g. disability benefit or option to receive an annuity.

    (*b*)   No allowance during period of deferment on '*deferred policies*'. [*Sec 266(3)(a)(d)*].

But neither (*a*) nor (*b*) applies to policies (i) in connection with *bona fide* employees' pension schemes as defined or for the benefit of persons engaged in any particular trade, profession, vocation or business, or (ii) taken out by teachers in secondary schools (as so called in 1918) pending setting up of a pension scheme. [*Sec 266(11)*].

    (*c*)   The insurance contract must be made with either (i) insurance company legally established in UK, *or lawfully carrying on business in UK,* (ii) underwriters, (iii) registered or incorporated friendly society, (iv) (deferred annuities) National Debt Commissioners. [*Sec 266(2)(a)(13); F(No 2)A 1992, 9 Sch 2*]. *Note.* Included under (i) is a policy issued and managed overseas but where the premium is paid to the UK branch of the insurance company (Revenue Press Release 4 February 1981).

45.4 Life Assurance Policies

(d)   Premiums allowed only so far as *paid* i.e. not covered by advances (*Hunter v A-G HL 1904, 5 TC 13*), nor repayment of advances (*R v Special Commissioners (ex parte Horner) KB 1932, 17 TC 362*). A premium paid otherwise than in the year in which it becomes due and payable is treated as paid in that year. [*Sec 266(4)*].

Non-residents must pay their premiums in full but will be given relief as appropriate under *Sec 278* (see 51.11 NON-RESIDENTS AND OTHER OVERSEAS MATTERS). Premiums to foreign life assurance companies etc. will be payable in full without relief but see Note in (c) above. A member of the armed forces or the wife or husband of such a member is treated as resident in the UK. [*Sec 266(8)(9), 14 Sch 6; FA 1988, 3 Sch 9; FA 1996, 18 Sch 11(2), 17(5)(7)*].

(e)   No allowance for joint insurance on two directors' lives (*Wilson v Simpson KB 1926, 10 TC 753*).

(f)   *Accident and Sickness Policies.* Relief allowed only on proportion of premium relative to death benefit.

(g)   *Children's Policies.* Premiums allowable if paid by parent for (i) life endowment on his own life, maturing when school fees begin, or when child may go into business, etc., or (ii) for securing series of payments on specified dates if parent dies earlier. But no relief to parent where policy is on life of *child* unless it is an industrial assurance policy or policy issued by a registered or incorporated friendly society on the life of a child or grandchild and the annual premiums do not exceed £64. [*14 Sch 2, 3; F(No 2)A 1992, 9 Sch 18*].

Policy by child on own life. The Board are of the opinion that no relief is in strictness due on premiums on a policy taken out by a child under age twelve, but are prepared to allow relief as follows. An industrial branch policy or friendly society policy as above will receive relief. Where an ordinary branch policy is taken out on the life of a child and is assigned to him or he possesses or acquires the whole interest in the policy, relief on premiums paid by him may be allowed (provided the other conditions are satisfied) where the policy was taken out (*a*) after the child had attained age twelve; (*b*) before 1 March 1979 and before the child attained age twelve; or (*c*) on or after 1 March 1979 before the child attained age twelve and he has attained that age. (Revenue Pamphlet IR 131, SP 11/79, 1 November 1979 relaxing SP 4/79, 28 February 1979.)

(h)   *Borrowings* (at intervals) against life policies may be treated as taxable income. Payments by way of loan under a contract or arrangement, made after 6 April 1949, providing (i) for such payments to be made at intervals during a period dependent on human life, (ii) that the loans, being secured on a life policy, are *not repayable* until the capital benefit accrues payable, and that (iii) the capital benefit *increases* with the length of the period (otherwise than by reason of the insured's right to share in profits of the insurer) are taxable as annual payments under Sch D, Case III, or Case V, if made to a resident under a foreign contract, as income from a foreign possession under *Sec 65(1)*. The section does not apply if the Board are satisfied that it is not one of the objects of the contract, etc., to secure for recipient the equivalent of an annuity equal to the periodic loan payments. [*Sec 554*]. But see 45.15 (*f*) below.

(j)   *Married persons.* Premiums paid by one spouse on the life of the other (in addition to relief on premiums paid on his or her own life) will be eligible for relief to the paying spouse even after divorce, unless the divorce was before 6 April 1979. [*14 Sch 1(1)*]. This treatment is extended to premiums paid by a divorced person on policies taken out prior to the marriage (Revenue Pamphlet IR 1, A31).

The premium relief limits in 45.2 above apply separately and in full to each spouse.

(*k*)   See 45.6 and 45.13 below regarding Qualifying and Non-Qualifying Policies respectively, effected after 19 March 1968.

45.5   WITHDRAWAL OF LIFE ASSURANCE PREMIUM RELIEF

(i)   **Clawback of relief on early surrender etc. within four years**
There was a 'clawback' of the tax relief given on premiums payable on a qualifying policy (see 45.6 below) issued in respect of an insurance made after 26 March 1974 and before 14 March 1984 (when relief ceased to be available) where within four years

(*a*)   the policy was wholly or partly surrendered (including certain loans, see 45.15 (*f*) below), or

(*b*)   there was a sum payable on the policy (other than on death) by way of participation in profits, or

(*c*)   the policy was wholly or partly made paid-up.

The body which issued the policy had to pay the clawback to the Revenue out of the sum falling due at the following rate for 1988/89 and earlier years.

Time of surrender etc.	Clawback of total premiums payable to date	Clawback limit
In year 1 or 2	3/6ths of 30% i.e. 15%	Surrender value less 85% of total premiums payable to date
In year 3	2/6ths of 30% i.e. 10%	Surrender value less 90% of total premiums payable to date
In year 4	1/6th of 30% i.e. 5%	Surrender value less 95% of total premiums payable to date

For partial surrenders etc. the clawback limit could not exceed the value withdrawn or the surrender value if the policy was made paid-up and account was taken of any earlier clawbacks on the same policy. If the annual premium on a policy was increased by more than 25% over the first annual premium (or the annual premium at 26 March 1974 where a policy was issued before that date), the additional premiums and rights obtained were treated as relating to a new policy.

The above provisions did not apply to policies issued in connection with sponsored superannuation schemes or certain approved retirement benefit schemes or if the event under (*a*) or (*c*) arose because of the winding-up of the issuing body. [*Sec 268*]. For replacement of one policy by another, see 45.12(*d*) below.

(ii)   **Clawback of relief on surrender etc. after four years**
If in the fifth or any later year from the making of an insurance either (*a*) or (*b*) (other than on death or maturity) in (i) above occurs and either event has occurred before, a clawback will be made of 12% (15% for 1988/89 and earlier years of assessment) on the lower of the premiums payable in that year and the sum payable by reason of the event.

If two or more events occur in the same year the total clawback is limited to the appropriate percentage (as above) of the premiums payable in that year. Account is taken of any clawback also due under *Sec 268* above on a policy treated as new because of an increase in premiums, see (i) above.

45.6   Life Assurance Policies

The above provisions apply to qualifying policies made after 26 March 1974 but not to industrial assurance policies. [*Sec 269*].

(iii)   **Reduction in relief where clawback occurs**
Where there has been a clawback under (i) or (ii) above, the tax relief on the relevant premiums is reduced by the same amount and the increased liability arising from the loss of the tax relief is set against the clawback suffered (earlier years first), with any excess clawback reclaimable by the taxpayer within six years after the end of the year of assessment in which the event happens.

The relevant premiums are, for (i) above, the total premiums payable under the policy up to the event giving rise to the clawback and, for (ii) above, the premiums payable in the year in which the event happens. [*Sec 270*].

(iv)   Provisions apply for the collection etc. of the clawback by the Revenue from the life office and for the taxpayer to be given, within 30 days by the life office, a statement of the clawback amount and how calculated. [*Sec 272*].

45.6   **QUALIFYING POLICIES**
A policy effected after 19 March 1968 qualifies for life assurance relief only if it provides no 'benefits' other than a capital sum (see 45.12(*a*) below for definition) payable only on death (or on death or earlier disability) or survival for specified term and it also fulfils the conditions set out in 45.7–45.9 below, subject to the exemptions in 45.10 below. [*Sec 266(3)(b), 15 Sch Pt I*].

By concession, free gifts offered as incentives in connection with life insurance policies are disregarded in determining whether a policy is a qualifying policy (and in computing any gain arising in respect of a non-qualifying policy, see 45.13 below), provided that the aggregate cost to the insurer of all gifts in connection with a policy (or a 'cluster' of policies) does not exceed £30. The concession applies in relation to all liabilities unsettled at 7 December 1993. (Revenue Pamphlet IR 1, B42).

See 45.17 below for conditions relating to 'new non-resident policies' issued in respect of an insurance made after 17 November 1983 by a company not resident in the UK.

Note. From 1 April 1976, the certification of new qualifying policies (other than friendly society policies) was transferred from the issuing body to the Revenue (with right of appeal if certificate refused). Certification of policies issued before 1 April 1976 but varied on or after that date remained the responsibility of the life office. [*15 Sch Pt II*]. Certification of policies is to be **abolished** altogether from a day to be appointed for the purpose by the Board, except for certification in relation to a time before that day, and subject to the rights of appeal in relation to refusals. A certificate issued under the old rules continues to be conclusive evidence that a policy is a qualifying policy. [*FA 1995, s 55(1)–(3); FA 1996, s 162(1)*].

45.7   **Policies payable only on death** (or earlier disability) **within a specified period** ('Term Assurance').

(*a*)   If the period *does not exceed ten years*, any surrender value must not exceed the return of premiums paid. [*15 Sch 1(4)*].

(*b*)   If the specified term *exceeds ten years*, premiums must be payable at yearly, or shorter intervals, during at least ten years or three-quarters of the term, whichever is less, or until the assured's earlier death (or disability), and those payable in any one year, excluding any loading for exceptional mortality risk, must not exceed

(i)   twice the amount of the premiums payable in any other year, nor

(ii)   one-eighth of the total premiums which would be payable if the policy ran for the full term (or, if appropriate, the sooner of ten years or three-quarters of the term). [*15 Sch 1(3)(8)*].

(c)   For policies issued on or after 1 April 1976, if the specified term ends after the age of 75 years and the policy provides for any payment on the whole or partial surrender of the policy, the capital sum payable on death must not be less than 75% of the total premiums payable if death occurred at 75 years of age. In the case of a policy payable on one of two lives, the age of the older is taken if the sum is payable on the death of the first, and the age of the younger is taken if payment arises on the death of the survivor. If limited to death after 16 (or some lower age) the benefit on earlier death must not exceed the return of premiums paid. [*15 Sch 1(5)*].

In calculating total premiums, there will be ignored any weighting due to premiums being payable at lesser than annual intervals (generally taken to be 10% if the reduction is not specified) and in calculating the capital sum, the smallest amount is used if more than one is payable. [*15 Sch 1(6)(9); FA 1996, s 167(7)*].

Short-term assurances. A policy will not be a qualifying policy under 45.6 above if the capital sum is payable only if death or disability occurs less than one year after making the insurance. [*15 Sch 10*].

45.8   **Endowment policies.** Term must be for at least ten years, or until the assured's earlier death (or disability). The policy must not provide for any capital benefit to be paid (other than on whole or part surrender of the policy or bonus additions to it or on disability) during its continuance, but it must guarantee on death (or death after 16 or some lower specified age) a sum at least equal to 75% of the total premiums (less any weighting due to premiums being paid at lesser than annual intervals, generally taken to be 10% if the reduction is not specified) which would be payable if the policy ran full term. For a policy effected on or after 1 April 1976 by a person over 55 years of age, the 75% requirement is reduced by 2% for each year the age exceeds 55. If limited to death after 16 (or some lower age) the benefit on earlier death must not exceed the return of premiums paid.

Premiums must be payable annually, or at shorter intervals, for a period of not less than ten years or until death, etc. Limitations (i) and (ii) under 45.7(*b*) above apply, but with exclusion of wording in brackets at end of (ii). For a policy payable on one of two lives, the rules under 45.7(*c*) above apply. [*15 Sch 2; FA 1996, s 167(7)*].

45.9   **Whole-life policies.** Premiums must be payable annually, or at shorter intervals, until the assured's death (or his earlier disability, if so provided) or for a specified period of at least ten years should he live longer than that period. Premium limitations (i) and (ii) under 45.7(*b*) above apply except that the total premiums under (ii) are those for the first ten years or for the specified period, as above, if longer. The provisions under 45.7(*c*) above also apply. [*15 Sch 1(2)*].

45.10   **Exemptions.** The above restrictions do not apply to the following.

(i)   Policies solely for the payment on an individual's death (or disability) of a sum substantially equal to the then balance of a mortgage (repayable by annual, or shorter, instalments) on his residence or business premises. [*Sec 266(10)(a)*].

(ii)   Policies under a sponsored superannuation scheme (as defined by *Sec 624*), if at least half the cost of the scheme is borne by the employer. [*ICTA 1970, s 19(4)(b)*]. This provision was repealed on 6 April 1980 [*FA 1971, 14 Sch Pt 1*] but is continued, for policies issued before that date, by extra-statutory concession (Revenue Pamphlet IR 1, A32).

45.11 Life Assurance Policies

(iii)   Policies issued in connection with approved occupational pension scheme under *Sec 590 et seq.* [*Sec 266(10)(b)*].

Although the above policies are not qualifying policies, relief under 45.1 to 45.4 above is available on premiums paid (subject to the general restrictions) and they are not subject to the charge on life assurance gains (see 45.13 and 45.15 below).

(iv)   Certain policies issued by a friendly society in the course of its tax-exempt life business are qualifying policies. See 31.3 FRIENDLY SOCIETIES.

45.11   **Disqualification of certain life policies.** A policy (issued in the UK or elsewhere) effected in the course of long-term business is not a 'qualifying policy' if it is 'connected with' another policy the terms of which provide benefits greater than would reasonably be expected if any policy 'connected with' it were disregarded.

A policy is 'connected with' another policy if

(*a*)   they are at any time simultaneously in force, and

(*b*)   either of them is issued with reference to the other, or with a view to enabling or facilitating the other to be issued on particular terms. (See Revenue Press Release 16 June 1980 for guidelines.)

This applies to policies issued in respect of insurances made after 25 March 1980 and to an insurance made on or before that date which is connected with one made after it, but not in relation to premiums paid before that date on the earlier policy.

In relation to policies issued in respect of insurances made after 22 August 1983, the above restriction applies where either of the policies concerned provides such excessive benefits as are mentioned above. With respect to payments made after 22 August 1983, this extension of the restriction also applies to insurances made before that date if further premiums exceeding £5 p.a. are made after that date.

A revised definition of 'long-term insurance business' applied before 23 August 1983.

A person issuing a policy which by virtue of the above is not a qualifying policy (or a policy which causes another policy to cease to be a qualifying policy) is required to give written notice of the fact to the Board within three months of issue. The Board may require any person who appears to them to be concerned in the issue of such a policy (but not a solicitor who only gave advice) to provide them with such information as they think necessary, and as that person has or can reasonably obtain, for the purposes of this provision within a specified time of not less than 30 days. The penalty provisions of *TMA s 98* apply. [*15 Sch 14*].

45.12   **Notes**

(*a*)   'Capital sum' includes a series of capital sums, or a sum varying with the circumstances. Bonus additions, an option to take an annuity, a payment on whole or part surrender, or a waiver of premiums in the event of disability *do not constitute* 'benefits'. [*15 Sch 1(7)(9)*].

(*b*)   For *Industrial assurance* policies and *Family Income and Mortgage Protection* policies, see *15 Sch 7–9*. After 1 April 1976, industrial insurance policies are generally regarded as qualifying policies although not within the appropriate conditions. In addition, industrial assurance policies issued in respect of insurances made after 13 March 1984 continue to attract premium relief (see 45.1 above) as if issued on or before that date provided that

(i)   the proposal form was completed on or before that date,

(ii)   the policy was prepared for issue before 1 April 1984, and

(iii)   before 1 April 1984 the policy was permanently recorded in the issuer's books in accordance with its normal business practice. [*14 Sch 8(3)*].

Industrial assurance ceases to be a distinct form of business for tax purposes for accounting periods beginning after 31 December 1995. However, the special treatment afforded to industrial assurance policies will continue to be given to policies issued by any company on or after a day to be appointed for the purpose by the Board, where the company had previously issued qualifying policies in the course of industrial assurance business and was, on 28 November 1995, offering such policies of the same type as those offered on or after the appointed day. [*15 Sch 8A; FA 1996, s 167(1)(8)*].

(c)   A variation after 19 March 1968 to a policy taken out before that date so as to increase benefits or extend term ranks as a new policy. [*14 Sch 8(1)(2)*].

(d)   Where, after 24 March 1982, a qualifying policy is replaced by another qualifying policy as a result of a variation in the life or lives assured (e.g. on marriage or divorce), both policies are treated for the following purposes as a single qualifying policy made at the time of the earlier policy provided that (*a*) any sum becoming payable in connection with the earlier policy is retained by the insurer and applied towards any premium on the later policy and (*b*) no consideration (apart from the benefits under the new policy) is received by any person in connection with the ending of the earlier policy. Any sum applied as in (*a*) is treated neither as a premium for premium clawback purposes (see 45.5 above) nor for the purposes of life assurance gain computations (see 45.13 below) nor as a capital sum received for the latter purposes. The replacement policy is also treated as made at the same time as the original policy for relief purposes (see 45.1 above) provided that the benefits conferred by the replacement policy are substantially equivalent to those under the original policy. [*14 Sch 8(6), 15 Sch 20*]. For the effect of other substitutions for and variations to policies generally, see *15 Sch 17–20* and note concession in Revenue Pamphlet IR 1, A45.

(e)   A body issuing a policy which is certified by the Board as being a qualifying policy (or which is in the appropriate standard form) must, within three months of receipt of a written request by the policyholder, supply a certificate to that effect. Such a certificate must similarly be supplied where a policy is varied in a significant respect, but continues to be a qualifying policy (although certain variations to pre-20 March 1968 policies are ignored for this purpose). [*15 Sch 22*]. This requirement will **cease to apply** following the abolition of certification (see 45.6 above). [*FA 1995, s 55(4); FA 1996, s 162(1)*].

(f)   Any option to vary a policy issued before 1 April 1976 is disregarded until it is exercised and the policy is then subject to the new qualifying conditions. A policy issued after 1 April 1976 with an option to vary the terms or to have another policy issued in substitution for it is only a qualifying policy if all the specified conditions would continue to be satisfied after the exercise of the option. [*15 Sch 19*].

(g)   As a result of legal advice received, the Revenue have not, since 24 February 1988, certified as a qualifying policy any new life assurance policy which may be converted or fundamentally restructured in such a way as to constitute, under contract law, a rescission of the original contract and the creation of a new one, e.g. the conversion of a whole life policy to an endowment policy or vice versa. Such conversions, etc. may arise by means of an agreement between the policyholder and the insurer or by the exercising of an option contained in the terms of the policy. Previously, such alterations were regarded as variations of the existing contract which did not, therefore, prejudice the qualifying status of the policy. Policies certified and sold

45.13 Life Assurance Policies

before 25 February 1988 will not lose their qualifying status even if subsequently converted or restructured. (Revenue Press Release 22 January 1988). Certification is to be abolished (see 45.6 above).

(h) The Revenue may concessionally disregard certain minor infringements of the conditions for recognition as a qualifying policy relating to:

    (i) policies back-dated by not more than three months, which may for certain purposes be treated as if the assurance was made on the earlier date;

    (ii) reductions in first year premiums which do not result in any value being credited to the policyholder;

    (iii) trivial non-recurring infringements of arithmetical tests; and

    (iv) policies which could have been certified as qualifying but which were not so certified when the assurance was made.

(Revenue Pamphlet IR 1, A41).

(i) *Status of certain life insurance policies.* Following a High Court decision in a non-tax case, certain types of contract entered into by life insurance companies and friendly societies, under which the return on death is no greater, or not significantly greater, than on a surrender at the same time, may not in law be life insurance policies. The previously accepted tax status of such policies is to be confirmed, by legislation if necessary. (Revenue Press Release 30 November 1994).

45.13 LIFE ASSURANCE GAINS

If a life policy effected after 19 March 1968 is not a qualifying policy (see 45.6 above), then

(a) no life assurance relief is granted on the premiums [*Sec 266(3)(b)*] (cf. 45.5 above re qualifying policies), and

(b) a gain is regarded as a 'chargeable event' and there is a charge to income tax at the excess of the higher rates over the basic rate on the 'gain' [*Secs 539 et seq.*] (and see (A) below as regards a charge on certain qualifying policies). The gain is for all other purposes treated as an addition to total income.

For the duty of insurers to inform the inspector of chargeable events, see *Sec 552.*

See 45.19 below for 'new non-resident policies' which are not qualifying policies.

A charge under (b) above does not arise if a new policy is issued on exercise of an option under a maturing policy and the proceeds of the maturing policy are fully applied to pay premium(s) under the new policy, *unless* the new policy is issued to a person who was an infant when the maturing policy was issued, and the maturing policy secured a capital sum within a month of his attaining age 25, or on the policy anniversary following his attaining that age. [*Sec 540(2)*].

The 'gain' (taxable as in (b) above) is the excess, over premiums paid, of

    (i) the surrender value of the policy *immediately prior to the death* plus any capital sums received previously (e.g. by surrender of bonus rights, etc.), or

    (ii) any sum received on the *maturity* of the policy, or for the *surrender*, or *assignment* for value, of rights under it (plus any prior capital sums). [*Sec 541*]. But see 45.12(d) above for replacement of a policy.

See 45.6 above as regards certain 'free gifts' given as incentives in relation to the issue of a policy, which are disregarded for these purposes.

See Revenue Pamphlet IR 131, SP 6/92, 3 July 1992 as regards certain accident insurance policies providing cover against dying as a result of an accident, which, from the date of issue of the Statement, are not regarded as life insurance policies for these purposes. The Statement of Practice applies mainly to group policies, under which a gain might otherwise arise on payment of a death benefit as a result of earlier payments under the policy.

See 45.15 below for computation of the gain realised on partial surrenders etc.

If the gain arises to a trust, the settlor is liable as under (b) above [Sec 547(1)(a)], but can recover from the trustees. [Sec 551]. If the gain arises to a close company, it is treated as distributable income for apportionment purposes. [Sec 547(1)(b)]. Following abolition of apportionment for company accounting periods beginning after 31 March 1989, this is replaced by a general charge on companies on gains on policies issued after 13 March 1989. [FA 1989, s 90, 9 Sch].

There is an exemption for gains arising on retirement annuities approved under Sec 621 and occupational pension schemes approved under Sec 590 et seq. See 65 RETIREMENT ANNUITIES AND PERSONAL PENSION SCHEMES, 66 RETIREMENT SCHEMES.

A charge on the gain, as under (b) above, also arises (if the policy was taken out after 19 March 1968 or varied, so as to increase benefits or extend term, after that date) on

(A) a qualifying policy if, within the lesser of ten years from inception or three-quarters of its term, it is surrendered or assigned for value, in whole or in part. Also, if it is converted to a paid-up policy within that period and any of the events as in (i) or (ii) above occur. [Sec 540(1)(b)]. See 45.15 below.

(B) life annuity contracts (including those issued in connection with 'Guaranteed Income Bonds'). The charge is on the total amount received up to and including surrender or assignment (excluding the proportion of any annual receipts already taxed as income) less premium etc. paid. [Secs 542, 543]. For contracts made after 26 March 1974, any gains will be chargeable at the basic rate under Schedule D, Case VI. This is in addition to the charge at the higher rates under the provisions above, and does not apply to gains on certain policies issued by non-UK resident companies within the charge to tax in a territory within the European Economic Area. [Sec 547(6)(6A); FA 1995, s 56(1)]. Capital sums payable on death under contracts made after 9 December 1974 are treated as a surrender of the contract. [Sec 542(2)]. See also 45.15 below.

(C) a capital redemption policy (under which a premium is paid for a return or returns on a specified date or dates in the future). The charge is on the total amounts received up to and including maturity, surrender or assignment (excluding the proportion of any annual receipts already taxed as income) less premium etc. paid. [Sec 545]. Also applicable to companies. See also 45.15(g) below.

Gains on certain policies issued by FRIENDLY SOCIETIES (31) may also be taxable at the basic rate. [Sec 547(7)].

'Assignment' for the above purposes does not include an assignment between spouses living together or by way of security for debt. [Sec 540(4)]. There are exemptions from the general charge under (b) above, and from the charge under (A) and (B) above, for assignees (for money or money's worth) in respect of policies or life annuity contracts issued or made before 26 June 1982 and assigned before that date, who will normally be liable to capital gains tax on their gains. But the original beneficial owner of a policy or contract which has been re-assigned to him is not exempt from the income tax charge on subsequent gains. Also, the exemption is denied where a policy or contract was assigned for money or money's worth before 26 June 1982 and, after 23 August 1982, either

(i) the policy is reassigned for money or money's worth (other than between spouses or as security for a debt or on the discharge of a debt so secured), or

(ii)   further capital is injected, or

(iii)   loans are taken against security of the policy, etc., except that (iii) does not apply

    (a)   unless the policy, etc. was issued in respect of an insurance or contract made after 26 March 1974, and the sum is lent to, or at the direction of, the individual who, at the time of the loan, owns the rights conferred by the policy, etc., or

    (b)   if the policy is a qualifying policy (see 45.6 above), and either a commercial rate of interest is payable on the sum lent, or it is lent to a full-time employee of the issuing body to assist in the purchase or improvement of his only or main residence.

[*Secs 540(3), 542(3), 544*].

Gains arising from partial surrenders prior to an assignment by gift are chargeable on the donor. [*Sec 541(4)*].

'**Top-slicing relief**'. An individual may claim that the additional tax payable by him as a result of (b) above shall be calculated as follows. Divide the gain by the number of *complete* years the policy has run (i) since the previous chargeable event (see 45.15(b) below) or (ii) since the start of the policy if there is no previous chargeable event, or on final termination of the policy. Calculate additional tax in the relevant year (of maturity etc.) payable on the gain as so divided treated as if it were the top slice of the taxpayer's income (but allowing a credit for tax at the basic and, where applicable, lower rates on that amount). Multiply the tax so calculated by the number of complete years the policy has run (as in (i) or (ii)). This gives the total liability on the full gain. This procedure will normally have the effect that the total gain is taxed at lower rates than if it was simply all brought in as additional income of one year. [*Sec 550; F(No 2)A 1992, s 19(2)*]. For this purpose the charge to basic rate income tax on gains under life annuity contracts (see (B) above) and friendly society policies (see above) will be ignored. [*Sec 547(6)(c)(7)*].

Non-residents will not be charged to tax if the proceeds of the policy or contract are not payable in the UK and the policy or contract was made outside the UK by either an overseas branch of a resident insurance company or by a non-resident insurance company (Revenue Pamphlet IR 131, SP 11/80, 9 October 1980).

45.14   *Example*

A single policyholder realises, in 1996/97, a gain of £2,600 on a non-qualifying policy which she surrenders after $2\frac{1}{2}$ years. Her other income for 1996/97 comprises earned income of £25,800 and dividends plus tax credits amounting to £2,425.

The tax chargeable on the gain is calculated as follows.

	Normal basis £	Top-slicing relief claim £
Policy gain	2,600	1,300
Earnings	25,800	25,800
Dividends	2,425	2,425
	30,825	29,525
Personal allowance	3,765	3,765
	£27,060	£25,760

Tax applicable to policy gain
Higher rate

	£	£
£1,560 at 40%	624.00	—
£260 at 40%	—	104.00
	624.00	104.00
Deduct		
Basic rate		
£1,560 at 24%	374.40	—
£260 at 24%	—	62.40
		£41.60

Appropriate multiple 2 × £41.60		£83.20
Tax chargeable lower of	£249.60 and	£83.20

Tax payable is therefore as follows.

3,900 @ 20%	780.00
18,135 @ 24%	4,352.40
2,425 @ 20%	485.00
1,040 @ 24%	249.60
25,500	
1,560 @ 40%	624.00
£27,060	
	6,491.00

Deduct: Tax credits on dividends (£2,425 @ 20%)	485.00	
Basic rate of tax on policy gain (£2,600 @ 24%)	624.00	
Top-slicing relief (£249.60 − £83.20)	166.40	1,275.40
Tax liability (subject to PAYE deductions)		£5,215.60

45.15   **Partial surrenders etc.** The following provisions apply in relation to the charging of income tax at the excess of the higher rates over the basic rate, plus the investment income surcharge (if applicable), on gains realised on the *partial surrender* (or *partial assignment* for money's worth) of life policies, capital redemption policies and annuity contracts.

(*a*)   '**Policy year**' is any twelve months reckoning from the commencement of the policy etc. and subsequent anniversaries. If the final policy year ends in the same year of assessment as the termination of the policy etc. by death, maturity or total surrender, the two periods shall be treated as the final year. [*Sec 546(4)*].

(*b*)   '**Chargeable event**'. Partial surrenders and assignments in any policy year may give rise to a taxable chargeable event at the end of that year. A chargeable event occurs where the 'reckonable aggregate value' (see below) exceeds the 'allowable aggregate amount' (see below).

On termination of a policy (by death, maturity, total surrender or assignment) all gains arising from previous chargeable events are deducted from the overall gain on that policy. A deficiency arising on termination is deductible from total income (but not for purposes of basic rate tax unless it relates to a life annuity contract made after 26 March 1974) insofar as it does not exceed the total gains on previous chargeable events. [*Secs 540–543, 545*].

45.16 Life Assurance Policies

(c) **'Reckonable aggregate value'** is the total value of all surrenders and assignments of the policy since its commencement (but excluding any policy year prior to the first such year falling wholly after 13 March 1975), less the total of such values which have been brought into account in earlier chargeable events. [*Sec 546(1)(2)*].

(d) **'Allowable aggregate amount'** is the total of annual fractions of one-twentieth (with a maximum of 20 twentieths) of the premiums, and lump sums, paid since the policy commenced (but excluding the fractions relating to policy years prior to the first such year falling wholly after 13 March 1975), less the total of such fractions which have been brought into account in earlier chargeable events. [*Sec 546(1)(3)*].

(e) **Bonuses.** Surrender (or automatic payment) of a bonus is treated as a surrender of rights with consequent calculation under (*b*) above. [*Sec 539(4)*].

(f) **Loans** by the body issuing the policy will be treated as surrenders (with consequent calculation under 45.5 (clawback) or (*b*) above (chargeable event)) on policies made after 26 March 1974, except where lent on qualifying policies at a commercial rate of interest or to assist in the purchase or improvement of an only or main residence of a full-time employee of the issuing body or of an insurance association serving the insurance market (see Revenue Pamphlet IR 1, A47). Any repayment of the loan will be treated as a premium when the calculation of any gain is made for the final year. [*Sec 548*]. By concession, a loan-back option exercised in connection with a concurrent retirement annuity contract with the same insurer may not be treated as a surrender. (Revenue Pamphlet IR 1, A42). There is no tax charge on a loan to an elderly person in connection with a life annuity contract to the extent that the interest is eligible for relief under *Sec 365* (see 43.24 INTEREST PAYABLE). [*Sec 548(3)(b)*].

(g) **Capital redemption policies.** Where the sums payable are chargeable as annual payments under Schedule D, no further charge to tax will arise under the above provisions. [*Sec 545(1)(a)*].

(h) **'Top-slicing relief'** applies as under 45.13 above.

45.16 *Example*

Jade takes out a policy on 4 February 1991 for a single premium of £15,000. The contract permits periodical withdrawals.

(i) Jade draws £750 p.a. on 4 February in each subsequent year.

There is no taxable gain because at the end of each policy year the 'reckonable aggregate value' (RAV) does not exceed the 'allowable aggregate amount' (AAA).

	£
At 3.2.95 withdrawals have been	2,250 (RAV)
Deduct $4 \times \frac{1}{20}$ of the sums paid in	3,000 (AAA)
	No gain

(ii) On 20.7.95 Jade withdraws an additional £3,500.

	£
At 3.2.96 withdrawals have been	6,500 (RAV)
Deduct $5 \times \frac{1}{20}$ of the sums paid in	3,750 (AAA)
Chargeable 1995/96	£2,750

(iii)   Jade makes no annual withdrawal on 4.2.96 but on 4.2.97 makes a withdrawal of £1,000.

In the year 1997/98 the position is

	£	£
At 3.2.98 withdrawals have been		7,500
Deduct Withdrawals at last charge		6,500
		1,000 (RAV)
Deduct 7 × $\frac{1}{20}$ of the sums paid in	5,250	
less amount deducted at last charge	3,750	
		1,500 (AAA)
		No gain

(iv)   Jade surrenders the policy on 1.7.98 for £13,250, having made a further £1,000 withdrawal on 4.2.98.

In the year 1998/99, the position is

	£	£
Proceeds on surrender		13,250
Previous withdrawals		8,500
		21,750
Deduct: Premium paid	15,000	
Gains previously charged	2,750	
		17,750
Chargeable 1998/99		£4,000

Notes

(*a*)   The gain on final surrender of the policy is calculated under *Sec 541* (see 45.13 above).

(*b*)   The gains in (ii) and (iv) above are subject to top-slicing relief (see 45.13 above).

45.17   OFFSHORE POLICIES

Conditions. A policy issued in respect of an insurance made after 17 November 1983 by a company resident outside the UK (a '*new non-resident policy*') will not be a qualifying policy under *15 Sch, Pt II* (see 45.6 above) until either

(*a*)   the premiums are payable to, and are business receipts of, a UK branch of the issuing company and the company is lawfully carrying on life assurance business in the UK; or

(*b*)   the policy holder is a UK resident and a portion of the issuing company's income from the investments of its life assurance fund is charged to corporation tax by virtue of *Sec 445*.

[*15 Sch 24; FA 1995, s 55(5)*].

Policies issued under insurances made before 18 November 1983 are not affected by the above unless they are varied after 17 November 1983 so as to increase the benefits secured or to extend the term of the insurance, in which event they are treated as issued after 17 November 1983. A variation includes the exercise of an option. [*15 Sch 27; FA 1995, s 55(7)*].

45.18   **Substitution of policies.** Where one policy is substituted for another and the old policy was a 'new non-resident policy' but the new policy is not, the rules in *15 Sch 17–20* (see 45.12(*d*) above) are modified as follows.

45.19 Life Assurance Policies

(*a*) If the old policy and any related policy (any preceding policy in a chain of substituted policies) would have been, or, where certification was required, would have been capable of being, a qualifying policy were it not for the 'new non-resident policy' rules, then it is assumed to have been a qualifying policy for the purposes of *15 Sch 17(2)*.

(*b*) If the new policy would otherwise be, or, where certification is still required, be capable of being, a qualifying policy, it will nevertheless not qualify unless the circumstances are those specified in *15 Sch 17(3)* (regarding residence, benefits, the issuing company etc.).

(*c*) The company issuing the new policy must certify that the old policy for which it is substituted was issued by a company outside the UK with whom they have arrangements for issuing substitute policies to persons coming to the UK.

The modification in (*c*) above also applied where the old policy was a qualifying policy issued on or before 17 November 1983 which would have been a non-qualifying 'new non-resident policy' if issued after that date while the new policy is issued after that date and is not a 'new non-resident policy'.

If the new policy confers an option to have another policy substituted for it or to have any of its terms changed and thereby falls within *15 Sch 19(3)* it is to be treated for the purposes of that sub-paragraph as having been issued in respect of an insurance made on the same day as the old policy. [*15 Sch 25, 26; FA 1995, s 55(6)*].

45.19   **Tax on chargeable events.** The income tax charge on gains from non-qualifying new non-resident policies is under Schedule D, Case VI and includes basic rate tax as well as the normal charge at higher rates (see 45.13 above). This also applies to '*new offshore capital redemption policies*', i.e. capital redemption policies issued in respect of contracts made after 22 February 1984 by non-UK resident companies. It does not apply to gains on new non-resident policies if the conditions in (*a*) or (*b*) in 45.17 above are fulfilled at all times between the date of issue and the date of the gain, or to gains on certain policies issued by non-UK resident companies within the charge to tax in a territory within the European Economic Area. [*Sec 553(6)(6A)(7)(10); FA 1995, s 56(2); FA 1996, s 168(5)*].

Except as below, the gain which would be chargeable is reduced by multiplying it by the fraction of which the denominator is the number of days for which the policy (and any preceding related policy) has run before the chargeable event and the numerator is the number of those days when the policy holder was a UK resident. No reduction is, however, made where, at any time during the life of the policy, it was held by a trustee resident outside the UK, or by two or more trustees any of whom was so resident, *unless* the policy was issued in respect of an insurance made on or before 19 March 1985 *and* it was on that date held by a trustee resident outside the UK or by two or more trustees any of whom was so resident. The gain thus reduced is chargeable to tax in full under Schedule D, Case VI (see above) but any top-slicing relief due under *Sec 550* (see 45.13 above) is computed by reference to higher (and additional) rate tax only. [*Sec 553(3)–(6)*].

The denominator in the 'appropriate fraction' in the top-slicing relief calculation is altered for these purposes to the number of complete years the policy has run before the chargeable event less any complete years in which the policy holder was not resident in the UK. [*Sec 553(8)*].

Where there is a substitution of policies within 45.18 above and the new policy is a qualifying policy there is no chargeable event on the surrender of rights under the old policy and the new policy is treated as having been issued in respect of an insurance made on the same day as the old policy. [*Sec 553(1)*].

If at any time a previously qualifying 'new non-resident policy' ceases to fulfil the conditions of either (*a*) or (*b*) in 45.17 above it is brought within the chargeable events legislation of *Sec 539 et seq.* from that time onwards. [*Sec 553(2); FA 1995, s 55(8)*].

The provisions of *Sec 550(5)* regarding the operation of top-slicing relief when there is more than one chargeable event do not apply to 'new non-resident policies' or to 'new offshore capital redemption policies'. [*Sec 553(9)*].

46 Losses

Cross-references. See 19 COMPENSATION FOR LOSS OF EMPLOYMENT; 51.12 NON-RESIDENTS AND OTHER OVERSEAS MATTERS for trade carried on and controlled abroad; 53 PARTNERSHIPS; 68.13 SCHEDULE A; 71.44 SCHEDULE D, CASES I AND II for loss of loans; 73.3 SCHEDULE D, CASES IV AND V for deficiencies on overseas lettings; 74 SCHEDULE D, CASE VI.

46.1 Restrictions on the use of losses apply to companies where control changes [*Secs 768, 769*] for which see Tolley's Corporation Tax. Also in relation to certain company partnership arrangements [*Sec 116*], see 53.14 PARTNERSHIPS. Loss relief cannot be claimed in respect of the special type of bonus issue described in *Sec 237* (see 3.18 ANTI-AVOIDANCE) nor for certain partnerships dealing in commodity futures (see 3.20 ANTI-AVOIDANCE). See also under 3 ANTI-AVOIDANCE generally for restrictions regarding certain transactions in securities etc. See Tolley's Capital Gains Tax for capital losses. See 46.10 below for other restrictions.

Headings in this chapter are as follows.

46.2 **TRADING ETC. LOSSES**

Relief may be obtained for trading losses

(a) by **Set-off** against other income in same year of assessment (and succeeding year if trade etc. still carried on, or preceding year where post-Finance Act 1994 provisions apply). See 46.3 to 46.11 below.

(b) by **Carry-forward** against subsequent profits of the same trade. See 46.13 below.

(c) by carry-back of **Losses in early years of a trade.** See 46.14 below.

(d) by carry-back of a **Terminal Loss.** See 46.16 below.

No part of any loss relieved under (a) or (c) above for a year of assessment is available for relief in subsequent years. [*Sec 382(3) as originally enacted*].

Where a loss can be relieved under more than one head and it is sufficiently large, the taxpayer can select the order in which the different heads are to be applied, but the whole of the income or profits available for relief under one head must be relieved before passing to the next (*Butt v Haxby Ch D 1982, 56 TC 547*).

For certain pre-trading expenses treated as a trading loss, see 71.75 SCHEDULE D, CASES I AND II. For other reliefs claimable by companies, see Tolley's Corporation Tax (under Losses).

Relief against income may be obtained for losses on shares in unquoted trading companies. See 46.19 below.

See 78.33 SELF-ASSESSMENT for further provisions regarding claims for a loss incurred in one year of assessment to be carried back to an earlier year.

46.3   **SET-OFF OF TRADING LOSSES ETC. AGAINST OTHER INCOME** [*Sec 380*]

Pre-Finance Act 1994. The following provisions apply **in respect of losses sustained in 1995/96 and earlier years in trades, etc. commenced before 6 April 1994. They do not apply to trades, etc. commenced on or after that date.** Subject as below, on a claim being made within two years of the end of any year of assessment, a taxpayer may elect to set against income of that year (i) **any loss he sustained in that year** in a trade, profession, employment or vocation carried on by him either solely or in partnership, or from woodlands assessed under Sch D [*Sec 380(4)*], and (ii) **any loss so sustained in the last preceding year** (so far as not already relieved, and provided the taxpayer still carries on the trade, etc.), and discharge or repayment of tax may be claimed accordingly. Where relief is claimed for a year under (ii) above, it is given in priority to relief under (i) above in respect of a loss sustained in that year. [*Sec 380(1)(2)*]. The order of priority of relief for a loss for which claims are made under both (i) and (ii) above is determined according to the order in which claims are made or, if they are made at the same time, as specified by the claimant. (Revenue Tax Bulletin May 1992 p 20).

For late claims see 46.11(*c*) below.

'*Losses*' means losses computed in the same way as trading profits are computed under Sch D, Case I or II. [*Sec 382(4)*]. This refers to computation of the amount of the loss, and not to the basis period by reference to which a loss is to be computed (*Gascoine v Wharton (Sp C 67) [1996] SSCD 135*). In practice, claims for losses of an accounting year ending in the year of assessment are generally accepted (see 46.11(*a*) below).

Post-Finance Act 1994. The following provisions apply **in respect of losses sustained in 1994/95 and subsequent years in trades, etc. commenced after 5 April 1994 and in respect of losses sustained in 1996/97 and subsequent years in trades, etc. commenced on or before that date.** [*FA 1994, s 209(7)(9); FA 1995, s 118*]. Where in a year of assessment a person sustains a loss in a trade, profession, vocation or employment, carried on solely or in partnership, he may make a claim, within, for 1996/97 and later years, twelve months after 31 January following that year of assessment (for earlier years, two years after the end of that year), for relief against income (i) of the year in which the loss is incurred, or (ii) of the year preceding that in which the loss is incurred. Where, against income of the same year, claims are made both under (i) in respect of that year's loss and under (ii) in respect of the following year's loss, (i) takes precedence. [*Sec 380(1)(2); FA 1994, s 209(1), 20 Sch 8*]. See above for the order of priority where both claims are made for the same loss.

For late claims see 46.11(*c*) below.

'*Losses*' means losses computed in the same way **and in respect of the same basis period** as profits are computed under Schedule D, Case I or II (see 71.11 to 71.19 SCHEDULE D, CASES I AND II for basis period rules). Where, as a result of basis periods overlapping, an amount of loss would otherwise fall to be included in the computations for two successive years of assessment, it is not to be so included for the second of those years. As regards trades, etc. commenced before 6 April 1994, this definition applies for 1997/98 and subsequent years ('losses' being defined as above for earlier years). [*Sec 382(3)(4); FA 1994, s 209(3)(8); FA 1995, s 118*].

Transition from pre- to post-Finance Act 1994 provisions. During the transitional period, relief under *Sec 380* may be claimed for the same year under both the old rules (e.g. under *Sec 380(1)*) and the new rules (e.g. under *Sec 380(1)(b)*). Since there is no statutory order of priority in these circumstances, reliefs are given in the order which saves most tax.

46.4 Losses

In practice, the taxpayer may choose the order in which reliefs are given. (Revenue Tax Bulletin December 1994 p 184).

46.4   *Examples*

Business commenced before 6 April 1994
Y, a single man, has been carrying on a trade for some years and prepares accounts to 31 December each year. His results as adjusted for tax for the three years to 31 December 1996 are as follows.

	Trading profit/(loss) £		Other income £
31.12.94	10,000	1995/96	5,000
31.12.95	(20,000)	1996/97	9,000
31.12.96	(6,000)	1997/98	6,000
31.12.97	12,000		

Y claims relief under *Sec 380(1)* and *(2)* (as originally enacted) for the 1995/96 loss, and under *Sec 380(1)(a)* (as amended) for the 1996/97 loss. The assessments for the relevant years are then as follows.

1995/96	£	£
Trading income (year ended 31.12.94)		10,000
Other income		5,000
Total income		15,000
Deduct Loss 1995/96 (*Sec 380(1)*)		15,000
		—

1996/97		
Trading income (note (*a*))		—
Other income		9,000
		9,000
Deduct Loss 1995/96 (balance) (*Sec 380(2)*)	5,000	
Loss 1996/97 (*Sec 380(1)(a)*)	4,000	9,000
		—

1997/98		
Trading income		12,000
Deduct Loss 1996/97 (balance b/f) (*Sec 385*)		2,000
		10,000
Other income		6,000
Assessable 1997/98		£16,000

Utilisation of losses

1995/96		
Loss available		20,000
Deduct Utilised 1995/96	15,000	
1996/97	5,000	20,000

	£	£
1996/97		
Loss available		6,000
Deduct Utilised 1996/97	4,000	
1997/98	2,000	6,000

Alternatively, L could claim relief for the 1995/96 loss only under *Sec 380(2)* (as originally enacted), and for the 1996/97 loss under *subsections (a)* and *(b)* of *Sec 380(1)* (as amended). The assessments for the relevant years would then be as follows.

	£
1995/96	
Trading income (year ended 31.12.94)	10,000
Other income	5,000
Total income	15,000
Deduct Loss 1996/97 (*Sec 380(1)(b)*)	6,000
Assessable 1995/96	£9,000

	£
1996/97	
Trading income (note *(a)*)	—
Other income	9,000
	9,000
Deduct Loss 1995/96 (*Sec 380(2)*)	9,000
	—

	£
1997/98	
Trading income	12,000
Deduct Loss 1995/96 (balance b/f)(*Sec 385*)	11,000
	1,000
Other income	6,000
Assessable 1997/98	£7,000

	£	£
Utilisation of losses		
1995/96		
Loss available		20,000
Deduct Utilised 1996/97	9,000	
1997/98	11,000	20,000

	£
1996/97	
Loss available	6,000
Deduct Utilised 1995/96	6,000

This could enable L to use his personal allowances and lower rate band in both 1995/96 and 1997/98, rather than only in 1997/98.

Note

(*a*) Under the current year basis transitional provisions (see 71.20 SCHEDULE D, CASES I AND II), the 1996/97 trading income assessment is based on the profits of the two years to 31.12.96. Since a loss was incurred in both those years, the assessment is nil.

46.4 Losses

Business commenced after 5 April 1994

L, a single woman, commences to trade on 1 July 1994, preparing accounts to 30 June, and has the following results (as adjusted for tax purposes and after capital allowances) for the first four years.

	Profit/(loss)
	£
Year ended 30 June 1995	9,000
Year ended 30 June 1996	3,000
Year ended 30 June 1997	(1,000)
Year ended 30 June 1998	(7,000)

L has other income of £6,000 for 1997/98 and £5,800 for 1998/99, having had no other income in the earlier years.

The taxable profits for the first four tax years of the business are as follows.

	£
1994/95 (1.7.94–5.4.95) (£9,000 × 9/12)	6,750*
1995/96 (y/e 30.6.95)	9,000
1996/97 (y/e 30.6.96)	3,000
1997/98 (y/e 30.6.97)	Nil
1998/99 (y/e 30.6.98)	Nil

* Overlap relief accruing – £6,750.

L claims relief under *Sec 380(1)(a)* (set-off against income of the same year) for the 1997/98 loss (£1,000). She also claims relief under *Sec 380(1)(b)* (set-off against income of the preceding year) for the 1998/99 loss (£7,000), with a further claim being made under *Sec 380(1)(a)* for the balance of that loss.

The tax position for 1997/98 and 1998/99 is as follows.

	£
1997/98	
Total income before loss relief	6,000
Deduct Claim under *Sec 380(1)(a)* note (a)	1,000
	5,000
Deduct Claim under *Sec 380(1)(b)*	5,000
Revised total income	Nil

	£
1998/99	
Total income before loss relief	5,800
Deduct Claim under *Sec 380(1)(a)*	2,000
Revised total income	3,800
Deduct Personal allowance	3,765
Taxable income	£35

Loss utilisation

	£
1997/98	
Loss available under *Sec 380(1)(a)*	1,000
Deduct Utilised in 1997/98	1,000
	══
Loss available under *Sec 380(1)(b)*	7,000
Deduct Utilised in 1997/98	5,000
Loss available for relief in 1998/99 under *Sec 380(1)(a)*	£2,000
	──
1998/99	
Balance of loss available under *Sec 380(1)(a)*	2,000
Deduct Utilised in 1998/99	2,000
	══

Note

(*a*)   Where losses of two different years are set against the income of one tax year, then, regardless of the order of claims, relief for the current year's loss is given in priority to that for the following year's loss (see 46.3 above). This is beneficial to the taxpayer in this example as it leaves £2,000 of the 1998/99 loss to be relieved in that year.

Losses in early years—business commenced after 5 April 1994

Q commenced trading on 1 February 1995 and prepared accounts to 31 December. He made a trading loss of £20,900 in the 11 months to 31 December 1995 and profits of £18,000 and £16,000 in the years to 31 December 1995 and 1996 respectively. He has substantial other income for 1994/95 and 1995/96 and makes claims under *Sec 380* for both years.

Taxable profits/(allowable losses) are as follows.

	£	£
1994/95 (1.2.95–5.4.95) (£20,900) × 2/11		(3,800)
1995/96 (1.2.95–31.1.96)		
1.2.95–31.12.95	(20,900)	
Less already allocated to 1994/95	3,800	
	(17,100)	
1.1.96–31.1.96 £18,000 × 1/12	1,500	
		(15,600)
1996/97 (y/e 31.12.96)		18,000
(Overlap relief accruing—£1,500)		
1997/98 (y/e 31.12.97)		16,000

Notes

(*a*)   Losses available for relief for 1994/95 and 1995/96 are £3,800 and £15,600 respectively. If both years' losses are carried forward under *Sec 385* instead of being set against other income (under either *Sec 380* or *Sec 381*), the aggregate loss of £19,400 will extinguish the 1996/97 profit and reduce the 1997/98 profit by £1,400. Note that although the actual loss was £20,900, there is no further amount available for carry-forward: the difference of £1,500 has been used in aggregation in 1995/96.

46.5 Losses

(b)   The net profit for the first three accounting periods is £13,100 (£18,000 + £16,000 − £20,900). The net taxable profit for the first four tax years is £14,600 (£18,000 + £16,000 − £3,800 − £15,600). The difference of £1,500 represents the overlap relief accrued (see 71.19 SCHEDULE D, CASES I AND II). Note that the overlap profit of £1,500 is by reference to an overlap period of *three* months, i.e. 1.2.95 to 5.4.95 (two months—overlap profit nil) and 1.1.96 to 31.1.96 (one month—overlap profit £1,500).

46.5   **SET-OFF OF TRADING LOSSES ETC. AGAINST CAPITAL GAINS** [*FA 1991, s 72*]

Where losses arise in 1991/92 and subsequent years and a person makes a claim under *Sec 380* as in 46.3 above, a further claim may be made in the same notice of claim for the determination of the '*relevant amount*', which is so much of the trading loss as

(a)   cannot be set off against the claimant's income for the year of claim, and

(b)   has not already been relieved for any other year.

A separate claim for relief under *FA 1991, s 72* will be accepted where (i) relief under *Sec 380* had previously been claimed and a claim under *FA 1991, s 72* could have been made, (ii) a separate claim under *FA 1991, s 72* is made within the time limits for the original *Sec 380* claim, (iii) after the *Sec 380* relief there is a balance of unrelieved trading losses, and (iv) all other conditions for *FA 1991, s 72* relief are satisfied. (Revenue Tax Bulletin August 1993 p 87).

The claim is not deemed to be determined until the relevant amount for the year can no longer be varied, whether by the Commissioners on appeal or on the order of any court.

The relevant amount, as finally determined, is to be treated for the purposes of capital gains tax as an allowable loss accruing to the claimant in the year up to the '*maximum amount*', i.e. the amount on which the claimant would be chargeable to capital gains tax for the year, disregarding the effect of this provision and of the capital gains tax annual exemption. In computing the maximum amount, no account is taken of any event occurring after the determination of the relevant amount and in consequence of which the maximum amount might otherwise be reduced by virtue of any capital gains tax legislation. Thus if, as a result of a subsequent reduction in the chargeable gains against which the maximum amount is set, the maximum amount exceeds those chargeable gains, the excess is carried forward as an allowable capital loss.

Losses claimed under this provision are relieved in priority to allowable capital losses brought forward.

No amount treated as an allowable loss under this provision may be deducted from chargeable gains accruing in a year of assessment which begins after the claimant has ceased to carry on the trade in which the loss was sustained.

Relief under this provision is treated in the same way as relief under *Sec 380* as regards prevention of double relief (see 46.2 above, 46.13 below) and set-off of capital allowances (see 46.7 below). [*FA 1991, s 72; FA 1994, 26 Sch Pt V(24)*].

46.6   *Example*

M has carried on a trade for some years, preparing accounts to 30 June each year. For the year ended 30 June 1995, he makes a trading profit of £20,000, and for the year ended 30 June 1996 he makes a trading loss of £17,000. His other income for 1996/97 amounts to £2,000. He makes a capital gain of £11,700 and a capital loss of £1,000 for 1996/97 and has capital losses brought forward of £5,800. He makes claims for loss relief, against income and gains of 1996/97, under *Sec 380(1)(a)* and *FA 1991, s 72* respectively.

Calculation of 'relevant amount'

	£
Trading loss—year ended 30.6.96	17,000
Relieved against income for 1996/97 (note (a))	12,000
Relevant amount	£5,000

Calculation of 'maximum amount'

	£
Gains for 1996/97	11,700
Deduct Losses for 1996/97	(1,000)
Unrelieved losses brought forward	(5,800)
Maximum amount	£4,900

Relief under *FA 1991, s 72*

	£	£
Gains for the year		11,700
Losses for the year	1,000	
Relief under *FA 1991, s 72*	4,900	
		5,900
Gain covered by annual exemption		£5,800
Capital losses brought forward and carried forward		£5,800

Loss memorandum

	£
Trading loss	17,000
Claimed under *Sec 380(1)(a)*	(12,000)
Claimed under *FA 1991, s 72*	(4,900)
Unutilised loss	£100

Note

(a) Under the current year basis transitional provisions (see 71.20 SCHEDULE D, CASES I AND II), the 1996/97 trading income assessment is based on one-half of the profits of the two years to 30.6.96. Since a loss was incurred in the year to 30.6.95, only the profit of the year to 30.6.96 is taken into account, so that the 1996/97 assessment on trading income is £10,000.

(b) In this example, £500 of the annual capital gains tax exemption is wasted, but the brought forward capital losses are preserved for carry-forward against gains of future years. If M had *not* made the claim under *FA 1991, s 72*, his net gains for the year of £10,700 would have been reduced to the annual exempt amount of £6,300 by deducting £4,400 of the losses brought forward. A further £1,400 would remain available for carry-forward against future gains and a further £4,900 of trading losses would have been available for carry-forward against future trading profits or for relief under *Sec 380(1)(b)* against income (and, if claimed, against gains) for 1995/96. So the effect of the claim is to preserve capital losses at the expense of trading losses.

46.7 TREATMENT OF CAPITAL ALLOWANCES

For 1996/97 and earlier years as regards businesses commenced before 6 April 1994 (see below for later years and as regards businesses commenced on or after that date), a loss for *Sec 380* purposes may be **increased**, or **created**, by treating as a deduction in computing the trading results for that year any **capital allowances** due for the *year of assessment for which the year of loss is the basis year* (so far as they exceed balancing charges for that year of assessment, as reduced by any capital allowances brought forward from earlier years which would, without those balancing charges, be ineffective in that year). [*Sec 383; FA 1994, s 214(1)(b)*]. For this purpose the basis year for any year of assessment is the tax year which coincides with, or contains the end of, the relevant basis period as defined for capital allowances by *CAA 1990, s 160*, but where, under this definition, a year of assessment would be the basis year for itself and also another year of assessment it is to be the basis year for the former year only. [*Sec 383(5)(a)*].

But where the capital allowances to be taken into account are (*a*) those for the year of claim itself, being its own basis year, or (*b*) where *Sec 380(2)* (*as originally enacted*) is invoked (see 46.3(ii) above), those for the preceding year, the allowances claimable are limited, under (*a*), to the amount of such allowances non-effective in the year of claim, or, under (*b*), to the amount non-effective in both that and the preceding year. [*Sec 383(3)*].

Capital allowances due for a year of assessment do not include such allowances brought forward from earlier years, but, for the purpose of offsetting profits, allowances for an earlier year are to be applied in priority to allowances for a later year. [*Sec 383(5)(b)(d)*].

On a cessation of business it is concessional practice, where this treatment would otherwise result in a loss of relief, to treat capital allowances brought forward as a *reduction* of the profits of the final year (instead of an offset against the assessment) (Revenue Pamphlet IR 1, A8).

Except as regards partners in cases of actual or notional discontinuance, or where a terminal loss claim is made under *Sec 388* (see 46.16 below), any capital allowances for a given year which are used as above for relief under *Sec 380* are, to that extent, treated as having been effectively allowed for all tax purposes.

Where a partner makes a *Sec 380* claim which includes capital allowances, the written consent is required of all persons (or their personal representatives) engaged in carrying on the trade from the end of the year of loss to the making of the claim, except if the loss occurred before an event treated as a discontinuance of the trade, no consent is required from any person so engaged in the trade only since the discontinuance. [*Sec 383(9)(10)*].

Order of use. Where a loss increased or created under the above provisions is not wholly used, the actual loss sustained, if any, is used first, then any capital allowances. [*Sec 383(6)*].

For 1994/95 and subsequent years as regards businesses commenced after 5 April 1994 and for 1997/98 and subsequent years as regards businesses commenced on or before that date, capital allowances are treated as trading expenses of periods of account (see 10.1, 10.2(vi) CAPITAL ALLOWANCES). They are thus automatically included in the amount of any trading loss (as adjusted for tax purposes).

Transitional position. Where, in a continuing business, there is a loss in the accounts for the year ending in 1995/96 (i.e. the year of loss is 1995/96), that year is not the basis period for 1996/97 (or any other year of assessment) under the current year basis transitional rules (see 71.20 SCHEDULE D, CASES I AND II), so that no capital allowances are strictly available to augment a loss claim for 1995/96. The Revenue will, however, not refuse a claim under *Sec 383* for 1995/96 provided that the allowances claimed are those which would have been available if the preceding year basis had continued to apply for 1996/97, and that the claim includes an undertaking that any allowances so relieved will be deducted from those available for claim in 1996/97, including any to be given effect by set-off against any balancing charges arising in that year. Where the allowances so claimed for 1995/96 exceed those available for 1996/97, the excess is recovered as a balancing charge for 1996/97. (Revenue Tax Bulletin February 1996 pp 286–289).

46.8   *Example*

A carries on a trade for which accounts are prepared to 31 December each year. The results for the two years ended 31 December 1994 are as follows.

Year	Sch D, Case I profit
31.12.93	£25,000
31.12.94	£4,500

	Capital Allowances
1994/95	£10,000
1995/96	£6,100

The assessment for 1994/95 would be as follows.

	£
Case I profit—year ended 31.12.93	25,000
Deduct Capital allowances	10,000
Adjusted Case I profit	15,000
Deduct Claim under *Sec 380(1)*	1,600
Taxable income	£13,400

Utilisation of losses under *Sec 380(1)*

Loss available for 1994/95

	£
1995/96 assessment	
Case I profit—year ended 31.12.94	4,500
Deduct Capital allowances (part) ·	4,500
	—
Available for claim under *Sec 380(1)*	
Capital allowances (balance)	£1,600

For the years ended 31 December 1995 and 31 December 1996, a Schedule D, Case I loss of £10,000 and profit of £15,000 arise respectively, and the capital allowance computation (all relating to plant and machinery) for 1996/97 is as follows.

	£
WDV b/f	36,000
additions (year to 31.12.95)	4,000
(year to 31.12.96)	8,000
disposals (year to 31.12.95	(6,000)
(year to 31.12.96)	(18,000)
	24,000
Writing down allowance	6,000
WDV c/f	18,000

46.9 Losses

The allowances which may be claimed in augmentation of the £10,000 loss for 1995/96 are those which would have been available if the preceding year basis had continued to apply for 1996/97, i.e. those which would have been available for a basis period year ended 31 December 1995, as follows.

	£
WDV b/f	36,000
additions	4,000
disposals	(6,000)
	34,000
Writing down allowance	8,500

The loss available for 1995/96 is thus (10,000 + £8,500 =) £18,500.

The capital allowances available for 1996/97 (£6,000 as above) are reduced by the allowance brought forward for relief in 1995/96 (£8,500), so that a balancing charge of £2,500 arises in 1996/97.

Note

(a) It is not obligatory to include capital allowances in a *Sec 380* claim, or, as in this example, to create a loss by taking capital allowances into account. If A's income had been lower, he might have wasted personal reliefs by claiming the loss relief of £1,600.

46.9 **ORDER OF SET-OFF AGAINST INCOME** [*Sec 380*]

A loss on a source which, had it been profitable, would have produced earned income (see 1.7 ALLOWANCES AND TAX RATES) was previously set first against the earned income of the taxpayer, then against his unearned income, then (unless specific claim was made) against, first, earned and then unearned income of the spouse. Similar, *but converse*, treatment for a loss on a source of unearned income, e.g. sleeping partnership. [*Sec 382(1)(2)*]. For this purpose, the income of the wife for the part of the year of marriage following the marriage was also treated as income of the husband. [*Sec 279(7)*]. These provisions are, however, repealed in relation to relief given for 1990/91 and subsequent years of assessment. [*FA 1988, 14 Sch Pt VIII*].

46.10 **RESTRICTIONS ON ABOVE RELIEFS**

(a) **Non-commercial basis** [*Sec 384; FA 1994, ss 214(1)(c), 216(3)(d); FA 1996, s 134, 20 Sch 25*]. As regards losses (and capital allowances) which would normally form the basis of relief as above, **relief under** *Sec 380* **will not be given unless**, for the year of assessment concerned (or by the end of it, if the trading method was changed during that year), the trade, profession or vocation was carried on

   (i) on a commercial basis, and

   (ii) with a view to realisation of profit in that trade, etc., or any larger undertaking of which it forms part.

The test is a subjective one – see *Walls v Livesey (Sp C 4), [1995] SSCD 12* on similar wording in *Sec 504(2)(a)*. In *Wannell v Rothwell Ch D, 1996 STI 605* an individual's speculative dealing in stocks and shares and commodity futures was held to be trading but not on a commercial basis.

A trade is treated as complying with the requirement at (ii) above if at the relevant time it was being carried on so as to afford a reasonable expectation of profit.

(The above restrictions do not apply to losses incurred in the exercise of functions conferred by or under any enactment, including a local or private Act.)

(b)   **Farming and market gardening** [*Sec 397; FA 1994, s 214(3); FA 1996, s 134, 20 Sch 27*]. Except as below, **relief will not be given under** *Sec 380* above for any loss (or any related capital allowances under *Sec 383* above) incurred in a trade of farming or market gardening if losses from that trade, computed under the normal Schedule D, Case I rules but ignoring capital allowances, were also incurred in each of the five years preceding the year of assessment. Similarly, if such a trade is carried on by a company a loss incurred in any accounting period may not be set off against total profits (under *Sec 393(2)* or *Sec 393A(1)*, see Tolley's Corporation Tax) if there would still be a loss if capital allowances were ignored and there was a loss (similarly computed) in each of the chargeable periods wholly or partly comprised in the five years preceding that accounting period.

Disallowance under *Sec 397* **does not apply if:**

(i)   the farming, etc., is part of, and ancillary to, a larger trading undertaking, or

(ii)   the farming, etc., activities in the year are carried on in a way which might reasonably be expected to produce profits in the future and the activities in the preceding five years could not reasonably have been expected to become profitable until after the year under review. [*Sec 397(3)(4)*].

See 71.56(d) SCHEDULE D, CASES I AND II for relief for repairs etc. on owner-occupied farms.

The Revenue concessionally extend the five year time limits above to eleven years from commencement in the case of a thoroughbred horse blood stock breeder, provided that the business is potentially profitable. (Revenue Inspector's Manual, IM 2350g).

(c)   **Leasing by individuals.** [*Sec 384(6)–(8); FA 1994, s 214(2)*]. Where an individual (alone or in partnership) incurs expenditure on machinery or plant for leasing in the course of a trade, any capital allowances are not to be included (either under *Sec 383* above or otherwise) in calculating loss relief under *Sec 380* above unless the individual carries on the trade for a continuous period of at least six months in, or beginning or ending in, the year of loss (i.e. the tax year in which the loss is sustained) and he devotes substantially the whole of his time to the trade throughout the year of loss or, if the trade begins or ceases (or both) in that year, for a continuous period of at least six months beginning or ending in that year. This prohibition also applies if the asset is not leased but payments in the nature of royalties or licence fees are to accrue from rights granted in connection with it. Any relief given will be withdrawn by assessment under Schedule D, Case VI. The foregoing provisions are without prejudice to *CAA 1990, s 142* (see 46.10(d) and (e) below). For capital allowances on assets not leased in the course of a trade, see 10.28(D) CAPITAL ALLOWANCES.

First-year allowances—

(d)   **Leasing partnerships.** [*CAA 1990, s 142(1)(4)*]. Where expenditure is incurred on machinery or plant for leasing in the course of a trade carried on, or to be carried on, by a partnership including a company and an individual (with or without other partners), any loss arising from a first-year allowance (where available—see 10.27 CAPITAL ALLOWANCES) on that expenditure will not be allowed as set-off against the general income of the individual under *Sec 380*. For this purpose, letting a ship on charter will be regarded as leasing.

46.11 Losses

(e) **First-year allowances—arrangements.** [*CAA 1990, s 142(2)*]. Where an individual incurs expenditure giving rise to a first-year allowance (see (d) above), no relief will be given to him for that allowance under *Sec 380* if, under an arrangement or scheme, a tax saving was expected as the sole or main benefit of the expenditure and (i) he was in partnership then or later, or (ii) he transferred the trade etc., or the relevant asset, to a connected person, or (iii) he transferred the asset to any person at lower than the open market price.

Any relief given will be withdrawn under (d) or (e) above by assessment under Schedule D, Case VI. [*CAA 1990, s 142(3)*].

46.11 **NOTES** [*Sec 380*]

(a) **Apportionments in arriving at amount of loss.** *The following comments apply as regards losses sustained in 1996/97 and earlier years in trades, etc. commenced before 6 April 1994.* Relief claimed under *Sec 380* is in strictness available for the loss which arose in the year of assessment, but by long-standing concessionary practice (confirmed by Revenue Pamphlet IR 1 (November 1995 Supplement), A87), relief is allowed for the loss of the year to the normal accounting date in the tax year (i.e. the 'accounts basis'). This does not, however, apply:

(i) to the first three years of assessment of a new business (or in the fourth year where the third year's assessment was adjusted under *Sec 62*, see 71.4 SCHEDULE D, CASES I AND II);

(ii) to any year of assessment immediately following a year for which relief under either *Sec 380* or *Sec 381* (see 46.14 below) has been allowed on the strict basis of the loss of the year to 5 April;

(iii) in the year of assessment of cessation; or

(iv) to a loss made by a partner in a year during which a partnership change has taken place for which a continuation election has been made under *Sec 113(2)* (see 53.6 PARTNERSHIPS) and relief under *Sec 381* (see 46.14 below) could be claimed by any partner for that year.

These exclusions are by reference to the year of assessment in which the loss was sustained, not that for which relief is claimed. Where an exclusion applies, or where the claimant does not wish the concessionary practice to be applied, the loss must be calculated on the strict basis. Where losses are apportioned on the strict basis, profits must be similarly apportioned in determining the loss (if any) available for relief. Any balance of loss unutilised is available for carry forward (see 46.13 below).

Example

A long-established business has the following agreed results.

Year ended 30 September 1991	Profit	£25,000
Year ended 30 September 1992	Profit	£20,000
Year ended 30 September 1993	Loss	£50,000
Year ended 30 September 1994	Profit	£30,000

If relief is claimed under *Sec 380* on the strict fiscal year basis, the loss sustained in 1992/93 is (£25,000 – £10,000 =) £15,000, which may be set against the £25,000 assessable on the preceding year basis for 1992/93. The loss sustained in 1993/94 is (£25,000 – £15,000 =) £10,000, which may be set against the £20,000 assessable on the preceding year basis for 1993/94. The balance of losses unrelieved (£25,000) may be carried forward and set against the 1995/96 assessment of £30,000.

If relief is instead claimed on the accounts year basis, the entire loss of £50,000 is available for 1993/94 against the £20,000 trading profits assessable for that year (and against any other 1993/94 and, if so claimed, 1994/95 income). Any unrelieved balance is then set against the 1995/96 assessment of £30,000.

Cessation adjustment. Where a business ceases in 1996/97 or earlier (or in 1997/98 where the Revenue have given a direction under *FA 1994, 20 Sch 3(2)* (see 71.24 SCHEDULE D, CASES I AND II) that the pre-*FA 1994* provisions shall continue to apply) and relief is claimed under *Sec 380* for the loss of the year of assessment of cessation, then if *Sec 380* relief has been allowed for the penultimate year on the accounts basis, the loss incurred in that year after the accounting date will not be relieved. In these circumstances, whether or not terminal loss relief is claimed under *Sec 388* (see 46.16 below), concessionary *Sec 380* relief is available. The following amounts will be calculated in terms of tax for those consecutive years before that of cessation for which relief has been allowed under *Sec 380* on the accounts basis.

(A)   The relief allowed for those years (up to a maximum of six).

(B)   The relief which would have been given for the same years if the losses had been computed on the strict basis.

(C)   If terminal loss relief has been allowed, the amount (if any) which would no longer be due following the computation at (B).

A repayment will then be made for the year of cessation of the lesser of

(1)   the excess of (B) over ((A) + (C)), and

(2)   tax at the claimant's marginal rate for the year of cessation on the part of the penultimate year's loss arising after the accounting date and not the subject of terminal loss relief.

A claim for the additional concessional relief arising from the recomputation should be made at the same time as the *Sec 380* claim for the year of cessation.

Where the recomputation at (B) creates a loss for the year preceding the first of the consecutive years for which claims were made, a late claim under *Sec 380* will be accepted for the loss of that year unless it is more than six years before the year of cessation. The claim should be made within 30 days of the date on which effect is given to the *Sec 380* claim for the year of cessation (as above).

(Revenue Pamphlet IR 1 (November 1995 Supplement), A88; Revenue Tax Bulletin June 1995 p 223).

Example

B ceases trading on 30 September 1995 and has the following agreed results for the last few years.

Year ended 30 September 1995	Loss	£9,000
Year ended 30 September 1994	Loss	£10,000
Year ended 30 September 1993	Loss	£12,000
Year ended 30 September 1992	Loss	£4,000
Year ended 30 September 1991	Profit	£3,000

B has other sources of income and claims relief under *Sec 380(1)* for each year's loss (including the final year) against other income of that year. No terminal loss relief is claimed. Losses are calculated on the accounts year basis apart from that for 1995/96 which has to be computed on the strict fiscal year basis. B's marginal tax rate for all years 1992/93 to 1995/96 (both before and after giving loss relief) is 25%. Relief is available under the above concession as follows.

46.11 Losses

(A) Relief allowed for consecutive years before year of cessation (in terms of tax)

		£
1994/95	£10,000 @ 25%	2,500
1993/94	£12,000 @ 25%	3,000
1992/93	£4,000 @ 25%	1,000
		£6,500

(B) Relief recalculated for those years on strict basis (in terms of tax)

		£
1994/95	£(5,000 + 4,500) @ 25%	2,375
1993/94	£(6,000 + 5,000) @ 25%	2,750
1992/93	£(2,000 + 6,000) @ 25%	2,000
		£7,125

The Revenue will repay the lesser of
(1) excess of (B) over (A) =	625
(2) £4,500 (1.10.94 to 5.4.95) @ 25%	1,125

They will therefore repay £625. In addition, they will accept a late *Sec 380* claim in respect of a loss calculated on the strict basis for 1991/92: £(2,000 − 1,500) = £500.

For losses sustained in 1994/95 and subsequent years in trades, etc. commenced after 5 April 1994 and those sustained in 1997/98 and subsequent years in trades, etc. commenced on or before that date, the loss for a year of assessment is taken to be that of the basis period for that year, which will normally be the account ending within that year (see 71.11 to 71.19 SCHEDULE D, CASES I AND II for basis period rules).

(*b*) **Effects of a claim.** The effect in particular cases of using *Sec 380* as regards personal allowances, higher rate income tax, etc. should be carefully considered. See 1 ALLOWANCES AND TAX RATES. The cancellation of the Sch D assessment may result in a *Sec 350* assessment on any annuities etc. paid less tax (see 1.9 ALLOWANCES AND TAX RATES). The section may advantageously be used when a business is declining and may cease, or the rate of tax is likely to fall; or when a partner or sole owner dies or retires.

(*c*) **Late claims.** Although there is no provision for the acceptance of late claims under *Sec 380* (or *Sec 381*), such relief may be granted as would have been due if a timeous claim had been made where the taxpayer or agent either:

(i) was misled by some relevant and uncorrected Revenue error; or

(ii) made an informal claim within the time limit which he or she reasonably believed to be an acceptable claim, and the need to formalise the claim was not pointed out by the Revenue within the time limit; or

(iii) was effectively prevented from making a timeous claim for reasons beyond his or her control,

and provided that the late claim is made within a reasonable period (not normally more than three months) after the expiry of the excuse. As regards (*c*) above, acceptable reasons do *not* normally include: delays in preparing the accounts (unless for reasons beyond the taxpayer's or agent's control); delays in the Revenue's agreeing the accounts (although valid claims may be made before the accounts are either submitted or agreed, provided that the loss is clearly identified); mis-understandings and failures to communicate between taxpayer and agent; oversight or neglect by current or previous agents; ignorance of the statutory time limits; or deliberate delays because it was unclear at the expiry of the time limit whether the claim was advantageous. (Revenue Tax Bulletin December 1994 p 183).

(d)   **No double allowance.** Losses claimed under *Sec 380* (to the extent they are allowed) cannot be also carried forward against future years' assessments under *Sec 385*, see below.

46.12   *Example*

Losses in transitional period on changeover to current year basis
K carries on a business which commenced before 6 April 1994 and continues beyond 5 April 1999. He has no other source of income. He prepares accounts to 31 August and has the following results (as adjusted for tax purposes, but before capital allowances) for the four years to 31 August 1997.

	Profit/(loss) £
Year ended 31 August 1994	13,000
Year ended 31 August 1995	20,000
Year ended 31 August 1996	(14,000)
Year ended 31 August 1997	5,300

Capital allowances are as follows.

	£
1995/96	2,000
1996/97	1,000
Year ended 31 August 1997	500

The taxable profits before taking account of loss reliefs are as follows

	£	£
1995/96 (y/e 31.8.94)	13,000	
Less capital allowances	2,000	
		11,000
1996/97 (y/e 31.8.95)	20,000	
(y/e 31.8.96)	Nil	
	£20,000	
£20,000 × 12/24	10,000	
Less capital allowances	1,000	
		9,000
1997/98 (y/e 31.8.97)		
(net of capital allowances)		4,800*

* Transitional overlap relief accrued (1.9.96–5.4.97):
£5,300 × 7/12 = £3,092.

The loss of £14,000 for the year ended 31 August 1996 may be treated under normal Revenue practice (see 46.11(*a*) above) as a loss for 1996/97. K wishes to obtain loss relief against the earliest possible income. *The tax position after taking into account the appropriate loss relief claims is as follows*

		£
1995/96	Total income before loss relief	11,000
	Deduct Claim under *Sec 380(1)(b)*	11,000
	Revised total income	Nil
1996/97	Total income before loss relief	9,000
	Deduct Claim under *Sec 380(1)(a)*	3,000
	Revised total income	£6,000

The position for 1997/98 is not affected.

Loss utilisation

	£
Loss for 1996/97	14,000
Used in 1995/96 under *Sec 380(1)(b)*	(11,000)
Used in 1996/97 under *Sec 380(1)(a)*	(3,000)

Notes

(*a*)   A loss in one part of the transitional period on changeover to current year basis (see 71.20 SCHEDULE D, CASES I AND II) is treated as nil for the purpose of averaging a profit in that period to arrive at the taxable profit for 1996/97. The profit is still averaged over the full length of the transitional period.

(*b*)   If the results for years ended 31 August 1995 and 1996 had been reversed, so that the loss were treated as a loss for 1995/96, the tax position before loss reliefs would have been the same. Loss relief could then have been claimed under *ICTA 1988, s 380(1)(2) as originally enacted* to achieve the same position as above.

46.13   LOSSES CARRIED FORWARD [*Sec 385; FA 1994, ss 209(4)(5)(8), 216(3)(e); FA 1995, s 118*]

Any balance of trading, etc. **loss not used as above** (or otherwise under the Act) may be carried forward without time limit as a set-off against the first following profits (or, if insufficient, the next, and so on) of the same business by the same owner. See *Bispham v Eardiston Farming Co Ch D 1962, 40 TC 322* as to effect of *Sec 53* (all farming by a person treated as one trade) on the carry forward of farming losses.

(*a*)   **Annual payments and interest.** See 46.18 below.

(*b*)   **Certain investment income.** Where full relief under *Sec 385* cannot be given for any year because of the insufficiency of the Sch D profits, these may be increased for the purpose by adding to them taxed interest and dividends on investments arising in that year which, had they not been taxed, would have formed part of the trading receipts. In that event repayment of tax may be due. [*Sec 385(4)*]. See 71.65 SCHEDULE D, CASES I AND II. See also *Sec 458(2)* for special provisions relating to capital redemption business.

(*c*)   **Private businesses converted into companies** [*Sec 386; FA 1994, s 216(3)(f)*]. Any unrelieved balance of loss from pre-conversion years may be made use of by individuals so transferring their business mainly for shares allotted to themselves or their nominees, as follows.

For any year *throughout which* they retain the beneficial ownership of the shares and the company carries on the business, the loss may be used as a set-off (under *Sec 385*) against any income derived from the company. The set-off must be used first against direct assessments (e.g. on director's fees, etc.) but any balance may be used to reclaim tax on dividends, etc. from the company. In practice, relief should not be refused so long as shares representing at least 80% of the consideration received for the business are retained. (Revenue Inspector's Manual, IM 3552).

(*d*)   **Partners.** In the case of partnerships, each partner's proportion of the loss belongs to him individually, and to the extent to which he does not use it in claims under *Sec 380* (see 46.3 above) it is carried forward and set against his individual statutory proportion of the subsequent year's assessments (even if there is a notional discontinuance [*Sec 385(5) as originally enacted*]). Consequently, when a partner dies or retires, his share of any unexhausted loss claims lapses. For 1994/95 and subsequent years as regards partnership trades, etc. commenced, or treated as commenced, after 5 April 1994 and for 1997/98 and subsequent years as regards those commenced on or before that date, each individual partner's share of a profit or loss is treated as derived from a trade carried on by him alone (see 53.3 PARTNERSHIPS), and loss reliefs, including that under *Sec 385*, are given accordingly.

(*e*)   **Carry forward of loss in first accounts.** A loss used to offset a profit in arriving at the opening years' assessments for businesses commenced before 6 April 1994 (see 71.4 SCHEDULE D, CASES I AND II) has been relieved and hence is not available for carry forward. Where so used twice, twice the amount is treated as relieved (*Scott Adamson CS 1932, 17 TC 679; Westward Television v Hart CA 1968, 45 TC 1*). As regards the opening years' assessments for businesses commenced after 5 April 1994 (see 71.12 SCHEDULE D, CASES I AND II), *Sec 382(3)(4)* apply (see 46.3 above) to prevent an amount of loss being taken into account twice where basis periods overlap. [*Sec 385(1); FA 1994, s 209(4)*].

(*f*)   **Use of loss against subsequent profits.** A loss carried forward must be set against the first subsequent profits, although the latter might otherwise have been completely offset by personal allowances, etc., for that year.

(*g*)   **Time limits for claims.** Claims relating to the amount of losses must be made within, for 1996/97 and subsequent years, five years after 31 January following the tax year in which they arose (for earlier years, six years after the end of that tax year). For 1994/95 and subsequent years as regards businesses commenced after 5 April 1994 and for 1997/98 and subsequent years as regards businesses commenced on or before that date, the loss is then relieved automatically with no further claim being necessary. Previously, a further claim for relief for losses carried forward had to be made within six years of the end of tax year for which relief is claimed. [*Sec 385(8); TMA s 43; FA 1994, ss 196, 199(2)(a), 209(5), 19 Sch 14*]. For a case turning on the failure to establish the year(s) in which losses from an abortive business venture arose, see *Richardson v Jenkins Ch D, [1995] STC 95.*

(*h*)   **Change of ownership of a company.** Restrictions on the carry forward of losses are contained in *Secs 768, 769*. See Tolley's Corporation Tax.

(*i*)   **Balancing charge on an industrial building after cessation of trade.** Trading losses may be set off against the charge arising in these circumstances. See 10.17 CAPITAL ALLOWANCES.

(*j*)   **Change of residence.** Where, on a sole trader becoming or ceasing to be UK resident, the trade is deemed to be permanently discontinued and a new one commenced, losses of the 'old' trade may be carried forward under *Sec 385* and set against profits of the 'new' trade. See 71.27 SCHEDULE D, CASES I AND II (and see 53.15 PARTNERSHIPS for a similar rule as regards an individual trading in partnership).

46.14 Losses

LOSSES IN EARLY YEARS OF A TRADE [*Secs 381, 382(3)(4); FA 1994, ss 209(2)(3)(7)–(9), 216(3)(c); FA 1995, s 118; FA 1996, ss 134, 135, 20 Sch 24, 21 Sch 10*]

If an individual (including a partner) sustains a loss in a trade, profession or vocation in any of the first four years of assessment from commencement of trading, he may claim relief for that loss against his other income of the preceding three years, earlier years first. The trade (or if part of a larger undertaking, the whole undertaking) must have been carried on during the period of loss on a commercial basis with a reasonable expectation of profits during that period or within a reasonable time thereafter (an objective test – see *Walls v Livesey (Sp C 4), [1995] SSCD 12*). The Revenue consider that, to satisfy this test, profits (calculated on normal accountancy principles) should, in normal circumstances, be realised within twelve months of commencement, and that the proprietor should be able to show that, when he commenced the business, he had available research or enquiry results demonstrating the likely viability of the project. (Tolley's Practical Tax 1983 p 158). There is no relief where the trade was previously carried on by the spouse earlier than the three years of assessment preceding the loss. Any change in a partnership is disregarded for an individual who is engaged in the trade immediately before and after that change.

Notes.

(*a*) **Claims** must be in writing within, for 1996/97 and later years, twelve months after 31 January following the year of assessment in which the loss occurred (for earlier years, two years after the end of that year of assessment). For late claims, see 46.11(*c*) above.

(*b*) **Order of set-off** against income of the appropriate year is as shown in 46.9 above.

(*c*) **Computation of losses** is as for *Sec 380* purposes (see 46.3 above) and, to the extent they are allowed, such losses cannot be claimed under any other relieving provision.

(*d*) **Capital allowances and stock relief** may be included in the loss in similar manner as described in 46.7 above and are subject to the restrictions in 46.10(*c*)(*d*)(*e*) above.

(*e*) **Overseas trades.** Individuals (including partners) carrying on trade abroad may claim relief.

(*f*) **Woodlands.** A claim under this section does not apply to woodlands brought within Schedule D by an election under *ICTA 1970, s 111* or *FA 1988, 6 Sch 4* (see 69.2 and 69.3 SCHEDULE B).

(*g*) See also 71.75 SCHEDULE D, CASES I AND II as regards **pre-trading expenditure**.

46.15 *Example*

F, a single person, commences to trade on 1 December 1994, preparing accounts to 30 November. The first four years of trading produce losses of £12,000, £9,000, £2,000 and £1,000 respectively, these figures being as adjusted for tax purposes and after taking account of capital allowances. For each of the four years of assessment 1991/92 to 1994/95, F had other income of £8,000.

The losses for tax purposes are as follows.

	£	£
1994/95 (1.12.94–5.4.95) (£12,000 × 4/12)		4,000
1995/96 (y/e 30.11.95)	12,000	
Less already allocated to 1994/95	4,000	
		8,000
1996/97 (y/e 30.11.96)		9,000
1997/98 (y/e 30.11.97)		2,000
1998/99 (y/e 30.11.98) note (*b*)		1,000

Loss relief under *Sec 381* is available as follows.

	1994/95	1995/96	1996/97	1997/98
	£	£	£	£
Losses available	4,000	8,000	9,000	2,000
Set against total income				
1991/92	4,000	—	—	—
1992/93	—	8,000	—	—
1993/94	—	—	8,000	—
1994/95	—	—	1,000	2,000
	£4,000	£8,000	£9,000	£2,000

Revised total income is thus £4,000 for 1991/92, nil for 1992/93 and 1993/94 and £5,000 for 1994/95.

Notes

(*a*)   Losses are computed by reference to the same basis periods as profits. Where any part of a loss would otherwise fall to be included in the computations for two successive tax years (as is the case for 1994/95 and 1995/96 in this example), that part is excluded from the computation for the second of those years.

(*b*)   The loss for the year ended 30 November 1998 in this example is not available for relief under *Sec 381* as it does not fall into the first four *tax years* of the business (even though it is incurred in the first four years of trading). It is of course available for relief under *Sec 380* (depending on other income for 1997/98 and 1998/99) or for carry-forward under *Sec 385*.

46.16   **TERMINAL LOSSES** [*Sec 388; FA 1994, ss 209(6)(7), 214(1)(d); FA 1995, s 118*]

On the permanent discontinuance of any trade, profession or vocation (or the occupation of woodlands assessed under Sch D), losses sustained in the twelve months before the date of discontinuance, so far as not otherwise relieved, may be carried back and set off against profits of the trade, etc., charged to income tax under Sch D (plus, in the case of a trade, interest or dividends arising which, had they not been taxed otherwise, would have been chargeable under Sch D, Case I as trading profits) for the three years of assessment prior to that in which the discontinuance occurs, relief being given first for the latest of those years, and so on. For 1994/95 and subsequent years as regards businesses commenced after 5 April 1994 and for 1996/97 and subsequent years as regards businesses commenced on or before that date, the eligible profits are those for the tax year in which the discontinuance occurs and the three tax years preceding it. Losses for this purpose include unrelieved capital allowances for the twelve months before discontinuance, but excluding any such allowances brought forward from earlier years. For 1994/95 and subsequent years as regards businesses commenced after 5 April 1994 and for 1997/98 and subsequent years as regards businesses commenced on or before that date, capital allowances are automatically included

46.17 Losses

in a trading loss (see 46.7 above) and are thus no longer considered separately. [*Secs 388(6)(7), 389(5)–(7); FA 1994, s 214(1)(d)(e)*].

(*a*)   So far as profits of any year were applied in making any payment from which tax was deducted but not accounted for because the payment was made out of taxed profits [*Sec 348*], those profits must, for relief purposes, be treated as reduced by the amount so applied. In such cases, losses available against prior years are reduced by a similar amount unless the payment is one which, had it not been paid out of taxed profits, could have been assessed under *Sec 350* and treated as a loss under *Sec 387*.

(*b*)   Losses for this purpose must be computed on the same basis as profits under Sch D, Cases I and II, and, insofar as they are relieved as terminal losses, cannot also be claimed under any other relieving provision.

(*c*)   On a partnership change treated as a permanent discontinuance (under *Sec 113*, see 53.6 PARTNERSHIPS) a retiring partner may claim his terminal loss against his share of partnership profits for the three preceding years as above (even if they include a period before a previous discontinuance), but no claim under this section may be made by a continuing partner. For 1994/95 and subsequent years as regards partnership trades, etc. commenced, or treated as commenced, after 5 April 1994 and for 1997/98 and subsequent years as regards those commenced on or before that date, each individual partner's share of a profit or loss is treated as derived from a trade carried on by him alone (see 53.3 PARTNERSHIPS), and terminal loss relief is available accordingly to an outgoing partner. All individual partners may claim terminal loss relief on a discontinuance or deemed discontinuance of the actual partnership trade, but the latter will occur only where there is no continuing partner (see 53.6 PARTNERSHIPS). [*Sec 389(3)–(5); FA 1994, ss 214(1)(e), 216(3)(g)(4)*]. For company partners see *Sec 114(3)(c)* and 53.14 PARTNERSHIPS.

(*d*)   Where the trade discontinued is, or includes, the working of a mine, oil well, etc., special provisions obviate dual claims under this section and *CAA 1990, s 17(1)*. [*Sec 389(2)*].

46.17   *Examples*

(A)

A carries on a trade and prepares accounts to 31 December each year. A ceases to trade on 30 September 1996 and the results for the four years and nine months to date of cessation are as follows.

Period	Trading Profit/(loss) £
31.12.92	3,500
31.12.93	5,000
31.12.94	600
31.12.95	(1,200)
30.9.96	(1,500)

Year of assessment	Capital Allowances £	Non-Trade Annual Payments £
1993/94	1,800	300
1994/95	1,500	300
1995/96	1,800	—
1996/97	1,600	—

The terminal loss available is as follows.

		£
1996/97 $\frac{6}{9}$ × £1,500		1,000
Capital allowances		1,600
1995/96 $\frac{3}{9}$ × £1,500	500	
$\frac{3}{12}$ × £1,200	300	800
Capital allowances		
$\frac{6}{12}$ × £1,800 note (*a*)		900
		£4,300

The assessments for these years are as follows.

Year	Assessment		*Sec 388* Relief	Revised
		£	£	£
1993/94	Profits	3,500		
	Capital allowances	1,800		
		£1,700	800	£900
1994/95	Profits	5,000		
	Capital allowances	1,500		
		£3,500	3,200	£300
1995/96	Profits	600		
	Capital allowances	600		
		—		Nil
1996/97		Nil		Nil
			£4,000	(see below)

	£
Terminal loss as above	4,300
Less: Utilised in 1994/95	3,200
	1,100
Less: Deduction for non-trade charges note (*b*)	300
	800
Less: Utilised in 1993/94	800
	Nil

Notes

(*a*)   The capital allowances of £900 for 1995/96 which are included in the terminal loss do not have to be restricted as only £600 of the total of £1,800 is set against the 1995/96 assessment. If £1,000 had been required to offset the 1995/96 assessment the 1995/96 capital allowances included in the terminal loss would have been restricted to £800.

(*b*)   The profits available for set-off against *Sec 388* loss relief are reduced by the annual payments which were paid out of income subject to tax. As they were non-trade charges, the terminal loss available against income of prior years is similarly reduced. See 46.16(*a*) above.

(*c*)   A could obtain more relief if he made a claim under *Sec 380(1)* for 1994/95 and then made a reduced claim for *Sec 388* terminal loss relief as follows

	£
Sec 380 relief 1994/95	
Profit for the year ended 31.12.94	600
Capital allowances (1995/96)	1,800
	£1,200

The terminal loss available would then be

	£
As calculated above	4,300
Deduct 1995/96 Capital allowances	
relieved under *Sec 380*	900
	£3,400

The position would then be

Year	Assessments	*Sec 380* relief	*Sec 388* relief	Revised
	£	£	£	£
1993/94	1,700		1,100	£600
1994/95	3,500	1,200	2,000	£300
1995/96	Nil			Nil
1996/97	Nil			Nil
		£1,200	£3,100	(see below)

	£
Terminal loss as above	3,400
Less: Utilised in 1994/95	2,000
	1,400
Less: Deduction for non-trade charges	300
	1,100
Less: Utilised in 1993/94	1,100
Balance	Nil

(B)

B, a trader with a 30 September year end, ceases to trade on 30 June 1996. Tax-adjusted results for his last two accounting periods are as follows.

	Trading Profit/(loss)
Year ended 30 September 1995	£28,000
Nine months to 30 June 1996	(£9,000)

There are no capital allowances due. Profits have been falling, and the Revenue do not revise the 1994/95 and 1995/96 assessments.

The terminal loss available is as follows.

		£	£
1996/97 (6.4.96 to 30.6.96)			
£9,000 × 3/9			3,000
1995/96 (1.7.95 to 5.4.96)			
1.10.95 to 5.4.96	£9,000 × 6/9	6,000	
1.7.95 to 30.9.95	(£28,000) × 3/12	(7,000)	
		(1,000)	Nil
Terminal loss			£3,000

Note

In determining the part of a terminal loss arising in a part of the final twelve months (the terminal loss period) that falls into any one year of assessment, a profit made in that period must be netted off against a loss in that period. In this example, no net loss is incurred in that part of the terminal loss period falling in 1995/96. However, the two different years of assessment are looked at separately, so that the 'net profit' of £1,000 falling within 1995/96 does not have to be netted off against the 1996/97 loss and is instead treated as nil.

46.18   **TREATMENT OF ANNUAL PAYMENTS AND INTEREST AS LOSSES**

(a)   **Assessments under Sec 350** in respect of annual payments, royalties, etc. not paid out of taxed income (see 23.3 DEDUCTION OF TAX AT SOURCE) may be treated as losses and carried forward under *Secs 385, 386* or allowed as terminal losses under *Sec 388* [*Secs 387, 389(1)*]. Further, where such payments are made to residents of a country with which a DOUBLE TAX RELIEF (25) agreement is in force and are thereby exempt from UK tax, so that no assessment under *Sec 350* is made in respect of them, the amounts thereof can nevertheless be similarly carried forward (*SI 1970 No 488*). But these provisions do not apply to *Sec 350* assessments arising from—

(i)   payments not made wholly and exclusively for the purposes of the trade etc.,

(ii)   payments charged to capital, or not ultimately borne by the person assessed,

(iii) certain rental payments to non-residents (see 25.6 DOUBLE TAX RELIEF),

(iv)   copyright royalties and design royalty and public lending right payments paid to non-residents (see *Secs 536–537B*),

(v)   sales of patent rights by non-residents (see *Sec 524* and 54 PATENTS),

(vi)   rents for cable wayleaves etc., paid by radio relay services (see *Sec 120(4)* and 23.14 DEDUCTION OF TAX AT SOURCE),

(vii) interest payments to purchaser re sales of securities falling under *Sec 737* (see 3.7 ANTI-AVOIDANCE).

(b)   *Interest payments.* Where relief is claimed under *Sec 353* (see 43.3 INTEREST PAYABLE) in respect of interest paid wholly and exclusively for the purposes of a trade etc. and full effect cannot be given to such relief due to an insufficiency of income, the amount unallowed may be carried forward as a loss under *Sec 385* or treated as a terminal loss under *Sec 388*. [*Sec 390*].

The above is *not* applicable to any interest paid less tax and assessed under *Sec 350* (see 23.3(ii) DEDUCTION OF TAX AT SOURCE). [*Sec 387(3)*]. (Such interest, if for business purposes, is deductible in computing business profits.)

46.19   **LOSSES ON SHARES IN UNLISTED TRADING COMPANIES** [*Secs 574–576; FA 1988, 14 Sch Pt VIII; FA 1989, 12 Sch 14; FA 1994, s 210, 20 Sch 8; FA 1995, s 119; FA 1996, 38 Sch 6*]

An individual may claim relief from income tax, instead of from capital gains tax, for an allowable loss (as computed for capital gains tax purposes) on a disposal of ordinary shares or stock in a qualifying trading company for which he subscribed and which were issued to him by the company in consideration of money or money's worth, or were transferred to him *inter vivos* by his spouse who had similarly subscribed for them. Where, for shares subscribed for before 10 March 1981, the consideration was deemed equal to the market value under *CGTA 1979, s 19(3)*, the loss allowable on disposal cannot exceed what the loss would have been without applying that subsection. For shares subscribed for after 9 March 1981, market value is not substituted where the consideration is less than market value. [*TCGA 1992, s 17(2)(b)*]. The temporary relief for indexation losses provided for by *FA 1994, s 93, 12 Sch* applies to losses claimed under these provisions [*FA 1994, 12 Sch 3(3), 6, 7*] (and see Tolley's Capital Gains Tax under Indexation).

A claim is available only if the disposal is at arm's length for full consideration or by way of a distribution on a winding-up or the value of the shares has become negligible and a claim to that effect made under *TCGA 1992, s 24(2)*. By concession, however, relief will not be denied by virtue of this requirement, provided that all the other conditions are fulfilled, where the company has no assets and is dissolved, the shareholder has not received a distribution in the course of dissolving or winding up the company (or an anticipated final distribution has not been made), and the shareholder has not made a deemed disposal of the shares under *TCGA 1992, s 24(2)*. (Revenue Pamphlet IR 1, D46).

A *'qualifying trading company'* is a company none of whose shares have at any time in the relevant period (i.e. ending with the date of disposal of the shares and beginning with the incorporation of the company, or, if later, one year before the date on which the shares were subscribed for) been listed on a recognised stock exchange and which

(*a*)   either (i) is a trading company (i.e. a company, other than an excluded company, whose business consists wholly or mainly of the carrying on of a trade or trades, or which is the holding company of a trading group) on the date of the disposal or (ii) has ceased to be a trading company within the previous three years and has not since that time been an investment company or an *'excluded company'* (i.e. a company whose trade consists mainly of dealing in shares, securities, land, trades or commodity futures or is not carried on on a commercial basis with a reasonable expectation of profit, or which is the holding company of a non-trading group, or which is a building society (see 9 BUILDING SOCIETIES) or a registered industrial and provident society within *Sec 486(12)*; and

(*b*)   either (i) has been a trading company for a continuous period of six years ending on the date of disposal of the shares or the time it ceased to be a trading company; or (ii) if shorter, a continuous period ending on that date or that time and had not before the beginning of that period been an excluded company or an investment company; and

(*c*)   it has been resident in the UK since incorporation until the date of disposal.

Securities on the Alternative Investment Market ('AIM') are treated as unlisted for these purposes. (Revenue Press Release 20 February 1995).

For losses incurred in **1993/94 and earlier years, claims** must be in writing within two years after the year of assessment *for which the loss is claimed*. A loss may be claimed against income

(i)   of the year in which the loss is incurred, or

(ii)   of the year following the year in which the loss is incurred.

Where both claims are made for the same loss, (i) takes precedence to the extent of the amount of the loss equal to the income of the year of loss. Where in the same year claims are made both under (ii) in respect of the preceding year's loss and under (i) in respect of the current year's loss, (ii) takes precedence. For 1989/90 and earlier years, a claim may stipulate that relief is given only by reference to the claimant's income without extending it to the income of his spouse, otherwise relief is given first against the claimant's earned income, then his other income, then against earned income of his spouse and then her other income.

For losses incurred in **1994/95 and subsequent years, claims** must be in writing within, for 1996/97 and later years, twelve months after 31 January following the year of assessment *in which the loss is incurred* (for 1994/95 and 1995/96, two years after the end of that year of assessment). A loss may be claimed against income.

(I)   of the year in which the loss is incurred, or

(II)   of the year preceding that in which the loss is incurred.

Where, against income of the same year, claims are made both under (I) in respect of that year's loss and under (II) in respect of the following year's loss, (I) takes precedence. Where both claims are made for the same loss, no order of priority is specified but it is considered that the Revenue would follow the same practice as for loss relief under *Sec 380* (see 46.3 above).

For **1993/94 and 1994/95**, relief under *Sec 574* may be claimed under both the old rules (under *Sec 574(1)* or *Sec 574(2)* respectively) and the new rules (under *Sec 574(1)(b)* or *Sec 574(1)(a)* respectively). Since there is no statutory order of priority in these circumstances, reliefs are given in the order which saves most tax. In practice, the taxpayer may choose the order in which reliefs are given. (Revenue Tax Bulletin December 1994 p 184).

Relief under the above provisions is given in priority to relief under *Sec 380* (see 46.3 above) and *Sec 381* (see 46.14 above) for the same year of assessment. The relief cannot also be allowed for capital gains tax purposes and appropriate adjustments will be made to avoid double relief.

Identification. Where an individual holds shares of the same class only some of which qualify for the above relief because they were subscribed for, then disposals are identified with acquisitions on a 'last in, first out' basis and relief is limited to the allowable loss relating solely to the qualifying shares.

Anti-avoidance. Any claim to relief will bring in the provisions of *TCGA 1992, s 30* (value-shifting to give a tax-free benefit) so that the relief may be adjusted for any benefit conferred whether tax-free or not.

Company reconstructions etc. Where the shares disposed of represent a new holding identifiable under *TCGA 1992, s 127* with 'old shares' after a reorganisation or reduction of share capital, relief is not available unless it could have been given (on the disposal of the old shares for full consideration) at the reorganisation etc. had this legislation been in force and had the reorganisation been a chargeable occasion producing a loss. Where the reorganisation did not so qualify, but new consideration was given for the new holding, relief is limited to such of that new consideration as is an allowable deduction. Where

46.20 Losses

TCGA 1992, s 137 operates to make a disposal of shares on a reconstruction etc., no relief is available under the above provisions. '*New consideration*' is money or money's worth but excluding any surrender or alteration to the original shares or rights attached thereto, and the application of assets of the company or distribution declared but not made out of the assets.

46.20   *Example*

X is a semi-retired business executive. Over the years he has acquired several shareholdings in unlisted companies and he has suffered the following losses.

(i)   500 shares in A Ltd (a qualifying trading company) which X subscribed for in 1987. Allowable loss for CGT purposes on liquidation in June 1995—£12,000.

(ii)   500 shares in B Ltd which X subscribed for in 1989 at £10 per share. B Ltd traded as a builder until 1992 when it changed its trade to that of buying and selling land. X received an arm's length offer for the shares of £3 per share in May 1995 which he accepted.

(iii) In 1984, X subscribed for 2,000 shares in C Ltd at £50 per share. In 1989 his aunt gave him a further 1,000 shares. The market value of the shares at that time was £60 per share.

The company has been a qualifying trading company since 1980 but has fallen on hard times recently. A company offered X £20 per share in June 1996. X accepted the offer to the extent of 1,500 shares.

The treatment of these losses in relation to income tax would be as follows.

(i)   Loss claim—*Sec 574*, 1995/96 or 1994/95—£12,000

(ii)   No loss claim under *Sec 574* is possible as company is an 'excluded company' (see 46.19 above).

(iii) Disposals are first identified with the most recent acquisitions

Date	Qualifying shares	Other shares
1984	2,000	
1989		1,000
1996	(500)	(1,000)

Loss claim—*Sec 574* for 1996/97 or 1995/96

	£
500 shares at £50 per share	25,000
Disposal proceeds	10,000
Allowable loss	£15,000

Utilisation of losses

X makes all possible claims under *Sec 574* so as to obtain relief against the earliest possible income. He is a single man and has total income, before *Sec 574* relief, of £7,000 for 1994/95, £11,500 for 1995/96 and £7,500 for 1996/97.

The *Sec 574* losses available as above are as follows.

	1995/96 disposals £	1996/97 disposals £
A Ltd shares	12,000	
C Ltd shares		15,000

Sec 574 claims are made as follows.

£

1994/95

Total income	7,000
Claim under *Sec 574(1)(b)*	(7,000)
Revised total income	Nil

1995/96

Total income	11,500
Claim under *Sec 574(1)(a)* note (*b*)	(5,000)
	6,500
Claim under *Sec 574(1)(b)*	(6,500)
Revised total income	Nil

1996/97

Total income	7,500
Claim under *Sec 574(1)(a)* (restricted)	(7,500)
Revised total income	Nil

Loss utilisation

£

1995/96 loss

Loss available	12,000
Relief claimed for 1994/95 (*Sec 574(1)(b)*)	(7,000)
Relief claimed for 1995/96 (*Sec 574(1)(a)*)	(5,000)

1996/97 loss

Loss available	15,000
Relief claimed for 1995/96 (*Sec 574(1)(b)*)	(6,500)
Relief claimed for 1996/97 (*Sec 574(1)(a)*)	(7,500)
Unused balance note (*c*)	£1,000

Notes

(*a*)   In this example, losses have been set against preceding year's income first, as X wished to obtain relief against earliest possible income, but this need not be the case.

(*b*)   Where two years' losses are set against one year's income, the current year's loss is relieved in priority to that of the following year.

(*c*)   The unused balance of the 1996/97 loss cannot be relieved under *Sec 574* due to insufficiency of income and therefore reverts to being a capital loss available to reduce chargeable gains.

47 Married Persons

(See also Revenue Pamphlets IR 80, 83, 90, 91.)

Cross-references. See 1.14, 1.15, 1.20–1.23 ALLOWANCES AND TAX RATES; 2 ALLOWANCES AND TAX RATES—EXAMPLES; 26.15, 26.28 ENTERPRISE INVESTMENT SCHEME (AND BES); 43.12 INTEREST PAYABLE; 64.5 RESIDENCE, ORDINARY RESIDENCE AND DOMICILE (residence); 53.13 PARTNERSHIPS.

The headings in this chapter are as follows.

47.1 **INDEPENDENT TAXATION**

For **1990/91** and subsequent years, married persons are treated separately for taxation purposes, subject to transitional provisions (see 47.5 below). See 47.6 *et seq.* below for aggregation of income under *Sec 279* for 1989/90 and earlier years. The operation of that section for earlier years does not, however, affect the question of the existence or amount of a married woman's income for 1990/91 or subsequent years. [*FA 1988, s 32, 3 Sch 25*].

47.2 **Personal reliefs. For 1990/91** and subsequent years, husband and wife are each entitled to the personal allowance (see 1.14 ALLOWANCES AND TAX RATES) in their own right. The husband is entitled to the married couple's allowance (see 1.15 ALLOWANCES AND TAX RATES) for a year of assessment at any time during which his wife is living with him. [*Secs 257, 257A; FA 1988, s 33; FA 1994, s 77; FA 1996, s 134, 20 Sch 14*].

Transfer of married couple's allowance. For **1993/94** and subsequent years of assessment, a wife may elect to be entitled to claim one-half of the married couple's allowance for any year of assessment (ignoring any age-related increase), the husband's entitlement being correspondingly reduced. Alternatively, they may jointly elect for the wife to be able to claim the full amount of the basic allowance, the husband's entitlement being restricted to any age-related increase, although the husband may then elect to be able to claim back one-half of the basic allowance (the wife's entitlement being correspondingly reduced). A woman may not, however, be entitled to more than one deduction under these provisions in any year of assessment. An election under these provisions has to be made in prescribed form (i.e. form 18) before the first year of assessment for which it is to have effect (or within the first 30 days of that year if prior notification of intention to elect has been given to the inspector before the beginning of that year), and has effect until withdrawn or until a different election is made. If an election is to have effect for the year of assessment of marriage, it may be made during that year, but will only apply for that year to the reduced basic allowance available. An election may be withdrawn with effect from the year following that in which notice of withdrawal is given. [*Sec 257BA; F(No 2)A 1992, 5 Sch 2; FA 1994, 8 Sch 2*].

For 1993/94, where a spouse's entitlement to married couple's allowance (including, in the case of the husband, any age-related increase in the basic allowance) exceeds his or her total income, the excess may, if he or she so notifies the inspector, be claimed as a deduction from the other spouse's total income (in addition to any part of the allowance to which she or he is entitled as above). The notification to the inspector must be given in prescribed form and is irrevocable. For 1996/97 and later years, it must be given within five years after 31 January following the year of assessment to which it is to apply. Previously, it had to be given within six years after the end of that year of assessment. For this purpose, total income is reduced by all deductions other than those in respect of investments under the business expansion scheme (see 26 ENTERPRISE INVESTMENT SCHEME (AND BES)) and in respect of payments for which relief is obtained by deduction of basic rate tax in respect of retirement benefit or personal pension scheme contributions (66.5(*a*) RETIREMENT SCHEMES, 65.2 RETIREMENT ANNUITIES AND PERSONAL PENSION SCHEMES), relevant loan interest (23.13 DEDUCTION OF TAX AT SOURCE), MEDICAL INSURANCE (48) premiums, and vocational training costs (71.87 SCHEDULE D, CASES I AND II, 75.42 SCHEDULE E). For 1994/95 and subsequent years, married couple's allowance may similarly be transferred where full effect cannot otherwise be given to the allowance because the surrendering spouse's total income tax liability (see 1.15 ALLOWANCES AND TAX RATES) is insufficient. [*Sec 257BB; F(No 2)A 1992, 5 Sch 2; FA 1994, 8 Sch 3; FA 1996, s 135, 21 Sch 4*].

For 1990/91, 1991/92 and 1992/93, a husband may surrender to his wife any part of the married couple's allowance (including any age-related increase in the basic allowance) in excess of his total income after all deductions (other than those referred to above in relation to later years). The husband must notify the inspector of the surrender in prescribed form (i.e. form 575) within six years after the end of the year of assessment to which it is to apply, and such notice is irrevocable. [*Sec 257B; FA 1988, s 33; FA 1989, ss 33(10), 57(4); FA 1991, s 32(4); F(No 2)A 1992, 5 Sch 2*].

Transfer of blind person's allowance. For 1990/91 and subsequent years of assessment, blind person's allowance (see 1.18 ALLOWANCES AND TAX RATES) may be transferred from husband to wife and *vice versa* subject to the same conditions as apply before 1993/94 in relation to transfers of married couple's allowance (see above). For this purpose, deductions from total income also exclude any married couple's allowance to which the surrendering spouse is entitled. For 1994/95 and subsequent years, references to deductions for relevant loan interest, medical insurance premiums and married couple's allowance are no longer relevant, as these items are not relieved by deduction from total income. The same time limits apply as for transfers of married couple's allowance above. [*Sec 265; FA 1988, 3 Sch 8; FA 1989, ss 33(10), 57(4); FA 1991, s 33(4); F(No 2)A 1992, 5 Sch 8; FA 1994, 8 Sch 10, 10 Sch 3, 26 Sch Pt V; FA 1996, s 135, 21 Sch 6*].

47.3   *Example*

Transfer of surplus married couple's allowance

Mr Grey is a sole trader and made a profit of £1,000 in the two years to 30 April 1996. Mr Grey has been married for some years. He has building society interest of £2,752 (net) for 1996/97 and his wife has a salary of £15,000 and building society interest of £1,600 (net). Mr and Mrs Grey receive interest of £1,120 (net) in 1996/97 from a bank deposit account in their joint names. Mr Grey makes an investment of £500 on 1 November 1996, which qualifies for enterprise investment scheme relief. Mr Grey elects under *Sec 257BB(2)* to transfer the unused balance of his married couple's allowance for 1996/97 to his wife.

47.4 Married Persons

The couple's tax position is as follows.

	Mr Grey £	Mrs Grey £
Schedule D, Case I $\left(£1,000 \times \dfrac{12}{24}\right)$	500	—
Schedule E	—	15,000
Building society interest (gross)	3,440	2,000
Bank deposit interest (gross)	700	700
Total income	4,640	17,700
Deduct Personal allowance	3,765	3,765
Taxable income	£875	£13,935
Tax payable:		
875/3,900 @ 20%	175.00	780.00
7,335 @ 24%		1,760.40
2,700 @ 20%		540.00
	175.00	3,080.40
Deduct EIS relief £500 @ 20%	100.00	
	75.00	
Deduct Married couple's allowance		
£1,790 @ 15% = £268.50, but restricted to	75.00	
Deduct Surplus married couple's allowance £(268.50 − 75.00)		193.50
Total tax liabilities	Nil	2,886.90
Deduct Tax at source:		
Building society interest	(688.00)	(400.00)
Bank deposit interest	(140.00)	(140.00)
Net tax (repayment)/liability (subject to wife's PAYE deductions)	£(828.00)	£2,346.90

47.4 **Jointly held property.** For 1990/91 onwards, special rules apply for the apportionment between spouses living together of income arising from property held in their joint names. Provided that at least one of them is beneficially entitled to that income, they are treated as beneficially entitled to it in equal shares, except in the following circumstances.

(i) Where the income is earned income or, not being earned income, is assessable in the name of a partnership.

(ii) To the extent that the income is by any other provision of the *Income Tax Acts* treated as the income either of the spouse who is not beneficially entitled to the income, or of a third party.

(iii) Where the husband and wife are not beneficially entitled to the income in equal shares, and they make a declaration of their beneficial interests in the income to which the declaration relates and the property from which that income arises, provided that the beneficial interests of the husband and wife in the property correspond to their beneficial interests in the income.

A declaration under (iii) above has effect in relation to income arising on and after the date of the declaration (except that a declaration made before 6 June 1990 had retrospective effect), and continues to have effect unless and until the beneficial interests of the spouses in either the income or the property cease to accord with the declaration. Notice of a declaration must be given to the inspector, in a prescribed form (i.e. form 17) and manner, within 60 days of the date of the declaration. [*Secs 282A, 282B; FA 1988, s 34*].

47.5 **Transitional reliefs.** Three transitional reliefs are available.

(a) *Husband with excess allowances.* Where a husband and wife are living together at any time during 1990/91, and for the whole or any part of 1989/90 the wife's income is aggregated with that of the husband for income tax purposes (and no election for separate taxation (see 47.10 below) is in force for 1989/90), the wife is entitled to a deduction from her total income for 1990/91 of an amount equal to the excess of the husband's 1989/90 allowances over the sum of the husband's total income for 1990/91 and the wife's allowances (apart from these transitional provisions) for 1990/91.

Where they were living together for part only of 1989/90, and the aggregation rules do not apply to them for any part of 1989/90, the wife is entitled to a deduction from her total income for 1990/91 of an amount equal to the excess of the husband's allowances (other than wife's earned income relief) for 1989/90 over his total income for 1990/91. The deduction is, however, reduced by the excess, if any, of the allowances to which the wife would be entitled for 1990/91 apart from these provisions over the lesser of

(i) her total income for 1989/90, and

(ii) her allowances for that year other than the additional relief for children, widow's bereavement allowance (see 1.17, 1.16 ALLOWANCES AND TAX RATES) and allowances transferred from her husband.

Transitional relief may also be available for 1991/92 or any subsequent year (the '*year in question*') at any time during which the husband and wife are living together, where they were also living together throughout the immediately preceding year of assessment, and the wife made a deduction from her total income under these transitional provisions for that immediately preceding year (see below). Where that deduction is greater than the excess of the wife's allowances given by deduction for the year in question over those for the immediately preceding year (in both cases apart from transitional relief under these provisions), and the husband's allowances given by deduction for the year in question (other than blind person's allowances (see 1.18 ALLOWANCES AND TAX RATES) and (before 1994/95) married couple's allowance (see 1.15 ALLOWANCES AND TAX RATES)) exceed his total income for that year, the wife is entitled to a deduction for the year in question of the lesser of

(A) the deduction under these transitional relief provisions for the immediately preceding year of assessment *less* any increase in her allowances (*other than* under these transitional relief provisions) for the year in question over those for the immediately preceding year, and

(B) the excess of her husband's allowances for the year in question (other than blind person's and married couple's allowances) over his total income for that year.

In determining for the above purpose the excess of the wife's allowances given by deduction for 1994/95 over those for 1993/94, deductions for 1993/94 in respect of allowances falling to be given by way of reduction in tax liability for 1994/95 are disregarded (so that like is compared with like). (In practice, this is likely to be

47.5 Married Persons

relevant only as regards married couple's allowance—see 1.15 ALLOWANCES AND TAX RATES.)

In determining whether the wife made a deduction from her total income under these transitional provisions for the immediately preceding year, and the amount thereof, it is assumed that such deduction is made after all other deductions except any in respect of business expansion scheme investments.

Total income for all the purposes of these transitional reliefs is as reduced by all deductions other than those in respect of investments under the business expansion scheme (see 26 ENTERPRISE INVESTMENT SCHEME (AND BES)) and in respect of payments for which relief is obtained by deduction of basic rate tax in respect of retirement benefit or personal pension scheme contributions (66.5(a) RETIREMENT SCHEMES, 65.2 RETIREMENT ANNUITIES AND PERSONAL PENSION SCHEMES), relevant loan interest (23.13 DEDUCTION OF TAX AT SOURCE), MEDICAL INSURANCE (48) premiums, and vocational training costs (71.87 SCHEDULE D, CASES I AND II, 75.42 SCHEDULE E). Any separate assessment election for 1989/90 (see 47.9 below) is similarly disregarded in determining the husband's excess allowances for that year. For 1994/95 and subsequent years, payments of relevant loan interest and medical insurance premiums are not relieved by deduction from total income, and are therefore no longer relevant.

Transitional relief under these provisions is available only if notice is given by the husband. The notice must be in writing and in prescribed form (i.e. form 575) to the inspector, and is irrevocable. For 1996/97 and later years, the notice must be given within five years after 31 January following the year of assessment to which it relates. Previously, it had to be given within six years after the end of that year of assessment. [*See 257D; FA 1988, s 33; FA 1989, ss 33(10), 57(4); F(No 2)A 1992, 5 Sch 3; FA 1994, 8 Sch 4, 10 Sch 3, 26 Sch Pt V; FA 1996, s 135, 21 Sch 5*].

(b) *The elderly.* Where, for 1989/90, a claimant is entitled (disregarding any separate assessment election) to the age allowance determined by reference to his wife's age and not his own (i.e. he was under 65 or under 75, as the case may be, throughout 1989/90), and the amount of that allowance exceeds the aggregate of the personal and married couple's allowances available for 1990/91 apart from these transitional provisions, then for any subsequent year at any time in which he has the same wife living with him, his personal allowance is £3,400 or £3,540, as appropriate (subject to restriction by reference to an income limit in the same way as the normal age increase, see above). The indexation provisions (see above) do *not* apply to these figures. The personal allowance is thus frozen at this figure until such time as the claimant becomes entitled himself to the increased personal allowance for those aged over 65 (or 75). [*See 257E; FA 1988, s 33; FA 1996, s 134, 20 Sch 15*]. These provisions are of no practical application for 1996/97 onwards as the normal personal allowance is higher than £3,540 (and has been higher than £3,400 since 1992/93).

(c) *Separated couples.* Where, before 6 April 1990, a husband and wife ceased to live together, but they continued to be married to one another and the wife is wholly maintained by the husband, then, subject to conditions as below, they may be treated as continuing to live together for the purposes of entitlement to married couple's allowance and the transitional relief for the elderly (see (b) above), although not for the purposes of transfer of excess allowances to the wife (see (a) above) or of married couple's allowance (see 47.2 above). This applies to any year of assessment for which the husband is not entitled to make a deduction in respect of maintenance payments in computing his income for tax purposes, provided that, for 1989/90, he was entitled to the married person's allowance, and that, in relation to years of assessment after 1990/91, he has been entitled to the married couple's allowance under this provision in each intervening year. [*Sec 257F; FA 1988, s 33; F(No 2)A 1992, 5 Sch 4; FA 1994, 8 Sch 5; FA 1996, s 134, 20 Sch 16*].

47.6   **AGGREGATION OF INCOME** [*Sec 279*]

For 1989/90 and earlier years, the income of a wife 'living with her husband' (see 47.12 below), whether earned or unearned, was deemed for tax purposes to be her husband's income, and had to be included in all returns of income made by him for such years (or, in certain circumstances, for 1990/91), unless (*a*) one spouse was resident abroad (see 47.12 below), or (*b*) separate taxation of wife's earnings had been claimed (see 47.10 below). See 47.11 below as to the position for the year of marriage. Any reliefs due to the husband but unallowed because of insufficiency of his own income were thus, in effect, allowed against the wife's income in addition to any other allowances available against her own income (e.g. wife's earned income relief, see 1.22 ALLOWANCES AND TAX RATES, which could, however, be set only against the wife's earned income assessable on the husband).

The husband was accordingly liable to pay income tax calculated by reference to the joint income unless (i) the Revenue required payment from the wife (see 47.8 below), (ii) the husband (or his executors, etc.) disclaimed liability under *Sec 286* (see 47.8 below), or (iii) separate assessment (see 47.9 below) or taxation (see 47.10 below) was claimed. PAYE (55) on a wife's earnings was deducted from her emoluments, and repayments generally made direct to the wife.

47.7   Each spouse enjoyed separately the exemption from income tax of the first £70 of certain National Savings Bank interest, see 29.11(iv) EXEMPT INCOME. Income apportioned under *Sec 423 et seq.* (close company apportionments) to married woman held correctly assessed on the husband (*Latilla v CIR (No 2) HL 1950, 32 TC 159*). Tax on wife's dividends, repaid under *Sec 380* on her farming losses, held to belong to wife (*Cameron's Exors v CIR Ch D 1965, 42 TC 539*).

A husband is not, however, liable on income which his wife receives entirely independent of him as trustee or guardian for others, and concerning which he has no interest or controlling power (unless either of them is the settlor and the trust is ineffective for tax purposes, see 80 SETTLEMENTS).

47.8   **Collection of tax from wife for 1989/90 and earlier years.** If income tax (or capital gains tax) assessed on husband (or his executors, etc.) remained unpaid 28 days after the due date, and the Revenue considered that had an election been made for separate assessment (see 47.9 below) an assessment could have been made on his wife (or former wife) or her trustees, etc., the Revenue could serve notice requiring payment of that unpaid tax by the wife (or by her trustees, etc.) up to the amount of the tax so notionally assessable on her. [*Sec 285; CGTA 1979, s 45(4)*]. The notice must be issued within the normal time limits (see 5.7 ASSESSMENTS) within which the tax could have been assessed under a separate assessment election (*Johnson v CIR CA 1977, 51 TC 258*).

A widower (or his executors, etc.) could disclaim liability for unpaid income tax or capital gains tax relating to his deceased wife's income or gains while they were living together, by giving notice to her executors, etc., and the inspector, within two months of the grant of probate (or later if executors consent). The Revenue were then required to collect the tax, calculated as under separate assessment (see 47.9 below), from the wife's estate. [*Sec 286; CGTA 1979, s 45(4)*].

Tax was also collectible from the wife if an election was made for separate assessment of wife's income (see 47.9 below) or separate taxation of wife's earnings (see 47.10 below).

47.9 Married Persons

47.9　**Separate assessment.** For 1989/90 and earlier years, separate assessment could be claimed, resulting in **apportionment of total tax payable** between husband and wife. The overall total tax payable was not affected.

(*a*)　If application made by either party within six months before 6 July in any year of assessment for which the husband's income would have included any income of his wife, separate income tax assessments were made on each, but the total amount of tax payable was not affected. [*Sec 283*].

　　　The application continued in force for subsequent years until notice given revoking it within the period allowed for making such application—i.e. within six months *before* 6 July in the year of assessment. [*Sec 283(3)–(5)*].

(*b*)　For 1988/89 and/or 1989/90, any 'qualifying interest' paid on an eligible property loan by either the husband or the wife, or by both, to which the 'residence basis' applied could, on their joint election, be apportioned between them as they chose in arriving at their respective incomes. Their respective 'sharer's limits' under *Sec 356A* could also be adjusted between them as they chose. See 43.10, 43.12 INTEREST PAYABLE. [*Sec 356B(4); FA 1988, s 42(1)*].

(*c*)　Relief for life assurance was given to the party paying the premiums (but see 45.4(*j*) LIFE ASSURANCE POLICIES) and, for dependants under *Secs 263, 264* to the party maintaining them. Any balance of reliefs was apportionable in proportion to the tax which each would have paid if no personal reliefs had been allowable. [*Sec 284*].

(*d*)　Any repayment of income tax due in respect of income of either spouse was made to the spouse whose income it was.

　　　But　(i)　allowances allocated to wife had to be not less, in terms of tax, than those which arose solely by reason of her earned income;

　　　　　(ii)　if the allowances allocated to the wife were more than sufficient to discharge her tax liability the excess went to the benefit of the husband, and vice versa.

(*e*)　Returns could be required from either party, or from both. [*Sec 284(4)*].

47.10　**Separate taxation of wife's earnings.** For 1989/90 and earlier years, an election could be made for the separate taxation of wife's earned income. This election normally resulted in a lower total overall tax liability where the wife had substantial earned income.

(*a*)　A married couple living together could jointly elect that the wife's earned income be assessed on her as if she were a single woman with no other income.

(*b*)　An election, in prescribed form, could be given not earlier than six months before the beginning, nor later than twelve months after the end, of the year of assessment (but Revenue could allow longer in cases of sickness or absence abroad of either spouse or where relevant information not available, see Revenue Pamphlet IR 133, A25) and continued for subsequent years until joint notice of revocation, which could be given up to twelve months after the end of the year to which the revocation was to apply or such further period as the Revenue allowed. Any election or revocation could be made jointly with personal representatives of deceased spouse within permitted time. [*Sec 288*].

(*c*)　If such an election was made, the husband continued to be assessed on his own income and any income of his wife other than her earned income, but he was given only the single personal allowance (in place of the higher personal allowance for a married man, plus the wife's earned income allowance). The wife was separately assessable, as a single woman, on her earnings and was given the single personal allowance.

(*d*)   For the above purposes a wife's earned income did not include any pension, superannuation, deferred pay or compensation arising from her husband's former employment nor any benefit under the *Social Security Acts* except a Category A retirement pension, invalid care allowance and (for 1987/88 and subsequent years) unemployment benefit. [*Sec 287(2)*].

(*e*)   All allowances were given as if the couple were two single persons, but no excess of one party's allowances was available to the other, and neither party could claim additional relief for children or age allowance. [*Sec 287(4)(5)*]. See 1 ALLOWANCES AND TAX RATES for particulars of these various allowances.

(*f*)   Charges paid by the wife (subject to (*g*) below) and her losses and capital allowances (which were primarily to be offset against her earned income) were available to reduce her earnings, but were not available to reduce her husband's income, including her unearned income. Any charges, losses, etc. of the husband were not available to reduce the wife's earnings. [*Sec 287(7)*]. However this rule did not affect relief for terminal losses [*Sec 388*] carried back to any year for which there was no election for separate taxation of wife's earned income. [*Sec 287(8)*].

(*g*)   For 1988/89 and/or 1989/90, any 'qualifying interest' paid on an eligible property loan by either the husband or the wife, or by both, to which the 'residence basis' applied could, on their joint election, be apportioned between them as they chose in arriving at their respective incomes. Their respective 'sharer's limits' under *Sec 356A* could also be adjusted between them as they chose. See 43.10, 43.12 INTEREST PAYABLE. [*Sec 356B(4); FA 1988, s 42(1)*].

(*h*)   Unless an application for separate assessment under 47.9 above was also in force, a wife's earnings election did not affect the duty of the husband to return his wife's income. [*Sec 287(10)*].

47.11   **Year of marriage.** For the year during which marriage takes place, the following special provisions apply for 1989/90 and earlier years.

(*a*)   The wife was assessed as a single person on the whole of her income for the year of marriage and any post-marriage income was *not* deemed to be the husband's for that year (unless married on 6 April). [*Sec 279(1)*].

(*b*)   Deeming the wife's income to be the husband's did not affect the year for which it was assessable nor the amount of the assessment. [*Sec 279(2)*]. Hence marriage (or the ending of marriage) did *not* cause the rules as to new and ceasing sources of income to apply.

(*c*)   In the year of marriage, the husband was entitled to the higher personal allowance for a married man, reduced for each complete month from 6 April to date of marriage by one-twelfth of the difference (i.e. of £1,590 for 1989/90) between this allowance and the single personal allowance. See 1.21 ALLOWANCES AND TAX RATES. He also received the benefit of any excess over his wife's income of claims by her to personal allowances for dependent relatives, son's or daughter's services and blindness, and to allowable interest paid after marriage. Also, if his life insurance premiums exceeded the limit of £1,500 or one-sixth of his income, the excess could be relieved up to any unused limitation on his wife's premiums. The wife could similarly benefit from any excess over her husband's income of claims by him to *any* personal allowances plus allowable interest and any unused limitation on his life insurance premiums. [*Sec 280*].

(*d*)   A wife's income from date of marriage was treated as income of her husband for purposes of setting off losses under *Sec 380* (see 46.9 LOSSES), *Sec 381* (see 46.14 LOSSES) and *CAA 1990, s 141* (which allows capital allowances in excess of profits etc. to be set off against general income). [*Sec 279(7)*].

47.12 Married Persons

47.12 'LIVING TOGETHER'

A married woman is treated as *'living with her husband'* unless they are

(a) separated under a Court Order or separation deed, or

(b) in fact separated in circumstances which render permanent separation likely.

[*Sec 282(1)*].

A husband and wife may be separated even though living under the same roof if they have become two households (*Holmes v Mitchell Ch D 1990, 63 TC 718*). But for 1989/90 and earlier years when, while still 'living together' under the above definition, one spouse is resident for the year and one is not, or both are resident but one is absent abroad throughout the year, then for that year they are treated as if permanently separated. Resident *for* the year includes residence during part of a year. Such treatment, however, is not to increase the net aggregate of tax which would be payable under the normal basis. [*Sec 282(2)(3); FA 1988, 3 Sch 11*]. This applies to CGT as well as income tax (*Gubay v Kington HL 1984, 57 TC 601*).

47.13 DECREE OF NULLITY

A decree of nullity does not operate retrospectively to disentitle the husband to the married allowance during the years the parties lived together (*Dodworth v Dale KB 1936, 20 TC 285*).

47.14 WHEN THE MARRIAGE ENDS

A marriage may end by death, by divorce or by separation (which for tax purposes is when the parties cease 'living together', as defined in 47.12 above). Effects are as below.

(a) The **husband** is entitled to the full married couple's allowance (see 1.15 ALLOWANCES AND TAX RATES) (before 1990/91, the full higher personal allowance, see 1.21 ALLOWANCES AND TAX RATES) for the year of assessment in which the marriage ends. If he remarries in the same year, the proportionate reduction in such allowances by reference to the length of the part of the year of assessment before the marriage took place does not apply.

(b) The **wife**, in addition to her personal allowance for the year of assessment and, if appropriate, the additional personal allowance for children (see 1.17 ALLOWANCES AND TAX RATES), is entitled to any of the married couple's allowance not used against her husband's income and, if the husband dies, to the widow's bereavement allowance (see 1.16 ALLOWANCES AND TAX RATES). All these allowances may be set against any income of the year or, where relevant, used to reduce the total tax liability for the year.

For 1989/90 and earlier years, the income of the wife up to the date the marriage ended was generally deemed to be that of her husband (see 47.6 above), against which wife's earned income relief (see 1.22 ALLOWANCES AND TAX RATES) may be available. The wife was entitled to the full single personal allowance against her income from the date the marriage ended to the following 5 April, and in addition, where appropriate, to the additional personal allowance for children and the widow's bereavement allowance. If a wife's earnings election (see 47.9 above) was in force for the year in which the marriage ended, the wife was also entitled to a single personal allowance against her earnings up to the date on which the marriage ended.

(c) See 71.9 SCHEDULE D, CASES I AND II for concessional continuation treatment of business previously carried on by, or in partnership with, deceased spouse. For 1989/90 and earlier years, the ending of the marriage other than by death (and the consequent ending of aggregation, see 47.6 above) does not cause the rules as to new and ceasing sources of income to apply (and see 47.10(*b*) above).

(*d*)   Interest payable by each former spouse on a property held on a joint tenancy or as tenants in common will be allowable, subject to the usual conditions, but the allowance may be restricted where the amount of the mortgage on which a former spouse pays interest exceeds the value of his/her interest in the property. (CCAB Memorandum TR 500, 10 March 1983).

47.15   **Alimony, maintenance, separation allowances, etc.**

See generally Revenue Pamphlet IR 93.

Payments of alimony and maintenance falling due **after 14 March 1988** and made other than under an 'existing obligation' (see 1.8(i) ALLOWANCES AND TAX RATES) are not charges on the income of the person making the payment and tax is not deductible at source. Such payments do not form part of the taxable income of the person to whom they are made or of any other person. Where such payments are 'qualifying maintenance payments', the payer obtains relief by reference to the lesser of

(*a*)   the aggregate amount of 'qualifying maintenance payments' made by him which fall due in that year, and

(*b*)   the amount of the married couple's allowance for that year (see 1.15 ALLOWANCES AND TAX RATES) (before 1990/91, the amount of the difference between the single person's allowance and the married man's allowance (see 1.20, 1.21 ALLOWANCES AND TAX RATES)).

For 1993/94 and earlier years, the relief was given as a deduction in arriving at the payer's total income, and thus saved tax at his marginal rate. If the payer also made other maintenance payments, under existing obligations, the deduction was reduced by the aggregate of such payments attracting tax relief for the year in question. For 1994/95 and subsequent years, relief is given at a reduced rate, 20% for 1994/95 and 15% thereafter. The relief is no longer given as a deduction from total income, but is given instead by means of a reduction in the payer's income tax liability. The reduction is the smaller of the specified percentage (i.e. 15% for 1995/96) of the amount established above and what would otherwise be the payer's total income tax liability. For this purpose, 'total income tax liability' is as defined in 1.15 ALLOWANCES AND TAX RATES, except that it is before any reductions on account of personal reliefs (where these are also given by way of reduction in income tax liability—see 1.15 to 1.17 ALLOWANCES AND TAX RATES).

For 1994/95 and subsequent years, so much of the aggregate of payments under existing obligations which attract tax relief as does not exceed the married couple's allowance is treated as if it were a qualifying maintenance payment made otherwise than under an existing obligation, and thus attracts the above relief subject to the overall limit.

A '*qualifying maintenance payment*' is a periodical payment (other than an instalment of a lump sum) which

(A)   is made under a UK (from 1992/93 a European Community, from 1 January 1994 a European Economic Area) Court Order, or under a written agreement the proper law of which is the law of a part of the UK (from 1992/93 a part of the European Community, from 1 January 1994 a part of the European Economic Area), or (after 5 April 1993) under a maintenance assessment made under the *Child Support Act 1991* (or NI equivalent),

(B)   is made by one party to a marriage (or former marriage) either

(i)   to or for the benefit of, and for the maintenance of, the other party, or

        (ii)   to the other party for the maintenance by that other party of a 'child of the family',

(C)   is due at a time when

        (i)   the two parties are not a married couple living together within *Sec 282(1)* and disregarding *Sec 282(2)* (see 47.12 above), and

        (ii)   the party to whom or for whose benefit the payment is made has not remarried, and

(D)   does not attract tax relief for the person making the payment, apart from the deduction specified above.

(B) above is treated as satisfied in relation to periodical payments made to or retained by the Secretary of State after 5 April 1993 under a maintenance assessment under the *Child Support Act 1991* (or NI equivalent) by one party to a marriage (whether or not dissolved or annulled) where the other party is, for the purposes of that *Act*, a parent of the child(ren) to whom the assessment relates. Assessments under *section 7* of that *Act* (right of child in Scotland to apply for maintenance assessment) are excluded from this treatment. Payments to the Secretary of State under *Social Security Administration Act 1992, s 106* or *Jobseekers Act 1995, s 23* (or NI equivalent of either) by one party to a marriage (whether or not dissolved or annulled) in respect of income support or an income-based jobseeker's allowance claimed by the other party are similarly treated as satisfying (B) above in relation to payments falling due after 5 April 1993.

A '*child of the family*' is a person under 21 who is either a child of both parties to a marriage or has been treated by them both as a child of their family, but excluding a child who has been boarded out with them by a public authority or voluntary organisation.

[*Sec 347B; FA 1988, ss 36, 38(3A), 40, 3 Sch 13; F(No 2)A 1992, ss 61, 62(1); FA 1994, s 79(1)(3)–(6)(8); SI 1992 No 2642; Jobseekers Act 1995, 2 Sch 15*].

Payments under 'existing obligations' (see 1.8(i) ALLOWANCES AND TAX RATES). For years of assessment before 1989/90, and except in the case of **small maintenance payments**, tax was deductible from payments, unless the Order directs them to be made in full, or without deduction of tax, or free of tax, in which cases the payments must be grossed up for all tax purposes. Under Scots law, an appropriately worded minute of agreement between the parties, registered for preservation and execution with the Court of Session, will have the same effect as a Court Order for these purposes (see Tolley's Practical Tax 1983 p 179).

Where an interim Court Order (which cannot apply to payments for a period exceeding three months) is made, it is understood that the Revenue treat payments under the Order as not being annual payments, so that tax could not be deducted or repaid.

Where maintenance payments to a divorced or separated spouse, or to the mother of his illegitimate child, are annual payments from which the spouse or father could deduct tax under *Sec 348*, but were made gross, the Revenue, by concession,

        (i)   allow to the payer against any tax retained in charge in respect of the maintenance payments a sum equal to the balance of any relief or repayment the recipient could have claimed had tax been deducted, but which cannot be allowed against the recipient's tax liability, and

        (ii)   regard the payments in the recipient's hands as taxed before receipt, but as not being available for repayment.

Similar concessional relief is available where payments are made direct to a child under a Court Order.

After 5 April 1989, the concession was of relevance only to payments under 'existing obligations' either due before 6 April 1989, or payable under a Court Order in favour of a child of 21 or over or, before 6 April 1995, under an agreement in favour of a child of 18 or over. The concession is of no relevance to payments made after 5 April 1996.

(Revenue Pamphlet IR 1, A52).

See 23.8(*b*) DEDUCTION OF TAX AT SOURCE for recovery of tax not deducted at time of payment and 23.16 for orders 'free of tax' and 25.5(*a*) DOUBLE TAX RELIEF where payer is resident abroad.

For 1988/89, a person in receipt of maintenance payments made in pursuance of an 'existing obligation' under a Court Order, in the UK or elsewhere, or under a written or oral agreement, which satisfy the conditions at (B) and (C) above, which are within the charge to SCHEDULE D, CASE III (72) or SCHEDULE D, CASE V (73) and which are not regarded under any provision of *Part XV* (see 80 SETTLEMENTS) as the income of the payer, may deduct, in computing his total income, the lesser of the aggregate amount of such payments and £1,490. [*FA 1988, s 37*].

For 1989/90 and subsequent years, payments satisfying the conditions set out below are to be made without deduction of tax and are not charges on income. For payments due in 1989/90 to 1993/94 inclusive, the payer may, in computing his total income, claim a deduction of the lesser of

(*aa*)   the aggregate amount of such payments falling due and made by him in the year of assessment, and

(*bb*)   the aggregate amount of payments due in 1988/89 which also satisfied the conditions set out below and for which he was entitled to tax relief for 1988/89.

The Revenue have in the past in practice allowed relief by reference to the full amount paid in 1988/89 notwithstanding that the payer's income was insufficient to allow full relief to be given for the payments. This practice is no longer applied (although claimants already receiving relief on this basis will not be affected by withdrawal of the practice). (Revenue Tax Bulletin February 1995 p 193).

For payments due in 1994/95 and subsequent years, the deduction is limited to the excess, if any, of the amount established as above over the amount of the married couple's allowance (see 1.15 ALLOWANCES AND TAX RATES). So much of the amount established as above as does *not* exceed the married couple's allowance is treated as if it were a qualifying maintenance payment made otherwise than under an existing obligation, and relief is thus given (subject to an overall limit) at a reduced rate and by way of a reduction in income tax liability rather than by deduction in computing total income (see above).

Such payments will form part of the recipient's taxable income and be chargeable under Schedule D, Case III (generally on a current year basis, see 72.4(*a*) SCHEDULE D, CASE III), or Case V if arising outside the UK, but only to the extent of the aggregate amount of payments received from the same payer which satisfied the conditions below and which formed part of his taxable income for 1988/89 (disregarding the above-mentioned deduction of up to £1,490 for that year). In addition, where the payments meet the conditions in (B) and (C) above, the recipient may claim, in respect of such payments, a deduction not exceeding an amount identical to that in (*b*) above. Where, for 1994/95 onwards, part of the aggregate payments falls to be treated, as regards the payer, as a qualifying maintenance payment (see above), this does *not* affect the tax position of the recipient, who continues to be taxed as if such part were a payment under an existing obligation.

These provisions apply to annual payments falling due in 1989/90 or any subsequent year which

(AA) are made in pursuance of an existing obligation under a Court Order, in the UK or elsewhere, or a written or oral agreement, or (after 5 April 1993) a maintenance assessment under the *Child Support Act 1991* (or NI equivalent),

(BB) are made by an individual either

    (i) to or for the benefit of, and for the maintenance of, his or her spouse or ex-spouse, or

    (ii) to any person under 21 for his own benefit, maintenance or education, or

    (iii) to any person for the benefit, maintenance or education of a person under 21, and

(CC) are, apart from these provisions, within the charge to tax under Schedule D, Case III or Case V and are not, under any provision of *Part XV* (see 80 SETTLEMENTS), regarded as the income of the payer.

[*FA 1988, s 38; F(No 2)A 1992, s 62(3); FA 1994, s 79(7)(8); SI 1992 No 2642*].

Before 6 April 1996, payments under a Court Order to, or for the maintenance of, a child aged 21 or over, continued to be made with deduction of tax (where such payments continued to be treated as made under an existing obligation—see 1.8(i) ALLOWANCES AND TAX RATES). Before 6 April 1995, payments under an agreement to, or for the maintenance of, a child aged 18 or over fell within *Sec 683* (see 80.28 SETTLEMENTS), and were thus within (CC) above, and made under deduction of tax. Where such payments are made on or after the said dates, they are disregarded for tax purposes. See also 23.9 DEDUCTION OF TAX AT SOURCE.

Where maintenance payments are made under existing obligations such that the above rules would apply, the payer may elect that they be treated in the same way as maintenance payments other than under existing obligations, and that *FA 1988, s 36* (see above) should thus apply thereto. The election must cover all such payments falling due in a year of assessment for which it has effect. It must be made in prescribed form (i.e. Form 142) and within, for 1996/97 and later years, twelve months after 31 January following the first year of assessment to which it is to apply (previously, twelve months after the end of that first year), will continue to have effect for subsequent years and is irrevocable. A person making such an election must, within 30 days of the date on which it is made, give notice thereof to every recipient of a payment affected by the election. [*FA 1988, s 39; FA 1996, s 135, 21 Sch 25*].

General matters. Court Orders for alimony generally take into account the income and tax liabilities of both parties.

Maintenance receipts, where taxable, are investment income.

If, under a **Divorce Court Order**, payments are made *to the wife* for the maintenance of children, such income is for tax purposes the wife's and not the children's (see *Stevens v*

Tirard CA 1939, 23 TC 321; Spencer v Robson KB 1946, 27 TC 198). Where a Court orders payment direct to the child, the income is that of the child. Under Scots law, where a child is entitled to aliment in his own right but payment is made to the parent with custody *qua tutrix* (or *tutor, curator, curatrix*), the income is that of the child for tax purposes. (*Huggins v Huggins 1981 SLT 179*). In strict law, the retrospective variation of an Order is not effective for tax purposes (*Morley-Clarke v Jones CA 1985, 59 TC 567*). In practice, however, where, before 1 July 1988, an Order, whether original or varying an existing Order, provides for payments for a period prior to the date of that Order, the Revenue will accept that such payments can be taken into account for tax purposes provided (i) the payments do not relate to a period before the date of application for the Order, (ii) the parties agree, and (iii) there has been no undue delay by the parties in pressing the application. (Revenue Pamphlet IR 131, SP 6/81, 8 September 1981). For Orders made or varied after 30 June 1988 which provide for retrospective payments, only payments made on or after the date of the Order count towards the limit on which tax relief is available in any year. Payments made under a legally binding written agreement before the Court Order may of course qualify in their own right. (Revenue Press Release 15 March 1988). Payments made under an agreement voluntarily entered into by a father in favour of his children, for their maintenance following separation, and later confirmed by a Court Order, were not made under that Order and were thus ineffective for tax purposes (*CIR v Craw CS 1985, 59 TC 56*).

Where the Court orders maintenance payments by a former spouse direct to his/her child who is living with the other spouse and an element is included to cover school fees, those fees may be paid direct to the school in *full* out of the *net* amount due under the maintenance order after tax at the basic rate has been deducted (assuming deduction at source to be still applicable) from the total amount payable, including the school fees. The payments will form part of the taxable income of the child, subject to the general rules outlined above. The Order normally includes: 'that part of the Order which reflects the school fees shall be paid to the (headmaster/bursar/school secretary) as agent for the said child and the receipt of that payee shall be sufficient discharge'.

The onus will be on the parties themselves to produce evidence, where requested, that the person receiving the school fees has agreed to act as agent for the child and that the contract for the payment of the fees (which is most easily proved if in writing) is between the child (not the spouse making the payments) and the school. (Revenue Pamphlet IR 131, SP 15/80, 14 November 1980 and see Tolley's Practical Tax 1983 p 124.)

See also *Sherdley v Sherdley HL, [1987] STC 217*, where the validity of such arrangements was considered and affirmed in a case where an Order was sought against himself by the parent having custody.

47.16   *Examples*

Maintenance payments: Court Orders before 15 March 1988
Mr Smith separated from his wife on 31 October 1987. For 1996/97 he has assessable Schedule D, Case I profits of £22,000 and building society interest of £4,000 (net). He pays mortgage interest of £2,400 on a home loan of under £30,000 which is outside the MIRAS scheme. Under a Court Order dated 5 March 1988, Mr Smith paid £50 per week maintenance directly to his son, Paul, aged 17 in 1996/97, who lives with Mrs Smith, and £70 per week maintenance to Mrs Smith. On 1 June 1990, the payments to Mrs Smith were increased by the Court to £100 per week. In 1996/97, Mrs Smith has earnings of £5,500. Paul Smith has no other income.

47.16   Married Persons

1996/97

Mr Smith

	£	£
Earned income		22,000
Building society interest	4,000	
Add Tax deducted at source	1,000	5,000
		27,000

Deduct: Maintenance payments:

	£	£
Wife £70 × 52 note (*a*)	3,640	
Son £50 × 52	2,600	
	6,240	
Less the first £1,790 note (*b*)	1,790	
		(4,450)
Total income		22,550
Deduct Personal allowance		3,765
Taxable income		£18,785

Tax payable:

3,900 @ 20%	780.00
9,885 @ 24%	2,372.40
5,000 @ 20%	1,000.00
	4,152.40
Deduct Mortgage interest relief £2,400 @ 15%	360.00
	3,792.40
Deduct Maintenance £1,790 @ 15% note (*b*)	268.50
Total tax liability	3,523.90
Deduct Tax paid on building society interest	1,000.00
Net tax liability	£2,523.90

Mrs Smith

	£	£
Earned income		5,500
Maintenance note (*a*)	3,640	
Deduction note (*a*)	1,790	
		1,850
Total income		7,350
Deduct Personal allowance note (*c*)		3,765
Taxable income		£3,585

Tax payable:

3,585 @ 20%	£717.00

474

Paul Smith	£
Maintenance	2,600
Deduct Personal allowance (restricted)	2,600
Taxable income	Nil
Tax payable/repayable	Nil

Notes

(*a*)   The tax relief and the amount chargeable on the recipient is limited to the relief obtainable and the amount forming part of the recipient's income for 1988/89. The recipient may then deduct from the amount otherwise chargeable an amount equal to the married couple's allowance for the year, providing the payments are from a divorced or separated spouse. See 47.15 above.

(*b*)   For 1996/97 and subsequent years, the first £1,790 of allowable maintenance payments attracts relief at 15%, such relief being given as an income tax reduction (see 47.15 above).

(*c*)   Mrs Smith may also be entitled to the additional personal allowance in respect of Paul if all the conditions of *Sec 259* are satisfied (see 1.17 ALLOWANCES AND TAX RATES).

Maintenance payments: Court Orders after 14 March 1988
Mr Green separated from his wife in June 1995 and, under a Court Order dated 15 July 1996, pays maintenance of £300 per month to his ex-wife and £100 per month to his daughter, payments being due on the first of each calendar month commencing 1 August 1996. Mr Green has earned income of £17,000 and dividends of £4,000 for 1996/97. He re-marries on 6 October 1996.

	£	£
1996/97		
Mr Green		
Earned income		17,000
Dividends	4,000	
Add Tax credits (£4,000 × 1/4)	1,000	5,000
Total income		22,000
Deduct Personal allowance		3,765
Taxable income		£18,235

48.1 Medical Insurance

	£
Tax payable:	
3,900 @ 20%	780.00
9,335 @ 24%	2,240.40
5,000 @ 20%	1,000.00
	4,020.40
Deduct Maintenance relief—wife:	
£2,700 paid, but restricted to £1,790 @ 15%	268.50
	3,751.90
Deduct Married couple's allowance	
£1,790 × 6/12 = £895 @ 15%	134.25
Total tax liability	3,617.65
Deduct Tax credits	1,000.00
Net tax liability (subject to PAYE deductions)	£2,617.65

48 Medical Insurance

(See Revenue Pamphlet IR 103.)

48.1   Where a UK resident individual makes a payment in respect of a private medical insurance premium under an 'eligible contract' insuring a UK resident individual or individuals who, or each of whom, is aged 60 or over at the date of the payment (or, where a married couple is insured, at least one of whom is aged 60 or over at that time), he may claim relief (see below) for the payment, provided that he is not entitled to any other relief or deduction in respect of the payment and does not make it out of resources provided by another person for the purpose of enabling it to be made. Crown employees treated as performing their duties in the UK under *Sec 132(4)(a)* (see 75.2(i) SCHEDULE E) are treated as UK resident for these purposes. Where a payment is made under a contract insuring a married couple one of whom is 60 or over, and the said spouse dies, a subsequent payment under the same contract is not disqualified from relief by virtue of the surviving spouse being under 60; this applies where the first or only payment after the death is made after 5 April 1994.

Payments made before 6 April 1994 were deductible in arriving at the individual's total income for the year of assessment in which the payment was made (and, consequently, relief was at the individual's marginal tax rate). For payments made after 5 April 1994, basic rate tax relief continues normally to be given by deduction at source (see below), but no further relief is available and the payment does not reduce the individual's total income. Where basic rate relief is not given at source, it is given by way of a reduction in the individual's total income tax liability and the relief is restricted to what would otherwise be the amount of that liability. For this purpose, 'total income tax liability' is as defined in 1.15 ALLOWANCES AND TAX RATES, except that it is before any reductions on account of personal reliefs, maintenance payments and interest payable (where such items are also relieved by way of reduction in income tax liability – see 1.15 to 1.17 ALLOWANCES AND TAX RATES, 47.15 MARRIED PERSONS and 43.3 INTEREST PAYABLE).

[*FA 1989, s 54(1)–(3C)(9); FA 1994, 10 Sch 2, 4*].

Regulations provide for the payment to be made under deduction of basic rate tax, the payee reclaiming the tax deducted from the Revenue, and for relief to be withdrawn, and the related tax accounted for, in prescribed circumstances. The Revenue consider that where a payment *may* be made under deduction of basic rate tax, basic rate relief can *only* be obtained by deduction. The tax deducted from payments is not clawed back where the individual is liable only at the lower rate of income tax or has no, or insufficient, income tax liability. For relief to be given by deduction at source, the individual must provide a notice of entitlement to relief, containing specified information and undertakings, etc., to the person to whom payments are made under the contract. That person must be either a 'qualifying insurer' (see 48.4 below) or a managing agent, either with Lloyd's or for a 'qualifying insurer'. The insurer (or agent) must have no reason to doubt any of the information given by the individual, must have undertaken to observe the requirements of the regulations (and, in the event of failure, must satisfy the Board that he is able and willing to observe them in future), and must have undertaken that, before entering into a further contract, he will give notice to the individual of his obligation to notify the insurer of any relevant changes in his (or the insured's) circumstances. Any refunded payments must not exceed the payment actually made, and any amount recovered from the Board in respect of tax deducted from payments which are refunded must be accounted for to the Board. There are detailed regulations for the recovery from the Board of tax deducted from payments, and for approval of standard forms of contract. [*FA 1989, s 54(4)–(8); FA 1996, s 129; SI 1989 No 2387; SI 1994 Nos 1518, 1527*].

The Inland Revenue Financial Intermediaries and Claims Office may be contacted in relation to private medical insurance on 0151–472 6172 as regards repayments or 0151–472 6157 for technical advice.

48.2   A contract is an '*eligible contract*' if, at the date it was entered into, the insurer was a 'qualifying insurer' approved by the Board for these purposes, and the period of insurance does not exceed one year from that date. As regards approval of qualifying insurers, see *SI 1989 No 2387, regs 12–14* as amended by *SI 1994 No 1527, reg 11*. No benefit other than an 'approved benefit' must have been provided by virtue of the contract, and the contract must not be, or have been, 'connected with' another contract.

As regards payments made before 1 July 1994, the contract must meet one or more of the following three conditions.

(*a*)   It is certified by the Board under *FA 1989, s 56*.

(*b*)   It is in a standard form certified by the Board.

(*c*)   It varied from a standard form so certified only by additions certified by the Board as compatible with that standard form.

(*b*) and (*c*) above are to be met at the time the contract was entered into or, in relation to a payment made after a variation of the contract, at the time it was varied. The other conditions for eligibility must be met at the time the payment is made under the contract.

After 30 June 1994, certification of contracts by the Board is abolished. Instead of meeting conditions (*a*) to (*c*) above, the contract must, at the time payment is made thereunder, meet the conditions at 48.6(*a*)–(*d*) below, which are very similar to those which were previously required for certification of a contract by the Board. Where a contract confers one or more 'material rights', but the total cost to the insurer of providing benefits in pursuance thereof would not exceed £30 (which amount is variable by Treasury order), this does not preclude eligibility. There is an anti-avoidance provision to prevent the above limit being by-passed by means of certain linked contracts. A '*material right*' is a right which does not otherwise meet the conditions for eligibility and is not a right to a cash benefit.

[*FA 1989, ss 55(1)–(6)(11)–(13), 56; FA 1994, 10 Sch 5, 6*].

There is no reason in principle why members of group schemes cannot come within the scope of the relief, provided that the scheme meets the qualifying conditions. (ICAEW Technical Release TAX 17/93, 28 September 1993).

48.3 A contract is '*connected with*' another contract at any time if they are both in force at that time; one was entered into with reference to the other or to enable the other to be entered into on particular terms or to facilitate the other being so entered into; and the terms on which one of the contracts was entered into would have been significantly less favourable to the insured but for the other being entered into. [*FA 1989, s 55(7)*].

48.4 A '*qualifying insurer*' is any insurer lawfully carrying on business in the UK of any of the classes specified in *Insurance Companies Act 1982, 2 Sch Pt I*, or an insurer not carrying on business in the UK but doing so in another EC country (or, from 1 January 1994, a country within the European Economic Area) and meeting certain other conditions as to status and location. [*FA 1989, s 55(8)*].

48.5 A benefit is an '*approved benefit*' if it is provided in pursuance of rights as under 48.6(*a*) below or as specified by regulations under 48.6(*b*) below. In relation to premiums paid after 30 June 1994, one or more benefits otherwise provided (and which are not cash benefits) are also approved benefits if their total cost to the insurer does not exceed £30 (which amount is variable by Treasury order). [*FA 1989, s 55(9)(10)(12)(13); FA 1994, 10 Sch 5(6)(7)*].

48.6 The conditions a contract must meet are that:

(*a*) it either provides indemnity in respect of all or any of the costs of all or any of the treatments, medical services and other matters prescribed by regulations for these purposes or, in addition to such indemnity, provides cash benefits falling within rules prescribed by such regulations;

(*b*) it confers no other right except as may be specified by regulations;

(*c*) the premium is reasonable; and

(*d*) it satisfies such other requirements as may be specified by regulations.

As regards (*a*) above, from 1 July 1994, the treatments, etc. specified in the regulations are the treatment of the insured consisting of medical or surgical procedures (including diagnosis, drugs and dressings) for the relief of illness or injury, and services for the purposes of or consequent upon such treatment consisting of:

(i) accommodation and other (including nursing) services in a hospital where the insured is a private patient charged for the accommodation or for treatments, etc. (as above);

(ii) home nursing;

(iii) accommodation for up to 14 days' convalescence following discharge from hospital;

(iv) transport by private ambulance (including by air ambulance) accompanied (where medically necessary) by one other person to or from hospital or to or from accommodation provided for convalescence; and

(v)   physiotherapy, occupational therapy, speech therapy, chiropody and podiatry, prosthesis and orthopty (including necessary equipment).

The treatment must either

(A)   be given to the insured as a private patient in a hospital by or under the supervision of a registered medical or dental practitioner, or

(B)   in the case of surgical procedures performed by a registered medical practitioner providing personal medical services for persons in a particular locality, be given to the insured as a private patient of that practitioner,

and physiotherapy services and equipment must be provided to the insured and must be associated with treatment given to the insured by or under the supervision of a registered medical practitioner.

Treatments are excluded if they were not provided free under the *National Health Service Act 1977* (or Scottish or NI equivalent), in the five years preceding the date the contract was entered into, more often than they were provided in the UK other than under that *Act*.

The allowable cash benefit may not exceed £5 for each night in a hospital as a private patient charged for the accommodation.

Other rights within (*b*) above are the right to terminate the contract and receive a refund in respect of the unexpired period of cover, waiver or refund by the insurer of payments for a period during which the insured is receiving treatment covered by the contract, and the right to enter into a further contract at the expiry of the current contract.

[*SI 1994 No 1518*].

Contracts are not permitted to cover charges for 'alternative medicine', dental procedures in a general dental practice, general ophthalmic procedures not carried out in hospital, and medical or surgical procedures (other than GP operations as above) not on an in-, out- or day-patient basis. (Revenue Press Release 19 July 1989).

48.7   Supplementary regulatory powers are provided, and the provisions of the *Taxes Management Act 1970* applied as necessary. [*FA 1989, s 57; FA 1996, s 129, 18 Sch 12, 17(1)–(4)(8)*].

49 Mineral Royalties

[Sec 122; TCGA 1992, ss 201–203]

49.1 Where a person resident or ordinarily resident in the UK is entitled to receive mineral royalties (i.e. so much of any rents, tolls, royalties or periodical payments as relates to the winning and working of minerals other than water, peat, topsoil, etc.) under a lease, licence or agreement conferring a right to win and work minerals in the UK or under a sale or conveyance of such minerals, only one-half of any such royalties receivable in any year of assessment or accounting period is treated as income for purposes of income tax or corporation tax on profits other than chargeable gains.

Management expenses available for set-off against those royalties, under *Sec 121* or under Schedule A, are similarly reduced by one-half.

Where Betterment Levy (which was abolished after July 1970) was not chargeable on the grant of the lease, or any subsequent renewal, extension or variation of it, the other half of the royalties receivable is treated as a chargeable gain for purposes of capital gains tax (or corporation tax on chargeable gains).

Where, on the last disposition (before 23 July 1970) affecting the lease, Betterment Levy was chargeable under Case B (as defined by *Land Commission Act 1967, Pt III*) the chargeable gain, as above, is limited to a fraction (base value of that disposition/ consideration received) of one-half of the royalties received. After 5 April 1988, this limitation applies only if it applied to a chargeable period ending on or before that date. But if such a lease is renewed, extended or varied after 22 July 1970, one-half of any subsequent royalty receipt is treated as a chargeable gain.

Where payments under a mineral lease, etc. relate both to the winning and working of minerals and to other matters, the part to be treated as mineral royalties for these purposes will be calculated under regulations made by the Board. See *SI 1971 No 1035*.

These chargeable gains are assessable in full, without any deduction on account of expenditure incurred.

Income tax was deductible from royalty payments made before 1 May 1995, but if the recipient was not a person chargeable to corporation tax the excess tax so suffered was set against CGT payable as above, any balance thereafter remaining being repaid.

Terminal Losses. If the mineral lease comes to an end while the person entitled to receive the royalties still has an interest in the land, and an allowable loss would then arise to him if he sold his interest for a price equal to its market value, he may claim to be treated for CGT (or corporation tax) purposes as if he had sold, and immediately reacquired, his interest at that price, the resultant loss being allowed, at his election, either (*a*) against CGT etc. for the year in which the lease expires, or (*b*) against chargeable gains, in respect of mineral royalties under the lease, within the previous 15 years.

50   Mutual Trading

50.1   A person cannot derive a taxable profit from trading with himself except in certain cases of self-supply by a trader of trading stock, see *Sharkey v Wernher HL 1955, 36 TC 275* and 71.82 SCHEDULE D, CASES I AND II. This is extended to a group of persons engaged in mutual activities of a trading nature, if there is an identifiable 'fund' for the common purpose with complete identity between contributors to, and participators in, the fund (the *mutuality principle*). A body not liable as regards transactions with members may nevertheless be liable under Schedule D, Case I on transactions with non-members and is liable in the ordinary way on any investment etc. income. Whether the mutuality principle applies depends on the facts. For mutual insurance see *Styles v New York Life Insce Co HL 1889, 2 TC 460* (an early leading case on the mutuality principle but there are now special provisions for life insurance companies—see Tolley's Corporation Tax); *Jones v South-West Lancs Coal Owners' Assn HL 1927, 11 TC 790; Cornish Mutual Assce Co Ltd HL 1926, 12 TC 841; Municipal Mutual Insce Ltd v Hills HL 1932, 16 TC 430; Faulconbridge v National Employers' Mutual General Insce Assn Ltd Ch D 1952, 33 TC 103.* For other cases see *Liverpool Corn Trade Assn Ltd v Monks KB 1926, 10 TC 442* (trade association providing corn exchange etc. held to be trading and not 'mutual'—but see 71.83 SCHEDULE D, CASES I AND II for special arrangement available for trade associations); *English & Scottish CWS Ltd v Assam Agricultural IT Commr PC 1948, 27 ATC 332* (wholesale co-operative with two members held to be trading and not mutual—there was no 'common fund'). Similarly a members' club is not trading and not liable on its surplus from the provision of its facilities for members (*Eccentric Club Ltd CA 1923, 12 TC 657*) but liable on the surplus attributable to non-members (*Carlisle and Silloth Golf Club v Smith CA 1913, 6 TC 48; NALGO v Watkins KB 1934, 18 TC 499; Doctor's Cave Bathing Beach (Fletcher) v Jamaica IT Commr PC 1971, 50 ATC 368*).

For distribution of assets by a company carrying on mutual business, see Tolley's Corporation Tax.

51   Non-residents and other Overseas Matters

Cross-references. See 64 RESIDENCE, ORDINARY RESIDENCE AND DOMICILE for the meaning of those terms. See also ANTI-AVOIDANCE at 3.8 regarding income payable to person abroad assessable on UK resident in certain circumstances; 3.9 for trading transactions with a non-resident under common control; 23 DEDUCTION OF TAX AT SOURCE for certain payments to non-residents; 24 DIPLOMATIC IMMUNITY, including international organisations etc.; 25 DOUBLE TAX RELIEF; 33.2 GOVERNMENT STOCKS for exemption on certain stocks held by non-residents; 47.12 MARRIED PERSONS where one spouse is resident abroad; 53 PARTNERSHIPS; 59 PENSIONS; 63 REMITTANCE BASIS; 70 SCHEDULE C regarding paying and collecting agents; 73 SCHEDULE D, CASES IV AND V under which assessments are raised on income from overseas securities and possessions; 75.3 to 75.6 SCHEDULE E for earnings from work done abroad and expenses.

Headings in this chapter are as follows.

51.1   **LIMIT ON INCOME CHARGEABLE ON NON-RESIDENTS**

For **1996/97 and subsequent years** (and see below as regards 1995/96), the income tax chargeable on the total income of a non-UK resident is not to exceed the aggregate of

(i)   the tax which would otherwise be chargeable if 'excluded income' and any personal allowances due (see 51.11 below) were both disregarded, and

(ii)   the tax deducted from so much of the 'excluded income' as is subject to deduction of income tax at source (including tax credits and tax treated as deducted at source).

Income is *'excluded income'* if it falls into one of the categories below and is not income in relation to which the non-resident has a UK representative for the purposes of the provisions at 51.5 to 51.7 below (i.e. income from or connected with a trade etc. carried on in the UK through a branch or agency, subject to the exclusions at 51.6). The categories are:

(*a*)   income chargeable under SCHEDULE C (70), SCHEDULE D, CASE III (72) or SCHEDULE F (76);

(*b*)   income chargeable under Schedule D, Case VI by virtue of *Sec 56* (see 13 CERTIFICATES OF DEPOSIT);

(*c*)   certain social security benefits (including state pensions);

(*d*)   income not falling within (*a*)-(*c*) above and not being Lloyd's underwriting profits, which arises as mentioned in 51.6(2)(3) below (certain income from trading in the UK through a broker or investment manager); and

(e)   any income designated for these purposes by Treasury regulations.

These provisions do not apply to limit the income tax chargeable on a settlement if any actual or potential beneficiary, whether his interest is absolute or discretionary, is an individual ordinarily resident in the UK or a UK resident company.

These provisions replace Revenue extra-statutory concessions B13 (which covered income within (a), (b) and, in practice, (c) above—see 51.3 below) and B40 (which covered broadly the same ground as (d) above—see 51.4 below). There may 'exceptionally' be arrangements set up before 29 November 1994 which fall outside the statutory provisions and to which ESC B40 will continue to apply until, at the latest, 5 April 2005 (see Revenue Press Release IR 31, 29 November 1994).

These provisions also have limited application for **1995/96** to income from certain transactions carried out through brokers and investment managers and to income within (c) above. In order to be excluded income, the income must arise after 5 April 1995 and must not be income in relation to which the non-resident would have a UK representative if the provisions in 51.5 to 51.7 below applied for 1995/96. The provisions apply to income within (a) or (b) above only if it arises from a transaction

(i)   which is carried out on the non-resident's behalf by a person then carrying on the business of a broker or, in the case of an investment transaction (as defined), of providing investment management services,

(ii)   which is carried out in the ordinary course of that business, and

(iii)   in respect of which the remuneration received by the broker or investment manager was at a rate not less than would have been customary for that class of business.

For the purposes only of applying (d) above, the provisions at 51.6 below are treated as applying for 1995/96. Extra-statutory concession B13 continues to apply for 1995/96 to income within (a) or (b) above which is not covered by the above provisions.

[*FA 1995, s 128*].

See Tolley's Corporation Tax under Residence for corresponding provisions applicable to non-resident companies.

51.2   *Example*

Hugh and Elizabeth are non-resident in the UK throughout 1996/97. They are each entitled to a UK personal allowance under the provisions in 51.11 below. Their tax liabilities on total UK income for 1996/97, disregarding the limit under *FA 1995, s 128* are as follows.

	Hugh £	Elizabeth £
Net rental income (Schedule A)	2,000	5,000
Bank interest (received gross)	4,265	565
Dividends	3,600	—
Tax credits	900	—
Total UK income	10,765	5,565
Deduct Personal allowance	3,765	3,765
Taxable UK income	£7,000	£1,800

51.3 Non-residents and other Overseas Matters

Tax on total UK income:

	£	£
£3,900/1,800 @ 20%	780.00	360.00
£3,100 @ 20% (savings income)	620.00	
	1,400.00	360.00
Deduct Tax credits	900.00	
	£500.00	£360.00

But tax is limited under *FA 1995, s 128* as follows.

	£	£
Schedule A	2,000	5,000

(Bank interest and dividends are 'excluded income'—see 51.1 above.)

	£	£
£2,000/3,900 @ 20%	400.00	780.00
£1,100 @ 24%		264.00
	£400.00	£1,044.00

Hugh's UK income tax liability is therefore restricted to £400.00 (plus £900.00 in tax credits, which cannot be reclaimed). Elizabeth's liability is not reduced under *FA 1995, s 128* and is thus £360.00.

51.3 COLLECTION OF TAX

The concession described below is replaced by the provisions at 51.1 above with effect as stated in that paragraph.

Although tax is legally assessable by notice served abroad, there are difficulties in collection. Where untaxed interest is paid to a person who for any year of assessment is regarded as non-resident, no action is taken to recover the tax unless a trustee or an agent or branch having the management and control of the interest is chargeable or a set-off is available against a claim to repayment of tax deducted from other UK income (unless repayment arises due to the other income being exempt from UK tax or treated as such under a double tax agreement). This applies equally to discounts, to profits on disposals of certificates of deposit, to building society dividends paid gross, to amounts representing interest on general client accounts, to 'income elements' chargeable in respect of a deep discount security and to 'deep gains' (see 44.5, 44.7 INTEREST RECEIVABLE) and to interest on quoted Eurobonds (Revenue Pamphlet IR 131, SP 8/84, 18 October 1984). (Revenue Pamphlets IR1, B13 and IR 20, para 7.8). In practice state pensions and small maintenance payments are similarly treated (see *Taxation* 24 August 1989, p 632). UK Courts will not enforce the Revenue laws of other countries. See *Govt of India v Taylor HL 1955, 34 ATC 10*, and *US Govt v Brokaw, Shaheen and Seatrain CA 1971, 50 ATC 95*.

51.4 NON-RESIDENTS TRADING IN UK—1995/96 AND EARLIER YEARS

The provisions of *TMA ss 78-85* described in (a)-(c) below no longer apply for 1996/97 and subsequent years for income tax and for company accounting periods beginning after 31 March 1996. They are replaced by provisions described at 51.5 to 51.7 below. See also 51.1 above (limitation on income chargeable on non-residents).

See DOUBLE TAX RELIEF (25) agreements generally. Subject to these the general position is as follows.

(a) **Assessability of UK profits.** The location of a business depends on from where it is managed and controlled (see 51.12 below) but a non-resident is liable on profits from a business 'exercised within' the UK [*Sec 18(1)(a)(iii)*] and is therefore liable if trading in the UK notwithstanding that the centre of control of his business is abroad (cf. *A-G v Alexander [1874] 10 Ex D 20*).

Where a non-resident carries on a trade partly in and partly outside the UK, the charge to UK tax is limited to the profits from the part of the trade carried on in the UK. The Revenue have reaffirmed that the profits from a part of a trade carried on in the UK are to be measured on the arm's length principle set out in the OECD model tax convention and explained in OECD publications, irrespective of whether a double tax agreement applies. (Revenue Tax Bulletin August 1995 pp 237–239).

The primary factors in deciding whether there is trading in the UK is whether or not the contracts for the sale of goods or performance of services are made in the UK, but each case depends on the facts. For cases illustrating this principle see *Erichsen v Last CA 1881, 1 TC 351, 537; 4 TC 422*, and the cases referred to at (*b*) below.

If profits 'cannot in any case be readily ascertained', the assessment will be made on percentage of turnover, particulars of which agent (see below) is obliged to disclose; if goods made abroad, on selling profits only. (With rights of appeal against percentage to Commissioners and from them to a board of referees to be appointed for this purpose by the Treasury.) [*TMA ss 80, 81*].

Provisions to prevent avoidance by sales at other than market price, where one of the parties is controlled by the other, are contained in *Sec 770* (see 3.9 ANTI-AVOIDANCE).

(*b*) **UK Agents.** A non-resident trading in the UK will generally do so through a UK agent or branch. Such an agent etc. is personally assessable on all profits arising directly or indirectly through a regular UK agency, branch, etc., whether in receipt of the profits or not but he may retain the tax out of money coming into his hands and be indemnified. Certain providers of investment management services are excluded from the operation of *TMA s 78(1)*. [*TMA ss 78, 79, 83, 84; FA 1985, s 50; FA 1991, s 81*]. For whether a lawyer acting for a non-resident company in a single trading transaction was the company's UK agent, see *Willson v Hooker Ch D, [1995] STC 1142*. For the Revenue's view on the effect of UK trading on the exclusion of investment managers from *TMA s 78*, the meaning of 'investment transactions' in that context, and the relevant factors in determining whether the active management of a portfolio on behalf of a non-resident client constitutes the exercise of a trade in the UK by that client, see Revenue Pamphlet IR 131, SP 15/91, 29 November 1991 and Revenue Tax Bulletin November 1992 p 44.

These provisions do not preclude assessment on the non-resident direct (if he can be served with a notice of assessment) whether or not he has an agent (cf. *Tischler v Apthorpe Q/B 1885, 2 TC 89*). For cases where a non-resident has been held to be trading in the UK and assessed through an agent, see *Wingate & Co v Webber C/E/S 1897, 3 TC 569* (Glasgow agent of foreign ship-owner); *Watson v Sandie & Hull Q/B 1897, 3 TC 611* (commission agent selling in own name); *Thomas Turner (Leicester) Ltd v Rickman Q/B 1898, 4 TC 25* and *Macpherson & Co v Moore SC/S 1912, 6 TC 107* (agent's sales subject to principal's approval and goods consigned to agent for delivery); *Wilcock v Pinto & Co C/A 1924, 9 TC 111* and *Belfour v Mace C/A 1928, 13 TC 539* (agent's sales subject to approval by principal and goods consigned by principal); *Brackett v Chater C/D 1986, 60 TC 134* (provision of consultancy services in UK to non-resident company). For cases in which the non-resident, assessed through an agent, was held not to be trading in the UK see *Grainger & Son v Gough H/L 1896, 3 TC 311, 462* (commission agent merely transmitted orders for execution by principal); *Smidth & Co v Greenwood H/L 1922, 8 TC 193* (contracts executed by principal abroad—*TMA s 79* is a machinery provision not extending the scope of the charge); *Boston Deep Sea Fishing v Farnham C/D 1957, 37 TC 505* (no agency).

But under *TMA s 82*, bona fide brokers or general commission agents, although they may act regularly for a non-resident, are not chargeable on the latter's profits, provided they receive not less than the remuneration customary in that class of business and provided they are not authorised persons carrying on the regular agency of the non-resident. See for this *Gavazzi v Mace K/B 1926, 10 TC 698; Tarn v Scanlan H/L 1927, 13 TC 91; Rowson v Stephen K/B 1929, 14 TC 543; Fleming v London Produce Co Ltd C/D 1968, 44 TC 582; Firestone Tyre & Rubber Co Ltd v Lewellin H/L 1957, 37 TC 111.*

Where an agent is specifically protected from assessment under *TMA s 78(1)* by the terms of the provisions described above relating to investment managers (*TMA s 78(2)*) or brokers and general commission agents (*TMA s 82(1)*), the Revenue, by concession, do not seek to assess the non-resident directly, or the agent under *TMA s 79* or *Sec 59* (income under Schedule D assessable on the person entitled to it). The concession does not apply to income on which a non-resident's liability is not pursued under extra-statutory concession B 13 (see 51.3 above), or if the employment of the UK agent exceeds the normal use of investment managers, brokers or general commission agents within the appropriate exemption, or if the non-resident has some other UK presence, not within those exemptions, carrying on activities related to the agency transactions. (Revenue Pamphlet IR 1, B40).

For 'double foreigner' transactions, i.e. sales etc. by one non-resident to another, see *TMA s 82(2)* and *Maclaine & Co v Eccott HL 1926, 10 TC 481* and *W H Muller & Co v Lethem HL 1927, 13 TC 126.*

See also 51.4(*d*) below.

(*c*) **Companies.** For the charge to corporation tax on non-resident companies, see *Sec 11* and Tolley's Corporation Tax. The provisions of *TMA ss 78–84*, described at (*a*) and (*b*) above, apply with any necessary adaptations to companies. [*TMA s 85; F(No 2)A 1987, 6 Sch 7*].

51.5   NON-RESIDENTS TRADING IN UK—1996/97 AND SUBSEQUENT YEARS

The provisions described below apply where a non-UK resident carries on a trade in the UK through a branch or agency (which means any factorship, agency, receivership, branch or management [*TMA s 118(1)*]). They establish the obligations and liabilities of UK representatives of such non-residents under self-assessment (and apply equally for corporation tax), and replace *TMA ss 78–85* (see 51.4 above). The new provisons have effect for 1996/97 and subsequent years for income tax and capital gains tax and for company accounting periods beginning after 31 March 1996. See also 78.43 SELF-ASSESSMENT.

Where a non-resident carries on a trade partly in and partly outside the UK, the charge to UK tax is limited, under general principles, to the profits from the part of the trade carried on in the UK (whether or not through a branch or agency). See also 51.4(*a*) above for assessability of UK profits generally. The Revenue have reaffirmed that the profits from a part of a trade carried on in the UK are to be measured on the arm's length principle set out in the OECD model tax convention and explained in OECD publications, irrespective of whether a double tax agreement applies. (Revenue Tax Bulletin August 1995 pp 237–239).

Meaning of 'UK representative'. For the purposes of 51.7 below and subject to 51.6 below (persons not treated as UK representatives), a branch or agency in the UK through which a non-resident carries on (solely or in partnership) a trade, profession or vocation is his UK representative in relation to the following:

(*a*)   such income from the trade etc. as arises, directly or indirectly, through or from the branch or agency;

(*b*)   any income from property or rights used by, or held by or for, the branch or agency;

(*c*)   capital gains arising in connection with the branch or agency and chargeable under *TCGA 1992, s 10* (see Tolley's Capital Gains Tax); and

(*d*)   certain other amounts where the non-resident is an overseas life insurance company.

Where the non-resident ceases to carry on the trade etc. through the branch or agency, it continues to be his UK representative for tax purposes in relation to amounts arising during the period of the agency. A UK representative is a legal entity distinct from the non-resident. Where the branch or agency is a partnership, the partnership is the non-resident's UK representative. If a trade etc. is carried on in the UK by a non-resident in partnership with at least one UK resident partner, the partnership itself is the UK representative in relation to the non-resident's share of UK profits. [*FA 1995, s 126*].

51.6   **Persons not treated as UK representatives for tax purposes.** The following are not treated as UK representatives for the purposes of 51.7 below.

(1)   *Casual Agents.* An agent is not treated as a non-UK resident's UK representative in relation to income etc. arising from so much of any business as relates to transactions carried out through the agent otherwise than in the course of carrying on a regular agency for the non-resident.

(2)   *Brokers.* A broker is not treated as a non-resident's UK representative in relation to income etc. arising from so much of any business as relates to transactions carried out through the broker and satisfying all the following conditions:

    (i)   the broker was carrying on the business of broker at the time of the transaction;

    (ii)   the transaction was carried out in the ordinary course of that business;

    (iii)   the remuneration for that transaction was at a rate not less than would have been customary for that class of business; and

    (iv)   the broker is not the non-resident's UK representative in relation to income chargeable to tax for the same chargeable period which is not excluded under these provisions.

(3)   *Investment managers.* An investment manager is not treated as a non-resident's UK representative in relation to income etc. arising from so much of any business as relates to investment transactions (as defined) carried out through the investment manager and satisfying all the following conditions:

    (i)   the manager was carrying on the business of providing investment management services at the time of the transaction;

    (ii)   the transaction was carried out in the ordinary course of that business;

    (iii)   the manager, when acting on the non-resident's behalf in that transaction, did so in an independent capacity;

    (iv)   the '20% condition' is satisfied in relation to the transaction (see below);

    (v)   the remuneration for the investment management services in question was at a rate not less than would have been customary for that class of business; and

(vi) the manager is not the non-resident's UK representative in relation to income chargeable to tax for the same chargeable period which is not excluded under these provisions.

A person is not to be regarded as acting in an independent capacity on behalf of the non-resident (see (iii) above) unless, having regard to its legal, financial and commercial characteristics, the relationship between them is a relationship between persons carrying on independent businesses that deal with each other at arm's length (and see Revenue Press Release 17 February 1995).

The '20% condition' (see (iv) above) is that, broadly, the investment manager and persons connected with him may not have a beneficial entitlement to more than 20% of the non-resident's excluded income (see 51.1 above) from transactions carried out by the investment manager on his behalf. The condition must be satisfied throughout a qualifying period which must at least consist of the chargeable period for which the income from the transaction in question is chargeable to tax and which may be no more than five years comprising two or more chargeable periods. Failure to satisfy the condition is disregarded if it was for reasons beyond the control of the manager and persons connected with him and they did not fail to take reasonable mitigating action. If a transaction satisfies the conditions at (i) to (vi) above except for the 20% condition, it is regarded as satisfying *all* conditions to the extent of any income etc. which does *not* represent excluded income to which the manager etc. has or has had a beneficial entitlement. Special rules apply to determine whether or not the 20% condition is satisfied in relation to a transaction carried out for a collective investment scheme (within *Financial Services Act 1986*) in which the non-resident is a participant; broadly, the condition is treated as satisfied by each participant if the scheme (were it taxable as a separate entity) would not be regarded as carrying on a trade in the UK or if it would be so regarded but the 20% rule is satisfied by reference to the scheme's taxable income.

Persons are connected if they are connected within *Sec 839* (see 20 CONNECTED PERSONS).

(4) *Lloyd's members' agents and managing agents.* A Lloyd's members' agent or syndicate managing agent is not treated as a non-resident Lloyd's underwriter's UK representative in relation to income etc. arising from his Lloyd's business (or, in the case of a managing agent, from the syndicate in question). See 89 UNDERWRITERS generally.

General. Where a person acts as broker or investment manager as part only of a business, that part is deemed to be a separate business for the purposes of (2) and (3) above. A person carries out a transaction on behalf of another where he either undertakes it himself or instructs a third party to do so. Income arising from so much of a business as results from transactions carried out through a branch or agency includes income from property or rights which as a result of the transactions are used by, or held by or for, that branch or agency.

[*FA 1995, s 127*].

51.7 **Obligations etc. imposed on UK representatives.** As regards the taxation of any amounts in relation to which a non-UK resident has a UK representative (see 51.5, 51.6 above), legislation making provision for, or in connection with, the assessment, collection and recovery of income tax, corporation tax and capital gains tax, and interest on tax, has effect as if the obligations and liabilities of the non-resident were *also* obligations and liabilities of the UK representative. The discharge of an obligation or liability by either the non-resident or the UK representative is treated as discharging the corresponding obligation or liability of the other. The non-resident is bound by any acts or omissions of his UK representative. Where an obligation or liability depends on the serving of a notice or other document or the making of a request or demand, it is not treated as having been imposed on the UK representative unless the notice etc. was served on or copied to him or he was notified of the request or demand. A person is not guilty of a criminal offence by virtue of these provisions except where he committed the offence himself or consented to or connived in its commission.

Independent agents. An *'independent agent'* of a non-resident is any person who is the non-resident's UK representative in respect of any agency from the non-resident in which he was acting on the non-resident's behalf in an independent capacity (see 51.6(3) above). The provisions above apply equally to independent agents as to other UK representatives, with the following applying in addition.

As regards his obligations to furnish information (including anything contained in a return, self-assessment, account, statement or report provided to the Revenue), the independent agent is not required to do anything beyond what is practicable by acting to the best of his knowledge and belief after having taken all reasonable steps to obtain the information. In such a case, the non-resident is not discharged from his own obligation to furnish the information, but is also not bound by any error or mistake in the information so furnished by the agent unless it results from the non-resident's own act or omission or one to which he consented or in which he connived. An independent agent is entitled to be indemnified in respect of any liability discharged by him on the non-resident's behalf under these provisions and to retain, out of monies due by him to the non-resident, amounts sufficient to cover any such liability, whether or not already discharged. An independent agent is not liable to any civil penalty or surcharge in respect of any act or omission which is neither his own nor one to which he consented or in which he connived, providing he can show that he could not recover the penalty etc. out of monies due to the non-resident after being indemnified for his other liabilities.

[*FA 1995, 23 Sch*].

51.8   NON-RESIDENT ENTERTAINERS AND SPORTSMEN

Any person making a payment or transfer (including by way of loan) for, in respect of, or which in any way derives either directly or indirectly from, the performance of a 'relevant activity' performed in the UK by an entertainer or sportsman (as broadly defined) who is not resident in the UK in the year of assessment in which that activity is performed, is required to deduct and account to the Revenue for an amount representing income tax, at a rate which may not exceed the basic rate of income tax for the year of assessment. In the case of a transfer, the actual worth of what is transferred is treated as being a net amount corresponding to a gross amount from which income tax at the basic rate has been deducted. That gross amount is treated as the value of the transfer and the net value is the cost to the transferor less any contribution made by the entertainer or sportsman.

A *'relevant activity'* is an activity performed in the UK by an entertainer or sportsman in his character as such on or in connection with (including promotion of) a commercial occasion or event (including participation in live or recorded transmissions of any kind) for which he is entitled to receive a payment or transfer or which is designed to promote commercial sales or activity by any means.

Payments or transfers from which tax need not be withheld under these provisions are as follows.

(i)   A payment subject to deduction of tax under some other provision of the *Taxes Acts* than *Sec 555(2)* and *The Income Tax (Entertainers and Sportsmen) Regulations 1987 (SI 1987 No 530)*.

(ii) An arm's length payment made to a person resident and ordinarily resident in the UK, who is not connected or associated with the payee, for services ancillary to the performance of a relevant activity.

(iii) Payments representing royalties from the sale of sound recordings.

(iv) Any total amount paid in a tax year by a payer, together with persons connected or associated with him, to a non-UK resident entertainer or sportsman, together with persons connected or associated with him, which does not exceed £1,000.

The *Regulations* provide for arrangements to be made in writing between the payer, the entertainer or sportsman, or other recipient of the payment, and the Board of Inland Revenue for a reduced tax payment representing, as nearly as may be, the actual liability of the entertainer or sportsman, to apply. Such application must be made not later than 30 days before the payment (or transfer) falls to be made and the full basic rate deduction must be made from any payment or transfer made before approval is given by the Board. There are provisions to prevent any payment suffering withholding tax more than once where it passes through an intermediary, and for reductions to apply where there is a double taxation agreement in force. Similarly, there are anti-avoidance provisions to prevent payments or transfers being routed through third parties such as controlled companies and similar entities.

The sum accounted for to the Revenue is treated as paid on account of the income or corporation tax liability of a person other than the person so accounting for it, whether a liability under the *Regulations*, under *Secs 555 et seq.* or under any other provision of the *Taxes Acts*. The charge under *Sec 555(2)* shall apply in place of any charge under Schedule E (any amount charged under which shall be treated as an expense of the 'Schedule 11 trade' (see below)), under *Secs 660–685* (Settlements) or under Schedule D (where the connected payment is a receipt falling to be included in the computation of profits of a company which provides the services of the entertainer or sportsman). A recipient is entitled to claim in writing that a tax payment deducted is excessive and *TMA s 42* (see 4 APPEALS) applies to such claims.

Computation of liability of entertainer or sportsman. Where a payment or other transfer is made within these provisions, the relevant activity is treated as performed in the course of a trade, profession or vocation (the '*Schedule 11 trade*', so called because these provisions were originally enacted in *FA 1986, 11 Sch*) exercised in the UK and thus chargeable to tax under Schedule D, Case I or II (to the extent that it would not otherwise be so treated) unless it is performed in the course of an office or employment.

Payment of tax is due, whether or not it has been withheld from the connected payment or transfer, before, or at the time when, a quarterly return (see below) is made, whether or not an assessment has been made.

Assessment to tax. An assessment may be made, in relation to a tax year or other period, on a current year (not a preceding year) basis and any apportionment, division or aggregation by reference to tax years or other periods may be made as is just and reasonable. The 'Schedule 11 trade' is thus treated separately from the 'world-wide trade' of an entertainer or sportsman, but for the purposes of loss relief under *Secs 381, 385* they are treated as the same trade, although losses in early years will be relieved only by reference to the date of commencement of the world-wide trade. Terminal loss relief under *Sec 388* will only be given in respect of the Schedule 11 trade if the world-wide trade ceases in the same period.

All other provisions of the *Taxes Acts* as to the time within which an assessment may be made apply to such an assessment as do the provisions for out of time assessments. Tax charged by an assessment is payable within 14 days of the issue of the notice, or by the due date of payment of the tax (see above) if this is earlier. The collection and recovery procedures and the provisions relating to interest on overdue tax in *TMA 1970* apply to such assessments. The penalty provisions of *TMA s 98* (see 58.4 PENALTIES) also apply.

Returns (including returns of payments for which a nil deduction rate applied) must be made quarterly in respect of the periods to 30 June, 30 September, 31 December and 5 April within 14 days of the end of each period. The Board may require, in writing, within a specified time, certain information regarding payments, payees and relevant activities. The penalty provisions of *TMA 1970* apply to failure to submit returns (see 67.2 RETURNS).

[*Secs 555–558; SI 1987 No 530*].

51.9 **NON-RESIDENT BANKS, INSURANCE COMPANIES AND DEALERS IN SECURITIES** carrying on business in the UK.

(i) For 1995/96 and earlier years and for accounting periods ending before 1 April 1996, such bodies are not exempt on income from overseas securities, stocks or shares, by reason of non-residence. [*Sec 474(1); FA 1995, 8 Sch 25(1); FA 1996, 7 Sch 18*]. (See *Owen v Sassoon Ch D 1950, 32 TC 101*). See now 72.1 SCHEDULE D, CASE III.

(ii) Where exempt on certain GOVERNMENT STOCKS (33) an amount equal to interest at the average rate for the period under review on all money borrowed for purposes of the business up to the total cost of any such tax-free securities held is disallowed in the computation of profits or losses and excluded from the definition of 'charges on income' for purposes of *Sec 338* (see Tolley's Corporation Tax). Expenses of acquiring, holding or dealing with the tax-free securities and any profits or losses arising therefrom are also excluded from computation. For 1996/97 and subsequent years, and for accounting periods ending after 31 March 1996, this applies only to $3\frac{1}{2}$% War Loan 1952 or later, and the prohibition on relief as a charge on income is replaced by a prohibition on relief as a loan relationship debit. [*Sec 475; FA 1995, 8 Sch 25(1); FA 1996, 14 Sch 27, 28 Sch 3*].

(iii) Where receipts of interest or dividends have been treated as tax-exempt under double taxation arrangements, they are not to be excluded from trading income etc. so as to give rise to losses for set-off against income etc. [*Sec 808*].

(iv) See also Tolley's Corporation Tax.

51.10 **PAYMENTS OF ANNUAL SUMS TO NON-RESIDENTS**

Copyright royalties, public lending right payments and **design royalties** (or 'sums paid periodically') paid '*by or through* any person' in the UK to **non-residents** are subject to deduction of tax on the net sum (i.e. less commission). [*Secs 536, 537, 537B; FA 1995, s 115(10)*].

Payment to foreign author for right to sell translation, held to be within *Sec 536* (*Longmans, Green KB 1932, 17 TC 272*). Also that solicitors of the payers remitting royalties to non-residents must deduct tax and account to Revenue (*Rye & Eyre v CIR HL 1935, 19 TC 164*).

The Inland Revenue may call for a return of payments. [*TMA s 16*]. See 67.6 RETURNS.

51.11 **PERSONAL ALLOWANCES FOR CERTAIN NON-RESIDENTS** [*Sec 278; FA 1988, s 31; FA 1996, ss 134, 145, 20 Sch 21*]

As mentioned under 64.3 RESIDENCE, ORDINARY RESIDENCE AND DOMICILE, a non-resident is liable to UK tax without any deduction for personal allowances etc. except under specific double tax treaties or in cases where the individual concerned is eligible for relief as below. (Foreigners resident here have the same rights to relief as British subjects, and where assessments are made on the ground of *'residence'* here, the taxpayer is entitled to the full allowances. But this does not apply to persons assessed because temporarily employed here, but not technically 'resident'.)

The non-resident individuals eligible for reliefs are as follows.

  (i) All Commonwealth citizens and citizens of Republic of Ireland.
 (ii) For 1996/97 onwards, all nationals of States within the European Economic Area (EEA), which comprises all EU States plus, as at 28 November 1995, Norway, Iceland and Liechtenstein.
(iii) Persons who are or who have been in service of the Crown.
 (iv) Missionaries.
  (v) Servants of British Protectorates.
 (vi) Residents in the Isle of Man or Channel Islands.
(vii) Persons abroad for health reasons (including health of wife or family) after residence in UK.
(viii) Widows or widowers of Crown Servants.

All personal reliefs under *ICTA 1988, Pt VII, Ch 1* are available in full to non-resident individuals within (i)–(viii) above, except that no relief is given to a wife under *Sec 257D* (see 47.5 MARRIED PERSONS) in respect of excess allowances of her husband where the husband is not UK resident.

Claimants should contact Inland Revenue, FICO (International), St John's House, Merton Road, Bootle, Merseyside, L69 9BB, except that Crown employees or Crown pensioners should contact Inland Revenue, Public Departments (Technical Unit) Foreign Section, Ty-Glas, Llanishen, Cardiff, Wales, CF4 5WN. A right of appeal to the Special Commissioners (and if necessary to the Courts) is given by *TMA s 42(3)*.

51.12   TRADES ETC. CARRIED ON AND CONTROLLED ABROAD

A trade, profession or vocation carried on by a UK resident is within Schedule D, Case I or II if carried on wholly or partly in the UK but within Case V if carried on wholly abroad [*Secs 18(1)(a)(ii), (3); FA 1995, 6 Sch 2*] subject to special rules as regards trades etc. in Eire. [*Sec 68; FA 1994, s 207(5)*]. This is so notwithstanding the wide wording of the Case I charging rule in *Sec 18(3)* (*Colquhoun v Brooks HL 1889, 2 TC 490*). A non-resident is chargeable on trading etc. in the UK (see 51.4 above).

Where a business is 'carried on' for this purpose depends on from where it is managed and controlled, irrespective of where the day-to-day business activities are conducted. See for this *Trustees of Ferguson, decd v Donovan Supreme Court (IFS) 1927, 1 ITC 214* (trustees delegated control of Australian business to Australian company and did not interfere in any way; held not within Case I) and contrast *Ogilvie v Kitton C/E/S 1908, 5 TC 338* (Canadian business managed by Canadians but 'head and brains' in UK where owners resided; Case I applied) and *Spiers v Mackinnon KB 1929, 14 TC 386*. For trades carried on by companies, see 51.9 above, and for trades carried on by partnerships, see 53.15 PARTNERSHIPS.

Where assessments are under Schedule D, Case V (see 73 SCHEDULE D, CASES IV AND V), income is nevertheless computed under the rules applicable to SCHEDULE D, CASES I AND II (71). For 1994/95 and subsequent years as regards businesses commenced after 5 April 1994 and for 1997/98 and subsequent years as regards businesses commenced on or before that date, the basis period rules in 71.11 to 71.19 SCHEDULE D, CASES I AND II apply, as does *Sec 113* (see 53.6 PARTNERSHIPS) (see also 73.9 SCHEDULE D, CASES IV AND V). [*Sec 65(3); FA 1994, ss 207(2)(6), 218*]. Loss relief under *Secs 380–386* and *388* (see 46 LOSSES) is available only against other overseas trading, etc. income, certain foreign emoluments (see 75.6 SCHEDULE E) or foreign pensions or annuities from which a deduction is allowable (see

59.1(iv), 59.2 PENSIONS). [*Sec 391*]. These provisions apply equally to income from Eire. [*ICTA 1970, 12 Sch Pt III; Sec 68*].

The REMITTANCE BASIS (63) applies to persons not domiciled in the UK and to persons who, being Commonwealth or Eire citizens, are not ordinarily resident in the UK. [*Sec 65(4); FA 1996, s 134, 20 Sch 3*].

Travelling expenses. A deduction may be claimed for expenses incurred in a business carried on abroad (and not assessable on the REMITTANCE BASIS (63)) in travelling between any place in the UK and any place where the business is carried on, either

(*a*)   for the individual, provided that his absence is wholly and exclusively for the performance of the functions of the business, or

(*b*)   where there is absence from the UK for a continuous period of 60 days or more, for the spouse and any children under 18 (at beginning of outward journey) accompanying the individual at the beginning of the period of absence or visiting him during that period, including the return journey, but with a limit of two outward and return journeys per person in any year of assessment.

Where (*a*) above applies, a deduction may also be claimed for expenditure incurred on board and lodging at the overseas location.

Where more than one business is carried on at the overseas location, travelling, etc., expenses are apportioned between them. [*Sec 80*].

Travelling between overseas businesses. Where more than one business is carried on abroad (and at least one is within *Sec 80*, as above), and absence from the UK is solely for business purposes, a deduction may be claimed for travelling between them. The deduction will normally be given in taxing the trade at the place of destination, but, exceptionally, where this trade is not within *Sec 80*, as above, it will be given in taxing the trade at the place of departure. Where more than one business is carried on at the place of destination or, exceptionally, at the place of departure, the expenses are apportioned between them. [*Sec 81*].

See 71.27 SCHEDULE D, CASES I AND II for provisions applying where an individual carrying on a business wholly or partly abroad **becomes or ceases to be UK resident.**

Partnerships abroad. See 53.15 PARTNERSHIPS.

51.13   **UNITED KINGDOM**

The United Kingdom for tax purposes comprises England, Scotland, Wales and Northern Ireland. The Channel Islands and the Isle of Man are not included. Great Britain comprises England, Scotland and Wales only.

Territorial extension of tax area. The territorial sea of the UK is regarded as part of the UK for tax purposes. Emoluments, profits and gains from exploration or exploitation activities in a designated area (under *Continental Shelf Act 1964, s 1(7)*), are treated as arising in the UK. A resident licence holder under *Petroleum (Production) Act 1934* may be held accountable for the liability of a non-resident and may be required by inspector to provide information concerning transactions with other persons and emoluments and other payments made. [*Sec 830; TCGA 1992, 276*]. As regards liability of non-resident lessors of mobile drilling rigs, vessels or equipment used in conjunction with exploration or exploitation activities, see Revenue Pamphlet IR 131, SP 6/84, 31 July 1984. See 25.2 DOUBLE TAX RELIEF as regards certain UK exemptions *not* extended to continental shelf workers.

51.14 UNREMITTABLE OVERSEAS INCOME

Where the *'income arising'* basis applies, such income which

(i) cannot, despite reasonable endeavour, be remitted to the UK, by reason of laws or executive action of, or the impossibility of obtaining foreign currency in, the territory concerned, and

(ii) the person chargeable has not realised outside that territory for sterling or an unblocked currency

may be omitted from assessments. For 1995/96 and earlier years, the taxpayer had to give written notice before the relevant assessments became final. For 1996/97 and later years, the relief must be claimed within twelve months after 31 January following the year of assessment in which the income arises.

When, for 1995/96 and earlier years, the Inland Revenue consider that the above conditions are no longer satisfied, the income becomes assessable (at its value at that date taking into account foreign taxes chargeable on it in the territory concerned), and assessments may be made within six years thereafter. When, for 1996/97 and later years, the conditions cease to be satisfied at any time, the income is treated as arising *at that time* and is taxable accordingly (valued as at that time, taking into account foreign taxes, and, if source of income ceased before that time, charged under SCHEDULE D, CASE VI (74)). Disputes are settled by appeal to the Special Commissioners. [*Sec 584; FA 1996, s 134, 20 Sch 33*].

Delayed remittances of overseas income. Where income under Schedule D, Cases IV or V or Schedule E, Case III is assessable on the REMITTANCE BASIS (63) the taxpayer may claim that so much of any remittance in the basis year for a year of assessment as consists of income which **arose before that basis year** shall be excluded from that year and treated as income of the basis year(s) for the year(s) of assessment in which it arose, provided that, despite reasonable endeavour, the income could not previously be remitted, by reason of the laws or executive action of, or the impossibility of obtaining foreign currency in, the territory of origin. The claim must be made within, for 1996/97 and later years, five years after 31 January following the tax year of remittance (for earlier years, six years after the end of that tax year). [*Sec 585; FA 1996, ss 134, 135, 20 Sch 34, 21 Sch 16*].

Interest does not run on the unpaid tax if Inland Revenue are informed promptly, see details under 42.4 INTEREST ON UNPAID TAX.

See 71.90 SCHEDULE D, CASES I AND II for relief for certain unremittable income forming part of the profits of trades within Case I of Schedule D.

52   Offshore Funds

52.1   INTRODUCTION

After 31 December 1983 'offshore income gains' arising on disposals of certain interests in offshore funds which are considered not to distribute sufficient income are charged to income tax or corporation tax under Schedule D, Case VI rather than to capital gains tax. Broadly, the present capital gains tax regime applies to any part of such a gain accruing before 1 January 1984 but the whole of the gain arising thereafter (without indexation) is taxed as income. Special provisions apply to funds operating equalisation arrangements.

Disposal of material interests in non-qualifying offshore funds. The offshore fund rules apply to a disposal by any person of an asset if

(*a*)   the disposal occurs after 31 December 1983 and, at that time, the asset constitutes a 'material interest' in an 'offshore fund' (see 52.3 below) which is or has at any 'material time' been a 'non-qualifying offshore fund' (see 52.4 below); or

(*b*)   the disposal occurs after 31 December 1984 and

    (i)   at that time, the asset constitutes an interest in a UK resident company or in a unit trust scheme within *Sec 469(7)* which has UK resident trustees; and

    (ii)   at a 'material time' after 31 December 1984 the company or unit trust was a 'non-qualifying offshore fund' and the asset constituted a 'material interest' in that fund. For this purpose the provisions of *CGTA 1979, s 78*, equating original shares with a new holding on reorganisation, apply.

[*Sec 757(1); FA 1984, s 92(1)*].

A '*material time*' is any time after 31 December 1983 or, if later, the earliest date on which any 'relevant consideration' was given for the acquisition of the asset. '*Relevant consideration*' is that given by or on behalf of the person making the disposal or a predecessor in title which would be taken into account in determining any gain or loss on disposal under *TCGA 1992*. [*Sec 757(7); FA 1990, 14 Sch 10*].

With some modifications, a disposal occurs for offshore fund purposes if there would be a disposal under *TCGA 1992*. Death is an occasion of charge as the deceased is deemed to have made a disposal at market value, immediately before his death, of any asset which was or had at any time been a 'material interest' in a 'non-qualifying offshore fund'. In addition, *TCGA 1992, s 135(3)* will not apply, and there will therefore be a disposal at market value, if an exchange or arrangement is effected under *TCGA 1992, s 135* or *s 136* in such a way that securities etc. in a company, which is or was at a material time a 'non-qualifying offshore fund', are exchanged for assets etc. which do not constitute interests in such a fund. [*Sec 757(2)–(6)*].

52.2   Offshore funds operating equalisation arrangements. There are specific provisions to enable funds operating 'equalisation arrangements' to satisfy the 'distribution test' (see 52.5 below) which the nature of such funds might otherwise preclude. As a corollary, provision is also made to ensure that the 'accrued income' paid to outgoing investors as part of their capital payments is treated as income for tax purposes when the fund qualifies as a distributor.

Definition. For these purposes, an offshore fund operates '*equalisation arrangements*' where the first distribution paid to a person acquiring a 'material interest' by way of 'initial purchase' includes a payment which is a return of capital (debited to the fund's 'equalisation account') determined by reference to the income which had accrued to the fund in the period before that person's acquisition. An acquisition is by way of '*initial* *purchase'* if it is by way of direct purchase from the fund's managers in their capacity as such.

'Accrued income' chargeable to income tax—application of offshore fund rules. A disposal is one to which the offshore fund provisions apply, subject to exception below, if it is a disposal by any person of a 'material interest' in an 'offshore fund' operating equalisation arrangements where

(i)   the disposal occurs after 5 April 1984 and the disposal proceeds are not a trading receipt; and

(ii)   the fund *is not*, and *has not been*, at any material time (see above) a 'non-qualifying offshore fund' (see 52.4 below)

(i.e. the provisions apply also to *distributing* funds (see 52.5 below) with equalisation arrangements).

Capital gains tax rules for disposals apply as they do for other offshore fund disposals (see 52.1 above) with some variations. Death is not treated as a disposal in this context. In addition, *TCGA 1992, s 127* (reorganisations etc.) (including that section as applied by *TCGA 1992, s 135* (exchange of securities) or by *TCGA 1992, s 132* (conversion of securities)) does not apply and there is a disposal at market value in such circumstances.

Exception. The offshore fund legislation does *not* apply as indicated above to a disposal where the fund's income for the period preceding the disposal is of such a nature that the part relating to the interest in question is in any event chargeable under Schedule D, Case IV or Case V on the person disposing of the interest (or would be so chargeable if residence/domicile/situation of assets requirements were met).

[*Secs 757(2)(3), 758; FA 1989, s 81*].

52.3   **MATERIAL INTERESTS IN OFFSHORE FUNDS**

An 'offshore fund' is

(*a*)   a company resident outside the UK; or

(*b*)   a unit trust scheme within *Sec 469(7)* which has non-UK resident trustees; or

(*c*)   any other arrangements taking effect under overseas law which create rights in the nature of co-ownership under that law,

in which any person has a 'material interest'. From 29 November 1994, it must also be a 'collective investment scheme' within *Financial Services Act 1986*. [*Sec 759(1)(1A); FA 1995, s 134(1)–(3)(8)*].

A **'material interest'** is one which, when acquired, could reasonably be expected to be realisable (by any means, either in money or in asset form) within seven years for an amount reasonably approximate to its proportionate share of the market value of the fund's assets. For these purposes, an interest in an offshore fund which at any time is worth substantially more than its proportionate share of the fund's underlying assets is not to be regarded as so realisable. [*Sec 759(2)–(4)*]. If shares in a quoted overseas company have habitually been traded at or near net asset value, and an investor in these shares had a reasonable expectation, on acquisition, of a future sale at or near such value, those shares are likely to represent a 'material interest'. (Revenue Pamphlet IR 131, SP 2/86, 7 March 1986).

Exceptions. The following are not material interests.

(i)   Interests in respect of loans etc. made in the ordinary course of banking business.

(ii)   Rights under insurance policies.

(iii) Shares in a company resident outside the UK where

(a)   the shares are held by a company and the holding is necessary or desirable for the maintenance and development of a trade carried on by the company, or by an associated company within *Sec 416*; and

(b)   the shares confer at least 10% of the voting rights and, on winding-up, a right to at least 10% of the assets after discharging all prior liabilities; and

(c)   the shares are held by not more than ten persons and all confer both voting rights and a right to assets on winding-up; and

(d)   at the time of acquisition of the shares the company could reasonably expect to realise its interest for market value within seven years only by virtue of (I) an arrangement requiring the company's fellow participators to purchase its shares and/or (II) provisions of either the overseas company's constitution or an agreement between the participators regarding that company's winding-up.

(iv)   Interests in companies resident outside the UK at any time when the holder is entitled to have the company wound up and to receive in that event in the same capacity more than 50% of the assets after discharging all prior liabilities.

[*Sec 759(5)–(8)*].

The Revenue have also indicated that normal commercial loans or other debt instruments entitling the lender to no more than a fixed return of principal on redemption, and which are not geared to the underlying asset value of the borrower's business, are not regarded as 'material interests'. (Revenue Pamphlet IR 131, SP 2/86, 7 March 1986).

'**Market value**' for the purposes of the offshore funds legislation is determined according to capital gains tax rules with necessary modifications of *TCGA 1992, s 272(5)* (market value in relation to rights in unit trust schemes) where appropriate. [*Sec 759(9)*].

52.4   NON-QUALIFYING OFFSHORE FUNDS

An offshore fund is '**non-qualifying**' except during an 'account period' in respect of which it is certified by the Board as a distributing fund pursuing a 'full distribution policy' (see 52.5 below). For these purposes, the first *'account period'* begins when the fund begins to carry on its activities or, if later, on 1 January 1984. An *'account period'* ends on the fund's accounting date or, if earlier, twelve months from the beginning of the period or on the fund's ceasing to carry on its activities. In addition, if the fund is a non-UK resident company, an *'account period'* ends when it becomes UK resident, and if the fund is a unit trust with non-UK resident trustees, it ends when those trustees become UK resident. [*Sec 760(1)(2)(8)–(10); FA 1984, s 95(8)*].

Conditions for certification. Subject to the modifications of conditions for certification in certain cases noted below, an offshore fund is not to be certified as a 'distributing fund' for any account period if, at any time in that period:

(a)   more than 5% by value of the fund's assets consists of interests in other offshore funds (but see below); or

(b)   more than 10% by value of the fund's assets consists of interests in a single company. For this purpose

(i)   the value of an interest in a single company is determined as at the most recent occasion (in that account period or earlier) on which the fund acquired an interest in that company for money or money's worth. However an occasion is disregarded if it is one on which *TCGA 1992, s 127* (equation of original shares and new holding) applied, including that *section* as applied by later provisions of *TCGA 1992* (reorganisations, conversion of securities etc.), and on which no consideration is given for the interest other than the interest in the original holding,

(ii) an interest is disregarded, except for determining the total value of the fund's assets, if it consists of a current or deposit account provided in the normal course of its banking business by a company whose business it is to provide such account facilities in any currency for members of the public and bodies corporate, and

(iii) Government-owned national or supra-national bodies whose activities are directed not with a view to commercial profits, but to the exercise of a wider social or economic function, are not regarded as companies for this purpose (Revenue Pamphlet IR 131, SP 2/86, 7 March 1986); or

(c) the fund's assets include more than 10% of the issued share capital, or any class of it, in any company; or

(d) there is more than one class of material interests (see 52.2 above) in the fund and, were each class and the assets represented by it in a separate offshore fund, each such separate fund does not pursue a 'full distribution policy'. For this purpose, interests held solely by persons involved in the management of the fund's assets are disregarded if they carry no right or expectation to participate in profits and no right to anything other than the return of the price paid on winding-up or redemption.

Where, however, the Board are satisfied that an apparent failure to comply with any of (a)–(c) above occurred inadvertently and was remedied without unreasonable delay, that failure may be disregarded.

[Sec 760(3)–(7), 27 Sch 14].

Modifications of conditions for certification. The conditions for certification in (a) to (d) above are modified in certain cases.

(A) **Investments in second tier funds.** If offshore funds ('primary funds') would fail to meet the conditions in (a) to (c) above because of investments in other offshore funds (referred to below as 'second tier funds') which could themselves be certified as qualifying distributing funds (without any modification of the (a) to (c) conditions), then the primary funds' interests in the second tier funds are left out of account, except for determining the total value of the primary funds' assets, in establishing whether the primary funds are prevented by (a) to (c) above from being certified as distributing funds. In addition, where the above applies, if at any time in a primary fund's account period that fund's assets include an interest in another offshore fund or in any company and the qualifying second tier fund's assets also include an interest in that other fund or company, then the primary fund's interest is aggregated with its proportionate share of the second tier fund's interest in determining whether the primary fund is within the limits in (a) to (c) above. Its share of the second tier fund's interest is the proportion which the average value during its account period of its own holding of interests in the second tier fund bears to the average value during the period of all interests in the second tier fund. [Sec 760(3), 27 Sch 6, 7, 9].

(B) **Investments in trading companies.** Where the assets of an offshore fund include an interest in a company whose business is wholly the carrying on of trade(s) the limit of 10% of a fund's assets invested in a single company in (b) above is increased to 20% and the 10% limit on the proportion of a class of share in any company in (c) above is increased to allow holdings of less than 50%. For these purposes companies are excluded if their business consists to any extent of banking or moneylending or of dealing, including dealing by way of futures contracts and traded options, in commodities, currency, securities, debts or other assets of a financial nature. [*Sec 760(3), 27 Sch 4(2), 10*]. Dealing in commodities, currency and financial assets incidental to the business of a company will be disregarded in determining whether the company is trading. (Revenue Pamphlet IR 131, SP 2/86, 7 March 1986).

(C)   **Wholly-owned subsidiaries.** Where an offshore fund has a wholly-owned subsidiary company, the receipts, expenditure, assets and liabilities of the fund and the subsidiary are aggregated so that the fund and the sudsidiary are treated as one for the purposes of determining whether the fund is within the limits in (*a*) to (*d*) above. In the same way, the interest of the fund in the subsidiary and any distributions or other payments between the fund and the subsidiary are left out of account. A wholly-owned subsidiary is one owned either directly and beneficially by the fund, or directly by the trustees of the fund for the benefit of the fund, or, in the case of a fund within 52.3(*c*) above, in some other equivalent manner. Where the subsidiary has only one class of issued share capital, ownership of at least 95% of that capital by the offshore fund constitutes the subsidiary a wholly-owned subsidiary for this purpose, and only a corresponding proportion of the subsidiary's receipts, expenditure, assets and liabilities are then aggregated with those of the offshore fund. [*Sec 760(3), 27 Sch 11*].

(D)   **Subsidiary dealing and management companies.** The investment restriction in (*c*) above does not apply to so much of an offshore fund's assets as consists of share capital of a company which is either

(1)   a wholly-owned subsidiary of the fund (as defined in (C) above) whose sole function is dealing in material interests in the offshore fund for management and administrative purposes and which is not entitled to any distribution from the fund; or

(2)   a subsidiary management company of the fund whose sole function is to provide the fund, or other funds with an interest in the company, with advisory services or administrative, management and related property holding services on arm's length commercial terms. For the purposes of determining whether a company is a subsidiary management company of a fund, that company and any wholly-owned subsidiary companies it may itself have are regarded as a single entity. [*Sec 760(3), 27 Sch 12*].

(E)   **Disregard of certain investments.** Certain holdings which would otherwise fall within the restriction at (*c*) above are not taken into account for the purposes of that restriction. This applies where no more than 5% of the value of the offshore fund's assets consists of such holdings and of interests in other non-qualifying offshore funds. [*Sec 760(3), 27 Sch 13*].

52.5   THE DISTRIBUTION TEST

An offshore fund pursues a '**full distribution policy**' with respect to an account period if

(*a*)   a distribution is made for that account period or for some other period falling wholly or partly within that period; and

(*b*)   subject to modifications below, the distribution represents at least 85% of the fund's income and not less than 85% of its 'UK equivalent profits' for that period; and

(*c*)   the distribution is made during or within six months after the end of the account period (the six month limit may be extended at the Board's discretion); and (*d*)   the distribution is in a form such that any part of it received in the UK by a UK resident which is not part of the profits of a trade etc. is chargeable under Schedule D, Case IV or Case V.

These conditions may equally be satisfied by any two or more distributions taken together. [*27 Sch 1(1)*].

The basic conditions in (*a*) to (*d*) above are modified in certain cases (see 52.6 below).

A fund is treated as pursuing a full distribution policy for any account period in which there is no income and no 'UK equivalent profits', or for account periods ending after 28 November 1994 for which gross fund income does not exceed 1% of the average value of fund assets during the period, but it will not be so treated for any account period for which no accounts are prepared. [*27 Sch 1(2)(3); FA 1995, s 134(4)(9)*].

Non-UK legal restrictions. Where in an account period an offshore fund is subject to non-UK legal restrictions on making distributions by reason of an excess of losses over profits as computed according to the law in question, a deduction is allowed from the fund's income of any amount which cannot be distributed but which would otherwise form part of the fund's income for that account period. [*27 Sch 1(6)*].

Apportionment of income and distributions between account periods. Where a period for which accounts are made up or for which a distribution is made covers the whole or part of two or more account periods of the fund, the income or distribution is apportioned on a time basis according to the number of days in each period. A distribution made out of specified income but not for a specified period is attributed to the account period in which the income arose. Where no period or income is specified, a distribution is treated as made for the last account period ending before the distribution. If the distribution made, or treated as made, for an account period exceeds the income of that period the excess is reallocated to previous periods, to later periods before earlier ones, until exhausted, unless the distribution was apportioned on a time basis as mentioned above in which case the excess is first reapportioned on a just and reasonable basis to the other account period(s). [*27 Sch 1(4)(5)*].

'**UK equivalent profits**' of an offshore fund are the total profits, excluding chargeable gains, on which, after allowing for any deductions available, corporation tax would be chargeable, assuming that

(i)   the offshore fund is a UK resident company in the account period in question, but in no other; and

(ii)   the account period is an accounting period of that company; and

(iii)   any dividends or distributions from a UK resident company are included.

The effects of *FA 1993, ss 125–133* (exchange gains and losses) and *FA 1994, ss 159, 160, 18 Sch 1* (profits and losses on interest rate and currency contracts) (see Tolley's Corporation Tax under Exchange Gains and Losses and Financial Instruments respectively) are ignored for this purpose, and it is assumed that income tax, rather than corporation tax, rules apply, as they do for unauthorised unit trusts, as regards certain creditor relationships of the fund (see generally Tolley's Corporation Tax under Gilts and Bonds).

Any UK government securities or securities of foreign states which are exempt from tax (see 33.2 GOVERNMENT STOCKS) must be brought into account in determining the fund's total profits.

Whether a fund is trading will turn on the particular facts, but in general a fund would not normally be regarded as trading in respect of relatively infrequent transactions, or where the intention was merely to hedge specific investments which were not associated with trading activities. (Revenue Pamphlet IR 131, SP 2/86, 7 March 1986).

Tolley's

NEW

Post-Budget Supplements

An invaluable update

This year, for the first time, you will be able to keep even more up to date on tax matters with the introduction of post-Budget tax supplements to the main Tolley tax annuals. Issued in December at little extra cost, they will cover all significant developments, including latest cases, Revenue announcements and Statutory Instruments, from this year's Finance Act up to Budget Day.

Address Details: PLEASE COMPLETE IN BLOCK CAPITALS

Surname _____ Initials _____

Company _____

Full Address _____

_____

_____ Post Code _____

R E T U R N   T H I S   C A R D   T O D A Y

PRIORITY ORDER FORM

Please supply Tolley Account details (if applicable)

Tolley Account No.

Remember to complete your address details overleaf

Tolley Publishing Co.Ltd
Telephone: Customer Services
0181-686 9141
Fax: 0181-686 3155

Title	No. of copies	Order Code	Price	Amount £
Tolley's New Post-Budget Supplements				
Tolley's Income Tax - 1996-97 post-Budget supplement		ITBS96	£14.95	
Tolley's Corporation Tax - 1996-97 post-Budget supplement		CTBS96	£13.95	
Tolley's Capital Gains Tax - 1996-97 post-Budget supplement		CGBS96	£13.95	
Tolley's Inheritance Tax - 1996-97 post-Budget supplement		IHBS96	£11.95	
Tolley's Value Added Tax - 1996-97 post-Budget supplement		VABS96	£12.95	
Tolley's National Insurance Contributions - 1996-97 post-Budget supplement		NIBS96	£15.95	

Full Refund Guarantee

Total £

If you are not satisfied with your order for any reason, simply return the book in saleable condition within 21 days and we will refund your payment in full upon request.

D94 / Z

Postage will be paid by licensee

BUSINESS REPLY SERVICE
Licence No.2501

TOLLEY PUBLISHING CO. LTD.
TOLLEY HOUSE
2 ADDISCOMBE ROAD
CROYDON
SURREY
CR9 5WZ

The deductions referred to above include a deduction equal to that allowed against a fund's income where non-UK legal restrictions prevent distribution (see above) and a deduction equal to any foreign capital tax allowed as a deduction in determining the fund's income for the account period in question.

Interest paid to a non-UK resident is deductible in the same way as if it were paid to a UK resident. UK income tax (whether suffered by deduction or by assessment) is available as a deduction. (Revenue Pamphlet IR 131, SP 2/86, 7 March 1986).

[*27 Sch 5; FA 1994, s 176(2); FA 1996, 10 Sch 3*].

52.6 MODIFICATIONS OF DISTRIBUTION TEST

The basic rules of the distribution test in 52.5(*a*) to (*d*) above are modified in various circumstances.

(*a*) **Funds operating equalisation arrangements.** Where an offshore fund operates such arrangements (see 52.2 above) throughout an account period (see 52.4 above), an amount equal to any 'accrued income' which is part of the consideration for certain disposals in that period is treated as a distribution for the purposes of the distribution test. This applies to a disposal

(i) which is a disposal of a material interest in the fund to either the fund or the fund managers in their capacity as such; and

(ii) which is one to which the offshore fund rules apply (whether or not by virtue of their application to disposals from distributing funds with equalisation arrangements—see 52.2 above), or which is one to which the rules would apply if the provisions regarding the non-application of *TCGA 1992, ss 127, 135* applied generally and not only for the purpose of determining whether a disposal from a distributing fund with equalisation arrangements is brought within the rules (see 52.2 above); and

(iii) which is not a disposal within the *exception* at 52.2 above (where the income of the fund is, or would be, chargeable to tax under Schedule D, Case IV or V in any event).

The '*accrued income*' referred to above is that part of the consideration which would be credited to the fund's equalisation account if the interest were resold to another person by way of 'initial purchase' (see 52.2 above) on the same day. However there are provisions to ensure that this accrued income figure is reduced where the interest disposed of was acquired by way of initial purchase (by any person) after the beginning of the account period by reference to which the accrued income is calculated. In addition, where an offshore commodity dealing fund (see also (*c*) below) operates equalisation and there is a disposal within (i) to (iii) above, one half of the accrued income representing commodity profits is left out of account in determining what part of the disposal consideration represents accrued income.

For the purposes of the distribution test, the distribution which the fund is treated as making on a disposal is treated as being paid to the person disposing of his interest, in the income form required by 52.5(*d*) above, out of the income of the fund for the account period of disposal. Where a distribution is made to the managers (in their capacity as such) of a fund operating equalisation arrangements it is disregarded for the purposes of the distribution test except to the extent that it relates to that part of the period for which the distribution is made during which the managers (in that capacity) held that interest. [*27 Sch 2, 4(4)*].

(*b*) **Funds with income taxable under Schedule D, Case IV or V on investors.** Where sums forming part of the income of an offshore fund within 52.3(*b*) or (*c*) above are chargeable to tax under Schedule D, Case IV or V on the holders of interests in the fund (or would be so chargeable were the necessary residence etc. rules met), any such sums which are not actually part of a distribution complying with the part of the distribution test in 52.5(c) and (d) above are treated as distributions which do so comply made out of the income of which they are part and paid to the holders of the interests in question. [27 Sch 3].

(c)   **Funds with commodity dealing income.** Where an offshore fund's income includes commodity dealing profits, half of those profits are left out of account in determining the fund's income and UK equivalent profits for the purposes of the distribution test in 52.5(b) above. '*Commodities*' are defined as tangible assets dealt with on a commodity exchange, excluding currency, securities, debts or other financial assets. '*Dealing*' includes dealing by way of futures contracts and traded options. Where the fund's income includes both commodity dealing profits and other income, its expenditure is apportioned on a just and reasonable basis and the non-commodity dealing business is treated as carried on by a separate company when determining what expenditure, if any, is deductible under *Sec 75* (management expenses of investment companies). See also (a) above for position where a commodity dealing fund operates equalisation arrangements. [27 Sch 4; FA 1988, 13 Sch 12].

(d)   **Wholly-owned commodity dealing subsidiaries.** In a situation within 52.4(C) above, the fund and the subsidiary dealing company are similarly treated as a single entity for the purposes of the distribution test. [27 Sch 11].

(e)   **Investments in second tier funds.** In a situation within 52.4(A) above, the UK equivalent profits of the primary fund for the period are increased by its 'share' of the 'excess income' (if any) of the second tier fund in determining whether not less than 85% of the primary fund's UK equivalent profits are distributed. The '*excess income*' of the second tier fund is the amount by which its UK equivalent profits exceeds its distributions. There are provisions for apportioning excess income between periods on a time basis when the account periods of the primary and second tier funds do not coincide. The primary fund's '*share*' of the excess income is the proportion which the average value during its account period of its own holding of interests in the second tier fund bears to the average value of all interests in that fund. [27 Sch 6, 8, 9].

52.7   **CERTIFICATION PROCEDURE**

Fund requesting certification. Application for certification as a distributing fund for an account period must be made within six months of the end of that period and should be sent to Inland Revenue Technical Division (Offshore Funds), Room 208, St John's House, Merton Road, Bootle, Merseyside, L69 9BB (tel 0151-922 6363 ext 2100). The application must be accompanied by a copy of the fund's accounts covering or including the account period for which certification is sought (including balance sheet, income and expenditure account, and, where prepared, the report for investors and the statement of source and application of funds), and provision of the following information in relation to the account period in question will assist the Board in its consideration of the application.

(1)   The fund's full name.

(2)   The account period for which certification is sought.

(3)   A copy of any fund prospectus or explanatory memorandum.

(4)   Details of any equalisation arrangements in force.

(5)   An analysis of the fund's investment portfolio at the last accounting date, unless supplied in the accounts. This should include the percentage value of the fund's

assets represented by each investment, and the percentage interest of the fund in each class of share capital of any unquoted company, and should identify any holding in other offshore funds (including whether they are considered to be distributing funds).

(6)   A copy of the accounts of any wholly-owned subsidiary of the fund dealing either in commodities or in material interests in the fund.

(7)   A copy of the accounts of any subsidiary management company in which the fund has an interest.

(8)   A computation of the fund's UK equivalent profits or, failing this, a summary analysis of surpluses on realisation taken directly to the fund reserves.

(9)   In respect of each class of share in the fund, the amount and date of each distribution (actual or projected) in respect of the account period, and the aggregate amount of deemed distributions made in respect of the period by way of equalisation.

(Revenue Press Release 31 July 1984).

Where the Board is satisfied that the necessary conditions are met it must certify the fund as a distribution fund for the period in respect of which application was made. The Board must give written notice if, after application, it determines that no certificate should be issued. It must also give notice where it appears that the accounts or other information provided do not make full and accurate disclosure of all relevant matters, in which case any notice of certification previously given is void. The fund may appeal to the Special Commissioners against Board decisions within ninety days. The Special Commissioners have jurisdiction to review any decision of the Board relevant to a ground of the appeal. [*27 Sch 15, 16*].

Investor requesting certification. No appeal may be brought against a tax assessment (see 52.8 below) on the grounds that a fund should have been certified as a distributing fund in respect of an account period. However, where a fund does not apply for certification, an investor, who is assessed to tax for which he would not be liable if the fund were certified, may by notice in writing require the Board to take action with a view to determining whether the fund should be so certified.

If more than one request from an investor is received, the Board is taken to have complied with each if it complies with one.

Broadly, the procedure is as follows.

(i)   The Board invites the fund to apply for certification. The time limit for application (see above) is then extended, if necessary, to 90 days from the date of the Board's invitation.

(ii)   If the fund does not then apply for certification the Board must determine the question as if such application had been made having regard to any accounts or information provided by the investor.

(iii)   If, after the Board has determined that the fund should not be certified, other accounts or information are provided which were not previously available, the Board must reconsider their determination.

(iv)   The Board must notify the investor who requested the Board to take action of their decision.

(v)   The Revenue has wide powers enabling it to disclose to interested parties information regarding Board or Special Commissioner decisions or details of any notice given to a fund regarding a lack of full and accurate disclosure of information (see above).

[*27 Sch 17, 18, 20*].

52.8 Offshore Funds

Postponement of tax. There are provisions to enable an investor to apply for tax assessed to be postponed pending the Board's determination of the question of certification. [*27 Sch 19*].

52.8 CHARGE TO INCOME OR CORPORATION TAX OF OFFSHORE GAIN

Where a disposal to which the offshore fund rules apply (including a disposal of a holding in a distributing fund operating equalisation arrangements—see 52.2 above) gives rise to an 'offshore income gain', then subject to below, that gain is treated for all purposes as income assessable under Schedule D, Case VI arising to the investor at the time of disposal.

For the Revenue practice as regards identification of part disposals out of mixed holdings where a non-qualifying offshore fund has subsequently obtained distributor status, see Revenue Inspector's Manual, IM 4121.

The following provisions have effect in relation to income tax or corporation tax on offshore income gains as they have in relation to capital gains tax (or corporation tax) on chargeable gains.

(*a*)   *TCGA 1992, s 2* (persons chargeable).

(*b*)   *TCGA 1992, s 10* (gains accruing to non-residents and non-resident companies carrying on a trade in the UK through a branch or agency) except that assets need not be situated in the UK.

(*c*)   *TCGA 1992, s 12* (foreign assets of UK resident or ordinarily resident persons with foreign domicile chargeable on remittance basis).

Charitable exemption applies similarly to that for capital gains (see 15.3(v) CHARITIES).

Where a disposal to which the offshore fund rules apply is one of settled property, any offshore income gain will escape the Schedule D, Case VI charge provided that the general administration of the trust is ordinarily carried on outside the UK and a majority of the trustees are not resident or not ordinarily resident in the UK. [*Sec 761; FA 1990, 14 Sch 11*].

52.9 COMPUTATION OF OFFSHORE INCOME GAIN

The computation of the gain depends upon whether the disposal is of an interest in a non-qualifying fund (see 52.10 below) or of an interest involving an equalisation element (see 52.11 below).

52.10 **Disposals of interests in non-qualifying funds.** A '*material disposal*' (one to which the offshore fund rules apply otherwise than by virtue of the provisions regarding distributing funds operating equalisation arrangements—see 52.2 above and 52.11 below) gives rise to an '*offshore income gain*' equal to the 'unindexed gain' or, if less, the 'post-1983 gain'.

Subject to the modifications to the CGT rules mentioned in 52.1 above and to exceptions below, the '*unindexed gain*' is the gain calculated under CGT rules without indexation allowance and without regard to any income tax or corporation tax charge arising under the offshore fund rules. The exceptions are as follows.

(*a*)   Where there has been indexation on an earlier disposal on a no gain/no loss basis within *TCGA 1992, s 56(2)*, the unindexed gain on the material disposal is computed as if indexation had not been available on the earlier disposal and, subject to that, as if the earlier disposal had produced neither gain nor loss.

(b)   If the material disposal forms part of a transfer to which *TCGA 1992, s 162* applies (rollover relief on transfer of business), the unindexed gain is computed without any deduction falling to be made under that section in computing a chargeable gain.

(c)   Any claim for relief under *FA 1980, s 79* (relief for gifts) does not affect the computation of the unindexed gain on the disposal. (See now *TCGA 1992, s 67*.)

(d)   In the case of an insurance company carrying on life assurance business, where a profit from overseas life assurance business, attributable to a material disposal, is taken into account in the computation under *Sec 441*, the unindexed gain, if any, accruing on disposal is computed as if *TCGA 1992, s 37(1)* did not apply. For accounting periods beginning before 1 January 1992, this applies equally where a profit arising from general annuity business attributable to a material disposal is taken into account (or would be but for the provisions relating to offshore income gains of insurance companies (see 52.12 below)) in the computation under *Sec 436*.

(e)   Where the computation of the unindexed gain would otherwise produce a loss, the unindexed gain is treated as nil so that no loss can arise on a material disposal.

[*28 Sch 1–3, 5; FA 1990, 7 Sch 7; FA 1991, 7 Sch 10*].

'Post-1983 gains'. A person making a material disposal who acquired, or is treated as having acquired, his interest in the offshore fund before 1 January 1984, is treated as having disposed of and immediately reacquired his interest at market value on that date. The offshore income gain from 1 January 1984 to the date of disposal is then calculated in the ordinary way. If the person making the material disposal acquired his interest by way of a deemed no gain/no loss disposal (other than those arising by virtue of the indexation provisions of *FA 1982, s 86(5), 13 Sch*) any previous owner's acquisition of the interest is treated as his acquisition of it. [*28 Sch 4*].

52.11   **Disposals involving an equalisation element.** A disposal is a '*disposal involving an equalisation element*' if it is a disposal to which the offshore fund rules apply by virtue of the provisions relating to distributing funds operating equalisation arrangements (see 52.2 above). Such a disposal gives rise to an '*offshore income gain*' of an amount equal, subject to below, to the 'equalisation element' relevant to the asset disposed of. [*28 Sch 6(1)(3)*].

The 'equalisation element' is the amount which would be credited to the fund's equalisation account in respect of accrued income if, on the date of the disposal, the asset disposed of were acquired by another person by way of 'initial purchase' (see 52.2 above). However, where the person making the disposal acquired the asset in question after the beginning of the account period by reference to which the accrued income is calculated, or at or before the beginning of that period where that period began before and ended after 1 January 1984, there are provisions to ensure that the equalisation element is reduced to exclude any part which accrued prior to either 1 January 1984 or to the investor's period of ownership. Where any of the accrued income represents commodity dealing profits (within 52.6(c) above) half of that income is left out of account in determining the equalisation element. [*28 Sch 6(2)(4)–(6)*].

'Part I gains'. Where the offshore income gain as computed above would exceed the 'Part I gain', the offshore income gain is reduced to the lower figure. If there is no 'Part I gain' there can be no offshore income gain. The '*Part I gain*' is, broadly, the amount which would be the offshore income gain on the disposal if the disposal were a 'material disposal' within 52.10 above (i.e. within *28 Sch Part I*) as modified by certain consequential amendments. [*28 Sch 7, 8*].

52.12 MISCELLANEOUS

Offshore income gains accruing to persons resident or domiciled abroad. There are consequential provisions made in connection with gains accruing to certain non-resident investors in offshore funds which modify, for the purposes of the offshore fund legislation, provisions relating to

(a) chargeable gains accruing to certain non-resident companies under *TCGA 1992, s 13*;

(b) gains of non-resident settlements under *TCGA 1992, ss 80–98*;

(c) avoidance of tax by the transfer of assets abroad under *Secs 739, 740*.

To the extent that an offshore income gain is treated by virtue of (a) or (b) above as having accrued to any person resident or ordinarily resident in the UK, that gain is not deemed to be the income of any individual under *Sec 739* or *Sec 740* or any provision of *Part XV* of *ICTA 1988* (settlements). [*Sec 762*].

Deduction of offshore income gain in determining capital gain. There are provisions to prevent a double charge to tax when a disposal gives rise to both an offshore income gain and a chargeable gain for capital gains tax purposes.

Where an offshore income gain arises on a 'material disposal' within 52.10 above, that gain is deducted from the sum which would otherwise constitute the amount or value of the consideration in the calculation of the capital gain arising under *TCGA 1992* (on 'the 1992 Act disposal'), although the offshore gain is not to be taken into account in calculating the fraction under *TCGA 1992, s 42(2)* (part disposal).

Where the 1992 Act disposal forms part of a transfer within *TCGA 1992, s 162* (rollover relief on transfer of business wholly or partly for shares) then, in determining the amount of the deduction from the gain on the old assets, the offshore income gain is deducted from the value of the consideration received in exchange for the business.

Where an exchange of shares or securities constitutes a disposal of an interest in an offshore fund (see 52.1 and 52.2 above), the amount of any offshore income gain to which the disposal gives rise is treated as consideration for the new holding.

Where the offshore fund provisions apply to a disposal of an interest in a fund operating equalisation arrangements (see 52.2 above) and the disposal

(a) is not to the fund or to its managers in their capacity as such, and

(b) gives rise to an offshore income gain in accordance with 52.11 above, and

(c) is followed subsequently by a distribution to either the person who made the disposal or to a person connected with him (within *Sec 839*, see 20 CONNECTED PERSONS) and that distribution is referable to the asset disposed of,

then the subsequent distribution (or distributions) is (are) reduced by the amount of the offshore income gain.

[*Sec 763*].

Offshore income gains of insurance companies. Income attributable to offshore income gains, so far as referable to general annuity business, is deducted from the receipts to be taken into account in computing the insurance company's profits from that business. [*Sec 437(2)(a); FA 1990, 6 Sch 6*].

Offshore income gains of trustees. Any offshore income gains arising to trustees and assessable under Schedule D, Case VI will be charged at the rate applicable to trusts (see 80.5 SETTLEMENTS) for the year in question. [*Sec 764; FA 1993, 6 Sch 13*]. However such tax paid is available for set-off against the amount assessable on discretionary trustees under *Sec 687(2)(b)* (see 80.5 SETTLEMENTS). [*Sec 687(3)(e)*].

Where trustees hold assets for a person who would be absolutely entitled as against the trustees but for being a minor, any offshore income gains liable to income tax which accrue on the disposal of those assets are deemed to be paid to that person for the purposes of the provisions regarding settlements on children in *Sec 660B* (for 1995/96 onwards—see 80.17 SETTLEMENTS) and, for earlier years, *Secs 663–670* (see 80.22 SETTLEMENTS). [*Secs 660B(4), 663(2) (repealed); FA 1995, 17 Sch 1*].

52.13   *Example*

R, who is resident, ordinarily resident and domiciled in the UK, invests in non-qualifying offshore funds as follows.

			£
(i)	**ABC fund**		
	30.11.82	1,000 shares purchased at £10 per share	10,000
	1.1.84	Market value per share = £20	20,000
	1.4.97	On amalgamation with XYZ fund (another non-qualifying offshore fund) the 1,000 original shares are exchanged for 2,000 new shares in XYZ which have a value of £15 per share	30,000
			£
(ii)	**DEF fund**		
	1.8.83	500 units purchased at £25 per unit	12,500
	1.1.84	Market value per unit = £20	10,000
	1.2.97	500 units sold for £40 per unit	20,000

R has offshore income gains and capital gains/losses in 1996/97 as follows.

Offshore income gains

Disposal on 1.2.97 of 500 DEF units	Post-1983 gain	Unindexed gain
	£	£
Disposal proceeds	20,000	20,000
Market value at 1.1.84	10,000	
Cost		12,500
	£10,000	£7,500

As the unindexed gain is less than the post-1983 gain, the offshore income gain chargeable under Schedule D, Case VI is £7,500.

Disposal on 1.4.97 of 1,000 ABC shares		
Disposal consideration	30,000	30,000
Market value at 1.1.84	20,000	
Cost		10,000
	£10,000	£20,000

The offshore income gain chargeable under Schedule D, Case VI is the £10,000 post-1983 gain as this is less than the unindexed gain.

52.13   Offshore Funds

Capital gains computation

Disposal on 1.2.97 of 500 DEF units

	£
Disposal proceeds	20,000
Offshore income gain	7,500
	12,500
Cost	12,500
Chargeable gain/allowable loss	Nil

Disposal on 1.4.97 of 1,000 ABC shares
There is no capital gains tax liability as the share exchange is not treated as a disposal for capital gains tax purposes. [*TCGA 1992, s 135*]. See Tolley's Capital Gains Tax.

Note

(*a*)   The £10,000 offshore income gain arising on the exchange of XYZ shares for ABC shares will be treated as part of the acquisition cost for capital gains tax purposes on a subsequent disposal of XYZ shares (see 52.12 above).

53 Partnerships

[*Secs 111–115*]

53.1   An English partnership is not a legal entity in the same way as a company, but a collection of separate persons. In Scotland, a firm is a legal person, see *Partnership Act 1890, s 4(2)*. However, the *Taxes Acts* are in general applied to Scottish partnerships in the same way as they are applicable to the rest of the UK.

For 1996/97 and earlier years as regards partnership trades, etc. commenced before 6 April 1994, the profits of a trade or profession carried on by a partnership are assessed jointly on the partnership (see 53.3 below) and to this extent it is treated for tax purposes as an entity distinct from its members. This does not apply for later years or as regards partnership trades, etc. commenced (or treated as commenced—see 53.6 below) after 5 April 1994; the taxable profits of the trade, etc. are apportioned between the partners, each of whom is then taxed on his own share. See also 78.5, 78.8, 78.9, 78.13, 78.16, 78.27 SELF-ASSESSMENT for provisions regarding partnership returns and general compliance; these apply to all partnerships, whenever trade commenced, but generally do not apply before 1996/97. For a general discussion of the tax treatment of partnerships, see *R v City of London Commrs (ex p Gibbs) HL 1942, 24 TC 221*.

Headings in this chapter are as follows.

53.2   **NATURE OF PARTNERSHIP**

Whether a partnership exists and, if so, from what date is a question of fact (*Williamson CS 1928, 14 TC 335; Calder v Allanson KB 1935, 19 TC 293*). The existence of a formal partnership agreement is not conclusive of the existence of a partnership (*Hawker v Compton KB 1922, 8 TC 306; Dickenson v Gross KB 1927, 11 TC 614*). Equally, whether a partnership can ante-date the date of the agreement is a question of fact (*Ayrshire Pullman Services v CIR CS 1929, 14 TC 754; Waddington v O'Callaghan KB 1931, 16 TC 187; Taylor v Chalklin KB 1945, 26 TC 463; Alexander Bulloch & Co v CIR CS 1976, 51 TC 563; Saywell v Pope Ch D 1979, 53 TC 40*).

Joint transactions may amount to a partnership or joint trading for tax purposes—see *Morden Rigg & Eskrigge v Monks CA 1923, 8 TC 450* (joint cotton transactions); *Gardner & Bowring Hardy v CIR CS 1930, 15 TC 602* (temporary joint coal merchanting); *Lindsay Woodward & Hiscox v CIR CS 1932, 18 TC 43* (joint transactions in whisky in violation of USA law); *Geo. Hall & Son v Platt Ch D 1954, 35 TC 440* (joint crop growing). See also *Fenston v Johnstone KB 1940, 23 TC 29*.

53.3 Partnerships

The *Limited Partnership Act 1907* allows the formation of limited partnerships, in which the liability of one or more (but not all) of the partners for the firm's debts is limited to a specified amount. See also 53.10 below.

Where a partnership terminated with open forward contracts, subsequently completed, it was held to continue trading notwithstanding that some of the partners had formed a new partnership to carry on a similar business (*Hillerns & Fowler v Murray CA 1932, 17 TC 77*). A doctor who sold his practice, helping the purchaser for a short time on a profit-sharing basis, was held not to be a partner (*Pratt v Strick KB 1932, 17 TC 459*).

A partnership set up for tax avoidance purposes may nevertheless be a true partnership (*Newstead v Frost HL 1980, 53 TC 525*).

A Rotary Club is not a partnership (*Blackpool Marton Rotary Club v Martin Ch D 1988, 62 TC 686*).

See 68.5 SCHEDULE A as regards joint ownership and exploitation of property.

53.3 ASSESSMENT AND COMPUTATION OF PROFITS

Pre-Finance Act 1994. For 1996/97 and earlier years as regards partnership trades, etc. commenced before 6 April 1994, the profits of a trade or profession carried on by a partnership are assessed in the first place as a whole, exactly as if it were the business of a sole trader. The assessment is computed in accordance with the basis period rules applicable to individuals (see 71.4 to 71.9, and, as regards 1996/97 only, 71.20, 71.24 SCHEDULE D, CASES I AND II by reference to the profits of the whole business. A 'joint assessment' is then made on the firm, and the Crown have the legal right (in default) to demand the whole of the tax from any partner. [*Sec 111 as originally enacted* and see *Stevens v Britten CA 1954, 33 ATC 399* and *Harrison v Willis CA 1965, 43 TC 61* (re deceased partner)]. See 53.12 below for excess liability.

Post-Finance Act 1994. For 1994/95 and subsequent years as regards partnership trades, etc. commenced (or treated as commenced—see 53.6 below) after 5 April 1994 and for 1997/98 and subsequent years as regards partnership trades, etc. commenced on or before that date, the partnership is not generally treated for tax purposes as an entity which is separate and distinct from its members. The profits or losses of the trade, profession or business are computed in like manner as if the partnership were a UK resident individual (for 1994/95 only, as if it were an individual). Each individual's share (see 53.5 below) of the profit or loss (as adjusted for tax purposes) is taxed or relieved as if it derived from a trade, etc. (the deemed trade) carried on by him alone. The deemed trade is treated as commencing at the time the individual becomes a partner, or, if the actual trade, etc. was previously carried on by him alone, at the time the actual trade commenced. Similar rules apply as regards cessations.

The deemed trade is taxed in accordance with the normal basis period rules (see 71.11 to 71.19 SCHEDULE D, CASES I AND II). A change of partnership accounting date results in a change of basis period of a partner's deemed trade only if it would have resulted in a change of basis period of the partnership if the partnership were taxed as a separate entity (see 71.15 SCHEDULE D, CASES I AND II). Where a change of accounting date in the second or third year of assessment of a partner's deemed trade fails to result in a change of basis period (because the necessary conditions are not satisfied), the 'opening years' rules (see 71.12 SCHEDULE D, CASES I AND II) are modified so as to determine the basis period for that year of assessment by reference to the old accounting date.

[*Sec 111(1)–(5)(10)–(13); FA 1994, s 215(1); FA 1995, s 117(1)(a)(2)(4)*].

For partnership trades commenced before 6 April 1994, the transitional rules at 71.20 to 71.24 SCHEDULE D, CASES I AND II apply, although as regards 1996/97 they apply to the partnership as a separate entity.

See 78.2 SELF-ASSESSMENT as regards anti-avoidance measures preventing exploitation of the transitional provisions, and in particular 43.22 INTEREST PAYABLE as regards artificial changes in partnership financing arrangements.

Non-trading income. Where the post-Finance Act 1994 rules apply to a trading or professional partnership to which non-trading income (or a relievable non-trading loss) accrues, each individual partner is taxed on his share, computed by reference to profit sharing ratios for the period of account of the trade etc. In the case of untaxed income (as defined) from one or more sources, the normal basis period rules (see 71.11 to 71.19 SCHEDULE D, CASES I AND II) apply as if each individual's share of the income (or loss) were profits (or losses) of a second deemed trade carried on by him alone. The second deemed trade is treated as commencing at the time the individual becomes a partner and ceasing when he ceases to be a partner, with each source of the income treated as continuing until he ceases to be a partner. The same comments apply as above as regards changes of partnership accounting date. Where overlap relief (see 71.19) in respect of untaxed income falls to be deducted in a year of assessment (because of a change of accounting date or a permanent discontinuance of the second deemed trade) and the deduction exceeds the partner's share of untaxed income for that year, the excess is deductible in computing his income for that year. [*Sec 111(7)–(9)(12)(13); FA 1994, s 215(1); FA 1995, s 117(1)(a)(2)*]. Strictly, in the case of income from property of a partnership commenced before 6 April 1994, the fiscal year basis applies for 1995/96 and 1996/97 (see 68.5 SCHEDULE A). If, however, an accounts basis (whether current or preceding year) was adopted for 1994/95 for Schedule A (or furnished lettings) income, the current year accounts basis may in practice be applied for 1995/96 and 1996/97 (to avoid a switch to the fiscal year basis just for those two years). (Revenue Tax Bulletin August 1995 p 242). See also 68.5 SCHEDULE A. For the treatment of any transitional adjustment needed because of gaps between the basis periods for 1994/95 and 1995/96, see generally 68.22 SCHEDULE A and, for further guidance, Revenue Tax Bulletin February 1996 pp 283–285. These special rules for non-trading untaxed income apply only where the associated trade or profession is carried on *in partnership*, so that, for example, if one partner is left to carry on the partnership business as a sole trader, his second notional trade ceases at that time and untaxed income is subsequently taxed on a fiscal year basis.

General. The assignment by a partner of part of his share in the partnership was ineffective for the purpose of displacing his liability to income tax on that part of his share of partnership profits (*Hadlee and Another v Commissioner of Inland Revenue (NZ) PC, [1993] STC 294*).

See *MacKinlay v Arthur Young McClelland Moores & Co HL 1989, 62 TC 704* as to prohibition on deduction of certain payments made to partners in connection with partnership business.

If a **company** is a partner, see 53.14 below.

Capital gains which arise from the disposal of partnership assets are charged on the partners separately. [*TCGA 1992, s 59; FA 1995, 29 Sch Pt VIII(16)*]. See Tolley's Capital Gains Tax.

Adjustments to profits will include items below.

(i) **Law costs** and stamps re partnership deeds are not normally permissible deductions.

53.4 Partnerships

(ii) **Partners'** salaries, domestic and personal expenses, interest credited on capital and any benefit of financial value given to a partner are not permissible deductions for tax purposes, being regarded as part of the taxable profits. But this does not necessarily apply to payments to a partner for goods or services 'altogether disconnected with the partnership business as such' and where the firm's premises are owned by a partner, *bona fide* rent paid to him under legal agreement is a proper deduction for tax purposes (*Heastie v Veitch CA 1933, 18 TC 305*). Contributions towards partners' removal expenses, where partner moved in the interests of the firm, are not deductible (*MacKinlay v Arthur Young McClelland Moores & Co HL 1989, 62 TC 704*).

(iii) **Taxed charges,** payable out of firm's income, are added back in computing the firm's taxable profits, and tax on them has to be accounted for. The Revenue accept the view that a partner's personal taxed investment income is available to cover his share of partnership charges. Should there be an excess of partnership taxed charges over partnership income, an assessment under *Sec 350* would therefore be made only to the extent that each individual partner's share of the excess is not covered by his own private investment income.

See also 71 SCHEDULE D, CASES I AND II for adjustments to profits generally and 75.24 SCHEDULE E for director's fees received by professional partnership.

53.4 *Example*

Partnership trading and investment income under current year basis

X and Y began to trade in partnership on 1 July 1995, preparing first accounts to 30 September 1996 and sharing profits equally. Z joins the firm as an equal partner on 1 October 1997. Y leaves the firm on 31 March 1999. Accounts are prepared to that date to ascertain Y's entitlement, but the accounting date then reverts to 30 September and the partnership does not give notice to the Revenue of a change of accounting date, so that there is no change of basis period. In addition to trading profits, the partnership had a source of lettings income which ceased in September 1998, and is in receipt of both taxed and untaxed interest, the latter from a source commencing in October 1996. Taxed interest is received on 31 March each year. Revised figures as adjusted for tax purposes are as follows.

	Schedule D, Case I	Schedule A	Schedule D, Case III	Taxed interest (gross)
	£	£	£	£
15 months to 30.9.96	30,000	4,500	—	750
Year to 30.9.97	24,000	5,000	1,000	1,500
Year to 30.9.98	39,000	3,000	600	300
6 months to 31.3.99	19,500	—	225	165
6 months to 30.9.99	14,000	—	140	—

The partners' shares of taxable income from the partnership for the years 1995/96 to 1999/2000 inclusive are as follows.

512

Schedule D, Case 1	X £	Y £	Z £
1995/96 1.7.95–5.4.96 (£30,000 × 9/15)	9,000	9,000	
1996/97 1.10.95–30.9.96 (£30,000 × 12/15)	12,000*	12,000*	
* Overlap relief accrued: 1.10.95–5.4.96 (£30,000 × 6/15)	6,000	6,000	
1997/98 Y/e 30.9.97	12,000	12,000	
1.10.97–5.4.98 (£39,000 × 6/12 × 1/3)			6,500
1998/99 Y/e 30.9.98	13,000	13,000	13,000*
1.10.98–31.3.99		6,500	
		19,500	
Less overlap relief		(6,000)	
		13,500	
* Overlap relief accrued 1.10.97–5.4.98 (as above)			6,500
1999/2000 Y/e 30.9.99 1.10.98–31.3.99 1.4.99–30.9.99	6,500 7,000		6,500 7,000
	13,500		13,500
Schedule A			
1995/96 1.7.95–5.4.96 (£4,500 × 9/15)	1,350	1,350	
1996/97 1.10.95–30.9.96 (£4,500 × 12/15)	1,800*	1,800*	
* Overlap relief accrued 1.10.95–5.4.96 (£4,500 × 6/15)	900	900	
1997/98 Y/e 30.9.97	2,500	2,500	
1.10.97–5.4.98 (£3,000 × 6/12 × 1/3)			500

53.5 Partnerships

	X £	Y £	Z £
1998/99			
Y/e 30.9.98	1,000	1,000	1,000*
1.10.98–31.3.99		—	
		1,000	
Less overlap relief		(900)	
		100	
* Overlap relief accrued			
1.10.97–5.4.98 (as above)			500
Schedule D, Case III			
1997/98			
Y/e 30.9.97	500	500	
1.10.97–5.4.98 (£600 × 6/12 × 1/3)			100
1998/99			
Y/e 30.9.98	200	200	200*
1.10.98–31.3.99		75	
		275	
* Overlap relief accrued			
1.10.97–5.4.98 (as above)			100
1999/2000			
Y/e 30.9.99			
1.10.98–31.3.99	75		75
1.4.99–30.9.99	70		70
	145		145
Taxed interest			
1995/96 (received 31.3.96)	375	375	
1996/97 (received 31.3.97)	750	750	
1997/98 (received 31.3.98)	100	100	100
1998/99 (received 31.3.99)	55	55	55
1999/2000	**	—	**

** Each to be based on one-half of interest received 31.3.2000.

Note

Taxed investment income is taxed on a fiscal year basis as for an individual, but is apportioned between the partners according to their shares for the accounting period in which the income arises.

53.5   **APPORTIONMENT BETWEEN PARTNERS**

Pre-Finance Act 1994. For 1996/97 and earlier years as regards partnership trades, etc. commenced before 6 April 1994, apportionment of the assessment on the firm is made between the individual partners according to their shares under the partnership agreement *for the year of assessment.*

Where partners have salaries, fluctuating commission or interest on capital, plus certain percentages of the balance of profits, each partner's proportion of the statutory assessment on the firm is his actual salary, commission and interest for the year of assessment, plus his percentage of the balance of the assessment after deducting all these salaries etc. This has been established in cases relating to appeals against super-tax assessments, including *Rutherford v CIR CS 1926, 10 TC 683* and *Lewis v CIR CA 1933, 18 TC 174.*

Each partner is entitled to have all reliefs due to him personally deducted from his share [*Sec 277 as originally enacted*] and the tax payable by the firm is reduced accordingly. If this does not exhaust all his allowances, any balance can be set against other income of his or, if the firm receives untaxed income or rents assessable under Schedule A, any unexhausted balance of allowances due to a partner may be set against his share of these.

Post-Finance Act 1994. For 1994/95 and subsequent years as regards partnership trades, etc. commenced (or treated as commenced—see 53.6 below) after 5 April 1994 and for 1997/98 and subsequent years as regards partnership trades, etc. commenced on or before that date, the taxable profits of the partnership for a period of account are apportioned between the individual members in accordance with their shares under the partnership agreement *for that period.* [*Sec 111(3); FA 1994, s 215(1)(4)(5); FA 1995, s 117*]. See 53.3 above as regards non-trading income.

General. The profit share of a partner actively engaged in the business is 'earned income', unlike that of a 'sleeping partner'. (In practice, however, it is treated as 'earned' whenever there is some degree of active participation and regular oversight.)

53.6   **CHANGES IN PARTNERS, ETC.**

Pre-Finance Act 1994. The following provisions apply for 1996/97 and earlier years as regards partnership trades, etc. commenced before 6 April 1994. Note that a deemed cessation and recommencement after 5 April 1994 (and before 6 April 1997) will immediately bring the 'new' partnership into the post-Finance Act 1994 regime.

In the event of any change in the persons comprising the partnership, the business is automatically treated as having ceased and a new business commenced at the date of change. [*Sec 113(1) as originally enacted*]. This means that the cessation and new business provisions set out in 71.3 SCHEDULE D, CASES I AND II will apply, subject to the special rules referred to below.

But, if *all partners* (or their executors) *before and after the change* (provided always there is one partner common to both periods) jointly so elect by notice to the inspector within two years of the change the continuing basis will apply. [*Sec 113(2) as originally enacted*]. The profit assessable for the year of change is then computed as if there had been no change, and is apportioned 'as may be just' (normally on a time basis) and the apportioned amounts assessed separately on the old and new firms. [*Sec 113(3) as originally enacted*]. Such an election can be made in the case of, e.g.

(*a*)   a sole proprietor taking in a partner, or

(*b*)   all partners going out except one, or

(*c*)   death of a partner,

but not where there is

(i)   a complete change of all the persons carrying on the business, or

(ii)   dissolution of partnership, each partner taking over part of the business.

A claim outside the two-year limit may be admitted where it is made as soon as is reasonably possible in all the circumstances and where it is late because of either

(A)   a relevant and uncorrected Revenue error resulting in the partners or their agent being misled as to whether the requirements of the legislation had been met, or

(B)   the unavailability at a crucial time, and for unforeseeable reasons (e.g. serious illness), of a required signatory (or of an agent for such a signatory where no-one else could reasonably be expected to stand in his shoes), or

(C)   some other difficulty in obtaining the required signatures, provided that, before the expiry of the time limit, the Revenue had been clearly notified that each signatory had decided to make the election and been given the reasons why the election could not be made in time.

An election will not be admitted where it was made late through oversight or negligence, or because of the temporary refusal of a partner to sign it, or where it was deliberately delayed because its effect on the partners' taxation liabilities was unclear when the time limit expired. (Revenue Pamphlet IR 131 (October 1995 Supplement), SP 9/92, 23 November 1992). See also Revenue Tax Bulletin February 1993 p 56 for an example of a Revenue decision on a late claim.

Where a partner has genuinely disappeared and all reasonable attempts to trace him or her have been exhausted, an election signed by the remaining partners will be accepted provided that they sign an indemnity. (Revenue Inspectors' Manual, IM 253).

Where an election is made it may be revoked provided the notice of revocation is signed by all interested parties and given within the limit of two years for making the election. (Revenue Pamphlet IR 131, A4).

But if a company is a partner, see 53.14(iii) below.

See 71.9 SCHEDULE D, CASES I AND II for concession on death of husband or wife who were in partnership.

Blanket continuation elections. By concession, a 'blanket' continuation election, covering all future partnership changes (until any or all of the partners withdraw from the arrangement), will be accepted where

(I)   the firm has at least 50 partners, or at least 20 non-UK resident partners, immediately after the first change under the election,

(II)   new partners add their names to the election, and

(III)   the Revenue are indemnified by all partners before the first change under the election, and by all subsequent new partners, against any loss of tax arising from a claim by any partner or former partner that the election was invalid so that the cessation basis should have been applied to a particular change or changes.

(Revenue Pamphlet IR 1, A80).

No continuation election. Where an election under *Sec 113(2)* as above could be, but is not, made in respect of a partnership change (other than a change from sole trader to partnership or vice versa) before 6 April 1994, the commencement rules of assessment (see 71.4 SCHEDULE D, CASES I AND II) are revised. For the year of assessment of the change and the following three years, the new partnership is assessed on the actual profits arising in the year of assessment in question. The new partners may, in addition, elect (within seven years after the end of the fifth year of assessment) for both the fifth and sixth years of assessment to be assessed on the actual profits arising in those years. [*Secs 61(4), 62(4)(5)*].

Post-Finance Act 1994. For 1994/95 and subsequent years as regards partnership trades, etc. commenced (or treated under the above provisions as commenced) after 5 April 1994 and for 1997/98 and subsequent years as regards partnership trades, etc. commenced on or before that date, a partnership trade, etc. is *not* treated as discontinued and recommenced on a change of partner providing there is at least one continuing partner (which also covers the situation where a sole trader begins to carry on the trade in partnership or a former partner begins to carry it on as a sole trader). The election under *Sec 113(2)* for the continuing basis is no longer relevant. [*Sec 113; FA 1994, ss 215(4)(5), 216(1)(2)*]. New partners are taxed on their profit share under the opening years provisions at 71.12 SCHEDULE D, CASES I AND II and outgoing partners are taxed on their share under the closing year provisions at 71.17 SCHEDULE D, CASES I AND II (see also 53.3 above).

53.7 *Examples*

General

P, Q and R have carried on a profession in partnership for a number of years, sharing profits in the ratio 2:2:1. Accounts are made up to 30 June. P leaves the partnership on 30 June 1994 and Q and R share profits 3:2 for the year to 30 June 1995 and equally thereafter. On 30 June 1997, Q leaves the partnership and on 1 July 1997, S becomes a partner. Profits are then shared between R and S in the ratio 2:1.

Results for relevant years up to 30 June 1999 are as follows.

Year ended	Partners' salaries				Adjusted Profit
	P	Q	R	S	
	£	£	£	£	£
30.6.91	9,000	9,000	4,500	—	40,000
30.6.92	12,000	12,000	6,000	—	70,000
30.6.93	4,000	4,000	2,000	—	72,000
30.6.94	18,000	13,000	11,500	—	60,000
30.6.95	—	12,500	12,500	—	80,000
30.6.96	—	12,000	17,000	—	85,000
30.6.97	—	4,000	11,000	—	95,000
30.6.98	—	—	5,000	—	101,000
30.6.99	—	—	2,000	—	110,000

The adjusted profit figures above are after adding back partners' salaries. There are no capital allowances to be taken into account.

53.7   Partnerships

The tax position for the years 1992/93 to 1999/2000 is as follows.

(i) if continuation election made on change in partners on 30.6.94

Assessments on partnership of P, Q & R

	£
1992/93 (y/e 30.6.91)	40,000
1993/94 (y/e 30.6.92)	70,000
1994/95 (y/e 30.6.93 × 3/12)	18,000

Assessments on partnership of Q & R

1994/95 (y/e 30.6.93 × 9/12)		54,000
1995/96 (y/e 30.6.94)		60,000
1996/97	£	
Y/e 30.6.95	80,000	
Y/e 30.6.96	85,000	
	£165,000	

£165,000 × 12/24 = 82,500

Taxable profits of Q, R & S individually from 1997/98

	Q £	R £	S £
1997/98			
Y/e 30.6.97			
Profits £(95,000 − 11,000 − 4,000)	40,000	40,000	
Salaries	4,000	11,000	
	44,000	51,000	
1.7.97–5.4.98			
£((101,000 − 5,000) × 1/3 × 9/12)			24,000
Less transitional overlap relief:			
(1.7.96–5.4.97 — £44,000 × 9/12)	33,000		
Schedule D, Case II	£11,000	£51,000*	£24,000
* Transitional overlap relief accrued:			
(1.7.96–5.4.97 — £51,000 × 9/12)	—	£38,250	—
1998/99			
Y/e 30.6.98			
Profits £(101,000 − 5,000)		64,000	32,000
Salary		5,000	—
Schedule D, Case II		£69,000	£32,000*
* Overlap relief accrued:			
(1.7.97–5.4.98 as above)			£24,000

	Q £	R £	S £
1999/2000			
Y/e 30.6.99			
Profits £(110,000 – 2,000)		72,000	36,000
Salary		2,000	—
Schedule D, Case II		£74,000	£36,000

(ii) if no continuation election made on change in partners on 30.6.94

Assessments on partnership of P, Q & R

	Preceding year £	Actual	£	£
1992/93	40,000	3/12 × 30.6.92	17,500	
		9/12 × 30.6.93	54,000	
				71,500
1993/94	70,000	3/12 × 30.6.93	18,000	
		9/12 × 30.6.94	45,000	
				63,000
	£110,000			£134,500

Higher figure of the two is £134,500, so assessments on actual.

1994/95	3/12 × 30.6.94	£15,000

Taxable profits of Q, R & S individually from 1994/95

	Q £	R £	S £
1994/95			
1.7.94–5.4.95			
Profits £(80,000 – 25,000) × 9/12	24,750	16,500	
Salaries × 9/12	9,375	9,375	
Schedule D, Case II	£34,125	£25,875	
1995/96			
Y/e 30.6.95			
Profits £(80,000 – 25,000)	33,000	22,000	
Salaries	12,500	12,500	
Schedule D, Case II	£45,500*	£34,500*	
* Overlap relief accrued:			
(1.7.94–5.4.95 as above)	£34,125	£25,875	
1996/97			
Y/e 30.6.96			
Profits £(85,000 – 29,000)	28,000	28,000	
Salaries	12,000	17,000	
Schedule D, Case II	£40,000	£45,000	

53.7 Partnerships

	Q £	R £	S £
1997/98			
Y/e 30.6.97			
Profits £(95,000 − 15,000)	40,000	40,000	
Salaries	4,000	11,000	
	44,000	51,000	
1.7.97–5.4.98			
£((101,000 − 5,000) × 1/3 × 9/12)			24,000
Less overlap relief (see 1995/96)	34,125		
Schedule D, Case II	£9,875	£51,000	£24,000
1998/99			
Y/e 30.6.98			
Profits £(101,000 − 5,000)		64,000	32,000
Salary		5,000	—
Schedule D, Case II		£69,000	£32,000*
* Overlap relief accrued:			
(1.7.97–5.4.98 as above)			£24,000
1999/2000			
Y/e 30.6.99			
Profits £(110,000 − 2,000)		72,000	36,000
Salary		2,000	—
Schedule D, Case II		£74,000	£36,000

Partnership assessments are allocated between partners as follows.

(iii) if continuation election made (see (i) above)

Partnership of P, Q & R

	P £	Q £	R £	Total £
1992/93				
Salaries 3/12 × 30.6.92	3,000	3,000	1,500	7,500
9/12 × 30.6.93	3,000	3,000	1,500	7,500
				15,000
Balance 2:2:1	10,000	10,000	5,000	25,000
Division of assessment	£16,000	£16,000	£8,000	£40,000

	P £	Q £	R £	Total £
1993/94				
Salaries 3/12 × 30.6.93	1,000	1,000	500	2,500
9/12 × 30.6.94	13,500	9,750	8,625	31,875
				34,375
Balance 2:2:1	14,250	14,250	7,125	35,625
Division of assessment	£28,750	£25,000	£16,250	£70,000
1994/95				
Salaries 3/12 × 30.6.94	4,500	3,250	2,875	10,625
Balance 2:2:1	2,950	2,950	1,475	7,375
Division of assessment	£7,450	£6,200	£4,350	£18,000
Partnership of Q & R				
1994/95				
Salaries 9/12 × 30.6.95		9,375	9,375	18,750
Balance 3:2		21,150	14,100	35,250
Division of assessment		£30,525	£23,475	£54,000
1995/96				
Salaries 3/12 × 30.6.95		3,125	3,125	6,250
Balance to 30.6.95 at 3:2		5,250	3,500	8,750
				15,000
Salaries 9/12 × 30.6.96		9,000	12,750	21,750
Balance from 1.7.95 at 1:1		11,625	11,625	23,250
Division of assessment		£29,000	£31,000	£60,000
1996/97				
Salaries 3/12 × 30.6.96		3,000	4,250	7,250
Salaries 9/12 × 30.6.97		3,000	8,250	11,250
				18,500
Balance 1:1		32,000	32,000	64,000
Division of assessment		£38,000	£44,500	£82,500

(iv) if continuation election not made (see (ii) above)

53.7   Partnerships

Partnership of P, Q & R

	P £	Q £	R £	Total £
1992/93				
Salaries 3/12 × 30.6.92	3,000	3,000	1,500	7,500
9/12 × 30.6.93	3,000	3,000	1,500	7,500
				15,000
Balance 2:2:1	22,600	22,600	11,300	56,500
	£28,600	£28,600	£14,300	£71,500
1993/94				
Salaries 3/12 × 30.6.93	1,000	1,000	500	2,500
9/12 × 30.6.94	13,500	9,750	8,625	31,875
				34,375
Balance 2:2:1	11,450	11,450	5,725	28,625
Division of assessment	£25,950	£22,200	£14,850	£63,000
1994/95				
Salaries 3/12 × 30.6.94	4,500	3,250	2,875	10,625
Balance 2:2:1	1,750	1,750	875	4,375
Division of assessment	£6,250	£5,000	£3,750	£15,000

A comparison can now be made of taxable profits under the two options under consideration.

(v) If continuation election made in respect of 30.6.94 change

	P £	Q £	R £	S £	Total £
1992/93	16,000	16,000	8,000		40,000 (1)
1993/94	28,750	25,000	16,250		70,000 (1)
1994/95 (PQR)	7,450	6,200	4,350		18,000 (1)
1994/95 (QR)		30,525	23,475		54,000 (1)
1995/96		29,000	31,000		60,000 (1)
1996/97		38,000	44,500		82,500 (1)
1997/98		11,000	51,000	24,000	86,000 (2)
1998/99			69,000	32,000	101,000 (2)
1999/2000			74,000	36,000	110,000 (2)
	£52,200	£155,725	£321,575	£92,000	£621,500
Overlap relief c/f			£38,250	£24,000	£62,250

(1) = Partnership to be assessed in one sum.
(2) = Partners to be taxed individually on their shares.

(vi) If no continuation election made in respect of 30.6.94 change

	P	Q	R	S	Total
	£	£	£	£	£
1992/93	28,600	28,600	14,300		71,500 (1)
1993/94	25,950	22,200	14,850		63,000 (1)
1994/95 (PQR)	6,250	5,000	3,750		15,000 (1)
1994/95 (QR)		34,125	25,875		60,000 (2)
1995/96		45,500	34,500		80,000 (2)
1996/97		40,000	45,000		85,000 (2)
1997/98		9,875	51,000	24,000	84,875 (2)
1998/99			69,000	32,000	101,000 (2)
1999/2000			74,000	36,000	110,000 (2)
	£60,800	£185,300	£332,275	£92,000	£670,375
Overlap relief c/f			£25,875	£24,000	£49,875

(1) = Partnership to be assessed in one sum.
(2) = Partners to be taxed individually on their shares.

Summary

The difference between (v) and (vi) above, after taking overlap relief into account, is £61,250 ((£621,500 − £62,250) − (£670,375 − £49,875)).

With a continuation election, 12 months' profits escape tax, being half the profits for the two-year period to 30.6.96, £82,500. In addition, 9 months' profits (1.7.96 to 5.4.97) attract transitional overlap relief, £71,250. Total drop-out of profits is thus £153,750 (£82,500 + £71,250).

With no continuation election, 21 months' profits escape tax, being profits for the period 1.7.90 to 5.4.92, a total of £92,500.

The difference in profits escaping tax is thus proved to be £61,250 (£153,750 − £92,500).

Transition to current year basis—new partner joining in 1996/97

A and B have traded in partnership since before 6 April 1994, preparing accounts to 30 June and sharing profits equally. C joins the firm on 1 January 1997 with a one-third profit share. The three partners make a continuation election. Profits as adjusted for tax purposes for relevant years are as follows.

	£
Year to 30.6.94	36,000
Year to 30.6.95	38,000
Year to 30.6.96	42,000
Year to 30.6.97	45,000
Year to 30.6.98	48,000

53.7 Partnerships

Assessments will be as follows.

	Total £	A £	B £	C £
Partnership assessments				
1995/96 (y/e 30.6.94)	36,000	18,000	18,000	N/A
1996/97 (2 yrs to 30.6.96 × ½ = 40,000)				
6.4.96 to 31.12.96(¾)	30,000	15,000	15,000	N/A
1.1.97 to 5.4.97 (¼)	10,000	3,334	3,333	3,333
	40,000	18,334	18,333	3,333

		A	B	C
Individual self-assessments				
1997/98				
A (y/e 30.6.97 × 1/3)		15,000		
B (y/e 30.6.97 × 1/3)			15,000	
C (1.1.97 to 31.12.97 × 1/3) see note (a) below				
1.1.97 to 30.6.97 × 1/3				7,500
1.7.97 to 31.12.97 × 1/3				8,000
				15,500
1998/99				
A (y/e 30.6.98 × 1/3)		16,000		
B (y/e 30.6.98 × 1/3)			16,000	
C (y/e 30.6.98 × 1/3)				16,000

		A	B	C
Overlap relief				
A & B (Transitional overlap relief)				
1.7.96 to 5.4.97—9/12 × £15,000 each		11,250	11,250	
C				
Transitional overlap relief:				
1.1.97 to 5.4.97—3/6 × £7,500				3,750
Actual overlap relief:				
1.7.97 to 31.12.97				8,000
Total overlap relief (overlap period—9 months each)		11,250	11,250	11,750

Notes

(a) 1997/98 is only C's second tax year of trading and his basis period must be determined in accordance with the opening years rules at 71.12 SCHEDULE D, CASES

I AND II. It is thus his first twelve months of trading. This is the case even though the concept of partners' individual basis periods did not apply to C's first year, 1996/97.

(b)   C's overlap relief is partly transitional and partly the result of a genuine overlap of basis periods. The distinction would be of importance only if the anti-avoidance rules at 71.22 SCHEDULE D, CASES I AND II came into play.

53.8   **Partnership mergers and demergers.** Where two businesses carried on in partnership merge, it is a question of fact whether the new partnership has succeeded to the businesses of the old partnerships, or whether the old businesses have ceased and a new business resulted from the merger which is different in nature from either of the two old businesses. Disparity of size between the old partnerships will not of itself be a significant matter. Clearly the former is more likely to be the case where the two old businesses carried on the same sort of activities, and the latter where they were themselves different in nature. Where the former is the case, *Sec 113* (see 53.6 above) applies, and the partners may elect in respect of one or both (or neither) of the old businesses for the continuation basis (where relevant—see 53.6 above) to apply. Apportionment of the profits of the new partnership will be necessary where a continuation election is made in respect of only one of the old businesses. Where the new partnership does not succeed to the old businesses, *Sec 113* has no application.

Similar considerations apply where a partnership is divided up and two or more partnerships are formed, in determining whether any of the separate partnerships has succeeded to the business of the original partnership. *Sec 113* will apply, and a continuation election (where relevant) be available, only where one of the businesses carried on after the division is so large in relation to the rest as to be recognisably the business previously carried on. If, however, it appears to the Revenue that a demerger has taken place for fiscal reasons, and is more apparent than real, they might wish to argue that the same trade is carried on after the demerger as before, so that a *Sec 113(2)* election could be made, with the result that the special rules referred to in 53.6 above apply.

Similar principles apply where sole traders merge into partnership or a partnership business is demerged and carried on by sole traders.

(Revenue Pamphlet IR 131 (October 1995 Supplement), SP 9/86, 10 December 1986).

See *C Connelly & Co v Wilbey Ch D, [1992] STC 783* for a case in which it was held that neither part of a demerged partnership succeeded to the former partnership trade (and in which legal costs relating to the dissolution were disallowed).

The amalgamation of two sole traders into partnership in *Humphries v Cook KB 1934, 19 TC 121* was held to result in the commencement of a new business and the cessation of both the old businesses, but this is applied sparingly by the Revenue, mainly where the new partnership business is of a different nature from those previously carried on.

For a discussion of the general principles outlined above and their interaction with current year basis of assessment and the transition thereto, see Revenue booklet SAT 1(1995), chapter 8. Under the post-Finance Act 1994 rules in 53.6 above, a continuation basis automatically applies on a *partial* change of ownership of a *continuing* business.

See 60.2 POST-CESSATION ETC. RECEIPTS AND EXPENDITURE for change in the basis of accounting.

53.9   **DOUBLE SUCCESSION**

Where there has been a change in partners in respect of which election for continuation basis has been given (where relevant — see 53.6 above), and between that change and the end of the second year of assessment following there is either a permanent discontinuance, or a further change treated as such, all the provisions of *Sec 63 as originally enacted* (as to basis of assessment for the final period and for the two years preceding discontinuance) apply to that discontinuance as if the earlier change had not occurred. [*Sec 113(3)(b) as originally enacted*]. A retiring partner who joins in a continuation election should therefore bear in mind that if a further change occurs within two years and a continuation election is not made on that occasion, there may be an increase in his assessable profits under *Sec 63*.

53.10   **LOSSES**

Partnership losses, as computed for tax purposes, are apportioned between the individual partners in the same way as are profits. The loss of each partner may (*a*) be set off against his other income [*Sec 380*] or (*b*) be carried forward against his share of subsequent profits of the partnership [*Sec 385*], including in certain circumstances where a partnership business is converted into a company [*Sec 386*] or (*c*) be used in a terminal loss claim. [*Sec 388*]. For further details of these loss claims, see under 46 LOSSES.

Similarly, losses made by a partner in other businesses may be set-off against his share of partnership profits under *Sec 380*.

Where the firm as a whole makes a profit (as computed for tax purposes) but, after the allocation of prior shares to other partners the result is that *an individual partner makes a loss*, the practice is not to allow that partner to claim relief for that loss, either against his other income under *Sec 380* or by carrying it forward under *Sec 385*; and that where there is a partnership loss, the aggregate amount carried forward cannot exceed that loss.

Limited partnerships. In *Reed v Young HL 1986, 59 TC 196*, it was held that the share of the loss of a limited partner (see 53.2 above) for *Sec 380* purposes was not restricted to the amount of her contribution to the partnership capital. The decision was, however, reversed by legislation. Where an individual 'limited partner' in a partnership sustains a loss or incurs capital expenditure in the partnership trade, or pays interest in connection with it, relief may be restricted. An allowance for capital expenditure which creates or augments a trading loss under *Sec 383(1)* (see 46.7 LOSSES) is for this purpose treated as made for the year of loss, and not for the year of assessment for which the year of loss is the basis year.

A '*limited partner*' is a partner carrying on a trade:

(*a*)   as a limited partner in a limited partnership registered under the *Limited Partnerships Act 1907*; or

(*b*)   as a general partner in a partnership, but who is not entitled to take part in the management of the trade, and who is entitled to have his liabilities for debts or obligations incurred for trade purposes discharged or reimbursed by some other person, in whole or beyond a certain limit; or

(*c*)   who, under the law of any territory outside the UK, is not entitled to take part in the management of the trade, and is not liable beyond a certain limit for debts or obligations incurred for trade purposes.

The restriction applies to any excess of the loss, etc. sustained by, or allowance for expenditure made to, a limited partner in respect of a trade as above for a year of assessment over his 'contribution' to the trade at the end of that year of assessment (or at the time he ceased to carry on the trade if he did so during that year of assessment). That excess may not be relieved under:

(i)   *Sec 380* (see 46.3 LOSSES);

(ii)   *Sec 381* (see 46.14 LOSSES);

(iii)   *CAA 1990, s 141* (see 10.17, 10.32 CAPITAL ALLOWANCES); or

(iv)   *Sec 353* (see 43.3 INTEREST PAYABLE),

other than against profits or gains arising from the same trade.

If relief has previously been given under any of the provisions at (i)–(iv) above to the individual for a loss, etc. or allowance in the partnership trade in any year of assessment at any time during which the individual carried on the trade as a limited partner, relief for the loss, etc. or allowance for the year of assessment in question is restricted by the excess of the sum of the loss, etc. or allowance for that year of assessment and earlier amounts so relieved, over the 'contribution'.

The partner's *'contribution'* to the trade at any time is the aggregate of:

(A)   capital contributed and not directly or indirectly withdrawn (excluding any the partner is or may be entitled to withdraw at any time he carries on the trade as a limited partner, or which he is or may be entitled to require another person to reimburse to him); and

(B)   any profits or gains of the trade to which he is entitled but which he has not received in money or money's worth.

Similar provisions apply to company partners (see Tolley's Corporation Tax under Partnerships).

[*Sec 117*].

53.11   **EFFECT OF PARTNERSHIP CHANGES ON LOSSES AND CAPITAL ALLOWANCES**

(*a*)   If, under the provision in 53.6 above, the business is *treated as continuing,*

(i)   continuing partners can bring forward their own shares of past losses under *Sec 380* and *Sec 385* but the shares of losses of outgoing partners lapse, and new partners do not share in any past losses; and

(ii)   unused capital allowances can be brought forward indefinitely.

(*b*)   If, under the above provisions or otherwise, the change is *treated as a discontinuance,*

(i)   each continuing partner can bring forward his share of past losses for use under *Secs 380, 385* (or, should it apply, *Sec 386*). Claims for carry-forward of losses under *Sec 385* only may be increased by adding to the loss capital allowances for the part of the year before the change. [*Secs 113, 380(3), 385(5), 386(4), all as originally enacted*]. Shares of losses of outgoing partners lapse; and

(ii)   all unused capital allowances (apart from above) lapse entirely.

See 10.22, 10.38(viii) CAPITAL ALLOWANCES.

The above rules apply for 1996/97 and earlier years as regards partnership businesses commenced before 6 April 1994. For 1997/98 and subsequent years as regards such businesses and for 1994/95 and subsequent years as regards partnership businesses commenced, or treated as commenced, after 5 April 1994, these rules cease to be directly relevant. A change of partner will not result in the business being treated as a discontinuance if there is a continuing partner (see 53.6 above). Capital allowances are given as trading expenses of the partnership business (see 10.1 CAPITAL ALLOWANCES), and, therefore, unused allowances are not carried forward as a separate item. Each partner's share of the business is treated separately for loss relief purposes (see 53.3 above). Where a person leaves a partnership, his own share of the business is treated as discontinued (see 53.3 above); he can claim loss reliefs (including terminal loss relief – see 46.16 LOSSES) to the same extent as if he ceased carrying on a business as a sole trader (see generally 46 LOSSES).

53.12   EXCESS LIABILITY

Any EXCESS LIABILITY (28) of the partners on the profits is included in the joint assessment on the firm under *Sec 111* (where applicable – see 53.3 above). See also 28.2(*e*) EXCESS LIABILITY.

53.13   WIFE AS PARTNER

This is treated as a case where a wife has separate earnings, and appropriate additional deductions and personal reliefs can be claimed. It is not necessary to prove actual payment if the fact of her partnership is established.

53.14   IF A COMPANY IS A PARTNER

(i)   **Assessments.** Where one of the partners carrying on a trade, profession or business in partnership is a company, the partnership profits are computed as under corporation tax (see Tolley's Corporation Tax) but ignoring distributions, charges on income, capital allowances, pre-trading expenditure (see 71.75 SCHEDULE D, CASES I AND II) and any losses brought forward, and without regard to any change in the partners carrying on the trade. The company is chargeable to corporation tax as if its apportioned share of profits, and of the other items as above, arose from a trade it carried on alone. For 1996/97 and earlier years as regards partnership trades, etc. commenced before 6 April 1994, the profits (computed as above) apportionable to individual partners are assessed to income tax as if they were those of a normal partnership of individuals (see above), capital allowances etc., for the accounting period being treated as for the tax years comprising that period, with apportionment where necessary. But, regardless of any difference between the partners' interests in the year of assessment and those in the basis year, the total assessed on the individual partners for any year of assessment for which those profits form the basis cannot be less than the amount of the total profits of the basis period, reduced by the company's share, as above. For 1994/95 and subsequent years as regards partnership trades, etc. commenced, or treated as commenced, after 5 April 1994 and for 1997/98 and subsequent years as regards those commenced on or before that date, individual partners are charged tax in respect of their profit shares and given relief for losses in the same way as if all the partners were individuals. [*Secs 111(2), 114, 115(1)–(3); FA 1994, s 215; FA 1995, ss 117, 125(4)*].

(ii)   Yearly interest of money chargeable to tax under SCHEDULE D, CASE III (72) (as it applies for income tax purposes) paid by a partnership of which a company is a member must be paid under deduction of income tax at the lower rate (before 1996/97, the basic rate) in force for the year in which the payment is made. [*Sec 349(2)(b)*].

(iii)   **On a partnership change** (see 53.6 above) *Sec 113(1)* applies only if an individual begins or ceases to be a partner (and in such a case an election for continuation basis may be made only if there is at least one continuing individual; notice under *Sec 113(2)* requiring signature solely by the individual partners before and after the change). This is of no application for 1994/95 and subsequent years as regards partnership trades, etc. commenced (or treated as commenced) after 5 April 1994 and for 1997/98 and subsequent years as regards those commenced on or before that date. [*Sec 114(3)(b); FA 1991, 15 Sch 3; FA 1994, s 215(3)–(5); FA 1995, 29 Sch Pt VIII(15)*].

(iv)   There are restrictions that apply in certain circumstances (where there are arrangements for transferring relief for losses etc.) on the use (*a*) by a partner company's losses in a partnership against its other income and (*b*) of a partner company's losses outside the partnership against its partnership profits. [*Sec 116*]. See Tolley's Corporation Tax (under Losses). See 3.20 ANTI-AVOIDANCE for withdrawal of losses from a company partnership dealing in commodity futures.

See 71.22 SCHEDULE D, CASES I AND II as regards the calculation of transitional overlap relief for individuals in partnership with a company.

53.15   **NON-RESIDENT   PARTNERS   AND   PARTNERSHIPS   CONTROLLED ABROAD**

Pre-Finance Act 1995. The following rules apply for 1996/97 and earlier years as regards partnership trades etc. commenced before 6 April 1994 and for 1994/95 only (where applicable) as regards those commenced, or treated as commenced, on or after that date. A partnership doing part of its business in the UK but *controlled and managed from abroad* is assessable to the extent only of its business in the UK. [*Sec 112 as originally enacted* (extended by *Sec 115(5)* to apply for corporation tax purposes where one of the partners is a company)]. But assessment not avoided by two firms, one in the UK and one abroad, trading jointly (*Morden, Rigg & Co v Monks CA 1923, 8 TC 450*). For *control and management*, see 51.12 NON-RESIDENTS AND OTHER OVERSEAS MATTERS. For European Economic Interest Groupings, see 53.19 PARTNERSHIPS.

Where a partnership business is carried on partly abroad and partly in the UK (**or wholly abroad**) and one or more partners are resident in the UK, then:

(*a*)   if control lies abroad, liability is under Case I on the whole of the profits made in UK and under Case V on UK residents' share of foreign profits (see *Colquhoun v Brooks HL 1889, 2 TC 490*);

(*b*)   if control lies in UK, liability is wholly under Case I on the full profits made in UK *plus* the resident partners' shares of foreign profits arising to them;

(*c*)   where a partnership business is controlled and managed abroad but one partner is a company resident in UK, that company may be assessed to corporation tax on its share of profits as if the partnership were itself resident.

A partnership set up abroad for tax avoidance purposes was held to be an overseas partnership in *Newstead v Frost HL 1980, 53 TC 525*.

Post-Finance Act 1995. The following rules apply for 1995/96 and subsequent years as regards partnership trades etc. commenced, or treated as commenced, after 5 April 1994 and for 1997/98 and subsequent years as regards those commenced on or before that date.

Partner non-UK resident. The general assessment and computation rules of *Sec 111* (see 53.3 above) are applied to a non-UK resident member of a trading etc. partnership in such a way as to ensure that he is taxed only on his share of profits earned in the UK (whereas UK resident partners are taxed on their share of worldwide profits). This mirrors and makes explicit the position under the pre-Finance Act 1995 regime. A similar rule applies to a non-resident company partner.

Individual partner's change of residence. Where a partnership trade or profession is carried on wholly or partly outside the UK and an individual partner becomes or ceases to be UK resident, he is treated for income tax purposes as ceasing to be a partner at that time and becoming a partner again immediately afterwards. His share of a loss sustained before the change may nevertheless be carried forward under *Sec 385* and set against his share of profits after the change.

Individual partner resident but not domiciled etc. in the UK. Where a partnership trade etc. is carried on wholly or partly outside the UK and controlled and managed outside the UK, an individual partner who is UK resident, but to whose overseas trading income the REMITTANCE BASIS (63.1) would normally apply, is taxed under Case V on that basis in respect of his share of the partnership profits earned outside the UK. This mirrors and confirms the position under the pre-Finance Act 1995 regime.

[*Secs 112(1)–(1B), 115(4); FA 1995, s 125(1)(2)(5)*].

Subject to the exception above, UK-resident partners are chargeable under Case I on both UK and foreign profits, regardless of where the partnership is controlled.

General. In the case of *Padmore v CIR CA 1989, 62 TC 352*, it was held that, where profits of a non-UK resident partnership were exempt under the relevant double tax treaty, the profit share of a UK resident partner was thereby also exempt. This decision is, however, reversed by *Sec 112(4)(5)*, to the effect that arrangements under a double tax treaty relieving partnership income or capital gains from UK tax are not to affect any UK tax liability in respect of a UK resident partner's share of such income or gains. Such a partner is similarly entitled to the corresponding share of the tax credit in respect of a UK company qualifying distribution to a share of which he is entitled. Where a partnership includes a company, these provisions apply equally for corporation tax purposes. In the case of a partnership falling within the post-Finance Act 1995 regime (see above), the provisions apply where the partnership either resides outside the UK or carries on any trade etc. the control and management of which is outside the UK (which effectively mirrors the position under the previous regime). [*Secs 112(4)–(6), 115(5); FA 1995, s 125(3)(5)*]. These changes are deemed always to have had effect. [*F(No 2)A 1987, s 62(2)*].

53.16   PARTNERSHIP RETIREMENT ANNUITIES

Annual payments for the benefit of a former partner (who has ceased to be a partner on retirement, because of age or ill-health, or on death), or the widow, widower or dependant of a former partner, are treated as earned income up to the limit below and, up to that limit, do not reduce the investment income of the payer.

The payments must be made under (*a*) the partnership agreement, or (*b*) an agreement replacing or supplementing the partnership agreement, or (*c*) an agreement with an individual who acquires the whole or part of the partnership business.

The limit referred to above is 50% of the average of the former partner's share of profits or gains (included in his tax return) in the best three of the last seven years of assessment in which he was required to devote substantially the whole of his time to the partnership (or to any other partnership of which he was a member—in which case the profits or gains of that partnership can be included in the calculations). Profits or gains not assessable to income tax are included in the calculation as if they were so assessable. [*Sec 628; FA 1988, 3 Sch 19*].

To the extent that they exceed or are outside the above provisions, partnership retirement annuities are investment income in the hands of the recipients.

Indexation. The above limit of profits on which the earned income element of the annuity is calculated can be increased by the same percentage increase as the increase in the retail prices index between the December in the year of assessment in which the former partner left the partnership and the December preceding the year in which the annuity income is assessed. [*Sec 628(4)*]. The first six years of the last seven years of assessment which are the basis for computing the limit (as above) are also to be increased by indexation. The increase for each of these six years is to be by the same percentage increase as the percentage increase in the retail prices index for the month of December in the seventh year over that for the month of December in each of the previous six years. [*Sec 628(3)*].

Incorporation. Where a partnership business is incorporated, or a company takes over a partnership, and the agreement in either case refers to the company assuming responsibility for payment of an annuity to a former partner, then provided that the annuity is commercial in amount, the payment is not prevented by *Sec 338(5)(b)* from being treated by the company as a charge on income. *Sec 125* (annual payments for non-taxable consideration, see 3.19 ANTI-AVOIDANCE) is not in practice considered to apply to such payments in respect of a *bona fide* commercial transaction. (Revenue Tax Bulletin August 1994 p 151).

See also 65 RETIREMENT ANNUITIES AND PERSONAL PENSION SCHEMES and 80.28(v) SETTLEMENTS.

53.17 LOANS FOR PURCHASING INTEREST IN PARTNERSHIP

See 43.22 INTEREST PAYABLE as regards relief for interest on a loan to an individual for purchasing a share of or making an advance to a partnership, and for anti-avoidance measures applying in connection with certain such loans on the changeover to the current year basis of assessment.

53.18 CAPITAL GAINS TAX ON PARTNERSHIPS

See Tolley's Capital Gains Tax.

53.19 EUROPEAN ECONOMIC INTEREST GROUPINGS [*FA 1990, s 69, 11 Sch*]

A European Economic Interest Grouping ('EEIG') within *EEC Directive No. 2137/85* (which, from 1 January 1994, applies to all EEIGs established within the European Economic Area), wherever it is registered, is regarded as acting as the agent of its members. Its activities are regarded as those of its members acting jointly, each member being regarded as having a share of EEIG property, rights and liabilities, and a person is regarded as acquiring or disposing of a share of the EEIG assets not only where there is an acquisition or disposal by the EEIG while he is a member but also where he becomes or ceases to be a member or there is a change in his share of EEIG property.

A member's share in EEIG property, rights or liabilities is that determined under the contract establishing the EEIG or, if there is no provision determining such shares, it will correspond to the profit share to which he is entitled under the provisions of the contract. If the contract makes no such provision, members are regarded as having equal shares.

Where the EEIG carries on a trade or profession, the members are regarded for the purposes of tax on income and gains as carrying on that trade or profession in partnership. The amount on which members are chargeable to income tax in respect of the trade or profession is computed (but not assessed) jointly, and the original provisions of *Sec 112* (see 53.15 PARTNERSHIPS) concerning partnerships controlled abroad are correspondingly amended in the case of EEIGS. [*Sec 510A; FA 1990, 11 Sch 1, 5; FA 1995, 29 Sch Pt VIII(16)*].

Contributions to an EEIG from its members are not assessable on the EEIG, and the members are not assessable on distributions from the EEIG (which is equally not obliged to account for ACT thereon). (Revenue EEIGs Manual, EEIG 34).

For the purposes of securing that members of EEIGs are assessed to income tax, corporation tax or capital gains tax, an inspector may, in the case of an EEIG which is registered, or has an establishment registered, in Great Britain or Northern Ireland, by notice require the EEIG to make a return containing such information as the notice may require, accompanied by such accounts and statements as the notice may require, within a specified time. In any other case, he may issue a similar notice to any UK resident member(s) of the EEIG (or if none is so resident, to any member(s)). Notices may differ from one period to another and by reference to the person on whom they are served or the description of EEIG to which they refer. Where a notice is given to an EEIG registered in Great Britain or Northern Ireland (or having an establishment registered there), the EEIG must act through a manager, except that if there is no manager who is an individual, the EEIG must act through an individual designated as a representative of the manager under the *Directive*. The return must in all cases include a declaration that, to the best of the maker's knowledge, it is correct and complete, and where the contract establishing the EEIG requires two or more managers to act jointly for the EEIG to be validly bound, the declaration must be given by the appropriate number of managers. [*TMA s 12A; FA 1990, 11 Sch 2; FA 1994, ss 196, 199, 19 Sch 2*]. See 67.1 RETURNS as regards the form and content of returns.

A penalty not exceeding £300 (and £60 per day for continued failure) may be imposed in the case of failure to comply with a notice under the above provisions. No penalty may be imposed after the failure has been remedied, and if it is proved that there was no income or chargeable gain to be included in the return, the maximum penalty is £100. Fraudulent or negligent delivery of an incorrect return, etc. or of an incorrect declaration may result in a penalty not exceeding £3,000 for each member of the EEIG at the time of delivery. For 1996/97 and subsequent years, the £300 and £60 penalties are multiplied by the number of members of the EEIG (but subject to the overall £100 maximum in the circumstances described above); the daily penalty may only be imposed by the Commissioners (on an application to them by the Revenue) and has effect from the day following notification of imposition. [*TMA s 98B; FA 1990, 11 Sch 3; FA 1994, ss 196, 199, 19 Sch 30*].

The provisions of *TMA ss 36, 40* for extended time limits for assessments in cases of fraudulent or negligent conduct (see 6.4, 6.5 BACK DUTY) are amended so that any act or omission on the part of the EEIG or a member thereof is deemed to be the act or omission of each member of the EEIG. [*TMA ss 36(4), 40(3); FA 1990, 11 Sch 4*].

54   Patents

[Secs 524–529]

Cross-references. See 10.50 CAPITAL ALLOWANCES for allowances on capital expenditure in acquiring patent rights; 23.15(*b*) DEDUCTION OF TAX AT SOURCE for patent royalties; 25.5(*l*) DOUBLE TAX RELIEF for DTR treatment of patent royalties from abroad and 71.72 SCHEDULE D, CASES I AND II for trading receipts and expenses re patents.

54.1   **Patent rights** means the right to do or authorise the doing of anything which would, but for the right, be an infringement of a patent. *[Sec 533(1)]*.

54.2   **Expenses** (otherwise than for the purpose of a trade) of devising inventions, agents' charges, patent office fees, etc. (including fees, expenses, etc. for rejected or abandoned applications) are allowable from income from patents with a right to carry forward indefinitely unallowed balances against future assessable patent income. *[Sec 526]*.

54.3   **Patent income** of inventors is treated as earned income. *[Sec 529]*.

54.4   **Patent royalties** are always assessable (*Kirke CA 1944, 26 TC 208*). Where royalties are received, less tax, for user of a patent which comprises two or more complete years, the income tax or corporation tax liabilities are reducible, on application, to the total that would have been payable if the royalties had been paid by equal instalments (corresponding to the number of complete years concerned, but not exceeding six years) made at yearly intervals ending with the date of actual receipt. *[Sec 527]*.

54.5   **Sales of patent rights** (including receipts for rights for which a patent has not yet been granted *[Sec 533(5)(6)]*) are treated according to the residence of the vendor.

(*a*)   **Resident** (*all patents*). Any capital sum received is assessable under Schedule D, Case VI (after deducting capital cost where purchased *[Sec 524(7)–(9)]*), but spread equally over year of receipt and five succeeding years thereafter, or wholly charged in year of receipt if written election made. *[Sec 524(1)(2)]*. See also *Green v Brace Ch D 1960, 39 TC 281*.

(*b*)   **Non-Resident** (*UK patents only*). Purchaser must deduct tax at basic rate from purchase money and account to Revenue under *Sec 349(1)* *[Sec 524(3)]*. But this procedure may be modified by DOUBLE TAX RELIEF (25) agreements. The non-resident may, however, (i) claim relief for the cost to him of acquiring the patent, and (ii) elect to have the net sum treated as arising over that and subsequent periods, to a total of six years. *[Sec 524(4)]*.

The election in (*a*) above must be made within, for 1996/97 and later years, twelve months after 31 January following the year of assessment in which the sum was received (for earlier years, two years after the end of that year of assessment) or, for corporation tax purposes, two years after the end of the accounting period in which it was received. The election in (*b*) above applies only for income tax, with the same time limits as above. *[Sec 524(2)(2A)(4); FA 1996, s 135, 21 Sch 15]*.

54.6   **On death, winding-up or partnership change,** any charges under *Sec 524* above for subsequent years become assessable, but personal representatives of deceased person, or each partner, may claim (within 30 days of the assessment) that such amount be spread back equally to the years beginning with the year of receipt and ending with the year in which the death or change occurred. *[Sec 525]*.

55 Pay As You Earn

[Sec 203]

Cross-reference. See also 78.42 SELF-ASSESSMENT.

55.1 Pay as you earn (PAYE) is a system of collection of tax from salaries, wages, etc. See under 75 SCHEDULE E for provisions regarding amount assessable, allowable deductions etc. and see 82.3 SOCIAL SECURITY for taxable benefits.

PAYE is subject to regulations which were consolidated in *The Income Tax (Employments) Regulations 1993 (SI 1993 No 744)* and which took effect on 6 April 1993. Subsequent amendments are made in *SI 1993 No 2276; SI 1994 Nos 775, 1212; SI 1995 Nos 216, 447, 853, 1284; SI 1996 Nos 804, 980*. References in this chapter to regulations are to those consolidated regulations (as amended).

See also Revenue Pamphlet P7 (Employer's Guide to PAYE) and IR 34 (Income tax—PAYE), IR 53 (Thinking of taking someone on?), IR 71 (Inspection of employers' records) and IR 109 (How settlements are negotiated). See Revenue Press Release 28 July 1989 for guidance on operation of PAYE under the receipts basis of assessment (see 75.1 SCHEDULE E). See also Revenue booklet SAT 3 'Self Assessment: what it will mean for employers', available free from tax offices.

The Revenue have published a Code of Practice (No 3, published February 1993 and available from local tax offices) setting out their standards for the way in which inspections of employers' records are conducted and the rights and responsibilities of taxpayers.

The outline of PAYE is stated below but reference should be made to the Revenue Pamphlets noted above.

55.2 **All payments of emoluments** assessable under SCHEDULE E (75) are subject to deduction of tax under the PAYE system, including lump sums and late commissions even though they may relate to earlier years. In the latter event, the earlier year's pay is subsequently carried back to that earlier year and all necessary adjustments of resultant tax liability are made. Emoluments received after 5 April 1989 are in any case assessable in the year of assessment of receipt (see 75.1 SCHEDULE E). The definition of 'emoluments' is wide enough to include certain deemed Schedule E income arising from share transactions (see 75.19 SCHEDULE E, 81.4 SHARE INCENTIVES AND OPTIONS) but does not include payments only part of which is assessable under Schedule E (*CIR v Herd HL 1993, 66 TC 29*).

Extension of scope. The following items are brought within the scope of PAYE from 25 May 1994 by virtue of regulations under *Secs 203F–203K* (introduced by *FA 1994, ss 127–131*).

(a) *'Tradeable assets'*, i.e. assets (including any property, subject to specific exclusions) capable of being sold or otherwise realised in specified markets, or in relation to which 'trading arrangements' exist at the time the asset is provided.

(b) 'Non-cash vouchers' (see 75.44(*a*) SCHEDULE E), not excluded by regulation, where, at the time the asset is provided, either the vouchers themselves, or the goods for which they can be exchanged, are capable of being sold or otherwise realised in specified markets, or are vouchers for goods for which 'trading arrangements' exist.

(c) 'Credit tokens' (see 75.44(*d*) SCHEDULE E), not excluded by regulation, on each occasion they are used to obtain money, or to obtain goods which, when they are obtained, are capable of being sold or otherwise realised in specified markets, or are goods for which 'trading arrangements' exist.

(d)   'Cash vouchers' (see 75.44(b) SCHEDULE E), not excluded by regulation, when received by the employee.

As regards (a), (b) and (c) above, '*trading arrangements*' are broadly arrangements, not excluded by regulation, which enable the recipient to obtain an amount not substantially less than the expense incurred in provision of the asset, goods or voucher concerned, including the use of an asset or goods as security for a loan or advance. Regulations exclude from (a) above shares, or rights over shares, in the employing company (or a company controlling that company), and from (c) and (d) above the use of cash vouchers and credit tokens to meet, or to obtain cash used to meet, allowable expenditure. [*Secs 203F–203L; FA 1994, ss 127–131; SI 1994 No 1212*]. See 55.4 below as regards accounting for tax in respect of items within (a)-(d) above.

Employee non-resident, or non-ordinarily resident, in the UK. Where such an employee works (or is likely to work) both inside and out of the UK in a year of assessment, and some of his income is assessable under Schedule E, Case II (see 75.1 SCHEDULE E) and an as yet unascertainable part may prove not to be assessable, an officer of the Board may, on application by the employer or a person designated by the employer, by notice direct that a proportion of any payment made in the year is to be dealt with as assessable income under PAYE. If no direction is made, the whole of any payment must be so dealt with. The direction may similarly be withdrawn (with at least 30 days notice) by a further notice. These provisions are without prejudice to any income assessment on the employee and to any rights to repayment, or obligations to repay, income tax over- or underpaid. [*Sec 203D; FA 1994, s 126*]. This provision has effect from 3 May 1994, but similar arrangements in force before that date are retrospectively validated by *FA 1994, s 133(3)*.

Assessments. Subject as follows, formal assessments under Schedule E are made each year to equate deductions with true liability and any overpayments are refunded by a payable order usually issued at the same time as the notice of assessment, while underpayments are collected in the next, or the next following, year, by coding adjustments. But see 41 INTEREST ON OVERPAID TAX for attribution of deductions and repayments.

Formal assessments need not be made in cases where both coding and deduction of tax under it are correct, unless taxpayer gives notice within five years after the end of the year of assessment. [*Sec 205*]. But see administrative practice at 56.7 PAYMENT OF TAX.

55.3   **All persons making payments of such emoluments** are required to deduct the appropriate amount of tax from each payment (or repay over-deductions) by reference to PAYE Tax Tables, which are so constructed that, as near as may be, tax deducted from payments to date from previous 5 April corresponds with the correct time proportion to date of the net total tax liability (after allowances and reliefs) of the recipient on those emoluments for the year. [*Sec 203; FA 1988, 3 Sch 4*]. See *Andrews v King Ch D 1991, 64 TC 332* as regards extended definition of 'employer' and *Booth v Mirror Group Newspapers plc QB, [1992] STC 615* as regards application of the PAYE regulations where emoluments are paid by a third party.

There are provisions to determine whether anything occurring after 26 July 1989 constitutes a payment for PAYE purposes. These equate to the rules in 75.1 SCHEDULE E for determining when emoluments are to be treated as received, but are not to apply if anything occurring on or before that date constituted a payment of, or on account of, the same income. [*Sec 203A; FA 1989, s 45*].

The 'total tax' may include adjustments for any previous year and it 'may be assumed' that payments to date bear the same proportion to the total emoluments as that part of the year bears to the whole. [*Sec 203(6)–(8)*]. Employers are also required to deduct national insurance contributions at the same time as PAYE tax is deducted.

55.4 Pay As You Earn

Employers may elect to operate separate PAYE schemes for different groups of employees. [*Reg 3*].

Payments by intermediaries. Where a payment of, or on account of, emoluments is made by an 'intermediary' of the employer (i.e. a person acting on behalf, and at the expense, of the employer or a person 'connected' (within *Sec 839*, see 20 CONNECTED PERSONS) with the employer, or trustees holding property for persons including the employer), then unless the intermediary deducts and accounts for tax under PAYE (whether or not the PAYE regulations apply to him), the employer is to be treated from 25 May 1994 as having made the payment (grossed up where the recipient is entitled to the amount after deduction of any income tax). [*Secs 203B, 203J, 203L; FA 1994, ss 125, 131; SI 1994 No 1212*]. See 55.4 below as regards the regulations required to deal with accounting for tax in respect of such notional payments.

Non-UK employer. Where, during any period, an employee works for a person (the 'relevant person') other than his employer, and any payment of, or on account of, his assessable income for work done in that period is made by the employer (or an intermediary of the employer, see above) outside the scope of PAYE, the relevant person is treated for PAYE as having made the payment (grossed up where the employee is entitled to the payment after deduction of any income tax). [*Sec 203C; FA 1994, s 126*]. This provision and *Sec 203E* (see below) replace *Reg 4* with effect from 3 May 1994, prior to which *Reg 4* is retrospectively validated by *FA 1994, s 133.*

Mobile UK workforce. Where a person (the 'relevant person') has entered, or is likely to enter, into an agreement that employees of another person (the 'contractor') will work for him, but not as his employees, for a period, and it is likely that PAYE will not be deducted or accounted for in accordance with the regulations on payments made by (or on behalf of) the contractor of, or on account of, assessable income of those employees for that period, the Board may by notice to the relevent person direct that he apply PAYE to any payments made by him in respect of work done in that period by such employees of the contractor. So much of the payment as is attributable to the work done by each such employee is treated for this purpose as a payment of assessable income of that employee. The notice must specify the relevant person and the contractor to whom it relates, and may similarly be withdrawn by further notice, and notices must, where reasonably practicable, be copied to the contractor. [*Sec 203E; FA 1994, s 126*]. This provision and *Sec 203C* (see above) replace *Reg 4* with effect from 3 May 1994, prior to which *Reg 4* is retrospectively validated by *FA 1994, s 133.*

55.4   **The tax deductions to be made** are those appropriate to the employee's 'code' (calculated by the inspector, and notified to both employer and employee, to take account of personal allowances and reliefs due, certain higher rate liabilities and reliefs, underpayments from earlier years, and emoluments such as benefits in kind from which deductions cannot be made). The code generally represents the total allowances due omitting the final digit. Notice of objection to a code or revised code may be made to the inspector and in default of agreement an appeal can be taken to General Commissioners.

Tax offices only notify an employer if there is a change in an employee's code. Until such notification an employer will continue to use the same code from year to year (subject to special provision for 1993/94 where code suffix F was in force for 1992/93 (see below)). [*Regs 6, 8, 13*].

Code suffixes H or L are to enable quicker adjustments for change in higher (married) or lower (single) allowances, but T will require special notification from the inspector. Suffixes P or V indicate that the full single or married age-related allowance is given.

The taxpayer may require that T is substituted for H, L, P or V. Prefix D indicates higher rates of tax applicable. For prefix F see 55.33 below.

From 6 April 1993, a new code, prefix K, is introduced which requires an *addition* to be made in arriving at taxable pay. This enables the correct tax to be deducted in cases where emoluments such as benefits in kind from which deduction cannot be made exceed allowances, but subject to a maximum deduction of 50% of cash pay. Prefix K codes replace prefix F codes previously applicable to certain pensioners (see 55.33 below).

Where a notional payment is brought within PAYE by regulations made by virtue of *Secs 203B, 203F–203I* or by *Sec 203C* (see 55.2, 55.3 above), the income tax thereon is to be deducted, at a prescribed time, from any actual payment(s) to the employee. Where, due to an insufficiency of actual payments, all or part of the tax cannot be so deducted, the employer must account to the Board, within a prescribed time, for any tax he is required, but unable, to deduct. The amount so deducted or accounted for is treated as an amount paid by the employee in respect of his own liability (for a prescribed year). As regards any amount the employer has accounted for (being unable to deduct it from any payments made to the employee), if the employee does not make good the amount to the employer within 30 days of the date on which the employer is treated as making the payment, the employee is treated as receiving emoluments of that amount on that date. [*Secs 144A, 203J; FA 1994, ss 131, 132; SI 1994 No 1212*]. The regulations, which came into force on 25 May 1994, also provide the rules for accounting for tax on notional payments.

55.5   **Tax Tables** show, in relation to each 'code', the cumulative 'free pay' for each weekly (or monthly) period, which is subtracted from the total gross pay down to that period leaving 'taxable pay' on which is calculated the tax due from (or refundable to) the employee.

Modified systems of deduction may be authorised by the inspector in cases of fixed salaries or wages. [*Reg 20*].

55.6   **Deductions working sheets** (Form P11 (New)) must be kept in each fiscal year by every employer in respect of each employee for recording the employee's pay, tax and related National Insurance contributions. An employer may use his own forms if approved by the Revenue. [*Reg 38*].

55.7   As to **recovery from employee** of tax under-deducted see *Reg 42(2)(3)* as amended by *SI 1995 No 447*. See also *Bernard & Shaw Ltd v Shaw KB 1951, 30 ATC 187*, and for wilful failure by employer to deduct correct tax, *R v CIR (ex p Chisholm) QB 1981, 54 TC 722, R v CIR (ex p Sims) QB 1987, 60 TC 398* and *R v CIR (ex p Cook) QB 1987, 60 TC 405*. In *R v CIR (ex p. McVeigh) QB, [1996] STC 91*, accounting entries purporting to deduct tax, where tax not paid over to Revenue, were held not to constitute deduction of tax for these purposes. For tax accounted for by employer in respect of certain notional payments, see 55.4 above.

55.8   **The net tax deducted by the employer and national insurance contributions must be paid to the Collector** within 14 days after the end of each month, except in certain cases where payment may be made quarterly. Quarterly payment applies where employees are on authorised fixed pay arrangements (see 55.5 above) and, after 5 April 1991, where the employer has reasonable grounds for believing that the average monthly total to be paid to the Collector in respect of deductions under PAYE and the CONSTRUCTION INDUSTRY TAX DEDUCTION SCHEME (21) and national insurance contributions will be less than £600 for the current year (£450 for 1994/95, 1993/94 and 1992/93, £400 for 1991/92). [*Regs 40–42; SI 1993 No 2276; SI 1995 No 216*]. A deduction may be made for payments of Statutory Sick and Maternity Pay. If no tax has been paid within that 14 days, or the Collector is not satisfied that any payment made satisfies the employer's liability, the Collector, if he is not aware of the amount the employer is liable to pay, can give notice requiring a return within

55.9 Pay As You Earn

14 days showing the amount of that liability. [*Reg 47*]. The inspector has powers to determine the amount of tax payable where it appears to him that tax may have been payable under these regulations but has not been paid. The determination applies as if it were an assessment to tax. [*Reg 49; SI 1995 No 447*].

Interest is charged at the prescribed rate (see 42.1 INTEREST ON UNPAID TAX) on tax unpaid in respect of determinations for 1991/92 and earlier years made after 19 April 1988, from 14 days after the end of the year of assessment to which the determination relates (or from 19 April 1988 if later). [*Sec 203(2)(d); FA 1988, s 128(1); Reg 50*]. In respect of tax payable for 1992/93 and subsequent years, interest is so charged on tax unpaid by 19 April in the tax year following that for which it was payable whether or not it is the subject of a determination. Also in respect of tax payable for 1992/93 and subsequent years, interest on overpaid tax runs at the prescribed rate (see 41.1 INTEREST ON OVERPAID TAX) from the end of the year after that in respect of which the payment was made (or in the case of a repayment of tax paid more than twelve months after the end of the year for which it was paid, from the end of the year in which the tax was paid) to the date of issue of the repayment order. [*Sec 203(2)(dd); FA 1988, s 128(1); FA 1994, ss 196, 199, 19 Sch 38; Regs 51, 53*]. In either case, such interest is paid without deduction of tax and is not taken into account in computing income for tax purposes. [*Sec 203(9); FA 1988, s 128(2)*]. Cheque payments are treated as made on the day of receipt by the collector (and see 56.1 PAYMENT OF TAX).

Interest may also arise in the case of late paid or overpaid Class 1 or 1A national insurance contributions (see *SI 1993 No 821*).

Employer is not entitled to charge Revenue with costs of PAYE collection (*Meredith v Hazell QB 1964, 42 TC 435*). Revenue have power to inspect wages sheets and other records to ensure regulations being observed. [*Sec 203(2)(b) and Reg 55*]. Where money is stolen, the employer is liable (*A-G v Antoine KB 1949, 31 TC 213*).

55.9 **After the end of each year the employer must**, in respect of each employee for whom he was required to maintain a deductions working sheet, send to the Inspector, or (in the case of (*a*), and if so required) the Collector of Taxes, the following.

(*a*)   Not later than 19 May

    (i)   an End of Year Return P14 (top and first copy),

    (ii)   a declaration on form P35 (including a nil return where appropriate).

(*b*)   Not later than 6 June (6 July starting with the return required for 1996/97)

    (i)   particulars on form P9D of emoluments given to an employee otherwise than in money; payments made on behalf of employee and not repaid; relocation expenses in excess of the tax-free limit (see 75.33 SCHEDULE E); and certain other payments etc. not treated as 'pay',

    (ii)   for all employees with emoluments at a rate of £8,500 p.a. or more and for all directors (except full-time service directors with no material interest in the company or employed by non-profit making companies or charities [*Sec 167(5)*] earning less than £8,500 p.a.), a return on form P11D showing additionally

        (A)   payments to employee for expenses,

        (B)   sums put at employee's disposal and paid away by him,

        (C)   expenses incurred by employer in connection with providing the employee with services, benefits or facilities falling under *Secs 154–165* (see 75.11 *et seq.* SCHEDULE E),

    but excluding relocation expenses (see (i) above) within the tax-free limit.

Supplementary returns (form P38A) must be submitted with form P35 for all employees for whom a deductions working sheet is not required.

[*Regs 43 – 46; SI 1993 No 2276, reg 8*]. See 58.4 PENALTIES as regards a period of grace for submission of returns under (*a*) above.

For the additional requirements for returns for 1996/97 and subsequent years, including information to be supplied to employees, see 78.42 SELF-ASSESSMENT.

Value added tax paid, if any, must be included in above. (Revenue Pamphlet IR 131, A7). See 55.42 below.

See 67.5 RETURNS and 78.42 SELF-ASSESSMENT for employers' returns generally.

55.10   Employers must also give each employee annually **a certificate** showing his total taxable emoluments for the year and total tax deducted therefrom, his appropriate code, National Insurance number, and the employer's name and address etc. [*Reg 39*]. This certificate is produced automatically as the third sheet of the End of Year Return, or a substitute form P60 may be used or other document approved by the Revenue.

55.11   For **Penalties** see 58.4 PENALTIES and *TMA ss 98, 98A*. See also Revenue Pamphlet IR 109.

55.12   **PAYE settlement agreements.** The Revenue and an employer may make a non-statutory agreement, known as an 'annual voluntary settlement', whereby the employer settles by way of lump sum an amount approximating to the tax otherwise payable by his employees on items covered by the settlement, which will be minor, incidental benefits and expenses payments, e.g. reimbursement of telephone expenses, late night taxis home and benefits shared between a number of employees. The employer is then relieved of including such benefits and expenses in the returns at 55.9(*b*) above and the employees do not have to declare them or include them in their total income.

A statutory framework is to be established for such arrangements, to be known as 'PAYE settlement agreements', by regulations provided for by *Sec 206A* (introduced by *FA 1996, s 110*) and expected to be made in 1996 and to have effect for 1996/97 and subsequent years. Separate legislation will enable national insurance contributions to be comprised in such settlements.

55.13   **Annual payments.** Tax on certain periodic redundancy and other similar payments by a former employer which are strictly assessable under Schedule D, Case III as annual payments, and payable under deduction of basic rate tax, may, where it is convenient and with the agreement of the parties and the inspector, be dealt with instead under PAYE (Revenue Tax Bulletin February 1995 p 196).

55.14   **Annuities** paid out of superannuation funds approved under *ICTA 1970, s 208* which have not sought approval under subsequent legislation and to which no contributions have been made since 5 April 1980 (see 66.13 RETIREMENT SCHEMES) continue to be charged under Schedule E and subject to PAYE. [*Sec 608*].

55.15   **Benefits in kind,** although not cash payments, are within PAYE and are usually dealt with by a deduction from the allowances in arriving at the coding (and see *R v Walton Commrs (ex p Wilson) CA, [1983] STC 464*). See 55.4 above as regards prefix K codes issued in certain cases where benefits etc. exceed allowances. See also 55.2 above as regards certain non-cash emoluments brought within PAYE.

55.16 **Cars provided for private use.** See 75.15(ii) SCHEDULE E for computation of the charge. Quarterly returns are required within 28 days of the end of the quarter on Form P46(car), starting with the quarter to 5 July 1994, showing employees first or no longer provided with a car, or provided with a change of car or an additional car, or already provided with a car but becoming a director or starting to earn at the rate of £8,500 p.a. or more during the quarter. [*Reg 46A; SI 1994 No 775*]. The Form asks in each case for details of the make, model and cubic capacity of the car (and whether it is petrol or diesel), of the list price of the car and accessories, of any capital contribution by the employee, and of the expected annual business mileage band. The pamphlet also explains the procedures for dealing with existing cars at the commencement of the new scheme.

Returns on Form P11D (see 55.9(ii) above) continue to be required.

55.17 **Charitable donations** up to £1,200 in any year of assessment (£900 in 1993/94, 1994/95 and 1995/96, £600 in 1990/91, 1991/92 and 1992/93) may be an allowable deduction for PAYE purposes. See 15.7 CHARITIES.

55.18 **Crown Priority.** The provisions of *Insolvency Act 1986, s 386, 6 Sch* apply to PAYE which the bankrupt was liable to deduct from emoluments paid in the twelve months before the date of the bankruptcy order or, if earlier, the date of appointment of an interim receiver. See 56.5 PAYMENT OF TAX.

55.19 **Director's remuneration.** Credit of remuneration voted to a director to an account with the company constitutes 'payment' for PAYE purposes. See generally ICAEW Technical Release TAX 11/93, 9 July 1993, as regards tax implications of payments to directors. [*Sec 203A(1)(c); FA 1989, s 45*]. See 55.3 above and 75.1 SCHEDULE E.

55.20 **Domestic workers and nannies.** A leaflet 'Thinking of Employing a Domestic Worker or Nanny?' is available from tax offices, setting out simple guidelines to the operation of PAYE by taxpayers likely to be employing domestic workers or nannies for the first time.

55.21 **Employee arriving.** A new employee should produce a form P45 and the employer should start a Deductions Working Sheet from the particulars on that form and send Part 3 to the tax office. If a form P45 (or other code authorisation) is not produced, the employer should complete form P46, ask the employee to sign the appropriate certificate on the back, and send to the tax office. A Deductions Working Sheet must be prepared and tax deducted in accordance with the instructions relating to the certificate signed by the employee. The employee should be given a Coding Claim form P15 to complete and this should be sent to the tax office. [*Regs 25, 28–34*]. See 55.39 below as regards tax refunds.

55.22 **Employee dying.** On death of employee, the employer must forthwith send all parts of P45 to inspector together with name and address of personal representative, if known. [*Reg 27*].

55.23 **Employee leaving** must be given certificate (form P45) by former employer showing code, pay and tax deductible to date of leaving (split, for 1996/97 onwards, if more than one employment). [*Reg 23; SI 1996 No 804, reg 3*]. This produced to new employer [*Reg 25*] ensures continuity and provides data for commencement of new deduction working sheet.

Payments to employees who have left and which are not included in P45 must have tax deducted at the basic rate. [*Reg 24*].

Employee retiring. At retirement on pension of an employee, the employer must, within 14 days, inform inspector on form P160 and continue operating code on Week 1/Month 1 basis. [*Reg 26(1)(2); SI 1996 No 804, reg 5*].

55.24   **Exemption.** Where the employee has no other employment and rate of payment is less than a weekly or monthly rate equal to 1/52nd or 1/12th respectively of the personal allowance, no tax is deductible. If employee has other employment this limit is reduced to £1 per week (£4 per month). [*Reg 28(1)(b)(2)*].

55.25   **Expense payments etc.** must (except as regards pure reimbursement to subordinate employees of specific outlay incurred) be included with pay and taxed with it, unless exempted by notification from the inspector under *Sec 166* (or under the earlier legislation in *ICTA 1970, s 199* or *FA 1976, s 70*).

55.26   **Free of tax payments, awards etc.** For remuneration payable free of tax, taxed incentive awards etc., see 75.40 SCHEDULE E.

55.27   **H.M. Forces.** Members of the reserve and auxiliary forces will generally have basic rate tax deducted from pay. [*Reg 61*].

55.28   **Holiday Pay.** Tax is normally deductible from holiday pay, but by arrangement with the employer it may be paid in full, compensating adjustments being made either in the coding, or by a system of credits which spreads the tax on the holiday pay over the whole year. Holiday pay paid to a participant in a holiday stamp scheme by the scheme management company is taxed at the basic rate at the time of payment. [*Reg 73*].

55.29   **Incapacity benefit,** where taxable (see 82.3 SOCIAL SECURITY), is brought within PAYE by *SI 1995 No 853.*

55.30   **Local councillors' attendance allowances.** The councillor may opt for deduction of basic rate tax from such allowances (net of an appropriate amount in respect of allowable expenditure) rather than deduction by reference to the appropriate code. [*SI 1993 No 744, regs 56–58*].

55.31   **Maternity pay** under **Employment Protection (Consolidation) Act 1978** is assessable under SCHEDULE E (75). The payment qualified for wife's earned income relief (see 1.22 ALLOWANCES AND TAX RATES). [*Sec 150*].

55.32   **Overseas Matters.** Where an employee works abroad, see Employer's Guide to PAYE. See *Reg 28(4)(b)(5)* as regards pensions. A non-resident employer must operate PAYE in respect of any emoluments of his employees within Schedule E if he has a 'trading presence' in the UK (*Clark v Oceanic Contractors Incorporated HL 1982, 56 TC 183*). See also *Bootle v Bye; Wilson v Bye (Sp C 61), [1996] SSCD 58*. See also 55.3 above as regards payments by intermediaries.

55.33   **Pensioners.** Before 6 April 1993, where a pensioner had a steady source of income to which PAYE could be applied, a special code with the prefix F enabled the tax on the excess State pension to be recovered through the PAYE system. The taxpayer had, however, the option to pay the tax in four instalments. See 5.8 ASSESSMENTS for tolerance limit in assessing certain pensions.

See 55.4 above as regards replacement of prefix F codes by prefix K codes after 5 April 1993.

55.34   **Records.** Wages sheets, deductions working sheets, certificates and other records required to be maintained under the PAYE regulations and not required to be sent to the Revenue must be retained by the employer for not less than three years after the end of the year to which they relate. [*Reg 55(12)*]. There are special provisions relating to inspection of computer records (see *FA 1988, s 127* and *Reg 55(7)*). See Revenue Pamphlets IR 71 and IR 109 as regards inspection of records and negotiation of settlements.

55.35   **Religious Centres.** If a Local Religious Centre does not expect to pay anyone £100 or more in a tax year, no action is required under PAYE. For anyone to whom the Centre does expect to pay £100 or more in a tax year, but who has no other job, records need to be kept for three years of name, address, national insurance number and the amount paid in the tax year. For any such person who has (or may have) another job, the Centre does not need to deduct tax, but should write to TIDO(LRC), Ty Glas, Llanishen, Cardiff CV4 5ZG giving details of name, address and national insurance number and of both the amount paid to the following 5 April and the amount expected to be paid in a full tax year. (Taxation, 16 February 1995, p 462).

55.36   **Seamen** are subject to standard PAYE procedures on wages from employment. Travelling expenses and subsistence allowances paid to seafarers making regular journeys to the same UK port are subject to PAYE. (Hansard 26 February 1981 Vol 999 Col 442).

55.37   **Suffixes to codes.** See 55.4 above.

55.38   **Superannuation contributions** ('net pay arrangement'). Employees' superannuation contributions authorised by the Pension Schemes Office are deducted from gross pay for PAYE purposes, but National Insurance contributions are calculated on gross pay. [*Reg 2*].

55.39   **Tax refunds** by employer to new employee are not to exceed £200 (£100 before 6 April 1991) unless authorised by inspector. [*Reg 25(6)*]. This requirement is abolished from 6 April 1996. [*SI 1996 No 804, reg 4(c)*].

Tax refunds arising during unemployment are made directly by inspector [*Reg 37*] but refunds are withheld from the unemployed who claim taxable state benefit and from strikers until the end of the strike. [*Sec 204* and *Reg 36*]. See 55.41 below.

55.40   **Tronc arrangements.** Gratuities and service charge shares under tronc arrangements are emoluments and the tronc-master is regarded as responsible for the tax deductions under PAYE. [*Reg 5; SI 1994 No 775*]. For a case in which informal arrangements, under which directors of the employing company collected gratuities and divided them between themselves and the employees, were held not to constitute a tronc, see *Figael Ltd v Fox CA 1991, 64 TC 441*.

55.41   **Unemployed persons and strikers receiving taxable social security etc. benefits.** The Department of Employment (the Department of Social Services for NI) maintain a record of the claimant's previous cumulative pay and tax in the tax year and of any taxable benefit paid to him. At the end of the claimant's period of benefit claim (or at the end of the tax year, if earlier) the Department calculate his tax position, make any repayments of tax due to him and notify the details to him and to his inspector of taxes. Detailed procedures apply to the provision of information between all the parties involved. [*Regs 81–93*]. See also 55.39 above and Revenue Pamphlets IR 41, IR 42 and IR 43.

55.42   **Value added tax.** Emoluments paid to a person holding an office in the course of carrying on a trade, profession or vocation and subject to VAT on services supplied by him should exclude the VAT element for PAYE purposes. (Revenue Pamphlet IR 131, A6). See also 55.9 above.

55.43   **Voluntary lifeboatmen** call-out fees, although taxable, are not subject to deduction of tax under PAYE. (Revenue Press Release 15 April 1986).

56   Payment of Tax

Cross-references. See 42 INTEREST ON UNPAID TAX and 55 PAY AS YOU EARN.

(See also Table at 57 PAYMENT OF TAX—DUE DATES.)

Note re self-assessment. For **1996/97 and subsequent years,** under self-assessment, income tax (on all sources of taxable income) for a year of assessment will be payable by means of two interim payments of equal amounts, based normally on the liability for the previous year and due on 31 January in the year of assessment (commencing on 31 January 1997) and the following 31 July, and a final balancing payment due on the following 31 January (on which date any capital gains tax liability will also be due for payment). Taxpayers will have the right to reduce their interim payments if they believe their liability will be less than that for the previous year or to dispense with interim payments if they believe they will have no liability. Interim payments will not in any case be required where substantially all of a taxpayer's liability is covered by deduction of tax at source, including PAYE, or where the amounts otherwise due are below *de minimis* limits to be prescribed by regulations. See 78.17 to 78.20 SELF-ASSESSMENT for details.

56.1   For **1995/96 and earlier years,** for **individuals and partnerships,** income tax (including higher rate income tax and investment income surcharge where applicable) and capital gains tax is payable as follows.

(*a*)   **On profits of**

(i)   trades and professions assessed under Schedule D, Cases I and II; or

(ii)   foreign businesses assessed under Schedule D, Case V

—as to one-half on 1 January falling within the tax year, and one-half on 1 July following the end of that year or, if later, 30 days after the date of issue of the notice of assessment. For partnerships which commenced before 6 April 1994, these payment dates continue to apply **for 1996/97.** [*Sec 5(2)(3); FA 1994, 26 Sch Pt V(23)*].

56.1 Payment of Tax

(b)   **On income charged under Schedule E**

    (i)   where PAYE is applied—by deduction from emoluments as and when paid [*Sec 203*] and

    (ii)   where the income is assessed—14 days after the first application by the Collector [*SI 1993 No 744, reg 105(2)*]. For payment by employers of tax deducted, see 55.8 PAY AS YOU EARN.

(c)   **On other income received gross**—on 1 January falling within the tax year, or 30 days after the date of issue of the notice of assessment, whichever is the later. [*Sec 5(1); FA 1994, 26 Sch Pt V(23)*]. For Schedule A for 1994/95 and earlier years, see 68.20 SCHEDULE A.

(d)   **On other income received under deduction of basic or lower rate income tax,** or which is treated as having been so received, or to which the 'tax credit' attaches under *Sec 231*—on 1 December following the end of the year for which assessed, or 30 days after the date of issue of the notice of assessment, whichever is the later. [*Sec 5(4); FA 1994, 26 Sch Pt V(23); FA 1996, 6 Sch 3, 28*].

(e)   **On capital gains**—on 1 December following the end of the year for which assessed, or 30 days after the date of issue of the notice of assessment, if later. [*TCGA 1992, s 7; FA 1995, 29 Sch Pt VIII(14)*].

Tax under the **paying and collecting agents** arrangements is payable within 14 days after the end of the month in which the dividend, etc. is paid. [*Sec 118F(2); FA 1996, 29 Sch 1*]. For 1995/96 and earlier years, see 70 SCHEDULE C.

Effective dates of payment. With effect generally from 6 April 1996, these are taken to be as follows.

(1)   *Cheques, cash, and postal orders* handed in at the Revenue office or received by post—the day of receipt by the Revenue *unless* received by post following a day on which the office was closed, in which case it is the day (or the first day) on which the office was closed.

(2)   *Electronic funds transfer*—one working day immediately before the date the value is received.

(3)   *Bank giro or Girobank*—three working days prior to the date of processing by the Revenue.

(Revenue Press Release 1 April 1996).

Previously, effective dates were considered to be as follows.

    (i)   *Cheques sent through the post*—the date on which an in-date cheque is posted but, because of the impossibility of referring to all postmarks, the practice is to take the third working day before the day on which the Collector received the cheque. First-class official paid envelopes or labels are enclosed with first applications for payment of tax and although there is no requirement for a taxpayer to make payment by first-class post, he has the means to do so without incurring any postal charge.

    (ii)   *Cash and in-date cheques tendered personally*—the date of the tender.

    (iii)   *Post-dated cheques*—the date of the cheque.

    (iv)   *Bank giro credit*—the date stamped on the payslip by the bank's cashier.

    (v)   *National Giro bank in-payment*—the date stamped on the payslip by the Post Office counter clerk.

    (vi)   *National Giro bank transfer*—the date of the Inland Revenue's National Giro bank statement on which the item appears.

(Tolley's Practical Tax 1981 p 42).

After 31 March 1993, where a payment of tax is made by electronic funds transfer, an effective date of payment one working day immediately before the date value is received by the Revenue is allowed. (Revenue Press Release 1 April 1993).

See 78.24 SELF-ASSESSMENT as regards cheques received by the Revenue after 5 April 1996.

56.2   PAYMENT OF TAX PENDING APPEAL

Where the appeal to the Commissioners is against an assessment, the full amount charged will be due and payable as in 56.1 above unless (except for 56.1(*b*)(ii) above—Schedule E) the appellant applies for the Commissioners to determine, in the same way as the appeal, the amount of tax to be postponed. The application must be made in writing to the inspector within thirty days after the date of the issue of the notice of assessment, stating the amount of tax believed to be overcharged, and the grounds for that belief. Application may be made outside the normal thirty day time limit if there is a change in the circumstances of the case giving grounds for belief that the appellant is overcharged. In the Revenue view, this requires a change in the circumstances in which the original decision not to apply for postponement was made, not just a change of mind, e.g. further accounts work indicating a substantially excessive assessment, or further reliefs becoming due. (Notes of CCAB meeting with Revenue on the 1982 Finance Bill, TR 477, 22 June 1982.) Any tax not postponed by the Commissioners shall be due and payable as if charged by an assessment issued at the time of the Commissioners' decision and against which no appeal is pending. If circumstances change, a further application to the Commissioners may be made by either party giving notice to the other. The appellant and an inspector may agree the amount of tax to be postponed and written confirmation of such agreement shall be treated as if the Commissioners had so determined. On determination of the appeal any tax overpaid is repaid; any tax postponed or not previously charged becomes due and payable as if charged under an assessment issued when the inspector issues to the appellant notice of the total amount payable. [*TMA ss 55, 56(9)(b), 59(6)(b); F(No 2)A 1975, s 45; FA 1982, s 68; FA 1989, s 156(2); FA 1990, s 104(2)(4)*]. For what is a determination of an appeal for this purpose, see 4.6(*a*) APPEALS. See also 42.2 INTEREST ON UNPAID TAX for interest which might run before the due date of payment of the tax. See 78.31 SELF-ASSESSMENT for the application of these provisions for 1996/97 and subsequent years.

In cases of appeals to the Courts, the tax must be paid first in accordance with the determination of the Commissioners. Tax overpaid consequent on the Court's decision is repaid (with, at the Court's discretion, interest) even though further appeal is possible (see e.g. *T & E Homes Ltd v Robinson CA 1979, 52 TC 567*), and any tax not previously charged is due and payable 30 days after the date of notification of the total amount payable. [*TMA s 56(9)*].

See also 42.2 INTEREST ON UNPAID TAX.

56.3   COLLECTION AND GENERALLY

The Collector may distrain (poind in Scotland). [*TMA ss 61–64; FA 1989, ss 152–155*]. See also *Herbert Berry Associates Ltd v CIR HL 1977, 52 TC 113*. Where amount due (or any instalment) is less than £1,000 (£500 before 1 September 1991, £250 before 11 September 1989), Collector may within six months of due date take summary magistrates' court proceedings. The limit is raised to £2,000 as respects 1996/97 and later years—see 78.40 SELF-ASSESSMENT. The Collector may recover the tax by proceedings in the County Court. [*TMA ss 65, 66; FA 1984, s 57; SI 1989 No 1300; SIs 1991, Nos 724, 1625*]. But for limitations in Scotland and N. Ireland see *TMA ss 65(4), 66(3)(4), 67; FA 1976, s 58; FA 1995, s 156*, and for time limits for proceedings see *Mann v Cleaver KB 1930, 15 TC 367* and *Lord Advocate v Butt C/S 1992, 64 TC 471*. Unpaid tax (and arrears) may also be recovered (with full costs) as a Crown debt in the High Court. [*TMA s 68*]. The amount of an assessment which has become final cannot be re-opened in proceedings to collect the tax (*Pearlberg CA 1953, 34 TC 57; CIR v Soul CA 1976, 51 TC 86*), and it is not open to the taxpayer to raise the defence that the Revenue acted *ultra vires* in raising the assessment (*CIR v Aken CA 1990, 63 TC 395*).

See 47.8 MARRIED PERSONS for collection from wife in certain circumstances and 53.3 PARTNERSHIPS for joint liability of firm. For whether unpaid tax is a business liability for commercial etc. purposes, see *Conway v Wingate CA 1952, 31 ATC 148; Stevens v Britten CA 1954, 33 ATC 399; R v Vaccari CCA 1958, 37 ATC 104; In re Hollebone's Agreement CA 1959, 38 ATC 142.*

56.4 COMPANIES

Companies resident in the UK pay corporation tax and are not assessable to income tax on their profits.

They must deduct income tax from payments of yearly interest (see 23.3(ii) DEDUCTION OF TAX AT SOURCE) as well as from other annual payments, and account for such income tax to the Revenue. See Tolley's Corporation Tax.

56.5 CROWN PRIORITY

Crown priority in bankruptcy was abolished with effect from 29 December 1986, except for sums due at the 'relevant date'

(*a*)   on account of net tax deductions the bankrupt was liable to make under PAYE (55) from emoluments paid during the twelve months before that date, and

(*b*)   in respect of deductions required to be made in the twelve months before that date under the CONSTRUCTION INDUSTRY TAX DEDUCTION SCHEME (21).

The '*relevant date*' is the date of the making of the bankruptcy order, or, if an interim receiver was appointed before that date, the date on which he was first appointed after presentation of the bankruptcy petition. [*Insolvency Act 1986, s 386, 6 Sch* and corresponding Scottish legislation].

Before the above provisions were brought into effect, the earlier provisions continued to apply. Under these, the Crown could claim priority of payment, subject to provision for administration costs, for one year's assessment out of taxes (including capital gains tax and corporation tax [*FA 1965, 10 Sch 15*]) assessed up to 5 April prior to the receiving order. [*Bankruptcy Act 1914, s 33(1)(a)* and similar legislation for Scotland and NI]. Tax unpaid on estimated assessments could be proved (*Calvert v Walker QB 1899, 4 TC 79; Moschi v CIR Ch D 1953, 35 TC 92*). Different years could be selected for different taxes and the actual assessments could be made before or after the receiving order. (See *Gowers v Walker Ch D 1929, 15 TC 165; In re Cockell, Jackson v A-G HL 1932, 16 TC 681; In re Pratt CA 1950, 31 TC 506* and *Purvis Industries CS 1957, 38 TC 155*). Similar provisions applied to insolvents' estates administered out of Court. [*Administration of Estates Act 1925, s 34(1)*]. PAYE and other tax deductions for twelve months prior to date of receiving order or death and not paid over by insolvent employer etc. had Crown priority under *FA 1952, s 30*.

56.6 REMISSION OR REPAYMENT OF TAX IN CASES OF OFFICIAL ERROR

Arrears of tax. Arrears of income or capital gains tax may be waived if they result from the Revenue's failure to make proper and timely use of information supplied by:

(*a*)   a taxpayer about his or her own income, gains or personal circumstances;

(*b*)   an employer, where the information affects a taxpayer's coding; or (*c*)   the DSS about a taxpayer's retirement, disability or widow's State pension.

The waiver will normally apply only where the taxpayer could reasonably have believed that his or her tax affairs were in order, and either:

(i)   was notified of the arrears more than twelve months after the end of the tax year in which the Revenue received the information indicating that more tax was due; or

(ii)   was notified of an over-repayment after the end of the tax year following the year in which the repayment was made.

Exceptionally, arrears notified less than twelve months after the end of the relevant tax year may be waived if the Revenue either failed more than once to make proper use of the facts they had been given about one source of income, or allowed the arrears to build up over two whole tax years in succession by failing to make proper and timely use of information they had been given.

(Revenue Pamphlet IR 1, A19; Revenue Press Release 11 March 1996).

Where the arrears were notified before 11 March 1996, a similar concession applies, but the proportion of the tax which can be remitted depends on the taxpayer's gross income, as follows.

Taxpayer's gross income	Tax remitted
£	£
0–15,500	All
15,501–18,000	Three-quarters
18,001–22,000	One-half
22,001–26,000	One-quarter
26,001–40,000	One-tenth

The income to be considered is that for the year in which the arrears are to be met, although in practice the preceding year's income is considered. If this produces an anomaly, income of the current year may be estimated. (ICAEW Technical Memorandum TR 627, August 1986).

These scales apply to arrears notified to the taxpayer on or after 17 February 1993. The scales apply separately to husbands and wives.

The concession is given only where the taxpayer was notified of the arrear after the end of the tax year following that in which it arose, unless (for cases settled after 25 April 1994) the Revenue had made repeated errors in that period or the arrear had built up over two whole years in succession as a direct result of the Revenue's failure to make proper and timely use of the information.

Special consideration will continue to be given to the exceptional case of a taxpayer with large family responsibilities whose income is just above the normal limits for full or partial remission.

(Revenue Pamphlet IR 1, A19; Revenue Press Release 26 April 1994).

Where an **overpayment** of tax has arisen because of official error, and there is no doubt or dispute as to the facts, claims to repayment of tax are accepted outside the statutory time limits. (Revenue Press Release 10 February 1992).

56.7   **OVERPAYMENT OF TAX**

The Revenue's administrative practice relating to repayments of tax is as below.

(i)   Where an assessment has been made and this shows a repayment due to the taxpayer, repayment is invariably made of the full amount.

(ii) Where the end of year check applied to Schedule E taxpayers shows an overpayment of £10 or less, an assessment is not normally made and the repayment is not made automatically.

(iii) Where tax has been paid to the Collector exceeding the amount due on an assessment and the discrepancy is not noted before the payment has been processed, the excess is not repaid automatically unless it is greater than £1.

The above tolerances are to minimise work which is highly cost ineffective, they cannot operate to deny a repayment to a taxpayer who has claimed it. (Revenue Pamphlet IR 131 (October 1995 Supplement), SP 6/95, 31 March 1995, superseding Revenue Pamphlet IR 131, SP 1/80, 16 January 1980 with effect from 6 April 1995). Provisional repayments will not be made during the tax year to which a claim or claims relate if the tax involved does not exceed £50 in total. (Revenue Press Release 29 March 1989).

See 56.6 above as regards claims in cases of official error. See 5.8 ASSESSMENTS for assessing tolerances on certain state pensions. See also 17.2 CLAIMS as regards repayment procedures.

Allocation of overpayments against underpayments. Where there are underpayments of tax, overpayments will, unless the taxpayer asks for them not to be, automatically be reallocated from the first to the second Schedule D instalment if the overpayment is after 1 June or if the amount involved is less than £1,000. In any other case, where there is an overdue charge, the Collector will suggest that the overpayment be reallocated against it if possible, and will do so unless the taxpayer confirms that the overpayment should not be reallocated.

The order of set-off for Schedule D payments is as follows:

Tax collectible—first instalment
NICs collectible—first instalment
Tax collectible—second instalment
NICs collectible—second instalment
Tax and NICs postponed in the same order as above

For payments made after the second instalment date, the order of set-off is as follows:

Tax collectible—first instalment
Tax collectible—second instalment
NICs collectible—first instalment
NICs collectible—second instalment
Tax and NICs postponed in the same order as above

If a payment relates to a particular instalment, it will only be used against liabilities relating to that instalment.

For the purposes of interest on unpaid and overpaid tax, the set-off gives the same result as if the overpaid tax had been repaid and then paid back against the other liability. Unallocated payments are held in a suspense account and, when the appropriate charge for set-off has been identified, treated as if allocated on the original payment date.

(ICAEW Memorandum TAX 13/92, 22 June 1992).

56.8   **OVER-REPAYMENTS OF TAX**

Tax over-repaid (by actual payment or set-off) and not assessable in the normal way under *TMA s 29* (see 5.1 ASSESSMENTS) may be recovered by assessment under Schedule D, Case VI as if it were unpaid tax. Any associated excess repayment supplement may be included in the assessment. The time limit for such assessment is, if necessary, extended to the end of the chargeable period following that in which the repayment was made (without prejudice to the extended time limits which apply in cases of fraudulent or negligent conduct, see 6.4 BACK DUTY). [*TMA s 30; FA 1982, s 149; FA 1989, s 149(3); FA 1990, s 105*]. See 78.39 SELF-ASSESSMENT as respects over-repayments for 1996/97 and subsequent years.

56.9   **EQUITABLE LIABILITY**

Where all other possible remedies have been exhausted by the taxpayer, the Revenue may be prepared to consider applying 'equitable liability' where it is clearly demonstrated that a liability assessed is greater than it would have been had the returns and supporting documentation been submitted at the proper time, provided that acceptable evidence is produced of what the correct liability should have been. It will not be sufficient to seek to replace the assessment with the taxpayer's (or accountant's) estimate of the liability. In such cases, the Revenue may be prepared to accept a reduced sum based on the evidence provided, having regard to all the relevant circumstances of the case, and not to pursue its right of recovery of the full amount. Full payment of the reduced sum would be expected.

The application of equitable liability is conditional on the taxpayer's affairs being brought fully up to date, and would be very unlikely to be applied more than once in favour of the same taxpayer.

Under self-assessment, even where, in the absence of a return, the Revenue has determined a taxpayer's liability, the taxpayer has until five years after the statutory filing date (or, if later, one year after the determination) to displace the determination with their own self-assessment (see 78.14 SELF-ASSESSMENT). The point should therefore not often be reached where a determination can no longer be replaced, but where that does occur and the above conditions are fulfilled, equitable liability may be extended to meet this situation.

(Revenue Tax Bulletin August 1995 pp 245, 246).

57 Payment of Tax—Due Dates

57.1   The Table below relates to tax for **1995/96 and earlier years** (and **for 1996/97** for Schedule D on partnerships which commenced before 6 April 1994). See 78.17 to 78.20 SELF-ASSESSMENT for due dates of interim and final payments for 1996/97 and subsequent years.

INDIVIDUALS AND PARTNERSHIPS	BASIC RATE AND HIGHER RATE	INVESTMENT INCOME SURCHARGE (1983/84 and earlier)
SCHEDULE D Cases I & II: Profits from trades and professions. Case V: Foreign business.	One-half on 1 January in tax year. One-half on 1 July following end of tax year.	—
SCHEDULE E Employment, PAYE	Deductible from emoluments as and when paid, or 14 days after first application by the Collector.	—
OTHER INCOME RECEIVED GROSS e.g. Rents, Development Gains.	1 January in tax year.	1 January in tax year.
OTHER INCOME RECEIVED UNDER DEDUCTION OF TAX, i.e. where basic or lower rate tax deducted or deemed to be deducted or if received with tax credits e.g. Dividends.	1 December following end of tax year.	1 December following end of tax year.

NOTES:

A. **If assessments are made later than dates in Table above,** see 56.1 PAYMENT OF TAX for due dates then applicable.

B. **If payments are made later than due dates,** see 42 INTEREST ON UNPAID TAX.

C. **Underwriters.** See 89 UNDERWRITERS.

58   Penalties

Cross-references. See 6 BACK DUTY. See also 67.1 RETURNS as regards reasonable excuse for failure to make returns. See also 78.10, 78.25 to 78.29 SELF-ASSESSMENT.

58.1   NOTIFICATION OF CHARGEABILITY

For 1988/89 to 1994/95 inclusive (see 78.4 SELF-ASSESSMENT as regards 1995/96 and subsequent years), a person chargeable to income tax for a year of assessment who has neither delivered a return for that year nor been required under TMA s 8 (see 67.2 RETURNS) to do so must, within one year after the end of that year, notify the inspector, in respect of each source of income (except as below), that he is so chargeable. The maximum penalty for failure is the tax liability in respect of income from each undeclared source for that year under assessments made more than twelve months after the end of the year. Partners are liable only in respect of their share of the income concerned. The sources of income which do not have to be so notified are those in respect of which

(a)   all payments, etc. are dealt with under PAYE (55), or

(b)   all income has been assessed or taken into account either in determining the chargeable person's liability to tax or under PAYE (55), or

(c)   the income is chargeable under Schedule F or is other income from which income tax has been, or is treated as having been, deducted (other than under the CONSTRUCTION INDUSTRY TAX DEDUCTION SCHEME (21)), provided that the chargeable person is not liable for that year other than at the basic or lower rate, or

(d)   the chargeable person could not become liable under assessments made more than twelve months after the end of the year.

Before 1988/89, the penalty for failure was £100 (in addition to any interest, etc. payable), and the exceptions referred to above were not specified. [TMA s 7; FA 1988, s 120; F(No 2)A 1992, s 19(1)].

Similar requirements apply in respect of notification of chargeable gains. [TMA s 11A; FA 1988, s 122; FA 1995, s 115(3)].

See 58.7 below as regards mitigation of penalties.

58.2   FAILURE TO RENDER RETURN

A person who fails to make a return when required to do so by notice under TMA s 8 (individual), TMA s 9 (partnership), TMA s 12 (capital gains) or (for 1989/90 and earlier years) Sec 284(4) (married person), may become liable to a penalty.

For notices served after 5 April 1989, the maximum penalty is £300. A penalty of up to £60 per day may in addition be incurred if the failure continues after such a penalty has been imposed (but not for any day for which such a daily penalty has already been imposed). Neither penalty may be imposed after the failure has been remedied. If the failure continues beyond the end of the tax year following that in which the notice was served, a further penalty may be imposed not exceeding the amount of tax charged under assessments made after that following year on income or gains which should have been included in the return. If, however, the defaulter proves that there was no income or chargeable gain to be included in the return, the penalty under these provisions may not exceed £100. [TMA s 93(1)(2)(5)(7); FA 1988, 3 Sch 28; FA 1989, s 162].

For notices served before 6 April 1989, the maximum initial penalty is £50. This penalty (and the daily penalty referred to below) is avoided if the return is rendered before penalty proceedings are commenced. If failure continues beyond the end of the tax year following that in which the notice was served, the amount of tax charged on assessments made after that year on income which should have been included in the return is added, as a penalty, to the £50 maximum, and without prejudice to the normal charge. A further penalty of £10 per day is incurred if failure continues after having been declared by Court or Commissioners before whom penalty proceedings have been commenced. If the defaulter can prove there was no income or chargeable gains to be included in the return, the total penalty cannot exceed £5. [*TMA s 93(1)(2)(5)(7) as originally enacted*].

In relation to all such notices, tax-based penalties may be reduced in respect of excess PAYE deductions, and partnership assessments are taken into account (other than in relation to partnership returns) only insofar as they relate to income of the defaulter. Assessments may not be taken into account in relation to more than one penalty, but assessments on personal representatives are taken into account following the death of the defaulter. [*TMA s 93(3)(4)(6)*].

Political objections do not justify failure to make returns (*Turton v Birdforth Commrs Ch D 1970, 49 ATC 346*), nor do objections to the system of taxation (*Walsh v Croydon Commrs Ch D 1987, 60 TC 442*). The submission of a return marked 'to be advised' or some similar phrase does not satisfy the requirements and penalties may be incurred (*Cox v Poole General Commrs Ch D 1987, 60 TC 445*).

See 58.7 below as regards mitigation of penalties.

58.3 NEGLIGENCE OR FRAUD

For negligently or fraudulently making or submitting an incorrect return, accounts, claim for allowance or relief, etc., the maximum penalty is the amount of income tax (including surtax) and capital gains tax underpaid by reason of the incorrectness, for the tax year in which return, etc., delivered, the year after, and any preceding year. For returns, etc. before 27 July 1989, the maximum penalty is £50 plus, in the case of negligence, the amount of the tax so underpaid or, in the case of fraud, twice that amount, and for this purpose, *negligence* includes any innocent error not rectified without unreasonable delay after discovery.

Accounts are deemed to have been submitted by taxpayer unless he proves they were submitted without his consent or connivance. [*TMA ss 95–97; FA 1989, s 163*].

For position if agent negligent etc., see *Mankowitz v Spec Commrs Ch D 1971, 46 TC 707* and cf. *Clixby v Pountney Ch D 1967, 44 TC 515*. Assisting in or inducing the preparation or delivery of any information, return, accounts or other document known to be incorrect and to be, or to be likely to be, used for any tax purpose carries a maximum penalty of £3,000. Before 27 July 1989, assisting in, or inducing, the making or delivery of a return or accounts known to be incorrect carried a maximum penalty of £500. [*TMA s 99; FA 1989, s 166*].

See 58.7 below as regards mitigation of penalties.

58.4 OTHER RETURNS ETC.

For failure to render any return, certificate, statement or other document required, whether by notice or otherwise, under the provisions listed in the Table in *TMA s 98*, the maximum penalty is £300, plus £60 for each day the failure continues after that penalty is imposed (but not for any day for which such a daily penalty has already been imposed). For failure, etc. before 27 July 1989, the penalties are £50 and £10 per day respectively, and the daily penalty applies for each day the failure continues after having been declared by the court or Commissioners before whom penalty proceedings were commenced.

The maximum penalty for fraudulently or negligently making an incorrect return, etc. is £3,000 (for failure, etc. before 27 July 1989, £250 in the case of negligence, £500 in the case of fraud).

Penalties for failure to render information etc. required by notice cannot be imposed after the failure is rectified, and daily penalties can similarly not be imposed where the information etc. was required other than by notice. For failure, etc. before 27 July 1989, penalties could not be imposed if the failure had been rectified before proceedings for recovery of the penalty had been commenced. [*TMA s 98; FA 1989, s 164*].

Special penalties are imposed for failure to make annual returns required under PAYE (see 55.9(*a*) PAY AS YOU EARN) or the construction industry scheme (see 21.4 CONSTRUCTION INDUSTRY TAX DEDUCTION SCHEME) by the statutory filing date, i.e. by 19 May following the end of the year of assessment for which the return is required. As regards returns required for 1994/95 and subsequent years, these are a penalty of £100 for each month or part month (up to twelve) during which the failure continues and for each 50 persons (or part where the total is not a multiple of 50) in respect of whom particulars should have been included in the return, and, if the failure continues beyond twelve months, an additional penalty of the amount payable for the year of assessment to which the return relates which remained unpaid at 19 April following that year. If an incorrect return is fraudulently or negligently made, the penalty is the difference between the amount payable under the return and the amount which would have been payable had the return been correct. [*TMA s 98A; FA 1989, s 165; SI 1993 No 743, reg 11; SI 1993 No 744, regs 43, 104; SI 1994 No 2508*]. For 1994/95 returns, a period of grace of 14 days from the statutory filing date was allowed during which the automatic penalties will not be charged. (Revenue Pamphlet IR 1 (November 1995 Supplement), B45). For subsequent returns, this will apply provided that the return is received on or before the last business day within seven days following the filing date. (Revenue Press Release 14 September 1995). For returns due for 1989/90 to 1993/94 inclusive, the Revenue are able to take proceedings before the Appeal Commissioners for an initial penalty of up to £1,200 per 50 employees, with penalties for continuing failure of up to £100 per 50 employees per month for up to twelve months. In the first year, no proceedings were taken in relation to returns submitted by 19 August 1990, but this three-month period of grace was successively reduced. (Revenue Press Release 14 March 1989). The final date for submission without penalty for 1992/93 returns was 19 June 1993, that for 1993/94 returns 19 May 1994. (Revenue Press Release 19 May 1993).

See 53.19 PARTNERSHIPS as regards penalties under *TMA s 98B* in relation to European Economic Interest Groupings.

Failure to allow access to computer records renders a person liable to a £500 penalty. [*FA 1988, s 127*].

For unlawfully possessing or disposing of an exemption certificate relating to a sub-contractor in the construction industry or making false statements relating thereto, the maximum fine is £5,000. [*F(No 2)A 1975, s 70(9)(10); Sec 561(10)–(13)*].

See 58.7 below as regards mitigation of penalties.

58.5   **COMMISSIONERS' PRECEPTS ETC.**

Summary penalties (to be treated as tax assessed and due and payable) may be determined by Commissioners against any party to proceedings before them who fails to comply with a precept, order for inspection etc. (see 4.6 APPEALS). The maximum penalty is £300 in the case of the General Commissioners, £10,000 in the case of the Special Commissioners (and in the case of the General Commissioners, a daily penalty up to £60 may also be imposed for continuing failure). A penalty up to £10,000 may similarly be imposed for failure to comply with any other direction of the Special Commissioners (including in relation to a

58.6 Penalties

preliminary hearing). [*SI 1994 No 1811, reg 24(1)(3); SI 1994 No 1812, reg 10(1)(3)(4)*]. If a person on whom a witness summons is served (see 4.6 APPEALS) fails to attend in obedience thereto, or attends but refuses to be sworn or to affirm, or refuses to answer any lawful question, or refuses to produce any document required by the summons, the Commissioners may summarily determine a penalty against that person, to be treated as tax assessed and due and payable. The maximum penalty is £1,000 in the case of the General Commissioners, £10,000 in the case of the Special Commissioners. [*SI 1994 No 1811, reg 24(2)(3); SI 1994 No 1812, reg 4(12)(13)*]. Before 1 September 1994, similar provisions applied under *TMA ss 51–53*, except that the maximum penalty for failure to comply with precepts etc. was in all cases £300 plus £60 per day (£3,000 in cases of fraudulently or negligently incorrect returns) under *TMA s 98* (see P6004 above), and the maximum penalty in relation to a witness summons was £50 in all cases.

Appeal against such summary penalties lies to the High Court (or Court of Session). [*TMA s 53 (as inserted by SI 1994 No 1813)*]. For the procedure on such appeals, see *QT Discount Foodstores Ltd v Warley Commrs Ch D 1981, 57 TC 268* and, for a case in which penalties were quashed because the taxpayer's evidence that he was unable to supply the information in question was not properly tested, *Boulton v Poole Commrs Ch D 1988, 60 TC 718*.

For appeals against penalties for non–compliance with precepts etc. see *Shah v Hampstead Commrs Ch D 1974, 49 TC 651; Chapman v Sheaf Commrs Ch D 1975, 49 TC 689; Toogood v Bristol Commrs Ch D 1976, 51 TC 634 and [1977] STC 116; Campbell v Rochdale Commrs Ch D 1975, 50 TC 411; B & S Displays Ltd v Special Commrs Ch D 1978, 52 TC 318; Galleri v Wirral Commrs Ch D 1978, [1979] STC 216; Beach v Willesden Commrs Ch D 1981, 55 TC 663; Stoll v High Wycombe Commrs and CIR Ch D 1992, 64 TC 587; Wilson v Leek Commrs and CIR Ch D 1993, [1994] STC 147*.

58.6 PROCEDURE

Events occurring after 26 July 1989. Except in the case of

(a) penalty proceedings instituted before the courts in cases of suspected fraud (see below), or

(b) penalties under

   (i) *TMA s 93(1)(a)* (see 58.2 above),

   (ii) *TMA s 94(1)* before the substitution by *F(No 2)A 1987, s 83*,

   (iii) *TMA s 98(1)(i)* (see 58.4 above),

   (iv) *TMA s 98A(2)(a)(i)* (see 58.4 above), or

   (v) *TMA s 98B(2)(a)* (see 58.4 above),

   (for which see further below),

an authorised officer of the Board may make a determination imposing any penalty under the *Taxes Acts* of an amount which he considers correct or appropriate. This does not apply to penalties awarded summarily by Commissioners (see 58.5 above).

The notice of determination must state the date of issue and the time within which an appeal can be made. It cannot be altered unless

(i) there is an appeal (see below), or

(ii) an authorised officer discovers that the penalty is or has become insufficient (in which case he may make a further determination), or

(iii) the penalty arises under *TMA s 94(6)*, and an authorised officer subsequently discovers that the amount of tax is or has become excessive (in which case it is to be revised accordingly).

A penalty under these provisions is due 30 days after the date of issue of the notice of determination, and is treated as tax charged under an assessment and due and payable. A determination which could have been made on a person who has died can be made on his personal representatives, and is then payable out of the estate. [*TMA ss 100, 100A; FA 1989, s 167; SI 1994 No 1813*].

Appeals. Subject to the following, the general APPEALS (4) provisions apply to an appeal against a determination as if it were an appeal against an assessment to tax. *TMA s 50(6)–(8)* (see 4.6(c)(e) APPEALS) do not, however, apply, and instead, on appeal, the Commissioners can

(A) in the case of a penalty which is required to be of a particular amount, set the determination aside, confirm it, or alter it to the correct amount, and

(B) in any other case, set the determination aside, confirm it if it seems appropriate, or reduce it (including to nil) or increase it as seems appropriate (but not beyond the permitted maximum, as above).

Without prejudice to any right to have a case stated by the General Commissioners for the opinion of the High Court, or to appeal against a Special Commissioners' decision (see 4.7 APPEALS), an appeal lies to the High Court (in Scotland, the Court of Session). [*TMA s 100B; FA 1989, s 167; SI 1994 No 1813*].

Proceedings before Commissioners. For a penalty within (b)(i)–(v) above, an authorised officer may commence proceedings before the General or Special Commissioners. The proceedings are by way of information in writing to the Commissioners, and upon summons issued by them to the defendant (or defender), and are heard and decided in a summary way. An appeal lies to the High Court (or Court of Session) on a question of law or, by the defendant (defender), against the amount. The court can set the determination aside, confirm it if it seems appropriate, or reduce it (including to nil) or increase it as seems appropriate (but not beyond the permitted maximum, as above). The penalty is treated as tax charged in an assessment and due and payable. [*TMA s 100C; FA 1989, s 167*].

Proceedings before court. If the Board consider that liability arises from fraud by any person, proceedings can be brought in the High Court (or Court of Session). If the court does not find fraud proved, it can nevertheless impose a penalty to which it considers the person liable. [*TMA s 100D; FA 1989, s 167*].

Events occurring before 27 July 1989. In the case of failure to make returns, etc. (see 58.2 to 58.4 above) inspector may himself commence penalty proceedings before General Commissioners (penalty then limited to £50, except where any further delay); penalties for failure to comply with precepts etc. are awarded by the Commissioners summarily (see 58.5 above). Subject to this, penalty proceedings require an order of CIR and may be commenced before General or Special Commissioners, High Court or Court of Session. On appeal, the court may confirm, reduce or increase any penalty imposed by the Commissioners. Any proceedings which were, or could have been, commenced against a deceased person may be commenced or continued against his personal representatives (any penalty being a debt of the estate). [*TMA s 100 as originally enacted*].

General matters. Non-receipt of notice of the hearing at which Commissioners awarded penalties cannot be raised by way of appeal to the Court (*Kenny v Wirral Commrs Ch D 1974, 50 TC 405, Campbell v Rochdale Commrs Ch D 1975, 50 TC 411*).

For validity of penalty proceedings while assessments open, see *A-G for Irish Free State v White 1931, 38 TC 666* and *R v Havering Commrs (ex p Knight) CA 1973, 49 TC 161*. For other procedural matters, see *Collins v Croydon Commrs Ch D 1969, 45 TC 566; Bales v Rochford Commrs Ch D 1964, 42 TC 17; Sparks v West Brixton Commrs Ch D, [1977] STC 212; Moschi v Kensington Commrs Ch D 1979, 54 TC 403*; and for other appeals against penalties for failure to make returns, see *Dunk v Havant Commrs Ch D 1976, 51 TC 519*;

58.7 Penalties

Napier v Farnham Commrs CA, [1978] TR 403; Garnham v Haywards Heath Commrs Ch D 1977, [1978] TR 303.

For variation, etc. of penalties by the court, see *Dawes v Wallington Commrs Ch D 1964, 42 TC 200; Salmon v Havering Commrs CA 1968, 45 TC 77; Williams v Spec Commrs Ch D 1974, 49 TC 670; Wells v Croydon Commrs Ch D 1968, 47 ATC 356; Taylor v Bethnal Green Commrs Ch D 1976, [1977] STC 44; Stableford v Liverpool Commrs Ch D 1982, [1983] STC 162; Sen v St. Anne, Westminster Commrs Ch D, [1983] STC 415; Willey v CIR and East Dereham Commrs Ch D 1984, 59 TC 640; Jolley v Bolton Commrs Ch D, [1986] STC 414; Lear v Leek Commrs Ch D 1986, 59 TC 247; Delapage Ltd v Highbury Commrs and CIR Ch D 1992, 64 TC 560.*

For the test used by the court in considering whether penalties excessive, see *Brodt v Wells Commrs Ch D 1987, 60 TC 436.* Per Scott LJ, penalties awarded by different bodies of Commissioners 'should, in relation to similar cases, bear some resemblance to one another'.

A mere denial of liability to penalties implies an intention by the taxpayer to set up a case in refutation, and details must be supplied (*CIR v Jackson CA 1960, 39 TC 357*).

Statements made or documents produced by or on behalf of a taxpayer are admissible as evidence in proceedings against him notwithstanding that reliance on CIR's practice in cases of full disclosure may have induced him to make or produce them. [*TMA s 105; FA 1989, s 168(5)*].

58.7 MITIGATION OR LIMITATION OF PENALTIES

CIR may mitigate penalties before or after judgment. [*TMA s 102; FA 1989, s 168(4)*]. In considering mitigation, credit will be given for co-operation of taxpayer (Revenue Press Release 1 August 1977). A binding agreement by a taxpayer to pay an amount in composition cannot be repudiated afterwards by him or his executors (*A-G v Johnstone KB 1926, 10 TC 758; A-G v Midland Bank Trustee Co KB 1934, 19 TC 136; Richards KB 1950, 33 TC 1*).

For the validity of tax amnesties see *R v CIR (ex p National Federation of Self-employed and Small Businesses Ltd) HL 1981, 55 TC 133.*

For power of Revenue to enter into agreements in full settlement of liabilities in investigation cases, see 6.11 BACK DUTY.

Where **two or more tax-geared penalties** relate to the same liability, the aggregate amount of the penalties is, for 1988/89 and subsequent years of assessment, limited to the greater or greatest penalty applicable. [*TMA s 97A; FA 1988, s 129*].

See also 67.1 RETURNS as regards 'reasonable excuse' for failure to fulfil obligations.

Negotiated settlements. In the case of tax-based penalties where a maximum penalty of 100% is in strict law exigible, the inspector will start with the figure of 100% and then take the following factors into account in arriving at the penalty element which he will expect to be included in any offer in settlement of liabilities.

(*a*) Disclosure. A reduction of up to 20% (or 30% where there has been full voluntary disclosure), depending on how much information was provided, how soon, and how that contributed to settling the investigation.

(*b*) Co-operation. A reduction of up to 40%, depending upon a comparison of the extent of co-operation given in the investigation with the co-operation which the inspector believes would have been possible.

(c)   Gravity. A reduction of up to 40%, depending upon the nature of the offence, how long it continued and the amounts involved.

(Revenue Pamphlet IR 73).

58.8   TIME LIMITS

Events occurring after 26 July 1989. The time within which a penalty can be determined, or proceedings commenced, depends on the penalty, as follows.

(a)   If the penalty is ascertainable by reference to tax payable, the time is

(i)   six years after the penalty was incurred, or

(ii)   a later time within three years after the determination of the amount of the tax (except that this alternative does not apply if the tax was payable by a person who has died, it is charged in an assessment made more than six years after the chargeable period for which it is charged (for 1996/97 and subsequent years, six years after 31 January following the chargeable period), and the determination would be made in relation to the personal representatives).

(b)   If the penalty arises under *TMA s 99* (see 58.3 above), the time is 20 years after the date when it was incurred.

(c)   In any other case, the time is six years from the time when the penalty was, or began to be, incurred.

[*TMA s 103; FA 1989, s 169; FA 1994, ss 196, 199, 19 Sch 32*].

Events occurring before 27 July 1989. Normally, penalty proceedings may be commenced within six years after the date the penalty was incurred, but in cases of fraud or wilful default this limit is extended to three years after final determination of tax liability, although this does not apply to personal representatives of a deceased defaulter. The time limit is also extended in cases where a penalty is calculated by reference to tax under an assessment for any year (see 58.2 and 58.3 above) made within six years thereafter. Proceedings may be commenced within three years of the final determination of that tax. But where proceedings could not have been commenced but for this extension, tax on assessments under *TMA ss 37, 39 or 40(2)* (see 6.4 and 6.5 BACK DUTY) is left out of account in penalty calculations. [*TMA s 103 as originally enacted*].

Final determination of tax. Provisional agreement of the amount due subject to the inspector's being satisfied with statements of assets, etc. is not final determination for these purposes (*Carco Accessories Ltd v CIR CS 1985, 59 TC 45*).

58.9   BANKRUPTS

Penalties awarded after a bankruptcy are provable debts, but in practice the Revenue does not proceed for penalties during a bankruptcy where there are other creditors. The trustee may agree to compromise any penalties awarded but the compromise must also be agreed by the bankrupt. (*Re Hurren Ch D 1982, 56 TC 494*).

58.10   LIABILITY UNDER CRIMINAL LAW

'False statements to prejudice of Crown and public revenue' are indictable as a criminal offence (*R v Hudson CCA 1956, 36 TC 561*).

Apart from the above, false statements in income tax returns, or for obtaining any allowance, reduction or repayment may involve liability to imprisonment for up to two years, under the *Perjury Act 1911, s 5*, for 'knowingly and wilfully' making materially false statements or returns for tax purposes. Also, in Scotland, summary proceedings may be taken under *TMA s 107.*

The Revenue practice as regards the seeking of civil penalties where a criminal prosecution has been brought for fraud are set out in Revenue Pamphlet IR 131, SP 2/88, 10 May 1988.

See 6.11 BACK DUTY as regards acceptance of money settlements instead of institution of criminal proceedings.

58.11 VALUE ADDED TAX AND EXCISE

VAT penalties and surcharge are not allowed as a deduction for tax purposes. [*Sec 827(1)*]. See Tolley's Value Added Tax under Penalties. Excise penalties under *FA 1994, ss 8–11* are similarly disallowed. [*Sec 827(1A); FA 1994, s 18(7)*].

58.12 INSURANCE PREMIUM TAX AND LANDFILL TAX

Penalties and interest under the insurance premium tax and landfill tax provisions are not allowed as a deduction for tax purposes. [*Sec 827(1B)(1C); FA 1994, 7 Sch 31; FA 1996, 5 Sch 40*].

59   Pensions

Cross-references. See also 65 RETIREMENT ANNUITIES AND PERSONAL PENSION SCHEMES and 66 RETIREMENT SCHEMES.

59.1   PENSIONS ASSESSABLE UNDER SCHEDULE E

The following pensions are assessable under Schedule E as earned income on the full amount of the pensions arising (even if paid to a non-UK resident except (iv) and subject to 59.3 below).

(i)   Retirement and widows' pensions etc. from UK government. [*Sec 617*]. See list at 82.3 SOCIAL SECURITY.

(ii)   Pensions payable by the Crown or out of UK public revenue. [*Sec 19(1)—para 2*].

(iii)   Other pensions—unless paid by or on behalf of a person outside the UK. [*Sec 19(1)—para 3*]. But see 59.4 below.

(iv)   Pensions payable in the UK to a resident of the UK by an agent of the government of a British dominion or protectorate or country mentioned in *British Nationality Act 1981, 3 Sch* in respect of foreign service [*Sec 19(1)—para 4*] as increased by exchange, and with no allowance for such deductions as costs of unsuccessful lawsuit against government (*Magraw v Lewis KB 1933, 18 TC 222*). A deduction of one-tenth is allowed. [*Sec 196*].

(v)   *Voluntary pensions* or 'annual payments' paid by employers or their successors to retired employees (or their relatives or dependants), notwithstanding that they are paid voluntarily and may be discontinued at any time [*Sec 133*]—except if from non-UK payer, see 59.2(ii) below.

(vi)   Pensions in respect of RETIREMENT SCHEMES (66) unless the Inland Revenue direct that Schedule D, Case III shall apply. [*Sec 597*].

(vii)   Periodical payments out of the House of Commons Members' Fund. [*Sec 613(3)*].

Disability payments from a company pension fund were assessable under Schedule E as pensions (*Johnson v Holleran Ch D 1988, 61 TC 428; Johnson v Farquhar Ch D 1991, 64 TC 385*).

A pension assessable under Schedule E is not an employment, so that no charge can arise on the provision of benefits in kind (see 75.13 SCHEDULE E) to retired employees. This applies in particular to the provision after retirement of medical insurance under the former employer's group medical scheme, other than in the exceptional case where the expense of providing such insurance represents a specific part of the retired person's pension or a supplementary pension. (Revenue Schedule E Manual, SE 3215).

59.2   PENSIONS ASSESSABLE UNDER SCHEDULE D, CASE V

The following pensions are assessable under Case V, as earned income.

(i)   Pensions paid by or on behalf of a person outside UK—unless 59.1(iv) above applies. [*Sec 58(1)*].

(ii)   Voluntary pensions in respect of former employment paid by or on behalf of a person outside UK. [*Sec 58(2)*].

The assessment is on 90% of the full amount arising in the preceding year of assessment (with adjustments in opening and closing years) or current year of assessment, whichever is applicable (see 73.9 SCHEDULE D, CASES IV AND V), *unless* the recipient is not domiciled in the UK, or being a British subject or Eire citizen is not ordinarily resident in the UK, in which case the assessment is on the amount remitted to the UK (see 63 REMITTANCE BASIS). [*Sec 65(1)(2)(4)–(9); FA 1974, s 22(2)*]. Arrears or retrospective increases of pensions chargeable on the arising basis may be taxed as if they arose in the years to which they relate. (Revenue Pamphlet IR 1, A55).

Where the UK government assumed responsibility under *Overseas Pensions Act 1973, s 1* for overseas pensions payable immediately before 6 April 1973, payments by them are treated as being from overseas, except as regards statutory increases. [*Sec 616(3)*]. See also Revenue Pamphlet IR 1, A49.

59.3   RELIEFS IN RESPECT OF PENSIONS FROM OR TO OVERSEAS

Relief may be claimable under the specific terms of a double tax treaty with the country concerned or by means of unilateral double tax relief granted in the UK. See 25 DOUBLE TAX RELIEF. Certain double tax reliefs are continued despite the British Government having assumed responsibility for payment. [*Sec 616(3)(4)*].

British and certain other persons resident abroad can claim UK personal allowances, see 51.11 NON-RESIDENTS AND OTHER OVERSEAS MATTERS.

59.4   EXEMPTIONS FROM UK TAX

(i)   Voluntary pensions not arising out of past employment or not paid by past employers or their successors. Where a voluntary pension is paid annually out of his own pocket by someone other than the employer (e.g. by one of the directors of a company) it does not fall under 59.1(v) above. But if the lump sum, or the total of periodic payments, exceeds £30,000, the recipient may be assessable on the excess under *Secs 148, 188, 11 Sch*, see 19 COMPENSATION FOR LOSS OF EMPLOYMENT.

(ii)   **Wound and Disability Pensions of members of Armed Forces** or retired pay of disabled officers (including nurses) and compensation paid to Mercantile Marine, or for injuries under War Compensation Acts. [*Sec 315*]. This exemption covers pensions given for causes attributable to or aggravated by naval, military or air-force service, and additions for that reason to ordinary pensions. But not e.g. pensions to parents for loss of sons. Where a member of Armed Forces invalided by service disability and awarded combined long service and disability pension, the whole pension is exempt because not possible to identify taxable part. (Hansard 29 June 1978 Cols 654/5).

(iii)   **Employees disabled at work.** Any pension awarded, on retirement through disability caused by injury on duty or by a work-related illness (or by war wounds), in addition to a retirement pension, or any excess above a normal pension on retirement through ill-health where the excess is attributable to such disablement. (Revenue Pamphlet IR 1, A62).

(iv)   Pensions payable to a non-UK resident under the *Pensions (India, Pakistan and Burma) Act 1955*; from the UK fund of a country mentioned in the *British Nationality Act 1981, 3 Sch* by virtue of a post-1956 enactment or of a British colony, protectorate etc., or under the Overseas Superannuation Scheme. The exemption does not apply to certain increases under *Pensions (Increase) Acts*. [*Sec 615(1)(2)(a)–(d)(4)*].

(v) Pensions paid to non-UK residents under *Overseas Service Act 1958* (if in respect of foreign service), from Central African Pension Fund or Overseas Service Pension Fund. [*Sec 615(1)(2)(e)–(g)*].

(vi) Lump sum 'relevant benefits' (see 66.1 RETIREMENT SCHEMES) received by an employee (or by his dependants or personal representatives) from

(*a*) a *superannuation fund* within *Sec 615(6)* (see 59.6 below), or

(*b*) an *overseas retirement benefits scheme* or *provident fund* where certain conditions as to the employee's foreign service are met.

As regards (*b*) above, exemption may be total or partial depending on the length of foreign service, and this is determined in the same way as the statutory exemption from charge under *Sec 148* for foreign service payments (see 19.6 COMPENSATION FOR LOSS OF EMPLOYMENT (AND DAMAGES)) (Revenue Pamphlet IR 1, A10).

(vii) For exemptions for pensions to *war widows etc.*, see 29.31 EXEMPT INCOME.

(viii) For exemption of pensions of *victims of Nazi persecution*, see 29.7 EXEMPT INCOME.

59.5 CONTRIBUTIONS TO SECURE PENSIONS

Social Security contributions are not allowed as a deduction for tax purposes unless made by a business employer in respect of an employee. [*Sec 617(3)(4)*]. See 82 SOCIAL SECURITY.

Superannuation Fund deductions are allowed as set out under 66 RETIREMENT SCHEMES.

Self-employed persons and those not in an occupational scheme can secure relief for contributions as set out under 65 RETIREMENT ANNUITIES AND PERSONAL PENSION SCHEMES.

59.6 OVERSEAS PENSIONS FUNDS

Pension Funds for Overseas Employees—Exemption (as for a person not domiciled, resident or ordinarily resident in UK) applies to income (including gains otherwise assessable to capital gains tax) from investments or other property of a fund (*a*) established under irrevocable trusts in connection with a trade carried on wholly or partly overseas (*b*) solely to provide superannuation benefits to overseas employees (incidental duties in UK ignored), and (*c*) recognised by both employer and employees. Annuities to non-residents are payable gross, and trustees are not liable under *Sec 349(1)*. [*Secs 614(5), 615(3)(6); TCGA 1992, s 271(1)(c)*].

Overseas Superannuation Scheme Fund, and pension funds established in UK by Government of *any colony, protectorate*, etc.—investment or deposit income and capital gains exempt. [*Sec 614(3); TCGA 1992, s 271(1)(c)*].

60 Post-Cessation Etc. Receipts and Expenditure (Trades, professions and vocations)

[*Secs 103–110; FA 1995, s 90*]

Cross-reference. See 12 CASH BASIS.

60.1 POST-CESSATION ETC. RECEIPTS

Earnings basis. Where a trade, etc., the profits of which are computed 'by reference to earnings' (as defined by *Sec 110(3)*) is permanently discontinued (or treated as such) all **sums received on or after the discontinuance** (other than those exempted below) arising from the carrying on of the trade, etc., during any period before its discontinuance (including the amount, or arm's length value, of any consideration for a transfer of the right to receive them, and any recoveries or releases of items previously allowed as bad or doubtful debts) which are not otherwise chargeable to tax nor already brought into account for any period before the discontinuance are chargeable under Schedule D, Case VI.

Where the profits are not computed 'by reference to earnings' there is a similar charge on amounts received after the discontinuance which, if the earnings basis had applied, would have been left out of account because the date on which they became due or the date on which the amount was ascertained fell after the discontinuance. [*Sec 103(1)(2)(4); FA 1994, s 144(3)*]. Receipts within the legislation will include, *inter alia*, royalties and similar amounts which under decisions such as *Carson v Cheyney's Exor HL 1958, 38 TC 240*, prior to the legislation, had been held not to be taxable.

The charge is for the year of receipt (or as if received on the date of discontinuance if received by the person who carried on the trade before the discontinuance (or his personal representatives) in a tax year beginning within six years after the discontinuance *and election made* within two years thereafter, or, for 1996/97 and later years, within one year after 31 January following the year of receipt). [*Sec 108; FA 1996, s 128(4)*]. See 78.33 SELF-ASSESSMENT for the way in which effect is given to this election.

Deductions. Deductions may be made of any expenses or losses (other than arising from the discontinuance) which are not otherwise allowable (and have not been allowed under any other provision) but which would have been allowable to the previous owner if the trade, etc., had not ceased (or changed its 'conventional' basis, see below) and any unused balance of his CAPITAL ALLOWANCES (10) down to the date of discontinuance (or change). [*Sec 105; FA 1995, s 78(6)*].

Exemptions

    (i)   Sums received by a non-resident (or his agent) for income arising outside the UK,

    (ii)   a lump sum received by an author's executor, etc., for total or partial assignment of copyright or public lending right in his literary, dramatic, musical or artistic work or of design right in his design,

    (iii)   sums realised for transfer of closing trading stock or professional work in progress (these are already dealt with by *Secs 100, 101* see 71.82 SCHEDULE D, CASES I AND II). [*Sec 103(3)*].

Deemed discontinuance. The above provisions also apply on a change of ownership which, under *Sec 113* (see 71.25 SCHEDULE D, CASES I AND II) or *Sec 337(1)* (company beginning or ceasing to carry on a trade), is treated as a permanent discontinuance, but if, on such a change, the right to receive sums as above is transferred from the previous owner to his successor the only liability under these sections is on the latter, who has to include as normal trade receipts, for the periods in which they are received, all such sums arising from the transfer. [*Sec 106(2)*]. Deduction may be made for any debts taken over on the discontinuance which prove bad, so far as not already allowed to the previous owner in computations for periods before the change. [*Sec 89*]. The provisions also apply to an individual leaving a partnership such that his deemed trade is permanently discontinued under the post-Finance Act 1994 provisions in 53.3 PARTNERSHIPS. [*Sec 110(2); FA 1994, s 215(1A); FA 1995, s 117(1)(b)(3)*].

60.2 **'Conventional' basis.** Where a trade, profession or vocation previously taxed on a 'conventional' basis, i.e. on the CASH BASIS (12) or otherwise than 'by reference to earnings' (see 60.1 above), is permanently discontinued (or treated as such), treatment as above applies to all receipts on or after the discontinuance arising from carrying on the trade etc. so far as their amount or value was not taken into account in computing the profits before the discontinuance. The charge does not extend to amounts otherwise chargeable (including amounts chargeable under 60.1 above) nor to the sums referred to in exemptions (i) and (ii) in 60.1 above. [*Sec 104(1)–(3)*].

Where a trade etc. changes from a 'conventional' basis to an earnings basis or to a different 'conventional' basis so that receipts drop out of computation, there is a similar charge on receipts after the change (and before any discontinuance). [*Sec 104(4)(5)*].

Professional work in progress. Where, in the case of a profession or vocation, there has been a change from a conventional basis to an earnings basis or a different conventional basis *and* the work in progress at the change has been allowed as a deduction after the change, the amount of that work in progress (if not counterbalanced by a previous credit) will be charged as above under Schedule D, Case VI. Similarly chargeable is any amount received for work in progress transferred or realised after discontinuance. [*Sec 104(6)(7)*].

Relief. In the case of an individual who was carrying on the trade, etc., on 18 March 1968 (profits of the trade, etc., not having been computed on an earnings basis at any time between that date and the discontinuance, or change, as above) any net amount chargeable on him under *Sec 104* above (but not any amount chargeable under *Sec 103*), is (subject as below) reduced by 5% for each year, or part year, by which his age at 5 April 1968 exceeded 51, up to a maximum of 75%, if he was then 65 or over. [*Sec 109*]. But the above reduction does not apply to any excess of a partner's share in post-cessation receipts over the amount which would have been apportioned to him had his share been calculated at the same rate as his average participation in partnership profits for the three tax years ending with that in which the discontinuance, or change, took place. [*Sec 109(5)*].

60.3 **Earned income.** Receipts assessable as above are treated as earned income if profits before the discontinuance or change of basis were previously so treated. [*Sec 107*].

60.4 **POST-CESSATION EXPENDITURE**

Relief against total income (and capital gains, see below) is available for certain payments made after 28 November 1994 in connection with a trade etc. which has been permanently discontinued (or treated as such—see 60.1 above) and within seven years after the discontinuance. Relief is given for the year in which the payment is made and unused relief cannot be carried forward (but may qualify as a deduction under *Sec 105* from post-cessation receipts of later years—see 60.1 above). The relief is not available to companies.

Payments qualifying for this relief are those made wholly and exclusively:

(a) in remedying defective work done, goods supplied or services rendered or by way of damages (awarded or agreed) in respect of defective work etc.;

(b) in meeting legal and professional fees in connection with a claim that work done etc. was defective;

(c) in insuring against such a claim or against the incurring of such legal etc. fees; or

(d) for the purpose of collecting a debt taken into account in computing profits of the former trade etc..

In addition, where an unpaid debt taken into account in computing profits of the former trade etc. proves to be bad in any part of the year of claim (and the claimant gives notice of that fact in making the claim) or is wholly or partly released as part of a voluntary arrangement or compromise (see 71.44 SCHEDULE D, CASES I AND II), then, to the extent that the former trader is entitled to the benefit of that debt, he is treated as making a payment qualifying for relief under these provisions and equal to the amount lost or released. To the extent that relief is then given under these provisions, any subsequent recovery of the debt is taxed as a post-cessation receipt (see 60.1 above) with no deduction available against it under *Sec 105*. (Where the claim was for 1994/95 or 1995/96, the Revenue had to be notified of a bad debt before the end of the year of claim.)

Where relief becomes available in respect of a payment within any of (a) to (d) above, the following are taxed as post-cessation receipts with no deduction available against them under *Sec 105*: (i) in the case of (a) or (b), any insurance proceeds, or similar, to allow the payment to be made or to reimburse it, (ii) in the case of (c), any refund of the insurance premium, or similar receipt, and (iii) in the case of (d), any sum received to meet the costs of collecting the debt. Where the receipt occurs in an earlier tax year than the related payment, it is treated as instead having been received in the year of payment.

Set-off of unpaid expenses against relief. Where a deduction was made in computing profits or losses of the former trade etc. in respect of an expense not actually paid, relief otherwise due and claimed under these provisions is reduced by the amount of any such expenses remaining unpaid at the end of the year to which the claim relates (to the extent that those expenses have not so reduced relief for an earlier year). If an unpaid expense has reduced relief but is subsequently paid, wholly or partly, the amount paid (or, if less, the amount of the reduction) is treated as a payment qualifying for relief under these provisions for the year of payment.

Exclusion of double relief. Relief is not available in respect of an amount for which income tax relief is otherwise available. In determining whether an amount could otherwise be relieved under *Sec 105* (deduction from post-cessation receipts—see 60.1 above), amounts not available for relief under these provisions are assumed to be relieved under *Sec 105* in priority to amounts that are so available.

Time limit. The relief must be claimed within two years after the year of assessment in which the payment is made where that year is 1994/95 or 1995/96. For later years, the time limit is twelve months after 31 January following the tax year of payment.

Relief against capital gains. Where a claim is made as above and the claimant's income for the year is insufficient to fully utilise the relief, he may include in his claim an additional claim to have the excess relief treated as an allowable loss for that year for capital gains tax purposes. The allowable loss may not exceed the amount of the claimant's gains for the year *before* deducting any losses brought forward, the capital gains tax annual exemption or any relief available under *FA 1991, s 72* for trading losses (see 46.5 LOSSES); any excess over that amount is *not* available to carry forward against gains of a later year.

[*Secs 109A, 110; FA 1995, s 90; FA 1996, s 134, 20 Sch 5*].

See generally Revenue Tax Bulletin October 1995 pp 256, 257.

60.5   *Example*

Simcock ceased trading in October 1995. In 1996/97 the following events occur in connection with his former trade.

(i)   He pays a former customer £9,250 by way of damages for defective work carried out by him in the course of the trade.

(ii)   He incurs legal fees of £800 in connection with (i) above.

(iii)   He incurs debt collection fees of £200 in connection with trade debts outstanding at cessation and which were taken into account as receipts in computing profits.

(iv)   He writes off a trade debt of £500, giving the Revenue notice of his having done so.

(v)   He incurs legal fees of £175 in relation to a debt of £1,000 owing by him to a supplier which, although disputed, was taken into account as an expense in computing his trading profits.

(vi)   He eventually agrees to pay £500 in full settlement of his liability in respect of the debt in (v) above, paying £250 in March 1997 and the remaining £250 in May 1997.

In 1997/98 he receives £3,000 from his insurers in full settlement of their liability with regard to the expense incurred in (i) above.

For 1996/97, his total income before taking account of the above events is £9,000, and he also has capital gains of £7,500 (with £1,000 capital losses brought forward from 1995/96).

He makes a claim under *Sec 109A* for 1996/97 and a simultaneous claim under *FA 1995, s 90(4)* to have any excess relief set against capital gains.

Simcock's tax position is as follows.

1996/97

	£	£
Income		
Total income before *Sec 109A* claim		9,000
Deduct post-cessation expenditure—		
(i)	9,250	
(ii)	800	
(iii)	200	
(iv)	500	
(v)	—	
(vi) *less* expenses unpaid at 5.4.97 (£1,000 − £250)	(750)	
	10,000	
Restricted to total income	(9,000)	(9,000)
Excess relief	£1,000	

60.5 Post-Cessation Etc. Receipts and Expenditure

	£	£
Capital gains		
Gains before losses brought forward and annual exemption		7,500
Deduct excess post-cessation expenditure (as above)		1,000
Net gains for the year		6,500
Losses brought forward	1,000	
Used 1996/97	200	200
Losses carried forward	£800	
Net gains (covered by annual exemption)		£6,300

1997/98

He will have taxable post-cessation receipts of £3,000 arising from the insurance recovery. He will be able to offset expenses of £175 under (v) above which, whilst not within *Sec 109A*, should qualify as a deduction under *Sec 105* (see 60.1 above). He will also have post-cessation expenditure of £250 in respect of the further payment under (vi) above, the 1996/97 post-cessation expenditure having been restricted by more than that amount.

61   Rationalisation Schemes

[Secs 568–572]

61.1   **Contributions,** paid for trade purposes, under schemes (certified by Board of Trade) for **rationalising industry** by eliminating redundant works, plant, machinery, etc. are deductible. [*Secs 568, 572*]. If contribution, or part, is repaid, the original deduction is adjusted. [*Sec 569*]. Where Secretary of State certificate withdrawn, the body carrying on the scheme is assessable, to the extent of its available resources, on contributions not repaid within one year. [*Sec 571*]. **Payments** under such a scheme to a person carrying on, or formerly carrying on a trade, to which the scheme relates are, except in certain circumstances, assessable on him as trading profits. [*Sec 570, 21 Sch Pt II; FA 1996, s 134, 20 Sch 31, 43*].

62   Regional Development Grants

62.1   Regional Development Grants, under *Industry Act 1972, Part I* or *Industrial Development Act 1982, Part II*, were payable on expenditure on certain buildings and certain new plant, machinery and mining works in special development areas, development areas, intermediate areas and derelict land clearance areas (which altogether cover a large part of UK outside S.E. England). Amount of grant does **not** operate to reduce capital expenditure on which CAPITAL ALLOWANCES (10) are claimable except where the grant results in a reduction in the expenditure allowable for the purposes of petroleum revenue tax. [*CAA 1990, s 153(1); Sec 495*]. Any such grant paid under *Industry Act 1972, s 7 or 8* (and certain NI payments made after 31 March 1984) is treated as a trading receipt unless designated as paid for specified capital expenditure or as compensation for the loss of capital assets. [*Sec 93*]. An 'interest relief grant' was held to be a trading receipt (*Burman v Thorn Domestic Appliances (Electrical) Ltd Ch D 1981, 55 TC 493*). See also 71.84 SCHEDULE D, CASES I AND II. Grants under *Industrial Development Act 1982, Part II* to traders, etc. or to investment companies are exempt from income tax. [*Sec 92*].

Similar provisions apply to corresponding grants in NI.

63 Remittance Basis

Cross-references. See RESIDENCE, ORDINARY RESIDENCE AND DOMICILE at 64.4 for domicile, 64.5 for residence, 64.6 for ordinarily resident; NON-RESIDENTS AND OTHER OVERSEAS MATTERS at 51.12 for trades etc. carried on abroad and 51.14 for unremittable overseas income; see 25.3 DOUBLE TAX RELIEF regarding Eire.

63.1 APPLICATION

The remittance basis (i.e. UK tax assessments are restricted to sums actually remitted to the UK out of such income or gains (grossed up in certain cases where credit for foreign tax is allowable, see 25.5(*b*)(i) DOUBLE TAX RELIEF)) applies to UK residents in respect of overseas income and gains as follows.

(A) **Persons not domiciled in the UK.**

   (i) **Capital gains** from disposal of assets abroad (with no allowance for losses arising abroad).

   (ii) **Emoluments** from an employer not resident in UK or Eire where the duties are performed wholly abroad (see 75.2, Case III(*a*) SCHEDULE E) but this only applies if the employee is also ordinarily resident in the UK (otherwise see (B) below).

   (iii) **Investment income etc.** from abroad assessable under SCHEDULE D, CASES IV AND V (73). [*Sec 65(4)(5); FA 1994, s 207(3); FA 1996, s 134, 20 Sch 3*]. But such income from Eire is assessable on the full amount arising, whether remitted or not. [*Sec 68; FA 1994, s 207(5)*].

   (iv) **Pensions** from overseas as described in 59.2 PENSIONS.

   (v) **Trades etc.** controlled abroad, see under 51.12 NON-RESIDENTS AND OTHER OVERSEAS MATTERS. Except trades etc. in Eire. [*Sec 68; FA 1994, s 207(5)*].

(B) **Persons not ordinarily resident in the UK.**
Emoluments in respect of duties performed wholly abroad, see Case III(*b*) in 75.2 SCHEDULE E.

(C) **Persons not ordinarily resident in the UK who are also either British subjects or Eire citizens.**

   Investment income etc.—per (A)(iii) above.
   Pensions—per (A)(iv) above.
   Trades etc.—per (A)(v) above.

Note. Employments are not treated as being abroad for the above purposes if they comprise certain Crown duties or sea or air duties. See 75.2 SCHEDULE E.

63.2 BASIS OF ASSESSMENT

Where assessment is under Schedule D, Cases IV or V (i.e. investment income etc., pensions and trades as under 63.1(A)(iii), (iv) and (v) and (C) above) the remittances to be taken into account are those of the preceding tax year subject to adjustments when a source commences or ceases, or, where the current year basis applies, those of the current year (see 73.9 SCHEDULE D, CASES IV AND V). Otherwise the assessment is on the actual remittances in the tax year (subject to the addition of any foreign tax for which credit is allowable, see 25.5(*b*)(i) DOUBLE TAX RELIEF).

See 25.5(*b*) DOUBLE TAX RELIEF for double tax relief claimable.

63.3   REMITTANCES—GENERAL

A remittance of capital is not taxable as such (unless within the provisions of capital gains tax, see Tolley's Capital Gains Tax) but a taxable remittance may include the proceeds of investments made abroad out of overseas income (*Scottish Provident Institution v Farmer CS 1912, 6 TC 34*). Where the proceeds were of investments made before the taxpayer came to reside in the UK, there was no liability (*Kneen v Martin CA 1934, 19 TC 33*). Similarly a remittance from a foreign bank into which overseas income had been paid may be assessable, dependent on the circumstances. For this see *Walsh v Randall KB 1940, 23 TC 55* (sterling draft on foreign bank in favour of London hospital received by taxpayer before handing to hospital, held to be remittance) and *Thomson v Moyse HL 1960, 39 TC 291* (dollar cheques on US bank sold to Bank of England held to be remitted) and compare *Carter v Sharon KB 1936, 20 TC 229* (drafts on foreign bank posted abroad to taxpayer's daughter for maintenance, held not to be remittance as, under relevant foreign law, gift to daughter completed on posting of draft). See also *Fellowes-Gordon v CIR CS 1935, 19 TC 683*. In *Harmel v Wright Ch D 1973, 49 TC 149* an amount received via two South African companies, ending as a loan from one of them, was held to be a remittance of South African emoluments within Schedule E, Case III. Where, contrary to the customer's instructions, a bank erroneously remitted untaxed overseas income to him, it was held there was no liability (*Duke of Roxburghe's Exors v CIR CS 1936, 20 TC 711*).

63.4   CONSTRUCTIVE REMITTANCES [*Sec 65(6)–(9)*]

Income arising abroad to a person *ordinarily resident* in the UK and which he applies abroad towards the satisfaction of

(*a*)   a debt (or interest thereon) for money lent him in the UK, or

(*b*)   a debt for money lent to him abroad and brought here, or

(*c*)   a loan incurred to satisfy such debts,

is treated as received by him in the UK.

Where an ordinarily resident person imports money lent to him abroad the debt for which has at that time already been wholly or partly satisfied, the loan is treated as a remittance at the date of importation to the extent that the debt is satisfied.

Income **hypothecated in any form to the lender** so that the amount of a loan debt, or the time of its repayment, depends directly or indirectly on the amount of property so available to the lender, is treated as having been applied towards satisfaction of the loan. '*Lender*' includes any person for the time being entitled to repayment.

These provisions regarding constructive remittances are contained in Schedule D, Cases IV and V legislation and are applied to emoluments assessable under Schedule E, Case III by *Sec 132(5)* and to capital gains tax by *TCGA 1992, s 12(2)*.

64   Residence, ordinary residence and domicile

Cross-reference. See 51 NON-RESIDENTS AND OTHER OVERSEAS MATTERS for situations in which the residence, ordinary residence or domicile of an individual may be of relevance for income tax purposes. See generally Revenue Pamphlets IR 20, to which reference is made throughout this chapter, IR 138 and IR 139.

64.1   UK tax liability may depend on a person's **domicile** (the country or state which is his 'natural home', see 64.4 below), on whether or not he is **resident** in the UK for tax purposes in a particular tax year (which is primarily a matter of physical presence, see 64.5 below) or, occasionally, on whether or not he is ordinarily resident in the UK (see 64.6 below). EEC law does not prevent a Member State from imposing more onerous fiscal charges on nationals resident in another Member State than those imposed on resident nationals (*Werner v Finanzamt Aachen-Innenstadt (Case C–112/91) CJEC, 1993 STI 376*).

64.2   A person who is **resident** in the UK is liable to UK tax on all his income and gains, whether from UK or overseas sources, subject to limited categories of EXEMPT INCOME (29).

Assessments are limited to remittances to the UK out of the income or gains in the circumstances listed under REMITTANCE BASIS (63).

Deductions are made from the amounts assessable as follows.

Emoluments. Employments wholly abroad where the employee is abroad for a qualifying period (as defined) of 365 days or more—a deduction of 100% is made (i.e. complete exemption). See 75.3 SCHEDULE E.

Overseas pensions. A deduction of 10% may be made, as set out in 59.1(iv) and 59.2 PENSIONS.

64.3   **Non-residents** are liable to UK tax on UK income, including income from property etc. in the UK, income from trades, professions etc. exercised in the UK [*Sec 18(1)(a)(iii)*] and on emoluments from offices or employments for duties performed in the UK (but see 75.6 SCHEDULE E regarding 'foreign emoluments', being emoluments of a non-domiciled person from a foreign employer). [*Sec 19(1)*].

See also 29.17 EXEMPT INCOME and 33.2 GOVERNMENT STOCKS for the special exemption to non-residents in respect of certain government stocks and 23.12 DEDUCTION OF TAX AT SOURCE for a similar relief in respect of the interest or dividends on certain foreign stocks and securities payable in the UK.

The appropriate double tax agreement should be examined for exemptions and for restrictions on the rates of tax to be borne. Otherwise non-residents are chargeable at the full rate and not entitled to personal or other reliefs. Thus a person carrying on a business in the UK but claiming to be non-resident may thereby have his tax allowances reduced or even refused. But see 51.11 NON-RESIDENTS AND OTHER OVERSEAS MATTERS for reliefs available to certain Commonwealth subjects and others.

Non-residents have no liability on overseas income.

64.4   **DOMICILE**

It may be necessary to determine domicile in relation, *inter alia*, to the assessment of income from foreign possessions and securities (see 73.5 SCHEDULE D, CASES IV AND V), of 'foreign emoluments' (see 75.6 SCHEDULE E) and of certain chargeable gains (see Tolley's Capital Gains Tax).

A person may have only one place of domicile at any given time denoting the country or state considered his permanent home. He acquires a **domicile of origin** at birth (normally that of his father). It may be changed to a **domicile of choice** (to be proved by subsequent conduct). If a domicile of choice is established but later abandoned (by actual action, not by intention or declaration only—see *Faye v CIR* below) reversion to domicile of origin is automatic.

Domicile is a highly technical matter and does not necessarily correspond with either residence or nationality (see *Earl of Iveagh v Revenue Commissioners Supreme Court (IFS) [1930] IR 431, Fielden v CIR Ch D 1965, 42 TC 501*, and *CIR v Cohen KB 1937, 21 TC 301*). This last case shows how difficult it is to displace a domicile of origin by a domicile of choice, but contrast *In re Lawton Ch D 1958 37 ATC 216*. A new domicile of choice may be acquired whilst continuing to be resident in the domicile of origin, but only if the residence in the domicile of choice is the 'chief residence' (*Plummer v CIR Ch D 1987, 60 TC 452*). See also *In re Wallach HC 1949, 28 ATC 486, Faye v CIR Ch D 1961, 40 TC 103, Buswell v CIR CA 1974, 49 TC 334, Steiner v CIR CA 1973, 49 TC 13, CIR v Bullock CA 1976, 51 TC 522, In re Furse decd., Furse v CIR Ch D, [1980] STC 597* and *Re Clore decd. (No 2) Ch D, [1984] STC 609*.

In determining domicile for tax purposes at any time **after 5 April 1996**, no action taken at any time in relation to registration as an 'overseas elector', or in voting as such, is taken into account in determining domicile, unless the person whose liability is being determined (whether or not the person whose domicile is in question) wishes it to be taken into account (in which case the domicile determination applies only for the purpose of ascertaining the liability in question). An '*overseas elector*' is broadly a non-resident British citizen to whom the parliamentary franchise is extended under *Representation of the People Act 1985, s 1* or *s 3*. [*FA 1996, s 200*].

See 64.5 below for administrative procedures for determination of domicile in certain cases.

Married women. Up to 31 December 1973, a woman automatically acquired the domicile of her husband on marriage. From 1 January 1974 onwards, the domicile of a married woman is to be ascertained 'by reference to the same factors as in the case of any other individual capable of having an independent domicile' except that a woman already married on that date will retain her husband's domicile until it is changed by acquisition or revival of another domicile. [*Domicile and Matrimonial Proceedings Act 1973, ss 1, 17(5)*]. But an American woman who married a husband with UK domicile before 1974 will be treated, for determining her domicile, as if the marriage had taken place in 1974. See Article 4(4) of the US/UK Double Tax Agreement. A **widow** retains her late husband's domicile unless she later acquires a domicile of choice (and see *CIR v Duchess of Portland Ch D 1981, 54 TC 648*).

Minors. The domicile of a minor normally follows that of the person on whom he is legally dependent. *Under Domicile and Matrimonial Proceedings Act 1973, s 3* (which does not extend to Scotland), a person first becomes capable of having an independent domicile when he attains 16 or marries under that age. Under *section 4* of that *Act*, where a child's father and mother are alive but living apart, his domicile is that of his mother if he has his home with her and has no home with his father.

64.5   **RESIDENCE**

General. There is relatively little statutory guidance on the determination of the 'residence' of an individual, despite its importance in determining the individual's tax liabilities (see 64.1–64.3 above). It has been held by the courts that residence is a question of fact for the Appeal Commissioners to decide on the particular circumstances of each case, and there are a number of important decisions indicative of the courts' views (see below). See also 64.8 below regarding appeals. A person can be resident for a particular tax year in more than one country for tax purposes (or may even be resident in none).

64.5 Residence, ordinary residence and domicile

For practical purposes, the Revenue's interpretation as set out in Pamphlet IR 20 and other sources referred to below is, subject to appeal, likely to determine the issue in any particular case.

There are three circumstances in which the residence status of an individual is subject to statutory provisions.

(a)   An individual in the UK for some temporary purpose only, and not with the intention of establishing his residence here, is UK resident for any year of assessment in which he is physically present in the UK for six months or more in aggregate, and is not resident for any year of assessment in which he is not physically present in the UK for six months or more. In determining whether the individual is in the UK for some temporary purpose only and not with the intention of establishing his residence here one of the considerations is that an individual is regarded as resident if visits to the UK average 91 days or more per tax year, calculated over a maximum of four years. (Revenue Pamphlet IR 131, SP 2/91, 19 March 1991). For 1993/94 and subsequent years, the question is determined without regard to any 'available accommodation' in the UK (see below). [Sec 336; FA 1993, s 208(1)(4)]. Strictly, periods of time in terms of hours are relevant in determining a period of presence in the UK (see *Wilkie v CIR Ch D 1951, 32 TC 495*) but in practice six months are regarded as 183 days, ignoring (normally) days of arrival and departure. (Revenue Pamphlet IR 20, para 1.2).

(b)   A Commonwealth or Eire citizen whose ordinary residence (see 99.6 below) has been in the UK, and who has left the UK for the purpose only of occasional residence abroad, continues to be UK resident. [Sec 334]. 'Occasional residence' is not defined, but generally refers to short stays on holiday or business trips (and see *Reed v Clark Ch D 1985, 58 TC 528*).

(c)   The residence of an individual working full time in a trade, profession or vocation no part of which is carried on in the UK, or in an office or employment all of the duties of which are performed outside the UK (other than any whose performance is merely incidental to the duties abroad), is determined without regard to any place of abode maintained for his use in the UK. [Sec 335]. As to whether duties are incidental, see *Robson v Dixon Ch D 1972, 48 TC 527* (airline pilot employed abroad but occasionally landing in UK where family home maintained, held UK duties more than incidental). See also Revenue Pamphlet IR 20, paras 6.7, 6.8. 'Full-time' employment (here and in relation to Revenue concession A11 referred to below), in an ordinary case involving a standard pattern of hours, requires an individual putting in what a layman would recognise as a full working week, typically 35–40 hours. See Revenue Tax Bulletin February 1993 p 57 for this and for the Revenue interpretation of the requirement in less straightforward cases.

'Available accommodation' does not depend on ownership but whether any accommodation is in fact maintained for occupation at any time by the individual concerned. A house owned and let out on a lease which denies availability is ignored, as is a renting of less than two years of furnished accommodation (or one year of unfurnished accommodation) during temporary stay. A house owned but left empty of furniture, or only available during a part of the year when the person is not in the UK, or situated too far away from a UK destination visited briefly on business for its use to be practical, may similarly be ignored. (Revenue Pamphlet IR 20, paras 4.2, 4.3, 4.4).

Case law. Resident in Eire making monthly visits to UK as director of British company (having no UK residence, but a permanent one in Eire) held to be resident and ordinarily resident in UK (*Lysaght v CIR HL 1928, 13 TC 511*) (but cf. *CIR v Combe CS 1932, 17 TC 405*). Officer succeeding to Eire estate, intending to return there permanently but prevented by military duties in UK, held on facts to be resident in both countries (*Lord Inchiquin v CIR CA 1948, 31 TC 125*). In *CIR v Brown KB 1926, 11 TC 292* and *CIR v Zorab KB 1926, 11*

TC 289, however, held that retired Indian civil servants making periodical visits to the UK, but having no business interests here, were not UK resident.

An American holding a lease of a shooting box in Scotland and spending two months there every year (*Cooper v Cadwalader CES 1904, 5 TC 101*), and a merchant usually resident and doing business in Italy but owning house in UK where he resided less than six months (*Lloyd v Sulley CES 1884, 2 TC 37*) were both held to be UK resident.

A Belgian who had at his disposal, for the visits he paid here, a house owned not by him but by a company which he controlled, so that it was in fact available whenever he chose to come, was held to be UK resident (*Loewenstein v De Salis KB 1926, 10 TC 424*). In *Withers v Wynyard KB 1938, 21 TC 724*, however, an actress (after 18 months abroad) performing in UK, and for $3\frac{1}{2}$ months in 1933/34 occupying a leasehold flat (unable to be disposed of and sublet when possible), was held to be non-resident for that year.

Where neither the individual nor spouse physically present in UK during tax year, although children here, the individual was non-resident (*Turnbull v Foster CES 1904, 6 TC 206*). See also *Reed v Clark Ch D 1985, 58 TC 528*, where individual held non-resident for tax year of absence from UK during which continuing trade carried on. If, however, either an individual or spouse, while they are still living together, has established a UK family home, any visit during a tax year, however short, to that home, may render the individual UK resident for that tax year (although cf. *Withers v Wynyard* above).

Revenue practice. Revenue Pamphlet IR 20 (to which paragraph numbers in the following text refer) considers the application of the above tests first generally, then in relation to those leaving the UK, then in relation to those coming to the UK.

General. Some physical presence in the UK during a tax year is normally required for an individual to be regarded as UK resident for that year, and the individual will invariably be so regarded where that physical presence is for six months or more in the year (as in (*a*) above). (para 1.2).

Strictly, residence status applies only by reference to whole tax years. By concession, however, an individual coming to the UK to take up permanent residence or to stay for at least two years, or leaving the UK for permanent residence abroad, is treated as UK resident only from the date of arrival or up to and including the date of departure, tax liabilities which are affected by residence status being calculated on the basis of the period of residence. In either case, the Revenue must be satisfied that the person was not ordinarily resident in the UK (see 64.6 below) prior to arrival or on departure. Similarly, subject to the further conditions as described below in relation to leaving the UK, an individual (and accompanying spouse) going abroad under a contract of employment will be so treated only up to and including the date of departure and from the date of return to the UK. The provisions limiting the income chargeable on non-residents (see 51.1 NON-RESIDENTS AND OTHER OVERSEAS MATTERS) do not apply to the non-resident part of a split year. This concession previously applied to temporary visitors coming to stay for at least three years, with a shorter period applying only in the case of those coming to the UK to take up employment expected to last at least two years, but by Revenue Press Release 29 January 1996 the concession was revised to apply the two year period for all temporary visitors. At the same time, an earlier requirement that employment abroad be 'full-time' (see (*c*) above) for the concession to apply was removed. (para 1.5; Revenue Pamphlet IR 1, A11 and A78). See also 73.11, 73.12 SCHEDULE D, CASE VI, 75.3 SCHEDULE E.

Full personal allowances are available for the year permanent residence begins or ends. (para 8.7).

For commentary on aspects of Revenue practice in relation to available accommodation, see ICAEW Technical Release TAX 20/94, 30 November 1994.

64.5 Residence, ordinary residence and domicile

Leaving the UK. Short trips abroad, e.g. on holiday or business trips, do not alter the residence status of a person who usually lives in the UK (see (*b*) above). (para 2.1).

An individual (and accompanying spouse) leaving to work abroad 'full-time' (see (*c*) above) under a contract of employment is treated as non-UK resident provided that both the absence from the UK and the employment cover a complete tax year; that any interim visits to the UK do not amount to either 183 days or more in any tax year or an average of 91 days or more per tax year (averaged over a maximum of four years, and ignoring days spent in the UK for exceptional circumstances beyond the person's control, for example own or family illness); and (for 1992/93 and earlier years) that all (other than incidental) duties of the employment were performed abroad. These conditions are applied separately in relation to the employee and the accompanying spouse, but must be satisfied by the employee for the concession to be available to the accompanying spouse. Also, in relation to the accompanying spouse, and for 1992/93 and earlier years, where accommodation was available in the UK, the concession applied only where there were no visits to the UK in the tax year, or after departure in the tax year of departure or before return in the tax year of return. See also 64.6 below as regards ordinary residence of the accompanying spouse. (paras 2.2–2.5).

An individual leaving the UK permanently is nevertheless treated as continuing to be UK resident if visits to the UK average 91 days or more per tax year. (For 1992/93 and earlier years, this also applied to any visit to the UK, however short, where accommodation was available in the UK for the individual's use (see below).) (para 2.6). Some evidence will normally be required in support of a claim to have become non-resident (and non-ordinarily resident, see 64.6 below), e.g. steps taken to acquire a permanent home abroad, and, if UK property is retained, a reason consistent with the stated aim of permanent residence abroad. If such evidence is satisfactory, UK residence (and ordinary residence) may provisionally be treated as ceasing on the day after departure from the UK. Such provisional treatment is confirmed (where appropriate) after a full tax year abroad (apart from permissible UK visits, as above). Otherwise, UK residence will provisionally be treated as continuing for up to three years, and the final decision will be based on what actually happened following departure from the UK. (paras 2.7, 2.8).

Coming to the UK. UK residence (and ordinary residence, see 64.6 below) will commence on the date of arrival in the UK where an individual whose home has been abroad comes to the UK to live here permanently or intending to stay for three years or more (or, in some cases, two years or more—see Revenue Press Release 29 January 1996). (para 3.1). Otherwise, the visitor will be treated as resident for a tax year in which they are in the UK for 183 days or more in the year (see (*a*) above), or from the fifth tax year where in the preceding four tax years regular visits have been made to the UK averaging 91 days or more per tax year (disregarding days spent in the UK due to exceptional circumstances beyond the individual's control, for example own or family illness). If such visits are clearly intended on arrival in the UK, residence will commence with the first of those four years. Otherwise, if the decision to make such visits is taken before the start of the fifth year, residence will commence with the year in which the decision was taken. (For 1992/93 and earlier years, a visitor for whose use available accommodation (see above) was maintained in the UK was treated as resident for any tax year in which a visit was made to the UK, however short.) (para 3.3).

The ownership, or acquisition on a lease of three years or more, of UK accommodation will be taken as indicating an intention to stay for three years or more (as above). (Revenue Press Release 16 March 1993).

It is understood that, in practice, an individual arriving in the UK with no fixed intentions regarding residence but who during the visit sets up a permanent residence in the UK is deemed resident and ordinarily resident from the date of arrival, provided that that date and the date of change of plan fall within the same tax year. Back assessments are understood to be made only where the visitor's intentions on arrival were admitted or quite clear.

An individual who comes to the UK not as a short-term visitor but with the intention of remaining in the UK may be regarded as UK resident even if UK visits are within the above limits. Whether an individual is a short-term visitor will depend on e.g. the reason for coming to the UK and the general background to the normal living pattern. An habitual visitor who stays in accommodation owned or available for less than 91 days in each tax year is unlikely to have the intention of remaining in the UK for at least three years and would, if this is so, be treated as a short-term visitor. (Taxation Practitioner October 1994, p 26).

An individual coming to the UK for employment of two years or more is treated as resident from the day of arrival to the day of departure (see above as regards split years generally). For shorter or uncertain periods of employment, UK residence will apply for a tax year only where 183 days or more are spent in the UK in the year (or, for 1992/93 and earlier years, where UK accommodation was available for the individual's use, see above). (para 3.6).

As regards visits for education, see 64.6 below.

Administrative procedures. Individuals who come to the UK to take up employment are asked to complete Form P86 to enable their residence status to be considered. This form also now includes a section on domicile so that, in straightforward cases (where, e.g., a person never domiciled in the UK comes here only to work and with the intention of leaving the UK when the employment ceases), the two matters may be dealt with together. In less straightforward cases, Form DOM1 has been introduced to obtain the information necessary to the determination of domicile. On leaving the UK, a shortened Form P85 (Form P85(S)) has been introduced to enable any repayment to be claimed in straightforward cases. Otherwise, Form P85 continues to be used.

As regards individuals who are not regarded as ordinarily resident in the UK on arrival, enquiries as to any change in circumstances now begin only after a complete tax year has elapsed since arrival, although individuals are expected to report any actual changes in their circumstances without delay, whether or not that period has elapsed. (Revenue Press Release 8 September 1994).

Residence of trustees and personal representatives. For 1989/90 onwards, where at least one of the trustees of a settlement is non-UK resident and at least one is UK resident, then provided that the settlor (including any person providing or undertaking to provide funds directly or indirectly for the settlement) satisfies a further condition (or, if there is more than one settlor, that at least one of them satisfies that condition), the non-UK resident trustee(s) is (are) treated as UK resident for income tax purposes. Otherwise, the UK resident trustee(s) is (are) treated as not resident in the UK and as resident elsewhere for those purposes.

Similar rules apply to determine the residence of personal representatives for 1989/90 onwards.

The condition to be met in relation to trustees is that the settlor is resident, ordinarily resident or domiciled in the UK at a 'relevant time'. A 'relevant time' is the time of the settlor's death in relation to a testamentary disposition or intestacy, otherwise it is the time, or each of the times, when he has provided funds for the settlement. In relation to personal representatives, the condition is that the deceased was resident, ordinarily resident or domiciled in the UK at the time of his death. For 1989/90 only, the condition as to residence, etc. is deemed not to have been satisfied, in the case of trustees if none of the trustees of a settlement is UK resident at any time in the period 1 October 1989 to 5 April 1990 inclusive, in the case of personal representatives if none of the personal representatives of the deceased is UK resident in that period.

See 3.8 ANTI-AVOIDANCE as regards certain circumstances in which the above rules do not apply. [*FA 1989, ss 110, 111*].

64.6 Residence, ordinary residence and domicile

Special provision is made for the assessment of trustees and personal representatives to income tax. See 80.3 SETTLEMENTS.

64.6 ORDINARY RESIDENCE

The term 'ordinary residence' is not defined in the *Taxes Acts*. See below for the case law on its interpretation. Broadly, it denotes greater permanence than the term 'residence' (see 64.5 above), and is equivalent to habitual residence; if an individual is resident year after year, he is ordinarily resident. An individual may be resident in the UK under the six months rule of *Sec 336* (see 64.5(*a*) above) without becoming ordinarily resident. Equally, he may be ordinarily resident without being resident in a particular year, e.g. because he usually lives in the UK but is absent on an extended holiday throughout a tax year. (Revenue Pamphlet IR 20, para 1.3).

An individual will be treated as ordinarily resident in the UK if he visits the UK regularly and either has available accommodation (see 64.5(*c*) above) or his visits average 91 days or more per tax year (ignoring days spent in the UK for exceptional circumstances beyond his control, for example his own or family illness). (Revenue Pamphlet IR 20, para 3.4).

If an individual regarded as ordinarily resident solely because of the availability of accommodation disposes of it and leaves the UK within three years of arrival, he is normally treated as not ordinarily resident for the duration of his stay (assuming this is to his advantage). (Revenue Pamphlet IR 20, para 3.12).

See 64.5 above for administrative procedures in certain cases.

Longer-term visitors—commencement of ordinary residence. The Revenue practice is to treat an individual coming to the UK, but not intending to stay more than three years (and not buying or leasing for three years or more accommodation for use in the UK), as ordinarily resident from the beginning of the tax year following the third anniversary of arrival. If, before the beginning of that tax year, either there is a change in the individuals' intention (i.e. to an intention to stay in the UK for three years or more in all) or accommodation for use in the UK is bought (or leased for three years or more), ordinary residence is treated as commencing at the beginning of the tax year in which either of those events happens (or from the date of arrival in the UK if later). For individuals coming to the UK before 6 April 1988, this practice applied only to those coming to the UK for employment. For other visitors, ordinary residence was treated as commencing either from the beginning of the tax year which included the third anniversary of arrival or from the beginning of the following tax year, depending on the amount of time spent in the UK in the tax year of arrival. (Revenue Pamphlet IR 131, SP 17/91, 4 December 1991 and Revenue Pamphlet IR 20, paras 3.8–3.11).

Education. A student who comes to the UK for a period of study or education and will be in the UK for less than four years will be treated as not ordinarily resident providing (i) he does not own or buy (or lease for three years or more) accommodation in the UK, and (ii) he will not, following his departure from the UK, be returning regularly for visits averaging 91 days or more per tax year. (Revenue Pamphlet IR 20, para 3.13).

Spouse accompanying employee working overseas. Where a person going abroad for full-time employment (see 64.5 above) was accompanied by a spouse who was within the concession (Revenue Pamphlet IR 1, A11) described at 64.5 above, and who retained available accommodation in the UK, the accompanying spouse was treated as not ordinarily resident throughout the period of absence, provided that the absence was three years or more and UK visits averaged less than 91 days per tax year. Where an intended period of absence of three years or more was cut to less than three years because of the unexpected termination of the spouse's employment, the shorter period might qualify provided that it included a complete tax year and UK visits averaged less than 91 days per tax year. (Revenue Pamphlet IR 1, A78).

Cases

In *Reid v CIR SC 1926, 10 TC 673*, British subject held '*ordinarily resident*' here although no fixed residence either here or abroad and regularly absent abroad $8\frac{1}{2}$ months every year. But she had here an address, family ties, banking account and furniture stored.

Levene v CIR HL 1928, 13 TC 486 was decided similarly. (British subject abroad for health reasons since 1918, no fixed residence here since (or abroad till 1925), but having ties with this country and in the 'usual ordering of his life', making habitual visits to UK 20 weeks yearly for definite purposes.) The judgments in this case interpreted the meaning of 'ordinarily resident' by the following phrases: 'habitually resident', 'residence in a place with some degree of continuity', and 'according to the way a man's life is usually ordered'. In *Peel v CIR CS 1927, 13 TC 443*, although appellant had his business and house in Egypt, he was held ordinarily resident here because he also had a house here, and spent an average of 139 days of each year in the UK.

In *Kinloch v CIR KB 1929, 14 TC 736*, a widow living mostly abroad with a son at school here, who had won an appeal in previous years but continued regular annual visits, was held to be resident and ordinarily resident.

In *Elmhirst v CIR KB 1937, 21 TC 381* appellant held on facts to have been ordinarily resident although denying any intention at the time to become so. And see *Miesegaes v CIR CA 1957, 37 TC 493* (minor at school here for five years, spending the occasional vacation with his father in Switzerland, held ordinarily resident). See also cases under 64.5 above.

In *R v Barnet London Borough Council (ex p. Nilish Shah) HL 1982, [1983] 1 AER 226* (a non-tax case), the words 'ordinarily resident' were held to mean 'that the person must be habitually and normally resident here, apart from temporary or occasional absence of long or short duration'.

64.7   **VISITS ABROAD AND CLAIMS TO NON-RESIDENCE (AND TO NON-ORDINARY RESIDENCE)**

Visits abroad are differentiated as follows.

(*a*)   **Absence from UK for full-time work abroad.** An individual working abroad in the circumstances specified in 64.5(*c*) above will normally be regarded as not resident and not ordinarily resident for his period of absence if the period includes at least one complete tax year and if his visits to the UK do not exceed the limits specified in 64.5(*a*) and (*b*) above. (Revenue Pamphlet IR 20 para 2.2).

(*b*)   **Absence from UK for other reasons.** Where an individual goes abroad and intends to remain abroad, he may claim to be treated, provisionally, as not resident and not ordinarily resident for the period of absence. Such a claim must be supported by suitable evidence (e.g. acquiring permanent living accommodation abroad and making appropriate arrangements in relation to any property owned in the UK) and will be reviewed after he has remained abroad throughout a complete tax year, with UK visits averaging less than 91 days per year. (Revenue Pamphlet IR 20, paras 2.6, 2.7).

If there is not sufficient evidence at the time of his departure abroad to support a claim for non-residence etc., the individual will be regarded as continuing to be resident and ordinarily resident for his first three years abroad. His position will then be reviewed and, if it is decided that he has been non-resident etc., his tax liabilities will be adjusted accordingly. (Revenue Pamphlet IR 20, para 2.8).

In any event, an individual will be regarded as resident in the UK in the circumstances described in 64.5(*a*) above, and as both resident and ordinarily resident in the circumstances described in 64.5(*b*) above. (Revenue Pamphlet IR 20, paras 3.3, 3.4).

64.8   Residence, ordinary residence and domicile

See 64.5 above as regards the relevance of available accommodation in the UK for 1992/93 and earlier years.

64.8   APPEALS

Ordinary residence and domicile in relation to Schedule E and CGT are determined by the Board. [*Sec 207*]. Claims to the remittance basis in respect of overseas income on the grounds of ordinary residence or domicile outside the UK (see 73.5 SCHEDULE D, CASES IV AND V), claims to the special reliefs referred to at 64.3 above and certain double tax claims (see 25.5(*e*) DOUBLE TAX RELIEF) are made to the Board. Any appeal from a Board decision is to the Special Commissioners [*TMA 2 Sch 3*] and the normal time limit of 30 days is extended to three months if on a question of residence, ordinary residence or domicile. [*TMA s 42(3)(b)*]. Other disputes regarding residence are settled by way of appeal against the relevant assessment in the ordinary way.

65   Retirement Annuities and Personal Pension Schemes

Cross-references. See 53.16 PARTNERSHIPS for partnership retirement annuities and 66 RETIREMENT SCHEMES generally.

General note. The provisions under *Secs 618–629* for retirement annuity contracts for the self-employed and those in non-pensionable employment are, for new schemes, replaced, after 30 June 1988, by the new regime for personal pension schemes under *Secs 630–655*, designed to encourage employees who wish to do so to opt out of company pension schemes in favour of independent arrangements not linked to any one employment. Retirement annuity schemes contracted before 1 July 1988 continue, however, to be dealt with under the earlier provisions now in *Secs 618–629*, and the new personal pension scheme provisions adopt many of the features of those earlier provisions.

The headings in this chapter are as follows.

<table>
<tr><td>65.1</td><td>Retirement annuities</td><td>65.9</td><td>Unused relief carried forward</td></tr>
<tr><td>65.2</td><td>Personal pension schemes</td><td>65.10</td><td>—example</td></tr>
<tr><td>65.3</td><td>Contract requirements</td><td>65.11</td><td>Cancellation of retirement</td></tr>
<tr><td>65.4</td><td>—retirement annuity contracts</td><td></td><td>annuity contract</td></tr>
<tr><td>65.5</td><td>—personal pension schemes</td><td>65.12</td><td>Relevant earnings</td></tr>
<tr><td>65.6</td><td>Limits of relief</td><td>65.13</td><td>Trust schemes</td></tr>
<tr><td>65.7</td><td>—example</td><td>65.14</td><td>Example</td></tr>
<tr><td>65.8</td><td>Premiums related back</td><td></td><td></td></tr>
</table>

65.1   RETIREMENT ANNUITIES

Where an individual pays a 'qualifying premium' in a year of assessment under a contract made before 1 July 1988 and approved by the Board of Inland Revenue under *Sec 620* or *Sec 621*, the amount of that premium may, subject to certain limits (see 65.6 below), be deducted from his 'relevant earnings' (see 65.12 below) as assessed for that year from a trade, profession, vocation, office or employment. [*Secs 618(1), 619(1), 620(1); FA 1988, s 54*]. These arrangements do not apply to income from a pensionable office or employment (see 65.12 below). Retirement annuity premiums are not deductible in arriving at profits for

Class 4 national insurance purposes (see 82.7 SOCIAL SECURITY). [*Social Security Contributions and Benefits Act 1992, 2 Sch 3(2)(f)*]. See 65.2 below as regards personal pension contributions.

Relief may be granted on a provisional basis in respect of renewal premiums, whether fixed or variable, without proof of payment being required before the due date for payment of tax (although proof of payment is of course required in due course). (Revenue Tax Bulletin May 1992 p 19).

An annuity payable under such a contract (so far as it derives from premiums in respect of which relief was given) is treated as earned income when received by an annuitant to whom it is made payable under the terms of the contract. [*Sec 619(1)*]. It will normally be paid under deduction of tax under Schedule D, Case III (see 23.11 DEDUCTION OF TAX AT SOURCE), although it is understood that the Revenue may accept its being dealt with under PAYE (55) where appropriate.

65.2   PERSONAL PENSION SCHEMES

With effect after 30 June 1988, relief similar to that available for retirement annuity premiums (see 65.1 above) is available in respect of contributions payable by an individual under arrangements made in accordance with a 'personal pension scheme' (see 65.5 below). The amount of such contributions paid in a year of assessment may, subject to certain limits (see 65.6 below), be deducted from the individual's 'relevant earnings' (see 65.12 below) as assessed for that year. In the case of Schedule E employees, and subject to conditions prescribed by regulations (see *SI 1988 No 1013*), relief is given by deduction of basic rate tax, which may be recovered by the scheme administrator. The Revenue consider that where a payment *may* be made under deduction of basic rate tax, basic rate relief can *only* be obtained by deduction. Relief other than by deduction at source, and higher rate relief in all cases, is given on a claim being made (on form PP120) by deduction or set off in an assessment. The tax deducted from valid contributions is not clawed back where the individual is liable only at the lower rate of income tax or has no income tax liability. The Inland Revenue Financial Intermediaries and Claims Office may be contacted in relation to personal pensions on 0151–472 6173 as regards repayments or 0151–472 6159 for technical advice.

In addition, any contribution to such a scheme by the employer is not chargeable to tax on the individual under Schedule E. There are provisions for adjustment of relief following alterations in the individual's liability to tax, and for the prevention of double relief. [*Secs 639, 640, 643(1), 655(4); FA 1988, s 54*].

Income and gains on scheme investments are exempt from income tax and capital gains tax, and there are similar reliefs in relation to authorised unit trusts which are also approved personal pension schemes. [*Sec 643(2); TCGA 1992, s 271(1)(h)(j)*]. See 71.32 SCHEDULE D, CASES I AND II as regards futures and options contracts.

There are special provisions relating to MPs' salaries. [*Sec 654*].

An annuity payable under such a scheme is treated as earned income of the annuitant to whom it is made payable by the terms of the arrangements. Annuity payments made after 5 April 1995 are dealt with under PAYE, rather than (as previously) being paid under deduction of tax under Schedule D, Case III (see 23.11 DEDUCTION OF TAX AT SOURCE) (unless the Board direct that Schedule D, Case III shall apply until a specified date). [*Secs 643(3)(4), 648A; FA 1994, s 109*]. Income withdrawals (within 65.5(ii) or (iv) below) are also earned income of the recipient assessable under Schedule E and dealt with under PAYE. [*FA 1995, 11 Sch 11*]. Payments, etc. from a scheme to or for the benefit of an individual who has made arrangements in accordance with the scheme, but which are not authorised under scheme rules, are chargeable under Schedule E on that individual [*See*

647], as are contributions by the employer to such a scheme where the arrangements are not approved (see 65.5 below). [*Sec 648*].

Where a lump sum refund of contributions is paid under 65.5(viii) below in a case where the member's death occurred after he had elected for income withdrawals under 65.5(ii) below, the scheme administrator is charged under Schedule D, Case VI on the gross payment at the rate of 35% (variable by Treasury order). [*Sec 648B; FA 1995, 11 Sch 12*].

Contributions to personal pension schemes are not deductible in arriving at profits for Class 4 national insurance purposes (see 82.7 SOCIAL SECURITY). [*Social Security Contributions and Benefits Act 1992, 2 Sch 3(2)(g)*]. See 65.1 above as regards retirement annuity premiums.

Information and penalties. The inspector may require information on scheme contributions and refunds, and copies of scheme accounts. There are penalties for giving false information in support of an application for approval (see 65.5 below) or for the purpose of obtaining relief from or repayment of tax under these provisions, or for failure to supply information as above or in relation to regulations regarding deduction of tax from contributions (see above). [*Secs 652, 653; TMA s 98; FA 1989, s 170(4)*].

See generally Revenue Pamphlet IR 78.

65.3   **CONTRACT REQUIREMENTS**

Broadly similar requirements as to the terms which must apply are laid down for retirement annuity contracts (see 65.4 below) and personal pension schemes (see 65.5 below).

65.4   **Retirement annuity contracts. For approval under Sec 620,** the annuity contract must have as its main object the provision for an individual of a life annuity in old age. It must be made by an individual with a person carrying on life annuity business in the UK, and, subject as follows, **must preclude**

(*a*)   any payment during the life of the individual other than a life annuity to him commencing not earlier than age 60 and not later than age 75, and

(*b*)   any payment after his death other than

    (i)   a life annuity (not greater than his original annuity) to his surviving spouse, or

    (ii)   if no annuity becomes payable either to the individual or his spouse, the return of premiums paid, with reasonable interest or bonuses out of profits.

An annuity under *Sec 620* may, if so provided and if the individual so elects before the annuity first becomes payable, be *partially commuted* for a lump sum not exceeding three times the annual amount of the remaining part of the annuity, but subject to this all annuities must be incapable of total or partial surrender, commutation or assignment.

For approved contracts made after 16 March 1987 (but before 1 July 1988), however, the maximum lump sum which may be paid to the individual is £150,000 (or such other sum as may be specified by Treasury order), regardless of the terms of the contract. Alternatively, the individual and the person(s) to whom premiums are payable were able jointly to elect (before the end of January 1988) for the approval of the contract to be cancelled *ab initio*.

But the Inland Revenue may, conditionally, approve a contract, otherwise satisfying the above, even though it contains one or more of the following provisions:

    (i)   the individual's life annuity to commence at age earlier than 60 in the event of his becoming incapacitated from carrying on his occupation, or any similar one,

(ii) the individual's life annuity to commence earlier than age 60 if his occupation is one in which retirement before that age is customary (see below),

(iii) a life annuity, after the individual's death, for a dependant other than the surviving spouse,

(iv) an annuity to continue for a term certain (not exceeding 10 years) despite death within that term, and for such an annuity to be capable of assignment by will, or by the annuitant's personal representatives in distributing his estate,

(v) suspension, or termination, of the annuity, in the event of marriage, remarriage, or otherwise,

(vi) the value of the accrued rights to be paid as a premium for another approved annuity contract or personal pension scheme, if required by the individual, widow, widower or dependant having the accrued rights.

[*Secs 618(2)(4), 620(1)–(4); FA 1988, s 54*].

As regards (ii) above, the following early retirement ages have been agreed by Super-annuation Funds Office.

30 Downhill skiers.

35 Athletes; badminton players; boxers; cyclists; dancers; footballers; models; National Hunt jockeys; real tennis players; Rugby League players; squash players; table tennis players; tennis players; wrestlers.

40 Cricketers; divers (saturation, deep sea and free swimming); golfers; motorcycle riders (motocross or road racing); motor racing drivers; speedway riders; trapeze artistes.

45 Flat racing jockeys; Royal Marine reservists (non-commissioned).

50 Croupiers; money broker dealers; newscasters (ITV); offshore riggers; Royal Naval reservists; Rugby League referees; Territorial Army members.

55 Air pilots; brass instrumentalists; distant water trawlermen; firemen (part-time); inshore fishermen; moneybroker dealer directors and managers responsible for dealers; nurses, physiotherapists, midwives or health visitors who are females; psychiatrists (who are also maximum part-time specialists employed within the NHS solely in the treatment of the mentally disordered); singers.

These pension ages apply only to arrangements funded by contributions in respect of relevant earnings from the occupation or profession in question. For professional sportsmen, the earnings must arise from activities as such, e.g. tournament earnings and appearance and prize money, and not from sponsorship or coaching (for which separate arrangements may be made).

(Revenue Pamphlet IR 76).

For approval under Sec 621, (term assurance or family income cover) the contract must be made by an individual with a person carrying on life annuity business in the UK. It must either

(*a*) have as its main object the provision of a life annuity for the surviving spouse or other dependants of the individual, or

(*b*) have as its sole object the provision of a lump sum on the death of the individual before age 75.

Unless the Revenue otherwise allow, a contract within (*a*) must also satisfy the following conditions:

65.5 Retirement Annuities and Personal Pension Schemes

    (i)   any annuity payable must be incapable of total or partial surrender, commutation or assignment;

    (ii)   if payable to the individual's surviving spouse or dependant, it must be a life annuity commencing on the individual's death;

    (iii)   if payable to the individual, it must be a life annuity commencing after the age of 60 and, unless payable as a result of the death of a person to whom an annuity would otherwise have been payable, commencing before the age of 75;

    (iv)   if, as a result of death, no annuity is payable, the only sums which may be paid under the contract are by way of return of premiums, reasonable interest on premiums or bonuses out of profits.

[*Sec 621(1)–(4)*].

65.5   **Personal pension schemes. For approval under Sec 631, a personal pension scheme must be established by:**

    (*a*)   a person authorised under *Financial Services Act 1986, Pt I, Ch III* to carry on investment business, and who carries on business either of issuing insurance policies or annuity contracts or of managing authorised unit trust schemes (see 90.1 UNIT TRUSTS);

    (*b*)   a building society (see 9 BUILDING SOCIETIES);

    (*c*)   a pension company which is an associate of a building society;

    (*d*)   an institution authorised under *Banking Act 1987* or a subsidiary or holding company (or a subsidiary of the holding company) of such an institution;

    (*e*)   a recognised bank or licensed institution within *Banking Act 1979*; or

    (*f*)   such other person as the Treasury may specify by order.

There must be a person responsible for administration of the scheme who is resident in the UK. These conditions do not apply to trust schemes established before 1 July 1988 (see 65.13 below). [*Secs 632, 638(1); FA 1988, s 54; SI 1988 No 993*].

The scheme may not provide for benefits to an individual participant other than the following.

    (i)   A life annuity payable to the participant, commencing not earlier than age 50 and not later than age 75 (subject to provision for earlier commencement in the same circumstances as apply in relation to retirement annuities, see 65.4 above) and which, · except as detailed at (v) below, must not be capable of assignment or surrender.

    (ii)   Where scheme (or amendments) are approved on or after 1 May 1995, income withdrawals, i.e. payments of income other than by way of annuity, during a period of deferral of the purchase of an annuity under (i) above, where the participant so elects. Income withdrawals may not commence before the participant attains the age of 50 (subject to provisions for earlier commencement as under (i) above) and must not continue after the participant attains the age of 75. The right to such income withdrawals must not be capable of assignment or surrender. The aggregate income withdrawals in each successive twelve month period starting with the 'pension date' must be between 35% and 100% (inclusive) of the annual amount of the annuity purchasable on the 'relevant reference date'. The *'pension date'* for this purpose is the date on which the member elects to make income withdrawals, and the *'relevant reference date'* is the pension date for the first three years of withdrawals, and thereafter the first day of each successive three year period. The annuity purchasable on any such date is determined by reference to the value on that date, as determined by the scheme administrator, of the accrued rights under the scheme (net of any lump sum payable on that date) and the Government Actuary's annuity rate tables (copies of which may be obtained free of charge from Supplies Section, Pension Schemes Office, Yorke House, PO Box 62, Castle Meadow Road, Nottingham NG2 1BG (tel. 0115–974 1670)).

(iii) A life annuity payable after the death of the participant to the surviving spouse or to a dependant, which, except as detailed at (v) below, must not be capable of assignment or surrender. Such an annuity may, however, cease on the marriage of the annuitant or, in the case of an annuity to a surviving spouse, if there ceases to be any dependant under the age of 18 before the surviving spouse attains age 45. An annuity to a dependant under 18 at the time the annuity first becomes payable *must* cease on his attaining age 18 or on the later of his attaining age 18 and ceasing full-time education, unless the dependancy was not only because of his being under age 18.

The aggregate of such annuities (or if they vary the initial aggregate) must not exceed the annuity (or highest annuity) payable to the participant under the scheme or, if he died before receiving an annuity under the scheme, the highest annuity that would have been payable under the scheme (ignoring any lump sum commutation, see (vi) below) had it been purchased on the day before his death.

An annuity to a surviving spouse who is under 60 at the time of the participant's death may be deferred to a time not later than the attainment of that age or, if an annuity is payable for a term certain under (v) below which terminates after attainment of that age, the termination of that annuity.

(iv) Where schemes (or amendments) are approved on or after 1 May 1995, income withdrawals (as under (ii) above) during a period of deferral of the purchase of an annuity under (iii) above, where the person entitled to the annuity so elects. (No such withdrawals could be made where an annuity had become payable under (i) above.) The limitations on the amount of withdrawals are as under (ii) above but by reference to the date of death of the participant rather than the date of election for income withdrawals. Withdrawals may not be made where an annuity under (iii) above has been deferred until the surviving spouse attains age 60, or after the payments under an annuity purchased under (iii) above by the person concerned would have ceased, or after the earlier of either that person or the participant attaining the age of 75. The right to such income withdrawals must not be capable of assignment or surrender.

(v) An annuity as at (i) or (iii) above may continue for a term certain not exceeding ten years if the original annuitant dies within that term, and such an annuity may be assigned by will or by the annuitant's personal representatives in distributing his estate. The annuity is regarded as being for a term certain even if it may terminate on the happening, after the original annuitant's death but within that term, of the marriage of the annuitant to whom it becomes payable, or of his attaining age 18, or of the later of his attaining age 18 and ceasing full-time education.

(vi) If the participant so elects, the benefits under the scheme may be partially commuted for a lump sum at the time when the annuity at (i) above is first payable or the time at which he elects to make income withdrawals under (ii) above. The lump sum must not exceed one-quarter of the difference between the total value at that time of the benefits under the scheme and the value at that time of the protected rights under *Social Security Act 1986* (or NI equivalent) (except that where the scheme came into existence before 27 July 1989, the protected rights reduction did not apply as regards arrangements made before that day), and must not be capable of assignment or surrender. In relation to schemes approved before 27 July 1989, the reduction for protected rights was not required, but is nevertheless treated as being included in the rules where the lump sum arrangements are made on or after that date. There was also an overriding limit on the lump sum of £150,000 (variable by Treasury order), but any scheme rule applying a fixed limit (other than in relation to lump sums payable out of transfer payments) is treated as not applying to lump sums payable on or after that date.

(vii) A lump sum may be payable on the death of the participant before age 75.

(viii) If no annuity under (i) or (iii) above has become payable at the time of the participant's death, a lump sum representing a return of contributions with reasonable interest or bonuses (or if contributions are invested in a unit trust scheme, the sale or redemption price of the units) may be payable. Where schemes (or amendments) are approved on or after 1 May 1995, the lump sum may be payable on or after the participant's death, but, where the death occurred after the participant had elected for income withdrawals (within (ii) above), within two years after the death (and see 65.2 above as regards charge to tax on lump sums so payable). Also in relation to such approvals, a refund of contributions is after allowing for any withdrawals within (ii) or (iv) above, no lump sum may be paid to a surviving spouse who has elected for deferral to age 60 under (iii) above, and the prohibition where an annuity has become payable under (iii) above applies only to a lump sum payable to the person who purchased the annuity. Where schemes (or amendments) are approved on or after 29 April 1996, a lump sum may also be payable (without time limit) on the death of a person who has deferred an annuity and taken income withdrawals under (iv) above (the lump sum being required to take account of any annuity purchased under (iii) above in favour of another person).

A scheme may also make provision for insurance against a risk relating to the non-payment of contributions.

Where a scheme is approved on or after 1 May 1995, it must (except in such cases as may be prescribed by regulations) prohibit the acceptance of further contributions and the making of transfer payments after the date on which an annuity within (i) above is first payable or the participant elects for income withdrawals within (ii) above. In the latter case, minimum contributions within (C) below may continue to be accepted with effect from 6 April 1996. [*SI 1996 No 805*].

An annuity within (i) or (iii) above or a lump sum within (vii) above must be payable by an authorised insurance company, which in the case of (i) and (iii) above may be chosen by the participant or the annuitant. For the definition of 'authorised insurance company', see *Sec 630* and, from 1 May 1995, *Sec 659B, 659C* introduced by *FA 1995, ss 59(4)(5), 60*.

[*Secs 630, 633–637A; FA 1989, 7 Sch 2, 11, 12; F(No 2)A 1992, 9 Sch 17; FA 1995, 11 Sch 1–8; FA 1996, s 172*].

A scheme must also satisfy any requirements laid down by the Board as to the making, acceptance and application of transfer payments. [*Sec 638(2)*]. See *The Personal Pension Schemes (Transfer Payments) Regulations 1988 (SI 1988 No 1014)* and *(Amendment) Regulations 1989 (SI 1989 No 1115)*.

Contributions may only be accepted from

(A)   the individual participants in the scheme,

(B)   their employers, and

(C)   in respect of certain minimum contributions (the 'contracted-out' rebate), the Secretary of State.

Contributions within (A) and (B) above by or in respect of a participant, together with those under any other schemes arranged by the participant, must not exceed the permitted maximum (see 65.6 below) for the year of assessment. Any excess must be repaid to the participant to the extent of his contributions, otherwise to the employer. A scheme must not accept contributions within (C) above in respect of service as a director whose emoluments are excluded from being relevant earnings (see 65.12 below), and such minimum contributions may only be accepted where either the participant is not in pensionable employment at the time the contributions are paid, or the scheme rules prohibit acceptance of contributions from the participant or employer.

[*Sec 638(3)–(8); FA 1988, s 55(2)(4); FA 1995, 11 Sch 9*].

Approval by the Board cannot be effective before 1 July 1988. Regulations provide for provisional approval to be granted. [*Sec 655(4)(5); FA 1988, s 54(2)(c); SI 1987 No 1765; SI 1988 No 1437; FA 1989, 7 Sch 9*].

Withdrawal of approval. If, in the Board's opinion, the facts concerning a personal pension scheme do not warrant the continuance of approval, it may be withdrawn. Approval may similarly be withdrawn in relation to any individual arrangements made under such a scheme. Withdrawal must be by written notice to the scheme administrator (and to the individual if appropriate), and must state the grounds for withdrawal and the date from which it is effective (which must not be before the date when the facts first warranted withdrawal). Approval may be withdrawn from the date on which arrangements were made where, in the Board's opinion, the securing of the provision of benefits under the arrangements was not the sole purpose of the individual in making them. [*Sec 650*].

Appeals against refusal or withdrawal of approval must be made to the Board within 30 days of the notice of refusal or withdrawal, and lie to the Special Commissioners. Their decision on an appeal against withdrawal may be to alter the effective date of the withdrawal. [*Sec 651*].

65.6   LIMITS OF RELIEF

Retirement annuity contracts. The amount of qualifying premiums which may be deducted from relevant earnings in any year of assessment is subject to an overall limit which is a percentage of 'net relevant earnings' in that year (see 65.12 below). See 65.9 below for relief carry-forward. [*Sec 619(2)(3)*].

The overall limit is $17\frac{1}{2}$% of net relevant earnings although older individuals are allowed a higher percentage (see below). Premiums paid under *Sec 621* approved contracts may not exceed 5% of net relevant earnings, and are included in the overall limit of $17\frac{1}{2}$%.

Increased limits for older individuals. The overall limits are increased as indicated in the following table where the individual is in the age range indicated at the beginning of a year of assessment.

51 to 55	20%
56 to 60	$22\frac{1}{2}$%
61 or more	$27\frac{1}{2}$%

[*Sec 626*].

Personal pension plans. A contribution paid by an individual under approved personal pension arrangements may be deducted from or set off against 'relevant earnings' for the year of assessment in which the payment is made. The maximum amount for which relief is available is $17\frac{1}{2}$% of 'net relevant earnings' (see 65.12 below), with increased limits for older individuals as indicated in the following table where the individual is in the age range indicated at the beginning of 1989/90 or any subsequent year of assessment.

36 to 45	20%
46 to 50	25%
51 to 55	30%
56 to 60	35%
61 or more	40%

65.7 Retirement Annuities and Personal Pension Schemes

For 1988/89, the limits were as for retirement annuities (see above). For 1989/90 onwards, any excess of 'net relevant earnings' over an allowable maximum is disregarded. The allowable maximum is the same as the 'permitted maximum' referred to at 66.4 RETIREMENT SCHEMES (i.e. £82,200 for 1996/97). Any employer contribution is deducted from the overall contribution limit, but minimum contributions within 65.5(C) above are ignored for this purpose. Within the overall limit, contributions to secure a lump sum payable on the death of the participant are limited to 5% of 'net relevant earnings'. [Secs 639(1), 640; FA 1989, 7 Sch 3, 4; FA 1995, 11 Sch 10].

Where relief is also available for qualifying retirement annuity premiums in a year of assessment, the relief available for personal pension contributions is correspondingly reduced. [Sec 655(1)(a)].

65.7   *Example*

C is an employee whose date of birth is 30 April 1944 and who does not participate in his employer's occupational pension scheme. His earnings, as computed for Schedule E purposes, for 1995/96 and 1996/97 are £80,000 and £84,000 respectively. C pays annual retirement annuity premiums of £6,000 under long-standing contracts. For all years up to and including 1994/95, he has paid additional retirement annuity premiums and personal pension scheme contributions so as to take maximum advantage of the relief available to him; he thus has no unused relief.

In August 1995, C makes a contribution of £12,900 (less basic rate tax) to a personal pension scheme. In December 1995, his employer contributes £750 to this scheme.

In the year ended 5 April 1997, C and his employer make contributions of £18,000 (less basic rate tax) and £1,000 respectively to the scheme.

The maximum relief is calculated as follows.

1995/96

	£	£
Maximum relief for personal pension contributions:		
25% of net relevant earnings of £78,600		19,650
Deduct retirement annuity relief claimed	6,000	
employer's contribution	750	6,750
Relief due		12,900
Amount paid		12,900
Unused relief		Nil

	£
Maximum relief for retirement annuity premiums:	
17½% of net relevant earnings of £80,000	14,000
Amount paid	6,000
	8,000
Less relief claimed for personal pension contributions	12,900
Unused relief	Nil
Total relief due (£12,900 + £6,000)	£18,900

1996/97

	£	£
Maximum relief for personal pension contributions:		
30% of net relevant earnings of £82,200		24,660
Deduct retirement annuity relief claimed	6,000	
employer's contribution	1,000	7,000
Relief due		17,660
Amount paid		18,000*
Unused relief		Nil

	£
Maximum relief for retirement annuity premiums:	
20% of net relevant earnings of £84,000	16,800
Amount paid	6,000
	10,800
Less relief claimed for personal pension contributions	17,660
Unused relief	Nil
Total relief due (£17,660 + £6,000)	£23,660

* For 1996/97, there are excess contributions of £340 which do not qualify for relief, and which must be repaid. Such an excess is deemed to relate primarily to contributions made by the individual rather than by his employer (see 65.5 above).

65.8   **PREMIUMS RELATED BACK**

Retirement annuity contracts. An individual who pays a qualifying premium in a year of assessment (whether or not he has relevant earnings for that year) may elect that the premium (or part of it, see Tolley's Practical Tax 1982 p 132) be treated as paid

(a)   in the last preceding year of assessment, or

(b)   if he had no net relevant earnings in the last preceding year, in the last preceding year but one.

For premiums paid in 1996/97 and later years, the election must be made on or before 31 January following the year of assessment in which the premium is paid. For earlier years, the election had to be made before the end of the year of payment although the Revenue normally allowed concessionally an additional three months, i.e. up to and including 5 July following the year of payment.

Where such an election is made, the premium is treated as having been paid in the year elected and not in the year actually paid. [*Sec 619(4); FA 1996, s 135, 21 Sch 17*]. An election is in practice treated by the Revenue as operative only up to the maximum available for relief for the year specified in the election. If the amount specified in the election becomes excessive as a result of an adjustment to the assessment for the year specified, the unrelievable proportion will fall back into the actual year of payment. (Tolley's Practical Tax 1984 p 158).

For years before 1997/98, *Lloyd's underwriters* may elect that a qualifying premium paid in the year may be related back to the third previous year of assessment before the year of payment (i.e. a premium paid in 1994/95 may be related back to relevant earnings assessed for 1991/92). The earlier year must have unused relief attributable to relevant earnings from Lloyd's underwriting activities. The election must be made before the end of the year of assessment in which the premium is paid. Where such an election is made the normal provisions for relating back premiums under *Sec 619(4)* above do not apply. The election ceases to be available for 1997/98 and subsequent years, for which the basis of assessment of Lloyd's underwriters is changed (see 89.2 UNDERWRITERS). [*Sec 627; FA 1993, s 183(3); FA 1994, s 228(2)(4)*].

Premiums (or parts) under **personal pension schemes** may similarly be related back. The election, whether under the general relief or in relation to Lloyd's underwriters, must be made, for premiums paid in 1996/97 and later years, on or before 31 January following the year of assessment in which the premium is paid (for earlier years, on or before 5 July following that year of assessment). [*Sec 641; FA 1993, s 183(3); FA 1994, s 228(2)(4); FA 1996, s 135, 21 Sch 18*]. Form PP43 is available from the inspector for the purpose of making such an election.

See 78.33 SELF-ASSESSMENT for provisions regarding claims for payments made in one year of assessment to be carried back to an earlier year.

65.9 **UNUSED RELIEF CARRIED FORWARD**

Retirement annuity contracts. Relief available for a year of assessment which is not used in that year may be carried forward and used to cover that part of a qualifying premium paid in any of the next six years which exceeds the relief limit (see 65.6 above) for that year. Relief is given in the year in which the premium is paid although the maximum relief for that year must be used first. Unused relief for earlier years must be used before that for later years.

Where an assessment on an individual's earnings becomes final and conclusive more than six years after the end of the year to which it relates, and as a result there is an amount of unused relief for that year, that amount shall not be available for any of the following six years. However that relief may be covered by a qualifying premium paid within six months of the date on which the assessment becomes final and conclusive. Relief is given in the year of assessment in which the premium is paid but is not allowed unless the maximum premium allowable for that year (see 65.6 above) is paid. Although the extra premium representing the unused relief must be paid within the specified six months, the maximum premium for the year of assessment in which the extra premium is paid may be paid at any time within the normal time limits for that year. If relief is given for a premium in this way, it may not be given under the normal carry-forward rule. [*Sec 625*]. Relief is given in a similar way where relevant earnings for a year which ended more than six years previously are not formally assessed but are taken into account in an offer in settlement in a back duty case. See 6.11 BACK DUTY.

Where contributions are made under approved personal pension arrangements (see 65.2 above) in a year of assessment, the unused relief that may be utilised in that year is correspondingly reduced. [*Sec 655(1)(b)*].

Relief is similarly available in respect of premiums under **personal pension schemes**. [*Sec 642*]. Form PP42 is available from the inspector for claiming such relief. Unused retirement annuity relief may be carried forward and used to cover personal pension scheme premiums. [*Sec 655(3)*].

65.10 *Example*

P, who was born in 1972, entered non-pensionable employment in September 1993 and his recent personal pension scheme contribution record, assuming no unused relief before 6 April 1993, is as follows.

Year	Net relevant earnings £	Maximum relief due £	Amount paid £	Unused relief £
1993/94	15,000	2,625	2,425	200
1994/95	19,000	3,325	2,200	1,125
1995/96	22,000	3,850	3,375	475

In 1996/97, P pays a personal pension scheme contribution of £5,000 (less basic rate tax). His net relevant earnings for that year are £24,000.

P has excess contributions for 1996/97 as follows.

Net relevant earnings	£24,000

	£
Maximum relief (£24,000 × 17½%)	4,200
Contributions made	5,000
Excess contributions	£800

Tax relief on the excess contributions can be obtained in the following way.

In 1995/96
£475 may be related back to 1995/96 and relief obtained in that year (see 65.8 above).

In 1996/97
The remainder (£325) is matched on a first in, first out basis with the unused relief brought forward (see 65.9 above).

	£	£
Excess contributions as above		800
Deduct amount related back to 1995/96		475
		325
Unused relief 1993/94	200	
Unused relief 1994/95	125	325

Thus, full relief is obtained for the £5,000 paid in 1996/97 and P's revised relief record is as follows.

Year	Net relevant earnings £	Maximum relief due £	Amount relieved £	Unused relief £	Unused relief c/f £
1993/94	15,000	2,625	2,425	200	200
1994/95	19,000	3,325	2,200	1,125	1,325
1995/96	22,000	3,850	3,850	—	1,325
1996/97	24,000	4,200	4,525	(325)	1,000

Notes

(a)   The balance of the 1994/95 unused relief, i.e. £1,000, will have to be utilised by 5 April 2002 (i.e. 6 years plus 1 year carry-back).

(b)   As an alternative to carrying back £475 to 1995/96, P could have utilised an additional £475 of his 1994/95 unused relief and obtained relief in 1996/97 for the whole of the £5,000 paid in that year. The £475 unused relief for 1995/96 would then be carried forward together with £525 of the 1994/95 relief. A further possibility is to carry back £1,800 to 1995/96, thus utilising all unused relief in that year and leaving £1,000 unused relief for 1996/97. This would be advantageous if the taxpayer's marginal tax rate were higher in the earlier year.

65.11   CANCELLATION OF RETIREMENT ANNUITY CONTRACT

The Pension Schemes Office has indicated that cancellation of a policy under a retirement annuity contract may be agreed to where there has been some fundamental misconception as to the nature of the policy. Where the Life Office accepts that a valid case of misapprehension by the taxpayer has arisen, and is anxious to cancel the policy *ab initio* and refund the premiums paid, the matter would be viewed sympathetically. Such a case may be settled on the basis that there was no valid contract at the outset, so that *Sec 620(2)* would not be breached. It is for the taxpayer to contact the Life Office, who should then approach the Pension Schemes Office. This would not extend to the case where a contract has been in existence for a number of years, and a premium is subsequently paid which for some reason is not fully tax-relieved. (Tolley's Practical Tax 1983 p 157, 1985 p 22).

See 65.5 above as regards refund of personal pension scheme contributions.

65.12   RELEVANT EARNINGS

Retirement annuities. '*Relevant earnings*' of an individual is chargeable income which is included in one of the following categories.

(a)   Income from an office or employment which is not a 'pensionable office or employment', and income from property which is either attached thereto or which forms part of the emoluments therefrom. This includes amounts assessed as benefits in kind. It would also appear to include any amounts charged in respect of profits on shares acquired under share incentive schemes (see 81.4 SHARE INCENTIVES AND OPTIONS), but averaged over three year periods (Tolley's Practical Tax 1983 p 157) and the excess over the exempt limit of any lump sum termination payment (see 19.6 COMPENSATION FOR LOSS OF EMPLOYMENT (AND DAMAGES)) (Tolley's Practical Tax 1986 p 165).

(b)   Income chargeable under Schedule D immediately derived from the carrying on, individually or in partnership, of his trade, profession or vocation. This includes enterprise allowances (see 71.84 SCHEDULE D, CASES I AND II) and POST-CESSATION RECEIPTS (60).

(c)   Income from patent rights treated as earned income under *Sec 529*.

It does not include remuneration of a controlling director of an investment company. A married woman's relevant earnings are her own and not her husband's for the purpose of determining entitlement to retirement annuity relief. The amount from each such source is the statutory income of the year of assessment (i.e. ignoring any 'conventional' basis of assessment—see Tolley's Practical Tax 1982 p 131) before deducting capital allowances (other than those actually deductible in computing profits) but inclusive of any balancing charges. [*Secs 623(1)(2)(5), 624(3); FA 1989, 12 Sch 15*]. See 75.32 SCHEDULE E as regards treatment as relevant earnings of certain payments to redundant steel workers.

As regards (b) above, for 1992/93 and earlier years, underwriting profits of non-working Names at Lloyd's are not 'relevant earnings' for these purposes (*Koenigsberger v Mellor CA, [1995] STC 547*). This ceases to apply from 1993/94 by virtue of *FA 1993, s 178* (see 89.3 UNDERWRITERS).

A '*pensionable office or employment*' is one to which any sponsored superannuation scheme applies which provides for retirement, etc., and under which any part of the cost is borne otherwise than by the holder of the office etc. (and is not assessable under Schedule E rules on him). An office or employment may be 'pensionable' even if the holder performs the duties partly outside the UK or is not chargeable to tax in respect of it. If the holder of such an office, etc., having an option, does not join the scheme, his office is treated, for this purpose, as non-pensionable. [Secs 623(3)(4), 624(1)(2)]. By concession, where an individual is treated as in pensionable employment solely because provision is made under a scheme or arrangement existing on 14 October 1980, fully or partly at the cost of the employer, for a benefit in pension form payable only on death or disability, the employment will be treated as non-pensionable for any tax year in which the individual has not become entitled to benefit as a result of that provision. Relief will be available on a year to year basis for the period of employment or until benefit becomes payable. Employment in the tax year in which such a contingency occurs will be regarded as pensionable and no retirement annuity relief will be available for that year, but relief given for previous years will not be affected. (Revenue Pamphlet IR 1, A38). The Pension Schemes Office has ruled that an office or employment is non-pensionable up to the date on which the employee, etc. first becomes entitled to benefits under a retirement scheme, even if these benefits are calculated by reference to earlier periods of service. (Tolley's Practical Tax 1982 p 131). It is, however, understood that where an employee receives a refund of contributions paid while in pensionable employment, that employment is *not* thereby rendered non-pensionable. (Tolley's Practical Tax 1986 p 135, 1990 p 95). See below, however, as regards personal pension schemes.

'*Net relevant earnings*' are relevant earnings, as above, less deductions which would be made therefrom in computing the individual's total income for income tax, being

(i)   deductions which but for *Sec 74(m), (p) or (q)* could be made in computing his profits or gains (i.e. various payments, subject to deduction of tax at source, made for business purposes—excluding e.g. annuities to former partners, which would be prohibited under *Sec 74(a)*—see Tolley's Practical Tax 1983 p 73), or

(ii)   deductions in respect of losses, or of capital allowances, relating to activities any profits from which would be relevant earnings of the individual (or, for 1989/90 and earlier years, the individual's spouse). [*Sec 623(6); FA 1988, 14 Sch Pt VIII*].

Other amounts deducted in charging the individual's income to tax (e.g. for earnings from work done abroad, see 75.3 SCHEDULE E, or under the current provisions) do not reduce net relevant earnings.

Where an individual has relevant earnings but no other income, and he obtains 100% capital allowances on the cost of constructing a small workshop for letting, the capital allowances will not reduce his net relevant earnings for retirement annuity relief purposes (Tolley's Practical Tax 1981 p 59).

If, in any year for which an individual claims relief, a deduction for a loss or allowance under (ii) above is treated as made to any extent out of income other than relevant earnings, his net relevant earnings for the next year are treated as reduced to that extent, any balance being carried forward to the third year, and so on. [*Sec 623(7)*].

In the case of partnership profits, net relevant earnings are the share of partnership income (as computed for tax purposes) after allowable deductions for partnership payments and capital allowances. [*Sec 623(9)*].

Personal pension schemes. '*Relevant earnings*' of an individual for the purposes of such schemes is chargeable income which is included in one of the following categories.

(A)   Income from an office or employment which is not 'earnings from pensionable employment', and income from property which is either attached thereto or forms part of the emoluments therefrom.

(B)   Income chargeable under Schedule D immediately derived from the carrying on, individually or in partnership, of his trade, profession or vocation. This includes enterprise allowances (see 71.84 SCHEDULE D, CASES I AND II) and POST-CESSATION RECEIPTS (60).

(C)   Income from patent rights treated as earned income under *Sec 529*.

It does not include any amount in respect of which tax is chargeable under Schedule E which arises from acquisitions or disposals of shares or interests in shares, or from rights to acquire shares, or any amount in respect of which tax is chargeable under *Sec 148* (see 19.5 COMPENSATION FOR LOSS OF EMPLOYMENT (AND DAMAGES)). Nor does it include income of the individual as director of a company whose income is wholly or mainly investment income and which is controlled (within *Sec 840*) by the individual, with or without past or present directors of the company. After 5 April 1989, it does not include emoluments of a person who is a 'controlling director' at any time in the year of assessment in question, or who has been one at any time during the period of ten years prior to that year, if at any time in the year of assessment any of the following circumstances apply to him.

(I)   He is in receipt of benefits under a 'relevant superannuation scheme' payable in respect of past service with the company.

(II)   He is in receipt of benefits under a personal pension scheme, the scheme has received a transfer payment from a 'relevant superannuation scheme', and the transfer payment was in respect of past service with the company.

(III) He is in receipt of benefits under a 'relevant superannuation scheme', the benefits are payable in respect of past service with another company, and the emoluments are for a period during which the company of which he is a 'controlling director' has carried on a trade or business previously carried on by the second company, which itself carried on the trade or business at any time during the period of service in respect of which the benefits are payable.

(IV)   He is in receipt of benefits under a personal pension scheme, the scheme received a transfer payment from a 'relevant superannuation scheme', the transfer payment was in respect of past service with another company, and the emoluments are for a period during which the company of which he is a 'controlling director' has carried on a trade or business previously carried on by the second company, which itself carried on the trade or business at any time during the period of service in respect of which the transfer payment was made.

A person is a *'controlling director'* if he is a director within *Sec 612(1)* and comes within the meaning of *Sec 417(5)(b)* (which broadly refers to ownership, or direct or indirect control, with or without associates, of 20% or more of ordinary share capital). *'Relevant superannuation scheme'* has the same meaning as in *Sec 645(1)* (see below). References to benefits and transfer payments payable in respect of past service include benefits and transfer payments partly so payable.

In determining 'net relevant earnings' (see below), relevant earnings are determined before deducting capital allowances (other than those deductible in computing profits) but inclusive of any balancing charges.

A married woman's relevant earnings are *not* relevant earnings of her husband for these purposes. [*Sec 644; FA 1989, 7 Sch 5, 12 Sch 16*].

See above under 'Retirement annuities' as regards earnings of Lloyd's underwriters.

'Earnings from pensionable employment' are earnings from an office or employment in respect of service in which the individual is a participant in a 'relevant superannuation scheme'. Such schemes under which benefits are restricted to an annuity to a surviving spouse or dependant and/or a lump sum on death in service are disregarded for this purpose, and for

1988/89 a scheme is similarly disregarded if any sums paid pursuant to it for the provision of benefits are treated as the individual's income for tax purposes. Where the only benefit paid under a scheme in respect of a period of employment was a refund of contributions (or where no benefit accrued in a non-contributory scheme), it is understood that earnings from that employment are relevant earnings for the purposes of carry-forward of unused relief (see 65.9 above) under a personal pension scheme. (Tolley's Practical Tax 1990 p 95). This does *not* apply in relation to retirement annuity contracts (see above).

A '*relevant superannuation scheme*' is a scheme established by a person other than the individual concerned, an object of which is the provision of retirement benefits, and which, in relation to 1989/90 and subsequent years, is (or, in the case of certain foreign emoluments, corresponds to) a scheme within 66.1(*a*)–(*c*) RETIREMENT SCHEMES.

It is irrelevant for this purpose where the duties of the office or employment are performed, and whether or not the individual is chargeable to tax in respect of it. [*Sec 645; FA 1989, 7 Sch 6*].

'*Net relevant earnings*' are generally defined in the same way as for retirement annuities (see above), except that deductions made by virtue of *Sec 198* (allowable expenses), *Sec 201* (professional subscriptions) or *Sec 332(3)* (clergymen's expenses) are made from relevant earnings. [*Sec 646*]. For 1989/90 and subsequent years of assessment, however, where an individual holds two or more 'associated' employments in a year, at least one of which is pensionable (as above) and one not, the earnings from the non-pensionable employment(s) are taken into account only to the extent that those from the pensionable employment(s) do not exceed the allowable maximum (see 65.6 above). Employments are '*associated*' if one employer controls the other, or both are controlled by a third person, directly or indirectly, at any time in the year. [*Sec 646A; FA 1989, 7 Sch 8*].

65.13   TRUST SCHEMES

The retirement annuity provisions also apply to contributions under a trust scheme, approved by the Inland Revenue, administered in the UK and established under irrevocable trusts by *a body representing a substantial proportion of the individuals engaged* (in UK, or in England, Scotland, Wales or NI) *in a particular occupation* (or group of occupations), for providing retirement annuities for them, with or without subsidiary benefits for their families or dependants. If the scheme is approved, income from investments or deposits of any fund maintained for the purpose of that fund is exempt from income tax. Gains are similarly exempt from capital gains tax. [*Secs 620(5)(6), 621(5); TCGA 1992, s 271(1)(d)*]. See 71.32 SCHEDULE D, CASES I AND II as regards futures and options contracts.

Relief ceases to be available under such schemes to a person by whom contributions are first paid after 30 June 1988, even though the scheme may have been established on or before that date. [*Sec 618; FA 1988, s 54*].

65.14   *Example*

Interaction between personal pension contributions and retirement annuity premiums
Y is self-employed and pays both retirement annuity premiums (RAPs), under a pre-1 July 1988 contract, and contributions to a personal pension scheme (PPCs). He had no unused relief brought forward at 6 April 1989, on which date he was 47 years of age. His net relevant earnings (NRE), RAPs paid and PPCs paid in each of the years 1989/90 to 1996/97 are as set out below. At no time does Y elect to carry back an RAP or a PPC to a previous year.

65.14 Retirement Annuities and Personal Pension Schemes

	NRE £	Earnings cap £	PPCs paid £	RAPs paid £
1989/90	58,000	60,000	—	10,000
1990/91	67,000	64,800	6,400	10,000
1991/92	72,000	71,400	7,000	10,000
1992/93	74,000	75,000	8,000	10,000
1993/94	78,000	75,000	12,000	10,000
1994/95	90,000	76,800	16,500	10,000
1995/96	120,000	78,600	14,000	10,000
1996/97	125,000	82,200	16,510	10,000

Y's records of amounts paid and tax relief given will look as follows

Personal pension contributions (PPCs)

	NRE £	Maximum PPC relief £	RAPs relieved £	PPCs paid £	Unused relief For year £	Cumulative £
1989/90	58,000	14,500 (1)	(10,000)	—	4,500	4,500
1990/91	64,800	16,200 (1)	(10,000)	(6,400)	(200)	4,300
1991/92	71,400	17,850 (1)	(10,000)	(7,000)	850	5,150
1992/93	74,000	18,500 (1)	(10,000)	(8,000)	500	5,650
1993/94	75,000	22,500 (2)	(10,000)	(12,000)	500	6,150
1994/95	76,800	23,040 (2)	(10,000)	(16,500)	(3,460)	2,690
1995/96	78,600	23,580 (2)	(10,000)	(14,000)	(420)	1,850 (3)
1996/97	82,200	24,660 (2)	(10,000)	(16,510)	(1,850)	Nil

(1) = Relief at 25%
(2) = Relief at 30%
(3) = £2,690 b/f *less* £420 relieved in 1995/96 *less* £420 remaining for 1989/90 which cannot be carried forward beyond 1995/96 (although relief for the £420 could have been obtained by an election to treat part of the 1996/97 premium as having been paid in 1995/96). The £1,850 consists of the aggregate unused relief for 1991/92, 1992/93 and 1993/94.

The aggregate for each year of the 'RAPS relieved' and 'PPCs paid' columns above represents the total relief given in each year.

Retirement annuity premiums (RAPs)

	NRE £	Maximum RAP relief £	RAPs relieved £	Unused relief £	PPCs paid £	Unused relief c/f £
1989/90	58,000	10,150 (4)	(10,000)	150	—	150
1990/91	67,000	11,725 (4)	(10,000)	1,725	(6,400)	(150)*
1991/92	72,000	12,600 (4)	(10,000)	2,600	(7,000)	Nil*
1992/93	74,000	12,950 (4)	(10,000)	2,950	(8,000)	Nil*
1993/94	78,000	15,600 (5)	(10,000)	5,600	(12,000)	Nil*
1994/95	90,000	18,000 (5)	(10,000)	8,000	(16,500)	Nil*
1995/96	120,000	24,000 (5)	(10,000)	14,000	(14,000)	Nil
1996/97	125,000	25,000 (5)	(10,000)	15,000	(16,510)	Nil*

(4) = Relief at 17.5%
(5) = Relief at 20%

* Unused relief carried forward cannot be reduced to a negative figure, so is merely reduced to nil.

Notes

(a)   The maximum relief for PPCs for any year is reduced by any RAPs relieved in that year (see 65.6 above). One effect of this is that if a combination of RAPs and PPCs is to be relieved in any year, the maximum relief available for that year (excluding unused relief brought forward) is restricted by reference to the earnings cap.

(b)   In computing unused retirement annuity relief for any year, any PPCs relieved in that year must be deducted (see 65.9 above).

(c)   The maximum relief for the eight years illustrated (taking the higher of the two maxima for each year) is £161,590. The total relief given is £160,410. Of the difference of £1,180, £420 is unused relief for 1989/90 which is lost under the six-year rule. The balance of £760 arises from the operation of the earnings cap for 1995/96 and 1996/97.

65.15   **MIS-SOLD PERSONAL PENSIONS ETC.**

See 29.3 EXEMPT INCOME for the exemption from income and capital gains tax of compensation awards for mis-sold personal pensions, etc. The Revenue will use their discretionary powers to permit such compensation to be paid in to top up the personal pension or supplement the retirement annuity contract. (Revenue Press Release REV 23, 28 November 1995).

66 Retirement Schemes for Employees

(See also Revenue Pamphlet IR 12 (1991) as amended by later Memoranda and Updates issued by the Inland Revenue Pension Schemes Office at Yorke House, PO Box 62, Castle Meadow Road, Nottingham NG2 1BG.

Cross-references. See 59 PENSIONS generally and in respect of overseas pension funds; 65 RETIREMENT ANNUITIES AND PERSONAL PENSION SCHEMES.

The headings in this chapter are as follows.

66.1 **WHETHER PAYMENTS BY EMPLOYER ARE ASSESSABLE ON EMPLOYEE**

Payments by an employer pursuant to a 'retirement benefits scheme' for the provision of 'relevent benefits' for an employee are treated as income of that employee unless

(a) the scheme is approved by the Inland Revenue, or

(b) the scheme is a 'relevant statutory scheme', or

(c) the scheme is set up by a non-UK government for the benefit (or primarily for the benefit) of its employees, or

(d) the employee exercises his employment outside the UK so that no tax is chargeable under Cases I or II of SCHEDULE E (75), or

(e) the employee receives 'foreign emoluments' (i.e. those of a non-domiciled person working for non-resident employer) and the scheme corresponds to (a), (b) or (c) above.

[Secs 595(1), 596(1)(2); FA 1989, 6 Sch 8].

See Revenue Explanatory Booklet 'The Tax Treatment of Top-Up Pension Schemes' for the Revenue view of when a charge arises under Sec 595(1). Where a payment has been the subject of such a charge, the employer should provide the employee with a notice of the charge, which the employee should retain in order to show that benefits arising under the scheme are not chargeable to tax under Sec 596A (see 66.9 below).

'Retirement benefits scheme' is defined in Sec 611 as including any scheme, deed or arrangement (even if for single employee and even if the pension is to commence immediately) providing 'relevant benefits'. Benefits payable to the employee's wife or widow, children, dependants or personal representatives are included. [Sec 595(5)]. A national scheme is not included. [Sec 611(1)].

'Relevant benefits' are any pension, lump sum, gratuity, etc. either (i) on retirement or death, or (ii) in anticipation of retirement, or (iii) in connection with past service, after retirement or death, or (iv) in anticipation of or in connection with any change in the nature of the employee's service, *other than* benefits afforded solely by reason of accidental disablement or death by accident during employment. [*Sec 612(1)*].

A '*relevant statutory scheme*' is a statutory scheme established before 14 March 1989 or established on or after that date and entered in the register maintained by the Board for that purpose. [*Sec 611A; FA 1989, 6 Sch 15*].

As regards certain lump sum payments on retirement, etc., see 66.12 below.

Employee is widely defined in *Sec 612(1)* and includes a director.

66.2   LIFE ASSURANCE RELIEF

Where approval was not obtained, and the payment by the employer is made under such an insurance or contract that life assurance relief (see 45.1 LIFE ASSURANCE POLICIES) would be obtained if made by the individual, then that individual is eligible for life assurance relief thereon. [*Sec 595(1)(b)*].

66.3   CONDITIONS FOR APPROVAL—HISTORY

Up to 5 April 1973, schemes for employees generally could be approved under *ICTA 1970, s 208* and a scheme for specific individuals (often referred to as a 'top-hat' scheme) could be approved under *ICTA 1970, s 222*.

After 5 April 1973, new schemes, or existing schemes materially altered, had to comply with new provisions which apply to *all* schemes after 5 April 1980 when *ICTA 1970, ss 208, 220–225* were repealed. [*FA 1971, 3 Sch*]. See 66.13 below.

Schemes existing at 5 April 1973 accordingly had to be amended to comply with the new provisions on or before 5 April 1980, in order for approval to be continued after that date.

66.4   CONDITIONS FOR APPROVAL AFTER 5 APRIL 1973 [*ICTA 1988, Pt XIV, Ch 1; FA 1988, 3 Sch 18; FA 1989, 6 Sch 3, 4; FA 1991, ss 34–36*]

Subject to provision for discretionary approval (see below), the following conditions apply.

(*a*)   The scheme must be established in connection with a trade or undertaking carried on in the UK by a UK resident, and there must be a UK resident who will be responsible for carrying out all statutory duties imposed on the administration of the scheme.

(*b*)   The employer must contribute to the scheme and both he and the employees to whom the scheme relates must recognise it, every employee who is, or has a right to be, a member of the scheme being given particulars of all essential features of it which concern him.

(*c*)   The sole purpose of the scheme must be to provide employees (or their widows (or, after 5 April 1990, widowers), children, dependants or personal representatives) with 'relevant benefits' (see 66.1 above)

   (i)   on, after, or in anticipation of, *retirement at a specified age*, which must be not later than 75 or earlier than 60 (before 25 July 1991, the upper and lower ages were 70 and 60, or 70 and 55 if the employee is a woman),

   (ii)   on, or after, *death*,

   (iii)   on, or in anticipation of, or in connection with, *a change in the nature* of the employee's service with the employer.

(*d*)   Employee's contributions must not be returnable in any circumstances (but see 66.5(*c*) below regarding existing schemes).

(*e*)   The employee's pension must not exceed *one-sixtieth* of his final remuneration for each year of service up to a maximum of 40. '*Final remuneration*' is the average annual remuneration of the last three years' service.

(*f*)   No pension may be commuted except where the scheme allows an employee to do so. A lump sum so obtained must not exceed *three-eightieths* of the employee's final remuneration for each year of service up to a maximum of 40; i.e. the maximum lump sum is $1\frac{1}{2}$ years' pay. (For schemes approved after 16 March 1987 and before 27 July 1989, and for any person who before 1 June 1989 became a member of a scheme which came into existence before 14 March 1989 but was not approved before 27 July 1989, there was excluded from final remuneration for this purpose any excess over £100,000.)

(*g*)   The normal pension payable to the widow (or, after 5 April 1990, widower) of an employee dying after retirement must not exceed *two-thirds of the pension*.

(*h*)   Approval may be withdrawn if in the Board's opinion its continuance is not warranted, from a specified date (not earlier than that on which the facts first ceased to warrant approval). An alteration to a scheme invalidates any earlier approval unless the alteration has been approved by the Board, either specifically or in general regulations.

(*i*)   Where more than one retirement benefits scheme applies to a particular class or description of employees, approval of any such scheme, so far as it relates to such employees, is considered by reference to all such schemes. The schemes to be considered are specified as schemes approved or seeking approval under these provisions, funds within *Sec 608* (see 66.13 below) and any relevant statutory schemes (see 66.1 above).

[*Secs 590, 591B, 612(1); FA 1989, 6 Sch 3(4); FA 1991, ss 34, 36*].

As regards (*a*) above, with effect from 3 May 1994, there are detailed provisions for determining who is the administrator of a scheme, responsible for all the tax affairs of the scheme. Broadly, the administrator of a scheme set up under a trust is the trustee or trustees of the scheme, and the administrator of a scheme not set up under a trust is the sponsor or sponsors of the scheme. In either case a different person or persons (who must be UK resident) may be appointed as administrator by written notice, and such person(s) must be so appointed if none of the trustees or sponsors, as the case may be, is UK resident. Such an appointment made after the establishment of the scheme is an alteration of the scheme requiring Revenue approval. [*Sec 611AA; FA 1994, s 103(1)*]. Previously, the administrator was the person or persons having the management of the scheme. [*Sec 612(1); FA 1994, s 103(2)*]. There are provisions dealing with the position where a scheme has no administrator (e.g. where the trustees or sponsors are non-UK resident and have made no appointment), or no administrator can be traced, or the administrator is in default (considered serious by the Board). In such cases responsibilities and liabilities pass to any UK resident trustee or sponsor who can be traced (where a different administrator has been appointed), or ultimately to the employer (provided that the employer is a contributor to the scheme—failing which, if the scheme is a trust scheme, they pass to the sponsor(s) of the scheme) or the UK branch or agent of a non-UK resident employer. [*Sec 606; FA 1994, s 104*].

Further restrictions are introduced by *FA 1989, 6 Sch* which apply to schemes approved after 26 July 1989 but, where a scheme came into existence before 14 March 1989, only as regards new members after 31 May 1989.

(i)   Where an employee is a member of a scheme by virtue of two or more 'relevant associated employments', or of a scheme which, in relation to the employee, is 'connected with' one or more other approved schemes, new limits on pension and commuted pension are applied by reference to a 'relevant amount' and to the aggregate payable in respect of all such employments or schemes.

(ii) In arriving at an employee's final remuneration for the purposes of (*e*) or (*f*) above, any excess over the 'permitted maximum' for the year in which his participation in the scheme ceases is disregarded. Where this restriction applies, the earlier permitted maximum referred to in (*f*) above is abolished.

Employments are '*relevant associated employments*' for this purpose if an employee has held both or all of them, and become entitled to benefits in respect of both or all of them, during a period during which both or all of the employers were 'associated', and a scheme is '*connected with*' another in relation to an employee if a period of service under both of two 'associated' employers gives rise to entitlement to benefits under one scheme by reference to service with one employer and under the other scheme by reference to service with the other employer. Employers are '*associated*' if one is 'controlled' by the other or both are 'controlled' by a third person. '*Control*' may be direct or indirect and in relation to companies is determined in accordance with *Sec 840* (or, if the company is a close company, *Sec 416*).

The '*relevant amount*' is, in the case of pensions, 1/60th, and in the case of commuted pension, 3/80ths of the 'permitted maximum' for the year of assessment in which the benefits become payable, for each year of qualifying service (up to a maximum of 40), with a corresponding allowance for part years. Where there are relevant associated employments, all periods counting for benefit at the time the benefits become payable are taken into account, but periods counting by virtue of more than one such employment are included only once. Where schemes are connected with one another in relation to the employee, all periods counting for benefit for the purposes of all the connected schemes at the time the benefits become payable are taken into account, but periods counting for the purposes of more than one scheme are included only once.

The '*permitted maximum*' is £60,000 for 1988/89 and 1989/90, and is thereafter increased in line with the retail prices index (unless Parliament sets a different figure), being £64,800 for 1990/91, £71,400 for 1991/92, £75,000 for 1992/93 and 1993/94, £76,800 for 1994/95, £78,600 for 1995/96 and £82,200 for 1996/97. It is not reduced if the retail prices index falls.

[*Secs 590(3), 590A–590C; FA 1989, 6 Sch 3(2)(3), 4; SI 1990 No 679; SI 1991 No 734; SI 1992 No 624; FA 1993, ss 106, 107; SI 1993 No 2950; SI 1994 No 3009; SI 1995 No 3034*].

Remuneration does not include anything chargeable under Schedule E arising from the acquisition or disposal of shares (or interests in shares) or from rights to acquire shares, nor anything in respect of which tax is chargeable under *Sec 148* (see 19.5 COMPENSATION FOR LOSS OF EMPLOYMENT (AND DAMAGES)). [*Sec 612(1)*].

Discretionary approval. The Board are given discretion, subject to regulations, to approve a scheme not fully complying with the above conditions (e.g. by allowing retirement up to 10 years before the ages prescribed in (*c*)(i) above, or earlier if incapacitated; by providing benefits in excess of the limits in (*e*) above on retirement after less than 40 years' service; by modifying the definition of 'final remuneration'; by providing a pension, and a lump sum up to four times final remuneration, for the widow or dependants of an employee dying in service; by providing for the commutation in full of trivial pensions (i.e. up to £260 p.a.); by including a trade carried on partly overseas or by a non-resident; or by allowing the return of employees' contributions in certain contingencies) and, in respect of schemes in existence on 6 April 1980, will exercise that discretion to preserve benefits earned, or rights arising out of prior service, before the date of the approval of the scheme under the new code or 5 April 1980, whichever is the earlier, and to preserve any rights to death-in-service benefits existing under the scheme at 26 February 1970. Discretion is also given to approve schemes which allow members to have their benefits secured by means of an annuity contract with an insurance company of their choice, and schemes to which the employer is not a contributor which provide benefits additional to those under the employer's scheme. A condition for discretionary approval is that the employee's contribution must not exceed 15% of remuneration (and see now 66.5(*a*) below). [*Sec 591; FA 1994, s 107; FA 1995, ss 59(2), 60(1)*]. Restrictions relating to the discretionary approval of small self-administered schemes (generally those with less than twelve members) are contained in *The Retirement Benefits Schemes (Restriction on Discretion to Approve) (Small Self-administered Schemes) Regulations 1991 (SI 1991 No 1614)*, and those relating to discretionary approval of additional voluntary contribution schemes in *The Retirement Benefits Schemes (Restriction on Discretion to Approve) (Additional Voluntary Contributions) Regulations 1993 (SI 1993 No 3016)*. See generally Revenue Pamphlet IR 12 (1991).

The Revenue have published model rules and guidance notes for simplified occupational pension schemes, satisfying certain specified criteria and aimed primarily at the smaller employer. There are two types of simplified scheme: 'final salary' and 'defined contribution'. The model scheme documents, if used unaltered, will enable schemes to obtain immediate tax approval. Copies may be obtained from the Pension Schemes Office (tel. 0115-974 0000). (Revenue Press Release 4 February 1988; SFO Memorandum No 94 February 1988).

Discretionary approval may be *withdrawn* in the same way as mandatory approval (see (*h*) above). Where regulations place certain restrictions on approval by reference to circumstances other than the provision of benefits, 36 months grace is given before withdrawal of approval after the regulations concerned come into effect. [*Secs 591A, 591B; FA 1991, ss 35, 36*].

The Board has wide information powers, including prescriptive regulation-making powers, in relation to approved and statutory schemes, and from 3 May 1994 penalties of up to £3,000 may be imposed in cases of fraudulent or negligent false statements or representations. [*Secs 605, 605A; FA 1994, ss 105, 106; SI 1995 Nos 3103, 3125*].

Tax on cessation of approval of certain schemes. A special charge to tax applies where approval of certain schemes is withdrawn on or after 2 November 1994 (under *Sec 591A* or *Sec 591B*, see above, but other than by a notice given before that day under *Sec 591B(1)*). This applies to any scheme which either:

(A)   immediately before the date of cessation of approval, had less than twelve individual members; or

(B)   at any time within the year preceding that date, had a member who has at any time been a controlling director (within *Sec 417(5)(b)*) of a company which has contributed to the scheme.

Any person to whom, at any particular time, a benefit under a scheme is being or may be provided in respect of his past or present employment is a member of the scheme at that time for these purposes.

Tax is charged under SCHEDULE D, CASE VI (74) at a rate of 40% on the value, as it stands immediately before the date approval ceases, of the assets held for the purposes of the scheme. The value of such assets is the market value, except that rights or interests in respect of money lent directly or indirectly to certain persons are valued at the amount owing (including unpaid interest). The charge is on the scheme administrator, except that where the scheme administrator is constituted by persons including a person who is an 'approved independent trustee', that person is not liable for the tax. An '*approved independent trustee'* is a person approved by the Board as a trustee of the scheme who is not connected (within *Sec 839*) with either a member or fellow trustee of the scheme or an employer who has contributed to the scheme.

For the purposes of taxation of capital gains, assets in respect of which a charge arises as above are treated as having been acquired immediately before the date of cessation of approval for a consideration equal to the amount on which tax is charged under these provisions, without any corresponding deemed disposal.

For the procedures leading to withdrawal of approval, see Revenue Tax Bulletin August 1995 p 233.

[*Secs 591C, 591D; FA 1995, s 61*].

See Pension Schemes Office Update No 10, 1 November 1995 or Revenue Tax Bulletin December 1995 p 266 as regards measures to prevent avoidance of a charge under *Sec 591C* by payment of a transfer value to a pension scheme subsequently transferred offshore.

An exempt approved scheme is any approved scheme as above which is established under irrevocable trusts, or any other approved scheme which the Board may direct as exempt. [*Sec 592(1)*].

66.5   **EFFECTS OF APPROVAL**

(*a*)   **Payments by employer** of ordinary annual contributions to an exempt approved scheme are deductible as an expense for tax purposes in the tax year (or chargeable period) in which paid. A payment by the employer to the scheme on or after 27 July 1993 discharging the employer's liability under *Social Security Pensions Act 1975, s 58B* or *Pension Schemes Act 1993, s 144* (or NI equivalent) is treated as a contribution to the scheme, and if the trade etc. has ceased before the payment is made, is deductible as if paid on the last day on which the trade etc. was carried on. Contributions other than ordinary annual contributions are also deductible, but Revenue may require these to be spread. For a year of assessment the basis period for which ends after 5 April 1993 (and for any accounting period ending after that date), tax relief is given only for contributions actually paid, and not e.g. for any provision for such contributions. Payments actually made after 5 April 1993 are not eligible for relief to the extent that the total amounts allowed for earlier chargeable periods exceed the total that would have been allowed if the above had always applied. A payment for which relief is spread is treated as made accordingly. [*Sec 592(4)–(6A); FA 1993, s 112*]. See Revenue Pamphlet IR 12 (1991) para 5.7 *et seq.* for practice on spreading of contributions (broadly over up to four years where special contributions exceed £25,000), and also Revenue Tax Bulletin November 1992 p 41 as regards transitional provisions for accounting periods straddling 31 August 1991. A Revenue decision on spreading is not subject to review on appeal (*Kelsall v Investment Chartwork Ltd Ch D 1993, 65 TC 750*). Where employer's business changes hands see *Clarke v Musker Ch D 1956, 37 TC 1*. Legal and other expenses of establishing a scheme and running expenses of revenue nature will be allowed. (Revenue Pamphlet IR 12 (1991) paras 5.9, 5.10). For repayments out of overfunded schemes, see 66.8 below.

Payments by employees of contributions to exempt approved schemes are allowed as an expense in the tax year in which paid, provided that they do not in total exceed 15% (or such higher percentage as the Board may prescribe) of remuneration of that year. For 1989/90 onwards, remuneration in excess of the permitted maximum (see 66.4 above) is disregarded for this purpose (although this limitation does not apply in the circumstances prescribed by regulation by the Board for this purpose, see *SI 1990 No 586; SI 1993 No 3221*), and where there is more than one employment, the

15% limit must not be exceeded in respect of any one of them. Where contributions are to a scheme to which the employer does not contribute, regulations provide for them to be made under deduction of basic rate tax. The tax deducted from payments is not clawed back where the individual is liable only at the lower rate of income tax or has no income tax liability. [*Secs 592(7)(8), 593; FA 1989, 6 Sch 5, 21; SI 1987 No 1749; SI 1990 No 585*].

(*b*) The exempt approved fund itself is exempt from income tax on income from investments or deposits held for the purposes of the scheme and from liability under capital gains tax on gains from disposals of investments so held. [*Secs 592(2)(3), 659; TCGA 1992, s 271(1)(g); FA 1996, s 134, 20 Sch 63*]. Exemption applies by concession to certain payments received in replacement of lost dividends or interest under approved stock lending arrangements (see 71.81 SCHEDULE D, CASES I AND II (Revenue Pamphlet IR 1, C19). See 71.32 SCHEDULE D, CASES I AND II as regards futures and options contracts. See also 66.13 below.

(*c*) **Repayments to employee.** Where contributions are repaid to an employee during his lifetime from an exempt approved scheme or a relevant statutory scheme, the administrator is chargeable at 20% under Schedule D, Case VI on lump sums and contributions repaid, and has no statutory right to deduct tax, but deduction may be made where the rules of the scheme so authorise. [*Sec 598; SI 1988 No 504; FA 1989, 6 Sch 10*].

The rate of 20% will also apply to any excess of a lump sum paid, in special circumstances, in commutation of an employee's entire pension over the sums specified in *Sec 599*.

Certain other unauthorised payments to employees may be the subject of charge under *Sec 600*.

As regards repayments from overfunded schemes, see 66.8 below.

(*d*) **Pensions payable** are assessable under Schedule E unless Inland Revenue direct that Schedule D, Case III, shall apply. Similarly where scheme funds are used to acquire an annuity for a member, annuity payments after 3 May 1994 are dealt with under PAYE rather than (as previously) being paid under deduction of tax under Schedule D, Case III (although it is understood that in practice the Revenue were previously prepared to agree to PAYE being applied where appropriate). [*Sec 597; FA 1994, s 110*]. Pensions under the unapproved voluntary pension scheme of a foreign company were held to be assessable under Case V (*Bridges v Watterson Ch D 1952, 34 TC 47*).

66.6 **SCHEMES APPROVED BEFORE 27 JULY 1989**

Approved schemes: general. *FA 1989, 6 Sch Pt II* came into effect on 14 March 1989, and applies in relation to any retirement benefits scheme approved by the Board before 27 July 1989, notwithstanding anything to the contrary in the scheme rules or (in relation to schemes approved before 23 July 1987, see 66.7 below) in *23 Sch*. The Board may, however, make regulations disapplying or modifying any of its provisions where appropriate (and certain such disapplications and modifications are contained in *The Retirement Benefits Schemes (Continuation of Rights of Members of Approved Schemes) Regulations 1990 (SI 1990 No 2101* and *(Amendment) Regulations 1993 (SI 1993 No 3220)*), which also give the Board power to disapply any of the provisions by direction in any particular case). Also, the administrator of a scheme may, before the end of 1989, elect for it not to apply and for approval of the scheme to cease from the date of approval or, if the scheme came into existence before 14 March 1989, from 1 June 1989 if earlier. [*FA 1989, 6 Sch 19*]. The revised rules are applied to all members of schemes which came into existence after 13

March 1989, but only as regards employees who became members after 31 May 1989 of schemes which were in existence on 13 March 1989. An employee who became a member of a scheme after 16 March 1987 and before 1 June 1989 may, for these purposes, elect (by written notice in prescribed form to the scheme administrator) to be treated as having become a member of the scheme on 1 June 1989. [*FA 1989, 6 Sch 29*].

Remuneration. Any excess of '*relevant annual remuneration*' (i.e. the annual remuneration on which scheme benefits are based) over the 'permitted maximum' (see 66.4 above) is disregarded in calculating benefits and any excess of remuneration over that maximum is disregarded for the purposes of any restriction on the aggregate of employee and employer contributions. The maximum allowable employee contribution is restricted as described in 66.5(*a*) above. [*FA 1989, 6 Sch 20, 22, 30*].

Accelerated accrual. If the scheme permits commutation of pension for a lump sum, that lump sum may not exceed the greater of 3/80ths of relevant annual remuneration for each year of service up to a maximum of 40 and the initial pension payable in the first year (assuming the employee survives the year and ignoring the effects of commutation or allocation to provide benefits for survivors) multiplied by 2.25. Where any lump sum is payable otherwise than by way of commutation, it must not exceed 3/80ths of relevant annual remuneration for each year of service up to a maximum of 40, or, if greater, the number of eightieths of relevant annual remuneration by reference to which the pension payable under the scheme is calculated (up to a maximum of 120). [*FA 1989, 6 Sch 23, 24*].

Associated employments and connected schemes. The provisions described in 66.4 above are applied in relation to pensions payable in respect of service in any of 'relevant associated employments' or in 'connected schemes', except that the permitted rate of accrual is 1/30th of the permitted maximum for each year of qualifying service, with a maximum of 20 years. [*FA 1989, 6 Sch 25, 26*].

Augmentation. Where an employee has contributed to an approved voluntary scheme to which the employer did not contribute, to supplement benefits under the main scheme, then in relation to any augmentation of benefits after the employee has ceased to be a member of the scheme, the limits on benefits under the main scheme rules are reduced by any benefits provided by the voluntary scheme. [*FA 1989, 6 Sch 27*].

Centralised schemes. In relation to such schemes, the references above to the date the scheme came into existence are replaced by a reference to the date the employee commenced participation in the scheme. A '*centralised scheme*' is a retirement benefits scheme established to enable any employer, other than an employer 'associated' with the person by whom the scheme is established, to participate in it as regards his employees. An employer is '*associated*' with a person if one controls the other or both are under the control of a third person (whether directly or indirectly). [*FA 1989, 6 Sch 28*].

Additional voluntary contributions. *FA 1989, 6 Sch Pt III* applies to schemes approved before 27 July 1989 which make provision for the payment by employees of voluntary contributions (again subject to variation by regulation by the Board) notwithstanding anything to the contrary in the scheme rules.

(*a*)   Where the employer does not contribute to the scheme and the provision for voluntary contributions is freestanding, a limit is imposed on benefits, equal to the main scheme limit on such benefits reduced by benefits under that scheme plus any similar benefits under other schemes providing additional benefits. This applies only to benefits provided after 26 July 1989. [*FA 1989, 6 Sch 32*].

(*b*)   The scheme administrator must repay surplus funds to the employee or his personal representatives (deducting therefrom the amount he is required to account for under *Sec 599A*, see 66.8 below), where total benefits exceed the relevant limits. The method of calculating the surplus is to be prescribed by regulations. [*FA 1989, 6 Sch 33, 34*].

66.7 **SCHEMES APPROVED BEFORE 23 JULY 1987**

23 Sch (or its predecessor) came into effect on 17 March 1987, and applies in relation to any retirement benefits scheme approved by the Board before 23 July 1987, notwithstanding anything to the contrary in the scheme rules. The Board may, however, make regulations disapplying or modifying any of its provisions where appropriate (and certain such disapplications and modifications are contained in *The Occupational Pension Schemes (Transitional Provisions) Regulations 1988 (SI 1988 No 1436)* and *(Amendment) Regulations 1993 (SI 1993 No 3219)*, which also give the Board power to disapply any of these provisions by direction in any particular case). Also, the administrator of a scheme could, before the end of 1987, elect for it not to apply, and for approval of the scheme to cease on and after 17 March 1987 (or the date of approval if later). [*23 Sch 1; FA 1988, s 56*]. See also 66.6 above for further supplementary rule changes which apply notwithstanding the provisions of *23 Sch*.

Accelerated accrual. Where an employee joins a scheme after 16 March 1987, the maximum rate of accrual of pension is one-thirtieth of '*relevant annual remuneration*' (i.e. the annual remuneration on which scheme benefits are based) for each year up to a maximum of 20. If commutation for a lump sum is allowed, a formula is laid down for determining the maximum lump sum which may be paid. This is in no case less than three-eightieths of relevant annual remuneration for each year of service up to a maximum of 40 (the '*basic rate lump sum*') and is increased by a percentage of the difference between the basic rate lump sum and a maximum rate lump sum as prescribed by the Board by regulation. That percentage derives from the ratio between the full pension under the scheme and the maximum allowable pension (as above), in both cases after deducting a pension of one-sixtieth of average annual remuneration for each year of service up to a maximum of 40. If the scheme provides for a lump sum other than by commutation of pension, similar limits apply, but with a somewhat faster accrual rate. [*23 Sch 2–4, 9; SI 1987 No 1513*].

Final remuneration. Where a scheme member retires after 16 March 1987, his relevant annual remuneration is determined with the meaning of 'remuneration' restricted as in 66.4 above. In the case of an employee who at any time in his last ten years of service has been a 'controlling director' of the employer company (broadly a director controlling 20% of its ordinary share capital), relevant annual remuneration is restricted to his highest average annual remuneration for any period of three or more years ending in his last ten years of service. A similar restriction applies to an employee whose relevant annual remuneration, so far as ascertained by reference to years beginning after 5 April 1987, would otherwise exceed £100,000 (or such other figure as is prescribed by Treasury order), but if he retires before 6 April 1991, a higher limit of his 1986/87 remuneration may apply where appropriate. [*23 Sch 5*].

Lump sums. Where an employee joins a scheme after 16 March 1987, any lump sum calculated by reference to relevant annual remuneration must disregard any excess of that remuneration over £100,000 (or such other figure as may be prescribed by Treasury order). [*23 Sch 6*].

Additional voluntary contributions. No commutation of a pension for a lump sum is permitted where an employee enters into arrangements to pay such contributions after 7 April 1987, to the extent that the pension is secured by those contributions. Benefits provided before 27 July 1989 from such voluntary contribution schemes acted to reduce any maxima otherwise applicable to benefits under the employer's scheme (and see now 66.6 above). [*23 Sch 7, 8; FA 1989, 6 Sch 17*].

66.8   PENSION SCHEME SURPLUSES

Payments to employers. A 40% charge may arise on any payment (or transfer of money's worth) out of a scheme which is or has been an exempt approved scheme (see 66.4 above). No charge arises where:

(a)   the employer is a charity (see 15 CHARITIES) or would otherwise be entitled to exemption in respect of the payment apart from the current provisions; or

(b)   the payment was made before the scheme was approved; or

(c)   the payment was made

    (i)   in winding up the scheme, provided the winding-up was commenced before 19 March 1986, or

    (ii)   following application to the Board before that date for assurance that the payment would not lead to withdrawal of approval; or

(d)   the payment was of a description prescribed for this purpose by regulation. Under *The Pension Scheme Surpluses (Administration) Regulations 1987 (SI 1987 No 352)*, this exclusion applies to reimbursement of certain expenditure by the employer on behalf of the scheme; commercial loans to, or repayment of loans or interest to, the employer; certain payments in respect of members' obligations to the employer; and reimbursement of a state scheme premium to which *Social Security Pensions Act 1975, s 42 or s 45* applies.

Where a charge arises, the payment to which it relates is treated neither as income for tax purposes nor as brought into charge to tax.

The amount charged is recoverable by the Board from the employer, and the Treasury is empowered to make regulations (see below) regarding the assessment and collection of the amount recoverable, which is treated for this purpose as an amount of income tax chargeable under Schedule D, Case VI (or, where the employer is a company, an amount of corporation tax). It is not, however, available for any exemption, relief or set-off. *The Pension Scheme Surpluses (Administration) Regulations 1987 (SI 1987 No 352)* require the scheme administrator to deduct the amount charged in making the payment to the employer, and, within 14 days of making the payment, to make a return to the Board and account for the amount deducted without the making of any assessment. An assessment may be made on the employer under which the tax due is reduced by any amount deducted and accounted for by the administrator, and if the full amount of tax and interest thereon is not paid within 60 days of the date of the notice of assessment, the tax and interest unpaid may be assessed on the administrator in the name of the employer, becoming due and payable within 14 days of the date of the notice of assessment. The administrator may recover any amount so assessed and paid from the employer.

The *Regulations* referred to above also provide for appeals and postponement applications to be made in the normal way against assessments under these provisions, and for interest on unpaid tax so assessed to run from the 15th day after the date of the payment to the employer. The Board may require information from the administrator or employer where there is reason to believe that a surplus payment has been made in respect of which no return, or an incorrect return, has been made. The penalty provisions of *TMA s 98* (see 58.4 PENALTIES) apply where information is not provided. [*Secs 601, 602*].

Certain payments out of an exempt approved scheme, to which the above provisions do not apply, are charged to tax on the employer as a trading receipt or, if the scheme did not relate to a trade, under Schedule D, Case VI. [*Sec 601(5)*].

Payments to employees. Where a payment or transfer of money's worth is made to or for an employee or to his personal representatives in pursuance of a duty to return surplus funds held for an exempt approved or relevant statutory scheme (see 66.6 above), the payment is grossed up at 34% (35% before 6 April 1996, variable by Treasury order) and the scheme administrator is charged to tax under Schedule D, Case VI at that rate on the grossed-up amount. Such a payment, etc. made to or for an employee is treated as income of the employee for the year of payment, etc., chargeable under Schedule D, Case VI, received under deduction of basic rate tax from a corresponding gross amount. No repayment of the tax notionally deducted may be made, and the income is chargeable only at rates other than the basic and lower rates. A payment so chargeable is not chargeable under *Secs 598, 599, 600* (see 66.5(*c*) above) or under certain regulations relating to old schemes. [*Sec 599A; FA 1989, 6 Sch 12; F(No 2)A 1992, s 19(2); FA 1996, s 122(7); SI 1996 No 830*].

Restriction of surpluses. *The Pension Scheme Surpluses (Valuation) Regulations 1987 (SI 1987 No 412)* (subsequently amended by *SI 1989 No 2290*) apply to all exempt approved schemes. The administrator of the scheme is required to provide, within three months of its being signed, either a written valuation of the scheme assets and liabilities (on the basis prescribed in those *Regulations*) or a certificate in prescribed form stating that such assets do not exceed such liabilities by more than 5%, with the signatory in either case being an actuary within the regulatory prescription. Such a valuation or certificate is required whenever scheme assets and liabilities are valued, and in any event within three and a half years (five years in certain cases) of the previous valuation (or the establishment of the scheme). Where such assets exceed such liabilities by more than 5%, the administrator must, within six months of the date of signature of the valuation or certificate, submit proposals for reducing or eliminating the surplus by any or all of the following means.

(A)   Making payments to the employer.

(B)   Suspending or reducing (for five years or less) employer's and/or employees' contributions.

(C)   Providing new or improved scheme benefits.

(D)   Any other way which may be prescribed by regulation.

The proposals must secure that, within a prescribed time, the excess will be reduced to not more than 5% (and where the proposals include any repayments to the employer, the excess must not be reduced *below* 5%). The prescribed time for this purpose is

(i)   where (A) applied, six months,

(ii)   where (B) applies, a maximum of five years,

(iii) where (C) applies, six months,

(iv)   in any other case, such period as is agreed with the Board,

beginning 30 days after the Board has notified its approval of the proposals (or 30 days after the final determination of an appeal). Under (D), a longer period is allowed in certain cases where a scheme has been in existence less than 15 years, or has ceased to admit new members, or has less than 30 members.

If proposals are not submitted within the prescribed time, or are not agreed, or are not carried out, only a fraction of the scheme income and gains attract exemption from the date of the valuation or certificate referred to above until the Board is satisfied that the excess no longer exceeds 5%. The fraction continuing to attract exemption is that obtained by dividing the Board's estimate of scheme liabilities, increased by 5%, by their estimate of scheme assets, both as at the date of the valuation or certificate.

The above provisions are modified in their application to schemes with twelve members or less and insured schemes (i.e. schemes the contributions to which (other than members' voluntary contributions) are invested wholly by way of insurance premiums) which require that contribution levels take account of surpluses. From 28 December 1989, they are similarly modified in their application to schemes approved by reference to limitations on aggregate contributions and lump sum and death benefits, and to insured schemes providing only lump sum death benefits before retirement age.

There are appeal provisions, and penalties apply under *TMA s 98* for failure to supply a valuation or certificate, or to furnish the Board with certain additional information. [*22 Sch*].

66.9   UNAPPROVED RETIREMENT BENEFIT SCHEMES

A charge applies in respect of any payment or benefit in kind provided pursuant to a funded unapproved retirement benefit scheme ('FURBS'), i.e. a scheme not within 66.1(*a*)–(*c*) above. The charge is under Schedule E or, where the recipient is not an individual, under Schedule D, Case VI (in the latter case being a charge on the administrator of the scheme at a special rate of 40% (variable by Treasury order)). There are various exemptions (see below). The charge is made for the year of assessment in which the payment or benefit is received, and, except as mentioned below, the amount of the charge is the amount received or the cash equivalent of the benefit (determined under the Schedule E rules, see 75.13, 75.29 SCHEDULE E, modified as appropriate in the case of living accommodation).

Where the scheme is entered into after 30 November 1993, or varied after that day with a view to the provision of the benefit, there is an exemption for any pension or annuity to the extent that it is chargeable under *Sec 19(1)* (see 75.1 SCHEDULE E), and for any pension or other benefit chargeable under *Sec 58* (see 59.2 PENSIONS). There is also an exemption for any lump sum provided under the scheme to the employee or certain other persons (which applies to the charge under *Sec 19(1)* or *Sec 148* (see 19.5 COMPENSATION FOR LOSS OF OFFICE) as well as to that under the current provisions) where the employee has been taxed under *Sec 595(1)* (see 66.1 above) in respect of contributions by the employer, except that if any of the income or gains of the scheme out of which the lump sum is provided is not brought into charge to UK tax (where the income or gains were chargeable to tax in the first place—see ICAEW Technical Release TAX 9/94, 7 June 1994), the exemption does not apply, although certain deductions may be made from the lump sum brought into charge in respect of employee contributions and employer contributions charged on the employee under *Sec 595(1)*. Income and gains are not for this purpose treated as brought into charge to tax merely because a tax charge arose on cessation of approval of the scheme under *Sec 591C* (see 66.4 above). A proportionate deduction is allowed where the lump sum is provided on the part disposal of an asset, and there is an expectation that a further lump sum will be received.

Where the scheme was entered into on or before 30 November 1993 and has not been varied after that day, there is an exemption to the extent that the payment or benefit is chargeable under Case I, II or III of Schedule E (see 75.1 SCHEDULE E), or can be shown to be attributable to the payment of a sum treated as income and charged to tax under *Sec 595(1)* (see 66.1 above).

[*Secs 591D(6), 596A, 596B; FA 1989, 6 Sch 9; FA 1994, s 108(1)–(6); FA 1995, s 61(1)*].

See 59.4(vi) PENSIONS as regards lump sum benefits from overseas schemes, and generally Revenue Explanatory Booklet 'The Tax Treatment of Top-Up Pension Schemes'.

66.10   DEDUCTIBILITY BY EMPLOYER

See 66.5(*a*) above regarding exempt approved schemes. Expenses incurred in, or with a view to, providing benefits pursuant to a non-approved scheme, i.e. a scheme not within 66.1(*a*)–(*c*) above, are not allowed as a SCHEDULE D, CASES I AND II (71) deduction (nor as a management expense under *Sec 75*) unless the benefits are within the charge to income tax on receipt or payments made are treated as income when paid by virtue of *Sec 595(1)* (see 66.1, 66.2, 66.9 above), and those exceptions do not apply unless the sums concerned have actually been expended. These restrictions do not, however, apply to contributions incurred on or after 29 April 1996 to overseas superannuation funds within *Sec 615(6)* (see 59.6 PENSIONS), or to retirement benefits schemes established outside the UK which correspond to schemes within 66.1(*a*)–(*c*) above and under which payments or provisions are made for the benefit either of employees in receipt of foreign emoluments or of employees not resident in the UK whose duties are performed wholly outside the UK or are incidental to duties so performed. (Similar relief was previously available by extra-statutory concession, see Revenue Pamphlet IR 1, B39.) [*FA 1989, s 76; FA 1996, 39 Sch 2*].

In cases not involving approved funds, a company's initial lump sum to cover past service on the setting up of a contributory pension scheme was disallowed as capital (*Atherton v British Insulated & Helsby Cables Ltd HL 1925, 10 TC 155*) as was a lump sum contribution to an employees' benevolent fund (*Rowntree & Co Ltd v Curtis CA 1924, 8 TC 678*). However, a series of payments to trustees to build up an indeterminate fund for the benefit of employees for whom pension arrangements might prove inadequate was allowable (*Jeffs v Ringtons Ltd Ch D 1985, 58 TC 680*). The cost of an annuity to replace a pension was allowed (*Hancock v General Reversionary & Investment Co Ltd KB 1918, 7 TC 358*) but not the cost of a policy for payment to a company of annuities equal to (allowable) pensions it paid (*Morgan Crucible Co Ltd v CIR KB 1932, 17 TC 311*). A gratuity on retirement was allowed (*Smith v Incorporated Council of Law Reporting KB 1914, 6 TC 477*) as was a lump sum in commutation of (allowable) premiums under a staff assurance scheme (*Green v Cravens Railway Wagon Co Ch D 1951, 32 TC 359*) but not premiums paid by a 'family company' to secure pensions for its directors (*Samuel Dracup & Sons Ltd v Dakin Ch D 1957, 37 TC 377*) nor payments to commute voluntary pensions on the cessation of trading (*Anglo Brewing Co Ltd KB 1925, 12 TC 803*).

A sum transferred from an unapproved fund on reconstruction as approved was allowed, under facts of that case (*Lowe v Peter Walker & R Cain CA 1935, 20 TC 25*).

66.11 **OTHER SCHEMES**

Doctors and Dentists. National Health Service superannuation contributions paid by practitioners who are assessable under Schedule D are treated as deductible in assessing those emoluments. Concessionally, where retirement annuity premiums are also paid, restrictions (as defined) are imposed either on the deduction for the NHS contribution or on the retirement annuity relief allowed. For 1980/81 onwards, the previous basis may be continued or (i) retirement annuity relief may be claimed on all relevant earnings (including NHS earnings) and no deduction allowed for the statutory contributions or (ii) deduction claimed for the NHS contributions and relief claimed on premiums related to non-NHS earnings (i.e. 'net relevant earnings' (see 65.12 RETIREMENT ANNUITIES AND PERSONAL PENSION SCHEMES) less sum produced by multiplying the NHS contributions by $16\frac{2}{3}$). (Revenue Pamphlet IR 1, A9). It is understood that this concession is treated as applying equally to personal pension scheme contributions.

Members of Parliament. For tax purposes, salaries are treated as reduced by contributions to House of Commons Members' Fund. [*Sec 613(1)*]. Periodical payments out of Fund are assessable under Schedule E. [*Sec 613(3)*].

Pilot's benefit fund. The Board may approve a fund established under the *Pilotage Act 1983* as if it were a retirement benefits scheme notwithstanding that some of the usual conditions are not satisfied. Contributions will be allowable as an expense under Schedule D and pensions paid out will be earned income. [*Sec 607*].

Relevant statutory scheme established under a public general Act (but not any national scheme). Employees' contributions are allowable deductions from income for purposes of Schedule E, subject to the same limits as under 66.5(*a*) above. [*Sec 594; FA 1989, 6 Sch 6*]. For contributions repaid to employees see 66.5(*c*) above.

66.12   **LUMP SUM ON RETIREMENT ETC.**

A lump sum benefit paid to a person, whether on his retirement or otherwise, will not be chargeable to tax under Schedule E if (*a*) it is from a scheme within *ICTA 1970, s 221(1)(2)* or *Sec 596(1)* and is neither an unauthorised payment under the scheme's rules chargeable to tax under *Sec 600*, nor a payment for premature retirement to which *Sec 188(2)* applies, or (*b*) it is a lump sum provided before 1 December 1993 (or on or after that date under a scheme entered into before that date and not varied on or after that date) for the provision of which the holder has been charged under *ICTA 1970, s 220* or *Sec 595* (see 66.1 above), or (*c*) it is paid under approved personal pension arrangements under *Sec 631* (see 65 RETIREMENT ANNUITIES AND PERSONAL PENSION SCHEMES). This exemption from tax shall be deemed always to have had effect. [*Sec 189; FA 1988, s 57; FA 1994, s 108(7)(8)*]. See also 59.4(iv)–(vi) PENSIONS and 19.3 and 19.6 COMPENSATION FOR LOSS OF EMPLOYMENT and, as regards the successor to (*b*) above, 66.9 above.

After 5 April 1980, *ICTA 1970, s 221(1)(2)* was repealed, but lump sums paid from *ICTA 1970, s 208* schemes which have not sought approval under the new code (see 66.3 and 66.4 above and 66.13 below) will by concession continue to enjoy exemption from tax under Schedule E. (Revenue Pamphlet IR 1, A33).

Ex gratia payments. With effect for payments after 31 October 1991, a revised Revenue practice came into effect in relation to *ex gratia* lump sum payments of 'relevant benefits' (see 66.1 above) on retirement or death. (Payments on redundancy or loss of office, or because of death or disability due to accident, are therefore not covered by the practice. This applies equally to cases of unfair dismissal (see Law Society Press Release 7 October 1992).) Where such payments are made by virtue of any 'arrangement', the arrangement will constitute a retirement benefits scheme, and unless that scheme has obtained Revenue approval, the benefits paid will be taxable under *Sec 596A* (see 66.1 above). Where Revenue approval has been obtained, the payments will not be chargeable to tax.

The question of what constitutes 'retirement' for these purposes depends on the facts of each particular case. See ICAEW Technical Release TAX 15/92, 23 October 1992 for the Revenue view of a number of borderline hypothetical cases.

'*Arrangement*' for these purposes includes any system, plan, pattern or policy connected with the payment, and this would include e.g. a decision at a meeting to make a payment on an employee's retirement, a decision to make a payment under a delegated authority, or the existence of a common practice for the making of such payments to a particular class of employee. Revenue approval may be given in relation to such non-contractual arrangements provided that:

(i)   the payment is the only lump sum relevant benefit potentially payable in respect of the employment (unless the payment is made on retirement and there is a scheme providing death in service benefits); and

(ii)   the normal requirements for approval of contractual retirement benefits schemes (e.g. as regards limits on benefits) are met.

Approval in these circumstances should be sought from the Pension Schemes Office, and PAYE applied to any payments made before such approval is received. Approval need *not* be sought for a single payment to a particular employee, provided that it meets the condition at (i) above and that the total of payments in connection with the retirement, etc. (including any from 'associated employers' (see 66.4 above)) does not exceed one-twelfth of the 'permitted maximum' for the year of payment (see 66.4 above). (Revenue Pamphlet IR 131 (October 1995 Supplement), SP 13/91, 31 October 1991). This Statement of Practice replaces a revised practice which came into effect on 1 March 1991, under which no provision was made for approval of 'arrangements' for *ex gratia* payments. (Joint Office of Pension Schemes Office and Occupational Pensions Board Memorandum No 104, March 1991).

Where exceptionally an *ex gratia* payment is made other than under an 'arrangement', the payment will, unless taxable under the general rules of Schedule E, be taxable under *Sec 148* (subject to the usual exemptions) (see 19.2 *et seq.* COMPENSATION FOR LOSS OF EMPLOYMENT (AND DAMAGES)).

66.13 SCHEMES CEASING TO BE APPROVED AT APRIL 1980

Where a scheme was an approved superannuation scheme under *ICTA 1970, s 208* immediately before 6 April 1980 and has not been approved under the new rules above and no contributions have been paid to it since 5 April 1980, exemption from income tax may be claimed on income from investments or deposits, underwriting commissions and transactions in certificates of deposit (otherwise taxable under Schedule D, Case VI), and from capital gains tax on gains from investments held for the purposes of the scheme. Any annuity paid out of such a scheme will be charged under Schedule E and PAYE applied. [*Sec 608; TCGA 1992, s 271(2); FA 1996, s 134, 20 Sch 63*]. By concession, certain minor rule amendments may be made to benefits provided under such schemes without the loss of tax exemptions (see Revenue Pamphlet IR 1 (November 1995 Supplement), B43).

See 71.32 SCHEDULE D, CASES I AND II as regards futures and options contracts.

66.14 OVERSEAS PENSIONS AND PENSION FUNDS

See under 59 PENSIONS.

66.15 SOCIAL SECURITY ACTS

Contributions by business employers in respect of employees are allowable for tax purposes, see 82.2 SOCIAL SECURITY.

67   Returns

Cross-reference. See also 78.5 to 78.9 SELF-ASSESSMENT.

67.1   The Revenue have considerable powers to obtain information and these are generally exercised initially by the requirement to complete and submit various returns, with PENALTIES (58) for non-compliance, omissions or incorrect statements. Explanatory notes are usually issued with the returns.

Following the changes introduced by *FA 1990* in the requirements in relation to the making of returns (see 53.19 PARTNERSHIPS, 67.2, 67.10 below, and 80.3 SETTLEMENTS), the principles followed by the Revenue in designing return forms and in determining the information required in them are explained in Revenue Pamphlet IR 131, SP 4/91, 1 May 1991.

It is generally provided that a person is deemed not to have failed to do anything required to be done where there was a reasonable excuse for the failure and, if the excuse ceased, provided that the failure was remedied without unreasonable delay after the excuse had ceased. Similarly, a person is deemed not to have failed to do anything required to be done within a limited time if he did it within such further time as the Board, or the Commissioners or officer concerned, may have allowed. [*TMA s 118(2); F(No 2)A 1987, s 94*]. See, however, 6.6 BACK DUTY. In *Creedplan Ltd v Winter (Sp C 54), [1995] SSCD 352*, the Special Commissioner, in confirming a penalty under *TMA s 94(1)(a)*, considered that 'there is no reasonable excuse . . . for sending in a return which was less than was required'.

67.2   ANNUAL RETURNS OF INCOME

For 1995/96 and earlier years (see 78.5 to 78.7 SELF-ASSESSMENT for the position thereafter), for the purposes of assessing a person to income tax, an inspector may by notice require that person to provide a return within a time limit specified in the notice and to supply with the return any information, accounts and statements relating to information contained in the return that may be required. The return must include a declaration that, to the best of the knowledge of the person making it, it is complete and correct. The information, accounts and statements required by the notice may differ in relation to different periods, or different sources of income, or different descriptions of person. [*TMA s 8; FA 1990, s 90(1)*]. Similar provisions apply in relation to returns by trustees. [*TMA s 8A; FA 1990, s 90(1)*].

In practice, soon after the commencement of each tax year forms are served on persons considered liable to tax and these must be completed within the time stipulated (30 days) although in practice further time is allowed. However tax returns are now often not issued every year to taxpayers whose only income is from an employment taxed under PAYE and it is accordingly especially important for such taxpayers to claim, by separate notice to their local inspector, any additional allowances to which they may become entitled.

All items comprising Total Income (see 1.6 ALLOWANCES AND TAX RATES) for the tax year must be included in the appropriate sections of the form and also computations of any chargeable gains. But where an individual's chargeable gains do not exceed the exempt amount for the year (i.e. £6,300 for 1996/97) on a total amount of related disposals not exceeding twice that exempt amount, a statement to that effect is sufficient entry on a return unless the inspector requires otherwise. [*TMA ss 12(1), 113(2); FA 1990, s 90(2); TCGA 1992, s 3*].

See 68.6, 68.19, SCHEDULE A, 71.28 SCHEDULE D, CASES I AND II for simplified accounts acceptable for smaller businesses, and the latter for rounding of profit computations.

67.2 Returns

Income subject to DEDUCTION OF TAX AT SOURCE (23) must be shown at the gross amounts and dividends must be shown with related tax credits. They are income of the tax year by reference to which the rate of tax deducted or of the tax credit is determined, irrespective of the period of accrual. [*Sec 835(6)*]. If shares or securities are sold, subsequent dividends etc. are normally income of the purchaser irrespective of the period of accrual (cf. *Wigmore v Thomas Summerson & Sons Ltd KB 1925, 9 TC 577; Oakley KB 1925, 9 TC 582*), but of the vendor if sold 'ex-dividend' (xd) through the Stock Exchange. See, however, 74.6 *et seq.* SCHEDULE D, CASE VI as regards certain income from securities treated as accruing on a day-to-day basis.

Each dividend received must be shown but only one figure need be shown for tax credit calculated on the total dividends received. Separate totals and credit figures should be given for husband and wife. (CCAB Statement 25 October 1977).

Interest and dividends on shares and deposits in Co-operative Societies must be included but not 'dividends' on purchases (but in *Pope v Beaumont KB 1921, 24 TC 78*, it was held that such a 'dividend' received by a trader on his purchases must be included in his profit computations). Building Society and bank deposit interest received net under the composite rate scheme must be included together with income from property owned and let, income from abroad, from trusts and all income not taxed by deduction.

Particulars must be given (but only where requested) of assets acquired where their disposal may give rise to capital gains tax (but excluding tangible movable property acquired for £6,000 or less). [*TMA s 12; FA 1989, s 123(1)*].

The return contains sections for claiming personal allowances and reliefs as applicable (see 1.14 to 1.18 ALLOWANCES AND TAX RATES) and relief for interest paid (see 43 INTEREST PAYABLE).

See 3 ANTI-AVOIDANCE for tax treatment in relation to certain types of transactions in securities etc.

Any person who is chargeable to tax for a tax year must, unless all his income and chargeable capital gains have been declared to the Revenue, in general give notice that he is so chargeable within one year after the end of that tax year, normally to the local inspector. [*TMA ss 7, 10, 11A; FA 1988, ss 120–122*]. See 58.1 PENALTIES.

Late returns. The Board have emphasised that an interest charge will be considered under *TMA s 88* (see 42.5 INTEREST ON UNPAID TAX) where a taxpayer delays the rendering of a return (or sends an incomplete return and delays providing any details required to complete it) if, in consequence, an assessment is made after the normal time to make good the tax on income, profits or capital gains reported late. Interest will not generally be charged as above unless the relevant return has not been made by the later of 30 days after the date of issue of the return and 31 October following the end of the tax year in which the income or chargeable gain arose. It will similarly not be charged where it is not possible to lodge the return but, within that time limit, information sufficient for the raising of an adequate estimated assessment is provided. In case of substantial delay, penalties may be considered under *TMA s 93* (see 58.2 PENALTIES). (Revenue Pamphlet IR 131, SP 6/89, 31 July 1989).

Where a new source of income is assessed on the current year basis, and could not have been assessed in time for tax to become due on the normal due date (e.g. because income first arose after that date), interest under *TMA s 88* will normally be treated as running from the earliest date tax would have become payable had the return been made within 30 days of the date of issue. Similarly where the information for making a Schedule E assessment would not have been available in time to give rise to a tax liability on 1 January (the normal due date), *TMA s 88* interest will normally be treated as running from the following 1 July. (Revenue Tax Bulletin August 1992 p 27).

A return is not completed until any relevant computations are also submitted (e.g. an entry in the capital gains section as 'To be advised' does not comply with the requirements even though the return may be accompanied by an investment schedule giving particulars of changes in holdings and proceeds of sale). See *Cox v Poole General Commissioners Ch D 1987, 60 TC 445*. The fact that information is not available to enable a full return to be made is not, however, an excuse for failure to comply with the statutory obligation to make a return (*Alexander v Wallington Commrs and CIR CA 1993, 65 TC 777*). See also 68.19 SCHEDULE A and 71.28 SCHEDULE D, CASES I AND II for simplified accounts acceptable for small businesses. Schedules may be used where appropriate, provided that every relevant section of the official return form is marked 'see schedule attached' or words to that effect. Alternatively, a return will be accepted if the official return form bears the taxpayer's declaration that it is correct and complete, and that

(i) schedules are attached to the official return form,

(ii) each schedule is numbered (or lettered) consecutively,

(iii) each page of the official return form is crossed through with a diagonal line and marked 'See schedules X–Y' (X and Y being the first and last schedules),

(iv) the headings to schedules indicate the number of sheets comprised in each schedule if more than one.

Claims for personal allowances and reliefs may be dealt with in the same way. (Revenue Pamphlet IR 131, SP 5/83, 28 April 1983).

The following matters continue to be relevant **for 1996/97 and later years**.

Signature of returns etc. The Revenue will accept returns signed by an attorney acting under a general or enduring power where the taxpayer is physically unable to sign (and not merely unavailable to do so). The attorney must have full knowledge of the taxpayer's affairs, and provide the original power or a certified copy when such a return is first made. In cases of mental incapacity, the signature of an attorney appointed under an enduring power registered with the Court of Protection (or of a receiver or committee appointed by that Court) will be accepted. Similar requirements apply to the signature of claims on behalf of physically or mentally incapacitated taxpayers, and to other documents such as applications for TESSAs or PEPs (see 29.11(iii), 29.20 EXEMPT INCOME) and certificates of eligibility under the MIRAS scheme (see 23.13 DEDUCTION OF TAX AT SOURCE). (Revenue Pamphlet IR 131, A13 and Revenue Tax Bulletin February 1993 p 51).

Substitute return forms. The Revenue have issued a Statement of Practice (Revenue Pamphlet IR 131, SP 5/87, 15 June 1987) concerning the acceptability of facsimile and photocopied tax returns. Whenever such a substitute form is used, it is important to ensure that it bears the correct taxpayers's reference.

Facsimiles must satisfactorily present to the taxpayer the information which the Board have determined shall be before him when he signs the declaration that the return is correct and complete to the best of his knowledge. They should be readily recognisable as a return when received in the Revenue office, and the entries of taxpayers' details should be distinguishable from the background text. Approval must be obtained from Inland Revenue, Corporate Communications Office, Room 9/3A, 9th Floor, NW Wing, Bush House, London WC2B 4PP before a facsimile return is used, and the facsimile must bear an agreed unique imprint for identification purposes. Copies of the major 1996 income tax return forms and an information sheet on the guidelines for production of substitute forms were made available in January 1996, so that modifications could be incorporated in computer produced facsimiles in time for their submission.

Photocopies must bear the actual, not photocopied, signature of the relevant person. They are acceptable provided that they are identical (except as regards use of colour) to the official form. Where double-sided copies are not available, it is sufficient that all pages are present and attached in the correct order. Although the copying of official forms is in strictness a breach of HMSO copyright, action will be taken only where forms are copied on a large scale for commercial gain.

Persons in receipt of taxable income belonging to others. Returns may also be required from any person who, in whatever capacity, receives money or value etc. belonging to another person who is chargeable to income tax in respect thereof, or could be so chargeable if resident in UK and not an incapacitated person (although information may not be sought in relation to years of assessment ending more than three years before the date of the notice). [*TMA s 13; FA 1988, s 123(1)*]. This applies where a person is in receipt of chargeable profits or gains of another, not of gross receipts representing an element in the determination of profits or gains (*Fawcett v Special Commrs and Lancaster Farmers' Auction Mart Co Ltd Ch D, [1995] STC 61*). In practice, returns may be restricted to receipts of the following nature:

(*a*)   those from Schedule A or D sources which have not suffered deduction of tax;

(*b*)   those exceeding £250 in aggregate in respect of any one person or estate;

(*c*)   those which have not been included on any other return or repayment claim;

(*d*)   those received by an agent acting on behalf of an individual not domiciled in, or (being a British subject) not ordinarily resident in, the UK.

(Law Society Press Release 29 May 1991).

67.3   **ELECTRONIC LODGEMENT OF TAX RETURNS, ETC.**

Certain returns required to be made to the Board or to an officer of the Board may, subject to the conditions detailed below, be lodged electronically. The provision under which the return is required must be specified for this purpose by Treasury order, which will also appoint a commencement day. Any supporting documentation (including accounts, statements or reports) required to be delivered with a return may similarly be lodged electronically if the return is so lodged (or may instead be delivered by the last day for submission of the return).

The normal powers and rights applicable in relation to returns, etc. delivered by post are applied to information transmitted electronically. A properly made and authenticated hard copy (see (*c*) below) is treated in any proceedings as if it were the return or other document in question, but if no such copy is shown to have been made, a hard copy certified by an officer of the Board to be a true copy of the information transmitted is so treated instead.

There are four conditions for electronic lodgement.

(*a*)   A person seeking approval must be given notice of the grant or refusal of approval, which may be granted for the transmission of information on the person's own behalf or on behalf of another person or persons. Approval may be withdrawn by notice from a given date, and any notice refusing or withdrawing approval must state the grounds. An appeal against refusal or withdrawal must be made within 30 days of such notice having been given, and lies to the Special Commissioners, who may grant approval from a specified date if they consider the refusal or withdrawal to have been unreasonable in all the circumstances.

(*b*)   The transmission must comply with any requirements notified by the Board to the person making it, including in particular any relating to the hardware or software to be used.

(c)   The transmission must signify, in an approved manner, that a hard copy was made under arrangements designed to ensure that the information contained in it is the information in fact transmitted.

(d)   The information transmitted must be accepted under a procedure selected by the Board for this purpose, which may in particular consist of or include the use of specifically designed software.

As regards (c) above, the hard copy must have been authenticated by the person required to make the return:

(i)   in the case of a return required by notice, by endorsement with a declaration that it is to the best of his knowledge correct and complete; or

(ii)   otherwise by signature.

[TMA s 115A, 3A Sch; FA 1995, s 153, 28 Sch].

67.4   **BANKERS ETC. RETURNS OF INTEREST**

On receipt of notice, any person (including the National Savings Bank and a building society) paying or crediting interest on money received or retained, in the UK, in the ordinary course of his business, and any bank (within Sec 840A, see 8.1 BANKS), must make a return, for any specified year of assessment (ending not more than three years previously), showing the names and addresses of the recipients and the gross amount of interest paid or credited to each and the amount (if any) of tax deducted therefrom. Where a declaration of non-ordinary residence has been given to the payer to enable interest to be paid gross (see 8.3 BANKS, 9.5 BUILDING SOCIETIES), and the person who made that declaration has so requested, the payer is not required to include the interest in the return under this provision. The payer may similarly exclude from that return interest paid to a person who has so requested and has given written notice that the person beneficially entitled to the interest is a non-UK resident company. Notices may be issued re parts or branches of a business. The Board have powers by statutory instrument to make regulations requiring further prescribed information with the return, or providing that prescribed information is *not* required. [TMA s 17; FA 1988, s 123(2); FA 1990, s 92; F(No 2)A 1992, s 29; FA 1996, 37 Sch 11; SI 1990 No 2231; SI 1992 No 2915]. The Inland Revenue Financial Intermediaries and Claims Office may be contacted in relation to *section 17* returns on 0151–472 6123 as regards submission arrangements or 0151–472 6156 for technical advice.

Returns may also be required from any other person paying interest (including building society dividends) [TMA s 18; FA 1988, s 123(3); FA 1990, s 92; FA 1991, 11 Sch 5; FA 1996, 37 Sch 11] and from persons collecting interest on securities on behalf of others who are resident in UK. [TMA s 24; FA 1996, 37 Sch 11].

67.5   **EMPLOYERS**

Employers (including deemed employers of agency workers) must on application furnish particulars, for employees (i.e. any person whose emoluments are assessable under Schedule E) and periods specified (but not earlier than six years before year of assessment in which application made), of remuneration including payments (a) for 'expenses', (b) on employees' behalf, (c) for services whether rendered in course of employment or not, and stating details of any apportionments made. Also, particulars of any assessable benefits provided to an employee, whether by the employer or another person (who must furnish information on application). [TMA ss 15, 16A]. See also 55 PAY AS YOU EARN and, for directors and employees with emoluments at the rate of £8,500 per annum or more, 75.11 et seq. SCHEDULE E. See 78.42 SELF-ASSESSMENT for the position for 1996/97 and later years.

Person in UK treated as employer. Where a person performs duties for a continuous period of not less than 30 days in the UK for a non-resident employer but for the benefit of a person resident or carrying on a trade etc. in the UK, then the latter person must include him in any returns of employees and the employee may be required to include any such emoluments in his tax return. [*FA 1974, s 24*].

67.6   FEES, COMMISSIONS, COPYRIGHTS, ETC.

Any person carrying on any trade, etc., and any body of persons carrying on any non-trading activity (including Crown departments, public or local authorities and any other public bodies), may, by notice, be required to give particulars of all payments made (including commissions or expenses), or valuable consideration given, for services rendered by persons not employed by him, including, in the case of a trade, etc., services in connection with the formation, acquisition, development or disposal thereof. Applies also to periodical or lump-sum payments in respect of any copyright or public lending right or design right. But returns are limited to payments from which tax is not deductible, and those (*a*) exceeding £15 in total to any one person, or (*b*) made during the three tax years ending prior to the notice. [*TMA s 16; FA 1983, s 27; FA 1988, s 124*]. See Revenue Pamphlet 46Q re payments to entertainers etc. for total payments exceeding £250 in a year.

67.7   GRANTS, SUBSIDIES, LICENCES ETC.

Any person paying grants or subsidies directly or indirectly out of public funds (whether UK or European Community), or issuing licences or approvals or maintaining entries in a register which subsist after that date, may be required to furnish particulars to the inspector where they may be relevant to the determination of any tax liability. [*TMA s 18A; FA 1988, s 125*].

67.8   HOTELS AND BOARDING HOUSES

Returns of all lodgers and inmates resident in any dwelling house must be made by the proprietor, if required by notice from the inspector. [*TMA s 14*].

67.9   ISSUING HOUSES, STOCKBROKERS, AUCTIONEERS, ETC.

For the purposes of obtaining particulars of chargeable gains, an inspector may require a return of parties to transactions and description and consideration of assets dealt with from (i) an issuing house or any other person concerned in effecting public issues or placing of shares etc. or (ii) a member of a stock exchange (other than a market maker) or any other person acting as an agent or broker in share transactions or (iii) any person or body managing a clearing house for any terminal market in commodities or (iv) an auctioneer and any person carrying on a trade of dealing in any description of tangible movable property or acting as agent in such where the value in the hands of the recipient exceeds £6,000. Returns are limited to transactions effected within three years prior to the issue of the notice requiring the return. [*TMA s 25; FA 1978, s 45(5); FA 1982, s 81*].

The Board may make regulations by statutory instrument, effective from a day to be appointed therein, making appropriate provision in regard to recognised investment exchanges other than the Stock Exchange. [*FA 1986, s 63, 18 Sch 8*].

See also *TMA s 21* as regards other transactions by market makers.

67.10   PARTNERSHIPS

Any partner may be required to complete and deliver a return of the profits or gains of the partnership and the names and residences of all partners, and of such other information etc.

as the inspector may require (the requirements being similar to those under *TMA s 8*, see 67.2 above). [*TMA s 9; FA 1990, s 90*].

67.11   **PAY AS YOU EARN**

See 55.9 PAY AS YOU EARN.

67.12   **TRUSTEES**

A return may be required from a trustee under *TMA ss 8A, 13*, see 67.2 above.

67.13   For forms of returns, see *TMA s 113* and 67.1, 67.2 above. For delivery and service of documents, see *TMA s 115*.

68   Schedule A—Property Income

[Secs 15, 21–43; FA 1995, s 39, 6 Sch]

(See also Tolley's Property Taxes and Revenue Pamphlet IR 150.)

68.1   Schedule A applies to **property income**. Tax is charged on rents etc. (see 68.4, 68.14 below) after deducting allowable expenses (see 68.5, 68.7, 68.15, 68.16 below). Certain lease premiums etc. are also taxable (see 68.27 below). 'Chargeable period' means a year of assessment or an accounting period of a company. *[Sec 832(1)]*. See 10.10 *et seq.* CAPITAL ALLOWANCES as regards relief available in respect of leased industrial buildings.

Headings in this chapter are as follows.

68.2   **HISTORY**

The legislation was introduced in *FA 1963* and assessments up to 1969/70 were made under Schedule D, Case VIII. From 1970/71 onwards, assessments have been made under Schedule A. A new regime, incorporating the concept of a 'Schedule A business' and *including furnished lettings* (previously chargeable under Schedule D, Case VI), was introduced by *FA 1995* for income tax purposes only, the previous regime continuing to apply for corporation tax purposes. The new provisions for income tax are covered at 68.3 to 68.13 below and the old provisions/current corporation tax provisions are covered at 68.14 to 68.21 below. See 68.22 below for Revenue guidelines on the transition from the old provisions to the new. The treatment of premiums and other matters common to both regimes are dealt with at 68.24 *et seq.* below.

68.3   **Commencement of Finance Act 1995 regime.** The provisions of *FA 1995* mentioned at 68.2 above have effect for 1995/96 and subsequent years of assessment, subject to the transitional provisions for 1995/96 described below. As stated above, they do not apply at all for corporation tax purposes.

Transitional provisions. The old provisions continue to apply for 1995/96 in relation to a source which is chargeable under Schedule A or Schedule D, Case VI (furnished lettings) for 1994/95 and which ceases to be such a source (assuming the continuation of the old regime) in 1995/96, *provided that* the person to whom the income arose does not commence a Schedule A business, i.e. he neither acquires a new source nor recommences the old, in 1995/96. See also 68.22 below.

[*FA 1995, s 39(4)(5)*].

68.4   **AMOUNTS CHARGEABLE**

With effect as in 68.3 above and otherwise than for corporation tax purposes, Schedule A applies to the annual profits or gains arising from any business carried on for the exploitation, as a source of rents or other 'receipts', of any estate, interest or rights in or over any land in the UK. To the extent that any transaction is entered into for such exploitation, that transaction is taken to have been entered into in the course of such a business; this brings into charge, for example, one-off or casual lettings. Income tax under Schedule A is charged on the persons receiving or entitled to the chargeable income. See below for exclusions from Schedule A and 68.5 below for computation of amounts chargeable.

'*Receipts*', in relation to any land, includes

(*a*)   any payment in respect of any licence to occupy or otherwise to use any land or in respect of the exercise of any other right over land; and

(*b*)   rentcharges, ground annuals and feu duties and any other annual payments reserved in respect of, or charged on or issuing out of, that land.

See also the case law mentioned in 68.14 below in relation to the old regime. Income from the letting of immobile caravans or permanently moored houseboats is specifically brought within the charge to Schedule A. Income from letting caravan pitches, i.e. site rents, is assessable under Schedule A to the extent that it arises from exploitation of land, but, by concession, where the site proprietor carries on associated activities (e.g. shops) which constitute trading and account for a substantial part of the income, the letting income may be included as receipts of the trade under Schedule D, Case I. (Revenue Press Release 17 May 1984 and see Revenue Pamphlet IR 1, B29).

A '*Schedule A business*' means any business the profits or gains of which are chargeable to income tax under Schedule A, including the business in the course of which any such transaction as is mentioned above is treated as entered into. All such businesses and transactions entered into by a particular person or partnership are treated as, or as transactions entered into in the course of carrying on, *a single business*.

Where any rent or other consideration is received for the use of **furnished** premises (including a caravan or houseboat) and any part of the amount received is within Schedule A, any part or additional sum relating to the use of the furniture is also within Schedule A. This does not apply to any amount falling to be taken into account as a trading receipt of a trade involving the making available of furniture for use in any premises.

Schedule A does not include the following.

(i)   *Woodlands.* Profits or gains arising from occupation of WOODLANDS (69) under commercial management with a view to profit.

(ii)   *Yearly interest.*

(iii)   *Farming, market gardening or other commercial occupation of land.* Profits or gains charged under *Sec 53* (Schedule D, Case I).

68.5 Schedule A—Property Income

(iv)   *Mineral rents, royalties etc.* charged under *Sec 55* (Schedule D, Case I), *119* or *120*, see under 23.2 and 23.14 DEDUCTION OF TAX AT SOURCE.

In addition, the provisions of *Sec 98* (tied premises—see 71.45 SCHEDULE D, CASE I) have priority over Schedule A.

[Secs 15, 21(1)(4), 832(1); FA 1995, s 39(1)(2), 6 Sch 1, 28].

68.5   COMPUTATION OF AMOUNTS CHARGEABLE

With effect as in 68.3 above and otherwise than for corporation tax purposes, tax under Schedule A is to be computed on the full amount of profits or gains arising in the year of assessment. *[Sec 21(2); FA 1995, s 39(2)].* The Revenue will no longer allow any deviation from a strict fiscal year basis (except as regards trading partnerships with ancillary Schedule A income, see below). The profit (or loss) should be arrived at by use of ordinary accounting principles and by applying the computational provisions of SCHEDULE D, CASE I (71) contained in *Pt IV, Chapter V* (*Sec 74 et seq.*) as if the Schedule A business were a trade (although Schedule A income continues to be investment income rather than trading income). Loan interest, to the extent that it is incurred wholly and exclusively for the purposes of the letting business, is deductible under general principles, replacing the previous special rules at 43.15 INTEREST PAYABLE. The restriction in *Sec 82* on deductibility of interest paid to non-UK residents does *not*, however, apply for the purposes of a Schedule A business (see 43.2(i) INTEREST PAYABLE). See 43.6 INTEREST PAYABLE as regards alternative concessionary relief for interest in certain cases of temporary absence from owner-occupied property, and see also below. The provisions relating to post-cessation receipts and expenditure (see 60 POST-CESSATION ETC. RECEIPTS AND EXPENDITURE) apply on the cessation of a Schedule A business as they do on that of a trade. *[Sec 21(2)(3)(5)(8); FA 1995, s 39(2), 6 Sch 13].* The following provisions relating to allowable expenditure of trades and professions also apply for Schedule A purposes.

(*a*)   *Sec 577(9)* (gifts to charitable bodies)—see 71.83 SCHEDULE D, CASES I AND II). (This also applies for corporation tax purposes with effect for accounting periods ending on or after 31 March 1995.)

(*b*)   *Sec 579* (redundancy payments), *Sec 588* (training courses for employees), and *Sec 589A* (counselling services for employees)—see 71.53 SCHEDULE D, CASES I AND II.

[FA 1995, 6 Sch 22–25].

A borrower who is eligible for mortgage interest relief in respect of a let property may choose each year whether to claim such relief (restricted to 15% on a maximum of £30,000) or to deduct the interest in computing the Schedule A business profits. As regards inclusion of the loan within MIRAS (mortgage interest relief by deduction at source), see 23.13 DEDUCTION OF TAX AT SOURCE. See also 43.2 INTEREST PAYABLE for concession available where part of a borrower's main residence is used for business (including a Schedule A business) purposes.

Partnerships. The post-Finance Act 1994 (current year basis) provisions for the assessment and computation of partnership profits and for changes in partners apply equally to a Schedule A business carried on in partnership (see 53.3, 53.6 PARTNERSHIPS). *[Sec 21(6)(7); FA 1995, s 39(2)].* Joint ownership of property does not, of itself, create a partnership. Where the letting is not ancillary to a trade or profession, there will only be a partnership if, exceptionally, the exploitation of property constitutes the carrying on of a business (using that term without regard to the concept of a Schedule A business) jointly with a view to profit. See Revenue Tax Bulletin December 1995 pp 271, 272.

68.6   **SIMPLIFIED RETURNS**

Landlords with a total annual gross income from property under £15,000 are required to state on their income tax returns only the gross property income, the total amount of allowable expenses and the net income or profit. There is, of course, still a need to keep accurate records to ensure the correctness of the three-line accounts. (Revenue Press Releases 7 November 1989, 1 November 1991).

68.7   **DEDUCTIONS—MISCELLANEOUS**

See also 68.5 above. The following apply with effect as in 68.3 above and, except for (c) and (d), otherwise than for corporation tax purposes.

(a)   *Pre-trading expenditure.* The provisions at 71.75 SCHEDULE D, CASES I AND II giving relief for otherwise allowable expenditure incurred in the seven years before trading commences applies also in respect of a Schedule A business. [*Sec 401(1B); FA 1995, 6 Sch 20*].

(b)   *Capital allowances* are available under *CAA 1990, Pt II* on *machinery or plant* provided for use, or used, by a person for the purposes of a Schedule A business as if that business were that person's trade. Allowances are given as expenses, and balancing charges treated as receipts, of the business. [*Sec 32; FA 1995, 6 Sch 8*]. But see also 68.8 below (capital allowances not due on plant let for use in a dwelling house, e.g. furniture).

See 10.25 CAPITAL ALLOWANCES as regards certain expenditure on industrial buildings treated as being on machinery or plant and 10.34 CAPITAL ALLOWANCES as regards entitlement to allowances for fixtures.

(c)   *Business entertaining. Sec 577* (non-deductibility of entertainment expenses—see 71.54 SCHEDULE D, CASES I AND II) also applies for Schedule A purposes (but see 68.5(a) above as regards gifts to charitable bodies).

(d)   *Expenditure involving crime. Sec 577A* (illegal payments etc.—see 71.62 SCHEDULE D, CASES I AND II) also applies for Schedule A purposes.

(e)   *Land managed as one estate.* Where, at 5 April 1963, land was in one ownership and managed as one estate, the owner may elect to be treated as receiving, for any part of the estate not let (other than premises he occupies for estate management or trade) and for any part let at less than its annual value, rent at a rate equal to its annual value. The estate is thus split into two parts, the part for which rent is determined as above (Part A) and the remainder (Part B). Expenditure relating to Part A must first be set against the rents as so determined (the deemed receipts); any balance is set against Part B receipts, with any excess treated as Part A expenditure for the following chargeable period. The excess cannot be set against income from outside the estate or form part of a Schedule A loss (see 68.13 below). Expenditure relating to Part B is deductible against any balance of Part A deemed receipts (after deducting Part A expenditure, including any excess brought forward as above). Any excess Part B expenditure is treated as a Schedule A loss.

Election, applying to all subsequent years in which the estate is in the same ownership, must be made within one year after the first tax year for which the owner could have made it, and then (except in the case of the first possible election) is valid only if the previous owner had made a similar election. Except in the case of certain trusts [*Sec 26(5)*] property acquired after 5 April 1963 does not form part of the estate. [*Sec 26(4)*]. The election will not generally cease to be effective because part of the estate becomes comprised in a maintenance fund (see 80.29 SETTLEMENTS), but also see *Sec 27; FA 1995, 6 Sch 6.* [*Sec 26; FA 1995, 6 Sch 5*].

Annual value, see Sec 837, is the rent reasonably to be expected from a letting on terms of the tenant paying tenant's rates etc. and the landlord bearing repairs, insurance and expenses necessary to maintain the property so as to command that rent. In practice, a property's gross rateable value is taken as its annual value. (Revenue Press Release 23 July 1985). In the case of Scottish estates, 1978 gross rateable values will continue to be used for this purpose, despite the 1985 rating revaluation, 'for the time being'. (Revenue Pamphlet IR 1, B30).

(f)   Sea walls. For allowances for expenditure on making sea walls, see Sec 30; FA 1995, 6 Sch 7 and Hesketh v Bray CA 1888, 2 TC 380.

68.8   FURNISHED LETTINGS

With effect as in 68.3 above and otherwise than for corporation tax purposes, furnished lettings are taxable as, or as part of, a Schedule A business (and the computational rules at 68.5 above thus apply), having previously been within Schedule D, Case VI (subject to the right of election referred to at 68.14(i) below). See 74.4 SCHEDULE D, CASE VI for coverage of the Case VI charge on furnished lettings (including the circumstances in which such letting may amount to a trade within Case I), and 68.9, 68.11 below for furnished holiday lettings and 'rent a room' relief respectively, both of which continue to be relevant under Schedule A.

CAPITAL ALLOWANCES (10) are not due on plant let for use in a dwelling house [CAA 1990, s 61(2)] (but see 68.9 below as regards furnished holiday lettings). Furniture and furnishing may be dealt with on the renewals basis but an alternative Revenue concession is to allow as depreciation 10% of the rents received as reduced by any council tax and water rates or material payments for services borne by landlord but normally a tenant's burden. Where the 10% deduction is allowed, no further deduction is given for the cost of renewing furniture or furnishings, nor for fixtures such as cookers, dishwashers or washing machines which, in unfurnished accommodation, the tenant would normally provide for himself. However, the cost of renewing fixtures which are an integral part of the building (e.g. baths, toilets, washbasins) may be claimed in addition, provided that they are revenue repairs to the fabric. Both bases, which applied under Case VI, are maintained under Schedule A. Any different basis in use for a particular case prior to 1975/76 will not normally be disturbed (Revenue Pamphlet IR 131, A19; Revenue Press Releases IR28, 29 November 1994 and 28 September 1995). See Abidoye v Hennessey Ch D 1978, [1979] STC 212.

68.9   Furnished holiday lettings.

In so far as a Schedule A business consists in the 'commercial letting' of 'furnished holiday accommodation' in the UK, it is treated for the following purposes as a trade.

(i)   Relief for losses under Secs 380–390 (see 46 LOSSES);

(ii)   Capital allowances for machinery and plant (see CAPITAL ALLOWANCES (10));

(iii)   Payment of tax in two equal instalments on 1 January in the year of assessment and 1 July following (no longer relevant after 1995/96);

(iv)   Classification as earned income;

(v)   Retirement annuity premium and personal pension contribution relief (see 65.9 RETIREMENT ANNUITIES AND PERSONAL PENSION SCHEMES).

Relief as at (i) above under Sec 381 (see 46.14 LOSSES) is not available for a year of assessment if any of the accommodation concerned was first let by the same person as furnished accommodation more than three years before the beginning of the year of assessment. Loss may not be relieved both under (i) above and under any other relief provision.

All such lettings by a particular person, body of persons or partnership are treated as a single trade.

All necessary adjustment may be made where a tax charge has previously been raised for such a year on some other basis.

Any necessary apportionments, where letting of accommodation only qualifies in part under these provisions, is on a just and reasonable basis.

'*Commercial letting*' is letting (whether or not under a lease) on a commercial basis and with a view to the realisation of profits, and accommodation is let '*furnished*' if the tenant is entitled to use of the furniture. For a case in which the 'commercial letting' test was satisfied despite a significant excess of interest over letting income, see *Walls v Livesey (Sp C 4)*, *[1995] SSCD 12*.

'*Holiday accommodation*' is accommodation which

(*a*)   must be available for commercial letting to the public generally as holiday accommodation for at least 140 days in a twelve month period (see below), and

(*b*)   is so let at least 70 such days.

It must, however, not normally be in the same occupation for more than 31 consecutive days at any time during a period (although not necessarily a continuous period) of seven months in that twelve month period which includes any months in which it is let as in (*b*) above. In the case of an individual or partnership, these conditions must be satisfied in the year of assessment in which the profits or gains arise, unless

(1)   the accommodation was not let furnished in the preceding year of assessment but is so let in the following year of assessment, in which case they must be satisfied in the twelve months from the date such letting commenced in the year of assessment, or

(2)   the accommodation was let furnished in the preceding year of assessment but is not so let in the following year of assessment, in which case they must be satisfied in the twelve months ending with the date such letting ceased in the year of assessment.

In the case of a company, the conditions must be satisfied in the twelve months ending on the last day of the accounting period in which the profits or gains arise, with similar variations as in (1) and (2) above where the accommodation was not let furnished in the twelve months preceding or following the period in question.

In satisfying the 70 day test (as above) averaging may be applied to letting periods of any or all of the accommodation let by the same person which would be holiday accommodation if it satisfied the 70 day test. A claim for averaging must be made within, for 1996/97 and later years, twelve months after 31 January following the year of assessment to which it is to apply (for earlier years, two years after the end of that year of assessment) or, for corporation tax purposes, two years after the end of the accounting period to which it is to apply. Only one such claim may be made in respect of accommodation in a year of assessment or accounting period.

[*Secs 503, 504; CAA 1990, s 29; FA 1995, 6 Sch 21, 31; FA 1996, ss 134, 135, 20 Sch 30, 44, 21 Sch 14*].

Furnished holiday accommodation may include caravans. (Revenue Press Release 17 May 1984).

See 74.4 SCHEDULE D, CASE VI as to the application of these provisions to corporation tax (and to income tax under that Case prior to the new Schedule A regime). See also Tolley's Capital Gains Tax as regards relief from capital gains tax in respect of furnished holiday lettings.

68.10 Schedule A—Property Income

Example

Mr B owns and lets out furnished holiday cottages. None is ever let to the same person for more than 31 days. Three cottages have been owned for many years but Rose Cottage was acquired on 1 June 1996 (and first let on that day) while Ivy Cottage was sold on 30 June 1996 (and last let on that day).

In 1996/97 days available for letting and days let are as follows.

	Days available	Days let
Honeysuckle Cottage	180	160
Primrose Cottage	130	100
Bluebell Cottage	150	60
Rose Cottage	150	60
Ivy Cottage	30	5

Additional information

Rose Cottage was let for 30 days between 6 April and 31 May 1997.
Ivy Cottage was let for 50 days in the period 1 July 1995 to 5 April 1996 but was available for letting for 110 days in that period.

Qualification as 'furnished holiday accommodation'

Honeysuckle Cottage qualifies as it meets both the 140-day availability test and the 70-day letting test.

Primrose Cottage does *not* qualify although it is let for more than 70 days as it fails to satisfy the 140-day test. Averaging (see below) is only possible where it is the 70-day test which is not satisfied.

Bluebell Cottage does not qualify by itself as it fails the 70-day test. However it may be included in an averaging claim.

Rose Cottage qualifies as furnished holiday accommodation. It was acquired on 1 June 1996 so qualification in 1996/97 is determined by reference to the period of twelve months beginning on the day it was first let, in which it was let for a total of 90 days.

Ivy Cottage was sold on 30 June 1996 so qualification is determined by reference to the period from 1 July 1995 to 30 June 1996 (the last day of letting). It does not qualify by itself as it was let for only 55 days in this period but it may be included in an averaging claim.

Averaging claim for 1996/97

	Days let
Honeysuckle Cottage	160
Bluebell Cottage	60
Rose Cottage	90
Ivy Cottage	55

$$\frac{16 + 60 + 90 + 55}{4} = 91.25 \text{ days} \quad \text{note } (a)$$

Note

(a) All four cottages included in the averaging claim qualify as furnished holiday accommodation as each is deemed to have been let for 91.25 days in the year 1996/97. If the average had been less than 70, any three of these cottages could have been included in an averaging claim leaving the other as non-qualifying. If this still did not produce the desired result, an average of any two could be tried. More than one averaging claim is possible for a year of assessment, but no cottage may be included in more than one claim.

68.11 **'Rent a room' relief for letting of rooms in private residence.** The taking in of domestic lodgers may be treated as the carrying on of a trade, where services other than accommodation are provided, or as furnished lettings. The relief described below applied for Schedule D, Case VI (as well as Case I) purposes prior to the introduction of the new Schedule A regime, and so applied for 1992/93 and subsequent years of assessment.

A special relief applies to an individual receiving sums for the use of furnished accommodation in a 'qualifying residence' or residences, or for ancillary services consisting of the provision of meals, cleaning, laundry etc., in respect of all of which the individual would otherwise be chargeable to income tax under Schedule D, Case I and/or Schedule A (previously and/or Case VI). Unless the taxpayer elects otherwise (see below), and provided that the gross sums received (i.e. without any deduction for expenses) do not exceed the individual's limit for the year (see below), the profits or gains (or losses) of the basis period for the year of assessment are treated as nil. No capital allowances or balancing charges are made to or on the individual in relation to the letting of the accommodation. If, however, the addition of such balancing charges which would otherwise be made for the year of assessment to the gross sums received would result in the individual's limit for the year being exceeded, the exemption does not apply. An election for the exemption not to apply for a year of assessment must be made, and may be withdrawn, within, for 1996/97 and later years, twelve months after 31 January following that year and, for earlier years, one year after the end of that year (or, in both cases, such longer time as the Board may allow—see Revenue Inspector's Manual, IM 1729g) by written notice, and any necessary assessment is not out of time if made within, for 1996/97 and later years, twelve months after 31 January following the tax year in which (for earlier years, one year after) the election was made (or withdrawal notice given). The exemption (and the further provisions described below) do not apply for a year of assessment for which the source(s) for income tax purposes of the gross sums concerned also include sums which are not within the reliefs.

Where the gross sums received exceed the individual's limit for the year of assessment, the individual may elect for the profits or gains of the basis period to be treated as equal to that excess. If the gross sums are treated for income tax purposes as arising from more than one source, the individual's limit is apportioned amongst those sources on the basis of the proportion of the gross sums taxable under each source. No capital allowances are made to the individual in relation to the letting of the accommodation. An election for this treatment to apply for a year of assessment must be made (and may be withdrawn) within, for 1996/97 and later years, twelve months after 31 January following that year and, for earlier years, one year after the end of that year (or, in both cases, such longer time as the Board may allow) by written notice, and the election (or withdrawal) applies for all subsequent years of assessment (but, in the case of a withdrawal, without prejudicing the right to make a fresh election). Any necessary assessment is not out of time if made within, for 1996/97 and later years, twelve months after 31 January following the tax year in which (for earlier years, one year after) the election was made (or withdrawal notice given). Where an election applies to a year of assessment for which the gross sums do *not* exceed the individual's limit, the individual is deemed to have withdrawn the election for that year and subsequent years of assessment (again without prejudicing the right to make a fresh election for a subsequent year).

A *'qualifying residence'* is a 'residence' which is the individual's only or main residence at any time in the basis period for the year of assessment in relation to the source in question. The Revenue consider that the basis period does not commence until the tenancy commences, and ceases when the tenancy ceases, so that the relief cannot apply during e.g. the absence of the taxpayer abroad, even during the years of departure and return (unless, exceptionally, there is a period of overlap between the tenant's and the taxpayer's occupation of the house as a residence, e.g. where part of the house is retained for the taxpayer's use, and used, *as his main residence* at some time during a basis period). (Revenue Inspector's Manual, IM 17291).

'*Residence*' means a building (or part) occupied or intended to be occupied as a separate residence (ignoring any temporary division into separate residences of a building (or part) designed for permanent use as a single residence), or a caravan or house-boat.

The individual's limit for a year of assessment is £3,250 (or such sum as may be specified by Treasury order), but is reduced to one-half of that amount in certain cases where sums accrue to another person in respect of use of furnished accommodation in the individual's only or main residence or in respect of services ancillary (as above) to that use.

[*F(No 2)A 1992, s 59, 10 Sch; FA 1995, 6 Sch 38; FA 1996, s 135, 21 Sch 47*].

The Revenue consider that 'rent a room' relief is inapplicable to the letting of a residence (or part) as an office or for other trade or business purposes (other than the business of providing furnished living accommodation). (Revenue Tax Bulletin August 1994 p 154).

68.12   *Example*

Frankie and Johnny are single persons sharing a house as their main residence. They have for some years taken in lodgers to supplement their income. Schedule D, Case VI assessments on the net rental income have been raised on a current year basis, with the 1991/92 assessments being based on the year ended 5 April 1992. As Frankie pays the greater share of the mortgage interest on the house, she and Johnny have an agreement to share the rental income in the ratio 2:1, although expenses are shared equally.

For each of the years ended 5 April 1993 and 1994, gross rents amounted to £4,200 and allowable expenses were £600. In the year ended 5 April 1995, the couple face a heavy repair bill after uninsured damage to one of the rooms. Gross rents for that year amount to £3,600 and expenses to £3,400. For the years ended 5 April 1996 and 1997, gross rents are £5,400 and expenses £2,400.

For 1992/93, the position is as follows

Normal Schedule D, Case VI computation

	Frankie £	Johnny £
Gross rents (y/e 5.4.93)	2,800	1,400
Allowable expenses	300	300
Net rents	£2,500	£1,100

Johnny's share of *gross* rents is less than his one half share (£1,625) of the basic amount (£3,250) for 1992/93. It is assumed that he would not make the election under *10 Sch 10* for the exemption under *10 Sch 9* ('rent a room' relief) not to apply. His share of net rents is thus treated as nil.

Frankie's share of gross rents exceeds £1,625, so the exemption in *10 Sch 9* cannot apply. She can, however, elect under *10 Sch 12* for *10 Sch 11* to apply, the election to be made by 5 April 1994. Under *10 Sch 11*, she is taxed on the excess of *gross* rents over £1,625. It is assumed that she will make the election as she will then be taxed on £1,175 rather than £2,500.

For 1993/94, the position is as for 1992/93.

For 1994/95, the position is as follows

Normal Schedule D, Case VI computation

	Frankie	Johnny
	£	£
Gross rents (y/e 5.4.95)	2,400	1,200
Allowable expenses	1,700	1,700
Net rents/(loss)	£700	£(500)

Johnny's share of gross rents continues to be less than his one half share of the basic amount. Under *10 Sch 9*, his share of net rents will be treated as nil. However, he will obtain no relief, by carry-forward or otherwise, for his loss. In order to preserve his loss, he could elect under *10 Sch 10* for *10 Sch 9* not to apply, the election to be made by 5 April 1996 and having effect for 1994/95 only.

Frankie's share of gross rents continues to exceed her one half share of the basic amount. Therefore, her previous election under *10 Sch 12* will not automatically be deemed to be withdrawn. She will be taxed under *10 Sch 11* on £775 (£2,400 – £1,625). However, this is greater than the amount taxable on a normal Schedule D, Case VI computation (£700), so it is assumed she would withdraw the election with effect for 1994/95 and subsequent years. The notice of withdrawal must be made by 5 April 1996 but does not prejudice the making of a fresh election for 1995/96 or any subsequent year.

For 1995/96, the position is as follows

Normal Schedule A computation

	Frankie	Johnny
	£	£
Gross rents (y/e 5.4.96)	3,600	1,800
Allowable expenses	1,200	1,200
Net rents	£2,400	£600

Johnny's share of gross rents now exceeds his share of the basic amount, so the exemption will not apply. He could elect for *10 Sch 11* to apply, and his assessment will then be reduced to £175 (£1,800 – £1,625). This is further reduced to nil (see the transitional provisions for Schedule A losses at 68.13(B) below) by the bringing forward of his £500 Case VI loss for 1994/95 (assuming that he has no other source of Case VI income in 1994/95 against which to relieve this loss). (Although a loss cannot enter into the ascertaining of the amount assessable under *10 Sch 11*, there appears to be no reason why a loss cannot be set off against the amount so ascertained.) If Johnny did not make the election, his assessment would be on £100 with the whole of his 1994/95 loss having been utilised.

Frankie can make a fresh election for *10 Sch 11* to apply, with effect from 1995/96, and her 1995/96 Schedule A assessment will then be £1,975 (£3,600 – £1,625).

For 1996/97, the position is as follows.

The normal Schedule A computation is as for 1995/96. Assuming Frankie and Johnny both elected under *10 Sch 11* for 1995/96, the elections will continue to apply for 1996/97, so that their respective 1996/97 Schedule A assessments are £1,975 and £175. Johnny's assessment is further reduced to nil by the brought forward balance of £325 of the 1994/95 Schedule D, Case VI loss (of which the balance of £150 is carried forward to 1997/98).

68.13 Schedule A—Property Income

LOSSES

Carry-forward. With effect as in 68.3 above and otherwise than for corporation tax purposes, where a loss (a '*Schedule A loss*'), computed in like manner as Schedule A profits, is incurred by any person in a Schedule A business, carried on alone or in partnership, it is carried forward without time limit as a set-off against the first following profits of the business, or, if insufficient, the next, and so on. [*Sec 379A(1)(7); FA 1995, 6 Sch 19(1)*].

Set-off against other income. Where a Schedule A loss is incurred in a year of assessment (the year of loss) and as regards that year,

(*a*)   there is a net amount of capital allowances, (i.e. capital allowances, with the exclusion mentioned below, exceed any balancing charges), *and/or*

(*b*)   the Schedule A business has been carried on in relation to land which consists of or includes an 'agricultural estate' to which 'allowable agricultural expenses' (see below) are attributable,

a claim may be made under *Sec 379A(3)* to set an amount of loss relief against total income for the year of loss or the following year. The amount of loss relief is restricted to the lowest of the following:

(i)   the loss,

(ii)   the 'relievable income' for the year to which the claim relates, and

(iii)   the net capital allowances (where (*a*) above applies) or the allowable agricultural expenses (where (*b*) applies) or the sum of those two items (where *both* (*a*) and (*b*) apply).

Relief cannot normally be claimed for both years in respect of the same loss, but where relief is restricted for one year by virtue of (ii) above, the balance (i.e. the excess of the lower of (i) and (iii) above over the relief given) may be claimed for the other year. A person's '*relievable income*' is his total income after taking into account any Schedule A loss brought forward under *Sec 379A(1)* (see above) from a year prior to the year of loss and, where the claim relates to the year of loss, after giving effect to any *Sec 379A(3)* claim in respect of a loss for the preceding year. A loss carried forward under *Sec 379A(1)* from the year of loss is restricted or extinguished by relief given for that loss under *Sec 379A(3)*.

A claim under *Sec 379A(3)* must be made within 12 months after 31 January following *the year to which the claim relates* (where that year is 1996/97 or a later year), and must be accompanied by any necessary amendments to the claimant's SELF-ASSESSMENT (78) for that year. If the claim relates to 1995/96, the time limit is extended to two years, i.e. the claim must be made by 5 April 1998.

In computing net capital allowances (see (*a*) above), there must be excluded any capital allowances on machinery and plant which is let to a person who does not use it or uses it for purposes other than those of a trade (with a proportionate amount being excluded where this applies for part only of the year). An '*agricultural estate*' (see (*b*) above) means any land (including any houses or other buildings) which is managed as one estate and which consists of or includes any agricultural land, i.e. land in the UK occupied wholly or mainly for husbandry. '*Allowable agricultural expenses*' (see (*b*) above) are any deductible disbursements or expenses attributable to the agricultural estate in respect of maintenance, repairs, insurance or estate management (but excluding loan interest). For these purposes, disbursements and expenses are taken into account only to the extent that they are attributable to the parts of it used for husbandry, with those attributable to parts used partly for other purposes being proportionately reduced.

[*Sec 379A(2)–(10); FA 1995, 6 Sch 19(1)(4)*].

Transitional provisions. The following are treated as Schedule A losses carried forward to 1995/96 (and, if necessary, to subsequent years) under *Sec 379A(1)*.

(A) Any excess expenditure brought forward to 1995/96 which under the old Schedule A regime would have been deductible from rents received and actually brought into account in that year (see 68.16 below).

(B) Any losses which could otherwise have been brought forward to 1995/96 under *Sec 392* in respect of *furnished lettings* (see 74.5 SCHEDULE D, CASE VI).

(C) Any unrelieved interest which could otherwise have been brought forward to 1995/96 under *Sec 355(4)* provided the Schedule A business relates to property that would have satisfied the conditions of *Sec 355(1)(b)* for 1995/96 (letting for 26 weeks out of 52 etc.) if those provisions had been extant for that year (see 43.15 INTEREST PAYABLE).

[*FA 1995, 6 Sch 19(2)(3)*].

68.14   **THE PRE-FINANCE ACT 1995 REGIME**

The provisions described below and in 68.15 to 68.21 below apply for income tax purposes for 1994/95 and earlier years (see also 68.2 above) and for 1995/96 where the transitional provisions at 68.3 above have effect. They continue to apply for corporation tax purposes.

Rents etc. [*Sec 15*]. Schedule A applies to profits or gains arising in respect of

(*a*) rents (including sums treated as such in respect of premiums, see 68.27 below) under leases (including any tenancy) of land (including buildings) in UK,

(*b*) rent-charges, ground annuals, feu duties and other annual payments reserved in respect of, or charged on or issuing out of, such land,

(*c*) any other receipts from an estate or interest in, or right over, such land or any incorporeal hereditament or incorporeal heritable subject in the UK,

generally on the basis of rents or receipts arising in the chargeable period, less allowable deductions as below. Receipts from sales of turf are within (*c*) although they may alternatively be taxed as trading receipts within Schedule D, Case I (*Lowe v J W Ashmore Ltd Ch D 1970, 46 TC 597*): but from sale of colliery dross bings held to be capital (*Roberts v Lord Belhaven's Exors CS 1925, 9 TC 501*). Sums received for licence to tip soil on land held capital (*McClure v Petre Ch D 1988, 61 TC 226*).

But Schedule A does not include the following.

(i) *Rents etc. from furnished lettings.* These are assessed under SCHEDULE D, CASE VI (74) unless the landlord elects for Schedule A in respect of the payment for use of the premises within two years of the end of the chargeable period. The inclusion in this provision of payments other than rents under leases is statutory for chargeable periods beginning after 5 April 1992, but was applied in practice for earlier periods. [*Sec 15(1)(2); F(No 2)A 1992, s 58*]. The rent for the furnishings, etc. then remains under Case VI. See, however, 74.4 SCHEDULE D, CASE VI and 68.9, 68.11 above as to holiday lettings and the letting of furnished accommodation in private residences. See 68.4 above as regards income from letting caravan pitches.

(ii) *Woodlands.* Profits or gains arising from occupation of WOODLANDS (69) under commercial management with a view to profit.

(iii) *Yearly interest.*

68.15 Schedule A—Property Income

(iv) *Mineral rents, royalties etc.* charged under *Secs 55* (Schedule D, Case I), *119* or *120*, see under 23.2 and 23.14 DEDUCTION OF TAX AT SOURCE. *[Sec 15(1); FA 1988, 6 Sch 6]*.

Rents etc. from connected persons. In relation to rents etc. chargeable under Schedule A which accrue after 9 March 1992, special provisions apply where the payer and recipient are 'connected' and the rents etc. accrue in a chargeable period of the recipient before that in which they are payable. If the payer is entitled to a deduction for the rents etc. in computing profits or gains for tax purposes, the recipient is regarded as becoming entitled to the rents etc. in the chargeable period in which they accrue (rather than that in which they become payable). For these purposes, rents etc. are treated as accruing at the same times and in the same amounts as they are so treated for the purposes of calculating the deduction to which the payer is entitled in respect of them, and the payer and recipient are 'connected' if they are CONNECTED PERSONS (20) within *Sec 839* either when the rents etc. accrue or at any earlier time after 9 March 1992 and after the making of the lease or agreement under which they accrue.

Similar provisions apply where the recipient of rents etc. in relation to land is connected with a person, other than the payer, who is entitled to a deduction for other rents etc. payable after they accrue under a lease or agreement relating to all or part of the same land, and those other rents etc. accrued before the rents etc. in question became payable. In such a case the rents etc. are treated as accruing, and hence chargeable, at the times and in the amounts they would be so treated if paid *by* rather than *to* the recipient and relieved as a trading deduction. *[Secs 33A, 33B; F(No 2)A 1992, s 57]*.

68.15 **Expenses deductible—specific items.** *[Secs 25–33]*. From *rent* (including sums treated as such in respect of premiums) to which the landlord becomes entitled in any chargeable period in respect of leased premises or land there may be deducted the aggregate of payments (but not interest, *Sec 25(2)*, nor items recoverable under insurance or from some other person, or (except in the case of a company) paid under deduction of tax) made by him for

(a) maintenance or repairs (arising from dilapidation during the currency of the lease and while he was landlord *[Sec 25(3)(b)]*), insurance or management (see below),

(b) other services the landlord was obliged, without separate consideration, to provide,

(c) rates or other charges on the occupier which the landlord was obliged to defray, and

(d) any rent (and see 68.28 below, re premiums), rent-charge, ground annual, feu duty or other periodical payment made by him in respect of the leased premises,

in that chargeable or any previous period, within the currency of the lease, during which he was the landlord.

In practice, relief under (b) above will be given for landlord's expenditure on services, amenities, etc. for tenants, even if not under an express lease covenant, but only if as under an arm's length agreement.

As regards (c), a deduction will normally be available for council tax (introduced on 1 April 1993) paid on let property (or for that part of any council tax paid which is attributable to the letting). (Revenue Press Release 16 March 1993). As regards the community charge, which was replaced by the council tax, a deduction is available for the standard community charge (payable in respect of premises which were not the sole or main residence of the occupier) where the property concerned was let. Similarly a deduction against rent is available for any amount of the collective community charge (payable by landlords in respect of certain houses in multiple occupation) which was not met by contributions from residents. (Revenue Press Release 10 November 1989). The deduction of business rates is unaffected by these changes.

Allowance for **maintenance and repairs** is limited to expenditure incurred by the taxpayer concerned in respect of current dilapidation [*Sec 25(3)*], and there is thus no allowance for remedying deterioration which occurred before he purchased the property except, by concession, where the immediately preceding owner was the spouse (or trustee for the spouse). (Revenue Pamphlet IR 1, A21). As regards pre-purchase dilapidation see *Law Shipping* and *Odeon Theatres* cases under 71.78 SCHEDULE D, CASES I AND II (but *Odeon* case does not displace *Sec 25(3)* for Schedule A purposes).

Expenditure on improvements, additions or alterations is not allowed, nor is any outlay which has been allowed otherwise in computing income—e.g. under Schedule D, Case I [*Sec 31(6)*], nor expenditure balanced by the receipt of insurance moneys or recovered from, or borne by, any person other than the taxpayer (except where the receipt itself is income chargeable under Sch A). [*Sec 31(5)*].

But, concessionally, the estimated cost of any maintenance and repairs obviated by alterations, etc., is allowed provided the alterations are not so extensive as to amount to reconstruction, and there has been no such change in the use of the property as would have rendered the repairs, etc., unnecessary. (Revenue Pamphlet IR 1, B4).

The following are types of expenditure normally allowable in respect of the property which is let.

(i)   Current repairs and redecorations, inside and out.

(ii)   Where falling under (*b*) above, upkeep of gardens of flats, and remuneration of porters, cleaners, etc.

(iii)   Expenditure, so far as incurred for the benefit of tenants, on keeping up private roads, drains, ditches, embankments, etc., on an estate containing property let by the landlord (but not road works payments by frontager, *Davidson v Deeks Ch D 1956, 37 TC 32*).

(iv)   Maintenance of common parts of blocks of offices, etc.

(v)   CAPITAL ALLOWANCES (10) under *CAA 1990, Pt II*, are given (if the taxpayer so elects in writing) on machinery or plant provided for use, or used, by a person entitled to rents or receipts falling under Sch A, for maintenance, repair, etc., of the properties concerned. See 10.25 CAPITAL ALLOWANCES as regards certain expenditure on industrial buildings treated as being on machinery or plant and 10.34 CAPITAL ALLOWANCES as regards entitlement to allowances for fixtures. An election as above, if made, has effect for the year of claim and all subsequent years, and may relate to all such machinery or, conditionally, to a specified class thereof only. Allowances or balancing charges are added to, or deducted from, total admissible outlay for the year; if a charge cannot be so dealt with it is assessed under Case VI. [*Sec 32*]. As an alternative to the above, renewals basis may be claimed.

(vi)   Insurance premiums against damage to the fabric of the property by fire, flood or tempest etc.

(vii)   Valuation fees for purposes of insurance (but not for sale, probate, etc.).

(viii)   Cost of rent collection. (But not rents embezzled by agent, *Pyne v Stallard-Penoyre Ch D 1964, 42 TC 183*. See also *Clapham's Trustees v Belton Ch D 1956, 37 TC 26*.)

(ix)   Upkeep of estate offices.

(x)   Salaries and wages of employees engaged full-time on estate management.

(xi) Pensions (not under covenant) customarily paid to retired employees or their widows so far as attributable to former services which were an allowable expense for Sch A purposes.

(xii) Legal costs relating to the drawing up of a lease or tenancy agreement, although strictly capital, are in practice allowed, provided that:

    (*a*) in the case of a first letting, the letting is for a period which does not exceed 21 years;

    (*b*) on a re-letting, the re-letting is for a period which does not (and could not at the lessee's option) exceed 50 years.

(xiii) Legal and accountancy costs for preparing accounts, tax computations, etc. for the property.

(xiv) As regards agricultural property, costs of arbitration to determine rent, obtaining certificate of bad farming, or making a record of the holding. (Costs and compensation under claims for disturbance, unexhausted manures, etc., are not allowed.)

(xv) Ordinary annual subscriptions to The Country Landowners' Association, The Scottish Landowners' Federation and The National Association of Property Owners.

See generally Revenue Assessment Procedures Manual, AP 1572 *et seq.*.

68.16 **Expenses and deficiencies deductible—general provisions.** See 68.13(A) above for the treatment of excess expenditure carried forward to 1995/96 where the new Schedule A regime for income tax has effect for that year.

(*a*) Expenditure on property the rent from which is assessable under Sch A is deductible, normally on the basis of actual payments made in the chargeable period. If the income for that period is insufficient to permit of full deduction, expenditure may be allowed for the period in which the payment became due. Any unrelieved excess may be carried forward during the currency of the lease and set against rents of the next subsequent period, and so on [*Secs 25, 31, 37(9)*], or, in the case of expenditure on maintenance, repair, insurance and management of agricultural property only, set against other income of the same year. [*Sec 33(1)*]. In the case of a property dealer, expenditure unrelieved under Schedule A in the current year may be allowed against Schedule D, Case I income. (Revenue Pamphlet IR 27, para 114, now withdrawn). There is also a limited right of offset against income from other properties in the same ownership, see below. See also 71.56 (*d*) SCHEDULE D, CASES I AND II as regards maintenance expenses of non-commercial owner-occupied farms.

(*b*) Where a lease is at a *full rent* (i.e. sufficient, on average, to cover the landlord's obligations, maintenance, repairs, insurance, etc.) deductions as above include unrelieved outlay incurred during (i) the period of any previous full-rent lease of the premises by the same landlord, or (ii) any void period which either immediately follows the end of such a lease, or which commences with the acquisition of the property by the present landlord. However expenditure in these earlier periods may not be deducted if there is a period which does not fall into either (i) or (ii) between the earlier period and the period in which the deduction is claimed. A *void period* is a period during which the owner is entitled to possession of the premises but during which he is not in occupation. [*Sec 25(2)(5)(6)*].

(*c*) There is further relief for excess expenditure as under (*a*) or (*b*) above on properties let at a full rent (or in void periods following such lettings). Any such excess may be set against rents receivable by the same landlord from other properties, provided that those other properties are let at *full rents* and *not* on *tenant's repairing leases*. Thus in effect all rents and expenses of properties let at full rents and not on tenant's repairing leases are pooled, and against any aggregate balance of receipts may be set:

(i)   excess expenditure of past years as under (*b*) above on properties in the pool; and

(ii)   excess expenditure of the same year and of past years as under (*b*) above on other properties of the same landlord let at full rents on tenant's repairing leases. [*Sec 25(7)*].

A *tenant's repairing lease* is one under which the lessee is obliged to maintain and repair the whole, or substantially the whole, of the premises. [*Sec 24(6)(c)*]. A lease under which all repair and maintenance work falls on the tenant apart from one structural item, such as maintenance of the foundations, is usually regarded as a tenant's repairing lease.

Deficiencies on leases not at '*full rent*' cannot be offset against any other source of income. They can only be carried forward for relief against income from the same property under the same lease while in the same ownership. [*Sec 25(3)(4)*].

(*d*)   For applying the above provisions to land which, at 5 April 1963, was in one ownership and *managed as one estate*, the owner may elect to be treated as receiving, for any part of the estate not let (other than premises he occupies for estate management or trade), rent at a rate equivalent to its annual value, and, for any part let at less than a full rent, rent at a rate at least equal to its annual value. He may then claim deduction of expenditure, as above, in respect of each of the properties in the estate. Any excess expenditure on such a property may not be set against rents from properties outside the estate, but excess expenditure on properties outside the estate let at full rent may be set against estate property rent, subject to the usual conditions at (*c*) above. For details of the election, meaning of 'annual value' and other matters, see 68.7(*e*) above.

(*e*)   From a receipt *other than rent* (rent charges, feu duties and other non-rental income) deductions may be made for payments as under 68.15(*a*) (*d*) above, and any other non-capital expenses, constituting expenses of the transaction under which the sum arose, or which could be, but have not been, deducted from sums arising from other similar transactions in the year of assessment or any previous year. [*Sec 28*]. For treatment of sporting rights, and allowances for expenditure on making sea walls, see *Secs 29, 30* and *Hesketh v Bray CA 1888, 2 TC 380*.

(*f*)   See 68.7(*c*) above (business entertaining) and 68.7(*d*) above (expenditure involving crime) both of which apply to prohibit deductions.

68.17   *Example*

Mr Grey lets out the following properties in 1994/95
Shop to B at full rent of £1,000 p.a., expenses £1,500 (landlord repairing lease)
Factor to C at full rent of £5,000 p.a., expenses £2,000 (landlord repairing lease)
Shop to D at full rent of £1,000 p.a., expenses £4,000 (tenant's repairing lease)
Shop to E at full rent of £6,000 p.a., expenses £500 (tenant's repairing lease)
House to F at less than full rent let at £200 p.a., expenses £500

68.18 Schedule A—Property Income

The tax position is as follows.

	Landlord repairing leases		Tenant's repairing leases		Lease at less than full rent
	£	£	£	£	£
Rents	1,000	5,000	1,000	6,000	200
Deduct Expenses	1,500	2,000	4,000	500	500
Profit (Loss)	(500)	3,000	(3,000)	5,500	(300)
Set-off	500	(500)	—	—	—
		2,500			
Set-off		(2,500)	2,500	—	—
Assessment			—	£5,500	—
Losses carried forward			£(500)	—	£(300)

68.18   **Lost rents etc.** Where any rent or receipt to which the landlord was entitled is not in fact received (by default of the payer, despite reasonable steps for enforcement, or by waiver reasonably made, without consideration, to avoid hardship) a claim may be made to leave that sum out of account. But if any sum so ignored is subsequently recovered the Revenue must be notified (under penalty) within six months thereafter and the relevant liabilities are then readjusted (but see 68.19 below where accounts basis applies). [*Sec 41*].

68.19   **Accounts basis and returns.** In appropriate cases where full accounts (including balance sheets) are made up annually to the same date the Revenue will accept computations based thereon, treating the items included in the accounts as being those for the tax year in which the accounting period ends. Both receipts and expenditure must be capable of analysis as relating to (*a*) properties let at full rents (see 68.16(*b*) above); (*b*) properties let at full rents on tenants' repairing leases; (*c*) properties let at other than full rents; and (*d*) other chargeable items. But separate figures for each individual property are not necessary where it is reasonably clear that total liability will not be affected. (Revenue Pamphlet IR 27 paras 102–104, now withdrawn).

Where accounts basis applies, lost rents (as under 68.18 above) may be treated as bad debts are for Case I purposes, i.e. allowed as deductions for the year in which written off in accounts, recoveries being treated as receipts of the year in which recovered.

See 68.22 below for Revenue guidelines on the transition to the Finance Act 1995 regime.

Simplified returns. Landlords with a total annual gross income from property under £15,000 (£10,000 for accounts submitted before 6 April 1992) are required only to state the gross income, the total amount of allowable expenses and the net income or profit. There will, of course, still be a need to keep accurate records to ensure the correctness of the three-line accounts. (Revenue Press Releases 7 November 1989, 1 November 1991).

68.20   **Assessments and payments of tax.** Made for income tax primarily on the basis of the net income as in the preceding tax year, tax being payable accordingly, but with automatic adjustment after the year end to the basis of the income to which the recipient became entitled in the actual year of assessment, less expenditure in that actual year (subject as above). [*Sec 22(2); FA 1995, 6 Sch 3*]. However, if, before 1 January (when the tax is normally due) in any year, the taxpayer shows that his actual rents and receipts (i.e. before any deductions) for that year will be less than those of the preceding year by reason of his having ceased to possess one or more sources of that income, the primary assessment, as above, will be reduced proportionately by the estimated reduction (with final adjustment after the end of the year). [*Sec 22(3); FA 1995, 6 Sch 3*].

68.21 **Collection from lessee or agent.** Income tax under Sch A is payable by the person entitled to the rents, etc. But if he does not pay, and is not in occupation of the property concerned, any lessee of the property whose interest derives from him may be required to pay, to the extent of any rent falling due. The lessee then has a right of recoupment when paying his rent. A person receiving rents, etc., on behalf of another may, in default of payment by the latter, be required, under penalty, to pay them to the Revenue in settlement. These provisions are repealed for corporation tax purposes with effect in relation to accounting periods ending on or after 31 March 1995. [*Secs 21, 23; FA 1995, s 39(4), 6 Sch 3*].

68.22 **TRANSITION TO FINANCE ACT 1995 REGIME**

The Revenue have, after consultation, published guidelines to its inspectors on how the transition for income tax from the old Schedule A regime or the Case VI charge on furnished lettings to the new Schedule A regime should be handled and the non-statutory adjustments that may be made so as far as possible to give a fair result, bearing in mind that the transition may involve changes in the basis of computation and/or changes of basis period (the new regime operating on a strict fiscal year basis). The adjustments will normally be made to the 1994/95 computation (but see below as regards loan interest). Where this cannot be done, because the 1994/95 assessment is already final, the adjustments should be made to the 1995/96 assessment, but not so as to affect the computation of the adjustment itself and not so as to increase the 1995/96 assessment (or reduce losses) beyond the strict statutory figure under the new regime. (Revenue Tax Bulletin December 1995 pp 268–271).

Basis of computation. The statutory basis of computation for 1994/95 and earlier for Schedule A was a receipts and payments basis, whereas that for 1995/96 onwards will be an accruals basis. By agreement between taxpayer and inspector in individual cases, (*a*) sources which first arise in 1994/95 may be dealt with as if the new regime applied for that year, thus avoiding any transition, (*b*) sources which cease soon after 1995/96 may continue to be dealt with under the old rules, and (*c*) for continuing sources a special computation may be produced for 1994/95, starting with the profit computed under the old rules and adding or deducting, as appropriate, items which would otherwise either fall into a gap between the 1994/95 and 1995/96 computations or be included in both. In some cases, by concession, an accruals basis may have operated previously, and in others (i.e. small landlords) a cash basis may continue to be acceptable under the new regime; therefore, an adjustment may not be necessary. The comments in this paragraph are not considered to be relevant for furnished lettings.

Basis periods. As mentioned at 68.19 above, an accounts basis was sometimes applied to Schedule A under the old regime. This was also the case for furnished lettings, for which a preceding year basis of assessment also often applied (see 74.3 SCHEDULE D, CASE VI). The Revenue's preferred option, in moving to a fiscal year (and current year) basis, is to invite the landlord to prepare accounts for a period starting with the end of the basis period for 1993/94 and ending with 5 April 1995 and to tax a time-based proportion of the profits. If, for example, the 1993/94 Schedule A assessment was based on accounts to 31 December 1993 under the old regime, the 1994/95 assessment will be based on 12/15 of the profit for the period 1 January 1994 to 5 April 1995 under these transitional rules and 1995/96 on the year to 5 April 1996 under the new regime. For capital allowances purposes, additions and disposals for the full transitional accounting period will be taken into account but only 12 months' writing-down allowance will be given.

Loan interest. Where loan interest relief was given for 1994/95 and earlier years under the rules in 43.15 INTEREST PAYABLE on an interest paid basis, a switch to an accruals basis under the new Schedule A regime may result in some interest being unrelieved. The inspector may allow 'some further relief' by deduction in arriving at the 1995/96 Schedule A profit. The principle to be followed is that if income and expenses are taken fully into account over the lifetime of the letting business, then relief should be given for all the interest paid over that period, but if income and expenses drop out on transition, as with a change of basis period as above, it may be appropriate for the overall position taking account of interest to be considered.

Absence of agreement. Where taxpayer and inspector cannot reach agreement on adjustments, the inspector will assess income under Schedule A for 1994/95 by reference to profits of the fiscal year (calculated under the old regime) and will determine a furnished lettings basis period under *Sec 69* (see 74.3 SCHEDULE D, CASE VI). Apportionment of profits of different accounting periods may be necessary. 1995/96 will then be assessed on the statutory basis (under the new regime) with no intervening adjustment. Similarly, on appeal, the Commissioners can only apply the strict statutory basis for either year.

(Revenue Press Release 10 February 1995).

See the examples at 68.23 below and see also Revenue Tax Bulletin December 1995 pp 268–271 for further commentary and examples, including an example where both computational and basis period adjustments arise in the same case.

68.23 *Examples*

Basis periods

Brown lets a number of furnished apartments and has in the past prepared furnished lettings accounts to 31 December. For tax years up to and including 1992/93, he has been assessed under Schedule D, Case VI on a preceding year basis. Both the choice of accounting date and the application of a preceding year basis are the result of a long-established practice agreed between Brown and his tax office. To facilitate the transition to the new Schedule A basis, Brown's inspector invites him to submit accounts covering the whole of the period from the end of 1993/94 basis period to 5 April 1995. Income and allowable expenditure are as follows.

	Income (£)	Expenditure (£)
Year ended 31 December 1992	14,000	3,000
27 months to 5 April 1995	36,000	9,450
Year ended 5 April 1996	17,000	4,000

Assessments will be as follows.

		£
1993/94	Schedule D, Case VI	11,000
1994/95	Schedule D, Case VI ((36,000 − 9,450) × 12/27)	11,800
1995/96	Schedule A	13,000

Basis of computation

The facts are as in the example above except that Brown also lets an unfurnished property, accounts having always been prepared to 5 April. Rent is receivable three months in advance on 6 December, 6 March, 6 June and 6 September, and was increased from £3,300 to £3,600 p.a. with effect from 6 March 1995, and to £3,720 p.a. from 6 March 1996. Gross rental income receivable as shown by the Schedule A computation to 5 April 1995, prepared on the statutory basis then prevailing, is as follows.

	£
3 × £825 (receivable 6 June, 6 September and 6 December 1994)	2,475
1 × £900 (receivable 6 March 1995)	900
	£3,375

The accounts for the year to 5 April 1996, prepared on an accruals basis in accordance with commercial accounting practice as for trades and professions, show rent receivable £3,610 calculated as follows.

	£
Rent received on the four due dates (3 × £900 + £930)	3,630
Less prepaid 6 April 1996 to 5 June 1996 (£930 × 2/3)	620
	3,010
Add prepaid 6 April 1995 to 5 June 1995 (£900 × 2/3)	600
	£3,610

Allowable expenses are £900 and £1,000 for the years to 5 April 1995 and 5 April 1996 respectively.

An adjustment to the 1994/95 computation may be agreed between the taxpayer and the inspector as follows.

	£
Gross rents as above	3,375
Deduct allowable expenditure	900
	2,475
Transitional adjustment	
Deduct rent for period 6 April 1995 to 5 June 1995 included in accounts to 5 April 1996	600
Schedule A taxable income	£1,875

The position for 1995/96 is as follows.

	£
Gross rents as above	3,610
Deduct allowable expenditure	1,000
	2,610
Furnished lettings (as in example above)	13,000
Profits of Schedule A business	£15,610

Note

For simplicity, the example immediately above considers only income. In practice, computational adjustments are also likely to arise as regards expenditure. See Revenue Tax Bulletin December 1995 pp 268–271 for examples.

68.24 **NON-RESIDENT LANDLORDS—COLLECTION FROM AGENTS OR TENANTS**

For 1996/97 and subsequent years, where a landlord is non-resident (i.e. his usual place of abode is outside the UK), tax is to be deducted at source by the agent for the property or, where there is no agent, the tenant, with a final settling up with the non-resident landlord. This applies for both income tax and corporation tax purposes, and so applies in relation to furnished letting income under Schedule D, Case VI as well as to Schedule A income (see 68.8 above). [*Sec 42A; FA 1995, s 40(1)–(3)(8)*]. The regulations giving effect to these requirements provide broadly as follows.

(i) Letting agents who receive or have control over UK property income of a non-resident must operate the scheme.

(ii) Where there is no letting agent acting, tenants of a non-resident must operate the scheme.

(iii) Tenants who pay less than £100 per week do not have to operate the scheme unless asked to do so by the Revenue.

(iv) Letting agents and tenants who have to operate the scheme must pay tax at the basic rate each quarter on the non-resident's UK property income less certain allowable expenses and deductions, and must give the non-resident an annual certificate showing details of tax deducted.

(v) Non-residents whose property income is subject to deduction of tax may set the tax deducted against their UK tax liability through their self-assessment.

(vi) Non-residents may apply to the Revenue for approval to receive their UK property income without deduction of tax provided that:

(*a*) their UK tax affairs are up to date;

(*b*) they have never had any obligations in relation to UK tax; or

(*c*) they do not expect to be liable to UK income tax,

and that they undertake to comply with all their UK tax obligations in the future. An appeal may be made against refusal or withdrawal of approval.

The regulations also make provision for interest on unpaid tax and for payments on account under self-assessment, and set out details of the annual information requirements on those operating the scheme, and of other information to be supplied on request. Penalties apply under *TMA s 98* for non-compliance with these return and information provisions.

[*Sec 42A(4)–(7); FA 1995, s 40(2); SI 1995 No 2902*].

The Revenue have issued detailed guidance notes to those required to operate the scheme. See also Revenue Pamphlet IR 140 'Non-resident landlords, their agents and tenants' and Revenue Tax Bulletin December 1995 pp 261–263.

For 1995/96 and earlier years, and for corporation tax as well as income tax purposes, agents for non-UK resident landlords were assessable (including at the higher rate) on their behalf and could retain the tax paid out of money coming into their hands and be indemnified. [*TMA ss 78, 83*]. Where, however, the payment of rent etc. was made (whether in the UK or elsewhere) *directly* to a person whose usual place of abode was outside the UK, the payer had to deduct tax at the basic rate and account for it to the Revenue as under *Sec 350* (see 23.3 DEDUCTION OF TAX AT SOURCE). If this resulted in an overcharge on the landlord, he could reclaim accordingly. [*Sec 43; FA 1995, s 40(3)*]. The tenant would not normally be held liable for tax not deducted at source if unaware of a landlord's change of abode (CCAB Memorandum TR 127, February 1974) or if he could reasonably plead ignorance of the requirement to deduct tax (Revenue Assessment Procedures Manual, AP 1268).

68.25   APPORTIONMENT OF RECEIPTS AND OUTGOINGS ON SALE OF LAND

Where a property is purchased or sold during the year, income or expenditure before contract, or between contract and completion, which is apportioned to the purchaser is treated as having arisen to him immediately after completion. Similarly, where part of a receipt or payment after completion is apportioned to the vendor that part is treated as if he had received or paid it in the period immediately before completion, and the purchaser is relieved accordingly. [*Sec 40; FA 1995, 6 Sch 4(f)*].

68.26   INFORMATION RE LEASES

Information, including consideration for their grant or assignment, etc., may be required, under penalty, from present or former lessees or occupiers, or from agents managing property or receiving rents, etc. [*TMA ss 19, 98; FA 1988, s 123(4)*].

68.27   PREMIUMS ETC. ON LEASES OF UP TO 50 YEARS—ASSESSABILITY ON RECIPIENT [*Secs 34–39; FA 1995, 6 Sch 9–12*]

Premiums. A premium receivable by the landlord (or by another person, see Note (ii) below) under a lease of land in the UK not exceeding 50 years, or otherwise under the terms subject to which a lease is granted, is treated as additional rent, receivable at the date the lease is granted (but see Notes (ii) and (v) below), equivalent to the amount of the premium less 1/50th for each full year (minus one) in the lease's duration (e.g. if the lease is for 10 years, 41/50ths of any premium will be chargeable). [*Sec 34(1)*, and see Note (ii) below]. For this purpose, where under the terms of the lease the tenant is required to carry out work on the premises (other than normal repairs or maintenance) the value of the benefit accruing to the landlord is treated as a premium receivable at the commencement of the lease. Similarly, any sum payable by the tenant (*a*) for varying or waiving any of the terms of a lease (even if granted before 1963/64), or (*b*), under the terms of the lease, for surrendering it, or in lieu of the whole or part of the rent, is treated as if it were a premium (falling due, under (*a*), at the date of the contract for variation or, under (*b*), when the sum is payable) on a lease for the period affected by the variation, etc. [*Secs 34(2)–(5); FA 1995, 6 Sch 9, 40(1)*]. Note that these provisions refer to leases granted and not to leases assigned. See *Banning v Wright* under 68.28 below. Also see 3.13 ANTI-AVOIDANCE concerning *Sec 780*, and under 71.65 SCHEDULE D, CASES I AND II.

Example (i): A person grants a 14 year lease of premises for a premium of £50,000. The amount chargeable on him in that year is

	£
Premium	50,000
Less $\frac{14-1}{50} \times 50,000$	13,000
Chargeable	£37,000

Note. Only complete years are taken into account. For allowance to payer, see 68.28 below.

But where a lease, etc., which gave rise to a liability as above (or would have done so but for relief as under Note (iii) below, or any exemption) is **subleased or sold**, any potential further liability on that latter event is compared with a fraction of the liability on the first transaction (proportionate to the period covered by the sublease, etc., as compared with that covered by the first lease, etc., with adjustment where the sub-lease relates to part only of the property) and only any *excess* is chargeable. [*Sec 37(1)–(3), (7); FA 1990, 14 Sch 2; FA 1995, 6 Sch 12*].

Example (ii): If, after 4 years, the payer of the premium in (*i*) above grants a sub-lease of 10 years for which he receives a premium of £60,000, the amount chargeable on him is

	£
Premium	60,000
Less $\dfrac{10-1}{50} \times 60,000$	10,800
	49,200
Less 'appropriate fraction' of amount chargeable on superior landlord (see (*i*) above) 10/14ths of £37,000	26,428
Chargeable	£22,772

For these purposes, the amount chargeable on the superior landlord is calculated ignoring any obligation on the tenant to carry out work on the premises in respect of which capital allowances have been or will be granted.

See also 68.28 below as regards relief where the 'appropriate fraction' of the amount chargeable on the superior landlord exceeds the amount of the premium chargeable on the intermediate landlord.

Anti-avoidance provisions. Where a lease granted at less than market value is assigned for a consideration exceeding any premium for which it was granted (or the consideration on any previous assignment) the excess, up to the limit of the amount of any premium, or additional premium, which the grantor forwent when granting the lease, is charged on the assignor to the same extent that an additional premium would have been charged on the grantor. Under the pre-Finance Act 1995 regime (see 68.14 above), the charge is under Schedule D, Case VI. [*Sec 35; FA 1995, 6 Sch 10*].

Similarly, where an interest in land is sold on terms requiring it to be subsequently reconveyed (or leased, later than one month after the sale) to the vendor, or a person connected with him, and the price at which the interest is sold exceeds that at which it is to be reconveyed (or, in the case of a lease-back, the value of the reversionary interest plus any premium for the lease), the excess less 1/50th for each full year (minus one) between the sale and the date (if at least two years after the sale) of the earliest possible reconveyance (or lease-back) is treated as a receipt of a Schedule A business carried on by the vendor, or, under the pre-Finance Act 1995 regime (see 68.14 above) is assessed on the vendor under Sch D, Case VI. [*Sec 36; FA 1995, 6 Sch 11*]. For the so-called 'Treasury Arrangement' to avoid a charge under *Sec 36* where there is a genuine commercial reason for the restricted sale, see Revenue Assessment Procedures Manual, AP 1560. See also 3.13 ANTI-AVOIDANCE.

Notes on above.

(i) For the above purposes the duration of a lease is governed by *Sec 38, 30 Sch 2–4*, and the tenant's rights of extension, or entitlement to a further lease, may be taken into account.

(ii) Where a premium, payment in lieu of rent or for surrender, is payable to a person other than the landlord, or where a payment for variation is due not to the landlord but to some person connected with him, then, under the pre-Finance Act 1995 regime (see 68.14 above), the recipient is not treated as receiving rent as above but is assessed on the whole receipt as profits or gains under Sch D, Case VI. Under the new regime (see 68.2 above), the receipt is treated as a receipt of a Schedule A business (see 68.4 above) carried on by the recipient. [*Sec 34(6)(7); FA 1995, 6 Sch 9*].

(iii) Where any premium etc., is receivable by instalments the recipient may, if he satisfies the Revenue that to pay tax on the whole premium as at the date the lease is granted would cause him undue hardship, pay the tax by instalments over a period not exceeding eight years (or the period during which the premium instalments are receivable if less). [*Sec 34(8)*].

(iv) Adjustment may be claimed under the pre-Finance Act 1995 regime to leave out of account any premium, etc., chargeable as above which is not received. (Terms as under 'Lost Rents', see 68.18 above.) [*Sec 41*]. (Under the new regime, bad debt relief would be available.)

(v) *No loss relief under* SCHEDULE D, CASE VI (74) may be claimed on a loss sustained on any transactions as above. [*Sec 392(4)*].

(vi) See Tolley's Capital Gains Tax for the treatment of chargeable gains arising from disposal by way of a lease. Note that the part of the premium chargeable to income tax is left out of the computation of chargeable gain.

68.28 **PREMIUMS ETC. ON LEASES OF UP TO 50 YEARS—ALLOWANCE TO PAYER**
[*Secs 37, 87; FA 1995, 6 Sch 12, 14*]

Where a premium paid on the grant of a lease, etc., gave rise to a charge on the recipient (see 68.27 above), or would have done so but for exemption, etc., the person for the time being entitled to that lease, etc., is treated as paying additional rent at a rate equivalent to the amount of that charge spread over the period to which it relates. See example below. In *Banning v Wright HL 1972, 48 TC 421* an agreed payment for waiving termination for subletting in breach of covenant was held to be a premium deductible from rents received. Adjustments arise in respect of sub-leases of the whole or part of the property.

The 'additional rent' so ascertained is allowable against property income, e.g. on a subletting [*Sec 37; FA 1995, 6 Sch 12*] or against profits if the property is used in connection with a trade, profession or vocation. [*Sec 87; FA 1995, 6 Sch 14*].

Example: For a premium paid as in example (i) in 68.27 above, the 'additional rent' is 1/14th of £37,000 which is £2,643 per annum (allocated on a daily basis). If, however, a sub-lease is granted for a premium (as in example (ii) in 68.27 above) the 'additional rent' is restricted to the 'appropriate fraction' not used to reduce the charge on that later premium. In the example, the 'appropriate fraction' is entirely used and no 'additional rent' is available.

Anti-avoidance provision. Relief under *Secs 37, 87* will not be allowed in respect of any amount which has become chargeable under *Sec 36* (see 68.27 above). [*Secs 37(1)(a), 87(1)(a); FA 1995, 6 Sch 12, 14*].

68.29 **SCHEDULE A ALLOWANCE ON SALE OF TRADING PREMISES**

Where a trader occupied property before 6 April 1963 for the purpose of his trade, and subsequently sells that property, or otherwise ceases to occupy it, he will normally be entitled (unless he permanently ceases to carry on the trade) to a special deduction from his profits amounting to the net annual value deductions for the years 1963/64 and 1964/65 to which he would have been entitled but for the Schedule A charge in *FA 1963* less the amounts mentioned under *30 Sch 5*. 'Trade' includes a profession or vocation. See Revenue Pamphlet IR 27 para 105, now withdrawn.

69 Schedule B—Woodlands

69.1 THE CHARGE

Schedule B applied to the 'occupation of woodlands in the UK managed on a commercial basis and with a view to the realisation of profit'. [*ICTA 1970, s 91*]. **It was abolished after 5 April 1988.** Where a company accounting period straddled that date, the Schedule B income was apportioned, and the part relating to the period commencing on 6 April 1988 was excluded from taxable income. [*FA 1988, s 65, 6 Sch 2*]. Profits or gains from such occupation are not chargeable under SCHEDULE A (68).

69.2 ELECTION FOR SCHEDULE D ASSESSMENT

Before 15 March 1988, an occupier of woodlands could elect, within two years after the end of the year of assessment (or company accounting period), to be assessed under Schedule D, rather than Schedule B. Such an election had to extend to all woodlands so occupied on the same estate, but woodlands planted or replanted within the previous ten years could be treated as a separate estate. The election remained in force for all subsequent years in which the woodlands continued to be occupied by the person making the election. [*ICTA 1970, s 111*]. CAPITAL ALLOWANCES (10) were available. [*CAA 1990, ss 27(1), 140(8)*]. An election for Schedule D treatment did not allow a claim under *Sec 381* (previously *FA 1978, s 30*, losses in early years of trade, see 46.14 LOSSES) to be made.

This election is abolished after 14 March 1988, subject to transitional provisions (see 69.3 below). Accordingly, profits or losses arising after that date from the occupation of commercial woodlands are, subject to the transitional provisions, not chargeable under Schedule D. Again subject to the transitional provisions, interest paid after that date by any person on a loan to buy an interest in a close company, an employee-controlled company or a partnership carrying on a business consisting of the occupation of commercial woodlands is not eligible for income tax relief (see 43.19, 43.21, 43.22 INTEREST PAYABLE), a just and reasonable apportionment being made where part only of the business so consists. A company's charges on income are similarly restricted where the company (or group) carries on such a business. [*FA 1988, s 65, 6 Sch 3*].

The management of woodlands in respect of which election for Schedule D assessment has been given does not necessarily constitute the carrying on of a trade, and standing timber is not stock for the purposes of *Sec 100* (*Coates v Holker Estates Ch D 1961, 40 TC 75*). See also *Sec 99(1)*, as to purchase and sales of woodlands by dealers in land, and *CGTA 1979, s 113*, for exclusion from capital gains tax of trees, standing or felled, on woodlands managed on a commercial basis. See also 71.82 SCHEDULE D, CASES I AND II (valuation of stock). As to profits from sawmills on an estate see *Christie v Davies KB 1945, 26 TC 398*, and *Williamson Bros CS 1950, 31 TC 370*. Felled timber processed in sawmill at some remove held covered by Schedule B assessment down to planking stage (*Collins v Fraser Ch D 1969, 46 TC 143*).

69.3 TRANSITIONAL PROVISIONS

Assessment under Schedule D and tax allowances for interest paid (see 69.2 above) continues to be available until 5 April 1993 where an election under *ICTA 1970, s 111* was made before 15 March 1988. An election subject to similar conditions and to the same effect could be made under *FA 1988, 6 Sch 4(1)* after 14 March 1988 and before 6 April 1993 where, in relation to a person's occupation of woodlands, either

(a) he had entered into a contract for occupation of the woodlands, or made arrangements evidenced by an instrument or document for such occupation, before 15 March 1988, or (*b*)   he was occupying them on that date, or

(*c*)   he occupies them after that date and had before that date entered into a contract or made arrangements for the afforestation (including the replanting) of the land, or

(*d*)   he occupies them after that date and a grant application by him under *Forestry Act 1979, s 1* (or NI equivalent) had been received by the Forestry Commissioners (or Department of Agriculture) before that date.

In the event of the death of the occupier, the election may be made by any other person occupying the woodlands by virtue of any disposition of property comprised in his estate immediately before his death.

A pre-15 March 1988 election is treated as if made under *FA 1988, 6 Sch 4(1)*. Where an election applies, profits or gains and losses are calculated disregarding any '*relevant grant*', (i.e. any grant under *Forestry Act 1979, s 1* (or NI equivalent) made on terms and conditions first published after 15 March 1988 and not supplementary to a grant made on terms and conditions first published before that date), and expenditure the subject of such a grant is not deductible. An election ceases to have effect for any chargeable period if, before the beginning of the period, a relevant grant has been made with respect to any woodlands on the same estate. For this purpose (and for the purposes of an election under *FA 1988, 6 Sch 4(1)*) woodlands may be treated as being on a separate estate by election within two years of their being planted or replanted.

Profits, etc. of a company accounting period straddling 5 April 1993 are apportioned for the purposes of such an election in force on that date.

For CAPITAL ALLOWANCES (10) purposes, any gap between the end of the basis period for the final year of assessment for which an election has effect and the beginning of the next year of assessment is treated as forming part of that basis period. If, however, a loss is incurred in that final year of assessment, so that the capital allowances in the basis period for the next following year of assessment may augment that loss, then it is that basis period which is extended to the end of the final year of assessment. [*FA 1988, s 65, 6 Sch 4, 5*].

70   Schedule C—Paying and Collecting Agents

[*Secs 17, 44–52, 3 Sch; FA 1996, s 79, 7 Sch*]

70.1   For **1995/96 and earlier years** (and for company accounting periods ending before 1 April 1996), **Schedule C** applies to paying agents (bankers and others) who are entrusted with the payment in the UK of 'interest, public annuities, dividends or shares of annuities' out of the public revenue of any government and the revenue of any public authority or institution outside UK. [*Secs 17(1) para 1, 45*]. 'Interest' in this context means interest on securities, and does not include interest on damages due from the Crown (*Esso Petroleum Co Ltd v Ministry of Defence Ch D 1989, 62 TC 253*). (Since the decision in the *Esso* case, payments of interest other than on securities by Government departments have been made without deduction of tax, but the Treasury announced that no steps would be taken to seek out, nor make further payments to, the recipients of earlier payments of such interest (see Revenue Press Release 2 February 1994).) The agents must deduct tax and pay the net amount to the persons entitled to the interest etc. Tax is to be deducted at the basic rate, except that, in relation to transactions after 5 April 1993, the lower rate applies in the case of a foreign dividend which is neither interest nor any other annual payment made otherwise than by way of dividend. For payments after 5 April 1996 and before 29 April 1996, deduction at the lower rate applies in all cases. Tax so accounted for is applied in the discharge of the tax liability of the person entitled to the related dividends or coupon proceeds. [*Sec 44, 3 Sch; FA 1993, 6 Sch 17; FA 1996, 6 Sch 25*]. This does not apply to dividends payable out of any non-UK public revenue in respect of securities held in a 'recognised clearing system' (see 23.3(ii) DEDUCTION OF TAX AT SOURCE). [*Sec 48(4)*]. The foregoing procedure also applies to amounts payable in Eire on UK government securities in the register of the Bank of Ireland [*Sec 17(1) para 2*] and to certain overseas coupons, including those held in a recognised clearing system. [*Sec 17(1) paras 3, 4; FA 1988, s 76(1)(2)*]. For dividends etc. paid after 30 September 1992, the paying agent must account for the tax deducted within 14 days after the end of the month in which the dividend etc. was paid, and deliver a return of payments within 30 days of the end of each calendar quarter. The Board may raise assessments where they consider tax which should have been accounted for has not been paid, and the tax is then due within 14 days after the date of issue of the notice of assessment. Interest runs on tax, whether assessed or not, from 14 days after the end of the month in which the dividend etc. was paid. [*3 Sch Pt III; F(No 2)A 1992, 11 Sch 2; SIs 1992 Nos 2073, 2075*]. For dividends paid before 1 October 1992, tax was due within 30 days after the date of issue of the notice of assessment. Interest on unpaid tax similarly ran from 30 days after issue of the notice of assessment, except that where an increased assessment resulted from determination of an appeal, interest ran, if earlier, from six months after the due date had there been no postponement. [*3 Sch Pt III as originally enacted; TMA s 86*].

Exemptions apply regarding (*a*) certain UK government stocks etc. (see under 33 GOVERNMENT STOCKS), (*b*) non-residents receiving payments in UK from foreign state securities [*Sec 48*], (*c*) non-resident central banks as specified [*Sec 516*], and (*d*) charities. [*3 Sch 4*]. See also under 43 INTEREST PAYABLE.

Schedule C is abolished for 1996/97 and subsequent years of assessment and for company accounting periods ending after 31 March 1996, the charge being transferred to Schedule D, Case III, IV or V as appropriate. [*Sec 18(3B)–(3E); FA 1996, s 79, 7 Sch, 14 Sch 5*]. The obligations under Schedule C are, however, in effect preserved until the date of Royal Assent to *FA 1996* by *FA 1996, 7 Sch 33–35* (and see above as regards deductions during this period). For the provisions for paying and collecting agents effective from that date, see *Secs 118A–118K* (introduced by *FA 1996, s 156, 29 Sch*) and regulations thereunder.

71   Schedule D, Cases I and II—Profits of Trades, Professions etc.

Cross-references. See subjects dealt with separately under 3 ANTI-AVOIDANCE; 10 CAPITAL ALLOWANCES; 12 CASH BASIS; 25 DOUBLE TAX RELIEF; 34 HERD BASIS; 43 INTEREST PAYABLE; 44 INTEREST RECEIVABLE; 46 LOSSES; 51 NON-RESIDENTS AND OTHER OVERSEAS MATTERS; 53 PARTNERSHIPS; 56 PAYMENT OF TAX; 60 POST-CESSATION ETC. RECEIPTS AND EXPENDITURE; 78 SELF-ASSESSMENT and 69 WOODLANDS.

For 'Whether a Trade Carried On', see 71.29 to 71.39 below and for 'Assessable Profits, Allowable Deductions Etc.' see 71.40 to 71.93 below. There is a sub-index preceding each of these divisions. The special provisions regarding stock relief are at Chapter 82.

The headings in this chapter are as follows.

71.1   CHARGE TO TAX

Tax is charged under **Schedule D, Case I and II** on the profits or gains of trades (Case I) and professions or vocations (Case II) carried on wholly or partly in the UK by UK residents or exercised within the UK by non-residents. [*See 18*]. Businesses carried on wholly abroad are 'possessions' within SCHEDULE D, CASES IV AND V (73) but a business controlled from the UK is within Cases I and II even though the day-to-day trading activities are carried on wholly abroad. For this see 51.12 NON-RESIDENTS AND OTHER OVERSEAS MATTERS and for trades exercised within the UK by non-residents see 51.4 NON-RESIDENTS AND OTHER OVERSEAS MATTERS.

Trade 'includes every trade, manufacture, adventure or concern in the nature of trade' [*Sec 832(1)*]. For what is a trade, see generally 71.29–71.39 below and in particular, in relation to isolated or speculative transactions, 71.35 below. There is no statutory definition of

71.2 Schedule D, Cases I and II—Profits of Trades etc.

'profession or vocation'. There are certain provisions applicable only to trades and others applicable only to professions or vocations but the distinction between the two is of limited practical importance. There is no reported case in which it was necessary to decide between the two for income tax purposes, but in a Hong Kong case it was held that stockbrokers were carrying on a trade, not a profession or business (*Kowloon Stock Exchange Ltd v Commr of Inland Revenue PC, [1984] STC 602*). There are a number of cases turning on whether a business was an exempt profession as specially defined for the purposes of excess profits duty and similar taxes. For these see Tolley's Tax Cases. For professions or vocations (e.g. actor) which necessarily involve carrying out numerous engagements see 71.43 below.

In the rest of this section 'trade' includes 'profession or vocation' unless the context indicates otherwise and similarly Case I includes Case II. For whether the liability is under Schedule D or Schedule E see 75.24 SCHEDULE E. See also 71.31 below for special treatment of certain divers and diving supervisors.

The Schedules are mutually exclusive, see 5.2 ASSESSMENTS. The general principle is that rents and other income derived from the exploitation of proprietary interests in land are within Schedule A and not income derived from a trade. The leading case is *Salisbury House Estate Ltd v Fry HL 1930, 15 TC 266*. For illustrations see *Sywell Aerodrome Ltd v Croft CA 1941, 24 TC 126; Webb v Conelee Properties Ltd Ch D 1982, 56 TC 149*. However, profits or gains arising out of land are charged under Case I in the case of mines, quarries, gravel pits, sand pits, brickfields, ironworks, gas works, canals, railways, rights of markets, fairs and tolls and like concerns. [*Sec 55*]. Farming and market gardening within the UK is treated as trading. [*Sec 53(1)*]. All the farming carried on by a particular person, partnership or body of persons is treated as one trade [*Sec 53(2)*] (*Bispham v Eardiston Farming Co Ch D 1962, 40 TC 322*) but this does not apply to farming outside the UK (*Sargent v Eayrs Ch D 1972, 48 TC 573*). See 69 SCHEDULE B for woodlands managed on a commercial basis.

71.2 COMPANIES

Companies (and other bodies corporate, unincorporated associations and authorised unit trusts—but not partnerships, local authorities or local authority associations [*Sec 832(1)(2)*]) are assessable to corporation tax on their trading income as computed under the law and practice applying to Schedule D, Case I or II. [*Sec 9*]. The provisions below, from 71.29 onwards (relating to Assessable Profits, Allowable Deductions and other Schedule D, Case I and II matters) apply generally to companies etc. (but by reference to actual income arising in the accounting period concerned as corporation tax is assessable on an actual basis [*Sec 12(1)*]). Items 71.3 to 71.9 below referring to the preceding year basis and the opening and closing year provisions do not apply to companies etc.. See 71.25 below for 'notional' commencements or cessations by companies. See Tolley's Corporation Tax.

71.3 INDIVIDUALS, PARTNERSHIPS ETC.—BASES OF ASSESSMENT— PRE-FINANCE ACT 1994

The basis period rules set out in detail in 71.4 to 71.9 below (the **preceding year basis of assessment**) apply for **1995/96 and earlier years as regards businesses commenced before 6 April 1994. They are of no application to businesses commenced after 5 April 1994.** See 71.11 to 71.19 below for new rules introduced by *Finance Act 1994*.

In summary the basis periods are generally as follows.

Opening Years (see 71.4 below)
Year 1   Actual
Year 2   First 12 months   } Taxpayer may elect for both to be based
Year 3   Preceding year basis } on actual profits (but not either alone).

Intermediate years (see 71.6 below)
Preceding year basis

Closing years (see 71.9 below)
Last year but 2 } Preceding year basis but actual profits if actual profits in aggregate
Last year but 1 } exceed profits on preceding year basis.
Last year   Actual profits

Preceding year basis normally means that the assessment is based on the profits shown by the annual accounts ended within the preceding tax year.

Power is given to apportion profits or losses, on a time basis in proportion to the number of days (before 1 May 1995, months, or fractions of months) in the respective periods, if necessary (but only where necessary, see *Marshall Hus & Partners Ltd v Bolton Ch D 1980, 55 TC 539*) for purpose of assessments under Cases I and II. [*Sec 72; FA 1995, s 121*].

71.4   **Opening years.** On the **commencement of a business** carried on by an individual or partnership (but not companies—see 71.2 above) the following rules apply. [*Sec 61*]. For what is a commencement, etc. see 71.25 below. See also 53.6 PARTNERSHIPS as regards special basis of assessment on certain partnership changes.

First tax year. The assessment will be on the profits (as adjusted for tax purposes) from the start to the following 5 April with any necessary apportionment if a trading account overlaps that date (see *Manson v Perrys (Ealing) Ltd KB 1931, 16 TC 60*).

Second tax year. The assessment will be on the profits of the first twelve months of the business with any necessary apportionment if a trading account overlaps the end of that period. (Thus, if the first account was for ten months to 31 May, followed by an account for twelve months, the assessment will be on the profits of the ten months, plus 2/12ths of the following year's profits.)

Third tax year. If the only account ending in the second tax year is for twelve months commencing either at the date the business started or at the end of the basis period for that year, the assessment will be on the profits of that account. Failing that, the basis period will be fixed by the Commissioners under *Sec 60(4)*. It will normally be taken as the twelve months to the date in the second year which will be the future accounting date or, if this is not possible, the first twelve months of trading.

Fourth tax year. If the only account ending in the third tax year is for twelve months commencing at the end of the basis period for that year, the assessment will be on the profits of that account. Failing that, the basis period will be fixed by the Commissioners under *Sec 60(4)*. It will normally be taken as the twelve months to the date in the third year which will be the future accounting date.

Where a loss enters into the apportionments for the opening years, see 46.13(*e*) LOSSES.

Relief in second and third year of assessment

(*a*)   Taxpayer may apply in writing within seven years of end of second year of assessment for assessments for both second and third years of assessment (but not for one year only) to be based on the actual profits of each of those years (apportioned to 5 April on a time basis). [*Sec 62(2)*]. Where the second and third years are 1989/90 and 1990/91, and the person liable to be charged for 1989/90 is a married man but for 1990/91 is his wife, the election is available to the wife and not to the husband. [*FA 1988, 3 Sch 2*].

(b)   He may give notice in writing revoking such previous notice, within six years of the end of third year of assessment. (His assessments for both years will then revert to the normal basis as explained above.) [*Sec 62(3)*].

(c)   Where, during the second and third years of assessment, there is a *change of partners*, or a sole trader enters into partnership, all notices given as above (after a change in respect of which notice has been given under *Sec 113(2)*, see 53.6 PARTNERSHIPS), must (where the notice is given within twelve months after the end of the second year) be signed by all persons engaged in the business at any time from the beginning of the second year to the date of signing; and all notices given after the end of the third year by all such persons so engaged at any time during the second and third years. (Personal representatives in case of deceased persons.) [*Sec 62(6)–(8)*]. For note re Double Succession see 53.9 PARTNERSHIPS.

71.5   *Example*

Roy commenced business on 1 January 1994. His Schedule D, Case I adjusted profits (before capital allowances) are

	£
16 months to 30.4.95	16,000
Year to 30.4.96	36,000
Year to 30.4.97	30,000

Capital allowances for the year to 30.4.97 are £3,000.

His first five years' assessments will be either of (i) or (ii) below

(i) No election under Sec 62(2) for actual basis in second and third year

	Basis period		£	£
1993/94	1.1.94 – 5.4.94	£16,000 × $\frac{3}{16}$		3,000
1994/95	1.1.94 – 31.12.94	£16,000 × $\frac{12}{16}$		12,000
1995/96	1.1.94 – 31.12.94	£16,000 × $\frac{12}{16}$		12,000
	Transitional period			
1996/97	1.1.95 – 30.4.96 (16 months):			
	1.1.95 – 30.4.95	£16,000 × $\frac{4}{16}$	4,000	
	1.5.95 – 30.4.96		36,000	
			£40,000	
	£40,000 × $\frac{12}{16}$			30,000
	Basis period			
1997/98	Y/e 30.4.97 (net of capital allowances)			27,000*
Total assessments for first five years**				£84,000

* Transitional overlap relief accrued (see 71.22 below):
  (1.5.96 – 5.4.97) £30,000 × $\frac{11}{12}$ £27,500

** Subject to capital allowances for 1993/94 to 1996/97 inclusive

(ii) With election under Sec 62(2) for actual basis in second and third year

	Basis period		£	£
1993/94	1.1.94 – 5.4.94	£16,000 × $\frac{3}{16}$		3,000
1994/95	6.4.94 – 5.4.95	£16,000 × $\frac{12}{16}$		12,000
1995/96	6.4.95 – 5.4.96:			
	6.4.95 – 30.4.95	£16,000 × $\frac{1}{16}$	1,000	
	1.5.95 – 5.4.96	£36,000 × $\frac{11}{12}$	33,000	
				34,000
	Transitional period			
1996/97	6.4.96 – 5.4.97:			
	6.4.96 – 30.4.96	£36,000 × $\frac{1}{12}$	3,000	
	1.5.96 – 5.4.97	£30,000 × $\frac{11}{12}$	27,500	
				30,500
	Basis period			
1997/98	Y/e 30.4.97 (net of capital allowances)			27,000*

Total assessments for first five years**   £106,500

* Transitional overlap relief accrued (see 71.22 below):
  (1.5.96 – 5.4.97) £30,000 × $\frac{11}{12}$ £27,500

** Subject to capital allowances for 1993/94 to 1996/97 inclusive

Notes

(*a*)   Roy would not make the election under *Sec 62(2)* (actual basis for second and third years) as taxable profits would thereby be greater. Note that where a business commenced in 1993/94, such an election affects not only 1994/95 and 1995/96 but also 1996/97 (the transitional year on the changeover to the current year basis of assessment—see 71.20 below and also note (*b*) below): therefore, one needs to compare the position for all three of those years.

(*b*)   Where 1995/96 is taxed on an actual basis, the transitional year 1996/97 is also taxed on an actual basis (with no averaging of profits) (see 71.20 below).

71.6   **Intermediate years.** (i.e. tax years for which the special rules for Opening Years, as in 71.4 above, or for Closing Years, as in 71.9 below, do not apply.)

Assessment on individuals and partnerships (but not companies etc., see 71.2 above) is on the preceding year basis, i.e. the profits (as adjusted for tax purposes) of the trading account ending in the preceding tax year if that account (i) is the only one ending in that year and (ii) is for twelve months commencing from the end of the basis period for that year. [*Sec 60(1)–(3)*]. If there is no account satisfying these requirements see 71.7 below.

71.7   **Change of accounting date.** Where the accounts made up do not satisfy the requirements of the preceding year basis (see 71.6 above), the following applies.

(i)   The Commissioners of Inland Revenue will decide 'what period of twelve months ending on a date within the year preceding the year of assessment shall be deemed to be the year the profits or gains of which are to be taken to be' the profits of that preceding year. [*Sec 60(4)*].

(ii)   They may also adjust the preceding year's assessment to correspond with any altered accounting date, and may make any necessary assessment or repayment, subject to a right of appeal to the General or Special Commissioners who may grant just relief and from them to the Courts. [*Sec 60(5)–(7)*].

There is no right of appeal against (i). See Revenue Pamphlet IR 26 as to the Revenue practice with examples. See also *CIR v Helical Bar Ltd HL 1972, 48 TC 221.*

In determining a basis period for 1995/96 (or an earlier year), these rules are applied as if the transitional rules for 1996/97 basis periods (see 71.20 below) did not apply, although any figure or basis period for 1996/97 is subsequently ignored. The transitional basis period for 1996/97 then commences immediately after the basis period determined for 1995/96. (Revenue Tax Bulletin August 1995 p 243, December 1995 p 271). This will normally apply only where accounts are prepared for a long period to a new accounting date falling within 1995/96, with no accounting date falling within 1994/95.

71.8   *Example*

Geoff, who has been trading for some years, has the following Schedule D, Case I adjusted profits

	£
Year to 30.9.92	24,000
Year to 30.9.93	15,000
15 months to 31.12.94	32,000

The assessable profit for 1995/96 is determined under *Sec 60(4)* and that for 1994/95 is considered for revision under *Sec 60(5).*

The assessments are calculated as follows.

1995/96
Sec 60(4) determination
The 1995/96 assessment is based on 12 months to 31.12.94
i.e. $\frac{12}{15}$ of £32,000   £25,600

1994/95
The accounting periods to be considered are those entering in whole or in part in to the *Sec 60(4)* basis period(s) or the 'corresponding period' under *Sec 60(5)*; viz

		Year of assessment
12 months to 30.9.93	15,000	1994/95
15 months to 31.12.94	32,000	1995/96
27 months	£47,000	24 months

Sec 60(5) consideration

The following tests are undertaken to see if the 1994/95 assessment should be amended.

(i)   Aggregate profit
        $\frac{24}{27}$ × £47,000   £41,777

(ii)   Sum of assessments for relevant years without revision for 1994/95

1994/95	£15,000
1995/96	25,600
	£40,600

(iii)   Sum of assessments for relevant years with revision for 1994/95
        1994/95 (revised to year to 31.12.93)

$\frac{9}{12}$ × £15,000	£11,250	
$\frac{3}{15}$ × £32,000	6,400	17,650
1995/96		25,600
Sum of assessments		£43,250

As the figure at (i) £41,777 is intermediate between (ii) £40,600 and (iii) £43,250 the revised assessment is

Figure at (i)	41,777
Assessed 1995/96	25,600
Revised assessment 1994/95	£16,177

Notes

(a)   If the difference between the figures at (i) and (ii) above was less than 10% of the average of the 1995/96 assessment and the unrevised 1994/95 assessment (i.e. £25,600 and £15,000) and, in addition, the difference was under £1,000, the 1994/95 assessment would not have been amended i.e. it would remain at £15,000.

(b)   If the figure at (i) was not intermediate between the figures at (ii) and (iii) above, the Inland Revenue would decide what revised assessments, if any, were necessary. This would also be the case if any year showed a loss.

(c)   In this example, assuming that Geoff continues to prepare accounts to 31 December, the transitional basis period on the changeover to the current year basis of assessment (see 71.20 below) will be the two years to 31 December 1996. For changes of accounting date within the transitional period, see 71.21 below.

71.9   **Closing years.** If there is a **discontinuance of a business** carried on by an individual or partnership (but not companies, see 71.2 above) the following rules apply. [*Secs 63, 113(1); FA 1988, 3 Sch 3*]. For what is a discontinuance, etc. see 71.25 below.

(i)   **Last Year.** Assessment to be adjusted to actual profits from 6 April to date of discontinuance.

(ii)   **Years preceding the last year.** If the aggregate of actual profits for the two years ending 5 April preceding the tax year in which the discontinuance occurs, arrived at by apportionment of the profits of the accounts as adjusted for tax purposes (*Manson v Wesley HL 1932, 16 TC 654*), exceeds the aggregate assessments for those years, assessments and adjustments may be made by Inland Revenue to bring into tax that excess, except where the trade is discontinued in consequence of the nationalisation of its trading assets (see *Sec 63(4)* and *CIR v Daniel Beattie CS 1955, 36 TC 379*). The inspector has no general discretion as to whether or not to make such assessments (*Baylis v Roberts Ch D 1989, 62 TC 384*). (*N.B.*—No similar option to taxpayer if the assessments exceed the profits.) In the case of a deceased person any additional tax will be a debt payable out of his estate.

See *Townsend v Electrical Yarns KB 1952, 33 TC 166*, re effect of balancing charges under *CAA 1968, ss 33, 41* and cf. *CIR v Lloyds Bank (Scott's Exors) Ch D 1963, 41 TC 294*.

See 46.16 LOSSES for terminal losses and 46.13(c) LOSSES for the carry forward of certain losses where a private business is converted into a company.

Death, retirement, etc. By concession, the above rules are not applied, unless claimed, to widow(er) continuing deceased spouse's business, but in any event no unrelieved losses, or unexhausted capital allowances applicable to the deceased can be carried forward. Capital allowances are, however, calculated as if assets had passed from the trader to the surviving spouse at open market value (the figure adopted for probate purposes being accepted for this purpose). (Revenue Capital Allowances Manual, CA 512). The concession, suitably adapted, is also extended to the survivor continuing a business previously carried on by husband and wife in partnership where no continuation election is made under *Sec 113(2)* (see 53.6 PARTNERSHIPS), and in such a case the losses and capital allowances which may be carried forward are restricted to the share appropriate to the surviving partner. (Revenue Pamphlet IR 1, A7). The concession is withdrawn following the introduction of the current year basis of assessment (see 71.11 *et seq.* below), from 6 April 1995 in respect of businesses commenced after 5 April 1994, and from a date to be announced (not earlier than 6 April 1997) for businesses already in existence on that date. (Revenue Press Release 4 April 1995). See also 72.4(*d*) SCHEDULE D, CASE III.

Where a person carrying on a business reduces the scope of his business and/or his hours of work in order to qualify for a National Insurance retirement pension (assessable under Schedule E), his business assessment will, if to his advantage, be computed as if his existing business had at that time discontinued and a new one commenced. (Revenue Pamphlet IR 1, A20). (This concession is of limited application following the abolition of the earnings rule from 1 October 1989.)

71.10   *Example*

Chris ceased business on 30 June 1996. His adjusted Schedule D, Case I profits were

		£
Year to 30.4.93		24,000
30.4.94		48,000
30.4.95		96,000
30.4.96		36,000
2 months to 30.6.96		5,000

His assessments will be

	Basis periods			
1996/97	6.4.96 – 30.4.96	$\frac{1}{12} \times 36,000$	3,000	
	1.5.96 – 30.6.96		5,000	
				£8,000

Then, either

1995/96	Year to 30.4.94		48,000
1994/95	Year to 30.4.93		24,000
			£72,000

Or

1995/96	6.4.95 – 30.4.95	$\frac{1}{12} \times 96,000$	8,000	
	1.5.95 – 5.4.96	$\frac{11}{12} \times 36,000$	33,000	
				41,000
1994/95	6.4.94 – 30.4.94	$\frac{1}{12} \times 48,000$	4,000	
	1.5.94 – 5.4.95	$\frac{11}{12} \times 96,000$	88,000	
				92,000
				£133,000

Note

(*a*)   The Inland Revenue would assess A on profits of £41,000 for 1995/96 and on £92,000 for 1994/95 as these figures are greater in total than the profits originally assessed for these years.

71.11   INDIVIDUALS, PARTNERSHIPS ETC.—BASES OF ASSESSMENT—POST-FINANCE ACT 1994

The basis period rules set out in detail in 71.11 to 71.19 below (the **current year basis of assessment**) apply **for 1996/97 and subsequent years as regards businesses commenced before 6 April 1994** (see 71.20 to 71.24 below for transitional provisions on the changeover from the preceding year basis of assessment). **They apply for 1994/95 and subsequent years as regards businesses commenced after 5 April 1994**. [*FA 1994, s 218(1)(2)(5)*]. See 53.3 PARTNERSHIPS as regards partnerships ceasing to be chargeable to income tax as a separate entity; the current year basis of assessment has no specific application to a partnership itself (although it applies as regards individual partners), except for 1996/97 as regards partnership businesses commenced before 6 April 1994.

A detailed Revenue booklet SAT 1(1995) 'The new current year basis of assessment—A guide for Inland Revenue officers and tax practitioners' should have been sent by tax offices to all tax practices with which they deal in August/September 1995. Further copies are available (price £7.50) from Inland Revenue Library, New Wing, Somerset House, Strand, London WC2R 1LB. Also, a series of explanatory articles on self-assessment have appeared in the Revenue Tax Bulletin from August 1993 onwards, many of which illustrate different aspects of the current year basis.

In summary the basis periods are generally as follows (subject to any change of accounting date—see 71.15 below).

Opening Years (see 71.12 below)

Year 1	Actual
Year 2	12 months ending with the accounting date in the year or, if the period from commencement to the accounting date in the year is less than 12 months, the first 12 months or, if there is no accounting date in the first or second year, actual
Year 3	Normally current year basis (see 71.12 below for exception)

See 71.19 below for relief (overlap relief) where the above rules have the effect of the same profits being taxed in each of two successive years of assessment.

Intermediate Years (see 71.14 below)
Current year basis.

Closing Year (see 71.17 below)
Period from the end of the basis period in the penultimate year to the date of cessation in the year (which may exceed 12 months).

General. Current year basis normally means that the assessment is based on the profits shown by the annual accounts ended within the current tax year.

Power to apportion profits or losses applies as in 71.3 above. In practice, the Revenue will accept any reasonable time-based apportionment that is applied consistently. If the taxpayer wishes, they will treat an accounting date of 31 March as being equivalent to one of 5 April. (Revenue booklet SAT 1(1995), paras 1.17, 1.98, 1.99).

71.12   Opening years. On the **commencement of a business** by an individual (which includes his commencing to carry on an existing business in partnership), the following rules apply. For what is a commencement, etc. see 71.25 below.

First tax year. The assessment will be on the profits (as adjusted for tax purposes) from the commencement date to the following 5 April. [*Sec 61(1); FA 1994, s 201*].

Second tax year. If there is an accounting date (i.e. a date to which accounts are made up) in the year, the assessment is based on the twelve months to that date. If the period from

71.13 Schedule D, Cases I and II—Profits of Trades etc.

commencement to the accounting date in the second year is less than twelve months, the assessment is based on the profits for the first twelve months of the business. If there is no accounting date in the first or second year, the second year's assessment will be on the actual profits for the year, i.e. 6 April to 5 April. Where there is more than one accounting date in the year, reference to the accounting date in the year is to the latest of such dates (see also the rules for changes of accounting date in 71.15 below). [*Secs 60(1(2)(3)(a)(5), 61(2)(a); FA 1994, ss 200, 201*].

Third tax year. If the year is the first year in which there is an accounting date falling not less than twelve months after the date of commencement, the assessment is based on the twelve months ending with the accounting date. Otherwise, the rule for intermediate years (see 71.14 below) apply as regards the third year. [*Sec 60(1)–(3); FA 1994, s 200*].

See 71.19 below for relief (overlap relief) where the above rules have the effect of the same profits being taxed in each of two successive years of assessment.

71.13   *Example*

Simon commences trade on 1 September 1994 and prepares accounts to 30 April, starting with an eight-month period of account to 30 April 1995. His profits (as adjusted for tax purposes and *after* capital allowances) for the first three accounting periods are as follows.

	£
Eight months to 30 April 1995	24,000
Year to 30 April 1996	39,000
Year to 30 April 1997	40,000

His taxable profits for the first four tax years are as follows.

	Basis period		£	£
1994/95	1.9.94 – 5.4.95	£24,000 × $\frac{7}{8}$		21,000
1995/96	1.9.94 – 31.8.95:			
	1.9.94 – 30.4.95		24,000	
	1.5.95 – 31.8.95	£39,000 × $\frac{4}{12}$	13,000	
				37,000
1996/97	Y/e 30.4.96			39,000
1997/98	Y/e 30.4.97			40,000

Overlap relief accrued:		
1.9.94 – 5.4.95 — 7 months		21,000
1.5.95 – 31.8.95 — 4 months		13,000
Total overlap relief accrued (see 71.19 below)		£34,000

71.14   **Intermediate years** (i.e. tax years for which the special rules for Opening Years, as in 71.12 above, or for the Closing Year, see 71.17 below, do not apply).

Assessment on individuals (including those trading in partnership) is on the current year basis, i.e. the profits (as adjusted for tax purposes) of the trading account ending in the current tax year (subject to changes of accounting date, see 71.15 below). [*Sec 60(1)(2)(3)(b); FA 1994, s 200*].

71.15   **Change of accounting date.** Where a change (an accounting change) from one accounting date (the old date) to another (the new date) is made in a year of assessment, the conditions below must be satisfied if the change of accounting date is to result in a change of basis period. (This does not apply if the year is the second or third year of assessment of the business.) An accounting change is made in a year of assessment if accounts are not made up to the old date in that year or are made up to the new date in that year. The conditions, *all of which must be satisfied*, are as follows.

(1)   The first accounting period (i.e. period for which accounts are made up) ending with the new date does not exceed 18 months.

(2)   Notice of the change is given to an officer of the Board in a personal (or, where appropriate, a partnership) tax return on or before the day on which that return is required to be delivered (see 78.5, 78.8 SELF-ASSESSMENT).

(3)   Either

  (i)   no accounting change resulting in a change of basis period has been made in any of the previous five years of assessment;

  or

  (ii)   the notice in (2) above sets out the reasons for the change and the Revenue do not, within 60 days of receiving the notice, give notice to the trader that they are not satisfied that the change is made for bona fide commercial reasons (which does not include the obtaining of a tax advantage). (An appeal may be made against such a Revenue notice, within 30 days beginning with the date of issue, and the Commissioners may either confirm the notice or set it aside.)

Where all the conditions are satisfied, or the accounting change is made in the second or third tax year of the business, the basis period for the year of assessment is as follows.

(*a*)   If the year is the second year of assessment of the business, the basis period is the twelve months ending with the new date in the year (unless the period from commencement of the business to the new date in the second year is less than twelve months, in which case the basis period is the first twelve months of the business).

(*b*)   If the 'relevant period' is a period of less than twelve months, the basis period is the twelve months ending with the new date in the year.

(*c*)   If the 'relevant period' is a period of more than twelve months, the basis period consists of the relevant period.

The '*relevant period*' is the period beginning immediately after the end of the basis period for the preceding year and ending with the new date in the year.

It will be seen that a basis period can be of more than twelve months' duration but cannot be less than twelve months. If not all of the above conditions are satisfied (and the year is not the second or third tax year of the business), the basis period for the year is the twelve months beginning immediately after the end of the basis period for the preceding year. However, the accounting change is then treated as made in the following year of assessment and can thus result in a change of basis period for that following year if all the above conditions are satisfied as regards that year. An accounting change can continue to be 'carried forward' in this way until such time, if any, as a change of basis period results or the old accounting date is reverted to.

[*Secs 60(3)(b), 61(2)(b), 62, 62A; FA 1994, ss 200–203; FA 1996, s 135, 21 Sch 1*].

See 71.19 below for relief (overlap relief) where the above rules in (*a*) or (*b*) above have the effect of the same profits being taxed in each of two successive years of assessment, and for the use of overlap relief brought forward in computing profits in a situation within (*c*) above.

For partnership trades, notice in (2) above and an appeal within (3)(ii) above may be given or brought by such one of the partners as may be nominated by them for the purpose (any resulting change of basis period affecting the deemed trades of individual partners—see 53.3 PARTNERSHIPS). [*Sec 111(6); FA 1994, s 215(1); FA 1995, s 117*].

71.16   *Examples*

(i) Change to a date earlier in the tax year
Miranda commenced trade on 1 September 1994, preparing accounts to 31 August. In 1997, she changes her accounting date to 31 May, preparing accounts for the nine months to 31 May 1997. The conditions of *Sec 62A* are satisfied in relation to the change. Her profits (as adjusted for tax purposes and *after* capital allowances) are as follows.

	£
Year ended 31 August 1995	18,000
Year ended 31 August 1996	21,500
Nine months to 31 May 1997	17,000
Year ended 31 May 1998	23,000

Taxable profits for the first five tax years are as follows.

	Basis period		£	£
1994/95	1.9.94 – 5.4.95	£18,000 × $\frac{7}{12}$		10,500
1995/96	Y/e 31.8.95			18,000
1996/97	Y/e 31.8.96			21,500
1997/98	1.6.96 – 31.5.97:			
	1.6.96 – 31.8.96	£21,500 × $\frac{3}{12}$	5,375	
	1.9.96 – 31.5.97		17,000	
				22,375
1998/99	Y/e 31.5.98			23,000

Overlap relief accrued (see 71.19 below)	
1.9.94 – 5.4.95 — 7 months	10,500
1.6.96 – 31.8.96 — 3 months	5,375
Total overlap relief accrued	£15,875

Note

(*a*)   In this example, the 'relevant period' is that from 1 September 1996 (the day following the end of the basis period for 1996/97) to 31 May 1997 (the new accounting date in the year 1997/98 — the year of change). As the relevant period is less than 12 months, the basis period for 1997/98 is the 12 months ending on the new accounting date.

(ii) Change to a date later in the tax year
Dennis starts a business on 1 July 1994, preparing accounts to 30 June. In 1997, he changes his accounting date to 31 December, preparing accounts for the six months to 31 December 1997. The conditions of *Sec 62A* are satisfied in relation to the change. His profits (as adjusted for tax purposes and *after* capital allowances) are as follows.

	£
Year ended 30 June 1995	18,000
Year ended 30 June 1996	21,500
Year ended 30 June 1997	23,000
Six months to 31 December 1997	12,000
Year ended 31 December 1998	27,000

Taxable profits for the first five years are as follows.

	Basis period		£	£
1994/95	1.7.94 – 5.4.95	$£18,000 \times \frac{9}{12}$		13,500
1995/96	Y/e 30.6.95			18,000
1996/97	Y/e 30.6.96			21,500
1997/98	1.7.96 – 31.12.97:			
	1.7.96 – 30.6.97		23,000	
	1.7.97 – 31.12.97		12,000	
			35,000	
	Deduct Overlap relief		9,000	
				26,000
1998/99	Y/e 31.12.98			27,000

	£
Overlap relief accrued:	
1.7.94 – 5.4.95 — 9 months	13,500
Less utilised in 1997/98	9,000
Carried forward	£4,500

Utilisation of overlap relief in 1997/98

Apply the formula: $A \times \dfrac{B - C}{D}$ (see 71.19 below)

where
A = aggregate overlap relief accrued (£13,500);
B = length of basis period for 1997/98 (18 months);
C = 12 months; and
D = the length of the overlap period(s) by reference to which the aggregate overlap profits accrued (9 months).

Thus, the deduction to be given in computing profits for 1997/98 is

$$£13,500 \times \frac{18-12}{9} = £9,000$$

Notes

(*a*) In this example, the 'relevant period' is that from 1 July 1996 (the day following the end of the basis period for 1996/97) to 31 December 1997 (the new accounting date in the year 1997/98—the year of change). As the relevant period is more than 12 months, the basis period for 1997/98 is equal to the relevant period. Note that a basis period of 18 months results in this case, even though accounts were prepared for a period of only 6 months to the new date.

(*b*) The overlap relief accrued (by reference to an overlap period of 9 months) is given on cessation or, as in this example, on a change of accounting date resulting in a basis period exceeding 12 months (the relief given depending on the extent of the excess). The balance of overlap relief (£4,500) is carried forward for future relief on the happening of such an event. See 71.19 below. If Dennis had changed his accounting date to 31 March or 5 April (instead of 31 December), the use of the formula in *Sec 63A(2)* would have resulted in overlap relief of £13,500 being given in full in 1997/98.

71.17 **Closing year.** If there is a **discontinuance of a business** carried on by an individual (which includes his ceasing to carry on an existing business in partnership), the following rule applies. For what is a discontinuance, etc. see 71.25 below.

The basis period for the **final year of assessment**, i.e. that in which cessation occurs, is the period beginning immediately after the end of the basis period for the penultimate year and ending with the date of cessation. [*Sec 63; FA 1994, s 204*]. The basis period may thus exceed twelve months, but see 71.19 below as regards the use of overlap relief brought forward in computing profits for the final year. Unlike the cessation rules under the preceding year basis of assessment (see 71.9 above), there are no special rules for the penultimate and ante-penultimate years of assessment (but see 71.24 below for transitional provisions where a business commenced before 6 April 1994 ceases in 1996/97, 1997/98 or 1998/99).

See 46.16 LOSSES for terminal losses and 46.13(*c*) LOSSES for the carry-forward of certain losses where a private business is converted into a company. See also the concession (A7) at 71.9 above where widow(er) continues deceased spouse's business (although this no longer has any practical application to partnerships).

71.18 *Example*

Robin commenced to trade on 1 May 1994, preparing accounts to 30 April. He permanently ceases to trade on 30 June 1998, preparing accounts for the two months to that date. His profits (as adjusted for tax purposes and *after* capital allowances) are as follows.

	£
Year ended 30 April 1995	24,000
Year ended 30 April 1996	48,000
Year ended 30 April 1997	96,000
Year ended 30 April 1998	36,000
Two months ended 30 June 1998	5,000
	£209,000

Taxable profits for the five tax years of trading are as follows.

	Basis period		£	£
1994/95	1.5.94 – 5.4.95	£24,000 × $\frac{11}{12}$		22,000
1995/96	Y/e 30.4.95			24,000
1996/97	Y/e 30.4.96			48,000
1997/98	Y/e 30.4.97			96,000
1998/99	1.5.97 – 30.6.98:			
	1.5.97 – 30.4.98		36,000	
	1.5.98 – 30.6.98		5,000	
			41,000	
	Deduct Overlap relief		22,000	
				19,000
				£209,000

Overlap relief accrued (see 71.19 below):		
1.5.94 – 5.4.95 — 11 months		22,000
Utilised in 1998/99		(22,000)

71.19   **Overlap relief.** An 'overlap profit' is an amount of profits which, by virtue of the basis period rules above, is included in the computations for two successive years of assessment. It may arise as a result of the opening year rules in 71.12 above or on a change of basis period within 71.15(*a*) or (*b*) above. An 'overlap period' in relation to an overlap profit is the number of days in the period for which the overlap profit arose. For example (working in terms of months for simplicity), if a business commences on 1 May 1995 and prepares its first accounts for the year to 30 April 1996 showing tax-adjusted profits of £24,000, the 1995/96 assessment is based on the period 1 May 1995 to 5 April 1996 (£24,000 × 11/12 = £22,000) and the 1996/97 assessment is based on the year ended 30 April 1996 (£24,000). The overlap profit is £22,000 by reference to an overlap period of 11 months.

Relief for an overlap profit is given, by way of a deduction in computing profits, on a change of accounting date resulting in a basis period of more than twelve months (see 71.15(*c*) above) and/or in the final year of assessment of the business (see 71.17 above). On the first such change of accounting date, if any, the deduction is

$$A \times \frac{B - C}{D}$$

where

A = the aggregate of any overlap profits;

B = the number of days in the basis period (i.e. more than 365 or 366);

C = the number of days in the year of assessment (365 or 366); and

D = the aggregate of the overlap periods by reference to which the overlap profits in A are calculated.

For example (working in terms of months for simplicity), if the overlap profit brought forward is £22,000 by reference to an overlap period of 11 months, and the basis period for a year of assessment is 15 months, the overlap relief deductible in computing profits for that year is £22,000 × 3/11 = £6,000, leaving an overlap profit of £16,000, by reference to an overlap period of eight months, to be carried forward. On subsequent applications of this formula, A and D are reduced by, respectively, the overlap profit previously relieved and the number of days referable to the previous relief.

On cessation, the deduction in computing profits for the final year of assessment is equal to the total overlap profits previously unrelieved.

[*Sec 63A(1)–(3)(5); FA 1994, s 205*].

The Revenue will accept a calculation of overlap relief by reference otherwise than to days, e.g. using months or fractions of months, providing the same method is used consistently so that, over the lifetime of the business, the total profits assessed exactly equal the profits made. (Revenue booklet SAT 1(1995), para 1.86).

See 71.22 below for overlap profits arising under the transitional rules for businesses commenced before 6 April 1994.

Overlap losses. Where an amount of loss would otherwise fall to be included in the computations for two successive years of assessment, that amount (the 'overlap loss') is not to be so included for the second of those years. [*Sec 63A(4); FA 1994, s 205*].

71.20 **Transitional rules for businesses commenced before 6 April 1994—Basis period for 1996/97.** A business commenced before 6 April 1994 is within the basis period rules in 71.3 to 71.9 above for all years up to and including 1995/96. In order to bridge what would otherwise be a gap between the basis periods for 1995/96 and 1996/97, the basis period for 1996/97 is determined as follows (subject to 71.24 below for businesses ceasing before 6 April 1999).

The standard basis period for 1996/97 is normally the twelve months ending with the accounting date (or latest accounting date) in that year. If there is no accounting date in that year (by virtue of a change of accounting date), the standard basis period is the twelve months ending on 5 April 1997 (and the change of accounting date is treated for the purposes of 71.15 above as made in the tax year in which accounts are made up to the new date).

The standard basis period as above is then extended by the period beginning immediately after the end of the basis period for 1995/96 and ending immediately before the beginning of the standard basis period (and taxpayers may, if they wish, draw up accounts to cover the whole of the extended basis period, although where there are losses this may be disadvantageous). **Tax is charged for 1996/97 on the 'appropriate percentage' of the profits of the extended basis period** (the 'transitional period'). The *'appropriate percentage'* is found by dividing 365 by the number of days in the transitional period, and expressing the result as a percentage. In a straightforward case with no change of accounting date, the transitional period will be a period of twenty-four months and 50% of the profits for that period will thus be charged to tax for 1996/97, the remaining 50% escaping tax completely. Exceptionally, if the assessment for 1995/96 is on an actual basis (6 April 1995 to 5 April 1996), e.g. because it commenced in 1993/94 and the taxpayer elected for the special rule in 71.4(*a*) above, there will be no gap and the 1996/97 assessment will also be on an actual basis (with no reduction in the profits charged).

[*FA 1994, 20 Sch 1, 2(1)–(3)(5)*].

Anti-avoidance measures have been introduced to deter and penalise attempts to exploit the transitional rules by moving profits into the transitional period so that they would not otherwise be fully charged to tax. Where any amount which is included in the aggregate profits of the transitional period (before applying the appropriate percentage) would not have been so included if any 'relevant change' made or any 'relevant transaction' entered into by the trader had not been made or entered into, the 1996/97 assessment is increased by 1.25 times the 'complementary percentage' (i.e. the difference between 100% and the appropriate percentage) of each amount so included. There are *de minimis* thresholds in that the said increase does not apply where the aggregate of the amounts so included or the proportion which that aggregate bears to the aggregate profits of the transitional period is less than an amount/proportion to be prescribed by regulations shortly before 5 April 1997, or where the appropriate percentage of turnover (i.e. amounts derived from ordinary activities, excluding VAT and after deducting trade discounts) for the transitional period is less than an amount to be so prescribed (and the regulations may make provision for partnerships different from that for individual traders). [*FA 1995, s 133, 22 Sch 1, 21(1)*]. There is no provision for the penalty to be mitigated or for any corresponding reduction to the assessment for any other year. Where voluntary disclosure is made in the tax return for 1996/97 (other than by amendment to the return), the adjustment is reduced by one-quarter of the complementary percentage of each amount so disclosed. [*FA 1995, 22 Sch 13*].

Any 'accounting change' or 'change of business practice' is a '*relevant change*' for the above purposes *unless* it is made exclusively for *bona fide* commercial reasons or the obtaining of a tax advantage is not the main benefit that could reasonably be expected to arise therefrom. An '*accounting change*' means any modification of an accounting policy or substitution of one such policy for another. This includes a change of accounting date *except* any such change which brings the end of the basis period for 1996/97 closer to 5 April 1997. A '*change of business practice*' means any change in an *established* business practice as to the *timing* of either supplies, invoicing, debt collection/settlement, the obtaining of goods or services or the incurring of business expenses or as to the obtaining or making of payments in advance or on account. [*FA 1995, 22 Sch 14*]. For further guidance as to their interpretation of these terms, see Revenue booklet SAT 1(1995), chapter 10.

A '*relevant transaction*' means any 'self-cancelling transaction' or any transaction with a 'connected person' *unless*, in either case, it is entered into exclusively for *bona fide* commercial reasons or the obtaining of a tax advantage is not the main benefit that could reasonably be expected to arise therefrom. An agreement by which a trader agrees to sell or transfer trading stock or work in progress is a '*self-cancelling transaction*' if by the same or any collateral agreement he either agrees to buy back or re-acquire the stock or work in progress or acquires or grants an option to do so which is subsequently exercised. '*Trading stock*' and '*work in progress*' are as defined, with necessary modifications in the latter case, by *Secs 100* and *101* respectively (see 71.82 below) and reference above to the sale or transfer of work in progress includes reference to the sale etc. of any benefits or rights accruing from the carrying out of the work. *Sec 839* (see 20 CONNECTED PERSONS) applies to determine whether persons are '*connected persons*' for these purposes, but disregarding the exception in 20.4 (commercial transactions in partnership assets). In addition, persons trading in partnership are connected with (i) an individual, if he controls the partnership, or (ii) a company, if the company controls the partnership or the same person controls both company and partnership, or (iii) members of another partnership, if the same person controls both partnerships. As regards a company, '*control*' is as defined by *Sec 416* (see Tolley's Corporation Tax, under Close Companies) and as regards a partnership it means the right to a share of more than half the partnership assets or income (see *Sec 840*). A person controls a company or partnership if he does so either alone or with one or more persons connected with him. [*FA 1995, 22 Sch 15–17*].

The obtaining of a tax advantage is not a *bona fide* commercial reason for the above purposes. [*FA 1995, 22 Sch 21(2)*].

If necessary, an assessment may be made, or a partnership statement amended, under the discovery provisions of *TMA s 29* or *s 30B* (see 78.15, 78.16 SELF-ASSESSMENT) to give effect to the above provisions. The normal exceptions at 78.15(1)(2) do not apply to prevent such an assessment/amendment until such time as a self-assessment or partnership

71.21 Schedule D, Cases I and II—Profits of Trades etc.

statement has been made for 1997/98 and is not still capable of being amended (see 78 SELF-ASSESSMENT generally). [*FA 1995, 22 Sch 11*].

See 43.22 INTEREST PAYABLE for anti-avoidance provisions aimed at the replacement of partnership borrowings by partners' personal borrowings during the transitional period.

71.21   *Examples*

Mandy has been in practice as a physiotherapist since the 1980s, preparing accounts to 30 September. In 1997, she changes her accounting date to 31 March, preparing accounts for the 18 months to 31 March 1997. It is accepted that there is no change of business practice and no transaction which would bring her within the anti-avoidance rules in 71.20 above. She ceases practice on 17 April 2000, preparing accounts for the 12 months and 17 days ending on that date. Her profits (as adjusted for tax purposes) for the six periods of account up to cessation are as follows.

	£
Year to 30 September 1994	26,000
Year to 30 September 1995	27,500
18 months to 31 March 1997	48,500
Year to 31 March 1998	31,000
Year to 31 March 1999	23,500
Period to 17 April 2000	16,500

The figures for the year to 31 March 1998 and subsequent periods are quoted net of capital allowances. Capital allowances for 1995/96 and 1996/97 are as follows.

	£
1995/96	1,800
1996/97	1,500

Mandy's taxable profits for the six tax years 1995/96 to 2000/2001 are as follows.

	£	£
1995/96 (PY basis — y/e 30.9.94)	26,000	
Deduct Capital allowances	1,800	
		24,200
1996/97 (transitional year)		
Y/e 30.9.95	27,500	
18 mths to 31.3.97	48,500	
Profits for 30 months	£76,000	
Average: £76,000 × $\frac{12}{30}$ (40%)	30,400	
Deduct Capital allowances	1,500	
		28,900
1997/98 (CY basis — y/e 31.3.98)		31,000
1998/99 (Y/e 31.3.99)		23,500
1999/2000 (1.4.99 – 31.3.2000) £16,500 × $\frac{12}{12.5}$		15,840
2000/2001 (1.4.2000 – 17.4.2000) £16,500 × $\frac{0.5}{12.5}$		660
		£124,100

Notes

(*a*)   In this case, the basis period for 1996/97 is the 12 months to 31 March 1997. This is extended by the gap between basis periods to give a 30-month transitional period of which 12 months are taxed.

(*b*)   The basis period for the year 1999/2000 (in which no period of account ends) is the 12 months beginning immediately after the end of the basis period for 1998/99 (see 71.15 above).

(*c*)   The change of accounting date does not bring the anti-avoidance rules into play as it brings the end of the basis period for 1996/97 closer to 5 April 1997 (see 71.20 above).

Application of anti-avoidance rules

The facts are as above except that the inspector discovers that there has been a change of business practice resulting in a decrease of £6,000 in the profits for the year to 30 September 1994 (which would otherwise have been £32,000) and a corresponding increase in the combined profits of the 30 months to 31 March 1997 (which would otherwise have been £70,000). Mandy is unable to show that the change was made for commercial reasons or other than mainly to obtain a tax advantage and the anti-avoidance provisions are therefore applied.

The addition to the 1996/97 taxable profits is calculated as follows.

$£6,000 \times (1.25 \times (100\% - 40\%)) = £4,500$

Without the anti-avoidance rules, there would have been a tax saving on profits of £3,600 (£6,000 × 60%). The adjustment cancels out the saving and adds a penalty of £900 (25% of the amount on which the taxpayer sought to avoid tax and, in this particular case, 15% of the amount shifted).

Taxable profits for the six years to 2000/2001 are now as follows.

	£	£
1995/96		24,200
1996/97 As above	30,400	
Anti-avoidance addition	4,500	
	34,900	
Deduct Capital allowances	1,500	
		33,400
1997/98		31,000
1998/99		23,500
1999/2000		15,840
2000/2001		660
		£128,600

71.22   **Transitional rules for businesses commenced before 6 April 1994—Overlap profit for 1997/98.** A business commenced before 6 April 1994 is treated as having a transitional overlap profit for 1997/98 (subject to 71.24 below for businesses ceasing before 6 April 1999). This is equal to the proportion of profits taxable for 1997/98, but before deduction/ addition of capital allowances/balancing charges (except in the case of a partnership with a corporate partner), which arises after the end of the basis period for 1996/97 and before 6 April 1997. For example, if accounts are regularly made up to 30 June and those for the year to 30 June 1997 show tax-adjusted profits of £20,000 before capital allowances, the 1997/98 assessment will be £20,000 *less* capital allowances and there will be a transitional overlap profit of £15,000 by reference to a transitional overlap period of nine months, 1 July 1996 to 5 April 1997 (working in terms of months rather than days, for simplicity). The transitional overlap profit is carried forward and relieved in the same way as other overlap profits (see 71.19 above). [*FA 1994, 20 Sch 2(4)–(4B); FA 1995, s 122(2)(3)*].

Anti-avoidance measures have been introduced to deter and penalise attempts to exploit the above rules by moving profits into the basis period for 1997/98, of which the transitional overlap period forms part, so as to otherwise increase the transitional overlap profit. Where any amount which is included in the transitional overlap profit would not have been so included if any 'relevant change' (see 71.20 above) made or any 'relevant transaction' (see 71.20 above) entered into by the trader had not been made or entered into, the transitional overlap profit is reduced by 1.25 times the aggregate of the amounts so included. (Any amount so included will itself be a proportion, dependent upon the accounting date, of an amount included in the 1997/98 basis period.) There are *de minimis* thresholds in that the said adjustment does not apply where the aggregate of the amounts so included or the proportion which that aggregate bears to the transitional overlap profit is less than an amount/proportion to be prescribed by regulations shortly before 5 April 1997, or where a percentage (based on the proportion which one year bears to the transitional overlap period) of the turnover (defined as for the anti-avoidance measures in 71.20 above) for the transitional overlap period is less than an amount to be so prescribed (and the regulations may make provision for partnerships different from that for individual traders). [*FA 1995, s 123, 22 Sch 3, 21(1)*]. There is no provision for the penalty to be mitigated or for any reduction in the assessment for 1997/98 or any other year, except that where voluntary disclosure is made in the tax return for 1997/98 (other than by amendment to the return), the adjustment is reduced by one-quarter of the aggregate amount so disclosed. [*FA 1995, 22 Sch 13*].

An officer of the Board cannot amend a self-assessment to give effect to the above anti-avoidance provisions unless he gives notice stating the aggregate of the amounts on which the adjustment is based. He may give such notice at any time until a self-assessment for 1998/99 has been made and is not still capable of being amended (see 78 SELF-ASSESSMENT generally). Such a notice is conclusive of the matters stated in it, subject to the right of the taxpayer to appeal within 30 days beginning with the date of the notice, the same procedures applying as for an appeal against an assessment, with the Commissioners able to confirm, set aside or modify the notice. [*FA 1995, 22 Sch 12*].

Where a trade to which the above anti-avoidance provisions apply is carried on in partnership and a partner leaves the firm during the transitional overlap period, he will be personally assessed under Schedule D, Case I or II for 1996/97 on the amount by which his share of transitional overlap profit would have been reduced had he continued to be a partner. [*FA 1995, 22 Sch 4*]. The discovery provisions of *TMA ss 29, 30B* apply with the same modifications and related time limits as in 71.20 above. [*FA 1995, 22 Sch 11*].

See 43.22 INTEREST PAYABLE for the potential reduction or further reduction of the transitional overlap profit where partnership borrowings are replaced by partners' personal borrowings during a period which includes the transitional overlap period.

71.23   *Example*

In the example at 71.5 above, Roy had profits of £27,000 (after deducting capital allowances of £3,000) for the year to 30 April 1997 (taxable in 1997/98) and had transitional overlap relief of £27,500 (£30,000 × 11/12). The inspector discovers that Roy entered into a self-cancelling transaction (see 71.20 above) with the result that profits of £6,000 were shifted from the year ended 30 April 1998 to the year ended 30 April 1997 (which would otherwise have been £24,000), and that he did so neither for commercial reasons nor otherwise than mainly to obtain a tax advantage. The anti-avoidance provisions are therefore applied.

Schedule D, Cases I and II—Profits of Trades etc.   71.25

The 1997/98 and 1998/99 assessments are unchanged. The transitional overlap relief is reduced as follows.

	£
Relief originally calculated at	27,500
Reduction £6,000 × 11/12 (1.5.96–5.4.97) = £5,500 × 1.25	6,875
Revised transitional overlap relief	£20,625

71.24 **Transitional rules for businesses commenced before 6 April 1994—cessation in 1996/97 to 1998/99.** A business commenced before 6 April 1994 and ceasing in the tax year 1996/97 is not subject to the basis period rules in 71.11 to 71.19 above. The cessation will be dealt with as under 71.9 above.

In the case of a business commenced before 6 April 1994 and ceasing in the tax year 1997/98, an officer of the Board may direct that neither the basis period rules in 71.11 to 71.19 above nor the transitional rules in 71.20, 71.22 should apply, in which case the cessation will be dealt with as under 71.9 above.

In the case of a business commenced before 6 April 1994 and ceasing in the tax year 1998/99, a comparison is made between the profits assessable for 1996/97 under the transitional rules in 71.20 above (ignoring any brought-forward losses) and those arising on an actual basis (6 April 1996 to 5 April 1997). If the latter figure is the greater, an officer of the Board may direct that 1996/97 should be taxed on an actual basis. The assessments for 1997/98 and 1998/99 are unaffected.

The Revenue may make all such adjustments, whether by assessment or otherwise, to give effect to either of the above-mentioned directions.

[*FA 1994, 20 Sch 3*].

71.25 **WHETHER OR NOT THERE HAS BEEN A COMMENCEMENT OR DISCONTINUANCE**

for purposes of 71.4, 71.9, 71.12 and 71.17 above.

The rules of 71.4 and 71.9 above for the opening and closing years apply (i) on the commencement of a new business or the permanent discontinuance of a business and (ii) on a change in the persons carrying on a business in which event there is a notional permanent discontinuance on the change and a notional commencement of a new business. [*See 113(1)*]. Where, however, the change is a partnership change (including where a sole trader acquires a partner and *vice versa*) there may be an election for the continuing basis to apply [*See 113(2)*], see 53.6 PARTNERSHIPS. Hence a notional discontinuance/commencement arises on partnership changes with no continuing basis election and on a transfer of the ownership of a business carried on by a sole trader, e.g. when it is sold or passes on death.

The rules of 71.12 and 71.14 above for the opening and closing years apply (i) on the commencement of a new business or the permanent discontinuance of a business and (ii) on an individual becoming or ceasing to be a member of a partnership (*but not so as to affect the continuing partners*)—see 53.3 PARTNERSHIPS.

See 53.8 PARTNERSHIPS as regards partnership mergers and demergers.

Although these rules do not apply to companies (see 71.2 above) the income of a company is to be computed on the basis of a commencement/cessation of a trade when it commences/ceases to carry on a trade whether or not there has been a permanent commencement/discontinuance. [*Sec 337(1)*]. This provision is necessary so that a provision operating on a notional cessation/commencement as well as a permanent one may, if required, be applied to companies as well as individuals. (For examples, see *Secs 102(2), 110(2)*.)

71.26 **Case law.** Whether or not a person has commenced/ceased trading and, if so, the date, are questions of fact. Preliminary activities in setting up a business do not amount to trading (*Birmingham & District Cattle By-Products Co Ltd v CIR KB 1919, 12 TC 92*). For pre-trading expenditure, see 71.75 below. For whether the sale of a business can be effective for tax purposes before the vending agreement, see *Todd v Jones Bros Ltd KB 1930, 15 TC 396* and contrast *Angel v Hollingworth & Co Ch D 1958, 37 TC 714*. 'Permanent discontinuance' does not mean a discontinuance which is everlasting (see *Ingram v Callaghan CA 1968, 45 TC 151*) but a trade may continue notwithstanding a lengthy break in active trading (*Kirk & Randall Ltd v Dunn KB 1924, 8 TC 663* but contrast *Goff v Osborne & Co (Sheffield) Ltd Ch D 1953, 34 TC 441*).

The trade was held to have been continuous when the owner of a drifter continued to manage it after its war-time requisition (*Sutherland v CIR CS 1918, 12 TC 63*); when a merchant sold stock on hand after announcing retirement (*J & R O'Kane v CIR HL 1922, 12 TC 303*); when a flour miller and baker gave up a mill (*Bolands Ltd v Davis KB(IFS) 1925, 4 ATC 532*); when a barrister took silk (*Seldon v Croom-Johnson KB 1932, 16 TC 740*); when a partnership was dissolved but completed open forward contracts (*Hillerns & Fowler v Murray CA 1932, 17 TC 77*); when a building partnership transferred construction activities to a company but retained building land and continued to sell land with houses built thereon by the company (*Watts v Hart Ch D 1984, 58 TC 209*). A new trade was held to have commenced when the vendor of a business retained the benefit of outstanding hire-purchase agreements (*Parker v Batty KB 1941, 23 TC 739*) and when the vendor of a business got commission on open contracts completed by the purchaser (*Southern v Cohen's Exors KB 1940, 23 TC 566*).

It is similarly a question of fact whether a trader expanding by taking over an existing business and operating it as a branch has succeeded to the trade. See e.g. *Bell v National Provincial Bank of England Ltd CA 1903, 5 TC 1* (bank succeeded to trade of single-branch bank taken over); *Laycock v Freeman Hardy & Willis Ltd CA 1938, 22 TC 288* (shoe retailer did not succeed to trade of manufacturing subsidiaries taken over); *Briton Ferry Steel Co Ltd v Barry CA 1939, 23 TC 414* (steel manufacturer succeeded to trade of tinplate manufacturing subsidiaries taken over); and *Maidment v Kibby Ch D, [1993] STC 494* (fish and chip shop proprietor did not succeed to trade of existing business taken over). See also *H & G Kinemas Ltd KB 1933, 18 TC 116* (cinema company disposed of existing cinemas and opened new one, held to commence new trade).

Whether or not there has been a commencement etc. has arisen in a number of cases where the activities of a company have altered on e.g. a change of shareholdings or a group reconstruction or on its absorption of another trade or part-trade. Such decisions are now of limited importance to companies (see 71.25 above) and where the facts are such that they are unlikely to arise in relation to individuals, they are not referred to here. For such cases, see Tolley's Tax Cases.

For a short article on the distinction between succession to a trade, extension of an existing trade and commencement of a new trade, see Revenue Tax Bulletin February 1996 pp 285, 286.

71.27 **Change of residence.** For 1995/96 and subsequent years as regards trades etc. commenced after 5 April 1994 and for 1997/98 and subsequent years as regards those commenced on or before that date, a special rule applies where a sole trader carrying on his trade wholly or partly outside the UK either becomes or ceases to be resident in the UK. The trade is deemed to have been permanently discontinued at the time of the change of residence and, in so far as the individual continues to carry on the actual trade, a new trade is deemed to have been set up immediately afterwards. This applies equally for the purposes of loss reliefs except that a loss incurred in the 'old' trade may be carried forward under *Sec 385* (see 46.13 LOSSES) and set against profits of the 'new' trade. [*Sec 110A; FA 1995, s 124*]. Previously, where a non-UK resident trader not within the charge to UK tax became UK resident, the date of commencement for UK tax purposes was taken to be the actual date that trading commenced and not the date of his becoming resident, i.e. the preceding year 'continuing' basis normally applied to the first UK assessment (see *Fry v Burma Corporation Ltd HL 1930, 15 TC 113*).

Similar rules apply to individuals trading in partnership (see 53.15 PARTNERSHIPS).

71.28   **ACCOUNTS**

Accounts are required by the inspector in order to assess business profits. The results shown by the accounts will usually need adjustments for items which are, or are not, allowable or assessable. Such adjustments are shown in a separate computation. See Revenue Pamphlet IR 28 (Starting in Business). Accounts may sometimes be re-opened to adjust profits and expenses attributable to past periods. The inspector will examine the accounts, computation and other information provided and will ask for further details to satisfy himself as to the correct assessment to make.

Simplified returns. Starting with the 1990/91 return (reporting income for the year ended 5 April 1990), small businesses with a total annual turnover under £15,000 (£10,000 for accounts submitted before 6 April 1992) are required only to state their total turnover, total business purchases and expenses, and the resultant net profit. There will, of course, still be a need to keep accurate business records to ensure the correctness of the three-line accounts, and such accounts will continue to be subject to investigation (see below) in the usual way. (Revenue Press Releases 7 November 1989, 1 November 1991). The Revenue have published three leaflets (IR 104, IR 105 and IR 106) explaining the new system of tax accounts for small businesses.

Rounding of tax computations. To reduce the compliance burden on large businesses whose statutory accounts are produced in round thousands, the Revenue are generally prepared to accept profit computations for tax purposes in figures rounded to the nearest £1,000 from single businesses or companies with an annual turnover of at least £5 million (including investment and estate income) in the accounts in question or in the preceding year, where rounding at least to that extent has been used in preparing the accounts. (Turnover of groups of companies is not aggregated for this purpose.) Such computations must be accompanied by a certificate by the person preparing the computations stating the basis of rounding, and confirming that it is unbiased, has been applied consistently and produces a fair result for tax purposes (and stating the program or software used where relevant), or, if there have been no changes from the previous year in these respects, confirming the unchanged basis. The rounding may not extend to the tax payable or other relevant figures of tax. Rounding is not acceptable where it would impede the application of the legislation, or where recourse to the underlying records would normally be necessary to do the computation. Thus it is not acceptable e.g. in computations of chargeable gains (except in relation to the incidental costs of acquisition and disposal), in accrued income scheme computations (see 74.6 SCHEDULE D, CASE VI), in computations of tax credit relief or in certain capital allowance computations. The inspector may exceptionally insist that roundings are not used in other circumstances, and any existing arrangements falling outside the above arrangements must cease for periods ending after 31 May 1995. (Revenue Pamphlet IR 131, SP 15/93, 18 May 1993).

In-depth examination. Since 1977, a more discriminating approach towards examining business accounts has been adopted by the Revenue by a more thorough enquiry into the records and underlying information of selected accounts exhibiting unsatisfactory features. 'It follows that accounts built up by qualified accountants from complete and reliable taxpayers' records will usually show a result that does not arouse the inspector's curiosity, and will accordingly be less likely to be chosen for investigation, possibly for many years.' (Revenue Press Releases 15 October 1976 and 1 August 1977 and CCAB Statement 18 October 1977). The Revenue affirmed that the selection of cases for in-depth examination was not on a random basis and that no lists of official gross profit percentages are issued to inspectors. See also CCAB Statements of 4 October 1978 and 25 September 1979. Complaints of unfair treatment etc. in a tax district should be made initially to the Regional Controller.

The Revenue have published a Code of Practice (No 2, published February 1993 and available from local tax offices) setting out their standards for the way in which investigations are conducted and the rights and responsibilities of taxpayers. Codes of Practice 8 and 9, dealing with Special Compliance Office Investigations in cases other than suspected serious fraud and cases of such fraud respectively, were published in January 1995 and are available from the Special Compliance Office, Angel Court, 199 Borough High Street, London SE1 1HZ.

See also 58.3, 58.7 PENALTIES. See generally Revenue Pamphlets IR 72 and IR 73.

Business Economic Notes relating to various trades, which are used by inspectors as background information in examining accounts, are available from Reference Room, Inland Revenue Library, Mid-Basement, Somerset House, London WC2R 1LB (price £1.50 post free). Those currently available are:

1. Travel agents.
2. Road haulage (revised 1995).
3. The lodging industry.
4. Hairdressers.
5. Waste materials reclamation and disposal.
6. Funeral directors.
7. Dentists.
8. Florists.
9. Licensed victuallers.
10. The jewellery trade.
11. Electrical retailers.
12. Antiques and fine art dealers.
13. Fish and chip shops.
14. The pet industry.
15. Veterinary surgeons.
16. Catering—general.
17.   —restaurants.
18.   —fast-foods, cafes and snack-bars.
19. Farming—stock valuation for income tax purposes.
20. Insurance brokers and agents.
21. Residential rest and nursing homes.
22. Dispensing chemists.

See 71.68 for allowability of accountancy expenses. For powers of Revenue to obtain accounts etc., see 6.8 BACK DUTY.

WHETHER A TRADE CARRIED ON

See also 50 MUTUAL TRADING and 83 STATUTORY BODIES. See 71.1 above for statutory definition of 'trade'; meaning of 'profession or vocation'; application of Cases I and II to overseas business activities; and the principle that income within Schedules A and B is not derived from trading. Special types of activity are dealt with below in alphabetical order.

71.29	Avoidance schemes	71.35	Isolated or speculative transactions
71.30	Betting	71.36	Liquidators etc. and personal
71.31	Divers etc.		representatives
71.32	Futures and options	71.37	Miscellaneous
71.33	Horse racing etc.	71.38	Property transactions
71.34	Illegal trading	71.39	Share dealing

71.29 AVOIDANCE SCHEMES

A line is drawn between transactions of a trading nature which remain trading even though entered into to secure tax advantages and transactions so remote from ordinary trading as to be explicable only as fiscal devices and hence not trading.

In *Ransom v Higgs* and *Kilmorie (Aldridge) Ltd v Dickinson, etc. HL 1974, 50 TC 1* the taxpayers entered into complex arrangements to siphon development profits into the hands of trustees. They succeeded, the Crown failing to establish that, looked at as a whole, the arrangements constituted trading. In *Johnson v Jewitt CA 1961, 40 TC 231* an elaborate and artificial device to manufacture trading losses was held not to amount to trading, but see *Ensign Tankers (Leasing) Ltd v Stokes HL 1992, 64 TC 617*, where the company's investment in two film production partnerships was entered into with a view to obtaining first-year capital allowances. See also *Black Nominees Ltd v Nicol Ch D 1975, 50 TC 229* and *Newstead v Frost HL 1980, 53 TC 525*. See generally ANTI-AVOIDANCE (3).

71.30 BETTING

Betting by professional bookmakers is assessable (*Partridge v Mallandaine QB 1886, 2 TC 179*) even if carried on in an unlawful way (*Southern v A B KB 1933, 18 TC 59*) but not private betting however habitual (*Graham v Green KB 1925, 9 TC 309*). Also exempt from CGT. [*TCGA 1992, s 51(1)*]. Receipts from newspaper articles based on betting system held assessable in *Graham v Arnott KB 1941, 24 TC 157*.

Lotteries and football pools promotion constitutes trading, but where a pool or small lottery is run by a supporters club or other society on terms that a specified part of the cost of the ticket is to be donated to a club or body within the purposes in *Lotteries and Amusements Act 1976, s 5(1)*, the donation element is not treated as a trading receipt. (Revenue Pamphlet IR 131, C1). See 15.3(iv) CHARITIES as regards charitable lotteries.

71.31 DIVERS AND DIVING SUPERVISORS

The emoluments of a person employed in the UK (including a designated area under *Continental Shelf Act 1964, s 1(7)*, see 51.13 NON-RESIDENTS AND OTHER OVERSEAS MATTERS) as a diver in operations to exploit the sea-bed, or as a supervisor in relation to such operations, are to be dealt with under Schedule D, Case I as if he were carrying on a trade and not under Schedule E. [*Sec 314*].

71.32 FUTURES AND OPTIONS

Any gain or loss arising in the course of dealing, other than in the course of trade, in commodity or financial futures or in traded or (after 28 April 1988) financial options on a recognised exchange is dealt with under the capital gains tax rules and is not chargeable to tax or relieved under Schedule D. [*Sec 128; TCGA 1992, s 143; FA 1994, s 95; SI 1988 No 744*]. See Tolley's Capital Gains Tax under Disposal.

Where dealing is in the course of a trade, any profit or loss is chargeable under Schedule D, Case I. In general, relatively infrequent transactions, and transactions to hedge specific investments, would not be regarded as trading, nor would purely speculative transactions.

For the Revenue view on what constitutes trading in this context, see Revenue Pamphlet IR 131, SP 14/91, 21 November 1991.

Special rules are to be applied (by regulation) to the market formed by the merger of the London International Financial Futures Exchange (LIFFE) and the London Traded Options Market (LTOM), which will operate outside the Stock Exchange. These relate to stock lending, bond-washing and manufactured dividends, and to stamp duty and stamp duty reserve tax. See *SIs 1992 Nos 568, 569, 570* and *572*.

Pension schemes etc. For the purposes of approved retirement benefit schemes (see 66.5(*b*), 66.13 RETIREMENT SCHEMES), personal pension schemes and retirement annuity trust schemes (see 65.2, 65.13 RETIREMENT ANNUITIES AND PERSONAL PENSION SCHEMES), futures and options contracts are, after 26 July 1990, treated as investments (and thus as attracting tax exemption for income and capital gains). Any income derived from transactions relating to such a contract is regarded as arising from the contract, and a contract is not excluded from these provisions by the fact that any party is, or may be, entitled to receive and/or liable to make only a payment of a sum in full settlement of all obligations, as opposed to a transfer of assets other than money. [*Sec 659A; TCGA 1992, s 271(10)(11); FA 1990, s 81(2)(3)(5)(6)*]. Previously, a contract entered into in the course of dealing in financial futures or traded options was regarded as an investment for those purposes by virtue of *Sec 659*, which is repealed following enactment of the more comprehensive provisions described above. [*Sec 659; FA 1990, s 81(4)(7)(8)*].

See 90.1 UNIT TRUSTS as regards similar exemption for trustees of authorised unit trusts in relation to futures and options contracts.

71.33   HORSE RACING ETC.

'Private' horse racing and training is not normally trading (cf. *Sharkey v Wernher HL 1955, 36 TC 275*). But racing and selling the progeny of a brood mare held within Schedule D in *Dawson v Counsell CA 1938, 22 TC 149* and in *Norman v Evans Ch D 1964, 42 TC 188* share of prize monies for letting racehorses held within Case VI. Profits from stallion fees are assessable and assessments under both Case I and Case VI have been upheld (*Malcolm v Lockhart HL 1919, 7 TC 99; McLaughlin v Bailey CA (I) 1920, 7 TC 508; Jersey's Exors v Bassom KB 1926, 10 TC 357; Wernher v CIR KB 1942, 29 TC 20; Benson v Counsell KB 1942, 24 TC 178*) but wear and tear allowances (the forerunner of modern capital allowances on plant, etc.) for stallions refused in *Derby v Aylmer KB 1915, 6 TC 665*. Profits from greyhound breeding held trading in *Hawes v Gardiner Ch D 1957, 37 TC 671*.

71.34   ILLEGAL TRADING

Crime, e.g. burglary, is not trading but the profits of a commercial business are assessable notwithstanding the business may be carried on in an unlawful way, e.g. 'bootlegging' (*Canadian Minister of Finance v Smith PC 1926, 5 ATC 621* and cf. *Lindsay Woodward & Hiscox v CIR CS 1932, 18 TC 43*), operating 'fruit machines' illegal at the time (*Mann v Nash KB 1932, 16 TC 523*), street bookmaking illegal at the time (*Southern v A B KB 1933, 18 TC 59*) and prostitution (*CIR v Aken CA 1990, 63 TC 395*). But penalties for trading contrary to war-time regulations held not deductible (*CIR v E C Warnes & Co KB 1919, 12 TC 227; CIR v Alexander von Glehn & Co CA 1920, 12 TC 232*). See also 71.30 above.

See 71.62 below as regards prohibition on deduction of expenditure involving crime.

71.35   ISOLATED OR SPECULATIVE TRANSACTIONS

For futures, property transactions and share dealing see 71.32, 71.38 and 71.39 respectively.

Whether the surplus on the purchase and resale of assets, otherwise than in the course of an established commercial enterprise, is derived from an 'adventure or concern in the nature of trade' (see 71.1 above) depends on the facts. Para. 116 of the Final Report of the Royal Commission on the Taxation of Profits and Income (1955 HMSO Cmd. 9474) lists six 'badges of trade': (i) the subject matter of the realisation; (ii) length of period of ownership; (iii) frequency or number of similar transactions; (iv) supplementary work on assets sold; (v) reason for sale; (vi) motive. Other relevant factors may be the degree of organisation, whether the taxpayer is or has been associated with a recognised business dealing in similar assets and how the purchases were financed. For a recent review of the factors to be considered, see *Marson v Morton Ch D 1986, 59 TC 381.*

Although in disputed cases the Revenue may make alternative Case I and Case VI assessments, it would seem from *Pearn v Miller KB 1927, 11 TC 610* and *Leeming v Jones HL 1930, 15 TC 333* (see 71.38 below) that as regards isolated transactions the income tax liability, if any, will be under Case I. As regards commodity futures, see 71.32 above.

Case I assessments were upheld on a purchase and resale of war surplus linen (*Martin v Lowry HL 1926, 11 TC 297*—a leading case); a purchase, conversion and resale of a ship (*CIR v Livingston CS 1926, 11 TC 538*); transactions in brandy (*Cape Brandy Syndicate v CIR CA 1921, 12 TC 358*), whisky (*Lindsay Woodward* at 71.34 above), whisky in bond (*P J McCall decd v CIR KB(IFS) 1923, 4 ATC 522; CIR v Fraser CS 1942, 24 TC 498*); 'turning over' cotton mills (*Pickford v Quirke CA 1927, 13 TC 251*); purchase and resale of cotton spinning plant (*Edwards v Bairstow & Harrison HL 1955, 36 TC 207*); and purchase and resale of toilet rolls (*Rutledge v CIR CS 1929, 14 TC 490*). But in *Jenkinson v Freedland CA 1961, 39 TC 636* the Commissioners' finding that a profit on the purchase, repair and sale (to associated companies) of stills was not assessable, was upheld, and in *Kirkham v Williams CA 1991, 64 TC 253*, the Commissioners' decision that the sale of a dwelling house built on land partly acquired for storage, etc. was an adventure in the nature of trade was reversed in the CA.

71.36 LIQUIDATORS ETC. AND PERSONAL REPRESENTATIVES

Whether a liquidator or receiver is continuing the company's trade or merely realising its assets as best he can, is a question of fact and similarly for the personal representatives of a deceased trader. For liquidators or receivers see *Armitage v Moore QB 1900, 4 TC 199; CIR v 'Old Bushmills' Distillery KB(NI) 1927, 12 TC 1148; CIR v Thompson KB 1936, 20 TC 422; Wilson Box v Brice CA 1936, 20 TC 736; Baker v Cook KB 1937, 21 TC 337.*

Personal representatives were held to be trading while winding up the deceased's business in *Weisberg's Executrices v CIR KB 1933, 17 TC 696; Wood v Black's Exor HC 1952, 33 TC 172; Pattullo's Trustees v CIR CS 1955, 36 TC 87* but not in *Cohan's Exors v CIR CA 1924, 12 TC 602* (completion of ship under construction at death) and *CIR v Donaldson's Trustees CS 1963, 41 TC 161* (sale of pedigree herd). For property sales after death of partner in property dealing firm, see *Marshall's Exors v Joly KB 1936, 20 TC 256* and contrast *Newbarns Syndicate v Hay CA 1939, 22 TC 461.*

71.37 MISCELLANEOUS

Assessments under Case I were upheld on a committee operating golf links owned by a Town Council (*Carnoustie Golf Course Committee v CIR CS 1929, 14 TC 498*); trustees under a private Act managing a recreation ground (*CIR v Stonehaven Recreation Ground Trustees CS 1929, 15 TC 419*); temporary joint coal merchanting (*Gardner and Bowring Hardy & Co v CIR CS 1930, 15 TC 602*); promotion of mining companies to exploit mines (*Murphy v Australian Machinery etc. Co Ltd CA 1948, 30 TC 244* and cf. *Rhodesia Metals v Commr of Taxes PC 1940, 19 ATC 472*); purchase and resale of amusement equipment (*Crole v Lloyd HC 1950, 31 TC 338*).

71.38 Schedule D, Cases I and II—Profits of Trades etc.

A company which made loans to another company to finance a trading venture was held not to be trading itself (*Stone & Temple Ltd v Waters; Astrawall (UK) Ltd v Waters Ch D, [1995] STC 1*).

The activities of the British Olympic Association (which included the raising of funds through commercial sponsorship and the exploitation of its logo, but many of which were non-commercial) were held as a whole to be uncommercial and not to constitute a trade (*British Olympic Association v Winter (Sp C 28), [1995] SSCD 85*).

See also *Smith Barry v Cordy CA 1946, 28 TC 250* in which a taxpayer was held liable on his surplus from the sale or maturing of endowment policies he had purchased, *J Bolson & Son Ltd v Farrelly CA 1953, 34 TC 161* (deals in vessels by company operating boat services held a separate adventure) and *Torbell Investments Ltd v Williams Ch D 1986, 59 TC 357* (dormant company revived for purpose of acquiring certain loans held to have acquired them as trading stock). But a company formed to administer a holidays with pay scheme for the building etc. industry was held not trading (*Building & Civil Engineering, etc. Ltd v Clark Ch D 1960, 39 TC 12*). Assessments on profits from promoting a series of driving schools were upheld in *Leach v Pogson Ch D 1962, 40 TC 585*; in concluding that the profit from *first* sale was assessable, Commissioners were entitled to take into account the subsequent transactions.

For circumstances in which the profits of a trade may not accrue to the proprietor, see *Alongi v CIR CS 1991, 64 TC 304*.

71.38 PROPERTY TRANSACTIONS

This paragraph relates to transactions in land and buildings otherwise than in the course of an established business of property development, building etc. For other sales of property see 71.76 below.

A line is drawn between realisations of property held as an investment or as a residence and transactions amounting to an adventure or concern in the nature of trade. The principles at 71.35 above apply suitably adapted.

In *Leeming v Jones HL 1930, 15 TC 333* an assessment on the acquisitions and disposal of options over rubber estates was confirmed by Commissioners. The Crown had defended the assessment under both Case I and Case VI. In a Supplementary Case the Commissioners found there had been no concern in the nature of the trade. The Court held there was no liability. Per Lawrence LJ 'in the case of an isolated transaction . . . there is really no middle course open. It is either an adventure in the nature of trade, or else it is simply a case of sale and resale of property.' See also *Pearn v Miller KB 1927, 11 TC 610* and *Williams v Davies* below.

Property transactions by companies held to be trading in *Californian Copper Syndicate v Harris CES 1904, 5 TC 159* (purchase of copper bearing land shortly afterwards resold); *Thew v South West Africa Co CA 1924, 9 TC 141* (numerous sales of land acquired by concession for exploitation); *Cayzer, Irvine & Co v CIR CS 1942, 24 TC 491* (exploitation of landed estate acquired by shipping company); *Emro Investments v Aller* and *Lance Webb Estates v Aller Ch D 1954, 35 TC 305* (profits carried to capital reserve on numerous purchases and sales); *Orchard Parks v Pogson Ch D 1964, 42 TC 442* (land compulsorily purchased after development plan dropped); *Parkstone Estates v Blair Ch D 1966, 43 TC 246* (industrial estate developed—land disposed of by sub-leases for premiums); *Eames v Stepnell Properties Ltd CA 1966, 43 TC 678* (sale of land acquired from associated company while resale being negotiated). See also *Bath & West Counties Property Trust Ltd v Thomas Ch D 1977, 52 TC 20*. Realisations were held to be capital in *Hudson's Bay v Stevens CA 1909, 5 TC 424* (numerous sales of land acquired under Royal Charter—contrast *South West Africa Co* above); *Tebrau (Johore) Rubber Syndicate v Farmer*

CES 1910, 5 TC 658 (purchase and resale of rubber estates—contrast *Californian Copper* above).

In *Rand v Alberni Land Co Ltd KB 1920, 7 TC 629* sales of land held in trust were held not trading but contrast *Alabama Coal Iron Land v Mylam KB 1926, 11 TC 232; Balgownie Land Trust v CIR CS 1929, 14 TC 684; St Aubyn Estates v Strick KB 1932, 17 TC 412; Tempest Estates v Walmsley Ch D 1975, 51 TC 305.* Sales of property after a period of letting held realisations of investments or not trading in *CIR v Hyndland Investment Co Ltd CS 1929, 14 TC 694; Glasgow Heritable Trust v CIR CS 1954, 35 TC 196; Lucy & Sunderland Ltd v Hunt Ch D 1961, 40 TC 132* but held trading in *Rellim Ltd v Vise CA 1951, 32 TC 254* (notwithstanding that company previously admitted as investment company); *CIR v Toll Property Co CS 1952, 34 TC 13; Forest Side Properties (Chingford) v Pearce CA 1961, 39 TC 665.* But sales by liquidator of property owned by companies following abandonment of plan for their public flotation held not trading in *Simmons v CIR HL 1980, 53 TC 461* (reversing Commissioners' decision).

Property transactions by individuals and partnerships. Profits held assessable in *Reynold's Exors v Bennett KB 1943, 25 TC 401; Broadbridge v Beattie KB 1944, 26 TC 63; Gray & Gillitt v Tiley KB 1944, 26 TC 80; Laver v Wilkinson KB 1944, 26 TC 105; Foulds v Clayton Ch D 1953, 34 TC 382* and *Kirkby v Hughes Ch D 1992, 65 TC 352;* in all of which the taxpayers were or had been associated with building or estate development, and contrast *Williams v Davies KB 1945, 26 TC 371* in which the taxpayers were closely associated with land development but a profit on transactions in undeveloped land in the names of their wives held not assessable. The acquisition and resale of land for which planning permission had been or was obtained held trading in *Cooke v Haddock Ch D 1960, 39 TC 64; Turner v Last Ch D 1965, 42 TC 517* and *Pilkington v Randall CA 1966, 42 TC 662* (and cf. *Iswera v Ceylon Commr PC 1965, 44 ATC 157*), but contrast *Taylor v Good CA 1974, 49 TC 277* in which a house bought as a residence was found unsuitable and resold to a developer after obtaining planning permission and held not an adventure. In *Burrell v Davis Ch D 1948, 38 TC 307; Johnston v Heath Ch D 1970, 46 TC 463; Reeves v Evans, Boyce & Northcott Ch D 1971, 48 TC 495* and *Clark v Follett Ch D 1973, 48 TC 677* the short period of ownership or other evidence showed an intention to purchase for resale at a profit and not for investment, but contrast *CIR v Reinhold CS 1953, 34 TC 389, Marson v Morton Ch D 1986, 59 TC 381* and *Taylor v Good* above. For other cases in which profits held assessable see *Hudson v Wrightson KB 1934, 26 TC 55* and *MacMahon v CIR CS 1951, 32 TC 311.*

For sales after a period of letting see *Mitchell Bros v Tomlinson CA 1957, 37 TC 224* and *Cooksey & Bibby v Rednall KB 1949, 30 TC 514.*

For sale of houses built by taxpayer and used as residences see *Page v Pogson Ch D 1954, 35 TC 545* and *Kirkham v Williams CA 1991, 64 TC 253.*

For sales after death of partner in property dealing transactions, see cases at 71.36 above. See also re partnership sales *CIR v Dean Property Co CS 1939, 22 TC 706* and *Dodd and Tanfield v Haddock Ch D 1964, 42 TC 229.*

71.39　**SHARE DEALING**

Share dealing with the public is strictly controlled by the *Financial Services Act 1986.* This paragraph is concerned with share transactions entered into (generally through the Stock Exchange) by persons not authorised to deal under that Act and the question arises whether they amount to an adventure or concern in the nature of trade. The principles of 71.35 above apply suitably adapted. The prudent management of an investment portfolio may necessitate changes in the holdings but this is not normally trading. Stock Exchange speculation, particularly by individuals, may be quasi-gambling and not trading—see Pennycuick J in *Lewis Emanuel & Son Ltd v White Ch D 1965, 42 TC 369* in which, reversing the Commissioners' finding, he held that the Stock Exchange losses of a fruit etc. merchanting company were from a separate trade of share dealing but observed that gambling by the company would have been *ultra vires*. In *Cooper v C & J Clark Ltd Ch D 1982, 54 TC 670*, the losses of a manufacturing company on its sale of gilts, in which it had invested temporarily surplus cash, were allowed as a set-off against its general trading profits. An individual speculating in stocks and shares and commodity futures was held to be trading in *Wannell v Rothwell Ch D, 1996 STI 605* (although loss relief was refused on the grounds that the trading was 'uncommercial', see 46.10(*a*) LOSSES), but the opposite conclusion was reached in *Salt v Chamberlain Ch D 1979, 53 TC 143*.

For share dealing by investment companies see *Scottish Investment Trust Co v Forbes CES 1893, 3 TC 231* and *Halefield Securities Ltd v Thorpe Ch D 1967, 44 TC 154*. For trading in secured loans, see *Torbell Investments Ltd v Williams Ch D 1986, 59 TC 357*.

For share sales connected with an existing business see 71.81 below.

ASSESSABLE PROFITS, ALLOWABLE DEDUCTIONS ETC.

See also 10 CAPITAL ALLOWANCES. Headings below after 71.40 are in alphabetical order.

71.40   GENERAL

The provisions for computing business profits are in *Secs 74–99*. The general rules for deductions are in *Sec 74*. These are few and simple and, in content and wording, little changed since Napoleonic times. There are no corresponding rules for receipts. Hence practice is largely based on principles evolved over the years and endorsed by the Courts.

Earnings basis. Although the Revenue will, on certain conditions, accept accounts for professions and vocations on a CASH BASIS (12) the legal basis is the earnings basis with provision for debtors, creditors, accruals and stock and work in progress (cf. *CIR v Gardner Mountain & D'Ambrumenil Ltd HL 1947, 29 TC 69*). Hence profits and losses which have not accrued cannot be anticipated (cf. *Willingale v International Commercial Bank Ltd HL 1977, 52 TC 242*) nor can future expenses. Conversely an expense actually incurred is allowable in full even though the benefit from it will not accrue until later years (*Vallambrosa Rubber Co Ltd v Farmer CES 1910, 5 TC 529; Duple Motor Bodies Ltd v Ostime HL 1961, 39 TC 537*). A provision for contingent liabilities may be permissible on certain conditions (*Owen v Southern Railway of Peru* at 71.48 below).

Accountancy principles. The starting figure in computing profits is that brought out by the accounts of the business and accountancy principles are therefore of the highest importance. They cannot however override established income tax principles (*Heather v P-E Consulting Group Ltd CA 1972, 48 TC 293; Willingale v International Commercial Bank Ltd HL 1977, 52 TC 242*; but see *Threlfall v Jones CA 1993, 66 TC 77; Johnston v Britannia Airways Ltd Ch D, [1994] STC 763*). See also *RTZ Oil & Gas Ltd v Elliss Ch D 1987, 61 TC 132*.

For clarification of Revenue practice following the decisions in *Threlfall v Jones* and *Johnston v Britannia Airways Ltd*, dealing in particular with provisions, alternative accounting policies, capitalised expenditure, and changes of accounting policy, see ICAEW Guidance Note TAX 10/95, 10 April 1995.

Capital receipts and expenses must, unless the Acts explicitly provide otherwise, be excluded. This principle is derived, as regards expenses, from *Sec 74(f)(g)* and generally because the charge to tax is on *income*. See also *Sec 817(2)*. 'No part of our law of taxation presents such almost insoluble conundrums as the decision whether a receipt or outgoing is capital or income for tax purposes' (Lord Upjohn in *Strick v Regent Oil Co Ltd HL 1965, 43 TC 1* q.v. for a comprehensive review of the law). A widely used test is the 'enduring benefit' one given by Viscount Cave in *Atherton v British Insulated & Helsby Cables Ltd HL 1925, 10 TC 155*. For a recent review of the cases, see *Lawson v Johnson Matthey plc HL 1992, 65 TC 39*. A gain or loss on the sale of a capital asset not included in trading profits is dealt with according to the provisions relating to capital gains tax. A sale of a fixed asset on which capital allowances have been claimed may result in a balancing charge or allowance, see 10 CAPITAL ALLOWANCES.

Wholly and exclusively. Any expense to be deductible must, *inter alia*, have been incurred 'wholly and exclusively . . . for the purposes' of the trade, etc. [*Sec 74(a)*]. This provision underlies, explicitly or implicitly, the very large number of 'expenses' cases noted in the paragraphs below. For a review of the leading cases see *Harrods (Buenos Aires) Ltd v Taylor-Gooby CA 1964, 41 TC 450* and for a frequently quoted analysis of the words see *Bentleys, Stokes & Lowless v Beeson CA 1952, 33 TC 491*. Since that case the *'dual purpose rule'* has figured prominently in Court decisions. If an expense is for a material private or non-business purpose, the whole is strictly disallowable as it is thereby not wholly and exclusively for business purposes. For examples of its application see 71.73 and 71.88 below. In practice, this rule is not always rigidly applied (and see para. 161 of Tucker Committee Report on Taxation of Trading Profits, 1951 HMSO Cmd. 8189, where the Revenue indicated to the Committee that the inspector would generally agree a fair apportionment where an expense had objects additional to those of a purely business nature). For rent etc. of premises used both for business and as residence, see 71.77 below. See *Mallalieu v Drummond* (71.73) for an important recent HL discussion of *Sec 74(a)*, in which it was held that the purposes of the relevant expenditure involved looking into the taxpayer's mind at the time of the expenditure, later events being irrelevant except as a reflection of that state of mind. However, the taxpayer's conscious motive at the time was not conclusive; an object, not a conscious motive (in this case the human requirement for clothing), could be taken into account. A purely incidental consequence of a business expense does not, however, preclude its being wholly and exclusively for business purposes. See, e.g., *Robinson v Scott Bader Ltd*, 71.53 below and *Stockbroker v McKnight*, 71.68, 71.73 below. *Mallalieu v Drummond* was applied in *Watkis v Ashford, Sparkes and Harward Ch D 1985, 58 TC 468*, where expenditure on meals supplied at regular partners' lunchtime meetings was disallowed, overruling the Commissioner's finding that the expenditure was exclusively for business purposes. Expenditure on accommodation, food and drink at the firm's annual weekend conference was, however, allowed. For deduction of payments by partnerships to individual partners generally, see *MacKinlay v Arthur Young McClelland Moores & Co HL 1989, 62 TC 704*.

See also 71.73 below as regards personal expenses.

It should be borne in mind that the trade for whose purposes the expenditure is incurred must be that in which the expense arose. For a case on this point, see *Vodafone Cellular Ltd v Shaw Ch D, [1995] STC 353*.

Schedule E income received by a trader should in law be excluded from his Case I and II income (see 5.2 ASSESSMENTS) but in practice the legal position is modified in certain circumstances. See *Walker v Carnaby Harrower Ch D 1969, 46 TC 561* and *CIR v Brander & Cruickshank HL 1970, 46 TC 574* for the inclusion in the Case II assessment of professions of remuneration as auditor, etc. For the tax treatment of directors' fees received by partnerships and other companies and the distinction between Schedule E and Schedule D, see 75.1(1) and 75.24 SCHEDULE E. See 75.32 SCHEDULE E as regards certain payments to redundant steel workers.

For **ancillary trading income** see 71.65 below.

71.41 ADVERTISING

Expenditure generally is allowable (but not capital outlay such as fixed signs (but see *Leeds Permanent Building Society v Proctor Ch D 1982, 56 TC 293*), nor initial costs, etc. of new business). Contribution to campaign for Sunday opening held allowable (*Rhymney Breweries Ch D 1965, 42 TC 509*). As to political campaign see *Tate & Lyle HL 1954, 35 TC 367*, contrasted with *Boarland v Kramat Pulai Ch D 1953, 35 TC 1*.

71.42 APPLICATION OF PROFITS

A requirement that a trading surplus is to be applied in a particular way does not remove the trade from Case I (*Mersey Docks and Harbour Board v Lucas HL 1883, 2 TC 25*) and applications of the profits under the requirement are not allowable deductions (*City of Dublin Steam Packet Co v O'Brien KB(I) 1912, 6 TC 101; Hutchinson & Co v Turner HC 1950, 31 TC 495; Young v Racecourse Betting Control Board HL 1959, 38 TC 426* and cf. *Pondicherry Rly Co PC 1931, 10 ATC 365; Tata Hydro-Electric Agencies PC 1937, 16 ATC 54; India Radio & Cable Communication Co PC 1937, 16 ATC 333*).

For circumstances in which the profits of a trade may not accrue to the proprietor, see *Alongi v CIR CS 1991, 64 TC 304*.

71.43 **AUTHORS AND ARTISTES**

For copyright, etc. see 71.50 below.

An actress based in the UK but with engagements abroad was held to be carrying on a single profession. Hence receipts from her overseas engagements fell to be included in her Case II assessment (*Davies v Braithwaite KB 1933, 18 TC 198* and compare *Withers v Wynyard KB 1938, 21 TC 724*). A taxpayer who, after spare time writing plays not sold, wrote a successful play was held to be carrying on the vocation of dramatist (*Billam v Griffith KB 1941, 23 TC 757*). Receipts from the occasional writing of articles are normally assessable under SCHEDULE D, CASE VI (74) but Case II assessments on a regular newspaper contributor were upheld in *Graham v Arnott KB 1941, 24 TC 157*. Receipts from the sale of an author's notebooks and memorabilia were held to be taxable as part of the fruits of his profession (*Wain v Cameron Ch D, [1995] STC 555*).

An artiste engaged by a theatre under a standard contract was held to be within Schedule E (*Fall v Hitchen Ch D 1972, 49 TC 433*), but see now 75.24 SCHEDULE E as regards application of Schedule D to artistes generally.

A sum received by an author on cancellation of his contract as script writer was held a revenue receipt (*Household v Grimshaw Ch D 1953, 34 TC 366*). See also *John Mills Productions Ltd v Mathias Ch D 1967, 44 TC 441*. Payment to actor for entering into restrictive covenant held not assessable (*Higgs v Olivier CA 1952, 33 TC 136*). Film writer's loss under guarantee of indebtedness of film company held allowable (*Lunt v Wellesley KB 1945, 27 TC 78*). Whether a literary prize is a receipt of the author's profession depends on the precise facts.

See 3.10 ANTI-AVOIDANCE for the treatment as income of certain capital sums received in lieu of earnings and 51.8 NON-RESIDENTS AND OTHER OVERSEAS MATTERS as regards certain non-resident entertainers and sportsmen.

71.44 **BAD AND DOUBTFUL DEBTS**

Bad debts (before 1996/97, proven bad debts), and doubtful debts to the extent they are estimated to be bad, are deductible. Where the debtor is bankrupt or insolvent, the debt is deductible except to the extent that any amount may reasonably be expected to be received on it. Debts (or parts) released wholly and exclusively for trade purposes after 29 November 1993 as part of a voluntary arrangement under or by virtue of *Insolvency Act 1986* or a compromise or arrangement under *Companies Act 1985, s 425* (or NI equivalent) are also deductible. [*Sec 74(j); FA 1994, s 144(1)(2)(6); FA 1996, s 134, 20 Sch 4*]. Otherwise, where a debt allowed in computing profits is subsequently released, the amount released is a trading receipt of the period in which it is released. [*Sec 94; FA 1994, s 144(3)(a)(7)*]. Where a trade is treated as notionally discontinued (see 71.25 above), the allowance extends to debts taken over by the successor, and similar treatment applies to recoveries. [*Secs 89, 106(2)*]. For debt recoveries and releases after the cessation of a trade, see 60 POST-CESSATION ETC. RECEIPTS AND EXPENDITURE. Bad debt allowances are not applicable where the business is assessed on a CASH BASIS (12). For VAT on bad debts, see 71.91 below.

The provision for a bad or doubtful debt for a period of account may reflect events after the balance sheet date insofar as they furnish additional evidence of conditions that existed at the balance sheet date. See Revenue Tax Bulletin August 1994 p 154, which also outlines the evidence which inspectors may require in support of the allowance of a provision.

Where as part of a transfer of assets and liabilities between group companies creditors consent to the release of the transferor company from its obligations in return for the transferee assuming those obligations, no charge arises under *Sec 94*. (Revenue Tax Bulletin August 1993 p 88).

Where an asset accepted in satisfaction of a trading debt is of market value (as at the date of acceptance) less than the outstanding debt, the deficit may be allowed as a deduction, provided that, on a disposal of the asset, any excess of disposal proceeds over that value (up to the amount by which the debt exceeds that value) is brought in as a trading receipt (such receipt being excluded from any chargeable gain computation on the disposal). (Revenue Inspectors' Manual, IM 642).

For the Revenue practice in relation to bad and doubtful international loans ('country-risk debts') see Revenue Pamphlet IR 131, SP 1/83, 25 January 1983. The principles apply whether the creditor is a bank or some other commercial organisation (Hansard Vol 36 Col 84, 1 February 1983). See also *Secs 88A–88C* introduced by *FA 1990, s 74*. These provisions were, however, repealed by *FA 1996, 41 Sch Pt V(3)* for 1996/97 onwards and for accounting periods ending after 31 March 1996. For the replacement corporation tax provisions in *FA 1996, 9 Sch 8, 9*, and the associated transitional provisions in *FA 1996, 15 Sch 17*, see Tolley's Corporation Tax under Gilts and Bonds.

An allowance agreed under conditions of full disclosure cannot be withdrawn because of a subsequent change in the circumstances (*Anderton & Halstead Ltd v Birrell KB 1931, 16 TC 200*) but an allowance for year 1 may be revised, upwards or downwards, in the year 2 computation by reference to the circumstances for year 2 and similarly for later years. The amount of the allowance depends on the likelihood of recovery. This is a question of fact but the fact that the debtor is still in business is not itself a reason for refusing an allowance (*Dinshaw v Bombay IT Commr PC 1934, 13 ATC 284*). See also *Lock v Jones KB 1941, 23 TC 749*.

The allowance is made in respect of a particular debt and general bad debt provisions are not allowed. However where there are a large number of comparatively small debts, making the 'valuation' of individual debts impracticable, the Revenue will normally agree to an allowance in accordance with a formula based on the bad debt experience of the business. Typical businesses are mail-order firms and firms with a large proportion of hire-purchase sales. Where hire-purchase is involved the formula may also cover the spread of the profit on hire-purchase sales. But no provision for the estimated cost of collecting future debt instalments is permissible (*Monthly Salaries Loan Co Ltd v Furlong Ch D 1962, 40 TC 313*).

For small credit traders who collect their debts by weekly instalments (sometimes called travelling drapers or Scotch drapers) a special arrangement is available. For details see Form 189 obtainable from inspectors.

Where a builder sold houses leaving part of the sale proceeds with Building Societies as collateral security for mortgages by the purchasers, held the amounts should be brought in at valuation and if practicable and otherwise when released by Building Society (*John Cronk & Sons Ltd v Harrison HL 1936, 20 TC 612* and cf. *Chibbett v Harold Brookfield & Son Ltd CA 1952, 33 TC 467*). A similar decision was reached in *Absalom v Talbot HL 1944, 26 TC 166* where amounts were left on loan to the purchasers. See also *Lock v Jones* above. The HL judgments in *Absalom v Talbot* are an important review of the treatment of trading debts.

The normal debt considered for allowance under *Sec 74(j)* is one for goods or services supplied or one in a business, such as banking or money-lending, which consists of advancing money. Losses on advances by a brewery company to its customers were allowed as on the evidence it habitually acted as banker for them in the course of its brewing business (*Reid's Brewery v Male QB 1891, 3 TC 279*). But losses on advances to clients by solicitors were refused as there was no evidence that they were money-lenders (*CIR v Hagart & Burn-Murdoch HL 1929, 14 TC 433; Rutherford v CIR CS 1939, 23 TC 8*. See also *Bury & Walkers v Phillips HC 1951, 32 TC 198* and contrast *Jennings v Barfield Ch D 1962, 40 TC 365*). An allowance was refused for an irrecoverable balance due from the managing director of a company as outside the company's trade (*Curtis v J & G Oldfield Ltd KB 1925, 9 TC 319*). See also *Roebank Printing Co Ltd v CIR CS 1928, 13 TC 864.*

Advances to finance or recoup the losses of subsidiary or associated companies are capital. Allowances were refused in *English Crown Spelter v Baker KB 1908, 5 TC 327* and *Charles Marsden & Sons v CIR KB 1919, 12 TC 217* for losses on advances to facilitate the supply of materials for the trade of the lender as were losses on an advance to a company under the same control (*Baker v Mabie Todd & Co Ltd KB 1927, 13 TC 235*), amounts written off in respect of the losses of a subsidiary (*Odhams Press Ltd v Cook HL 1940, 23 TC 233*) and payments to meet the operating losses of a subsidiary (*Marshall Richards Machine Co Ltd v Jewitt Ch D 1956, 36 TC 511*). See also *CIR v Huntley & Palmers Ltd KB 1928, 12 TC 1209; Henderson v Meade-King Robinson & Co Ltd KB 1938, 22 TC 97;* and *Stone & Temple Ltd v Waters; Astrawall (UK) Ltd v Waters Ch D, [1995] STC 1.* (N.B. The loss of subsidiary may now be eligible for group relief—see Tolley's Corporation Tax.)

Payments by the purchaser to discharge the unpaid liabilities of the vendor to preserve goodwill, etc. allowed in *Cooke v Quick Shoe Repair Service KB 1949, 30 TC 460.*

See 71.90 below for relief for certain unremittable overseas debts of trades within Schedule D, Case I.

Note. Loans made after 11 April 1978 to a trader for the setting up or purposes of his trade and irrecoverable are in certain circumstances allowable as a loss for capital gains tax. See Tolley's Capital Gains Tax.

For losses under guarantees see 71.60 below.

71.45   BREWERIES, DISTILLERIES, LICENSED PREMISES

Rents received by brewery from **tied houses** are trading receipts and rents paid deductible, but no allowance for 'rent forgone' if rent received is less than a full commercial rent. [*Sec 98; FA 1995, 6 Sch 16*]. Repairs, rates, insurance premiums paid on behalf of tied tenants allowable (*Usher's Wiltshire Brewery v Bruce HL 1914, 6 TC 399*) but not extra expenditure incurred to keep licensed houses open while undergoing rehabilitation (*Mann Crossman & Paulin Ltd v Compton KB 1947, 28 TC 410*) or compensation to a tenant displaced on a licence transfer (*Morse v Stedeford KB 1934, 18 TC 457*). For compensation paid on the termination of tenancies of tied houses, see *Watneys (London) Ltd v Pike Ch D 1982, 57 TC 372.* Losses on advances to 'customers and connections' held allowable (*Reid's Brewery v Male QB 1891, 3 TC 279*).

The expenses of an unsuccessful application for licences were held not allowable (*Southwell v Savill Bros KB 1901, 4 TC 430*—it was conceded that expenses of successful applications are capital) nor expenses of applying for licence transfers (*Morse v Stedeford* above; *Pendleton v Mitchells & Butlers Ch D 1968, 45 TC 341*). Contributions by a brewer to a trade association to promote Sunday opening in Wales allowed in *Cooper v Rhymney Breweries Ch D 1965, 42 TC 509.* Compensation Fund levies deductible (*Smith v Lion Brewery HL 1910, 5 TC 568*) but not monopoly value payments (*Kneeshaw v Albertolli KB 1940, 23 TC 462; Henriksen v Grafton Hotels Ltd CA 1942, 24 TC 453*).

Damages paid to hotel guest injured by falling chimney held not allowable—see *Strong & Co v Woodifield* at 71.46 below. For accrued whisky storage rents see *Dailuaine-Talisker Distilleries v CIR CS 1930, 15 TC 613; CIR v Oban Distillery Co CS 1932, 18 TC 33* and *CIR v Arthur Bell & Sons CS 1932, 22 TC 315.*

Where a brewery company ceased brewing but continued to sell beer brewed for it by another company it was held to have discontinued its old trade and commenced a new one (*Gordon & Blair Ltd v CIR CS 1962, 40 TC 358*).

71.46   **COMPENSATION, DAMAGES ETC.—PAYMENTS**

For compensation and redundancy payments to directors or employees see 71.53 below. An important case is *Anglo-Persian Oil Co Ltd v Dale CA 1931, 16 TC 253* in which a substantial payment by a company for the cancellation of its principal agency, with ten years to run, was held to be allowable. It was not for a capital asset nor to get rid of an onerous contract (cf. *Mallett v Staveley Coal CA 1928, 13 TC 772*) but to enable it to rationalise its working arrangements. See also *Vodafone Cellular Ltd v Shaw Ch D, [1995] STC 353* (payment for release from onerous agreement), in which the principle underlying the decision in *Van den Berghs Ltd v Clark* (see 71.47(*b*) below) was applied, but cf. *Tucker v Granada Motorway Services Ltd HL 1979, 53 TC 92*, where a payment to modify the method of calculating the rent was held to be capital, and *Whitehead v Tubbs (Elastics) Ltd CA 1983, 57 TC 472*, where a payment to alter the terms of a capital loan by removing borrowing restrictions on borrower was held to be capital.

A payment by a shipping company for cancelling an order it had placed for a ship was held capital (*'Countess Warwick' SS Co Ltd v Ogg KB 1924, 8 TC 652* and contrast *Devon Mutual Steamship Insce v Ogg KB 1927, 13 TC 184*). A payment to an associated company in return for its temporarily ceasing production held allowable (*Commr of Taxes v Nchanga Consolidated Copper Mines PC 1964, 43 ATC 20*) as were statutory levies on a brewery for a Compensation Fund where a licence is not renewed (*Smith v Lion Brewery Co Ltd HL 1910, 5 TC 568*) and a payment to secure the closure of a rival concern (*Walker v The Joint Credit Card Co Ltd Ch D 1982, 55 TC 617*). Payments by a steel company to secure the closure of railway steel works were held capital (*United Steels v Cullington (No 1) CA 1939, 23 TC 71*) as were payments to safeguard against subsidence on a factory site (*Bradbury v United Glass Bottle Mfrs CA 1959, 38 TC 369*; compare *Glenboig Union Fireclay* at 71.47(*c*) below) and a payment for cancelling electricity agreement on closure of a quarry (*CIR v Wm Sharp & Son CS 1959, 38 TC 341*). For compensation paid on the termination of tied houses of breweries, see *Watneys (London) Ltd v Pike Ch D 1982, 57 TC 372*.

Where damages awarded by a Court against a solicitor were later compounded, the compounded amount (accepted as allowable) was held to be an expense of the year in which the Court award was made (*Simpson v Jones Ch D 1968, 44 TC 599*). See also *CIR v Hugh T Barrie Ltd CA(NI) 1928, 12 TC 1223*.

Damages paid by a brewery to a hotel guest injured by a falling chimney were held to have been incurred by it *qua* property owner and not *qua* trader and not deductible (*Strong & Co of Romsey Ltd v Woodifield HL 1906, 5 TC 215*). Penalties for breach of war-time regulations and defence costs not allowed (*CIR v Warnes & Co KB 1919, 12 TC 227; CIR v Alexander von Glehn & Co Ltd CA 1920, 12 TC 232*), nor fines imposed by professional regulatory body (*Stockbroker v McKnight (Sp C 65), [1996] SSCD 103*), nor damages for breach of American 'anti-trust' law (*Cattermole v Borax & Chemicals Ltd KB 1949, 31 TC 202*). See also *G Scammell & Nephew v Rowles CA 1939, 22 TC 479; Fairrie v Hall KB 1947, 28 TC 200; Golder v Great Boulder Proprietary HC 1952, 33 TC 75; Knight v Parry Ch D 1972, 48 TC 580; Hammond Engineering v CIR Ch D 1975, 50 TC 313*.

71.47   **COMPENSATION, DAMAGES ETC.—RECEIPTS**

(*a*)   **Capital sums** (i.e. sums not taken into account in computing income) received as compensation for damage, injury, destruction or depreciation of assets are subject to capital gains tax [*TCGA 1992, s 22(1)*] (or corporation tax in the case of a company), but this does not apply to compensation or damages to an individual for wrong or injury to his person or in his profession or vocation. [*TCGA 1992, s 51(2)*].

(*b*)   **Cancellation or variation of trading contracts and arrangements.** An important case is *Van den Berghs Ltd v Clark HL 1935, 19 TC 390* in which a receipt on the termination of a profit-sharing arrangement was held to be capital. The arrangement related to the whole structure of the recipient's trade, forming the fixed framework within which its circulating capital operated. Compensation, etc. receipts were also held to be capital in *Sabine v Lookers Ltd CA 1958, 38 TC 120* (varying car distributor's agreement); *British-Borneo Petroleum v Cropper Ch D 1968, 45 TC 201* (cancelling a royalty agreement); *Barr Crombie & Co Ltd v CIR CS 1945, 26 TC 406* (terminating agreement as ship-managers). A payment by the liquidator of a shipping company to its managers as authorised by the shareholders held not assessable (*Chibbett v Robinson & Sons KB 1924, 9 TC 48*).

Compensation, etc. receipts on the cancellation of contracts receipts from which, if completed, would have been trading receipts are normally themselves trading receipts, to be credited in the computations for the period in which cancelled. See *Short Bros Ltd v CIR* and *Sunderland Shipbuilding Co Ltd v CIR CA 1927, 12 TC 955* (cancellation of order for ships); *CIR v Northfleet Coal Co KB 1927, 12 TC 1102*; *Jesse Robinson & Sons v CIR KB 1929, 12 TC 1241* (cancellation of contracts for sale of goods, etc.); *Greyhound Racing Assn v Cooper KB 1936, 20 TC 373* (cancellation of agreement to hire greyhound track); *Shove v Dura Mfg Co Ltd KB 1941, 23 TC 779* (cancellation of commission agreement). Similarly compensation to a merchanting company on cancellation of a contract to supply goods to it was held a trading receipt (*Bush, Beach & Gent Ltd v Road KB 1939, 22 TC 519*). See also *United Steel v Cullington (No 1) CA 1939, 23 TC 71; Shadbolt v Salmon Estates KB 1943, 25 TC 52; Sommerfelds Ltd v Freeman Ch D 1966, 44 TC 43; Creed v H & M Levinson Ltd Ch D 1981, 54 TC 477.*

Compensation received on the termination of agencies is a trading receipt unless the agency, by reason of its relative size, etc., is part of the 'fixed framework' (see *Van den Berghs* above) of the agent's business. See *Kelsall Parsons CS 1938, 21 TC 608; CIR v Fleming & Co CS 1951, 33 TC 57; CIR v David MacDonald & Co CS 1955, 36 TC 388; Wiseburgh v Domville CA 1956, 36 TC 527; Fleming v Bellow Machine Co Ch D 1965, 42 TC 308; Elson v James G Johnston Ltd Ch D 1965, 42 TC 545* (in all of which the compensation, etc. was held to be a trading receipt). See also *Anglo-French Exploration Co Ltd v Clayson CA 1956, 36 TC 545.*

For payments received on termination of building society agencies, see Revenue Capital Gains Tax Manual, CG 13050 *et seq.*.

The treatment of compensation on the termination of posts held in the course of a business (particularly a profession), the yearly remuneration having been included in the business receipts (see 75.24 SCHEDULE E), has arisen in a number of cases. In *Blackburn v Close Bros Ltd Ch D 1960, 39 TC 164*, compensation on the cancellation of an agreement by a merchant banker to provide secretarial services was held to be a trading receipt but in *Ellis v Lucas Ch D 1966, 43 TC 276* compensation on the termination of an auditorship was held to be within the ambit of the Schedule E 'golden handshake' legislation [*Sec 148*—see 19.4 COMPENSATION FOR LOSS OF EMPLOYMENT] and hence could not be included in the profits for Case II purposes (except a small part of the payment held to be compensation for the loss of general accountancy work). Similar decisions were reached in *Walker v Carnaby Harrower, Barham & Pykett Ch D 1969, 46 TC 561* (loss of auditorship by firm of accountants) and *CIR v Brander & Cruikshank HL 1970, 46 TC 574* (loss of company secretaryships by firm of Scottish advocates) and in *Carnaby Harrower* the payment was also held not to be a professional receipt because of its *ex gratia* nature. For *ex gratia* payments, see also (*e*) below. For compensation on cancellation of contracts of authors, etc. see 71.43 above.

(*c*) **Compensation, etc. relating to capital assets.** Compensation to a company making fireclay goods for refraining from working a fireclay bed under a railway line was held to be capital (*Glenboig Union Fireclay Co Ltd v CIR HL 1922, 12 TC 427* and cf. *Thomas McGhie & Sons v BTC QB 1962, 41 ATC 144* and *Bradbury v United Glass Bottle CA 1959, 38 TC 369*), but compensation to a colliery from the Government for requisition of part of its mining area was held to be a trading receipt (*Waterloo Main Colliery v CIR (No 1) KB 1947, 29 TC 235*). Compensation to a shipping company for delay in the overhaul of a ship was held to be a trading receipt (*Burmah Steam Ship Co v CIR CS 1930, 16 TC 67*) as was compensation to a jetty owner for loss of its use after damage by a ship (*London & Thames Haven v Attwooll CA 1966, 43 TC 491*) and compensation for the detention of a ship (*Ensign Shipping Co v CIR CA 1928, 12 TC 1169* but contrast *CIR v Francis West CS 1950, 31 TC 402*).

For insurance recoveries see 71.63 below.

(*d*) **Compensation on compulsory acquisition, etc.** Where compensation is paid for the acquisition of business property by an authority possessing powers of compulsory acquisition, any amounts included as compensation for temporary loss of profits or losses on trading stock or to re-imburse revenue expenditure, such as removal expenses and interest, are treated as trading receipts. (See Revenue Pamphlet IR 131, SP 8/79, 18 June 1979. This Statement of Practice was originally issued as consequence of *Stoke-on-Trent City Council v Wood Mitchell & Co Ltd CA 1978, [1979] STC 197*.)

(*e*) **Other compensation, etc. receipts.** Voluntary payments to an insurance broker on the loss of an important client company (made by its parent company) were held, approving *Chibbett v Robinson* and *Carnaby Harrower* (see (*b*) above), not to be assessable (*Simpson v John Reynolds & Co CA 1975, 49 TC 693*) and similarly for voluntary payments from a brewer to a firm of caterers for the surrender of the leases of tied premises (*Murray v Goodhews CA 1977, 52 TC 86*) but *ex gratia* payments to an estate agent who had not been given an agency he expected were held, on the facts, to be additional remuneration for work already done and assessable. (*McGowan v Brown & Cousins (Stuart Edwards) Ch D 1977, 52 TC 8*). A payment to a diamond broker under informal and non-binding arbitration as damages for the loss of a prospective client was held assessable (*Rolfe v Nagel CA 1981, 55 TC 585*). Compensation for 'loss of profits' following the destruction of the premises of a business not recommenced was held to be of a revenue nature in *Lang v Rice CA (NI) 1983, 57 TC 80*. For compensation receipts relating to the terms on which business premises are tenanted, see 71.77 below.

Financial loss allowances paid to e.g. jurors, members of certain local authorities and magistrates to compensate them for loss of profit in their trade or profession are assessable under Schedule D, Case I or II as trading receipts. (Revenue Tax Bulletin May 1992 p 20). Such payments are not taxable under Schedule E (see 75.7 SCHEDULE E).

Damages awarded to a theatrical company for breach of a licence it had, were held to be assessable (*Vaughan v Parnell & Zeitlin KB 1940, 23 TC 505*) as was compensation received by a development company under legislation for restricting development (*Johnson v W S Try Ltd CA 1946, 27 TC 167*). A retrospective award for a war-time requisition of trading stock was held to be a trading receipt of the year of requisition (*CIR v Newcastle Breweries Ltd HL 1927, 12 TC 927*).

71.48   CONTINGENT AND FUTURE LIABILITIES

For forward contracts see 71.49 below.

Where a company is required under overseas legislation to make leaving payments to its employees, a provision in its accounts for its prospective liability is permissible if capable of sufficiently accurate calculation (*Owen v Southern Railway of Peru HL 1956, 36 TC 602*). The allowance each year is the actual payments as adjusted for any variation between the opening and closing provisions but the deductible provision for the year in which the legislation was enacted may include an amount in respect of previous services of the employees (*CIR v Titaghur Jute Factory Ltd CS 1978, 53 TC 675*).

No deduction is permissible for future repairs or renewals (*Clayton v Newcastle-under-Lyme Corpn QB 1888, 2 TC 416; Naval Colliery Co Ltd v CIR HL 1928, 12 TC 1017; Peter Merchant Ltd v Stedeford CA 1948, 30 TC 496*) or the future cost of collecting debts (*Monthly Salaries Loan Co v Furlong Ch D 1962, 40 TC 313*) or for future payments of damages in respect of accidents to employees unless liability has been admitted or established (*James Spencer & Co v CIR CS 1950, 32 TC 111*). See also *Albion Rovers Football Club v CIR HL 1952, 33 TC 331* (wages deductible when paid). A provision for regular major overhaul work accrued due on aircraft engines was, however, allowed in *Johnston v Britannia Airways Ltd Ch D, [1994] STC 763*.

For provisions by insurance companies for unexpired risks, etc., see *Sun Insurance Office v Clark HL 1912, 6 TC 59*. For the liability of cemetery companies in receipt of lump sums for the future maintenance of graves, see *Paisley Cemetery Co v Reith C/E/S 1898, 4 TC 1* and *London Cemetery Co v Barnes KB 1917, 7 TC 92*.

A provision by a company engaged in the exploitation of a North Sea oil field, for anticipated future expenditure on the completion of the exploitation, in dismantling installations used and (as required under its licence) in 'cleaning up' the sea bed, was disallowed as capital when incurred in *RTZ Oil & Gas Ltd v Elliss Ch D 1987, 61 TC 132*.

71.49   CONTRACTS

For compensation, etc. on the cancellation or variation of contracts see 71.46 and 71.47 above. For work in progress under contracts see 71.82 below.

Where a taxpayer took over a coal merchanting business on the death of his father, an amount paid for the benefit of contracts between his father and suppliers was held capital (*John Smith & Son v Moore HL 1921, 12 TC 266* and see *City of London Contract Corpn v Styles CA 1887, 2 TC 239*). The completion of outstanding contracts following a partnership dissolution (*Hillerns & Fowler v Murray CA 1932, 17 TC 77*) and on a company going into liquidation (*Baker v Cook KB 1937, 21 TC 337*) held to be trading.

Where under a long-term contract goods were invoiced as delivered, the sale proceeds are receipts of the year of delivery (*J P Hall & Co Ltd v CIR CA 1921, 12 TC 382*). If contract prices are varied retrospectively the resultant further sums are assessable or deductible for the years applicable to the sums at the original prices (*Frodingham Ironstone Mines Ltd v Stewart KB 1932, 16 TC 728; New Conveyor Co Ltd v Dodd KB 1945, 27 TC 11*). Compare *English Dairies Ltd v Phillips KB 1927, 11 TC 597; Isaac Holden & Sons Ltd v CIR KB 1924, 12 TC 768* and contrast *Rownson Drew & Clydesdale Ltd v CIR KB 1931, 16 TC 595*.

Losses because of a fall in prices fixed under forward contracts, etc. cannot be anticipated (*Edward Collins & Sons Ltd v CIR CS 1924, 12 TC 773; Whimster & Co v CIR CS 1925, 12 TC 813*) and cf. *Wright Sutcliffe Ltd v CIR KB 1929, 8 ATC 168; J H Young & Co v CIR CS 1924, 12 TC 817; CIR v Hugh T Barrie Ltd CA(NI) 1928, 12 TC 1223*.

71.50   COPYRIGHT ETC.

For the assessment of authors and artistes see 71.43 above.

Where copyrights or public lending rights in literary, dramatic, musical or artistic works, taking more than twelve months to produce, are assigned for a lump sum in circumstances which would render the proceeds assessable as profits of a single year of assessment, an option is given to spread the sum retrospectively (as set out in *Sec 534(2)(3)*) over that and the preceding tax year and (if the work took more than 24 months to produce) the tax year before that. [*Secs 534, 537*]. This treatment applies also to sale prices, etc., of paintings, sculptures or other works of art taking more than twelve months to produce [*Sec 538; FA 1996, s 128(10)*)] and to periodical payments, including royalties, due within two years of date of first publication, etc. A claim for 1995/96 and earlier years in relation to such periodical payments must be made by 5 April following expiration of eight years from date of publication. For claims in relation to lump sum payments, the general six-year time limit at 17.4 CLAIMS applies. A claim relating to 1996/97 or a subsequent year must be made witihin one year after 31 January following the year of assessment (or in the case of periodical payments the latest year of assessment) into whose basis period the payments would otherwise have fallen. Where the claim relates to periodical payments, it must cover all such payments from the same work, and for 1996/97 onwards, where payments fall into more than one year of assessment, the claim is treated as if it were two or more separate claims, being one for each of the years concerned. [*Sec 534(4)(b)(5)–(5B); FA 1996, s 128(5)*]. See 78.33 SELF-ASSESSMENT for the method of giving effect to claims.

Broadly similar provisions apply in the case of design rights in a design. [*See 537A; Copyright, Designs and Patents Act 1988, 7 Sch 36(6); FA 1996, s 128(9)*]. See also *Sec 537B* as regards taxation of design royalties where the owner of such rights does not have his usual place of abode in the UK.

Alternatively, where an author assigns, wholly or partially, for *two years or more* (or similarly grants by licence an interest in) the copyright or public lending right in a literary, dramatic, musical or artistic work of his (first published ten or more years previously) for a lump sum which would normally be treated as profits of a single year, he may claim to treat that sum as receivable by equal yearly instalments (up to a maximum of six) during the period covered by the assignment or licence, the first of such sums being treated as due on the date the lump sum became receivable. But if the author permanently discontinues his profession, or dies, any subsequent instalments as above are treated as having been receivable together with the last instalment due before the cessation or death unless, within two years after that event, the author (or his personal representatives) elects for recomputation as if the assignment, etc., had been for a lesser period ending with the day before the cessation or death. This election is abolished for 1996/97 and later years. A claim under these provisions relating to 1996/97 or a subsequent year must be made within one year after 31 January following the year of assessment into whose basis period the lump sum would otherwise have fallen. Previously, the six-year time limit at 17.4 CLAIMS applied. [*Sec 535; FA 1996, s 128(7)(8)*].

Sec 534 and *Sec 535* are mutually exclusive. [*Secs 534(6), 535(9)*].

None of the above provisions apply for corporation tax, nor, as regards any receipt after 5 April 1996, can any claim be made by a partnership. [*Sec 534(6A); FA 1996, s 128(6)*].

Amounts held to be assessable include advance payments of gramophone royalties to a singer (*Taylor v Dawson KB 1938, 22 TC 189*); commutations of future royalties paid to an authoress (*Glasson v Rougier KB 1944, 26 TC 86*); receipts from sale of film rights in books (*Howson v Monsell HC 1950, 31 TC 529*); sales of copyright in novels written when the author was non-resident (with no deduction for his expenses then incurred—*Mackenzie v Arnold CA 1952, 33 TC 363*). But contrast *Mitchell v Rosay CA 1954, 35 TC 496. Sharkey v Wernher* (see 71.82 below) does not apply to a gift of copyright (*Mason v Innes CA 1967, 44 TC 326*). Royalties, etc. arising after an author, etc. dies or otherwise ceases to carry on his profession or vocation may be chargeable as POST-CESSATION ETC. RECEIPTS AND EXPENDITURE (60).

Copyright and design royalties or public lending right payments paid by publisher, etc. are deductible in computing their profits but royalties to non-residents must be paid less tax, the tax being accounted for to the Revenue under *Sec 536* or *Sec 537B*.

For the treatment of expenditure on producing films and certain similar assets, see 71.57 below and 10.25 CAPITAL ALLOWANCES.

71.51   **DEDUCTION OF TAX AT SOURCE—AMOUNTS PAID UNDER**

The combined effect of *Sec 74(m)(p)(q)* is to prohibit the deduction in computing profits of annuities, annual payments (other than interest), patent royalties, etc. payable under DEDUCTION OF TAX AT SOURCE (23) but see 23.13 re certain mortgage interest. For interest see 71.64 below and for copyright royalties see 71.50 above. For the treatment of such payments as 'charges on income' for companies see Tolley's Corporation Tax. See 46.18 LOSSES where payments exceed the profits.

Sec 74(m) applies only to amounts 'payable out of the profits or gains' (cf. similar wording in *Sec 348*). Payments made before the profits can be ascertained are not payable out of the profits and therefore not within the *Sec 74(m)* prohibition. For this see *Gresham Life Assce v Styles HL 1890, 3 TC 185* and *Paterson Engineering Co Ltd v Duff KB 1943, 25 TC 43*. See also *Ogden v Medway Cinemas Ltd KB 1934, 18 TC 691* and *Moss Empires Ltd v CIR HL 1937, 21 TC 264*.

71.52   **EMBEZZLEMENT ETC.**

Losses allowed but not misappropriation by partner or director. See *Bamford v ATA Advertising Ch D 1972, 48 TC 359* and cf. *Curtis v J & G Oldfield Ltd KB 1925, 9 TC 319*. Where defalcations were made good by the auditor who admitted negligence, refund held to be a trading receipt for the year in which made (*Gray v Penrhyn KB 1937, 21 TC 252*).

See 71.62 below as regards prohibition on deduction of expenditure involving crime.

71.53   **EMPLOYEES (AND DIRECTORS)**

Bona fide remuneration is deductible including bonuses, commissions, tax deducted under PAYE and the cost of board, lodging, uniforms and benefits provided. The deduction is for the remuneration etc. payable; future payments cannot be anticipated (*Albion Rovers Football Club v CIR HL 1952, 33 TC 331*). The remuneration etc. must be shown to be wholly and exclusively for the purposes of the trade. In *Stott & Ingham v Trehearne KB 1924, 9 TC 69* an increase in the rate of commission payable to the trader's sons was disallowed as not on a commercial footing. See also *Johnson Bros & Co v CIR KB 1919, 12 TC 147*, *Copeman v Wm Flood & Sons Ltd KB 1940, 24 TC 53* and *Earlspring Properties Ltd v Guest CA, [1995] STC 479*. Payments by a farming couple to their young children for help on the farm were disallowed in *Dollar v Lyon Ch D 1981, 54 TC 459*. For excessive payments to 'service company' see *Payne, Stone Fraser* at 71.71 below. For wife's wages see *Thompson v Bruce KB 1927, 11 TC 607; Moschi v Kelly CA 1952, 33 TC 442*. The salary etc. of an employee for service in an overseas subsidiary was allowed in computing the profits of the parent in *Robinson v Scott Bader & Co Ltd CA 1981, 54 TC 757*. The secondment was wholly and exclusively for the purposes of the parent's business, notwithstanding the benefit to the subsidiary's business.

Any excess of the market value over the par value of shares issued to employees at par is not deductible (*Lowry v Consolidated African Selection Trust Ltd HL 1940, 23 TC 259*). For payments to trustees to acquire shares for the benefit of employees, see *Heather v P-E Consulting Group CA 1972, 48 TC 293, Jeffs v Ringtons Ltd Ch D 1985, 58 TC 680* and

71.53 Schedule D, Cases I and II—Profits of Trades etc.

E Bott Ltd v Price Ch D 1985, 59 TC 437, and contrast *Rutter v Charles Sharpe & Co Ltd Ch D 1979, 53 TC 163.* See also 81 SHARE INCENTIVES AND OPTIONS.

For periods of account ending **after 5 April 1989**, 'relevant emoluments' and 'potential emoluments' which would otherwise be deductible may be deducted only if they are paid before the end of the period of nine months beginning with the end of the period of account. Emoluments paid at a later date are deductible for the period of account *in which* they are paid. For periods of account beginning before 6 April 1989 and ending before 6 April 1990, the nine-month period is extended to eighteen months. The time at which emoluments are paid is to be determined in accordance with the same rules as in 75.1 SCHEDULE E as to when emoluments are to be treated as received. Computations prepared before the end of the said nine-month (or eighteen-month) period must be prepared on the basis that any unpaid 'relevant emoluments' will not be paid before the expiry of that period and are therefore not deductible for that period of account. If, in fact, such emoluments *are* paid within the said nine-month (or eighteen-month) period, the computation can be adjusted accordingly on a claim being made to the inspector within two years after the end of the period of account concerned. For periods of account ended before 30 June 1993, the nine-month (or eighteen-month) and two-year periods referred to above are increased by three years in the case of an authorised Lloyd's underwriting agent.

'*Relevant emoluments*' are emoluments for a period after 5 April 1989 allocated specifically or in general to offices or employments (or both). '*Potential emoluments*' are amounts or benefits reserved in the employer's accounts (or held by an intermediary) with a view to their becoming relevant emoluments, and are paid when they become relevant emoluments which are paid. [*FA 1989, s 43; FA 1993, s 181*].

Similar provisions apply in relation to investment and insurance companies. [*FA 1989, s 44*].

Council tax and community charge. An employer who pays the council tax or community charge (or Scottish community water charge) for an employee will normally be able to claim a deduction for it. If such payments are also made on behalf of members of the employee's family, they too are deductible if part of the employee's remuneration package (which would normally mean they were paid under the contract of employment). (Revenue Press Releases 10 November 1989, 16 March 1993).

Employee share ownership trusts. Payments made after 26 July 1989 by a UK resident company by way of contribution to a trust which at the time of payment is a qualifying employee share ownership trust (ESOT) from which at least some of its employees (or those of a company which it controls (within *Sec 840*)) are eligible to benefit are allowable on a claim to that effect being made within two years after the end of the period of account in which the payment is charged as an expense. In order for the payment to qualify for relief, the sum received must be expended by the trustees within nine months (or such longer period as the Board may, by notice, allow) after the end of the said period of account (all sums received by the trustees being deemed to be expended by them on a first in/first out basis) for one or more of the following qualifying purposes:

(*a*)   the acquisition of shares in the company which established the trust;

(*b*)   the repayment of borrowings;

(*c*)   the payment of interest on borrowings;

(*d*)   the payment of sums to beneficiaries;

(*e*)   the meeting of expenses (including income or capital gains tax, see Revenue Inspector's Manual, IM 680e).

[*FA 1989, s 67*].

Contributions received are deemed to be used first to meet expenditure for qualifying purposes, expenditure for non-qualifying purposes being treated as far as possible as met out of other income (e.g. dividends or interest). (Revenue Inspector's Manual, IM 680f).

See 81.11 SHARE INCENTIVES AND OPTIONS for the definition of a qualifying ESOT and for provisions enabling a charge to tax to be made, in certain circumstances, on the trustees, but recoverable also from the company, where the above relief has previously been given.

Expenditure after 31 March 1991 on establishing a qualifying ESOT is deductible in computing the company's trading profits (or as a management expense). If the deed establishing the trust is executed more than nine months after the end of the period of account in which the expenditure is incurred, it is treated as incurred in the period in which the deed is executed. [Sec 85A; FA 1991, s 43].

Profit sharing and share option schemes. Expenditure after 31 March 1991 on establishing an approved profit sharing or share option scheme (see 81.6, 81.8, 81.9, 81.10 SHARE INCENTIVES AND OPTIONS) is deductible in computing the company's trading profits (or as a management expense) provided that:

(a) in the case of a profit sharing scheme, the trustees acquire no shares under the scheme before it is approved; or

(b) in the case of a share option scheme, no employee or director obtains rights under the scheme before it is approved.

If the scheme is approved more than nine months after the end of the period of account in which the expenditure is incurred, it is for these purposes treated as incurred in the period in which the approval is given. [Sec 84A; FA 1991, s 42].

In the case of an approved profit sharing scheme, a similar deduction is available for payments made to the scheme trustees which are either necessary to meet their reasonable administration expenses or applied by them, within nine months after the end of the period of account in which the expense is charged (or such longer time as the Revenue may allow), in acquiring shares for appropriation to participants. [Sec 85].

Retirement and benevolent provisions for employees. See 66.5(a), 66.10 RETIREMENT SCHEMES for the deductibility of payments by the employer under such schemes. Bona fide voluntary pensions and retirement gratuities, including pensions to widows, are allowed (*Smith v Incorporated Council of Law Reporting KB 1914, 6 TC 477*). The cost of an annuity to replace a pension is allowed but not the cost of a policy to secure payment *to the employer* of an annuity equal to pensions payable by him (*Hancock v General Reversionary & Investment Co Ltd KB 1918, 7 TC 358; Morgan Crucible Co Ltd v CIR KB 1932, 17 TC 311*). For provisions for directors of 'family companies' see *Samuel Dracup & Sons Ltd v Dakin Ch D 1957, 37 TC 377*.

Payments directly or indirectly for the benefit of employees are allowable including donations to hospitals and charities (see 71.83 below) unless capital or abnormal (*Rowntree & Co v Curtis CA 1924, 8 TC 678; Bourne & Hollingsworth v Ogden KB 1929, 14 TC 349*). See also *Hutchinson & Co v Turner HC 1950, 31 TC 495*. Subscriptions to BUPA and similar group schemes for employees are allowed (see 75.37 SCHEDULE E for position regarding the employees).

Redundancy payments, or other employer's payments, under *Employment Protection (Consolidation) Act 1978* (or NI equivalent) allowable. Rebates recoverable are trading receipts. [Secs 579, 580].

Non-statutory redundancy and similar payments are normally allowable unless made on the cessation of trading (but now see following paragraph) (*CIR v Anglo-Brewing Co Ltd KB 1925, 12 TC 803; Godden v Wilson's Stores CA 1962, 40 TC 161; Geo Peters & Co v Smith Ch D 1963, 41 TC 264*) or part of the bargain for the sale of shares of the company carrying

71.53 Schedule D, Cases I and II—Profits of Trades etc.

on the business (*Bassett Enterprise Ltd v Petty KB 1938, 21 TC 730; James Snook & Co Ltd v Blasdale CA 1952, 33 TC 244*). See also *Overy v Ashford Dunn & Co KB 1933, 17 TC 497* and contrast *CIR v Patrick Thomson Ltd CS 1956, 37 TC 145*. A payment to secure the resignation of a life-director who had fallen out with his co-directors was allowed in *Mitchell v B W Noble Ltd CA 1927, 11 TC 372*. See also *O'Keeffe v Southport Printers Ltd Ch D 1984, 58 TC 88*. For provisions for future leaving payments see 71.48 above.

Payments in addition to the statutory payment made on cessation of trading (including deemed cessation on a partnership change) will be allowed if would have been allowed had there been no cessation. Allowance is up to three times the statutory payment and payment made after cessation is treated as made on last day business carried on. [*Sec 90*]. In practice, allowance will also be given for such payments on a partial cessation (i.e. where an identifiable part of a trade is discontinued). (Revenue Pamphlet IR 131, SP 11/81, 6 November 1981).

Relief under *ICTA 1988, s 579* or *s 90* (as above) is due for the period of account in which the payment is made (or, if paid after discontinuance, for the last day on which the business is carried on). Where instead relief is due under general principles, a provision for future payments may be allowed for a period of account provided that:

(*a*)   it appears in the commercial accounts in accordance with generally accepted accounting principles;

(*b*)   it was accurately calculated (normally requiring the identification of the individual employees affected) using the degree of hindsight permitted by SSAP 17;

(*c*)   a definite decision to proceed with the redundancies was taken during the period; and

(*d*)   payment was made within nine months of the end of the period.

(Revenue Tax Bulletin February 1995 p 195).

Counselling services. Expenditure on outplacement counselling which falls within the Schedule E exemption under *Secs 589A, 589B* in relation to employments terminated (or expenditure incurred) after 15 March 1993 (see 75.42 SCHEDULE E) is deductible either in computing the profits or gains of the employer's trade or as a management expense under *Sec 75*. [*Sec 589A(7)–(10); FA 1993, s 108*].

Key employee insurance. Premiums on policies in favour of the employer insuring against death or critical illness of key employees are generally allowable, and the proceeds of any such policies trading receipts.

National Insurance contributions. Deduction allowed for whole amount of employers' contributions in respect of employees. [*Sec 617(4)*].

Technical Education. Payments by trader for technical education, requisite to employees in his trade, at a university, technical institution, etc., approved by Secretary of State (or NI equivalent), are allowable. [*Sec 84*]. And see *Wickwar v Berry CA 1963, 41 TC 33* (farmer's payments re own sons allowable). (N.B. This relief is given only to trades and not to professions or vocations.)

This relief is replaced, for payments after 18 March 1991, by a relief for certain gifts to educational establishments (see 71.59 below). [*FA 1991, s 68*]. The technical education relief had already effectively been superseded by the reliefs for charitable contributions, including gift aid (see 15.8 CHARITIES). (Revenue Press Release 19 March 1991).

Training costs. Expenditure which falls within the Schedule E exemption under *Secs 588, 589* for training costs (see 75.42 SCHEDULE E) is deductible either in computing the profits or gains of the employer's trade or as a management expense under *Sec 75*. The provisions relating to assessments, information and penalties in relation to the Schedule E exemption apply equally in relation to this deduction. [*Sec 588(3)–(5); FA 1996, 18 Sch 10, 17(1)(2)*]. See 71.83 below as regards contributions to training and enterprise councils, and 71.87 below as regards relief for self-employed.

Employees seconded to charities or educational bodies. If an employer seconds an employee temporarily to a charity (as defined in *Sec 506*, see 15.1 CHARITIES), any expenditure attributable to the employment incurred by the employer is deductible in computing its profits to the extent to which it would have been deductible if the employee's services had continued to be available for its business. This relief is extended to secondments to certain educational bodies in respect of employment before 1 April 1997. The bodies concerned include education authorities and educational institutions maintained by such authorities, and certain other approved educational bodies. [*Sec 86*].

Payroll deduction scheme. See 15.7 CHARITIES.

71.54 **ENTERTAINMENT EXPENSES**

Entertainment expenses not allowed (and no capital allowances on cars, etc., used for entertaining) except for staff entertainment. See below as regards entertainment of an overseas customer. Covers gifts unless (*a*) carrying prominent advertisement, (*b*) not food, drink, etc., and (*c*) no more than £10 worth per person p.a. [*Sec 577*]. Deductions allowed for items provided in the ordinary course of a trade of providing entertainment (see *Fleming v Associated Newspapers Ltd HL 1972, 48 TC 382*) or provided gratuitously for advertising to the public generally. [*Sec 577(10)*]. See also the VAT cases of *C & E Commissioners v Shaklee International and Another CA, [1981] STC 776* and *Celtic Football and Athletic Co Ltd v C & E Commissioners CS, [1983] STC 470*.

Overseas customers. Expenditure on reasonable entertainment of 'overseas customers' (as defined) is allowed (subject to provision of full particulars, if required) where the entertainment was provided before 15 March 1988 (or the expenditure incurred under a contract entered into before that date). [*ICTA 1970, s 411(2)(4)(6); FA 1988, s 72*].

See 71.83 below as regards gifts to charitable bodies.

71.55 **EXCHANGE GAINS AND LOSSES**

See Tolley's Corporation Tax under Exchange Gains and Losses for special provisions applying in the case of transactions by certain 'qualifying companies'.

In general, exchange differences are taken into account in computing trading profits if they relate to the circulating capital of the business but not otherwise. In *Overseas Containers (Finance) Ltd v Stoker CA 1989, 61 TC 473*, exchange losses arising on loans transferred to a finance subsidiary set up to convert the losses to trading account were held not to arise from trading transactions.

In *Davies v The Shell Co of China Ltd CA 1951, 32 TC 133*, a petrol marketing company operating in China required agents to deposit Chinese dollars with it, repayable on the ending of the agency. Exchange profits it made on repaying the deposits were held to be capital. In *Firestone Tyre & Rubber Co Ltd v Evans Ch D 1976, 51 TC 615*, a company repaid in 1965 a dollar balance due to its US parent, the greater part of which represented advances in 1922–1931 to finance the company when it started. The Commissioners' finding that 90% of the resultant large exchange loss was capital and not allowable, was upheld. A profit by an agent on advances to the principal to finance purchases by the agent on behalf of the principal, was held to be a trading receipt (*Landes Bros v Simpson KB 1934, 19 TC 62*) as was a profit by a tobacco company on dollars accumulated to finance its future purchases (*Imperial Tobacco Co v Kelly CA 1943, 25 TC 292*). See also *McKinlay v H T Jenkins & Son KB 1926, 10 TC 372; Ward v Anglo-American Oil KB 1934, 19 TC 94;*

71.55 Schedule D, Cases I and II—Profits of Trades etc.

Beauchamp v F W Woolworth plc HL 1989, 61 TC 542; and contrast *Radio Pictures Ltd v CIR CA 1938, 22 TC 106.* Where a bank operated in foreign currencies and aimed at, and generally succeeded in, matching its monetary assets and liabilities in each currency, it was held that there could be no profit or loss from matched transactions where there were no relevant currency conversions (*Pattison v Marine Midland Ltd HL 1983, 57 TC 219*). In *Whittles v Uniholdings (No 3) Ch D, [1995] STC 185* it was held that there was sufficient interdependence between a dollar loan and a simultaneous foward contract with the same bank for dollars sufficient to repay the loan for them to be treated, for tax purposes, as a single composite agreement, only the small net profit being taxable.

Following the *Marine Midland Ltd* case (above) the Revenue issued a statement setting out their views on the general treatment of exchange differences for tax purposes. Broadly these are as follows.

Where currency assets are matched by currency liabilities in a particular currency, so that a translation adjustment on one would be cancelled out by a translation adjustment on the other, no adjustment is required for tax purposes.

Where currency assets are not matched, or are incompletely matched, with currency liabilities in a particular currency, the adjustment required to the net exchange difference debited or credited in the profit and loss account is determined along the following lines:

(i)   the aggregate exchange differences, positive and negative, on capital assets and liabilities in the profit and loss account figure are ascertained;

(ii)   if there are no differences as at (i), no adjustment is required;

(iii) if the net exchange difference as at (i) is a loss, and the net exchange difference in the profit and loss account is also a loss, the smaller of the two losses is the amount disallowed for tax purposes as relating to capital transactions;

(iv)   if the net exchange difference as at (i) is a profit, and the net exchange difference in the profit and loss account is also a profit, the smaller of the two profits is allowed as a deduction for tax purposes;

(v)   if the net exchange difference as at (i) is a loss, and the net exchange difference in the profit and loss account is a profit, or vice versa, no adjustment is required for tax purposes.

Where net exchange differences are taken to reserve rather than to the profit and loss account, the nature of the assets and liabilities will need to be considered to determine whether or not a tax adjustment is required, applying the principles as above.

In considering whether a trader is matched in a particular foreign currency, *forward exchange contracts* and *currency futures* entered into for hedging purposes may be taken into account, provided the hedging is reflected in the accounts on a consistent basis from year to year and in accordance with accepted accountancy practice. *Currency swap agreements* are treated as converting the liability in the original currency into a liability in the swap currency for the duration of the swap. Hedging through *currency options* does not result in any matching.

The statement also indicates that the accounts treatment of financial assets held on the 'realisation' basis (i.e. where profits are assessable only on their disposal) will be acceptable for tax purposes where the profits or losses on realisation are in effect recognised for accounts purposes net of exchange differences.

Where an *overseas trade*, or an *overseas branch* of a trade, is carried on primarily in a non-sterling economic environment, the Revenue will accept computations based on (*a*) local currency accounts, with the adjusted profit (before capital allowances) translated into sterling at either average or closing rate, or

(*b*) the sterling equivalent of local currency accounts, translated using the 'net investment/closing rate' method, or

(*c*) sterling accounts produced by the 'temporal' method (see SSAP 20 paras 4–12),

provided the same method is applied consistently from year to year. The principles outlined in this Statement of Practice should be applied in considering any adjustment necessary in respect of exchange differences in the foreign currency accounts.

Where *roundabout loan arrangements* are employed in unmatched or partly matched situations, the Revenue consider that, applying the *Ramsay* principle (see 3.1 ANTI-AVOIDANCE), such arrangements may fall to be treated for tax purposes by reference to their composite effect, depending on the facts of the particular case. It will generally be for the trader to justify the adoption of any basis other than that outlined above in the particular circumstances of his case.

(Revenue Pamphlet IR 131, SP 1/87, 17 February 1987).

If not taken into account in computing trading profits, a profit/loss on the sale of currency is within the ambit of CGT unless exempted by *TCGA 1992, s 269* as currency required for an individual's (or his dependant's) personal expenditure abroad (including provision or maintenance of a residence abroad).

71.56 **FARMING AND MARKET GARDENING**

(*a*) **Averaging of profits.** Where for two consecutive years of assessment the profits of an individual or partnership from a trade of farming or market gardening in the UK for one year are less than 75% of the profits for the other, a claim for relief may be made as described below. The relief does not extend to corporation tax.

'*Farming*' for this purpose includes the intensive rearing of livestock or fish on a commercial basis for the production of food for human consumption. (Revenue Pamphlet IR 1, A29).

If the profits for either year do not exceed seven-tenths of the profits of the other (or are nil), the profits for each year are adjusted to half the total of both. If either year's profits exceed seven-tenths of the other's, but are less than three-quarters, the profits are adjusted by adding to the lower and subtracting from the higher the amount obtained by multiplying the difference by three and deducting three-quarters of the higher figure. (Thus, if the profits are £21,900 and £30,000, the adjusted profits after relief would be £23,700 and £28,200.)

'*Profits*' for this purpose are those before any adjustment for losses and for stock relief. Previously, no adjustment was made for capital allowances or balancing charges either (save insofar as these were taken into account in the computation of profits), and, in the case of partnerships (see also below), the relevant profits were those assessed jointly on the partnership. However, neither of these rules applies where the first of the two years to which the averaging claim relates is 1995/96 or a subsequent year as regards trades commenced after 5 April 1994 or 1996/97 or a subsequent year as regards trades commenced on or before that date.

The adjustments made under the relief are effective for all income tax purposes except that they are disregarded in reviewing the years preceding a year of discontinuance (under the pre-Finance Act 1994 basis period rules—see 71.9 above) (but see below as regards the further claim for relief which may be made where the profits of those years are adjusted under the cessation provisions). Further, they do not prevent any claim for loss relief. (Thus, if there was a loss of £5,000 in the basis period for one year and a profit of £15,000 in that for the other, the profits chargeable for each year become £7,500 but the loss of £5,000 remains eligible for loss relief in the normal way.)

A claim must be made to the inspector in writing within two years after the end of the second year of assessment to which it relates, but once a claim has been made, no new claim is open for earlier years. Where the first of the two years to which the claim relates is 1996/97 or a subsequent year, the time limit is twelve months from 31 January following the second year. If a claim has been made for years 1 and 2, a claim may also be made for years 2 and 3, the profits for year 2 being taken as those adjusted on the first claim, and similarly for subsequent years. In the case of partnerships, where the first of the two years to which the averaging claim relates is 1995/96 or a subsequent year as regards trades commenced after 5 April 1994 or 1996/97 or a subsequent year as regards trades commenced on or before that date, an individual partner may make his own claim, based on his share of profits, regardless of whether or not other partners make claims. For earlier years, a partnership claim must be made jointly by all the partners who are individuals and if there is a change in the partners (with an election for continuance) all the individual partners engaged in the trade before and after the change must join in making the claim (including the personal representatives of any deceased). See 78.33 SELF-ASSESSMENT for further provisions regarding claims.

No claim is available for a year of assessment in which the trade was commenced or discontinued or treated as having been discontinued.

If, after a claim, the profits of either or both years are adjusted for some other reason, the claim lapses but a new one may then be made, in respect of the adjusted profits, within the year of assessment following the year in which the adjustment is made. Where the first of the two years to which the original claim relates is 1996/97 or a subsequent year, the deadline for the new claim is 31 January following the year immediately after that in which the adjustment is made.

Where a claim is made as above for 1995/96 or earlier, any claim for relief for the same year under any other provisions of the *Income Tax Acts* may be made, revoked or amended within the same time limits as above but not after the claim as above is determined. Under self-assessment, a claim for other relief for either of the two years affected by an averaging claim can be made, amended or revoked within the period during which the averaging claim can be revoked by amendment of a return or otherwise (which, other than in enquiry cases, will normally end twelve months after the filing date for the return in which the averaging claim is made—see 78.7 SELF-ASSESSMENT). See also 78.33 SELF-ASSESSMENT for the way in which claims for other relief are given effect. [*Sec 96; FA 1994, ss 196, 214(1)(a)(7), 216(3)(a)(5), 19 Sch 37, 26 Sch Pt V(24); FA 1995, 6 Sch 15; FA 1996, s 128(3)*].

Example

A, who has been farming for several years, earns the following profits as adjusted for Schedule D, Case I and *before* capital allowances.

Year ended	Schedule D, Case I Profit/(loss)
	£
30.9.92	20,000
30.9.93	14,000
30.9.94	(5,000)
30.9.95	8,000
30.9.96	16,000

Averaged profits for all years would be

		No averaging claims £	Averaging claims for all years £
1993/94	note (a)	20,000	17,000
1994/95	notes (b)(d)	14,000	8,500
1995/96	note (c)	Nil	10,000
1996/97 (transitional year)	note (e)	12,000	10,500
		£46,000	£46,000

Notes

(a)
1993/94	20,000
1994/95	14,000
	£34,000 ÷ 2 = £17,000

As £14,000 does not exceed $\frac{7}{10}$ × £20,000, the straight average applies.

(b)
1994/95	17,000
1995/96	Nil
	£17,000 ÷ 2 = £8,500

(c)
1995/96	8,500
1996/97	12,000
	£20,500

As £8,500 exceeds $\frac{7}{10}$ of £12,000 but does not exceed $\frac{3}{4}$, the adjustment is computed as follows.

Difference £3,500 × 3	10,500	
Deduct $\frac{3}{4}$ × £12,000	9,000	
Adjustment	1,500	1,500
Existing 1995/96	8,500	
Existing 1996/97		12,000
	£10,000	£10,500

(d)   The loss for the year to 30 September 1994 is not taken into account for averaging, but would be available to reduce the averaged profits for 1994/95 on a claim under *Sec 380(1) as originally enacted*.

(e)   The assessment for 1996/97 before averaging is based on 12/24 of the profits for the two years to 30 September 1996 (the transitional period) (see 71.20 above).

(b)   **Compensation for compulsory slaughter.** Where compensation is received for compulsory slaughter of animals to which the HERD BASIS (34) does not apply, any excess of the amount received over the book value or cost of those animals may, by concession, be excluded from the year of receipt and treated, by equal instalments, as profits of the next three years. (Revenue Pamphlet IR 1, B11). In practice, the profit on an animal born in the year of slaughter is deemed to be 25% of the compensation received. For examples of the arrangements for spreading of compensation, see Revenue Inspector's Manual, IM 2268a *et seq.*.

(c)   **Drainage.** Where land is made re-available for cultivation by the restoration of drainage or by re-draining, the net expenditure incurred (after crediting any grants receivable) will be allowed as a revenue expenditure in farm accounts provided it excludes (i) any substantial element of improvement (e.g. the substitution of tile drainage for mole drainage) and (ii) the capital element in cases in which the present owner is known to have acquired the land at a depressed price because of its swampy condition. (Revenue Pamphlet IR 131, SP 5/81, 8 September 1981).

(d)   **Farmhouses.** The apportionment of the running costs of a farmhouse between business and private use should be based on the facts of the case for the year of account in question, and may require revision to reflect the fact that many farmhouses are now used only to a limited extent for business purposes. The long-standing practice of accepting a one-third business/two-thirds private split will in many cases no longer be appropriate. (Revenue Tax Bulletin February 1993 p 54).

Maintenance expenses of owner-occupied farms not carried on on a commercial basis. Where a loss claim against general income is precluded by *Secs 384, 397* (see 46.10 LOSSES) or *Sec 393A(3)* (see Tolley's Corporation Tax under Losses), relief for maintenance etc. of land, houses etc. may be claimed under *Sec 33* (see 68.16(a) SCHEDULE A). (Revenue Pamphlet IR 1, B5).

(e)   **Gangmasters.** A special unit within the Revenue monitors compliance by agricultural gangmasters, in relation to PAYE and national insurance in respect of their workers and their own returns. It is the Agricultural Compliance Unit, Sovereign House, 40 Silver Street, Sheffield S1 2EN (tel. 01142 739099). (Revenue Press Release 2 September 1988). For whether a worker also responsible for selection of other workers acts as gangmaster, see *Andrews v King Ch D 1991, 64 TC 332.*

(f)   **Grants and subsidies.** See generally 71.84 below. As regards the time at which a receipt should be brought in for tax purposes, a distinction should be drawn between grants to meet particular costs and those subsidising the sale proceeds of a specific crop. The former should reduce the costs in question (and if those costs are included in the closing stock valuation, the net cost should be used), whereas the latter should be recognised as income of the year in which the crop is sold. (Revenue Tax Bulletin February 1993 p 53). A grant subsidising trading income generally is a trading receipt of the period when the entitlement to the grant was established, provided that it can be quantified with reasonable accuracy. As regards instalments of grant, the tax treatment should follow accounting practice, which provides that information available before accounts are completed and signed should be taken into account as regards those to which entitlement arose in the period of account. (Revenue Tax Bulletin February 1994 p 108).

As regards animal grants and subsidies, these are generally recognised either at the end of the retention period or on receipt. Either of these bases will be accepted for tax purposes provided that it is consistently applied, as will any other basis which reflects generally accepted accounting practice provided that it does not conflict with tax law. A change of basis should be made only where the need for change outweighs the requirement for accounts to be prepared on a consistent basis, and will be dealt with in accordance with Revenue Statement of Practice SP 3/90 (see 71.82 below) (and regard should be had to the anti-avoidance provisions under the current year basis transitional rules, see 78.2 SELF-ASSESSMENT). (Revenue Tax Bulletin December 1994 p 182).

The following relate to specific types of farm support payment.

(i)   *Advances under British Sugar Industry (Assistance) Act 1931,* linked with sugar production and prices, were held to be assessable as trading receipts (*Smart v Lincolnshire Sugar Co Ltd HL 1937, 20 TC 643*).

(ii)   *Arable area payments.* Payments under the 1992 scheme for land set aside may be treated as sales subsidies, and hence recognised when the crops are sold. Valuations based on 75% of market value (see (*j*) below) should include the same proportion of the related arable area payments. (Revenue Tax Bulletin February 1994 p 109). See (*f*) (v) below for specific comment on oilseed support payments.

(iii)   *Dairy herd conversion scheme.* Grants for changing from dairying to meat production were held to be assessable as trading receipts (*White v G & M Davis Ch D 1979, 52 TC 597; CIR v Biggar CS 1982, 56 TC 254*).

(iv)   *Flood rehabilitation grants* in excess of rehabilitation costs (admitted to be capital) were held to be capital receipts (*Watson v Samson Bros Ch D 1959, 38 TC 346*).

(v)   *Oilseed support scheme.* Payments of aid under the 1992 scheme are a subsidy towards the selling price, and as such should be recognised as income at the time of sale. If the final amount is not known when the accounts are prepared, but it is reasonably certain that a further payment will be received, the tax computations should be kept open to admit the final figure. If a reasonable estimate is included in the accounts and the difference when the final amount is known has only a small effect on the overall tax liability, the inspector may agree to recognise the difference in arriving at profits of the following year. (Revenue Tax Bulletin February 1993 p 53).

(vi)   *Ploughing subsidies* were held to be assessable as trading receipts (*Higgs v Wrightson KB 1944, 26 TC 73*).

(g)   **Milk quotas.** *SLOM compensation.* The Revenue view is that such compensation is on revenue account, and should be recognised for income tax purposes in one sum in the accounting period in which legal entitlement to it arises and the amount can be quantified with reasonable certainty using information available at the time of preparation of the accounts. Additions for interest to the date of payment should be dealt with under the normal Schedule D, Case III rules. (Revenue Tax Bulletin May 1994 p 127).

Superlevy. The Revenue view is that superlevy is an allowable Schedule D, Case I deduction, but that the purchase of additional quota to avoid superlevy does not give rise to a deduction for either the superlevy thus avoided or the sum which would have been paid to lease rather than purchase the additional quota. (Revenue Tax Bulletin August 1994 p 151).

For capital gains tax considerations, see Tolley's Capital Gains Tax under Land and Rollover Relief.

(h)   **Share farming.** The Inland Revenue consider that both parties to a share farming agreement based on the Country Landowners Association model may be considered to be carrying on a farming trade for tax purposes. In the case of the landowner, he must take an active part in the share farming venture, at least to the extent of concerning himself with details of farming policy and exercising his right to enter onto his land for some material purpose, even if only for the purposes of inspection and policy-making. (Country Landowners Association Press Release 19 December 1991). This reverses an earlier Revenue decision to deny such treatment in respect of the landowner's share of income under a share farming agreement, which was itself a change of view from that previously held by the Revenue.

(i)   **Short rotation coppice.** With effect from 29 November 1994, the cultivation of 'short rotation coppice' (i.e. a perennial crop of tree species planted at high density, the stems of which are harvested above ground level at intervals of less than ten years) is treated for tax purposes as farming and not as forestry, so that UK land under such cultivation is farm or agricultural land and not woodlands. [*FA 1995, s 154*]. For the Revenue view of the taxation implications of short rotation coppice, see Revenue Tax Bulletin October 1995 p 252.

(*j*)   **Single trade.** All farming carried on by any particular person or partnership or body of persons is treated for all tax purposes as one trade. [*Sec 53(2)*]. This applies, however, only to farming of land in the UK (see *Sec 832(1)* and *Sargent v Eayrs Ch D 1972, 48 TC 573*).

(*k*)   **Stock valuations.** See generally Business Economic Notes No 19 'Farming—stock valuations for income tax purposes' (for which see 71.28 above) and, for a commentary thereon relating particularly to changes in the basis of valuation, Revenue Tax Bulletin May 1993 p 63. See also 34 HERD BASIS and, for trading stock generally, 71.82 below. In general, livestock is treated as trading stock unless the herd basis applies, and home-bred animals may be valued, if there is no adequate record of cost, at 75% for sheep and pigs (60% for cattle) of open market value. Deadstock may be taken at 75% of market value (85% before 31 March 1993).

Where an animal grant or subsidy for which application has been made has not been taken into account for a particular period but has been applied for, and that application materially affects the value of the animal, the grant or subsidy should be taken into account as a supplement to the market value when deemed cost is computed. Grants or subsidies applied for but not recognised as income in the period concerned should also be taken into account in arriving at net realisable value for stock valuation purposes. (Revenue Tax Bulletin December 1994 p 182).

Effect of BSE on stock valuations. Against the background of bovine spongiform encephalopathy (BSE), the Revenue have clarified their approach to the valuation of livestock for stock-taking. In particular, although the principles set out in the Business Economic Notes continue to apply, a special basis of arriving at market value will be accepted for normal stock-taking dates between 20 March 1996 and 31 May 1996. See Revenue Press Release 29 April 1996 for the detailed arrangements.

(*l*)   **Subscriptions** to the **National Farmers Union** are allowable in full.

(*m*)   **Trading profits.** Proceeds from the sale of trees (mostly willows planted by the taxpayer) were held to be farming receipts (*Elmes v Trembath KB 1934, 19 TC 72*), but no part of the cost of an orchard with nearly ripe fruit purchased by a fruit grower was an allowable deduction in computing his profits, which included receipts from the sale of the fruit (*CIR v Pilcher CA 1949, 31 TC 314*). Proceeds from sales of turf were held to be trading receipts from farming (*Lowe v J W Ashmore Ltd Ch D 1970, 46 TC 597*).

71.57   FILM ETC. PRODUCTION

In the absence of special legislation, the master negative and soundtrack of a film (or the electronic equivalent) would generally be plant for tax purposes, so that the production costs would attract capital allowances (see 10.24 *et seq.* CAPITAL ALLOWANCES), although this would not apply to e.g. expenditure on the acquisition of exhibition rights in a film. Under *CAA 1990, s 68* however, expenditure on the production or acquisition of a film, tape or disc which would otherwise be so treated is to be regarded as revenue rather than capital expenditure, and any receipts from the disposal of any interest or right or insurance or compensation or other similar moneys derived from the film etc. are revenue receipts. See below, however, as regards certain 'qualifying films' etc. References to a film, tape or disc are references to the original master negative and soundtrack of the film and to the original tape or disc masters of the film, and acquisition of a film etc. includes acquisition of any description of rights in the film etc.

Neither the provisions of *CAA 1990, s 68*, nor the relief under *F(No 2)A 1992, s 42* (see below), apply to revenue expenditure in relation to trades in which the film etc. concerned constitutes trading stock under *Sec 100(2)* (see 71.82 below).

Under *CAA 1990, s 68(3)–(6B)* as amended by *F(No 2)A 1992, s 69*, all revenue expenditure on the production etc. of films etc. is allocated to periods of account on a just and reasonable basis having regard to the expenditure unallocated at the beginning of a period, the proportion which the estimated value of the film etc. realised in the period (whether by way of income or otherwise) bears to the aggregate of the value so realised and the estimated remaining value at the end of the period, and the need to bring the whole expenditure into account over the time during which the value of the film etc. is expected to be realised. Additional expenditure (so far as not previously allocated to the period or to any earlier period) may be claimed for a period bringing the total expenditure allocated to the period up to the value of the film etc. which is realised in the period (whether by way of income or otherwise). The claim must be made (i) for income tax for 1996/97 onwards, within twelve months after 31 January following the tax year in which the period in question ends, and (ii) for income tax for earlier years and for corporation tax, within two years after the end of the period in question. [*FA 1996, s 135, 21 Sch 32(2)(3)*]. For an explanation and examples of how these provisions are applied in practice, see Revenue Pamphlet IR 131, SP 1/93, 11 January 1993, paras 1–25. Expenditure in respect of which a deduction has been made for a period of account under *F(No 2)A 1992, s 42* (see below) is not allocated under these provisions, and where this applies, no expenditure on the film etc. concerned is allocated to that period.

Qualifying films etc. A person carrying on a trade or business consisting of, or including, the exploitation of films etc. may elect for the provisions of *CAA 1990, s 68* not to apply to expenditure which is incurred on the production or acquisition of a film etc. which is certified by the Secretary of State as being a 'qualifying film' etc., and the value of which is expected to be realisable over a period of not less than two years. [*CAA 1990, s 68(9)–(9B); F(No 2)A 1992, s 69; FA 1996, s 135, 21 Sch 32(4)–(6)*]. The election, which is irrevocable, must relate to the whole of the expenditure on the film etc. concerned. The election must be made (i) for income tax for 1996/97 onwards, within twelve months after 31 January following the tax year in which ends the period of account in which the film etc. is completed, and (ii) for income tax for earlier years and for corporation tax, within two years after the end of such period. A film etc. is completed when it can reasonably be regarded as ready for copies to be made and distributed for exhibition or, in relation to expenditure incurred on acquisition of a film etc., the time of that acquisition, if later. No election is available in respect of expenditure in relation to any of which a claim has been made under *F(No 2)A 1992, s 41* or *s 42* (see below). In relation to films completed before 10 March 1992, the exclusion of the provisions of *CAA 1990, s 68* applies in the circumstances described above without election.

A film etc. is a '*qualifying film*' etc. if it is within the definition applied for this purpose by *Films Act 1985, s 6, 1 Sch*, broadly a film meeting certain criteria as to EEC and Commonwealth content. See Leaflet FB1 'Evidence of British Nature of a Film', available from Department of National Heritage, 2nd Floor, Grey Core, 151 Buckingham Palace Road, London SW1W 9SS. Regulations relating to certification are contained in *The Films (Certification) Regulations 1985 (SI 1985 No 994)*.

In relation to qualifying films etc. completed (as above) **after 9 March 1992**, an alternative deduction may be claimed for a period, in respect of any expenditure incurred in producing a film completed in or before the period, of up to one-third (proportionately reduced for periods of less than twelve months) of the total production expenditure (reduced by any preliminary expenditure already deducted under *F(No 2)A 1992, s 41*, see below), subject to a maximum of the total such expenditure not already deducted. Similar relief is available in respect of expenditure on the acquisition of, or of any description of rights in, a film etc. completed (see above) in the period to which the claim relates (or in an earlier period), provided that it is a qualifying film etc. These provisions do not apply where an election has been made in respect of the expenditure under *CAA 1990, s 68(9)* (see above), or where a deduction has been made in respect of it under *CAA 1990, s 68(3)–(6)* (see above), and where a deduction has been allowed for a period under *section 68(3)–(6)*, no deduction is allowed under these provisions for that period in respect of any expenditure on the film concerned. A claim is irrevocable and must be made within, for 1996/97 and later years, twelve months after 31 January following the tax year in which ends the period to which the claim relates (for income tax for earlier years and for corporation tax purposes, two years after the end of the period to which it relates). [*F(No 2)A 1992, ss 42, 43; FA 1996, s 135, 21 Sch 46*]. See Revenue Pamphlet IR 131, SP 1/93, 11 January 1993, paras 26–42 for guidance on procedural points in relation to this relief.

Preliminary expenditure. For expenditure payable **after 9 March 1992**, a deduction may be claimed for a period for any expenditure payable in the period (or in an earlier period) which can reasonably be said to have been incurred in deciding whether or not to make a film (as defined in *Films Act 1985, 1 Sch 1*), and which is not payable under a contract etc. whereby it may be repaid if the film is not made. If the decision taken is to make the film, this applies to expenditure incurred before commencement of principal photography, up to a maximum of 20% of the budgeted expenditure as at the first day of principal photography, provided that the film etc. is a qualifying film etc. or, if it has not been completed at the time the claim is made, it is reasonably likely that, if completed, it would be a qualifying film etc. If the decision taken is not to make the film, it applies only where it is reasonably likely that it would have been a qualifying film etc. had it been completed. No relief may be claimed where a deduction has previously been made for the expenditure, or an election made in respect of it under *CAA 1990, s 68(9)* (see above). A claim must be made within, for 1996/97 and later years, twelve months after 31 January following the tax year in which ends the period in which the expenditure becomes payable (for income tax for earlier years and for corporation tax purposes, two years after the end of such period). [*F(No 2)A 1992, ss 41, 43; FA 1996, s 135, 21 Sch 45*]. See Revenue Pamphlet IR 131, SP 1/93, 11 January 1993, paras 26–42 for guidance on procedural points in relation to this relief.

71.58   FRANCHISING

Under a business system franchising agreement (i.e. an agreement under which the franchisor grants to the franchisee the right to distribute products or perform services using that system), there is generally an initial fee (payable in one sum or in instalments) and continuing, usually annual, fees.

The capital or revenue treatment of the initial fee depends on what it is for. To the extent that it is paid wholly or mainly for substantial rights of an enduring nature, to initiate or substantially extend a business, it is a capital payment (as are any related professional fees). (See 71.40 above for general principles.) It is immaterial that the expenditure may prove abortive, and the treatment of the payment in the hands of the franchisor is irrelevant. However, where goods or services of a revenue nature are supplied at the outset (e.g. trading stock or staff training), the Revenue will accept that an appropriate part of the initial fee is a revenue payment, provided that the sum claimed fairly represents such items, and that it is clear that the items are not separately charged for in the continuing fees. The costs of the franchisee's own initial training are not normally allowable.

The continuing fee payable by the franchisee is generally a revenue expense.

(Revenue Tax Bulletin June 1995 p 224).

71.59   GIFTS AND OTHER NON-CONTRACTUAL RECEIPTS AND PAYMENTS

The fact that a receipt is gratuitous is not in itself a reason for its not being a trading receipt. See *Severne v Dadswell Ch D 1954, 35 TC 649* (payments under war-time arrangements held trading receipts although *ex gratia*); *CIR v Falkirk Ice Rink CS 1975, 51 TC 42* (donation to ice rink from associated curling club held taxable); *Wing v O'Connell Supreme Court (IFS) 1926, [1927] IR 84* (gift to professional jockey on winning race taxable).

In recent years the problem has arisen in relation to *ex gratia* payments on the termination of long-standing business arrangements. A distinction is drawn between parting gifts as personal testimonials (not taxable as business receipts) and payments which, on the facts, can be seen as additional rewards for services already rendered or compensation for a loss of future profits (taxable). For cases see 71.47(*e*) above and compare the position for employees, see 75.26 SCHEDULE E. For gifts and donations made, see 71.83 below.

Cremation fees ('ash cash') assigned in advance, and paid directly, to a medical charity may escape liability under Schedule D, Case VI where the doctor entitled to them is not assessed under Case II, but liability under Case II is not affected by such assignment. See Revenue Inspector's Manual, IM 2203.

Gifts to educational establishments. After 18 March 1991, a relief is available for certain gifts by traders for the purposes of 'designated educational establishments'.

Where the gift is of an article manufactured by the trader, or of a type sold by him, in his trade, and would have been classified as machinery or plant for capital allowance purposes if the educational establishment had incurred expenditure on it for the purposes of a trade carried on by it, the trader is not required to bring in any amount as a trading receipt in respect of the gift.

Similarly, where the gift is of an article on which the trader has claimed machinery and plant capital allowances, he is not required to bring in any disposal value in respect of the article in his capital allowances computation.

For 1996/97 and later years, the relief must be claimed within twelve months after 31 January following the year of assessment in whose basis period the gift was made (or, for corporation tax where self-assessment applies, within two years after the end of the accounting period in which it was made). Previously, the claim had to be made within two years after the making of the gift. The claim must specify the article and educational establishment concerned. The value of any benefit received by the donor or by a person connected with him (see 20 CONNECTED PERSONS), which is in any way attributable to the making of a gift for which relief has been given, will be assessed on the donor under Case I, Case II or Case VI of Schedule D, as appropriate.

'*Designated educational establishment*' means any educational establishment designated (or of a category designated) in regulations, broadly all UK universities, public or private schools and further and higher educational institutions (see *SI 1992 No 42* as amended by *SI 1993 No 561*).

[*Sec 84; FA 1991, s 68; FA 1996, s 135, 21 Sch 2*].

(*Note.* This relief is substituted for the relief for payments for technical education previously available under *Sec 84*, for which see 71.53 above.)

See also generally 71.53 above, 71.83 and 71.84 below and CHARITIES (15).

71.60   GUARANTEES

Losses under guarantees of the indebtedness of another are analogous to bad debt losses (see 71.44 above) and similar principles apply. Losses allowed to a solicitor under the guarantee of a client's overdraft (*Jennings v Barfield Ch D 1962, 40 TC 365*) and to a film-writer under guarantee of loans to a film company with which he was associated (*Lunt v Wellesley KB 1945, 27 TC 78*) but refused to a company under a guarantee of loans to an associated company with which it had close trading connections (*Milnes v J Beam Group Ltd Ch D 1975, 50 TC 675*). See also *Bolton v Halpern & Woolf CA 1980, 53 TC 445* and *Garforth v Tankard Carpets Ltd Ch D 1980, 53 TC 342*.

A loss by an asphalt contractor under a guarantee to an exhibition (for which he hoped but, in the event, failed to work) allowed (*Morley v Lawford & Co CA 1928, 14 TC 229*). For commission paid to guarantors see *Ascot Gas Water Heaters Ltd* at 71.64 below.

Payments under guarantees made to a trader for the setting up or the purposes of his trade and irrecoverable are in certain circumstances allowable as a loss for capital gains tax if the guarantee was made after 11 April 1978. [*TCGA 1992, s 253; FA 1996, 21 Sch 40*]. See Tolley's Capital Gains Tax.

71.61   HIRE-PURCHASE

Where assets are purchased under hire-purchase agreements, the charges (the excess of the hire-purchase price over the cash price, sometimes called interest but not true interest) are, appropriately spread, allowable deductions (*Darngavil Coal Co Ltd v Francis CS 1913, 7 TC 1*). See 71.44 above for the bad debt etc. provisions of hire-purchase traders. For relief on capital element, see 10.38(vi) CAPITAL ALLOWANCES.

For whether goods sold under hire-purchase are trading stock, see *Lions Ltd v Gosford Furnishing Co Ltd & CIR CS 1961, 40 TC 256* and cf. *Drages Ltd v CIR KB 1927, 46 TC 389*.

71.62   ILLEGAL PAYMENTS ETC.

In computing profits or gains chargeable under Schedules A or D, no deduction may be made in respect of expenditure (including incidental costs) incurred in making a payment after 10 June 1993 the making of which constitutes the commission of a criminal offence. A deduction is similarly denied for any payment after 29 November 1993 induced by a demand constituting blackmail or extortion. Relief as a management expense is similarly denied. [*Sec 577A; FA 1993, s 123; FA 1994, s 141*]. For a discussion of the circumstances in which these provisions may apply, see Revenue Inspector's Manual, IM 666–667f.

71.63   INSURANCE

Premiums for business purposes are normally allowable including insurance of assets, insurance against accidents to employees, insurance against loss of profits and premiums under mutual insurance schemes (cf. *Thomas v Richard Evans & Co HL 1927, 11 TC 790*; for trade associations see 71.83 below). See also 65 RETIREMENT ANNUITIES AND PERSONAL PENSION SCHEMES and 66 RETIREMENT SCHEMES, and for war risk premiums see *Sec 586*.

Any corresponding recoveries are trading receipts (or set off against trading expenses (see *Sec 74(l)*) or capital, according to the nature of the policy. If capital, the recovery may be taken into account, where appropriate, for the purposes of CAPITAL ALLOWANCES (10) or capital gains tax. The whole of a recovery in respect of the destruction of trading stock is a trading receipt of the year of destruction, notwithstanding that it exceeds the market value of the stock lost or not all the stock was replaced (*Green v J Gliksten & Son Ltd HL 1929, 14 TC 364; Rownson Drew & Clydesdale Ltd v CIR KB 1931, 16 TC 595*). The total recovery under a loss of profits was held a trading receipt although in excess of the loss suffered (*R v British Columbia Fir & Cedar PC 1932, 15 ATC 624*). See also *Mallandain Investments Ltd v Shadbolt KB 1940, 23 TC 367*. For recoveries under accidents to employees see *Gray & Co v Murphy KB 1940, 23 TC 225; Keir & Cawder Ltd v CIR CS 1958, 38 TC 23*. Where a shipping company insured against late delivery of ships being built for it, both premiums and recoveries held capital (*Crabb v Blue Star Line Ltd Ch D 1961, 39 TC 482*).

Premiums on policies in favour of the employer insuring against death or critical illness of key employees are generally allowable, and the proceeds of any such policies trading receipts.

For mutual insurance trading, see 50 MUTUAL TRADING.

Health insurance. By concession, compensation for loss of income from self-employment under an individual's policy covering sickness or disability is exempt from tax for the first twelve months, provided that the benefit entitlement commences on or after 6 April 1994. Exemption does not apply where, exceptionally, the benefits are chargeable under Schedule E or the premiums have wholly or partly qualified for relief as pension contributions. (Revenue Pamphlet IR 1, A83). See also 75.37 SCHEDULE E. In practice, tax has not been collected where insurance benefits are provided in times of sickness, disability or unemployment to meet existing specified obligations such as loan repayments. (Revenue Press Release REV 6, 28 November 1995). The concession is effectively superseded by statutory provisions applicable to annual payments falling to be made after 5 April 1996 under certain insurance policies. Any payments falling to be taken into account in computing business profits are excluded, as are payments under policies the premiums on which have qualified for tax relief (as a deduction in computing business profits or otherwise). Subject to further conditions, the provisions also apply to payments falling due on or before that date, thereby giving statutory effect to the above-mentioned practice. See 29.10 EXEMPT INCOME for the detailed provisions.

Locum insurance. No tax relief is available for premiums paid by doctors and dentists on policies to meet locum and/or fixed overhead costs in the event of their illness. Proceeds of such policies are not trading receipts. (Revenue Inspector's Manual, IM 2207).

Professional indemnity insurance premiums are normally allowable on general principles, and the Revenue will not seek to disallow a premium paid prior to cessation of trading on the grounds that the cover extends to claims lodged after cessation. (Premiums paid after cessation will generally be relievable as post-cessation expenditure, see 60.4 POST-CESSATION ETC. RECEIPTS AND EXPENDITURE.) (Revenue Tax Bulletin October 1995 p 257).

Commissions. Revenue Statement of Practice SP 5/95, 31 March 1995, sets out the Revenue view of the taxation consequences of commissions which are:

(*a*)   received;

(*b*)   netted-off (i.e. only a net premium is paid);

(*c*)   invested (i.e. used to obtain additional benefits); or where

(*d*)   a discounted premium is paid (i.e. the premium is reduced without any explicit entitlement to commission).

This applies to any insurance policies, capital redemption policies, life annuity contracts and personal pension schemes. The Statement applies both to intermediaries (e.g. brokers or professional agents) and to policy holders in respect of policies effected for their own benefit (the latter having previously been the subject of Revenue Pamphlet IR 131, SP 3/79, 19 February 1979, which is superseded).

(Revenue Pamphlet IR 131 (October 1995 Supplement), SP 5/95, 31 March 1995).

The Revenue intend, after further consultation, to issue a revision to this Statement of Practice, to the effect that ordinary policyholders are not considered taxable on commissions in respect of their own policies. (Revenue Press Release 19 October 1995).

71.64 Schedule D, Cases I and II—Profits of Trades etc.

See also Revenue Tax Bulletin April 1995 pp 201–204 for background to and reasoning behind the views expressed in the Statement of Practice.

71.64 INTEREST AND OTHER PAYMENTS FOR LOANS

Interest paid for business purposes if not claimed as a relief under *Sec 353* is deductible, subject to certain restrictions, as described at 43.2 INTEREST PAYABLE. For 'hire-purchase interest' see 71.61 above.

Premium on repayment of mortgage (*Arizona Copper Co v Smiles CES 1891, 3 TC 149*) and on repayment of loan to finance estate development (*Bridgwater v King KB 1943, 25 TC 385*) held not allowable, as were exchange losses attendant on foreign borrowings by a company to finance its purchase of a controlling interest in another company (*Ward v Anglo-American Oil Co Ltd KB 1934, 19 TC 94*). A share of profits paid as partial consideration for a loan was held to be distribution of profits and not allowed in *Walker & Co v CIR KB 1920, 12 TC 297*.

Prior to *FA 1969*, interest paid in full on capital advances was disallowed (cf. *European Investment Trust Ltd v Jackson CA 1932, 18 TC 1*). The legislation was amended by *FA 1969*. In a case under the old law, commission paid for a guarantee of a trading liability was allowed but not for guarantee of a debenture loan (*Ascot Gas Water Heaters Ltd v Duff KB 1942, 24 TC 171*).

INTEREST ON UNPAID TAX (42) is not an allowable deduction in computing profits or losses. This applies equally to interest on unpaid or under-declared value added tax, insurance premium tax or landfill tax. [*TMA s 90; Sec 827(1)(1B)(1C); FA 1994, 7 Sch 31; FA 1996, 5 Sch 40*].

For the treatment of the incidental costs of obtaining loan finance, see 71.69 below. See also 43.16 INTEREST PAYABLE regarding interest relief for persons living in job-related accommodation.

Companies. For the special provisions applicable for accounting periods ending after 31 March 1996 to all profits and losses in respect of company 'loan relationships', see Tolley's Corporation Tax under Gilts and Bonds.

71.65 INVESTMENT INCOME (DIVIDENDS, INTEREST, RENTS, ROYALTIES)

Income received under deduction of tax may not be included in a Case I or II assessment (cf. *F S Securities Ltd v CIR HL 1964, 41 TC 666; Bucks v Bowers Ch D 1969, 46 TC 267; Bank Line Ltd v CIR CS 1974, 49 TC 307*) nor, subject to the Crown option between Cases (see 5.2 ASSESSMENTS), may income received in full from sources within Cases III, IV or V (cf. *Northend v White & Leonard & Corbin Greener Ch D 1975, 50 TC 121*) and also from sources *explicitly* within Case VI. See 46 LOSSES for treatment of certain investment income as trading profits for loss relief purposes and Tolley's Corporation Tax for similar provisions for companies. Rents receivable within Schedule A may not be assessed under Schedule D (see 5.2 ASSESSMENTS) but in practice the Revenue do not generally object to the inclusion in trading profits of rents from the letting of business accommodation temporarily surplus to requirements, provided that the premises in question continue to be partly used for the business and the rental income is comparatively small (see Revenue Tax Bulletin February 1994 p 115). See also 71.77 below.

Investment income may be treated as a trading receipt where it is the fruit derived from a fund employed and risked in the business (see *Liverpool and London and Globe Insurance Co v Bennett HL 1913, 6 TC 327*). This treatment is not confined to financial trades, but the making and holding of investments at interest must be an integral part of the trade. See *Nuclear Electric plc v Bradley HL, [1996] STC 405*, in which (in refusing the company's claim) the crucial test was considered to be whether the investments were employed in the business (of producing electricity) in the year of assessment in question. The Court of Appeal, whose judgment was approved, considered decisive the facts that the liabilities against which the investments were provided were liabilities to third parties, not to customers, and that, in view of the long-term nature of the liabilities, the business could be carried on for a long period without maintaining any fund of investments at all. See also *Bank Line Ltd v CIR* (above).

Payments received in lieu of dividends in contango operations held trading receipts (*Multipar Syndicate Ltd v Devitt KB 1945, 26 TC 359*); also co-operative society 'dividends' on trading purchases (*Pope v Beaumont KB 1941, 24 TC 78*). For interest received by underwriters on securities deposited with Lloyd's see *Owen v Sassoon HC 1950, 32 TC 101* and for discount receivable on bills see *Willingale v International Commercial Bank Ltd HL 1978, 52 TC 242*.

For the purposes of the excess profits tax and similar taxes it was necessary to determine whether rents and royalties were 'investment income'. For cases dealing with this, not involving the Case I or II treatment of the income, see Tolley's Tax Cases.

71.66   **KNOW-HOW**

'Know-how' is any industrial information and techniques of assistance in (*a*) manufacturing or processing goods or materials, (*b*) working, or searching for, etc., mineral deposits, or (*c*) agricultural, forestry or fishing operations. [*Sec 533(7)*]. Where know-how which has been used in the vendor's trade (the trade thereafter continuing) is disposed of, the consideration received (including any consideration for a restrictive covenant connected with the disposal) is a trading receipt (if not already taxable). [*Sec 531(1)*]. It should, however, be noted that, in relation to know-how on which expenditure is incurred after 31 March 1986, a balancing adjustment will normally be made in these circumstances (see 10.23 CAPITAL ALLOWANCES). [*Sec 530(5); FA 1994, 26 Sch Pt V(24)*]. A non-trading vendor is assessable under Schedule D, Case VI, on his net gain (treated as earned income if he devised the know-how) after deducting expenditure on acquisition or disposal. [*Sec 531(4)–(6)*].

But the above provisions do not apply to a sale between bodies of persons (which includes partnerships) under the same control. [*Sec 531(7)*].

If know-how is sold together with a trade, or part trade, both the vendor and the purchaser are treated as if the consideration for the know-how were a payment for goodwill. They may, however, jointly elect (within two years of the disposal, and provided they are not bodies under common control) for allowances instead to be made to the purchaser as if the know-how had been acquired for use in a trade he previously carried on. Such treatment will in any event apply where the trade acquired was previously carried on wholly outside the UK. [*Sec 531(2)(3)(7)*]. If goodwill, capital gains tax may apply.

For capital allowances on purchases of know-how, see 10.23 CAPITAL ALLOWANCES.

In *Delage v Nugget Polish Co Ltd KB 1905, 21 TLR 454*, payments for the use of a secret process, payable for 40 years and based on receipts, were held to be annual payments subject to deduction of tax at source. See also *Paterson Engineering v Duff KB 1943, 25 TC 43*.

For patents, see 71.72 below.

71.67   **LEASE RENTAL PAYMENTS**

In relation to finance leases entered into after 11 April 1991, the Revenue practice described below applies to rentals payable by a lessee under a finance lease, i.e. a lease which transfers substantially all the risks and rewards of ownership of an asset to the lessee while maintaining the lessor's legal ownership of the asset. The treatment of such rentals depends upon whether or not SSAP 21 has been applied. This practice has no implications for the tax treatment of rentals receivable by the lessor, nor for the availability of capital allowances to the lessor. (Revenue Pamphlet IR 131, SP 3/91 and Revenue Press Release 11 April 1991).

Finance lease rentals are revenue payments for the use of the asset, and, both under normal accounting principles and for tax purposes, should be allocated to the periods of account for which the asset is leased in accordance with the accruals concept. Where there is an option for the lessee to continue to lease the asset after expiry of the primary period under the lease, regard should be had, in allocating rentals to periods of account, to the economic life of the asset and its likely period of use by the lessee, as well as to the primary period.

Under SSAP 21, the lessee is required to treat a finance lease as the acquisition of an asset subject to a loan, to be depreciated over its useful life, with rentals apportioned between a finance charge and a capital repayment element. This treatment does not, however, affect the tax treatment, which remains as described above.

Where SSAP 21 has not been applied, the lessee's accounting treatment of rental payments is normally accepted for tax purposes, provided that it is consistent with the principles described above. If not, computational adjustments are made to secure the proper spreading of the rental payments.

Where SSAP 21 has been applied, the finance charge element of the rental payments for a period of account is normally accepted as a revenue deduction for that period. In determining the appropriate proportion of the capital repayment element to be deducted for tax purposes, a properly computed commercial depreciation charge to profit and loss account will normally be accepted. Where, however, the depreciation charge is not so computed, the appropriate proportion for tax purposes will be determined in accordance with the principles described above.

For comment on the principles set out in SP 3/91, and on their application to particular arrangements, see Revenue Tax Bulletin February 1995 pp 189–193. This considers in particular: sums paid before the asset comes into use; depreciation of leased assets (and the interaction with SSAP 21); long-life assets; termination adjustments; fixtures leases; and the interaction of SP 3/91 with statutory restrictions on relief for rental payments.

71.68   LEGAL AND PROFESSIONAL EXPENSES

The costs of forming a company are capital but in so far as they relate to loan capital may qualify for relief by virtue of *Secs 77, 401* (see 71.69 and 71.75 below).

The expenses of a company incorporated by charter in obtaining a variation of its charter, etc. were allowed (*CIR v Carron Co HL 1968, 45 TC 18*). See also *McGarry v Limerick Gas HC(IFS) [1932] IR 125* and contrast *A & G Moore & Co v Hare CS 1914, 6 TC 572*. In general, the costs of maintaining existing trading rights and assets are revenue expenses (*Southern v Borax Consolidated KB 1940, 23 TC 597; Bihar etc. IT Commr v Maharaja of Dharbanga PC 1941, 20 ATC 337* and compare *Morgan v Tate & Lyle Ltd HL 1954, 35 TC 367*). But the incidental costs of acquiring new assets, etc. are part of their capital cost. The expenses of obtaining or renewing a lease of business premises are strictly capital but, in practice, the expenses of renewing leases under 50 years are generally allowed (although a proportionate disallowance may apply where a lease premium is involved, see Revenue Inspector's Manual, IM 803b). The cost of an unsuccessful application to vary a carrier's licence was disallowed (*Pyrah v Annis & Co CA 1956, 37 TC 163*) as was the cost of an unsuccessful application for planning permission (*ECC Quarries Ltd v Watkis Ch D 1975, 51 TC 153* but see 10.11(*b*) CAPITAL ALLOWANCES). For excise licenses, see 71.45 above.

Legal expenses in defending charges brought by a professional regulatory body were allowed on the grounds that they were incurred to prevent suspension or expulsion and thus to protect the taxpayer's business (citing *Tate & Lyle Ltd* above), although the fines imposed were disallowed (*Stockbroker v McKnight (Sp C 65), [1996] SSCD 103*).

The cost of tax appeals even though successful is not allowable (*Allen v Farquharson Bros & Co KB 1932, 17 TC 59; Smith's Potato Estates v Bolland HL 1948, 30 TC 267; Rushden Heel Co v Keene HL 1948, 30 TC 298*). Where an accountant, etc. agrees the tax liabilities based on the accounts he prepares, normal annual fees are allowed but not fees for a special review of settled years (*Worsley Brewery Co v CIR CA 1932, 17 TC 349*) or fees for additional work on 'back duty' investigations.

Costs incurred by a partner in connection with the dissolution of the partnership were disallowed in *C Connelly & Co v Wilbey Ch D, [1992] STC 783*.

Additional accountancy expenses incurred as a result of an 'in-depth' examination by the Revenue of a particular year's accounts (see 71.28 above) will normally be allowed if the investigation does not result in an adjustment to the profits of any earlier year or in the imposition of interest or interest and penalties in relation to the current year. Where the investigation reveals discrepancies and additional liabilities for earlier years, or results in a settlement for the current year including interest (with or without penalties), the expenses will be disallowed. (Revenue Pamphlet IR 131, SP 16/91, 3 December 1991).

71.69   **LOAN FINANCE INCIDENTAL COSTS**

Expenditure may qualify for relief under *Sec 77*. The relief applies to the incidental costs of obtaining finance by means of a loan or issue of loan stock (*a*) the interest on which would be deductible in computing profits (see 71.64 above and 43.2 INTEREST PAYABLE), or, as regards companies, allowable as a charge on income, and (*b*) which does not carry a right, exercisable within three years, of conversion into, or to the acquisition of, shares or other (non-qualifying) securities.

(*b*) does not apply if the right is not wholly exercised within the three-year period, and where part only of the loan, etc. is so converted, only the corresponding part of the incidental costs is disallowed. For this purpose, incidental costs incurred before the end of the three-year period are treated as incurred immediately after that period. [*Sec 77*].

The incidental costs deductible are those incurred wholly and exclusively for the purpose of (i) obtaining the loan finance, whether actually obtained or not, or (ii) providing security for it, or (iii) repaying it. They include fees, commissions, advertising, printing, and other incidental matters but not stamp duty nor does the relief extend to exchange losses (or sums paid for protection against them) or a premium on repayment. [*Sec 77(6)*]. Costs incidental to the taking out of a life insurance policy as a condition of obtaining the loan finance are deductible, but not premiums payable on such a policy. (Revenue Tax Bulletin February 1992 p 13).

Where loan finance costs are incurred on the formation of a company before it commences trading, see 71.75 below.

These provisions do not apply for corporation tax purposes for accounting periods ending after 31 March 1996. [*Sec 77(8); FA 1996, 14 Sch 9*]. See now Tolley's Corporation Tax under Gilts and Bonds.

71.70   **MINES, QUARRIES, ETC.**

See 10.39 *et seq.* CAPITAL ALLOWANCES for mining etc. expenditure so allowable. The relevant legislation which applied before 1 April 1986 originated from 1945 and may therefore affect any pre-1945 decisions below.

The cost of sinking (*Coltness Iron Co v Black HL 1881, 1 TC 287*), deepening (*Bonner v Basset Mines KB 1912, 6 TC 146*) or 'de-watering' (*United Collieries v CIR CS 1929, 12 TC 1248*) a pit is capital.

A lump sum paid at the end of a mining lease for surface damage was held capital (*Robert Addie & Sons v CIR CS 1924, 8 TC 671*) but not periodic payments during the currency of the lease based on acreage worked (*O'Grady v Bullcroft Main Collieries KB 1932, 17 TC 93*). *Bullcroft* was decided before the enactment of what is now *Sec 119* and rents and tonnage payments for the right to withdraw surface support are easements within *Sec 119* (*CIR v New Sharlston Collieries CA 1936, 21 TC 116*). For the deduction of tax under *Sec 119* see 23.14 DEDUCTION OF TAX AT SOURCE and also for periodic payments for rights to minerals, sand and gravel, etc. For shortworkings, see *Broughton & Plas Power v Kirkpatrick QB 1884, 2 TC 69; CIR v Cranford Ironstone KB 1942, 29 TC 113*. Provision for the future costs of abandoning an oil field and of restoring hired equipment used therein to its original state held capital (*RTZ Oil and Gas Ltd v Elliss Ch D 1987, 61 TC 132*).

In practice, actual land restoration costs (but not provisions for future restoration expenditure) in a continuing business are generally allowable. (Revenue Inspectors' Manual, IM 2795).

Purchase of unworked deposits by sand and gravel merchant held capital (*Stow Bardolph Gravel Co Ltd v Poole CA 1954, 35 TC 459*) as was purchase of land with nitrate deposits by chemical manufacturer (*Alianza Co v Bell HL 1905, 5 TC 172*) and payment by oil company for unwon oil in wells it took over (*Hughes v British Burmah Petroleum KB 1932, 17 TC 286*). See also *Golden Horse Shoe v Thurgood CA 1933, 18 TC 280* (purchase of tailings for gold extraction, allowable) and *CIR v Broomhouse Brick CS 1952, 34 TC 1* (purchase of blaes for brick manufacture, allowable).

71.71   MISCELLANEOUS EXPENSES AND RECEIPTS

Card winnings of club proprietor, trading receipts (*Burdge v Pyne Ch D 1968, 45 TC 320*). For lotteries and football pools, see 71.30 above.

Computer software. The Revenue's views on the treatment of expenditure on computer software are summarised as follows.

Software acquired under licence. Regular payments akin to a rental are allowable revenue expenditure, the timing of deductions being governed by correct accountancy practice (see 71.40 above). A lump sum payment is capital if the licence is of a sufficiently enduring nature to be considered a capital asset in the context of the licencee's trade (see 71.40 above), e.g. where it may be expected to function as a tool of the trade for several years. Equally the benefit may be transitory (and the expenditure revenue) even though the licence is for an indefinite period. Inspectors will in any event accept that expenditure is on revenue account where the software has a useful economic life of less than two years. Timing of the deduction in these circumstances will again depend on correct accountancy practice.

Where the licence is a capital asset, capital allowances are available (see 10.25 CAPITAL ALLOWANCES).

Expenditure on a package containing both hardware and a licence to use software must be apportioned before the above principles are applied.

Software owned outright. The treatment of expenditure on such software (including any in-house costs) follows the same principles as are described above in relation to licensed software.

(Revenue Tax Bulletin November 1993 p 99).

Purchases/sales of assets. See *T Beynon & Co v Ogg KB 1918, 7 TC 125* (profits of colliery agent from deals in wagons held trading receipts); *Gloucester Railway Carriage v*

CIR HL 1925, 12 TC 720 (sale by wagon manufacturer of wagons previously let, held trading receipts); *Bonner v Frood KB 1934, 18 TC 488* (sale of rounds by credit trader, held trading receipts).

Reimbursements of capital expenditure spread over 30 years held capital as regards both payer and recipient (*Boyce v Whitwick Colliery CA 1934, 18 TC 655*). For allowances from railway in respect of traffic on sidings paid for by trader see *Westcombe v Hadnock Quarries KB 1931, 16 TC 137; Legge v Flettons Ltd KB 1939, 22 TC 455.*

Excessive payments to **service company** of professional firm held not deductible (*Stephenson v Payne, Stone Fraser & Co Ch D 1967, 44 TC 507*).

Solicitor's fees as trustee held professional receipts (*Jones v Wright KB 1927, 13 TC 221*) even though also a beneficiary (*Watson & Everitt v Blunden CA 1933, 18 TC 402*).

Timber purchases and sales. For purchases and sales of standing timber by timber merchants see *Murray v CIR CS 1951, 32 TC 238; McLellan, Rawson & Co v Newall Ch D 1955, 36 TC 117; Hood Barrs v CIR (No 2) HL 1957, 37 TC 188; Hopwood v C N Spencer Ltd Ch D 1964, 42 TC 169; Russell v Hird and Mercer Ch D 1983, 57 TC 127.* For sales of trees by farmer see *Elmes v Trembath KB 1934, 19 TC 72.*

Trade marks or designs. Fees and expenses of applications for registration and extensions are allowable. [*Sec 83*].

Video tape rental. Relief for the cost of acquiring video tapes for hire may be obtained by way of either:

(i)   capital allowances (provided the useful economic life is at least two years);

(ii)   valuation basis (where the useful economic life is two years or less); or

(iii)   renewals basis.

See Revenue Tax Bulletin October 1995 pp 254, 255 for a discussion of each of these methods in this context.

General. See also *Thompson v Magnesium Elektron CA 1943, 26 TC 1* (payments based on purchases, held trading receipts); *British Commonwealth International Newsfilm v Mahany HL 1962, 40 TC 550* (payments to meet operating expenses, trading receipts); *CIR v Pattison CS 1959, 38 TC 617* (weekly instalments for business, capital).

71.72   PATENTS

Expenses (agent's charges, patent office fees, etc.) in obtaining, or extending the term of, a patent for the purposes of a trade (including rejected or abandoned applications) are allowable. [*Sec 83*]. For capital expenditure on the purchase of patent rights see 10.50 CAPITAL ALLOWANCES.

Sums received on the sale of patent rights may, dependent on the facts, be trading receipts (*Rees Roturbo Development v Ducker HL 1928, 13 TC 366; Brandwood v Banker KB 1928, 14 TC 44; CIR v Rustproof Metal Window CA 1947, 29 TC 243* and cf. *Harry Ferguson (Motors) v CIR CA(NI) 1951, 33 TC 15*). Other sums are taxable under *Sec 524*, see 54 PATENTS.

Where a company held a patent for renovating car tyres, lump sums received by it under arrangements for giving the payer a *de facto* franchise in his area, were held to be capital receipts (*Margerison v Tyresoles Ltd KB 1942, 25 TC 59*).

Patent royalties are payable less tax and not deductible—see 71.51 above. For spreading of patent royalties received less tax, see 54 PATENTS and for DTR treatment of royalties from abroad, see 25.5(*l*) DOUBLE TAX RELIEF.

For copyright, know-how and trade marks, see 71.50, 71.66 and 71.71 respectively.

71.73   PERSONAL EXPENSES

Expenditure for domestic and private purposes is explicitly disallowable under *Sec 74(b)* and is, in any event, not wholly and exclusively for business purposes and disallowable under *Sec 74(a)*. The 'dual purpose rule' (see 71.40 above) is relevant here. Hence the cost of treatment at a nursing home was disallowed even though motivated by need for room from which to conduct business (*Murgatroyd v Evans-Jackson Ch D 1966, 43 TC 581*) as was the cost of a minor finger operation to enable a professional guitarist to continue playing as, on the evidence, he also played the guitar as a hobby (*Prince v Mapp Ch D 1969, 46 TC 169*). Medical expenses where illness said to be due to working conditions were not allowed in *Norman v Golder CA 1944, 26 TC 293*. Expenditure on ordinary clothing is not normally allowable, the leading case here being *Mallalieu v Drummond HL 1983, 57 TC 330*, in which, reversing the decisions in the lower Courts, it was held that the cost of sober clothing worn by a lady barrister to comply with Bar Council guidelines was for the dual purpose of her profession and her requirements as a human being, and not allowable. See also 71.40 above and the 'clothing' cases at 75.10(*b*) SCHEDULE E. In *Watkis v Ashford, Sparkes and Harward Ch D 1985, 58 TC 468*, expenditure on meals at regular partners' lunchtime meetings was disallowed, whilst expenditure on accommodation, food and drink at the firm's annual weekend conference was allowed. In *Stockbroker v McKnight (Sp C 65), [1996] SSCD 103*, legal expenses in defending charges brought by a professional regulatory body were allowed despite the fact that the taxpayer's 'personal reputation was inevitably involved'. In *MacKinlay v Arthur Young McClelland Moores & Co HL 1989, 62 TC 704*, contributions towards the removal expenses of a partner moved in the interests of the firm were not allowed. For rent, etc. of premises used both as residence and for business see 71.77 below and for travelling and subsistence expenses see 71.88 below. See also *Mason v Tyson Ch D 1980, 53 TC 333* (expenses of occasional use of flat).

The personal costs (e.g. accommodation, food and drink) of a UK resident individual assessable under Schedule D, Case I or Case II (and of accompanying partner) of living abroad on business are not disallowed under *Sec 74(a)* or (*b*). (Revenue Inspectors' Manual, IM 825).

71.74   POOLING OF PROFITS

Where traders pool profits or act together in consortia but so as not to form PARTNERSHIPS (53) or trade jointly (cf. *Gardner and Bowring Hardy v CIR CS 1930, 15 TC 602; Geo Hall & Son v Platt Ch D 1954, 35 TC 440*) each trader's share of the pooled profits will normally be treated as a receipt of his main trade and any payment under the arrangement by one trader to another will be deductible in computing his profits (*Moore v Stewarts & Lloyds Ltd CS 1905, 6 TC 501* and cf. *United Steel v Cullington (No 1) CA 1939, 23 TC 71*). In *Utol Ltd v CIR KB 1943, 25 TC 517* payments by one company to another under a profit sharing arrangement were held to be dividends payable less tax under the law in force before SCHEDULE F (76). For compensation received on the termination of a profit sharing arrangement see *Van den Berghs* at 71.47(*b*) above.

71.75   PRE-TRADING EXPENDITURE

The general rule is that trading expenditure is deductible when incurred and hence is not allowable if incurred before trading commenced (cf. *Birmingham & District Cattle By-Products Ltd v CIR KB 1919, 12 TC 92*). The rule is modified for certain pre-trading capital expenditure, including scientific research expenditure and abortive exploration expenditure by mining concerns (see 10 CAPITAL ALLOWANCES).

There is also a special relief on expenditure incurred by a person in the seven years (five years where the trade commenced after 31 March 1989 and before 1 April 1993, three years where the trade was commenced before 1 April 1989) before he commenced to carry on a trade which, had it been incurred after he commenced, would have been deductible in computing the profits. The relief does not extend to expenditure already deductible in computing profits, e.g. pre-trading purchases of stock or advance payments of rent. For income tax purposes as regards trades commenced before 6 April 1995, such expenditure may be treated as a trading loss of the year of assessment in which the trade commenced (see (46) LOSSES, including the relief for losses in the early years of trade), to be claimed separately from any other loss relief. For income tax purposes as regards trades commenced after 5 April 1995 and for corporation tax purposes, the expenditure is treated as incurred on the day the person commences the trade. Where the company carries on the trade in partnership, see 53.14 PARTNERSHIPS. [*Sec 401; FA 1989, s 114; FA 1993, s 109(1)(4); FA 1995, s 120*].

See 68.7(*a*) SCHEDULE A as regards Schedule A businesses.

For commencements after 31 March 1993, the relief is extended to unrelieved trade charges paid by companies before commencement. However, for accounting periods ending after 31 March 1996 this is replaced by a special relief for non-trading debits arising under the loan relationship provisions introduced in *FA 1996* (see Tolley's Corporation Tax under Gilts and Bonds). [*Sec 401(1A)–(1AC); FA 1993, s 109(2)(4); FA 1996, 14 Sch 20*].

71.76   **PROPERTY SALES AND OTHER PROPERTY RECEIPTS**

For property dealing see 71.38 above and for rents received see 71.65 above.

Sales of property by builders in special circumstances have been considered in a number of cases. Profits held trading receipts in *Spiers & Son v Ogden KB 1932, 17 TC 117* (building activities extended); *Sharpless v Rees KB 1940, 23 TC 361* (sale of land acquired for hobby abandoned for health reasons); *Shadford v H Fairweather & Co Ch D 1966, 43 TC 291* (sale of site after development plan dropped); *Snell v Rosser, Thomas & Co Ch D 1967, 44 TC 343* (sale of land surplus to requirements); *Bowie v Reg Dunn (Builders) Ch D 1974, 49 TC 469* (sale of land acquired with business); *Smart v Lowndes Ch D 1978, 52 TC 436* (sale of land in wife's name). Sales of property built but let meanwhile held trading in *J & C Oliver v Farnsworth Ch D 1956, 37 TC 51; James Hobson & Sons v Newall Ch D 1957, 37 TC 609; W M Robb Ltd v Page Ch D 1971, 47 TC 465* and this notwithstanding active building given up (*Speck v Morton Ch D 1972, 48 TC 476; Granville Building Co v Oxby Ch D 1954, 35 TC 245*). But in *Harvey v Caulcott HC 1952, 33 TC 159* the sales were held realisations of investments and in *West v Phillips Ch D 1958, 38 TC 203* some houses were treated as investments and others as trading stock. See also *Andrew v Taylor CA 1965, 42 TC 557.* Sales of houses retained after business *transferred* held sales of investments in *Bradshaw v Blunden (No 1) Ch D 1956, 36 TC 397; Seaward v Varty CA 1962, 40 TC 523.* See also *Hesketh Estates v Craddock KB 1942, 25 TC 1* (profit on sale of brine baths held trading receipt of mixed business including land development).

For house sales subject to ground rents, etc., see *CIR v John Emery & Sons HL 1936, 20 TC 213; B G Utting & Co Ltd v Hughes HL 1940, 23 TC 174; McMillan v CIR CS 1942, 24 TC 417; Heather v Redfern & Sons KB 1944, 26 TC 119.* For ground rents (England) and feu duties (Scotland) there should be credited the lower of their market value and cost, the cost being taken as the proportion of the cost of the land and building in the ratio of the market value to the sum of the market value and the sale price. For ground annuals (Scotland) which are perpetual the realisable value is brought in. The right to receive the rent then becomes part of the fixed capital of the trade, whose subsequent sale is not taken into account for income tax purposes. Any premiums on the grant of leases are part of the sale proceeds.

Turf sales by a farmer were held to be farming receipts in *Lowe v J W Ashmore Ltd Ch D 1970, 46 TC 597.* For timber sales see 71.71 above and for woodlands managed on a commercial basis see 69 SCHEDULE B.

Any excess of SCHEDULE A (68) deductions over rent received by a builder from property held as trading stock may be allowed as a trading expense. (Revenue Inspectors' Manual, IM 1959).

Annuities under *Agriculture Act 1967* for giving up (after attaining age of 55) uncommercial agricultural land are treated as earned income [*Sec 833(5)(d)*] and receipts of grants under the same *Act* for the same reason are exempt from capital gains tax. [*TCGA 1992, s 249*].

Where sales of land, etc., are capital, the profits on assets disposed of are liable to capital gains tax. See also 3.11 ANTI-AVOIDANCE for provisions affecting land or land development. [*Sec 776*].

For transactions not at market value see 71.82 below.

71.77   RENTS, ETC. FOR BUSINESS PREMISES
are allowable. For repairs see 71.78 below.

Where partly used privately (e.g. shop with residential accommodation above), *Sec 74(c)* provides for the allowance of not more than two-thirds of the rent unless the circumstances justify a higher proportion. In practice, the allowance is normally two-thirds for retail businesses and, although not provided for in the legislation, rates and 'common' repairs are similarly apportioned. For this see *Wildbore v Luker HC 1951, 33 TC 46*. For allowance for use of home for business, see *Thomas v Ingram Ch D 1979, 52 TC 428*. See also *Mason v Tyson Ch D 1980, 53 TC 333* (expenses of flat used occasionally to enable professional man to work late not allowed).

For rents from letting surplus business accommodation see 71.65 above. Where premises became redundant or were closed down, continuing rents (less sub-letting receipts) were allowed (*CIR v Falkirk Iron CS 1933, 17 TC 625; Hyett v Lennard KB 1940, 23 TC 346*) but not payments to secure the cancellation of leases no longer required (*Mallett v Staveley Coal & Iron CA 1928, 13 TC 772* (the leading case here); *Cowcher v Richard Mills & Co KB 1927, 13 TC 216; Union Cold Storage v Ellerker KB 1939, 22 TC 547; Dain v Auto Speedways Ch D 1959, 38 TC 525*). See also *West African Drug Co v Lilley KB 1947, 28 TC 140*. Where the rent of a motorway service station was calculated by reference to takings, a lump sum payment for the exclusion of tobacco duty from takings was held capital (*Tucker v Granada Motorway Services HL 1979, 53 TC 92*), but, distinguishing *Granada Motorways*, an amount received by a company in respect of its agent's negligent failure to serve its landlord with counter-notice of an increase in its rent, was held to be a trading receipt in *Donald Fisher (Ealing) Ltd v Spencer CA 1989, 63 TC 168*. Rent for a building not required for occupation for business purposes but to control access to the lessee's works was held deductible (less sub-let rents) in *Allied Newspapers v Hindsley CA 1937, 21 TC 422*.

Additional rent liability incurred to obtain the freehold reversion to premises already rented held capital (*Littlewoods Mail Order v McGregor CA 1969, 45 TC 519* following *CIR v Land Securities HL 1969, 45 TC 495*), as were periodical payments to reimburse capital expenditure incurred by landlord (*Ainley v Edens KB 1935, 19 TC 303*) and payments based on production for grant of sisal estates (*Ralli Estates v East Africa IT Commr PC 1961, 40 ATC 9*). But payments for the use of a totalisator calculated by reference to its cost were allowed (*Racecourse Betting Control Board v Wild KB 1938, 22 TC 182*) as were rents subject to abatement dependent on profits (*Union Cold Storage v Adamson HL 1931, 16 TC 293*). For Scottish duplicands see *Dow v Merchiston Castle School CS 1921, 8 TC 149*. Rent paid by partnership to partner owning business premises allowed (*Heastie v Veitch & Co CA 1933, 18 TC 305*). For excessive payments to professional 'service company' see *Payne, Stone Fraser* at 71.71 above.

Rates, council tax and community charge. Business rates are deductible in the same way as rent, and before their replacement by the community charge and subsequently by the council tax, domestic rates were deductible to the extent that domestic premises were used for trade purposes. Council tax may similarly be deducted where it is attributable to premises (or part) used for trade purposes. No deduction is available for the personal community charge. Where, however, the standard community charge was payable in respect of premises which were not the sole or main residence of the occupier, and which were used for trade purposes, an appropriate proportion of the charge is deductible in ascertaining the profits of the trade. Similarly, where the collective community charge was payable in respect of houses in multiple occupation, and the landlord carries on a trade (e.g. of providing accommodation), he may claim as a trading deduction any part of the charge not met by contributions from residents. No deduction is available in respect of their contribution to the collective charge to any of the residents who used the premises for business purposes, as their contribution is in lieu of the personal community charge. (Revenue Press Releases 10 November 1989, 16 March 1993).

Premiums. Certain lease premiums, etc., in relation to leases not exceeding 50 years are assessable on the landlord to an extent which varies with the length of the lease (see 68.27 SCHEDULE A). For any part of the 'relevant period' (the duration of the lease, etc. as defined in *Sec 87(9)*) during which the lessee occupies the premises for purposes of a trade, etc. or (with certain limitations) deals with his interest therein as property employed for trade, he is treated as paying *additional rent* for the property, allowable against profits under Schedule D, Case I or II, at a rate calculated by spreading over the relevant period the amount in respect of which the landlord is assessed (or would be assessed but for certain claims which he can make) proportionately reduced for any part of the premium, etc. paid which gives rise to an allowance under *CAA 1990, s 105(1)(b)* (mineral depletion), or in respect of which any other CAPITAL ALLOWANCES (10) have been, or will be, made. Partial allowance is given where part only of the property is occupied for trade etc. purposes [*Sec 87; FA 1995, 6 Sch 14*], otherwise lease premiums not allowable. Lease premiums not within the legislation are not allowable (cf. *MacTaggart v Strump CS 1925, 10 TC 17*).

General. See 3.12 ANTI-AVOIDANCE [*Sec 779*] regarding restrictions where there is a lease-back at a non-commercial rent and 3.13 ANTI-AVOIDANCE [*Sec 780*] for taxation of capital sums received on certain lease-backs after 21 June 1971.

For deductibility of rents for wayleaves paid by Radio Relay services see 23.14 DEDUCTION OF TAX AT SOURCE.

71.78　**REPAIRS AND RENEWALS**

(a)　**General.** Expenditure held to be capital as described at (*b*) and (*c*) below may now qualify for CAPITAL ALLOWANCES (10). Any allowable expenditure is deductible in the period when incurred and not when the repairs, etc. accrued (*Naval Colliery Co Ltd v CIR HL 1928, 12 TC 1017*) and provisions for future repairs and renewals are not allowable (*Clayton v Newcastle-under-Lyme Corpn QB 1888, 2 TC 416; Peter Merchant Ltd v Stedeford CA 1948, 30 TC 496*). A provision for regular major overhaul work accrued due on aircraft engines was, however, allowed in *Johnston v Britannia Airways Ltd Ch D, [1994] STC 763*.

(b)　**Business premises.** The general rule is that expenditure on additions, alterations, expansions or improvements is capital but the cost of repairs, i.e. restoring a building to its original condition, is allowable. But the use of modern materials in repairing an old building does not make the expenditure capital (*Conn v Robins Bros Ltd Ch D 1966, 43 TC 266*). If the expenditure is capital, the estimated cost of 'notional repairs' obviated by the work is not allowable (see *Wm P Lawrie* and *Thomas Wilson (Keighley)* below).

A renewal of a building, i.e. a complete re-construction, is capital (*Fitzgerald v CIR Supreme Court (IFS) 1925, 5 ATC 414; Wm P Lawrie v CIR CS 1952, 34 TC 20*). The cost of rebuilding a factory chimney was held capital in *O'Grady v Bullcroft Main Collieries KB 1932, 17 TC 93* but allowed in *Samuel Jones & Co v CIR CS 1951, 32 TC 513* where the chimney was an integral part of the building. For roof replacements see *Wm P Lawrie* (above) and *Thos Wilson (Keighley) v Emmerson Ch D 1960, 39 TC 360*. The replacement of the ring in a cattle auction mart and of a stand in a football ground were held not to be repairs in *Wynne-Jones v Bedale Auction Ltd Ch D 1976, 51 TC 426* and *Brown v Burnley Football Co Ltd Ch D 1980, 53 TC 357* respectively in which the problem is reviewed.

Cost of barrier against coastal erosion held capital (*Avon Beach & Cafe v Stewart HC 1950, 31 TC 487*); also replacing a canal embankment (*Phillips v Whieldon Sanitary Potteries HC 1952, 33 TC 213*) and building new access road (*Pitt v Castle Hill Warehousing Ch D 1974, 49 TC 638*).

Where on taking a lease of dilapidated property the dilapidations were made good under a covenant in the lease, the cost was held disallowable as attributable to the previous use of the premises (*Jackson v Laskers Home Furnishers Ch D 1956, 37 TC 69*) but when cinemas were acquired in a state of disrepair (but still fit for public showings) because of war-time restrictions on building work, the cost of the repairs was allowed (*Odeon Associated Theatres Ltd v Jones CA 1971, 48 TC 257*). See also (*c*) below. In practice, expenditure on repairing and redecorating newly acquired premises is allowed unless abnormal (and likely to be reflected in the purchase price or rent payable).

Dilapidations of a repair nature on the termination of a lease are generally allowed.

For repairs to tied premises see 71.45 above.

(*c*)   **Plant and other business assets, etc.** The general rules at (*b*) above apply to plant with the important modification that expenditure on the renewal of plant is allowed as an alternative to capital allowances. For this see 10.38(x) CAPITAL ALLOWANCES. Renewals of utensils and loose tools are allowable, see *Sec 74(d)*. The cost of additional utensils and loose tools is capital but if not ranking for capital allowances (cf. *Hinton v Maden & Ireland Ltd HL 1959, 38 TC 391*) the Revenue may in suitable cases agree to spread the cost forward.

For repairs soon after the acquisition of an asset see *Law Shipping v CIR CS 1923, 12 TC 621* and *CIR v Granite City SS Co CS 1927, 13 TC 1* in which the cost of repairs to ships attributable to their use before acquisition, was held capital. But see *Odeon Associated Theatres* at (*b*) above in which *Law Shipping* was distinguished. See also *Bidwell v Gardiner Ch D 1960, 39 TC 31* in which the replacement of the furnishings of a newly acquired hotel was held capital.

Expenditure on renewal of railway tracks was allowed in *Rhodesia Railways v Bechuanaland Collector PC 1933, 12 ATC 223*, distinguishing *Highland Railway v Balderston CES 1889, 2 TC 485* in which held capital. Abnormal expenditure on dredging a channel to a shipyard was held capital in *Ounsworth v Vickers Ltd KB 1915, 6 TC 671* but the cost to a Harbour Board of removing a wreck (*Whelan v Dover Harbour Board CA 1934, 18 TC 555*) and of renewing moorings (*In re King's Lynn Harbour CES 1875, 1 TC 23*) was allowed. For shop fittings see *Eastmans Ltd v Shaw HL 1928, 14 TC 218; Hyam v CIR CS 1929, 14 TC 479*. See also *Lothian Chemical v Rogers CS 1926, 11 TC 508*.

71.79   **SCIENTIFIC RESEARCH**

Revenue expenditure incurred by a trader on scientific research, undertaken directly or on his behalf, in relation to his trade (as defined), is allowable as a deduction from profits. Similarly, any sum paid to an approved scientific association having as its object such research in relation to the class of trade concerned, or to any approved university, etc. for such scientific research, is allowed. Approval of an association rests with the appropriate Secretary of State who may also give a final decision on what is scientific research. [*CAA 1990, ss 136, 139(1)(3)*]. For *capital* outlay, see 10.52 CAPITAL ALLOWANCES. The relief is given to trades and not to professions or vocations.

71.80   **SECURITY**

A deduction may be allowed from profits of a trade etc. carried on by an individual (or partnership of individuals) for certain expenditure incurred after 5 April 1989 in connection with the provision for or use by the individual (or any of them) of an asset or service which improves personal security. The asset or service must be provided or used to meet a special threat to the individual's personal physical security arising wholly or mainly by virtue of the trade, profession or vocation, and the sole object of the provider must be the meeting of that threat. In the case of an asset, relief is available only to the extent that the provider intends the asset to be used solely to improve personal physical security (ignoring any other incidental use), and in the case of a service, the benefit to the individual must consist wholly or mainly in such an improvement. Any improvement in the personal physical security of the individual's family resulting from the asset or service provided is disregarded for these purposes.

Excluded from relief is provision of a car, ship or aircraft, or of a dwelling (or grounds appurtenant thereto); but relief may be obtained in respect of equipment or a structure (such as a wall), and it is immaterial whether or not an asset becomes affixed to land and whether or not the individual acquires the property in the asset or (in the case of a fixture) an estate or interest in the land. [*FA 1989, ss 112, 113*]. See also 10.25 CAPITAL ALLOWANCES, 75.35 SCHEDULE E.

71.81   **SHARE, SECURITY ETC. ISSUES, PURCHASES, SALES AND EXCHANGES**

For whether a trade of 'share dealing' carried on see 71.39 above. For transactions not at market value see 71.82 below.

Profits and losses on realisations of investments by a bank in the course of its business enter into its Case I profits (*Punjab Co-operative Bank v Lahore IT Commr PC 1940, 19 ATC 533* and see *Frasers (Glasgow) Bank v CIR HL 1963, 40 TC 698*) and similarly for insurance companies (*Northern Assce Co v Russell CES 1889, 2 TC 551; General Reinsurance Co v Tomlinson Ch D 1970, 48 TC 81* and contrast *CIR v Scottish Automobile CS 1931, 16 TC 381*). Profits/losses held capital in *Stott v Hoddinott KB 1916, 7 TC 85* (investments acquired by architect to secure contracts); *Jacobs Young & Co v Harris KB 1926, 11 TC 221* (shares held by merchanting company in subsidiary wound up); *Alliance & Dublin Consumers' Gas Co v Davis HC(IFS) 1926, 5 ATC 717* (investments of gas company earmarked for reserve fund). A profit by a property dealing company on the sale of shares acquired in connection with a property transaction was held a trading receipt (*Associated London Properties v Henriksen CA 1944, 26 TC 46*) but contrast *Fundfarms Developments v Parsons Ch D 1969, 45 TC 707* and see now 3 ANTI-AVOIDANCE.

Shares allotted for mining concessions granted by company dealing in concessions held trading receipts at market value (*Gold Coast Selection Trust v Humphrey HL 1948, 30 TC 209*). See also *Murphy v Australian Machinery & Investment Co CA 1948, 30 TC 244* and *Scottish & Canadian Investment Co v Easson CS 1922, 8 TC 265*.

71.81 Schedule D, Cases I and II—Profits of Trades etc.

For options, see *Varty v British South Africa Co HL 1965, 42 TC 406* (no profits or loss until shares sold). See also *Walker v Cater Securities Ch D 1974, 49 TC 625*.

Conversion etc. of securities held as circulating capital. Where a new holding of securities (as defined) is issued in exchange for an original holding beneficially owned by a person carrying on a business of banking, insurance or dealing in investments, the transaction, for purposes of Schedule D, Case I, shall be treated as not involving any disposal of the original holding; the new holding being treated as the same asset. This applies to securities where a profit on their sale would normally be a trading profit and to transactions which otherwise would result in the new holding being equated with the original holding under *TCGA 1992, ss 132, 136* (capital gains rollover relief in cases of conversions etc.) and *TCGA 1992, s 134* (compensation stock) but does not apply to a transaction under *Sec 471* (see below) whether or not a notice has been given under that section. Where there is consideration in addition to the new holding, apportionment will apply. [*Sec 473*]. By concession, this treatment may also be claimed where the capital gains tax provisions referred to would not have applied but could have been treated as applying under the concession relating to earn-outs. (Revenue Pamphlet IR 1 (November 1995 Supplement), D 27). See Tolley's Capital Gains Tax under Shares and Securities for details of the earn-out concession.

Exchange of securities by share dealers in connection with conversion operations, nationalisation etc. by Government. The securities received, together with any additional consideration, will take the place of the securities given up without involving any disposal until the new securities are realised. Election may be made for these provisions not to apply. For 1996/97 and later years, it must be made within twelve months after 31 January following the year of assessment in whose basis period the exchange takes place (or, for corporation tax where self-assessment applies, within two years after the end of the accounting period in which the exchange takes place). Previously, election had to be made within two years after the end of the relevant chargeable period. [*Sec 471; FA 1996, s 135, 21 Sch 12*].

Gilt-edged securities: stripping and reconsolidation. Where the computation of profits and gains from a trade, etc. requires amounts in respect of the acquisition or redemption of a gilt-edged security to be brought into account, there are special provisions dealing with the exchange of such a security for strips of the security and for reconsolidation on the exchange of strips for the security from which they derived.

On an exchange for strips, the security is treated as having been redeemed at its market value, and the strips as having been acquired at that market value apportioned *pro rata* to their market value at the time of the exchange. Similarly on a consolidation, each strip is treated as having been redeemed at its market value, and the security as having been acquired at the aggregate market value of the strips. The Treasury may make regulations for determining market value for these purposes.

Sec 473 (conversion etc. of securities held as circulating capital, see above) does not apply where these provisions apply.

These provisions do not apply for the purposes of corporation tax, for which see Tolley's Corporation Tax under Gilts and Bonds (special cases).

[*Sec 730C; FA 1996, 40 Sch 7*].

Stock lending. Where arrangements are made under which securities, including stocks and shares, are transferred to a person (or his nominee) to enable him to fulfil a contract for sale of securities, and in return securities of the same kind and amount are to be transferred to the lender (or his nominee), the transfers under the arrangements are disregarded in computing trading profits or losses and for the purposes of capital gains tax. By concession, this treatment is extended to arrangements under which a loan of gilt-edged securities falls due for redemption and an appropriate cash sum is paid instead of the stock being returned, or where a loan is made to replace an existing stock loan rather than to meet a sale. (Revenue Pamphlet IR 1, B35, B36). The same exemptions apply where, to enable him to fulfil such arrangements, the lender himself enters into similar arrangements with a third party. For transfers made after 30 September 1993, the exemptions also apply to arrangements made as part of a chain of arrangements all having the effect of enabling the lender to make the transfer to the seller. The exemptions are statutory for transfers after 18 August 1989, and are subject to the various conditions as to Revenue approval of the arrangements and of the participants set out in *The Income Tax (Stock Lending) Regulations 1989 (SI 1989 No 1299)* as amended by *SI 1990 No 2552, SI 1992 No 572, SI 1993 No 2003, SI 1995 No 1283* and *SI 1995 No 3219*. Regulations may also provide for the exemptions to apply in cases where the arrangements under which the securities are transferred are for purposes other than enabling a contract for sale to be fulfilled (and see *SI 1995 No 3219* for such provision in relation to gilt-edged securities from 2 January 1996). *SI 1995 No 3219* also makes provision from that date for the exemptions to apply where the arrangements terminate on redemption of the securities. [*Sec 129; FA 1991, s 57; TCGA 1992, s 271(9); FA 1995, s 84*]. Before 19 August 1989, exemption was by extra-statutory concession (Revenue Pamphlet IR 1, B15), and that concession continues to apply where stock was lent before that date and the borrower has not returned stock of the same kind by that date. (Revenue Press Release 28 July 1989). See also 44.5(*f*) INTEREST RECEIVABLE, 74.26, 74.27 SCHEDULE D, CASE VI.

Cash collateral arrangements. Special provisions apply where, in relation to a stock lending arrangement within the above provisions entered into **on or after 1 May 1995**, the borrower of the stock pays to the lender an amount of 'cash collateral' by way of security for the performance of the obligation under the arrangement. Where the lender earns interest (paid without deduction of tax) on the whole of the cash collateral for the period he holds it, and pays to the borrower an amount of 'rebate interest' equal to the interest so earned by the lender (and identified as such separately from any other amount payable in connection with the arrangement):

(A)   the interest earned by the lender is treated as income of the borrower and not of the lender;

(B)   tax is not deductible from the payment of rebate interest;

(C)   no relief is available to the lender in respect of the payment of rebate interest; and

(D)   the rebate interest is not treated as income of the borrower.

This applies equally to a nominee acting for the borrower or lender, and, with appropriate modification, to a chain of arrangements. [*Sec 129A, 5A Sch; FA 1995, s 85, 19 Sch*].

Stock lending fees relating to investments eligible for relief under *Sec 592(2), 608(2)(a), 613(4), 614(3), 620(6)* or *643(2)* (pension scheme funds, etc., see 66.5, 66.13, 66.11 RETIREMENT SCHEMES, 59.6 PENSIONS, 65.13, 65.2 RETIREMENT ANNUITIES AND PERSONAL PENSION SCHEMES) are also eligible for relief under those *sections*, where the stock lending arrangement is entered into after 1 January 1996. [*FA 1996, s 157*].

Purchase of company's own shares from dealer. Where a company pays a sum to a 'dealer in securities' for the redemption, repayment or purchase of its own shares, or for the purchase of rights to acquire its own shares,

(i)   the sum so paid, including any element of distribution, is brought into account in computing the dealer's Schedule D, Case I or II profits,

(ii)   income tax under Schedule F is not chargeable, and no tax credit is available, in respect of any element of distribution in the payment,

(iii)   the normal exemption from corporation tax of UK company distributions [*Sec 208*] does not apply.

The above provisions do not include the redemption of fixed-rate preference shares (i.e. issued wholly for new consideration and carrying no right to conversion into, or to the acquisition of, any other shares or securities and carrying no right to dividends unless they are at a fixed amount or fixed rate and the dividends plus any redemption money represent no more than a reasonable commercial return on the consideration for which the shares were issued), or the redemption on terms settled before 6 April 1982 of other preference shares issued before that date, if (in either case) the shares were issued to and continuously held by the person from whom they are redeemed.

A '*dealer in securities*' for the above purposes is a person in computing whose profits under Schedule D, Case I or II the profit on sale of the shares would have been brought into account had he sold the shares other than to the company. [*Sec 95*].

Extra return on new issues of securities. Where

(*a*)   securities of a particular kind are issued (being the original issue of securities of that kind),

(*b*)   new securities of the same kind are issued subsequently, and after 18 March 1991,

(*c*)   a sum (the 'extra return') is payable by the issuer in respect of the new securities, to reflect the fact that interest is accruing on the old securities and calculated accordingly, and

(*d*)   the issue price of the new securities includes an element (separately identified or not) representing payment for the extra return,

the extra return is treated for all tax purposes (except, for new issues after 31 March 1996, corporation tax) as a payment of interest, but the issuer is not entitled to tax relief, either as a deduction in computing profits or otherwise as a deduction or set-off, for the payment. [*Sec 587A; FA 1991, 12 Sch 1, 5; FA 1996, 14 Sch 33*].

General. See also 3 ANTI-AVOIDANCE, including transactions in securities to obtain tax advantage [*Sec 703*], bond washing [*Sec 729*], dividend-stripping [*Sec 736*].

For share transactions entered into to secure tax advantages see 71.29 above and for transactions in dividend-stripping before the enactment of existing legislation see Tolley's Tax Cases.

71.82   **STOCK IN TRADE AND WORK IN PROGRESS**

For relief for increase in value, see 85 STOCK RELIEF.

Basis of valuation. The general rule is that stock is to be valued at the lower of cost and market value and this is so notwithstanding that accounts use, and accountancy principles permit, a different basis. Leading cases are *Minister of National Revenue v Anaconda American Brass Co PC 1955, 34 ATC 330* and *BSC Footwear v Ridgway HL 1971, 47 TC 495*. Market value held to be replacement price for a merchant (*Brigg Neumann & Co v CIR KB 1928, 12 TC 1191*) and retail price for a retailer in *BSC Footwear* above (Revenue prepared to take price net of any selling commission). Stock may be valued partly at cost and partly at market value where lower (*CIR v Cock Russell & Co KB 1949, 29 TC 387*). The base stock method is not permissible (*Patrick v Broadstone Mills CA 1953, 35 TC 44*) nor is 'LIFO' (*Anaconda American Brass* above). See also *Ryan v Asia Mill HL 1951, 32 TC 275*. The cost should include as a minimum the cost of materials and direct labour but the accounts treatment of overheads is normally accepted (*Duple Motor Bodies v Ostime HL 1961, 39 TC 537*).

For accepted accountancy practice see SSAP 9 (revised September 1988) (issued by Institute of Chartered Accountants in England and Wales), and for Revenue's view see Pamphlet IR 131, SP 3/90, 10 January 1990.

For the use of formulae in computing stock provisions and write-downs, see Revenue Tax Bulletin December 1994 p 184. Broadly, inspectors will accept formulae which reflect a realistic appraisal of future income from the particular category of stock and which result in the stock being included at a reasonable estimate of net realisable value. Where computations are accepted without enquiry, it is on the assumption that profits are arrived at in accordance with such principles. (Revenue Tax Bulletin December 1994 p 184).

For motor dealer stock valuations, see Revenue Tax Bulletin August 1994 p 156.

Changes in basis of valuation. Where the stock was found to be grossly undervalued it was held that an assessment to rectify the closing undervaluation must be reduced by the opening undervaluation to bring out the true profits (*Bombay IT Commr v Ahmedabad New Cotton Mills Co PC 1929, 9 ATC 574*). But where a company altered its method of dealing with accrued profits on long-term contracts and the closing work in progress in the year 1 accounts on the old basis was substantially below the opening figure in the year 2 accounts on the new basis, held, distinguishing *Ahmedabad*, the difference must be included in the year 2 profits (*Pearce v Woodall-Duckham Ltd CA 1978, 51 TC 271*). See also Revenue Pamphlet IR 131, SP 3/90, 10 January 1990.

Where there is a change in the basis of valuation in accounts for a period ending after 9 January 1990, the following practice is applied for tax purposes. If the bases of valuation both before and after the change are acceptable, the opening figure for the period of change must be the same as the closing figure for the preceding period. If the change is from an unacceptable basis to an acceptable one, the opening figure for the period of change must be arrived at on the same basis as the closing figure for that period, and liabilities for earlier years will be reviewed. However, if there is no question of fraudulent or negligent conduct, tax for past years will not be recovered on an amount greater than that resulting from the uplift of the opening figure for the year of change. (Revenue Pamphlet IR 131, SP 3/90, 10 January 1990). Previously (unless the taxpayer requests that the new basis be applied to earlier open years), where there was a change between acceptable bases of valuation, the opening figure was not adjusted to the previous year's closing figure, and the Revenue did not normally either seek to revise earlier years or admit 'error or mistake relief' claims (see 17.6 CLAIMS). See, however, *Woodall-Duckham Ltd* (above) as regards long-term contracts, and *Sec 104(7)* (60 POST-CESSATION ETC. RECEIPTS AND EXPENDITURE) as regards professional work-in-progress.

Long-term contracts. Revenue practice permits provision for a proportion of an overall loss, calculated either on a time basis or by reference to expenditure, provided that all contracts, profitable or otherwise, are similarly dealt with. Provisions for foreseeable further expenditure, representing obligations up to final delivery, are normally allowed where work substantially completed (which is likely to require at least 90% completion—see Revenue Inspector's Manual, IM 569) and financial outcome of contract reasonably certain. Reasonable provision for future expenditure under guarantees or warranties also normally allowed. But, beyond these limits, no provision is permitted for future loss, apportionable to remainder of contract. Payments on account should be credited when receivable. (Revenue Pamphlet IR 131, SP 3/90, 10 January 1990). See above for changes of basis. This practice does not apply to professional work in progress. In *Symons v Weeks and Others Ch D 1982, 56 TC 630*, it was held that progress payments under the long-term contracts of a firm of architects did not fall to be brought into account for tax before the relevant contract was completed, notwithstanding that they exceeded the figure brought in for work in progress, calculated on the correct principles of commercial accounting.

Goods sold subject to reservation of title. Where the supplier of goods reserves the title in them until payment is made (as a protection should the buyer become insolvent) and meanwhile the goods are treated by both parties for accountancy purposes as having been sold/purchased, the Revenue will follow the accounts treatment. (Revenue Pamphlet IR 131, B6).

Goods on consignment stock are normally treated as stock in the hands of the supplier until disposed of by the consignee (e.g. sale or return). (Revenue Pamphlet IR 131, B6).

For forward contracts, see 71.49 above.

Insurance recoveries. See 71.63 above.

Transactions not at market value. Where trading stock is disposed of otherwise than by way of trade, the realisable value is to be credited for tax purposes. This was established by *Sharkey v Wernher HL 1955, 36 TC 275* approving *Watson Bros v Hornby KB 1942, 24 TC 506*. It applies, *inter alia*, to goods taken out of stock by a retailer for his own use (see below). It was applied in *Petrotim Securities Ltd v Ayres CA 1963, 41 TC 389* to a disposal of shares at gross under-value as part of a tax avoidance scheme, but in *Ridge Securities Ltd v CIR Ch D 1963, 44 TC 373*, dealing with the other end of the same scheme, it was held that the same principle applied to acquisitions of trading stock otherwise than by way of trade, market price being substituted for the actual purchase price. But the principle is not applicable to sales or purchases by way of trade notwithstanding not at arm's length. Hence when a share dealing company acquired shares at substantial overvalue from an associated company, the claim by the Revenue for market value failed (*Craddock v Zevo Finance Co HL 1946, 27 TC 267*), and when a property dealing company acquired property from its controlling shareholder at substantial undervalue, its claim to substitute market value failed (*Jacgilden (Weston Hall) v Castle Ch D 1969, 45 TC 685*). See also *Skinner v Berry Head Lands Ch D 1970, 46 TC 377* and *Kilmorie (Aldridge) v Dickinson HL 1974, 50 TC 1*.

Appropriations to trading stock of assets held in another capacity are generally treated as a disposal and reacquisition at market value. Where a chargeable gain or allowable loss would otherwise arise for capital gains tax purposes under *TCGA 1992, s 161(1)*, the trader may elect for the market value to be reduced for these purposes by the amount of the chargeable gain (or increased by the amount of the allowable loss), the trading profits being computed accordingly and the appropriation being disregarded for capital gains tax purposes. The election must be made within, for 1996/97 and later years, twelve months after 31 January following the tax year in which ends the period of account in which the asset is appropriated, or for corporation tax purposes where self-assessment applies, two years after the end of the accounting period in which the asset is appropriated. Previously, the general six-year time limit at 17.4 CLAIMS applied. [*TCGA 1992, s 161(3)(3A); FA 1996, s 135, 21 Sch 36*].

Stock taken for own use or disposed of otherwise than by sale in the normal course of trade. The case of *Sharkey v Wernher HL 1955, 36 TC 275* established the principle that such a transfer should be treated as if it were a sale at market value. Inspectors have been authorised to take a reasonably broad view in applying this principle. The case is not considered to apply to

(*a*)   services rendered to the trader personally or to his household the cost of which should be disallowed under *Sec 74(b)*;

(*b*)   the value of meals provided for proprietors of hotels, boarding houses, restaurants etc. and members of their families, the cost of which should be disallowed under *Sec 74(b)*;

(*c*)   expenditure incurred by a trader on the construction of an asset which is to be used as a fixed asset in the trade.

(Revenue Pamphlet IR 131, A32).

What constitutes stock. Greyhounds kept by greyhound racing company not trading stock (*Abbot v Albion Greyhounds (Salford) KB 1945, 26 TC 390*). Payments by cigarette manufacturer for cropping trees (not owned by it) for leaves used in manufacture, held to be for materials (*Mohanlal Hargovind of Jubbulpore v IT Commr PC 1949, 28 ATC 287*). For payments for unworked minerals, sand and gravel, etc., (including tailings, etc.) by mines, quarries etc. see 71.70 above. For payments for oil by oil companies, see *Hughes v British Burmah Petroleum KB 1932, 17 TC 286; New Zealand Commr v Europa Oil (NZ) PC 1970, 49 ATC 282; Europa Oil (NZ) v New Zealand Commr PC, [1976] STC 37*. For timber see 71.71 above and *Coates v Holker Estates Co Ch D 1961, 40 TC 75.*

Valuation on discontinuance of business. Under *Sec 100* where a trade is discontinued (or so treated for tax purposes by *Sec 113* or *Sec 337(1)*) otherwise than on the death of a sole trader—

(1)   Where the stock is '*sold or transferred for valuable consideration*' to a person carrying on (or intending to carry on) a trade in the UK who can deduct the cost as an expense for tax purposes, the stock is normally to be valued at the amount realised on the sale (or the value of the consideration). However, for cessations of trade **after 28 November 1994**, where the two parties to the sale or transfer are connected persons (defined more broadly than by *Sec 839*—see *Sec 100(1F)*), arm's length value is to be taken instead. The connected persons rule does not apply in the case of certain sovereign debts, and neither rule applies to a transfer of farm animals where the anti-avoidance rules at 34.9 HERD BASIS apply. Where arm's length value exceeds both (i) actual sale price and (ii) acquisition value (broadly, the amount that would have been deductible in respect of the stock had it been sold in the course of trade immediately before cessation), connected persons may jointly elect to substitute the greater (taking all the stock sold or transferred together) of (i) and (ii), the election to be made within two years after the end of the chargeable period in which cessation occurs. The stock valuation determined under these provisions applies both to transferor and transferee.

See *Moore v Mackenzie Ch D 1971, 48 TC 196*. If both trades are within the jurisdiction of the same body of General Commissioners appeals are dealt with by them, otherwise by Special Commissioners [*Sec 102(1); FA 1996, 22 Sch 11*] and see *Bradshaw v Blunden (No 2) Ch D 1960, 39 TC 73; CIR v Barr (No 2) CS 1955, 36 TC 455.*

Sec 100 not applicable to woodlands managed on a commercial basis (*Coates v Holker Estates* above). For application to 'hire-purchase debts' see *Lions Ltd v Gosford Furnishing Co Ltd & CIR CS 1961, 40 TC 256.*

(2)   In all other cases stock is to be valued at the price it would have realised if sold in open market at date of discontinuance.

This section applies to all kinds of property real or personal sold in usual course of the trade, materials used in manufacture etc. and services etc., which would be treated as work in progress if the trade were a profession (see below).

[*Sec 100; FA 1995, s 141*].

On the death of a sole trader, trading stock is valued at cost, although if the executors continue trading, or if the business passes direct to a beneficiary, the opening stock may be brought in at market value. (Revenue Inspector's Manual, IM 571).

Similar provisions are applied, *mutatis mutandis*, to work in progress at the date when a profession or vocation is, or is treated as, discontinued. But taxpayer may elect that for computing his profits to the date of cessation w.i.p. shall be taken at cost, and that any realised excess over cost shall be treated as POST-CESSATION ETC. RECEIPTS (60) under *Sec 103*. For 1996/97 and later years, the election must be made within twelve months after 31

January following the year of assessment of cessation (or, for corporation tax where self-assessment applies, within two years after the end of the accounting period of cessation). Previously, the election had to be made within twelve months after the discontinuance. [*Sec 101; FA 1996, s 135, 21 Sch 3*].

See ICAEW Technical Release TAX 7/95, 15 February 1995, for a guidance note on the taxation implications of various treatments of transfers of work in progress and debtors on incorporation of a professional partnership.

71.83   SUBSCRIPTIONS, ETC. INCLUDING TRADE ASSOCIATION CONTRIBUTIONS

Gifts to charitable bodies are deductible under general rules of business expenses (i.e. requiring the outlay to be wholly and exclusively for purposes of the trade etc.) notwithstanding *Sec 577(8)* (see 71.54 above). [*Sec 577(9)*]. Concessionally, other gifts are allowed provided that they are (i) wholly and exclusively for the purposes of the business, (ii) made for the benefit of a body or association established for educational, cultural, religious, recreational or benevolent purposes which is local to the donor's business activities and not restricted to persons connected with the donor and (iii) reasonably small in relation to the sale of the donor's business. (Revenue Pamphlet IR 1, B7). In *Bourne & Hollingsworth v Ogden KB 1929, 14 TC 349* an abnormally large donation was disallowed. For donations of part of cost of ticket in football pools and lotteries, see 71.30 above. See 15.6 CHARITIES for three year covenants to charities, and see 15.7, 15.8 CHARITIES as regards certain other donations by individuals. See Tolley's Corporation Tax as regards qualifying donations by companies to charities.

Trade and professional associations. Ordinary annual subscriptions to local associations, including Chambers of Commerce, are normally allowed. Subscriptions to larger associations are allowable, and receipts therefrom assessable, if the association has entered into an arrangement with the Revenue under which it is assessed on any surplus of receipts over allowable expenditure (the association should be asked). Most associations enter into the arrangement but if not the allowance is restricted to the proportion applied by the association for purposes such that it would have been allowed if so applied by the subscriber (*Lochgelly Iron & Coal Co Ltd v Crawford CS 1913, 6 TC 267*). For other cases see Tolley's Tax Cases. Subscriptions to the Economic League are not allowed (*Joseph L Thompson & Sons Ltd v Chamberlain Ch D 1962, 40 TC 657*).

Contributions to mutual insurance associations are allowable even though used to create a reserve fund (*Thomas v Richard Evans & Co Ltd HL 1927, 11 TC 790*). See also 50 MUTUAL TRADING.

Local enterprise agencies. Expenditure incurred in making any contribution (whether in cash or kind) before 1 April 2000 to an 'approved local enterprise agency' is allowable if not otherwise deductible. There is no allowance if any related benefit is receivable by the contributor, or any person connected with him (see 20 CONNECTED PERSONS), from the agency or from any other person, and any relief already given will be recovered by a charge under Schedule D, Cases I or II or VI to the extent of the benefit.

'*Approved local enterprise agency*' is any body approved by the Secretary of State who is satisfied (i) its sole objective is the promotion or encouragement of industrial and commercial activity or enterprise in a particular area of the UK and with particular reference to small businesses, or (ii) one of its principal objectives is as in (i) *and* it maintains a separate fund for that objective. The agency must be precluded from making dividends, gifts etc. to its members or managers. Approval may be conditional and may be withdrawn retrospectively. [*Sec 79; FA 1990, s 75; FA 1994, s 145(1)*].

Training and enterprise councils, local enterprise companies and business link organisations. Identical provisions to those described above in relation to local enterprise agencies apply to a contribution after 31 March 1990 and before 1 April 2000 to a training and enterprise council which has an agreement with the Secretary of State to act as such, or to a local enterprise company which has an agreement with the Scottish Development Agency, the Highlands and Islands Development Board, Scottish Enterprise or Highlands and Islands Enterprise to act as such, or after 29 November 1993 and before 1 April 2000 to a business link organisation authorised by the Secretary of State to use a service mark designated for these purposes. [*Sec 79A; FA 1990, s 76; FA 1994, s 145*].

71.84 SUBSIDIES, GRANTS ETC.

Enterprise allowance, paid to assist unemployed people in setting up their own businesses, is paid under *Employment and Training Act 1973, s 2(2)(d)* or *Enterprise and New Towns (Scotland) Act 1990, s 2(4)(c)* (or NI equivalent). Payments are charged to tax under Schedule D, Case VI. This treatment does not, however, prevent the payments being treated as earned income or as 'relevant earnings' for retirement annuity purposes (see 65.12 RETIREMENT ANNUITIES AND PERSONAL PENSION SCHEMES). They may also continue to give rise to liability to Class 4 national insurance contributions. [*Sec 127, 29 Sch 14*]. From 1991/92, the responsibility for payment of such allowances was transferred to the Training and Enterprise Councils (in Scotland, Local Enterprise Councils). They are now more commonly known as **business start up allowances**, but provided that they retain the essential characteristics of enterprise allowances (in particular that the recipient is unemployed or working notice and that the allowance is a flat rate weekly amount), they are in practice treated in the same way for tax purposes. (Revenue Inspector's Manual, IM 392).

Farming support payments. See 71.56 above.

Fishing grants. For the tax treatment of decommissioning grants, laying-up grants, exploratory voyage grants and joint venture grants under *SI 1983 No 1883*, see Revenue Inspector's Manual, IM 2363.

Football pools promoters. Certain contributions to the Football Trust 1990 by pools promoters for football ground improvements are allowable as deductions in the pools promoter's trade, as are certain payments by them to other trustees established mainly for the support of athletic sports or games (but with power to support the arts). [*FA 1990, s 126; FA 1991, s 121*]. See also 10.2 (ii) CAPITAL ALLOWANCES..

Industry Act 1972, s 7. See above and 62.1 REGIONAL DEVELOPMENT GRANTS for 'interest relief' and other similar grants.

Regional development grants. Grants under *Industry Act 1972, ss 7, 8* (and similar NI legislation) and certain other NI payments, not made towards specified capital expenditure or compensation for loss of capital assets, are trading receipts. [*Sec 93*]. An earlier interest relief grant under the *Act* was held to be assessable in *Burman v Thorn Domestic Appliances (Electrical) Ltd Ch D 1981, 55 TC 493*, as was a similar grant undifferentiated between revenue and capital in *Ryan v Crabtree Denims Ltd Ch D 1987, 60 TC 183*, applying *Gayjon Processes Ltd* (below) and distinguishing *Seaham Harbour* (below). Grants under *Industrial Development Act 1982, Part II* to traders, etc. or investment companies are exempt from income tax. [*Sec 92*]. See also 62 REGIONAL DEVELOPMENT GRANTS.

Research grant by trading company to medical practitioner held assessable (*Duff v Williamson Ch D 1973, 49 TC 1*).

Temporary employment subsidy was paid under *Employment and Training Act 1973, s 5* (as amended by *Employment Protection Act 1975, 14 Sch 2*) as a flat-rate weekly payment or (in the textile, clothing and footwear industries) by way of reimbursement of payments made to workers on short time.

Such payments were held to be taxable as trading receipts in *Poulter v Gayjon Processes Ltd Ch D 1985, 58 TC 350*, distinguishing the grants made by the Unemployment Grants Committee in *Seaham Harbour* (below).

Unemployment grants. Subsidy to dock company (from Unemployment Grants Committee) for extension work to keep men in employment held, although grant made in terms of interest, not a 'trade receipt' for tax purposes (*Seaham Harbour v Crook HL 1931, 16 TC 333*).

See 10.2(ii) CAPITAL ALLOWANCES for effect thereon of grants and subsidies.

See 67.7 RETURNS as regards returns of certain grant and subsidy payments.

71.85   TAXATION

Income tax and corporation tax are not deductible in computing profits (cf. *Allen v Farquharson Bros & Co KB 1932, 17 TC 59*). Overseas taxes may be subject to DOUBLE TAX RELIEF (25) but any such tax not relieved by credit on overseas income included in the profits may be deducted [*Sec 811*] but not on UK income, e.g. profits of UK branches (*CIR v Dowdall O'Mahoney & Co Ltd HL 1952, 33 TC 259*).

In *Harrods (Buenos Aires) v Taylor-Gooby CA 1964, 41 TC 450* an annual capital tax imposed by the Argentine on foreign companies trading there was not a tax on the profits and was allowable.

For deduction of part of Class 4 National Insurance contributions from total income, see 1.9 ALLOWANCES AND RATES.

For taxation appeals see 71.68 above. For VAT see 71.91 below.

71.86   TIED PETROL STATIONS, ETC.

For tied licensed premises see 71.45 above.

'Exclusivity payments' by petrol company to retailers undertaking to sell only its goods were allowed in computing its profits in *Bolam v Regent Oil Co Ltd Ch D 1956, 37 TC 56* (payments for repairs carried out by retailer), *BP Australia Ltd PC 1965, 44 ATC 312* (lump sums paid for sales promotion) and *Mobil Oil Australia Ltd PC 1965, 44 ATC 323*, but held capital in *Strick v Regent Oil HL 1965, 43 TC 1* where the payment took the form of a premium to the retailer for a lease of his premises (immediately sub-let to him).

In the hands of the retailer exclusivity payments were held capital when for capital expenditure incurred by him (*CIR v Coia CS 1959, 38 TC 334; McLaren v Needham Ch D 1960, 39 TC 37; Walter W Saunders Ltd v Dixon Ch D 1962, 40 TC 329*) but revenue when for repairs, etc. (*McLaren v Needham above*) or sales promotion (*Evans v Wheatley Ch D 1958, 38 TC 216*).

For a summary of the Revenue view of such arrangements, see Revenue Tax Bulletin August 1993 p 88.

71.87   TRAINING

Costs incurred by an employer in respect of employee training are generally allowable as a trade expense under *Sec 74(a)* (see 71.40 above). See 71.53 above as regards certain other allowable employee training costs and 71.83 above as regards contributions to training and enterprise councils. A broader relief is introduced for trainees undergoing certain courses for 1992/93 and subsequent years of assessment. See also 75.42 SCHEDULE E.

In general, the expenses of a training course undertaken by a self-employed person are allowed as a trade deduction under general principles only where the training is undertaken for the purposes of the trade and relates to the updating of existing expertise rather than the acquisition of new skills.

Where, **after 5 April 1992**, a UK-resident individual pays fees in connection with his own training under a 'qualifying course of vocational training', he is entitled to a deduction from or set-off against his income of the year of the amount so paid, provided that

(*a*) at the time of the payment, he has not received, and is not entitled to receive, public financial assistance (as defined by Treasury order, see *SI 1992 No 734; SI 1993 No 1074; SI 1995 No 3274*) in relation to the course, and

(*b*) he is not otherwise entitled to tax relief in respect of the payment,

and, in relation to payments made *after 31 December 1993*, provided also that

(*c*) at the time the payment is made, the individual is aged 16 or over, and, if under 19, he is not being provided with full-time education at a school (including any institution at which such education is provided to persons at least some of whom are under 16), and

(*d*) he undertakes the course neither wholly nor mainly for recreational purposes or as a leisure activity.

Subject to conditions specified by the Board in regulations (see *SI 1992 No 746; SI 1993 Nos 1082, 3118*), basic rate relief may be obtained by deduction of basic rate tax from the payment, with the recipient recovering the amount deducted from the Board on a claim. The Board consider that where a payment *may* be made under deduction of basic rate tax, basic rate relief can *only* be obtained by deduction. Where relief may not be obtained by deduction, and for higher rate purposes, relief must be claimed by the individual. The tax deducted from payments is not clawed back where the individual is liable only at the lower rate of income tax or has no income tax liability.

The Treasury may make regulations for the withdrawal of relief in whole or in part in prescribed circumstances, and requiring either the individual or the recipient of the fees (as the regulations may prescribe) to account for the tax from which relief was given. The first such regulations (*SI 1992 No 734*) deal with payments refunded to the trainee by the training provider, and with awards by the training provider to the trainee by virtue merely of the course being undertaken, completed or completed successfully.

A '*qualifying course of vocational training*' is any programme of activity capable of counting towards a qualification accredited as a National or Scottish Vocational Qualification by the appropriate Council, except, in relation to payments made before 1 January 1994, a qualification at level 5, the highest of the levels defined by those Councils. (Level 5 extends to senior managerial and professional skills, including degree-standard qualifications.)

In relation to payments made *after 5 May 1996* by individuals *aged 30 or over* at the time the payment is made, a '*qualifying course of vocational training*' also includes any course of training, whether or not leading towards a qualification as above, which

(i) is designed to impart or improve skills or knowledge relevant to, and intended to be used in the course of, gainful employment (including self-employment) of any description,

(ii) is devoted entirely to the teaching and/or practical application within the UK of such skills or knowledge (treating time devoted to study in connection with the course as such practical application),

(iii) requires participation on a full-time, or substantially full-time, basis, and

(iv) extends for a period consisting of or including four *consecutive* weeks but does not last more than one year.

The Revenue have appropriate regulatory powers. Penalties under *TMA s 98* apply for failure to furnish information etc. required under such regulations, and various assessment, interest and penalty provisions apply in relation to invalid claims by the recipients of fees for repayment of tax deducted therefrom. [*FA 1991, ss 32, 33; FA 1994, s 84; FA 1996, ss 129, 144, 18 Sch 14, 17(1)–(4)(8)*].

A Training Pack is available from Inland Revenue, FICO (Savings and Investment) (Vocational Training Unit), St John's House, Merton Road, Bootle, Merseyside L69 9BB, containing details of the scheme and the appropriate Forms for registration of the training provider (VTR 21), for a declaration of entitlement by the trainee (VTR 1), and for annual and interim claims by the provider for repayment of tax deducted from fees (VTR 14, VTR 10).

The Revenue have published a Code of Practice (No 4, published July 1993) setting out their standards for the carrying out of inspections of tax relief at source schemes operated by financial intermediaries.

The Inland Revenue Financial Intermediaries and Claims Office may be contacted in relation to vocational training relief on 0151–472 6109 as regards repayments or 0151–472 6159 for technical advice.

See generally Revenue Leaflet IR 119.

71.88   **TRAVELLING AND SUBSISTENCE EXPENSES**

The cost of travelling in the course of the business activities is allowable but not that of travelling between home and the place at or from which the business is conducted. For this see *Newsom v Robertson CA 1952, 33 TC 452* in which the expenses of a barrister between his home and his chambers were refused and contrast *Horton v Young CA 1971, 47 TC 60* in which a 'self-employed' bricklayer was allowed his expenses between his home and the sites at which he worked as, on the evidence, his business was conducted from his home. Compare the position for employees—see 75.43 SCHEDULE E. Any expenses of an employment ancillary to a profession not allowable in the Schedule E assessment may not be deducted in computing the profits of the profession (*Mitchell & Edon v Ross HL 1961, 40 TC 11*).

The 'dual purpose rule' (see 71.40 above) entails the disallowance of *all* travelling expenses with a material private purpose, i.e. the part attributable to business purposes is not allowable. Thus the expenses of a solicitor in travelling abroad partly for a holiday and partly to attend professional conferences were disallowed in *Bowden v Russell & Russell Ch D 1965, 42 TC 301* (but the expenses of an accountant to attend a professional conference abroad were allowed in *Edwards v Warmsley, Henshall & Co Ch D 1967, 44 TC 431*). Similarly the expenses of a dentist in travelling between his home and surgery were disallowed even though he collected dentures from a laboratory on the way (*Sargent v Barnes Ch D 1978, 52 TC 335*). The expenses of a farmer in visiting Australia with a view to farming there were held inadmissible (*Sargent v Eayrs Ch D 1972, 48 TC 573*). In practice, the Revenue normally allow a fair proportion of overseas trips partly for holidays if there was a genuine business purpose. (In *Bowden v Russell* above, the Revenue considered the business purpose too remote to justify apportionment.) Car expenses are also apportioned if used partly for private purposes. Parking and other motoring fines are normally disallowed in their entirety either under the 'dual purpose rule' (see 71.40 above) or under the general principles applicable to allowable trading deductions (see *CIR v Alexander von Glehn & Co Ltd CA 1920, 12 TC 232*, in which penalties for breach of wartime regulations were disallowed), although reimbursement of employee normally allowable (but see 75.7 SCHEDULE E as regards employee's liability).

Similar principles apply to hotel, etc. expenses incurred when travelling for business purposes. The reasonable cost of overnight stays is allowed but not the cost of lunches

(*Caillebotte v Quinn Ch D 1975, 50 TC 222*). In practice, reasonable costs of evening meals and breakfast taken in conjunction with overnight accommodation are similarly allowed, and this treatment is extended to such costs incurred by long distance lorry drivers who sleep in their cabs. (Revenue Tax Bulletin August 1993 p 88). Normally there is no restriction for 'home saving' (cf. 75.43 SCHEDULE E). Nor will there be any disallowance of personal living expenses (i.e. accommodation, food and drink of self but not family or other dependants) incurred on longer business trips abroad. (Revenue Pamphlet IR 131, A16).

See 51.12 NON-RESIDENTS AND OTHER OVERSEAS MATTERS for extended relief for travelling expenses in overseas trade.

71.89   UNCLAIMED BALANCES

for which firm liable to account, held not assessable although distributed to partners (*Morley v Tattersall CA 1938, 22 TC 51*). But such balances held by pawnbroker assessable when claimants' rights expire (*Jay's, the Jewellers v CIR KB 1947, 29 TC 274*), and deposits on garments not collected held trade receipts assessable when received (*Elson v Prices Tailors Ch D 1962, 40 TC 671*). See 71.44 above for releases of debts owing.

71.90   UNREMITTABLE RECEIPTS, DEBTS ETC.

Where a trade is carried on partly in the UK and partly overseas, so that liability to tax arises on all trade profits, the following amounts will be included in profits, with no relief being available under *Sec 584* (unremittable overseas income, see 51.14 NON-RESIDENTS AND OTHER OVERSEAS MATTERS) or *Sec 74(j)* (bad and doubtful debts, see 71.44 above):

(*a*)   amounts received overseas but not remittable to the UK;

(*b*)   amounts owed to the trader overseas which temporarily cannot be paid; and

(*c*)   amounts owed to the trader overseas which, even when paid, will not be remittable to the UK.

By concession, where any of (*a*)–(*c*) above applies solely as a result of local foreign exchange control restrictions, and continues to apply twelve months after the end of the accounting period in which the amount concerned was received or the debt arose, relief may be claimed, provided that:

(i)   the assessment in question is not final and conclusive;

(ii)   all reasonable endeavours have been made to secure payment and remittance to the UK of funds;

(iii)   receipts or debts have not been used to finance expenditure or investment outside the UK;

(iv)   (in the case of debts) the debt cannot be discharged in the UK; and

(v)   the taxpayer agrees to the withdrawal of relief by an addition to profits for the period in which the concessional relief ceases to be available (see below).

As regards (iii) above, debts are regarded as having been used to finance expenditure outside the UK where they are used, or might have been used, to meet expenditure or guarantee a liability incurred in the same territory by the trader or by a person with whom the trader has a special relationship, or where they remain unpaid by reason of such a relationship.

Relief for debts is available only to the extent that they are not insured. Relief is given by a deduction from trading profits for the accounting period in which the receipt or debt is recognised as unremittable. Any excess may be carried forward against trading profits of subsequent periods.

Relief is withdrawn where (*a*)–(*c*) or (iii) above cease to apply, or the receipt or debt is otherwise applied outside the UK or exchanged for or discharged in a remittable currency.

This concession also applies to unremittable bank interest in appropriate circumstances.

(Revenue Pamphlet IR 1, B38).

71.91   **VALUE ADDED TAX**

For treatment in computing business profits see Revenue Pamphlet IR 131 (October 1995 Supplement), B1.

In general, if the trader is not a 'taxable person' for VAT his expenditure *inclusive* of any VAT on it, is treated in the ordinary way.

If he is a taxable person, the receipts and expenses (including capital items) to be taken into account will generally be exclusive of VAT but if he suffers VAT on any expenditure which does not rank as 'input tax' (e.g. entertaining expenses and certain expenditure relating to motor cars) that expenditure inclusive of VAT will be taken into account for income tax, etc. purposes (although any such inclusive sum in respect of entertaining expenses may also be disallowed for income tax purposes). Any allowance for bad debts (see 71.44 above) is inclusive of any VAT not recovered but accounted for to HM Customs and Excise. (*VATA 1994, s 36* and regulations made thereunder now provide for VAT on bad debts to be refunded in certain cases.)

VAT interest, penalties and surcharge are not allowed as a deduction for income tax purposes, and repayment supplement is disregarded for income tax purposes. [*Sec 827*].

VAT refunds. See Revenue Tax Bulletin October 1995 pp 255, 256 for the timing of the recognition, for the purposes of computing trading profits, of certain VAT refunds (specifically, of refunds to opticians following acceptance by Customs and Excise that they had incorrectly required VAT to be charged on certain outputs).

See, generally, Tolley's Value Added Tax.

71.92   **WASTE DISPOSAL**

Expenditure on purchase and reclamation of tipping sites by a company carrying on a waste disposal business was held to be capital in *Rolfe v Wimpey Waste Management Ltd CA 1989, 62 TC 399*, as were instalment payments for the right to deposit waste material in *CIR v Adam CS 1928, 14 TC 34*. See also *McClure v Petre Ch D 1988, 61 TC 226*, where the receipt of sum for licence to tip soil was also held to be capital.

Site preparation and restoration expenditure. A person making a 'site restoration payment' **after 5 April 1989**, in the course of carrying on a trade, may deduct the payment in computing profits for the period of account (i.e. a period for which an account is made up) in which the payment is made. A payment will not qualify for relief to the extent that it represents either expenditure allowed as a trading deduction for prior periods or capital expenditure qualifying for capital allowances.

A '*site restoration payment*' is a payment made

(*a*)   in connection with the restoration of a site (or part thereof), and

(*b*)   in order to comply with any condition of a 'relevant licence', or any condition imposed on the grant of planning permission to use the site for the carrying out of 'waste disposal activities', or any term of a 'relevant agreement'.

'*Waste disposal activities*' are the collection, treatment, conversion and final depositing of waste materials, or any of those activities.

A 'relevant licence' is a disposal licence under the *Control of Pollution Act 1974, Pt I* (or NI equivalent), a waste management licence under the *Environmental Protection Act 1990, Pt II* (or NI equivalent) or (for trades commenced after 31 March 1993) an authorisation for the disposal of radioactive waste or a nuclear site licence.

A 'relevant agreement' is an agreement under *Town and Country Planning Act 1971, s 52, Town and Country Planning (Scotland) Act 1972, s 50* or *Town and Country Planning Act 1990, s 106* (or NI equivalent) regulating the development or use of land. [*Sec 91A; FA 1990, s 78; FA 1993, s 110(1)(3)*].

For periods of account ending **after 5 April 1989**, a deduction is available of the 'allowable amount' where a person incurs, in the course of a trade, 'site preparation expenditure' in relation to a 'waste disposal site', and, at the time when he first deposits waste materials on the site in question, he holds a relevant licence (as above) which is in force. A claim for the relief to apply will have to be made in the prescribed manner and the Board may also require plans and other documents to verify it. For trades commenced after 31 March 1993, expenditure incurred for trade purposes by a person about to carry on the trade is for this purpose treated as incurred on the first day of trading.

A 'waste disposal site' is a site used (or to be used) for the disposal of waste materials by their deposit on the site, and in relation to such a site, 'site preparation expenditure' is expenditure on preparing the site for the deposit of waste materials (and may include expenditure on earthworks). This includes expenditure incurred before the relevant licence is granted, and in particular expenses associated with obtaining the licence itself. (Revenue Tax Bulletin November 1992 p 45).

In relation to the period of account in question, the 'allowable amount' of the expenditure is

$$(A - B) \times \frac{C}{C + D}$$

where 'A' is the site preparation expenditure incurred by the person at any time before the beginning of, or during, the period in question in relation to the site in question and in the course of carrying on the trade. It does not include any expenditure which either has been allowed as a trading deduction for a prior period or is capital expenditure qualifying for capital allowances. In addition, where any expenditure which would otherwise be included in 'A' was incurred before 6 April 1989, 'A' is reduced by an amount determined by

$$E \times \frac{F}{F + G}$$

where 'E' is so much of the initial expenditure (that is, the expenditure which would otherwise be included in 'A') as was incurred before 6 April 1989,

'F' is the volume of waste materials deposited on the site in question before 6 April 1989,

'G' is the capacity (expressed in volume) of the site in question not used up for the deposit of waste materials immediately before 6 April 1989;

'B' is the amount (or aggregate of amounts) allowed as a trading deduction under this provision in prior periods and as regards expenditure incurred in relation to the site in question;

'C' is the volume of waste materials deposited on the site in question during the period in question, excluding any deposited before 6 April 1989;

71.93 Schedule D, Cases I and II—Profits of Trades etc.

'D' is the capacity of the site in question not used up for the deposit of waste materials as at the end of the period in question.

[*Sec 91B; FA 1990, s 78; FA 1993, s 110(2)(3)*].

71.93 WOODLANDS

See 69.2, 69.3 SCHEDULE B as regards the election for Schedule D treatment of profits arising from the commercial occupation of woodlands, and for the transitional provisions following its abolition after 14 March 1988.

With effect from 29 November 1994, short rotation coppice cultivation is treated for tax purposes as farming and not as forestry, so that UK land under such cultivation is not woodlands. [*FA 1995, s 154*]. See 71.56 above.

71.94 GENERAL EXAMPLE

A UK trader commences trading on 1 October 1995. His profit and loss account for the year to 30 September 1996 is

	£	£
Sales		110,000
Deduct Purchases	75,000	
Less Stock and work in progress at 30.9.96	15,000	
		60,000
Gross profit		50,000
Deduct		
Salaries (all paid by 30.6.97)	15,600	
Rent and rates	2,400	
Telephone	500	
Heat and light	650	
Depreciation	1,000	
Motor expenses	2,700	
Entertainment	600	
Bank interest	900	
Hire-purchase interest	250	
Repairs and renewals	1,000	
Accountant's fee	500	
Bad debts	200	
Sundries	700	
		27,000
Net profit		23,000
Gain on sale of fixed asset		300
Rent received		500
Bank interest received (net)		150
Profit		£23,950

Further Information

(i) Rent and rates. £200 of the rates bill relates to the period from 1.6.95 to 30.9.95.

(ii) Telephone. Telephone bills for the trader's private telephone amount to £150. It is estimated that 40% of these calls are for business purposes.

(iii) Motor expenses. All the motor expenses are in respect of the proprietor's car. 40% of the annual mileage relates to private use and home to business use.

(iv)	Entertainment	Staff	£ 100
		UK customers	450
		Overseas customers	50
			£600

(v)   Hire-purchase interest. This is in respect of the owner's car.
(vi)   Repairs and renewals. There is an improvement element of 20% included.
(vii)   Bad debts. This is a specific write-off.
(viii)   Sundries. Included is £250 being the cost of obtaining a bank loan to finance business expenditure, £200 for agent's fees in obtaining a patent for trading purposes and a £50 bribe to a local official.
(ix)   Other. The proprietor obtained goods for his own use from the business costing £400 (retail value £500) without payment.
(x)   Capital allowances for the year to 30 September 1996 amount to £1,520.

Schedule D, Case I Computation — Year to 30.9.96

	£	£
Profit per the accounts		23,950
Add		
Repairs — improvement element		200
Hire-purchase interest (40% private)		100
Entertainment note (*e*)		500
Motor expenses (40% private)		1,080
Depreciation		1,000
Telephone (60% × £150)		90
Goods for own use		500
Illegal payment note (*f*)		50
		27,470
Deduct		
Bank interest received — Taxed income	150	
Rent received — Schedule A	500	
Gain on sale of fixed asset	300	
		950
		26,520
Less Capital allowances		1,520
Schedule D, Case I profit		£25,000

Notes

(*a*)   Costs of obtaining loan finance are specifically allowable (see 71.69 above).

(*b*)   For businesses commenced after 5 April 1994, capital allowances are deductible as a trading expense (see 10.1 CAPITAL ALLOWANCES).

(*c*)   The adjusted profit of £25,000 would be subject to the commencement provisions for assessment purposes (see 71.12 above).

(*d*)   Pre-trading expenses are treated as incurred on the day on which trade is commenced if they are incurred within seven years of the commencement and would have been allowable if incurred after commencement. Different rules applied for trades commenced before 6 April 1995. See 71.75 above.

(*e*)   All entertainment expenses, other than staff entertaining, are non-deductible (see 71.54 above).

(*f*)   Expenditure incurred after 10 June 1993 in making a payment which itself constitutes the commission of a criminal offence is specifically disallowed. This includes bribes which are contrary to the Prevention of Corruption Acts. See 71.62 above.

72   Schedule D, Case III—Interest Receivable etc.

[Secs 18, 64, 66, 67]

Cross-references. See generally under 23 DEDUCTION OF TAX AT SOURCE; 33 GOVERNMENT STOCKS; 44 INTEREST RECEIVABLE; 71.50 SCHEDULE D, CASES I AND II re copyrights and royalties.

72.1   Case III of Schedule D is principally concerned with the taxation of interest and annual payments. There are, however, significant changes following the abolition of SCHEDULE C (70), and the introduction of a new corporation tax regime for the taxation of most profits and gains from securities (by reference to 'loan relationships', for which see Tolley's Corporation Tax under Gilts and Bonds). Both of these changes take effect for 1996/97 and subsequent years and for accounting periods ending after 31 March 1996, and the charges under Cases III to V of Schedule D are accordingly now defined separately for income tax and for corporation tax purposes.

For corporation tax, Case III now includes all profits and gains from loan relationships, any annuity or other annual payment (not chargeable under Schedule A) payable in or out of the UK, and at whatever intervals, in respect of anything other than a loan relationship and any discount arising other than in respect of a loan relationship. Thus, for corporation tax purposes, Case IV is subsumed into Case III, and Case V is redefined to exclude profits or gains from loan relationships.

For income tax purposes, the abolition of Schedule C has led to the inclusion under Case III of income from the UK (and NI) public revenue previously dealt with under that Schedule. Case IV is similarly extended to include all income from securities out of the UK (including foreign public revenue income previously within Schedule C), and Cases IV and V now include income realised by disposal of coupons on overseas holdings (again previously within Schedule C). Thus, for **1996/97 and subsequent years**, income tax is charged under Schedule D, Case III in respect of:

(i)   any interest of money, and any annuity or other annual payment (not chargeable under SCHEDULE A (68)), either as a charge on or reservation out of property of the payer or as a personal contractual debt or obligation, whether payable in or out of the UK and at whatever intervals received and payable;

(ii)   all discounts; and

(iii)   income from securities payable out of UK (or NI) public revenue.

Previously, (iii) comprised all income from securities bearing interest payable out of the public revenue unless within Schedule C.

[Sec 18(3)–(3E); FA 1996, 7 Sch 4(2)(3), 14 Sch 5].

The following items are additionally brought within the charge under Case III.

(a)   Profits and losses from discounts on securities. *[FA 1996, 13 Sch].* See 72.2 below. (These provisions apply for 1996/97 and subsequent years. Previously, there was a Case III (or Case IV) charge on disposal of 'deep discount', 'deep gain' or 'qualifying convertible' securities (see 44.5–44.8 INTEREST RECEIVABLE).)

(b)   Share or loan interest paid by a registered industrial and provident society. *[Sec 486(4)].*

(c)   Borrowings against life policies in certain circumstances. *[Sec 554].* See 45.4(h) LIFE ASSURANCE POLICIES.

(d)   Certain mining rents and royalties and electric line wayleaves. *[Secs 119(2), 120(3)].* See 23.14 DEDUCTION OF TAX AT SOURCE.

72.2 Schedule D, Case III—Interest Receivable etc.

For general exemptions from charge to tax, see EXEMPT INCOME (29). The following items are additionally excluded from Case III.

(1)   Distributions within SCHEDULE F (76). [*Sec 20(2)*].

(2)   Certain annual payments by individuals. [*Sec 347A*]. See 1.8(i) ALLOWANCES AND TAX RATES.

(3)   The capital portion of purchased life annuity payments. [*Sec 656*]. See 23.11(*c*) DEDUCTION OF TAX AT SOURCE.

(4)   Certain payments to redundant steel workers, see 75.32 SCHEDULE E.

(5)   Certain payments to theatrical angels, see 74.2 SCHEDULE D, CASE VI.

Various of the above items are payable after deduction of tax by the payer under *Secs 348, 349*. See under 23 DEDUCTION OF TAX AT SOURCE for the provisions relating to such deductions and for annuities and annual payments etc. See also under 43 INTEREST PAYABLE.

For 1996/97 and subsequent years, most types of Case III income, including interest and discounts, are chargeable to income tax at the lower rate (to the extent that they do not fall within an individual's higher rate band). See 1.8(iii) ALLOWANCES AND TAX RATES for the full provisions.

Chargeability under Case III depends upon there being a UK source. The Revenue regard the most important factors supporting the existence of a UK source of interest to be (i) the debtor's residence (i.e. the place in which the debt will be enforced), (ii) the source from which interest is paid, (iii) where the interest is paid, and (iv) the nature and location of the security for the debt. If all of these are located in the UK, it is likely that the interest will have a UK source. (Revenue Tax Bulletin November 1993 p 100).

Income from overseas securities and possessions is assessable under SCHEDULE D, CASES IV AND V (73).

72.2   DISCOUNTS ON SECURITIES

Charge to and relief from tax for profits and losses realised on discounts on securities. For any year of assessment **1996/97 onwards** in which a person transfers a 'relevant discounted security', or becomes entitled, as holder, to any payment on its redemption, and where the amount payable on the transfer or redemption exceeds the amount he paid for its acquisition, he is chargeable under Schedule D, Case III (or Case IV as appropriate) on the amount of the excess net of any 'relevant costs'. A loss arising disregarding relevant costs (together with any such costs) may be relieved against income of the year of assessment of the transfer or redemption. Relief must be claimed by 31 January next but one following the end of that year. '*Relevant costs*' are those incurred by that person in connection with the acquisition and the transfer or redemption of the security.

'Transfer' for these purposes means transfer by way of sale, exchange, gift or otherwise. A transfer or acquisition under an agreement is treated as taking place when the agreement is made if entitlement to the security passes at that time. A conditional agreement is treated as made when the condition is satisfied. Where the holder dies, he is treated as having tranferred the security at market value immediately before his death, and his personal representative as acquiring it at that value on his death. Except in relation to certain gilt strips (see below), 'redemption' includes the extinguishment of a security (under rights conferred by the security) by conversion into shares in a company or into any other securities, the amount payable on that deemed redemption being the market value of the replacement shares or securities.

A '*relevant discounted security*' is, except as below, any security such that the amount payable on redemption (excluding interest) is or might be an amount involving a '*deep gain*', i.e. the issue price is less than the amount payable on redemption by 15% of that amount or, if less, by 1/2% per annum of that amount (counting months and part months as 1/12th of a year) to the earliest possible redemption date. This comparison is made as at the time of issue of the security and assuming redemption in accordance with the terms of issue. 'Redemption' for these purposes refers to redemption on maturity or, if the holder of the security may opt for earlier redemption, the earliest occasion on which the holder may require redemption. Exclusions are:

(a)   shares in a company;

(b)   gilt-edged securities (other than strips, see below);

(c)   'excluded indexed securities';

(d)   LIFE ASSURANCE POLICIES (45);

(e)   capital redemption policies (see 45.13(C) LIFE ASSURANCE POLICIES); and

(f)   securities issued under the same prospectus as other securities issued previously but not themselves relevant discounted securities.

Gilt strips (see 33.3 GOVERNMENT STOCKS) are always relevant discounted securities, without regard to their issue terms. As regards (f) above, if none of the securities originally issued under a prospectus would otherwise be a relevant discounted security, and some of those subsequently issued under the prospectus would be but for (f) above, and the aggregate nominal value of the latter at any time exceeds that of all other securities issued under the prospectus, then all securities issued under that prospectus are, from that time, treated as relevant discounted securities acquired as such.

A security is an '*excluded indexed security*' within (c) above if, in pursuance of any provision having effect for the purposes of the security, the amount payable on redemption is determined by applying to the amount for which the security was issued a percentage change, over the 'relevant period', in the value of chargeable assets of any particular description (or in an index of the value of such assets – the retail prices index or similar foreign general prices index is not such an index). If, however, there is such a provision which is made subject to any other provision applying to the determination of the amount payable on redemption, whose only effect is to place a lower limit on the discharge payment of a specified percentage (which must not be more than 10%) of the amount for which the security is issued, then that other provision is disregarded for this purpose. An asset is for these purposes a chargeable asset if any disposal gain would be a chargeable gain (assuming the asset (not being trading stock, etc.) to belong to the person in question (and that that person does not have the benefit of exemption under *TCGA 1992, s 100* (authorised unit trusts, etc.)), and disregarding gains previously deferred under *TCGA 1992, s 116* on a capital reorganisation, etc. involving a qualifying corporate bond, see Tolley's Capital Gains Tax under Qualifying Corporate Bonds). The '*relevant period*' is the period between the time of issue and redemption, or any other period in which almost all of that period is comprised and which differs from it exclusively for valuation purposes.

These provisions do not apply for corporation tax purposes. For accounting periods ending after 31 March 1996, a separate regime is enacted for corporation tax, broadly dealing with all interest and profits or losses on securities on revenue account, either on an accruals basis or on a mark-to-market basis. See Tolley's Corporation Tax under Gilts and Bonds.

Treatment of losses where income exempt. A loss under the current provisions may only be relieved against income chargeable for the same year under the current provisions where a profit under these provisions on that transfer or redemption would have been an exempt profit for the year of assessment in which the loss is sustained. An 'exempt profit' for this purpose is income:

72.2 Schedule D, Case III—Interest Receivable etc.

(1) which is eligible for relief under *Sec 505(1)* (or which would be so eligible but for *Sec 505(3)*) (charitable exemptions and restrictions, see 15.3, 15.5 CHARITIES); or

(2) which is eligible for relief under *Sec 592(2), 608(2)(a), 613(4), 614(2)–(5), 620(6)* or *643(2)* (pension scheme funds, etc., see 66.5, 66.13, 66.11 RETIREMENT SCHEMES, 59.6 PENSIONS, 65.13, 65.2 RETIREMENT ANNUITIES AND PERSONAL PENSION SCHEMES).

As regards (2) above, where the exemption under *Sec 592(2)* applies, there is special provision for the interaction with the pension fund surplus provisions of *22 Sch* (see 66.8 RETIREMENT SCHEMES).

[*FA 1996, ss 102, 105(1)(b), 13 Sch 1–5, 7, 10, 13, 14(1), 16*].

Trustees. Amounts chargeable under these provisions on the transfer or redemption of a security by trustees are treated for the purposes of *Secs 660A–682A* (see 80.13–80.18 SETTLEMENTS) as income arising under the settlement from the security, and for the purposes of *Secs 686 et seq.* (see 80.5 SETTLEMENTS) as income arising to the trustees. To the extent that tax on such an amount is chargeable on the trustees, it is chargeable at the rate applicable to trusts (see 80.5 SETTLEMENTS). This does not apply to trustees of unauthorised unit trusts (see 90.2 UNIT TRUSTS) to the extent that the amount is treated as income in the scheme accounts.

Relief for losses under these provisions may, in the case of trustees, be given only against income chargeable under these provisions. Where, in any year of assessment, losses exceed amounts chargeable, the excess is carried forward and treated as a loss sustained under these provisions in the next year of assessment (although this does not apply to the extent that the loss arises in circumstances such that a profit would have been exempt, see above).

Non-resident trustees. Charges and reliefs under these provisions do not apply to securities held under a settlement the trustees of which are non-UK resident.

[*FA 1996, 13 Sch 6(1)–(6), 7(2)*].

Personal representatives. On the transfer of a relevant discounted security to a legatee, personal representatives are deemed to obtain market value consideration. A 'legatee' is any person taking under a testamentary disposition or on an intestacy or partial intestacy (including an appropriation in or towards satisfaction of a legacy or other interest or share in the deceased's property). [*FA 1996, 13 Sch 6(7)(8)*].

Gilt strips. (See 33.3 GOVERNMENT STOCKS and Tolley's Corporation Tax under Income Tax in Relation to a Company as regards gilt strips generally.) Every gilt strip is a relevant discounted security within these provisions. For these purposes:

(A) on the exchange of a gilt-edged security for strips of that security, the acquisition cost of each strip is determined by apportioning the market value of the security *pro rata* to the market value of each strip;

(B) when a person consolidates strips into a gilt-edged security by exchanging them for that security, each strip is treated as being redeemed at market value;

(C) any person holding a strip on 5 April in any year of assessment, and not transferring or redeeming it on that day, is deemed to have transferred it at market value on that day and to have re-acquired it at the deemed disposal value on the following day (without incurring any relevant costs); and

(D) the Treasury has wide powers by regulation to modify these provisions in their application to gilt strips.

[*FA 1996, 13 Sch 14*].

Market value transfers. In addition to the deemed transfer on death and in relation to personal representatives and gilt strips (see above), the following transfers of relevant discounted securities are deemed to take place at market value.

(i)   Transfers between CONNECTED PERSONS (20) (within *Sec 839*).

(ii) Where the consideration for the transfer is not all money or money's worth.

(iii) Where the transfer is not by way of a bargain made at arm's length.

[*FA 1996, 13 Sch 8, 9*].

Accrued income scheme. Where the current provisions apply on the transfer of a security, *Secs 710–728* (accrued income scheme, see 74.6 *et seq.* SCHEDULE D, CASE VI) do not apply. [*FA 1996, 13 Sch 11*].

Transfer of assets abroad. For the purposes of *Secs 739, 740* (transfer of assets abroad, see 3.8 ANTI-AVOIDANCE), a profit chargeable under these provisions realised by a person resident or domiciled outside the UK is taken to be income of that person.

For 1995/96 and earlier years, a number of separate provisions dealt with discounts on securities, in addition to the accrued income scheme referred to above. See in particular 44.5, 44.7, 44.8 INTEREST RECEIVABLE and 33.4 GOVERNMENT STOCKS. These applied equally for corporation tax purposes, but see above as regards the separate regime for corporation tax introduced by *FA 1996*.

72.3   **SCOPE AND ASSESSMENT**

(a)   **Assessment.** Certain interest and certain annuities and annual payments are payable under deduction of tax at source. If so paid, the deduction is treated as tax paid by the recipient who is then liable, if his total income is high enough, at the excess of the higher rate(s) of tax over the basic or lower rate (whichever is applicable) on the gross amount.

If the payer omits to deduct tax an assessment may be made on either the payer or payee. See 23.8 DEDUCTION OF TAX AT SOURCE for omission to deduct tax.

All other income not taxed at source is charged by direct assessment on the recipient. Loss relief and capital allowances are not applicable.

For years before 1996/97, for purposes of assessment, income under Case III may be assessed and charged in one sum [*Sec 73; FA 1995, s 115(9)*] but where there are changes in particular items they will be treated separately under the rules of new source and disposals (where applicable) in 72.4 below. [*Secs 66(3), 67(1)(a); FA 1994, ss 207(4), 218*]. The person receiving or entitled to the income is assessable. [*Sec 59(1)*]. See also *Aplin v White Ch D 1973, 49 TC 93*. A non-resident may be assessed under Case III through an agent under *TMA s 82* (*Scales v Atalanta SS Co KB 1925, 9 TC 586*) (and see also 51.5 to 51.7 NON-RESIDENTS AND OTHER OVERSEAS MATTERS).

Bank interest is generally received when credited to the account (*Dunmore v McGowan Ch D 1978, 52 TC 307; Peracha v Miley CA 1990, 63 TC 444*), but there may be no receipt or entitlement if the bank has the right to refuse payment out of the account and the interest is not in fact paid out (*Macpherson v Bond Ch D 1985, 58 TC 579*). Interest paid by cheque is received when the sum is credited to the recipient's account, not when the cheque is received. (*Parkside Leasing Ltd v Smith Ch D 1984, 58 TC 282*).

(b)   **Interest and discount.** Whether an amount described as interest in a Court or arbitration award is true interest or an element entering into the calculation of the award and capital depends on the facts. See *Schulze v Bensted (No 1) CS 1915, 7 TC 30; Westminster Bank Ltd v Riches HL 1947, 28 TC 159* and *Barnato CA 1936, 20 TC 455* and contrast *Ballantine CS 1924, 8 TC 595*. A premium on the repayment of a loan was held to be interest in *Davies v Premier Investment Co Ltd KB 1945, 27 TC 27*, but a premium on the repayment of securities quoted on the Stock Exchange or issued on terms similar to those of quoted securities is normally regarded as capital and similarly as regards the discount on securities issued at a discount. A discount within Case III is a profit of an income nature received on a discounting transaction. See *National Provident Institution v Brown HL 1921, 8 TC 57* and *Ditchfield v Sharp CA 1983, 57 TC 555* and contrast *Lomax v Peter Dixon & Son Ltd CA 1943, 25 TC 453*.

Payments in pursuance of a guarantee of the capital of a company were held to be interest in *Blake v Imperial Brazilian Rly Co CA 1884, 2 TC 58*. See also *Wilson v Mannooch KB 1937, 21 TC 178* and *Ruskin Investments Ltd v Copeman CA 1943, 25 TC 187*. The interest element in loan repayments after the death of a money-lender was held to be assessable on his administrator under Case III (*Bennett v Ogston KB 1930, 15 TC 374*). Accrued interest on securities sold (if not sold 'ex-dividend') is income of the purchaser (*Wigmore v Thomas Summerson & Sons Ltd KB 1925, 9 TC 577* and *Schaffer v Cattermole CA 1980, 53 TC 499*) but see 3.3 ANTI-AVOIDANCE if arrangement to repurchase. Arrears of interest are not assessable until received—see *St Lucia Usines v Colonial Treasurer PC 1924, 4 ATC 112* and the cases noted in 28.2(*d*) EXCESS LIABILITY.

See now the special provisions for 1996/97 and subsequent years at 72.2 above.

(*c*)   **Annual payments and annuities.** For cases where deduction of tax is involved, see 23.9 and 23.10 DEDUCTION OF TAX AT SOURCE.

Case III assessments were upheld in respect of periodical payments to a newspaper company after a merger (*Morning Post Ltd v George KB 1940, 23 TC 514*), payments to an actress from the exploitation of a film (*Mitchell v Rosay CA 1954, 35 TC 496*) and annual payments to the executors of a deceased director pursuant to an agreement entered into by him relating to special services he had rendered (*Westminster Bank Ltd v Barford Ch D 1958, 38 TC 68*). Compensation payments by the USA Government to a wounded American soldier were held not to be assessable in *Laird v CIR CS 1929, 14 TC 395* but in *Forsyth v Thompson KB 1940, 23 TC 374* periodical disability payments from a mutual insurance society were held to be assessable. But see now 75.37 SCHEDULE E.

(*d*)   **Deductions.** The full amount of the income is assessable without any deduction. Cf. *Lord Inverclyde's Trustees v Millar CS 1924, 9 TC 14* and *A B (Committee of) v Simpson KB 1928, 14 TC 29*.

72.4   **BASIS OF ASSESSMENT**

The rules at (a)–(d) below apply for 1995/96 and earlier years as regards income from a source first arising before 6 April 1994—see (e) and (f) below for the position for later years. They have no application to income from a source first arising after 5 April 1994, for which see (e) below.

(*a*)   **Preceding year basis.** Assessment is normally on actual income of preceding year without any deduction [*Sec 64*] but subject to changes in items as below.

If the source is still retained, assessment to income tax continues on preceding year's income even if no profits from that source in the year of assessment. [*Sec 71*]. This held to apply even when interest waived for year of assessment, if money still kept on deposit and not transferred to current account (*Cull v Cowcher KB 1934, 18 TC*

449). Conversely, no liability arises unless the source is held in the year of assessment. But see (*c*)(i) and (ii) below and *National Provident Instn v Brown HL 1921, 8 TC 57; Grainger v Maxwell's Exors CA 1925, 10 TC 139.*

Income received under deduction of tax is, however, income of the year of assessment by reference to the basic or lower rate of tax for which tax is deducted from the income, without regard to the period of accrual. [*Sec 835(6); FA 1996, 6 Sch 24, 28*]. See 23.1 DEDUCTION OF TAX AT SOURCE.

For corporation tax purposes, assessment is on the actual income of the accounting period.

The preceding year basis and the rules in (*b*) and (*c*) below do not apply to maintenance payments under 'existing obligations' (see 47.15 MARRIED PERSONS). The charge under Case III is computed on the payments falling due in the year of assessment, providing they are actually made but regardless of whether or not they are made in the year for which they are due. [*FA 1988, s 38(8)*].

See 72.3(*a*) above as regards when interest is received for the purposes of Case III.

(*b*)   **New Source**
If any new source or an addition to any source is acquired or if loan interest previously taxable by deduction becomes receivable gross the following rules apply.

If income first arose **on** 6 April in the first year of assessment

First tax year assessed on first year's income.
Second tax year assessed on first year's income, with option to taxpayer to substitute second year's income if claimed within six years from end of year of assessment.
Third tax year assessed on second year's income.

If income first arose **after** 6 April in the first year of assessment

First tax year assessed on first year's income.
Second tax year assessed on second year's income.
Third tax year assessed on second year's income with option to taxpayer to substitute third year's income if claimed within six years from end of year of assessment.

Each item newly acquired is to be treated separately. [*Sec 66*].

Large addition to bank account held to be acquisition of new source (*Hart v Sangster CA 1957, 37 TC 231*) but in practice small changes are ignored and all bank accounts owned by a taxpayer may generally be treated as one source unless the taxpayer requires that they be treated as separate sources. See also *Beese v MacKinlay Ch D, [1980] STC 228.*

(*c*)   **Disposals etc.** If any particular source of income or any part thereof ceases to be possessed by the taxpayer or if loan interest previously receivable gross becomes taxable by deduction the following rules apply.

Last year —Assessment to be adjusted to actual income from 6 April to date of disposal.

Year before the last —If the income arising within the twelve months to 5 April of that year is greater than the assessment for that year, the excess is chargeable by assessment. [*Sec 67(1)(b)*].

See (*b*) above as regards all bank accounts being treated as a single source.

72.4 Schedule D, Case III—Interest Receivable etc.

(i)   *If no income arose during the last two years of ownership,* taxpayer may claim to be treated as if he had ceased to possess the source in the year in which income last arose provided this was not more than eight years before the claim. *[Sec 67(1)(c), (4)]*.

(ii) *If a source, having produced income, does not do so for six consecutive years of assessment thereafter,* taxpayer may claim to be treated as above as if he had ceased to possess it at the end of the those six years and immediately thereafter acquired it as a new source. *[Sec 67(5)]*.

Time limits for claims under (i) and (ii) are two years after end of year of actual cessation, or assumed cessation under (ii). The claims are also available to personal representatives. *[Sec 67(1)(c), (5)(8)]*.

(*d*) **Death of spouse.** Where on the death of a spouse a source of income passes in its entirety from the deceased to the surviving spouse, cessation and commencement adjustments (see (*b*) and (*c*) above) will not be made unless requested by the personal representative or by the survivor. (Revenue Pamphlet IR 1, A7). See 71.9 SCHEDULE D, CASES I AND II as regards the application of this concession to trading profits. The concession is withdrawn following the introduction of the current year basis of assessment (see (*e*) below), from 6 April 1995 in respect of sources commencing after 5 April 1994, and from a date to be announced (not earlier than 6 April 1997) for sources already in existence on that date. (Revenue Press Release 4 April 1995).

(*e*) **Current year basis.** For 1994/95 and subsequent years as regards income from a source first arising after 5 April 1994, and for 1996/97 and subsequent years as regards income from a source first arising on or before that date (see (*f*) below for transitional rules), the assessment is on actual income of the current year without any deduction. *[Sec 64; FA 1994, s 206]*. There are no special rules for opening and closing years as in (*b*) and (*c*) above.

(*f*) **Transitional rules on changeover to current year basis.** The following rules apply to income from a source first arising before 6 April 1994 and continuing (without interruption) beyond 5 April 1996. If the source ceases in 1996/97 or 1997/98, the rules in (*a*)–(*d*) above apply throughout. If the source continues beyond 5 April 1998, the assessment for 1996/97 is on 50% of the income arising in 1995/96 and 1996/97, the other 50% escaping tax. This does not apply if income first arose in 1993/94 and taxpayer opts for the actual basis for 1995/96 (see (*b*) above); in this case, the 1996/97 assessment is on a current year basis with no reduction. *[FA 1994, s 218, 20 Sch 4, 5, 14(1)]*.

Anti-avoidance measures have been introduced to deter and penalise attempts to exploit the transitional rules by moving income into the transitional period, i.e. 1995/96 and 1996/97, so that it would not otherwise be fully charged to tax. Where any amount is included in *interest* arising to a person within 1995/96 and 1996/97 (otherwise than where 1996/97 is on an actual basis) and would not have been so included if any 'relevant arrangements' made between that person and another had not been made, the 1996/97 assessment is increased by 62.5% of each amount so included. There are *de minimis* thresholds in that the increase does not apply where the aggregate of the amounts so included or the proportion which that aggregate bears to the aggregate interest arising in 1995/96 and 1996/97 is less than an amount/proportion to be prescribed by regulations shortly before 5 April 1997. Any arrangements under which interest arises at irregular intervals, or there are 'artificial variations' in the rate of interest applicable, during the years 1994/95 to 1997/98 are 'relevant arrangements' for these purposes unless the obtaining of a tax advantage is not the main benefit that could reasonably be expected to arise therefrom. All variations are 'artificial variations' unless based on variations in a variable and regularly published rate of interest. *[FA 1995, s 123, 22 Sch 9, 18]*. Similar measures apply as regards Case III *income other than interest* except that (i) *'relevant arrangements'* means any arrangements under which income arises at irregular intervals during the years 1994/95 to 1997/98 unless they are made exclusively for *bona fide* commercial reasons or the obtaining of a tax advantage is not the main benefit that could reasonably be expected to arise, and (ii) the measures also apply where the taxpayer has entered into any 'relevant transaction' which results in an amount being included in income for 1995/96 and 1996/97 which would not otherwise have been so included. Any transaction with a connected person (within *Sec 839*—see 20 CONNECTED PERSONS) is a *'relevant transaction'* for these purposes unless it is entered into exclusively for *bona fide* commercial reasons or the obtaining of a tax advantage is not the main benefit that could reasonably be expected to accrue therefrom. [*FA 1995, 22 Sch 10, 19, 20*]. The obtaining of a tax advantage is not regarded as a *bona fide* commercial reason for the above purposes. The discovery provisions of *TMA ss 29, 30B* apply with the same modifications and related time limits as in 71.20 SCHEDULE D, CASES I AND II. [*FA 1995, 22 Sch 11, 21(2)*]. There is no provision for any penalty to be mitigated or for any corresponding reduction to the assessment for any other year, except that where voluntary disclosure is made in the tax return for 1996/97 (other than by amendment to the return), the adjustment is reduced to 50% of each amount so included. [*FA 1995, 22 Sch 13*].

The Revenue have also announced their intention to counter movements between accounts after 30 March 1994, designed to increase the income qualifying for transitional relief, by strictly applying the law so as to treat such additional deposits into a pre-6 April 1994 account as new sources and thus subject to current year basis. This will apply where it appears that pre-existing sources taxed on current year basis have been depleted and sources taxed on preceding year basis correspondingly increased. (Revenue Press Release 31 March 1994).

72.5   *Example*

Patrick has the following sources of untaxed interest, chargeable under Schedule D, Case III.

	Opened/acquired	Closed
(1) National Savings income bonds	21.6.93	—
(2) National Savings Bank ordinary account	6.8.93	29.4.98
(3) National Savings Bank investment account	8.1.94	—

His wife, Judy, also opens a National Savings Bank ordinary account (Source (4)) on 21 June 1993, but closes it on 31 December 1997.

Interest credited/received in each of the tax years 1993/94 to 1998/99 is as follows.

	Source (1) £	Source (2) £	Source (3) £	Source (4) £
1993/94	800	520	—	520
1994/95	700	470	600	470
1995/96	600	550	800	550
1996/97	650	350	825	350
1997/98	575	335	775	335
1998/99	550	100	725	—

There are no 'relevant arrangements' or movements between accounts so as to bring into play the anti-avoidance measures in 72.4(*f*) above.

The interest chargeable under Schedule D, Case III for each year is as follows

(NB: the first £70 of National Savings Bank ordinary account interest for each tax year is exempt (see 29.11(iv) EXEMPT INCOME).

72.5 Schedule D, Case III—Interest Receivable etc.

	Source (1)	Source (2)	Source (3)	Source (4)
1993/94 (1st year — CY)	£800	£450	—	£450
1994/95 (2nd year — CY)	700	400		400
(CY basis)			600	
	£700	£400	£600	£400
1995/96 (3rd year — election				
for CY basis)	600			
(3rd year — PY)		400		400
(CY basis)			800	
	£600	£400	£800	£400
1996/97 (CY basis)	650		825	
(transitional year)		380		
(PY basis)				480
	£650	£380	£825	£480
1997/98 (CY basis)	575	265	775	
(Final year — CY)				265
	£575	£265	£775	£265
1998/99 (CY basis)	£550	£30	£725	—

Notes

(a)   *Source 1.* Income first arose in 1993/94. Because an election is made under *Sec 66(1)(c)* (third year — actual), the averaging rule does not apply for 1996/97, to which the current year basis therefore applies.

(b)   *Source 2.* Transitional rules apply for 1996/97. The amount chargeable is 50% of the aggregate income arising in 1995/96 and 1996/97. (As the source is a National Savings Bank ordinary account, the first £70 of the amount otherwise chargeable is exempt.)

(c)   *Source 3.* Income first arises after 5 April 1994. Therefore the source goes directly onto the current year basis.

(d)   *Source 4.* Because income last arises before 6 April 1998, the current year basis and transitional provisions do not apply, the source being taxed throughout on the preceding year basis rules.

73 Schedule D, Cases IV and V—Overseas Income

[*Secs 18, 65–67*]

Cross-references. See INTEREST RECEIVABLE at 44.5 for deep discount securities, 44.7 for deep gain securities and 44.8 for qualifying convertible securities; RESIDENCE, ORDINARY RESIDENCE AND DOMICILE at 64.4 for domicile, 64.5 for residence; NON-RESIDENTS AND OTHER OVERSEAS MATTERS at 51.12 for trades etc. carried on and controlled abroad, 51.14 for unremittable overseas income; 53.15 PARTNERSHIPS for partnerships abroad; 56 PAYMENT OF TAX; 59.2 PENSIONS for foreign pensions; 63 REMITTANCE BASIS for remittances; 75.6 SCHEDULE E for foreign employment.

73.1 Persons resident in the UK are assessable under Schedule D, Cases IV and V on overseas income, except from the carrying on in the UK of a trade, profession or vocation, either solely or in partnership (assessable under Schedule D, Cases I or II) or employment income (assessable under Schedule E).

Case IV applies to interest on overseas **securities,** other (for 1995/96 and earlier years) than income assessable under SCHEDULE C (70).

Case V applies to income from overseas **possessions.** [*Sec 18(3); FA 1996, 6 Sch 4(2)(b)*].

See 72.1, 72.2 SCHEDULE D, CASE III for interaction with that Case, and for variations for corporation tax purposes.

73.2 'Securities' are debts or claims secured on some fund or property, i.e. debenture or mortgage. (Cf. dicta in *Williams v Singer HL 1920, 7 TC 419*).

'Possessions' include all sources of income other than securities. The distinction between the two has ceased to be of any general practical importance.

73.3 **Overseas income** within Cases IV or V includes foreign bank interest; income as partner (*Colquhoun v Brooks HL 1889, 2 TC 490; Padmore v CIR CA 1989, 62 TC 352*); alimony paid under a foreign decree (*Anderstrom CS 1927, 13 TC 482*) (and see below); annuity paid under foreign deed of separation (*Chamney v Lewis KB 1932, 17 TC 318*); interest on unpaid instalments of a debt (*Hudson's Bay Co v Thew KB 1919, 7 TC 206*). Where the aggregate face value of foreign promissory notes exceeded the consideration for them, the excess was held to be interest within Case V (*Lord Howard de Walden v Beck KB 1940, 23 TC 384*).

Alimony, maintenance payments, etc. arising outside the UK which fall due after 14 March 1988 and are made in pursuance of 'existing obligations' (see 1.8(i) ALLOWANCES AND TAX RATES) are within the charge to tax under Case V, but subject (for 1988/89 and subsequent years) to the deductions and limitations described at 47.15 MARRIED PERSONS. Other maintenance payments falling due after 14 March 1988 which, if they had arisen in the UK, would not have been within the charge to tax under Case III (see 47.15 MARRIED PERSONS) are similarly exempted from charge under Case V if arising abroad. [*Sec 347A(4); FA 1988, ss 36(1), 38(8)*].

Promissory notes issued in satisfaction of arrears were held to be assessable (*Lilley v Harrison HL 1952, 33 TC 344*) and in *Westminster Bank v National Bank of Greece HL 1970, 46 TC 472* interest on foreign bonds paid, as guarantor, by the London branch of a foreign bank was held to be within Case IV. A dividend from a foreign company out of a capital profit was held to be within Case V (*Reid's Trustees HL 1949, 30 TC 431*) but see *Lazard Inv Co v Rae HL 1963, 41 TC 1*, where different treatment by application of Maryland law. In *Lawson v Rolfe Ch D 1969, 46 TC 199*, bonus shares received, by operation of Californian law, by the UK resident life tenant under a US will trust were held not assessable under Case V. And see *Courtaulds Investments v Fleming Ch D 1969, 46 TC 111*, distribution out of the share premium reserve of an Italian company (released, under Italian law, by accumulating out of profits a corresponding reserve fund) held a return of capital. See also *Pool v Guardian Investment Trust Co Ltd KB 1921, 8 TC 167* and *Associated Insulation Products Ltd v Golder CA 1944, 26 TC 231.* Compensation paid by a foreign government, following redundancy, in substitution for a proportion of salary was held to be assessable as income (*Beveridge v Ellam (Sp C 62), [1996] SSCD 77*).

Whether **premiums and discounts** are assessable to income tax depends upon whether recipient received altogether more than commercial interest reasonable on a sound investment (*Lomax v Peter Dixon CA 1943, 25 TC 353*, compared with *Thomas Nelson & Sons Ltd CS 1938, 22 TC 175*, and *Davis v Premier Investment KB 1945, 27 TC 27*). If exempt from income tax they may be assessable to capital gains tax. See 44.5–44.7 INTEREST RECEIVABLE for the charge on disposal of a 'deep discount' or 'deep gain security'.

Overseas lettings of property, caravans and houseboats are assessed under Case V. See 73.4 below. For foreign pensions, see 59.2 PENSIONS and cf. *Bridges v Watterson Ch D 1952, 34 TC 47.* For foreign trust income, see 80.10 SETTLEMENTS. For Crown option between Cases of Schedule D, see 5.2 ASSESSMENTS. For treatment of blocked currency cases, see 51.14 NON-RESIDENTS AND OTHER OVERSEAS MATTERS and *Secs 584, 585.*

73.4   **Overseas lettings.** For 1995/96 and subsequent years of assessment (but see the transitional provisions below) and otherwise than for corporation tax purposes or where the REMITTANCE BASIS (63) applies (see 73.5 below), income arising from any business (other than a trade, profession or vocation) carried on for the exploitation, as a source of rents or other receipts, of any estate, interest or rights in or over land outside the UK is chargeable under Case V but is to be computed under the rules applicable to a Schedule A business (including those for capital allowances). The question of whether income falls within this description is also determined as for Schedule A purposes. See 68.4, 68.5 SCHEDULE A. The following do *not*, however, apply as they would under Schedule A: (i)   *Secs 80, 81*—travelling expenses (see 51.12 NON-RESIDENTS AND OTHER OVERSEAS MATTERS), but see below, and (ii) *Secs 503, 504* and *CAA 1990, s 29*—special rules for furnished holiday lettings (see 68.9 SCHEDULE A). Where a person carries on both a Schedule A business and an overseas lettings business treated as such by virtue of the above, each is treated as a separate business without regard to the other. [*Secs 65(2A)(2B)(4), 65A; CAA 1990, s 161(2A); FA 1995, s 41(1)–(3)(10); FA 1996, s 134, 20 Sch 3*]. Under general principles, relief is available for travelling expenses incurred wholly and exclusively for the purposes of the overseas letting business. Interest on a loan to purchase an overseas property is deductible as an expense to the extent that it is incurred wholly and exclusively for the purposes of the letting business, with the interest being apportioned accordingly where the owner occupies the property, or it is otherwise unavailable for letting, for part of the year or if only part of the property is used exclusively for letting. (Revenue booklet SAT 1(1995), paras 9.151–9.153). Although all overseas let properties are regarded as a single letting business, the income from each must be calculated separately for the purposes of computing DOUBLE TAX RELIEF (25) (SAT 1(1995), para 9.160).

Transitional provisions.

(1)   The above rules do not apply in any case which would be within the Schedule A transitional provisions (see 68.3 SCHEDULE A) if the land were in the UK (i.e. where the source ceases in *1995/96* without a new source being acquired).

(2)   For *1995/96* and *1996/97*, where a person lets more than one overseas property, the letting of each property is treated as a separate Schedule A business without regard to the other properties.

Schedule D, Cases IV and V—Overseas Income 73.5

(3) If, had it not been for the introduction of the above rules, a source would have been chargeable on the preceding year basis for *1995/96* and under the transitional rules for *1996/97* (see 73.9 below), that basis and those rules are preserved for those years (see also (6) below). However, where those rules so apply to income from any property, no capital allowances or balancing charges can be made for those years in connection with that property.

(4) The relief for SCHEDULE A losses at 68.13 does *not* apply to an overseas letting business for any of the years *1995/96, 1996/97* or *1997/98* (see also below).

[*FA 1995, s 41(5)–(9)*].

(5) *Basis of computation.* In moving onto an accruals basis for 1995/96 from some other basis (for example, receipts and payments) in 1994/95, the guidelines at 68.22 SCHEDULE A should be followed.

(6) *Basis periods.* Where an accounting date other than 5 April has previously been used to assess overseas letting income, it is necessary to move to a statutory fiscal year basis under the new rules. The Revenue's preferred option is to adjust the basis period for 1996/97 (the transitional year—see 73.9 below) to run from the end of the 1995/96 basis period to 5 April 1997, with accounts being prepared to cover that period and a proportion equivalent to twelve months' profits being taxed.

(Revenue booklet SAT 1(1995), paras 9.150, 9.161–9.164).

For years before 1998/99, deficiencies of income from overseas lettings may by concession be carried forward for set-off against future income from the same property (and this will continue for corporation tax purposes). For 1998/99 onwards, the loss regime at 68.13 SCHEDULE A will operate instead, but any unrelieved losses at 5 April 1998 (including any incurred after 5 April 1995 on properties where letting ceases before 1998/99) may by concession be carried forward against future profits of the single overseas letting business. (Revenue Pamphlet IR 1, B25; Revenue Booklet SAT 1(1995), paras 9.157–9.159).

Interest payable on a loan used to purchase a flat in Gibraltar for furnished letting was held not deductible in *Ockendon v Mackley Ch D 1982, 56 TC 2* (but this has no application under the new rules above).

73.5 **Assessment** on income chargeable under Cases IV and V is normally on **income arising** whether remitted to this country or not but the **remittance basis** (see 63 REMITTANCE BASIS) applies to

(*a*) persons not domiciled in the UK.

(*b*) Commonwealth subjects, or citizens of Republic of Ireland, not ordinarily resident in the UK.

[*Sec 65(1)(4)(5); FA 1994, s 207(1)(3); FA 1996, s 134, 20 Sch 3*].

But income from whatever source in the Republic of Ireland is assessable on the amount arising in the year of assessment whether remitted to this country or not, subject to certain deductions in the case of income not remitted. [*Sec 68; F(No 2)A 1992, s 60; FA 1994, s 207(5)*].

In arriving at the amount assessable on the arising basis, deductions are made of 10% in respect of certain pensions (see 59.1(iv) and 59.2 PENSIONS).

For 1996/97 and subsequent years and other than where the remittance basis applies, interest, discounts etc. within Case IV or V are chargeable to income tax at the lower rate

73.6 Schedule D, Cases IV and V—Overseas Income

(to the extent that such income does not fall within an individual's higher rate band). See 1.8(iii) ALLOWANCES AND TAX RATES for the full provisions.

73.6 **Aggregation of income.** For years before 1996/97, for purposes of assessment, income arising (including remittances) under Case IV or V may respectively be assessed in one sum. [*Sec 73; FA 1995, s 115(9)*].

73.7 **Deductions.** In general the assessment is on the full amount of the income with no deductions (cf. *Aikin v Macdonald Trustees CES 1894, 3 TC 306*), but where the assessment is on the arising basis (see 73.5 above) there may be deducted from income not received in the UK (*a*) the same deductions and allowances as if it had been so received, and (*b*) any annuities or other annual payments (not being interest) payable out of the income to a resident abroad. No deduction is permitted either in respect of any annuity or annual payment falling due after 14 March 1988 which would not have been chargeable under Schedule D, Case III if made to a UK resident, nor, with effect for 1989/90 and subsequent years, in respect of any payment of maintenance within *FA 1988, s 38* (see 47.15 MARRIED PERSONS). [*Secs 65(1), 347A(5); FA 1988, ss 36(1), 38(9); FA 1994, s 207(1)*].

Foreign tax for which no double tax credit is allowable (see 25.2 DOUBLE TAX RELIEF) may be deducted where the arising basis applies. [*Secs 811, 795(2)*]. Where the remittance basis applies, see *Sec 795(1)*.

73.8 No assessment can be made for years during which the source of income was taxed by **deduction at source.** See 5.4 ASSESSMENTS (and cf. *Bradbury v Eng. Sewing Cotton HL 1923, 8 TC 481*).

73.9 **BASIS OF ASSESSMENT**

Preceding year basis. For 1995/96 and earlier years, as regards income from a source first arising (or, where the remittance basis applies, see 73.5 above, income first remitted to the UK) before 6 April 1994, the basis of assessment under Schedule D, Cases IV and V, is the same as set out under 72.4 SCHEDULE D, CASE III (i.e. preceding year basis normally applies [*Sec 65*] with special rules for new sources [*Sec 66*] and disposals etc. [*Sec 67*]), subject to variations as follows.

(*a*)   If the remittance basis applies to the recipient (see 73.5 above)—then all assessments will be made on the basis of remittances to the UK (in the preceding year etc.) instead of on income arising. [*Secs 65(4)(5), 66(6), 67(6)*]. It is understood, however, that any sums received derived from income which arose in a year of non-residence (other than a basis year for a preceding year basis assessment) are excluded from assessment.

(*b*)   If income from any foreign security or possession previously taxed by deduction ceases to be so treated—new source rules apply. [*Sec 66(5)*].

(*c*)   If income previously assessed under Cases IV and V becomes taxable by deduction —disposal etc. rules apply. [*Sec 67(3)*].

(*d*)   Income arising in Eire is assessed on a current year basis. [*Sec 68*].

(*e*)   See also 73.11 and 73.12 below.

Current year basis. For 1994/95 and subsequent years (1996/97 and subsequent years as regards income from a source first arising (or, where the remittance basis applies, see 73.5 above, income first remitted to the UK) before 6 April 1994), the assessment under Case

IV or V is on the income arising (or, where applicable, remitted) in the year of assessment. [*Sec 65; FA 1994, ss 207(1)(3)(4), 218(1)(4)*]. Generally, there are no special rules for new sources or disposals. In the case of a trade, profession or vocation chargeable under Case IV or V, the basis period rules in 71.11 to 71.19 SCHEDULE D, CASES I AND II and *Sec 113* (see 53.6 PARTNERSHIPS) apply (for 1997/98 and subsequent years as regards trades, etc. commenced before 6 April 1994). [*Sec 65(3); FA 1994, s 207(2)(6)*].

Transitional rules on changeover to current year basis. The following rules apply to income from a source first arising (or, where the remittance basis applies, see 73.5 above, income first remitted to the UK) before 6 April 1994 and continuing (without interruption) beyond 5 April 1996. If the source ceases in 1996/97 or 1997/98, the rules in 72.4(*a*)–(*d*) SCHEDULE D, CASE III apply throughout. If the source continues beyond 5 April 1998, the assessment for 1996/97 is on 50% of the income arising (or, where applicable, remitted) in 1995/96 and 1996/97, the other 50% escaping tax. This does not apply if income first arose in 1993/94 and taxpayer opts for the actual basis for 1995/96 (see 72.4 SCHEDULE D, CASE III); in this case, the 1996/97 assessment is on a current year basis with no 50% reduction. In the case of a trade, profession or vocation chargeable under Case IV or V, a transitional overlap profit may arise for 1997/98 in the same way as in 71.22 SCHEDULE D, CASES I AND II. [*FA 1994, s 218, 20 Sch 6, 7, 14*].

Anti-avoidance measures have been introduced to deter and penalise attempts to exploit the transitional rules by moving income into the transitional period, i.e. 1995/96 and 1996/97, so that it would not otherwise be fully charged to tax. They do not apply where the remittance basis applies. For interest and other income other than trading etc. profits, the provisions are identical to those described at 72.4 SCHEDULE D, CASE III. [*FA 1995, s 123, 22 Sch 9, 10, 13*]. For trades, professions or vocations within Case IV or V, the anti-avoidance provisions mirror those at 71.20 SCHEDULE D, CASES I AND II with the transitional period being the tax years 1996/96 and 1996/97, and there are also measures more or less identical to those at 71.22 SCHEDULE D, CASES I AND II aimed at manipulation of the transitional overlap profit. [*FA 1995, 22 Sch 6–8, 13*].

73.10   *Example*

In July 1993 S inherited shares in X, a company resident outside the UK. S is resident, ordinarily resident and domiciled in the UK and is not liable to higher rate tax. The dividends which arise and tax deducted therefrom are as follows (the dividends arising on or after 1 October 1998 have UK tax deducted by a UK paying agent).

	Gross	Foreign tax at 15%	UK tax (at lower rate less foreign tax)
	£	£	£
1993/94	120	18.00	—
1994/95	175	26.25	—
1995/96	190	28.50	—
1996/97	180	27.00	—
1997/98	240	36.00	—
Period 6.4.98 – 30.9.98	135	20.25	—
		£156.00	
Period 1.10.98 – 5.4.99	145	21.75	7.25

73.10   Schedule D, Cases IV and V—Overseas Income

S's assessments are as follows.

		£	£
1993/94 (1st year — CY)		£120	
		—	
Tax thereon at 20%		24.00	
Deduct Tax credit relief		18.00	18.00
		—	
UK tax payable		£6.00	
1994/95 (2nd year — CY)		£175	
		—	
Tax thereon at 20%		35.00	
Deduct Tax credit relief		26.25	26.25
		—	
UK tax payable		£8.75	
1995/96 (3rd year — PY)		£175	
		—	
Tax thereon at 20%		35.00	
Deduct Tax credit relief		26.25	26.25
		—	
UK tax payable		£8.75	
1996/97 (transitional year)			
Income arising in 1995/96		190	
Income arising in 1996/97		180	
		—	
		£370	
		—	
£370 × 50%		£185	
		—	
Tax thereon at 20%		37.00	
Deduct Tax credit relief:			
£(28.50 + 27.00) × 50%		27.75	27.75
		—	
UK tax payable		£9.25	
1997/98 (CY)		£240	
		—	
Tax thereon at 20%		48.00	
Deduct Tax credit relief		36.00	36.00
		—	
UK tax payable		£12.00	
1998/99 (period 6.4.98 to 30.9.98 — CY)		£135	
		—	
Tax thereon at 20%		27.00	
Deduct Tax credit relief		20.25	20.25
		—	
UK tax payable		£6.75	
		—	
Total tax credit relief			£154.50

Notes

(a) S would choose to have the assessment for 1995/96 assessed under the preceding year basis since the income for 1994/95 is lower than that for 1995/96. [*See* *66(1)(c)*].

(b) The income of £145 for the period 1.10.98–5.4.99 would normally be assessed for 1998/99 as foreign dividends. However, no assessment need be raised as S is not liable to higher rate tax and the income has effectively suffered lower rate tax at source.

(c) For 1993/94 onwards, dividends which are assessable under Schedule D, Case V are charged at the lower rate of 20% except to the extent that the dividend income brings the recipient into the higher rate band (see 1.3 ALLOWANCES AND TAX RATES).

(d) *Double taxation relief.* Tax credit relief for 1996/97 (the transitional year on the changeover to the current year basis of assessment) is restricted to 50% of the aggregate foreign tax paid on income arising from the source in question in 1995/96 and 1996/97 (see 25.5(n)(1) DOUBLE TAX RELIEF).

The total tax credit relief given (£154.50) is less than the total foreign tax paid (£156.00). No adjustment is made for the difference. If total tax credit relief had exceeded total foreign tax paid, an amount would have become chargeable under Schedule D, Case VI. Such amount is the excess of (A) tax credit relief given more than once because of the opening years rules (£26.25 in this example) (see *ICTA 1988, s 804(1) as originally enacted*) over (B) the tax credit relief foregone because of the 50% restriction in 1996/97 (£27.75 in this example). (In this example, there is clearly no such excess.) See 25.5(n)(2) DOUBLE TAX RELIEF. Where a source is subject to the current year basis throughout (i.e. where income first arises after 5 April 1994), no such adjustment will be relevant.

73.11   **NEW RESIDENTS**

As regards a trade, profession or vocation carried on by an individual wholly or partly outside the UK, the comments and concessions below are superseded by the statutory provisions at 71.27 SCHEDULE D, CASES I AND II which apply for 1995/96 onwards as regards trades etc. commenced after 5 April 1994 and for 1997/98 onwards as regards those commenced on or before that date.

Strictly, an individual who becomes resident (see 64.5 RESIDENCE, ORDINARY RESIDENCE AND DOMICILE) in the UK during a tax year is treated as resident throughout that year. He is assessable on income arising or remitted as appropriate (see 73.5 above) on the preceding year basis, unless income first arose or was first remitted to the UK less than two years before the start of the tax year of his arrival in the UK, in which case the usual commencement provisions apply (see 73.9 above and *Back v Whitlock KB 1932, 16 TC 723; Carter v Sharon KB 1936, 20 TC 229; Joffe v Thain Ch D 1955, 36 TC 199*).

For the year in which an individual whose home has previously been abroad becomes permanently resident in the UK, however, certain concessions are generally available, provided that he was not previously ordinarily resident in the UK. (These concessions will require revision by the Revenue in view of the introduction of a current year basis of assessment—see 73.9 above.)

(i)   The individual may be treated as resident only from the date of his arrival in the UK to take up permanent residence.

(ii)   No assessment is made in respect of a source ceasing before the date of arrival in the UK to take up permanent residence.

(iii)   Where income is assessable on the 'arising' basis (see 73.5 above),

(a)   if the source ceases in the period between arrival and the end of the tax year of arrival, assessment will be restricted to the amount arising in that period;

(b)   if the source ceases in the tax year following that of arrival, assessment for the year of arrival will be on a proportion of the greater of the income for the year of arrival and that for the preceding year. The proportion is that which corresponds to the period of UK residence in the year of arrival. For the following year, assessment will be on the income arising during that year;

(c)   if income from a continuing source first arose in the tax year of arrival but before arrival, or in the previous tax year, assessment for the year of arrival is restricted to the same proportion as in (b) above of the income of that year. If it first arose in an earlier year, assessment is on the same proportion of income of the year before that of arrival.

(iv)   Where income is assessable on the 'remittance' basis (see 73.5 above),

(a)   if the source ceases in the period between arrival and the end of the tax year of arrival, assessment is restricted to the amount assessable under (iii) (a) above as if the income was assessable on the 'arising' basis;

(b)   if the source ceases in the tax year following that of arrival, the assessment for the year of arrival is restricted to the amount assessable under (iii) (b) above as if the income was assessable on the 'arising' basis ('A'). The sum of the assessments for the year of arrival and the following year is then restricted to the sum of 'A' and the amount of income arising from 6 April in the year of cessation to the date the source ceases.

These concessions do not, however, apply to income received from a source in the Republic of Ireland (see 73.5 above) and are of limited application to individuals previously resident in the Republic.

(Revenue Pamphlet IR 20, paras 1.5, 6.4, 7.15, 7.16).

73.12   INDIVIDUALS PERMANENTLY LEAVING UK

As regards a trade, profession or vocation carried on by an individual wholly or partly outside the UK, the comments and concessions below are superseded by the statutory provisions at 71.27 SCHEDULE D, CASES I AND II which apply for 1995/96 onwards as regards trades etc. commenced after 5 April 1994 and for 1997/98 onwards as regards those commenced on or before that date.

Strictly, an individual who is resident in the UK (see 64.5 RESIDENCE, ORDINARY RESIDENCE AND DOMICILE) continues to be so for the remainder of the tax year after his permanent departure from the UK. Certain concessions are, however, available, provided that he ceases to be ordinarily resident in the UK on his departure.

(i)   Where income is assessable on the 'arising' basis (see 73.5 above), the assessment for the year in which permanent residence ceases is restricted to the lesser of

(a)   income arising between 6 April in that year and the date of his departure, and

(b)   the proportion of the income otherwise assessable for the year (whether on the current or preceding year basis, see 73.9 above) corresponding to the period of UK residence in the year.

(ii)   Where income is assessable on the 'remittance' basis (see 73.5 above), concessions apply as in (i) above, substituting 'remitted' for 'arising'.

These concessions do not, however, apply to income received from a source in the Republic of Ireland (see 73.5 above), and are of limited application to persons leaving to take up residence in the Republic.

(Revenue Pamphlet IR 20, paras 1.5, 6.4, 7.12, 7.13).

74 Schedule D, Case VI—Miscellaneous Income

[*Secs 18, 69*]

74.1 Tax is charged under Schedule D, Case VI in respect of any annual profits or gains not falling under any other case of Schedule D and not charged by virtue of any other Schedule. [*Sec 18(3)*].

Case VI is also specifically applied to other kinds of income to include: various charges under ANTI-AVOIDANCE (3); withdrawal of relief under 26.12, 26.26 ENTERPRISE INVESTMENT SCHEME (AND BES); sale of patent rights, see 54 PATENTS; CERTIFICATES OF DEPOSIT (13); easements not falling under *Secs 119, 120* and certain under-deductions where tax rate changed, see 23 DEDUCTION OF TAX AT SOURCE; interest paid by issue of bonds, see 32 FUNDING BONDS; gains on certain offshore life insurance policies, see 45.17–45.19 LIFE ASSURANCE POLICIES; formerly unremittable overseas income where source has ceased, see 51.14 NON-RESIDENTS AND OTHER OVERSEAS MATTERS; offshore income gains, see 52 OFFSHORE FUNDS; recovery of tax over-repaid, see 56.8 PAYMENT OF TAX; certain POST-CESSATION ETC. RECEIPTS (60); lease premiums and assignments at under-value etc. see 68.27 SCHEDULE A; certain furnished lettings—see 74.4 below; certain settlement income, see 80.14 SETTLEMENTS; charges on trustees of employee share ownership trusts, see 81.11 SHARE INCENTIVES AND OPTIONS; recovery of various excess reliefs for double taxation [*Secs 788, 790, 804*], losses [*Sec 383(11)*], capital allowances [*CAA 1990, ss 9(6), 15(2), 23(2), 142(3); Sec 32(4)*] etc.

74.2 Following held to be income within Case VI: commission for guaranteeing overdrafts (*Ryall v Hoare KB 1925, 8 TC 521* and *Sherwin v Barnes KB 1931, 16 TC 278*); underwriting commission (*Lyons v Cowcher KB 1926, 10 TC 438*); commission for negotiating a sale of shares (*Grey v Tiley CA 1932, 16 TC 414*); commission from an insurance company (*Hugh v Rogers Ch D 1958, 38 TC 270* and see *Way v Underdown CA 1974, 49 TC 648*); shipping dues (the two *Forth Conservancy Board* cases *HL 1928, 14 TC 709, HL 1931, 16 TC 103*); share of prize monies for letting racehorses (*Norman v Evans Ch D 1964, 42 TC 188*).

Held to be capital were shares allotted to members of a mining finance development scheme (*Whyte v Clancy KB 1936, 20 TC 679*) and shares allotted for a guarantee of dividends (*National United Laundries v Bennet KB 1933, 17 TC 420*).

A payment to an architect for his services relating to a property deal was held income within Case VI in *Brocklesby v Merricks KB 1934, 18 TC 576*, but payments for services in deals are not income if made gratuitously in such circumstances that the recipient has no enforceable right to them. For cases in which such payments held *not* income see *Bradbury v Arnold Ch D 1957, 37 TC 665; Bloom v Kinder Ch D 1958, 38 TC 77; Dickinson v Abel Ch D 1968, 45 TC 353*. See also *Scott v Ricketts CA 1967, 44 TC 303* in which a payment to an estate agent linked with a development scheme was held not to be income even though embodied in a contract.

Receipts of the use of copyright material were held income within Case VI in *Hobbs v Hussey KB 1942, 24 TC 153* (sale of rights in life story to newspaper) and *Housden v Marshall Ch D 1958, 38 TC 233* and *Alloway v Phillips CA 1980, 53 TC 372* (receipt for material for newspaper articles by 'ghost writer') but held capital in *Earl Haig Trustees v CIR CS 1939, 22 TC 725* (payment to trustees for permission to use diaries of deceased); *Beare v Carter KB 1940, 23 TC 353* (payment for permission to re-print book); *Nethersole v Withers HL 1948, 28 TC 501* (sale of film rights in work by deceased author).

For other copyright sales see 71.43 and 71.50 SCHEDULE D, CASES I AND II. For the line between Cases I and VI as regards surpluses on the sales of assets see 71.35 SCHEDULE D, CASES I AND II.

Volunteer drivers (e.g. hospital car service drivers) are taxable in the normal way under Case VI on the profit element in any mileage allowances. Arrangements to collect such tax have been made with effect from 6 October 1991, but, by concession, the profit is taxed as to one-quarter only for the period from 6 October 1991 to 5 April 1992 and for 1992/93, as to one-half only for 1993/94 and as to three-quarters only for 1994/95. Tax is payable in full on the profit element for 1995/96 and subsequent years. This concession does not apply to taxi and mini-cab drivers and similar operators who drive for the hospital car service and other volunteer organisations. (Revenue Pamphlet IR 1, A77). See also Revenue explanatory leaflet IR 122.

Theatrical angels. UK-resident backers of theatrical productions ('angels'), although strictly assessable under SCHEDULE D, CASE III (72) on any return over and above their original investment (with the capital gains tax rules applicable to any losses), may treat the profit or loss arising on any particular transaction as within Case VI, thereby being able to utilise such losses against similar (or any other) Case VI profits. Losses so utilised cannot also qualify as capital losses. The Revenue will not insist on deduction of tax being applied to payments to angels whose usual place of abode is in the UK where it is strictly required under *Sec 349*. (Non-resident angels may apply for authority for tax not to be deducted, see 25.6 DOUBLE TAX RELIEF.) This concessional treatment reflects a long-standing Revenue practice. (Revenue Press Release 8 February 1996).

74.3 **ASSESSMENT**

For 1994/95 and subsequent years (1996/97 and subsequent years as regards income from a source first arising before 6 April 1994), the income tax assessment under Case VI is made on the profits arising in the year of assessment. Previously, it was made either on the profits arising in the year of assessment, or on the average of such period, not being greater than one year, as Commissioners direct. [*Sec 69; FA 1994, ss 208, 218(1)*]. In practice, if the income is of a recurrent nature, e.g. furnished letting profits (see 74.4 below) the assessment is often on the preceding year's income and may be on Case I or Case III lines (see 71.3 SCHEDULE D, CASES I AND II, 72.4 SCHEDULE D, CASE III) for the opening and closing years. In other cases the assessment is on the current year's income. But for corporation tax the assessment is on the actual income of the accounting period.

Where a preceding year accounting period basis has been used for 1995/96 and earlier years, an averaging computation analogous to that described at 71.20 SCHEDULE D, CASES I AND II will be used to determine the assessable income for 1996/97, with the current year basis applying thereafter. (Revenue Booklet SAT 1, para 6.63). See 68.22 SCHEDULE A for Revenue guidelines on the transition from the Case VI charge on furnished lettings to a charge under Schedule A (and see also 74.4 below).

Assessments under Case VI are not earned income unless specifically provided e.g. in *Sec 107* (POST-CESSATION ETC. RECEIPTS (60)), in *Sec 491(5)* (distribution of assets of mutual companies), in *Sec 531(6)* (sale of know-how, see 71.66 SCHEDULE D, CASES I AND II), in *Sec 775(2)* (capitalisation of earnings, see 3.10 ANTI-AVOIDANCE).

74.4 **FURNISHED LETTINGS**

With effect for 1995/96 and subsequent years (subject to the transitional provisions at 68.3 SCHEDULE A) *and for income tax purposes only,* income from furnished lettings is within SCHEDULE A (see 68.8). Previously, and with continuing effect for corporation tax purposes, such income was normally within Case VI (and see 68.22 for Revenue guidelines on the

74.5 Schedule D, Case VI—Miscellaneous Income

transition from Case VI to SCHEDULE A). However, dependent on the nature of the lettings including their frequency and the extent to which the landlord provides services, e.g. cleaning, laundry and meals, the letting may amount to a trade of provision of serviced accommodation within Case I. The letting of caravans may similarly be within Case I or Case VI. (Revenue Press Release 17 May 1984 and see Revenue Pamphlet IR 1, B29). Alternatively the provision of services may be a separate trade (cf. *Salisbury House Estate Ltd v Fry HL 1930, 15 TC 266*). In *Gittos v Barclay Ch D 1982, 55 TC 633*, the letting of two villas in a holiday village was held not to amount to trading. A similar decision was reached in *Griffiths v Jackson; Griffiths v Pearman Ch D 1982, 56 TC 583* in relation to the extensive letting of furnished rooms to students. Where use of furniture is charged under Case VI, the Case VI assessment also includes payments for use of the premises *unless* the landlord elects in writing within two years after end of year of assessment for Schedule A to apply to that rent (see 68.14 SCHEDULE A). [*Sec 15(1)(2); F(No 2)A 1992, s 58; FA 1995, s 39*].

Assessment is on rents received less rent paid, repairs, rates, commission and any other expenses relating to the letting (which may include interest on money borrowed to purchase the property). Apportionment is necessary where only part of premises is let or personally occupied or only let for part of a year.

Expenses of residence (or loss on billeting) elsewhere not allowable (*Wylie v Eccott CS 1912, 6 TC 128* and *Smith v Irvine KB 1946, 27 TC 381*).

CAPITAL ALLOWANCES (10) are not due on plant let for use in a dwelling house [*CAA 1990, s 61(2)*] (but see below as regards furnished holiday lettings). Furniture and furnishing may be dealt with on the renewals basis but an alternative Revenue concession is to allow as depreciation 10% of rents received as reduced by any council tax and water rates or material payments for services borne by landlord but normally a tenant's burden. Where the 10% deduction is allowed, no further deduction is given for the cost of renewing furniture or furnishings, nor for fixtures such as cookers, dishwashers or washing machines which, in unfurnished accommodation, the tenant would normally provide for himself. However, the cost of renewing fixtures which are an integral part of the building (e.g. baths, toilets, washbasins) may be claimed in addition, provided that they are revenue repairs to the fabric. Any different basis in use for a particular case prior to 1975/76 will not normally be disturbed. (Revenue Pamphlet IR 131, A19; Revenue Press Release 28 September 1995). See *Abidoye v Hennessey Ch D 1978, [1979] STC 212*.

Furnished holiday lettings. See 68.9 SCHEDULE A for the full provisions relating to treatment of the commercial letting of furnished holiday accommodation as a trade for certain purposes. Those provisions also applied to the income tax charge under Case VI and the said purposes also included relief for pre-trading expenditure (see 71.75 SCHEDULE D, CASES I AND II) (and such relief applies automatically to a Schedule A business). The provisions continue to apply, where relevant, to furnished holiday lettings chargeable under Case VI for corporation tax purposes and also cover relief for company trading losses under *Secs 393* and *393A(1)* (and covered terminal loss relief under *Sec 394* prior to its abolition). See Tolley's Corporation Tax for these reliefs. For both income tax and corporation tax purposes, expenses are deductible according to SCHEDULE D, CASES I AND II (71) principles as if the letting were a trade. [*Secs 503, 504; CAA 1990, s 29; FA 1996, ss 134, 135, 20 Sch 30, 44, 21 Sch 14*].

'Rent a room' relief for letting of rooms in private residence. See 68.11 SCHEDULE A.

74.5 LOSSES

Losses on transactions which, if profitable, would have been assessable under Schedule D, Case VI (other than losses on transactions falling under *Secs 34–36*, see 68.27 SCHEDULE A), can be set off against any profit or gains charged under Case VI for the same year of assessment or carried forward against the next subsequent profits chargeable under that Case. Claims relating to the amount of losses must be made within, for losses sustained in 1996/97 and later years, five years after 31 January following the tax year in which they arose. A further claim for relief for losses brought forward must be made within five years after 31 January following the tax year for which relief is claimed. For earlier years, the time limit in both cases was six years after the end of the tax year in question. [*Sec 392; FA 1996, s 135, 21 Sch 11*].

Under transitional provisions, a Case VI loss in respect of furnished lettings (see 74.4 above) can be carried forward against Schedule A income of 1995/96 and subsequent years. See 68.13(B) above.

74.6   **ACCRUED INCOME SCHEME (BONDWASHING)**

Introduction. Provisions to counteract bondwashing took effect on 28 February 1986. Bondwashing is the practice of converting income into capital gains by disposing of securities at a time when the price obtained reflects a significant element of accrued interest. Under the accrued income provisions, interest on securities is treated as accruing on a day to day basis between 'interest payment days', and on transfer of the securities a person is charged to income tax on the interest that accrues during the 'final interest period' of his ownership with appropriate adjustments to the taxable incomes of transferor and transferee. There were transitional provisions, intended to limit forestalling before the accrued income scheme came into operation, which applied between 28 February 1985 and 27 February 1986 (for which see Tolley's Income Tax 1992/93 or earlier). The above dates are varied for UNDERWRITERS (89), see 74.27 below.

For **1996/97 onwards**, the accrued income scheme provisions do not apply on a transfer to which *FA 1996, 13 Sch* applies (charge to or relief from tax on the profit or loss realised from the discount on a relevant discounted security, see 72.2 SCHEDULE D, CASE III).

A Revenue Pamphlet (IR 68) is available describing in brief terms the basic rules of the scheme.

These provisions are disapplied for the purposes of corporation tax for accounting periods ending after 31 March 1996, except as respects transfers taking place on or before that date, and subject to transitional provisions. [*Sec 710(1A); FA 1996, 14 Sch 36, 15 Sch 18*]. For the corporation tax securities regime introduced for accounting periods ending after 31 March 1996, and for the transitional provisions, see Tolley's Corporation Tax under Gilts and Bonds.

74.7   The **main definitions** of terms used in the accrued income legislation are in *Secs 710–712*.

'*Securities*' include any loan stock or similar security of any government, or public or local authority, or any company, or other body, whether or not secured or carrying a right to interest of a fixed amount or at a fixed rate per cent and whether or not in bearer form. Not included are shares in a company (other than certain building society shares); securities on which the whole of the return is a distribution under *Sec 209(e)(iv)(v)* (issued by a subsidiary to its non-resident parent, see Tolley's Corporation Tax under Distributions); national and war savings certificates (including Ulster savings certificates); CERTIFICATES OF DEPOSIT (13) and certain other rights for which a certificate of deposit could be, but has not been, issued (see 13.3 CERTIFICATES OF DEPOSIT); and redeemable zero coupon securities (see 44.5, 44.7 INTEREST RECEIVABLE). [*Sec 710(2)(3); FA 1991, 10 Sch 2; F(No 2) A 1992, 8 Sch 5*].

Securities are '*of the same kind*' if so treated by a recognised stock exchange or if they would be so treated if dealt with on such an exchange. [*Sec 710(4)*].

'*Transfer*' in relation to securities means transfer by way of sale, exchange, gift or otherwise, but does not include their vesting in personal representatives on a death after 5 April 1996, or exchanges of gilt-edged securities for strips (or reconsolidation of strips) except as provided by *Sec 722A* (see 74.25 below). A transfer takes effect when an agreement for transfer is made and not at any later date. Except for this, a person '*acquires*' securities when he becomes entitled to them and '*holds*' them on any day if he is entitled to them at the end of that day. Partners in Scottish partnerships are treated as being entitled to securities held by the firm and as carrying out themselves any partnership dealings. [*Sec 710(5)–(9), (10); FA 1996, s 158(1)(5)*].

'*Interest*' includes dividends and any other return (however described) except a return consisting of the excess of a security's redemption amount over its issue price. [*Sec 711(9)*].

An '*interest payment day*' is a day on which interest is payable or, where payment may be made on more than one day, the first such day. [*Sec 711(2)*].

An '*interest period*' is normally the period beginning with the day after one interest payment day (or the day after issue) and ending with the next (or first) such day. If, however, an interest period would otherwise exceed twelve months, it is divided into successive twelve month interest periods with any remaining months also a separate interest period. [*Sec 711(3)(4)*].

The '*interest applicable to securities*' for an interest period is that due at the end of the period, unless the period does not end on an interest payment day. Where the interest period is part of a long period as above, or it is an interest period only by virtue of *Sec 725(9)* (see 74.27 below), the interest applicable is a pro rata proportion of that due at the end of the long period of which the interest period is part. [*Sec 711(7)(8)*].

The '*settlement day*', where securities are transferred through a recognised market such as the Stock Exchange, is the agreed settlement day or, if the transferee may settle on more than one day, the day he settles. If the transfer is not through such a market and the consideration is money alone and there is no interest payment day between the agreement for transfer and the agreed payment day or days, that day (or the latest such day) is the settlement day. If the transfer is not through such a market and either there is no consideration, or it is treated as a transfer by virtue of special provisions in *Secs 710(13), 715(3), 717(8), 720(4), 721, 722, 722A or 724(1A)* (see 74.17, 74.21, 74.19, 74.12, 74.15, 74.16, 74.25 or 74.29 below), the settlement day is the day of transfer. There are also special rules fixing the settlement day for Lloyd's underwriters, see 74.27 below. If the settlement day is not established by one of the above, it is decided by an inspector, subject to review by the General or Special Commissioners on appeal. [*Sec 712; FA 1990, 6 Sch 9, 11; FA 1996, 40 Sch 5*].

74.8   **Determination of accrued income.** When securities are transferred, the 'interest applicable to the securities' for 'the interest period' in which the 'settlement day' falls is apportioned between the old and new owners so that the former is charged to income tax on the interest accrued up to the date of transfer while the latter is similarly charged on the interest accruing from that date. For 1996/97 onwards, a transfer to which *FA 1996, 13 Sch* applies (relevant discounted securities, see 72.2 SCHEDULE D, CASE III) is treated for these purposes as not being a transfer.

The interest actually received is chargeable to tax in the normal way. It may, however, be reduced, or a further charge may arise, as below.

Subject to exceptions in 74.10 below, if the transfer is *with accrued interest* (i.e. with the right to receive the next interest due, or 'cum div'), the transferor is treated as entitled to a sum equal to the 'accrued amount' while the transferee is treated as entitled to relief of the same amount. If, on the other hand, the transfer is *without accrued interest* (i.e. 'ex div') the transferor is treated as entitled to relief equal to the 'rebate amount' while the transferee is treated as entitled to a sum of the same amount.

The *'accrued amount'* is either the gross interest accruing to the settlement day (see 74.7 above) where this is accounted for separately by the transferee (as happens with short-dated gilts), or the 'accrued proportion' of the interest applicable for that interest period (see 74.7 above) in any other case. The *'accrued proportion'* is A/B where A is the number of days in the interest period up to and including the settlement day and B is the number of days in the whole period.

Conversely, the *'rebate amount'* is either the gross interest accruing from the settlement day to the next interest payment date where the transferor accounts to the transferee for this, or the 'rebate proportion' of the interest applicable for that interest period in any other case. The *'rebate proportion'* is (B − A)/B where A and B have the same meanings as for the accrued proportion above. [*Secs 711(5), 713*].

74.9   **Tax charge (or relief).** The various sums and reliefs to which a person is deemed to be entitled as in 74.8 above and which relate to securities of a particular kind in an interest period (see 74.7 above) are aggregated. If the overall result is a sum chargeable to tax, it is taxed under Schedule D, Case VI as if it were income received at the end of the interest period. If, on the other hand, the overall result shows entitlement to relief, the relief is given by way of a reduction in the actual interest received at the end of the interest period so that only the reduced amount is charged to tax. If this reduction is not possible because no interest is received at the end of the interest period, the relief is carried forward to be taken into account in calculating the accrued income or relief in the next interest period. Provision is also made (where relevant) to ensure that a company does not escape liability where the date on which an interest period ends does not fall within an accounting period. [*Sec 714; FA 1996, 41 Sch Pt V(3)*].

74.10   **Exceptions to deeming provisions.** The following are excluded from the accrued income scheme.

(*a*)   Transfers by persons who account for such transfers in the computation of their trading profits or losses (e.g. financial traders).

(*b*)   Transfers by individuals, personal representatives and trustees of mentally disabled persons or persons in receipt of attendance allowance, provided that the nominal value of securities held in the capacity in question does not exceed £5,000 on any day in the year of assessment in which the interest period ends or in the preceding year of assessment. Before 6 April 1990, husband and wife were treated as one for this purpose.

(*c*)   Transfers by persons neither resident nor ordinarily resident in the UK in the chargeable period in which the transfer is made, unless trading in the UK through a branch or agency. However, where such a person does so trade in the UK, the accrued income scheme only applies to securities used, or held, or acquired for use, for the purposes of the branch or agency, if the person is a company, and only to such of those securities as are situated in the UK (within the meaning of *TCGA 1992, s 275*) in other cases.

(*d*)   Transfers of FOTRA securities (see 33.2 GOVERNMENT STOCKS) where the appropriate conditions are met.

74.11 Schedule D, Case VI—Miscellaneous Income

(e) For foreign securities only, transfers by individuals who would be liable to tax on the remittance basis on actual interest on the securities under Schedule D, Case IV or V (i.e. persons not domiciled in the UK, or Commonwealth subjects or citizens of the Republic of Ireland not ordinarily resident in the UK).

The exceptions apply separately by reference to the circumstances of the transferor and the transferee. [*Secs 710(9), 715; FA 1996, s 154, 41 Sch Pt V(18)*].

74.11   *Example*

The following transactions take place between individuals during the year ended 5 April 1997.

Settlement day	Sale by	Purchase by	Securities
15.6.96	X (cum div)	Y	£2,000 15% Exchequer 1997
8.9.96	X (ex div)	P	£3,000 15½% Treasury Loan 1998
15.3.97	S (cum div)	Y	£1,000 9% Treasury Loan 2012

Interest payment days are as follows.

15% Exchequer 1997	27 April, 27 October
15½% Treasury Loan 1998	30 March, 30 September
9% Treasury Loan 2012	6 February, 6 August

Both X and Y owned chargeable securities with a nominal value in excess of £5,000 at some time in either 1995/96 or 1996/97, and both are resident and ordinarily resident in the UK. P is not resident and not ordinarily resident in the UK throughout 1996/97. The maximum value of securities held by S at any time in 1996/97 and 1997/98 is £4,000.

15.6.96 transaction

The transaction occurs in the interest period from 28.4.96 to 27.10.96 (inclusive).

Number of days in interest period	183
Number of days in interest period to 15.6.96	49
Interest payable on 27.10.96	£150

The accrued amount is

$$£150 \times \frac{49}{183} = £\underline{40}$$

X is treated as receiving income (chargeable under Schedule D, Case VI) of £40 on 27.10.96.
Y is given credit for £40 against the interest of £150 he receives on 27.10.96. £110 remains taxable.

8.9.96 transaction

The transaction occurs in the interest period from 31.3.96 to 30.9.96 (inclusive).

Number of days in interest period	184
Number of days in interest period to 8.9.96	162
Interest payable on 30.9.96	£233

The rebate amount is

$$£233 \times \frac{184 - 162}{184} = £28$$

X is given credit for £28 against the interest of £233 he receives on 8.9.96. £205 remains taxable.

P is not assessed on any notional income as he is neither resident nor ordinarily resident in the UK.

15.3.97 transaction
The transaction occurs in the interest period from 7.2.97 to 6.8.97 (inclusive).

Number of days in interest period	181
Number of days in interest period to 15.3.97	37
Interest payable on 6.8.97	£45

The accrued amount is

$$£45 \times \frac{37}{181} = £9$$

S is not assessed on any notional income. He is not within the accrued income scheme provisions as his holdings do not exceed £5,000 at any time in 1996/97 or 1997/98 (the year in which the interest period ends).

Y is given credit for £9 against the interest of £45 he receives on 6.8.97. £36 remains taxable.

74.12   **ACCRUED INCOME SCHEME: SPECIAL CASES**

Nominees and trustees. Transfers made by or to a nominee, or by or to a trustee of a person or persons absolutely entitled as against the trustee (including persons who would be so entitled if not an infant or under a disability), are treated for accrued income scheme purposes as being made by or to the person on whose behalf the nominee or trustee acts. [*Sec 720(1)(2)*].

A person who becomes entitled to securities as trustee immediately after holding them in another capacity is treated as making a transfer within the new legislation. Such a transfer is 'with accrued interest' (see 74.8 above) if the person was entitled to receive any interest payable on the day of transfer or on the next interest payment day. [*Secs 711(6), 720(4)*].

Trustees' accrued income (i.e. excluding that deemed to be that of a beneficiary, see above) is chargeable at the rate applicable to trusts (see 80.5 SETTLEMENTS). This tax is set against any subsequent tax charge under *Sec 687* (payments by trustees of discretionary trusts). The charge does not apply to certain funds in court within *Sec 328*, and special rules apply to calculation of the income of such funds in receipt of interest on securities. [*Sec 720(5); FA 1993, 6 Sch 13*].

Where a trustee is treated as receiving accrued income (see 74.9 above), or where he would have been treated as receiving, or receiving a greater amount of, accrued income if he had been UK resident or domiciled, the SETTLEMENTS (80) provisions apply with the effect that the accrued amount is, broadly, treated as income of the settlor where any actual income would be so treated. Similarly, any actual income received in those circumstances is reduced where the trustee is entitled to relief under the accrued income scheme (see 74.9 above). [*Sec 720(6)–(8); FA 1995, 17 Sch 17*].

74.13 **Interest payable in foreign currency.** Provision is made for establishing the rate of exchange to be used in converting into sterling certain figures used in calculating the accrued income charge.

The accrued amount and the rebate amount (see 74.8 above). Where accrued interest is accounted for separately and the parties specify a sterling equivalent themselves, this figure is used. Otherwise accrued interest is converted at the rate of exchange (the London closing rate) on the settlement day.

Nominal values are converted at the London closing rate for the day in question.

[*Secs 710(12), 713(7)–(9)*].

74.14 **Foreign securities: delayed remittances.** A person (or his personal representatives) may claim to postpone all or part of sums which would be chargeable under the accrued income provisions if

(*a*)   he makes a claim within six years of the end of the interest period in which the transfer occurred, and

(*b*)   he was unable (through no want of reasonable endeavour) to remit the proceeds of transfer(s) to the UK, either because of the laws or government action of the territory in question or because of the impossibility of obtaining foreign currency there.

The postponed sums are taken into account in the chargeable period in which (*b*) above ceases to apply. [*Sec 723*].

74.15 **Death**, subject to below and to special provisions for Lloyd's underwriters (see 74.27 below), is, for deaths **before 6 April 1996**, treated as the occasion of a transfer of all securities to the deceased's personal representatives. The transfer is 'with accrued interest' (see 74.8 above) if the deceased was entitled to receive any interest payable on the day of death or on the next interest payment day thereafter. Any taxable accrued income is deemed to arise on the day of death. Where the transfer to personal representatives and the latters' transfer (with accrued interest) to a legatee takes place in the same interest period, the transfer on death is regarded as being made to the legatee and the transfer by the personal representatives is disregarded. Where death occurs **after 5 April 1996**, the death is *not* treated as giving rise to a transfer to the personal representatives. Where a transfer by the personal representatives to a legatee takes place in the interest period in which the death occurs, the transfer is disregarded for the purposes of the current provisions. [*Secs 711(6), 721; FA 1996, s 158*].

74.16 **Trading stock: appropriations, etc.** A transfer is deemed to be made under the new provisions where a person appropriates to trading stock securities previously held as investments, and vice versa. The transfer is 'with accrued interest' (see 74.8 above) if the person was entitled to receive any interest payable on the day of transfer or on the next interest payment day thereafter. [*Secs 711(6), 722*].

74.17 **Conversions.** On a conversion of securities within *TCGA 1992, s 132*, the person entitled to them immediately before the conversion is treated as transferring them on the day of the conversion (if there is no actual transfer). The transfer is 'with accrued interest' (see 74.8

above) if the person was entitled to receive any interest payable on the day of conversion or on the next interest payment day thereafter. The 'interest period' (see 74.7 above) in which the conversion is made is treated as ending on the day on which it would have ended but for the conversion. [*Secs 710(13), 711(6)*].

74.18 **Transfer of unrealised interest (bearer securities).** Provision is made to ensure that accrued interest which has already become payable before the settlement day (e.g. on bearer securities) does not escape the accrued income scheme. The transferor is treated as entitled to that interest and taxed accordingly while the transferee is not taxed when he actually receives the interest. The exceptions at 74.10 above apply to a charge so arising on the transferor and to the relief arising to the transferee. The capital gains tax calculation of the gain on the disposal by the transferor is adjusted to exclude the accrued interest from the consideration received and the transferee's base cost is similarly reduced by the amount of the relief obtained as above. Where necessary, the unrealised interest is converted into sterling at the London closing rate of exchange on the settlement day. [*Sec 716; TCGA 1992, s 119(4)*]. See also 74.20 below where there is a default in interest payments.

74.19 **Variable rate bonds.** Special rules apply to the transfer of securities unless either

(*a*) they carry interest from issue to redemption at one, and only one, of the following rates:

    (i) a constant fixed rate; or

    (ii) a rate fixed in relation to a standard published base rate or the retail prices index (or foreign equivalent), or

(*b*) they are deep discount securities for which the rate of interest for each interest period does not exceed the yield to maturity (see 44.5 INTEREST RECEIVABLE).

Where securities not within (*a*) or (*b*) above are transferred at any time between issue and redemption, then:

(1) if they are transferred without accrued interest, they are treated as transferred with accrued interest;

(2) the transferor is treated as entitled to a sum equal to such amount (if any) as is just and reasonable (for 1995/96 and earlier years, such amount, if any, as an inspector (or the Commissioners on appeal) decides is just and reasonable);

(3) no relief is available to the transferee; and

(4) the person entitled to the securities immediately before their redemption is treated as transferring them with accrued interest on the day of redemption, giving rise to a charge as in (2) and (3) above.

Where there is a deemed transfer as a result of (4) above, in relation to which the settlement day falls after the end of the only or last interest period in relation to the securities the period from the day following that interest period to the settlement day (inclusive) is treated as an interest period (even if it is longer than twelve months). [*Sec 717; FA 1996, s 134, 20 Sch 35*].

74.20 **Interest in default.** Where there has been a failure to pay interest on the securities, the charge under the accrued income scheme on transfer is calculated by reference to the value of the right to receive the interest on the interest payment day in question rather than the full amount of the interest payable. The provisions regarding transfers of unrealised interest (see 74.18 above) similarly apply by reference to the value of the right to receive the interest (if less than the amount of the unrealised interest). If the transferee subsequently receives the unrealised interest, the assessment on the interest is reduced by the amount of the value of the right to receive the interest at the time of purchase (i.e. the relief given to him at that time). If he transfers the securities with the unrealised interest, the charge on him under the current provisions is restricted to any increase in the value of the right to receive the interest between purchase and re-sale. Special rules apply where unrealised interest is partially repaid and where part of a holding of securities is transferred. [*Secs 718, 719; TCGA 1992, s 119(5)*].

74.21   **Charities** are excluded from the accrued income scheme if any interest actually received would be exempt under *Sec 505(1)(c)(d)*, but where securities cease to be subject to charitable trusts the trustees are treated for the purposes of the legislation as making a transfer at that time. Such a transfer is 'with accrued interest' (see 74.8 above) if the trustees were entitled to receive any interest payable on the day of transfer or on the next interest payment day thereafter. [*Secs 711(6), 715(1)(d), (2)(3)*].

74.22   **Retirement schemes.** Transfers to or by pension funds are excluded from the accrued income scheme as regards the pension fund if any interest received would be exempt under *Sec 592(2)*. [*Sec 715(1)(k), (2)*].

74.23   **Building society bonds.** For 1990/91 and earlier years, where interest was within the composite rate scheme then applicable to building societies (see 9.3 BUILDING SOCIETIES) and was not payable gross, the accrued income scheme applied generally by reference to the grossed-up equivalent of the interest (i.e. the interest grossed up at the basic rate of tax). This applied equally to unrealised interest (see 74.18 above). For the purposes of calculating the income and tax credit for corporation tax or higher rate income tax, the reduction allowed in the amount of interest where a charge arose under these provisions (see 74.9 above) was ignored. [*Sec 726; CGTA 1979, s 33A(5)(c); FA 1991, 19 Sch Pt V*].

74.24   **Sale and repurchase of securities.** Where, under an agreement or agreements entered into under the same arrangement, securities are sold and the transferor, or a person connected with him (within *Sec 839*), either buys them (or similar securities) back or acquires an option to do so which he subsequently exercises, the accrued income scheme provisions are disapplied to both transfers. Securities are 'similar' for this purpose if they entitle the holder to the same rights against the same persons as to capital and interest, and to the same enforcement remedies. The exclusion of such transfers applies where the sale agreement is entered into **on or after 1 May 1995**, except that in relation to any description of securities for which the appointed day under the manufactured payments provisions of *Sec 737A* (see 3.7 ANTI-AVOIDANCE) falls after 1 May 1995, it applies instead to sale agreements entered into on or after that appointed day. [*Sec 727A; FA 1995, s 79*].

The Treasury has broad powers to make regulations providing for the above provisions to apply with modifications (including exceptions and omissions) in relation to cases involving any arrangement for the sale and repurchase of securities where the obligation to repurchase is not performed, or the repurchase option not exercised, or where provision is made by or under any agreement:

(*a*)   for different or additional securities to be treated as, or included with, securities which, for the purposes of the repurchase, are to represent securities transferred in pursuance of the original sale; or

(*b*)   for any securities to be treated as not included with securities which, for repurchase purposes, are to represent securities transferred in pursuance of the original sale; or

(c)   for the sale or repurchase price to be determined or varied wholly or partly by reference to fluctuations, in the period from the making of the agreement for the original sale, in the value of securities transferred in pursuance of that sale, or in the value of securities treated as representing those securities, or for any person to be required, where there are such fluctuations, to make any payment in the course of that period and before the repurchase price becomes due.

Regulations may also make such modifications in relation to cases where corresponding arrangements are made by an agreement, or by related agreements, in relation to securities which are to be redeemed in the period after their sale, those arrangements being such that the vendor (or a person connected with him), instead of being required to repurchase the securities or acquiring an option to do so, is granted rights in respect of the benefits that will accrue from their redemption.

[Sec 737E; FA 1995, s 83(1)].

74.25   **Gilt strips.** Where a person exchanges a gilt-edged security for strips of that security, that person is deemed to have transferred the security with accrued interest (unless the exchange is after the balance has been struck for a dividend on the security but before the day the dividend becomes payable), without any person being treated as the transferee within *Sec 713(2)(b)* (see 74.8 above), and without affecting the end of the interest period in which the exchange takes place. Similarly where strips are reconstituted by any person into the security from which they derived, the security is deemed to have been transferred to that person with accrued interest (unless the reconstitution is after the balance has been struck for a dividend on the security but before the day the dividend becomes payable) without any person being treated as the transferor, and the interest period in which the reconstitution takes place is deemed to have begun on the day specified for that purpose in the security. [Secs 710(13A)(13B), 722A; FA 1996, 40 Sch 3, 4, 6].

74.26   **Stock lending.** The exclusion from the accrued income scheme of transfers by financial traders, etc. (see 74.10(a) above) is not affected by *Sec 129(3)*, which enables certain stock lending transactions to be ignored in computing profits or gains (see 71.81 SCHEDULE D, CASES I AND II). For transfers not within the exclusion, the accrued income scheme provisions are specifically disapplied in relation to such stock lending transactions. [Sec 727].

74.27   **Underwriters.** The accrued income scheme is modified to make it workable within the framework of the special rules which apply to UNDERWRITERS (89). However, with effect for the underwriting year 1994 and subsequent years, the scheme has no application to underwriters' premiums trust funds. [Sec 725; FA 1993, 23 Sch Pt III(12)]. It also has no effect for new-style special reserve funds under *FA 1993* for 1992/93 and subsequent years (see 89.8(b) UNDERWRITERS). Special terms used below are as defined in *Sec 457* and *FA 1993, s 184*, see 89 UNDERWRITERS below. [Sec 710(14); FA 1993, s 183(4)].

For the underwriting year 1993 and earlier years, an underwriter is treated as if he himself made the transfers made by the trustees of his premiums trust fund. For 1991/92 and earlier years of assessment, this also applied with respect to an underwriter's special reserve fund. It continues to apply with respect to an ancillary trust fund (see 89.3 UNDERWRITERS). [Sec 720(3); FA 1993, ss 176(1), 183(5), 23 Sch Pt III(12)].

For the underwriting year 1993 and earlier years, there is a deemed transfer of securities forming part of a premiums trust fund between one calendar year and the next, with accrued interest where appropriate, and with the settlement day being 31 December. This paragraph does not apply where 31 December is an interest payment day for the securities (as the normal provisions will then cater adequately for underwriters). [Sec 725(1)–(6); FA

74.28 Schedule D, Case VI—Miscellaneous Income

1993, 23 Sch Pt III(12)]. For the purposes of these provisions, certain transfers within *Sec 129* (stock lending—see 71.81 SCHEDULE D, CASES I AND II) made by the trustees of a premiums trust fund are, effectively, to be regarded as not having taken place. *[Sec 725(10)(11); FA 1989, s 91; TCGA 1992, s 207(4)(5); FA 1993, 23 Sch Pt III(12)].*

Division of periods straddling year end. Where securities of a premiums trust fund are transferred in a period straddling the end of a calendar year which would otherwise be an interest period (see 74.7 above), that period is not itself an interest period but is instead divided into two interest periods, with the first ending on 31 December and the second beginning on the following 1 January (although this does not apply to other parties to such transfers unless themselves trustees of such funds). *[Sec 725(7)–(9); FA 1993, 23 Sch Pt III(12)].*

Death. When an underwriter dies the normal rules on death (see 74.15 above) do not apply to securities which form part of his premiums trust fund (for 1993 and earlier years), special reserve fund (for 1991/92 and earlier years) or ancillary trust fund (see 89.3 UNDER-WRITERS). Instead his personal representatives are treated as carrying out the deceased's transfers in the interest period in which he died. *[Sec 721(5)(6); FA 1993, s 176(3)(a)(4), 23 Sch Pt III(12)].*

Special reserve fund transfers. As far as the calculation of his annual transfer to an old-style special reserve fund (see 89.8 UNDERWRITERS) is concerned, any accrued income which arises from the underwriter's premiums trust fund, special reserve fund or other required or authorised trust fund is treated as if it were actual income. *[Sec 452(8); FA 1993, 23 Sch Pt III(12)].*

74.28 **Interest etc. on debts between associated companies or to associates of banks.** For accounting periods ending before 1 April 1996, certain debts owed by non-UK resident companies (or certain third parties) to UK resident 'associated' companies (within *Sec 416*), or by any company to a UK resident company associated with a company carrying on a UK banking business, are classed as 'qualifying debts'. Where the debt on a 'security' (within 74.7 above) is a qualifying debt, it is treated as transferred for the purposes of the accrued income scheme on becoming or ceasing to be a qualifying debt, at the end of each accounting period, and on the provisions in question coming into force. *[FA 1993, ss 61–63, 66; FA 1995, ss 88, 89; FA 1996, 41 Sch Pt V(3)].* See Tolley's Corporation Tax under Profit Computations for the detailed provisions, and under Gilts and Bonds for the provisions substituted for later accounting periods.

74.29 **Insurance companies.** For accounting periods ending before 1 April 1996, there are also special provisions dealing with insurance companies. See *Sec 724* as amended. See now Tolley's Corporation Tax under Gilts and Bonds.

74.30 **New issues.** Where

(a) securities of a particular kind are issued (being the original issue of securities of that kind),

(b) new securities of the same kind are issued subsequently, and after 18 March 1991,

(c) a sum (the 'extra return') is payable by the issuer in respect of the new securities, to reflect the fact that interest is accruing on the old securities and calculated accordingly, and

(d) the issue price of the new securities includes an element (separately identified or not) representing payment for the extra return,

then, for the purposes of the accrued income scheme,

(i)   the new securities are treated as having been issued on the '*relevant day*' (being the last 'interest payment day' (see 74.7 above) prior to the actual day of issue, or, if there is no such day, the day on which the original securities were issued);

(ii)   they are treated as transferred *to* the person to whom they are issued, but are not treated as transferred *by* any person; and

(iii)   the transfer is treated as being 'with accrued interest' (see 74.8 above) and as made on the actual day of issue of the new securities, that day being treated as the settlement day (notwithstanding *Sec 712*—see 74.7 above).

If *Sec 717* (see 74.19 above) applies to the new securities, after applying (i) above, (ii) and (iii) above do not apply.

The 'accrued amount' (see 74.8 above) in respect of the transfer in (ii) above is the 'accrued proportion' (see 74.8 above) of the interest applicable for the interest period in which the settlement day falls. If, however, the new securities are issued under an arrangement whereby the 'extra return' (see (*c*) above) is accounted for separately to the issuer by the person to whom the securities are issued, the accrued amount is equal to the extra return so accounted for (or to its sterling equivalent calculated by reference to the London closing rate of exchange on the settlement day, in cases where interest on the new securities is payable in a foreign currency).

[*Sec 726A; FA 1991, 12 Sch 2, 5*].

74.31   INTERACTION WITH OTHER TAXES AND PROVISIONS

Income tax. For 1996/97 onwards, the accrued income scheme provisions do not apply on a transfer to which *FA 1996, 13 Sch* applies (charge to or relief from tax on the profit or loss realised from the discount on a relevant discounted security, see 72.2 SCHEDULE D, CASE III).

Corporation tax. The accrued income scheme provisions are disapplied for the purposes of corporation tax for accounting periods ending after 31 March 1996, except as respects transfers taking place on or before that date, and subject to transitional provisions. [*Sec 710(1A); FA 1996, 14 Sch 36, 15 Sch 18*]. For the corporation tax securities regime introduced for accounting periods ending after 31 March 1996, and for the transitional provisions, see Tolley's Corporation Tax under Gilts and Bonds.

Capital gains tax. Adjustments are necessary to capital gains tax computations where the accrued income scheme applies. The consideration for the disposal is adjusted to exclude or add the accrued or rebate amounts as appropriate (see 74.8 above) and the sums allowed as a deduction to the transferee on a future disposal are correspondingly adjusted. [*TCGA 1992, s 119(1)–(3)*]. Where there is a CGT disposal which is not a transfer (see 74.7 above) for accrued income scheme purposes but which would be within the scheme if it were such a transfer, a transfer is deemed to be made on the day of the disposal and the capital gains tax consideration and sums deductible are adjusted accordingly as above. [*TCGA 1992, s 119(6)–(9)*]. Where there is a conversion of securities within *TCGA 1992, s 132* or an exchange not involving a disposal within *TCGA 1992, Pt IV, Ch II* (reorganisations, etc.) a capital gains tax adjustment is made to allow for the effect of the accrued income scheme. Any accrued amount which the transferor is treated as receiving (see 74.8 above) is first treated as reducing any consideration receivable on the conversion, etc., and then as consideration given for the conversion, etc., while any rebate amount is treated as consideration received for the conversion, etc. [*TCGA 1992, s 119(10)(11)*].

74.32   Double taxation relief.

Where a person is treated as receiving accrued income taxable under Schedule D, Case VI (see 74.9 above) and any interest actually received would be

74.33 Schedule D, Case VI—Miscellaneous Income

liable both to UK tax under Schedule D, Case IV or V (foreign securities) and to foreign tax, he is allowed credit against UK tax on accrued income for foreign tax at the rate at which tax would be payable on interest on the securities. The credit is treated as if it were allowed under *Sec 790(4)*. See 25.4 DOUBLE TAX RELIEF.

Where a person is entitled to double tax relief under *Secs 788, 790(4)* against UK tax on interest which is treated as reduced under the accrued income scheme (see 74.9 above), the credit is reduced to the same proportion that the interest actually taxable bears to the interest which would have been taxable without the reduction. There is a similar reduction where relief is allowed by way of deduction of foreign tax from interest received under *Sec 811(1)*. The proportionate reduction in the credit does not apply if the person entitled to it is an individual unless the interest arises from securities to which he became or ceased to be entitled during the interest period.

[*Sec 807*].

Sec 807 does not apply for corporation tax purposes for accounting periods ending after 31 March 1996 [*Sec 807(6); FA 1996, 14 Sch 45*], but an equivalent corporation tax relief is provided for such periods by *Sec 807A* introduced by *FA 1996, 14 Sch 46*.

74.33 **Anti-avoidance.** Several anti-avoidance measures are affected by this legislation.

Transfer of assets abroad. Where a non-UK resident or non-UK domiciled person would have been treated as receiving income under the accrued income scheme (see 74.9 above) if he had been so resident or domiciled, the accrued income which he would have been treated as receiving is treated as income becoming payable to him for the purposes of *Secs 739–741* (transfer of assets abroad). A corresponding reduction in interest payable for these purposes is made where it would have been made under the accrued income scheme. See 3.8 ANTI-AVOIDANCE. [*Sec 742(4)–(7)*].

Sale and repurchase of securities. Securities within the accrued income scheme are excluded from *Sec 729* (see 3.3 ANTI-AVOIDANCE). [*Sec 729(10)(b)*].

Sec 734 (see 3.6 ANTI-AVOIDANCE) similarly does not apply. [*Sec 731(9)*].

Sec 737 and (after 29 November 1993) *23A Sch* (manufactured dividends and interest, see 3.7 ANTI-AVOIDANCE) take precedence over the accrued income scheme and the latter does not apply to the extent that the transfer is covered by those provisions [*Sec 715(6)(7); FA 1994, s 123(1)(6)*].

74.34 **POWER TO REQUIRE INFORMATION**

Inspectors have power by notice in writing to require Stock Exchange members and other persons acting as UK agents or brokers to provide information about transactions in securities effected by them. Information may not be required about transactions effected more than three years before service of the inspector's notice.

Market makers are excluded from these information requirements. The Board has powers, by regulation by statutory instrument, to broaden the scope of information requirements to include other recognised investment exchanges.

Similarly, any person in whose name securities are registered can be required to state who is the beneficial owner.

The penalty provisions of *TMA s 98* (failure to comply with notices etc.) apply. See 58.4 PENALTIES.

[*Sec 728*].

75   Schedule E—Emoluments

[*Secs 19, 131–207*]

Cross-references. See 19 COMPENSATION FOR LOSS OF EMPLOYMENT; 25 DOUBLE TAX RELIEF; 64 RESIDENCE, ORDINARY RESIDENCE AND DOMICILE for definitions of those terms; 55 PAY AS YOU EARN; 56 PAYMENT OF TAX; 59 PENSIONS; 63 REMITTANCE BASIS; 65 RETIREMENT ANNUITIES AND PERSONAL PENSION SCHEMES; 66 RETIREMENT SCHEMES; 81 SHARE INCENTIVES AND OPTIONS; 82 SOCIAL SECURITY for taxation of benefits.

The headings in this chapter are as follows.

75.1   Basic principles—assessment
75.2   —the three Cases
75.3   Earnings from work done abroad
75.4   —example
75.5   Work done abroad—travelling expenses etc.
75.6   Employees of non-UK domicile
75.7 to 75.46 Assessable income, allowable deductions etc. (see separate index before 75.7)

75.1   **BASIC PRINCIPLES—ASSESSMENT**

Tax is chargeable under Schedule E on the emoluments of offices and employments [*Sec 19*] including 'all salaries, fees, wages, perquisites and profits whatsoever'. [*Sec 131(1)*]. For what constitutes an office see *Edwards v Clinch HL 1981, 56 TC 367*. See also 75.24 below. The charge is under three 'Cases', see 75.2 below. Where, as is normally the case, the employment is held by a person resident and ordinarily resident in the UK and the duties are wholly performed in the UK for a UK employer, the assessment is under Case I.

All the relevant legislation extends to 'offices' as well as employments held.

Basis of assessment after 5 April 1989—receipts basis. Emoluments which are received after 5 April 1989 are assessable in the year of assessment in which they are received (or, in the case of Case III emoluments, received in the UK), regardless of whether or not the office or employment is held at the time of receipt (or receipt in the UK) and whether the emoluments relate to the year of receipt or to a different year (including a year before 1989/90). Emoluments received after the death of the person entitled to them may be assessed and charged on his executors or administrators, and the tax thereon is payable out of the estate. These rules do not, however, apply where the death was before 6 April 1989. [*Sec 202A; FA 1989, s 37*].

For the purposes of the receipts basis, in its application to Schedule E, Cases I and II, emoluments are to be treated as received at the earliest of the following times ((*c*)–(*e*) apply only where the person concerned is a 'director' of a company at any time in the year of assessment in which the event occurs and the emoluments are from an office or employment with that company, whether or not the office or employment is that of director):

(*a*)   when payment is actually made of, or on account of, emoluments;

(*b*)   when a person becomes entitled to such payment;

(*c*)   when sums on account of emoluments are credited in the company's accounts or records, regardless of any restrictions on the director's right to draw those sums;

(*d*)   when a period of account ends and the amount of emoluments for that period has already been determined;

(*e*)   when the amount of emoluments for a period of account is determined and that period has already ended.

75.1 Schedule E—Emoluments

A *'director'* is defined as being any of the following:

(i) a member of a board of directors, or similar body, which manages the company;

(ii) a single director, or similar person, who manages the company;

(iii) a member of the company, in cases where the company is managed by its members;

(iv) a person on whose advice, given other than in a professional capacity, the directors, as defined in (i)–(iii) above, are accustomed to act.

These rules for determining time of receipt do not apply to emoluments in the form of benefits not consisting of money. These are generally treated as received at the time when, or in the year or period in which, the benefit is provided. See also 19.5 COMPENSATION FOR LOSS OF EMPLOYMENT (AND DAMAGES) for the time at which terminal payments within *Sec 148* are treated as being received. [*Sec 202B; FA 1989, s 37*].

Prospective and retrospective remuneration. Without prejudice to the application of the receipts basis, where emoluments would otherwise be for a year of assessment, being the year 1989/90 or any subsequent year, in which a person does not hold the office or employment concerned, then

(A) if the office or employment has never been held, the emoluments are treated as emoluments of the first year of assessment in which it is so held, and

(B) if the office or employment is no longer held, the emoluments are treated as emoluments of the last year of assessment in which it was so held,

except that emoluments cannot be treated under these rules as emoluments of a year of assessment before 1989/90. [*Sec 19(1); FA 1989, s 36(3)(5)*].

Exception: pensions etc. Pensions and social security benefits generally continue to be assessable by reference to the amount accruing in respect of the year of assessment, irrespective of the time of payment. [*FA 1989, s 41*].

See Revenue Press Release 28 July 1989 for guidance on operation of PAYE (55) under the receipts basis, and ICAEW Technical Release TAX 11/93, 9 July 1993 for a review of the tax implications of certain payments to directors.

Basis of assessment before 6 April 1989. As regards emoluments for the year 1988/89 or any earlier year the statutory basis of assessment was the actual amount *earned* during the year and not the amount paid during that year (see *Dracup v Radcliffe KB 1946, 27 TC 188*, and also *Heasman v Jordan Ch D 1954, 35 TC 518*, in which a bonus was spread back to years in which earned). In practice, the payments in the year were used where the remuneration was paid regularly weekly or monthly.

Where remuneration, commission, bonus etc. was based on the trading results of the employer and was not known until after the preparation of annual accounts, this could hold up the assessment, and apportionment of the income between fiscal years could lead to further delay. In these circumstances an 'accounts basis' could be adopted by agreement with the inspector so that the amount of the remuneration shown in the employer's accounts was treated as the income of the tax year in which the accounts ended. If the accounts basis was adopted, the statutory 'earnings' basis had still to apply to

(i) the first year of assessment for which the emoluments were earned;

(ii) the following year of assessment where the emoluments payable for the accounting period ending in that second year related to a period of less than twelve months; and

(iii) the year of cessation and the penultimate year.

The position was subject to review by the Revenue (including a review of earlier years where appropriate) if the accounting date changed or a claim was made by the taxpayer for the earnings basis to apply. Either basis could be applied to a separate source of income. (Tolley's Practical Tax 1981 p 101).

Directors' remuneration was legally assessable for the year in which earned with time apportionment when voted for an accounting period. In practice, the accounts year basis was largely used.

Retrospective remuneration etc. The normal time limits for assessment (see 5.7 ASSESSMENTS) are modified as regards emoluments for 1988/89 and earlier years received before 6 April 1989 but subsequent to the year in which they are assessable; assessments on them can be made up to six years after the tax year in which they were received. (But for deceased persons this time limit expires at the end of the third year after death.) [*TMA ss 35, 40(1)*]. An emolument was, *prima facie*, assessable in the year it was received, unless grounds existed for attributing it to a specific previous period or periods. If the source had then ceased, no liability arose other than, possibly, under *Sec 148* (see 19.5 COMPENSATION FOR LOSS OF EMPLOYMENT (AND DAMAGES)) (*Bray v Best HL 1989, 61 TC 705*).

Basis of assessment—transitional provisions. *FA 1989, ss 38–40* contain transitional provisions consequent on the introduction of the receipts basis of assessment (as above).

Where Case I or II emoluments for a year of assessment before 1989/90 are not paid before 6 April 1989 but are received (as defined by *Sec 202B*—see above) after 5 April 1989 and before 6 April 1991, they are, on written notice (stating the amount involved) being given before 6 April 1991 to the inspector by or on behalf of the employee concerned, to be charged to tax only by reference to the year of assessment in which they are received. The references to 6 April 1991 may be replaced by references to a later date specified by the Board for these purposes in a particular case (see below), and are replaced by a reference to 6 April 1994 (or a later date specified by the Board in a particular case) in the case of an office or employment under or with a Lloyd's underwriting agent to whose business the duties of the office or employment wholly or mainly relate. These provisions do not, however, apply where the only emoluments not paid before 6 April 1989 are for a period consisting of, or falling within, the period from 5 March 1989 to 5 April 1989 inclusive, or if the person entitled to the emoluments died before 6 April 1989. Where the accounts basis was in force for 1987/88, whether or not it was also in force for other years, it will be deemed, in determining (for the purpose of these transitional provisions) the year to which emoluments relate, also to have been in force for 1988/89. Unless already revoked in writing before 6 April 1989, any request to revoke the accounts basis will be ignored in applying these provisions. [*FA 1989, s 38*].

The Revenue will normally exercise its discretion to extend the 6 April 1991 time limit referred to above (for payment of emoluments and claim for the transitional relief) in any case where written notice of the claim is given within three months of the date of issue of an assessment for 1988/89 or 1989/90, whichever is the later, provided the inspector has not already drawn the attention of the taxpayer or his agent to the transitional provision. For the discretion to be exercised in any other cases, taxpayers would have to satisfy the Revenue that, for reasons clearly beyond their control, they were unable to meet the 6 April 1991 deadline or to give written notice within three months of the 1988/89 or 1989/90 assessment. (Revenue Pamphlet IR 131, SP 1/92, 3 January 1992).

Case III emoluments for 1988/89 and earlier years which are received in the UK after 5 April 1989 are not treated as emoluments for any year before 1989/90, but are treated as emoluments for the year of assessment in which they are so received and assessed for that year on the receipts basis. [*FA 1989, s 39*].

Where emoluments for a year of assessment after 1988/89 were paid (or, in the case of Case III emoluments, received in the UK) before 6 April 1989, they will be treated as having been received (or received in the UK) on 6 April 1989 and will thus be assessable for 1989/90 on the receipts basis. [*FA 1989, s 40*].

Other matters:

(1) *Directors' fees received by other companies.* Where a company has the right to appoint a director to the board of another company and the director is required to hand over to the first company any fees or emoluments received from the second company and does so, and the first company agrees to accept liability to corporation tax on the fees, the director is not charged to tax on those fees. Where the first company is not chargeable to corporation tax but to income tax (e.g. a non-resident company not trading through a branch or agency in the UK) and agrees to accept liability, tax is deducted at the basic rate from the fees. This practice is extended to the case where the first company has no formal right to appoint the director to the board but the director is required to, and does, hand over his fees, provided the first company is (*a*) chargeable to corporation tax on its income and (*b*) not a company over which the director has control. '*Control*' for this purpose has the meaning given by *Sec 840* (see 20.8 CONNECTED PERSONS), but in determining whether the director has control of the company the rights and powers of his spouse, his children and their spouses and his parents, will also be taken into account (Revenue Pamphlet IR 1, A37). For directors' fees received by professional partnerships, see 75.24 below.

(2) *Formal assessments* need not be made in cases where the tax collected under PAY AS YOU EARN (55) is correct, unless the taxpayer gives notice within five years after the end of the year of assessment. [*Sec 205*]. In other cases an assessment will be issued in the usual manner. See *SI 1993 No 744, Regs 102–104* for payment by instalments in certain cases. In practice, assessments with tax liability of £75 or less will not be made on National Insurance pensioners and war widows with small tax liabilities which cannot be collected in any other way. (Revenue Pamphlet IR 131, A12).

(3) *Changes in practice.* Where emoluments, dealt with under PAYE, were received more than twelve months before the beginning of the year *in* which the assessment on them is made, that assessment, if made after the period of twelve months following the year *for* which it is made, is to accord with the practice generally prevailing at the end of that period. [*Sec 206; FA 1995, s 111(2)*]. Section 206 cannot, however, displace an unqualified statutory exemption relating to the income in question (*Walters v Tickner CA, [1993] STC 624*).

(4) *Error or Mistake.* Subject to the above, *TMA s 33* (see 17.6 CLAIMS) applies to Schedule E.

(5) *Repayments of tax.* See 41 INTEREST ON OVERPAID TAX for attribution of deductions and repayments and 56.7 PAYMENT OF TAX for administrative practice.

(6) *Divers.* See 71.31 SCHEDULE D, CASES I AND II for treatment of certain divers etc. under Schedule D, Case I.

75.2 **BASIC PRINCIPLES—THE THREE CASES**

The emoluments of an employment are charged under one or more of three Cases, the Case applicable being dependent on the residence and ordinary residence of the employee and where he performs the duties and also, as regards 'foreign emoluments' (see 75.6 below), on his domicile and the residence of the employer. [*Sec 19(1)*].

Case I applies to employees **resident and ordinarily resident** in the UK wherever the duties are performed (but with the exclusion of those receiving 'foreign emoluments', see 75.6 below, in respect of duties performed wholly abroad). The liability is on the total emoluments subject to deductions, see 75.3 to 75.6 below, from earnings from work done abroad and from 'foreign emoluments'. [*Secs 19(1), 192–195*].

Case II applies to employees **not resident (or if resident, not ordinarily resident)** in the UK. The liability is on emoluments from duties performed in the UK subject to a deduction, see 75.6 below, from 'foreign emoluments'. [*Secs 19(1), 195*].

But see 25.2 DOUBLE TAX RELIEF regarding non-resident employees working in the UK for an overseas employer.

Case III applies to employees **resident in the UK (whether ordinarily resident or not)** so far as the emoluments do not fall within Case I or II. The liability is on emoluments received in the UK (i.e. on the REMITTANCE BASIS (63)). [*Sec 19(1)*]. Thus, Case III applies to

(*a*)   employees not domiciled in the UK in respect of emoluments from a non-resident employer (i.e. 'foreign emoluments', see 75.6 below)—*where the duties are performed wholly abroad* and where the employee concerned is resident and ordinarily resident in the UK, and

(*b*)   employees (wherever domiciled) resident but not ordinarily resident in the UK—*in respect of duties performed abroad* (whether for a resident or non-resident employer), including the part abroad if the employment is carried on partly in the UK and partly abroad.

Tax is not chargeable under Case III on emoluments which, had the new legislation had effect for years before 1974/75, would have fallen under Case I or Case II. [*30 Sch 19*].

Remittances include, for 1988/89 and earlier years, (*a*) remittances in that year of emoluments for that year, or for any previous year in which the taxpayer was resident, and (*b*) emoluments for that year of assessment remitted in an earlier year. See 75.1 above for the receipts basis of assessment applying with effect for 1989/90 and subsequent years. Remittances continue to include any sums paid, used or enjoyed in the UK, and any 'constructive remittances', see 63.4 REMITTANCE BASIS. Capital allowances are not applicable, but expenses which would have been allowable (under *Sec 198(1)*, see 75.10 below), had the remuneration been assessable under Schedule E, Case I in the year it arose, may be deducted. [*Secs 132(5), 198(2)(3)*].

Apportionment of emoluments. Where a person resident but not ordinarily resident in the UK performs duties of a single employment both inside and outside the UK, the emoluments will be taxable in full under Case II in respect of the UK duties, but under Case III on amounts remitted to the UK in respect of the non-UK duties. Apportionment of the emoluments between UK and non-UK duties is a question of fact, but time apportionment based on working days inside and outside the UK will normally be applied, unless clearly inappropriate. Where part of the emoluments is paid in the UK, the Revenue practice is to accept that, where a reasonable apportionment has been made between emoluments assessable under Case II and Case III, liability arises under Case III only on any excess of the aggregate of emoluments paid and benefits received in the UK and emoluments remitted to the UK over the amount assessable under Case II. Where none of the emoluments is paid in the UK, remittances are generally taken in the first instance as out of income liable under Case II. (Revenue Pamphlet IR 131, SP 5/84, 28 March 1984).

Duties deemed to be performed in the UK (for the above purposes)

(i)   Offices and employments under the *Crown* of a public nature remunerated out of UK public revenue [*Sec 132(4)(a)*] including civil servants (*Graham v White Ch D 1971, 48 TC 163* and *Caldicott v Varty Ch D 1976, 51 TC 403*) and HM Forces. See 75.27 below, 29.5 and 29.30 EXEMPT INCOME. Certain educational allowances under the Overseas Services Aid Scheme, and daily subsistence allowances paid to Detached National Experts on secondment to the European Commission, are exempt from income tax. (Revenue Pamphlet IR 1, A44, A84). No UK tax is charged in the case of locally engaged unestablished staff working abroad who are not UK resident if the maximum pay for their grade is less than that of an executive officer in UK Civil Service in Inner London. (Revenue Pamphlet IR 1, A25). See also 43.6 INTEREST PAYABLE as regards concessional mortgage interest relief.

(ii)   Duties by *seafarers and members of aircraft crews* if (i) the voyage does not extend to a port outside the UK or (ii) the person concerned is resident in UK and (*a*) the voyage or flight begins or ends in the UK, or (*b*) it is a part, beginning or ending in the UK, of a voyage which does not so begin or end. [*Sec 132(4)(b)*]. But see 75.3 Note (C) below.

Incidental duties in the UK (for the above purposes). If the employment is substantially one where the duties for the year are due to be performed abroad, any duties incidental thereto performed in UK are treated as if performed abroad. [*Sec 132(2)*]. As to whether duties 'incidental' to foreign duties see *Robson v Dixon Ch D 1972, 48 TC 527* (airline pilot employed abroad but occasionally landing in UK where family home maintained, held UK duties more than incidental). But Revenue will normally disregard a single take-off and landing on *de minimis* grounds. (Revenue Pamphlet IR 131, A10). See also Revenue Pamphlet IR 20, paras 6.7, 6.8, and 75.3 Note (D) below.

Leave periods, etc. Emoluments of periods of absence from an employment, all or part of the duties of which are ordinarily performed in the UK, are treated as emoluments for duties performed in the UK, except insofar as, but for that absence, they would have been for duties performed outside the UK. [*Sec 132(1); FA 1996, s 134, 20 Sch 6*]. An airline pilot, the great majority of whose work was performed outside the UK, could not rely on this provision to treat his days of absence from work as days of absence from the UK in the same proportion as his working days (*Leonard v Blanchard CA 1993, 65 TC 589*). It is understood that the Revenue will, by concession, normally regard a university or college lecturer during a period of study leave abroad as performing his duties wholly abroad for the purposes of relief under *Sec 193(1)* (see 75.3 below).

75.3   **EARNINGS FROM WORK DONE ABROAD**

Deductions are made as below from *emoluments within Case I.*

(i)   *Duties performed wholly or partly outside the UK in the course of a qualifying period of* **365 days or more** (which can include days outside the tax year concerned). A deduction is made of **100%** of the emoluments for the duties attributable to the period, i.e. they are completely relieved from UK tax.

A qualifying period consists either (*a*) entirely of consecutive days of absence from the UK or (*b*) of days of absence from the UK *plus* any earlier qualifying period *plus* the intervening period in the UK, provided that the total number of days in the UK in the intervening period and in the earlier qualifying period is not more than one-sixth of the total number of days in the new qualifying period, and that no intervening period is of more than 62 days. Successive intervening periods and periods of absence may continue to qualify as long as these conditions are met in relation to each new period of absence. Overseas duties merely incidental to a UK employment are treated for this purpose as performed in the UK.

The employee must have been resident and ordinarily resident in the UK for tax purposes throughout the qualifying period, although this restriction is applied only to employees who become UK resident and ordinarily resident after 5 April 1992. Previously, persons who had been UK resident but who returned to the UK after having become non-UK resident could count days of absence during which they were non-UK resident as part of a qualifying period. (Revenue Pamphlet IR 131, SP 18/91, 6 December 1991). Following this change of practice, it may be more favourable for a taxpayer departing from or returning to the UK to be treated, in strict accordance with the statute, as UK resident throughout the year of assessment of departure or return, rather than only being so treated for the part of that year falling before the departure or after the return under Revenue Extra-statutory Concession A11 (see 64.5 RESIDENCE, ORDINARY RESIDENCE AND DOMICILE). Schedule E liabilities are normally calculated on the basis that the concession applies unless the application of the statutory basis is requested. (Revenue Tax Bulletin November 1992 p 40).

In the case of seafarers (i.e. where employment consists of performance of duties on a ship, or of such duties and other duties incidental to them), the figures of one-sixth and 62 days above are increased to one-quarter and 90 days for 1988/89 to 1990/91 inclusive, and to one-half and 183 days for 1991/92 and subsequent years. For these increased figures to apply in determining whether a period and an earlier qualifying period, together with the intervening days, are to be a qualifying period, at least one of the intervening days must fall after 5 April 1988 or 5 April 1991 respectively.

A period spent in the UK during a contract of employment but not followed by a period abroad may not be included in the qualifying period (*Robins v Durkin Ch D 1988, 60 TC 700*).

A day of absence means absent from the UK at the end of it.

Emoluments for duties attributable to a qualifying period include emoluments from that employment for a period of leave immediately following that period (and so qualify for the 100% deduction) but not so as to make emoluments for one year of assessment emoluments for another. [*Sec 193(1), 12 Sch 3, 4, 6; FA 1988, s 67; FA 1991, s 45*]. See Notes below.

Gulf war: workers in Kuwait or Iraq. Where the following conditions are satisfied:

(a)   a person was in Kuwait or Iraq at any time in the period of 62 days ending on 2 August 1990;

(b)   he was at that time engaged in performing the duties of an office or employment which were to be performed to a substantial extent in Kuwait or Iraq;

(c)   he returned to the UK after that time;

(d)   the period of absence from the UK ending with his return is not, and is not part of, a qualifying period consisting of at least 365 days; and

(e)   he satisfies the Revenue (or, on appeal, the Commissioners) that it is likely that the period of absence would have been part of such a qualifying period but for events leading up to, or arising from, the invasion of Kuwait on 2 August 1990,

then so much of the period before his return to the UK as would, but for those events, have been part of a qualifying period of at least 365 days is treated as a qualifying period consisting of at least 365 days.

In the case of employment as a seafarer (see above), this provision has effect as if '62 days' read '90 days'. [*FA 1991, s 46*].

(ii)   '*Foreign emoluments*'. See 75.6 below.

Notes to above

(A)   The 100% deduction under (i) above is, for 1992/93 and subsequent years of assessment, applied to the emoluments as reduced by capital allowances and allowable deductions (e.g. expenses, superannuation contributions, foreign travel and accommodation expenses (see 75.5, 75.6 below) and certain 'corresponding' foreign deductions (see 75.6 below)). *[12 Sch 1A; F(No 2)A 1992, s 54]*. This provision was enacted to correct a change inadvertently introduced into the legislation in 1984, which did not come to light until 1992, and which allows the relief to be calculated by reference to gross emoluments, thus enabling a deduction to be made in certain cases from earnings fully taxable in the UK. Claims to relief for 1990/91 and 1991/92 by reference to the gross emoluments will be accepted, and any tax overpaid in settled cases for those years may be repaid under *TMA s 33* (error or mistake relief, see 17.6 CLAIMS). Claims for earlier years will only be accepted where there is an open appeal against an assessment, and the assessment was made before the end of the year following the year of assessment to which it relates, or where an assessment was based on a return made after 5 April 1991. The Revenue consider that any assessment for such earlier years may continue to be made in accordance with the earlier practice (i.e. by reference to the net emoluments) by virtue of *Sec 206* (but see *Walters v Tickner CA, [1993] STC 624,* 75.1(3) above). (Revenue Press Release 8 June 1992).

(B) *Emoluments eligible for relief.* Where the duties of the employment *or* any associated employment are not performed wholly outside the UK, then in (i) above the emoluments relievable are not to exceed a reasonable proportion of the total emoluments having regard to the nature of and the time devoted to duties performed outside and in the UK and to all other relevant considerations.

Employments are associated if the employers are under common control or one controls the other, control being as in *Sec 416* (for companies) and *Sec 840* (for individuals and partnerships, see 20.8 CONNECTED PERSONS). *[12 Sch 2; FA 1996, s 134, 20 Sch 42]*.

(C) Duties performed on a ship or aircraft on any part of a voyage, etc. (or the whole if there is no intervening place of call) beginning or ending in the UK and ending or beginning abroad, are to be treated as performed abroad notwithstanding they may fall to be treated as performed in the UK under *Sec 132(4)(b)* (see 75.2 above). *[12 Sch 5]*.

(D) The question under (i) above as to where any duties are performed or whether a person is absent from the UK shall not be affected by *Sec 132(2)* (incidental duties in the UK, see 75.2 above). *[Sec 132(3)]*.

(E) For deductions for travelling expenses etc., see 75.5, 75.6 below and for seafarers regularly travelling to the same UK port, see 55.36 PAY AS YOU EARN.

See generally Revenue Pamphlet IR 58.

75.4 *Example*

F is sales director of G (UK) Ltd, a UK resident company. He is resident in the UK and made a number of business trips abroad, as follows.

Departed UK	D1	30.9.95
Returned UK	R1	23.12.95
Departed UK	D2	3.1.96
Returned UK	R2	31.5.96
Departed UK	D3	30.6.96
Returned UK	R3	18.12.96
Departed UK	D4	16.1.97
Returned UK	R4	31.3.97

F then worked in the UK for the next three months.

The following steps must be considered.

(i)   The period D1-R1 consists of 84 consecutive days of absence and will therefore be a qualifying period.

(ii) The period D1-R2 must next be considered to establish if the period R1-D2 exceeds 62 days or if that period exceeds $\frac{1}{6}$th of the number of days in the period D1-R2. Period R1-D2 comprises 11 days; it is therefore not more than 62 days and not more than $\frac{1}{6}$th of 244 days and so D1-R2 becomes a qualifying period.

(iii) The period D1-R3 is then examined on the same basis as the previous period. Period R2-D3 comprises 30 days; it is therefore not more than 62 days and since R1-D2 (11 days) and R2-D3 (30 days), or 41 days in total, are not more than $\frac{1}{6}$th of D1-R3 (445 days), D1-R3 becomes a qualifying period (and is a qualifying period of at least 365 days).

(iv) The final period D1-R4 (548 days) is then examined. Period R3-D4 comprises 29 days; it is therefore not more than 62 days and since the previous 41 days (see (iii) above) and the 29 days (70 days in total) are not more than $\frac{1}{6}$th of 548 days, D1-R4 becomes a qualifying period.

The position can be summarised as follows.

		Total	1995/96	1996/97	Days in UK	1/6 of total
Abroad	D1-R1	84	84			
In UK	R1-D2	11	11		11	
Abroad	D2-R2	149	94	55		
	D1–R2	244			11	40
In UK	R2-D3	30		30	30	
Abroad	D3-R3	171		171		
	D1–R3	445			41	74
In UK	R3-D4	29		29	29	
Abroad	D4-R4	74		74		
	D1–R4	548	189	359	70	91

Note

(a)   D1–R3 is itself a 365-day qualifying period, so the 100% deduction becomes due at this point. However, the qualifying period can be extended by R3–R4, thus enabling further emoluments to qualify. As F then spent three months (i.e. more than 62 days) in the UK, the qualifying period D1–R4 cannot be further extended even if there are subsequent periods of working abroad.

75.5   WORK DONE ABROAD—TRAVELLING EXPENSES ETC.

For travelling expenses generally, see 75.43 below. For certain expenses of MPs, see 29.15 EXEMPT INCOME.

Where the duties of an employment by an employee resident and ordinarily resident in the UK are performed abroad, the following deductions may be made from his emoluments (if not 'foreign emoluments', see 75.6 below).

75.6   Schedule E—Emoluments

(i)   **Where duties performed wholly outside the UK**

(*a*)   Travelling expenses incurred by the employee from any place in the UK to take up the overseas employment and to return on its termination.

(*b*)   Board and lodging outside the UK provided or reimbursed by the employer (so far as included in the assessable emoluments) to enable the employee to perform the duties of the overseas employment.

[*Sec 193(2)–(4)*].

(ii)   **More than one employment**

Where two or more employments are held and at least one of them is performed wholly or partly outside the UK, and travelling expenses are incurred by the employee in travelling from one place where duties of one employment were performed to another place to perform duties of another, and either or both places are outside the UK, the expenses are deductible from the emoluments of the second employment (if not 'foreign emoluments', see 75.6 below). [*Sec 193(5)(6)*].

Apportionment applies where expenses are partly for performing the duties and partly for another purpose.

(iii)   **Where duties are performed partly outside the UK**

Travel facilities, provided or reimbursed by the employer (so far as included in the assessable emoluments), between any place in the UK and the place of performance of any of the duties outside the UK, either

(*a*)   for the employee, provided that the duties concerned can only be performed outside the UK, and that the absence from the UK is wholly and exclusively for the purpose of performing the duties concerned, or

(*b*)   where there is absence from the UK for a continuous period of 60 days or more, for the spouse and any children under 18 (at beginning of outward journey) accompanying the employee at the beginning of the period of absence or visiting him during that period, including the return journey, but with a limit of two outward and return journeys per person in any year of assessment.

For these purposes, duties performed on a ship or aircraft on a voyage or flight extending to a port outside the UK are not treated under *Sec 132(4)* (see 75.2(ii) above) as performed in the UK, and the requirements as to place of performance of duties are suitably modified.

[*Sec 194*].

For travel on leave by HM Forces, see 75.27 below.

See generally Revenue Pamphlet IR 58.

75.6   **EMPLOYEES OF NON-UK DOMICILE**

UK resident employer. A deduction may be allowed from emoluments for duties performed in the UK for the cost of certain travel facilities provided or reimbursed by the employer (so far as included in assessable emoluments) for a period of five years beginning with the date of arrival in the UK to perform the duties of the employment. This applies to facilities provided

(a)   for any journey between the employee's usual place of abode (i.e. the country outside the UK where he normally lives) and any place in the UK in order to perform, or after performing, any duties of the employment, and

(b)   where the employee is in the UK for the purpose of performing the duties of any such employment for a continuous period of 60 days or more, for any outward and return journey by his spouse or child (under 18 at the beginning of the journey to the UK) between his usual place of abode and the place where any of those duties are performed in the UK, either to accompany him at the beginning of the period or to visit him during it (but limited to two outward and return journeys by any person in a year of assessment).

No deduction is, however, available unless, on a date on which he arrives in the UK to perform the duties, either

(i)   he was not resident in the UK in either of the two immediately preceding years of assessment, or

(ii)   he was not in the UK for any purpose at any time in the two years ending immediately before that date.

If this condition is satisfied on more than one date in a year of assessment, relief is given by reference to the first such date only. [*Sec 195(1)–(12)*].

Non-UK resident employer. Emoluments of a person not domiciled in the UK from an employer not resident in the UK (other than emoluments of a UK resident from an employer resident in Eire) are '*foreign emoluments*'. [*Sec 192(1)*]. The existence of a branch or agency of an overseas employer does not normally of itself make the overseas employer UK resident for this purpose, even where profits of the branch or agency are liable to UK tax (Tolley's Practical Tax 1983 p 156).

Foreign emoluments are excepted from Case I but remain within Case III where the duties are performed *wholly abroad*. Where the duties are performed *wholly or partly in the UK*, the normal rules apply and they are within Case I, II or III as appropriate (see 75.2 above). [*Sec 192(2)*].

Certain payments made by an employee out of 'foreign emoluments' 'in circumstances corresponding to those in which the payments would have reduced his liability to income tax' may be allowed as a deduction in computing the amount of the emoluments. [*Sec 192(3); F(No 2)A 1992, s 60*].

Travelling expenses. The conditions for relief for travelling expenses described above in relation to employments with UK resident employers apply equally to employments with non-resident employers, except that

(1)   the condition for relief at (i) or (ii) above does not apply before 6 April 1986, and

(2)   where relief is available in 1984/85 or 1985/86 only by virtue of (1) above, relief continues to be available until 5 April 1991, but condition (i) or (ii) above must be satisfied for relief to be available thereafter.

[*Sec 195*].

75.7 Schedule E—Emoluments

ASSESSABLE INCOME, ALLOWABLE DEDUCTIONS ETC.

Main headings below are in alphabetical order.

75.7 ASSESSABLE INCOME GENERALLY

The income assessable as *emoluments* of an office or employment includes 'all salaries, fees, wages, perquisites and profits whatsoever'. [*Sec 131(1)*]. (For other income assessable under Schedule E, see 59 PENSIONS; 82 SOCIAL SECURITY; 19 COMPENSATION FOR LOSS OF EMPLOYMENT and 81 SHARE INCENTIVES AND OPTIONS.) See 3.10 ANTI-AVOIDANCE regarding capital sums received in lieu of earnings. [*Sec 775*]. The emoluments assessable are those arising from the office or employment, regardless of by whom they are provided (see e.g. *Shilton v Wilmshurst HL 1991, 64 TC 78*).

In general terms, where there is no explicit legislation to the contrary, the assessable income is what comes to the employee in respect of the employment in money or money's worth. For an early and important statement of this, see *Tennant v Smith HL 1892, 3 TC 158*. Where an employee was granted a share option, the emolument was the granting of the option (any subsequent increase in value not being an emolument) (*Abbott v Philbin HL 1960, 39 TC 82*). See, however, *Bootle v Bye; Wilson v Bye (Sp C 61), [1996] SSCD 58*, where payments under an agreement with a third party, and not the rights under the agreement, were held to be emoluments.

Whether 'money's worth' received by an employee comes to him as an emolument may be a difficult question of fact. For modern examples see *Hochstrasser v Mayes HL 1959, 38 TC 673* (compensation for loss on sale of house on transfer, held not assessable); *Wilcock v Eve Ch D, [1995] STC 18* (payment for loss of rights under share option scheme, held not assessable), and contrast *Hamblett v Godfrey CA 1986, 59 TC 694* (payment for loss of trade union, etc. rights, held assessable); *Laidler v Perry HL 1965, 42 TC 351; Brumby v Milner HL 1976, 51 TC 583; Tyrer v Smart HL 1978, 52 TC 533*. The meeting by the employer of a pecuniary liability of the employee constitutes money's worth, see e.g. *Hartland v Diggines HL 1926, 10 TC 247* (tax liability), *Nicoll v Austin KB 1935, 19 TC 531* (rates, etc. of employee's residence), and *Glynn v CIR PC 1990, 63 TC 162* (payment direct to school of child's school fees); this applies to payment of the employee's community charge (and, in Scotland, community water charge) (Revenue Press Release 10 November 1989) or council tax (Revenue Press Release 16 March 1993), and to payment of parking etc. fines of employees (although certain fixed penalties relating to company cars may be the employer's liability) (Tolley's Practical Tax 1988 p 120, 1990 p 63). For specific items and legislation modifying the general rule, see 75.8 onwards below.

Hence, subject to any special legislation, board, lodging, uniforms, etc. provided by the employer and not convertible into money are not assessable, but cash allowances *in lieu* are assessable, e.g. a clothing allowance to a 'plain-clothes' policeman (*Fergusson v Noble CS 1919, 7 TC 176*); a meals allowance when working abnormal hours (*Sanderson v Durbridge Ch D 1955, 36 TC 239*); lodging allowances to army personnel (*Nagley v Spilsbury Ch D 1957, 37 TC 178*); an allowance to meet extra cost of living abroad (*Robinson v Corry CA 1933, 18 TC 411*). See 75.30 below for luncheon vouchers. See also 29.15 EXEMPT INCOME as regards accommodation allowances for Members of Parliament and 75.29 below as regards living accommodation generally. Where deductions were made from salary for board etc., held gross amount assessable (*Cordy v Gordon KB 1925, 9 TC 304; Machon v McLoughlin CA 1926, 11 TC 83*). Where a higher salary may be taken in lieu of the provision of free board and lodging, the value of the provision is taxable, but see Revenue Pamphlet IR, A60 as regards concessional treatment of agricultural workers. It is understood that a similar concession is applied to stable lads employed by racehorse trainers.

Where an employee used his car in the course of his duties, a lump sum and mileage allowances were held to be emoluments (*Perrons v Spackman Ch D 1981, 55 TC 403*). See 75.43 below as regards mileage allowances and travelling and subsistence allowances generally. 'Garage allowances' to salesmen with company cars were held to be assessable in *Beecham Group Ltd v Fair Ch D 1983, 57 TC 733*, but expenditure on the provision of car parking facilities for an employee at or near his place of work does not constitute an emolument. [*Sec 197A*].

Financial loss allowances, or payments for loss of earnings, to members of public bodies, or to magistrates or those on jury service, are not taxable under Schedule E (although when received by the self-employed they are taxable as business receipts, see 71.47(*e*) SCHEDULE D, CASES I AND II). (Revenue Schedule E Manual, SE 1165). For the PAYE treatment of local councillors' attendance allowances, see 55.30 PAY AS YOU EARN.

By concession, cash allowances to miners in lieu of free coal are not assessed. (Revenue Pamphlet IR 1, A6).

Employer's gift of clothing assessable on *second-hand* value (*Wilkins v Rogerson CA 1960, 39 TC 344*), but gift voucher available for use only in specified shop assessable on face value (*Laidler v Perry HL 1965, 42 TC 351*) but see 75.44 below for legislation now applicable although the case remains an important authority on what constitutes an emolument. Also see *Heaton v Bell HL 1969, 46 TC 211* (assessment on free use of car connected with reduction in wages but see company car legislation at 75.15 below).

Interest on money loaned interest-free, subject to conditions and repayable on demand, by the employer to a trust for the benefit of an employee held to be emoluments within Schedule E (*O'Leary v McKinlay Ch D 1990, 63 TC 729*).

Endowment premiums paid by employers are assessable (*Richardson v Lyon KB 1943, 25 TC 497*). But trustees' payments out of fund set up by employers for assisting education of employees' children held not assessable on parent (*Barclays Bank v Naylor Ch D 1960, 39 TC 256*) but see now educational scholarships under 75.20 below. In *Ball v Johnson Ch D 1971, 47 TC 155*, a discretionary payment to employee for passing an examination was held not assessable (but see 75.13 below for treatment of such awards as benefits-in-kind). Commission applied in taking up shares held assessable (*Parker v Chapman CA 1927, 13 TC*

677). In *Clayton v Gothorp Ch D 1971, 47 TC 168*, a loan to a former employee for improving qualifications, which became non-repayable when the employee returned to employer's service after qualification, was held assessable for year in which it became non-repayable. Where wages paid in gold sovereigns, held their market value to be taken as the measure of the emoluments (*Jenkins v Horn Ch D 1979, 52 TC 591*).

Whether lump sum payments, etc. on taking up an employment are emoluments of the employment or non-taxable inducements is a question of fact. Signing-on fees to an amateur footballer on joining a Rugby League club were held to be assessable in *Riley v Coglan Ch D 1967, 44 TC 481*, distinguishing *Jarrold v Boustead CA 1964, 41 TC 701*. It is, however, understood that any fee not exceeding £8,500 (£6,000 before 8 October 1993) paid for surrender of amateur status to a rugby player turning professional (insofar as that distinction still applies) will be treated as free of tax, although a fee exceeding that figure will be taxable in full. In *Shilton v Wilmshurst HL 1991, 64 TC 78*, a transfer fee paid by his old club to a professional footballer was taxable as an emolument of his new employment. The value of shares allotted to an accountant on becoming managing director of a company was held not to be assessable in *Pritchard v Arundale Ch D 1971, 47 TC 680*, but an opposite conclusion was reached on the facts in *Glantre Engineering Ltd v Goodhand Ch D 1982, 56 TC 165*. See now 75.34 below. A lump sum payment for giving up rights to trade union representation was assessable (*Hamblett v Godfrey CA 1986, 59 TC 694*).

For the Revenue view of the taxation implications of guaranteed selling price (or similar) schemes for houses as part of employee relocation packages, see Revenue Tax Bulletin May 1994 p 122 and April 1995 p 211.

75.8   **BENEFITS**

Generally, if an employee receives money or money's worth from his employment he is chargeable to tax on that amount. However, he or his family may receive benefits by reason of his employment where special legislation is required if taxation is to apply. For benefits derived by directors and certain employees from their employment, see 75.11 *et seq.* below. For other benefits of general application, see under the appropriate heading of this chapter. A benefit provided by a third party (e.g. a car provided by a car dealer to a football player for promotional purposes) is potentially within the benefits charging provisions where it is provided by reason of the employment.

See 59.1 pensions as regards the provision of benefits to retired employees.

Certain of the exceptions listed at 75.13 below from the special charge on benefits apply also where a charge would otherwise arise under the general Schedule E provisions. See in particular 75.13(v)–(viii), (x)–(xii), (xxii).

See 55.12 pay as you earn as regards PAYE settlement agreements whereby employer accounts for tax on minor benefits, which do not then count as employees' income.

75.9   **CLERGYMEN, ETC.**

By *Sec 332*, a clergyman is not assessable on any sums paid for or refunded to him in respect of any 'statutory amounts' payable or 'statutory deductions' made in connection with the residence made available to him by a charity or ecclesiastical corporation for carrying out his duties (except in so far as they relate to any part of the premises which he lets). This exemption applies to the meeting of the Scottish community water charge, but not to the personal community charge (Revenue Press Release 10 November 1989). In addition (unless he is in 'director's or higher-paid' employment, see 75.11 below) no account is taken of the value of any expenses relating to his own living accommodation so provided [*Sec 332(2)(c)*], and, by concession, no liability arises in respect of payment or reimbursement of his heating, lighting, cleaning or gardening expenses (Revenue Pamphlet IR 1, A61). Up to one-quarter of the aggregate of any expenses of maintenance, repair, insurance or management of the premises borne by him may be allowed as a deduction from his emoluments.

If he pays rent in respect of a dwelling-house any part of which is used mainly or substantially for his duties, up to one-quarter thereof may be deducted from emoluments, under *Sec 332(3)(b)*. Also, expenses necessarily etc., incurred in performance of duties (e.g. postage, stationery, telephone, car, etc.) may be deducted. Concessionally, regard is had to the cost of *locum tenens* for illness or holidays and (sometimes) lighting, heating, cleaning and rates of study. The expenses of a minister in visiting his congregation were allowed (*Charlton v CIR CS 1890, 27 SLR 647*) but not expenses of a curate in moving from one curacy to another (*Friedson v Glyn-Thomas KB 1922, 8 TC 302*). In *Mitchell v Child KB 1942, 24 TC 511*, cost of opposing a Bill which would have dispossessed rector of parsonage was allowed.

Gifts to a clergyman including voluntary subscriptions and collections (*In re Strong C/E/S 1878, 1 TC 207; Slaney v Starkey KB 1931, 16 TC 45*), Easter offerings (*Cooper v Blakiston HL 1908, 5 TC 347*) and grants (*Herbert v McQuade CA 1902, 4 TC 489; Poynting v Faulkner CA 1905, 5 TC 145*) are assessable but not where in recognition of past service (*Turner v Cuxson QB 1888, 2 TC 422*). The cost of maintenance of a priest living in communal presbytery held not assessable as not convertible into money (*Daly v CIR CS 1934, 18 TC 641*).

An unbeneficed clergyman was held to be within Schedule E (*Slaney v Starkey* above) as was a professed nun employed as a teacher (*Dolan v K Supreme Court (IFS), 2 ITC 280*) but not the headmaster of a school established by a congregation of secular priests (*Reade v Brearley KB 1933, 17 TC 687*).

For the treatment of contemplative religious communities, see Revenue Pamphlet IR 131, B10.

75.10   **DEDUCTIONS GENERALLY**

(*a*)   A deduction is allowed for money 'necessarily' as regards travelling expenses, and 'wholly, exclusively and necessarily' as regards other expenses, expended 'in the performance of duties' of the employment or office. [*Sec 198(1)*]. The inclusion of 'necessarily' and 'in the performance of the duties' imposes an additional restriction on the allowability of items under Schedule E as compared with those generally deductible under Schedule D. It follows that expenses incurred prior to entering upon duties or merely in preparation for them are not allowed. See *Nolder v Walters KB 1930, 15 TC 380*, air pilot allowed hotel expenses because incurred *in course of duty*, but not car and telephone *merely in preparation for it*, and *Bhadra v Ellam Ch D 1987, 60 TC 466* where a doctor's travelling and secretarial expenses in relation to locum posts obtained through medical agencies were not allowed, as his duties commenced only on arrival at the hospital concerned. But contrast *Pook v Owen HL 1969, 45 TC 571* where a GP with a part-time Schedule E hospital appointment was allowed his expenses of travelling to the hospital from his home (where his surgery was), not covered by his mileage allowance, because, on the facts, his home as well as the hospital was a place where he carried out the duties of his appointment. See also *Gilbert v Hemsley Ch D 1981, 55 TC 419* and 75.43 below generally.

Use of room at home for business purposes allowed (*Newlin v Woods CA 1966, 42 TC 649*) but not alternative room for son's homework (*Roskams v Bennett Ch D 1950, 32 TC 129*). No deduction was allowable for any part of the employee's personal community charge liability, but a deduction may be due for a proportion of the council tax payable where a room or rooms are used exclusively for work purposes. (Revenue Press Releases 10 November 1989, 16 March 1993).

75.11 Schedule E—Emoluments

Expenses of a part-time Schedule E appointment not allowable under Schedule E may not be deducted in computing the profits of an associated business within Schedule D (*Mitchell & Edon v Ross HL 1961, 40 TC 11*).

(b) **Expenses not allowed** include: employment agency fees (*Shortt v McIlgorm KB 1945, 26 TC 262*); meal expenses paid out of meal allowances (*Sanderson v Durbridge Ch D 1955, 36 TC 239*); living expenses paid out of living allowances when working away from home (*Elderkin v Hindmarsh Ch D 1988, 60 TC 651*); headmaster's course to improve background knowledge (*Humbles v Brooks Ch D 1962, 40 TC 500*); articled clerk's examination fees (*Lupton v Potts Ch D 1969, 45 TC 643*); cost of ordinary clothing (*Hillyer v Leeke Ch D 1976, 51 TC 90; Woodcock v CIR Ch D 1977, 51 TC 698; Ward v Dunn Ch D 1978, 52 TC 517*); rental of telephone installed at employer's behest, but not used *wholly* and *exclusively* in performance of duties (*Lucas v Cattell Ch D 1972, 48 TC 353*); telephone and other expenses of consultant anaesthetist (*Hamerton v Overy Ch D 1954, 35 TC 73*); and journalists' expenditure on newspapers and periodicals (*Fitzpatrick v CIR and related appeals (No 2), Smith v Abbott and related appeals HL, [1994] STC 237*).

Any excess cost of living in place where required by work (*Bolam v Barlow KB 1949, 31 TC 136; Collis v Hore (No 1) KB 1949, 31 TC 173; Robinson v Corry CA 1933, 18 TC 411*); cost of domestic assistance where wife employed (*Bowers v Harding QB 1891, 3 TC 22*); cost of looking after widower's children (*Halstead v Condon Ch D 1970, 46 TC 289*). Entertaining expenses are not allowed [*Sec 577*], but see 71.54 SCHEDULE D, CASES I AND II for exceptions. However where an employer is not allowed a deduction for expenditure on business entertainment paid by him, directly or indirectly, to a member of his staff, and that sum is also taxable as emoluments of the employee (see 75.12 below) the employee is allowed an equivalent deduction from taxable emoluments for expenses defrayed out of that sum. [*Sec 577(3)*].

(c) For travelling, subsistence and incidental overnight expenses etc., see 75.43 below, and for other specific deductions, see below at 75.25 (flat rate expenses), 75.39 (subscriptions) and 75.42 (training, etc.).

(d) For provision of security assets and services for employees, see 75.35 below.

(e) For capital allowances where plant or machinery is provided for the purposes of an employment, see 10.24 CAPITAL ALLOWANCES. See also 75.43 below.

(f) For expenditure by Members of Parliament on accommodation, see 75.29 below.

(g) For charitable donation payroll deduction scheme, see 15.7 CHARITIES.

(h) For deduction of agents' fees by artistes, see 75.24 below.

(j) For expenditure on indemnity insurance and on certain liabilities such as legal costs in relation to the employment, see 75.23 below.

75.11 DIRECTORS OR HIGHER-PAID EMPLOYEES

(*Note.* The term 'higher-paid employee' was replaced by a reference to employment with emoluments at the rate of £8,500 p.a. or more by *FA 1989, s 53*. No alteration to the import of the benefits legislation results from the change, and the term 'higher-paid employee' is for convenience retained in the coverage of that legislation in this section.)

The provisions of *Secs 153–168* apply to

(I) every director, except if he has no material interest (i.e. broadly if his and/or his associates' interests in the company do not exceed 5%) in the company *and either* is a full-time working director *or* the company is non-profit-making (i.e. it does not carry on a trade nor is its main function the holding of investments or other property) *or* the company is a charity,

780

(II) any person with emoluments at the rate of £8,500 a year or more including all chargeable benefits etc. (together with certain amounts otherwise covered by the special car benefit rules, and a modified amount in respect of certain beneficial home loans) and before any deduction for necessary expenses of employment etc., but after deducting any contributions to approved superannuation funds in respect of which the individual is entitled to tax relief as an expense (see 66.5(a) RETIREMENT SCHEMES), any exempt profit-related pay (see 75.31 below) and any contributions under an approved payroll giving scheme (see 15.7 CHARITIES). For 1995/96 onwards, where an alternative is offered to a company car such that if it had been chargeable under general Schedule E rules the taxable amount would have exceeded the car and fuel benefits computed as in 75.15(i)(iv) below, the excess is taken into account in ascertaining emoluments for this purpose. All employments with the same employer are treated as director's or higher-paid if (i) the total of emoluments from those employments is at the rate of £8,500 a year or more or (ii) one or more of those employments is director's or higher-paid. An individual, partnership or body is deemed to be the employer where he or it controls the employing partnership or body. [Secs 167, 168(8)–(12); FA 1991, 6 Sch 2; FA 1993, 6 Sch 1; FA 1995, s 43(3)(4)].

A person under (I) or (II) above will be assessable under Schedule E on payments and benefits (so far as not refunded or paid for by him) received *and not otherwise taxable*, but may claim relief under *Sec 198* (expenses 'wholly and necessarily incurred', see 75.10 above), *Sec 201* (see Subscriptions at 75.39 below), *Sec 201AA* (see Employee liabilities and indemnity insurance at 75.23 below) and *Sec 332(3)* (see Clergymen at 75.9 above).

No amount will be assessable where a payment or provision is made by an employer, being an individual, in the normal course of his domestic, family or personal relationships. [*Secs 153, 154, 168(3); FA 1995, s 91(2); FA 1996, s 134, 20 Sch 10(1)*].

See 75.22 below for dispensations.

A director excluded from (I), e.g. by working for a charity, may nevertheless be within (II), e.g. if his emoluments exceed the prescribed amount.

Detailed application of the provisions is covered in 75.12–75.22 below.

75.12 **Expenses.** All payments for expenses, including sums put at employee's disposal and paid away by him, are assessable. [*Sec 153*]. Includes use of employer's credit card. See also the exceptions at 75.13 below. See 55.12 PAY AS YOU EARN as regards PAYE settlement agreements whereby employer accounts for tax on minor payments of expenses within the agreement, which do not then count as employeees' income.

75.13 **Benefits-in-kind generally.** All benefits provided (including to employee's family or household) of accommodation (other than living accommodation, for which see 75.29 below), entertainment, domestic or other services and other benefits and facilities whatsoever are assessable. See 75.15–75.20 for special charging provisions. The amount to be assessed is the cash equivalent of the benefit (see below). Included are benefits provided by reason of an employment by someone other than the employer. [*Secs 154, 155(1)*].

In relation to the timing of a benefit, 'provided' refers to the fulfilment by the employer of the conditions necessary for the benefit to be made available, rather than to its being made available to the employee (*Jacobs v Templeton (Sp C 25), [1995] SSCD 150*).

See 59.1 PENSIONS as regards benefits provided to retired employees.

Following the decision in *Wicks v Firth HL 1982, 56 TC 318*, payments of cash are potentially within the benefits legislation, so that for example examination awards which would otherwise not be taxable following *Ball v Johnson* (see 75.7 above) fall within the benefits charge. (ICAEW Technical Memorandum TR 786, 15 March 1990).

Legal expenses incurred by a company in defending a dangerous driving charge against a director were held to be a benefit (*Rendell v Went HL 1964, 41 TC 641*). Parking, etc. fines met by employer would generally constitute a benefit.

Exceptions are

(i)   Provision of accommodation, supplies, services, etc. in premises occupied by the employer or other provider and used solely in performing duties. [*Sec 155(2)*].

(ii)   Provision of living accommodation and connected expenses in certain circumstances, see 75.29 below. [*Secs 154(2), 155(3), 163*].

(iii)   Provision of any pension, annuity, lump sum, gratuity or other like benefit to employee or his dependants to be given on his death or retirement. (But see under 66.1 RETIREMENT SCHEMES.) [*Sec 155(4)*]. This is extended by concession to include provision of death or retirement benefits to any member of the employee's family or household, e.g. including a parent or a son- or daughter-in-law. (Revenue Pamphlet IR 1, A72).

(iv)   Provision of meals in any canteen in which meals are provided for staff generally. [*Sec 155(5)*]. Relief is extended by concession to all free or subsidised meals provided on the business premises, and to the use of any ticket or token to obtain such meals, if meals are provided on a reasonable scale and either free or subsidised meals are available on a reasonable scale to all employees, whether on the business premises or elsewhere, or free or subsidised meal vouchers are provided for staff for whom meals are not provided. The concession does not extend to provision in a hotel or catering, etc. business of staff meals in a restaurant or dining-room at a time when meals are being served to the public, unless part of it is designated for staff use only. (Revenue Pamphlet IR 1, A74).

(v)   Provision of travel, accommodation and subsistence during public transport disruption caused by industrial action. (Revenue Pamphlet IR 1, A58). See also 75.43 below.

(vi)   Provision of transport between home and place of employment for severely disabled employees. (Revenue Pamphlet IR 1, A59). See also 75.15, 75.43 below.

(vii)   Provision of transport for occasional late night journeys from work to home, subject to certain conditions. (Revenue Pamphlet IR 1, A66). See also 75.43 below.

(viii)   Provision of transport between mainland and offshore rig, etc., and necessary overnight accommodation on the mainland, for offshore oil and gas workers. (Revenue Pamphlet IR 1, A65).

(ix)   Travelling expenses (including reasonable hotel expenses) of

(A)   a director of two or more companies within a group of companies, between his main place where he acts as director and other places within the UK in the course of his duties as a director. Similarly where a person is a director of one company and an employee of another company in the same group;

(B)   an unremunerated director of a company not managed with a view to dividends (e.g. a club);

(C)   a director who holds the position as part of a professional practice, provided no claim is made to a deduction under Schedule D;

(D)   a spouse accompanying a director on his or her duties abroad because of his or her precarious health.

(Revenue Pamphlet IR 1, A4). See also 75.43 below.

(x)   In relation to changes of job or job location before 6 April 1993 (or before 3 August 1993 under a firm commitment entered into before 6 April 1993), removal expenses borne by employer where employee has to change residence in order to take up a new employment or on transfer within employer's organisation, provided cost is reasonable and payment properly controlled. The Revenue take the view that the terms of the concession had always required that the former residence be disposed of, but the concession was amended (see Revenue Press Release 23 November 1993) to include a specific provision that the employee must relinquish or dispose of all interest in his or her main home at the previous location. The amended concession states that provisional relief will be given prior to disposal, provided that the property is being actively marketed, but may be wholly or partly withdrawn if the employee does not in the event change his or her residence. However, following the replacement of the concession by a statutory relief which does *not* incorporate such a requirement (see below), the Revenue announced (see Revenue Press Release 16 March 1993) that, where the employer or agent had been informed of the Revenue's interpretation of the (unamended) concession on this point, liabilities in unsettled cases would be pursued only for 1987/88 and subsequent years. The Revenue later announced (see Revenue Press Release 23 November 1993) their agreement with representatives of the main employers and accountancy firms involved that tax in unsettled cases would be sought only for 1990/91 and subsequent years where, before the start of the year in question, either the employer or agent had been informed of the Revenue's interpretation of the concession on this point, or it was clear from the facts already available to the Revenue that the employer or agent knew of the Revenue's interpretation even though neither of them may have been specifically informed of it. The same terms are available to other employers with unsettled cases.

'Removal expenses' includes related items such as temporary subsistence allowance while the employee is looking for accommodation at the new station, and also a disturbance allowance of, from 1 April 1993 (figures from 5 April 1992/1991 in brackets) up to £2,705 (£2,655/£2,550) for a married person, £1,645 (£1,615/£1,550) for a single householder or £635 (£625/£600) for a single non-householder. It also includes reimbursement of the net interest (after tax relief) payable on a bridging loan, and the provision of a cheap or interest-free bridging loan otherwise chargeable under *Sec 160* (see 75.17 below). For a loan to be a bridging loan for these purposes:

(A)   it must be used only to bridge an unavoidable gap between the incurring of expenditure on the new property and receipt of the sale proceeds of the old property;

(B)   it must be used only to pay off the mortgage on the old property, to fund the purchase of the new property or to meet immediately related incidental expenditure;

(C)   in the case of reimbursement of interest, the interest must be payable by the employee within twelve months of the making of the loan;

(D)   in the case of a cheap or interest-free loan, the loan must be outstanding for no more than twelve months,

and it will in any event only be so treated to the extent that it does not exceed a reasonable estimate of the market value of the old property (although the excess may nevertheless attract concessional relief as described at 75.17 below). The twelve month time limits referred to at (C) and (D) above may be extended at the Revenue's discretion.

(Revenue Pamphlet IR 1, A5(*a*)).

The concession also covered the reimbursement of any standard (*not* personal) community charge incurred either at the old or at the new location as a result of the move. (ICAEW Guidance Note TR 795, 14 June 1990).

The concession is replaced in relation to changes after 5 April 1993 or 2 August 1993 (as above) by a statutory relief (see 75.33 below). Dispensations (see 75.22 below) in relation to payments which continue to be made under the concession are cancelled with effect from 14 April 1993. (Revenue Press Releases 16 March 1993, 14 April 1993).

For the Revenue view of the taxation implications of guaranteed selling price (or similar) schemes for houses as part of employee relocation packages, see Revenue Tax Bulletin May 1994 p 122 and, in relation in particular to the application of the concession at (xxi) below, April 1995 p 211.

(xi)   Miners' free coal and allowances in lieu thereof. (Revenue Pamphlet IR 1, A6).

(xii)   Luncheon vouchers. See 75.30 below.

(xiii)   Medical insurance for treatment and medical services where the need for treatment arises while abroad in performance of duties. [*Sec 155(6)*].

(xiv)   Car parking facilities. No benefit arises from the provision for the employee of a car parking space at or near his place of work. [*Sec 155(1A)*]. See also 75.7 above, 75.44 below.

(xv)   Entertainment by third parties. No benefit arises from the provision of entertainment for the employee (or for his family or household), unless it is provided either

(*a*)   in recognition or anticipation of particular services by the employee in the course of the employment, or

(*b*)   directly or indirectly by the employer or by any person connected with the employer (within *Sec 839*, see 20 CONNECTED PERSONS).

[*Sec 155(7)*].

See also 75.44 below and, as regards concessionary relief in respect of gifts from third parties, 75.26 below.

(xvi)   Christmas parties, etc. The Revenue will not seek tax on modest expenditure on an annual Christmas party or similar annual function open to the staff generally. Expenditure of up to £75 (£50 for 1994/95 and earlier years) per head per annum, including VAT and any transport or accommodation costs, will be regarded as modest, and where expenditure exceeds this amount the full amount will be taxable. The total cost is for this purpose divided by the total number of people attending the function to determine whether the limit is exceeded. For 1995/96 and subsequent years, the expenditure may be split between more than one annual event, and where the total expenditure for the year exceeds the £75 limit, a function or functions whose cost or the sum of whose costs is within the limit will not be taxed, the cost of the remaining functions being taxed in full. Casual hospitality is not regarded as constituting an annual function for these purposes. No P11D return (see 55.9 PAY AS YOU EARN) is required in respect of expenditure not exceeding the limit. (Revenue Pamphlet IR 1, A70; Revenue Press Release 1 November 1995).

(xvii)   Child care facilities. No benefit arises from the provision of care for a child to the extent that

  (a)   either the employee has parental responsibility (within *Children Act 1989, s 3(1)*) for the child or the child is resident with or (being a child or step child of the employee) maintained by the employee,

  (b)   the care is provided other than on premises wholly or mainly used as a private dwelling,

  (c)   the care is provided either on premises made available by the employer alone or under arrangements made by persons who include the employer, on premises made available by one or more of them, with the employer being wholly or partly responsible for financing and managing the provision of the care, and

  (d)   the premises or the person providing the care are registered if so required under *Nurseries and Child-Minders Regulation Act 1948, s 1* (or NI equivalent) or *Children Act 1989, s 71*.

'Care' means any form of care or supervised activity, whether or not provided on a regular basis, other than supervised activity provided primarily for educational purposes. 'Child' means a person under 18.

[*Sec 155A; FA 1990, s 21*].

(xviii)   Certain training and counselling expenses, see 75.42 below.

(xix)   It is understood that the provision of driver training courses for employees will not be taxed as a benefit.

(xx)   Medical check-ups. The provision of routine health checks or medical screening for employees does not confer a chargeable benefit, whether carried out by the employer's own medical staff or by an outside firm. (Revenue Tax Bulletin May 1993 p 74). This applies also to such provision for members of the employee's family or household. (Revenue Schedule E Manual, SE 3216).

(xxi)   For 1994/95 and subsequent years, normal purchaser's costs in relation to the sale or transfer of an asset by the employee to the employer (or to some other person by reason of the employment) are by concession disregarded in calculating any benefit arising to the employee. (Revenue Pamphlet IR 1 (November 1995 Supplement), A85). See Revenue Tax Bulletin April 1995 p 210 as regards the application of this concession in relation to guaranteed selling price (or similar) schemes for houses as part of employee relocation packages (and see (x) above).

(xxii)   Incidental overnight expenses. For 1995/96 and subsequent years, a benefit is exempt from tax where its provision is incidental to the employee's being away from home on business during a 'qualifying absence' in relation to which the authorised maximum (£5 per night spent in the UK and £10 per night spent abroad) is not exceeded, being a benefit the cost of which is not otherwise deductible from emoluments. [*Sec 155(1B)(1C); FA 1995, s 93(3)*]. See also 75.43 below.

See 75.35 below as regards provision of security assets and services for employees.

75.13 Schedule E—Emoluments

See 55.12 PAY AS YOU EARN as regards PAYE settlement agreements whereby employer accounts for tax on minor benefits within the agreement, which do not then count as employees' income.

Cash equivalent of the benefit is the cost (including a proper proportion of any expense relating partly to the benefit and partly otherwise) less any part made good by the employee to those providing the benefit. [*Sec 156(1)(2)*]. VAT is included whether or not recoverable by the employer. (Revenue Pamphlet IR 131, A7). The cost of 'in-house' benefits (i.e. those consisting of services or facilities enjoyed by the employee which it is part of the employer's business to provide to members of the public) is the additional or marginal cost of their provision to the employee, rather than a proportionate part of total costs incurred in their provision both to employees and to the public. See *Pepper v Hart HL 1992, 65 TC 421*, in which only the marginal cost of providing school places for the children of masters at the school was assessable, regardless of whether or not the children occupied places which would otherwise have been provided to members of the public. (*Note.* This decision was based on consideration of statements by the Financial Secretary to the Treasury in Standing Committee debates on the enacting legislation. See 4.7 APPEALS as regards the circumstances in which this is permissible.) For how the Revenue proposed to deal with repayments etc. arising from this decision, see Revenue Press Release 21 January 1993, which also offers the Revenue's view of how the marginal cost rule should apply in practice. In particular, nil or negligible cost arises in the case of:

(i)   rail or bus travel by employees (provided fare-payers are not displaced);

(ii) goods sold to employees for not less than the wholesale price; and

(iii) provision of professional services not requiring additional staffing (excluding disbursements).

It is accepted that no additional benefit arises where teachers pay 15% or more of normal school fees.

The decision also affects the calculation of the benefit of the provision of assets for part business, part private use. Fixed costs need not now be taken into account where the private use is incidental to the business use. The cash equivalent is the proper proportion of the 'annual value' of the asset (see below) together with any *additional* running expenses.

(Revenue Press Release 21 January 1993).

See 75.44(*a*) below as regards valuation of incentive awards.

Where the benefit is the *use of an asset* other than a car or (from 1993/94) a van (as to which see 75.15 below), the cash equivalent is the annual value (or if higher, the rent or hire charge paid by those providing the benefit) plus any expenses related to the asset's provision (excluding the cost of acquiring or producing it and excluding also any rent or hire charge payable for the asset by those providing the benefit). [*Sec 156(5)(7)*].

Where the benefit is the transfer of an asset after it has been used or depreciated since the transferor acquired it, the cost of the benefit is the market value at the time of the transfer. However, if the asset (not a car or, from 1993/94, a van) was first applied for the provision of any benefit for a person or for members of his family or household by reason of his employment after 5 April 1980 and a person (whether or not the present transferee) has been chargeable to tax on its use, the cost of the benefit (unless a higher benefit is obtained by taking market value at the time of transfer) is its market value when it was first so applied less the total amounts charged to tax for its use in the years up to and including the year of transfer. [*Sec 156(3)(4)*].

Annual value of the use of an asset is:

for land, its annual value under *Sec 837*, see 68.7(*e*) SCHEDULE A;

for any other case, 20% of market value (10% for assets provided before 6 April 1980) at time asset was first provided as a benefit. [*Sec 156(6)*].

75.14   *Example*

During 1996/97 P Ltd transferred to R a television set which it had previously leased to him for a nominal rent of £2 per month. The company also leased a suit to R under the same arrangements. R's salary is £30,000 p.a..

Television

First leased to R in May 1995 (when its market value was £350); transferred to R in March 1997 for £50, the market value at that time being £125.

R's benefits are		£	£
1995/96			
Cost of benefit	20% × £350		70
Deduct Rent paid by R (11 months)			22
Cash equivalent of benefit			£48
1996/97			
Cost of benefit	20% × £350		70
Deduct Rent paid by R (12 months)			24
Cash equivalent of benefit			46
Greater of			
(i)	Market value at transfer	125	
	Deduct Price paid by R	50	
		£75	
	and		
(ii)	Original market value	350	
	Deduct Cost of benefits note (*b*)	140	
		210	
	Deduct Price paid by R	50	
		£160	
			160
Total			£206

Suit
First leased to R in November 1996 (when its market value was £200).

R's benefit for 1996/97 is		
Cost of benefit	20% × £200	40
Deduct Rent paid by R (5 months)		10
Cash equivalent of benefit		£30

Notes

(*a*)   Although each asset was either leased to R or transferred to him after the start of a fiscal year, he will be assessed on the full cost of the benefit for that year (as reduced by any rent paid). There is no time apportionment as in the case of cars made available for private use.

(*b*)   On the transfer of the television set, the cost of the benefits to date (2 × £70), not the cash equivalents, is deducted from the original market value.

(*c*)   It is assumed that the television set and suit have been bought by P Ltd and are not goods provided from within its own business. If the latter was the case, R would be assessed on the marginal cost to P Ltd in providing the benefit (in accordance with *Pepper v Hart*—see 75.13 above).

75.15   **Motor vehicles provided for private use.** The provision by an employer of a car or (from 1993/94) a van partly or wholly for 'private use' by an employee (or a member of his family or household), without the transfer of any property in it, is the subject of a special basis of charge. '*Private use*' means any use for travel other than that necessary to the performance of the employee's duties, and a car or van is deemed to be available for private use unless the terms on which it is made available prohibit such use *and* there was no such use. [*Secs 157(1), 159AA(1), 168(5)(5A)(6); FA 1993, 4 Sch 4, 6; FA 1996, s 134, 20 Sch 10(2)*]. See 75.43 below as regards business use where more than one place of work. See also *Gilbert v Hemsley Ch D 1981, 55 TC 419*. Where a car salesman or demonstrator has to take a car home as part of his normal duties in order to call on a prospective customer, this will not of itself make the car available for his private use. The use of test or experimental cars by engineers in the motor and components industries will be considered on the facts of each particular case. (Revenue Booklet 480).

A car provided by a third party (e.g. by a car dealer to a football player for promotional purposes) is within these provisions where it is provided by reason of the employment. (Revenue Schedule E Manual, SE 3413).

Where such a special basis of charge applies, no other charge arises in respect of any expenses or reimbursements etc. in relation to the vehicle. It appears that this would not normally apply to the payment of fines etc. by the employer (although certain parking fines may be the liability of the employer, see 75.7 above). The provision of a driver is a separate benefit under 75.13 above (subject to an expense claim for business use). [*Secs 154(2), 155(1), 157(3), 159AA(3); FA 1993, 4 Sch 2–4*]. Before 1991/92, the provision of a car telephone did not give rise to a separate charge (Revenue Pamphlet IR 131, SP 5/88, 22 July 1988), but see now 75.16 below for flat rate charge on mobile telephones. The provision of a personalised registration number does not enter into the computation under the special basis of charge, whether under (i) or (ii) below, and is normally exempt as above. (Revenue Tax Bulletin December 1994 p 177).

For 1995/96 and subsequent years, the mere fact that an employee is offered an alternative (for example, a cash alternative) to a company car does not make the benefit chargeable under the general Schedule E rules as opposed to the special company car provisions. [*See 157A; FA 1995, s 43(1)(4)*]. Previously, the benefit *was* so chargeable where use of a company car was freely exchangeable for cash (see *Heaton v Bell HL 1969, 46 TC 211*). The new rule is aimed principally at avoidance of national insurance contributions (see Revenue Press Release 21 July 1994).

A *car* is any mechanically propelled road vehicle *except* (i) a vehicle constructed primarily for carrying goods, (ii) a vehicle of a type unsuitable and not commonly used as a private vehicle, (iii) a motor cycle and (iv) an invalid carriage. [*Sec 168(5)(a)*]. A car owned by the fire brigade and equipped with a flashing light and other emergency equipment was held to be within (ii) (*Gurney v Richards Ch D 1989, 62 TC 287*).

A *van* is a mechanically propelled road vehicle, other than a motor cycle, of a construction primarily suited for the conveyance of goods or burden and designed (or adapted) not to exceed a laden weight of 3,500 kgs. in normal use. [*Sec 168(5A)(a)(e); FA 1993, 4 Sch 6*].

Excluded from charge, by concession, is any specially adapted vehicle provided for a severely and permanently disabled employee provided that private use is prohibited and no such use is made other than for the employee's travel from home to work (and, if the vehicle is available for private use, such travel is treated as business use). (Revenue Pamphlet IR 1, A59 and Booklet 480). See also 75.13(vi) above, 75.43 below.

The provision of parking facilities for an employee at or near his place of work (including such provision in relation to a privately-owned vehicle) constitutes neither an emolument nor a benefit. [*Sec 155(1A); FA 1988, s 46*].

Where two members of the same family are each supplied with a car for their private use by the same employer, and each is in director's or higher-paid employment, each will be charged separately according to his/her own usage but, by concession, will not be charged in respect of the car supplied to the other. Similarly, if one of them is not in such employment, but is supplied with the car in his/her own right in equivalent circumstances to other employees in similar employment and in accordance with normal commercial practice for a job of that kind, the other will not be charged in respect of the car supplied to the lower-paid employee. Where two or more persons are chargeable in respect of their shared use of the same car, a single charge will be apportioned between them. (Revenue Pamphlet IR 1, A71).

Compensation to an employee from whom a company car was withdrawn following a change of policy by the employer was held to be an assessable emolument in *Bird v Martland; Bird v Allen Ch D 1982, 56 TC 89*.

Where the special basis of charge applies to provision of a car, a separate charge also arises in respect of provision of any fuel for private use (see (iv) below). In the case of provision of a van, no separate charge arises on provision of fuel.

(i)   *Cars for private use: 1994/95 onwards*. For 1994/95 and subsequent years, the cash equivalent of the benefit of provision of a company car for private use is 35% of the 'price of the car as regards a year'. This is reduced by two-thirds where the employee is required by the nature of his employment to use, and does use, the car for at least 18,000 miles of business travel in the year concerned, or by one-third where such use amounts to at least 2,500 but less than 18,000 business miles. Where an employee is taxable in respect of the benefit of the provision of two or more cars available concurrently, for all such cars other than the one used to the greatest extent for business travel in the period of concurrent availability the reduction for 18,000 or more business miles is reduced to one-third, and no reduction is made where business miles are less than 18,000. The figures of 2,500 and 18,000 are reduced *pro rata* where the car is 'unavailable' for part of the year.

The cash equivalent is reduced, or further reduced, by one-third where the car is four or more years old at the end of the year of assessment in question. It is similarly reduced *pro rata* where the car is 'unavailable' for part of the year.

Where the employee is required, as a condition of the car being available for private use, to pay for that use, the cash equivalent determined as above for a year is reduced (or extinguished) by the amount so paid in respect of the year. No reduction was allowed for a payment made to the employer to obtain a better car (*Brown v Ware (Sp C 29) [1995] SSCD 155*) or for a payment made for the insurance of the car for both private and business use (*CIR v Quigley CS, [1995] STC 931*).

75.15 Schedule E—Emoluments

A car is '*unavailable*' on a day falling before the first day on which it is made available to the employee (or a member of his family or household) or after the last day on which it is made so available, or on a day falling within a period of 30 or more consecutive days throughout which it is not so available. See below as regards regulations modifying these provisions in cases where a replacement car is provided during a period in which the car normally available to an employee is not so available for a period of less than 30 days.

The '*price of a car as regards a year*' is its 'list price' (or its 'notional price' if it has no list price) on the '*relevant day*', i.e. the day immediately before the date on which the car was first registered under the *Vehicle Excise and Registration Act 1994* or corresponding legislation, plus the price of certain accessories and net of certain capital contributions, and the age of a car commences with the date of its first registration.

The '*list price*' of a car is the price published by the manufacturer, importer or distributor (as the case may be) as the inclusive price (including delivery charges and taxes, but not vehicle excise duty) appropriate for a car of that kind (including any standard accessories) sold in the UK singly in an open market retail sale, plus the price so published (including any fitting charges) of any optional accessories with the car when it was first made available to the employee (or to a member of his family or household). The price advertised by a car dealer cannot be used instead of that published by the manufacturer, etc. (see Revenue Tax Bulletin December 1994 p 177). If no such price is available for an optional accessory, no adjustment is made to the list price in respect of the accessory (which may, however, be the subject of a separate addition, see below). The accessories taken into account for these purposes are those attached to the car (whether or not permanently) for use with the car (without any transfer of the property) and not necessarily provided for use in the performance of the employee's duties. Mobile telephones (see 75.16 below) are excluded, as is, for 1995/96 onwards, equipment either designed solely for use by a chronically sick or disabled person or made available to enable an employee holding, at the time the car is first made available to him, a disabled person's badge (an 'orange badge') to use the car in spite of the disability which entitles him to hold that badge at that time.

The charge is based on the list price of an individual car at the time it is first registered, not on average prices. For existing cars, the Revenue will accept prices based on the list price of the car and major accessories, or from published guides of actual list prices where the manufacturer's price list is not available. Estimates of the price, including major accessories, should be provided to the inspector where, exceptionally, the price of an existing car cannot be found. (Revenue Press Release 27 September 1993).

The '*notional price*' of a car is that which might reasonably be expected to have been its list price (as above) (including accessories) had such a price been published.

There is, however, an overall limit of £80,000 (or such greater sum as the Treasury may specify by order) on the price, whether list or notional, after taking account of accessories (as below), to be taken into account under these provisions.

Optional accessories not having a list price and hence not taken into account as above, are the subject of a separate addition to the price of the car equal to their price delivered and fitted (list or notional, as above, as appropriate). A separate addition is similarly made where such accessories are fitted after the car is first made available to the employee (or to a member of his family or household), and after 31 July 1993 (but ignoring any accessory whose price is less than £100 (or such greater sum as the

Treasury may specify by order) for this purpose). Again, mobile telephones and accessories designed solely for use by the disabled are excluded.

The Treasury may make regulations (which may make different provision for different cases) as regards the fitting of replacement accessories, to provide either that the price of the car will remain the same as if the accessory replaced had continued in use, or that the above provisions are to be modified in some other way to take account of the replacement.

Where the employee makes a capital contribution to the cost of the car or accessories taken into account as above, the price of the car for the purposes of the charge for the year in which the contribution is made and subsequent years is reduced by the lesser of the amount of the contribution (or the sum of such contributions) and £5,000 (or such greater sum as may be specified by Treasury order). An agreement for the employee to receive a proportionate return of his capital contribution on disposal of the car will not prejudice relief in respect of the contribution, and will not give rise to any Schedule E charge on the amount repaid. An agreement to refund the contribution in full will result in the contribution being disregarded. (Revenue Tax Bulletin December 1994 p 177).

[Secs 157(2), 168A–168E, 168G, 6 Sch; FA 1993, 3 Sch 1–5, 7; FA 1995, s 44; FA 1996, s 134, 20 Sch 40].

Classic cars. There are special provisions substituting market value for the price determined as above where the market value is at least £15,000 (or such greater sum as the Treasury may specify by order) and exceeds that price, and the car is 15 years or more old at the end of the year concerned. Capital contributions are taken into account on a similar basis to that described above, and the £80,000 overall limit similarly applies. [Secs 168F, 168G; FA 1993, 3 Sch 4].

Replacement cars and accessories. Regulations provide for the situation where a double charge would otherwise arise where a temporary replacement car is provided while the normal car is unavailable for use for less than 30 days. The replacement car is ignored, and mileage in it treated as mileage in the normal car, provided that it is of a similar quality to the normal car and is not provided as part of an arrangement to supply a better car. Similarly, where an accessory is fitted which replaces another, regulations provide that the 'price' of the car will not be affected where the replacement is of the same kind and does not cost more than the price of the old accessory (or, if greater, the current price of an equivalent to the old accessory). The addition to the 'price' in respect of a more costly replacement accessory is restricted to the excess cost over the amount (if any) included in the 'price' in respect of the old accessory. [SI 1994 Nos 777, 778].

Administration. Revenue Pamphlet IR 132 provides an employers' guide to the new scheme, and sets out the compliance requirements. See also 55.16 PAY AS YOU EARN.

Example

A, B and C are employees of D Ltd. Each earns at least £8,500 per annum and each is provided with a company car throughout 1996/97. The company also bears at least part of the cost of petrol for private motoring (see (iv) below).

A is provided with a 1,800 cc car first registered in October 1993 with a list price (including VAT, car tax (but not road tax), delivery charges and standard accessories) of £19,000. The car was made available to A in April 1994. An immobilisor was fitted in September 1994 at a cost of £200. A's business mileage is 20,000 for 1996/97. He is required to pay the company £250 per year as a condition of using the car for private motoring, and duly pays this amount.

B is provided with a 1,400 cc car first registered in March 1992 with a list price of £9,000. B drives 8,000 business miles in 1996/97. He was required to make a capital contribution of £1,000 on provision of the car in January 1995.

C is provided with a luxury car first registered in February 1995 with a list price of £85,000 (which includes optional accessories). He made a capital contribution of £3,000 in 1994/95. C's business mileage was 2,000 in 1996/97.

Car and fuel benefits for 1996/97 are as follows.

	A £	B £	C £
List price	19,000	9,000	85,000
Later optional accessories	200	—	—
	19,200		
Capital contributions	—	(1,000)	(3,000)
			£82,000
Price cap for expensive cars			80,000
Price of car	£19,200	£8,000	£80,000
Cash equivalent — 35% of price of car	6,720	2,800	28,000
Discount for high business mileage (2/3)	(4,480)	—	—
Discount for moderate business mileage (1/3)	—	(933)	—
		1,867	
Discount for older cars (1/3)	—	(622)	—
	2,240		
Contribution for private use	(250)	—	—
Car benefit	1,990	1,245	28,000
Fuel benefit (see (iv) below)	890	710	1,320
Total car and fuel benefits	£2,880	£1,955	£29,320

(ii) *Cars for private use: 1993/94 and earlier years.* A scale charge applies for each year of assessment as follows.

Table for 1993/94

	Age of car at end of relevant year of assessment	
	Under 4 years	4 years or more
Original market value up to £19,250		
(a) with cylinder capacity of	£	£
Up to 1,400 cc	2,310	1,580
1,401 cc to 2,000 cc	2,990	2,030
2,001 cc or more	4,800	3,220

		Age of car at end of relevant year of assessment	
		Under 4 years	4 years or more
(b)	without a cylinder capacity but an original market value of	£	£
	Up to £5,999	2,310	1,580
	£6,000 to £8,499	2,990	2,030
	£8,500 to £19,250	4,800	3,220

Original market value over £19,250

	£19,251 to £29,000	6,210	4,180
	£29,001 or more	10,040	6,660

[*FA 1993 s 70*]

Also for 1993/94

(1) The flat rate will be increased by one-half if the employee uses the car for business travel of 2,500 miles or less, proportionately reduced if the car is available for only part of the year.

(2) Where the employee uses the car for business travel of 18,000 miles or more in a year, the rate will be reduced by one-half. The 18,000 mile threshold is proportionately reduced if the car is available for only part of the year.

(3) Where a person is taxable on two or more cars made available concurrently, the Table rate is increased by one-half for each car other than the one used to the greatest extent for the employee's business travel.

(4) The flat rate will be reduced by time-apportionment, where the car was not made available to the employee for part of the year, or where it was incapable of being used at all throughout a period of not less than 30 consecutive days.

(5) The flat rate will be reduced by any amount paid by the employee for private use of the car provided that its payment is a condition of the car being made available for private use. No reduction was allowed for a payment made to the employer to obtain a better car (*Brown v Ware (Sp C 29) [1995] SSCD 155*) or for a payment made for the insurance of the car for both private and business use (*CIR v Quigley CS, [1995] STC 931*).

(6) The '*original market value*' of a car is the price, inclusive of customs or excise duty, car tax and value added tax, which it might reasonably have been expected to fetch if sold singly in the UK in a retail sale in the open market immediately before its first registration in the UK (or elsewhere under corresponding legislation), and its age commences with the date of its first registration. [*Sec 168(5)(b)(d)(e)*]. The Revenue are understood to consider that the market value should take account of all accessories fitted prior to delivery, but not the delivery charges. Accessories fitted after delivery and not necessary to the functioning of the car may be subject to a charge on the cash equivalent of the benefit of their provision (see 75.13 above).

[*Sec 157, 6 Sch as originally enacted*].

75.15 Schedule E—Emoluments

Table for 1992/93

	Age of car at end of relevant year of assessment	
	Under 4 years	4 years or more

Original market value up to £19,250

	£	£
(a) with cylinder capacity of		
Up to 1,400 cc	2,140	1,460
1,401 cc to 2,000 cc	2,770	1,880
2,001 cc or more	4,440	2,980
(b) without a cylinder capacity but an original market value of		
Up to £5,999	2,140	1,460
£6,000 to £8,499	2,770	1,880
£8,500 to £19,250	4,440	2,980

Original market value over £19,250

£19,251 to £29,000	5,750	3,870
£29,001 or more	9,300	6,170

[SI 1992, No 731]

Table for 1991/92

	Age of car at end of relevant year of assessment	
	Under 4 years	4 years or more

Original market value up to £19,250

	£	£
(a) with cylinder capacity of		
Up to 1,400 cc	2,050	1,400
1,401 cc to 2,000 cc	2,650	1,800
2,001 cc or more	4,250	2,850
(b) without a cylinder capacity but an original market value of		
Up to £5,999	2,050	1,400
£6,000 to £8,499	2,650	1,800
£8,500 to £19,250	4,250	2,850

Original market value over £19,250

£19,251 to £29,000	5,500	3,700
£29,001 or more	8,900	5,900

[FA 1991, s 29]

Table for 1990/91

	Age of car at end of relevant year of assessment	
	Under 4 years	4 years or more

Original market value up to £19,250

	£	£
(a) with cylinder capacity of		
Up to 1,400 cc	1,700	1,150
1,401 cc to 2,000 cc	2,200	1,500
2,001 cc or more	3,550	2,350

	Age of car at end of relevant year of assessment	
	Under 4 years	4 years or more
(b) without a cylinder capacity but an original market value of		
Up to £5,999	1,700	1,150
£6,000 to £8,499	2,200	1,500
£8,500 to £19,250	3,550	2,350

Original market value over £19,250

	£	£
£19,251 to £29,000	4,600	3,100
£29,001 or more	7,400	4,900

[*FA 1990, s 22*]

Table for 1989/90

	Age of car at end of relevant year of assessment	
	Under 4 years	4 years or more

Original market value up to £19,250

	£	£
(a) with cylinder capacity of		
Up to 1,400 cc	1,400	950
1,401 cc to 2,000 cc	1,850	1,250
2,001 cc or more	2,950	1,950
(b) without a cylinder capacity but an original market value of		
Up to £5,999	1,400	950
£6,000 to £8,499	1,850	1,250
£8,500 to £19,250	2,950	1,950
£19,251 to £29,000	3,850	2,600
£29,001 or more	6,150	4,100

[*FA 1989, s 49*]

The notes (1)–(5) in the Table for 1993/94 above also apply to earlier years.

(iii) *Vans for private use.* For 1993/94 and subsequent years of assessment, where a van is available for an employee's private use, the employee is to be taxed on the benefit in accordance with a standard scale.

Unless the van is a 'shared van' (see below) for all or part of the year, the scale benefit is £500, reduced to £350 for a van aged four years or more at the end of the year. The scale benefit is reduced pro-rata if for any part of the year it is either 'unavailable' or is a shared van. A van is '*unavailable*' on a day falling before the first day on which it is made available to the employee (or a member of his family or household) or after the last day on which it is made so available, or on a day falling within a period of 30 or more consecutive days throughout which it is not so available. The scale benefit is reduced (or extinguished) by any monetary contribution which the employee is required to make, and does make, as a condition for private use. The age of a van commences with the date of its first registration.

A van is a '*shared van*' for any period throughout which it is available concurrently or otherwise to two or more employees of the same employer, and in which there is no period exceeding 30 consecutive days during which it is exclusively available to one employee. A van shared for part of a day is treated as shared throughout that day. Each employee to whom one or more shared vans are available for private use while they are shared vans and who makes private use of the van (or at least one of them) while it is a shared van is a '*participating employee*'.

Scale benefits of £500 or £350 (depending on the van's age) are allocated to each shared van, these amounts being reduced pro-rata where for any part of the year the van is not a shared van or where the van is incapable of use for 30 or more consecutive days. The aggregate scale benefit for all shared vans is then divided equally among the participating employees, and the result is the amount on which each such employee is taxed for the year, except that if that amount is more than £500 it is reduced to £500.

A participating employee may claim an alternative method of calculation (such a claim being counted as a claim for relief for the purposes of penalties under *TMA s 95*, see 58.3 PENALTIES), as follows.

(*a*)   For each van involved, take the number of days in the year of assessment during which the employee (or a member of his family or household) makes private use of a van while it is a shared van.

(*b*)   Aggregate the numbers arrived at under (*a*) (where more than one van is involved).

(*c*)   Multiply the number in (*a*) or, where applicable, the number in (*b*) by £5.

The result is the amount on which the employee is taxed.

The amount on which the employee would otherwise be taxed, whether calculated under the standard or the alternative method, is reduced, or extinguished, by any monetary contribution which the employee is required to make, and does make, as a condition for private use of a shared van while it is a shared van. Where more than one van is involved, the aggregate of such contributions is taken.

Where, in respect of the same van, an employee has a taxable benefit for a year under both the non-shared van and the shared van provisions as above, the benefits are aggregated to arrive at his total taxable benefit for the year.

There is an overall limit of £500 on the charge under these provisions on an employee for a year at no one time during which more than one van was available for the private use of the employee or a member of his family or household.

[*Secs 159AA(1)(2), 168(5A), 6A Sch; FA 1993, 4 Sch 4, 6–8*].

Revenue Pamphlet IR 136 provides an employees' and employers' guide to the taxation of company vans.

Example

L is an employee of N Ltd, earning £18,000 per annum. From 1 October 1996 to 5 April 1997, L is provided by his employer with exclusive use of a one-year old company van (Van A) on terms which do not prohibit private use and which provide for a deduction of £4 per month to be made from his net salary at the end of each month in consideration for private use. For the period 6 April 1996 to 30 September 1996 inclusive, L had shared the van with another employee, M. Either L or a member of his family or household had made private use of the shared van for 42 days during that period, and M also made private use of the van. No payment for private use was required.

In addition to the van mentioned above, four other company vans are shared between five employees of N Ltd (excluding L and M) throughout the year ended 5 April 1997, three of which vans are aged less than four years at the end of that year. All the employees make some private use of one or more of the vans. One of the vans is off the road and incapable of use for three weeks in March 1997.

All vans mentioned have a normal laden weight not exceeding 3,500 kilograms.

The taxable benefit to L for 1996/97 of company vans is calculated as follows.

Non-shared van

	£
Cash equivalent of benefit before adjustment	500
Exclude Period for which van is a shared van:	
$£500 \times \dfrac{178}{365}$ (6.4.96 – 30.9.96)	244
	256
Deduct Payment for private use (6 × £4 per month)	24
Cash equivalent of benefit	£232

Shared van

	£	£
Basic values:		
Van A	500	
Exclude Period for which van is not a shared van:		
$£500 \times \dfrac{187}{365}$ (1.10.96 – 5.4.97)	256	
		244
Other vans ((3 × £500) + (1 × £350))		1,850
Sum of basic values		£2,094
Divide £2,094 equally between seven participating employees		£299
Cash equivalent of benefit to L (maximum £500)		£299

Total benefits to L

	£
Non-shared van	232
Shared van	299
Total cash equivalent of benefit	£531
But restricted by *6A Sch 11* to	£500

L will thus be taxed on a van benefit of £500 for 1996/97.

75.15 Schedule E—Emoluments

In relation to the shared van, L then makes a claim for the alternative calculation under 6A Sch 8.

Number of relevant days for Van A	42
Number of relevant days for other shared vans	Nil
Aggregate number of relevant days	42
Cash equivalent of benefit to L (42 × £5 per day)	£210

Total benefits to L (revised)

	£
Non-shared van	232
Shared van	210
Total cash equivalent of benefit	£442

L will thus be taxed on a van benefit of £442 for 1996/97.

(iv) *Fuel for private use.* A scale charge applies to free fuel provided for private motoring in 'company' cars. The charge varies with the cylinder capacity of the car. For 1992/93 onwards, separate scales apply for petrol and diesel cars. The scale charge does not apply to fuel provided for vans.

The scale charges are as follows.

Table for 1996/97

(a) with cylinder capacity of	Petrol (£)	Diesel (£)
Up to 1,400 cc	710	640
1,401 cc to 2,000 cc	890	640
2,001 cc or more	1,320	820

(b) without a cylinder capacity	£1,320

[*SI 1995 No 3035*]

Table for 1995/96

(a) with cylinder capacity of	Petrol (£)	Diesel (£)
Up to 1,400 cc	670	605
1,401 cc to 2,000 cc	850	605
2,001 cc or more	1,260	780

(b) without a cylinder capacity	£1,260

[*SI 1994 No 3010*]

Table for 1994/95

(a) with cylinder capacity of	Petrol (£)	Diesel (£)
Up to 1,400 cc	640	580
1,401 cc to 2,000 cc	810	580
2,001 cc or more	1,200	750

(b) without a cylinder capacity	£1,200

[*FA 1994, s 87*]

Table for 1993/94

		Petrol (£)	Diesel (£)
(a)	with cylinder capacity of		
	Up to 1,400 cc	600	550
	1,401 cc to 2,000 cc	760	550
	2,001 cc or more	1,130	710
(b)	without a cylinder capacity but an original market value of	£	
	Up to £5,999	600	
	£6,000 to £8,499	760	
	£8,500 or more	1,130	

[*FA 1993, s 71(1)(3)*]

Table for 1992/93

		Petrol (£)	Diesel (£)
(a)	with cylinder capacity of		
	Up to 1,400 cc	500	460
	1,401 cc to 2,000 cc	630	460
	2,001 cc or more	940	590
(b)	without a cylinder capacity but an original market value of	£	
	Up to £5,999	500	
	£6,000 to £8,499	630	
	£8,500 or more	940	

[*F(No 2)A 1992, s 53(2)*]

Table for 1987/88 to 1991/92 inclusive

		£
(a)	with cylinder capacity of	
	Up to 1,400 cc	480
	1,401 cc to 2,000 cc	600
	2,001 cc or more	900
(b)	without a cylinder capacity but an original market value of	£
	Up to £5,999	480
	£6,000 to £8,499	600
	£8,500 or more	900

[*SI 1986 No 702*]

Where the rate for private use of a car is reduced by note (4) in the Table for 1993/94 under (ii) above, the scale rate for private fuel is similarly reduced. For 1992/93 and earlier years, this also applied in relation to note (2) in that Table (50% reduction where annual business mileage is 18,000 miles or more), but this ceases to apply for 1993/94 and subsequent years. There are no special rules for second cars, cars with low business mileage or older cars. If the employee is required to make good to his employer the cost of *all* company fuel used for private purposes (including travel between home and work), and in fact does so during the year in question (or without unreasonable delay thereafter), the scale charge is cancelled, but there is no reduction where fuel is provided for part only of a year. Fuel provided only for home-to-work travel of severely and permanently disabled employees is ignored for this purpose (see Revenue Booklet 480). Where the scale charge applies, there is no charge under other provisions (e.g. on expense allowances or use of credit cards or vouchers which enable the employee to obtain private fuel) and, accordingly, the *method* by which private fuel is obtained does not affect the employee's tax liability. The rates do not apply to fuel provided for use in individuals' own cars, hire cars etc. where the existing rules continue to apply (i.e. the employer will notify the Revenue on form P11D of the actual cost of fuel provided by him). The Treasury may alter the Table by statutory instrument.

[*Sec 158; F(No 2)A 1992, s 53; FA 1993, s 71(2)(3), 3 Sch 6, 7; FA 1995, s 43(2)*].

(v)   *Pooled vehicles.* Cars or, from 1993/94, vans provided as *pooled cars* or *pooled vans* will not be treated as being available for private use by any employee.

Conditions are

(*a*)   the vehicle must have been included for the year in a car or van pool for use of employees of one or more employers and actually used by more than one of those employees by reason of their employment and not ordinarily used by one of them to the exclusion of the others, and

(*b*)   any private use of the vehicle in the year by an employee was merely incidental to his other use of it, and

(*c*)   the vehicle was not normally kept overnight at or near any of the residences of the employees concerned (except on the employer's premises).

As regards (*b*) above, the Revenue interpret the requirement that private use is 'merely incidental to' other use as a qualitative test requiring consideration, in the case of each employee using the vehicle during the year, of whether the private use is independent of the employee's business use (so that it is not 'merely incidental' to it) or follows from the business use (so that it is). Thus if a business journey requiring an early start cannot reasonably be undertaken starting from the normal place of work, the journey from work to home the previous day (although private) is merely incidental to the business use. Similarly minor private use (e.g. to visit a restaurant) while away from home on a business trip is merely incidental to the business use. On the other hand use for an annual holiday would not be merely incidental to business use, no matter how small in comparison to business travel in the year. As regards cars with drivers, carrying and working on confidential papers, whilst a factor in determining whether a journey is business or private (and if private whether merely incidental to business use), is not determinative of the issue. The need to deliver papers to a client, or to have them available for a meeting at the employee's home, may be additional relevant factors. (Before 1996/97, it was accepted that all such journeys could be merely incidental to business use, without regard to their frequency or length or to other use of the car.) Where a chauffeur is obliged to take the car home for the night, in order to collect or deliver passengers, this does not disqualify the car from treatment as a pooled vehicle. (Revenue Statement of Practice SP 2/96, 29 March 1996).

For 1995/96 and earlier years, claims may be made to the inspector by any employee concerned or by employer on behalf of all and any determination arising from an appeal is binding on all for that car or van in that year. For 1996/97 onwards, claims are unnecessary. [*Secs 159, 159AB; FA 1993, 4 Sch 4; FA 1996, s 134, 20 Sch 8*].

The Revenue accept that condition (*c*) above is satisfied if the occasions on which the vehicle is taken home by employees do not amount to more than 60% of the year. However, where a vehicle is garaged at employees' homes on a large number of occasions (although less than 60% of the year), they consider it 'unlikely' that all home-to-work journeys would satisfy the 'merely incidental' test in (*b*) above. Such use by a chauffeur employed to drive a car does not prevent its being a pooled car. (Revenue Booklet 480).

(vi)   *Heavier commercial vehicles.* For 1993/94 and subsequent years of assessment, where a 'heavier commercial vehicle' is made available to an employee in such circumstances that had it been a van it would have been chargeable under the provisions described at (iii) above, no charge will arise in respect of its provision unless the vehicle is wholly or mainly used for private purposes. A benefit will, however, arise on the provision of any driver for the vehicle. A *'heavier commercial vehicle'* is defined in the same terms as a van under (iii) above, but with a design laden weight limit exceeding 3,500 kgs. in normal use. [*Sec 159AC; FA 1993, s 74*].

75.16   **Mobile telephones.** For 1991/92 and subsequent years of assessment, where a 'mobile telephone' is made available to a director or employee (or to a member of his family or household) by the employer, and is available for private use, an amount of £200 (which may be increased by Treasury order) is treated as an emolument of the employment (unless the benefit is otherwise chargeable to tax as income). If in any year there is no private use, or the employee is required to, and does, make good the full cost of private use, the charge is reduced to nil. The full cost of private use for this purpose is the cost of private calls, plus a proportionate share of the higher of the equipment rental and 20% of the market value of the equipment when first used to provide a benefit (plus, unless the purpose of the provision of the telephone was to make it available for business use, a proportionate share of any other expenses incurred, e.g. line rental, in connection with its provision) (see Revenue Tax Bulletin August 1994, p 158). Only outgoing private calls (and incoming reversed charge private calls) are taken into account for this purpose. A call is private unless made wholly, exclusively and necessarily in the performance of the duties of the employment. Although the requirement to reimburse must be imposed in advance, where the telephone is provided for business use only but a non-business call is made entirely due to an exceptional and genuine emergency, reimbursement for that call by the employee will be regarded as satisfying the condition. (Revenue Tax Bulletin May 1992 p 20).

The charge is reduced *pro rata* for days on which the telephone is unavailable, either before or after it is provided at all or during a period of 30 consecutive days on which it is incapable of being used at all. A further charge applies for each additional mobile telephone made available, but the fact that different apparatus may be supplied on different days is disregarded.

'Mobile telephone' is defined to include provision in connection with a car or, from 1993/94, a van or heavier commercial vehicle, whether or not a company car etc., but to exclude cordless extensions to fixed telephones and certain short-range radio apparatus. [*Sec 159A; FA 1991, s 30; FA 1993, s 74(2), 4 Sch 5*].

75.17   **Beneficial loan arrangements.** Where a director or employee within 75.11 above and in employment the emoluments from which are assessable under Schedule E (or a 'relative' of the employee) obtains a loan (which includes any form of credit) from the employer (or prospective employer), and the loan (or any part) is outstanding at any time during a year of assessment, the employee is chargeable to tax on the difference between the interest (if any) he pays and interest calculated by reference to an official rate prescribed by the Treasury by statutory instrument (see below). The charge applies to a loan made by a company controlling, or under the control of, the employer company or where a person controls both companies, and similarly for a partnership, and, if any of those companies is a close company, where the loan is by a person having a material interest in any of those companies. It also applies to arranging, guaranteeing or in any way facilitating the continuation of an existing loan as it does to the making of a loan. A loan made to replace a beneficial loan used to be treated in the same way as the original loan, but this no longer generally applies for 1995/96 onwards (although there are now more specifically targeted rules on replacement loans).

It is not necessary for the application of these provisions that there be any benefit from the loan in terms of something of an advantage to the employee (*Williams v Todd Ch D 1988, 60 TC 727*). A loan secured by a charge on a house purchased by a relocated employee, with an agreement that when the charge was called in the employing company would receive the same proportion of the sale price or valuation as the loan bore to the purchase price, was within these provisions (*Harvey v Williams (Sp C 49), [1995] SSCD 329*). The prescribed rate is as follows.

    15% p.a. from 6 May 1980 to 5 October 1982
    12% p.a. from 6 October 1982 to 5 April 1987
  11.5% p.a. from 6 April 1987 to 5 June 1987
  10.5% p.a. from 6 June 1987 to 5 September 1987
  11.5% p.a. from 6 September 1987 to 5 December 1987
  10.5% p.a. from 6 December 1987 to 5 May 1988
   9.5% p.a. from 6 May 1988 to 5 August 1988
    12% p.a. from 6 August 1988 to 5 October 1988
  13.5% p.a. from 6 October 1988 to 5 January 1989
  14.5% p.a. from 6 January 1989 to 5 July 1989
  15.5% p.a. from 6 July 1989 to 5 November 1989
  16.5% p.a. from 6 November 1989 to 5 November 1990
  15.5% p.a. from 6 November 1990 to 5 March 1991
  14.5% p.a. from 6 March 1991 to 5 April 1991
  13.5% p.a. from 6 April 1991 to 5 May 1991
 12.75% p.a. from 6 May 1991 to 5 July 1991
 12.25% p.a. from 6 July 1991 to 5 August 1991
 11.75% p.a. from 6 August 1991 to 5 October 1991
 11.25% p.a. from 6 October 1991 to 5 March 1992
 10.75% p.a. from 6 March 1992 to 5 June 1992
  10.5% p.a. from 6 June 1992 to 5 November 1992
  9.75% p.a. from 6 November 1992 to 5 December 1992
    9% p.a. from 6 December 1992 to 5 January 1993
  8.25% p.a. from 6 January 1993 to 5 March 1993
  7.75% p.a. from 6 March 1993 to 5 January 1994
   7.5% p.a. from 6 January 1994 to 5 November 1994
    8% p.a. from 6 November 1994 to 5 October 1995
  7.75% p.a. from 6 October 1995 to 5 February 1996
  7.25% p.a. from 6 February 1996 onwards.

[*SI 1978 No 28; SI 1980 No 439; SI 1982 No 1273; SI 1987 Nos 512, 886, 1493, 1989; SI 1988 Nos 757, 1279, 1622, 2186; SI 1989 No 1001; SI 1991 Nos 889, 1120, 1377, 1695, 2070; SI 1992 Nos 265, 1338, 2075, 2451, 2818, 3167; SI 1993 Nos 222, 3171; SI 1994 No 2657; SI 1995 No 2436; SI 1996 No 54*].

The average rate for 1995/96 is thus 7.79% (1994/95 7.70%, 1993/94 7.688%, 1992/93 9.75%, 1991/92 11.81%, 1990/91 16%, 1989/90 15.67%).

For 1994/95 and subsequent years, regulations may provide for a different official rate of interest in relation to a loan in the currency of a country or territory outside the UK, the benefit of which is obtained by reason of the employment of a person who normally lives in that country or territory and who has lived there at some time in the year in question or the preceding five years. In this context, 'lives' and 'has lived' are considered to connote a degree of continuance if not permanence, i.e. more than a return for a short holiday. (Revenue Tax Bulletin October 1994 p 162). The following different rates are applicable.

Japan	3.9% p.a. from 6 June 1994 onwards.
Switzerland	5.7% p.a. from 6 June 1994 to 5 July 1994.
	5.5% p.a. from 6 July 1994 onwards.

[*SI 1994 Nos 1307, 1567*]. The average rates for 1994/95 are thus 4.50% (Japan) and 5.85% (Switzerland). For the circumstances in which loans taken out prior to an employee coming to work in the UK are within the beneficial loan provisions, see Revenue Tax Bulletin October 1994 p 161.

(The rates listed above from 6 November 1989 to 5 April 1991 were set by reference to a formula based on bank lending rates and were announced in Revenue Press Releases. [*SI 1989 No 1297*]. The system of prescription by statutory instrument was reintroduced from 6 April 1991. (Revenue Press Release 5 April 1991).)

The amount chargeable in respect of the loan for a year of assessment is treated as an emolument chargeable under Schedule E. For 1994/95 and subsequent years, the employee is treated as having paid interest on the loan in that year of that amount. It is not treated as 'relevant loan interest' (i.e. it is not within MIRAS, see 23.13 DEDUCTION OF TAX AT SOURCE), nor is it treated as income of the lender, but it is treated as accruing during, and paid at the end of, the year (or, if different, the period during the year when the employee was in the employment and the loan was outstanding). For 1995/96 and earlier years, all loans in the same currency outstanding at any time in a year between the same employer and employee had to be treated as a single loan, but excluding

(*a*)   loans for interest on which relief is available under *Sec 353* (or would be so available but for exceeding the qualifying maximum under *Sec 357(1)(b)*) (see 43.5, 43.10 INTEREST PAYABLE), and

(*b*)   loans interest on which is deductible under Schedule D, Case I or II,

or on which such relief would be available if interest were payable. See further below as to relief for notional interest for 1993/94 and earlier years. For 1996/97 and subsequent years, as regards all loans whenever made, such aggregation of loans no longer applies, except that, where the lender is a close company (see Tolley's Corporation Tax under Close Companies) and the borrower a director, the lender may elect, on or before 6 July following the tax year, to treat as a single loan all loans with that borrower which are in the same currency, are not within (*a*) or (*b*) above, were obtained by reason of employment and the rate of interest on which has been below the official rate throughout the year.

The above provisions do not apply as regards a loan to a 'relative' if the employee derived no benefit from the loan, or if the loan was made by an individual in the normal course of domestic, family or personal relationships (for 1993/94 and earlier years, only where that individual was the employer). They also do not apply where a loan made for a fixed and unvariable period and at a fixed and unvariable rate of interest (originally not less than the official rate) becomes a beneficial loan only by reason of an increase in the official rate, or on similar unvariable loans made before 6 April 1978 where the rate of interest is not less than could have been expected to apply between persons not connected with each other.

For 1994/95 and subsequent years, the above provisions are also disapplied in relation to loans made in the ordinary course of a business which includes the lending of money and which is carried on by the lender, if

(A)   at the time the loan was made, loans made for the same or similar purposes, and on the same terms and conditions, were available to all the lender's usual customers,

(B)   of all such loans (including the loan in question) made at or about the same time by the lender, a substantial proportion were made at arm's length to members of the public,

(C)   the loan in question and all arm's length loans referred to in (B) are held on the same terms, and

(D)   if the terms on which the loan in question is held are altered, such alteration was imposed in the ordinary course of business.

As regards (A), (C) and (D) above, for loans made before 1 June 1994, differences in fees, commission or other incidental expenses incurred by the borrower for the purpose of obtaining the loan are disregarded in determining whether the same terms and conditions apply to that and other loans.

For loans made on or after 1 June 1994, the terms and conditions must be exactly the same, so that the exemption would *not* apply where e.g. the lending criteria were relaxed in favour of employees or any normal application or loan fees or charges were waived or reduced in their favour. For this and generally, see Revenue Tax Bulletin August 1994 p 157.

A claim may be made for late payments of interest to be related to the year to which they apply, and for assessments to be adjusted accordingly.

[*Secs 160, 161(1A)(1B)(2)(3)(4), 7 Sch 1–3; FA 1994, s 88; FA 1995, s 45(2); FA 1996, ss 107(1)(4), 134, 20 Sch 9, 41*].

De minimis exemption. For 1994/95 and subsequent years, no amount is treated as emoluments (or as interest paid) in respect of a loan under the above provisions if the loan (or aggregate loans) at no time in the year exceed £5,000. Similarly if a loan (or the aggregate loans) not falling within (*a*) or (*b*) above does not exceed £5,000, the above provisions do not apply to that loan or those loans. For 1993/94 and earlier years, this exemption applied where the amount chargeable (or the sum of the amounts chargeable) under these provisions for a year did not exceed £300 (£200 for 1990/91 and earlier). [*Sec 161(1); FA 1994, s 88(3)(6)*].

'*Relative*' for these purposes means spouse of the employee, or parent, ancestor, lineal descendant, brother or sister (or those persons' spouses), of the employee or spouse. [*Sec 160(6)*].

Bridging loans. By concession, reimbursement by an employer of the net interest on a bridging loan is not charged to tax, nor is the benefit of a bridging loan advanced by an employer in excess of the relief limit. See 75.13(*b*)(x) above.

Relief is also given from a charge under *Sec 160* on another loan which is chargeable only because of the existence of the bridging loan. (Revenue Pamphlet IR 1, A5(*b*)).

There is also no charge, in practice, on advances for employee's expenses necessarily incurred in employment provided (*a*) the maximum amount at any one time does not exceed £1,000; (*b*) the advances are spent within six months; and (*c*) the employee accounts to his employer at regular intervals for the expenditure of the sum advanced. Where there are good reasons for exceeding the limits, they will not, in practice, be charged. Where the conditions are met, no entry is required on form P11D for beneficial loans but details of expense payments are still necessary. (Revenue Pamphlet IR 131, SP 7/79, 11 April 1979).

Relief for interest: 1993/94 and earlier years. Where the amount chargeable under these provisions, had it been interest paid, would have been eligible for relief (or would have been so but for *Sec 353(2)*, see 23.13 DEDUCTION OF TAX AT SOURCE), no charge arises. Special provisions apply for 1991/92, 1992/93 and 1993/94 where a beneficial loan is accordingly exempt from charge by virtue of being a 'home loan', i.e. a loan in respect of which higher rate relief is denied (see 43.5 INTEREST PAYABLE). Where, disregarding the exemption, the employee would be liable to higher rate income tax for a year, the exemption does not apply, but the amount brought into charge is treated as interest eligible for relief under *Secs 353, 355(1)(a)* (so that higher rate relief is denied thereon). The exemption continues to apply, however, where it is only the removal of the exemption which gives rise to higher rate liability, and the aggregate of certain amounts of, or treated as, income does not exceed the basic rate limit by more than the *de minimis* amount referred to above. Special rules apply where interest is or would be partly eligible for relief. [*7 Sch 7, 14–18*].

The following further provisions apply for 1993/94 and earlier years where there is an interest-free loan in conjunction with an interest-bearing loan.

(i)   Where a person has an interest-free loan (interest on which would have qualified for relief if it had been interest-bearing) obtained by reason of his, or any other person's, employment (the 'employer's loan') and, at the same time or later, another loan on the same land, caravan or houseboat is made to that person (or to that person's spouse) on which interest is wholly or partly eligible for relief (see 43.6 *et seq.* INTEREST PAYABLE), the employer's loan is treated as having been made later for the purpose of determining whether interest at the official rate on the employer's loan would be eligible for relief. The beneficial loan provisions of *Secs 160, 161, 7 Sch* are then applied accordingly, relief being restricted or denied if necessary with effect from the date of the second loan.

(ii)   Where a person has, alone or with spouse, two or more loans on which interest is not paid and which relate to the same land, caravan or houseboat, then, for the purpose of determining whether interest at the official rate on those loans would have been eligible for relief, the loans are treated as a single loan and any relief on interest which would have been paid on that single loan is attributed to the earliest actual loan first and then any balance to later loans in order of time.

The priorities in (i) are not affected by (ii). 'Spouse' does not include a separated husband or wife. [*7 Sch 10–12*].

Calculation of interest at the official rate. The normal method for any year of assessment ('the relevant year') is (*a*) to take the average of the amounts of the loan outstanding at the commencement and end of the relevant year (or at the date the loan was made or discharged if falling within that year), (*b*) multiply that figure by the number of whole months (a month begins on sixth day of each calendar month) during which the loan was outstanding in that year and divide by twelve, (*c*) multiply the result by the official rate of interest in force, or if the rate changed, the average rate. [*7 Sch 4(1)*]. For 1995/96 and subsequent years, a replacement loan (whenever made) is treated for averaging purposes as being the same loan as the original if it is a 'further employment-related loan' which replaces (i) the original loan or (ii) a non-employment related loan which itself replaced the original, the second replacement occurring in the same tax year, or within 40 days thereafter, as the first. A '*further employment-related loan*' is a loan the benefit of which is obtained by reason of the same employment or other employment with the same employer or a person connected with him (within *Sec 839*—see (20) CONNECTED PERSONS). [*7 Sch 4(2)–(4); FA 1995, s 45(4)(5)*].

An alternative method may be required by the inspector or elected by the employee. For 1996/97 and subsequent years, as regards all loans whenever made, notice of requirement or election must be given within twelve months after 31 January following the relevant year of assessment (previously, the inspector had to give notice of requirement when raising or amending an assessment and the employee had to elect within thirty days of an assessment, or longer if the inspector agreed, or if no assessment made, within six years after end of the relevant year). The alternative method is to calculate the figures by reference to the daily amounts of the loan and official rates of interest. [*7 Sch 5; FA 1996, s 107(2)–(4)*].

For 1993/94 and earlier years, certain modifications apply to both methods where part of the interest is, or would be, eligible for relief under *Sec 353*. [*7 Sch 8, 9*].

General. See ICAEW Technical Release TAX 11/93, 9 July 1993 as regards loans to directors.

Interest on money loaned interest-free, subject to conditions and repayable on demand, by the employer to a trust for the benefit of an employee held to be emoluments within Schedule E (*O'Leary v McKinlay Ch D 1990, 63 TC 729*).

Loans written off. Any amount released from, or written off, a loan (whenever made and including any form of credit) obtained by reason of employment will be charged as an emolument, unless otherwise taxable as income. Where however it would be taxable under *Sec 148* (see 19.5 COMPENSATION FOR LOSS OF EMPLOYMENT) it will instead be taxable under *Sec 160(2)* and where the loan is one which is a capital sum within *Sec 677* (see 80.18 SETTLEMENTS) the charge will be on the excess of the amount released over sums previously treated as the employee's income under *Sec 677*. These provisions continue to apply after termination of employment, and to a loan replacing the original loan, but they cease on death of the employee. They apply if the loan is to a relative (see above) unless the employee shows he derived no benefit himself. They do not apply to arrangements to protect a person from a fall in value of shares acquired before 6 April 1976. [*Secs 160(2)–(7), 161(4)–(7); FA 1995, s 45(3)*].

Where the lender is a company in which the employee is also a participator and a charge arises under *Sec 160(2)*, the Revenue would not seek to treat the amount written off as a distribution. Similarly, where the lending company is close and a charge arises under *Sec 421* (see 28.3 EXCESS LIABILITY), the Revenue would not seek to treat the amount written off as a distribution or to raise an assessment under *Sec 160(2)*. (Tolley's Practical Tax 1993 p 144).

75.18   *Examples*

(i)

D, who is an employee of A Ltd earning £25,000 per annum, obtained a loan of £10,000 from the company on 10 October 1995 for the purpose of buying a car. Interest at a nominal rate is charged on the outstanding balance while the principal is repayable by instalments of £1,000 on 31 December and 30 June commencing 31 December 1995. The interest paid by D in 1995/96 amounted to £50 and, in 1996/97 to £250. The official rates of interest were as listed below.

From 6.10.95 to 5.2.96   7.75% p.a.
From 6.2.96   7.25% p.a.

It is assumed *purely for the purposes of the example* that the rate is increased to 8% p.a. from 6 December 1996 and that there are no further changes before 6 April 1997.

D will be assessed in 1995/96 as follows.

Normal method (averaging)	£
Average balance for period $\dfrac{£10,000 + £9,000}{2}$	£9,500
$£9,500 \times \frac{5}{12}$ note (*a*)	£3,958
$£3,958 \times 7.75\% \times \frac{119}{179}$	204
$£3,958 \times 7.25\% \times \frac{60}{179}$	96
	300
Deduct Interest paid in year	50
Cash equivalent of loan benefit	£250

Alternative method

Period	Balance of loan in period	Interest at official rate on balance	
	£		£
10.10.95 – 31.12.95	10,000	£10,000 × 7.75% × $\frac{83}{366}$	176
1.1.96 – 5.2.96	9,000	£9,000 × 7.75% × $\frac{36}{366}$	69
6.2.96 – 5.4.96	9,000	£9,000 × 7.25% × $\frac{60}{366}$	107
			352
Deduct Interest paid in year			50
Cash equivalent of loan benefit			£302
Amount chargeable to tax note (*b*)			£302

D will be assessed in 1996/97 as follows.

Normal method (averaging)   £

Average balance for year $\dfrac{£9,000 + £7,000}{2}$ £8,000

	£
£8,000 × 7.25% × $\frac{244}{365}$	388
£8,000 × 8% × $\frac{121}{365}$	212
	600
Deduct Interest paid in year	250
Cash equivalent of loan benefit	£350

Alternative method

Period	Balance of loan in period	Interest at official rate on balance	
	£		£
6.4.96 – 30.6.96	9,000	£9,000 × 7.25% × $\frac{86}{365}$	154
1.7.96 – 5.12.96	8,000	£8,000 × 7.25% × $\frac{158}{365}$	251
6.12.96 – 31.12.96	8,000	£8,000 × 8% × $\frac{26}{365}$	46
1.1.97 – 5.4.97	7,000	£7,000 × 8% × $\frac{95}{365}$	146
			597
Deduct Interest paid in year			250
Cash equivalent of loan benefit			£347
Amount chargeable to tax note (*b*)			£350

75.18 Schedule E—Emoluments

Notes

(a) The period 10 October 1995 to 5 April 1996 is, for the purpose of calculating the average balance, five complete months (months begin on the sixth day of each calendar month). However, for the purpose of applying the changing interest rates, the full number of days (179) during which the loan was outstanding is taken into account.

(b) The inspector will probably require the alternative method to be applied for 1995/96. It is assumed that the employee will not elect for the alternative method in 1996/97 as the difference is negligible.

(ii)

B, another employee of A Ltd, earns £30,000 per annum and obtained a loan from the company of £50,000 in January 1996 for house purchase (B's principal private residence). At 5 April 1996, no capital had been repaid but on 1 August 1996 B repays £10,000 of the loan. The rate of interest on the loan is 2.5% per annum on the daily outstanding balance and interest paid in 1996/97 is £1,080. The official rates of interest are as in the Example above. B has no other source of taxable income for 1996/97. He is a single man.

A Ltd also gives B a season ticket loan of £2,400, interest-free and repayable in equal monthly instalments, on 10 January 1997.

The cash equivalent of the loan benefit for 1996/97 is computed as follows.

(i)   Normal method (averaging)

		£
Average balance for year $\dfrac{£50,000 + £40,000}{2}$		45,000
$£45,000 \times 7.25\% \times \frac{244}{365}$		2,181
$£45,000 \times 8\% \quad \times \frac{121}{365}$		1,193
		3,374
Deduct Interest paid in year		1,080
Cash equivalent of loan benefit		£2,294

(ii)   Alternative method

Period	Balance of loan in period £	Interest at official rate on balance	£
6.4.96 – 1.8.96	50,000	$£50,000 \times 7.25\% \times \frac{118}{365}$	1,172
2.8.96 – 5.12.96	40,000	$£40,000 \times 7.25\% \times \frac{126}{365}$	1,001
6.12.96 – 5.4.97	40,000	$£40,000 \times 8\% \quad \times \frac{121}{365}$	1,061
			3,234
Deduct Interest paid in year			1,080
Cash equivalent of loan benefit			£2,154

	£
Amount chargeable to tax (on assumption that B elects for the alternative method)	£2,154

B is also treated as having paid notional interest on the loan of an amount equal to that chargeable to tax. Interest eligible for tax relief is as follows.

(i) Interest actually paid

Interest paid		Interest eligible for relief	
	£		£
6.4.96 – 1.8.96 (118 days)			
£50,000 × 2.5% × $\frac{118}{365}$	404	£404 × $\dfrac{30,000}{50,000}$	243
2.8.96 – 5.4.97 (247 days)			
£40,000 × 2.5% × $\frac{247}{365}$	676	£676 × $\dfrac{30,000}{40,000}$	507
	£1,080		£750

(ii) Notional interest paid

Interest paid		Interest eligible for relief	
	£		£
6.4.96 – 1.8.96	1,172	£1,172 × $\dfrac{30,000}{50,000}$	703
2.8.96 – 5.12.96	1,001	£1,001 × $\dfrac{30,000}{40,000}$	751
6.12.96 – 5.4.97	1,061	£1,061 × $\dfrac{30,000}{40,000}$	796
	3,234		2,250
Deduct actual interest	1,080		750
	£2,154		£1,500

B's tax liability for 1996/97 is computed as follows.

	£
Salary	30,000
Benefit (home loan)	2,154
Schedule E income	32,154
Other income	—
Total income	32,154
Deduct Personal allowance	3,765
Taxable income	£28,389

Tax payable:

3,900 @ 20%	780.00
21,600 @ 24%	5,184.00
2,889 @ 40%	1,155.60
	c/f 7,119.60

75.19 Schedule E—Emoluments

	£	£
		b/f 7,119.60
Deduct Interest relief:		
Actual interest	750	
Notional interest	1,500	
	£2,250	
£2,250 @ 15%		337.50
Tax liability		£6,782.10

Note

(a) The season ticket loan does not give rise to a taxable benefit as it is not a qualifying loan and at no time in the tax year does the amount outstanding exceed £5,000.

75.19 Employee shareholdings. Where an employee or person connected with him (see 20 CONNECTED PERSONS) acquires shares in any company at an under-value in pursuance of a right or opportunity available by reason of the employment, then he will be treated as if he had the benefit of an interest-free notional loan, with the effect that

(i) termination of that loan under (b) or (c) below will give rise to a charge under *Sec 160(2)* (see 75.17 above) and such a charge will be deductible for capital gains, and

(ii) a charge will arise on notional interest under *Sec 160(1)* (see 75.17 above).

A right, etc. is 'available' to the taxpayer although he may himself have stipulated its being granted (*CIR v Herd CS 1992, 66 TC 77*).

The initial amount of the notional loan is so much of the market value of fully paid-up shares of that class (less any payments then made) as is not otherwise chargeable as an emolument. The loan may be reduced by later payments or terminated by

(a) payments to clear the loan,

(b) if shares not fully paid up at acquisition, the release etc. of any outstanding or contingent obligation to pay for them,

(c) disposal of the shares,

(d) death of employee.

Where shares are acquired as above, *but whether or not at an under-value*, and disposed of at more than market value, the excess is treated as emoluments of the employment for the year of disposal.

These provisions continue to apply up to the death of the employee notwithstanding any prior termination of employment. Where there is less than full beneficial ownership of the shares, the provisions apply proportionately. [*Sec 162; TCGA 1992, s 120(3)*].

See also 75.36 below.

75.20 Scholarships. Where payments are made under scholarship awards *Sec 331* is not to be construed as conferring exemption from tax on any person other than the holder of the scholarship. If a scholarship (including an exhibition, bursary or other similar educational endowment) is provided to a member of the family or household of a director or higher-paid employee by reason of the latter's employment the payments are assessable on such director etc. as a benefit under *Sec 154*. A scholarship is to be taken to have been provided by reason of a person's employment if provided, directly or indirectly, under arrangements entered into by, or by a person connected with, his employer.

However *Sec 154* will not bring into charge as a benefit a payment under a scholarship awarded

(i)   out of a trust fund, or under a scheme, to a person receiving full-time instruction at an educational establishment, where 25% or less of the payments made out of the fund, etc. in any year of assessment are scholarship payments provided, or treated as provided, by reason of a person's employment (regardless of whether or not the employment is director's or higher-paid or in the UK).

Payments which are *in fact* provided by reason of a person's employment are taxable even if the fund meets the 25% test.

(ii)   before 15 March 1983, provided that the first payment was made before 6 April 1984. For payments made after 5 April 1989, there is an additional requirement for the person holding the scholarship to continue to receive full-time instruction at the same educational establishment he was attending on 15 March 1983 or, if later, at the time of the first payment. As regards this last condition, the Revenue have commented that in general an integrated course—e.g. a course of study for a first degree—will count as a single period of study whether or not part of it is spent abroad, as in the case of language students. (CCAB Memorandum TR 511, 26 August 1983). [*Sec 165*].

See also 29.25 EXEMPT INCOME for payments to employees to attend sandwich courses.

75.21   **Sporting and recreational facilities.** For 1993/94 and subsequent years, the provision to an employee (or to a member of his family or household) of

(*a*)   any benefit consisting in, or in a right or opportunity to make use of, any sporting or other recreational facilities made available generally to, or for use by, the employees of the employer in question, or

(*b*)   any non-cash voucher (see 75.44 below) capable of being exchanged only for such a benefit

is exempted from any charge to tax under Schedule E.

Excluded from the relief (unless prescribed by regulation) is any benefit consisting in

(i)   an interest in, or the use of, any mechanically propelled vehicle (including ships, boats, aircraft and hovercraft),

(ii)   an interest in, or the use of, any holiday or other overnight accommodation or associated facilities,

(iii) a facility provided on domestic premises (i.e. premises used wholly or mainly as a private dwelling, or belonging to or enjoyed with such premises),

(iv)   a facility available to, or for use by, the general public,

(v)   a facility not used wholly or mainly by persons whose right or opportunity to use it derives from employment, or

(vi)   a right or opportunity to make use of any facility within (i)–(v) above.

As regards (v) above, a right or opportunity derives from employment only if it derives from the person's being (or having been) an employee of a particular employer (or a member of such a person's family or household) and the facility is available generally to employees of that employer.

The Treasury may by regulation prescribe exceptions from, and conditional inclusions in, this relief.

[*Sec 197G; FA 1993, s 75*].

75.22 Schedule E—Emoluments

75.22 **Dispensations** (Notices of nil liability). If an employer supplies the inspector with a statement of the cases and circumstances in which particular types of expense payments and benefits are made or provided by him for any employees (whether his own or those of anyone else) and the inspector is satisfied that such benefits etc. give rise to no tax liability, he shall issue a notice of nil liability, but this can be revoked later. [*Sec 166*]. Dispensations are frequently given for e.g. travelling and subsistence expenses on an approved scale for business journeys in the UK (but not generally 'round sum' expense allowances). The effect is to exclude such items from the PAYE scheme, returns, etc. They are not given, however, where the effect would be to remove the employee from liability under the benefits legislation (see 75.11 above). See Revenue Pamphlets IR 69 for conditions and 480 generally.

Provided that the circumstances under which a dispensation was issued have not changed, it will also be accepted as evidence that the expenses covered are not earnings for national insurance contributions purposes. (Revenue Tax Bulletin August 1995 p 245).

75.23 **EMPLOYEE LIABILITIES AND INDEMNITY INSURANCE**

For 1995/96 and subsequent years of assessment, there may be deducted from Schedule E emoluments out of which they are paid

(*a*)   any amount paid in or towards the discharge of a 'qualifying liability' of the employee;

(*b*)   costs or expenses incurred in connection with any claim that the employee is subject to a 'qualifying liability' or with any related proceedings; and

(*c*)   so much of any premium (or similar payment) paid under a 'qualifying contract' of insurance as relates to the indemnification of the employee against a 'qualifying liability' or to the payment of such costs and expenses as in (*b*) above.

Where any amount in (*a*)–(*c*) above is met by the employer or a third party, there may be made a deduction to offset a resultant taxable benefit (see 75.11 above). However, no deduction may be made for any such liability, costs or expenses if it would have been unlawful for the employer to insure against them (for example, costs arising from criminal convictions, and see Revenue Tax Bulletin October 1995 p 258).

A liability is a '*qualifying liability*' of the employee if it is imposed either

(i)   in respect of any acts or omissions of the employee in his capacity as such or in any other capacity in which he acts in the performance of his duties, or

(ii)   in connection with any proceedings relating to or arising from claims in respect of such acts or omissions.

A '*qualifying contract*' of insurance is one

(A)   which, as regards the risks insured against, relates exclusively to one or more of the following

(i)   indemnification of any employee against any qualifying liability,

(ii)   indemnification of any person against any vicarious liability in respect of acts or omissions giving rise to a qualifying liability of another,

(iii) payment of costs and expenses in connection with any claim that a person is subject to a liability to which the insurance relates or with related proceedings, and

(iv)   indemnification of any employer against any loss from the payment by him to an employee of his of any amount in respect of either a qualifying liability or costs and expenses as in (iii) above;

(B)   which is not 'connected' with any other contract (see below);

(C) a significant part of the premium for which does not relate to rights to payments or benefits other than cover for the risks insured against and any right of renewal; and

(D) the period of insurance under which is not more than two years (disregarding renewals) and which the insured is not required to renew.

Two contracts are '*connected*' (see (B) above) if either was entered into by reference to the other or to enable the other to be, or to facilitate the other being, entered into on particular terms *and* the terms of either contract would have been significantly different if it had not been for the other. Connected contracts, each of which satisfy (A), (C) and (D), are qualifying contracts despite (B) above, where the only significant difference in terms consists in certain premium reductions.

Where applicable, for the purposes of these provisions, an insurance premium may be reasonably apportioned as between the different risks, persons or employments to which the contract relates.

[*Sec 201AA; FA 1995, s 91*].

For clarification of certain points on operation of the relief, see Revenue Tax Bulletin October 1995 pp 257, 258.

Post-employment deductions. Relief against total income (and capital gains, see below) may be claimed for payments made by a former employee which are made after the employment ceases and no later than six years after the end of the year of assessment in which it ceased and which would have been deductible under *Sec 201AA* (see above) if the employment had continued and if the payment had been made out of the emoluments. Relief is given for the year in which the payment is made and unused relief cannot be carried forward. In determining whether the payment would have been deductible under *Sec 201AA*, only acts or omissions relating to the actual period of employment are taken into account.

Relief is not available for any payment the cost of which is ultimately borne by the former employer, by a successor to the former employer's business or to his liabilities, by a person connected with either of those (see (20) CONNECTED PERSONS) or out of related insurance proceeds. However, where such a payment falls to be treated as a taxable emolument of the former employee or as a taxable benefit provided under an unapproved retirement benefit scheme (see 66.9 RETIREMENT SCHEMES), he is treated as having paid an equivalent amount out of that emolument or benefit, so as to effectively cancel the tax charge (providing the payment qualifies for relief under these provisions). No tax is charged under *Sec 148* (see 19.5 COMPENSATION FOR LOSS OF EMPLOYMENT) in respect of any amount paid, or valuable consideration given, to reimburse the former employee for a payment, which, had he not been reimbursed, would have attracted relief under these provisions; the same applies as regards amounts paid etc. to the former employee's executors or administrators.

Relief against capital gains. Where a claim is made as above and the claimant's income for the year is insufficient to fully utilise the relief, he may make a claim to have the excess relief treated as an allowable loss for that year for capital gains tax purposes. The allowable loss may not exceed the amount of the claimant's gains for the year *before* deducting any losses brought forward, the capital gains tax annual exemption, any relief available under *FA 1991, s 72* for trading losses (see 46.5 LOSSES) or any relief available to a former trader etc. for post-cessation expenditure (see 60.4 POST-CESSATION ETC. RECEIPTS AND EXPENDITURE); any excess over that amount is *not* available to carry forward against gains of a later year.

[*FA 1995, s 92*].

75.24 **EMPLOYMENT OR PROFESSION?**

Whether a person holds an office or employment or carries on a profession or vocation depends on the facts including the relevant contract(s). A distinction is drawn between a contract *of service* (Schedule E) and a contract *for services* (Schedule D). A vision mixer engaged under a series of short-term contracts was within Schedule D (*Hall v Lorimer CA 1993, [1994] STC 23*), as was an artiste who entered into a series of engagements (*Davies v Braithwaite KB 1933, 18 TC 198*), but contrast *Fall v Hitchen Ch D 1972, 49 TC 433* in which a ballet dancer engaged by a theatrical management under a standard form of contract, but able to work elsewhere when not required by the management, was held to be within Schedule E. See now below as regards artistes. A barristers' clerk was not the holder of an office (*McMenamin v Diggles Ch D 1991, 64 TC 286*), but in *Horner v Hasted Ch D, [1995] STC 766* an unqualified accountant contributing capital to, and sharing profits of, a firm of accountants was held not to be a partner. See *Andrews v King Ch D 1991, 64 TC 332* as regards agricultural gangmasters.

Problems may arise in relation to part-time activities. A part-time medical appointment of a doctor in private practice assessable under Schedule D was held to be within Schedule E (*Mitchell & Edon v Ross HL 1961, 40 TC 11*) as were the lecture fees of a full-time consultant within Schedule E (*Lindsay v CIR CS 1964, 41 TC 661*) and a non-practising barrister (*Sidey v Phillips Ch D 1986, 59 TC 458*), the evening class fees of a teacher (*Fuge v McClelland Ch D 1956, 36 TC 571*) and the remuneration as lecturer of a professional singer (*Walls v Sinnett Ch D 1986, 60 TC 150*), but *ad hoc* Crown appointments were held to be within Schedule D (*Edwards v Clinch HL 1981, 56 TC 367*). Salaries of sub-postmasters carrying on a retail trade from the same premises as the sub-post office are in practice treated as part of their Schedule D income. It is understood that, where a company operates sub-post offices in its shops with its directors as nominee sub-postmasters, and the directors are required to, and do, hand over their salaries as sub-postmasters to the company, the salaries will similarly be brought into the company's Schedule D, Case I computation and not assessed on the directors under Schedule E. (Tolley's Practical Tax 1986 p 23).

Certain appointments, such as auditorships and registrarships, are strictly offices within Schedule E but if held by practising accountants or solicitors the annual remuneration therefrom is, in practice, usually included in the Schedule D assessment on the profession. Fees from directorships of professional partnerships may be included in Schedule D assessment provided that the directorship is a normal incident of the profession and the practice concerned, and that the fees are only a small part of total profits and are pooled for division among the partners under partnership agreement. A written undertaking must be given that the full fees received will be included in gross income of the basis period whether or not the directorship is still held in the year of assessment or the partner concerned is still a partner. (Revenue Pamphlet IR 1 (1992) A37). For directors' fees received by other companies see 75.1(1) above. However any compensation etc. payments on the termination of such appointments are dealt with under *Sec 148*, see 19.4 COMPENSATION FOR LOSS OF EMPLOYMENT and *Brander & Cruickshank HL 1970, 46 TC 574* and the cases referred to therein.

See generally Revenue Pamphlet IR 56.

Artistes (i.e. actors, singers, musicians, dancers and theatrical artists). It is understood that, for 1994/95 and subsequent years, the Revenue accept that the earnings of most artistes should be assessed under Schedule D, Case 1. Circumstances in which Schedule E and PAYE should be applied would e.g. be where the artiste is engaged for a regular salary to perform in a series of different productions at the direction of the engager, and with a period of notice stipulated before termination of the contract. This might apply e.g. to permanent members of an opera, ballet or theatre company or an orchestra. (*Taxation 8 September 1994, p 553*).

Individuals now accepted to be within Schedule D, Case 1, but previously assessed under Schedule E (as below), can apply to have their tax liabilities for 1990/91, 1991/92, 1992/93 and 1993/94 recomputed, and all those concerned should have been contacted by their local tax office inviting the submission of revised computations and repayment requests where appropriate.

Under the practice previously applied by the Revenue, artistes working under standard Equity contracts were, after 5 April 1990, generally brought within Schedule E, and (55) PAYE applied in the usual way. The normal Schedule E rules as regards deductions, etc. applied (except in relation to agents' fees, see below), but see ICAEW Guidance Note TR 796, 25 June 1990, for their application in these particular circumstances, and for the transition from self-employed to employed status. Artistes could claim a deduction of up to $17\frac{1}{2}\%$ of their Schedule E emoluments in respect of percentage fees (and VAT thereon) paid out of those emoluments to a licensed employment agency within *Employment Agencies Act 1973* or to a *bona fide* non-profit-making co-operative society acting as agent for the artiste. [*Sec 201A; FA 1990, s 77; FA 1991, s 69*].

By concession, certain artistes qualified for 'reserved Schedule D status', and continued to be taxed under Schedule D on all income from theatrical performances so long as they continued their professional activities without a cessation for Schedule D purposes and continued to meet their taxation obligations satisfactorily. A nil tax code was issued to employers in such cases. Reserved Schedule D status applied where either:

(*a*)   Schedule D assessments had been made on such income for 1986/87, 1987/88 and 1988/89, one at least of which was based on a return submitted before 31 May 1989; or

(*b*)   such assessments had been made for at least three years between 1979/80 and 1988/89 inclusive, and

(i)   the Schedule D history had been satisfactory,

(ii)   returns were made before 31 May 1989 for all relevant years before 1987/88, and

(iii)   the last engagement starting before 6 April 1990 was dealt with under Schedule D.

(Revenue Pamphlet IR 1, A75 and ICAEW Guidance Note TR 796, 25 June 1990).

Taxation of earnings under reserved Schedule D status did not prevent any compensation payments received for termination of contracts from attracting the £30,000 exemption under *Sec 148* (see 19.6 COMPENSATION FOR LOSS OF EMPLOYMENT (AND DAMAGES)). (Tolley's Practical Tax 1994, p 15).

A **dentist** employed by a Panamanian company, which contracted with a UK practice to supply his services in return for a proportion of the NHS fees and a management charge, was held to be within Schedule E, although the legality of the arrangements was in question (*Cooke v Blacklaws Ch D 1984, 58 TC 255*).

Divers etc. employed in UK area of the Continental Shelf are assessed under Schedule D, Case I, see 71.31 SCHEDULE D, CASES I AND II.

Film, etc. technicians. From 6 April 1983, the Revenue reclassified certain grades of such technicians as employed persons liable under Schedule E, subject to the usual rights of appeal. (Revenue Press Release 30 March 1983). A vision mixer was, however, held to be self-employed in *Hall v Lorimer CA 1993, [1994] STC 23*.

75.25   **FLAT RATE EXPENSES FOR EMPLOYEES**

Deductions are allowed for tools, special clothing etc. necessarily provided by an employee without reimbursement, and which the employer does not make available. If tools or protective clothing are supplied, but not both, or if some of the tools are provided, the rate of allowance may be reduced accordingly. These are mostly agreed with trade unions, but the agreed rates do not preclude further claims, if justified, under *Sec 198(1)*. See Revenue Pamphlet IR 1 (November 1995 Supplement), A1 Appendix (which also includes figures from 6 April 1987 to 5 April 1991) and *Ward v Dunn Ch D 1978, 52 TC 517*.

75.25 Schedule E—Emoluments

Industry Code	Industry Group	Occupation		Allowances from 6 April 1995 (1991) £
10	Agriculture	All Workers		70 (60)
20	Forestry	All Workers		70 (60)
30	Seamen	a. Carpenters (Seamen)	Passenger Liners	135 (140)
		b. Carpenters (Seamen)	Cargo Vessels, Tankers, Coasters and Ferries	130 (110)
50	Iron Mining	a. Fillers, Miners and Underground Workers		100 (85)
		b. All Other Workers		75 (65)
60	Quarrying	All Workers		70 (60)
70	Iron and Steel	a. Day Labourers, General Labourers, Stockmen, Timekeepers, Warehouse Staff and Weighmen		60 (50)
		b. Apprentices		45 (40)
		c. All Other Workers		120 (105)
90	Brass and copper	All Workers		100 (85)
100	Aluminium	a. Continual Casting Operators, Process Operators, De-Dimplers, Driers, Drill Punchers, Dross Unloaders, Firemen, Furnace Operators and their helpers, Leaders, Mouldmen, Pourers, Remelt Department Labourers, Roll Flatteners		130 (110)
		b. Cable Hands, Case Makers, Labourers, Mates, Truck Drivers and Measurers, Storekeepers		60 (50)
		c. Apprentices		45 (40)
		d. All Other Workers		100 (85)
110	Engineering	a. Pattern Makers		120 (105)
		b. Labourers, Supervisory and Unskilled Workers		60 (50)
		c. Apprentices and Storekeepers		45 (40)
		d. Motor Mechanics in Garage Repair Shops		100 (85)
		e. All Other Workers		100 (85)
120	Shipyards	a. Blacksmiths and their Strikers, Boilermakers, Burners, Carpenters, Caulkers, Drillers, Furnacemen (Platers), Holders Up, Fitters, Platers, Plumbers, Riveters, Sheet Iron Workers, Shipwrights, Tubers and Welders		115 (95)
		b. Labourers		60 (50)
		c. Apprentices and Storekeepers		45 (40)
		d. All Other Workers		75 (65)
130	Vehicles	a. Builders, Railway Wagon etc. Repairers, and Railway Wagon Lifters		105 (90)

Industry Code	Industry Group	Occupation	Allowances from 6 April 1995 (1991) £
		b. Railway Vehicle Painters and Letterers, Railway Wagon etc. Builders' and Repairers' Assistants	60 (50)
		c. All Other Workers	40(30)
140	Particular Engineering	*a.* Pattern Makers	120 (105)
		b. All Chainmakers–Cleaners, Galvanisers, Tinners and Wire Drawers in the Wire Drawing In-dustry–Toolmakers in the Lockmaking Industry	100 (85)
		c. Apprentices and Storekeepers	45 (40)
		d. All Other Workers	60 (50)
150	Constructional Engineering	*a.* Blacksmiths and their Strikers, Burners, Caulkers, Chippers, Drillers, Erectors, Fitters, Holders Up, Markers Off, Platers, Riggers, Riveters, Rivet Heaters, Scaffolders, Sheeters, Template Workers, Turners and Welders	115 (95)
		b. Banksmen Labourers, Shop-helpers, Slewers and Straightenders	60 (50)
		c. Apprentices and Storekeepers	45 (40)
		d. All Other Workers	75 (65)
160	Precious Metals	All Workers	70 (60)
170	Electrical and Electricity Supply	*a.* Those workers incurring laun-dry costs only (generally CEGB employees)	25 (20)
		b. All Other Workers	90 (75)
180	Textiles	*a.* Carders, Carding Engineers, Overlookers (all), and Technicians in Spinning Mills	85 (70)
		b. All Other Workers	60 (50)
190	Clothing	*a.* Lacemakers, Hosiery Bleachers, Dyers, Scourers and Knitters, and Knitwear Bleachers and Dyers	45 (40)
		b. All Other Workers	30 (25)
200	Textile Prints	All Workers	60 (50)
210	Leather	*a.* Curriers (Wet Workers), Fell-mongering Workers and Tanning Operatives (Wet)	55 (45)
		b. All Other Workers	40 (30)
220	Food	All Workers	40 (30)
230	Printing	*a.* The following occupations in the Letterpress Section:- Elec-trical Engineers (Rotary Presses), Electro-typers, Ink and Roller Makers, Machine Minders (Rotary), Maintenance Engineers (Rotary Presses) and Stereotypers	105 (90)

75.25   Schedule E—Emoluments

Industry Code	Industry Group	Occupation	Allowances from 6 April 1995 (1991) £
		b. Bench Hands (P&B), Compositors (Lp), Readers (Lp), T&E Section Wireroom Operators, Warehousemen (PprBox)	30 (25)
		c. All Other Workers	70 (60)
240	Glass	All Workers	60 (50)
250	Building Materials	a. Stone Masons	85 (70)
		b. Tile Makers and Labourers	40 (30)
		c. All Other Workers	55 (45)
260	Wood and Furniture	a. Carpenters, Cabinet Makers, Joiners, Wood Carvers and Woodcutting Machinists	115 (95)
		b. Artificial Limb Makers (other than in wood), Organ Builders and Packaging Case Makers	90 (75)
		c. Coopers not providing own tools, Labourers, Polishers and Upholsterers	45 (40)
		d. All Other Workers	75 (65)
270	Building	a. Joiners and Carpenters	105 (95)
		b. Cement Works, Roofing Felt and Asphalt Labourers	55 (45)
		c. Labourers and Navvies	40 (30)
		d. All Other Workers	85 (70)
280	Heating	a. Pipe Fitters and Plumbers	100 (90)
		b. Coverers, Laggers, Domestic Glaziers, Heating Engineers and their Mates	90 (75)
		c. All Gas Workers and All Other Workers	70 (60)
290	Railways	All Workers except Craftsmen (For craftsmen see the appropriate industry code lists e.g. engineering)	70 (60)
300	Public Service	i. Dock and Inland Waterways	
		a. Dockers, Dredger Drivers and Hopper Steerers	55 (45)
		b. All Other Workers	40 (30)
		ii. Public Transport	
		a. Garage Hands (including Cleaners)	55 (45)
		b. Conductors and Drivers	40 (30)
320	Prisons	Uniformed Prison Officers	55 (45)
330	Banks	Uniformed Bank Employees	40 (30)
355	Police Force	Uniformed Police Officers (ranks up to and including Chief Inspector)	55 (45)

It is understood that an allowance of £18 p.a. is available to nurses to cover the cost of shoes and tights. (Tolley's Practical Tax 1993 p 72).

Notes.

1. Industry Code is an industry identification term used for Inland Revenue computer purposes.
2. The expressions 'all workers' and 'all other workers' refer only to manual workers, or certain other workers who have to bear the cost of upkeep of tools or special clothing. They do not extend to other employees such as office staff.
3. 'Cost of upkeep' means the cost of replacement, repair or cleaning, but not the initial cost of providing the tools or special clothing.
4. 'Special clothing' means overalls or other protective clothing or uniform, but does not include ordinary clothing of the sort which is also worn off duty.

75.26   **GIFTS, AWARDS ETC. RECEIVED**

Gifts etc. are taxable when they arise out of the employment but not if they are given to the recipient in a personal capacity. The line between the two may be fine. Although emoluments may be voluntary and irregular, they are assessable. Also all commissions, Xmas presents, 'cost of living', cash and other bonuses. For 'tax-free' payments and awards, see 75.40 below. For payments to clergymen, see 75.9 above.

Bonus to a director described as a gift held assessable (*Radcliffe v Holt KB 1927, 11 TC 621*). Proceeds of a *public benefit match* for a cricketer held to be a gift and not chargeable (*Reed v Seymour HL 1927, 11 TC 625*), but see *Moorhouse v Dooland CA 1954, 36 TC 1* re collections. In *Davis v Harrison KB 1927, 11 TC 707, Corbett v Duff and other cases KB 1941, 23 TC 763*, payments to professional football players *in lieu of benefit* or on *transference to another club*, held assessable. World Cup bonus to professional footballer not assessable (*Moore v Griffiths Ch D 1972, 48 TC 338*). Present to *successful jockey* by owner of racehorse assessable (*Wing v O'Connell Supreme Court (Ireland) 1926, 1 ITC 170*) also *taxi-driver's tips* (*Calvert v Wainwright KB 1947, 27 TC 475*) and gifts to Hunt servant (*Wright v Boyce CA 1958, 38 TC 160*). Betting winnings on own games by professional golfer not assessable (*Down v Compston KB 1937, 21 TC 60*).

Gift to employee by company to which his services were lent by employer held not assessable, *Morris CS 1967, 44 TC 685*. But amount to company secretary, agreed by directors for negotiating sale of works and paid by liquidator, held assessable (*Shipway v Skidmore KB 1932, 16 TC 748*) as were payments to a director for negotiating sale of a branch (*Mudd v Collins KB 1925, 9 TC 297*) and to a director for special services abroad (*Barson v Airey CA 1925, 10 TC 609*). Commission for work outside ordinary duties assessable (*Mudd v Collins KB 1925, 9 TC 297*). Sums paid as compensation for loss of benefit under an abandoned salvage scheme held assessable (*Holland v Geoghegan Ch D 1972, 48 TC 482*), also assets distributed to employees on termination of profit-sharing trust fund before termination of employment (*Brumby v Milner HL 1976, 51 TC 583*). See, however, *Bray v Best HL 1989, 61 TC 705* as regards such a distribution after termination of employment.

See 75.36 below regarding gifts of shares.

Pensions (voluntary or otherwise) to retired employees are assessable (see 59.1(v) PENSIONS) as are certain payments in consideration of, in consequence of, or in connection with the termination, or change, of employment (see 19 COMPENSATION FOR LOSS OF EMPLOYMENT).

Suggestion scheme awards are, by concession, not taxed under Schedule E provided that there is a formally constituted scheme open to all employees on equal terms, and that the suggestion concerned is outside the scope of the employee's normal duties. Suggestions put forward at meetings held for that purpose are excluded. Awards under the scheme must either be 'encouragement' awards of £25 or less for meritorious suggestions not implemented, or must follow a decision to implement the suggestion. In the latter case, the decision to make the award must relate to the benefit expected to flow from implementation, and the amount of the award must not exceed 50% of the first year's expected net benefit, or 10% of the expected benefit over a period of up to five years, with an overriding maximum of £5,000. Any excess over £5,000 is not covered by the concession. Where a suggestion is put forward by more than one employee, the award must be divided on a reasonable basis. (Revenue Pamphlet IR 1, A57).

Long service awards, of tangible articles or of shares in the employing company (or in another group company), to employees, including directors, for service of 20 years or more, will not be taxed provided cost to employer does not exceed £20 for each year of service and no similar award has been made to recipient within previous 10 years. (Revenue Pamphlet IR 1, A22). Cash awards are assessable (*Weston v Hearn KB 1943, 25 TC 425*).

Gifts from third parties. Gifts (other than cash) costing not more than £150 (inclusive of VAT) in any tax year (£100 for 1994/95 and earlier years) received from a person other than the employer are, by concession, exempt from tax, subject to similar conditions as apply to the provision of entertainment by third parties (see 75.13(xv) above) and provided that they are not made under any sort of reciprocal arrangement. (Revenue Pamphlet IR 1, A70; Revenue Press Release 1 November 1995).

75.27   **HM FORCES**

Mess and ration allowances and certain bounties and gratuities are exempt. [*Sec 316*]. No tax allowance may be claimed for lodging expenses paid out of assessable lodging allowance (*Evans v Richardson, Nagley v Spilsbury Ch D 1957, 37 TC 178*), nor for mess expenses (*Lomax v Newton Ch D 1953, 34 TC 558*).

Territorial Army pay assessable but not annual bounty and training expenses. [*Sec 316(4)*]. Terminal grants, gratuities (including commutation of annual sums) are exempt. [*Sec 188(1)(e)*]. See also 29.5 and 29.30 EXEMPT INCOME and 59.4 PENSIONS. Travel facilities (including allowances, vouchers and warrants) for going on, or returning from, leave are exempt from tax. [*Sec 197*].

Uniform allowances. Serving officers may claim the cost of their uniforms as being money spent wholly, exclusively and necessarily in the performance of their duties. [*Sec 199*]. The amounts agreed for **1995/96** are

Army	£
Officers serving at full mounted duty	1,012.88
Male dismounted Officers, Colonels and above	749.78
Female Officers, Colonels and above (except QARANC (below))	499.84
Dismounted Officers (Household Division) below Colonel	673.19
Male dismounted Officers below Colonel (except Household Division)	589.29
Female Officers below Colonel (except QARANC (below))	488.30
QARANC: Female Nursing Officers, Colonels and above	671.48
Female Nursing Officers below Colonel	652.87
Male SSLC and SSVC Officers	186.55
Female SSLC and SSVC Officers	201.20

Royal Air Force	£
Male RAF Officers (including PMRAFNS)	
Air Officers	422.76
Group Captains	402.72
Wing Commander and below	361.10
Female officers of PMRAFNS	
Air Officers	589.16
Group Captains	586.00
Wing Commander and below	579.70
Female RAF Officers	
Air Officers	477.98
Group Captains	460.74
Wing Commander and below	421.69
Royal Navy and Royal Marines	£
Officers Flag and equivalent ranks	1,071.00
Officers below Flag rank	792.12
WRNS Officers: seagoing only	853.80
non-seagoing	680.52
Women Medical and Dental Officers: seagoing	792.60
non-seagoing	567.48
QARNNS Officers (female)	
Matron and above	544.68
Below Matron	828.00
QARNNS Officers (male)	
Chief Nursing Officer and above	489.36
Below Chief Nursing Officer	456.48

75.28   LEGAL

In *Eagles v Levy KB 1934, 19 TC 23* held (*a*) costs of action to recover remuneration not an allowable deduction, and (*b*) lump sum amount in settlement of action for balance remuneration assessable in full.

Where company had special need of director's services and paid more than necessary in legal costs of defence on motoring charge, no apportionment between benefits to company and employee and all assessable (*Rendell v Went HL 1964, 41 TC 641*).

75.29   LIVING ACCOMMODATION ETC.

Provision of living accommodation etc., for an employee may be taxable emoluments under general principles (see 75.7 above), but see below as regards 1996/97 onwards. In *Nicoll v Austin KB 1935, 19 TC 531*, a company maintained a large house owned and occupied by its managing director and controlling shareholder, paying the rates, fuel bills and other outgoings. The expenditure was held to be assessable on him as emoluments of his office.

There may also be liability under special legislation as described below. For 1996/97 and subsequent years, the charge under this legislation takes priority over any charge under general principles, the latter applying only if, and to the extent that, the charge would exceed that under *Secs 145* and *146* below. [*Sec 146A; FA 1996, s 106(2)(3)*]. This is an anti-avoidance measure aimed at salary sacrifices.

75.29 Schedule E—Emoluments

Basic charge

For any employee, any living accommodation provided to him, or to members of his family or household, by his employer (and, before 1996/97, not otherwise taxable), is treated as an emolument equal to the value of the accommodation to him for the period, less any sum made good by the employee to those providing the accommodation, *unless* it is provided in the normal course of domestic, family and personal relationships, or by a local authority under its usual terms for non-employees.

The value of the accommodation is normally the annual value ascertained under *Sec 837* (which is equivalent to the gross rateable value, see 68.7(*e*)(*d*) SCHEDULE A), or any actual rent, if greater, paid by those providing the benefit, reduced by any amount which would be deductible as an expense under *Sec 198* (see 75.10 above) or *Sec 332(3)* (see 75.9 above, Clergymen) if the employee had paid for the accommodation himself. [*Sec 145(1)–(3), (6); FA 1996, s 106(1)(3)*]. In Scotland, where the 1985 rating revaluation produced annual values out of line with those in the rest of the UK, a figure lower than the gross rateable value is, by concession, used as annual value. The 1985 valuation figure is scaled back by the average increase in Scottish rateable values between 1978 and 1985 (170%), e.g. a 1985 value of £270 becomes £100 for this purpose. (Revenue Pamphlet IR 1, A56). For new properties which do not appear on the domestic rating lists, and for those where there has been a material change since the lists ceased to be maintained, estimates will be agreed of what the gross annual value would have been had domestic rates been continued. In the case of Scotland these will then be scaled back to 1978 values. (Revenue Press Releases 10 November 1989, 19 April 1990).

Where a property is provided as living accommodation to more than one employee or director in the same period, the total amounts charged under *Sec 145* and *Sec 146* (see below) will, by concession, not exceed the amount which would have been chargeable if the property had been provided to a single employee in that period. (Revenue Press Release (REV 35) 28 November 1995).

Exemptions to the above charge are

(a) where it is necessary for the proper performance of his duties for the employee to reside in the accommodation;

(b) where the employment is such that it is customary for employees to be provided with accommodation for the better performance of their duties;

(c) where there is a special threat to the employee's security, and he resides in the accommodation as part of special security arrangements in force;

(d) where the employer is an individual and the provision of accommodation is made in the normal course of his domestic, family or personal relationships;

(e) where the employer is a local authority and the accommodation provided is on no better terms than those for similar accommodation to non-employees.

[*Sec 145(4)(7); FA 1996, s 134, 20 Sch 7*].

See *Vertigan v Brady Ch D 1988, 60 TC 624* as regards the scope of (a) and (b) above.

Notes to above

(A) *Rates.* Where (a), (b) or (c) applies, there is also no liability if the rates are paid or reimbursed by the employer (otherwise there could be liability under general principles, see above). [*Sec 145(4)*]. The exemption does not apply to payments of the community charge (and, in Scotland, the community water charge), which are the employee's (or his family's) personal liability. (Revenue Press Release 10 November 1989).

(B) *Directors.* Neither (a) nor (b) above applies to accommodation provided by a company, or associated company, to its director unless for each such directorship he has no material interest in the company (i.e. broadly if his and/or his associates' interests in the company do not exceed 5%) *and either* he is a full-time working director *or* the company is non-profit-making (i.e. it does not carry on a trade nor is its main function the holding of investments or other property) *or* the company is a charity. [*Sec 145(5)(8)*].

Additional charge in respect of certain properties

For all employees, if there is a liability to tax on living accommodation under *Sec 145* (or there would be a liability if the employee's contributions towards the cost were disregarded) and the cost of providing the accommodation exceeds £75,000, the employee will, in addition to any charge under *Sec 145* (see above), be assessed under Schedule E on the 'additional value' to him of the accommodation. Where, however, the charge under *Sec 145* is based on the full open market rent the property might fetch, the Revenue will, by concession, not seek to impose an additional charge under *Sec 146*. (Revenue Press Release (REV 35) 28 November 1995). Any rent paid by the employee which exceeds the value of the accommodation as determined under *Sec 145* is deducted from the additional value. The '*additional value*' is the rent which would have been payable for the period if the annual rent was the 'appropriate percentage' of the amount by which the cost of providing the accommodation exceeds £75,000. The '*appropriate percentage*' is the 'official rate' in force for the purposes of the beneficial loan arrangements of *Sec 160* (see 75.17 above) at the beginning of the year of assessment.

The cost of providing the accommodation is the aggregate of expenditure incurred by any 'relevant person' in acquiring the property together with any improvement expenditure incurred before the year of assessment in question *less* any payments by the employee to any relevant person as reimbursement of such expenditure or as consideration for the grant of a tenancy, or subtenancy, to him. Where the employee first occupies the property on a date after 30 March 1983 and any estate or interest in the property was held by any relevant person throughout the period of six years ending with that date (i.e. the date of first occupation), then the cost of providing the accommodation, for the purposes of calculating the additional value, is the aggregate of the market value of the property at that date, together with any improvement expenditure incurred after that date and before the year of assessment, less any employee contributions as above. A '*relevant person*' is the person providing the accommodation, or, if different, the employee's employer, and any person, other than the employee, connected with such persons under *Sec 839* (see 20 CONNECTED PERSONS). '*Market value*' is open market value assuming vacant possession and disregarding any options on the property held by the employee, a person connected with him or any relevant person as defined above.

Where an employee is provided with more than one property, the £75,000 limit is applied separately to each property. (Revenue Press Release 22 November 1990). Where a property is provided as living accommodation to more than one employee or director in the same period, the total amounts charged under *Sec 145* (see above) and *Sec 146* will, by concession, not exceed the amount which would have been chargeable if the property had been provided to a single employee in that period. (Revenue Press Release (REV 35) 28 November 1995).

It is understood that the Revenue would not normally seek to revise the cost of providing the accommodation for these purposes where the property in question happens to be transferred for administrative reasons within a group, although continuing to be provided for the same employee. (Tolley's Practical Tax 1985 p 120).

Any surplus of amounts deductible as necessary expenses from assessable emoluments under *Sec 145* may be deducted from any assessment on the additional value of the accommodation. [*Sec 146*].

75.29 Schedule E—Emoluments

Example

S, the founder and managing director of S Ltd, a successful transport company, has for four years occupied a mansion house owned by S Ltd. The house was acquired by S Ltd in August 1986 for £150,000 and, since acquisition, but before 6 April 1995, £80,000 has been spent by S Ltd on alterations and improvements to the house. The gross annual value of the house for rating purposes before 1 April 1990 (when the community charge replaced general rates) was £1,663. S pays annual rental of £2,000 to the company in respect of 1996/97 only. He pays all expenses relating to the property.

S will have assessable benefits in respect of his occupation of the house for 1995/96 and 1996/97 as follows.

	£	£
1995/96		
Gross annual value		1,663
Additional charge		
Acquisition cost of house	150,000	
Cost of improvements	80,000	
	230,000	
Deduct	75,000	
Additional value	£155,000	
Additional value at 8%		12,400
		£14,063
1996/97		
Gross annual value		Nil*
Additional charge		
Acquisition cost of house	150,000	
Cost of improvements	80,000	
	230,000	
Deduct	75,000	
Additional value	£155,000	
Additional value at 7.25%		11,237
		11,237
Rental payable by S	2,000	
Deduct Gross annual value	1,663	
		337*
		£10,900

* No taxable gross annual value arises in 1996/97 because the rental of £2,000 payable by S exceeds the gross annual value of £1,663. The excess is deductible from the amount of the benefit arising under the additional charge.

Directors and certain employees

For 'directors or higher-paid employees' the provision of living accommodation is excluded as a benefit under the special legislation applying to them (see 75.11 above) but they are chargeable under the provisions above.

Expenses connected with living accommodation discharged or borne on behalf of the employee may be benefits-in-kind (see 75.13 above), but

(i) *Alterations and repairs* to accommodation provided for directors and higher-paid employees will not be treated as benefits if

(A) the alterations or additions are of a structural nature, or

(B) the repairs would be the obligation of the lessor if the premises were leased and *Landlord and Tenant Act 1985, s 11* applied. [*Sec 155(3)*].

(ii) *Other expenses.* Where one of the exemptions in (*a*), (*b*) or (*c*) above applies, any amount to be treated as emoluments in respect of expenditure on heating, lighting, cleaning, repairs, maintenance, decoration, provision of furniture etc. normal for domestic occupation is limited to 10% of the net emoluments of the employment for the period concerned less any sum made good by the employee. *Emoluments* include any from an associated company (i.e. where one company has control of the other or both are under control of the same person). *Net emoluments* are (ignoring the benefit in question) after deducting capital allowances, allowable expenses, superannuation, retirement annuities and approved pension scheme payments. [*Sec 163*]. The emoluments concerned are those for the year under review, regardless of the year in which they are assessed (i.e. the year of receipt, see 75.1 above). (Revenue Schedule E Manual, SE 3192).

Example

N is employed by the G Property Co Ltd, earning £12,000 p.a. He occupies, rent-free, the basement flat of a block of flats for which he is employed as caretaker/security officer. The annual value of the flat is determined at £250. In 1996/97, G Ltd incurred the following expenditure on the flat.

	£
Heat and light	700
Decoration	330
Repairs	210
Cleaning	160
Conversion of large bedroom into two smaller bedrooms	3,000

In addition, the company pays N's council tax which amounts to £500.

As the company does not have a pension scheme, N pays a personal pension premium of £200 (net) on 31 October 1996, but apart from his personal allowance, he has no other reliefs.

N's taxable income for 1996/97 is	£
Salary	12,000
Annual value of flat	—
Heat and light, decoration, repairs, cleaning	
£1,400 restricted to	1,200
	13,200
Deduct	
Personal allowance	3,765
Taxable	£9,435

Notes

(*a*)   N is not assessed on the annual value of the flat as long as he can show that it is necessary for the proper performance of his duties for him to reside in the accommodation.

(*b*)   The structural alterations costing £3,000 will not be regarded as a benefit.

(*c*)   The emoluments treated as having arisen in respect of the heat and light, decoration, repairs and cleaning costs will be restricted to the lesser of

(i)	the expenses incurred	£1,400
(ii)	10% × £12,000 (net emoluments)	£1,200

The personal pension contribution is not deductible in arriving at net emoluments for this purpose, although retirement annuity premiums and occupational pension scheme contributions are so deductible. (The contribution is not shown above as a deduction from taxable income as basic rate relief has been given at source and higher rate relief is not applicable.)

(*d*)   Where the benefit of living accommodation is exempt under *Sec 145(4)*, the payment by the employer of the employee's council tax is also exempt. (Revenue Press Release 16 March 1993).

Case law

The following cases, decided under earlier legislation, may be relevant to a charge under *Sec 154* in respect of expenses related to living accommodation. *Butter v Bennett CA 1962, 40 TC 402* ('representative occupier' held to be assessable on provisions for fuel and gardening); *Doyle v Davison QB(NI) 1961, 40 TC 140* (repairs paid for by employer held to be benefits); *McKie v Warner Ch D 1961, 40 TC 65* (flat provided at reduced rent held to be benefit); *Luke HL 1963, 40 TC 630* (certain expenses held not to be benefits—house owned by employer); *Westcott v Bryan CA 1969, 45 TC 476* (apportionment approved where company house provided to accommodate company guests).

Other matters relating to living accommodation etc.

(A)   **Compulsory transfers**

(i)   **Guarantee payments** making good loss on sale of employee's house when compulsorily transferred were held not assessable in *Hochstrasser v Mayes, Jennings v Kinder HL 1959, 38 TC 673*.

(ii)   **Allowances for higher accommodation costs.** In relation to changes of job location before 6 April 1993 (or before 3 August 1993 under a firm commitment entered into before 6 April 1993), where an employee is compulsorily transferred, and as a result has to move to an area of higher accommodation costs, an allowance paid for a limited period by the employer to meet such additional costs (e.g. additional net mortgage interest, rent, rates, etc.) is, by concession, regarded as non-taxable provided that:

(*a*)   allowances are restricted by reference to the price or rent of accommodation roughly equivalent to that previously owned or rented;

(*b*)   allowances are restricted to reimbursement of outgoings of a revenue rather than a capital nature;

(*c*)   any tax allowances claimable (e.g. mortgage interest relief) are taken into account;

(*d*)   allowances are payable for a limited period and taper as the years progress;

(*e*)   allowances are not in the form of a lump sum at the time of, or in relation to, transfer;

(*f*)   the total of allowances is limited according to the date of the move as follows:

1 April 1987 to 31 May 1987	£18,270
1 June 1987 to 29 March 1988	£17,220
30 March 1988 to 30 September 1988	£15,750
1 October 1988 to 31 January 1989	£20,160
1 February 1989 to 30 November 1989	£21,210
1 December 1989 to 5 April 1990	£22,890
6 April 1990 to 30 November 1990	£24,150
1 December 1990 to 31 May 1991	£22,680
1 June 1991 to 31 October 1991	£20,370
1 November 1991 to 1 February 1993	£18,060
2 February 1993 onwards	£13,440

Excessive allowances within (*a*) to (*e*) above will be taxed pro-rata for each of the years concerned.

The Revenue take the view that the terms of the concession had always required that the former residence be disposed of, but the concession was amended (see Revenue Press Release 23 November 1993) to include a specific provision that the employee must relinquish or dispose of all interest in his or her main home at the previous location. The amended concession states that provisional relief will be given prior to disposal, provided that the property is being actively marketed, but may be wholly or partly withdrawn if the employee does not in the event change his or her residence. However, following the replacement of the concession by a statutory relief which does *not* incorporate such a requirement (see below), the Revenue announced (see Revenue Press Release 16 March 1993) that, where the employer or agent had been informed of the Revenue's interpretation of the (unamended) concession on this point, liabilities in unsettled cases would be pursued only for 1987/88 and subsequent years. The Revenue later announced (see Revenue Press Release 23 November 1993) their agreement with representatives of the main employers and accountancy firms involved that tax in unsettled cases would be sought only for 1990/91 and subsequent years where, before the start of the year in question, either the employer or agent had been informed of the Revenue's interpretation of the concession on this point, or it was clear from the facts already available to the Revenue that the employer or agent knew of the Revenue's interpretation even though neither of them may have been specifically informed of it. The same terms are available to other employers with unsettled cases.

(Revenue Pamphlet IR 1, A67 and Revenue Press Releases 28 October 1987, 30 March 1988, 8 November 1988, 22 February 1989, 27 November 1989, 9 April 1990, 20 November 1990, 30 May 1991, 30 October 1991, 29 January 1993, 16 March 1993, 23 November 1993; Revenue Pamphlet IR 131, SP 1/85, 18 January 1985).

The concession is replaced in relation to job location changes after 5 April 1993 or 2 August 1993 (as above) by a statutory relief (see 75.33 below). Dispensations (see 75.22 below) in relation to payments which continue to be made under the concessions are cancelled with effect from 14 April 1993. (Revenue Press Releases 16 March 1993, 14 April 1993).

Payments in respect of the community charge do not fall within the terms of the concession, as the charge is a personal and not a housing cost. (Revenue Press Release 10 November 1989). For employees who move after 31 March

1993, but to whom the concession still applies (under the transitional arrangements where the move is after 5 April 1993), council tax may be taken into account in calculating the additional housing cost payments. (Revenue Press Release 16 March 1993).

For removal expenses, see 75.13(x) above and 75.33 below.

(B) **Members of Parliament.** MPs are not allowed a deduction for expenditure incurred on residential or overnight accommodation to enable duties to be performed. [*Sec 198(4)*]. See 29.15 EXEMPT INCOME as regards exempt accommodation allowances.

As regards board and lodging allowances, see 75.7 above and for subsistence allowances, see 75.43 below. For deductibility of the cost of living accommodation etc., see 75.10(*b*) above.

75.30 LUNCHEON VOUCHERS

No assessment on employee if vouchers are (i) non-transferable, (ii) used for meals only, (iii) limited to 15 pence per working day, (iv) if limited in issue, available to lower-paid staff.

The value of any voucher or part voucher not satisfying these conditions is assessable. (Revenue Pamphlet IR 1, A2). See 75.13(iv) above for canteen meals.

75.31 PROFIT-RELATED PAY [*Secs 169–184, 8 Sch; FA 1989, s 61, 4 Sch; FA 1991, s 37; FA 1994, ss 98, 99; FA 1995, ss 136, 137(1)(6)*].

Profit-related pay is charged in accordance with the receipts basis (see 75.1 above) subject to the exemption from tax of so much of the profit-related pay as does not exceed the lower of:

(*a*) one-fifth of the aggregate, for the employment to which the scheme relates, of non-profit-related pay (within PAYE but excluding benefits) in the '*profit period*' (i.e. the accounting period by reference to which the profit-related pay is calculated), or in the part of that period by reference to which eligibility for profit-related pay arises, and the profit-related pay itself, and

(*b*) £4,000 (proportionately reduced where the profit period is less than twelve months or the employee is entitled to profit-related pay by reference to part only of that period).

Example

E is employed by C Ltd and receives, on 1 May 1996, profit-related pay of £4,200 for the year to 31 March 1996 (the profit period). His earnings received in the year to 31 March 1996, excluding profit-related pay, amounted to £16,600 and he was also provided with a company car on which both car and fuel benefits arise.

The amount of profit-related pay to be included in E's taxable emoluments for 1996/97 is as follows.

	£	£
Amount received		4,200
Deduct tax-free amount, being the *lower* of		
(i) 20% of £20,800	4,160	
(ii) Overriding maximum	4,000	
	——	4,000
Taxable profit-related pay		£200

For profit periods beginning before 1 April 1991, only one-half of such profit-related pay is exempt.

The profit-related pay must be paid under a registered scheme (see below) under which a part of the emoluments in the 'employment unit' to which the scheme relates is determined by reference to the profits in a profit period of that 'employment unit'. '*Employment unit*' means the undertaking (or part) to which a scheme relates.

[*Secs 169–171; FA 1989, s 42(4), 4 Sch 2, 17 Sch Pt IV; FA 1991, s 37*].

Relief is denied where either

(i)   the profit-related pay relates to a period when the employee had another employment in respect of which he receives profit-related pay which is exempt under these provisions, or

(ii)   no Class 1 National Insurance contributions are payable by the employer in respect of the profit-related pay (unless they are not payable only because the employee's earnings are below the lower earnings limit—see 82.7 SOCIAL SECURITY). [*Sec 172*].

Excluded employments. Crown and local authority employments (as widely defined) cannot be covered by a scheme seeking registration (see below). [*Sec 174*].

Conditions for registration. To qualify for registration, a scheme must satisfy the following conditions.

(A)   Its terms must be set out in writing.

(B)   It must identify

(i)   the 'scheme employer' and any other person by whom emoluments of scheme employees are paid, and

(ii)   the undertaking (or distinct part) to which the scheme relates (which must be carried on with a view to profit).

(C)   It must enable employees to whom it relates to be identified.

(D)   It must exclude employees (or their associates, as defined) with a 'material interest' (broadly, a 25% interest) in the company throughout a profit period.

(E)   It must ensure that payments are not made under the scheme by reference to any profit period at the beginning of which less than 80% of the employees in the employment unit are covered by the scheme (ignoring employees excluded under (D) above and certain short service and (in relation to schemes registered before 1 May 1995) part-time employees who are excluded from the scheme).

(F)   It must identify the accounting period(s) by reference to which profit-related pay is to be calculated. Any such period must be of twelve months' duration unless either the scheme is cancelled with effect from a date after the start of the period, or the scheme is a 'replacement scheme' in which case it may only provide for two periods, the first of which may be less than twelve months. Some leeway is allowed where an employer makes up his financial accounts to slightly varying dates; the twelve month period may be increased or reduced by up to seven days. (Revenue Press Release 22 December 1987).

(G)   It must provide for a method for calculating the '*distributable pool*' (i.e. the amount which may be paid to scheme employees in respect of a profit period). Except in the case of a 'replacement scheme', one of two methods must be specified. These are set out as 'Method A' and 'Method B' in *8 Sch 13–14A*, which broadly allow the distributable pool to be equal *either* to a fixed percentage of the profits of the employment unit in the profit period *or* to a percentage of the distributable pool for the previous profit period (with a notional pool being specified for the first profit period). In either case, there is a formula for ensuring that, where profits remain unchanged, the pool is at least 5% of the annual equivalent of scheme employees' pay (within PAYE but excluding benefits) at the beginning of the first profit period (as reasonably estimated at the time of application for registration). Equally, either method may provide for profit increases in excess of 60% (or a specified higher figure) to be disregarded in arriving at the pool, and for there to be no pool when profits are below a specified level (which must be below that giving rise to the 5% minimum referred to above). Where there is accordingly no pool for a profit period and the following year's pool is to be a set percentage of the earlier year's pool, the percentage is applied to the pool that would have arisen but for the special provision for there to be no pool.

The requirement for a 5% minimum is abolished in relation to schemes registered after 2 February 1989. (Revenue Press Release 3 February 1989). In consequence, the requirement to be met for there to be no distributable pool is replaced by a requirement that the profits limit below which there is to be no pool must not exceed profits representing a zero increase. Any of the rules included in a scheme which moderate the effect of profit changes on the distributable pool may take effect either from the first profit period or from any later profit period determined in accordance with the scheme.

For schemes registered after 2 August 1992, the requirement that the scheme specify a fixed percentage (Method A) or the amount of a notional pool (Method B) will *not* be met where a formula is specified rather than an actual figure, unless the factors used in the formula are ascertained at the time the scheme is written, so that the actual figure derived from the formula may be fully and finally identified at that time. (Revenue Pamphlet IR 131, SP 7/92, 3 August 1992).

Schemes registered after 30 November 1993 which include a 60% (or higher) limit on profit increases to be taken into account in arriving at the pool must also include a provision for that upper limit to be increased where there is a fall in the taxable pay (ignoring PRP) by comparison with the previous profit period (or the base year) (or, in the case of Method B, the previous twelve months). The percentage decrease must be applied as an increase in the amount of the 160% (or higher) limit. Also, where a scheme registered after 30 November 1993 includes provision for either a 60% (or higher) upper profits limit or a lower profits level below which there is no pool, profit-related pay and secondary Class 1 national insurance contributions must be accorded the same accountancy treatment in arrriving at the profits for both the current and the previous profit period (or the base year) (or, in the case of Method B, the previous twelve months).

A 'replacement scheme' must provide for the distributable pool to be a specified percentage of the profits of the profit period.

(H) It must provide for the whole of the distributable pool to be paid to employees in the employment unit, and for the timing of such payments.

(J) Its provisions must ensure that employees participate on similar terms, although payments may vary according to objective factors such as length of service or level of remuneration.

(K) It must provide for the preparation of a profit and loss account giving a true and fair view of the profit or loss of the employment unit to which the scheme relates in respect of each profit period (and any other necessary period). *Companies Act 1985, 4 Sch* (or NI equivalent) applies, with appropriate modification, to such accounts which must not, however, include a deduction for the remuneration (as widely defined) of any person excluded from the scheme as having a material interest (see above). Certain other restrictions apply as to what the scheme may require to be included in or excluded from the accounts notwithstanding *Companies Act* requirements, and as to what changes in accounting policy between periods may be permitted (see *8 Sch 19–20 as amended* and Revenue Pamphlet IR 1 (November 1995 Supplement), B44).

(L)   In relation to schemes registered after 26 July 1989, where the employment unit is part of an undertaking, and the scheme requires the profits to be taken as equivalent to those of the whole (identified) undertaking, the provisions of *8 Schedule* apply as if those profits were the profits of the employment unit. The scheme must, however, contain provisions ensuring that no payments are made under it by reference to a profit period unless, at the beginning of the period, the number of scheme employees does not exceed 33% of the total number of employees in other registered schemes relating to employees of the same undertaking (disregarding other schemes whose rules require the profits for scheme purposes to be taken as equivalent to those of the whole undertaking, or under which no payments could be made for the profit period concerned by virtue of the rules required by (E) above). Where two or more schemes relating to employment units which are parts of the same undertaking both have rules requiring their profits for scheme purposes to be taken as equivalent to those of the whole undertaking, an employee to whom another scheme relates cannot be included for the purposes of the above 33% test in connection with more than one of those schemes.

For schemes registered after 30 November 1993, there is a further condition that the scheme must ensure that its fixed percentage (in the case of schemes employing Method A) or notional or distributable pool (in the case of schemes employing Method B) (see (G) above) does not exceed a limit calculated by reference to the ratio of PRP to total pay in the other scheme or schemes registered for the business. The ratio is calculated by reference to the figures for pay and PRP paid for a specified earlier period.

The '*scheme employer*' is the person by whom the emoluments of all employees to whom the scheme relates are paid or, if there is no one such person, the parent company of the group of companies (i.e. consisting of the parent company and its 51% subsidiaries) where all the persons paying such emoluments are members of the group. Changes in the members of a partnership which is a scheme employer are ignored for these purposes.

A scheme is a '*replacement scheme*' if it relates to employees to not less than one-half of whom another registered scheme (or schemes) applied, and the registration of the previous scheme was cancelled because of changes in the employment unit or in the circumstances relating to the scheme which occurred within the three months before the start of the first profit period of the new scheme. The Board must also be satisfied as to certain other matters.

[*Secs 169, 173, 183, 8 Sch; FA 1989, 4 Sch 9–15; FA 1994, ss 98, 99; FA 1995, s 136*].

Registration. Application for registration of a profit-related pay scheme must be in such form, and supported by such information, as the Board may require, and must specify the profit period(s) to which it relates. It must be made to the Board by the scheme employer, and must contain an undertaking that any requirements under minimum wage legislation will be met without taking profit-related pay into account, and a declaration that the scheme complies with the conditions referred to above. It must also be accompanied by a report by an 'independent accountant', in a form prescribed by the Board, to the effect that, in his opinion, the scheme complies with the conditions referred to above, and the books and records are adequate for preparation of the annual return required (see below). If it is made more than three months before the beginning of the period (or first period) to which the scheme relates, it is guaranteed that the scheme will, if approved, be registered from the beginning of that period. There is provision for further information in support of the application to be sought by the Board. If the Board are not satisfied that the application meets the various requirements, the application will be refused (subject to appeal, see below). Later applications may, if the Board are satisfied, lead to registration before the beginning of the first period to which they relate, but will otherwise be regarded as having been refused (again, subject to appeal). Notice of registration or refusal must be in writing.

An '*independent accountant*' is a qualified auditor who does not employ scheme employees and who is not (and is not an employee of) a partner, officer, employee or partner of an employee of a person who employs scheme employees or whose subsidiary or holding company or fellow subsidiary employs scheme employees. A report may be signed in the name of a firm of accountants, provided that all partners meet these qualifications. (Revenue Press Release 22 December 1987).

[*Secs 173, 175, 176, 184; FA 1989, 4 Sch 10(2); SI 1991 No 1997*].

Change of employer. Where there is a change in the scheme employer, and the successor would be eligible to apply for registration, and there is no other material change in the employment unit to which the scheme relates or in the circumstances affecting the scheme, the predecessor and successor may, within one month of the change, jointly elect for the scheme registration to be amended by substitution of the successor for the predecessor. Provided that there are not other grounds for cancellation of the scheme, it will continue to operate under the amended registration as if the successor had been the original applicant. [*Sec 177*]. After 26 July 1989, a scheme registration may be amended following the death of the scheme employer to substitute his personal representatives, on written application within one month of the grant of probate, etc., provided that there would be no grounds apart from the death for cancellation of the registration. The provisions then apply as if the personal representatives had been the scheme employer throughout. The scheme registration may be cancelled with effect from the date of death if the personal representatives so request within the same period. [*Secs 177A, 178(5A); FA 1989, 4 Sch 3, 4(4)*].

Alteration of scheme terms. After 26 July 1989, where the terms of a registered scheme are altered, the Board may cancel the registration with effect from the beginning of the profit period during which the alteration took place or any later profit period, although such alteration does not of itself invalidate the registration. The scheme employer may, however, apply to the Board, in a prescribed form and within one month of the alteration, for registration of the alteration, which precludes cancellation of the registration by virtue of the alteration. Provided that the alteration meets one of the conditions listed below, and the scheme employer declares (and a report in a prescribed form by an independent accountant confirms) that it does so and that the scheme as altered complies with *8 Schedule* (as at the date the scheme was registered subject to any specified subsequent amendments to that *Schedule*), the Board will register such an alteration. The Board's decision on the application must in any event be given within three months of receipt and notified to the scheme employer. If it subsequently appears to the Board that the application did not meet the above requirements or that the declaration by the scheme employer was false, the registration may be cancelled with effect as if the alteration had not been registered.

The conditions referred to above are that the alteration either:

(*a*)   relates to a term not relevant to the scheme's complying with the requirements of *8 Schedule*; or

(*b*)   relates to a term identifying any person (other than the scheme employer) who pays scheme employees' emoluments; or

(c)   consists of the addition of a term providing for an abbreviated profit period following cancellation of registration; or

(d)   amends the provisions identifying scheme employees for subsequent profit periods; or

(e)   relates to a scheme provision dealing with the computation under Method A or Method B (see (G) above) for subsequent profit periods; or

(f)   amends the provisions as to when payments are made to employees for subsequent profit periods; or

(g)   is made to bring the scheme into compliance with the requirements of *8 Schedule* (as it had effect either at the time of registration or at the date of application for registration of the alteration) if it did not so comply at the time of registration, provided that

    (i)   it is made for the purposes of all profit periods to which the scheme relates,

    (ii)   it is made within two years of the beginning of the first profit period, and

    (iii)   it does not wholly or partly invalidate any payment of profit-related pay already made under the scheme.

[*Secs 177B, 178(3A)(3B); FA 1989, 4 Sch 3, 4(3)*].

Cancellation of registration. The Board may (subject to appeal, see below) cancel registration of a scheme, by notice in writing, where certain conditions have not been complied with or where losses have arisen, or if the scheme employer so requests in writing. The cancellation generally applies from the beginning of the profit period in which the change giving rise to the cancellation takes place. Any shortfall in tax deducted from profit-related pay as a result of cancellation of registration is payable by the scheme employer (or by his personal representatives or by the UK payer if the scheme employer is non-UK resident) to the Board, and PAYE regulations provide for collection and recovery and interest on unpaid amounts. [*Secs 178, 179; FA 1989, 4 Sch 4, 5, 10(2); SI 1995 No 917*]. With effect from 14 July 1995, interest is charged on tax recovered from employers in respect of payments incorrectly made tax-free under PRP schemes for 1994/95 and subsequent years. Penalties will be sought where there has been fraud or negligence in making late or incorrect returns for such years. (Revenue Press Release 14 July 1995).

See also the preceding paragraphs as regards death of the scheme employer and scheme alterations.

Appeals. An appeal against refusal or cancellation of registration, or against refusal to register an alteration or amend a registration on the death of the scheme employer, must be made within 30 days of notification of the refusal, etc., and lies to the Special Commissioners. [*Sec 182; FA 1989, 4 Sch 8*].

Returns and other information. An annual return and a report by an independent accountant (including confirmation that the scheme terms have been complied with in the period) are required, as laid down by the Board (see Revenue Press Release 1 February 1988), within ten months of the end of each scheme accounting period (seven months in the case of public companies). The time limit may be extended by three months in certain cases where a company has overseas interests.

There is a general requirement to provide relevant information requested by the Board, and for the scheme employer to notify the Board of anything of which he becomes aware which may be a ground for cancellation of that registration. The personal representatives of a deceased scheme employer must inform the Board of his death within one month of the grant of probate, etc. [*Secs 180, 181; FA 1989, 4 Sch 6, 7*].

Penalties apply for failure to furnish information as above. [*TMA s 98*].

Guidance notes and model rules on profit-related pay schemes are available from Profit Related Pay Office, Inland Revenue, St Mungo's Road, Cumbernauld, Glasgow G67 1YZ.

75.32 **REDUNDANCY PAYMENTS**

Amounts received under *Employment Protection (Consolidation) Act 1978*, or NI equivalent, may be taken into account for purposes of *Sec 148*, see 19.5 COMPENSATION FOR LOSS OF EMPLOYMENT, but are otherwise exempt under Schedule E. [*Secs 579, 580*]. Other redundancy payments may be assessable emoluments, see 19.5 *et seq.* COMPENSATION FOR LOSS OF EMPLOYMENT.

Payments to redundant steel workers under British Steel Corporation schemes or under the various articles of the Iron and Steel Employees Readaptation Benefit Scheme are treated as Schedule E income, although strict assessment under Schedule D, Case III may be claimed in the case of BSC scheme payments. Concessionary inclusion of such payments in Schedule D, Case I or II computations ceased as from 24 February 1984 (with some exceptions), although where retirement annuity relief had been allowed in respect of such benefits as at that date, it will continue to be allowed as long as entitlement to benefit continues. (Revenue Pamphlet IR 131, SP 2/84, 24 February 1984).

75.33 **RELOCATION PACKAGES**

Certain payments and benefits received in connection with job-related residential moves are exempted from charge under Schedule E. This applies in relation to changes in employment after 5 April 1993, and replaces the reliefs previously provided by concession, which are contained in Revenue Pamphlet IR 1, A5, A67, and which are dealt with at 75.13(x) and 75.29(A)(ii) above respectively.

Those concessions continue to apply for employees who started a job in a new location before 6 April 1993, and for those who had entered into a firm commitment to a job-related move before 6 April 1993 and who started the job at the new location before 3 August 1993. To establish such a commitment, the Revenue will require evidence either that the employer has given formal notification of the job transfer or that the employee is committed to accepting the job transfer. (Revenue Press Releases 16 March 1993, 23 November 1993).

The statutory exemption applies to

(*a*)   any sums paid to the employee, or to another person on behalf of the employee, in respect of 'qualifying removal expenses', and

(*b*)   any 'qualifying removal benefit' provided for the employee or to members of his family or household (including sons- and daughters-in-law, servants, dependants and guests),

provided they do not exceed a 'qualifying limit'.

'*Qualifying removal expenses*' are 'eligible removal expenses' reasonably incurred by the employee, and '*qualifying removal benefits*' are 'eligible removal benefits' reasonably provided, on or before the 'relevant day' on a change of the employee's sole or main residence 'in connection with the employment'. The change of residence does not require the disposal of the former residence, but the new residence must, on the facts of the particular case, become the main residence of the employee. (Revenue Press Release 14 April 1993).

For a change of residence to be 'in connection with the employment', it must result from the employee commencing employment with the employer, or from an alteration of his duties in the employment, or from an alteration of the place where those duties are normally to be performed. The change must be made wholly or mainly to bring the employee's residence within a reasonable daily travelling distance of the place he normally performs, or is to perform, those duties. What is a 'reasonable daily travelling distance' is not defined, but is a matter for common sense, taking account of local conditions. It may depend on either or both travelling time or distance. (Revenue Tax Bulletin November 1993 p 94).

The '*relevant day*' is the last day of the year of assessment following that in which the commencement or change of duties etc. took place, unless the Board grants an extension in a particular case to the end of a later year of assessment.

'*Eligible removal expenses*' fall into seven different categories.

(i)   Expenses of disposal, i.e. legal expenses, loan redemption penalties, estate agents' or auctioneers' fees, advertising costs, disconnection charges, and rent and maintenance etc. costs during an unoccupied period, relating to the disposal of his interest (or of the interest of a member of his family or household) in the employee's former residence. Expenses of a sale which falls through are eligible provided that the residence is in fact still changed.

(ii)   Expenses of acquisition, i.e. legal expenses, procurement fees, insurance costs, survey fees, Registry fees, stamp duty and connection charges, relating to the acquisition by the employee (or by a member of his family or household) of an interest in his new residence.

(iii)   Expenses of abortive acquisition, i.e. expenses which would have been within (ii) above but for the interest not being acquired, for reasons beyond the control of the person seeking to acquire it or because that person reasonably declined to proceed with it.

(iv)   Expenses of transporting belongings, i.e. expenses, including insurance, temporary storage and disconnection and reconnection of appliances, connected with transporting domestic belongings of the employee and of members of his family or household from the former to the new residence.

(v)   Travelling and subsistence expenses (subsistence meaning food, drink and temporary accommodation). These are restricted to:

    (*a*)   such costs of the employee and members of his family or household on temporary visits to the new area in connection with the change;

    (*b*)   the employee's travel costs between his former residence and new place of work;

    (*c*)   (other than in the case of a new employment) the employee's travel costs, before the change in the employment, between his new residence and old place of work;

    (*d*)   the employee's subsistence costs (not within (*a*));

    (*e*)   the employee's travel costs between his old residence and any temporary living accommodation;

    (*f*)   (other than in the case of a new employment) the employee's travel costs, before the change in the employment, between his new residence and any temporary living accommodation;

    (*g*)   the travel costs of the employee and members of his family or household between the former and new residences;

    (*h*)   certain costs incurred to secure continuity of education for a member of the employee's family or household who is under 19 at the beginning of the year of assessment in which the commencement or change of duties etc. takes place.

Expenses for which a deduction is allowable under *Secs 193–195* (certain foreign travel expenses, see 75.5, 75.6 above) are excluded.

(vi) Bridging loan expenses, i.e. interest payable by the employee (or by a member of his family or household) on a loan raised at least partly because there is a gap between the incurring of expenditure in acquiring the new residence and the receipt of the proceeds of disposal of the former residence. Interest on so much of the loan as either

    (*a*) exceeds the market value of his interest (or the interest of a member of his family or household) in the former residence (at the time the new residence is acquired), or

    (*b*) is not used for the purpose of either redeeming a loan raised by the employee (or by a member of his family or household) on his former residence or acquiring his interest (or the interest of a member of his family or household) in the new residence

is excluded.

(vii) Duplicate expenses, i.e. net expenses incurred as a result of the change on the replacement of domestic goods used at the former residence but unsuitable for use at the new residence.

The Treasury may by regulation amend these categories so as to add any expenses from a day to be specified in the regulations, with effect for commencements or changes of duties etc. taking place on or after that day.

'*Eligible removal benefits*' fall into six different categories, consisting of the benefit of services corresponding, as applicable, to the expenses specified under (i)–(v) and (vii) above in relation to eligible removal expenses (but, under (v), excluding the provision of a company car or van also available for general private use). They may include administration fees of a relocation management company charged to the employer. The Treasury has similar powers to those applicable in the case of eligible removal expenses.

The '*qualifying limit*' as regards any change of residence applies to the aggregate of qualifying removal expenses paid and the value of qualifying removal benefits received in respect of the change. The value attributed to such benefits is their cash equivalent under the general benefits legislation (75.13 above) or, as appropriate, the amount of the living accommodation charge under *Sec 145* and, where applicable, *Sec 146* (net of any attributable contribution by the employee and of any amount which would have been deductible under *Sec 198* or *Sec 332(3)* (see 75.10, 75.9 respectively)) (see 75.29 above).

The amount of the '*qualifying limit*' is £8,000. This may be varied upwards by Treasury order from a day to be specified in the order, with effect for commencements or changes of duties etc. taking place on or after that day.

Bridging loan finance obtained before the relevant day (as above) by reason of the employment within *Sec 160* (see 75.17 above) on a move meeting the above conditions may attract a measure of relief where the expenses and benefits for which relief is obtained in respect of the move are in total less than the £8,000 (or increased) limit. Relief is obtained by delaying the implementation of *Sec 160* for a number of days after the making of the loan such that the interest (at the official rate at the time the loan was made, see 75.17 above) on the maximum sum borrowed for those days would equate to the amount by which the £8,000 (or increased) limit exceeds the amount of expenses and benefits otherwise relieved. If the loan is discharged before those days have expired, no charge arises under *Sec 160*. An assessment made under *Sec 160* for a year of assessment ending before the relevant day on the assumption that the maximum relief would be utilised by the payment of qualifying removal expenses and benefits may be adjusted as necessary if that turns out not to be the case.

Commencement. These provisions apply to changes of residence resulting from commencements, changes of duties etc. taking place after 5 April 1993 (but see above as regards transitional arrangements in certain cases where a new job commenced before 3 August 1993).

[*Secs 191A, 191B, 11A Sch; FA 1993, s 76, 5 Sch*].

PAYE should not be applied to payments made under a relocation package, even if the qualifying limit is exceeded. Flat rate allowances may be paid gross, provided that the inspector is satisfied that they do no more than reimburse employees' eligible expenses. Any taxable payments are to be included in the annual return of benefits. See *SI 1993 No 2276* and Revenue Press Release 14 April 1993.

75.34 RESTRICTIVE COVENANTS

Where, after 8 June 1988, the present, past or future holder of an office or employment, the emoluments of which are within Cases I or II of Schedule E, gives, in connection therewith, an undertaking (whether qualified or legally valid or not) restricting his conduct or activities, any sum paid to any person in respect of the giving or fulfilment (in whole or part) of the undertaking is, if it would not otherwise be so, treated as an emolument of the office or employment for the year of assessment of payment. If such a payment is made after the death of the individual concerned, it is treated as having been paid immediately before his death. Where valuable consideration rather than money is given, a sum equal to the value of that consideration is treated as having been paid. Sums to which this section applies may be deducted as an expense in computing the profits of the trade, profession or vocation of the payer, or treated as a management expense if paid by an investment company.

For such sums paid in respect of undertakings given before 9 June 1988, the grossed-up equivalent of the sum paid is treated as part of the individual's total income received after deduction of basic rate tax. No assessment is raised in respect of basic rate tax, no repayment may be made thereof, and the gross amount may not be used to cover charges under *Secs 348, 349* (see 23.2, 23.3 DEDUCTION OF TAX AT SOURCE). The payer of such a sum must give particulars to the inspector within one month of the end of the year of assessment of the payment, subject to penalties under *TMA s 98*. [*Sec 313; FA 1988, s 73*].

Termination settlements. Financial settlements relating to the termination of an employment may require the employee to undertake that the agreement is in 'full and final settlement' of his claims relating to the employment, and/or not to commence, or to discontinue, legal proceedings in respect of those claims. They may also reaffirm undertakings about the employee's conduct or activity after termination which formed part of the employment terms. The Revenue accept that such undertakings do not give rise to a charge under *Sec 313*, without prejudice to the treatment of other restrictive undertakings, whether or not contained in the settlement. (Revenue Statement of Practice SP 3/96, 4 April 1996).

75.35 SECURITY OF EMPLOYEES

Where an asset or service which improves personal security is provided for an employee by reason of his employment, or is used by the employee, and the expenditure was (wholly or partly) borne by (or for) a person other than the employee, then a Schedule E deduction is allowed to the extent that the provision gives rise to emoluments chargeable under Schedule E on the employee. The asset or service must be provided or used to meet a special threat to the employee's personal physical security arising wholly or mainly by virtue of the employment, and the sole object of the provider must be the meeting of that threat. In the case of an asset, relief is available only to the extent that the provider intends the asset to be used solely to improve personal physical security (ignoring any other incidental use), and in the case of a service, the benefit to the employee must consist wholly or mainly in such an improvement. Any improvement in the personal physical security of the employee's family resulting from the asset or service provided is disregarded for these purposes.

Excluded from relief is provision of a car, ship or aircraft, or of a dwelling (or grounds appurtenant thereto) or living accommodation; but relief may be obtained in respect of equipment or a structure (such as a wall), and it is immaterial whether or not an asset becomes affixed to land and whether or not the employee acquires the property in the asset or (in the case of a fixture) an estate or interest in the land.

Similar relief applies where the employee incurs the expenditure out of his emoluments and is reimbursed by some other person, and to office holders. [*FA 1989, ss 50–52*].

See also 10.25 CAPITAL ALLOWANCES, 71.80 SCHEDULE D, CASES I AND II.

75.36   SHARES ETC.

The value of a gift or transfer of shares to a director or employee, if regarded as a reward for services or part of his emoluments, is assessable on him. Held, liability did not arise in *Bridges v Bearsley CA 1957, 37 TC 289* (because gift of shares in default of legacy held to be testimonial not remuneration). Where shares were issued to employees at par value which was less than market value, the difference was held assessable (*Weight v Salmon HL 1935, 19 TC 174; Ede v Wilson KB 1945, 26 TC 381; Patrick v Burrows Ch D 1954, 35 TC 138; Bentley v Evans Ch D 1959, 39 TC 132; Tyrer v Smart HL 1978, 52 TC 533*). See also 75.19 above.

A payment received from the parent company of a group after the employing company left the group, in consideration of loss of rights under the parent company's savings-related share option scheme (see 81.8 SHARE INCENTIVES AND OPTIONS), was not assessable (*Wilcock v Eve Ch D, [1995] STC 18*).

For capital gains tax, such gifts are treated as an acquisition for nil consideration where there is no corresponding disposal of the shares, i.e. where the shares are issued by the company concerned. [*TCGA 1992, s 17*].

For the circumstances in which the Revenue will accept that shares or share options were acquired by a director or employee in a different capacity and not by reason of the office or employment, see Revenue Inspector's Manual, IM 5329.

Priority allocations for employees, etc. Where a director or employee (or future or past director or employee) is entitled, as such, to priority allocation of shares in a *bona fide* public offer at fixed price or by tender made after 22 September 1987, there is no charge to tax under Schedule E on any benefit arising thereby provided that

(*a*)   the shares reserved for such priority allocation do not exceed

    (i)   10% of the total shares subject to the offer, or

    (ii)   in relation to an offer made after 10 October 1988 which is part of arrangements under which shares of the same class are offered to the public under more than one offer, either 40% of the total shares subject to the offer or 10% of all the shares of that class subject to any such offers,

(*b*)   all persons entitled to priority allocation are so entitled on similar terms (which may, however, vary according to level of remuneration, length of service or similar factors), and

(*c*)   the persons entitled to priority allocation are not restricted to directors or to those whose remuneration exceeds a particular level.

As regards offers made on or after 26 July 1990, (*b*) above is still satisfied where allocations to directors and employees of the company are greater than those to other persons, provided that

(A)   the aggregate value of priority allocations made under the offer and under other public offers made at the same time in respect of the shares of other companies to those persons, and

(B)   the aggregate value of the shares allocated to comparable directors and employees of the company

are, as nearly as practicable, the same.

In relation to offers made after 10 October 1988, the benefit of a discount on the fixed price or lowest price successfully tendered is not covered by this exemption. Previously, no exemption at all was available where such a discount applied. After 15 January 1991, any 'registrant discount' is disregarded for this purpose. Broadly, the '*registrant discount*' is any discount which, subject to any conditions imposed, may be available in respect of all or some part of the shares allocated to any person, whether a member of the public or an employee or director applying for shares as such. For this to apply, at least 40% of the shares allocated to members of the public (other than employees or directors of the company) must be allocated to individuals entitled either to the discount or to some benefit of similar value.

In relation to offers made after 15 January 1991, relief is extended to cases where there is a *bona fide* offer to the public of a combination of shares in two or more companies at a fixed price or by tender, and at the same time there is such an offer of shares in any one or more, but not all, of those companies to directors and employees (with or without others) of any company, any of whom is entitled, by reason of his office or employment, to priority in the allocation of shares over members of the public subscribing as such. The limits in (*a*) above must be satisfied in relation to each of the companies whose shares are included in the combination. The extension of relief is achieved by treating both the public offer and the employee offer as being a single offer of shares to the public. Where the extended relief applies, the denial of exemption on any employee discount on the offer price (see above) is imposed by reference to an '*appropriate notional price*' for shares in each company concerned, i.e. the fixed price at which the shares might have been expected to be offered in a separate offer to the public, proportionately varied where the sum of the notional prices for all the companies concerned would otherwise differ from the combined offer price to the public.

For capital gains tax purposes, the market value rules do not apply to shares so acquired, which are thus treated as acquired for the actual consideration paid. [*FA 1988, s 68; FA 1989, s 66; FA 1990, s 79; FA 1991, s 44*].

See also 81 SHARE INCENTIVES AND OPTIONS.

75.37   SICK PAY AND HEALTH INSURANCE

Continuing pay from an employer during sickness or other absence from work is taxable under the general Schedule E provisions. Any payments of statutory sick pay under *Social Security Contributions and Benefits Act 1992, s 15* are similarly taxable. [*Sec 150(c)*].

Any employed person assessable under Schedule E is chargeable to tax under that Schedule on any sum not otherwise chargeable paid to him (or to his spouse, to a son or daughter or spouse of a son or daughter, or to a parent or dependant) as a result of any arrangements entered into by the employer, in respect of his absence from work by reason of sickness or disability. There is no charge under *Sec 154* (benefits, see 75.13 above) on the right to receive such sums, and these provisions do not apply to the extent that the contributions are paid by the employee. [*Secs 149, 154(2)*]. See further below as regards treatment of self-funded arrangements.

A lump sum received under a life, accident or sickness or insurance policy is not normally taxable.

By concession (and see now the statutory provisions mentioned below), benefits under an individual's permanent health or other insurance policy providing benefits which compensate for loss of income from employment or self-employment during ill-health or disability are exempt from income tax for the first twelve months (unless, exceptionally, the benefits are chargeable under Schedule E or the policy premiums have wholly or partly qualified for relief as pension contributions). The concession does not apply to benefits payable to the employer, nor where the premiums are paid by the employer. Tax will not be deducted from payments covered by the concession. The concession applies where a policy holder first becomes entitled to benefit on or after 6 April 1994, and replaces the previous concession A26 (see below). The previous concession will continue to apply to benefits to which a policy holder first became entitled before 6 April 1994, and also where entitlement first arises on or after that date but in relation to a period of absence extending before that date and for which benefit entitlement had arisen under one or more policies before that date. (Revenue Pamphlet IR 1, A83).

For benefits to which a policy holder first became entitled before 6 April 1994 (and as above), the previous concession referred to above continues. This applies to exempt continuing benefits otherwise chargeable under Schedule D, Case III under policies taken out by individual taxpayers on their own behalf, unless the benefit has continued for at least twelve months prior to commencement of the year of assessment. It is thus not restricted to benefits compensating for lost earnings. (Revenue Pamphlet IR 1, A26).

In practice, tax has not been collected where insurance benefits are provided in times of sickness, disability or unemployment to meet existing specified obligations such as loan repayments. (Revenue Press Release REV 6, 28 November 1995).

The above-mentioned concessions are effectively superseded by statutory provisions applicable to annual payments falling to be made after 5 April 1996 under certain insurance policies. Subject to further conditions, the provisions also apply to payments falling due on or before that date, thereby giving statutory effect to the practice mentioned immediately above. See 29.10 EXEMPT INCOME for the detailed provisions.

See also 71.63 SCHEDULE D, CASES I AND II.

75.38   SOCIAL SECURITY BENEFITS

See 82 SOCIAL SECURITY.

75.39   SUBSCRIPTIONS

Professional Subscriptions etc. [*Sec 201*]. There may be deducted from Schedule E assessments on emoluments out of which they are paid

(*a*)   provided the registration, retention etc. is a condition of the performance of the duties, statutory fees payable for the retention of name on the Register of Architects, or registers of dentists, ancillary dental workers, ophthalmic opticians, dispensing opticians or pharmaceutical chemists; annual fees payable by registered patent agents, registered veterinary surgeons or persons on the Supplementary Veterinary Register; fee (and contribution to the Compensation Fund or Guarantee Fund) payable on issue of solicitor's practising certificate;

(*b*)   annual subscription, or part thereof, to bodies approved by the Board as being conducted, otherwise than for profit, for advancing or spreading knowledge, maintaining or improving professional conduct and competence, or indemnifying or protecting professional persons against claims incurred in exercising their profession, provided the activities of the body concerned are relevant to the office or employment and the body is not of a mainly local character.

As to approval of bodies by the Board, withdrawal of approval, apportionment of subscription and appeals generally see *Sec 201(3)(4)(6)(7)*. Applications for approval should be made in writing to Inland Revenue, SP 1 (Schedule E), Sapphire House, 550 Streetsbrook Road, Solihull, West Midlands B91 1QU. A list of bodies approved by the Board for this purpose is available, price £5.00, from Inland Revenue Reference Library, New Wing, Somerset House, London WC2R 1LB.

Other Subscriptions. Bank manager's club subscriptions reimbursed by bank not allowed, *Brown v Bullock CA 1961, 40 TC 1*, but subscriptions to clubs to obtain cheaper accommodation on visits to London were allowed, *Elwood v Utitz CA (NI) 1965, 42 TC 482*.

75.40   **'TAX-FREE PAYMENTS'**

If an employer pays an employee without deducting tax under PAY AS YOU EARN (55), the employee's gross emoluments will be that gross figure which includes tax paid, or deemed to be paid, on his behalf. The employer should account for PAYE tax on that gross amount so that the employee effectively 'pays tax on tax'. (*Income Tax (Employments) Regulations 1993, SI 1993 No 744, Regulation 22* and see *North British Rly v Scott HL 1922, 8 TC 332; Hartland v Diggines HL 1926, 10 TC 247; Jaworski v Institution of Polish Engineers CA 1950, 29 ATC 385*). See also Revenue Pamphlet P7 (Employer's Guide to PAYE).

Special forms and tax tables are available to assist employers who pay employees on a 'net of tax' basis to calculate how much tax is due. (Revenue Press Release 2 March 1984).

Where an employer paying emoluments of a director fails, in whole or in part, to deduct and account for PAYE tax at the proper time, and that tax is subsequently accounted for by someone other than the director, such tax paid, less so much as is made good by the director, will be treated as an emolument chargeable under Schedule E unless the director has no material interest in the company and either he is a full-time working director or the company is non-profit-making.

Any amounts accounted for after cessation of employment are treated as having arisen in the year of assessment in which the employment ended but no amounts accounted for after the death of the director will be chargeable. [*Sec 164*].

An agreement to reimburse tax as 'expenses' was held not to be enforceable as the contract was illegal (*Miller v Karlinski CA 1945, 24 ATC 483*, and see also *Napier v National Business Agency CA 1951, 30 ATC 180*).

Taxed award schemes. Employers may, if they wish, enter into arrangements with the Revenue to meet the liability of employees on the grossed-up value of non-cash incentive prizes and awards. The arrangements involve a legally binding contract for payment of the related tax together with simplified reporting arrangements. The arrangements may involve payment of tax at the basic rate or at the higher rate or both, although separate contracts are required in relation to basic rate and higher rate schemes. Previously only basic rate schemes were permitted. Where only basic rate liabilities are met, higher rate liabilities continue to be collected from employees in the usual way. Valuation of an award will depend on details of the scheme and whether or not the recipient is in director's or higher-paid employment (see 75.11 above). Details of the arrangements may be obtained from Inland Revenue, Incentive Valuation Unit, Room 417 Angel Court, 199 Borough High Street, London SE1 1HZ (tel. 0171-234 3715 or 3745). (Revenue Press Releases 2 November 1984, 18 January 1990).

75.41 Schedule E—Emoluments

For the valuation of incentive awards generally, see 75.44 below and Revenue Pamphlet IR 131, SP 6/85, 29 July 1985.

75.41 TERMINATION PAYMENTS

See 19.3 COMPENSATION FOR LOSS OF EMPLOYMENT (AND DAMAGES) for the assessment of such payments under general Schedule E principles (see 75.7 above). See also 75.32 above for statutory redundancy payments and 75.45 below for wages in lieu of notice.

Certain payments to Members of the European Parliament standing unsuccessfully for re-election, and to Ministers, etc. in the House of Lords leaving office, are exempted from the general Schedule E charge. They are, however, liable in the normal way under *Sec 148* (see 19 COMPENSATION FOR LOSS OF EMPLOYMENT (AND DAMAGES)). [*Sec 190*].

75.42 TRAINING, COUNSELLING ETC.

Employer training costs. Expenditure incurred by the employer in paying or reimbursing 'relevant expenses', incurred in connection with a 'qualifying course of training' undertaken by a past or present employee, does not give rise to any emoluments forming part of the employee's income for any purpose of Schedule E. The course must be undertaken '*with a view to retraining*' the employee, which requires that the employee begins the course during, or within one year of leaving, the employment, and has left that employment by two years after the end of the course, and that he is not re-employed by the employer within two years of leaving. If, after the relief has been given, any of these conditions fail to be met, an assessment may be raised to withdraw the relief within six years of the end of the year of assessment in which the failure occurred. The employer must notify such failure to the inspector within 60 days of coming to know of it, and the inspector may require information from the employer in relation to any such failure where he has reason to believe that the employer has failed to give such notice. Penalties apply under *TMA s 98* for failure to give such notice or furnish such information.

A '*qualifying course of training*' must

(a) be designed to impart or improve skills or knowledge relevant to, and intended to be used in the course of, gainful employment (or self-employment) of any description, and

(b) be devoted entirely to the teaching and/or practical application within the UK of such skills or knowledge, and

(c) not last more than one year, and

(d) be available on similar terms to all, or to a particular class or classes of, past or present employees,

and the employee must

(i) attend the course on a full-time or substantially full-time basis, and

(ii) be employed full-time by the employer throughout the two years prior to starting the course (or prior to his earlier leaving that employment—see above).

'*Relevant expenses*' are

(A) course attendance fees, and

(B) course examination fees, and

(C) costs of essential course books, and

(D) travelling expenses which would be deductible as a Schedule E expense if attendance at the course was a duty of the employment, and if the employee was in that employment when the expenses were incurred.

[*Secs 588, 589; FA 1996, 18 Sch 10, 17(1)(2)*].

For relief to the employer, see 71.53 SCHEDULE D, CASES I AND II.

Concessional relief from any charge to tax on the employee is available where the costs (and certain associated expenses) of external training courses in the UK, e.g. day release courses, attended by an employee are borne by the employer, provided that the course either

(*a*)   is a course of general education for young employees (i.e. under 21 at commencement) of a type commonly undertaken at school, or

(*b*)   leads to the acquisition of job-related knowledge or skills.

The course need not lead to any qualification.

A similar concession applies where an employee bears the costs of attending an external training course relating to his employment, but is not reimbursed by the employer. In this case, however, the course must be full-time and the course (or each block) must last four weeks or more. Provided that he continues to receive full salary and attends the course during normal working hours, the costs incurred may be allowed as a deduction from his emoluments. Expenses relating to 're-sit' courses are excluded.

In the case of both concessions, additional costs of travelling and subsistence may be included where the course requires the employee temporarily to be absent from his normal place of work, and fees for which tax relief is due under *FA 1991, s 32* (see below) are excluded. An employee can only be regarded as temporarily away from his normal place of work if the period away will not exceed twelve months, after which he will return to the normal place of work.

(Revenue Pamphlet IR 1, A63, A64).

Employee training costs. Where, **after 5 April 1992**, a UK-resident individual (or a Crown employee whose duties are for tax purposes treated as performed in the UK, see 75.2(i) above) pays fees in connection with his own training under a 'qualifying course of vocational training', he is entitled to a deduction from or set-off against his income of the year of the amount so paid, provided that

(*a*)   at the time of the payment, he has not received, and is not entitled to receive, public financial assistance (as defined by Treasury order, see *SI 1992 No 734; SI 1993 No 1074; SI 1995 No 3274*) in relation to the course, and

(*b*)   he is not otherwise entitled to tax relief in respect of the payment,

and, in relation to payments made *after 31 December 1993*, provided also that

(*c*)   at the time of the payment, the individual is aged 16 or over, and, if under 19, he is not being provided with full-time education at a school (including any institution at which such education is provided to persons at least some of whom are under 16), and

(*d*)   he undertakes the course neither wholly nor mainly for recreational purposes or as a leisure activity.

Subject to conditions specified by the Board in regulations (see *SI 1992 No 746; SI 1993 Nos 1082, 3118*), basic rate relief may be obtained by deduction of basic rate tax from the payment, with the recipient recovering the amount deducted from the Board on a claim. The Board consider that where a payment *may* be made under deduction of basic rate tax, basic rate relief can *only* be obtained by deduction. Where relief may not be obtained by deduction, and for higher rate purposes, relief must be claimed by the individual. The tax deducted from payments is not clawed back where the individual is liable only at the lower rate of income tax or has no income tax liability.

75.42 Schedule E—Emoluments

The Treasury may make regulations for the withdrawal of relief in whole or in part in prescribed circumstances, and requiring either the individual or the recipient of the fees (as the regulations may prescribe) to account for the tax from which relief was given. The first such regulations (*SI 1992 No 734*) deal with payments refunded to the trainee by the training provider, and with awards by the training provider to the trainee by virtue merely of the course being undertaken, completed or completed successfully.

A '*qualifying course of vocational training*' is any programme of activity capable of counting towards a qualification accredited as a National or Scottish Vocational Qualification by the appropriate Council, except, in relation to payments made before 1 January 1994, a qualification at level 5, the highest of the levels defined by those Councils. (Level 5 extends to senior managerial and professional skills, including degree-standard qualifications.)

In relation to payments made *after 5 May 1996* by individuals *aged 30 or over* at the time the payment is made, a '*qualifying course of vocational training*' also includes any course of training, whether or not leading towards a qualification as above, which

(i) is designed to impart or improve skills or knowledge relevant to, and intended to be used in the course of, gainful employment (including self-employment) of any description,

(ii) is devoted entirely to the teaching and/or practical application within the UK of such skills or knowledge (treating time devoted to study in connection with the course as such practical application),

(iii) requires participation on a full-time, or substantially full-time, basis, and

(iv) extends for a period consisting of or including four *consecutive* weeks but does not last more than one year.

The Revenue have appropriate regulatory powers. Penalties under *TMA s 98* apply for failure to furnish information etc. required under such regulations. [*FA 1991, ss 32, 33; FA 1994, s 84; FA 1996, ss 129, 144, 18 Sch 14, 17(1)–(4)(8)*].

A Training Pack is available from Inland Revenue, FICO (Savings and Investment) (Vocational Training Unit), St John's House, Merton Road, Bootle, Merseyside L69 9BB, containing details of the scheme and the appropriate Forms for registration of the training provider (VTR 21), for a declaration of entitlement by the trainee (VTR 1), and for annual and interim claims by the provider for repayment of tax deducted from fees (VTR 14, VTR 10).

The Inland Revenue Financial Intermediaries and Claims Office may be contacted in relation to vocational training relief on 0151–472 6109 as regards repayments or 0151–472 6159 for technical advice.

See generally Revenue Leaflet IR 119.

Youth training scheme. A trainee allowance paid to a non-employee under the YTS is tax-free. Travel and accommodation payments to trainees in receipt of such allowances are also tax-free. (Hansard 6 June 1989, Vol 154, Col 120).

See also 29.25 EXEMPT INCOME as regards sandwich courses.

Counselling services provided by employers. Exemption is provided from Schedule E tax in respect of 'qualifying counselling services' and necessary related travelling expenses provided for, or paid or reimbursed on behalf of, an employer in connection with the termination of his employment, where either

(*a*) the employment terminates after 15 March 1993, or

(*b*) in relation to a termination on or before that date, the relevant expenditure is incurred after that date.

This applies whether or not the services or expenses are provided or paid by the employer.

'*Qualifying counselling services*' are services provided in the UK consisting wholly of giving advice and guidance, imparting or improving skills, and providing or making available the use of office equipment or similar facilities to enable an employee to adjust to his job loss and/or find other employment. The employee must have been employed by the employer full-time throughout the period of two years to the date the services are provided or, if earlier, the time he ceases to be employed. The opportunity to receive the services must be generally available to employees or a particular class of employees. Where services are provided partly outside the UK, a just and reasonable apportionment can be made.

[*Secs 589A, 589B; FA 1993, s 108*].

For relief to the employer, see 71.53 SCHEDULE D, CASES I AND II.

75.43   **TRAVELLING, SUBSISTENCE ETC.**

Travelling expenses deductible are those necessarily incurred in the performance of the duties (see 75.10(*a*) above) and hence exclude those of travelling to the place of employment from home or from a place at which a business or another employment is carried on. A leading case here is *Ricketts v Colquhoun HL 1925, 10 TC 118* in which a barrister practising in London was refused his expenses of travelling to Portsmouth where he was employed as Recorder. See also *Cook v Knott QB 1887, 2 TC 246; Revell v Directors of Elworthy Bros & Co Ltd QB 1890, 3 TC 12; Nolder v Walters KB 1930, 15 TC 380; Burton v Rednall Ch D 1954, 35 TC 435; Bhadra v Ellam Ch D 1987, [1988] STC 239* (see 75.10(*a*) above); *Parikh v Sleeman CA 1990, 63 TC 75; Smith v Fox Ch D 1989, 63 TC 304; Miners v Atkinson Ch D, 1995 STI 1724* and contrast *Pook v Owen* (see below and 75.10(*a*) above) and *Taylor v Provan HL 1974, 49 TC 579* in both of which *Ricketts v Colquhoun* was distinguished. The deduction is refused notwithstanding that the taxpayer is unable to live nearer his place of employment (*Andrews v Astley KB 1924, 8 TC 589; Phillips v Keane HC(IFS), 1 ITC 69*). No allowance to an assistant required to attend classes (*Blackwell v Mills KB 1945, 26 TC 468*). For extra-statutory concession for directors and employees of two or more group companies, see 75.13(ix) above.

If an employee with a normal place of work travels directly from home to another place at which he is required to perform duties of the employment, or *vice versa*, the allowable travel and subsistence expenditure (including business mileage) is the lesser of that actually incurred and that which would have been incurred if the journey (by the same mode of transport) had started or finished at the normal place of work. In general, business travel by a route other than the shortest possible is acceptable, provided that the longer route was selected for good business reasons. (Revenue Booklet 480; Revenue Tax Bulletin December 1994 p 185).

If an emergency call-out requires an employee to travel from home to the normal place of employment, reimbursed travel expenses will be chargeable emoluments unless the conditions underlying the decision in *Pook v Owen H/L 1969, 45 TC 571* (for which see also 75.10(*a*) above) are met, i.e. (i) advice on handling the emergency is given on receipt of the telephone call; (ii) responsibility for those aspects appropriate to the employee's duties is accepted at that time; and (iii) the employee has a continuing responsibility for the emergency whilst travelling to the normal place of employment. A claim for a deduction for expenses not reimbursed will be allowed on the same basis. Where an emergency call-out requires travel from home to a place other than the normal place of employment, reimbursed expenses are not chargeable emoluments, and a claim for expenses not reimbursed should be allowed. (Revenue Schedule E Manual, SE 1410, 1411).

By concession, reasonable reimbursement of expenses of home to work travel is not taxed where the expenses are incurred either (*a*) as a result of public transport disruption owing to industrial action, or (*b*) by severely disabled employees unable to use public transport. (Revenue Pamphlet IR 1, A58, A59). See also 75.13(v)(vi) above.

By concession, the provision by an employer of private transport, e.g. taxis, hired cars, etc., for the journey home of employees required to work late will not result in a charge to tax on the employee, providing (*a*) the employee is occasionally required to work late, i.e. until 9 p.m. or later, but those occasions are neither regular, i.e. following a predictable pattern, nor frequent, i.e. occurring on more than 60 occasions in a tax year, and (*b*) either public transport between the employee's place of work and his home has ceased for the day or it would not be reasonable to expect him to use it, for example if the journey would take much longer than usual due to low availability or reliability of services at that hour. (Revenue Press Release 25 September 1987).

Travel and subsistence expenditure is allowed, and reimbursement thereof not taxed, when working temporarily away from home and normal place of employment. This is intended to cover the extra cost of travelling and subsistence incurred because of being away on duty—but not the cost of travelling from home to normal place of work or usual expenses on food or meals taken when at normal place of work. (Revenue Pamphlet IR 131, SP 16/80, 20 November 1980). It also covers any reimbursement of the standard (*not* personal) community charge on temporary accommodation occupied near the temporary place of work. (ICAEW Guidance Note TR 795, 14 June 1990). An absence is regarded as temporary where it is not expected to, and does not, exceed twelve months, and the employee returns to the normal place of work at the end of it. Where it becomes clear during such a period that the absence will extend beyond twelve months, the exemption will apply only to amounts paid up to the date the change of circumstances became known. (Revenue Tax Bulletin May 1994 p 130). As regards what is meant by the 'normal place of employment', the Revenue normally accept that it is the place where an employee spends more than 50% of his working time, and a lower proportion may be acceptable depending on the circumstances of each business and the employee's pattern of work. Employers should be able to agree with their local inspector to divide employees into groups for these purposes. (ICAEW Technical Memorandum TR 760, 6 September 1989). A claim for a deduction corresponding to living allowances paid while working away from home was refused where an engineer without a permanent work base was required to undertake assignments necessitating his living away from home for long periods (*Elderkin v Hindmarsh Ch D 1988, 60 TC 651*).

In addition, reasonable reimbursement of expenditure on subsistence, etc. is, by concession, not taxed where (*a*) an employee occupies overnight accommodation near his normal place of work as a result of public transport disruption owing to industrial action, or (*b*) it is necessary for an offshore oil or gas worker to take overnight accommodation near the point of his departure from the mainland for the offshore rig, etc. (Revenue Pamphlet IR 1, A58, A65). See also 75.13(v)(vi) above.

See 75.13(x) as regards certain removal expenses.

Private car used for office or employment. A proportion of the expenses of running a privately-owned car used partly in the performance of the duties of an office or employment is allowable as a deduction from emoluments where the normal requirements of *Sec 198* are met (see 75.10 above). Similar proportionate relief is available by way of capital allowances (under *CAA 1990, s 27*, see 10.24 CAPITAL ALLOWANCES), for expenditure incurred on provision of the car, and interest relief (under *Sec 359*, see 43.18 INTEREST PAYABLE), for interest on a loan for its purchase.

In considering capital allowances and interest relief, there is no requirement that the car be 'necessarily' provided for use in the office or employment (i.e. that the duties of the office or employment could not be carried out without its provision, see 75.10(*a*) above). Any balancing allowance (see 10.30 CAPITAL ALLOWANCES) on the car being disposed of, or starting to be used wholly for purposes other than those of the office or employment, is reduced to the proportion that the number of years of assessment for which capital allowances have been claimed for use of the car in the office or employment bears to the number of years of assessment for which allowances were available for such use. [*Sec 359(3); CAA 1990, s 27; FA 1990, s 87*].

As an alternative to keeping detailed records of costs, employees may, for 1996/97 and subsequent years, apply the 'tax-free' rates under the Fixed Profit Car Scheme (see below) to their business mileage to support a tax deduction for allowable motoring expenses (after allowing for any mileage allowances received). (Revenue Press Release (REV 32) 28 November 1995).

Mileage allowances. As a general rule, the excess of such allowances paid to an employee (or office-holder) over the costs necessarily incurred in travelling in the performance of the duties of the employment is taxable on the employee, but the treatment of a particular payment will depend on the facts of the case. In *Pook v Owen HL 1969, 45 TC 571* (see 75.10(*a*) above) the mileage allowance paid to a doctor was held not to be part of his emoluments, and this decision was applied in *Donnelly v Williamson Ch D 1981, 54 TC 636* (mileage allowance paid to a schoolteacher for use of her car when attending parents' meetings) but distinguished in *Perrons v Spackman Ch D 1981, 55 TC 403* (lump sum and mileage allowances to a county council employee treated as part of his emoluments, but he was allowed to deduct his actual car expenses on official duties, including a proportion of his repairs and standing expenses). Deductions for car expenses in excess of the employer's allowance were refused to a Regional Hospital Board employee (*Hamerton v Overy Ch D 1954, 35 TC 73*) and a civil servant (*Marsden v CIR Ch D 1965, 42 TC 326*).

Strictly, the employer should return the full amount of such allowances paid, and the employee submit a detailed claim for relief based on actual expenses and business/private mileage. The Revenue, however, operate with some employers a simplified administrative arrangement known as the Fixed Profit Car Scheme (FPCS) under which an employee's taxable business mileage profit is determined by reference to engine size and the excess of the mileage allowance paid over the FPCS 'tax-free' rates, which are as follows (*a*) for the first 4,000 miles in the year and (*b*) for mileage in excess of 4,000.

Capacity	Up to 1,000cc		1,001–1,500cc		1,501–2,000cc		Over 2,000cc	
	(*a*)	(*b*)	(*a*)	(*b*)	(*a*)	(*b*)	(*a*)	(*b*)
1990/91	24.5p	9.5p	30p	11.5p	34p	13.5p	43p	16.5p
1991/92	24.5p	11p	30p	13p	34p	16p	45p	20.5p
1992/93	25p	14p	30p	17p	38p	21p	51p	27p
1993/94	26p	15p	32p	18p	40p	22p	54p	30p
1994/95	27p	15p	33p	19p	41p	23p	56p	31p
1995/96	27p	15p	34p	19p	43p	23p	60p	32p
1996/97	27p	16p	34p	19p	43p	23p	61p	33p

Banded payments by employers are matched as closely as possible to the FPCS bands, and where uniform allowances are paid, the average of the two middle FPCS bands is used. Relief for interest on a loan for purchase of the car (see 43.18 INTEREST PAYABLE) is not included in the FPCS rates, and needs to be claimed separately. (Revenue Press Releases 21 June 1990, 26 March 1991, 10 March 1992, 23 March 1993).

Before 6 April 1990, the above FPCS rates for 1990/91 up to 4,000 miles applied to *all* business mileage (except that the 34p rate applied to all cars over 1,500 cc). Transitional provisions apply to prevent higher mileage claimants suffering too abrupt an increase in their taxable mileage profit. Broadly, these limit the chargeable mileage profit of an employee for 1990/91 to the amount on which tax was paid for 1989/90, and subsequent increases in the chargeable mileage profit to an additional £1,000 each year. Adjustments are made where there is additional business mileage in 1990/91 and subsequent years.

Transitional relief will *not*, however, apply where the allowances paid increase out of line with the costs incurred.

The transitional reliefs apply equally to those not within a Fixed Profit Car Scheme. [*Secs 197B–197F; FA 1990, s 23, 4 Sch*].

Where the employer has not entered into the FPCS, employees may, for 1996/97 and subsequent years, nevertheless use the FPCS rates to calculate any taxable profit on mileage allowances received. (Revenue Press Release (REV 32) 28 November 1995).

For cars provided by the employer ('company cars'), see 75.15 above. Expenditure on the provision of car parking facilities for an employee at or near his place of work (whether for a company or a private car) does not constitute an emolument. [*FA 1988, s 46*].

Volunteer drivers (e.g. hospital car service drivers). See 74.2 SCHEDULE D, CASE VI.

See generally Revenue Pamphlet IR 125.

Incidental overnight expenses. For 1995/96 and subsequent years, payments made to or on behalf of an employee in respect of his overnight personal incidental expenses (e.g. laundry, newspapers, telephone calls home) while away from home on business are exempt from tax up to certain limits. Payments above the limits are taxable in full. The exemption covers expenses incidental to the employee's being away from home during a 'qualifying absence' other than one in relation to which the 'authorised maximum' is exceeded, being expenses which would not otherwise be deductible. A *'qualifying absence'* is a continuous period throughout which the employee is obliged to stay away from home and which includes at least one overnight stay but does not include any such stay at a place the expenses of travelling to which would not be deductible under normal rules. The *'authorised maximum'*, in relation to a qualifying absence, is £5 for each night spent in the UK and £10 for each night any part of which is spent outside the UK (such amounts being subject to increase by Treasury Order from a date specified therein). In determining whether the authorised maximum is exceeded, payments by non-cash voucher or credit token and the providing of benefits are taken into account as well as cash payments. [*Sec 200A; FA 1995, s 93(4)(5)*]. Inland Revenue guidance notes for employers on the practical application of these provisions (to be included in Revenue Booklet 480 and the Employer's Guide to PAYE (P7) in due course) are available (see Revenue Press Release 16 May 1995).

Working Rule Agreements. Where Working Rule Agreements are drawn up between employers and trade unions and include payments of allowances for daily travel and subsistence, the Revenue have agreed that certain of these payments (or part) should not be taxed because of the high degree of mobility required in the industries concerned. Consistent treatment is accorded to site-based staff who work alongside operatives who are covered by a Working Rule Agreement and who have broadly the same working circumstances. Employers must obtain authority from their local tax district before making any such tax-free payments. (Revenue Press Release 13 February 1981).

Lodging allowances may generally be paid tax-free to an employee engaged under the terms of a Working Rule Agreement, provided that he is married, or has dependants living with him, and incurs extra expense while working away from home in addition to the cost of maintaining a permanent home. This treatment is extended to single men without dependants who maintain a permanent home. (ICAEW Memorandum TR 713, August 1988).

Travelling appointments. Excess expenditure on meals away from home may be claimed by employees holding full-time travelling appointments (e.g. lorry drivers) not restricted to a limited area. Bills, receipts etc. must be produced as evidence. Estimated figures will not be accepted. Relief is not restricted by amount saved by not having meals at home or a fixed place of work. (Revenue Pamphlet IR 131, SP 16/80, 20 November 1980). It is understood that the Revenue has agreed a tax-free overnight subsistence allowance of £19.90 (for calendar year 1994 – £19.50 for 1993, £19.00 for 1992, £18.15 for 1991) (reduced by 25% where a sleeper cab is available) under certain industry agreements.

Employment abroad. Tax will not be charged on the reimbursement to an employee, whose duties are carried on wholly abroad and who retains an abode in the UK, of expenses, including reasonable hotel expenses necessarily incurred, in travelling (whether alone or with his wife and family) to the country where his duties are performed and returning to the UK. Similar concession for persons receiving 'foreign emoluments' and travelling between UK and abode in home country. See 75.5 and 75.6 above. For allowances for travelling etc. expenses to members of the European Parliament, see *Lord Bruce of Donington v Aspden CJEC, [1981] STC 761.*

For overseas trips see *Newlin v Woods CA 1966, 42 TC 649* (cost of journey for health reasons disallowed); *Maclean v Trembath Ch D 1956, 36 TC 653* (business trip accompanied by wife; expenses attributable to wife disallowed); *Thomson v White Ch D 1966, 43 TC 256* (expenses of farmers and wives on organised trip partly for sightseeing and partly to see farms overseas disallowed); *Owen v Burden CA 1971, 47 TC 476* (expenses of county surveyor voluntarily to attend overseas road conference disallowed). Expenses of spouse of director or higher-paid employee who accompanies director on business journey abroad because his or her health is too precarious for travel alone are not assessable on employee. (Revenue Pamphlet IR 1, A4). See 29.15 EXEMPT INCOME as regards certain overseas travel costs of MPs.

75.44   VOUCHERS AND CREDIT-TOKENS

The following, when provided for an employee (or his spouse, parent, child or spouse of his child or any dependant of the employee), are taxable as emoluments of his employment. For the application of PAYE, see 55.2 PAY AS YOU EARN.

(*a*)   **Non-cash vouchers** (i.e. vouchers, stamps or similar documents or tokens capable of being exchanged, either singly or together, immediately or later, for money, goods or services or any combination of these but excluding cash vouchers, see below). The tax charge is on the expense incurred by the person at whose cost the voucher, and the money, goods or services for which it is capable of being exchanged, are provided, and in or in connection with that provision (before 3 May 1994, the expense incurred by the employer in providing the voucher and the money, goods or services for which it may be exchanged), with 'just and reasonable' apportionment in the case of schemes relating to groups of employees, and less any amounts made good by the employee. The charge is reduced to the extent that relief would have been claimable by the employee under *Sec 198* (necessary expenses etc., see 75.10(*a*) above), *Sec 201* (professional subscriptions, see 75.39 above), *Sec 201AA* (employee liabilities and indemnity insurance, see 75.23 above) or *Sec 332(3)* (re clergymen, see 75.9 above) if he had incurred the cost himself. The year of assessment is the year in which the expense is incurred by the employer or, if different and later, the year in which the voucher is received by, or appropriated to, the employee but, for cheque vouchers, it is the year in which the voucher is handed over in exchange for money, goods or services (time of posting is treated as time of handing over). [*Secs 141(1)–(5), (7), 144(3); FA 1994, s 89(1)(2); FA 1995, s 91(2)*]. This provision does not affect the treatment of luncheon vouchers as in 75.30 above.

Expense incurred by the employer in providing vouchers or any other incentive awards includes expenses beyond the direct cost of buying the goods or services provided where the expenses contribute more or less directly to the advantage enjoyed by the employee, e.g. costs of selecting and testing goods or services, or of after-sales service, or of storage and distribution. More remote expenses, e.g. costs of planning or administering a scheme or of promotional literature, etc., are excluded. See Revenue Pamphlet IR 131, SP 6/85, 29 July 1985.

Transport vouchers are specifically included in the above provisions but *not included* is a voucher provided for an employee of a passenger transport undertaking under arrangements in operation on 25 March 1982 to enable that employee (including spouse or family, as above) to obtain passenger transport services from his employer or his employer's subsidiary or parent company or another passenger transport undertaking. 'Transport voucher' means any ticket, pass or other document or token intended to enable a person to obtain passenger transport services (whether or not in exchange for it). [*Sec 141(6)(7)*].

Cheque vouchers are also included in the above provisions. '*Cheque voucher*' means a cheque provided for an employee and intended for his use wholly or mainly for payment for particular goods or services or for goods or services of one or more particular classes. [*Sec 141(7)*].

A voucher used by an employee to obtain the use of a *car parking space* at or near his place of work is excluded from these provisions [*Sec 141(6A)*], and a voucher provided neither by the employer nor by a person connected with the employer (within *Sec 839*, see 20 CONNECTED PERSONS) and used to obtain *entertainment* for the employee (or a relation) is similarly excluded, subject to the same conditions as are specified in 75.13(xv) above. [*Sec 141(6B); FA 1994, s 89(3)*]. See also 75.21 above for the exclusion of vouchers relating to certain sports and recreational facilities.

Incidental overnight expenses. For 1995/96 and subsequent years, there is excluded from these provisions a voucher used to obtain goods or services (or to obtain money to buy goods or services) incidental to the employee's being away from home on business during a 'qualifying absence' in relation to which the authorised maximum (£5 per night spent in the UK and £10 per night spent abroad) is not exceeded, where the cost of such goods or services is not otherwise deductible from emoluments. [*Sec 141(6C)(6D); FA 1995, s 93(1)*]. See also 75.43 above.

General. The above provisions do not apply if a person supplies the inspector with a statement of the cases and circumstances in which vouchers are provided to any employee (whether his own or not) and the inspector is satisfied that no additional tax is payable under these provisions and notifies that person accordingly. Such notification may be revoked retrospectively. [*Sec 144(1)(2)*].

(*b*)   **Cash vouchers** (as defined below). Where, as in some holiday pay schemes, a cash voucher is provided for an employee (including spouse or family as for non-cash vouchers, see (*a*) above) for redemption for cash which will be an emolument, tax is to be charged on the redemption amount when the voucher is received by, or appropriated to, the employee, with 'just and reasonable' apportionment in the case of schemes relating to groups of employees, *unless* the voucher is issued under a scheme which is approved by the Board as being practicable for PAYE to be applied at the time the vouchers are exchanged for cash. (Before 3 May 1994, PAYE was applied where tax was to be charged on receipt of the voucher, but see now 55.2 PAY AS YOU EARN.)

'*Cash voucher*' means any voucher, stamp or similar document capable of being exchanged, either singly or together, immediately or later, for a sum of money not substantially less than the cost to the person at whose cost it is provided, but excluding any document for a sum which would not have been chargeable under Schedule E if paid to the employee directly and excluding any savings certificate on which accumulated interest is exempt from tax. Where the sum of money is substantially less than the cost, any part of the difference representing benefits in connection with sickness, personal injury or death will be disregarded in deciding if the voucher is a cash voucher.

With effect from 3 May 1994, the above provisions do not apply if a person supplies the inspector with a statement of the cases and circumstances in which cash vouchers are provided to any employee (whether his own or not) and the inspector is satisfied that no additional tax is payable under these provisions and notifies that person accordingly. Such notification may be revoked retrospectively. [*Secs 143, 144(1)–(3); FA 1994, s 89(8)–(14)*].

(*c*)   **Luncheon Vouchers.** See 75.30 above.

(*d*)   **Credit-tokens** (as defined below). Tax is charged, when the employee uses a credit token to obtain money, goods or services, on the expense incurred by the person at whose cost the money, goods or services are provided (before 3 May 1994, by the person providing the credit token), in or in connection with that provision, with 'just and reasonable' apportionment in the case of schemes relating to groups of employees. See (*a*) above as regards valuation of expenses incurred. The money, goods or services obtained by the employee are disregarded (to avoid a double charge). The charge is reduced by any amounts made good by the employee and by any amounts for which relief would have been claimable under *Sec 198, Sec 201, Sec 201AA* or *Sec 332(3)* (see (*a*) above) if he had purchased the goods etc. himself. *Sec 142* does not apply if a person supplies the inspector with a statement of the cases and circumstances in which credit-tokens are provided to any employee (whether his own or not) and the inspector is satisfied that no additional tax is payable under *Sec 142* and notifies that person accordingly. Such notification may be revoked retrospectively. [*Secs 142(1)–(3), 144(1)(2); FA 1994, s 89(5)(6); FA 1995, s 91(2)*].

A token used by an employee to obtain the use of a *car parking space* at or near his place of work is excluded from these provisions [*Sec 142(3A)*], and a token provided neither by the employer nor by a person connected with the employer (within *Sec 839*, see 20 CONNECTED PERSONS) and used to obtain *entertainment* for the employee (or a relation) is similarly excluded, subject to the same conditions as are specified in 75.13(xv) above. [*Sec 142(3B); FA 1994, s 89(7)*].

Incidental overnight expenses. For 1995/96 and subsequent years, there is excluded from these provisions a token used to obtain goods or services (or to obtain money to buy goods or services) incidental to the employee's being away from home on business during a 'qualifying absence' in relation to which the authorised maximum (£5 per night spent in the UK and £10 per night spent abroad) is not exceeded, where the cost of such goods or services is not otherwise deductible from emoluments. [*Sec 142(3C)(3D); FA 1995, s 93(2)*]. See also 75.43 above.

'*Credit-token*' means a card, token or other thing given to a person by another person who undertakes that (*a*) on the production of it (whether or not some other action is also required) he will supply money, goods or services on credit or (*b*) on similar production to a third party, he will pay that third party for the money etc. supplied (whether or not taking any discount or commission). '*Production*' includes the use of an object provided to operate a machine. Not included is a cash voucher and a non-cash voucher already chargeable in (*b*) or (*c*) above. [*Sec 142(4)(5)*].

75.45   WAGES IN LIEU OF NOTICE

The taxation treatment of payments in lieu of notice is governed by the general principles applying to payments on cessation of employment, for which see 19.3 *et seq.* COMPENSATION FOR LOSS OF EMPLOYMENT. Where the payment is not within the general Schedule E charge, it will generally fall within *Sec 148*, subject to the exemptions from charge under that *section*. The application of the general principles (as above) depends on the circumstances in which a payment is made.

(*a*)   Dismissal without proper notice, with payment in lieu of notice. The payment would not normally be within the general Schedule E charge.

(*b*)   Agreement following proper notice that employee will be paid during notice period, although not required to work. The payment would normally be within the general Schedule E charge.

(*c*)   Immediate termination of employment, either by agreement or at employer's option under contract, with payment in lieu of proper notice. It would seem that such a payment should not fall within the general Schedule E charge, as not being for 'acting as or being' an employee, but the Revenue may seek to impose general Schedule E treatment in view of the contractual nature of the payment.

The non-tax case *Delaney v Staples [1992] 2 WLR 451* provides a useful analysis of such payments.

75.46   WORKERS SUPPLIED BY AGENCIES

Where an individual worker (including a partner in a firm and a member of an unincorporated body) has a contract or arrangement with another person (e.g. with an agency, which term includes an unincorporated body of which the worker is a member) under which he is obliged to render personal services to the client which are subject to supervision, direction or control, he will be chargeable under Schedule E (if not already so chargeable) on the remuneration received for those services. '*Remuneration*' includes every form of payment, perquisites, benefits etc. but not anything which would not otherwise be chargeable under Schedule E if receivable from an office or employment. [*Sec 134*]. For the existence of a contract, see *Brady v Hart Ch D 1985, 58 TC 518.*

For the general application of these provisions, see *Bhadra v Ellam Ch D 1987, 60 TC 466*, where a doctor obtaining locum posts through medical agencies was held to be within *Sec 134*.

The above provisions do not apply (*a*) to entertainers or fashion etc. models, or (*b*) if the services are wholly rendered in the worker's own home or at other premises which are neither under the control or management of the client nor at which the services are required by their nature to be rendered, or (*c*) if the worker is a sub-contractor within the CONSTRUCTION INDUSTRY TAX DEDUCTION SCHEME (21). [*Sec 134(5)*].

The person paying the remuneration (i.e. the agency or the client) must include the worker in his return of employees under *TMA s 15*, see 67.5 RETURNS. Where a worker is engaged through a foreign agency which does not have a branch or permanent agency operating PAYE, the client is deemed to be the employer and is responsible for operating PAYE and National Insurance arrangements. See *Sec 203C* (55.3 PAY AS YOU EARN).

76   Schedule F—Dividends etc.

76.1   Schedule F commenced on 6 April 1966 and applies to dividends and other distributions of UK companies. [*Sec 20; FA 1993, s 183(1)*].

76.2   Up to 5 April 1973, the company was required to account (to the Revenue) for the standard rate of income tax on the dividends etc.

76.3   After 5 April 1973, the company pays (to the Revenue) Advance Corporation Tax (at a prescribed rate) on paying the dividend etc. and the recipient gets an equivalent 'tax credit' (subject to special provisions for 1993/94) except in the case of certain 'foreign income dividends'—see 1.8(iii) ALLOWANCES AND TAX RATES. [*Secs 231, 246C; FA 1993, s 78(3); FA 1994, 16 Sch 1*].

See also Tolley's Corporation Tax under Advance Corporation Tax and Distributions.

77   Scientific Research Associations

77.1   Scientific research associations are, on a claim, granted the same exemptions from tax as CHARITIES (15), including exemptions from tax on capital gains, if

(*a*)   object is scientific research which may lead to extension of any class(es) of trade, and association is approved for this purpose by the Secretary of State, and

(*b*)   the Association is prohibited by Memorandum or similar instrument from distribution of income or property, in any form, to its members (other than reasonable payments for supplies, labour, power, services, interest and rent). [*Sec 508; TCGA, s 271(6)(b)*].

78 Self-Assessment

(See also Revenue Pamphlet IR 142.)

The headings in this chapter are as follows.

78.1 INTRODUCTION

Self-assessment will have effect generally for 1996/97 and subsequent years of assessment, although certain aspects of the system come into effect in earlier or later years. The term 'self-assessment' refers to the system whereby the annual tax returns filed by individuals and trustees should include a self-assessment of the taxpayer's liability for income tax and capital gains tax. Payment of tax will then be due automatically, based on the self-assessment. The main body of legislation is contained in *Finance Act 1994*, although there have been further provisions in subsequent Finance Acts.

Two detailed Revenue booklets, SAT 1 'The new current year basis of assessment' and SAT 2 'Self Assessment: the legal framework', both guides for Inland Revenue officers and tax practitioners, should have been sent by tax offices to all practices with which they deal in

August/September 1995. Further copies are available (price £7.50 and £5.00 respectively) from Inland Revenue Reference Library, New Wing, Somerset House, Strand, London, WC2R 1LB. A booklet SAT 3 'Self Assessment: what it will mean for employers' should also have been sent to employers as part of an information pack in July 1995. Further copies are available free from tax offices, as are the following explanatory pamphlets:

SA/BK1   Self Assessment: a general guide

SA/BK2   Self Assessment: a guide for the self-employed

SA/BK3   Self Assessment: a guide to keeping records for the self-employed

SA/BK4   Self Assessment: a general guide to keeping records

A series of articles has been published in the Revenue Tax Bulletin from August 1993 onwards on various aspects of self-assessment.

Returns. The first returns to be affected will be those covering the tax year 1996/97, normally sent out by the Revenue in April 1997. Such returns must normally be filed by 31 January following the year of assessment (see 78.5 below). Taxpayers who would prefer not to compute their own liabilities will not have to do so providing they file their return early, normally by 30 September following the year of assessment (see 78.6 below). Penalties will be imposed for late submission of returns, subject to appeal on the grounds of reasonable excuse (see 78.26 below). There are provisions for making amendments to self-assessments (see 78.7 below). The Revenue are given broadly one year from the filing date to give notice of their intention to enquire into the return (see 78.11 below). A formal procedure is laid down for such enquiries (see 78.11 to 78.13 below). If they do not give such notice, the return becomes final and conclusive, subject to any 'error or mistake' claim by the taxpayer (see 78.37 below) or 'discovery' assessment by the Revenue (see 78.15 below). In the event of non-submission of a return, the Revenue will be able to make a determination of the tax liability; there will be no right of appeal but the determination may be superseded upon submission of the return (see 78.14 below). Capital losses must be quantified if they are to be allowable losses (see Tolley's Capital Gains Tax).

A new style of return will have to be filed by partnerships. This must include a statement of the allocation of partnership income between the partners. See 78.8, 78.9 below.

Payment of tax. Income tax (on all sources of taxable income) for a year of assessment will be payable by means of two interim payments of equal amounts, based normally on the liability for the previous year and due on 31 January in the year of assessment and the following 31 July, and a final balancing payment due on the following 31 January (on which date any capital gains tax liability will also be due for payment). Taxpayers will have the right to reduce their interim payments if they believe their liability will be less than that for the previous year or to dispense with interim payments if they believe they will have no liability. Interim payments will not in any case be required where substantially all of a taxpayer's liability is covered by deduction of tax at source, including PAYE, or where the amounts otherwise due are below *de minimis* limits to be prescribed by regulations. See 78.17 to 78.20 below.

Interest on overdue payments will run from the due date to the date of payment (see 78.22 below). There will also be a 5% surcharge on any tax unpaid by 28 February following the year of assessment and a further 5% surcharge on any tax unpaid by the following 31 July, such surcharges being subject to appeal on the grounds of reasonable excuse (see 78.21 below). Interest on tax overpaid will run from the due date (or date of payment if later) to the date of repayment (see 78.23 below); the rate of interest will be lower than that on overdue tax.

Miscellaneous. Numerous consequential amendments are made to taxes management provisions and time limits. There is a new statutory requirement for taxpayers to keep records for the purpose of making returns and to preserve such records for specified periods (see 78.10 below).

The above changes are covered in this chapter, except for changes to time limits and other consequential amendments which are dealt with in the appropriate chapters.

78.2   **Changes to facilitate self-assessment.** Fundamental changes are made by *Finance Act 1994* to the system of computing tax liabilities under Schedule D. The principal change involves a move from a preceding year basis of assessment to a current year basis, but they also involve amendments to the provisions on, for example, trading loss reliefs, capital allowances and to the means by which members of partnerships are charged to tax. The provisions are summarised below and covered in detail in the appropriate chapters.

As regards businesses commenced, and other sources of income first arising, after 5 April 1994, the new provisions have effect for 1994/95 and subsequent years of assessment. As regards businesses commenced, and other sources of income first arising, before 6 April 1994, they generally come into effect for 1996/97 and subsequent years. For such businesses, etc., there are transitional provisions to facilitate the changeover from the old system to the new. Some of the provisions affecting partnerships do not have effect until 1997/98.

Current year basis. Subject to special rules for opening years (see 71.12 SCHEDULE D, CASES I AND II) and the closing year (see 71.17 SCHEDULE D, CASES I AND II), individuals carrying on a trade, profession or vocation will be taxed for a year of assessment on the profits made in the period of account ending in that year (see 71.14 SCHEDULE D, CASES I AND II). There are statutory rules for determining the basis period in the event of a change of accounting date; these can produce a basis period of more than 12 months but not one of less than 12 months (see 71.15 SCHEDULE D, CASES I AND II).

The broad intention is that over the lifetime of a business the profits taxed should equate to the profits earned (as adjusted for tax purposes). Profits will, in fact, sometimes be taxed twice (as a result of the opening year rules or certain changes of accounting date). However, the amount taxed twice can be deducted (known as overlap relief) in computing profits for the year of cessation or for a year of assessment the basis period for which is longer than 12 months, i.e. as a result of a change of accounting date. See 71.19 and 71.22 SCHEDULE D, CASES I AND II.

Income chargeable under Schedule D, Cases III to VI will be taxed for a year of assessment on the basis of the income arising in that year. See 72.4(*e*) SCHEDULE D, CASE III, 73.9 SCHEDULE D, CASES IV AND V and 74.3 SCHEDULE D, CASE VI.

Transitional provisions. For businesses commenced before 6 April 1994, 1996/97 will be a transitional year. The basis period will run from the end of the basis period for 1995/96 (on a preceding year basis) to the end of the basis period for 1996/97 (applying the current year basis). Assuming no change of accounting date, this will be a two-year period and the taxable profit will be one half of the profits for that period, the other half escaping tax. Where this transitional period is more or less than two years, the profits will be apportioned so that twelve months' profits are taxed and the balance escapes tax. A trading loss for any part of the transitional period will qualify for relief in full, with no apportionment. See 71.20 SCHEDULE D, CASES I AND II.

For businesses commenced before 6 April 1994, the current year basis and the transitional rules above will not apply if the business ceases before 6 April 1997. Special rules, based on the closing year rules under the preceding year basis, may be applied as regards 1995/96 and 1996/97 where such a business ceases in 1997/98 and as regards 1996/97 only for a cessation in 1998/99. See 71.24 SCHEDULE D, CASES I AND II.

Similar rules will apply to other sources of Schedule D income on the changeover to a current year basis. See 72.4(*f*) SCHEDULE D, CASE III and 73.9 SCHEDULE D, CASES IV AND V.

There are anti-avoidance provisions designed to deter and penalise attempts to exploit the transitional rules by shifting income either into the transitional basis period so that it will not be fully charged to tax (see 71.20 SCHEDULE D, CASES I AND II, 72.4(*f*) SCHEDULE D, CASE III and 73.9 SCHEDULE D, CASES IV AND V) or (for trading etc. profits only) into the transitional overlap period (see 71.22 SCHEDULE D, CASES I AND II and 73.9 SCHEDULE D, CASES IV AND V). There are various triggers which automatically bring these measures into play, subject to statutory let-outs based on motive and benefit and to *de minimis* limits to be announced shortly before 5 April 1997. The counteraction is to increase the assessment for the transitional year 1996/97 or reduce the transitional overlap profit (see 71.22) by 1.25 times the amount on which the taxpayer sought to avoid tax (reduced by 0.25 times that amount to the extent that disclosure is made voluntarily in the tax return). There are also provisions aimed at the refinancing of partnership borrowings for the transitional basis period or transitional overlap period by means of loans taken out by individual partners after 31 March 1994 (see 43.22 INTEREST PAYABLE).

Losses. Under the current year basis, trading losses will always be computed for tax purposes on an accounts basis (as was usually the case in practice under the preceding year basis of assessment) rather than a fiscal year basis. Loss relief under *Sec 380* (against other income) will be available against income of the tax year in which the loss is incurred and/or the previous year. See 46.3 LOSSES. This also applies, for 1994/95 onwards, to income tax relief for losses on unquoted shares (see 46.19 LOSSES). Other consequential changes are made to loss relief provisions (see 46 LOSSES generally).

Capital allowances. Capital allowances are to be treated as trading expenses (and balancing charges as trading receipts) in the same way as has long since applied for corporation tax purposes (see 10.1 CAPITAL ALLOWANCES). The chargeable period for capital allowances purposes will be the period of account rather than the year of assessment (see 10.2(vi) CAPITAL ALLOWANCES). For businesses commenced before 6 April 1994, these changes apply for 1997/98 and later years. Other consequential changes are made to capital allowances provisions (see 10 CAPITAL ALLOWANCES generally).

Partnerships. A partnership will no longer be taxed as a separate entity. Instead, each individual partner's share of profits, after all partnership expenses and capital allowances, will fall to be included in his or her self-assessment. Profits will be allocated between partners by reference to the sharing ratios for the period of account (rather than those for the year of assessment). A change in the members of a partnership will no longer be regarded as a cessation for tax purposes (provided there is at least one continuing partner), and continuation elections under *Sec 113(2)* will thus be defunct. The commencement and cessation provisions will instead apply to partners individually. For partnership businesses commenced before 6 April 1994, these changes apply for 1997/98 and later years. A deemed cessation and recommencement after 5 April 1994 will bring the new rules into effect immediately as regards the new partnership. See 53 PARTNERSHIPS.

Double taxation relief. Special rules are introduced to ensure that all relief available for foreign tax on business profits is given over the lifetime of a business. See 25.5 (*j*)(*n*) DOUBLE TAX RELIEF.

78.3 INTERPRETATION OF REFERENCES TO ASSESSMENTS, ETC.

Following the introduction of self-assessment, references to an individual (or trustee) being assessed to tax, or being charged to tax by an assessment, are to be construed as including a reference to his being so assessed, or being so charged, by a self-assessment under *TMA s 9* (see 78.6 below) or by a determination under *TMA s 28C* (see 78.14 below) which has not been superseded by a self-assessment. [*FA 1994, s 197*].

78.4 **NOTICE OF CHARGEABILITY**

For *1995/96 and subsequent years*, a person chargeable to income tax or capital gains tax for a year of assessment who has not been required by a notice under *TMA s 8* (see 67.2 RETURNS for 1995/96 and 78.5 below for later years) to deliver a return for that year must, within six months after the end of that year, notify an officer of the Board that he is so chargeable. The maximum penalty for non-compliance is the amount of tax in which the person is assessed for that year which is not paid on or before 31 January following that year. A person is not required to give notice under these provisions if his total income for the year consists of income from the sources below and he has no chargeable gains. The said sources are those in respect of which

(*a*)   all payments, etc. are dealt with under PAYE, or

(*b*)   all income has been or will be taken into account either in determining the chargeable person's liability to tax or under PAYE, or

(*c*)   the income is chargeable under Schedule F or is other income from which income tax has been, or is treated as having been, deducted, provided that the chargeable person is not liable for that year other than at the basic or lower rate, or

(*d*)   all income for that year is income on which the chargeable person could not become liable to tax under a self-assessment under *TMA s 9* (see 78.6 below) in respect of that year (or, as regards 1995/96 only, under assessments made more than six months after the end of that year).

These provisions also apply with the appropriate modifications to 'relevant trustees' (as defined in 78.41 below) of settlements.

[*TMA s 7; FA 1994, s 196, 19 Sch 1; FA 1995, ss 103(1)(2), 115(1), 21 Sch 1*].

As regards items within (*b*) above, the Revenue will normally accept that employees in receipt of copy form P11D (or equivalent particulars) from their employer (see 78.42 below) can assume that any items on it not already taken into account for PAYE will be so taken into account, so there is no need to notify chargeability in respect of such items. Notice of chargeability is, however, necessary to the extent that the P11D is incorrect or incomplete or if the employee knows that the actual form has not been submitted to the Revenue. Employees are not relieved of any obligation to notify chargeability if they have not received a copy P11D or in respect of non-P11D items which ought to have been reported by the employer to the Revenue on other returns. For 1995/96, as there is no statutory obligation on the employer to provide employees with particulars of P11D items, the Revenue will take the absence of such information into account as a mitigating factor in determining penalties for failure to notify such items. (Revenue Statement of Practice SP 1/96, 1 February 1996).

78.5 **ANNUAL RETURNS OF INCOME AND CHARGEABLE GAINS**

For the purposes of establishing a person's income, chargeable gains and net income tax liability for 1996/97 or a subsequent year of assessment, an officer of the Board may by notice require that person to deliver a return on or before 31 January following the year or, if later, within three months beginning with the date of the notice. The return must contain such information and be accompanied by such accounts, statements and documents as may reasonably be required. The return must include a declaration that, to the best of the knowledge of the person making it, it is complete and correct. The information, accounts and statements required by the notice may differ in relation to different periods, or different sources of income, or different descriptions of person. [*TMA s 8; FA 1990, s 90(1); FA 1994, ss 178(1), 199(2)(a); FA 1995, s 104(1)(3); FA 1996, s 121(1)–(3)*]. Similar provisions apply in relation to returns by trustees, by reference to any 'relevant trustee' (see 78.41 below). [*TMA s 8A; FA 1990, s 90(1); FA 1994, ss 178(2), 199(2)(a); FA 1995, ss 103(3), 104(1); FA 1996, s 121(1)–(3)*].

In practice, business accounts are not normally required with the return except in 'particularly large or complex' cases. Instead, the return will include a special section in which the relevant accounts information can be entered. Accounts should be retained in cases of enquiry (see 78.11 below). (Revenue booklet SAT 2(1995), para 2.22). It has been suggested by professional bodies and commentators that accounts should be submitted even if not 'required', so as to minimise the risk of a discovery assessment (see 78.15 below).

In the case of a person carrying on a profession, trade or business in partnership, a return under *TMA s 8* must include each amount, which according to any 'relevant statement' is his share of any income, loss, tax, credit or charge for the period covered by the statement. A *'relevant statement'* is a statement falling to be made, as respects the partnership, under *TMA s 12AB* (see 78.9 below) for a period which includes, or includes any part of, the year of assessment or its basis period. [*TMA s 8(1B)(1C); FA 1994, s 178(1); FA 1995, s 104(2)*].

The Revenue will, on request, issue a return before the end of the tax year

(*a*)   in which the taxpayer dies (or administration of the estate is completed), to the personal representatives of the deceased, or

(*b*)   in which a trust is wound up, to the trustees.

(Revenue Press Release 4 April 1996). See also 78.11 below as regards enquiries into such returns.

See 78.26 below as regards penalties for non-compliance.

See 67.2 RETURNS as regards signature of returns and use of substitute return forms.

78.6   **SELF-ASSESSMENTS**

For 1996/97 and subsequent years, every return under *TMA s 8* or *8A* (see 78.5 above) must include, subject to the exception below, an assessment (a self-assessment) of the amounts in which, based on the information in the return and taking into account any reliefs and allowances claimed therein, the person making the return is chargeable to income tax and capital gains tax for the year of assessment and of his net income tax liability for the year, taking into account tax deducted at source and tax credits on dividends. In the event of non-compliance, an officer of the Board *may* make the assessment on his behalf, based on the information in the return, and send the person a copy.

A person need not comply with this requirement if he makes and delivers his return on or before 30 September following the year of assessment or, if later, within two months beginning with the date of the notice to deliver the return. For returns submitted outside these time limits, the Revenue will still, if the taxpayer so requests, carry out the computations based on the return, but will not guarantee that the relevant filing date will be met. In the event of a person making no self-assessment under this option, an officer of the Board *must* make the assessment on his behalf, based on the information in the return, and send the person a copy. If, by reason only of Revenue delay, the assessment is made less than 30 days before the due date for payment of the tax, the date from which any interest or surcharge is triggered (see 78.21, 78.22 below) is 30 days after the issue of the assessment. (ICAEW Technical Release TAX 9/94, 7 June 1994).

Assessments made as above by an officer of the Board are treated as self-assessments by the person making the return.

A self-assessment must not show as repayable any notional tax treated as deducted from certain income deemed to have been received after deduction of tax, for example STOCK DIVIDENDS (84).

[*TMA s 9(1)–(3); FA 1994, ss 179, 199(2)(a); FA 1995, ss 104(4), 115(2); FA 1996, ss 121(4), 122(1)*].

The Revenue need not give notice to deliver a return under 78.5 above, and thus a self-assessment will not be required, in cases where tax deducted under PAY AS YOU EARN (55) equates to the total tax liability for the year. The taxpayer may, however, give notice requiring a return to be issued so that he can make a self-assessment, such notice to be given within the five years after 31 October following the year of assessment. [*Sec 205; FA 1995, s 111(1)*].

SCHEDULE E (75) taxpayers who wish to have their liability coded out through PAYE (55) will be encouraged to comply with the earlier date of 30 September whether or not they choose to complete their own self-assessment. (Revenue booklet SAT 2(1995), para 2.37).

A return and self-assessment containing an estimated figure will be accepted providing the figure is clearly identified as such and details given as to how it is calculated and when the final figure should be available (at which time it should be notified without unreasonable delay). A return omitting a figure or stating 'to be agreed' will be an incomplete return. (SAT 2(1995), paras 2.53, 2.54).

78.7   **Amendments of self-assessments other than where enquiries made**

At any time within nine months beginning with the delivery of a person's return, an officer of the Board may by notice to that person amend his self-assessment to correct ('repair') obvious errors (whether of principle, arithmetical or otherwise).

At any time within twelve months beginning with the filing date (i.e. the date by which the return must be delivered, as in 78.5 above), that person may by notice to an officer of the Board amend his self-assessment to give effect to any amendments to his return which he has notified to such an officer.

However, no such amendment of a self-assessment may be made (by the taxpayer or the Revenue) after an officer of the Board has given notice of intention to enquire into the return (see 78.11 below) and before his enquiries are completed.

[*TMA s 9(4)–(6); FA 1994, s 179*].

See 78.13 below for amendments to self-assessments where the Revenue make enquiries into the return.

78.8   **PARTNERSHIP RETURNS**

The following provisions apply for 1996/97 and subsequent years or, as regards corporate partners, for accounting periods ending on or after an appointed day (which will be no earlier than 1 April 1996).

Any partner may be required by notice to complete and deliver a return of the partnership profits together with accounts, statements, documents, etc. (see also 78.9 below). The return must include information as to taxable partnership income, reliefs and allowances claimed, tax at source and tax credits plus the names, residences and tax references of all persons (including companies) who were partners during the period specified in the notice and such other information as may reasonably be required by the notice, which may include information relating to disposals and acquisitions of partnership property. The general requirements are similar to those for personal returns under *TMA s 8* (see 78.5 above). The notice will specify the period (the relevant period) to be covered by the return and the date by which the return should be delivered (the filing date). For a partnership including at least one individual, the filing date will be no earlier than 31 January following the year of assessment concerned (normally that in which the relevant period ends). For a partnership including at least one company, the filing date will be no earlier than the first anniversary of the end of the relevant period. In both cases, the filing date will be deferred until, at the earliest, the last day of the three-month period beginning with the date of the notice, if this is a later date than that given above.

Where the partner responsible for dealing with the return ceases to be available, a successor may be nominated for this purpose by a majority of the persons (or their personal representatives) who were partners at any time in the period covered by the return. A nomination (or revocation of a nomination) does not have effect until notified to the Revenue. Failing a nomination, a successor will be determined according to rules on the return form or will be nominated by the Revenue.

[*TMA s 12AA; FA 1994, ss 184, 199; FA 1995, ss 104(6), 115(4); FA 1996, ss 121(6)(7), 123(1)–(4)*].

See 78.27 below as regards penalties for non-compliance.

It will not be possible for individual partners to make, in their personal tax returns, supplementary claims for expenses incurred on the partnership's behalf or capital allowances on personal assets used in the partnership. If not included in the accounts, adjustments for such expenditure etc. must be included in the tax computation forming part of the partnership return. (Revenue booklet SAT 1(1995), para 5.17).

78.9   **PARTNERSHIP STATEMENTS**

Every partnership return under 78.8 above must include a statement (a partnership statement) showing, in respect of the period covered by the return and each period of account ending within that period,

(*a*)   the partnership income or loss from each source, after taking into account any relief or allowance due to the partnership and for which a claim is made under any of the provisions in *TMA s 42(7)* (see 78.32 below),

(*b*)   the amount of consideration for each disposal of partnership property,

(*c*)   the amounts of any tax deducted at source from or tax credits on partnership income, and

(*d*)   the amount of each charge on partnership income,

and each partner's share of that income, loss, consideration, tax, credit or charge. Provisions similar to those in 78.7 above apply as regards amendments to partnership statements. Where a partnership statement is so amended, the partners' self-assessments will be amended by the Revenue accordingly, by notice to each partner concerned. [*TMA s 12AB; FA 1994, s 185; FA 1995, s 104(7)(8); FA 1996, s 123(5)(6)*].

78.10   **RECORDS**

Any person who may be required to make and deliver a return under 78.5 above (personal and trustee's returns) or 78.8 (partnership returns) or a corporation tax return for a year of assessment or other period will be statutorily required to keep all necessary records and to preserve them until the end of the 'relevant day'. The *'relevant day'* is normally

(*a*)   in the case of a person carrying on a trade (including, for these purposes, any letting of property), profession or business alone or in partnership or a company, the fifth anniversary of 31 January following the year of assessment or, for partnership or company returns, the sixth anniversary of the end of the period covered by the return; and

(*b*)   in any other case, the first anniversary of 31 January following the year of assessment.

Where notice to deliver the return is given before the day in whichever is the applicable of (*a*) or (*b*) above, the '*relevant day*' is the *later* of that day and whichever of the following applies:

(i)   where Revenue enquiries are made into the return (or into an amendment of the return), the day on which the enquiries are statutorily treated as completed (see 78.13 below);

(ii)   where no such enquiries are made, the day on which the Revenue no longer have power to enquire (see 78.11 below).

Where notice to deliver the return is given *after* the day in whichever is the applicable of (*a*) and (*b*) above, (i) and (ii) above still apply to determine the relevant day but only in relation to such records as the taxpayer has in his possession at the time the notice is given.

In the case of a person within (*a*) above, the records in question include records concerning business receipts and expenditure and, in the case of a trade involving dealing in goods, all sales and purchases of goods. All supporting documents (including accounts, books, deeds, contracts, vouchers and receipts) relating to such items must also be preserved. Generally, copies of documents may be preserved instead of the originals and are admissible in evidence in proceedings before the Commissioners. (See Revenue Tax Bulletin February 1996 p 283 as regards the use of optical imaging to preserve records.) Exceptions to this are vouchers, certificates etc. which show tax credits or deductions at source of UK or foreign tax, e.g. dividend vouchers, interest vouchers (including those issued by banks and building societies) and evidence of tax deducted from payments to sub-contractors under the CONSTRUCTION INDUSTRY TAX DEDUCTION SCHEME (21), which, with effect on or after 29 April 1996, must be preserved in their original form.

The maximum penalty for non-compliance in relation to any year of assessment or accounting period is £3,000. This penalty does not apply where the failure relates to records which might have been requisite only for the purposes of claims, elections or notices which are *not* included in the return (but see 78.34 below for the requirement as regards records relating to such claims etc. and the penalty for non-compliance), or to vouchers, certificates etc. showing UK tax credits or deductions at source (e.g. dividend vouchers and interest certificates) where the inspector is satisfied that other documentary evidence supplied to him proves any facts he reasonably requires to be proved and which the voucher etc. would have proved.

[*TMA s 12B; FA 1994, s 196, 19 Sch 3; FA 1995, s 105; FA 1996, s 124(2)–(5)(9)*].

The Revenue have published guidance notes as to the type of records to be kept. The above-mentioned penalty will not be charged for any failure to keep records in accordance with those notes which occurred before 6 April 1996. (Revenue Pamphlet SA/BK3).

78.11   **ENQUIRIES INTO RETURNS**

Power to enquire. An officer of the Board may enquire into a return (or amendment of a return) on the basis of which a person's self-assessment under *TMA s 9* (see 78.6 above) has been made (or amended by that person), or into any claim or election included in a return (by amendment or otherwise). The officer must give notice in writing of his intention to so enquire, such notice to be given,

(a)   in the case of a return delivered or amendment made on or before the filing date (i.e. the date on or before which the return must be delivered – see 78.5 above), within twelve months beginning with that date; and

(b)   otherwise on or before the quarter day (meaning 31 January, 30 April, etc.) next following the first anniversary of the day of delivery or amendment.

A return or amendment cannot be enquired into more than once. [*TMA s 9A; FA 1994, s 180; FA 1996, 19 Sch 2*].

In the case of a return by the personal representatives of a deceased taxpayer (for the year of death or of completion of administration of the estate), the Revenue will give early written confirmation if they do not intend to enquire into the return (although, in exceptional circumstances, an enquiry at a later date would not thereby be precluded if the return was discovered to be incomplete or incorrect). Such early confirmation will also be given to trustees in relation to the return for the year in which the trust is wound up. (Revenue Press Release 4 April 1996). See also 78.5 above as regards early issue of returns in such cases.

Similar provisions apply as regards a partnership return on the basis of which a partnership statement (see 78.9 above) was made and to claims or elections included therein. The notice of intention to enquire may be given to a successor (see 78.8 above) of the person who made the return or amendment. The giving of such notice is deemed to include the giving of notice under *TMA s 9A* (see above) (or, where applicable, the equivalent corporation tax provision) to each partner affected. [*TMA s 12AC; FA 1994, s 186; FA 1996, s 123(7), 19 Sch 2*].

78.12   **Power to call for documents.** At the same time as giving notice under 78.11 above to any person, or subsequently, an officer of the Board may by notice in writing require that person, within a specified period of at least 30 days, to produce to the officer such documents (as are in the person's possession or power) and such accounts or particulars as the officer may reasonably require to check the validity of the return or amendment. Copies of documents may be produced but the officer has power to call for originals, and may himself take copies of, or make extracts from, any document produced. A person is not obliged under these provisions to produce documents, etc. relating to the conduct of any pending appeal by him. There is provision for a person to appeal, within 30 days beginning with the date of the notice, against any requirement imposed by a notice as above. In restricted cases, an officer may, alternatively or in addition, require documents, accounts etc. to enable him to exercise the 'Crown Option' (see 78.13 below). [*TMA s 19A; FA 1994, s 187; FA 1996, 19 Sch 3, 22 Sch 2*]. See 76.28 below as regards penalties for non-compliance.

78.13   **Amendment of self-assessment or partnership statement where enquiries made.** Where notice has been given by an officer of the Board under 78.11 above of intention to enquire into the taxpayer's return, amendment, claim or election, the officer's enquiries are treated as completed at such time as he, by notice, informs the taxpayer that he has completed his enquiries and states his conclusions as to the amount of tax which should be contained in the taxpayer's self-assessment and as to any claims or elections into which he has enquired. The taxpayer may before that time apply to the Commissioners for a direction that the officer shall give such notice within a period specified in the direction, such application to be heard and determined in the same way as an appeal against an amendment of a self-assessment and the Commissioners to give such a direction unless they are satisfied that the officer has reasonable grounds for not giving such notice.

The taxpayer is given 30 days beginning with the date of completion of the officer's enquiries to amend his self-assessment in accordance with the officer's conclusions. Where the enquiry was into a return rather than an amendment, and the return was made before the expiry of twelve months beginning with the due date for delivery (see 78.5 above), the taxpayer also has this 30-day period to amend his self-assessment in accordance with any amendments to the return which he has notified to the officer. The officer then has a further 30 days in which to amend the self-assessment himself.

If, in the officer's opinion, there is otherwise likely to be a loss of tax to the Crown, the officer may by notice amend the self-assessment before his enquiries are completed.

Similar provisions allow firstly the taxpayer and then the officer to amend or omit, within the same time limits, claims and elections included in the return which do not directly affect the self-assessment, for example a claim to carry forward trading losses, but which the officer thinks should be wholly or partly disallowed, and this is notwithstanding any statutory provision under which the claim or election would otherwise be unamendable or irrevocable.

Where the enquiry is into an amendment by the taxpayer to the return, rather than into the return itself, any amendment by the officer of the self-assessment, whether before or after completion of the enquiry, must be restricted to any deficiency or excess of tax as is attributable to the taxpayer's amendment.

[*TMA s 28A; FA 1994, s 188; FA 1996, 19 Sch 2, 4(1)(2), 22 Sch 3*].

Similar provisions apply in the case of an enquiry into a partnership return etc., taking references above to the self-assessment as references to the partnership statement (see 78.9 above) based on the return. However, there is no provision for the officer to amend the partnership statement before completion of his enquiries. Where a partnership statement is amended under these provisions, the officer will, by notice, make any necessary consequential amendments to the self-assessments of the partners (including company partners).

[*TMA s 28B; FA 1994, s 189; FA 1996, 19 Sch 2, 5(1)*].

See 78.31 below for right of appeal against an amendment by the Revenue to a self-assessment or partnership statement.

There are provisions concerning enquiries into a personal or partnership return which includes amounts which may be taxed using more than one method, with the Revenue having the right to choose which method is to be used (the 'Crown Option'). These are restricted to cases where amounts may be taxed either under Case I or II or under any of Cases III to V of Schedule D (applicable normally to dividends and interest forming part of a financial trader's profits) and to life assurance companies taxable either under Case I or under the so-called I minus E basis. [*TMA ss 28A(7A)–(7C), 28B(6A)(6B); FA 1994, ss 188, 189; FA 1996, 19 Sch 4(3), 5(2)*].

78.14   DETERMINATION OF TAX WHERE NO RETURN DELIVERED

Where a notice has been given under *TMA s 8, 8A* (notice requiring an individual or trustee to deliver a return—see 78.5 above) and the return is not delivered by the due date (the filing date), an officer of the Board may make a determination of the amounts of taxable income, capital gains and income tax payable which, to the best of his information and belief, he estimates for the year of assessment. The officer must serve notice of the determination on the person concerned. Tax is payable as if the determination were a self-assessment, with no right of appeal. No determination may be made after the expiry of five years beginning with the filing date.

A determination is automatically superseded by any self-assessment made (whether by the taxpayer or the Revenue), based on information contained in a return. Such self-assessment must be made within the five years beginning with the filing date or, if later, within twelve months beginning with the date of the determination. Any tax payable or repayable as a result of the supersession is deemed to have fallen due for payment or repayment on the normal due date, usually 31 January following the year of assessment (see 78.19 below).

Any recovery proceedings commenced before the making of such a self-assessment may be continued in respect of so much of the tax charged by the self-assessment as is due and payable and has not been paid.

[*TMA ss 28C, 59B(5A); FA 1994, s 190; FA 1996, s 125*].

78.15   **DISCOVERY ASSESSMENTS**

If, as regards 1996/97 and subsequent years, an officer of the Board or the Board 'discover', as regards any person (the taxpayer) and a chargeable period (i.e. for income tax and capital gains tax purposes, a year of assessment), that

(*a*)   any income or chargeable gains which ought to have been assessed to tax (see 78.3 above) have not been assessed, or

(*b*)   an assessment is or has become insufficient, or

(*c*)   any relief given is or has become excessive,

then with the exceptions below, an assessment (a discovery assessment) may be made to make good to the Crown the apparent loss of tax.

No discovery assessment may be made in respect of a chargeable period, where a return under *TMA s 8* or *8A* (see 78.5 above) or *11* has been delivered,

(1)   if it would be attributable to an error or mistake in the return as to the basis on which the liability ought to have been computed and the return was, in fact, made on the basis, or in accordance with the practice, generally prevailing at the time when it was made; or

(2)   unless either

    (*a*)   the loss of tax is attributable to fraudulent or negligent conduct by the taxpayer or a person acting on his behalf, or

    (*b*)   at the time when an officer of the Board either ceased to be entitled to enquire (see 78.11 above) into the return or informed the taxpayer of the completion of his enquiries, he could not have been reasonably expected, on the basis of the information so far made available to him (see below), to be aware of the loss of tax.

For the purposes of (2)(*b*) above, information is regarded as having been made available to the officer if it has been included in

   (i)   the return (or accompanying accounts, statements or documents) for the chargeable period concerned or for either of the two immediately preceding it, or

  (ii)   a partnership return (see 78.8 above), where applicable, in respect of the chargeable period concerned or either of the two immediately preceding it, or

 (iii)   any claim for the chargeable period concerned, or

 (iv)   documents, etc. produced for the purposes of any enquiries into such a return or claim,

or is information the existence and relevance of which could reasonably be expected to be inferred from the above-mentioned information or are notified in writing to the Revenue.

An objection to a discovery assessment on the grounds that neither (*a*) nor (*b*) in (2) above applies can be made only on an appeal against the assessment. (See 78.31 below for right of appeal.)

[*TMA s 29; FA 1994, ss 191(1), 199(2)(a)*].

See 78.20 below as regards due date of payment. The above provisions supersede the existing discovery assessment provisions of *TMA s 29(3)(4)* (see 5.3 ASSESSMENTS). As regards partnership businesses commenced (or deemed to commence) before 6 April 1994, the existing provisions continue to apply for all years of assessment before 1997/98. [*FA 1994, s 191(2)*].

78.16   **Amendment of partnership statement where loss of tax discovered.** Provisions broadly similar to those described in 78.15 above apply, for 1996/97 and subsequent years, as regards an understatement of profits or excessive claim for relief or allowance in a partnership statement (see 78.9 above), although the Revenue's remedy in this case is to amend the partnership statement, with consequent amendment of partners' self-assessments. [*TMA s 30B; FA 1994, ss 196, 199(2)(a), 19 Sch 6; FA 1995, s 115(5)*]. See 78.31 below for right of appeal.

78.17   **INTERIM PAYMENTS OF TAX ON ACCOUNT**

For 1997/98 and subsequent years (see below as regards 1996/97), where, as regards the year immediately preceding the year of assessment in question,

(*a*)   a person is assessed to income tax under *TMA s 9* (self-assessment—see 78.6 above),

(*b*)   the assessed amount exceeds any income tax deducted at source (including tax deducted under PAYE, taking in any deduction in respect of that year but to be made in a subsequent year but subtracting any amount paid in that year but in respect of a previous year, tax treated as deducted from, or as paid on, any income, and tax credits on dividends), and

(*c*)   the said excess (the relevant amount) and the proportion which the relevant amount bears to the assessed amount are not less than, respectively, a *de minimis* limit and a *de minimis* proportion, both to be prescribed by regulations,

the person must make two interim payments on account of his income tax liability for the year of assessment in question, each payment being equal to 50% of the relevant amount (see (*c*) above) and the payments being due on or before, respectively, 31 January in the year of assessment and the following 31 July. If the preceding year's self-assessment is made late or is amended, the relevant amount is determined as if the liability as finally agreed had been shown in a timeous self-assessment, with further payments on account then being required where appropriate. If a discovery assessment (see 78.15 above) is made for the preceding year, each payment on account due is deemed always to have been 50% of the relevant amount plus 50% of the tax charged by the discovery assessment as finally determined.

At any time before 31 January following the year of assessment, the taxpayer may make a claim stating his belief that he will have no liability for the year or that his liability will be fully covered by tax deducted at source and his grounds for that belief, in which case each of the interim payments is not, and is deemed never to have been, required to be made. Within the same time limit, the taxpayer may make a claim stating his belief that his liability for the year after allowing for tax deducted at source will be a stated amount which is less than the relevant amount, and stating his grounds for that belief, in which case each of the interim payments required will be, and deemed always to have been, equal to 50% of the stated amount. The maximum penalty for an incorrect statement made fraudulently or negligently in connection with either claim is the amount or additional amount he would have paid on account if he had made a correct statement. Interim payments of tax are subject to the same recovery provisions as any other payments of tax.

An officer of the Board may direct, at any time before 31 January following a year of assessment, that a person is not required to make payments on account for that year, such adjustments being made as necessary to give effect to the direction.

[*TMA s 59A; FA 1994, s 192; FA 1995, s 108; FA 1996, s 126(1), 18 Sch 2, 17(1)*].

Special provisions apply to determine the amount of interim payments in respect of 1996/97. Broadly, such payments are based on the excess of income tax assessed (as finally determined) for 1995/96, disregarding any excess of higher rate tax over basic rate tax on taxed investment income, over tax deducted at source for that year. That excess is then reduced by any amount by which any Schedule E liability exceeds tax deducted under PAYE or otherwise collected during 1995/96, to give the '*relevant amount*'. The first interim payment due, on 31 January 1997, is equal to such part of the relevant amount as consists of tax under Schedule A or any of Cases III to VI of Schedule D plus 50% of the balance of the relevant amount. The amount due on 31 July 1997 is equal to the remaining 50% of the balance of the relevant amount. Claims may be made as above to eliminate interim payments or make reduced payments. [*FA 1995, s 116(1), 21 Sch 2*]. The effect is that payment on account of tax under Schedule A and Schedule D, Cases III to VI is made in one instalment on 31 January 1997 and payment on account of tax under Schedule D, Case I or II (and Class 4 national insurance—see below) is made in two equal instalments on 31 January and 31 July 1997, no payment on account being required in respect of Schedule E tax or higher rate tax on taxed income (see the example at 78.18 below).

A personal pension payment (or retirement annuity contribution) made in 1996/97 but related back to 1995/96 (see 65.8 RETIREMENT ANNUITIES AND PERSONAL PENSION SCHEMES), although given effect in 1996/97 (see 78.33 below), is taken into account in determining the interim payment required for 1996/97. (Revenue Press Release 21 March 1996).

These provisions (and those described at 78.19–78.21 below) apply equally to Class 4 national insurance contributions. [*Social Security Contributions and Benefits Act 1992, s 16(1)(b); FA 1994, 19 Sch 45*].

78.18 *Example*

Calculation of interim payments for 1996/97

Kylie is a single person with the following income and gains for 1995/96.

	£
Profit as freelance writer (year to 30.4.94)	9,000
Salary and benefits from employment (tax paid under PAYE £3,350)	19,001
Rental income net of expenses	3,000
Untaxed interest (year to 5 April 1995)	400
Dividends (including tax credits £200)	1,000
Taxed interest (tax deducted £375)	1,500
Capital gains	6,300

She makes payments of £150 in 1995/96 under charitable covenants.

Assessments for 1995/96 are raised and agreed showing the following amounts of tax due.

Schedule D, Case II	2,250.00
Schedule E	359.00
Schedule A	1,196.40
Schedule D, Case III	160.00
Higher rate tax on dividends and taxed interest	425.00
Capital gains tax	120.00

Assuming she makes no claim either to eliminate or reduce interim payments (see 78.17 above), Kylie's interim payments under self-assessment for 1996/97 are calculated as follows.

(A) Relevant amount £(2,250 + 1,196.40 + 160.00)—the Schedule E liability and higher rate liability on taxed income being excluded for this transitional year only, the capital gains tax liability always being excluded £3,606.40

(B) Part of relevant amount consisting of tax under Schedule A or any of Cases III to VI of Schedule D £(1,196.40 + 160.00) £1,356.40

(C) Balance of relevant amount (i.e. Schedule D, Case II liability) £2,250.00

First interim payment due 31.1.97 ((B) + ½ of (C)) 2,481.40
Second interim payment due 31.7.97 (½ of (C)) 1,125.00

£3,606.40

A balancing payment/repayment will be due on 31.1.98 equal to the difference between the net income tax liability self-assessed for 1996/97 plus any capital gains tax liability and £3,606.40 paid on account (see 78.19 below).

Note

(a) This example disregards any liability for 1995/96 to Class 4 national insurance contributions. Any such liability should be added to the figures at (A) and (C), each interim payment for 1996/97 thus being increased by ½ the previous year's Class 4 liability.

78.19 FINAL PAYMENT (REPAYMENT) OF TAX

For 1996/97 and subsequent years, a final payment is due for a year of assessment if a person's combined income tax and capital gains tax liabilities contained in his self-assessment (see 78.6 above) exceed the aggregate of any payments on account (whether under *TMA s 59A*, see 78.17 above, or otherwise) and any income tax deducted at source. If the second total exceeds the first, a repayment will be made. Tax deducted at source has the same meaning as in 78.17(*b*) above (but see below as regards partnership tax for 1996/97).

The due date for payment (or repayment) is 31 January following the year of assessment. The one exception is where the person gave notice of chargeability under *TMA s 7* (see 78.4 above) within six months after the end of the year of assessment, but was not given notice under *TMA s 8* or *s 8A* (see 78.5 above) until after 31 October following the year of assessment; in such case, the due date is the last day of the three months beginning with the date of the said notice.

[*TMA s 59B(1)–(4)(7)(8); FA 1994, ss 193, 199(2)(a); FA 1996, ss 122(2), 126(2)*].

As regards partnership businesses commenced (or deemed to commence) before 6 April 1994, each partner's share of income tax assessed on the partnership for 1996/97 is treated for the purposes of determining that partner's final payment or repayment for that year as if it were tax deducted at source. [*FA 1995, s 116(1), 21 Sch 3*].

78.20   **Due date: further provisions.** Where a person's self-assessment is amended under the relevant provisions in 78.7, 78.13 or 78.16 above, the due date for the final payment (or repayment) is normally as in 78.19 above but is deferred, as regards any tax payable (or repayable) by virtue of the amendment and subject to the appeal and postponement provisions in 78.31 below, until, if later, 30 days after the date of notice of the amendment (but note that this does not defer the date from which interest accrues on unpaid tax—see 78.22 below).

Where an officer of the Board enquires into the return (see 78.11 above) and a repayment is otherwise due, the repayment is not required to be made until the enquiry is completed (see 78.13 above) although the officer may make a provisional repayment at his discretion. This does not affect the due date of repayment for interest purposes (see 78.23 below).

Unless otherwise provided, the due date for payment of tax charged by any assessment other than a self-assessment, e.g. a discovery assessment under *TMA s 29* (see 78.15 above), is 30 days after the date of the assessment (but see 78.22 below as regards interest on unpaid tax).

[*TMA s 59B(4A)(5)(6); FA 1994, ss 193, 199(2)(a); FA 1995, s 115(6); FA 1996, s 127*].

78.21   **SURCHARGE ON UNPAID TAX**

For 1996/97 and subsequent years, where income tax or capital gains tax has become payable in accordance with *TMA s 59B* (see 78.19 and 78.20 above) or *TMA s 55* (payment and postponement of tax pending appeal—see 78.31 below) and any of the tax remains unpaid more than 28 days after the due date, the taxpayer will be liable to a surcharge of 5% of the unpaid tax. A further 5% surcharge will be levied on any tax still unpaid more than six months after the due date. Interest will accrue on an unpaid surcharge with effect from the expiry of 30 days beginning with the date of the notice imposing the surcharge. An appeal may be made, within that same 30-day period, against the imposition of a surcharge as if it were an assessment to tax. The Commissioners may, on appeal, set aside the surcharge if it appears to them that, throughout the period from the due date until payment, the taxpayer had a reasonable excuse for not paying the tax. Inability to pay the tax will not be regarded as a reasonable excuse.

There are provisions to prevent a double charge where tax has been taken into account in determining certain tax-geared penalties; such tax will not be subject to a surcharge. The Board have discretion to mitigate, or to stay or compound proceedings for recovery of, a surcharge and may also, after judgment, entirely remit the surcharge.

These surcharge provisions also apply to an assessment for 1995/96 or an earlier year which is made on or after 6 April 1998.

[*TMA s 59C; FA 1994, ss 194, 199(2)(a); FA 1995, s 109*].

78.22   **INTEREST ON UNPAID TAX**

For 1996/97 and subsequent years (1997/98 and subsequent years as regards partnerships whose business commenced before 6 April 1994), interest is chargeable as follows on interim payments (see 78.17 above) and final payments (see 78.19 and 78.20 above) of income tax and capital gains tax which are made late, on tax chargeable on any assessment other than a self-assessment and on tax becoming payable under *TMA s 55* (payment and postponement of tax pending appeal—see 78.31 below). Interest accrues from the 'relevant date' (even if a non-business day) to the date of payment. For the two interim payments under 78.17 above, the *'relevant dates'* are the due dates, i.e. 31 January in the year of assessment and the following 31 July respectively. In any other case, the *'relevant date'* is 31 January following the year of assessment (with the one exception that where the due date of a final payment is deferred until three months after notice is given to deliver a return—see 78.19 above—the relevant date is identically deferred).

There are provisons to remit interest charged on interim payments to the extent that an income tax repayment is found to be due for the year. There are also provisions covering the situation where a taxpayer makes a claim to dispense with or reduce his interim payments (see 78.17 above) and the total income tax liability for the year is found to be such that interim payments should have been made or should have been greater. Interest is chargeable as if each interim payment had been equal to half the current year's liability or half the previous year's liability, whichever is less.

Interest is also chargeable under these provisions in respect of an income tax or capital gains tax assessment **for 1995/96 or an earlier year which is made on or after 6 April 1998,** the *'relevant date'* being 31 January following the year of assessment.

[*TMA s 86; FA 1995, s 110; FA 1996, s 131, 18 Sch 3, 17(1)(2)*].

Interest is also chargeable on late payment of surcharges (see 78.21 above) and penalties (see 78.25 below).

The rate of interest charged on unpaid tax will be in line with the average rate for borrowing. The rate paid on overpaid tax (see 78.23 below) will be in line with the average return on profits. (Revenue booklet SAT 2(1995), para 3.114).

Where the above provisions of *Sec 86* have effect, *Sec 88* (interest on tax recovered to make good loss of tax due to taxpayer's fault—see 6.6 BACK DUTY) no longer has effect. [*FA 1996, 18 Sch 4, 17(3)(4)*].

78.23   **INTEREST ON OVERPAID TAX**

The provisions of *Sec 824* (see 41 INTEREST ON OVERPAID TAX) are amended for 1996/97 and subsequent years (1997/98 as regards partnership businesses commenced (or deemed to commence) before 6 April 1994). A repayment of income tax (including an amount paid on account as in 78.17 above), or of a surcharge under *TMA s 59C* (see 78.21 above) or of a penalty incurred by an individual under any provision of *TMA* will be increased by an amount (a repayment supplement) equal to interest on the amount repaid for the period (if any) between the 'relevant time' and the date of repayment. The *'relevant time'* is,

(*a*)   as regards interim payments (see 78.17 above), the due date for the payment,

(*b*)   as regards income tax (other than that paid by way of interim payment), 31 January following the year of assessment, and

(*c*)   as regards a penalty or surcharge, the date following the expiry of 30 days from the date it was incurred or imposed,

or, in all cases, if later than the date given above, the date of payment. Other amendments are made to *Sec 824*, consequential to the introduction of self-assessment. [*Sec 824; FA 1994, ss 196, 199(2)(a), 19 Sch 41*]. Although the legislation is not clear on the matter, the Revenue have confirmed that, if interim payments for any year exceed the income tax liability for the year, repayment supplement runs from the due date for each of the interim payments (or, if later, the date on which they were paid).

The rate of interest paid on overpaid tax will be in line with the average return on profits. The rate charged on unpaid tax (see 78.22 above) will be in line with the average rate for borrowing. (Revenue booklet SAT 2(1995), para 3.114).

78.24   DATE OF PAYMENT BY CHEQUE

For the purposes of *TMA* and *Secs 824* (see 78.23 above), *825* and *826*, where any payment to an officer of the Board or the Board is received by cheque after 5 April 1996 and the cheque is paid on its first presentation to the bank on which it is drawn, the payment is treated as made on the date of receipt of the cheque by the officer or the Board. [*TMA s 70A; FA 1994, s 196, 19 Sch 22*]. See also 56.1 PAYMENT OF TAX.

78.25   PENALTIES

The penalty provisions described at 78.26 to 78.30 below apply for 1996/97 and subsequent years. See also 78.4 above for the penalty for failing to give notice of chargeability to tax and see 78.10 above and 78.34 below for penalties for failing to keep and preserve records. Penalties for special returns (see 58.4 PENALTIES) continue to apply as before, as do the statutory provisions on mitigation and limitation of penalties described at 58.7 PENALTIES.

For 1996/97 and subsequent years, a penalty under 78.4 above (notice of chargeability), 78.10 above (records), 78.17 above (payments on account), 78.34 below (records relating to claims) or any penalty under *TMA Pt X* (*ss 93–107*) carries *interest*, calculated from the due date to the date of payment. [*TMA s 103A; FA 1994, 19 Sch 33; FA 1995, s 115(8)*].

Consequential amendments are made to *TMA s 100B* (appeals against penalty determinations—see 58.6 PENALTIES). [*TMA s 100B; FA 1994, ss 196, 199(2)(a), 19 Sch 31; FA 1995, s 115(7)*]. See 53.19 PARTNERSHIPS as regards penalties under *TMA s 98B* in relation to European Economic Interest Groupings.

78.26   Failure to make return for income tax and capital gains tax. A person (the taxpayer) who fails to deliver a return when required to do so by notice under *TMA s 8* or *8A* (see 78.5 above) is liable to a penalty of £100. For continuing failure, a further penalty of up to £60 per day may be imposed by the Commissioners (but not at any time after the failure has been remedied) on application by an officer of the Board, such daily penalty to start from the day after the taxpayer is notified of the Commissioners' direction (but not for any day for which such a daily penalty has already been imposed). If the failure continues for more than six months beginning with the filing date (i.e. the due date for delivery of the return—see 78.5 above), and no application for a daily penalty was made within those six months, the taxpayer is liable to a further £100 penalty. If failure continues after the anniversary of the filing date, and there would have been a liability under *TMA s 59B* (see 78.19 above), based on a proper return promptly delivered, the taxpayer is liable to a further penalty of an amount not exceeding that liability. See 78.41 below as regards trustees.

If the taxpayer proves that his liability under *TMA s 59B*, based on a proper return promptly delivered, would not have exceeded a particular amount, his liability to penalties other than the daily and tax-geared penalties is reduced to that amount. On an appeal against either of the £100 penalties (reduced where appropriate), the Commissioners may either confirm the penalty or, if it appears to them that throughout the period of failure the taxpayer had a reasonable excuse for not delivering the return, set it aside.

[*TMA s 93; FA 1994, ss 196, 199(2)(a), 19 Sch 25*].

78.27   Failure to make partnership return. The same fixed penalties (including the daily penalty) as in *TMA s 93* (see 78.26 above) apply in the case of failure to submit a partnership return as required by a notice under *TMA s 12AA* (see 78.8 above). However, there is no tax-geared penalty and no provision for reducing the £100 penalties. Each person who was a partner at any time during the period in respect of which the return was required is separately liable to each penalty. The penalties apply by reference to failure by the representative partner, i.e. the partner required by the notice under *TMA s 12AA* to deliver the return, or his successor (see 78.8 above). Where penalties are imposed on two or more partners, an appeal cannot be made otherwise than by way of composite appeal by the representative partner (or successor). The same reasonable excuse provisions apply as under *TMA s 93* but by reference to the representative partner (or successor). [*TMA s 93A; FA 1994, ss 196, 199(2)(a), 19 Sch 26; FA 1996, s 123(8)–(11)*].

78.28   **Fraud or negligence.** The provisions of *TMA s 95* (tax-geared penalty for fraudulently or negligently delivering an incorrect return, accounts, etc.—see 58.3 PENALTIES) continue to apply, with consequential amendments, under self-assessment. [*TMA s 95; FA 1994, ss 196, 199(2)(a), 19 Sch 27*].

Similar provisions will apply as regards partnerships. They apply where a partner (the representative partner) delivers an incorrect partnership return (see 78.8 above), or, in connection with such a return, makes an incorrect statement or declaration or submits incorrect accounts, and either he does so fraudulently or negligently or his doing so is attributable to fraudulent or negligent conduct on the part of a 'relevant partner' (i.e. any person who was a partner at any time in the period covered by the return). Each relevant partner is liable to a penalty not exceeding the income tax (or corporation tax) underpaid by him as a result of the incorrectness. Where penalties are imposed on two or more partners, an appeal cannot be made otherwise than by way of composite appeal by the representative partner, or his successor (see 78.8 above). [*TMA s 95A; FA 1994, ss 196, 199(2)(a), 19 Sch 28; FA 1996, s 123(12)(13)*].

78.29   **Failure to produce documents.** A new penalty applies where a person fails to comply with a notice or requirement under *TMA s 19A* (notice requiring production of documents, etc. for purpose of Revenue enquiry into a return—see 78.12 above). He is liable to a fixed penalty of £50 and, for continuing failure after the fixed penalty is imposed, a daily penalty not exceeding the 'relevant amount'. No penalty may be imposed after the failure has been remedied. An officer of the Board may determine the daily penalty under *TMA s 100* (see 58.6 PENALTIES), in which case the '*relevant amount*' is £30, or may commence proceedings under *TMA s 100C* (see 58.6 PENALTIES) for determination of the penalty by the Commissioners, in which case the '*relevant amount*' is £150. [*TMA s 97AA; FA 1994, ss 196, 199(2)(a), 19 Sch 29; FA 1996, 19 Sch 3(4)*].

78.30   **ASSESSMENTS: PROCEDURE AND TIME LIMIT**

The procedure for the raising of assessments other than self-assessments is set out in *TMA s 30A*. All income tax falling to be charged by such an assessment may, even if chargeable under more than one Schedule, be included in one assessment. [*TMA s 30A; FA 1994, ss 196, 199(2)(a), 19 Sch 5*].

The normal time limit for the making of an assessment to income tax and capital gains tax for 1996/97 or a subsequent year is five years after 31 January following the year of assessment. [*TMA s 34(1); FA 1994, ss 196, 199(2)(a), 19 Sch 10*]. The extended time limit in cases of fraudulent or negligent conduct is twenty years after 31 January following the year of assessment. [*TMA s 36(1); FA 1994, ss 196, 199(2)(a), 19 Sch 11(1)*]. The latest time for assessing the personal representatives of a deceased person is three years after 31 January following the year of assessment in which death occurred. [*TMA s 40(1)(2); FA 1994, ss 196, 199(2)(a), 19 Sch 12*]. (For time limits applying before 1996/97, see 5.7 ASSESSMENTS and 6.4, 6.5 BACK DUTY.)

78.31 APPEALS

For 1996/97 and subsequent years, a right of appeal is conferred by *TMA s 31* against

(*a*) any assessment other than a self-assessment,

(*b*) an amendment by an officer of the Board of a self-assessment or partnership statement on enquiry into the return on which it is based (see 78.13 above),

(*c*) an amendment of a partnership statement where loss of tax is 'discovered' (see 78.16 above), and

(*d*) a disallowance, in whole or in part, of a claim or election included (by amendment or otherwise) in a return.

Written notice of appeal must be given within 30 days after the issue of the notice of assessment, amendment or disallowance. An appeal within (*b*) above against an amendment to a self-assessment cannot be heard and determined before the officer gives notice that he has completed his enquiries, if he has not already done so (see 78.13 above). An appeal within (*b*) to (*d*) above cannot question the exercise by the Revenue of the 'Crown Option' (see 78.13 above).

[*TMA s 31(1)–(3); FA 1994, ss 196, 199(2)(a), 19 Sch 7; FA 1996, 19 Sch 6, 22 Sch 4*].

Consequential amendments are made to *TMA s 50* (procedure on appeals heard by Commissioners—see 4.6 APPEALS). The Commissioners are given the power to vary the extent to which a claim or election included in a return is disallowed. [*TMA s 50(6)–(9); FA 1994, ss 196, 199(2)(a), 19 Sch 17; FA 1996, 19 Sch 7*]. Otherwise, the provisions in 4 APPEALS generally continue to apply.

Payment of tax pending appeal. The provisions of *TMA s 55* (payment and postponement of tax pending appeal—see 56.2 PAYMENT OF TAX) continue to apply in respect of

(i) an assessment other than a self-assessment, and

(ii) an amendment by an officer of the Board of a self-assessment on enquiry into the return on which it is based (see 78.13 above).

[*TMA s 55; FA 1994, ss 196, 199(2)(a), 19 Sch 18; FA 1996, 18 Sch 1, 17(1)(2)*]. See 78.22 above as to the date from which interest on unpaid tax will accrue.

78.32 CLAIMS, ETC.

A new formal procedure applies for 1996/97 and subsequent years as regards the making of claims and elections. A claim for a relief, allowance or tax repayment (other than one to be given effect by a PAYE coding adjustment) must be for an amount quantified at the time of the claim. Where notice has been given by the Revenue requiring the delivery of a return (see 78.5, 78.8 above), a claim, etc. (other than one to be given effect by a PAYE coding adjustment) can only be made at any time by inclusion in such a return (or by virtue of an amendment to a return) *unless it could not be so included* either at that time or subsequently. In the case of a partnership business, a claim or election under any of numerous provisions specified in *TMA s 42(7)* must be made by a partner nominated by the partnership if it cannot be included in a partnership return (or amendment thereto). See 78.34 below for provisions applying where a claim, etc. is made otherwise than by inclusion in a return.

Where a claimant discovers an error or mistake has been made in a claim (whether or not made in a return), he may make a supplementary claim within the time allowed for making the original claim.

[*TMA s 42; FA 1994, ss 196, 199(2)(a), 19 Sch 13; FA 1995, s 107(1)–(3)(7)(9); FA 1996, ss 128(1), 130*].

78.33   **Claims for relief involving two or more years.** The provisions described below are introduced to facilitate the administration under self-assessment of claims, elections etc. which affect more than one tax year. They generally deem the claim to be that of the later year (with consequent effect on the dates from which interest on unpaid and overpaid tax will run) and have effect where the year to which the claim relates, or is so deemed to relate, is 1996/97 or a subsequent year of assessment.

Relief for losses and other payments. A claim, under whatever provision, for a loss incurred or payment made (for example, a personal pension contribution) in one year of assessment to be carried back to an earlier year need not be made in a return, is treated as a claim for the year of loss or payment (the later year), must be for an amount equal to what would otherwise have been the tax saving for the earlier year (after taking into account any associated claims, see below, to which effect has already been given) and is given effect *in relation to the later year* by repayment, set-off etc. or by treating the said amount for the purposes of 78.19 above as a tax payment made on account.

See 78.17 above as regards special treatment of personal pension/retirement annuity payments for 1996/97 only. The Revenue have also confirmed that such payments made in 1996/97 and carried back will amend the 1995/96 assessment, thus preserving the pre-self-assessment treatment for a further year.

Averaging of farming or market gardening profits. Where a farmer or market gardener makes a claim under *Sec 96* to average the profits of two consecutive years of assessment (see 71.56(*a*) SCHEDULE D, CASES I AND II), the claim is treated as a claim for the later of those years. To the extent that the claim would otherwise have affected the profits of the earlier of those years, it must be for an amount equal to the tax that would consequently have become payable or repayable for that earlier year (after taking into account any associated claims, see below, to which effect has already been given) and is given effect *in relation to the later year* by increasing the tax payable or treating the said amount for the purposes of 78.19 above as a tax payment made on account, whichever is appropriate. Where the later year is included in a subsequent averaging claim, i.e. it is then averaged with the following year, the application of these provisions to the first claim is ignored in computing the effect of the subsequent claim.

Where, having made an averaging claim, a person then makes, amends or revokes any other claim for relief for either of the two years affected, which would be out of time but for the provisions of *Sec 96*, the claim, amendment or revocation is treated as relating to the later of the two years. To the extent that it relates to income for the earlier year, the amount claimed (or, as appropriate, the increase or reduction therein) must be equal to the tax that would consequently have become payable or repayable for that earlier year (after taking into account any associated claims, see below, to which effect has already been given) and is given effect *in relation to the later year* by increasing the tax payable or treating the said amount for the purposes of 76.18 above as a tax payment made on account, whichever is appropriate.

Election for post-cessation receipts to be treated as if received on date of discontinuance. Where a person elects under *Sec 108* (see 60.1 POST-CESSATION ETC. RECEIPTS AND EXPENDITURE) for a post-cessation receipt to be treated as if received on the date of cessation of trade rather than in the year of receipt (the later year), the election is treated as a claim for the later year, must be for an amount equal to what would otherwise have been the additional tax payable for the year of assessment (the earlier year) in which the sum is treated as received (after taking into account any associated claims, see below, to which effect has already been given) and is given effect *in relation to the later year* by increasing the tax payable for that year.

Backward spreading of lump sums for copyright etc. Where a claim is made under *Secs 534, 537A* or *538* to spread back lump sum receipts for copyrights etc. over more than one year of assessment (see 71.50 SCHEDULE D, CASES I AND II), the claim is treated as a claim for the year of assessment into whose basis period the lump sum would have fallen had the claim not been made (the payment year). To the extent that the claim would otherwise have affected the profits of an earlier year of assessment, it must be for an amount equal to the additional tax that would consequently have become payable for that earlier year (after taking into account any associated claims, see below, to which effect has already been given) and is given effect *in relation to the payment year* by increasing the tax payable for that year.

For the purposes of all the above provisions, two claims, elections etc. (including, where appropriate, amendments and revocations) by the same person are '*associated*' in so far as the same year of assessment is the earlier year in relation to both.

[*TMA s 42(11A), 1B Sch; FA 1996, s 128(2), 17 Sch*].

78.34 **Claims, etc. not included in returns.** Subject to any specific provision requiring a claim, etc. to be made to the Board, a claim or election made otherwise than in a return (see 78.32 above) must be made to an officer of the Board. The claim, etc. must include a declaration by the claimant that all particulars are correctly stated to the best of his information or belief. No claim requiring a tax repayment can be made unless the claimant has documentary proof that the tax has been paid or deducted. The claim must be made in a form determined by the Board and may require, *inter alia*, a statement of the amount of tax to be discharged or repaid and supporting information and documentation. In the case of a claim by or on behalf of a person who is not resident (or who claims to be not resident or not ordinarily resident or not domiciled) in the UK, the Revenue may require a statement or declaration in support of the claim to be made by affidavit.

A person who may wish to make a claim must keep all such records as may be requisite for the purpose and must preserve them until such time as the Revenue may no longer enquire into the claim (see below) or such enquiries are treated as completed. There is a maximum penalty of £3,000 for non-compliance in relation to any claim *actually made*. Similar provisions and exceptions apply as in 78.10 above as to the preservation of copies of documents instead of originals and the exception from penalty for non-compliance in relation to dividend vouchers, interest certificates etc. .

Provisions similar to those in 78.7 above (amendments of self-assessments) apply to enable a claimant (within twelve months of the claim) or officer of the Board (within nine months of the claim) to amend a claim, etc. The Revenue have power of enquiry into a claim, etc. (or amendment thereof) similar to that in 78.11 above (enquiries into returns). Notice of intention to enquire must be given by the first anniversary of 31 January following the year of assessment (or where the claim relates to a period other than a year of assessment the first anniversary of the end of that period) or, if later, the quarter day (meaning 31 January, 30 April etc.) next following the first anniversary of the date of claim, etc.. In the event of such an enquiry, they have power to call for documents similar to that in 78.12 above. Where an enquiry is in progress, an officer of the Board may give provisional effect to the claim, etc. (or amendment thereof) to such extent as he thinks fit. Provisions similar to those in 78.13 above apply as regards amendments of claims upon completion of an enquiry. The Revenue must give effect to such an amendment, by assessment if necessary, within 30 days after it is made. An appeal may be made against a Revenue amendment to a claim following an enquiry, written notice of appeal to be given normally within 30 days after the amendment is made (extended to three months where certain specified issues concerning residence are involved). If an amendment is varied on appeal, the Revenue have a further 30 days to give effect to the variation. Where a claim, etc. does not give rise to a discharge or repayment of tax (for example, a claim to carry forward trading losses), there are provisions as to disallowance of such claims on enquiry similar to those in 78.13 above in respect of claims, etc. included in returns, with appeal procedures similar to those above.

Appeals against amendments to claims are normally made to the General Commissioners. Where the claim was made to the Board or under certain specified provisions, appeal is to the Special Commissioners, and in other cases, there are rules, similar to those in 4.3 APPEALS, enabling the taxpayer to elect to bring the appeal before the Special Commissioners. If the taxpayer also has an appeal pending concerning an assessment and the appeals relate to the same income, both appeals must be to the same body of Commissioners.

[*TMA s 42(11), 1A Sch; FA 1994, ss 196, 199(2)(a), 19 Sch 13, 35; FA 1995, s 107(10)(11), 20 Sch; FA 1996, ss 124(4), 130(6)–(8), 19 Sch 8–10, 22 Sch 9*].

78.35 **General time limit for claims.** *Unless otherwise prescribed*, a claim relating to 1996/97 or a subsequent year with respect to income tax or capital gains tax must be made within five years after 31 January following the year of assessment to which it relates. [*TMA s 43(1); FA 1994, ss 196, 199(2)(a), 19 Sch 14*]. (See 17.4 CLAIMS and 86.6 TIME LIMITS—5 APRIL 1997 for the position as regards earlier years and as regards corporation tax.)

78.36 **JURISDICTION OF COMMISSIONERS**

As regards any proceedings relating to 1996/97 or a subsequent year (or for corporation tax any accounting period to which self-assessment applies), certain questions which may be in dispute on appeal (but not necessarily the entire appeal) must be determined by the Special Commissioners.

The questions concerned mirror those previously contained in *TMA s 31(3)* (see 4.3 APPEALS) and *s 47* and involve the application of provisions on SETTLEMENTS (80), DECEASED ESTATES (22), liability on transfers of assets abroad (see 3.8 ANTI-AVOIDANCE) and in respect of controlled foreign companies (see Tolley's Corporation Tax under Controlled Foreign Companies), and liability in relation to territorial sea and designated areas (see 51.13 NON-RESIDENTS AND OTHER OVERSEAS MATTERS). They also include any question as to the value for the purposes of capital gains tax or corporation tax on chargeable gains of any unquoted shares or securities in a UK resident company (any question for those purposes as to the value of any land or lease of land being determined by the relevant Lands Tribunal).

The above applies as regards appeals against a Revenue amendment, following enquiry, of a self-assessment, partnership statement (including an amendment on discovery—see 78.16 above), claim or election or a complete or partial disallowance of a claim or election (see 78.13 above and, as regards claims etc. not in returns, 78.34 above) and appeals against assessments other than self-assessments.

[*TMA ss 46B, 46D; FA 1996, 22 Sch 7*].

An appeal against an assessment made by the Board or under *Sec 350* (assessment to collect tax deducted from payments made—see 23.3 DEDUCTION OF TAX AT SOURCE) *must*, as previously, be to the Special Commissioners. [*TMA s 31(3); FA 1996, 22 Sch 4*]

Where, on an appeal against an amendment of a self-assessment or partnership statement, the question in dispute concerns a claim made to the Board or made under any one or more specified provisions, the question must be determined by the Special Commissioners. This effectively continues the rules previously in *TMA 2 Sch 2, 3*. The specified provisions cover double taxation relief, management expenses of the owner of mineral rights, exemptions for certain friendly societies, trade unions and employers' associations, and reliefs in respect of royalties, copyright payments etc. [*TMA s 46C; FA 1996, 22 Sch 7*].

Rules for assigning procedures to General Commissioners. Where the General Commissioners have jurisdiction, the rules for prescribing the appropriate division are adapted for self-assessment (see 4.3 APPEALS as regards previous rules and general practice). For proceedings relating to income tax or capital gains tax (except those concerning PAYE or partnerships or where the Board otherwise direct, see below), either the taxpayer or an officer of the Board (whichever commences the proceedings) may elect by notice to the other in writing for the proceedings to be heard in the division in which is situated either the taxpayer's place of residence, his place of business (as defined) or his place of employment (as defined and regardless of whether the proceedings are in connection with the employment). An officer may make the election if the taxpayer fails to exercise his right to do so when giving notice of appeal or otherwise commencing proceedings or at such later time as the Board allow. The taxpayer's election is irrevocable. The division for PAY AS YOU EARN (55) appeals is governed by the *Income Tax (Employments) Regulations 1993 (SI 1993 No 744)* except to the extent that the appellant elects as above. Proceedings relating to a partnership to which a partner is a party are brought before the division in the place where the partnership business is, or is mainly, carried on. For proceedings relating to corporation tax (or income tax where a UK resident company is a party), there are rules similar, but suitably modified, to those above for income tax and capital gains tax.

Notwithstanding the above, the Board may direct that specified proceedings be brought before the General Commissioners for a specified division. An officer of the Board must serve on the taxpayer written notice stating the effect of the direction, and the taxpayer may object in writing within 30 days of the notice being served, in which case the direction has no effect. The Board may also give directions for determining the appropriate division, other than in PAYE appeals, where there is no place of residence, business or employment (or corporation tax equivalents) as described above, or where that place would otherwise be outside the UK; procedure is as above except that the taxpayer has no right of objection.

The parties to proceedings may supersede the above rules by coming to an agreement that the proceedings be brought before the General Commissioners for a division specified therein. The rules are also subject to specified provisions in relation to which two or more parties other than the Revenue are involved (which have their own rules), to regulations under *TMA s 46A* (see 4.3, 4.6 APPEALS) and to regulations for capital gains tax appeals (see Tolley's Capital Gains Tax under Appeals).

[*TMA s 44(1)(2), 3 Sch; FA 1988, s 133(2); FA 1996, 22 Sch 10; 41 Sch Pt V(12)*].

78.37   ERROR OR MISTAKE RELIEF

The error or mistake relief provisions of *TMA s 33* (see 17.6 CLAIMS) continue to apply for 1996/97 and subsequent years. They apply by reference to an overcharge to tax under a self-assessment as well as under any other assessment. The time limit for claiming error or mistake relief, in the case of an income tax or capital gains tax assessment, is five years after 31 January following the year of assessment to which the return in question relates. No relief is available in respect of an error or mistake in a claim which is included in a return (but see 78.32 above as regards supplementary claims). [*TMA s 33; FA 1994, ss 196, 199(2)(a), 19 Sch 8*].

78.38   Error or mistake in partnership statement.

Error or mistake in partnership statement. Error or mistake relief is extended to cover an error or mistake in a partnership statement (see 78.9 above) by reason of which the partners allege that their self-assessments were excessive. The claim to relief must be made by one of the partners within five years after the filing date for the partnership return (see 78.8 above). Where the claim results in an amendment to the partnership statement, the Board will, by notice, make any necessary amendments to the self-assessments of all persons who were partners at any time in the period covered by the partnership statement. Otherwise, provisions similar to those in 17.6 CLAIMS apply, with appropriate modifications. [*TMA s 33A; FA 1994, ss 196, 199(2)(a), 19 Sch 9; FA 1996, 22 Sch 5*].

78.39   OVER-REPAYMENTS OF TAX

TMA s 30 (assessments to recover tax over-repaid—see 56.8 PAYMENT OF TAX) continues to apply but subject, for 1996/97 and subsequent years, to the same exceptions (modified as appropriate) as in 78.15 above (discovery assessments). The normal time limit for such an assessment is extended, if necessary, to the later of the end of the chargeable period following that in which the repayment was made and, where relevant, the day on which an officer of the Board's enquiries into a return (or amendment of a return) delivered by the person concerned are treated as completed (see 78.13 above). [*TMA s 30(1B)(5); FA 1994, ss 196, 199(2)(a), 19 Sch 4*].

78.40   COLLECTION AND RECOVERY

For 1996/97 and subsequent years, miscellaneous amendments are made to provisions covering the collection and recovery by the Revenue of tax, interest on tax, surcharges and penalties. The limit of £1,000 referred to in 56.3 PAYMENT OF TAX is raised to £2,000. [*TMA ss 65, 69, 70; FA 1994, ss 196, 199(2)(a), 19 Sch 19–21*].

78.41   LIABILITY OF RELEVANT TRUSTEES

In relation to income and chargeable gains, the *'relevant trustees'* of a settlement are the persons who are the trustees when the income arises or in the year of assessment in which the chargeable gain accrues and, in both cases, any persons who subsequently become trustees. Where the relevant trustees are liable to a penalty under the self-assessment regime, to interest on a penalty, to a surcharge and/or interest thereon, to make interim and final payments of income tax and payments on an assessment to recover tax over-repaid, or to interest on unpaid tax, the penalty etc. may be recovered (but only once) from any one or more of them. As regards penalties and surcharges (and interest on either), the liability of any relevant trustee is, however, restricted to those incurred after the day that he became a relevant trustee (a daily penalty being regarded as incurred on a daily basis). The 'reasonable excuse' provisions in 78.21 and 78.26 above have effect by reference to each of the relevant trustees. [*TMA ss 7(9), 107A; FA 1995, s 103*].

78.42   EMPLOYERS' OBLIGATIONS AND RETURNS

With effect for 1996/97 and later years, amendments are made to *The Income Tax (Employments) Regulations 1993 (SI 1993 No 744)*, i.e. the PAYE (55) Regulations, to ensure that sufficient information is given to employees, and in good time, to enable them to complete their self-assessments. The Revenue have undertaken to provide an education and assistance programme for employers, which includes a booklet SAT 3 'Self Assessment: what it will mean for employers' sent out to employers as part of an information pack in July 1995 and available free from tax offices. The amendments are as follows.

(a)   A time limit is introduced for providing an employee with form P60 (certificate of pay and tax deducted—see 55.10 PAYE). It must be provided no later than 31 May following the tax year to which it relates, commencing with 31 May 1997. [*SI 1993 No 744, reg 39; SI 1995 No 1284, reg 3*].

(b)   The deadline for submitting to the Revenue forms P9D and P11D (returns of benefits and expenses payments—see 55.9 PAYE and (c) below) is extended to no later than 6 July (previously 6 June) following the tax year, commencing with 6 July 1997. Within the same time limit, there is a new requirement for the employer to provide each employee for whom such a form is relevant with particulars of the information stated therein. Where an employer operates the Fixed Profit Car Scheme (FPCS) (see 75.43 SCHEDULE E), he must provide each scheme employee with either his taxable business mileage profit figure or the figures for allowances paid and mileage covered. An employer is not obliged to provide any of the above particulars to an employee who left during the tax year in question unless requested to do so within three years after the end of that tax year, the information to be provided within 30 days of receipt of the request if later than the normal 6 July deadline. [*SI 1993 No 744, regs 46(1), 46AA; SI 1995 No 1284, reg 4*].

(*c*)   In addition to the information specified at 55.9 PAYE, forms P11D and P9D must contain the following information:

    (i)   whether emoluments relating to business entertainment (see 71.54 SCHEDULE D, CASES I AND II) have been or will be disallowed as a deduction in the employer's business tax computations (see also 75.10(*b*) SCHEDULE E);

    (ii)   the cash equivalent of benefits provided, i.e. the amount chargeable to tax under the relevant legislation disregarding certain deductions which may be claimed by the employee in his own return, e.g. expenses 'wholly and necessarily incurred' and allowable professional subscriptions; and

    (iii)   particulars, including cash equivalents as in (ii) above, of payments made and benefits provided by third parties *by arrangement with the employer*. 'Arranging' includes guaranteeing or facilitating the payment or provision of the benefit—see Revenue booklet SAT 3(1995), paras 2.10 to 2.21. See also (*d*) below.

[*SI 1993 No 744, reg 46; SI 1995 No 1284, reg 4*].

(*d*)   Where a third party makes payments or provides benefits which if done by arrangement with the employer would have fallen to be included on forms P11D and P9D (see (*c*)(iii) above), he must provide particulars, including cash equivalents, to the *employee* by 6 July following the tax year. The third party is not obliged to provide such particulars to the Revenue unless required to do so by notice under *TMA s 15* (see below). [*SI 1993 No 744, reg 46AB; SI 1995 No 1284, reg 4*].

There are also changes to form P45 (for employees changing jobs—see 55.21 to 55.23 PAYE) from 6 April 1996. The form will contain an additional part for retention by the employee.

Penalties under *TMA s 98* for failure to provide information to the Revenue (see 58.4 PENALTIES) apply equally to failure to comply with the above requirements for providing particulars to employees.

The following amendments are made to the provisions of *TMA s 15* (employers' returns of employees' emoluments etc.—see 67.5 RETURNS) as respects payments made or benefits provided on or after 6 April 1996.

(i)   An employer will not have to include in his return information relating to any year of assessment if notice to deliver the return is given more than five years after 31 January following that year (replacing the six year rule previously in force).

(ii)   The return must include particulars of payments made/benefits provided to employees by third parties by arrangement with the employer, plus the name and business address of the third party; also, the name and business address of any person who, to the employer's knowledge, has made payments/provided benefits to an employee in respect of the employment other than by such arrangement.

(iii)   When providing particulars of benefits, cash equivalents must be given as at (*c*)(ii) above.

(iv)   The Revenue's power to require returns by third parties is extended.

[*TMA s 15; FA 1995, s 106*].

TAXATION OF NON-RESIDENTS

Non-UK residents are taxed on the shoreline principle, i.e. on income arising in or connected with the UK. New rules were introduced by *Finance Act 1995* to simplify the procedures for taxing non-residents and align them with self-assessment. See 51.5 to 51.7 NON-RESIDENTS AND OTHER OVERSEAS MATTERS for rules under *FA 1995, ss 126, 127, 23 Sch* which apply where a non-resident carries on a trade in the UK through a branch or agency and for the obligations and liabilities of his UK representative. See 68.24 SCHEDULE A for provisions of *FA 1995, s 40* on income from UK property. See 51.1 NON-RESIDENTS AND OTHER OVERSEAS MATTERS for provisions of *FA 1995, s 128* which limit the income tax chargeable on a non-resident's total UK income, and Tolley's Corporation Tax under Residence for corresponding provisions applicable to non-resident companies. See Revenue Tax Bulletin August 1995 p 237 for a summary of the rules for taxing various types of income of non-residents under self-assessment.

---

79   Self-Employed Persons

79.1   The individual in business, whether full-time or part-time, on his own or in partnership with others, is subject to particular tax legislation and practices. Such legislation etc. is included in this book under various subject headings and the following paragraphs indicate where the detailed provisions are to be found.

See also 37 INLAND REVENUE EXPLANATORY PAMPHLETS for the pamphlets which are obtained free from Inspectors of Taxes, etc. (including Pamphlets IR 28 'Starting in Business' and IR 57 'Thinking of Working for Yourself?').

See 75.24 SCHEDULE E—EMOLUMENTS as regards the distinction between employment and self-employment.

79.2   **ASSESSMENTS, ETC.**

Profits and income are assessed under SCHEDULE D, CASES I AND II (71). Special provisions relate to the opening and closing years of a business. Particular items of expenditure or receipt may, or may not, be included in the computation of taxable profits. Where a business is discontinued, see also 60 POST-CESSATION ETC. RECEIPTS AND EXPENDITURE. Partnership matters are dealt with under 53 PARTNERSHIPS. Farmers may elect for the HERD BASIS (34) to apply to their animals. Special provisions apply to UNDERWRITERS (89).

Where the accounts of a business do not include accruals and unbilled work, assessment may be on the CASH BASIS (12). Some transactions may result in an assessment because they contravene legislation on ANTI-AVOIDANCE (3).

For general assessment procedure, see SELF-ASSESSMENT (78). See also 5 ASSESSMENTS and 4 APPEALS.

Property. For 1995/96 and subsequent years, property income is assessed under SCHEDULE A (68). Previously, income from furnished letting was generally assessed under SCHEDULE D, CASE VI (74) but other property income was under Schedule A.

Assets. The acquisition or ownership of business assets may give rise to CAPITAL ALLOWANCES (10) as the tax substitute for the disallowable depreciation charge (if any) in the accounts. The disposal of assets may result in balancing adjustments, and also to an assessment to capital gains tax unless certain exemptions and reliefs apply.

Overseas. Income from trades etc. carried on wholly abroad is assessed under SCHEDULE D, CASES IV AND V (73). See 51.4 NON-RESIDENTS AND OTHER OVERSEAS MATTERS for non-residents trading in the UK.

Losses. If trading losses are incurred, relief may be obtained by various alternatives, see under 46 LOSSES.

79.3 EMPLOYEES

If staff are employed, then the regulations under the PAY AS YOU EARN (55) system must be complied with.

79.4 PAYMENT OF TAX

For times of payment, see under SELF-ASSESSMENT (78). See also 56 PAYMENT OF TAX and 42 INTEREST ON UNPAID TAX. Special provisions relate to the construction industry, see CONSTRUCTION INDUSTRY TAX DEDUCTION SCHEME (21).

See 14 CERTIFICATES OF TAX DEPOSIT for a method of payment.

79.5 PROVISION FOR RETIREMENT

Special legislation allows tax relief for payments made for RETIREMENT ANNUITIES AND PERSONAL PENSION SCHEMES (65).

79.6 SOCIAL SECURITY

Class 4 contributions will be levied and included with certain assessments of business profits, see 82 SOCIAL SECURITY. For partial deduction from total income, see 1.9 ALLOWANCES AND TAX RATES.

79.7 VALUE ADDED TAX

The detailed provisions of VAT are outside the scope of this book but registration is generally required when the 'taxable turnover' of the business will exceed £47,000 (£46,000 before 29 November 1995) in a year. For detailed information, see Tolley's Value Added Tax.

80 Settlements

Cross-references. See 3.8 ANTI-AVOIDANCE for transfer of assets abroad; 23 DEDUCTION OF TAX AT SOURCE generally and at 23.10 for annuities etc. and 23.17 for tax-free annuities under wills etc.; 64.5 RESIDENCE, ORDINARY RESIDENCE AND DOMICILE for residence of trustees; 78.4, 78.5, 78.41 for management provisions relating to trustees under SELF-ASSESSMENT.

80.1   Legislation providing specially for the tax treatment of settlements is dealt with at 80.13 to 80.29 below. The general tax treatment of trust income and trustees is in 80.2 to 80.12 below and, where appropriate, is applicable to trusts created by a will. For the income of estates of deceased persons in course of administration, see 22 DECEASED ESTATES.

The headings in this chapter are as follows.

80.2   **GENERAL POINTS ON TRUST TAXATION**

(a)   **Trustees** of settlements are taxed in their representative capacities under the Schedule appropriate to the income received (see 80.3 below). The income tax so charged is at the basic rate, but this is increased by 10% on the income of discretionary and accumulation trusts as described in 80.5 below. From 6 April 1993, dividends are generally taxed at the lower rate, with an additional charge being applied in the case of discretionary and accumulation trusts. From 6 April 1996, this is extended to 'savings income' generally (see 1.8(iii) ALLOWANCES AND TAX RATES).

(b)   **Beneficiaries** receive income from settlements which is treated as net of basic rate income tax (lower rate in the case of dividend income arising after 5 April 1993) because the trust etc. has suffered such tax. In the case of the trusts mentioned in 80.5 below, the income is regarded as having suffered tax at the sum of the basic and additional rates. The grossed-up amount of the income is treated as part of the total income of the beneficiary for tax purposes. If the total income of a beneficiary is high enough, he will suffer income tax at the excess of the higher rate(s) over the basic (or lower) rate on this grossed-up amount of the trust etc. income he receives. On the other hand he may be entitled to repayment of all or part of the tax accounted for by the trustees where that tax exceeds his own liability on the grossed-up amount of the income received. See also 80.5 below for tax repayments to non-residents.

For 1993/94 and subsequent years, in determining the income of beneficiaries, trustees' expenses, so far as properly chargeable to income (or so chargeable but for any express provisions of the trust) are to be treated as set against, broadly, income chargeable at the lower rate (see 1.8(iii) ALLOWANCES AND TAX RATES) in priority to other income. [Sec 689B; FA 1993, s 79(3); FA 1996, 6 Sch 16, 28, 41 Sch Pt V(1)]. See also 80.3, 80.5 below for rules on trustees' expenses.

(c)   **Scottish trusts.** For 1993/94 onwards, provided that the trustees are UK resident, the rights of a beneficiary of a Scottish trust are deemed to include an equitable right in possession to any trust income to which such a right would have arisen if the trust had effect under the law of England and Wales. [FA 1993, s 118]. This enables such beneficiaries to obtain the benefit of the application of the lower rate of tax to dividend income for 1993/94 onwards.

(d)   **Demergers.** For the income and capital gains tax treatment of shares received by trustees as a result of exempt demergers under Sec 213 (for which see Tolley's Corporation Tax under Groups of Companies), see Revenue Tax Bulletin October 1994 pp 162–165 and Revenue Capital Gains Tax Manual, CG 33900 et seq..

(e)   Trustees are also liable to capital gains tax.

80.3   **ASSESSMENTS ON TRUST INCOME**

General. Income may be assessed and charged on and in the name of any one or more of the trustees to whom settlement income arises and any subsequent trustees of the settlement. [FA 1989, s 151].

The untaxed income of a trust within Schedules A or D may be assessed on the trustee as the person receiving it [Secs 21(1), 59(1) and cf. Reid's Trustees v CIR CS 1929, 14 TC 512] but if, under his authority, it is paid direct to the beneficiary and he returns it under TMA s 13, he will not be assessable. [TMA s 76]. See also Williams v Singer HL 1920, 7 TC 387 (trustees not assessable where overseas income paid direct to non-resident beneficiary) and compare Kelly v Rogers CA 1935, 19 TC 692 (UK trustee of foreign trust held assessable in respect of overseas income as there was no ascertainable non-resident beneficiary entitled to the income) and Dawson v CIR HL 1989, 62 TC 301 (sole UK resident trustee of foreign trust with three trustees held not assessable in respect of income not remitted). See, however, 64.5 RESIDENCE, ORDINARY RESIDENCE AND DOMICILE as regards special residence provisions. Held in Pakenham HL 1928, 13 TC 573 that settlement trustees not assessable in respect of beneficiary's super-tax liability; presumably this will apply to excess liability.

Expenses of administering the trust are not deductible in the assessments on the trustee (Aikin v Macdonald Trustees C/E/S 1894, 3 TC 306; Inverclyde's Trustees v Millar CS 1924, 9 TC 14) even though deductible in arriving at the beneficiaries' income as at 80.8 below.

In computing the amount of a beneficiary's taxable income from a trust, for 1996/97 and subsequent years, and subject to Sec 689A (see below), trust expenses, in so far as they are properly chargeable to income (or would be so chargeable but for any express provisions of the trust) are to be set firstly against certain specified types of income (for example, foreign income dividends, stock dividends) which carry a notional and non-repayable tax credit, secondly against other 'savings income' chargeable at the lower rate (see 1.8(iii) ALLOWANCES AND TAX RATES) and finally against other income. [*Sec 689B; FA 1996, 6 Sch 16, 28*]. For 1993/94 to 1995/96 inclusive, expenses were set against dividend income chargeable at the lower rate (see 1.8(ii) ALLOWANCES AND TAX RATES) in priority to other income. [*FA 1993, s 79(3); FA 1996, 41 Sch Pt V(1)*]. See the examples at 80.4 below.

For 1996/97 and subsequent years, where a beneficiary is not liable to income tax on part of his share of the trust income, by virtue wholly or partly of his being non-UK resident or being deemed under a double tax agreement to be resident in a territory outside the UK, the management expenses otherwise deductible in computing his income are reduced in the same proportion as that which such non-taxable income bears to his full share of income (using in each case the income net of UK and foreign tax). Where the beneficiary's income tax liability is limited under the provisions at 51.1 NON-RESIDENTS AND OTHER OVERSEAS MATTERS, excluded income (see 51.1), other than that which is subject to deduction of tax at source, must be included in non-taxable income for the purposes of this apportionment. [*Sec 689A; FA 1996, 6 Sch 16, 28*].

A trustee may be required to make a return under *TMA s 8A* (as inserted by *FA 1990, s 90(1)*) of the income chargeable on him or on the settlor or beneficiaries. In practice, trustees normally make an annual statement of all the trust income, expenses, etc. from which is ascertained any tax payable by the trustees and each beneficiary's share of the net trust income. For 1996/97 and subsequent years, trustees are within the self-assessment regime (see 78.5, 78.6, 78.41 SELF-ASSESSMENT).

See 80.5 below for trustees' liability where trust income is accumulated.

80.4   *Examples*

A is sole life-tenant of a settlement which has income and expenses in the year 1996/97 of

	£	£
Property income		500
Taxed investment income (tax deducted at source £300)		1,500
Dividends	800	
Add Tax credits	200	
	—	1,000
		£3,000
Expenses chargeable to revenue		£400

The tax assessable on the trustees will be £120 (£500 at 24%). The expenses are not deductible in arriving at the tax payable by the trustees. The 20% lower rate band applies only to individual taxpayers and not to trustees, although the 20% rate on 'savings income' (see 1.8(iii) ALLOWANCES AND TAX RATES) does apply to trustees.

A is sole life-tenant of the above settlement and as such is absolutely entitled to receive the whole settlement income.

A's income for 1996/97 will include the following.

	£	£
Trust dividend and interest income (gross)	2,500	
Other trust income		500
Deduct: Lower rate tax (20%)	(500)	
Basic rate tax (24%)		(120)
	2,000	380
Deduct Expenses (note (*b*))	400	
Net income entitlement	£1,600	£380
Grossed-up amounts: £1,600 × $\frac{100}{80}$	£2,000	
£380 × $\frac{100}{76}$		£500

Notes

(*a*)   This income falls to be included in A's return even if it is not actually paid to him, as he is absolutely entitled to it. He will receive a tax certificate (form R185E) from the trust agents, showing two figures for gross income (£2,000 and £500), tax deducted (£400 and £120) and net income (£1,600 and £380).

(*b*)   The trust expenses are deducted from income falling within *Sec 1A* (savings income) in priority to other income (see 80.3 above).

(*c*)   That part of A's trust income which is represented by savings income (£1,600 net) is treated in A's hands as if it were savings income received directly by A. It is thus chargeable at the lower rate only, the liability being satisfied by the 20% tax credit, except to the extent, if any, that it exceeds his basic rate limit.

80.5   **DISCRETIONARY AND ACCUMULATION TRUSTS**

Income received by a trust which is to be accumulated, or payable at the discretion of the trustees or some other person, is, for 1993/94 and subsequent years, taxed at the 'rate applicable to trusts' rather than at the basic or (where otherwise applicable, see 1.8(ii)(iii) ALLOWANCES AND RATES) lower rate. The '*rate applicable to trusts*' is the sum of the basic and additional rates for the year, currently 34%. Before 1993/94, income was charged separately at the basic and additional rates. The special charge does not apply where (*a*) the trust is exempt as a charity (see 15 CHARITIES), (*b*) the income arises from property held for the purposes of certain retirement benefit or personal pension schemes, or (*c*) the income is income of any person other than the trustees or treated as income of a settlor (see 80.13 to 80.29 below). As regards (*c*), for 1995/96 onwards, the position is considered *before* the income is distributed, so that income paid to the settlor's unmarried minor children does not fall within the exemption. See also 44.5, 44.7 INTEREST RECEIVABLE as regards a similar charge in respect of deep discount and deep gain securities. The trustees may offset management expenses against trust income for the purpose of determining income chargeable at the rate applicable to trusts (before 1993/94, for determining income chargeable at the additional rate), although income so relieved remains subject to basic or lower rate tax. They must, however, be expenses properly chargeable to income (or which would be so chargeable but for any express provisions of the trust) (see *Carver v Duncan; Bosanquet v Allen HL 1985, 59 TC 125*). The order of set-off, subject to the apportionment of expenses in the circumstances described below, is determined by *Sec 689B* or, before 1996/97, by *FA 1993, s 79(3)* (see 80.3 above), disregarding for this purpose the fact that all income is in fact chargeable at the rate applicable to trusts (the tax saving being the difference between that rate and either the basic or lower rate—see the examples at 80.6 below). For 1993/94 and subsequent years, where the trust has income not chargeable to income tax, by virtue wholly or partly of the trustees being non-UK resident or being deemed under a double tax agreement to be resident in a territory outside the UK, the management expenses otherwise available for offset are reduced in the same proportion as that which such non-taxable income bears to the total trust income for the year. For 1996/97 and later years, where the trustees' income tax liability is limited under the provisions at 51.1 NON-RESIDENTS AND OTHER OVERSEAS MATTERS, excluded income (see 51.1), other than that which is subject to deduction of tax at source, must be included in non-taxable income for the purposes of this apportionment. 'Income' of the trustees for the purposes of these provisions includes income receipts by trustees (which will be treated as net of tax at the applicable rate (before 1993/94, basic rate tax)) (i) from personal representatives during administration of estate or (ii) consisting of building society interest and dividends paid or credited before 6 April 1991. It also included income apportioned from close companies prior to abolition of apportionment. [*Secs 686, 832(1); FA 1988, ss 24(4), 55(3); FA 1989, 17 Sch Pt V; FA 1990, 5 Sch 13; FA 1993, 6 Sch 8; FA 1995, 17 Sch 13; FA 1996, 6 Sch 13, 15, 28*].

Where the income of the trustees includes a non-qualifying distribution (within *Sec 233(2)*), liability is restricted to the difference between the rate applicable to trusts (as above) and the lower rate on so much of the distribution as otherwise falls to be assessed at the rate applicable to trusts. [*Sec 233(1B); FA 1993, 6 Sch 2*]. Where the income of non-resident trustees includes a qualifying distribution which is grossed up at the lower rate (see 1.8(iii) ALLOWANCES AND RATES), a credit is allowed for the lower rate tax (which may not, however, be repaid). [*Sec 233(1)(1A); FA 1993, 6 Sch 2; FA 1996, s 122(3)(4)*]. See *Sec 246D(4)* (introduced by *FA 1994, 16 Sch 1*) as regards receipt of foreign income dividends within *ICTA 1988, Pt VI, Ch VA*.

Discretionary payments by trustees, if treated for tax purposes as income of the payee, are treated as net after tax at the rate applicable to trusts (as above). For 1995/96 and later years, this also applies to payments to the settlor's unmarried minor children which are treated under *Sec 660B* as the settlor's income (see 80.17 below). [*Sec 687(1), (2)(a); FA 1995, 17 Sch 14*]. For whether a payment is received as income, see *Stevenson v Wishart and Others (Levy's Trustees) CA 1987, 59 TC 740*.

The tax treated as deducted from the payments is assessable on the trustees but the amount will be reduced by

(a)   tax already suffered by them at the rate applicable to trusts (or at the basic and additional rates) (or, in certain cases, at the excess of that rate over the lower rate of tax), and

(b)   tax suffered up to 5 April 1973, which for this purpose is deemed to be two-thirds of net amount of income available for distribution at 5 April 1973. [*Sec 687(2)(b), (3); FA 1989, s 96(2); FA 1990, 5 Sch 14; FA 1993, s 79(2), 6 Sch 9; FA 1994, 16 Sch 15; FA 1996, 14 Sch 35*].

By concession, tax paid by trustees of a non-resident trust may, subject to conditions, similarly be set against any liability of the settlor under *Sec 660B*. (Revenue Press Release 25 January 1996).

Employee trusts which are discretionary trusts are, by concession, and subject to conditions as regards returns and evidence, able to reclaim from the Revenue tax at the rate applicable to trusts on payments to employee beneficiaries made in any year which are taxed under Schedule E as emoluments in the hands of the employees without credit being available for the tax deducted from the payments (but limited to the total tax which the trustees would have available to set against their liability in respect of payments to beneficiaries in the year). (Revenue Pamphlet IR 1, A68).

Taxed overseas income included in payments by trustees may be certified as such by them and recipient may claim appropriate double tax relief within six years of the end of the tax year in which the income arose to the trustees. [*Sec 809*].

Payments to beneficiaries—concessionary reliefs. A non-resident beneficiary of a UK resident discretionary trust who receives income treated as net of tax may claim relief in respect of the tax exemption on certain UK or foreign securities (see 33.2 GOVERNMENT STOCKS, 23.12 DEDUCTION OF TAX AT SOURCE) or under the terms of a double taxation agreement, where such relief would have been available had the beneficiary received the income directly instead of through the trustees. Repayment may similarly be claimed where the beneficiary would not have been chargeable to UK tax in those circumstances. Relief is granted provided that the payment is out of income which arose to the trustees not earlier than six years before the end of the year of assessment in which the payment was made to the beneficiary. The trustees must have submitted trust returns supported by tax certificates and relevant information.

A similar concession applies where a beneficiary receives a payment from discretionary trustees which is income arising from a foreign possession (e.g. from a non-resident trust). A non-resident beneficiary who, had he received the income out of which the payment was made, would have been liable to UK tax thereon may claim relief under *Sec 278* (personal reliefs, see 51.11 NON-RESIDENTS AND OTHER OVERSEAS MATTERS) and may be treated as if he received the payment from a UK resident trust, but credit may be claimed only for UK tax actually paid by the trustees on the income out of which the payment was made. A UK resident beneficiary of a non-UK resident trust may similarly claim credit for tax actually paid by the trustees on the income out of which the payment was made as if the payment were from a UK resident trust. In all cases, the trustees must have submitted trust returns supported by tax certificates and relevant information, and have paid tax under *Sec 686* (see above) at the rate applicable to trusts on the UK income of the trust. No credit is given for tax treated as paid on income received by the trustees which would not be available for set-off under *Sec 687(2)* (see above) if that section applied, and that tax is not repayable.

(Revenue Pamphlet IR 1 (November 1995 Supplement), B18).

However, where the beneficiary is resident in a country with which the UK has a double taxation agreement, and the 'Other Income' Article in that agreement gives sole taxing rights in respect of such income to that country, the above concession does not apply, and the tax paid by the trustees will be repaid in full to the beneficiary, subject to the conditions in the Article being met. (Revenue Pamphlet IR 131, SP 3/86, 2 April 1986).

80.6   *Examples*

An accumulation and maintenance settlement set up by W for his grandchildren in 1979 now comprises quoted investments and an industrial property. The property is let to an

80.6   Settlements

engineering company. Charges for rates, electricity etc. are paid by the trust and recharged yearly in arrears to the tenant. As a result of the delay in recovering the service costs, the settlement incurs overdraft interest.

The relevant figures for the year ended 5 April 1997 are as follows.

	£
Property rents (Schedule A)	40,000
UK dividends (including tax credits of £1,000)	5,000
Taxed interest (tax deducted at source £700)	3,500
	£48,500

	£
Trust administration expenses—proportion chargeable to revenue	1,350
Overdraft interest	1,050
	£2,400

The tax liability of the trust for 1996/97 is as follows

	£	£
Schedule A £40,000 at 34%		13,600
Taxed interest (net)	2,800	
Net dividends	4,000	
Deduct Expenses	(2,400)	
	£4,400	
£4,400 grossed at $\frac{100}{80}$ = £5,500 @ 14% (34 – 20)		770
Tax payable by assessment		14,370
Add: Tax deducted at source		700
Tax credits		1,000
Total tax borne		£16,070

Notes

(a)   Expenses (including in this example the overdraft interest) are set firstly against income falling within *Sec 1A* (savings income). The effect is that the expenses, grossed-up at 20%, save tax at 14% (the difference between the 20% rate applicable to savings income and the rate applicable to trusts).

(b)   The net revenue available for distribution to the beneficiaries, at the trustees' discretion, will be £30,030 (£48,500 – £16,070 – £2,400).

M, the 17-year old grandson of W, is one of the beneficiaries to whom the trustees can pay the settlement income. The trustees make a payment of £3,000 to M on 31 January 1997. He has no other income in the year 1996/97 and is unmarried.

M's income from the trust is

	£
Net income	3,000.00
Tax at $\frac{34}{66}$	1,545.45
Gross income	£4,545.45

He can claim a tax repayment for 1996/97 of

	£
Total income	4,545
Deduct Personal allowance	3,765
	£780

Tax thereon at 20% (within lower rate band)	156.00
Tax accounted for by trustees	1,545.45
Repayment due	£1,389.45

Note

(a)   Unlike the position with interest in possession trusts (see 80.4 above), no distinction is made between dividend and interest income and other income in the beneficiary's hands, the full amount of the payment to him having suffered tax at a single rate of 34% in the hands of the trustees.

80.7   PERSONAL POSITION OF TRUSTEE

Annual remuneration paid to a trustee under a will or settlement is an annual payment within Case III of Schedule D from which tax is deductible at source, and is not chargeable on him under any other case or schedule (*Baxendale v Murphy KB 1924, 9 TC 76; Hearn v Morgan KB 1945, 26 TC 478* and cf. *Clapham's Trustees v Belton Ch D 1956, 37 TC 26*). Where a trustee is empowered to, and does, charge for his professional services, his fees are part of his receipts for Schedule D, Case II purposes (*Jones v Wright KB 1927, 13 TC 221*) even where he is also a beneficiary (*Watson & Everitt v Blunden CA 1933, 18 TC 402*).

80.8   INCOME OF BENEFICIARIES

In the case of life-tenants and those with similar interests in trust income, the beneficiary's income for tax purposes (see 80.2(*b*) above) is the grossed-up amount of the net income after deducting any trust outgoings payable out of the income (*Lord Hamilton of Dalzell CS 1926, 10 TC 406; Murray v CIR CS 1926, 11 TC 133; MacFarlane v CIR CS 1929, 14 TC 532*)—see 80.3 above re trust expenses generally. In other cases, the tax treatment of payments under a trust depends on the circumstances. Payments to a parent for the maintenance of children were held to be income of the children assessable on the parent in *Drummond v Collins HL 1915, 6 TC 525* (remittances to mother as guardian of minors, all resident in UK, of income of American trust) and *Johnstone v Chamberlain KB 1933, 17 TC 706*. Payments for the rates etc. and the super-tax of a beneficiary and payments for the maintenance of beneficiaries were held to be income in their hands in *Lord Tollemache v CIR KB 1926, 11 TC 277; Shanks v CIR CA 1928, 14 TC 249; Waley Cohen v CIR KB 1945, 26 TC 471*. In a number of cases, the outgoings of a residence provided for the beneficiary, grossed-up, have been held to be income of the beneficiary (*Donaldson's Exors v CIR CS 1927, 13 TC 461; Sutton v CIR CA 1929, 14 TC 662; Lady Miller v CIR HL*

80.9 Settlements

1930, 15 TC 25). Income applied in reducing charges on the trust fund was held not to be income of the life-tenant (*Wemyss CS 1924, 8 TC 551*). Shares allotted to trustees in consideration of arrears of dividends were held to be income and not capital of the trust fund (*In re MacIver's Settlement Ch D 1935, 14 ATC 571*).

Interest on money loaned interest-free, subject to conditions and repayable on demand, by the employer to a trust for the benefit of an employee held to be emoluments within Schedule E (*O'Leary v McKinlay Ch D 1990, 63 TC 729*).

The tax treatment of income accumulated (e.g. during the minority of a beneficiary) has arisen in a number of cases. The test is whether the beneficiary's interest under the trust is vested or contingent. If vested, the accumulated income is his income as it arises. (N.B. If the accumulated income is the beneficiary's, 80.5 above does not apply. If the interest was contingent, see 80.12 below). Decision involves the general law of trusts, outside the scope of this book. For tax cases in which the accumulated income has been treated as income of the beneficiary, see *Gascoigne v CIR KB 1926, 13 TC 573; Stern v CIR HL 1930, 15 TC 148*, and *Brotherton v CIR CA 1978, 52 TC 137*; for cases where the income was held not to be the beneficiary's, see *Stanley v CIR CA 1944, 26 TC 12* (where the position under the *Trustee Act 1925, s 31* was considered); *Cornwell v Barry Ch D 1955, 36 TC 268*, and *Kidston CS 1936, 20 TC 603*. For the release of accumulated income on the termination of a trust, see *Hamilton-Russell's Exors v CIR CA 1943, 25 TC 200*, and on termination of legally permissible period of accumulation, see *Duncan v CIR CS 1931, 17 TC 1*.

See also 22 DECEASED ESTATES.

80.9 ANNUITIES AND OTHER ANNUAL PAYMENTS

Annuities and other annual payments under settlements or wills are subject to the normal rules for DEDUCTION OF TAX AT SOURCE (23). Annual remuneration to a trustee is an annual payment for this purpose (see 80.7 above). Where the annuity etc. is paid out of the capital of the trust fund, the tax deducted is assessed on the trustees under *Sec 350*. (Where tax is not deducted, the beneficiary may be assessed under Case III.) Payments out of capital may be directed or authorised by the settlor or testator, as where he directs a stipulated annual amount to be paid out of capital (*Jackson's Trustees v CIR KB 1942, 25 TC 13; Milne's Exors v CIR Ch D 1956, 37 TC 10*) or authorises the beneficiary's income to be augmented to a stipulated amount out of capital (*Brodie's Trustees v CIR KB 1933, 17 TC 432; Morant Settlement Trustees v CIR CA 1948, 30 TC 147*), or direct payments out of capital for the maintenance etc. of the recipient (*Lindus & Hortin v CIR KB 1933, 17 TC 442; Esdaile v CIR CS 1936, 20 TC 700*) even though discretionary (*Cunard's Trustees v CIR CA 1945, 27 TC 122*). For position if annuity exceeds income of fund on which charged, see *Lady Castlemaine KB 1943, 25 TC 408*. Annuities directed to be paid out of capital but paid out of accumulated income forming part of the capital were held to have been paid out of income (*Postlethwaite v CIR Ch D 1963, 41 TC 244*).

For 'free of tax' annuities, see 23.17 DEDUCTION OF TAX AT SOURCE.

80.10 FOREIGN TRUST INCOME

There are no special provisions for the income tax treatment of foreign trust income. For the liability of trustees within the jurisdiction as regards foreign trust income, see the case of *Williams v Singer, Dawson v CIR* and *Kelly v Rogers* at 80.3 above.

The income of a life-tenant of a foreign trust fund depends first on the nature of his interest under the relevant foreign law. See for this the cases of *Archer-Shee v Baker HL 1927, 11 TC 749* and *Garland v Archer-Shee HL 1930, 15 TC 693*, dealing with the same life-tenancy. In the first, with no evidence as to the foreign law, the life-tenant was held to be assessable on the basis that the investments forming part of the fund were separate foreign possessions or securities. In the second case, relating to later years, it was held that having regard to evidence given as to the foreign law, she was assessable on the basis that the income was from a single foreign possession. (N.B. The decisions have lost some of their practical importance because of subsequent changes in the basis rules of Schedule D, Cases IV and V, but the principles established remain important.) See also *Nelson v Adamson KB 1941, 24 TC 36* and *Inchyra v Jennings Ch D 1965, 42 TC 388*. Stock dividends received by trustees of an American trust fund were part of the trust income under the relevant American law but held not to be income of a UK life-tenant, as not of an income nature under UK principles (*Lawson v Rolfe Ch D 1969, 46 TC 199*).

Discretionary remittances from foreign trustees are assessable and become income when the discretion is exercised (*Drummond v Collins HL 1915, 6 TC 525*) but cf. *Lawson v Rolfe*, see 73.3 SCHEDULE D, CASES IV AND V.

See 51.14 NON-RESIDENTS AND OTHER OVERSEAS MATTERS for unremittable foreign income and 73 SCHEDULE D, CASES IV AND V for assessments on overseas income generally.

80.11 **CLAIMS BY TRUSTEES AND BENEFICIARIES**

Only such claims as relate to the Trust can be made by the trustee—except as regards incapacitated persons for whom he is assessable, e.g., under *TMA s 72*. [*TMA s 42(6)*]. Beneficiaries other than these must claim in their own (or husband's) name. See 80.2(*b*) and 80.5 above. Beneficiaries claiming refund on their share of trust income must each make a separate claim showing their total income from all sources and tax paid on it.

In claim by non-resident life-tenants of residue subject to annuity, held that (where no 'appropriation') latter not to be treated as paid out of UK taxed income but rateably out of all investments. (*Crawshay CA 1935, 19 TC 715*).

80.12 **CLAIMS FOR PERSONAL ALLOWANCES ETC. ON INCOME UP TO 1968/69—from specified 'Contingent Interests' on obtaining a specified age or marrying.**

Under *ITA 1952, s 228*, where an individual has an interest under a will or settlement that is contingent on his or her attaining a specified age or marrying, and income is directed to be accumulated meantime, claims by that individual for personal allowances etc. may be made within six years after the end of the tax year in which the contingency happens, in respect of all income so compulsorily accumulated prior to 6 April 1969. [*ICTA 1970, 14 Sch 1*]. Such claims cannot be made in respect of income which is deemed to be the income of the settlor as below. See 41 INTEREST ON OVERPAID TAX.

Where income is legally vested in beneficiaries, relief as above is refused; it is important, therefore, to ascertain whether income legally vested or contingent (*Roberts v Hanks KB 1926, 10 TC 351; Jones v Down KB 1936, 20 TC 279*), and when the 'contingency' happens (*Stonely v Ambrose KB 1925, 9 TC 389*, and *Lynch v Davies Ch D 1962, 40 TC 511*).

The section applies only when the contingency is the claimant's attainment of a specified age or marriage (*Bone CS 1927, 13 TC 20* and *White v Whitcher KB 1927, 13 TC 202*). Claimant's right must depend solely on happening of one of these contingencies *and on nothing else*, and no claim can be made if right to receive income is wholly at trustee's discretion (*Dain v Miller KB 1934, 18 TC 478*, and see *Maude-Roxby CS 1950, 31 TC 388*). See also *Cusden v Eden KB 1939, 22 TC 435* as to accumulations.

Tax on income accumulated but directed to be capitalised on happening of contingency may nevertheless be claimed under this section (*Dale v Mitcalfe CA 1927, 13 TC 41*).

The amount recovered belongs to the beneficiary (*Fulford v Hyslop Ch D 1929, 8 ATC 588*). In *Chamberlain v Haig Thomas KB 1933, 17 TC 595* where accumulations directed (from

80.13   Settlements

1913 onwards) for infant children subject to power of appointment (which not in fact exercised until 1922), section held to apply to income of intervening period.

80.13   **LIABILITY OF SETTLOR**

In 80.16, 80.17 below, there are set out the provisions of *Secs 660A, 660B*, introduced by *FA 1995, s 74, 17 Sch*, which treat the income of settlements as the income of the settlor in certain circumstances. **These provisions apply for 1995/96 and subsequent years to all settlements, whenever made.** [*FA 1995, s 74(2)*]. They are intended as a simplification of those in *Secs 660–676, 679–681* and *683–685* which applied for 1994/95 and earlier years and which they replaced (the earlier rules being covered at 80.20, 80.28 below). The rules in *Secs 677, 678* dealing with loans etc. to the settlor continue to apply and are covered at 80.18 below. The Finance Act 1995 provisions are divided into two areas:

(*a*)   income under settlements where settlor retains an interest [*Sec 660A*] (see 80.16 below); and

(*b*)   payments out of a settlement to unmarried minor children of the settlor [*Sec 660B*] (see 80.17 below).

Settlors have an obligation to notify their tax office of any liability under the new provisions even if they do not normally receive a tax return. (Revenue Press Release 4 January 1995).

80.14   **The charge to tax** under *Secs 660A, 660B* is under **Schedule D, Case VI**. Income treated under these provisions as income of the settlor is deemed to be the top slice of his income, but before taking into account income chargeable under *Sec 148* (payments on loss of office, see 19.5 COMPENSATION FOR LOSS OF EMPLOYMENT) or *Sec 547(1)(a)* (life assurance gains, see 45.13 LIFE ASSURANCE POLICIES). The same deductions and reliefs are allowed as if the income had actually been received by the settlor. [*Sec 660C; FA 1995, 17 Sch 1*]. The settlor is entitled to recover the tax paid from any trustee or any person to whom the income is payable under the settlement, and to that end can obtain from the Revenue a certificate specifying the amount of income charged on him and the tax paid. If the settlor receives a tax repayment by virtue of setting an allowance or relief against income chargeable on him under these provisions, he must pay it over to the trustee or any person(s) to whom the income is payable under the settlement, with the General Commissioners having the final decision on any question as to the amount payable or how it should be apportioned. Nothing in these provisions precludes tax being charged on the trustees as persons by whom any income is received. [*Sec 660D; FA 1995, 17 Sch 1*].

Revenue information powers. An officer of the Board can, by notice, require from any party to a settlement such particulars as he thinks necessary (subject to penalty under *TMA s 98* for non-compliance). [*Sec 660F; FA 1995, 17 Sch 1, 23*]. See *Cutner v CIR QB 1974, 49 TC 429* and *Wilover Nominees v CIR CA 1974, 49 TC 559* in connection with similar information powers under the pre-Finance Act 1995 provisions.

80.15   **Definitions etc.** The following apply for the purposes of *Secs 660A, 660B*, covered in 80.16, 80.17 below.

(*a*)   '*Settlement*' includes any disposition, trust, covenant, agreement, arrangement or transfer of assets. [*Sec 660G(1); FA 1995, 17 Sch 1*]. The latter includes a gift of shares (*Hood Barrs v CIR CA 1946, 27 TC 385*) or of National Savings Bank deposit (*Thomas v Marshall HL 1953, 34 TC 178*). For shares in new company issued at par, see *Butler v Wildin Ch D 1988, [1989] STC 22*. See also *Yates v Starkey CA 1951, 32 TC 38* re Court Orders and *Harvey v Sivyer Ch D 1985, 58 TC 569* re provision for children whether under compulsion or not. The creation of a new class of preference shares in a company, and their allotment to the wives of the directors, who had previously also been the sole shareholders, was held to be a settlement by the directors (*Young v Pearce; Young v Scrutton Ch D, 1996 STI 541*).

Parent's release of expectant life interest is a settlement (*Buchanan CA 1957, 37 TC 365*) and see *D'Abreu v CIR Ch D 1978, 52 TC 352*.

A distinction can be made between arrangements which amount to a settlement and bona fide commercial transactions without any element of bounty which do not (*Copeman v Coleman KB 1939, 22 TC 594; Bulmer v CIR Ch D 1966, 44 TC 1*) and this notwithstanding that tax avoidance was a motive for the transactions (*CIR v Plummer HL 1979, 54 TC 1*). See also *CIR v Levy Ch D 1982, 56 TC 67*. For whether 'arrangements' are a settlement, see also *Prince-Smith KB 1943, 25 TC 84; Pay Ch D 1955, 36 TC 109; Crossland v Hawkins CA 1961, 39 TC 493; Leiner Ch D 1964, 41 TC 589; Wachtel Ch D 1970, 46 TC 543; Mills v CIR HL 1974, 49 TC 367; Chinn v Collins HL 1980, 54 TC 311; Butler v Wildin Ch D 1988, 61 TC 666.*

For 'property comprised in a settlement', see *Vestey v CIR HL 1949, 31 TC 1*. Where the settlement is of shares in a company controlled by the settlor, the assets of the company are not comprised in the settlement (*Chamberlain v CIR HL 1943, 25 TC 317; Langrange Trust v CIR HL 1947, 28 TC 55*).

Where the trust is imperfect, income not disposed of reverts to the settlor (*Hannay's Exors v CIR CS 1956, 37 TC 217*).

A foreign settlement of UK income by a non-resident was held to be within the ambit of the pre-Finance Act 1995 settlements legislation (*Kenmare HL 1957, 37 TC 383*).

(*b*) 'Settlor', in relation to a settlement, means any person by whom the settlement was made. A person is deemed to have made a settlement if he has made or entered into it directly or indirectly and/or has provided or undertaken to provide funds directly or indirectly for the purpose of the settlement or has made reciprocal arrangements for another person to make or enter into the settlement. [*Sec 660G(1)(2); FA 1995, 17 Sch 1*]. See *Crossland v Hawkins CA 1961, 39 TC 493, Leiner Ch D 1964, 41 TC 589* and *Mills HL 1974, 49 TC 367.*

(*c*) If there is *more than one settlor*. Each is to be treated as the sole settlor, but only in respect of income or property he has himself provided, directly or indirectly. [*Sec 660E; FA 1995, 17 Sch 1*].

(*d*) 'Income arising under a settlement' includes any income chargeable to income tax, by deduction or otherwise, or which would have been so chargeable if received in the UK by a person domiciled, resident and ordinarily resident in the UK, but not income on which the settlor, if he were himself entitled to it, would not have been chargeable by reason of non-domicile, non-residence etc. (but such income *is* treated as arising under the settlement in a year of assessment in which it is subsequently remitted to the UK if, were the settlor entitled to the income when remitted, he would be chargeable to income tax by reason of his UK residence). [*Sec 660G(3)(4); FA 1995, 17 Sch 1*].

(*e*) *Payment of inheritance tax by trustees on assets put into settlement by settlor*. Where the trustees have power to pay, or do in fact pay, inheritance tax on assets which the settlor puts into the settlement, the Revenue will not argue that such a power renders that income the settlor's income for income tax purposes. This is because both the settlor and the trustees are liable for such inheritance tax. (Revenue Pamphlet IR 131, SP 1/82, 6 April 1982).

80.16 Settlements

SETTLOR RETAINING AN INTEREST [*Sec 660A; FA 1995, 17 Sch 1*]

See also 80.13, 80.15 above.

Income arising under a settlement during the life of the settlor is treated for all income tax purposes as the income of the settlor (and not of any other person), *unless* the income arises from property in which the settlor has no interest (see below).

For the purposes of these provisions, a settlement does not include:

(*a*)   an outright gift between spouses of property from which income arises (but a gift which does not carry a right to the whole of that income is not excluded, nor is a gift of a right to income); or

(*b*)   an irrevocable allocation of pension rights between spouses under a relevant statutory scheme (see 66.1 RETIREMENT SCHEMES).

As regards (*a*) above, a gift is not an outright gift if it is conditional or if the property or any 'derived property' could in any circumstances become payable to the donor or be applied for his benefit.

The following income is excluded from these provisions:

(i)   income arising under a marriage settlement made between spouses after separation, divorce or annulment, being income payable to or for the benefit of the spouse being provided for;

(ii)   annual payments by an individual for *bona fide* commercial reasons in connection with his trade, profession or vocation; and

(iii)   covenanted payments to charity (as defined at 15.6 CHARITIES).

A settlor has an *interest in property* if that property or any 'derived property' could in any circumstances become payable to the settlor or his spouse or be applied for the benefit of either. For this purpose, a spouse does not include a possible future spouse, a separated spouse or a widow/widower of the settlor. A settlor does *not* have an interest in property if it could become so payable or be so applied only in the event of

(A)   the bankruptcy of a current or potential beneficiary,

(B)   an assignment of, or charge on, the property or 'derived property' being made or given by a current or potential beneficiary,

(C)   in the case of a marriage settlement, the death of both spouses and all or any of their children, or

(D)   the death of a child of the settlor who has become beneficially entitled to the property etc. at an age not exceeding 25,

or if (and so long as) there is a beneficiary alive under the age of 25 during whose life the property etc. cannot become so payable etc. except in the event of the beneficiary becoming bankrupt or assigning or charging his interest.

'*Derived property*', in relation to any property, means income from that property or any other property directly or indirectly representing proceeds of, or of income from, that property or income therefrom.

CHILDREN'S SETTLEMENTS [*Sec 660B; FA 1995, 17 Sch 1*]

See also 80.13, 80.15 above.

Income arising under a settlement which during the life of the settlor is paid to or for the benefit of an unmarried minor child (i.e. a child under 18, including a stepchild or illegitimate child) of the settlor in any year of assessment is treated for all income tax purposes as income of the settlor (and not of any other person) for that year. However, this does *not* apply for any tax year if the aggregate amount that would otherwise be treated as the settlor's income for that year in relation to any particular child does not exceed £100. Nor does it apply if the income falls to be treated under 80.16 above as that of the settlor.

Retained or accumulated income. Any payment under the settlement to or for the child is taken into account as above to the extent that there is available retained or accumulated income, i.e. aggregate income arising since the settlement was entered into exceeds the aggregate amount of such income which has been

(*a*)   treated as income of the settlor or a beneficiary, or

(*b*)   paid (as income or capital) to or for a beneficiary other than an unmarried minor child of the settlor, or

(*c*)   used to pay expenses of the trustees which were properly chargeable to income (or would have been so chargeable but for express provisions of the trust).

Any provision by a parent for his child may create a settlement, whether made under compulsion or merely under parental obligation (*Harvey v Sivyer Ch D 1985, 58 TC 569*), although in practice the Revenue do not treat payments made under a Court Order as being under a settlement for this purpose. '*Stepchild*' includes a child of the wife by a previous marriage (*CIR v Russell CS 1955, 36 TC 83*).

80.18   **CAPITAL SUMS, LOANS and REPAYMENTS OF LOANS TO SETTLOR from SETTLEMENT OR CONNECTED BODY CORPORATE—**
treated as income of settlor to extent that settlement has undistributed income.
[*Secs 677, 678*]

Where in any year of assessment the trustees of a settlement pay any 'capital sum' to the settlor or spouse (or to the settlor jointly with another person), such an amount (grossed up at the rate applicable to trusts) is treated as income of the settlor to the extent that it falls within the amount of 'income available in the settlement' up to the end of that year of assessment or, to the extent that it does not fall within that amount, to the end of the next and subsequent years of assessment up to a maximum of eleven years after the year of payment. [*Sec 677(1)(6)(9); FA 1993, 6 Sch 7*]. There is a corresponding deduction for any amount included in the settlor's income under *Sec 421* (see 28.3(*a*) EXCESS LIABILITY) in respect of a loan. [*Sec 677(3)*]. See also 80.29 below.

Any 'capital sum' paid before 6 April 1981 and not treated as income under these provisions before that date is for these purposes treated as having been paid on that date. [*FA 1982, s 63(4)*].

'*Income available in the settlement*' up to the end of any tax year is the aggregate amount of income arising under the settlement (see 80.15 above), for that and any previous year, which has not been distributed (see 80.20 below), less

(*a*)   any amount of that income which has already been 'matched' against a capital payment for assessment on the settlor (see above), and

(*b*)   any income taken into account under these provisions in relation to capital sums previously paid to the settlor, and

(*c*)   sums treated as income of the settlor under *Secs 671–674A, Sec 683* (see 80.23–80.26, 80.28 below) or *Secs 660A, 660B* (see 80.13–80.17 above), and

(*d*)   sums not allowed as an income deduction to the settlor under *Sec 676* (see 80.27 below), and (*e*) sums from an accumulation settlement for children treated as income of the settlor under *Sec 664(2)(b)* (see 80.22(iv) below), and

(*f*) sums included in the income arising under the settlement as amounts which have been apportioned (under *Sec 681(1)*, see 80.20(*e*) below) to a beneficiary out of the income of a close company, or could have been so apportioned if the company were incorporated and resident in the UK, and

(*g*) the tax at the rate applicable to trusts on the accumulated undistributed income less the amounts in (*c*) to (*f*) above. [*Sec 677(2); FA 1993, 6 Sch 7; FA 1995, 17 Sch 9*].

'*Capital sum*' includes a loan or loan repayment and any other sum (other than income) paid otherwise than for full consideration (but excluding sums which could not have become payable to the settlor except in one of the events mentioned in 80.24 above or, in the case of sums paid after 5 April 1995, in 80.16(A)–(D) above (or on the death under the age of 25 of the person referred to in the paragraph following 80.16(A)–(D) above). [*Sec 677(9); FA 1995, 17 Sch 9*]. As regards loans and repayment of loans, see *Potts' Exors v CIR HL 1950, 32 TC 211; De Vigier HL 1964, 42 TC 24; Bates v CIR HL 1966, 44 TC 225; McCrone v CIR CS 1967, 44 TC 142; Wachtel Ch D 1970, 46 TC 543* and *Piratin v CIR Ch D 1981, 54 TC 730*.

There is also treated as a capital sum paid to the settlor any sum paid to a third party at the settlor's direction or by assignment of his right to receive it (where the direction or assignment is after 5 April 1981) and any other sum otherwise paid or applied for the settlor's benefit. [*Sec 677(10)*].

Loan to settlor. Where the capital sum represents a loan to the settlor, there will be no tax charge on him for any tax year after the year in which the loan is repaid. If previous loans have been made and wholly repaid, any new loan will only be charged on its excess, if any, over so much of the earlier loans as have been treated as his income. [*Sec 677(4)*].

Repayment to settlor of loan. Where the capital sum is repayment of a loan by a settlor, a charge arises on him but will not apply for any year after the year in which he makes a further loan at least equal in amount to the loan repaid. [*Sec 677(5)*].

The tax charge under Schedule D, Case VI on the settlor is at the rate or rates in excess of the rate applicable to trusts (i.e. he will receive credit for the grossing up at that rate). Such deductions and reliefs are allowed as would have been given if the sum treated as income had actually been received as income. [*Sec 677(7)(8); FA 1993, 6 Sch 7*].

Secs 660E (more than one settlor—see 80.15 above), *660F* (Revenue information powers —see 80.14 above) and *660G* (definitions—see 80.15 above) apply for the purposes of these provisions as they apply for those of *Secs 660A, 660B*. [*Sec 682A; FA 1995, 17 Sch 11*].

Payment of IHT by trustees, see 80.15 above.

Connected companies. A capital sum (as above) paid to a settlor by a company connected with the settlement (see 20.8 CONNECTED PERSONS) is treated as paid to him by the trustees of the settlement irrespective of whether or not the funds originated from that settlement if there has been an 'associated payment' (made directly or indirectly) to the company (or to another company associated with that company under *Sec 416* at that time) from the settlement (which, before 6 April 1995, was assumed to be the case unless the settlor showed otherwise). Such company payments to the settlor in a tax year will be 'matched' with associated payments from the trustees to the company up to the end of that year (less any amounts already 'matched') in order to determine the amount deemed paid to the settlor by the trustees in the year, any 'unmatched' balance being 'matched' with associated payments in subsequent years. Such amounts are then 'matched' with the 'income available in the settlement' as above. [*Sec 678(1)(2)(4)(5)(7); FA 1995, 17 Sch 10*].

'*Associated payment*' is any capital sum paid, or any other sum paid or asset transferred for less than full consideration, to the company by the trustees within five years before or after the capital sum paid to the settlor by the company. [*Sec 678(3)*].

Loans. The above provisions do not apply to any payment to the settlor by way of loan or repayment of a loan if (i) the whole of the loan is repaid within twelve months and (ii) the total period during which loans are outstanding in any period of five years does not exceed twelve months. [*Sec 678(6)*].

80.19   *Example*

The trustees of a settlement with undistributed income of £1,375 at 5 April 1994 made a loan of £15,000 to B, the settlor, on 30 September 1994.

B repays the loan on 31 December 1996. Undistributed income of £3,500 arose in 1994/95, £6,500 in 1995/96 and £5,500 in 1996/97. B has taxable income of £30,000 in each year (excluding dividend income).

B will be treated as receiving the following income.

		£
1994/95	£4,875 × $\dfrac{100}{65}$	7,500
1995/96	£6,500 × $\dfrac{100}{65}$	10,000
1996/97	£3,625 × $\dfrac{100}{66}$ note (*a*)	5,492

B will pay additional tax of

		£
1994/95	£7,500 at 5% (40% – 35%)	375
1995/96	£10,000 at 5% (40% – 35%)	500
1996/97	£5,492 at 6% (40% – 34%)	329
		£1,204

Note

(*a*)   The amount treated as income in 1996/97 is limited to the amount of the loan less amounts previously treated as income (£15,000 – (£4,875 + £6,500)).

80.20   **LIABILITY OF SETTLOR—1994/95 AND EARLIER YEARS**

The provisions in *Secs 660–685* are not mutually exclusive, and if a disposition etc. falls under any one (or more) of them it is invalid for tax purposes to the extent provided by each section (*Gillies v CIR CS 1928, 14 TC 329*). However, to prevent double assessment, there are provisions whereby an assessment under a particular provision below is reduced by any assessments on the same amounts made under preceding provisions. The Revenue may require information from any party to a settlement [*Secs 669, 680*] and see the cases mentioned at 80.14 above.

80.21   Settlements

(a)   '*Settlement*' includes any disposition, trust, covenant, agreement or arrangement, and also, as regards settlor's own children, any transfer of assets. [*Secs 660(3), 670, 681(4)*]. See also the cases mentioned at 80.15(*a*) above.

A foreign settlement of UK income by a non-resident was held to be within the ambit of the settlements legislation (*Kenmare HL 1957, 37 TC 383*).

(b)   '*Settlor*' includes a person by whom the settlement was made, or who has directly or indirectly provided the funds, or who has made reciprocal arrangements. [*Secs 670, 681(4)*]. See also the cases mentioned at 80.15(*b*) above.

(c)   If there is *more than one settlor*. Each to be treated as a sole settlor, but only in respect of income or property he has himself provided, directly or indirectly. [*Secs 662, 668, 679*].

(d)   '*Wife of settlor*' in legislation now in *Secs 672, 673* does not include his widow (*Vestey v CIR HL 1949, 31 TC 1*).

(e)   '*Income arising under a settlement*' (under 80.23–80.28 below) includes any income chargeable to income tax, whether by deduction or otherwise, or which would have been so chargeable if received in UK by a person domiciled, resident and ordinarily resident, but not income on which the settlor, if he were himself entitled to it, would not have been chargeable by reason of non-domicile, non-residence, etc.

Where applicable, it also includes any income of a close company apportioned under *ICTA 1988, Pt XI, Ch III* to the trustees or any beneficiary or which could have been so apportioned had the company been incorporated in the UK. This definition is extended to include sub-apportionments through another company and to include residence in the UK as well as incorporation. Income so apportioned is increased by the rate of advance corporation tax applicable to a distribution made at the end of the accounting period to which the apportionment relates. [*Sec 681(1)–(3)*]. Apportionment was abolished for company accounting periods beginning after 31 March 1989. [*FA 1989, s 103, 17 Sch Pt V*].

Income apportioned or sub-apportioned to a foreign company held not to be within above definition (*Howard de Walden v CIR HL 1948, 30 TC 345*).

In calculating '*undistributed*' income, deductions are made for (i) sums other than interest paid to beneficiaries, etc., as income for tax purposes, (ii) trustees' expenses properly chargeable to income, and (iii) exempt income of charitable trusts. Interest may not be included in (ii) if otherwise eligible for tax relief (see 43 INTEREST PAYABLE) or payable to the settlor or spouse. A proportion of other interest may be allowable corresponding to the proportion of total income (after expenses including interest) represented by payments within (i) other than to settlor or spouse. [*Sec 682*].

(f)   *Recovery by Settlor from Trustees*. Additional income tax paid by the settlor by reason of income attributed to him under 80.21–80.26 below may be recovered by him from the trustees, and for this purpose he may require the inspector to supply him with a certificate. On the other hand, an additional repayment must be handed over to the trustees. [*Secs 661, 667, 675(3), 30 Sch 10(6)*].

(g)   *Payment of inheritance tax by trustees on assets put into settlement by settlor*. See 80.15(*e*) above.

80.21   **Disposition which cannot exceed six (or three) years—income is treated as that of settlor.** [*Secs 660–662*]. Where under a disposition (including trust, deed of covenant, agreement or arrangement) income is payable to, or for the benefit of, any person for a period which cannot exceed six years (or three years, see below), that income is treated for all tax purposes as income of the disponor if living (and of no other person) unless the disposition was made for valuable and sufficient consideration. [*Sec 660*]. In *Becker v Wright Ch D 1965, 42 TC 591* held that *Sec 660* applies only to income which could be deemed income of a UK resident settlor, and does not displace income received by a UK beneficiary from a short-term settlement made by a non-resident. See *Racal Group Services Ltd v Ashmore CA, [1995] STC 1151* for an unsuccessful attempt retrospectively to amend a deed to achieve the intended effect for tax purposes.

For 'valuable and sufficient consideration', see *CIR v Plummer HL 1979, 54 TC 1* (but substantive decision has been superseded by *Sec 125*, see 3.19 ANTI-AVOIDANCE). See also 15.6 CHARITIES.

Deeds of covenant executed after 14 March 1988 (other than those providing for payments either to charity or for *bona fide* commercial reasons in connection with the payer's trade, profession or vocation) are ineffective for tax purposes, payments thereunder being ineligible for tax relief and not forming part of the taxable income of any person. [*Sec 347A; FA 1988, s 36*]

Six years. Notwithstanding that a deed may be for seven years, yet if the last payment under it is due less than six years from the date of the deed, it is void for tax purposes under *Sec 660 (Hostel of St Luke CA 1930, 15 TC 682)*. But see *Verdon-Roe CA 1962, 40 TC 541*. The restriction must also be considered where some of the provisions in a deed are in force for a period of less than seven years, although the others cover a longer period. See also *Nicolson and Bartlett Ch D 1953, 34 TC 354* dealing with supplemental deeds extending seven year period; and *D'Ambrumenil v CIR KB 1940, 23 TC 440*, where held that there 'must be some constant element in yearly payment', but that the same fractional part of income might be sufficient. But cf. *Black CA 1940, 23 TC 715*, when also held immaterial that period which could have exceeded six years did not, in fact, do so. If payments are to continue after settlor's death, they are legally payable out of capital unless contrary direction in Will (see 80.9 above).

Three years. For covenanted payments to charity, the period of six years stated above is reduced to three years. A '*covenanted payment to charity*' means a payment under a covenant in favour of a body of persons or trust established for charitable purposes only and under which the annual payments become payable for a period which can exceed three years. The covenant must not be for a consideration in money or money's worth and can only be terminable within the three year period with the consent of the charity. [*Sec 660*]. See also 80.28(vii) *et seq.* below regarding restrictions on higher-rate relief for covenantor.

Other requirements. A deed of covenant, other than in favour of a charity, made before 15 March 1988 had to reach the inspector of taxes by the end of June 1988 in order for payments after 14 March 1988 thereunder to be effective for tax purposes by virtue of their being made in pursuance of an existing obligation. [*FA 1988, s 36(4)(b)*]. See 1.8(i) ALLOWANCES AND TAX RATES. In examining deeds of covenant for validity and repayment claims, the Revenue had to satisfy themselves as to

(*a*) *evidence of payment* and deduction of tax;

(*b*) *non-reciprocity*. A declaration may be required from the covenantor that there are no arrangements for the direct or indirect return of any part of the benefit of the deed;

(*c*) *evidence of sealing*. The attestation clause of the deed includes the word 'sealed'. (This does not apply in Scotland.)

(Revenue Pamphlet IR 131, A1).

As regards (*c*) above, with effect from 31 July 1990 the sealing requirement disappeared in England and Wales. (Revenue Press Release 20 March 1990).

80.22 Settlements

80.22 **Settlement by parent in favour of own child—income is treated as that of parent while child is unmarried and under 18** (but note exceptions below). [*Secs 663–670*]. Where under a settlement (see definition in 80.20(*a*) above) income is, or may become, payable to, or for the benefit of, a child of the settlor, that income is treated for all tax purposes as the income of the parent if living (and not of the child). This rule only applies if at the time of payment the child is unmarried and also under 18. [*Secs 663(1), 664(1)*].

Exceptions to the above rule are as follows.

(i) Irrevocable settlements made before 22 April 1936. [*Sec 663(3), 30 Sch 10*]. For meaning of 'irrevocable', see *Sec 665*. See also cases in 80.23 below.

(ii) If the aggregate amount in any tax year for one child does not exceed £100 (£5 for 1990/91 and earlier years). [*Sec 663(4); FA 1990, s 82*].

(iii) If the parent is not taxable as a UK resident. [*Sec 663(5)*].

(iv) 'Accumulation settlements' which are irrevocable as defined in *Sec 665*. The rule above (i.e. income treated as that of parent) only applies to such settlements to the extent that (*a*) settlement income consists of or represents sums (e.g. annual payments) allowable as deductions from settlor's total income, or (*b*) income (or capital in lieu) is paid to, or for the benefit of, the child, so assessment on the parent can generally be avoided by accumulating all the capital and income of the settlement. [*Sec 664*].

'*Child*' includes stepchild, adopted child and illegitimate child. [*Sec 670(1)*]. '*Stepchild*' includes a child of the wife by a previous marriage (*CIR v Russell CS 1955, 36 TC 83*). Any provision by a parent for his child may create a settlement, whether made under compulsion or merely under parental obligation (*Harvey v Sivyer Ch D 1985, 58 TC 569*), although in practice the Revenue do not treat payments made under a Court Order as being under a settlement for this purpose.

If the trustees pay any interest (other than to the settlor or his spouse) on which they are not entitled to tax relief (see 43 INTEREST PAYABLE), payments to, or for, an unmarried infant child (as above) of the settlor, are deemed to be increased by an amount equal to the part of that interest bearing the same proportion to the total interest paid as payments to or for such children bear to the total income of the settlement (net of trustees' expenses properly chargeable to income) for that year of assessment. [*Sec 666*].

80.23 **Revocable (or diminishable) settlements—income is treated as that of settlor.** [*Secs 671, 672*]. So long as an *income settlement* is subject to a power of revocation (or of diminution of payments under the settlement) which, if exercised, would enable the settlor (or spouse) to cease to make (or reduce) annual payments due under the settlement, those payments (or the part corresponding to the potential diminution) are treated as income of the settlor (and of no other person). [*Sec 671*]. Similarly, if a *capital settlement* is subject to a power of revocation (or of diminution of the settlement property or of payments under the settlement) which, if exercised, would, or might, entitle the settlor (or spouse) to the whole or part of the income or capital of the settled property, the whole (or a corresponding part) of the settlement income is treated as income of the settlor (and of no other person). [*Sec 672*].

But where the power of revocation, etc., cannot be exercised within six years (three years in the case of a 'covenanted payment to charity') from the date of the first annual payment (such payments being continuous), or from the date of the first transfer of property to the settlement, the above does not apply so long as the power remains unexercisable (in the case of a 'covenanted payment to charity' under a covenant made on or after 7 May 1992 or where the revocation power cannot be exercised before that day, unexercised rather than unexerciseable). [*Secs 671(2), 672(2); F(No 2)A 1992, s 27*]. Cf. *Nicolson and Bartlett Ch D 1953, 34 TC 354.* As regards a 'covenanted payment to charity', see 80.21 above for definition. [*Sec 671(2)(a)*].

For certain settlements made before 16 April 1958, see *30 Sch 11.* For certain payments of IHT by trustees, see 80.20(*g*) above.

Power to revoke or determine. A power of appointment is a power of determination (*Jamieson v CIR HL 1963, 41 TC 43*). See also *Warden CS 1938, 22 TC 416; Delamere KB 1939, 22 TC 525; Payne CA 1940, 23 TC 610; Morton CS 1941, 24 TC 259; Rainsford-Hannay CS 1941, 24 TC 273; Dalgety v CIR KB 1941, 24 TC 280; Prince-Smith KB 1943, 25 TC 84; Eastwood CA 1943, 25 TC 100; Vestey HL 1949, 31 TC 1; Wolfson HL 1949, 31 TC 141* and *Cookson CA 1977, 50 TC 705.*

80.24   **Where settlor retains an interest—income is treated as that of settlor.** [*Sec 673*]. So long as the settlor has an interest in the income or property of a settlement (i.e. if any income or capital may *in any circumstances* be paid or applied for the benefit of the settlor or spouse) the income under the settlement, or a part proportionate to the interest retained, is to be treated as that of the settlor (and not of any other person) to the extent that it remains undistributed (and so long as the settlor is alive).

Exceptions to the above rule are as follows.

(*a*)   Where settlor's interest can arise only on

    (i)   bankruptcy of beneficiary, or charge or assignment by him, or

    (ii)   in a marriage settlement, death of both parties and all or any of the children, or

    (iii)   in a contingent trust, beneficiary's death before vesting age (25 or less).

(*b*)   If and so long as some person is alive and under 25 during whose life (unless bankrupt etc.) settlor cannot benefit. [*Sec 673(3)*].

See *Glyn KB 1948, 30 TC 321; Tennant KB 1942, 24 TC 215; Barr's Trustees v CIR CS 1943, 25 TC 72; Jenkins CA 1944, 26 TC 265; Vestey HL 1949, 31 TC 1; Vandervell HL 1966, 43 TC 519.* Cf. *Muir CA 1965, 43 TC 367; Wachtel Ch D 1970, 46 TC 543.*

As to power of advancement see *CIR v Bernstein CA 1960, 39 TC 391.* For certain payments of IHT by trustees, see 80.20(*g*) above.

See also 80.25 and 80.29 below.

80.25   **Discretionary trusts that could possibly benefit settlor or spouse—income treated as that of settlor.** [*Sec 674*]. Income arising under a settlement (wherever made) is treated as that of the settlor, and not of any other person, to the extent that it, or property comprised in the settlement, is capable, by exercise of a discretionary power, of being paid or applied for the benefit of the settlor (or the wife or husband of the settlor), except where the conditions in 80.24(*a*) or (*b*) above apply. Where the discretionary power cannot be exercised within six years from the time income first arose to, or property became comprised in, the settlement, the above does not apply to that income, or the income from that property, so long as the power remains unexercisable. [*Sec 674*]. See *Blausten v CIR CA 1971, 47 TC 542,* regarding trustees' power to add to class after wife excluded by Deed of Appointment. See *30 Sch 12* as regards certain settlements made before 9 July 1958.

Under the Revenue interpretation of the decision in *CIR v Tennant KB 1942, 24 TC 215,* both *Sec 673* (80.24 above) and *Sec 674* apply if (*a*) the settlor being presently unmarried, benefit could arise to any person whom he might marry in the future, or (*b*) whether settlor presently married or not, if the terms of the settlement indicate a specific intention to benefit a future wife (or husband). (Revenue Pamphlet IR 131, A30).

80.26 **Income settlements—income treated as that of settlor.** [*Sec 674A; FA 1989, s 109*]. Income arising under a settlement (other than income consisting of annual payments under 'existing obligations' within *FA 1988, s 36(3)* (see 1.8(i) ALLOWANCES AND TAX RATES)) payable to a person other than the settlor is treated as income of the settlor. The conditions and exemptions are identical to those applicable for the purposes of higher rate liability (see 80.28 below), except that the exemption for covenanted payments to charity in 80.28(vii) applies without the restriction where *Sec 505(3)* applies.

80.27 **Income payments by settlor to trustees—are not allowed as a deduction from the income of the settlor to the extent that there is undistributed income in the settlement at the end of a tax year.** [*Sec 676*]. Where the settlor (or spouse) makes payments (e.g. under covenant) to the trustees of a settlement that would otherwise be eligible for deduction from his income for tax purposes, such payments are not so deductible to the extent that there is undistributed income in the settlement at the end of a tax year. [*Sec 676(1)*].

Sums paid by the settlor to a body corporate which is connected with the settlement (see 20.8 CONNECTED PERSONS for meaning) are treated as if paid to the trustees. [*Sec 676(2)*].

See *Pay Ch D 1955, 36 TC 109* re mortgage interest paid to trustees by the settlor. See also 80.29 below.

Trust income equivalent to the amounts disallowed is not available for tax relief. [*Sec 676(3)*]. *Sec 676* applies for all income tax purposes. However, it does not apply to settlements made before 27 April 1938 except for certain revocable settlements varied on or after that date. [*Sec 676(4)*].

80.28 **Settlements (e.g. covenants) of income only (i.e. capital not divested) are generally ineffective for purposes of excess liability (i.e. excess of higher rates of income tax over basic and lower rates, and (for 1983/84 and earlier) investment income surcharge).** [*Secs 683–685*]. The definition of 'settlement' in 80.20(*a*) above is, for the purposes of *Sec 683*, modified in two respects for 1990/91 onwards.

(*a*) It does not include an unconditional outright gift between spouses of property from which income arises unless either the gift does not carry the right to the whole of the income, or the property given is wholly or substantially a right to income, or the donor retains any actual or potential benefit.

(*b*) It does not include the irrevocable allocation between spouses of pension rights under a relevant statutory scheme (see 66.1 RETIREMENT SCHEMES). [*FA 1989, s 108*].

As regards (*a*) above, preference shares created in a company, and given to the wives of the directors, were held to be property consisting wholly or substantially of a right to income (*Young v Pearce; Young v Scrutton Ch D, 1996 STI 541*).

'Divestment of capital'. In order to fall outside the scope of *Sec 683*, the settlor must divest himself completely of the property from which the income arises, so that in no circumstances can benefit come to himself or spouse [*Secs 683(1)(d), 685(1)*] subject to exceptions in 80.24(*a*) above. [*Sec 685(2)*]. See *Watson v Holland Ch D, [1984] STC 372*.

Otherwise, the income is treated for excess liability purposes as that of the settlor (and not of any other person) unless one of the following exceptions applies (and see also 80.21 above for deeds of covenant non-effective for tax purposes).

(i) The settlement was made before **7 April 1965** [*Sec 683(1)*] but certain restrictions apply to settlements made between 10 April 1946 and 6 April 1965 (the main restriction being that covenants etc. in favour of charities are not effective for surtax or excess liability purposes). [*Sec 684*].

(ii) The income consists of *annual payments* made for full consideration **under a partnership agreement** to a **former partner** or, if he is dead, to his widow (or, after 5 April 1990, widower) or dependants, or to a person who receives a right to the payments on the former partner's death (but limited in this case to a period of ten years since the partner ceased to be a member of the partnership). [*Sec 683(1)(a), (8); FA 1988, 3 Sch 20(1)(2)*].

(iii) The income consists of *annual payments* made for full consideration by an individual in connection with the **acquisition of a business, or part, from a partnership** to

    (*a*)   a former partner (or widow, etc. as in (ii) above) of that or any 'preceding partnership', or

    (*b*)   an individual (or, on the individual's death, to widow, etc.) whose business, or part, was acquired by that or any 'preceding partnership',

but only if such annual payments are in substitution for, or matched by reductions in, payments which would themselves be eligible for relief under (ii) above in the case of (*a*) and (iv) below in the case of (*b*).

A '*preceding partnership*' is one that transfers its business, or part, to another if one or more partners are members of both. [*Sec 683(6)(b), (7), (8), (10)(b); FA 1988, 3 Sch 20(4)*].

(iv) The income consists of *annual payments* made by an individual for full consideration, **in connection with the acquisition of a business,** to, or for the benefit of, the individual from whom the business was acquired, or the widow, etc. as in (ii) above if the individual is dead. [*Sec 683(6)(a); FA 1988, 3 Sch 20(3)*].

(v) *Where* (ii), (iii) *or* (iv) *above applies* to an annual payment to a former partner or, if dead, to the widow, etc. as in (ii) above and the payment falls short of the limit for the year under *Sec 628* (amount of partnership retirement annuity treated as earned income, see 53.16 PARTNERSHIPS), any additional annual payment up to that limit will be similarly treated notwithstanding that it is not given for full consideration. [*Sec 683(9); FA 1988, 3 Sch 20(5)*].

(vi) The income is under a **marriage settlement** made by one party to a marriage as provision for the other after separation etc. or dissolution or annulment of marriage. [*Sec 683(1)(c)*]. (But see 47.15 MARRIED PERSONS for the tax treatment of maintenance payments generally.)

(vii) The income consists of '**covenanted payments to charity**' (see definition in 80.21 above). There is no restriction on the overall amount of the covenanted payments made, but where £1,000 or more of such payments in the year is, in the hands of the charity or charities receiving them, denied relief by *Sec 505(3)* (see 15.5 CHARITIES), the amount on which relief is so denied is similarly denied excess liability relief under these provisions. [*Sec 683(3)–(5)*]. See also 15.8 CHARITIES as regards donations treated as covenanted payments.

A covenanted payment within *Sec 683* remains as a deduction in computing the settlor's income for basic or lower rate tax purposes but it must then be added back for the purpose of establishing liability at the higher and additional rates. Any amount so added back under *Sec 683* is income arising under a settlement and thus investment income, despite the fact that the actual payment may have been made out of earned income. (*Ang v Parrish Ch D 1980, 53 TC 304*).

For the deductibility of annual payments for which the consideration is a capital amount, see *Sec 125* (3.19 ANTI-AVOIDANCE) and for the position before that legislation, see *CIR v Plummer HL 1979, 54 TC 1*.

80.29 MAINTENANCE FUNDS FOR HISTORIC BUILDINGS— tax exemption for settlors etc. [*Sec 691*]

Where the Treasury has directed under *IHTA 1984, 4 Sch 1* that funds put into a settlement for the maintenance, repair or preservation of qualifying property are exempt for inheritance tax purposes, the trustees may elect in writing for any year of assessment that (*a*) any income arising shall not be treated as income of the settlor (see 80.13 to 80.28 above) and (*b*) any sum applied for the purposes (as above) of the settlement shall not be treated as income of any person by virtue of his interest in, or occupation of, the building or land or by virtue of *Sec 677* (see 80.18 above). The election must be made within, for 1996/97 and later years, twelve months after 31 January following the year of assessment to which it relates (for earlier years, two years after the end of that year of assessment). If no election made, then (*b*) still applies to any sums so applied in excess of the income for that tax year. Under certain circumstances, an election (as above) may be made separately for different parts of a year of assessment. [*Secs 690, 691; FA 1996, s 135, 21 Sch 19*].

An income tax charge will arise when any property (whether capital or income) of a fund is applied for purposes other than within a Treasury direction as above (i.e. (i) the maintenance of, or public access to, the property, or (ii) for the benefit of specified national bodies, or (iii) for charities whose sole or main object is the preservation for public benefit of buildings, land etc. of historic, national etc. interest) or when any settlement property devolves on any body or charity other than mentioned in (ii) or (iii). The charge will also apply if property devolves on a body or charity mentioned in (ii) and (iii) *and* at or before that time an interest under the settlement is or has been acquired for money or money's worth by that or another such body or charity (but any acquisition from another such body or charity will be disregarded). The charge is on all income which has arisen from the property since the last charge under this provision or, otherwise, since the creation of the settlement, and has not been applied as in (i), (ii) or (iii) above. The charge will not apply to income which is treated as income of the settlor under *Secs 660–689* (see 80.13 *et seq.* above) and sums applied otherwise than in (i) to (iii) above will be treated as paid first out of such income treated as the settlor's and only the excess charged in this way. There is no charge where the whole of the settlement property is transferred to another exempt settlement within 30 days of any charge otherwise arising as above or where immediately before and after the transfer the property is subject to a Treasury direction as above. The charge is assessed on the trustees and is in addition to tax charged under any other provision. The rate of charge is the higher rate of income tax *less* the rate applicable to trusts, i.e. 5%. [*Sec 694; FA 1993, 6 Sch 10; FA 1995, 17 Sch 16*].

Reimbursement of settlor. Where a settlor incurs expenditure on the maintenance of an historic building which the Treasury has approved for the purposes of capital transfer or inheritance tax (under *IHTA 1984, 4 Sch 1*, see above) and the settlor is carrying on a trade of showing the property to the public or, for 1995/96 onwards, a SCHEDULE A (68) business, and that expenditure is reimbursed to the settlor by the trustees of the settlement, then the reimbursement will not reduce the expenditure deductible in computing the profits of the trade or business and will only be taxed as income of the settlor under *Secs 660–685* (see 80.13 to 80.28 above). [*Sec 692; FA 1995, 6 Sch 26*].

81   Share Incentives and Options

(See Revenue Pamphlets IR 16, 17 and 95 to 100).

81.1   For general tax liability in respect of shares given to directors or employees as part of their emoluments, see 75.19 and 75.36 SCHEDULE E.

81.2   Legislation applies where there are arrangements to allow employees to acquire shares in their employing companies, as follows.

(*a*)   Share options under *Sec 135*, see 81.3 below.

(*b*)   Share incentives under *Sec 138* or *FA 1988, Pt III, Ch II*, see 81.4 below.

(*c*)   Profit sharing schemes under *Sec 186*, see 81.6 below.

(*d*)   Savings-related share options under *Sec 185(1)(a)*, see 81.8 below.

(*e*)   Executive share option schemes under *Sec 185(1)(b)*, see 81.9 below. Now superseded by (*f*) below.

(*f*)   Company share option plans under *Sec 185(1)(b)* and *FA 1996*, see 81.10 below.

(*g*)   Employee share ownership trusts under *FA 1989, ss 67–74, 5 Sch*, see 71.53 SCHEDULE D, CASES I AND II and 81.11 below.

'*Shares*' includes stocks [*Secs 136(5)(d), 139(11), 187(2); FA 1988, s 87(1)*] and, for (*b*) above, also includes securities as defined in *Sec 254(1)*. [*Secs 139(11), 140(3); FA 1988, s 87(1)*].

A *jointly owned company* (or subsidiary of such a company) cannot strictly participate in an approved scheme under (*c*), (*d*), (*e*) or (*f*) which is a group scheme established by either of its joint owners, because it will not be controlled by the company which established the scheme as the legislation requires. By concession, a group scheme expressed to extend to a jointly owned company will normally be approved upon application by the company establishing the scheme, provided that:

(i)   the jointly owned company is not controlled (under *Sec 840*) by any single person;

(ii)   it is controlled between them by two persons, one of whom established the scheme; and

(iii)   in relation to each of (*c*), (*d*), (*e*) and (*f*) it only participates in a scheme established by one of the companies controlling it.

A similar concession applies in relation to subsidiaries of a jointly owned company which satisfies (i) and (ii) above, provided that (iii) above would also be satisfied if it related both to the jointly owned company and to its subsidiaries.

Such concessionary approval is conditional upon the scheme ceasing to apply to the jointly owned company or its subsidiaries where (i) or (ii) above ceases to be satisfied (unless the companies thereby pass into the control of the company which established the scheme). It must similarly cease to apply to a company which ceases to be a subsidiary of the jointly owned company (again, unless it thereby passes into the control of the company which established the scheme). The company establishing the scheme for which the concession is sought must undertake to notify the Revenue of any change of control of any of the companies concerned.

(Revenue Pamphlet IR 1, B27).

81.3 Share Incentives and Options

For *capital gains tax* purposes, when shares acquired under the above arrangements are disposed of, any sum assessed to income tax under (*a*), (*b*), (*e*) or (*f*) above is treated as a cost of acquiring the shares but for (*c*) above capital gains tax is charged without deduction for any amount charged to income tax. [*TCGA 1992, ss 120(1)(4)–(6), 238(2); FA 1993, s 105*]. For (*d*) above, the consideration given will be the cost of acquisition. [*See 185(3)(b)*].

81.3 SHARE OPTIONS—CHARGE TO TAX

(*a*) Where a person realises a gain by exercising, assigning or releasing an option to acquire shares in a company which he obtained at any time as a present, past or prospective director or employee, within Case I of Schedule E, of that, or of any other, company, he is assessable under Schedule E on the difference between

    (i)   the then open-market value of those shares (or, in the case of an assignment or release, the consideration received for the assignment or release) and

    (ii)   the consideration (apart from services in his office or employment) which he gave for the option (if any) plus that for the acquisition of the shares.

For the circumstances in which the Revenue will accept that shares or share options were acquired by a director or employee in a different capacity and not by reason of the office or employment, see Revenue Inspector's Manual, IM 5329.

The charge is independent of any charge on grant of the option, and depends solely on the above conditions being satisfied (*Ball v Phillips Ch D 1990, 63 TC 529*).

A person is treated as assigning or releasing a right for this purpose if he receives money or money's worth in connection with omitting, or undertaking to omit, to exercise the right, or granting, or undertaking to grant, to another a right to acquire the shares or an interest therein. Further application of these provisions is not prevented, but any consideration given for the original grant of the right may be taken into account only once for this purpose.

Provisions prevent avoidance by having the option granted, or assigned, to a third party, or by assigning the option, in whole or in part, for another option, or by entering into joint arrangements with another person or persons having chargeable options. There are reporting requirements relating to any of the events which may give rise to a charge under these provisions. For 1993/94 and subsequent years, information should be sent to Inland Revenue, Employee Share Schemes Unit, Savings and Investment Division, First Floor, SW Wing, Bush House, Strand, London WC2B 4RD. (Revenue Tax Bulletin February 1994 p 110).

PAY AS YOU EARN (55) need not be applied to payments for the surrender, cancellation, assignment or release of options, irrespective of whether any payment was made for the grant of the option and by whom the payment was made. (Revenue letter to Share Scheme Lawyers Group, see press release 17 July 1995).

(*b*) If a right, as under (*a*) above, can be exercised more than seven years after being obtained, tax liability can arise at the time the right is obtained, as well as on exercise of the right. Any tax so charged is deducted from the charge under (*a*) above. Otherwise no liability arises on receipt of a right as under (*a*) above.

(*c*) No charge arises under these provisions where an option is exercised after the death of the grantee by his personal representative or legatee. When shares so acquired are disposed of, a capital gains tax charge arises by reference to a base cost of the market value of the option at the date of death plus the price paid for the shares on its exercise. (Revenue Pamphlet IR 16, para 2.10).

(d)   For options exercised before 6 April 1994, no charge arises under these provisions where an option is exercised by an individual neither resident nor ordinarily resident in the UK, and the option is over shares in the overseas parent of a UK subsidiary for which the individual (being normally resident and employed outside the UK) was working for a brief period when the option was granted. Similarly for options so exercised, where the individual was entitled to a foreign earnings deduction (see 75.3 SCHEDULE E) for the year of assessment of the exercise in respect of earnings from the employment for which the option was granted, the gain on exercise attracts a similar deduction (the gain being treated for this purpose, where relevant, as accruing evenly over the year of assessment). (Revenue Pamphlet IR 16 (September 1991), paras 5.3, 5.5). These practices are withdrawn for options exercised after 5 April 1994.

[*Secs 135, 136, 140(1)(a)*].

Example

An employee is granted an option exercisable within 5 years to buy 1,000 shares at £5 each. The option costs 50p per share. He exercises the option in 1996/97 when the shares are worth £7.50. The option is not granted under an approved scheme.

He is chargeable to income tax under Schedule E in 1996/97 as follows

	£	£
Open market value of shares 1,000 × £7.50		7,500
Price paid 1,000 × £5 — shares	5,000	
1,000 × 50p — option	500	
		5,500
Assessable		£2,000

Notes

(a)   The result would be the same if, instead of exercising the option, the employee transferred his option to a third party for £2,500.

(b)   The capital gains tax base cost of the shares will be £7,500. [*TCGA 1992, s 120(4)*]. See Tolley's Capital Gains Tax.

Payment of tax. Tax on a charge under *Sec 135*, on a gain realised by the exercise of a right to acquire shares obtained before 6 April 1984, may be paid by instalments if (i) the acquisition of the shares was for a consideration not less than the market value (determined as for capital gains tax) of shares of that class when the right was granted (or, if granted before 6 April 1982, 90% of that market value) and (ii) the tax payable exceeds £250 and (iii) an election to pay by instalments is made in writing to the inspector within 60 days after the end of the year of assessment in which the right was exercised. In such cases the tax is payable in equal instalments: for options exercised before 6 April 1983, by three instalments, the first 14 days after the tax is demanded under PAYE regulations, the third on the last day of the third year after the end of the year in which the right was exercised and the second on the date midway between the first and third instalments; for options exercised after 5 April 1983, by five instalments, the first as before, the fifth on the last day of the fifth year after the end of the year in which the right was exercised, the intermediate instalments at regular intervals between. If the first instalment is not due until after the final instalment is due, then all tax becomes due on the later date. All tax may be paid early and will become due immediately if the taxpayer becomes bankrupt. The gain is to be treated as being the highest part of the taxpayer's income of the year of assessment in which the right was exercised, subject to any other provisions for determining the highest part of his income. If the consideration is less than required in (i) above only because the shares are diminished in market value solely because the share capital of the issuing company was varied after the right to acquire the shares was granted, the consideration is treated as being not less than that required under (i). [*Sec 137*]. Where the tax charged under the Schedule E assessment for the year in which the gain arises is less than that attributable to the gain (because e.g. of offset losses), the instalment arrangements apply only to the tax payable under the assessment (i.e. it is not possible to claim instalment payment of the full amount of the tax attributable to the gain and a refund of tax deducted under PAYE) (*Hunt v Murphy Ch D 1991, 64 TC 427*).

81.4   **'SHARE INCENTIVES'—CHARGE TO TAX**

Shares acquired before 26 October 1987. The provisions in *Secs 138–140* do not apply to shares acquired after 25 October 1987, for which see the provisions of *FA 1988, Pt III, Ch II* described below. In relation to shares acquired before 26 October 1987, the following continues to apply, but see the transitional provisions under the *FA 1988* scheme.

Where (unless exempted as below) the holder of an office or employment, the emoluments from which are chargeable to tax under Case I of Schedule E, acquires shares (or an interest in shares) in a company under a right or opportunity given him by reason of that office or employment, he is chargeable to income tax under Schedule E, as earned income,

(*a*)   on the value of any benefit, not applicable to the majority of the ordinary shareholders, which he receives in respect of such shares acquired after 5 April 1972 and before 26 October 1987, and

(*b*)   at the end of seven years from the acquisition (or, if earlier, when he parts with the shares or they cease to be subject to specified restrictions (see *Sec 138(6), (9)(c)*)) on any excess of their market value then over their value when acquired. [*Secs 138(1)(9)(12), 140(1)(a)*].

A right, etc. is 'offered' to the taxpayer although he may himself have stipulated its being granted (*CIR v Herd C/S, [1992] STC 264*).

For the circumstances in which the Revenue will accept that shares or share options were acquired by a director or employee in a different capacity and not by reason of the office or employment, see Revenue Inspector's Manual, IM 5329.

Neither (*a*) nor (*b*) above applies if the shares are acquired:

(i)   in pursuance of an offer to the public [*Sec 138(1)*]; or

(ii)   under an arrangement whereby a company gives its employees, as part of their emoluments, shares as a predetermined participation in profits, and for new schemes (or existing schemes modified) after 22 March 1973 if (A) equal participation is allowed to all full-time employees taxable under Case I of Schedule E over 25 years of age and with five years continuous service, (B) shares are in a company which is either quoted on a recognised stock exchange or not controlled by another company, (C) shares have no restrictions which may result in subsequent increase in value and (D) shares cannot be exchanged or converted into shares subject to such restrictions [*Sec 138(2)(4)*],

and (*b*) above does not apply:

(1)   where immediately after the shares were acquired (A) the shares were not subject to specified restrictions (see *Sec 138(6)*), nor exchangeable into such shares, and the

majority of available shares (exclusive of associated company shareholdings) of the same class were acquired otherwise than as under *Sec 138(1)* (see above), or (B) the shares were not subject to specified restrictions (see *Sec 138(6)(a)(b)*), nor exchangeable into such shares, and the majority of the available shares of the same class (as above) were acquired by present or past employees or directors (of the company or a subsidiary) who together had control of the company [*Sec 138(3)(a)*]; or

(2)   for acquisitions after 5 April 1984 of shares in authorised unit trusts (see 90.1 UNIT TRUSTS) approved by the Board for this purpose, provided that shares in the employer company (or in any associated company) do not make up more than 10% of the value of the trust investments for a continuous period of one month or more throughout which a director or employee of the employer company has such a right as is dealt with under these provisions to acquire unit trust shares, or retains an interest in shares so acquired. [*Sec 138(3)(b), (7)*].

Before 19 March 1986, the ending of the restrictions specified in *FA 1972, s 79(2A)* (the predecessor to *Sec 138(6)*) triggered the charge under (*b*) above, but where such restrictions cease after 18 March 1986, the charge is triggered only if, had the shares been acquired immediately after the restrictions were lifted, they would have been excluded from the operation of (*b*) above by virtue of (1) above. [*Sec 138(9)(c)*].

Additional shares (or an interest therein), acquired after 18 March 1986 by virtue of a holding of (or of an interest in) shares which are not excluded from (*b*) above, are for the purposes of (*b*) above treated with the original holding as one holding acquired at the same time and in the same circumstances as the original holding, the market value of the original holding being attributed proportionately over all shares in the new holding. Any consideration given for the additional shares is treated as an increase in the consideration for the original holding and thus as reducing any charge arising under (*b*) above. [*Sec 138(10)(11)*].

The Board has information and penalty powers as regards approval of authorised unit trusts under (2) above. [*Sec 139(6); TMA s 98*].

As regards (i) above, shares (or an interest in shares) acquired by a director or employee are treated as acquired in pursuance of an offer to the public where

(A)   they were acquired at a discount under an offer (the 'discount offer') to directors or employees in their capacity as such;

(B)   the discount offer was made in conjunction with an offer to the public on the same terms but without the discount;

(C)   the director or employee is chargeable under Schedule E on an amount equal to the discount on shares acquired by him; and

(D)   at least 75% of the shares acquired under the discount offer and the offer to the public together were acquired under the offer to the public.

[*Sec 139(1)(2)*].

The amount of the charge under (*b*) is reduced where, under acquisition terms, any increased consideration is subsequently payable or the shares are disposed of at less than market value. [*See 138(8)*].

A profit on the sale of shares was held to be assessable under the legislation, notwithstanding that the employee had purchased the shares through the Stock Exchange (*Cheatle v CIR Ch D 1982, 56 TC 111*).

Company reconstructions, etc. Where shares are disposed of after 18 March 1986 in circumstances such that a 'new holding' of shares is acquired which is treated as the same asset as the original holding under *TCGA 1992, ss 127–130*, the new holding is similarly treated for the purposes of *Sec 138*. Any consideration given for the new holding is treated as an increase in the consideration for the original holding, and thus as reducing any charge under (*b*) above. Any consideration received for the original holding, other than the new holding, is treated as proportionately increasing the market value of the shares comprised in the new holding at any subsequent time. [*Sec 139(13)*].

Shares acquired after 25 October 1987. The above provisions cease to apply in respect of shares acquired after 25 October 1987, and are replaced by the following.

Where a person acquires shares, or an interest in shares, in a company in pursuance of a right conferred on him, or opportunity offered him, by reason of his being a director or employee, past, present or future, within Case 1 of Schedule E, of that or any other company, a charge to tax may arise on him (as below) unless the acquisition is made in pursuance of an offer to the public. Where such a right is assigned to a person, and the right was conferred on some other person by reason of the assignee's office or employment, the assignee is treated as having acquired the shares in pursuance of a right conferred on him by reason of that office or employment. [*FA 1988, ss 77, 87(4)*]. An option to acquire shares does not constitute an interest in the shares for this purpose. (ICAEW Memorandum TR 739, para 32, 13 February 1989). A right, etc. is 'offered' to the taxpayer although he may himself have stipulated its being granted (*CIR v Herd CS 1992, 66 TC 77*).

The Revenue consider that all share acquisitions by employees potentially fall within these provisions, regardless of any investment element in the acquisition (e.g. in a management buy-out). (Revenue Schedule E Manual, SE 2908). For the circumstances in which the Revenue will accept that shares or share options were acquired by a director or employee in a different capacity and not by reason of the office or employment, see Revenue Inspector's Manual, IM 5329.

Where, after 15 January 1991, combinations of shares in two or more companies are offered to the public, and at the same time shares in one or more but not all of those companies are offered to directors or employees, and the offers are treated for the purposes of *FA 1988, s 68* as a single offer to the public (see 75.36 SCHEDULE E), they are similarly treated for these purposes. [*FA 1991, s 44(9)*].

A charge under Schedule E will arise in the following situations.

(*a*) *Removal of restrictions, etc.* If a 'chargeable event' occurs while he still has a beneficial interest in the shares, and the shares are in a company which was not a 'dependent subsidiary' at the time either of this acquisition or of the 'chargeable event', the charge will be made for the year in which the 'chargeable event' occurs on the amount by which that event increases the value of the interest (or would do so but for some other event).

A '*chargeable event*' is the removal or variation of a restriction, or the creation or variation of a right, relating to the shares, or the imposition or variation of a restriction, or removal or variation of a right, relating to other shares in the company, which increases (or would do so but for another event) the value of the shares. This does not normally apply on the triggering of certain kinds of performance-related rights or restrictions attached at the outset to the shares acquired (known as 'equity ratchets') which are commonly found in management buy-outs. Under these, the managers' share of the company's equity is increased on some predetermined basis by reference to the company's performance. (Revenue Press Release 14 April 1988). It is understood that this applies equally to such arrangements in situations other than management buy-outs. (Tolley's Practical Tax 1995 p 15).

An event is *not* a '*chargeable event*' unless, at any time within the previous seven years, the person acquiring the shares was a director or employee of the company, or of the company as director or employee of which he acquired the shares, or of an 'associated company' of either. Nor is it a *'chargeable event'* if, in relation to all shares of the same class, it is a removal, etc. as above and, at the time of the event, either

(i)   the majority of shares of that class are held otherwise than by, or for the benefit of, directors or employees of the company or an 'associated company', or the 'associated company' itself, or

(ii) the company is 'employee-controlled' by virtue of holdings of shares of that class, or

(iii) the company is a subsidiary other than a 'dependent subsidiary', and its shares are of a single class.

[*FA 1988, s 78*].

(*b*)   *Shares in dependent subsidiaries.* If the shares are in a company which

(i)   was a 'dependent subsidiary' at the time of the acquisition, or

(ii) became one before the person acquiring the shares ceased to have a beneficial interest in them,

and there is a 'chargeable increase' in the value of the shares, the charge is made, for the year in which ends the period for which the 'chargeable increase' is determined, on the amount of the increase (or appropriate part where the interest in the shares is less than full beneficial ownership). If, under the terms of the acquisition, the consideration is subsequently increased, the amount taxable is correspondingly reduced. If, under those terms, the person acquiring the shares subsequently ceases to have any beneficial interest in them by a disposal for consideration less than the value of the shares at the time of the disposal, the amount taxable is reduced by the excess of that value over that consideration.

Where (*b*)(i) above applies, there is a *'chargeable increase'* if the value of the shares, at the earlier of seven years from acquisition and the time when the person acquiring the shares ceases to have any beneficial interest in them, exceeds their value at the time of acquisition.

Where (*b*)(ii) above applies, there is a *'chargeable increase'* if the value of the shares, at the earliest of

(A)   seven years from the time of the company becoming a 'dependent subsidiary',

(B)   the time when the person acquiring the shares ceases to have any beneficial interest in them, and

(C)   the time when the company ceases to be a dependent subsidiary,

exceeds their value at the time when the company became a 'dependent subsidiary', but only if, at some time during the seven years before the company became a 'dependent subsidiary', that person was a director or employee of the company, or of the company as a director or employee of which he acquired the shares, or of an 'associated company' of either of them. [*FA 1988, s 79*].

(*c*)   *Special benefits.* If the person acquiring the shares receives a 'special benefit' through his ownership of them, and was at some time during the previous seven years a director or employee as mentioned under (*b*) above, then unless the benefit is taxable under another provision of the *Taxes Acts*, the charge is made for the year in which the benefit is received on the value thereof.

A benefit received when the company is a 'dependent subsidiary' whose shares are of a single class is a *'special benefit'*. In any other case, a benefit is a *'special benefit' unless*, when it becomes available, it is available to at least 90% of holders of shares of the same class and, when it is received, either

(i)   the majority of shares in respect of which the benefit is received are held otherwise than by, or for the benefit of, directors or employees of the company or an 'associated company', or the 'associated company' itself, or

(ii)   the company is 'employee-controlled' by virtue of holdings of shares of the class, or

(iii)   the company is a subsidiary which is not a 'dependent subsidiary', and the majority of its shares in respect of which the benefit is received are held otherwise than by, or for the benefit of, directors or employees of the company or of an 'associated company', or by, or for the benefit of, an 'associated company' other than a company of which it is a subsidiary.

In relation to benefits received before 12 November 1991, a benefit is a 'special benefit' unless it is received in respect of all shares of the same class and, when it is received, meets one of the conditions at (i)–(iii) above, but with the amendments that (i) refers to the majority of shares of the same class rather than to the majority of shares in respect of which the benefit is received, and (iii) requires that the company be a subsidiary, other than a 'dependent subsidiary', with shares of a single class.

[FA 1988, s 80; F(No 2)A 1992, s 37].

Any increase or reduction in a person's interest in shares is for these purposes treated as a proportionate acquisition or disposal of a separate interest. [FA 1988, s 81].

A company is 'employee-controlled' for these purposes by virtue of shares of a class if the majority of shares of that class (other than those held by or for an 'associated company') are held by or for employees or directors of the company or a company which it controls, and those employees and directors as holders of the shares are together able to control the company. Control is defined by Sec 840. [FA 1988, s 87(2)(3)]. 'Associated company' is as defined by Sec 416.

A subsidiary is a 'dependent subsidiary' throughout a period of account unless

(i)   the whole (or substantially the whole) of its business during that period is carried on with persons who are not members of the same group (i.e. the principal company, which is not itself a subsidiary, and all its subsidiaries), and

(ii)   during that period, any increase in the value of the company from intra-group transactions not on arm's length terms (other than group relief payments) does not exceed 5% of the company's value at the beginning of the period (or pro rata for periods other than twelve months), and

(iii)   the directors of the principal company give the inspector, within two years of the end of the period, a certificate that in their opinion (i) and (ii) are satisfied for that period, and attached to that certificate is a report from the subsidiary's auditors that, after enquiry, they are not aware of anything to indicate that the directors' opinion is unreasonable. [FA 1988, s 86(1)].

As regards (i) above, business carried on by a company with a subsidiary is treated as carried on with a non-member of the group unless all (or substantially all) of the business of that or any other subsidiary during the period of account is carried on with members of the group other than the company and its subsidiaries. [FA 1988, s 86(2)]. Also as regards (i) above, the Revenue consider that, to meet this condition, at least 90% of the company's business must be carried on outside the group, although a higher percentage may be required in any particular case. (Revenue Schedule E Manual, SE 2923).

Connected persons. Shares acquired by a person connected with a director or employee (within *Sec 839*, see 20 CONNECTED PERSONS) are deemed to be acquired by the director or employee for these purposes, as is any benefit received by such a connected person. A disposal, other than by an arm's length bargain with a non-connected person, is disregarded for these purposes until there is an onward disposal by such a bargain (except that this does not apply if the disposal is to the company concerned under the terms on which the shares were acquired), and any benefit received during such deemed ownership is deemed to be received by the person who originally acquired the shares. [*FA 1988, s 83*].

Company reorganisations. Any additional shares acquired by virtue of a holding within these provisions is treated as having been acquired at the same time, and in like manner, as the originally-acquired shares (whether or not consideration was given for the additional shares). As regards (*b*) above, all the shares are treated as one holding, their value being determined accordingly and the acquisition value allocated proportionately, and any consideration given for the additional shares is treated as additional consideration for the originally-acquired shares under the terms of the original acquisition.

If the shares originally acquired are converted into a new holding (within *TCGA 1992, ss 127–130*), the original and new holdings are equated for the purposes of these provisions, any new consideration *given* is treated as additional consideration under the terms of the original acquisition, and any consideration *received* is apportioned among the shares in the new holding, whose value is increased accordingly. [*FA 1988, s 82*].

Capital gains tax. Any amount charged under these provisions is treated as allowable expenditure for capital gains tax purposes on the first disposal (subject to the CONNECTED PERSONS (20) rules, see above). [*TCGA 1992, s 120(1)*].

Information. The company whose shares are acquired (and, if different, the company as a director or employee of which they were acquired) must, under penalty, notify the inspector of the acquisition and of any chargeable event or special benefit (see (*a*), (*c*) above) in relation to those shares. [*FA 1988, s 85*]. For 1993/94 and subsequent years, information should be sent to Inland Revenue, Employee Share Schemes Unit, Savings and Investment Division, First Floor, SW Wing, Bush House, Strand, London WC2B 4RD. (Revenue Tax Bulletin February 1994 p 110).

Transitional provisions. If tax is chargeable under the earlier provisions applying to shares acquired before 26 October 1987 (see above) by reference to the market value after that date of shares in a company which is not a dependent subsidiary (see above) on that date, and that market value is greater than the market value on that date, the latter is substituted.

Except as regards (*b*) and (*c*) above, the new provisions apply to shares acquired before 26 October 1987, unless the company was a dependent subsidiary on that date. However, the removal of a restriction on such shares is not a chargeable event (see (*a*) above) if it would have been excluded from being a chargeable event before that date by *FA 1973, 8 Sch 7*. [*FA 1988, s 88*].

81.5   *Example*

E, an employee of Perks Ltd, exercised, on 1 June 1987, an option, conferred on him by reason of his employment, to acquire 3,000 shares in that company, their open market value at that time being £12,000. He was duly charged to tax under Schedule E under the rules in 81.3 above. The shares were subject to one of the restrictions in *Sec 138(6)*. Market value per share at 26 October 1987 and at 1 June 1994 was £4.50 and £4.75 respectively. On 1 November 1996, a chargeable event under *FA 1988, s 78(2)* occurs by virtue of the restriction being removed. Removal of the restriction increases the value per share from £5.00 to £7.50. E has remained in the company's employment throughout the period and at no time has the company been a 'dependent subsidiary'.

81.6   Share Incentives and Options

E will be charged to income tax under Schedule E as follows.

			£	£
(i)	*Charge under ICTA 1988, s 138(1)(a) in 1994/95*			
	Market value at 26.10.87	note (*a*)	13,500	
	Less market value at 1.6.87		12,000	
				£1,500
(ii)	*Charge under FA 1988, s 78(3) in 1996/97*			
	Increase in market value resulting from chargeable event (3,000 × £2.50)	note (*b*)		£7,500

Notes

(*a*)   A charge arises on the seventh anniversary of acquisition (1 June 1994), but under the transitional provisions of *FA 1988, s 88(2)* it is calculated by reference to market value at 26 October 1987 as this is less than market value at 1 June 1994.

(*b*)   The charge under *FA 1988, s 78(3)* is on the increase in value as a result of the chargeable event. Note that the increase between 26 October 1987 and 31 October 1996 escapes any charge to income tax. If the value had decreased, no relief would have been available for the decrease.

(*c*)   On a sale of the shares, the capital gains tax base cost would include the amounts chargeable under (i) and (ii) above, such amounts being regarded as consideration given for the acquisition of the shares under *TCGA 1992, s 120(5)* and *s 120(1)* respectively (see Tolley's Capital Gains Tax).

81.6   PROFIT SHARING SCHEMES—APPROVAL

The provisions of *Secs 186, 187, 9 Sch* allow directors and employees of companies to receive shares free of income tax under certain conditions.

Under a scheme approved by the Board a company provides funds to UK resident trustees who purchase certain defined shares (see below) and appropriate such shares to eligible employees (see below). The limit on the market value of shares which may be appropriated to any one individual in any year of assessment is 10% of his salary (net of pension contributions—CCAB Memorandum TR 511, 26 August 1983) for PAYE purposes (less any benefits taxable, see 75.11 *et seq.*, 75.29 SCHEDULE E) for that year (or for the preceding year if greater), with a minimum limit of £3,000 and a maximum of £8,000 (£2,000 and £6,000 respectively for 1989/90 and 1990/91, £1,250 and £5,000 respectively for 1988/89 and earlier years). An employee to whom the trustees have appropriated shares ('a participant') contracts (i) not to assign or dispose of his beneficial interest in the shares within a 'period of retention' (see below); (ii) to permit the trustees to retain his shares for that period; (iii) to pay to the trustees a sum equal to income tax at the basic rate on the 'appropriate percentage' of the 'locked-in value' (see 81.7 below) should he direct them to transfer the shares to him before the 'release date', and (iv) not to direct them to dispose of his shares before the release date other than by sale for the best consideration obtainable or, if the shares are redeemable shares in a 'workers' co-operative', by redemption. The participant may, however, at any time direct the trustees to accept, in respect of his shares, certain share exchanges or other offers (including, in certain cases, qualifying corporate bonds) made to all holders of the same class of shares. Any contravention of (i) above renders him ineligible for the tax relief (and he is charged to tax as at the time the shares were appropriated to him). Alterations to the scheme must be approved. Approval of a scheme may be withdrawn if Board ceases to be satisfied with conditions. Appeal is available to the Special Commissioners within thirty days of notification of the Board's decision to refuse approval of a scheme or of an alteration in a scheme or in the trust deed. [*Secs 186(1), 187(2)(5), 9 Sch 2(2), 3(2), 4–6, 10 Sch 1, 6(1)(2); FA 1989, s 63; FA 1991, s 41; FA 1994, s 101*]. See *CIR v Burton Group plc Ch D 1990, 63 TC 191*, where an appeal against Revenue refusal of approval of a share option scheme under identical statutory provisions was upheld.

'*Period of retention*' begins on the date the shares are appropriated to the participant and ends two years later or, if earlier, at cessation of employment due to injury, disability, redundancy or death, or on reaching the 'relevant age' or, if the shares are redeemable shares in a 'workers' co-operative', on his ceasing to be employed by, or by a subsidiary of, the co-operative. [*10 Sch 2; FA 1991, s 38(3)*].

The '*relevant age*' must be specified in the scheme rules, must be the same for men and women, and must not be less than 60 or more than 75. In relation to schemes approved before 25 July 1991, it is the normal state pensionable age (although in practice the Revenue have permitted the alteration of scheme rules to make the relevant age 60 for both men and women for this purpose). [*9 Sch 8A; FA 1991, s 38(5)*].

The '*release date*' is the third anniversary of the date of appropriation of the shares to the participant if that anniversary occurs on or after 29 April 1996. Previously, it was the fifth anniversary of the date of appropriation, except that 29 April 1996 is itself the release date if it falls after the third anniversary but before the fifth anniversary. [*Sec 187(2); FA 1996, s 116*].

A '*workers' co-operative*' is a registered industrial and provident society within *Sec 486* (see Tolley's Corporation Tax under Industrial and Provident Societies) which is a co-operative society whose rules restrict membership to employees of the society, or of a subsidiary of the society, and trustees of its profit-sharing scheme, all of whom must be entitled to membership subject to any qualifications as regards age, length of service or other factors. The changes necessary to allow workers' co-operatives to set up profit-sharing schemes apply with effect after 24 July 1986, and where the rules of the society include provisions to enable it to set up such a scheme, these provisions are disregarded in determining whether the society is a *bona fide* co-operative society within the *Industrial and Provident Societies Act 1965* (or NI equivalent). [*Sec 187(10); FA 1986, s 24*].

A specimen set of scheme documents is included in Revenue Pamphlet IR 96, available free of charge from Public Enquiry Room, West Wing, Somerset House, London WC2R 1LF.

The shares must be (*a*) quoted on a recognised stock exchange or (*b*) in a company not controlled by another company or (*c*) in a company controlled by a quoted company (other than a company which is, or would be if resident in the UK, a close company); and they must be ordinary shares of the company concerned, its controlling company or a company (or its controlling company) which is a member of a consortium owning the company concerned (or its controlling company). Before 27 July 1989, it was additionally required that such a consortium member own not less than three-twentieths of the ordinary share capital of the company concerned or its controlling company. The shares must be fully paid up, not redeemable (unless they are shares in a workers' co-operative) and (except as below) not subject to any restrictions differing from those attaching to other shares of the same class. For shares appropriated after 24 July 1986, certain restrictions connected with cessation of employment may apply to scheme shares without applying to all shares of the same class. The articles of association may impose a restriction requiring all shares held by directors or employees to be disposed of on cessation of the employment, and all shares acquired by persons who are not directors or employees, but which were acquired in pursuance of rights or interests obtained by directors or employees, to be disposed of immediately they are so acquired. The required disposal must be by sale for money on specified terms, and the articles must also provide that any person disposing of shares of the same class (however acquired) may be required to sell them on the same terms. The restriction must not, however, require a disposal before the release date of shares the ownership of which has not been transferred to the participant, unless the shares are redeemable shares in a workers' co-operative. For earlier appropriations, the Revenue considered that the prohibition of restrictions did not preclude a company's Articles requiring an employee who left the company to transfer his shares after their legal ownership had passed to him (see Revenue Press Release 11 June 1985). Where there is more than one class of shares, the majority of the class of shares appropriated under the scheme must either (i) be held by persons other than directors or employees who received special rights of acquisition, or trustees for such persons or where shares are within (*c*) above and not within (*a*) above, companies which control the company whose shares are in question or of which that company is an associated company (as defined), or (ii) for shares appropriated after 24 July 1986, be '*employee-control shares*', i.e. shares held by persons who are or have been directors or employees, and who are together able to control the company by virtue of their holdings. [*9 Sch 10–12, 14; FA 1989, s 64*].

Persons eligible must include all employees (for schemes approved before 1 May 1995, all full-time employees) and full-time directors subject to tax under Case I of Schedule E (and may include any person who was such during the eighteen months preceding appropriation of shares to him, part-timers, and those chargeable under Case II or Case III of Schedule E) and employed for a maximum qualifying period of five years by the company or group concerned and all those who do participate must do so on similar terms (although variations by reference to salary, length of service, etc. do not prevent this condition being met). The terms must not in effect either discourage any description of eligible participant, or confer benefits wholly or mainly on directors or the highest-paid employees in a group scheme. A person is not eligible if, in the same year of assessment, shares have been appropriated to him under another approved scheme by the company or group concerned, or if within the preceding twelve months he and/or certain associates of his had a material (broadly more than 25% of ordinary share capital) interest in such a company which was a close company or would be if it were resident in the UK or if its shares were not publicly quoted. [*Sec 187(3), 9 Sch 2(3)(4), 8, 35–40; FA 1989, s 65; FA 1995, s 137(4)(7)*].

See 71.53 SCHEDULE D, CASES I AND II as regards deduction available to company for expenses in setting up the scheme and in meeting expenses of trustees in administering the scheme and acquiring shares under the scheme.

Personal equity plans. See 29.20 EXEMPT INCOME for the transfer of shares emerging from profit-sharing schemes into personal equity plans.

81.7　　**PROFIT SHARING SCHEMES—CHARGE TO TAX**

There is no charge to income tax on an eligible employee when the shares are appropriated to him. [*Sec 186(2)*]. On disposal or other chargeable event before the 'release date', tax is chargeable under Schedule E for the year of assessment in which the disposal or event takes place on a percentage of the 'locked-in' value (see below) as follows.

Disposals etc. on or after 29 April 1996:

Before third anniversary of appropriation	100%

Disposals etc. before 29 April 1996:

Before fourth anniversary of appropriation	100%
On or after fourth anniversary and before fifth anniversary	75%
On or after fifth anniversary	No charge

The '*release date*' is the third anniversary of the date of appropriation of the shares to the participant if that anniversary occurs on or after 29 April 1996. Previously, it was the fifth anniversary of the date of appropriation, except that 29 April 1996 is itself the release date if it falls after the third anniversary but before the fifth anniversary.

If the participant ceases employment with the company because of injury, disability, redundancy or reaching the 'relevant age' before the disposal and before the third anniversary (for disposals before 29 April 1996, before the fifth anniversary), the appropriate percentage is 50%. The '*relevant age*' in relation to schemes approved on or after 25 July 1991 must be specified in the scheme rules, must be the same for men and women, and must not be less than 60 or more than 75. For schemes approved before that date, it is generally the normal state pensionable age. However, in practice, such older schemes have been permitted to alter their rules to make 60 the relevant age for men as well as women for the purposes of the period of retention rules (see 81.6 above), and where this has been the case, for events occurring after 29 November 1993 (and after the scheme rules were altered), the relevant age for men for the purposes of determining the appropriate percentage is also 60.

[*Secs 186(4), 187(2), 10 Sch 3; FA 1991, s 38; FA 1994, s 100; FA 1996, ss 116, 117*].

Locked-in value of shares is their initial market value when appropriated to the employee (or any earlier dates as agreed in writing between the Board and the trustees) as reduced by any capital receipt charged to income tax under these provisions (see below), or the disposal proceeds, if less.

Proceeds are reduced by any payment to the trustees previously made for a rights issue but payments received from a disposal of rights are disregarded. Disposals are allocated to appropriations on a first in, first out basis. [*Secs 186(5)–(10), 187(8), 9 Sch 30(4); FA 1996, ss 117(2), 134, 20 Sch 11*].

Any **excess or unauthorised shares** (i.e. in excess of the limit (see 81.6 above) or appropriated to a person not eligible (see 81.6 above)) are chargeable to tax on the market value at whichever is the earlier: date of disposal; release date; or death. The charge on anniversary of appropriation is applied by reference to authorised shares before excess or unauthorised shares. [*10 Sch 6*].

Capital receipts are charged on the appropriate percentage (as above) and after any appropriate allowance (see below) for the year in which the trustees or the participant become entitled to them but do not include (*a*) taxable income in hands of recipient or (*b*) disposal proceeds on any of the chargeable events referred to above or (*c*) new shares issued in a company reconstruction under *TCGA 1992, ss 132, 136* (except redeemable shares not issued for new consideration or bonus issues following repayment of share capital and stock dividends) or (*d*) proceeds of rights used to exercise other rights. Capital receipts are charged only on the excess over the 'appropriate allowance', which, for any tax year, is £20 multiplied by one plus the number of years which fall within the three years (before 1997/98, five years) immediately preceding the year in question and in which the shares were appropriated to the participant, up to a maximum of £60 (before 1997/98, £100). If more than one capital receipt arises to the trustees or the participant in any year (before the release date), the receipts are set against the appropriate allowance in the order received. [*Sec 186(3)(12), 10 Sch 4, 5; FA 1978, s 56(6); FA 1980, s 46(6); FA 1982, s 42(1)(2); FA 1985, s 45(4); FA 1996, s 118*].

PAYE applies to disposals as above. The trustees shall pay to the company out of the disposal proceeds, the sum of money on which tax is chargeable and the company must deduct tax under PAYE and pay the balance to the participant. The company is the employing company or, if more than one, whichever company the Board directs. If there is no appropriate company, the Board may direct the trustees to apply PAYE as if the participant were a former employee of theirs. [*10 Sch 7*].

Capital gains tax is chargeable on disposal of the shares by the participants, without deduction for any amount determined for purposes of charging income tax under the above provisions. For this purpose, a participant is absolutely entitled to his shares as against the trustees. The allowable cost is the initial market value of the shares. No CGT arises to the trustees if they appropriate shares to participants within eighteen months of acquisition. [*TCGA 1992, s 238(1)(2)*].

Dividends received on shares by the trustees are not liable to the additional rate if the shares are appropriated within eighteen months of acquisition. [*Sec 186(11)*].

81.8 SAVINGS-RELATED SHARE OPTION SCHEMES

Savings-related schemes were introduced by *FA 1980, s 47, 10 Sch* and are now contained in *Sec 185, 9 Sch*. A company may establish a scheme for its directors and employees to obtain options to acquire shares in itself or another company without any charge to income tax on the receipt of the options and on any increase in value of the shares between the date of the option being granted and the date on which it is exercised (see 81.4 above) and, for capital gains tax purposes, the market value of the shares will not be substituted for the consideration given. Reliefs are withdrawn where option is exercised within three years of being obtained in the circumstances described at (*j*) or (*l*) below, except that for options acquired after 31 December 1991, the exemption from charge on receipt of the option continues to apply in those circumstances.

The scheme must be linked to an approved savings scheme (see 29.11(vi) EXEMPT INCOME), on which interest and bonuses are exempt from tax, to provide the funds for the acquisition of the shares when the option is exercised. Monthly contributions to all such schemes must not be permitted to exceed £250, and the minimum monthly contribution set for any scheme must not exceed £10 (but see below). The limits may be altered by the Treasury, as may the interest and bonuses on the associated savings scheme, but not so as to affect existing contracts. The requirements for approval of the share option scheme and its participants etc. are stated below. [*Sec 185(1)(a), (2)–(4), 9 Sch 24; FA 1991, ss 39(3)(4)(8), 40; SI 1991 No 1741*].

See 71.53 SCHEDULE D, CASES I AND II as regards deduction available to company for expenses in setting up the scheme.

The Treasury will be issuing a new contractual sharesave scheme prospectus in Spring 1996 providing for a new three-year savings contract in addition to the existing five- and seven-year contracts. The minimum monthly contribution is to be reduced from £10 to £5. (Revenue Press Release REV 7, 28 November 1995).

Approval of scheme is by the Board (on application in writing by the company which has established the scheme, 'the company concerned') if the following conditions are included.

(*a*) The directors and employees may obtain rights to acquire 'scheme shares', see below.

(*b*) The scheme shares are to be paid for out of savings (and interest) with a certified contractual savings scheme (SAYE) (under *Sec 326*) which is approved by the Board for this purpose.

(*c*) Rights under the scheme must not (save as permitted under (*d*) to (*m*) below) be exercisable before the 'bonus date' i.e. the date on which the SAYE repayments fall due. For this purpose, the repayments may be taken as including, or as not including, a bonus, and the decision on this must be taken when options under the scheme are acquired. Where repayments are taken as including the maximum bonus, the time when the repayments fall due is the earliest date on which the maximum bonus is payable and in any other case, the earliest date on which a bonus is payable.

(*d*)   If a participant dies before the bonus date, the rights must be exercised, if at all, within twelve months after his death and if he dies within six months after the bonus date, the rights may be exercised within twelve months after the bonus date.

(*e*)   If a participant ceases to hold the office or employment which makes him eligible for the scheme because of injury, disability, redundancy or retiring on reaching a 'specified age', his rights must be exercised, if at all, within six months of his so ceasing, and if he so ceases for any other reason within three years of obtaining the rights, they cannot be exercised at all (except as under (*l*) below). If he so ceases for any other reason more than three years after obtaining the rights, the scheme must provide for forfeiture of the rights or their exercise within six months of so ceasing.

(*f*)   A participant continuing in employment after reaching a 'specified age' may exercise his rights under the scheme within six months.

(*g*)   Rights under the scheme must not be transferable or capable of being exercised later than six months after the bonus date (except as under (*d*) above).

(*h*)   The participant's contribution under the SAYE contract must secure, as nearly as may be, repayment equal to the amount required for purchase of the shares in the option acquired. See (*c*) above for determining the repayments.

(*i*)   The price at which scheme shares may be acquired under the option must be stated when the option is obtained and not be manifestly less than 80% of the market value of shares of the same class at that time or, if Board and company agree in writing, at some earlier time. The scheme may provide for such variation of the stated price as may be necessary to take account of any variation in the share capital of which the scheme shares form part.

As regards (*e*) and (*f*) above, the '*specified age*' must be specified in the scheme rules, must be the same for men and women, and must not be less than 60 or more than 75. In relation to approvals before 25 July 1991, it was the normal state pensionable age.

The scheme *may* also include the following provisions.

(*j*)   If a person obtains control of the company whose shares are scheme shares as a result of making a general offer to acquire the whole of its issued share capital or of all the shares of the same class as the scheme shares, rights under the scheme to acquire shares may be exercised within six months of that person obtaining control. Rights under the scheme may also be exercised at any time when a person becomes bound or entitled to acquire shares in the company under the *Companies Act 1985, s 428* (or NI equivalent) (power to acquire shares of dissenting shareholders). Where the court sanctions a compromise or arrangement with creditors and members under the *Companies Act 1985, s 425* (or NI equivalent) or if the company passes a resolution for voluntary winding-up, rights under the scheme to acquire shares may be exercised within six months of the sanction or the resolution. If these rights are exercised within three years of their being obtained, then the exemption from income tax as above will not apply.

(*k*)   If any other company (the 'acquiring company') obtains control of the company whose shares are scheme shares, or is bound or entitled to acquire shares in the company, in the circumstances described in (*j*) above, the scheme may provide for the rights to acquire scheme shares to be exchanged for rights to acquire shares in the acquiring company, or in another company falling within (i) below in relation to the acquiring company, which are equivalent, as regards value and conditions, to the rights under the existing scheme. The new rights are then treated as having been granted at the time the original rights were granted, and the exchange is not treated itself as the acquisition of a right. The exchange must take place within six months of the company taking unconditional control, or of the court sanctioning the compromise or arrangement, or within the period during which the acquiring company remains bound or entitled to acquire the shares. Where a scheme approved before 1 August 1987 was altered before 1 August 1989 to include such a provision, the alteration may apply to rights obtained before the date on which the alteration took effect, and may permit an exchange where the event on which it depends occurs after 16 March 1987 but before the date on which the alteration took effect. An exchange may be permitted in a case where, following the event in question, the rights would otherwise have ceased to be exercisable. The approval of the Board is required in the normal way for an alteration to a scheme permitting such exchanges.

(*l*)   Where the office or employment giving rise to eligibility under the scheme is in a subsidiary of which the company which established the scheme ceases to have control, or if it relates to a business (or part) which is transferred to a person other than a subsidiary or associated company, the rights under a scheme approved or altered after 24 July 1986 may be exercised within six months of the change. Where a scheme approved before 1 August 1986 is altered in this respect before 1 August 1988, the alteration may apply to rights acquired before the date on which the alteration takes effect, and the scheme may also allow rights to be exercised where such a change took place before the alteration was made but after 17 March 1986.

(*m*)   The scheme may extend to other companies of which the company concerned has control and is then a 'group scheme' with 'participating companies' (for which see *CIR v Reed International plc and cross-appeal CA, [1995] STC 889*).

(*n*)   If at the bonus date, rights under a scheme are held by a person who is then employed by a company which is not a participating company (see (*m*) above) but which is an associated company of or under the control of the company which established the scheme, the rights may be exercised within six months of that date. This applies to options granted on or after 29 April 1996 but, if the scheme is altered accordingly (subject to the Board's approval) before 5 May 1998, it may also be applied to options granted before the alteration and before 29 April 1996 (whether or not the bonus date falls before that date). Such alteration is not regarded as giving rise to the acquisition of new rights by an option holder.

The Board need not approve a scheme if it appears to them that there are features which are neither essential nor reasonably incidental to its purpose, or which are designed to discourage an eligible person from participating. Where the company establishing the scheme is a member of a group of companies, the scheme must not in effect be restricted wholly or mainly to directors or the more highly-paid employees in the group. If, after approval, any of the above conditions cease to be satisfied or any unapproved alteration is made to the scheme or information is not provided, approval is withdrawn but existing right to tax-free exercise of option remains. There is a right of appeal to the Special Commissioners within thirty days of notification of the Board's decision to withhold or withdraw approval of a scheme or of an alteration to a scheme. [*9 Sch 1–6, 9, 15–25; FA 1989, s 62(3); FA 1991, s 38; FA 1996, s 113*]. See *CIR v Burton Group plc Ch D 1990, 63 TC 191* where an appeal against a Revenue refusal to approve an alteration imposing performance conditions was upheld. In *CIR v Reed International plc and cross-appeal CA, [1995] STC 889*, a similar decision was reached where the amendment removed a contingency on which options would be exerciseable and would be required to be exercised within a specified period. This did not amount to the acquisition of a new and different right to acquire scheme shares. See also *CIR v Eurocopy plc Ch D 1991, 64 TC 370*.

A specimen set of scheme documents is contained in Revenue Pamphlet IR 98, available free of charge from Public Enquiry Room, West Wing, Somerset House, London WC2R 1LF.

'Scheme shares' must

(i)   form part of the ordinary share capital of the company concerned; or a company which has control of the company concerned; or a company which either is, or has control of, a company which is a member of a consortium owning either the company concerned or a company controlling that company;

(ii)   be (*a*) quoted on a recognised stock exchange or (*b*) shares in a company not under the control of another company or (*c*) be shares in a company under the control of a quoted company (other than a company which is, or would be if resident in the UK, a close company);

(iii)   be fully paid and not redeemable and not subject to any restrictions (as defined but excluding any provisions similar to the Stock Exchange Model Code for Securities Transactions by Directors of Listed Companies (November 1984)) other than restrictions which attach to all shares of the same class. For shares appropriated after 24 July 1986, certain restrictions connected with cessation of employment may apply to scheme shares without applying to all shares of the same class. The articles of association may impose a restriction requiring all shares held by directors or employees to be disposed of on cessation of the employment, and all shares acquired by persons who are not directors or employees, but which were acquired in pursuance of rights or interests obtained by directors or employees, to be disposed of immediately they are so acquired. The required disposal must be by sale for money on specified terms, and the articles must also provide that any person disposing of shares of the same class (however acquired) may be required to sell them on the same terms;

(iv)   except where the scheme shares are in a company whose ordinary share capital is all one class, the majority of shares of the same class must be held either (1) by persons other than (*a*) shareholders who acquired their shares as directors or employees of that or any other company and not in pursuance of an offer to the public and (*b*) trustees for such shareholders and (*c*) where shares are within (ii)(*c*) above and not within (ii)(*a*) above, companies which control the company whose shares are in question or of which that company is an associated company; or (2) for shares appropriated after 24 July 1986, be '*employee-control shares*', i.e. shares held by persons who are or have been directors or employees, and who are together able to control the company by virtue of their holdings. [*9 Sch 10–14; FA 1989, s 64*].

As regards (iii) above, for appropriations before 24 July 1986, the prohibition on restrictions did not preclude a company's Articles giving its directors a discretionary veto on share transfers, provided that a declaration was made (and publicised to employees) that the veto would not be exercised to discriminate against shares acquired under the scheme. It did, however, prevent approval being given to a scheme where a company could compel employees leaving the company to sell their shares to another shareholder. (Revenue Press Release 11 June 1985).

Persons eligible to participate must include every person who

(A)   is an employee (for schemes approved before 1 May 1995, a full-time employee) or a full-time director of the company concerned or, in the case of a group scheme, a participating company, and

(B)   has been such an employee or director at all times during a qualifying period, not exceeding five years, and

(C)   is chargeable to tax in respect of his office or employment under Case I of Schedule E.

It may include part-time directors or employees and those whose emoluments are not chargeable under Case I of Schedule E.

The above persons must be able to obtain and exercise rights on similar terms, and those who do participate must actually do so on similar terms, but there may be variation of rights between participants according to their remuneration, length of service or similar factors. A person must not be eligible if he, and/or certain associates of his, has, or at any time within the preceding twelve months has had, a material interest (broadly more than 25% of ordinary share capital) in a close company (within meaning of *Sec 414*) which is a company whose shares may be obtained under the scheme or that company's holding company or a member of a consortium owning such a company. For this purpose 'close company' includes a non-resident company which would otherwise be close and a company which would be close except for its stock exchange quotation. [*Sec 187(3), 9 Sch 8, 26, 37–40; FA 1989, s 65; FA 1995, s 137(2)(7); FA 1996, s 113(3)*].

Transitional arrangements. A person who already had a SAYE contract before 15 November 1980 and has obtained rights under an existing scheme (see below) to acquire shares in a company of which he is an employee or director (or a company of which such a company has control) using repayments made under that contract, may come under the scheme described above and tax relief will be restricted to the proceeds which would have been available if the terms of that contract had corresponded to those of a scheme approved as above. [*9 Sch 16(2)(3)*].

Information. The Board may by notice in writing require any person to provide (in not less than thirty days) such information as the Board think necessary, and as the person to whom the notice is addressed has or can reasonably provide, for the performance of their functions under these provisions. [*9 Sch 6*].

'Associated company'. For the above purposes, a company is an 'associated company' of another at a given time, if at that time (or, except in (*e*) or (*l*) above, at any time in the previous twelve months), one of the two has control of the other, or both are under the control of the same person or persons. [*Sec 187(2)*].

Personal equity plans. See 29.20 EXEMPT INCOME for the transfer of shares emerging from SAYE share option schemes into personal equity plans.

81.9   EXECUTIVE SHARE OPTION SCHEMES

(Note. Reliefs under the type of scheme described below are **withdrawn** by *FA 1996* for options granted **on or after 17 July 1995**, unless they were granted within 30 days of a written offer or invitation to apply for them made before that date. Relief is, however, available under a type of scheme introduced by *FA 1996* (Company Share Option Plans) which is more restrictive than, but which retains many of the features of, the type of scheme described below. See 81.10 below for details of the *FA 1996* scheme and of the transition from the old type of scheme to the new.)

FA 1984, s 38, 10 Sch introduced a more flexible type of share option scheme, now contained in *Sec 185, 9 Sch*. Where an individual obtains, as a director or employee of a company, the right to acquire shares in that or any other company, under a scheme approved under *9 Sch* (see below), a liability will arise under Schedule E (as earned income) on any excess of the market value at that time of a similar quantity of the shares in question over the aggregate of the consideration given for the right and the price at which the shares may be acquired under the right. (See, however, (vi) below as regards certain options acquired after 31 December 1991.) Otherwise no tax is chargeable in respect of receipt of the right. Similarly, no tax is chargeable on exercise of the right, and for capital gains tax purposes the shares are treated as acquired for the actual consideration given plus the amount of any charge on receipt of the right (as above), provided that:

(*a*)   it is not exercised less than three or more than ten years after it was obtained by the individual; and

(b)   it is not exercised by the individual within three years of his exercise of a right under the same or any other scheme approved under these provisions attracting relief from income tax treatment (although other rights exercised on the same day may be disregarded for this purpose).

In the case of rights exercised by a personal representative not more than ten years after they were obtained by the deceased individual, (a) and (b) above do not have to be satisfied.

Where a charge arises on receipt of the right (as above), and a charge subsequently arises under *Sec 135* (see 81.3 above) or *Sec 162* (see 75.19 SCHEDULE E) (e.g. because the scheme has ceased to be approved under *9 Sch* (below)), relief is given for the charge previously borne. [*Sec 185(1)–(3), (5)–(8), 9 Sch 27(3)*].

The conditions for approval by the Board of a company share option scheme under *9 Sch* are as follows.

(i)   The scheme must provide for directors and employees to obtain rights to acquire shares (see (iv) below). [*9 Sch 9(1)*].

(ii)   Only full-time directors and 'qualifying employees' of participating companies (see (vii) below) may participate, although a scheme may permit exercise of rights by persons who have ceased to be full-time directors or qualifying employees, and by personal representatives of deceased participants (not more than one year after the date of death). 'Full-time' generally means working 25 or more hours per week excluding meal breaks (see *Explanatory notes* referred to below), and an employee is a '*qualifying employee*' if he is not a director of the company or of any other participating company in a group scheme (see (vii) below) (and, for schemes approved before 1 May 1995, if he is required under his terms of employment to work for the company for at least 20 hours per week (again excluding meal breaks)). Schemes approved before 1 May 1995 may be altered after that date to admit part-time employees. A person must not be eligible to participate (i.e. to obtain or exercise rights) if he, and/or certain associates of his, has, or at any time in the preceding twelve months has had, a 'material interest' (broadly more than 10% of ordinary share capital) in a close company which is a company whose shares may be obtained under the scheme or that company's holding company or a member of a consortium owning such a company. For this purpose, 'close company' includes a non-resident company which would otherwise be close and a company which would be close except for its stock exchange quotation. [*Sec 187(3), 9 Sch 8, 27, 37–40; FA 1989, s 65; FA 1995, s 137(3)(7)*]. Shares which the participant may acquire under an option are included when considering the 'material interest' test, i.e. the total holding including such shares must, if appropriate, be brought down to the 10% level or below twelve months before the exercise of the option (see *Explanatory notes* referred to below).

(iii)   The value (at the time of grant of the right) of shares over which an individual may hold unexercised rights must not exceed the greater of £100,000 and four times his emoluments (within PAYE but excluding benefits-in-kind and after deducting employee's superannuation contributions to which net pay arrangement applies) of the current or preceding year. Where there were no such emoluments in the preceding year, the alternative limit is four times such emoluments for the twelve months from the first day in the current year for which there were such emoluments. [*9 Sch 28*].

(iv)   The shares over which options are granted must meet identical conditions to those relating to scheme shares under 81.8 above [*9 Sch 10–14; FA 1989, s 64*], except that the restrictions referred to in 81.8(iii) do not include any terms for repayment of, or security for, a loan. [*FA 1988, s 69*].

(v) Rights must be non-transferable (but see (ii) above as regards personal representatives of deceased participants and (viii) below as regards certain changes of control). [*9 Sch 27(2)*].

(vi) Except as detailed below for options granted after 31 December 1991, the price to be paid must be fixed at the time of grant of the right, and must not be manifestly less than the market value of the shares at that time (or at any earlier time if the Board and company so agree). The scheme may provide for such variation of the stated price as may be necessary to take account of any variation in the share capital of which the shares subject to the option form part. The market value will normally be fixed at a date not more than 30 days prior to grant of the option. If the market value is, or should have been, known at the date of grant of the option to exceed the aggregate of any consideration for the option and the option price, then no option can be granted on such terms in accordance with an approved scheme. Only where an accidental error occurs in valuing the shares (within the normal tolerances for such valuations) can that aggregate be less than market value without being 'manifestly' so. The involvement of Shares Valuation Division should prevent such errors in practice. See above as regards the income tax liability on grant of an option at less than market value. No such charge will, however, arise solely because of an increase in market value between an agreed valuation date and the date of grant of the option. (See *Explanatory notes* referred to below.)

After **31 December 1991**, shares may in certain circumstances be acquired at a price not manifestly less than 85% of the market value at the time the option is granted (or such earlier time as is agreed with the Board, as above). This applies where:

(*a*)   the company has established, or (at the time the option is granted) is a participating company in relation to, an approved savings-related share option scheme (see 81.8 above) or an approved profit sharing scheme (see 81.6 above) (a '*qualifying scheme*') (although there is no requirement for the scheme to have been put into operation); and

(*b*)   either

(i)   where there is only one qualifying scheme, every employee eligible to participate in that scheme at the time the option under the approved share option scheme is granted has, in the preceding twelve months, been informed of the existence of the qualifying scheme by either the employing company, the company establishing the scheme or (in the case of a group scheme) any participating company, or

(ii)   where there is more than one qualifying scheme, the condition in (i) above is satisfied in relation to each of them.

As regards (*a*) above, withdrawal of approval of a qualifying scheme after the date of grant of the option is disregarded even if it applies retrospectively from a time before that date. As regards (*b*) above, the annual return for the scheme will be required to set out how the notification requirement has been fulfilled. (Revenue Tax Bulletin November 1991 p 2). Both (*a*) and (*b*) above must be satisfied, where the approved share option scheme is a group scheme (see (vii) below) at the time the option is granted, as respects each company to which the scheme is expressed to extend at that time; otherwise they must be satisfied as respects the company establishing the scheme. The provision for an income tax charge, in the exceptional case where the aggregate of any consideration for the option and the option price is less than the market value of the shares (see above), is correspondingly amended in cases where options are granted at 85% of market value. [*Sec 185(6B); 9 Sch 29; FA 1991, s 39*].

(vii)   The scheme may extend to other companies of which the company setting up the scheme has control, and all companies in such a 'group scheme' are 'participating companies'. [*9 Sch 1(3)(4)*]. See also *Explanatory notes* referred to below.

(viii)   The scheme may also include a provision for exchange of options following a change of control, etc., subject to the same conditions as apply in relation to *FA 1980* schemes (see 81.8(*k*) above). [*9 Sch 15*].

The Board need not approve a scheme if it appears to them that there are features which are neither essential nor reasonably incidental to its purpose. If, after approval, any of the above conditions cease to be satisfied, or any unapproved alteration is made to the scheme, or information required by the Board (see below) is not provided, approval may be withdrawn. There is a right of appeal to the Special Commissioners within thirty days of notification of the Board's decision to withhold or withdraw approval of a scheme or of an alteration to a scheme. [*9 Sch 2(1), 3(1), 4, 5*]. The Board's refusal to accept an amendment to the rules of an approved scheme, allowing for the imposition or variation, after the date of grant of options, of 'key task' conditions on whose fulfilment the number of shares to which an employee was entitled under the scheme depended, was reversed on appeal in *CIR v Burton Group plc Ch D 1990, 63 TC 191*. A similar conclusion was reached in *CIR v Reed International plc and cross-appeal CA, [1995] STC 889*, where the amendment removed a contingency on which options would be exerciseable and would be required to be exercised within a specified period. This did not amount to the acquisition of a new and different right to acquire scheme shares. In *CIR v Eurocopy plc Ch D 1991, 64 TC 370*, however, the Board's refusal to accept (in relation to existing options) an amendment to a scheme, bringing forward the earliest date on which options could be exercised, was upheld. A different right would be acquired as a result of the amendment, so that the option price set at the time of the original grant would be 'manifestly less' (see (vi) above) than the market value of the shares at the time the new right was acquired.

The existence of a 'phantom' scheme alongside an approved scheme, designed to provide the employee with the cash needed to subscribe for shares under the approved scheme, does not affect either the approval of the option scheme or the tax relief on exercise of the option. (Revenue Tax Bulletin May 1992 p 19).

The Board may, by notice in writing, require any person to provide (in not less than thirty days) such information as the Board consider necessary, and as the person to whom the notice is addressed has or can reasonably provide, for the performance of the Board's functions under these provisions. [*9 Sch 6*].

See 71.53 SCHEDULE D, CASES I AND II as regards deduction available to company for expenses in setting up the scheme.

Explanatory notes on the setting up of a scheme under these provisions, including a specimen set of scheme rules, are in Revenue Pamphlet IR 100, available free of charge from Public Enquiry Room, West Wing, Somerset House, London WC2R 1LF.

81.10   **COMPANY SHARE OPTION PLANS**

Company share option plans are discretionary share option schemes approved under *ICTA 1988, 9 Sch* and subject to the provisions of *Sec 185, 9 Sch* (see 81.9 above) as amended by *FA 1996*. They are designed to replace executive share option schemes (see 81.9 above). They retain most of the rules and features of such schemes but are more restrictive, being aimed particularly at employees in the middle and lower income ranges. The provisions described below apply to rights granted on or after 29 April 1996 but see also the transitional provisions below as regards existing executive schemes.

The provisions relating to company share option plans differ from those relating to executive schemes and described in 81.9 above in the following respects.

81.11 Share Incentives and Options

(*a*)   It is a condition of approval of a scheme by the Board (replacing the condition at 81.9(iii) above) that the aggregate market value (at the time of the grant of the right) of shares over which an individual may hold unexercised rights under the scheme (or any other approved share option scheme, other than a savings-related scheme, established by the company or an associated company) must not exceed £30,000.

(*b*)   It is a further condition of approval that the price to be paid must be fixed at the time of the grant and must not be manifestly less than the market value of the shares at that time (or at any earlier time if the Board and company so agree). Whilst this duplicates the principal condition at 81.9(vi) above, the further possibility therein mentioned of granting options at a discount of up to 15% in specified circumstances is not permitted under the company share option plan provisions. The possibility of the scheme providing for necessary variations in the stated price is retained. See 81.9(vi) above as regards meaning of 'manifestly less' and further comment.

(*c*)   Amendments purely consequential to the removal of the right to grant options at a discount are made to *Sec 185* and *TCGA 1992, s 120*.

[*Sec 185(6), 9 Sch 28, 29; TCGA 1992, s 120(6); FA 1996, s 114, 41 Sch Pt V(5)*].

Transitional provisions. As regards rights granted on or after 29 April 1996, executive share option schemes (see 81.9 above) approved before that date (existing schemes) are deemed to have incorporated into their rules the conditions at (*a*) and (*b*) above, notwithstanding anything included in the scheme to the contrary. Such deemed alterations to schemes are treated as having been approved by the Board before 29 April 1996. If, however, a company does not wish to adopt both conditions into its scheme, it may give notice to that effect to the Board before 1 January 1997. The scheme will then cease to be an approved scheme as from the date of the notice. [*FA 1996, s 114(9), 16 Sch*].

As regards rights obtained by a person on or after 17 July 1995 and before 29 April 1996 under an existing scheme, the conditions at (*a*) and (*b*) above must be satisfied as if they applied in respect of rights granted during that period and as if the scheme had adopted them accordingly. In the event of the conditions not being met, the rights in question are treated as having been obtained otherwise than under an approved scheme. In considering whether or not the £30,000 limit at (*a*) above is breached, the value of unexercised options granted before 17 July 1995 must be taken into account. [*FA 1996, s 115(1)–(3)(5)*].

In the case of an executive scheme approved before 17 July 1995, rights obtained on or after that date but within 30 days of a written offer or invitation to apply for them made before that date are regarded as having been obtained before that date (so that the above provision does not apply and the options fall within 81.9 above). [*FA 1996, s 115(4)*].

81.11   EMPLOYEE SHARE OWNERSHIP TRUSTS

Under provisions introduced by *FA 1989, ss 67–74, 5 Sch*, companies may claim an allowable deduction, for corporation tax, for payments to qualifying employee share ownership trusts (ESOTs), being, broadly, trusts set up to acquire shares in the employer company and distribute them to employees. After 31 March 1991, a deduction is also available for the costs of setting up such a trust. See 71.53 SCHEDULE D, CASES I AND II for details of these deductions. Investment companies may also obtain the deduction by treating payments as management expenses. Neither the ESOT nor its beneficiaries qualify for any special income tax or capital gains tax reliefs, although such a trust may be used in conjunction with an approved profit sharing scheme (see 81.6 above) or, for trusts established on or after 29 April 1996, an approved savings-related share option scheme (see 81.8 above), thus enabling beneficiaries to receive shares free of income tax. In certain circumstances (see below), where the above-mentioned deduction has been made, the tax relief given to the company may, effectively, be clawed back by means of a charge under

Schedule D, Case VI on the trustees, with powers to recover the tax so charged from the company.

Definition. A trust is an ESOT at any time (the relevant time) if it was a 'qualifying ESOT' at the time it was established, regardless of whether or not it is a qualifying ESOT at the relevant time. A '*qualifying ESOT*' is a trust established, by means of a trust deed, by a UK resident company (the 'founding company') which is not controlled by another company, and which, at the time of establishment, satisfies the conditions in *FA 1989, 5 Sch 3–11* as summarised below. A trust is established when the deed under which it is established is executed. [*FA 1989, 5 Sch 1, 2, 13, 17; FA 1994, 13 Sch 8*].

The trust deed must deal with the appointment, retirement, removal and replacement of **trustees.** The trustees must number at least three, must all be UK resident and must include a trust corporation or a solicitor (or member of such other professional body as the Board may allow). Most of the trustees must be employees, either of the founding company or of a UK resident company controlled by it, who have never had a material interest (broadly more than 5% of ordinary share capital) in any such company, and those trustees must be selected by a majority of employees or by the employees' elected representatives. Most of the trustees must never have been directors of either the founding company or a UK resident company controlled by it.

For ESOTs set up after 3 May 1994, two other possible trust structures are permitted: a 'paritarian' trust structure; or a UK resident corporate trustee controlled by the founding company and with directors composed in the same way as the trustees in a 'paritarian' trust structure. The 'paritarian' trust structure requires three or more UK resident trustees, of whom at least one must be, and at least two must not be, 'professional' trustees. A '*professional*' trustee is a trust corporation or a solicitor (or member of such other professional body as the Board may allow), other than an employee or director of the founding company (or of a UK resident company controlled by it), selected by the non-professional trustees. Also, at least half of the non-professional trustees must be employees of the founding company (or of a UK resident company controlled by it) who have never had a material interest (as above) in any such company and who are selected either by election (with all such employees being able to stand for election or to vote) or by selection by elected representatives of those employees.

A trust is not a qualifying ESOT at any time when the requirements as to trustees are not satisfied.

[*FA 1989, 5 Sch 3–3C, 12, 12A; FA 1994, s 102, 13 Sch 2–5*].

The terms of the trust deed must be such that a person is a **beneficiary** at a particular time if

(*a*) he is then an employee or director of the founding company or a UK resident company then under its control, and

(*b*) he has been an employee or director of such a company throughout a period specified in the trust deed, which must not be more than five years (and which, for trusts established before 29 April 1996, had to be at least one year), ending at that time, working for at least twenty hours a week (ignoring holidays and sickness). (For trusts established under deeds executed on or after 1 May 1995, the minimum hours restriction applies only to directors.)

The trust deed *may* provide that where a person has been an employee or director as required under (*a*) above throughout a period of the length specified in the trust deed as under (*b*) above and ending when the employment/directorship ceased or the company ceased to be controlled by the founding company, that person may continue to be a beneficiary for 18 months thereafter. For trusts established on or after 29 April 1996, the deed *may* also provide for a person to be a beneficiary at a given time if at that time he is eligible to participate in an approved savings-related share option scheme (see 81.8 above) established by a member of the founding company's group; the deed must then provide that the only powers and duties the trustees may exercise in relation to such beneficiaries (if they would not otherwise be beneficiaries) are those exercisable under such a scheme. A trust deed *may* also provide for a charity to be a beneficiary if the trust is being wound up in consequence of there being no qualifying beneficiaries under the deed. All persons not satisfying these conditions at a particular time must be excluded from being beneficiaries at that time. Notwithstanding the fact that a person satisfies these conditions, he cannot be a beneficiary at a particular time if he then has, or has had at any time in the previous twelve months, a material interest (broadly more than 5% of ordinary share capital) in the founding company (but this restriction does not apply to persons who qualify as beneficiaries only by virtue of their being eligible to participate in a savings-related scheme).

[*FA 1989, 5 Sch 4; FA 1995, s 137(5)(9); FA 1996, ss 119, 120(1)(5)–(7)(12)*].

The **general functions of trustees** must be to receive sums and to acquire, retain and manage and eventually to transfer sums or securities (i.e. shares and debentures) to beneficiaries or transfer securities at not less than market value to trustees of approved profit sharing schemes (see 81.6 above) or, for trusts established on or after 29 April 1996, grant rights to acquire shares (i.e. under approved savings-related share option schemes —see 81.8 above) to beneficiaries. Any sum received, whether from the founding company or by way of loan or otherwise, must be expended, within the 'relevant period', for a qualifying purpose (see 71.53 SCHEDULE D, CASES I AND II), being retained in cash or in a bank or building society account in the meantime. The '*relevant period*' is the period of nine months after the end of the period of account, of the company making the payment to the trust, for which the payment is charged as an expense, or, in the case of sums received other than from the founding company or a company under its control, nine months from the date of receipt of the sum in question.

Sums received are to be treated as being expended on a first in/first out basis, and all sums paid to different beneficiaries at the same time must be paid on similar terms (although variations according to remuneration, length of service or similar factors are permitted). The trust deed must not contain features which are not essential or reasonably incidental to the purposes herein described as being the general functions of the trustees. [*FA 1989, 5 Sch 5, 6, 10; FA 1996, s 120(8)(11)(12)*].

The **securities** to be acquired by the trust must be fully paid up, non-redeemable ordinary shares in the founding company which are free of restrictions other than those attaching to all shares of the same class or certain restrictions imposed by the company's articles of association. The deed must preclude the trustees from acquiring shares either at greater than open market value or at a time when the founding company is under the control of another company. It *may* allow for the trustees to acquire securities other than shares in the founding company if they are acquired as a result of a company reorganisation or reconstruction within *TCGA 1992, s 126* or *s 135* and the shares originally held were shares in the founding company. The trustees must transfer securities to beneficiaries within seven years (twenty years in the case of trusts established under deeds executed after 3 May 1994) of their acquisition (securities acquired being deemed to be transferred on a first in/first out basis) and on 'qualifying terms'. A transfer is made on '*qualifying terms*' if

(i)   all securities transferred at the same time (other than to savings-related share option scheme participants—see below) are transferred on similar terms (allowing, if desired, for differences in levels of remuneration, length of service or similar factors),

(ii)   securities have been offered to all existing beneficiaries (disregarding those who would be not be beneficiaries but for their being participants in a savings-related scheme) at the time of transfer, and

(iii) securities are transferred to all such persons who have accepted.

As regards trusts established on or after 29 April 1996, a transfer of securities is also made on '*qualifying terms*' if made to a person exercising a right to acquire shares under an approved savings-related share option scheme (see 81.8 above) established by the founding company or a company under its control, where the consideration for the transfer is payable to the trustees.

The trust deed must contain specified provisions determining the time at which the trustees are deemed to acquire and transfer securities and when they are considered to retain securities.

[*FA 1989, 5 Sch 7, 8, 9, 11; FA 1994, 13 Sch 7; FA 1996, s 120(9)(10)(12)*].

See *FA 1989, 5 Sch 14-16* as regards interpretation of the provisions of *Schedule 5*.

Clearance. Requests for clearance that a trust is a qualifying ESOT, supported by copies of the trust deed or draft deed and any other relevant information, should be sent to Inland Revenue, Business Profits Division (Employee Share Schemes), Room 111A, New Wing, Somerset House, Strand, London WC2R 1LB.

Tax charge on trustees. Where a 'chargeable event' occurs in relation to the trustees of an ESOT, they will be charged tax under Schedule D, Case VI, for the year of assessment in which the event occurs, on the 'chargeable amount' at the rate applicable to trusts (see 80.5 SETTLEMENTS) for that year. If they fail to pay the tax in full within six months of the assessment's becoming final and conclusive, a notice of liability for the unpaid tax may be served either on the founding company or on any company which has previously made a payment to the trust and obtained tax relief thereon. The company is also liable for any interest, accruing before or after the date of the notice, on the unpaid tax. If any tax and/or interest still remains unpaid three months after the date of notice, it may be recovered from the trustees without prejudice to the right to recover it instead from the company.

A '*chargeable event*' occurs whenever the trustees of an ESOT do any of the following:

(A)   make a transfer, other than a 'qualifying transfer', of securities;

(B)   make a transfer of securities, other than on 'qualifying terms' (see above), to beneficiaries;

(C)   retain securities for more than seven years (for ESOTs established under deeds executed after 3 May 1994, more than twenty years);

(D)   make a payment other than for a 'qualifying purpose' (see 71.53 SCHEDULE D, CASES I AND II).

A '*qualifying transfer*' is a transfer made either to a beneficiary, or at not less than open market value to the trustees of an approved profit sharing scheme (see 81.6 above), or (after 31 December 1991) by way of exchange of shares within *TCGA 1992, s 135(1)*.

The '*chargeable amount*' is determined as follows:

(I)   if the event falls within (A), (B) or (C) above, the chargeable amount, if the event constitutes a disposal for capital gains tax purposes, is the amount of allowable expenditure under *TCGA 1992, s 38(1)(a)(b)*, or, if the event does not constitute such a disposal, is the amount that would have been so allowable if it did so;

(II) if the event falls within (D) above, the chargeable amount is the amount of the payment made;

but see below for limitation on the chargeable amount.

Once a chargeable event as defined above has occurred, then if at that time there was outstanding any principal of any borrowings by the trustees and if the chargeable amount was limited as described below, a further chargeable event will occur at the end of any year of assessment in which any part of such principal is repaid by the trustees. Amounts borrowed earlier are for these purposes taken to be repaid before amounts borrowed later. The chargeable amount in this case is the amount repaid (but subject to limitation, see below) and is chargeable and recoverable in the same way as on other chargeable events. There are provisions to prevent a double charge in respect of the same borrowings where two or more chargeable events, of the kind first described above, occur at different times.

The chargeable amount, however arising, is limited to the total amount of payments received by the trustees before the chargeable event in question which have either qualified for corporation tax relief or would so qualify if a claim to that effect were made immediately before the occurrence of the event. For the purpose of determining whether or not the limit has been exceeded, any previous chargeable amounts must be aggregated with the chargeable amount in question. There is also a limitation on the chargeable amount in respect of repaid borrowings by reference to earlier chargeable amounts.

[*FA 1989, ss 68–72; F(No 2)A 1992, s 36; FA 1993, 6 Sch 20; FA 1994, 13 Sch 6; FA 1996, s 120(3)(4)(12)*].

Capital gains relief on introduction of shares. A form of capital gains rollover relief may be available on the transfer of shares into a qualifying ESOT. The relief is available where:

(*a*) the claimant makes a disposal of, or of his interest in, shares to the trustees of the trust, and, immediately after the disposal, the founding company was a 'trading company' or the 'holding company' of a 'trading group' (those terms being defined as under *TCGA 1992, 6 Sch 1*);

(*b*) the shares meet the conditions for acquisition by the trust (as above);

(*c*) at any time in the 'entitlement period', the trustees are beneficially entitled to at least 10% of the ordinary share capital of the founding company and of any 'profits available for distribution to equity holders' therein, and would be beneficially entitled to at least 10% of any of the founding company's 'assets available for distribution to equity holders' on a winding-up;

(*d*) the claimant obtains consideration for the disposal and, at any time in the 'acquisition period', applies all the consideration in acquiring assets (or an interest therein) which are, immediately thereafter, 'chargeable assets' in relation to the claimant and which are not shares in, or debentures issued by, the founding company or a company which, at the time of the acquisition, is in the same 'group' (as under *TCGA 1992, s 170*) as the founding company. The requirement that the consideration be applied in the 'acquisition period' is satisfied if the acquisition is made pursuant to an unconditional contract entered into in that period. Partial relief may be available where only part of the consideration is applied as above;

(*e*) at all times in the 'proscribed period', there are no 'unauthorised arrangements' under which the claimant or a person connected with him may be entitled to acquire any of the shares, or an interest in or right deriving from any of the shares, which are the subject of the disposal by the claimant;

(*f*) no chargeable event (see above) occurs in relation to the trustees in the chargeable period(s) in which the claimant makes the disposal and acquisition or in any other chargeable period between those of the disposal and the acquisition, 'chargeable period' meaning year of assessment or (if the claimant is a company) claimant company accounting period.

The *'entitlement period'* is the period starting with the disposal and ending twelve months after the date of the disposal.

The *'acquisition period'* is the period starting with the disposal and ending six months after the date of the disposal or, if later, after the date on which the condition at (*c*) above first becomes fulfilled.

The *'proscribed period'* is the period starting with the disposal and ending on the date of the acquisition or, if later, the date on which the condition at (*c*) above first becomes fulfilled.

Arrangements are *'unauthorised arrangements'* unless either they arise wholly from a restriction authorised by *FA 1989, 5 Sch 7(2)* (as above in relation to permissible securities), or they only allow, as regards shares, interests or rights, acquisition by a beneficiary under the trust and/or appropriation under an approved profit sharing scheme.

An asset is a *'chargeable asset'* at a particular time in relation to the claimant if:

(i) he is at that time UK resident or ordinarily resident and, were the asset to be disposed of at that time, a gain accruing to him would be a chargeable gain; or

(ii) were it to be disposed of at that time, any gain accruing to him would be a chargeable gain chargeable under *TCGA 1992, s 10(1)*

but not if, were he to dispose of it at that time, double tax relief arrangements under *ICTA 1988, s 788* would render him not liable to UK tax on any gain accruing to him on the disposal. However, dwelling-houses or land, or options to acquire dwelling-houses or land, are not treated as chargeable assets for these purposes where they attract the private residence relief under *TCGA 1992, s 222*. Similarly shares in respect of which relief under the enterprise investment scheme or the business expansion scheme (see 26 ENTERPRISE INVESTMENT SCHEME (AND BES)) is claimed are not treated as chargeable assets.

As regards the condition at (*c*) above, the provisions of *ICTA 1988, 18 Sch* apply as appropriate.

For details of the relief and of the circumstances in which relief may be withdrawn, see Tolleys Capital Gains Tax under Shares and Securities.

[*TCGA 1992, ss 227–234*].

Information. Where any payments to an ESOT have been allowed for tax purposes, the inspector must notify the trustees, stating the amount involved. He may, by written notice to the trustees, require the submission by them, with penalties for failure to comply, of a return containing such further information as is specified in the notice. This may include information about sums received, sums borrowed, expenditure incurred, assets acquired, transfers of assets made, etc. [*FA 1989, s 73*]. Similar provisions apply in relation to claims for capital gains tax relief on the introduction of shares. [*TCGA 1992, s 235*].

82 Social Security

82.1 The *Social Security Acts of 1973* and *1975* were designed to assimilate earlier national insurance and industrial injuries legislation. Subsequent *Acts* have introduced many detailed changes and extended the scope of the social security system. The legislation was consolidated in 1992.

82.2 **Contributions** by an employee are not allowable for tax purposes. A business employer is allowed his contributions for employees as a business expense. [*Sec 617(3)(4)*]. See also 1.9 ALLOWANCES AND TAX RATES as regards Class 4 contributions.

82.3 **Benefits taxable** (as earned income under Schedule E) are

Incapacity benefit (1995/96
  onwards) (see below)
Industrial death benefit (if paid
  as pension)
Invalid care allowance
Invalidity allowance when paid
  with retirement pension
Jobseeker's allowance (up to 'taxable
  maximum')
Job release allowance

Old persons' pension
Retirement pension
Statutory maternity pay
Statutory sick pay
Income support when paid to
  unemployed and strikers (see below)
Unemployment benefit
Widowed mother's allowance
Widow's pension

[*Secs 151A, 617(1)(2)(6); FA 1994, s 139*]. See 29.31 EXEMPT INCOME for certain exemptions on war widow's pension and 29.27 for other exemptions. See inside back cover for **rates** of main taxable benefits.

To reduce the administration of receiving returns before assessing retirement pensions and widow's pensions, the Revenue are generally notified by the DSS of the amounts each year. (Revenue Press Release 26 July 1979).

Incapacity benefit (which replaces invalidity benefit from 6 April 1995) is taxable under Schedule E (and may be within PAYE) *except for* short-term benefit payable otherwise than at the higher rate, i.e. benefit payable for the first 28 weeks of incapacity (and except for any child addition). There is also an exclusion for certain payments where invalidity benefit was previously payable in respect of the same period of incapacity. [*FA 1994, s 139; FA 1995, s 141*]. For the application of PAYE to taxable payments of incapacity benefit, see *SI 1995 No 853*.

Income support is taxable under Schedule E only if the entitlement to it is subject to the condition specified in the *Social Security Act 1986, s 20(3)* (or NI equivalent) as regards availability for employment, or if the claimant is one of a couple (whether or not married) and *Social Security Act 1986, s 23* (or NI equivalent) (trade disputes) applies to the claimant but not to the other person (i.e. broadly if the claimant is unemployed or on strike). There is a maximum amount in any period which is taxable, and this maximum applies to the sum of income support and unemployment benefit where both are in payment. There is provision for notification of, and objection to, determination of the taxable amount by the benefit officer. [*Secs 151, 152*]. See Revenue Pamphlets IR41 (Income Tax and the Unemployed), IR42 (Income Tax: Lay-offs and Short-time Work) and IR43 (Income Tax and Strikes).

See also 55.41 PAY AS YOU EARN regarding the withholding of tax refunds from the unemployed and strikers.

Statutory sick pay and **statutory maternity pay** paid by employers is taxable. See 75.37 SCHEDULE E.

82.4   **Benefits not taxable** are

Means-tested benefits

Educational maintenance allowance
Family credit
Hospital patients' travelling expenses
Housing benefit
Income support (if not taxable as in 82.3 above)
Social fund payments
Student grants
Uniform and clothing grants

Industrial injury benefits

Industrial death benefit child allowance
Disablement benefit, including
  Constant attendance allowance
  Exceptionally severe disablement allowance
  Reduced earnings allowance
  Retirement allowance
  Unemployability supplement

Short-term benefits

Incapacity benefit (not at the higher rate, see 82.3 above)
Maternity allowance
Sickness benefit

War disablement benefits

Disablement pension, including
  Age allowance
  Allowance for lowered standard of occupation
  Clothing allowance
  Comforts allowance
  Constant attendance allowance
  Dependant allowance
  Education allowance
  Exceptionally severe disablement allowance
  Invalidity allowance
  Medical treatment allowance
  Severe disablement occupational allowance
  Unemployability allowance

Other benefits

Attendance allowance
Back to work bonus (paid by way of jobseeker's allowance or income support)
Child benefit
Child dependency additions *paid with* widowed mother's allowance, retirement pension, invalid care allowance or unemployment benefit
Child's special allowance
Christmas bonus for pensioners
Disability living allowance
Disability working allowance
Employment rehabilitation allowance
Fares to school
Guardian's allowance
Home improvement, repair and insulation grants
Invalidity allowance when paid with invalidity pension
Invalidity pension
Jobfinder's grant
Jobmatch payments and training vouchers
Jobseeker's allowance (in excess of 'taxable maximum')
Job search allowances
Mobility allowance
One parent benefit
Severe disablement allowance
Employment training allowance
War orphan's pension
War widow's pension
Widow's payment

82.5 Social Security

Youth training scheme allowance (unless trainee has employee status)

[*Secs 315, 614(1), 617(1)(2); FA 1996, s 152*]. See also 82.3 above.

Foster care allowances. Foster parents may receive many different types of allowances and grants. The National Foster Care Association of Francis House, Francis Street, London SW1P 1DE has published guidelines agreed with the Revenue on the taxation treatment of these allowances etc. In general, to the extent that local authority payments made to a foster carer do no more than meet the actual costs of caring, the payments are not taxable. (Hansard 26 October 1994, Vol 248, Col 628).

Payments by foreign governments to UK residents which correspond to UK child benefit or to benefits exempt under *Sec 617(1)* will also be exempt from tax (with special rules in relation to incapacity benefit, see 82.3 above). (Revenue Pamphlet IR 1 (November 1995 Supplement), A24).

82.5   **Benefits under Government pilot schemes.** For 1996/97 and later years, the question as to whether or not, or to what extent, any benefit under a Government pilot scheme is to be within the charge to income tax is to be determined by Treasury Order. The Treasury may also by order provide for any such benefit to be wholly or partly left out of account in determining whether expenditure otherwise qualifying for capital allowances has been subsidised by the Crown etc. (see 10.2(ii) CAPITAL ALLOWANCES). For these purposes, a Government pilot scheme means, broadly, any arrangements made for a trial period by the Government which provide for new social security benefits or benefits under work incentive schemes. [*FA 1996, s 151*].

82.6   For 1989/90 and earlier years, for the purposes of (i) wife's earned income relief, see 1.22 ALLOWANCES AND TAX RATES [*Sec 257(6)*] and (ii) wife's earned income if an election is made for it to be treated separately, see 47.10 MARRIED PERSONS [*Sec 287(1)*], **earned income of a wife does not include** any payment of benefit under the *Social Security Acts 1975* except a Category A retirement pension, unemployment benefit and invalid care allowance. Under (ii), unemployment benefit is included only after 5 April 1987. [*Secs 257(7), 287(2); FA 1987, s 27*].

82.7   **National Insurance contributions** for **1996/97** (1995/96 where different) are as follows.

Class 1 (earnings-related)

Not contracted out

The employee contribution is payable where earnings exceed £60.99 (£57.99) p.w., and is 2% of earnings up to £61 (£58) p.w. plus 10% of earnings between £61 (£58) p.w. and £455 (£440) p.w. The employer contribution is as follows.

Weekly earnings	Employer contribution (% payable on all earnings)
0–£60.99 (0–£57.99)	—
£61.00–£109.99 (£58.00–£104.99)	3.00%
£110.00–£154.99 (£105.00–£149.99)	5.00%
£155.00–£209.99 (£150.00–£204.99)	7.00%
Over £209.99 (£204.99)	10.20%

Contracted out

The 'not contracted out' rates are reduced on the band of earnings from £61 (£58) per week to £455 (£440) per week by:

for employees   1.80%
for employers   3.00%

Married women

The reduced employee rate for certain married women and widows with a certificate of election is **3.85%**.

Class 1A (cars and car fuel)

Employer contributions at **10.2%** are required on a scale charge value of cars and fuel made available to employees for private use.

Class 2 (self-employed, flat rate)

The flat weekly rate of contribution is **£6.05** (£5.75). The annual limit of net earnings for exception from Class 2 liability is **£3,430** (£3,260).

Class 3 (voluntary contributions)

The flat weekly rate of contribution is **£5.95** (£5.65).

Class 4 (self-employed, profit-related) (see Revenue Pamphlet IR 24)

The 1996/97 contribution rate is 6% on the band of profits between **£6,860** and **£23,660**. See below for earlier years' figures. Class 4 contributions are levied, generally, on profits assessed under Schedule D, Cases I and II (plus any enterprise allowance, see 71.84 SCHEDULE D, CASES I AND II) and are shown separately on the notice of assessment for payment at the same time as the tax. Profits for this purpose are after capital allowances and certain interest and annual payments for trade purposes. [*Social Security Contributions and Benefits Act 1992, 2 Sch 2, 3(5)*]. Trading losses set against other income may, *for Class 4 purposes*, be carried forward and set against the first available profits. [*SSCBA 1992, 2 Sch 3(4)*]. Contributions to personal pension schemes and retirement annuity premiums are not deductible in arriving at profits for Class 4 purposes by virtue of *Social Security Contributions and Benefits Act 1992, 2 Sch 3(2)(f)(g)*. For 1995/96 and earlier years, 50% of Class 4 contributions is deductible in arriving at total income. There are various exceptions from Class 4 liability, including persons over State pensionable age, divers etc. assessed under Schedule D (see 71.31 SCHEDULE D, CASES I AND II) and, on application, those under 16 at the beginning of the year of assessment. [*SI 1979 No 591, regs 58-60*]. Non-UK residents and sleeping partners are not within the scope of Class 4.

From 19 April 1993, interest is chargeable on overdue Class 4 contributions under *TMA s 86* and *s 88* as it is for income tax purposes (see 42.1 INTEREST ON UNPAID TAX), and repayment supplement (see 41.1 INTEREST ON OVERPAID TAX) is similarly available. [*SSCBA 1992, 2 Sch 6; SI 1993 No 1025*]. Previously, interest was chargeable only under *TMA s 88* and no repayment supplement was available.

The Class 4 rates and bands for earlier years are as follows.

	Rate	Band
1995/96	7.3%	£6,640 – £22,880
1994/95	7.3%	£6,490 – £22,360
1993/94	6.3%	£6,340 – £21,840
1992/93	6.3%	£6,120 – £21,060
1991/92	6.3%	£5,900 – £20,280
1990/91	6.3%	£5,450 – £18,200

82.8 See Tolley's Social Security and State Benefits and Tolley's National Insurance Contributions for full details of this subject.

83 Statutory Bodies

83.1   *Marketing Boards.* Payments by Marketing Boards into certain compulsory reserve funds for maintaining guaranteed prices etc., allowed (on conditions) as deductions, and withdrawals (generally) treated as trading receipts. [*Sec 509*].

83.2   *Atomic Energy Authority* and *National Radiological Protection Board* are entitled to certain exceptions. [*Sec 512; TCGA 1992, s 271(7)*].

83.3   *Harbour reorganisation schemes* are subject to special tax treatment. [*Sec 518; TCGA 1992, s 221*].

83.4   *Local authorities, local authority associations* and *health service bodies* are exempt from tax. [*Secs 519, 519A, 842A as amended; TCGA 1992, s 271(3)*].

83.5   Subject to the special provisions above and, where appropriate, to the Crown exemption (see 30.6 EXEMPT ORGANISATIONS), statutory bodies are liable in the ordinary way to corporation tax on their income and capital gains. Whether their activities amount to trading depends on the facts. See *Mersey Docks and Harbour Board v Lucas HL 1883, 1 TC 385, 2 TC 25* (held to be chargeable under legislation now in *Sec 55*) and *Port of London Authority v CIR CA 1920, 12 TC 122* and contrast the *Forth Conservancy Board* cases, *14 TC 709, 16 TC 103* (liable under Case VI on surplus from shipping dues) and *British Broadcasting Corporation v Johns CA 1964, 41 TC 471* (liable under Case I on profits from publications etc. but not on rest of surplus; not entitled to Crown exemption). See also *Sowrey v King's Lynn Harbour Mooring Commrs QB 1887, 2 TC 201; Humber Conservancy Board v Bater KB 1914, 6 TC 555*.

83.6   *Statutory corporation borrowing in foreign currency.* Interest on securities issued by, or on a loan to, a statutory corporation (as defined) in foreign currency (for securities issued before 6 April 1982, in a currency outside the scheduled territories) shall, if the Treasury directs, be paid without deduction of income tax and be exempt from income tax (but not corporation tax) in the hands of a non-resident beneficial owner of such securities or, in the case of a loan, in the hands of the person for the time being entitled to repayment or eventual repayment of the loan. [*Sec 581*].

84 Stock Dividends

84.1   Shares issued by a UK company in lieu of a cash dividend are chargeable on the individual beneficial shareholder to higher rate tax on an amount equal to the cash they replace grossed up at the lower rate (for 1992/93 and earlier years, the basic rate) of tax, as if that amount were a dividend (see 1.8(iii) ALLOWANCES AND RATES). No charge to, or repayment of, the lower (or basic) rate tax is made (and for 1992/93, the income is treated as not chargeable at the lower rate of tax), and the gross amount is not available to cover charges. Where there is no cash equivalent or this equivalent is substantially above or below (i.e. more than one or two percentage points outside 15% either way: Revenue Pamphlet IR 131

(October 1995 Supplement), A8) the market value of shares issued, the market value is used. Similarly chargeable are bonus shares issued in respect of shares held under terms which carry the right to the bonus. The shareholder is treated as receiving the shares on the due date of issue i.e. the earliest date the company was required to issue the shares. Where more than one person is entitled to the shares issued, apportionment is made according to their respective interests. [Secs 249(1)–(4), 251; F(No 2)A 1992, s 19(4); FA 1993, s 77(3); FA 1996, s 122(5), 6 Sch 6, 28, 41 Sch Pt V(1)].

84.2   **Capital Gains Tax.** Stock dividends received subject to tax are deemed to be acquired for a consideration equal to the relevant cash dividend or market value and treated as a rights issue taken up. [TCGA 1992, s 141]. This applies also to a person who is absolutely entitled, at the time of the issue of the stock dividend, to shares held by a trustee. [TCGA 1992, s 142].

84.3   **Companies.** For provisions affecting companies issuing and receiving stock dividends, see Tolley's Corporation Tax.

84.4   **Deceased estates.** Stock dividends issued to personal representatives during the administration period are grossed as in 84.1 above and deemed part of the aggregate income of the estate, see 22 DECEASED ESTATES. [Sec 249(5)].

84.5   **Discretionary and accumulation trusts.** The provisions in 84.1 above apply, but the additional rate tax may be set off against payments to beneficiaries, see 80.2 and 80.5 SETTLEMENTS. [Sec 249(6)].

84.6   **Enhanced stock dividends received by trustees of interest in possession trusts.** Where the trustees of an interest in possession trust have concluded that either

(a)   an enhanced stock dividend belongs to the income beneficiary, or

(b)   it forms part of the trust's capital, or

(c)   while adding the enhanced stock dividend to capital, the trustees should compensate the income beneficiary for the loss of the cash dividend he would otherwise have received,

and the view they have taken of the trust law position is supportable on the facts, the Revenue will not seek to challenge what the trustees have done. The income tax consequences of each view are as follows.

(a)   Since the beneficiary is beneficially entitled to the shares comprised in the dividend, the provisions described at 84.1 above apply.

(b)   Since the stock dividend is regarded as capital, there is no income tax liability.

(c)   The payment to the beneficiary is an annual payment from which basic rate tax must be deducted.

For full details of this treatment and of the capital gains tax consequences, and for differences under Scottish law, see Revenue Pamphlet IR 131 (October 1995 Supplement), SP 4/94, 17 May 1994.

85   Stock Relief

Cross-reference. See 71.82 SCHEDULE D, CASES I AND II for stock in trade and work in progress generally.

85.1   Tax relief for an increase in trading stock values was introduced by *F(No 2)A 1975, 10 Sch* for individuals and partners carrying on a trade, profession or vocation within Schedule D, Cases I and II. The relief was continued with some changes by *FA 1976, 5 Sch* and subsequent legislation, with substantial modification by *FA 1980, 7 Sch.*

A revised scheme of relief, which applied to all periods of account ending after 13 November 1980 and beginning before 13 March 1984, was introduced by *FA 1981, s 35, 9 and 10 Schs.* Stock relief was finally abolished by *FA 1984, s 48.*

85.2   The following provisions continue to be of relevance following the abolition of stock relief.

Carry-forward of unused relief. Relief under the *FA 1981* provisions may be carried forward for a maximum of six years, measured by the interval between the end of the period of account in which relief arose and the beginning of the period of account for whose 'relevant year of assessment' relief is to be given. The '*relevant year of assessment*' is generally the year of assessment for which the period of account is the basis period.

Relief under the *FA 1976* provisions may be carried forward without restriction. [*FA 1981, 9 Sch 7, 9, 10; 30 Sch 18*].

In determining whether losses brought forward include unused relief under either the *FA 1981* or the *FA 1976* provisions, deductions from profits in earlier years which include capital allowances, stock relief or trading losses brought forward are made in the following order:

(*a*)   current year capital allowances;

(*b*)   capital allowances brought forward from years of assessment not earlier than that for which the basis period ended on or included 14 November 1980;

(*c*)   stock relief under the *FA 1981* provisions (later years being relieved before earlier);

(*d*)   capital allowances brought forward from years earlier than those within (*b*) above;

(*e*)   stock relief under the *FA 1976* provisions;

(*f*)   trading losses brought forward.

For this purpose, capital allowances for any year are treated as being deducted in the following order:

(i)   allowances as in (*a*) above;

(ii)   allowances as in (*b*) above;

(iii)   allowances as in (*d*) above.

[*FA 1981, 9 Sch 5; 30 Sch 18; CAA 1990, s 140(5) as originally enacted*].

86   Time Limits—5 April 1997

See also 87 TIME LIMITS—MISCELLANEOUS.

86.1   **TIME LIMITS OF ONE YEAR OR LESS**

(a)   **Advance time limit**
i.e. action in respect of 1997/98 must be taken by 5 April 1997.

Transfer of married couple's allowance. Election by wife to receive one-half of the allowance, or by spouses jointly for wife to receive the whole of the allowance, or by husband to receive one-half where a joint election has been made for wife to receive the whole of the allowance, must be made before the start of the first year of assessment to which the election is to apply (subject to a 30 day extension where notice of intention to elect was given to the inspector before the start of that year). Withdrawals of such elections similarly do not have effect until the year of assessment after that in which notice of withdrawal was given. See 47.2 MARRIED PERSONS.

(b)   **60 days**
i.e. action in respect of 1996/97 must be taken by 4 June 1997.

Exercise of option to acquire shares. Election to pay tax by instalments. See 81.3 SHARE INCENTIVES AND OPTIONS.

(c)   **Three months**
i.e. action in respect of 1996/97 must be taken by 5 July 1997.

Election to treat personal pension contributions as paid in earlier year must be made within three months of end of tax year of payment. See 65.8 RETIREMENT ANNUITIES AND PERSONAL PENSION SCHEMES.

(d)   **Six months**
i.e. action in respect of 1995/96 must be taken by 5 October 1996.

Notification of chargeability. Any person who is chargeable to tax for a year of assessment must give notice to the Revenue that he is so chargeable within six months after the end of that year, unless his income comes solely from certain sources (e.g. income dealt with under PAYE or Schedule F) and he has no chargeable gains. [*TMA s 7 as amended*]. See 78.4 SELF-ASSESSMENT.

(e)   **Twelve months**
i.e. action in respect of 1995/96 must be taken by 5 April 1997.

(i)   *Claims following late assessments.* A claim (including a supplementary claim) which could not have been allowed but for the making of an assessment to income tax or capital gains tax after the year of assessment to which it relates may be made before the end of the year of assessment following that in which the assessment was made. [*TMA s 43(2)*].

(ii)   *Qualifying interest.* Election for interest paid by one spouse to be treated as paid by the other, and for the sharer's limit to be adjusted between them, where the 'residence basis' applies. See 43.10, 43.12 INTEREST PAYABLE.

(iii) *Maintenance payments.* Election for payments under 'existing obligations' to be brought within the *FA 1988* rules. See 47.15 MARRIED PERSONS.

(iv)   *'Rent a room' relief.* Election (or withdrawal of election) for exemption not to apply, or for exemption to apply to amount of gross income in excess of individual limit. See 68.11 SCHEDULE A.

    (v)   *Land managed as one estate at 5 April 1963.* Election to include notional rents and deduct certain expenses. See 68.7(*e*) SCHEDULE A.

86.2   TWO-YEAR TIME LIMITS

i.e. action in respect of 1994/95 must be taken by 5 April 1997.

(*a*)   *Capital allowances.* The following two-year limits apply.

    (i)   Claims to offset allowances against income other than that against which they are primarily to be given. See 10 CAPITAL ALLOWANCES *passim.*

    (ii)   *Agricultural buildings and works.* Election for balancing adjustments to apply on a disposal, etc. See 10.3 CAPITAL ALLOWANCES.

    (iii)   *Ships.* Writing-down allowances may, on a claim, be postponed to a later period, and an election made for the 'single ship trade' provisions not to apply. See 10.28(B) CAPITAL ALLOWANCES.

    (iv)   *Short-life assets.* Expenditure on certain machinery or plant may, by election, be treated as on short-life assets, and certain transfers between connected persons treated as at tax written-down value. See 10.28(F) CAPITAL ALLOWANCES.

    (v)   *Equipment leasing.* An election may in certain circumstances be made for fixtures to be treated as belonging to the lessor and not the lessee. See 10.34(*b*) CAPITAL ALLOWANCES.

(*b*)   HERD BASIS (34) election where farming commenced in 1994/95, or there is a loss claim in 1994/95, or where a herd was slaughtered compulsorily and compensation is receivable in the base year for 1994/95.

(*c*)   *Claim for loss in trade etc.* incurred during the year 1993/94 to be set off against general income (see 46.3 LOSSES) or carried back (see 46.14 LOSSES).

(*d*)   *Claim for losses on shares* in unlisted companies. See 46.19 LOSSES.

(*e*)   *Patent rights* election where capital sum received. See 54.5 PATENTS.

(*f*)   *Spreading back* of POST-CESSATION RECEIPTS (60).

(*g*)   *Claim for rent to be assessed under Schedule A* when furniture also supplied. See 68.14(i) SCHEDULE A.

(*h*)   *Farming.* Claim to average profits, see 71.56(*a*) SCHEDULE D, CASES I AND II.

(*i*)   *Films.* Certain expenditure on production or acquisition may be reallocated to other periods. See 71.57 SCHEDULE D, CASES I AND II.

(*j*)   *Furnished holiday lettings.* Election for averaging treatment. See 74.4 SCHEDULE D, CASE VI.

(*k*)   *Share dealers.* Rejection of rollover relief on exchange of securities by government in connection with conversion operations, nationalisation etc. See 71.81 SCHEDULE D, CASES I AND II.

(*l*)   SCHEDULE D, CASE III (72). Election for cessation rules to apply in certain circumstances.

(*m*)   SCHEDULE D, CASES IV AND V (73). Election for cessation rules to apply in certain circumstances.

(*n*)   *Settlements for maintenance of historic buildings.* Election for tax exemption on income. See 80.29 SETTLEMENTS.

(*o*)   *Valuation of trading stock on discontinuance.* Election for transfers between CON-
NECTED PERSONS (20) to be reduced below market value in certain cases. See 71.82
SCHEDULE D, CASES I AND II.

86.3   THREE-YEAR TIME LIMITS

i.e. action in respect of 1993/94 must be taken by 5 April 1997.

(*a*)   *Claim for loss in trade etc.* incurred during the year 1993/94 to be set against general
income of the year 1994/95, providing the taxpayer still carries on the trade etc. See
46.3 LOSSES.

(*b*)   *Deceased estates.* Claim for adjustment of assessments where administration was
completed in 1993/94. See 22.3 DECEASED ESTATES.

(*c*)   *Lloyd's underwriters* may relate back to 1993/94 qualifying premiums paid in
1996/97 for retirement annuities and personal pension contributions. See 65.8
RETIREMENT ANNUITIES AND PERSONAL PENSION SCHEMES.

86.4   FOUR-YEAR TIME LIMITS

There are no four-year time limits, so 1992/93 need not be considered in the present
context.

86.5   FIVE-YEAR TIME LIMITS

Schedule E formal assessment request in respect of 1991/92, see 75.1(2) SCHEDULE E.

86.6   SIX-YEAR TIME LIMITS

Except where other time limits are prescribed, claim must be made within six years of the
end of the year of assessment to which it relates. [*TMA s 43(1)*]. Such claims, as listed
below, for 1990/91 must accordingly be made by 5 April 1997.

(*a*)   *Error or mistake claims.* See 17.6 CLAIMS.

(*b*)   *Claim for additional personal allowances etc.* omitted from the taxpayer's tax return.

(*c*)   *Claim against double assessment* where the same person has been assessed 'for the same
cause' in the same year. [*TMA s 32*].

(*d*)   DOUBLE TAX RELIEF (25).

(*e*)   INTEREST PAYABLE (43).

(*f*)   LOSSES (46) except where shorter time limits apply.

(*g*)   MINERAL ROYALTIES (49).

(*h*)   NON-RESIDENTS AND OTHER OVERSEAS MATTERS at 51.14. Delayed remittances of
overseas income or gains.

(*i*)   RETIREMENT ANNUITIES AND PERSONAL PENSION SCHEMES (65). Unused relief may be
claimed.

(*j*)   SCHEDULE D CASES I AND II at 71.4. Claim for actual basis for the second and third
years of assessment must be made within six years of the end of the third year of
assessment (i.e. where a business commenced in 1988/89 claims may be made up to
5 April 1997).

(*k*)   SCHEDULE D, CASES I AND II at 71.50. Spreading of lump sums received for
copyrights.

(*l*)   SCHEDULE D, CASE III (72) and SCHEDULE D, CASES IV AND V (73). Claim for actual basis to apply for the first year of assessment to which the preceding year basis would otherwise apply. Claim for cessation basis may be made if there is no income from a source for six years or if no income arose in the last three years of ownership (see *Sec 67(4)(5)* for full details).

(*m*)   SETTLEMENTS at 80.12. Claims for personal allowances etc. up to 1968/69 in respect of specified contingent interests must be made by 5 April 1997 if the contingency occurred in 1990/91.

(*n*)   Any other matter not specified in 86.1–86.6 above for which relief from income tax is claimed.

86.7   **COMPANIES**

Claims and elections in respect of companies, where applicable, usually have the same time limits as shown above except that the expiry date is by reference to the end of the company's accounting period instead of the end of the year of assessment.

87   Time Limits—Miscellaneous

See also 86 TIME LIMITS—5 APRIL 1997 above. Time limits other than to 5 April are set out below. In some (but not all) cases, the periods can be extended at the discretion of the Inland Revenue.

87.1   TIME LIMITS OF ONE YEAR OR LESS

(a)   **30 days**

(i)   Appeals against assessments. Lodging of formal notice of appeal. See 4 APPEALS.

(ii)   Appeals to High Court. See 4.7 APPEALS.

(iii)   Returns of income etc. See 67 RETURNS.

(iv)   Tax generally becomes due and payable 30 days after the issue of the notice of assessment and interest begins to run. See 56 PAYMENT OF TAX and 42 INTEREST ON UNPAID TAX.

(v)   Patent rights election after death, winding-up or partnership change. See 54.6 PATENTS.

(vi)   There are many instances in which Revenue information powers and clearance procedures require a response within 30 days, see e.g. 3.2 ANTI-AVOIDANCE.

(b)   **60 days**
There are a number of circumstances in which information is required to be provided within 60 days, see e.g. 26.16, 26.29 ENTERPRISE INVESTMENT SCHEME (AND BES).

(c)   **Three months**

(i)   Appeals against Board's decision regarding (i) personal reliefs for non-residents, (ii) residence, ordinary residence or domicile, (iii) pension funds for service abroad. [TMA s 42(3); Sec 207].

(ii)   Application for judicial review must be made within three months of the date when the grounds for application arose. See 4.8 APPEALS.

(d)   **Six months**
Payment of retirement annuity and personal pension payments by an individual (if not made during the tax year) may be made within six months of the agreed assessment for that year, together with an election, in certain circumstances. See 65.9 RETIREMENT ANNUITIES AND PERSONAL PENSION SCHEMES.

(e)   **Twelve months**

(i)   *Lloyd's underwriters.* Payment into an underwriter's Special Reserve Fund must be notified to the inspector within twelve months of the deemed date of closing the account of an underwriting year. See 89 UNDERWRITERS. [Sec 452(6)].

(ii)   *Work in progress.* Election for valuation at cost on discontinuance of profession or vocation must be made within twelve months of discontinuance. See 71.82 SCHEDULE D, CASES I AND II.

(iii)   *Enterprise investment scheme* relief must be claimed within twelve months after the authorisation by the inspector of the issue of Form EIS 3 by the company. See 26.11 ENTERPRISE INVESTMENT SCHEME (AND BES).

87.2 Time Limits—Miscellaneous

87.2 TWO-YEAR TIME LIMITS

(a) *Industrial buildings.* Election for allowances to apply to holder of long lease out of relevant interest within two years of lease taking effect. See 10.14 CAPITAL ALLOWANCES.

(b) *Sales without change of control.* Election for transfer of assets at tax written-down value. See 10.22(i) CAPITAL ALLOWANCES.

(c) *Equipment leasing.* Election for certain fixtures on which expenditure incurred by incoming lessee to be treated as belonging to lessee within two years of date of lease taking effect. See 10.34(*d*) CAPITAL ALLOWANCES.

(d) *Successions.* Election for transfers between 'connected persons' to be at tax written-down value. See 10.38(xi) CAPITAL ALLOWANCES.

(e) *Partnership changes.* Election for continuation basis within two years of change. See 53.6 PARTNERSHIPS.

(f) *Lump sums received by authors etc.* Election for adjustment of period of spread must be made within two years of death or discontinuance. See 71.50 SCHEDULE D, CASES I AND II.

(g) *Know-how payment.* Election within two years of disposal for it not to be treated as a payment for goodwill. See 71.66 SCHEDULE D, CASES I AND II.

(h) *Qualifying films.* Claims for special treatment within two years of end of period of account of expenditure or completion. See 71.71 SCHEDULE D, CASES I AND II.

88 Trade Unions

88.1 Trade Unions are entitled to the tax exemptions below providing they are registered (which means listed under the *Trade Union and Labour Relations Act 1974* or NI equivalent) and providing they are precluded from assuring more than £4,000 by way of gross sum or £825 by way of annuity (excluding retirement annuities approved under *Sec 620(9)*) in respect of any one person. Before 1 April 1991, the sums assurable were £3,000 and £625 respectively. The limits may be increased by the Treasury by order. [*Sec 467; ICTA 1970, s 338; FA 1987, s 31; FA 1991, s 74*].

Exemption is then granted on income which is not trading income and is applicable and applied to *provident benefits* (as defined in *Sec 467(2)* as amended by *FA 1988, 3 Sch 17*) which include legal expenses incurred in representing members at Industrial Tribunal hearings of cases alleging unfair dismissal, or in connection with a member's claim in respect of accident or injury suffered, and general administrative expenses of providing such benefits. (Revenue Pamphlet IR 131, SP 1/84, 17 February 1984). See also *R v Special Commrs (ex p NUR) QB 1966, 43 TC 445*. Similar exemption is granted on capital gains so applied. [*Sec 467(1)(b)*].

Similar provisions apply to employers' associations registered as trade unions [*Sec 467(4)(b)*] and to the Police Federations for England and Wales, Scotland and Northern Ireland and other police organisations with similar functions. [*Sec 467(4)(c)*].

89 Underwriters

For a detailed treatment of this subject, see Tolley's Taxation of Lloyd's Underwriters.

89.1 Special tax provisions for Lloyd's underwriters were contained in *Secs 450–457* and *19A Sch*. With effect generally for 1992/93 and subsequent years, but with some changes taking effect later than 1992/93, these provisions are repealed and replaced with a new tax regime for underwriters contained in *FA 1993, ss 171–184, 19, 20 Schs*. The new regime partly mirrors the old but also includes substantive changes. Further changes in *FA 1994, s 228, 21 Sch* facilitate the introduction of self-assessment by revising the relationship between the underwriting year and the year of assessment. Various further provisions are contained in *SI 1974 Nos 896, 1330* (amending), *SI 1990 No 2524* (amending) and in annual regulations as noted in 89.5 below. See also 74.27 SCHEDULE D, CASE VI for the application of the accrued income and forestalling charges ('bondwashing') to underwriters for underwriting years before 1994.

Following the admission of corporate members to Lloyd's from 1 January 1994, special provisions are contained in *FA 1994* for the application of corporation tax to such members. Broadly, the effect of these is as follows.

(*a*) Corporation tax will continue to be chargeable, and Pay and File to apply, in the normal way.

(*b*) Schedule D, Case I rules apply in determining the income from the Lloyd's underwriting trade, and in addition profits and gains from syndicate participation, premium trust funds, ancillary funds, etc. are included.

(*c*) Profits and gains from syndicate participation are treated as accruing uniformly over the underwriting year in which they are declared and apportioned to the concurrent accounting periods.

(*d*) Non-syndicate income and gains are taxable as income (as for corporate insurers generally).

(*e*) There are special rules for items such as stop-loss insurance, reinsurance to close, premiums trust fund assets and cessation.

(*f*) There is no provision for a special reserve fund.

See *FA 1994, ss 220–227, 229, 230, 248; FA 1996, 11 Sch 7*.

89.2 **Self-assessment.** To enable the self-assessment rules to be applied for 1997/98 and subsequent years, a revised basis of assessment applies to profits or losses from syndicate membership, including syndicate investment income, and arising from assets forming part of the premiums trust fund. The profits or losses in a year of assessment are those declared in the underwriting year ending in the year of assessment, i.e. profits of underwriting year 1994 will generally be declared in 1997 and assessed for 1997/98. Profits of 1993 will continue to be assessed for 1993/94, and there will be no assessments for 1994/95, 1995/96 or 1996/97. [*FA 1993, s 172(1); FA 1994, 21 Sch 2*]. The statutory instrument laying down the transitional administrative arrangements up to and including 1997/98 had not been published at the time of publication, but the Revenue have indicated that they will operate as follows.

(i) Tax in respect of the 1992 underwriting year, assessable 1992/93, will be due on 1 January 1996 (basic rate, as previously) and 31 January 1997 (higher rate, previously 1 July 1996). The dates for underwriting year 1993, assessable 1993/94, will be 1 January 1997 and 31 January 1998 respectively. For underwriting year 1994, assessable 1997/98, tax will be due under the normal self-assessment rules on 31 January 1998, 31 July 1988 and 31 January 1999, and so on for subsequent years.

(ii) For 1994/95, 1995/96 and 1996/97, for which no underwriting profits, etc. fall to be assessed, tax in respect of personal receipts (such as ancillary fund income) will be due on 31 January 1998.

(iii) Information relating to underwriting years 1992 and 1993 will be required with the income tax returns issued in April 1996 and April 1997 respectively, one year later than under current rules. Information relating to 1994/95, 1995/96 and 1996/97 will also be sought with the latter return, although for convenience it may be noted on earlier returns as it becomes available. If it is clear that a loss has arisen in any of those years, relief will be allowed on submission of a claim as soon as the figures are available, and early relief may similarly be allowed where the results for 1992/93 and 1993/94 show a loss, provided that all the information that would have been required in the tax return is given.

(Revenue Press Release 17 December 1993).

For these purposes, an individual commencing underwriting business at Lloyd's during underwriting year 1994 is treated as having commenced business on 6 April 1994. [*FA 1994, s 218(3)*].

89.3 UNDERWRITING PROFITS

For 1986/87 and subsequent years, the aggregate of a member's **underwriting profits** is chargeable under Schedule D, Case I. Underwriting profits include income from premiums trust fund assets and income arising after 5 April 1993 from 'ancillary trust fund' assets. An '*ancillary trust fund*' does not include a premiums trust fund or special reserve fund but otherwise means any trust fund required or authorised by Lloyd's rules or required by an underwriter's member's agent or (before 1994/95) the managing agent of a syndicate of which he is a member. [*Sec 450(2); FA 1988, s 58(1); FA 1993, ss 171(1)(2)(4), 184(2)(b); FA 1994, 21 Sch 8(1)*].

Foreign income dividends within *ICTA 1988, Pt VI, Ch VA* are included in premiums trust fund income for 1992/93 and subsequent years at the actual amount received. [*FA 1993, s 171(2A); FA 1994, 21 Sch 1(1)(3)(a)*].

After 31 December 1993, annual appreciation in value of and profits on disposal of premiums trust fund assets are included in underwriting profits for income tax purposes and annual depreciation in value and losses on disposal are deducted in arriving at such profits. For the purposes of computing appreciation and depreciation in value of premiums trust fund assets, certain transfers within *Sec 129* (stock lending—see 71.81 SCHEDULE D, CASES I AND II) are, effectively, regarded as not having taken place, and there is an exemption similar to that in 74.10(*d*) SCHEDULE D, CASE VI (FOTRA securities). [*FA 1993, ss 174, 184(2); FA 1994, 21 Sch 3; FA 1996, s 154, 41 Sch Pt V(18)*]. Before 1 January 1994, such appreciation, profits etc. constitute gains and losses for capital gains tax purposes. [*Sec 450(6); TCGA 1992, ss 206–209; FA 1993, 23 Sch Pt III(12)*]. Under Lloyd's rules, gains and losses on disposals and deemed disposals for the underwriting year 1994 are apportioned between the 1992, 1993 and 1994 underwriting accounts and those for 1995 to the 1993, 1994 and 1995 accounts. Thus, a proportion of total gains and losses allocated to 1992 and 1993 will qualify for income tax treatment. There are transitional provisions affecting the calculation of syndicate profits for income tax purposes for those two years. [*FA 1993, 19 Sch 10(2)(b)(c)(3)(c)(d)(4)*]. Gains and losses on ancillary trust fund assets remain within the capital gains tax regime. [*FA 1993, s 176(2)*].

For 1993/94 and subsequent years, underwriting profits are treated as derived from the carrying on of a business and thus as **earned income**. [*FA 1993, s 180*]. For earlier years, underwriting profits are treated as earned income only where the underwriter is a 'working name', i.e. is actively engaged in the business of underwriting and is employed full-time (i.e. at least 75% of a full working week) in the Room at Lloyd's or in the office of an underwriting agent or broker. Where this was not the case, such profits are not 'relevant earnings' for the purposes of contributions to RETIREMENT ANNUITIES AND PERSONAL PENSION SCHEMES (65) (*Koenigsberger v Mellor CA, [1995] STC 547*).

Stop-loss insurance premiums are allowable as an expense in computing underwriting profits, and insurance money received in respect of a loss is a trading receipt of the year of assessment corresponding to the underwriting year in which the loss arose or, in relation to underwriting year 1997 onwards, was declared. This treatment is extended to payments into and receipts out of the High Level Stop Loss Fund, i.e. the fund of that name established under Lloyd's rules for the underwriting year 1993 and subsequent years. For 1992/93 and subsequent years, a repayment of insurance money received etc. is likewise allowed as an expense, as is any amount payable under a quota share contract, i.e. a contract made in accordance with Lloyd's rules and practice between the underwriter and another person which provides for that other person to take over any rights and liabilities of the underwriter under any of his syndicates. Also for 1992/93 onwards, the treatment of insurance receipts etc. is modified where the inspector is not notified of the receipt in time to raise the necessary assessment for the year corresponding to that in which the loss arose; in such a case, the trading receipt is treated as arising in the year of assessment corresponding to the underwriting year in which the payment of insurance money etc. was made to the underwriter. [*Sec 450(4); FA 1988, s 59; FA 1993, ss 178, 184(1); FA 1994, 21 Sch 5*].

Reinsurance premiums. A restriction is placed on relief for such premiums payable in respect of liabilities outstanding at the end of an underwriting year for the purpose of closing the accounts for the underwriting year, where the member by whom the premium is payable is also a member of the syndicate as a member of which the reinsurer is entitled to receive it. Relief is restricted to an amount which must not exceed an assessment, arrived at with a view to producing neither profit nor loss to the member to whom it is payable, of the value of the liabilities in respect of which it is payable, and a corresponding reduction is made in his profits or gains as a member of the reinsurer syndicate. [*Sec 450(5)(5A); FA 1988, s 60; FA 1993, s 177; FA 1994, 21 Sch 4*].

Bank guarantee fees paid initially to secure membership as a Lloyd's underwriter are not deductible, but annual payments for the maintenance of such facilities are deductible.

Association of Lloyd's members. It is understood that subscriptions to the Association are allowable, as is the cost of League Tables and Syndicate Results. Two-thirds of the cost of prospective names seminars, and one-half of the cost of most other conferences and meetings, is also allowable, with proportionate allowance of travelling expenses other than to or from London (the place of business).

For the 1993 Account and thereafter, **personal accountancy fees** are allowed on the usual 'wholly and exclusively' basis applicable to traders generally, by reference to the amount paid in the year of account. For 1993 only, a Name may instead either claim the amount paid in the period 6 April to 31 December 1993 against the 1993/94 Schedule D, Case I assessment, or opt for a scale fee equal to two-thirds of the 1992 scale fee (as below). For the 1992 Account and earlier, personal accountancy fees are in most cases given automatically on a non-statutory Revenue scale according to the number of syndicates of which the individual is a member. Formal claims must be submitted for any higher allowance. For the 1991 and 1992 Accounts, the scale allowance is £300 for the first syndicate, £90 for each of the next five and £37.50 for each of the next twenty-one. For the 1987, 1988, 1989 and 1990 Accounts, it is £400 for the first syndicate, £120 for each of the next five and £50 for each of the next twenty-one. For the 1985 and 1986 Accounts, it is £350 for the first syndicate, £120 for each of the next five and £50 for each of the next nineteen.

Compensation payments from managing or members' agents are likely to be treated as trading receipts of the underwriting year in which the entitlement to compensation arises, and thus as not being chargeable to capital gains tax. Any legal fees incurred, together with any payments out of the compensation to stop-loss insurers, are deductible for tax purposes. (Revenue Tax Bulletin May 1992 p 17). For confirmation that such compensation payments are taxable, see *Deeny and others v Gooda Walker Ltd HL, [1996] STC 299*.

89.4   **ASSESSMENT AND COLLECTION**

For 1993/94 and earlier years, underwriting profits are assessed on a current year basis by reference to the underwriting year corresponding with the year of assessment (i.e. underwriting year 1993, the year to 31 December, is assessed for 1993/94). However, an underwriting year is generally kept open for two years before it is closed and the profit ascertained. Assessments are, under administrative arrangements (see 89.5, 89.6 below), delayed until the account is closed. For 1997/98 and subsequent years, underwriting profits are assessed by reference to the underwriting year whose profits are declared in the year of assessment (i.e. underwriting year 1994, whose profits are declared in 1997, is assessed for 1997/98), and, subject to transitional provisions (see 89.2 above), the normal self-assessment payment dates apply. No underwriting profits are, accordingly, assessed for 1994/95, 1995/96 or 1996/97. [*Secs 450(1), 457(2); FA 1993, ss 172, 184(2)(a); FA 1994, 21 Sch 2*].

On cessation (on death or otherwise), the final year of assessment is that which corresponds to the underwriting year in which the underwriter's Lloyd's deposit is paid over to him or his personal representatives or assigns, except that if the underwriter dies before 6 April 1994 and before the end of that underwriting year, his final year of assessment is that in which he dies. Any underwriting profits or losses which do not fall to be taken as profits or losses of an earlier year of assessment are taken to be profits or losses of the final year of assessment. These provisions do not apply where the payment of the Lloyd's deposit to the underwriter etc. was made before 1 January 1993. [*FA 1993, s 179; FA 1994, 21 Sch 6(1)(2)*]. Where a member dies after 5 April 1994

(a)   he is treated for these purposes as having died on 5 April in the underwriting year in which he actually died, and

(b)   the business is treated as continuing until the member's deposit is paid over to his personal representatives, whose carrying on of the business is not treated as a change in the persons so engaged. [*FA 1993, s 179A; FA 1994, 21 Sch 6(2)(3)*].

If underwriting commenced before 2 January 1971 and a cessation occurs, a claim may be made for assessments (a) for the penultimate year to be reduced to the lesser of (i) the whole of the profits of that year and (ii) the profits for the underwriting year 1972, and (b) for the final year to be based on actual profits from 6 April to the date of cessation. [*SI 1974 No 896, reg 21*].

For 1996/97 and earlier years, *retirement annuity premiums and personal pension contributions* may be related back to the third previous year of assessment, see 65.8 RETIREMENT ANNUITIES AND PERSONAL PENSION SCHEMES for special provisions.

89.5   The general administrative arrangements for assessment and collection of tax (see below) are contained in *FA 1993, 19 Sch* (before 1992/93, *19A Sch*). Annual arrangements for 1986/87 are contained in *SI 1989 No 421*, those for 1987/88 in *SI 1990 No 627*, those for 1988/89 in *SI 1991 No 851*, those for 1989/90 in *SI 1992 No 511*, those for 1990/91 in *SI 1993 No 415*, those for 1991/92 in *SI 1994 No 728*, those for 1992/93 to 1996/97 inclusive in *SI 1995 Nos 351, 352* (as amended by *SI 1996 Nos 781, 782*) and those for 1997/98 onwards in *SI 1995 No 351*.

These arrangements broadly enable the inspector to require a return of syndicate profits at any time after the beginning of a year of assessment (before 1997/98, after the end of the closing year (i.e. the year of assessment next but one following the year of assessment concerned)), and a payment on account of basic rate tax. Penalties apply for failure to comply with a notice requiring such a return.

The return must be submitted by 1 September in the year of assessment (before 1997/98, by 1 September following the end of the closing year) or three months after service of the notice requiring the return if later. The inspector may determine the syndicate profit or loss either in accordance with the return or, subject to the usual appeal procedures, to the best of his judgment if he is not satisfied with the return, and the determination is conclusive as regards the tax liability of each member. A return may be required apportioning the profits so determined between syndicate members, again subject to penalty for failure to comply.

For 1988/89 and subsequent years of assessment, the return of syndicate profit or loss is to be made by the managing agent, who may also, within six years from 1 March next following the end of the closing year (i.e. the underwriting year next but one following the underwriting year concerned), claim repayment of tax suffered by deduction on syndicate investment income and, for 1992/93 onwards, tax credits in respect of qualifying distributions forming part of such income (and for this purpose, a non-resident member is treated as entitled to tax credits as if he were UK resident, and for all individual members the tax credit will be treated as income from premiums trust fund assets (see 89.3 above)). Any such repayment must be apportioned and, where there is a syndicate profit available for distribution, paid to the members' agents within 90 days of receipt. No repayment supplement is available.

For 1993/94 and earlier years of assessment, the member's agent may also (and subject to similar conditions) be required to make a return of the member's profit in respect of those syndicates in relation to which he is the agent of the member, including a statement of tax at the basic rate for the year of assessment on such profit. Certain additions and deductions in arriving at the profit so returned are specified, and the return is to be made by 1 October in the year of assessment following the closing year (or three months after service of notice requiring the return, if later). The payment on account (i.e. the basic rate liability, if any, stated in the return) must be made by the members' agent on or before 1 January following the end of the closing year for the year of assessment concerned, and may be the subject of assessment and interest by reference to that date if not made in accordance with the above provisions. Any discrepancy between the payment on account and the amount deducted by the members' agent in accounting to the member is adjusted between them.

For 1992/93 onwards, there are special provisions relating to stop-loss insurance, to reasonable excuse for certain failures to deliver returns, to determinations and to cessations. For 1992/93 and 1993/94, there are also provisions relating to members' agents, to error or mistake relief claims, to extended time limit assessments and to payment of tax. The extended time limit provisions apply also for 1994/95, and the payment provisions for 1994/95 to 1996/97 inclusive. For underwriting years 1994 and 1995 there are special provisions for running-off syndicates.

For 1988/89, 1989/90 and 1990/91, there are special provisions for the date of payment of assessed tax, for reasonable excuse for certain failures by the managing agent or members' agent, for error or mistake relief, and for the amendment of various provisions of the *Taxes Acts* in their application to underwriters.

For 1986/87 and 1987/88, only the return by the managing agent was required, and this had to include a statement of tax at the basic rate on the syndicate profit (if any). The managing agent was then required to make the payment on account in the amount of that basic rate tax. Where a member's own agent notifies the syndicate managing agent that the amounts returned for the Name for all his syndicates give rise to an overall loss on his Lloyd's income, the managing agent may, by concession, deduct from the amount due to the Revenue, and pass direct to the Name, any tax which he has withheld from income due to the Name. This concession applies only where the total amount withheld for the Name from all his Lloyd's income exceeds £1,000 and the amount withheld in the syndicate concerned exceeds £200. (Revenue Pamphlet IR 1, A73).

Member's liability. The amount of basic rate tax apportioned to a member as above is regarded as a payment on account of the member's liability in respect of his share of the profits, any additional liability or repayment being dealt with directly between the member and the Revenue. Tax is due in respect of profits from all a member's syndicates on or before 1 July in the year of assessment next but one following the closing year, with credit being given for the basic rate tax accounted for as above by the member's agents. Thus for underwriting year 1990, for which the closing year is 1992/93, the basic rate tax is due on 1 January 1994 and the balance of the member's liability on 1 July 1994.

For the purposes of assessment in cases involving fraudulent or negligent conduct, anything done or omitted to be done by the managing agent is treated as having been done or omitted by each syndicate member. [*19A Sch; FA 1988, s 58(4), 5 Sch; FA 1989, ss 149(6), 170(5); SI 1990 No 2524; FA 1993, ss 173, 184(1), 19 Sch; FA 1994, 21 Sch 9–11*].

89.6   For 1985/86 and earlier years, only the underwriting profits of a member are assessable under Schedule D, Case I, and there is no provision requiring returns or a payment on account by agents (although in practice agents make the necessary returns and agree tax computations with the Revenue). Basic rate tax on income from premiums trust fund assets is accounted for by the agent. Liability of the member falls due on 1 January in the year next following the closing year in respect of basic rate tax, and on the following 1 July in respect of higher rate tax (e.g. for underwriting year 1985, for which the closing year is 1987/88, on 1 January 1989 and 1 July 1989 respectively). [*SI 1974 No 896, Pt II*].

89.7   **LOSSES**

An underwriting loss can be **carried forward** for relief against underwriting profits in subsequent tax years (under the normal provisions for carry-forward of losses under *Sec 385(1)*).

An underwriting loss for a tax year can also be **offset against other income** of the underwriter of the same tax year under the normal tax provisions of *Sec 380(1)*. Note that, for 1989/90 and earlier years, if the underwriter is not a working name, a loss will be set off first against unearned income. For 1996/97 and earlier years, the loss can also be offset against other income of the immediately preceding tax year providing he was an underwriter during that preceding tax year, so far as relief cannot be given against income of the tax year in which the loss was sustained and can be given after any relief for a loss in that preceding tax year. However, similarly for 1996/97 and earlier years, an underwriting loss cannot be carried forward for use against other income of the underwriter in the succeeding tax year under *Sec 380(2)*. [*Sec 450(3); FA 1993, s 171(3)*].

An underwriting loss in the early years of the business may be carried back and offset against other income under *Sec 381*.

A claim to relief under *Secs 380* or *381* must normally be made within two years of the end of the year of assessment in which the loss is incurred, but prior to the introduction of a revised basis of assessment for 1997/98 onwards (see 89.2 above), this was generally extended for Lloyd's underwriters, by annual regulations, to four years.

See 46 LOSSES.

89.8   **SPECIAL RESERVE FUND**

An underwriter may set up a Special Reserve Fund into which he may make payments (eligible for tax relief—see below) for the purpose of meeting future losses.

(a)   **1991/92 and earlier years**

The arrangements must satisfy the requirements of *Secs 452 et seq.*, be approved by the Revenue and certified by the Board of Trade. [*Sec 452(1)*]. The funds must be vested in trustees, who may invest them and income from these investments must be held on trust for the underwriter. An underwriter carrying on business personally and also through an agent, or through more than one agent, may have more than one special reserve fund. [*Sec 452(2), (3), (4)(a)*].

Payments into the fund. The underwriter may pay into the fund(s) annually amounts limited, in aggregate, to (when grossed-up at the basic rate) the lesser of £7,000 or 50% of his underwriting profit (inclusive of investment income on all trust and reserve funds). [*Sec 452(5)(7)(8); FA 1988, s 61(1)(d); FA 1989, s 96(1)(4)*]. Such payments are treated as 'annual payments', from which tax has been deducted at the basic rate, in the year of assessment in which the underwriting year ends, deductible from underwriting income (and from underwriting investment income last). [*Secs 454, 457(2)*]. Thus the underwriter receives relief (where relevant) for income tax at the higher rates in excess of the basic rate and at the additional rate.

No election is necessary for making payments into a special reserve fund but the amount of any such payment must be notified to the inspector within twelve months after the deemed date of closing the accounts of an underwriting year. The payment must be made not more than 30 days after the inspector has notified his agreement, or 30 days after the expiration of the aforesaid twelve months, if later. [*Sec 452(6)*].

Payments out of the fund. There will be made out of the capital of the special reserve fund (into the underwriter's 'premiums trust fund') payments which, when grossed-up at the basic rate equal underwriting losses (as certified by the inspector, with right of appeal—*Sec 453(4)*). These payments may be made on a provisional basis pending final adjustment of the loss, whereafter adjustment will be made. [*Sec 453*]. Such payments (other than provisional amounts) are treated as 'annual payments' receivable by the underwriter from which tax has been deducted at the basic rate, in the year of assessment in which the underwriting year ends [*Sec 454(3)*] and relief for a loss is given as far as possible against the income represented by the payment (for which see *Peterson v De Brunner (Sp C 64), [1996] SSCD 91*). [*Sec 454(4)*].

On the underwriter ceasing to carry on business, the capital of his special reserve fund (so far as not required for a loss as above) shall be paid over to him, or his personal representatives or assigns. [*Sec 452(4)(b)*]. Tax consequences are as follows.

(i)   *If he ceases to carry on business before his death*—payment out is treated as an 'annual payment' to him, from which tax has been deducted at the basic rate, on the last day on which he carried on business. [*Sec 454(5)*].

(ii)   *If he dies while carrying on business*—there is to be ascertained that part of the fund which represents the excess in the fund (after withdrawals for losses) over what would be in the fund if payments in had been limited to amounts which, when grossed-up, had not in any year exceeded £5,000 or 35% of the profit, whichever was the less. This excess, grossed-up at the rates of tax applicable to the relevant years, is treated as an annual payment to him in the relevant year of assessment in which each part of the excess was deemed to be paid in. [*Sec 455(1)(2)*].

Any withdrawal for a loss made at any time is, for the above purpose, treated as having been met (*a*) out of payments made into the fund for years before that loss was incurred, and before withdrawal for any later loss, (*b*) primarily out of payments made for any underwriting year up to limits of £5,000 or 35%, and (*c*) out of excess payments over £5,000 or 35%, but taking those of later years before earlier years. [*Sec 455(1)(3)*]. In cases where the income of an underwriter falls to be treated as investment income, transfers out of the fund shall be treated as investment income to the extent of any transfer not offset by reliefs. [*Sec 456(1)*].

(*b*)   **1992/93 and subsequent years**

Special reserve funds within (*a*) above cease to apply with effect for 1992/93 and subsequent years and must be closed (see (*c*) below). For those years, a new-style special reserve fund may be set up in relation to each underwriter under arrangements complying with the requirements of *FA 1993, 20 Sch Pt I* and approved by the Revenue (who may consent to any variation of the arrangements). The fund must be vested in trustees who have control over it, and there must be appointed a fund manager, authorised under Lloyd's rules, and who may be the trustees or one or more of them, to invest the capital and vary the investments. Payments into and out of the fund (which, unless a contrary intention appears in the legislation, must be in money) must be allowed only where required or permitted (expressly or by necessary implication) by the provisions of *Schedule 20*. Otherwise, the income arising from the fund must be added to capital and retained in the fund. The underwriter is absolutely entitled as against the trustees to the fund assets, but (for 1994/95 onwards) without affecting the operation of capital gains tax on a disposal of an asset by the underwriter to the trustees. The fund manager must value the fund in a manner to be prescribed by regulations (see *SI 1995 No 353*) as at the end of each underwriting year, commencing with the underwriting year 1994, and must report the value (and such other matters as may be prescribed by regulations) to the underwriter. [*FA 1993, s 175(1)(2), 20 Sch 1(1), 2, 6(1), 8; FA 1994, 21 Sch 12(1), 13; FA 1995, s 143*].

Payments into and out of the special reserve fund are, respectively, deductions and additions in arriving at the underwriter's profit (to be included, for 1992/93 and 1993/94, in the member's agent's return, see 89.5 above). [*FA 1993, 19 Sch 10(2)(a)(3)(a), 20 Sch 10*]. This does not apply for 1994/95, 1995/96 or 1996/97, for which no underwriting profits fall to be assessed (see 89.2 above). [*FA 1994, 21 Sch 14(3)*]. See also below.

Tax exemption. Profits arising from special reserve fund assets are exempt from both income tax and capital gains tax, and losses are not allowable. The fund manager may, at any time after the end of an underwriting year, claim repayment of income tax deducted from such profits for that year and of tax credits in respect of qualifying distributions forming part of the fund income for that year. [*FA 1993, 20 Sch 9*].

For the purposes of the provisions described below, an underwriter's '*syndicate profit*' for an underwriting year is the excess of his aggregate profits over his aggregate losses, profits or losses being those shown in syndicate accounts as arising to him and disregarding payments into or out of the special reserve fund. Profits of a run-off underwriting year are attributable to the last underwriting year but one preceding the run-off year. An underwriter's '*syndicate loss*' is to be construed accordingly. [*FA 1993, 20 Sch 1; SI 1995 No 353*].

Payments into the fund out of syndicate profits. If an underwriter has made a syndicate profit for an underwriting year, he may pay into his special reserve fund, before the end of a period to be prescribed by regulations (see *SI 1995 No 353*), the lesser of

(i)   50% of that profit, and

(ii)   the excess, if any, of an amount equal to 50% of the underwriter's 'overall premium limit' for the closing year (i.e. the year next but one following the underwriting year) over the value of the fund at the end of that year.

An underwriter's *'overall premium limit'* for an underwriting year means the maximum amount which, under Lloyd's rules, he may accept by way of premiums in that year. If the underwriter did not accept premiums in the closing year, the reference in (ii) above to the closing year is to be taken as a reference to the latest underwriting year in which he did so. The above provisions are not to apply, in the case of any underwriter, to any year of assessment after a year of assessment in which the Revenue cancel their approval of the arrangements referred to above, having first given notice to Lloyd's of their intention to do so.

The payment into the fund in respect of an underwriting year is deductible as an expense in arriving at underwriting profits. For 1992/93 and 1993/94, it is made for the year of assessment to which the underwriting year corresponds (i.e. 1992 and 1993 respectively). From 1997/98 onwards, it is made for the year of assessment next but two after that year (i.e. a payment made in underwriting year 1994 is deducted in 1997/98). [*FA 1993, s 175(3), 20 Sch 1(1), 3, 10(1); FA 1994, 21 Sch 14*].

Payments out of the fund. Payments *must* be made out of the fund in the following circumstances.

(1)   To cover 'cash calls'. A *'cash call'* means a request for funds made to the underwriter by an agent of a syndicate of which he is a member, being made in pursuance of a contract made in accordance with Lloyd's rules and practices. If a cash call is made in respect of an underwriting year, there must be paid out of the underwriter's special reserve fund into a premiums trust fund of his an amount equal to the amount of the call (or, if less, the amount of the special reserve fund). There are provisions for a payment to be made back into the special reserve fund if a stop-loss payment (i.e. a payment of insurance money under a stop-loss insurance or a payment out of the High Level Stop Loss Fund—see 89.3 above) is made to the underwriter, and for a further payment out of the fund if a stop-loss payment is wholly or partly repaid. [*FA 1993, 20 Sch 4; SI 1995 No 353*].

(2)   To cover syndicate losses. If an underwriter sustains a syndicate loss for an underwriting year, there must be paid out of his special reserve fund into a premiums trust fund of his an amount equal to the 'net amount of the loss' (or, if less, the amount of the special reserve fund). The *'net amount of the loss'* is the amount of the syndicate loss as reduced by any payment made out of the special reserve fund for the year to cover a cash call (see (1) above). As in (1) above, there are provisions for payments into and out of the special reserve fund in the event of stop-loss payments and repayments of stop-loss payments. If a stop-loss payment is made in respect of the loss before any payment out of the special reserve fund in respect of the loss, no payment is required into the fund but the said payment out of the fund is determined as if the net amount of the loss were reduced by the amount of the stop-loss payment. [*FA 1993, 20 Sch 5*].

(3)   To eliminate excess amounts. If on the valuation (see above) of the special reserve fund at the end of the underwriting year, it is found that the value of the fund exceeds 50% of the underwriter's overall premium limit (see above) for that year (or for the last year in which he accepted premiums), the excess must be paid to the underwriter (or to his personal representatives or assigns). [*FA 1993, 20 Sch 6(2)*].

(4)   On cessation. On a person ceasing to be an underwriter (on death or otherwise), the amount of his special reserve fund (net of any amount required to be paid out to cover cash calls or syndicate losses) must be paid over to the underwriter (or to his personal representatives or assigns), the payment to be in money or in assets forming part of the fund, as the recipient may direct. [*FA 1993, 20 Sch 7; FA 1994, 21 Sch 12(2)*].

Any payments required to be made out of or into the fund under (1)–(3) above must be made before the end of a period to be prescribed in each case by regulations (see *SI 1995 No 353*). [*FA 1993, 20 Sch 4(8), 5(10), 6(3)*].

In computing underwriting profits for a year of assessment, payments into the special reserve fund under (1) and (2) above in respect of the corresponding (for 1997/98 onwards, the 'relevant') underwriting year are deductible as expenses, and the following are treated as trading receipts:

(A)   payments out of the fund in respect of the corresponding or 'relevant' underwriting year to cover cash calls and losses;

(B)   payments out of the fund as a result of the repayment of stop-loss payments (see (1) and (2) above) in the corresponding or 'relevant' underwriting year; and

(C)   any payment out of the fund under (3) above in respect of the corresponding or 'relevant' underwriting year's closing year (i.e. the underwriting year next but one following the corresponding or 'relevant' underwriting year).

The '*relevant*' underwriting year for this purpose (which applies for 1997/98 onwards) is the underwriting year next but two before the corresponding underwriting year, i.e. for 1997/98, for which the corresponding underwriting year is 1997, the relevant underwriting year is 1994.

[*FA 1993, 20 Sch 10(2)–(4); FA 1994, 21 Sch 14*].

Cessation. Any payment made out of the special reserve fund under (4) above is treated, in computing underwriting profits for the 'relevant year of assessment', as made immediately after the end of the 'relevant underwriting year' and as being a trading receipt. The amount of the trading receipt is the value of the fund at the end of the 'penultimate underwriting year' as reduced by subsequent payments out (other than under (3) or (4) above) and as increased by subsequent payments in (other than out of syndicate profits) and by any subsequent repayment of tax or tax credits in respect of special reserve fund income. The transfer of an asset under (4) above is treated for capital gains purposes as an acquisition at market value as at the end of the 'penultimate underwriting year'.

For 1994/95 and subsequent years, the '*relevant year of assessment*' is the final year of assessment except that, where a member dies before the occurrence of certain events, it is the year of assessment at the end of which he is treated as having died (see 89.4 above). The events in question are where the member's deposit is paid over to any person (or a substituted arrangement ceases) or the last open year of account of any syndicate of which he was a member is closed or is regarded as having closed. The '*relevant underwriting year*' is the underwriting year corresponding to the year of assessment immediately preceding the final year of assessment except that, where the member dies before the occurrence of certain events (as above), it is the underwriting year immediately preceding that corresponding to the relevant year of assessment (as above). The '*penultimate underwriting year*' is the underwriting year corresponding to the year of assessment immediately preceding the final year of assessment. Before 1994/95, the '*relevant year of assessment*' was the final year of assessment in all cases, and the '*relevant underwriting year*' and the '*penultimate underwriting year*' were in all cases the underwriting year immediately preceding that in which the member's deposit was paid over to him or his personal representatives or assigns. [*FA 1993, 20 Sch 11; FA 1994, 21 Sch 15; SI 1995 No 353, reg 8; SI 1995 No 1185, reg 5*].

Death. Where a member dies after 5 April 1994 and his personal representatives carry on his underwriting business after his death, the above provisions are modified to apply to the personal representatives. [*SI 1995 No 353, regs 7, 7A; SI 1995 No 1185, reg 4*].

(c) **Winding-up of old-style funds**

The following provisions have effect as respects the winding-up of any special reserve fund set up under the arrangements in (*a*) above (an '*old-style fund*') and which belongs to an underwriter for whom a special reserve fund may be set up under the arrangements in (*b*) above (a '*new-style fund*').

An underwriter may, at any time before the end of the 'relevant period', direct that so much of the capital of any old-style fund of his as represents sums paid into it under *Sec 452* (see (*a*) above) be transferred at the end of that period into his new-style fund, such transfer to be made in money or in assets forming part of the fund or both, as he may direct (the transfer of an asset being treated as a disposal at market value by the underwriter for capital gains tax purposes). Where such a transfer is made, the Revenue will make a payment to the new-style fund representing basic rate tax on the gross equivalent of the amount transferred (i.e. an amount equal to one-third of the amount transferred).

If an underwriter does not direct that a transfer be made, so much of the capital of any old-style fund of his as represents sums paid into it under *Sec 452* must be paid over to the underwriter at the end of the 'relevant period'. In computing for income tax purposes the underwriter's profits for 1992/93, the amount paid is to be grossed up by reference to the basic rate of tax (25%) and the gross amount treated as a trading receipt.

Whether or not the transfer is made, any remaining capital of the old-style fund is to be paid over to the underwriter at the end of the 'relevant period'.

For the above purposes, any withdrawals made from the old-style fund under *Sec 453* (see (*a*) above) are treated as having been made primarily out of payments into the fund under *Sec 452*.

The '*relevant period*' is the period of three months beginning with the 'closing date'. The '*closing date*' is the earliest date on which each of the following has occurred as respects 1991/92 and earlier years of assessment:

(i) the time for making payments into the fund under *Sec 452* has expired, or the underwriter has given notice to the inspector that he will not be making any (or any further) payments; and

(ii) any withdrawals from the fund under *Sec 453* have been made.

References above to items being paid over to the underwriter include references to their being paid over to his personal representatives or assigns. [*FA 1993, s 175(4), 20 Sch 12–14; FA 1994, 21 Sch 16*].

90 Unit Trusts

Cross-references. For corporation tax provisions applicable to authorised unit trusts, see Tolley's Corporation Tax under Unit and Investment Trusts. See 52 OFFSHORE FUNDS for unit trusts which are offshore funds.

90.1 AUTHORISED UNIT TRUSTS

An *'authorised unit trust'* is a 'unit trust scheme' which is the subject of an order under *Financial Services Act 1986, s 78* for the whole or part of an accounting period. A *'unit trust scheme'* is as defined under *Financial Services Act 1986*, but subject to certain exclusions by Treasury order (see *SI 1988 No 267, SI 1992 Nos 571, 3133, SI 1994 No 1479*). *[Secs 468(6), 469(7); TCGA 1992, s 99(2)]*. The *Tax Acts* have effect as if the trustees were a company resident in the UK, and the rights of unit holders were shares in the company (but without prejudice to the making of 'interest distributions' (see below) for distribution periods beginning after 31 March 1994). Expenses of management (including managers' remuneration) are allowed as if the company were an investment company. *[Sec 468(1) (4); FA 1994, 14 Sch 3]*. For capital gains purposes, any unit trust scheme is treated as if the scheme were a company and the rights of the unit holders shares in the company, and, in the case of an authorised unit trust, as if the company were UK resident and ordinarily resident. *[TCGA 1992, s 99(1)]*.

A special rate of corporation tax applies to the trustees of an authorised unit trust. For financial year 1996 and subsequent years, the rate is equivalent to the lower rate of income tax (currently 20%) for the year of assessment beginning in the financial year concerned. *[Sec 468(1A); FA 1996, 6 Sch 10(1)(2)]*. Previously, the rate was equivalent to the basic rate of income tax for the year of assessment beginning in the financial year concerned, except that in certain cases (see below) it was the lower rate of income tax that applied, and for financial year 1993 only, the rate was set at 22.5%. Relief for interest as a charge on income was denied in respect of certain borrowings breaching duties imposed under *Financial Services Act 1986, s 81* (or such borrowings as might be specified in substitution by Treasury regulation). *[Sec 468E; FA 1994, s 111; FA 1996, 6 Sch 10(3)]*. For the special corporation tax loan relationship provisions, see Tolley's Corporation Tax under Gilts and Bonds (special cases).

For financial years 1994 and 1995, the corporation tax rate was equivalent to the lower rather than the basic rate of income tax (as above) where, on a claim for an accounting period all or part of which fell in the financial year concerned, the inspector was satisfied that, throughout the accounting period, no more than 60% of the market value of the investments subject to the trusts (disregarding cash awaiting investment) was represented by 'qualifying investments'. The claim had to be made within twelve months of the end of the accounting period. *'Qualifying investments'* are defined as

(*a*)   money placed at interest,

(*b*)   building society shares,

(*c*)   securities (other than company shares) of any Government, public or local authority or company, whether secured or unsecured, and including any loan stock or similar security, and

(*d*)   an entitlement to a share in the investments of another authorised unit trust unless, throughout the accounting period in question, no more than 60% of the market value of that other unit trust's investments is represented by investments falling within (*a*)–(*c*) above, but the Treasury may, by order, extend or restrict the meaning of 'qualifying investments', including any necessary or expedient transitional provisions. [*Sec 468EE; FA 1994, s 111(2); FA 1996, 6 Sch 10(3)*].

For corporation tax regime applicable for accounting periods ending *on or before 31 December 1990* (31 December 1989 in the case of certain 'certified unit trusts'), and for transitional provisions, see Tolley's Income Tax 1993/94 or earlier.

'*Umbrella schemes*' (i.e. schemes which provide separate pools of contributions between which participants may switch) which are authorised unit trusts may treat each of the separate pools as an authorised unit trust. This applies from 1 April 1994, subject to transitional arrangements for schemes which were umbrella schemes immediately before that date. [*Sec 468(7)–(9); FA 1994, s 113*].

Futures and options. Income derived from transactions relating to futures or options contracts after 26 July 1990 is exempt from tax under Schedule D, Case I in the hands of the trustees. A contract is not excluded from this exemption by the fact that any party is, or may be, entitled to receive and/or liable to make only a payment of a sum (rather than a transfer of assets other than money) in full settlement of all obligations. [*Sec 468AA; FA 1990, s 81(1)*].

For **distribution periods beginning before 1 April 1994** (except in the case of an authorised unit trust which is an approved personal pension scheme, see 65.2 RETIREMENT ANNUITIES AND PERSONAL PENSION SCHEMES), any income available for distribution or investment for a distribution period is treated as dividends on the deemed shares held by unit holders paid to them in proportion to their rights, the date of payment, in the case of income not paid to unit holders, being the latest (or only) date for distribution under the terms of the trust or, if there is no such date, the last day of the distribution period. [*Sec 468(2)*]. Special provisions apply as regards distributions to unit holders within the charge to corporation tax generally and to unit holders which are investment trusts (see *Secs 468F, 468G,* repealed by *FA 1994, 14 Sch 4*).

For **distribution periods beginning after 31 March 1994**, the total amount available for distribution to unit holders is to be shown in the distribution accounts as available for distribution either as dividends which are not foreign income dividends within *ICTA 1988, Ch VI, Pt VA* (a 'dividend distribution'), or (in relation to distribution dates (see below) after 30 June 1994) as foreign income dividends (a 'foreign income distribution'), or as yearly interest (which may not include any amount deriving from Schedule A income) (an 'interest distribution') or as divided between the first two categories (in which case no discrimination between unit holders is permitted). These provisions do not apply to an authorised unit trust which is an approved personal pension scheme (see 65.2 RETIRMENT ANNUITIES AND PERSONAL PENSION SCHEMES). [*Secs 468H(5), 468I; FA 1994, 14 Sch 2, 7*].

For these purposes, the making of a distribution includes the investment of an amount on behalf of the unit holder in respect of his accumulation units. [*Sec 468H(2); FA 1994, 14 Sch 2*].

As regards dividend distributions, they are treated as dividends on shares paid on the '*distribution date*' (i.e. the date specified under the trust or, if there is no such date, the last day of the distribution period), in respect of which no foreign income dividend election may be made. See 1.8(iii) ALLOWANCES AND TAX RATES as regards taxation of dividends. [*Sec 468J; FA 1994, 14 Sch 2*]. Special provisions apply to dividend distributions to unit holders within the charge to corporation tax (see *Sec 468Q* introduced by *FA 1994, 14 Sch 2*).

As regards foreign income distributions, they are treated as foreign income dividends on shares paid on the '*distribution date*' (as above) to which *Secs 246A, 246B* (elections for foreign income dividend treatment), *246K–246M* (subsidiaries) and *246S–246W* (international headquarters companies) do not apply (and for which provisions see Tolley's Corporation Tax under Foreign Income Dividends). [*Sec 468K; FA 1994, 14 Sch 2*]. Special provisions apply where, on the distribution date, the unit holder is within the charge to corporation tax (see *Sec 468R* introduced by *FA 1994, 14 Sch 2*).

As regards interest distributions, they are treated as payments of yearly interest made on the '*distribution date*' (as above). They are not charges on income within *Sec 338(1)*, but if paid under deduction of tax (see below) they are deductible from total profits (see *Sec 468L(5)–(7)* (as amended), introduced by *FA 1994, 14 Sch 2*). Lower rate tax (for 1995/96 and earlier years, basic rate tax) is deductible under *Sec 349(2)* except in certain cases where the unit holder to whom the payment is made satisfies the residence condition of *Secs 468O, 468P* (introduced by *FA 1994, 14 Sch 2*) on the distribution date, broadly that a valid declaration is made in prescribed form that either he is non-UK ordinarily resident or, if he holds the units as personal representative of a deceased unit holder, at the time of his death the unit holder was non-UK ordinarily resident. In relation to company unit holders, the declaration must be that the company is not UK resident. In the case of distributions made to or received under a trust, under regulations effective from 27 September 1994 (see *SI 1994 No 2318*), the requirement is for a valid declaration from the trustees both that they are non-UK resident and that each beneficiary known to them satisfies the individual or company residence conditions as appropriate (except that where the whole of the distribution is, or is treated as, income of a person other than the trustees, the residence conditions apply only to that person). If the gross income in the distribution accounts derives entirely from 'eligible income', payments to unit holders satisfying the appropriate residence condition may be made without deduction of tax. There is a formula for determining the amount which may be paid without deduction of tax where the gross income does not derive entirely from 'eligible income' (see *Sec 468N(4)–(6)* introduced by *FA 1994, 14 Sch 2*). *SI 1994 No 2318* also provides the Revenue with the appropriate powers to determine whether interest distributions have properly been paid gross. '*Eligible income*' is defined in *Sec 468M(4)(5)* (introduced by *FA 1994, 14 Sch 2*) as amended, and is broadly income which would not be subject to deduction if received directly by a non-resident.

Interest distributions made after 5 April 1996 are subject to tax deductions at source at the lower rate, under the general principle at 1.8(iii) ALLOWANCES AND TAX RATES (previously the basic rate). For *distribution periods ending after 31 March 1996*, an interest distribution may be made only if the authorised unit trust satisfies the qualifying investments test throughout the distribution period, which it does if, at all times in that period, the market value of 'qualifying investments' exceeds 60% of the market value of all the investments of the trust (disregarding cash awaiting investment). The definition of '*qualifying investments*' is equivalent to that given above (i.e. for determining the corporation tax rate for financial years 1994 and 1995) and may be extended or restricted by Treasury Order.

[*Secs 468L, 468M, 468N; FA 1994, 14 Sch 2; FA 1996, 6 Sch 11, 7 Sch 17, 14 Sch 26*].

90.2 UNIT TRUSTS NOT TREATED AS AUTHORISED UNIT TRUSTS

Special provisions apply to the income of a unit trust scheme not within 90.1 above (and to certain other unit trusts for distribution periods beginning before 1 January 1991—see Tolley's Income Tax 1993/94 or earlier) unless the trustees are non-UK resident. Such a trust is outside the scope of *Sec 468* (see 90.1 above), and is subject to basic rate tax on its income. Capital allowances are available to the trustees (but, since the trustees are not treated as a company, there is no relief for management expenses). The unit holders are treated as receiving annual payments, under deduction of basic rate tax, equal to their respective entitlements to the grossed-up income available for distribution or investment. The date the payment is treated as having been made is the latest (or only) date for distribution under the terms of the trust or (if there is no such date or it is more than twelve months after the end of the distribution period) the last day of the distribution period. For the definition of 'distribution period', see *Sec 469(6)* as amended by *FA 1994, 14 Sch 5*.

For 1996/97 and later years, the income of the trustees, and thus of the unit holders, continues to be chargeable at the basic rate, as opposed to the lower rate, even if the nature of the income is such that it would otherwise constitute 'savings income' within 1.8(iii) ALLOWANCES AND TAX RATES.

The liability of the trustees to account for tax deducted from annual payments treated as made by them, so far as not covered by tax deducted from income received, is reduced where there is a cumulative uncredited surplus of income on which they are chargeable to tax over such annual payments. [*Sec 469; FA 1988, s 71; FA 1994, 14 Sch 5; FA 1996, 6 Sch 12, 28, 41 Sch Pt V(1)*].

91 Venture Capital Trusts

91.1 From 6 April 1995, the venture capital trust scheme described at 91.2 *et seq.* below is introduced to encourage individuals to invest in unquoted trading companies through such trusts. The provisions dealing with the approval of companies as venture capital trusts, and with the reliefs for investors, are introduced in *FA 1995, ss 70–72, 14–16 Schs.* The Treasury has wide powers to make regulations governing all aspects of the reliefs applicable to venture capital trust investments, and for the requirements as regards returns, records and provision of information by the trust. [*FA 1995, s 73; FA 1996, 18 Sch 16, 17(1)(3)*]. See now *SI 1995 No 1979*.

91.2 **CONDITIONS FOR APPROVAL** [*Sec 842AA; FA 1995, s 70*]

A '*venture capital trust*' ('VCT') is a company approved for this purpose by the Board, close companies being excluded. The time from which an approval takes effect is specified in the approval, and may not be earlier than the time the application for approval was made or, for approvals given in 1995/96, 6 April 1995.

Except as detailed further below, approval may not be given unless the Board are satisfied that the following conditions are met.

(a)   The company's income in its most recent complete accounting period has been derived wholly or mainly from shares or securities, and not more than 15% of its income from shares and securities has been retained.

(b)   Throughout that period at least 70% by value of the company's investments has been represented by shares or securities in 'qualifying holdings' (see 91.3 below), at least 30% of which (by value) has been represented by holdings of '*eligible shares*', i.e. ordinary shares carrying no present or future preferential right to dividends, to assets on a winding up or to redemption.

(c)   The company's ordinary shares (or each class thereof) have been listed in the Official List of the Stock Exchange throughout that period.

(d)   No holding in any company other than a VCT (or a company which could be a VCT but for (c) above) has at any time in that period represented more than 15% of the value of the company's investments.

'Securities' includes liabilities in respect of certain loans not repayable within five years, and any stocks or securities relating to which are not re-purchasable or redeemable within five years of issue. Provided that the loan is made on normal commercial terms, the Revenue will not regard a standard event of default clause in the loan agreement as disqualifying a loan from being a security for this purpose. If, however, the clause entitled the lender (or a third party) to exercise any action which would cause the borrower to default, the clause would not be regarded as 'standard'. (Revenue Statement of Practice SP 8/95, 14 September 1995).

As regards the 15% limits in (a) and (d) above, the provisions which apply to the similar restrictions on investment trusts (see Tolley's Corporation Tax under Unit and Investment Trusts) apply modified as appropriate.

Where (a)–(d) above are met, the Board must also be satisfied that they will be met in the accounting period current at the time of application for approval. Where any of (a)–(d) above are not met, approval may nevertheless be given where the Board are satisfied as to the meeting of those conditions (and in certain cases other conditions imposed by regulations) in future accounting periods.

Where the 70% limit in (b) is breached inadvertently, and the position corrected without delay after discovery, approval will in practice not be withdrawn on this account. Full details of any such inadvertent breach should be disclosed to the Revenue as soon as it is discovered. (Revenue Press Release 14 September 1995).

The value of any investment for the purposes of (*b*) and (*d*) above is the value when the investment was acquired, except that where it is added to by a further holding of an investment of the same description, or a payment is made in discharge of any obligation attached to it which increases its value, it is the value immediately after the most recent such addition or payment.

Approval may be **withdrawn** where there are reasonable grounds for believing that either:

(A)   the conditions for approval were not satisfied at the time the approval was given; or

(B)   a condition that the Board were satisfied (as above) would be met has not been or will not be met; or

(C)   in either the most recent complete accounting period or the current one, one of conditions (*a*)–(*d*) above has failed or will fail to be met (unless the failure was allowed for as above).

The withdrawal is effective from the time the company is notified of it, except that:

(1)   where approval is given on the Board's being satisfied as to the meeting of the relevant conditions in future accounting periods, and is withdrawn before all the conditions (*a*)–(*d*) above have been satisfied in relation to either a complete twelve-month accounting period or successive complete accounting periods constituting a continuous period of twelve months or more, the approval is deemed never to have been given; and

(2)   for the purposes of relief for capital gains accruing to a VCT under *TCGA 1992, s 100* (see 91.11 below), withdrawal may be effective from an earlier date, but not before the start of the accounting period in which the failure occurred (or is expected to occur).

An assessment consequent on the withdrawal of approval may, where otherwise out of time, be made within three years from the time notice of the withdrawal was given.

For the detailed requirements as regards granting, refusal and withdrawal of approval, and appeals procedures, see *SI 1995 No 1979, Pt II*.

91.3   **Qualifying holdings.** Shares or securities in a company are comprised in a VCT's '*qualifying holdings*' at any time if they were first issued to the VCT, and have been held by it ever since, and the following conditions are satisfied at that time.

(*a*)   The company is an '*unquoted company*' (whether or not UK resident), i.e. none of its shares, stocks, debentures or other securities is

(i)   listed on a recognised stock exchange, or a designated exchange outside the UK, or

(ii)   dealt in on the Unlisted Securities Market, or outside the UK by such means as may be designated for the purpose by order.

Securities on the Alternative Investment Market ('AIM') are treated as unquoted for these purposes. (Revenue Press Release 20 February 1995).

If the company ceases to be an unquoted company at a time when its shares are comprised in the qualifying holdings of the VCT, this condition is treated as continuing to be met, in relation to shares or securities acquired before that time, for the following five years.

(*b*)   Either

      (i)   the company must exist wholly for the purpose of carrying on one or more 'qualifying trades' (disregarding any purpose having no significant effect on the extent of its activities as a whole), or

      (ii)   its business must consist entirely in holding shares in or securities of, or making loans to, one or more 'qualifying subsidiaries' (for which see *28B Sch 10*, introduced as *FA 1995, 14 Sch 10*), with or without the carrying on of one or more 'qualifying trades'.

In addition, the company, or a qualifying subsidiary, must, when the shares were issued to the VCT and ever since, have been carrying on a 'qualifying trade' wholly or mainly in the UK, or preparing to carry on such a trade intended to be carried on wholly or mainly in the UK. In the latter case, there is a time limit of two years from the issue of the shares for the trade to be commenced as intended.

A trade is a '*qualifying trade*' if it meets the same conditions as apply in relation to the Enterprise Investment Scheme (see 26.7 ENTERPRISE INVESTMENT SCHEME (AND BES)), but without the exclusion of oil extraction activities, and taking references to the 'relevant period' in relation to that scheme as references to the period since issue of the shares to the VCT. The definition of 'controlling interest' in relation to those conditions is also revised to permit holdings of non-voting fixed-rate preference shares, and rights as a loan creditor, to be disregarded. Research and development (i.e. activity intended to result in a patentable invention or a computer program) from which it is intended that there will be derived a qualifying trade carried on wholly or mainly in the UK is treated as the carrying on of a qualifying trade.

In considering whether a trade is carried on 'wholly or mainly in the UK', the totality of the trade activities is taken into account. Regard will be had, for example, to the locations at which assets are held, and at which any purchasing, processing, manufacturing and selling is done, and to the places at which the employees customarily carry out their duties. No one of these factors is itself likely to be decisive in any particular case. Accordingly a company may carry on some such activities outside the UK and yet satisfy the requirement, provided that the major part of them, that is over one-half of the aggregate of these activities, takes place within the UK. Thus relief is not excluded solely because some or all of a company's products or services are exported, or because its raw materials are imported, or because its raw materials or products are stored abroad, or because its marketing facilities are supplied from abroad. Similar principles apply in considering the trade(s) carried on by a company and its qualifying subsidiaries.

In the particular case of a ship chartering trade, the test is satisfied if all charters are entered into in the UK and the provision of crews and management of the ships while under charter take place mainly in the UK. If these conditions are not met, the test may still be satisfied depending on all the relevant facts and circumstances.

(Revenue Pamphlet IR 131, SP 2/94, 9 May 1994 as revised by Revenue Press Release 14 September 1995).

(*c*)   The money raised by the issue of shares to the VCT must have been employed wholly for the purposes of, or of preparing for the carrying on of, the qualifying trade (disregarding insignificant amounts used for other purposes), or be intended to be so employed. In the latter case, the money must actually be so employed within twelve months of the later of the issue of the shares to the VCT and the date the qualifying trade was commenced.

(*d*)   The aggregate of money raised from shares issued by the company to the VCT must not have exceeded the 'maximum qualifying investment' of £1 million in the period from six months before the issue in question (or, if earlier, the beginning of the year of assessment of the issue) to the time of the issue in question. Disposals are treated as far as possible as eliminating any such excess. The £1 million limit is proportionately reduced where, at the time of the issue, the qualifying trade is carried on, or to be carried on, in partnership or as a joint venture, and one or more of the other parties is a company.

(e)   The value of the company's 'relevant assets' did not exceed £10 million immediately before the issue or £11 million immediately thereafter. '*Relevant assets*' are the gross assets of the company and, at any time when it has one or more qualifying subsidiaries, of all such subsidiaries. In the latter case, assets consisting in rights against, or shares in or securities of, another member of the group consisting of the company and its qualifying subsidiaries are disregarded.

The general approach of the Revenue is that the value of a company's gross assets is the sum of the value of all the balance sheet assets. Where accounts are actually drawn up to a date immediately before or after the issue, the balance sheet values are taken provided that they reflect usual accounting standards and the company's normal accounting practice, consistently applied. Where accounts are not drawn up to such a date, such values will be taken from the most recent balance sheet, updated as precisely as practicable on the basis of management information available to the company. Regard will also be had to the value in the accounts for the period in which the issue is made—where this differs from the value in the previous period (e.g. because of revaluation or a change in the method of valuation), this may indicate that the value at the time of issue should reflect the revised treatment. The company's assets immediately before the issue do not include any advance payment received in respect of the issue. Where shares are issued partly paid, the right to the balance is an asset, and, notwithstanding the above, will be taken into account in valuing the assets immediately after the issue regardless of whether it is stated in the balance sheet. (Revenue Statement of Practice SP 7/95, 14 September 1995).

(f)   The company must not 'control' (with or without 'connected persons') any company other than a qualifying subsidiary, nor must another company (or another company and a person connected with it) control it. Neither must arrangements be in existence by virtue of which such control could arise. For these purposes, '*control*' is as under *Sec 416*, except that possession of, or entitlement to acquire, fixed-rate preference shares (within *Sec 95*) of the company which do not, for the time being, carry voting rights is disregarded, as is possession of, or entitlement to acquire, rights as a loan creditor of the company. '*Connected persons*' are as under *Sec 839* (see 20 CONNECTED PERSONS) except that the definition of 'control' therein is similarly modified.

(g)   Where the company is being wound up, none of conditions (a)–(f) above are regarded on that account as not being satisfied provided that those conditions would be met apart from the winding up, and that the winding up is for *bona fide* commercial reasons and not part of a scheme or arrangement a main purpose of which is the avoidance of tax.

As regards (c) and (d) above, where either condition would be met as to only part of the money raised by the issue, and the holding is not otherwise capable of being treated as separate holdings, it is treated as two separate holdings, one from which that part of the money was raised, the other from which the rest was raised, with the value being apportioned accordingly to each holding. In the case of (c), this does not require an insignificant amount applied for non-trade purposes to be treated as a separate holding.

As regards (c) above, in relation to buy-outs (and in particular management buy-outs), the Revenue will usually accept that where a company is formed to acquire a trade, and the funds raised from the VCT are applied to that purchase, the requirement that the funds be employed for the purposes of the trade is satisfied. Where the company is formed to acquire another company and its trade, or a holding company and its trading subsidiaries, this represents an investment rather than employment for the purposes of the trade. However, the Revenue will usually accept that the requirement is satisfied if the trade of the company, or all the activities of the holding company and its subsidiaries, are hived up to the acquiring company as soon as possible after the acquisition. In the case of a holding company and its subsidiaries, to the extent that the trades are not hived up, the holding cannot be a qualifying holding. (Revenue Tax Bulletin August 1995 pp 243, 244).

The Treasury have power by order to modify the requirements under (*b*) above as they consider expedient, and to alter the cash limits referred to in (*d*) and (*e*) above.

[*Sch 28B; FA 1995, 14 Sch; FA 1996, s 161*].

91.4   **INCOME TAX RELIEFS** [*Sec 332A, 15B Sch; FA 1995, s 71, 15 Sch*].

Relief from income tax is granted for 1995/96 and subsequent years in respect of both investments in VCTs and distributions from such trusts.

91.5   **Relief in respect of investments.** Subject to the conditions described below, an individual may claim relief for a year of assessment for the amount (or aggregate amounts) subscribed by him on his own behalf for 'eligible shares' issued to him in a year of assessment by a VCT (or VCTs) for raising money. There is a limit of £100,000 on the relief which may be claimed for any year of assessment.

'*Eligible shares*' means new ordinary shares in a VCT which, throughout the five years following issue, carry no present or future preferential right to dividends or to assets on a winding up or to be redeemed.

Relief is given by a reduction in what would otherwise be the individual's income tax liability for the year of assessment by the lesser of

(i)   tax at the lower rate (currently 20%) on the amount(s) subscribed, and

(ii)   an amount sufficient to reduce that liability to nil.

In determining what would otherwise be the individual's income tax liability for the year of assessment for this purpose, no account is taken of:

(A)   any income tax reduction in respect of enterprise investment scheme investments (see 26.8 ENTERPRISE INVESTMENT SCHEME (AND BES)), personal reliefs (see 1.15, 1.16, 1.17 ALLOWANCES AND TAX RATES), qualifying maintenance payments (see 47.15 MARRIED PERSONS), interest relief (see 43.5 INTEREST PAYABLE) or medical insurance (see 48.1 MEDICAL INSURANCE);

(B)   any reduction of liability to tax by way of DOUBLE TAX RELIEF (25); or

(C)   any basic rate tax on income the tax on which the individual is entitled to charge against any other person or to deduct, retain or satisfy out of any payment.

Where relief is given by repayment of tax more than twelve months after the end of the year of assessment in which the shares were issued, interest under *Sec 824* (see 41.1 INTEREST ON OVERPAID TAX) is payable.

An individual is **not** entitled to relief where:

(a)   he was under 18 years of age at the time of issue of the shares;

(b)   circumstances have arisen which, had the relief already been given, would have resulted in the withdrawal or reduction of the relief (see 91.7 below);

(c)   the shares were issued or subscribed for other than for *bona fide* commercial purposes or as part of a scheme or arrangement a main purpose of which was the avoidance of tax; or

(d)   a loan is made to the individual (or to an 'associate' within *Sec 417*, but excluding a brother or sister) by any person at any time in the period beginning with the incorporation of the VCT (or, if later, two years before the date of issue of the shares) and ending five years after the date of issue of the shares, and the loan would not have been made, or would not have been made on the same terms, if he had not subscribed, or had not been proposing to subscribe, for the shares. The granting of credit to, or the assignment of a debt due from, the individual or associate is counted as a loan for these purposes.

[*15B Sch 1, 2, 6; FA 1995, 15 Sch 1, 2, 6*].

As regards (d) above, for this restriction to apply, the test is whether the lender makes the loan on terms which are connected with the fact that the borrower (or an associate) is subscribing for eligible shares. The prime concern is why the lender made the loan rather than why the borrower applied for it. Relief would not be disallowed, for example, in the case of a bank loan if the bank would have made a loan on the same terms to a similar borrower for a different purpose. But if, for example, a loan is made specifically on a security consisting of or including the eligible shares (other than as part of a broad range of assets to which the lender has recourse), relief would be denied. Relevant features of the loan terms would be the qualifying conditions to be satisfied by the borrower, any incentives or benefits offered to the borrower, the time allowed for repayment, the amount of repayments and interest charged, the timing of interest payments, and the nature of the security. (Revenue Pamphlet IR 131 (October 1995 Supplement), SP 3/94, 9 May 1994, as revised by Revenue Press Release 14 September 1995).

An individual subscribing for eligible shares may obtain from the VCT a certificate giving details of the subscription and certifying that certain conditions for relief are satisfied. [*SI 1995 No 1979, reg 9*].

91.6   *Example*

On 1 May 1996, Miss K, who is 66 and whose pension is £16,265 p.a., subscribes for 40,000 eligible £1 shares issued at par to raise money by VCT plc, an approved venture capital trust. On 1 September 1996 she purchases a further 90,000 £1 shares in VCT plc for £70,000 on the open market. The trust makes no distribution in 1996/97. Miss K's other income for 1996/97 consists of dividends of £14,400. She pays qualifying MEDICAL INSURANCE (48) premiums of £800 under deduction of basic rate tax, and £200 interest on a private mortgage (outside MIRAS) for the purchase of her home. PAYE tax deducted is £2,850.

Miss K's tax computation for 1996/97 is as follows.

		£
Pension		16,265
Dividends	14,400	
Add Tax credit	3,600	18,000
Total income		34,265
Deduct Personal allowance		3,765
Taxable income		£30,500
Tax payable:		
3,900 @ 20%		780
8,600 @ 24%		2,064
13,000 @ 20%		2,600
5,000 @ 40%		2,000
c/f		7,444

91.7 Venture Capital Trusts

	b/f	7,444

Deduct Relief for investment in
VCT plc, 20% of £40,000 subscribed,
but restricted to   7,444

Net tax payable   —

Income tax £6,450 (PAYE £2,850 + tax credits £3,600) is repayable. There is no clawback of the basic rate tax deducted from the medical insurance premiums, but no relief is obtained for the mortgage interest.

91.7 **Withdrawal of relief on investment.** *Disposal of investment.* Where an individual disposes of eligible shares, in respect of which relief has been claimed as under 91.5 above, within five years of their issue (other than to a spouse when they are living together, see below), then:

(*a*)   if the disposal is otherwise than at arm's length, relief given by reference to those shares is withdrawn;

(*b*)   if the disposal is at arm's length, the relief given by reference to those shares is reduced by an amount equivalent to tax at the lower rate (for the year for which relief was given) on the consideration received for the disposal (or withdrawn if the relief exceeds that amount).

Relief is **not** withdrawn where the disposal is by one spouse to the other at a time when they are living together. However, on any subsequent disposal the spouse to whom the shares were transferred is treated as if he or she were the person who subscribed for the shares, as if the shares had been issued to him or her at the time they were issued to the transferor spouse, and as if his or her liability to income tax had been reduced by reference to those shares by the same amount, and for the same year of assessment, as applied on the subscription by the transferor spouse. Any assessment for reducing or withdrawing relief is made on the transferee spouse.

Identification of shares. For the above purposes, disposals of eligible shares in a VCT are identified with those acquired earlier rather than later. As between eligible shares acquired on the same day, shares by reference to which relief has been given are treated as disposed of after any other eligible shares.

Withdrawal of approval. Where approval of a company as a VCT is withdrawn (but not treated as never having been given) (see 91.2 above), relief given by reference to eligible shares in the VCT is withdrawn as if on a non-arm's length disposal immediately before the withdrawal of approval.

Assessments withdrawing or reducing relief, whether because relief is subsequently found not to have been due or under the above provisions, are made under SCHEDULE D, CASE VI (74) for the year of assessment for which the relief was given. No such assessment is, however, to be made by reason of an event occurring after the death of the person to whom the shares were issued.

Information. Particulars of all events leading to the reduction or withdrawal of relief must be notified to the inspector by the person to whom the relief was given within 60 days of his coming to know of the event. Where the inspector has reason to believe that a notice so required has not been given, he may require that person to furnish him, within a specified time not being less than 60 days, with such information relating to the event as he may reasonably require. The requirements of secrecy do not prevent the inspector disclosing to a VCT that relief has been given or claimed by reference to a particular number or proportion of its shares. Penalties under *TMA s 98* apply for failure to comply with these requirements.

[*15B Sch 3–5; FA 1995, s 71(3), 15 Sch 3–5*].

91.8   *Example*

On 1 May 1999, Miss K in the *Example* at 91.6 above, who has since 1996/97 neither acquired nor disposed of any shares in VCT plc, gives 25,000 shares to her son. On 1 January 2000, she disposes of the remaining 105,000 shares for £80,000. The relief given as in 91.6 above is withdrawn as follows.

Disposal on 1 May 1999

The shares disposed of are identified with 25,000 of those subscribed for, and, since the disposal was not at arm's length, the relief given on those shares is withdrawn.

£

$$\text{Relief withdraw } \frac{25,000}{40,000} \times 7,444 = \qquad\qquad 4,652$$

Disposal on 1 January 2000

The balance of £2,792 of the relief originally given was in respect of 15,000 of the shares disposed of. The disposal consideration for those 15,000 shares is

$$80,000 \times \frac{15,000}{105,000} = £11,428$$

The relief withdrawn is the lesser of the relief originally given and 20% of the consideration received, i.e.

20% of £11,428 = £2,286

Relief withdrawn is therefore   2,286

The 1996/97 Schedule D, Case VI
assessment is therefore   £6,938

91.9   **Relief on distributions.** A 'relevant distribution' of a VCT to which a 'qualifying investor' is beneficially entitled is not treated as income for income tax purposes, provided that certain conditions are fulfilled as regards the obtaining of an 'enduring declaration' from the investor, and that the VCT claims the related tax credit, which it is required to pass on to the investor.

A '*qualifying investor*' is an individual aged 18 or over who is beneficially entitled to the distribution either as the holder of the shares or through a nominee (including the trustees of a bare trust).

A '*relevant distribution*' is a dividend (including a capital dividend) in respect of ordinary shares in a company which is a VCT which were acquired at a time when it was a VCT by the recipient of the dividend, and which were not shares acquired in excess of the 'permitted maximum' for the year. It does not include any dividend paid in respect of profits or gains of any accounting period ending when the company was not a VCT.

Shares are acquired in excess of the '*permitted maximum*' for a year where the aggregate value of ordinary shares acquired in VCTs by the individual or his nominee(s) in that year exceeds £100,000, disregarding shares acquired other than for *bona fide* commercial reasons or as part of a scheme or arrangement a main purpose of which is the avoidance of tax. Shares acquired later in the year are identified as representing the excess before those acquired earlier, and in relation to same-day acquisition of different shares, a proportionate part of each description of share is treated as representing any excess arising on that day. Shares acquired at a time when a company was not a VCT are for these purposes treated as disposed of before other shares in the VCT. Otherwise, disposals are identified with earlier acquisitions before later ones, except that as between shares acquired on the same day, shares acquired in excess of the permitted maximum are treated as disposed of before any other shares. There are provisions for effectively disregarding acquisitions arising out of share exchanges where, for capital gains purposes, the new shares are treated as the same assets as the old.

[*15B Sch 7–9; FA 1995, 15 Sch 7–9; SI 1995 No 1979, reg 10*].

For the detailed requirements as regards obtaining relief for distributions, including the obtaining of the 'enduring declaration' and the claiming of tax credits, see *SI 1995 No 1979, Pt III, Ch II*.

91.10   *Example*

In 1997/98, Miss K in the *Example* at 91.6 above, whose circumstances are otherwise unchanged, receives a distribution from VCT plc of 4p per share. The company has claimed the tax credit in respect of the distribution, and distributes this as a further 1p per share.

The shares in VCT plc were acquired in 1996/97 for £110,000, so that distributions in respect of shares representing the £10,000 excess over the permitted maximum of £100,000 are not exempt. The 40,000 shares first acquired for £40,000 are first identified, so that the shares representing the excess are one-seventh of the 90,000 shares subsequently acquired for £70,000, i.e. 12,857 of those shares.

Miss K's tax computation for 1997/98 is as follows.

		£
Pension		16,265
Dividends (other than VCT plc)	14,400	
Add Tax credit	3,600	18,000
VCT plc distribution in respect of 12,857 shares	514	
Add Further distribution in respect of tax credit reclaimed by company	128	642
Total income		34,907
Deduct Personal allowance (say)		3,765
Taxable income		£31,142

Tax payable (say):	£
4,200 @ 20%	840
8,300 @ 22%	1,826
14,000 @ 20%	2,800
4,642 @ 40%	1,857
	7,323
Deduct Mortgage interest £200 @ 15%	30
Tax payable	7,293
Deduct Tax credit	3,600
Net tax liability	£3,693

91.11   **CAPITAL GAINS TAX RELIEFS** [*TCGA 1992, ss 151A, 151B, 5C Sch; FA 1995, s 72, 16 Sch*]

From 6 April 1995, the capital gains of a VCT are not chargeable gains. [*TCGA 1992, s 100(1); FA 1995, s 72(2)*]. In addition, for 1995/96 and subsequent years, individual investors in VCTs are entitled to two reliefs:

(*a*)   on disposal of VCT shares (see 91.12 below); and

(*b*)   by deferral of chargeable gains on re-investment in VCT share issues (see 91.14 below).

Various provisions of *TCGA 1992* which are superseded for these purposes by specific provisions (as below) are disapplied or applied separately to parts of holdings which do not fall within the reliefs.

Withdrawal of approval. Where approval of a company as a VCT is withdrawn (but not treated as never having been given) (see 91.2 above), shares which (apart from the withdrawal) would be eligible for the relief on disposal (see 91.12 below) are treated as disposed of at their market value at the time of the withdrawal. For the purposes of the relief on disposal, the disposal is treated as taking place while the company is still a VCT, but the re-acquisition is treated as taking place immediately after it ceases to be so.

91.12   **Relief on disposal.** A gain or loss accruing to an individual on a 'qualifying disposal' of ordinary shares in a company which was a VCT throughout his period of ownership is not a chargeable gain or an allowable loss. A disposal is a '*qualifying disposal*' if:

(*a*)   the individual is 18 years of age or more at the time of the disposal;

(*b*)   the shares were not acquired in excess of the 'permitted maximum' for any year of assessment; and

(*c*)   the shares were acquired for *bona fide* commercial purposes and not as part of a scheme or arrangement a main purpose of which was the avoidance of tax.

The identification of those shares which were acquired in excess of the '*permitted maximum*' is as under 91.9 above (in relation to income tax relief on distributions—broadly those in excess of an annual limit of £100,000), and the identification of disposals with acquisitions for this purpose is similarly as under 91.9 above.

[*TCGA 1992, ss 151A, 151B; FA 1995, s 72(3)*].

See 91.11 above as regards relief on withdrawal of approval of the VCT.

91.13 Venture Capital Trusts

91.13   *Example*

On the disposals in the *Example* at 91.8 above, a chargeable gain or allowable loss arises only on the disposal of the shares acquired in excess of the permitted maximum for 1996/97. As in the *Example* at 91.10 above, these are 12,857 of the shares acquired for £70,000 on 1 September 1996. The disposal identified with those shares is a corresponding proportion of the 105,000 shares disposed of for a consideration of £80,000 on 1 January 2000.

Miss K's capital gains tax computation for 1999/2000 is therefore as follows.

Disposal consideration for 12,857 shares—

	£
$80,000 \times \dfrac{12,857}{105,000} =$	9,796

Deduct Cost—

$70,000 \times \dfrac{12,857}{90,000} =$	10,000
Allowable loss	£204

(No indexation allowance is available to enhance a loss.)

91.14   **Deferred charge on re-investment.** *TCGA 1992, 5C Sch* (introduced as *FA 1995, 16 Sch* by *FA 1995, s 72(4)*) applies where:

(a)   a chargeable gain accrues to an individual after 5 April 1995 on the disposal of any asset (or on the occurrence of certain events in relation to enterprise investment scheme investments, see *TCGA 1992, 5B Sch 4, 5* introduced as *FA 1995, 13 Sch 4(3)*, or under the current provisions, see below);

(b)   the individual makes a 'qualifying investment'; and

(c)   the individual is UK resident or ordinarily resident both when the chargeable gain accrues to him and when he makes the 'qualifying investment', and is not, at the latter time, regarded as resident outside the UK for the purposes of any double taxation arrangements the effect of which would be that he would not be liable to tax on a gain arising on a disposal, immediately after their acquisition, of the shares comprising the 'qualifying investment', disregarding the exemption under *TCGA 1992, s 151A(1)* (see 91.12 above).

A '*qualifying investment*' is a subscription for shares in a company which is a VCT, by reference to which relief is obtained under 91.5 above, within twelve months (extendible by the Board) before or after the time of the accrual of the chargeable gain in question, and, if before, provided that the shares are still held at that time.

Broadly, the provisions allow a claim for the chargeable gain to be rolled over into the VCT shares, and for the gain to become chargeable on certain events in relation to those shares (including, in particular, on their disposal). For the detailed provisions, see *TCGA 1992, 5C Sch 2–6*, introduced as *FA 1995, 16 Sch 2–6*, and see Tolley's Capital Gains Tax under Venture Capital Trusts.

92   Finance Act 1996—Summary of Provisions

(Royal Assent 29 April 1996)

INCOME TAX MATTERS

s 72   **Charge and rates of income tax for 1996/97.** The basic rate is reduced from 25% to 24%, the lower and higher rates remaining at 20% and 40% respectively. The lower rate band is increased from £3,200 to £3,900, and the basic rate band limit is increased to £25,500. See 1.3 ALLOWANCES AND TAX RATES, 21.1 CONSTRUCTION INDUSTRY TAX DEDUCTION SCHEME.

s 73,   **Application of lower rate to income from savings.** For 1996/97 onwards, most forms
6 Sch   of savings income are taxable at the lower rather than the basic rate. See 1.8(iii) ALLOWANCES AND TAX RATES and *passim.*

s 74   **Personal allowances for 1996/97** are increased to £3,765 for those aged under 65, £4,910 for those aged 65 to 74 and £5,090 for those aged 75 and over. See 1.14 ALLOWANCES AND TAX RATES.

s 75   **Blind person's allowance** for 1996/97 onwards is increased to £1,250. See 1.18 ALLOWANCES AND TAX RATES.

s 76   **Limit on relief for interest.** The qualifying maximum remains at £30,000 for 1996/97. See 43.10, 43.24 INTEREST PAYABLE.

s 79,   **Abolition of Schedule C charge etc..** The charge is transferred to Schedule D. See 70
7 Sch   SCHEDULE C and *passim.*

ss 80–105,   **Loan relationships.** A new corporation tax regime for the taxation of profits and gains
8–15 Schs   from gilts and bonds is introduced. This does not apply for income tax, but a new simplified regime for the taxation of discounts on securities is introduced for 1996/97 onwards for income tax purposes (see *Schedule 13*). See INTEREST RECEIVABLE (44), 72.2 SCHEDULE D, CASE III and *passim.*

s 106   **Living accommodation provided for employees.** Changes are made to the Schedule E benefits charge to counter salary sacrifice schemes. See 75.29 SCHEDULE E.

s 107   **Beneficial loans.** Changes are made to the Schedule E benefits charge in relation to the introduction of self-assessment, in particular ending the compulsory aggregation of loans. See 75.17 SCHEDULE E.

s 108   **Incidental benefits for holders of certain offices etc..** Provision of transport and subsistence to ministers and other government office-holders is exempted from tax. See 29.15 EXEMPT INCOME.

s 109   **Charitable donations: payroll deduction scheme.** The annual limit is increased to £1,200 for 1996/97 onwards. See 15.7 CHARITIES.

s 110   **PAYE settlement agreements.** A statutory framework is introduced for annual voluntary settlements. See 55.12 PAY AS YOU EARN.

s 113   **SAYE share option schemes: exercise of rights by employees of non-participating companies** is permitted where the non-participating company is associated with or controlled by the company which set up the scheme. See 81.8 SHARE INCENTIVE AND OPTIONS.

ss 114, 115, **Non-SAYE share option schemes: requirements to be satisfied by approved**
16 Sch   **schemes and transitional provisions.** A new relief for options acquired under Company Share Option Plans replaces the previous Executive Share Option Scheme. The

main differences are that there is a £20,000 limit on shares options over which may be held under the new relief, and options may not be granted at a discounted exercise price. There are provisions dealing with the transition between the two reliefs. See 81.10 SHARE INCENTIVE AND OPTIONS.

ss 116–118 **Profit sharing schemes: the release date, the appropriate percentage and the appropriate allowance.** The period during which shares must be held in trust is reduced from five years to three, with consequential changes. See 81.6, 81.7 SHARE INCENTIVE AND OPTIONS.

ss 119, 120 **Employee share ownership trusts: removal of requirement for at least one year's service, and grant and exercise of share options.** The one-year service requirement is removed, as are various incompatibilities precluding the use of ESOTs in conjunction with SAYE share option schemes. See 81.11 SHARE INCENTIVE AND OPTIONS.

ss 121–142, **Self-assessment, general management etc..** More detailed provisions for the intro-
17–25 Schs duction of self-assessment relating to income tax, corporation tax and capital gains tax. See SELF-ASSESSMENT (78) generally and *passim*.

s 143 **Annual payments under certain insurance policies.** Exemption from tax is provided for benefits paid under certain accident, sickness, disability, infirmity or unemployment policies. See 29.10 EXEMPT INCOME.

s 144 **Vocational training.** The scope of the reliefs available is extended. See 71.87 SCHEDULE D, CASES I AND II, 75.42 SCHEDULE E.

s 145 **Personal reliefs for non-resident EEA nationals.** Entitlement to UK personal reliefs is extended to all EEA nationals even where they are non-UK resident. See 51.11 NON-RESIDENTS AND OTHER OVERSEAS MATTERS.

s 146 **Exemptions for charities.** The exemption of certain investment income (previously given by concession) is enacted. See 15.3, 15.4 CHARITIES.

s 147 **Withdrawal of relief for Class 4 contributions.** The income tax relief for one-half of Class 4 national insurance contributions is withdrawn for 1996/97 onwards (the rate being cut from 7.3% to 6% in compensation). See 82.7 SOCIAL SECURITY.

s 148 **Mis-sold personal pensions etc..** Certain compensation payments are relieved from income tax and capital gains tax. See 29.3 EXEMPT INCOME.

s 149 **Annual payments in residuary cases.** From 6 April 1996, certain payments under 'existing obligations' to persons who reached the age of 21 before 6 April 1994 are disregarded for tax purposes. See 1.8(i) ALLOWANCES AND TAX RATES, 23.9 DEDUCTION OF TAX AT SOURCE.

s 150, **Income tax exemption for periodical payments of damages and compensation**
26 Sch **for personal injury.** The relief introduced by *FA 1995* is extended. See 29.4 EXEMPT INCOME.

s 151 **Benefits under pilot schemes.** Regulation-making powers are granted to the Treasury in relation to the tax treatment of payments under Government pilot schemes. See 82.5 SOCIAL SECURITY.

s 152 **Jobfinder's grant** payments are exempted from income tax (with retrospective effect). See 82.4 SOCIAL SECURITY.

s 154, **FOTRA securities.** The Treasury powers to issue securities 'free of tax to residents
28 Sch abroad' are updated, with consequential changes to the related tax provisions. See 33.2 GOVERNMENT STOCKS.

s 155 **Directions for payment without deduction of tax.** Minor technical change. See 33.3 GOVERNMENT STOCKS.

s 156,
29 Sch
Paying and collecting agents etc.. New arrangements are introduced following the abolition of Schedule C. See SCHEDULE C (70).

s 157
Stock lending fees received by pension funds are exempted from tax. See 71.81 SCHEDULE D, CASES I AND II.

s 158
Transfers on death under the accrued income scheme. The accrued income ceases to apply to transfers to personal representatives on deaths occurring after 5 April 1996. See 74.15 SCHEDULE D, CASE VI.

s 159
Manufactured payments, repos, etc.. A number of changes are made to the anti-avoidance provisions. See 3.3, 3.6, 3.7, 3.15(ii) ANTI-AVOIDANCE.

s 161
Venture capital trusts: control of companies etc.. In relation to qualifying investments, the definition of 'control' is amended to disregard certain holdings etc.. See 91.3 VENTURE CAPITAL TRUSTS.

s 162
Qualifying life insurance policies: certification. The abolition of certification is deferred. See 45.6, 45.12(*e*) LIFE ASSURANCE POLICIES.

s 171
Friendly societies: life or endowment business. The definition is revised, and certain consequential changes made. See 45.3(ii) LIFE ASSURANCE POLICIES.

s 172
Personal pension schemes: return of contributions on or after death of member. The circumstances in which a return of contributions may be made are extended. See 65.5(viii) RETIREMENT ANNUITIES AND PERSONAL PENSION SCHEMES.

s 175
Cancellation of tax advantages: transactions in certain securities. The securities concerned are redefined. See 3.2 ANTI-AVOIDANCE.

s 178
Sub-contractors in the construction industry. Mandatory registration cards are to be introduced for those without an exemption certificate (probably in August 1998). See 21.5 CONSTRUCTION INDUSTRY: TAX DEDUCTION SCHEME.

s 179,
35 Sch
Capital allowances: roll-over relief in respect of ships. The conditions for the relief are eased. See 10.30 CAPITAL ALLOWANCES.

s 198,
37 Sch
Banks. A new definition is introduced for certain purposes. See 8.1 BANKS.

s 199,
38 Sch
Quotation or listing of securities. A wide range of legislative references is updated following changes to Stock Exchange rules.

s 200
Domicile for tax purposes of overseas electors. Actions in relation to voting registration may be disregarded. See 64.4 RESIDENCE, ORDINARY RESIDENCE AND DOMICILE.

s 201,
39 Sch
Enactment of Inland Revenue concessions. See 10.17, 10.28(A) CAPITAL ALLOWANCES, 46.13(*i*) LOSSES, 66.10 RETIREMENT SCHEMES and concessions B19, B28, B39, D1, D19, D28, D36, D43, D48, G1 and G2.

s 202,
40 Sch
Gilt stripping. Consequential changes are made to tax legislation to facilitate the market in gilt-edged strips. See 71.81 SCHEDULE D, CASES I AND II, 74.25 SCHEDULE D, CASE VI.

s 204
Interpretation.

s 205,
41 Sch
Repeals.

s 206
Short title.

OTHER MATTERS

ss 1–24, 1, 2 Schs	**Customs and Excise.**
ss 25–38, 3, 4 Schs	**Value added tax.**
ss 39–71, 5 Sch	**Landfill tax.**

ss 77, 78   **Corporation tax.** For financial year 1996, the full rate remains at 33%, the small companies rate being reduced to 24%. The upper and lower marginal relief limits remain at £1,500,000 and £300,000 respectively, the marginal relief fraction accordingly being nine four-hundredths. See Tolley's Corporation Tax under Introduction and Rates of Tax and Small Companies Rate.

ss 111, 112   **Capital gains tax: share options.** Changes are made to the amount taken into account as consideration for unapproved share options, and removing the charge on the release and replacement of options. See Tolley's Capital Gains Tax under Disposal.

s 153,
27 Sch   **Foreign income dividends.** A number of amendments are made to the foreign income dividend arrangements. See 1.8(ii) ALLOWANCES AND TAX RATES and Tolley's Corporation Tax under Foreign Income Dividends.

s 160,
30 Sch   **Investments in housing** by investment trusts are permitted. See Tolley's Corporation Tax under Unit and Investment Trusts.

ss 163–170,
31–34 Schs   **Insurance companies.** Changes are made to the taxation of life insurance companies, in particular removing the distinction of industrial assurance business. See 45.1, 45.7, 45.8, 45.12(*b*) LIFE ASSURANCE POLICIES and Tolley's Corporation Tax under Life Insurance Companies.

s 173   **Close companies: loans to participators etc..** Changes are made to the timing of charges and reliefs under these provisions. See Tolley's Corporation Tax under Close Companies and Interest on Overpaid Tax.

s 174   **Close companies: attribution of gains to participators in non-resident companies.** The rules for apportionment of gains are revised. See Tolley's Capital Gains Tax under Overseas Matters.

ss 176,
177   **Chargeable gains: reliefs.** Changes are made to retirement and reinvestment reliefs. See Tolley's Capital Gains Tax under Retirement Relief and Reinvestment in Shares Relief.

ss 180, 181   **Oil taxation.**

s 182,
36 Sch   **Controlled foreign companies.** A number of changes are made to the CFC legislation. See Tolley's Corporation Tax under Controlled Foreign Companies.

ss 183–185   **Inheritance tax.**

ss 186–196   **Stamp duty and stamp duty reserve tax.**

s 197   **Indirect taxation: setting of rates of interest.**

s 203   **Modification of the Agriculture Act 1993** in connection with privatisation tax rules. See Tolley's Corporation Tax under Capital Gains and Losses.

93   Table of Leading Cases

This Table lists those of the approximately 2,000 cases referred to in this book which are considered to be of most general application and interest. For fuller details of these cases, and of all other tax cases relevant to current or recent legislation, see Tolley's Tax Cases.

A

AB, Southern v	71.30; 71.34
KB 1933, 18 TC 59; [1933] 1 KB 713.	
Abbott v Philbin	75.7
HL 1960, 39 TC 82; [1961] AC 352; [1960] 2 All ER 763.	
Absalom v Talbot	71.44
HL 1944, 26 TC 166; [1944] AC 204; [1944] 1 All ER 642.	
Alexander von Glehn & Co Ltd, CIR v	71.34; 71.46; 71.88
CA 1920, 12 TC 232; [1920] 2 KB 553.	
Allen, Bosanquet v	80.5
HL 1985, 59 TC 125; [1985] STC 356; [1985] 2 WLR 1010; [1985] 2 All ER 645.	
Allen v Farquharson Bros & Co	4.9
KB 1932, 17 TC 59.	
Anderton & Halstead Ltd v Birrell	71.44
KB 1931, 16 TC 200; [1932] 1 KB 271.	
Andrews, Rignell v	1.21
Ch D 1990, 63 TC 312; [1990] STC 410.	
Ang v Parrish	80.28
Ch D 1980, 53 TC 304; [1980] STC 341; [1980] 1 WLR 940; [1980] 2 All ER 790.	
Anglo Brewing Co Ltd, CIR v	66.10; 71.53
KB 1925, 12 TC 803.	
Anglo-Persian Oil Co Ltd v Dale	71.46
CA 1931, 16 TC 253; [1932] 1 KB 124.	
Archer-Shee, Garland v	80.10
HL 1930, 15 TC 693; [1931] AC 212.	
Archer-Shee v Baker	80.10
HL 1927, 11 TC 749; [1927] AC 844.	
Arthur Young McClelland Moores & Co, MacKinlay v	53.3; 71.40; 71.73
HL 1989, 62 TC 704; [1989] STC 898; [1989] 3 WLR 1245; [1990] 1 All ER 45.	
Atherton v British Insulated & Helsby Cables Ltd	66.10; 71.40
HL 1925, 10 TC 155; [1926] AC 205.	
Attorney-General v Metropolitan Water Board	23.3(i)
CA 1927, 13 TC 294.	
Attwooll, London & Thames Haven Oil Wharves Ltd v	71.47(c)
CA 1966, 43 TC 491; [1967] Ch 772; [1967] 2 All ER 124.	

B

BP Oil Northern Ireland Refinery Ltd, Elliss v	10.28
CA 1986, 59 TC 474; [1987] STC 52.	
BSC Footwear Ltd v Ridgway	71.82
HL 1971, 47 TC 495; [1972] AC 544; [1971] 2 All ER 534.	
Bairstow & Harrison, Edwards v	4.7; 71.35
HL 1955, 36 TC 207; [1956] AC 14; [1955] 3 All ER 48.	
Baker, Archer-Shee v	80.10
HL 1927, 11 TC 749; [1927] AC 844.	
Banin v Mackinlay	4.6(a)
CA 1984, 58 TC 398; [1985] STC 144; [1985] 1 All ER 842.	
Banning v Wright	68.28
HL 1972, 48 TC 421; [1972] 1 WLR 972; [1972] 2 All ER 987.	
Barnet London Borough Council (ex p. Nilish Shah), R v	64.6
HL 1982, [1983] 2 WLR 16; [1983] 1 All ER 226.	

C

M

93   Table of Leading Cases

94   Table of Statutes

95 Index

This index is referenced to the chapter and paragraph number.
The entries printed in bold capitals are main subject headings in the text.

95　Index

Purchased life annuities, 23.11(c)
loans for, interest on, 43.24
savings income, 1.8(iii)
Purchase of property, relief for interest paid,
43.6

Q

Qualifying convertible securities, 44.8
Qualifying deposit rights, 9.5
Quarantine premises, 10.25(iv)
Quarries, 71.1
rent payable in connection with, 23.14

R

Rates, 71.77
of income tax, 1.3, 1.5
Sch A, 68.15
Sch D, 71.77
RATIONALISATION SCHEMES, 61
Receipts basis (Schedule E), 71.53, 75.1
Reckonable date, 42.2
Records,
PAYE, 55.34
production of, 4.6(b), 6.8
Recovery of tax,
Court proceedings, 56.3
distraint, 56.3
lessee, from, 68.21
poinding, 56.3
repayment claims, 17.2
third parties, from, 68.21
Redundancy payments,
deduction for additional payments, 71.53
exempt, 19.5, 29.22, 75.32
non-statutory, 19.5
paid, 71.53
received, Sch E, 75.32
REGIONAL DEVELOPMENT GRANTS, 62
Relevant earnings, 65.12
Religious centres,
PAYE, 55.35
Religious communities, 38.B10
Religious societies, 15.2(i)
Relocation packages, 75.33
Remission for official error, 56.6
REMITTANCE BASIS, 63
application, 63.1
basis of assessment, 63.2
constructive remittances, 63.4
double tax relief, 25.5(b)
general, 63.3
Remittances,
basis, 63
constructive, 63.4
double tax relief, 25.5(b)
new residents, by, 73.11

unremittable overseas income, 51.14
unremittable trade receipts, 71.90
Removal expenses, 75.13(x)
Remuneration, 71.53, 75
Renewals, 71.78
capital allowances, 10.38(x)
Rent-a-room relief, 68.11, 74.4
Rents,
business premises, 71.77
connected persons, from, 68.14
deductions from, 68.4, 68.15, 68.16
— of tax from, 23.14
electric line wayleaves, 23.2, 23.14
furnished lettings, 68.2, 68.14, 74.4
land managed as one estate, 68.16(d)
lost, 68.18
mines and quarries, 23.2, 23.14
non-residents, payments to, 68.24
premiums, 68.27, 68.28
Sch A, 68
Sch D, 71.77
tied premises, 71.45
unfurnished lettings, 68.14
Repairs, 71.78
Sch A, 68.15
Repayment,
annuitants, to, 23.17(c)
charities, to, 15.6
claims, 17.2
example, 2.2
interest on, 41
official error, cases of, 56.6
PAYE, 55.39
provisional, 56.7
supplement, 29.23, 41
tax overpaid, 41, 56.7
Repos, 3.5, 33.3
RESIDENCE, ORDINARY RESIDENCE
AND DOMICILE, 64
administrative procedures, 64.5
appeals, 64.8
change of residence,
— losses on, 46.13(j)
— partnerships, 53.15
— traders, 71.27
domicile, 64.4
double tax relief, 25, 64.3
house, see Private residence
husband and wife, 47.12
ordinarily resident, 64.6
residence, 64.2, 64.5, 64.6
— company, 51.4(c)
— part of year, 64.5, 73.11, 73.12
— temporary, 64.5
— working abroad, 64.5, 75.2, 75.3
visits abroad, 64.7
Residuary income, 22.3
Residuary legatees, 22.3
Restrictive covenants, 75.34
excess liability, 28.3(a)(iii)